821

881

Mt. St. Joseph.

THE

POETICAL WORKS

OF

ALFRED, LORD TENNYSON

(POET LAUREATE).

From the Author's Text.

ILLUSTRATED BY CHURCH, DIELMAN, FREDERICKS, FENN,
MURPHY, SCHELL, TAYLOR, AND OTHER
EMINENT ARTISTS.

———

NEW YORK: 46 EAST 14TH STREET.

THOMAS Y. CROWELL & CO.

BOSTON: 100 PURCHASE ST.

CONTENTS.

—o-o-o-o-o—

TO THE QUEEN.

Revered, beloved — O you that hold
    A nobler office upon earth
    Than arms, or power of brains, or birth
Could give the warrior kings of old,

Victoria, — since your Royal grace
    To one of less desert allows
    This laurel greener from the brows
Of him that utter'd nothing base;

And should your greatness, and the care
    That yokes with empire, yield you time
    To make demand of modern rhyme
If aught of ancient worth be there;

Then — while a sweeter music wakes,
    And thro' wild March the throstle calls,
    Where all about your palace-walls
The sun-lit almond-blossom shakes —

Take, Madam, this poor book of song;
    For tho' the faults were thick as dust

In vacant chambers, I could trust
Your kindness.   May you rule us long,

And leave us rulers of your blood
   As noble till the latest day!
   May children of our children say,
" She wrought her people lasting good;

" Her court was pure; her life serene;
   God gave her peace; her land reposed ;
   A thousand claims to reverence closed
In her as Mother, Wife, and Queen;

" And statesmen at her council met
   Who knew the seasons when to take
   Occasion by the hand, and make
The bounds of freedom wider yet

" By shaping some august decree,
   Which kept her throne unshaken still,
   Broad-based upon her people's will,
And compass'd by the inviolate sea."

March, 1851.

JUVENILIA.

CLARIBEL.

A MELODY.

I.

Where Claribel low-lieth
The breezes pause and die,
    Letting the rose-leaves fall:
But the solemn oak-tree sigheth,
    Thick-leaved, ambrosial,
With an ancient melody
Of an inward agony,
Where Claribel low-lieth.

II.

At eve the beetle boometh
    Athwart the thicket lone:
At noon the wild bee hummeth
    About the moss'd headstone;
At midnight the moon cometh
    And looketh down alone.
Her song the lintwhite swelleth,
The clear-voiced mavis dwelleth,
    The callow throstle lispeth,
The slumbrous wave outwelleth,
    The babbling runnel crispeth,
The hollow grot replieth
    Where Claribel low-lieth.

NOTHING WILL DIE.

When will the stream be aweary of
        flowing
    Under my eye?
When will the wind be aweary of
        blowing
    Over the sky?
When will the clouds be aweary of
        fleeting?
When will the heart be aweary of
        beating?
    And nature die?
Never, oh! never, nothing will die;
    The stream flows,
    The wind blows,
    The cloud fleets,
    The heart beats,
        Nothing will die.

Nothing will die;
All things will change
Thro' eternity.
'Tis the world's winter;
Autumn and summer
Are gone long ago;
Earth is dry to the centre,
But spring, a new comer,
A spring rich and strange,
Shall make the winds blow
Round and round,
Thro' and thro',
    Here and there,
    Till the air
And the ground
Shall be fill'd with life anew.

The world was never made;
It will change, but it will not fade.
So let the wind range;
For even and morn
    Ever will be
    Thro' eternity.
Nothing was born;
Nothing will die;
All things will change.

ALL THINGS WILL DIE.

CLEARLY the blue river chimes in its
 flowing
  Under my eye;
Warmly and broadly the south winds
  are blowing
   Over the sky.
One after another the white clouds are
  fleeting;
Every heart this May morning in joy-
  ance is beating
   Full merrily;
    Yet all things must die.
The stream will cease to flow;
The wind will cease to blow;
The clouds will cease to fleet;
The heart will cease to beat;
  For all things must die.
   All things must die.
Spring will come never more.
  Oh! vanity!
Death waits at the door.
See! our friends are all forsaking
The wine and the merrymaking.
We are call'd — we must go.
Laid low, very low,
In the dark we must lie.
The merry glees are still;
The voice of the bird
Shall no more be heard,
Nor the wind on the hill.
  Oh! misery!
Hark! death is calling
While I speak to ye,
The jaw is falling,
The red cheek paling,
The strong limbs failing;
Ice with the warm blood mixing;
The eyeballs fixing.
Nine times goes the passing bell:
Ye merry souls, farewell.
  The old earth
  Had a birth,
  As all men know,
  Long ago.
And the old earth must die.
So let the warm winds range,
And the blue wave beat the shore;
For even and morn
Ye will never see
Thro' eternity.

All things were born.
Ye will come never more,
For all things must die.

LEONINE ELEGIACS.

LOW-FLOWING breezes are roaming
  the broad valley dimm'd in the
  gloaming:
Thoro' the black-stemm'd pines only
  the far river shines.
Creeping thro' blossomy rushes and
  bowers of rose-blowing bushes,
Down by the poplar tall rivulets babble and fall.
Barketh the shepherd-dog cheerly; the
  grasshopper carolleth clearly;
Deeply the wood-dove coos; shrilly
  the owlet halloos;
Winds creep; dews fall chilly: in her
  first sleep earth breathes stilly:
Over the pools in the burn water-gnats
  murmur and mourn.
Sadly the far kine loweth: the glimmering water out-floweth:
Twin peaks shadow'd with pine slope
  to the dark hyaline.
Low-throned Hesper is stayed between
  the two peaks; but the Naiad
Throbbing in mild unrest holds him
  beneath in her breast.
The ancient poetess singeth, that Hesperus all things bringeth,
Smoothing the wearied mind: bring
  me my love, Rosalind.
Thou comest morning or even; she
  cometh not morning or even.
False-eyed Hesper, unkind, where is
  my sweet Rosalind?

SUPPOSED CONFESSIONS
OF A SECOND-RATE SENSITIVE MIND.

O GOD! my God! have mercy now.
I faint, I fall. Men say that Thou
Didst die for me, for such as *me*,
Patient of ill, and death, and scorn,
And that my sin was as a thorn

Among the thorns that girt Thy brow,
Wounding Thy soul. — That even now,
In this extremest misery
Of ignorance, I should require
A sign! and if a bolt of fire
Would rive the slumbrous summer
    noon
While I do pray to Thee alone,
Think my belief would stronger grow:
Is not my human pride brought low?
The boastings of my spirit still?
The joy I had in my freewill
All cold, and dead, and corpse-like
    grown?
And what is left to me, but Thou
And faith in Thee? Men pass me by;
Christians with happy countenances —
And children all seem full of Thee!
And women smile with saint-like
    glances
Like Thine own mother's when she
    bow'd
Above Thee, on that happy morn
When angels spake to men aloud,
And Thou and peace to earth were
    born,
Goodwill to me as well as all —
I one of them: my brothers they:
Brothers in Christ — a world of peace
And confidence, day after day;
And trust and hope till things should
    cease,
And then one Heaven receive us all.

How sweet to have a common faith!
To hold a common scorn of death!
And at a burial to hear
The creaking cords which wound and
    eat
Into my human heart, whene'er
Earth goes to earth, with grief, not
    fear,
With hopeful grief, were passing
    sweet!

Thrice happy state again to be
The trustful infant on the knee!
Who lets his rosy fingers play
About his mother's neck, and knows
Nothing beyond his mother's eyes.
They comfort him by night and day;
They light his little life alway;

He hath no thought of coming woes;
He hath no care of life or death;
Scarce outward signs of joy arise,
Because the Spirit of happiness
And perfect rest so inward is;
And loveth so his innocent heart,
Her temple and her place of birth,
Where she would ever wish to dwell,
Life of the fountain there, beneath
Its salient springs, and far apart,
Hating to wander out on earth,
Or breathe into the hollow air,
Whose chillness would make visible
Her subtil, warm, and golden breath,
Which mixing with the infant's blood,
Fulfils him with beatitude.
Oh! sure it is a special care
Of God, to fortify from doubt,
To arm in proof, and guard about
With triple-mailèd trust, and clear
Delight, the infant's dawning year.

Would that my gloomed fancy were
As thine, my mother, when with brows
Propt on thy knees, my hands upheld
In thine, I listen'd to thy vows,
For me outpour'd in holiest prayer —
For me unworthy! — and beheld
Thy mild deep eyes upraised, that knew
The beauty and repose of faith,
And the clear spirit shining thro'.
Oh! wherefore do we grow awry
From roots which strike so deep? why
    dare
Paths in the desert? Could not I
Bow myself down, where thou hast
    knelt,
To the earth — until the ice would
    melt
Here, and I feel as thou hast felt?
What Devil had the heart to scathe
Flowers thou hadst rear'd — to brush
    the dew
From thine own lily, when thy grave
Was deep, my mother, in the clay?
Myself? Is it thus? Myself? Had I
So little love for thee? But why
Prevail'd not thy pure prayers? Why
    pray
To one who heeds not, who can save
But will not? Great in faith, and
    strong

Against the grief of circumstance
Wert thou, and yet unheard. What if
Thou pleadest still, and seest me drive
Thro' utter dark a full-sail'd skiff,
Unpiloted i' the echoing dance
Of reboant whirlwinds, stooping low
Unto the death, not sunk! I know
At matins and at evensong,
That thou, if thou wert yet alive,
In deep and daily prayers would'st strive
To reconcile me with thy God.
Albeit, my hope is gray, and cold
At heart, thou wouldest murmur still —
"Bring this lamb back into Thy fold,
My Lord, if so it be Thy will."
Would'st tell me I must brook the rod
And chastisement of human pride;
That pride, the sin of devils, stood
Betwixt me and the light of God!
That hitherto I had defied
And had rejected God — that grace
Would drop from his o'er-brimming love,
As manna on my wilderness,
If I would pray — that God would move
And strike the hard, hard rock, and thence,
Sweet in their utmost bitterness,
Would issue tears of penitence
Which would keep green hope's life. Alas!
I think that pride hath now no place
Nor sojourn in me. I am void,
Dark, formless, utterly destroyed.

Why not believe then? Why not yet
Anchor thy frailty there, where man
Hath moor'd and rested? Ask the sea
At midnight, when the crisp slope waves
After a tempest, rib and fret
The broad-imbased beach, why he
Slumbers not like a mountain tarn?
Wherefore his ridges are not curls
And ripples of an inland mere?
Wherefore he moaneth thus, nor can
Draw down into his vexed pools
All that blue heaven which hues and paves

The other?   I am too forlorn,
Too shaken: my own weakness fools
My judgment, and my spirit whirls,
Moved from beneath with doubt and fear.

"Yet," said I in my morn of youth,
The unsunn'd freshness of my strength,
When I went forth in quest of truth,
"It is man's privilege to doubt,
If so be that from doubt at length,
Truth may stand forth unmoved of change,
An image with profulgent brows,
And perfect limbs, as from the storm
Of running fires and fluid range
Of lawless airs, at last stood out
This excellence and solid form
Of constant beauty. For the Ox
Feeds in the herb, and sleeps, or fills
The horned valleys all about,
And hollows of the fringed hills
In summer heats, with placid lows
Unfearing, till his own blood flows
About his hoof. And in the flocks
The lamb rejoiceth in the year,
And raceth freely with his fere,
And answers to his mother's calls
From the flower'd furrow. In a time,
Of which he wots not, run short pains
Thro' his warm heart; and then, from whence
He knows not, on his light there falls
A shadow; and his native slope,
Where he was wont to leap and climb,
Floats from his sick and filmed eyes,
And something in the darkness draws
His forehead earthward, and he dies.
Shall man live thus, in joy and hope
As a young lamb, who cannot dream,
Living, but that he shall live on?
Shall we not look into the laws
Of life and death, and things that seem,
And things that be, and analyze
Our double nature, and compare
All creeds till we have found the one,
If one there be?" Ay me! I fear
All may not doubt, but everywhere
Some must clasp Idols. Yet, my God,
Whom call I Idol? Let Thy dove
Shadow me over, and my sins

Be unremember'd, and Thy love
Enlighten me. Oh teach me yet
Somewhat before the heavy clod
Weighs on me, and the busy fret
Of that sharp-headed worm begins
In the gross blackness underneath.

O weary life! O weary death!
O spirit and heart made desolate!
O damned vacillating state!

THE KRAKEN.

BELOW the thunders of the upper
deep;
Far, far beneath in the abysmal sea,
His ancient, dreamless, uninvaded
sleep
The Kraken sleepeth: faintest sun-
lights flee
About his shadowy sides: above him
swell
Huge sponges of millennial growth
and height;
And far away into the sickly light,
From many a wondrous grot and
secret cell
Unnumber'd and enormous polypi
Winnow with giant arms the slumber-
ing green.
There hath he lain for ages and will lie
Battening upon huge seaworms in his
sleep,
Until the latter fire shall heat the
deep;
Then once by man and angels to be
seen,
In roaring he shall rise and on the
surface die.

SONG.

THE winds, as at their hour of birth,
Leaning upon the ridged sea,
Breathed low around the rolling earth
With mellow preludes, "We are
free."

The streams through many a lilied row
Down-carolling to the crisped sea,
Low-tinkled with a bell-like flow
Atween the blossoms, "We are
free."

LILIAN.

I.

AIRY, fairy Lilian,
Flitting, fairy Lilian,
When I ask her if she love me,
Clasps her tiny hands above me,
Laughing all she can;
She'll not tell me if she love me,
Cruel little Lilian.

II.

When my passion seeks
Pleasance in love-sighs,
She, looking thro' and thro' me
Thoroughly to undo me,
Smiling, never speaks:
So innocent-arch, so cunning-simple,
From beneath her gathered wimple
Glancing with black-beaded eyes,
Till the lightning laughters dimple
The baby-roses in her cheeks;
Then away she flies.

III.

Prithee weep, May Lilian!
Gayety without eclipse
Wearieth me, May Lilian:
Thro' my very heart it thrilleth
When from crimson-threaded lips
Silver-treble laughter trilleth:
Prithee weep, May Lilian.

IV.

Praying all I can,
If prayers will not hush thee,
Airy Lilian,
Like a rose-leaf I will crush thee,
Fairy Lilian.

ISABEL.

I.

EYES not down-dropt nor over-bright,
but fed
With the clear-pointed flame of
chastity,
Clear, without heat, undying, tended
by
Pure vestal thoughts in the trans-
lucent fane

Of her still spirit ; locks not wide-dis-
  pread,
  Madonna-wise on either side her
  head ;
  Sweet lips whereon perpetually
  did reign
The summer calm of golden charity,
Were fixed shadows of thy fixed mood,
  Revered Isabel, the crown and
  head,
The stately flower of female fortitude,
  Of perfect wifehood and pure
  lowlihead.

II.

The intuitive decision of a bright
  And thorough-edged intellect to part
  Error from crime ; a prudence to
  withhold ;
  The laws of marriage character'd
  in gold
Upon the blanched tablets of her
  heart ;
A love still burning upward, giving
  light
To read those laws ; an accent very
  low
In blandishment, but a most silver flow
  Of subtle-paced counsel in dis-
  tress,
Right to the heart and brain, tho'
  undescried,
  Winning its way with extreme
  gentleness
Thro' all the outworks of suspicious
  pride ;
A courage to endure and to obey ;
A hate of gossip parlance, and of sway,
Crown'd Isabel, thro' all her placid life,
The queen of marriage, a most perfect
wife.

III.

The mellow'd reflex of a winter moon ;
A clear stream flowing with a muddy
  one,
  Till in its onward current it absorbs
  With swifter movement and in
  purer light
  The vexed eddies of its wayward
  brother:
A leaning and upbearing parasite,

Clothing the stem, which else had
  fallen quite
With cluster'd flower-bells and am-
  brosial orbs
Of rich fruit-bunches leaning on
  each other —
  Shadow forth thee : — the world
  hath not another
(Tho' all her fairest forms are types
  of thee,
And thou of God in thy great charity)
Of such a finish'd chasten'd purity.

MARIANA.

"Mariana in the moated grange."
Measure for Measure.

WITH blackest moss the flower-plots
  Were thickly crusted, one and all :
The rusted nails fell from the knots
  That held the pear to the gable-
  wall.
The broken sheds look'd sad and
  strange :
  Unlifted was the clinking latch ;
Weeded and worn the ancient thatch
Upon the lonely moated grange.
  She only said, " My life is dreary,
  He cometh not," she said ;
  She said, " I am aweary, aweary,
  I would that I were dead !"

Her tears fell with the dews at even ;
  Her tears fell ere the dews were
  dried ;
She could not look on the sweet heaven,
  Either at morn or eventide.
After the flitting of the bats,
  When thickest dark did trance the
  sky,
  She drew her casement-curtain by,
And glanced athwart the glooming flats.
  She only said, "The night is dreary,
  He cometh not," she said ;
  She said, " I am aweary, aweary,
  I would that I were dead !"

Upon the middle of the night,
  Waking she heard the night-fowl
  crow :
The cock sung out an hour ere light :
  From the dark fen the oxen's low

"She said, 'I am aweary, aweary,
I would that I were dead!'"

Page 8.

Came to her: without hope of change,
  In sleep she seem'd to walk forlorn,
  Till cold winds woke the gray-eyed
    morn
About the lonely moated grange.
    She only said, "The day is dreary,
      He cometh not," she said;
    She said, "I am aweary, aweary,
      I would that I were dead!"

About a stone-cast from the wall
  A sluice with blacken'd waters slept,
And o'er it many, round and small,
  The cluster'd marish-mosses crept.
Hard by a poplar shook alway,
  All silver-green with gnarled bark:
For leagues no other tree did mark
  The level waste, the rounding gray.
    She only said, "My life is dreary,
      He cometh not," she said;
    She said, "I am aweary, aweary,
      I would that I were dead!"

And ever when the moon was low,
  And the shrill winds were up and
    away,
In the white curtain, to and fro,
  She saw the gusty shadow sway.
But when the moon was very low,
  And wild winds bound within their
    cell,
The shadow of the poplar fell
Upon her bed, across her brow.
    She only said, "The night is dreary,
      He cometh not," she said;
    She said, "I am aweary, aweary,
      I would that I were dead!"

All day within the dreamy house,
  The doors upon their hinges creak'd;
The blue fly sung in the pane; the
    mouse
  Behind the mouldering wainscot
    shriek'd,
Or from the crevice peer'd about.
  Old faces glimmer'd thro' the doors,
  Old footsteps trod the upper floors,
Old voices called her from without.
    She only said, "My life is dreary,
      He cometh not," she said;
    She said, "I am aweary, aweary,
      I would that I were dead!"

The sparrows chirrup on the roof,
  The slow clock ticking, and the sound
Which to the wooing wind aloof
  The poplar made, did all confound
Her sense; but most she loathed the
    hour
When the thick-moated sunbeam lay
Athwart the chambers, and the day
Was sloping toward his western bower.
    Then, said she, "I am very dreary,
      He will not come," she said;
    She wept, "I am aweary, aweary,
      Oh, God, that I were dead!"

MARIANA IN THE SOUTH.

WITH one black shadow at its feet,
  The house thro' all the level shines,
Close-latticed to the brooding heat,
  And silent in its dusty vines:
A faint-blue ridge upon the right,
  An empty river-bed before,
  And shallows on a distant shore,
In glaring sand and inlets bright.
    But "Ave Mary," made she moan,
      And "Ave Mary," night and
        morn,
      And "Ah," she sang, "to be all
        alone,
        To live forgotten, and love for-
          lorn."

She, as her carol sadder grew,
  From brow and bosom slowly down
Thro' rosy taper fingers drew
  Her streaming curls of deepest
    brown
To left and right, and made appear
  Still-lighted in a secret shrine,
  Her melancholy eyes divine,
The home of woe without a tear.
    And "Ave Mary," was her moan,
      "Madonna, sad is night and
        morn,"
      And "Ah," she sang, "to be all
        alone,
        To live forgotten, and love for-
          lorn."

Till all the crimson changed, and past
  Into deep orange o'er the sea,

Low on her knees herself she cast,
  Before Our Lady murmur'd she;
Complaining, " Mother, give me grace
  To help me of my weary load."
And on the liquid mirror glow'd
The clear perfection of her face.
    " Is this the form," she made her
      moan,
      " That won his praises night
        and morn ? "
    And " Ah," she said, " but I wake
      alone,
      I sleep forgotten, I wake for-
      lorn."

Nor bird would sing, nor lamb would
  bleat,
  Nor any cloud would cross the vault,
But day increased from heat to heat,
  On stony drought and steaming salt;
Till now at noon she slept again,
  And seem'd knee-deep in mountain
    grass,
  And heard her native breezes pass,
And runlets babbling down the glen.
    She breathed in sleep a lower
      moan,
      And murmuring, as at night and
      morn,
    She thought, " My spirit is here
      alone,
    Walks forgotten, and is forlorn."

Dreaming, she knew it was a dream :
  She felt he was and was not there.
She woke : the babble of the stream
  Fell, and, without, the steady glare
Shrank one sick willow sear and small.
  The river-bed was dusty-white ;
  And all the furnace of the light
Struck up against the blinding wall.
    She whisper'd, with a stifled moan
      More inward than at night or
      morn,
    " Sweet Mother, let me not here
      alone
      Live forgotten, and die forlorn."

And, rising, from her bosom drew
  Old letters, breathing of her worth,
For " Love," they said, " must needs
  be true,

To what is loveliest upon earth."
An image seem'd to pass the door,
  To look at her with slight, and say
  " But now thy beauty flows away,
So be alone forevermore."
    " O cruel heart," she changed her
      tone,
      " And cruel love, whose end is
      scorn,
    Is this the end to be left alone,
      To live forgotten, and die for-
      lorn ? "

But sometimes in the falling day
  An image seem'd to pass the door,
To look into her eyes and say,
  " But thou shalt be alone no more."
And flaming downward over all
  From heat to heat the day decreased,
  And slowly rounded to the east
The one black shadow from the wall.
    " The day to night," she made her
      moan,
      " The day to night, the night to
      morn,
      And day and night I am left alone
      To live forgotten, and love for-
      lorn."

At eve a dry cicala sung,
  There came a sound as of the sea ;
Backward the lattice-blind she flung,
  And lean'd upon the balcony.
There all in spaces rosy-bright
  Large Hesper glitter'd on her tears,
  And deepening thro' the silent
    spheres
Heaven over Heaven rose the night.
And weeping then she made her moan,
  " The night comes on that knows
    not morn,
When I shall cease to be all alone,
  To live forgotten, and love forlorn."

———

TO ——.

I.

CLEAR-HEADED friend, whose joyful
  scorn,
  Edged with sharp laughter, cuts
  atwain

The knots that tangle human
　　creeds,
The wounding cords that bind and
　　strain
The heart until it bleeds,
Ray-fringed eyelids of the morn
　　Roof not a glance so keen as thine :
Thou wilt not live in vain.

II.

Low-cowering shall the Sophist sit ;
　　Falsehood shall bare her plaited
　　　brow :
　　Fair-fronted Truth shall droop not
　　　now
With shrilling shafts of subtle wit.
Nor martyr - flames, nor trenchant
　　swords
　　Can do away that ancient lie ;
　　A gentler death shall Falsehood die,
Shot thro' and thro' with cunning
　　words.

III.

Weak Truth a-leaning on her crutch,
　　Wan, wasted Truth in her utmost
　　　need,
　　Thy kingly intellect shall feed,
　　Until she be an athlete bold,
And weary with a finger's touch
　　Those writhed limbs of lightning
　　　speed ;
Like that strange angel which of old,
　　Until the breaking of the light,
Wrestled with wandering Israel,
　　Past Yabbok brook the livelong
　　　night,
And heaven's mazed signs stood still
In the dim tract of Penuel.

MADELINE.

I.

THOU are not steep'd in golden lan-
　　guors,
　　No tranced summer calm is thine,
　　Ever varying Madeline.
Thro' light and shadow thou dost
　　range,
　　Sudden glances, sweet and strange,
Delicious spites and darling angers,
　　And airy forms of flitting change.

II.

Smiling, frowning, evermore,
Thou art perfect in love-lore.
Revealings deep and clear are thine
Of wealthy smiles : but who may know
Whether smile or frown be fleeter ?
Whether smile or frown be sweeter,
　　Who may know ?
Frowns perfect-sweet along the brow
Light-glooming over eyes divine,
Like little clouds sun-fringed, are
　　thine,
　　Ever varying Madeline.
Thy smile and frown are not aloof
　　From one another,
　　Each to each is dearest brother ;
Hues of the silken sheeny woof
　　Momently shot into each other.
　　All the mystery is thine ;
Smiling, frowning, evermore,
Thou art perfect in love-lore,
　　Ever varying Madeline.

III.

A subtle, sudden flame,
　　By veering passion fann'd,
　　　About thee breaks and dances :
When I would kiss thy hand,
The flush of anger'd shame
　　O'erflows thy calmer glances,
And o'er black brows drops down
A sudden-curved frown :
But when I turn away,
Thou, willing me to stay,
　　Wooest not, nor vainly wranglest ;
　　But, looking fixedly the while,
　　All my bounding heart entanglest
　　In a golden-netted smile ;
Then in madness and in bliss,
If my lips should dare to kiss
Thy taper fingers amorously,
Again thou blushest angerly ;
And o'er black brows drops down
A sudden-curved frown.

SONG : THE OWL.

I.

WHEN cats run home and light is come,
　　And dew is cold upon the ground,
　　And the far-off stream is dumb,

And the whirring sail goes round,
And the whirring sail goes round ;
    Alone and warming his five wits,
    The white owl in the belfry sits.

II.

When merry milkmaids click the latch,
    And rarely smells the new-mown
        hay,
And the cock hath sung beneath the
        thatch
    Twice or thrice his roundelay,
    Twice or thrice his roundelay ;
        Alone and warming his five wits,
        The white owl in the belfry sits.

SECOND SONG.
TO THE SAME.
I.

Thy tuwhits are lull'd, I wot,
    Thy tuwhoos of yesternight,
Which upon the dark afloat,
    So took echo with delight,
    So took echo with delight,
        That her voice untuneful grown,
        Wears all day a fainter tone.

II.

I would mock thy chant anew ;
    But I cannot mimic it ;
Not a whit of thy tuwhoo,
    Thee to woo to thy tuwhit,
    Thee to woo to thy tuwhit,
        With a lengthen'd loud halloo,
        Tuwhoo, tuwhit, tuwhit, tuwhoo-
            o-o.

RECOLLECTIONS OF THE
ARABIAN NIGHTS.

When the breeze of a joyful dawn
        blew free
In the silken sail of infancy,
The tide of time flow'd back with me,
    The forward-flowing tide of time ;
And many a sheeny summer-morn,
Adown the Tigris I was borne,
By Bagdat's shrines of fretted gold,
High-walled gardens green and old ;
True Mussulman was I and sworn,

For it was in the golden prime
    Of good Haroun Alraschid.

Anight my shallop, rustling thro'
The low and bloomed foliage, drove
The fragrant, glistening deeps, and
        clove
The citron-shadows in the blue :
By garden porches on the brim,
The costly doors flung open wide,
Gold glittering thro' lamplight dim,
And broider'd sofas on each side :
    In sooth it was a goodly time,
    For it was in the golden prime
        Of good Haroun Alraschid.

Often, where clear-stemm'd platans
        guard
The outlet, did I turn away
The boat-head down a broad canal
From the main river sluiced, where all
The sloping of the moon-lit sward
Was damask-work, and deep inlay
Of braided blooms unmown, which
        crept
Adown to where the water slept.
    A goodly place, a goodly time,
    For it was in the golden prime
        Of good Haroun Alraschid.

A motion from the river won
Ridged the smooth level, bearing on
My shallop thro' the star-strown calm,
Until another night in night
I enter'd, from the clearer light,
Imbower'd vaults of pillar'd palm,
Imprisoning sweets, which, as they
        clomb
Heavenward, were stay'd beneath the
        dome
    Of hollow boughs. — A goodly time,
    For it was in the golden prime
        Of good Haroun Alraschid.

Still onward ; and the clear canal
Is rounded to as clear a lake.
From the green rivage many a fall
Of diamond rillets musical,
Thro' little crystal arches low
Down from the central fountain's flow
Fall'n silver-chiming, seemed to shake
The sparkling flints beneath the prow.

A goodly place, a goodly time,
For it was in the golden prime
   Of good Haroun Alraschid.

Above thro' many a bowery turn
A walk with vary-color'd shells
Wander'd engrain'd.   On either side
All round about the fragrant marge
From fluted vase, and brazen urn
In order, eastern flowers large,
Some dropping low their crimson bells
Half-closed, and others studded wide
   With disks and tiars, fed the time
   With odor in the golden prime
      Of good Haroun Alraschid.

Far off, and where the lemon grove
In closest coverture upsprung,
The living airs of middle night
Died round the bulbul as he sung;
Not he: but something which possess'd
The darkness of the world, delight,
Life, anguish, death, immortal love,
Ceasing not, mingled, unrepress'd,
   Apart from place, withholding time,
   But flattering the golden prime
      Of good Haroun Alraschid.

Black the garden-bowers and grots
Slumber'd: the solemn palms were
      ranged
Above, unwoo'd of summer wind:
A sudden splendor from behind
Flush'd all the leaves with rich gold-
      green,
And, flowing rapidly between
Their interspaces, counterchanged
The level lake with diamond-plots
   Of dark and bright.   A lovely time,
   For it was in the golden prime
      Of good Haroun Alraschid.

Dark-blue the deep sphere overhead,
Distinct with vivid stars inlaid,
Grew darker from that under-flame.
So, leaping lightly from the boat,
With silver anchor left afloat,
In marvel whence that glory came
Upon me, as in sleep I sank
In cool soft turf upon the bank,
   Entranced with that place and time,
   So worthy of the golden prime
      Of good Haroun Alraschid.

Thence thro' the garden I was drawn—
A realm of pleasance, many a mound,
And many a shadow-checker'd lawn
Full of the city's stilly sound,
And   deep myrrh-thickets blowing
      round
The stately cedar, tamarisks,
Thick rosaries of scented thorn,
Tall orient shrubs, and obelisks
   Graven with emblems of the time,
   In honor of the golden prime
      Of good Haroun Alraschid.

With dazed visions unawares
From the long alley's latticed shade
Emerged, I came upon the great
Pavilion of the Caliphat.
Right to the carven cedarn doors,
Flung inward over spangled floors,
Broad-based flights of marble stairs
Ran up with golden balustrade,
   After the fashion of the time,
   And humor of the golden prime
      Of good Haroun Alraschid.

The fourscore windows all alight
As with the quintessence of flame,
A million tapers flaring bright
From twisted silvers look'd to shame
The hollow-vaulted dark, and stream'd
Upon the mooned domes aloof
In inmost Bagdat, till there seem'd
Hundreds of crescents on the roof
   Of night new-risen, that marvellous
      time
   To celebrate the golden prime
      Of good Haroun Alraschid.

Then stole I up, and trancedly
Gazed on the Persian girl alone,
Serene with argent-lidded eyes
Amorous, and lashes like to rays
Of darkness, and a brow of pearl
Tressed with redolent ebony,
In many a dark delicious curl,
Flowing beneath her rose-hued zone;
   The sweetest lady of the time,
   Well worthy of the golden prime
      Of good Haroun Airaschid.

Six columns, three on either side,
Pure silver, underpropt a rich
Throne of the massive ore, from which

Down-droop'd, in many a floating fold,
Engarlanded and diaper'd
With inwrought flowers, a cloth of
   gold.
Thereon, his deep eye laughter-stirr'd
With merriment of kingly pride,
  Sole star of all that place and time,
  I saw him — in his golden prime,
    THE GOOD HAROUN ALRASCHID.

ODE TO MEMORY.
ADDRESSED TO ——.

I.

  THOU who stealest fire,
From the fountains of the past,
To glorify the present; oh, haste,
  Visit my low desire!
Strengthen me, enlighten me!
I faint in this obscurity,
Thou dewy dawn of memory.

II.

Come not as thou camest of late,
Flinging the gloom of yesternight
On the white day; but robed in soft-
  en'd light
  Of orient state.
Whilom thou camest with the morn-
  ing mist,
  Even as a maid, whose stately brow
The dew-impearled winds of dawn
  have kiss'd.
  When, she, as thou,
Stays on her floating locks the lovely
  freight
Of overflowing blooms, and earliest
  shoots
Of orient green, giving safe pledge of
  fruits,
Which in wintertide shall star
The black earth with brilliance rare.

III.

Whilom thou camest with the morning mist,
  And with the evening cloud,
Showering thy gleaned wealth into my
  open breast
(Those peerless flowers which in the
  rudest wind

    Never grow sear,
When rooted in the garden of the
  mind,
  Because they are the earliest of the
    year).
  Nor was the night thy shroud.
In sweet dreams softer than unbroken
  rest
Thou leddest by the hand thine infant
  Hope.
The eddying of her garments caught
  from thee
The light of thy great presence; and
  the cope
  Of the half-attain'd futurity,
  Tho' deep not fathomless,
Was cloven with the million stars
  which tremble
O'er the deep mind of dauntless in-
  fancy.
Small thought was there of life's dis-
  tress;
For sure she deem'd no mist of earth
  could dull
Those spirit-thrilling eyes so keen and
  beautiful:
Sure she was nigher to heaven's
  spheres,
Listening the lordly music flowing
  from
  The illimitable years.
  O strengthen me, enlighten me!
  I faint in this obscurity,
  Thou dewy dawn of memory.

IV.

Come forth, I charge thee, arise,
Thou of the many tongues, the myriad
  eyes!
Thou comest not with showers of
  flaunting vines
  Unto mine inner eye,
  Divinest Memory!
  Thou wert not nursed by the water-
    fall
Which ever sounds and shines
A pillar of white light upon the wall
Of purple cliffs, aloof descried:
Come from the woods that belt the
  gray hill-side,
The seven elms, the poplars four
That stand beside my father's door,

And chiefly from the brook that loves
To purl o'er matted cress and ribbed
    sand,
Or dimple in the dark of rushy coves,
Drawing into his narrow earthen urn,
    In every elbow and turn,
The filter'd tribute of the rough wood-
    land,
    O! hither lead thy feet!
Pour round mine ears the livelong
    bleat
Of the thick-fleeced sheep from wat-
    tled folds,
    Upon the ridged wolds,
When the first matin-song hath
    waken'd loud
Over the dark dewy earth forlorn,
What time the amber morn
Forth gushes from beneath a low-hung
    cloud.

v.

Large dowries doth the raptured eye
    To the young spirit present
      When first she is wed;
      And like a bride of old
    In triumph led,
      With music and sweet showers
    Of festal flowers,
Unto the dwelling she must sway.
Well hast thou done, great artist
    Memory,
    In setting round thy first experiment
    With royal frame-work of wrought
      gold;
Needs must thou dearly love thy first
    essay,
And foremost in thy various gallery
    Place it, where sweetest sunlight
      falls
    Upon the storied walls;
      For the discovery
And newness of thine art so pleased
    thee,
That all which thou hast drawn of
    fairest
Or boldest since, but lightly weighs
With thee unto the love thou bearest
The first-born of thy genius. Artist-
    like,
Ever retiring thou dost gaze
On the prime labor of thine early days:

No matter what the sketch might be;
Whether the high field on the bush-
    less Pike,
Or even a sand-built ridge
Of heaped hills that mound the sea,
Overblown with murmurs harsh, ·
Or even a lowly cottage whence we see
Stretch'd wide and wild the waste
    enormous marsh,
Where from the frequent bridge,
Like emblems of infinity,
The trenched waters run from sky to
    sky;
Or a garden bower'd close
With plaited alleys of the trailing rose,
Long alleys falling down to twilight
    grots,
Or opening upon level plots
Of crowned lilies, standing near
Purple-spiked lavender:
Whither in after life retired
From brawling storms,
From weary wind,
With youthful fancy re-inspired,
    We may hold converse with all
    forms
Of the many-sided mind,
And those whom passion hath not
    blinded,
Subtle-thoughted, myriad-minded.

My friend, with you to live alone,
Were how much better than to own
A crown, a sceptre, and a throne!

O strengthen me, enlighten me!
I faint in this obscurity,
Thou dewy dawn of memory.

SONG.
I.

A SPIRIT haunts the year's last hours
Dwelling amid these yellowing
    bowers:
    To himself he talks;
For at eventide, listening earnestly,
At his work you may hear him sob and
    sigh
    In the walks;
    Earthward he boweth the heavy
    stalks

Of the mouldering flowers:
  Heavily hangs the broad sunflower
  Over its grave i' the earth so
    chilly;
  Heavily hangs the hollyhock,
    Heavily hangs the tiger-lily.

II.

The air is damp, and hush'd, and close,
As a sick man's room when he taketh
    repose
    An hour before death;
My very heart faints and my whole
    soul grieves
At the moist rich smell of the rotting
    leaves,
    And the breath
    Of the fading edges of box
      beneath,
And the year's last rose.
  Heavily hangs the broad sunflower
  Over its grave i' the earth so
    chilly;
  Heavily hangs the hollyhock,
    Heavily hangs the tiger-lily

A CHARACTER.

WITH a half-glance upon the sky
At night he said, "The wanderings
Of this most intricate Universe
Teach me the nothingness of things."
Yet could not all creation pierce
Beyond the bottom of his eye.

He spake of beauty; that the dull
Saw no divinity in grass,
Life in dead stones, or spirit in air;
Then looking as 'twere in a glass,
He smooth'd his chin and sleek'd his
    hair,
And said the earth was beautiful.

He spake of virtue: not the gods
More purely, when they wish to charm
Pallas and Juno sitting by:
And with a sweeping of the arm,
And a lack-lustre dead-blue eye,
Devolved his rounded periods.

Most delicately hour by hour
He canvass'd human mysteries,
And trod on silk, as if the winds
Blew his own praises in his eyes,
And stood aloof from other minds
In impotence of fancied power.

With lips depress'd as he were meek,
Himself unto himself he sold:
Upon himself himself did feed:
Quiet, dispassionate, and cold,
And other than his form of creed,
With chisell'd features clear and sleek.

THE POET.

THE poet in a golden clime was born,
  With golden stars above;
Dower'd with the hate of hate, the
    scorn of scorn,
  The love of love.

He saw thro' life and death, thro'
    good and ill,
  He saw thro' his own soul,
The marvel of the everlasting will
  An open scroll,

Before him lay: with echoing feet he
    threaded
  The secretest walks of fame:
The viewless arrows of his thoughts
    were headed
  And wing'd with flame,

Like Indian reeds blown from his sil-
    ver tongue,
  And of so fierce a flight,
From Calpe unto Caucasus they sung
  Filling with light

And vagrant melodies the winds which
    bore
  Them earthward till they lit;
Then, like the arrow-seeds of the field
    flower,
  The fruitful wit

Cleaving, took root, and springing
    forth anew
  Where'er they fell, behold,

Like to the mother plant in sem-
    blance, grew
    A flower all gold,

And bravely furnish'd all abroad to
    fling
    Thy winged shafts of truth,
To throng with stately blooms the
    breathing spring
    Of Hope and Youth.

So many minds did gird their orbs
    with beams,
    Tho' one did fling the fire.
Heaven flow'd upon the soul in many
    dreams
    Of high desire.

Thus truth was multiplied on truth,
    the world
    Like one great garden show'd,
And thro' the wreaths of floating dark
    upcurl'd,
    Rare sunrise flow'd.

And Freedom rear'd in that august
    sunrise
    Her beautiful bold brow,
When rites and forms before his burn-
    ing eyes
    Melted like snow.

There was no blood upon her maiden
    robes
    Sunn'd by those orient skies;
But round about the circles of the
    globes
    Of her keen eyes

And in her raiment's hem was traced
    in flame
    WISDOM, a name to shake
All evil dreams of power — a sacred
    name.
    And when she spake,

Her words did gather thunder as they
    ran,
    And as the lightning to the thun-
    der
Which follows it, riving the spirit of
    man,
    Making earth wonder,

So was their meaning to her words.
    No sword
    Of wrath her right arm whirl'd,
But one poor poet's scroll, and with
    his word
    She shook the world.

THE POET'S MIND.

I.

VEX not thou the poet's mind
    With thy shallow wit:
Vex not thou the poet's mind;
    For thou canst not fathom it.
Clear and bright it should be ever,
Flowing like a crystal river;
Bright as light, and clear as wind.

II.

Dark-brow'd sophist, come not anear;
    All the place is holy ground;
    Hollow smile and frozen sneer
        Come not here.
    Holy water will I pour
    Into every spicy flower
Of the laurel-shrubs that hedge it
    around.
The flowers would faint at your cruel
    cheer.
    In your eye there is death,
    There is frost in your breath
    Which would blight the plants.
        Where you stand you cannot hear
        From the groves within
            The wild-bird's din.
In the heart of the garden the merry
    bird chants.
It would fall to the ground if you came
    in.
    In the middle leaps a fountain
        Like sheet lightning,
        Ever brightening
    With a low melodious thunder;
All day and all night it is ever drawn
    From the brain of the purple moun-
    tain
    Which stands in the distance yon-
    der:
It springs on a level of bowery lawn,
And the mountain draws it from
    Heaven above,

And it sings a song of undying love ;
And yet, tho' its voice be so clear and
    full,
You never would hear it; your ears
    are so dull ;
So keep where you are : you are foul
    with sin ;
It would shrink to the earth if you
    came in.

THE SEA-FAIRIES.

Slow sail'd the weary mariners and
    saw,
Betwixt the green brink and the run-
    ning foam,
Sweet faces, rounded arms, and bosoms
    prest
To little harps of gold ; and while they
    mused
Whispering to each other half in fear,
Shrill music reach'd them on the mid-
    dle sea.

Whither away, whither away, whither
    away ? fly no more.
Whither away from the high green
    field, and the happy blossoming
    shore ?
Day and night to the billow the foun-
    tain calls :
Down shower the gambolling water-
    falls
From wandering over the lea :
Out of the live-green heart of the dells
They freshen the silvery-crimson
    shells,
And thick with white bells the clover-
    hill swells
High over the full-toned sea :
O hither, come hither and furl your
    sails,
Come hither to me and to me :
Hither, come hither and frolic and
    play ;
Here it is only the mew that wails ;
We will sing to you all the day :
Mariner, mariner, furl your sails,
For here are the blissful downs and
    dales,
And merrily, merrily carol the gales,

And the spangle dances in bight and
    bay,
And the rainbow forms and flies on
    the land
Over the islands free ;
And the rainbow lives in the curve of
    the sand ;
Hither, come hither and see ;
And the rainbow hangs on the poising
    wave,
And sweet is the color of cove and
    cave,
And sweet shall your welcome be :
O hither, come hither, and be our
    lords,
For merry brides are we :
We will kiss sweet kisses, and speak
    sweet words :
O listen, listen, your eyes shall glisten
With pleasure and love and jubilee :
O listen, listen, your eyes shall glisten
When the sharp clear twang of the
    golden chords
Runs up the ridged sea.
Who can light on as happy a shore
All the world o'er, all the world o'er ?
Whither away ? listen and stay :
    mariner, mariner, fly no more.

THE DESERTED HOUSE.

I.

Life and Thought have gone away
    Side by side,
    Leaving door and windows wide :
Careless tenants they !

II.

    All within is dark as night ·
    In the windows is no light ;
    And no murmur at the door,
    So frequent on its hinge before.

III.

Close the door, the shutters close,
    Or thro' the windows we shall see
    The nakedness and vacancy
Of the dark deserted house.

IV.

Come away : no more of mirth
    Is here or merry-making sound.

"The nakedness and vacancy of the dark, deserted house."

The house was builded of the earth,
  And shall fall again to ground.

v.

Come away: for Life and Thought
  Here no longer dwell;
    But in a city glorious —
A great and distant city — have bought
A mansion incorruptible.
Would they could have staid with us!

THE DYING SWAN.

i.

THE plain was grassy, wild and bare,
Wide, wild, and open to the air,
Which had built up everywhere
  An under-roof of doleful gray.
With an inner voice the river ran,
Adown it floated a dying swan,
  And loudly did lament.
It was the middle of the day.
Ever the weary wind went on,
  And took the reed-tops as it went.

ii.

Some blue peaks in the distance rose,
And white against the cold-white sky,
Shone out their crowning snows.
  One willow over the river wept,
And shook the wave as the wind did
    sigh;
Above in the wind was the swallow,
    Chasing itself at its own wild will,
    And far thro' the marish green
      and still
The tangled water-courses slept,
Shot over with purple, and green, and
    yellow.

iii.

The wild swan's death-hymn took the
    soul
Of that waste place with joy
Hidden in sorrow: at first to the ear
The warble was low, and full and
    clear;
And floating about the under-sky,
Prevailing in weakness, the coronach
    stole

Sometimes afar, and sometimes anear;
But anon her awful jubilant voice,
With a music strange and manifold,
Flow'd forth on a carol free and bold;
As when a mighty people rejoice
With shawms, and with cymbals, and
    harps of gold,
And the tumult of their acclaim is
    roll'd
Thro' the open gates of the city afar,
To the shepherd who watcheth the
    evening star.
And the creeping mosses and clamber-
    ing weeds,
And the willow-branches hoar and
    dank,
And the wavy swell of the soughing
    reeds,
And the wave-worn horns of the echo-
    ing bank,
And the silvery marish-flowers that
    throng
The desolate creeks and pools among,
Were flooded over with eddying song.

A DIRGE.

i.

Now is done thy long day's work;
Fold thy palms across thy breast,
Fold thine arms, turn to thy rest.
    Let them rave.
Shadows of the silver birk
Sweep the green that folds thy grave.
    Let them rave.

ii.

Thee nor carketh care nor slander;
Nothing but the small cold worm
Fretteth thine enshrouded form.
    Let them rave.
Light and shadow ever wander
O'er the green that folds thy grave.
    Let them rave.

iii.

Thou wilt not turn upon thy bed;
Chanteth not the brooding bee
Sweeter tones than calumny?
    Let them rave.

Thou wilt never raise thine head
From the green that folds thy grave.
    Let them rave.

IV.

Crocodiles wept tears for thee;
The woodbine and eglatere
Drip sweeter dews than traitor's tear.
    Let them rave.
Rain makes music in the tree
O'er the green that folds thy grave.
    Let them rave.

V.

Round thee blow, self-pleached deep,
Bramble roses, faint and pale,
And long purples of the dale.
    Let them rave.
These in every shower creep
Thro' the green that folds thy grave.
    Let them rave.

VI.

The gold-eyed kingcups fine;
The frail bluebell peereth over
Rare broidry of the purple clover.
    Let them rave.
Kings have no such couch as thine,
As the green that folds thy grave.
    Let them rave.

VII.

Wild words wander here and there:
God's great gift of speech abused
Makes thy memory confused:
    But let them rave.
The balm-cricket carols clear
In the green that folds thy grave.
    Let them rave.

LOVE AND DEATH.

WHAT time the mighty moon was
    gathering light
Love paced the thymy plots of Para-
    dise,
And all about him roll'd his lustrous
    eyes;
When, turning round a cassia, full in
    view,
Death, walking all alone beneath a
    yew,

And talking to himself, first met his
    sight:
"You must begone," said Death,
    "these walks are mine."
Love wept and spread his sheeny vans
    for flight;
Yet ere he parted said, "This hour is
    thine:
Thou art the shadow of life, and as
    the tree
Stands in the sun and shadows all
    beneath,
So in the light of great eternity
Life eminent creates the shade of
    death;
The shadow passeth when the tree
    shall fall,
But I shall reign forever over all."

THE BALLAD OF ORIANA.

My heart is wasted with my woe,
    Oriana.
There is no rest for me below,
    Oriana.
When the long dun wolds are ribb'd
    with snow,
And loud the Norland whirlwinds
    blow,
    Oriana,
Alone I wander to and fro,
    Oriana.

Ere the light on dark was growing,
    Oriana,
At midnight the cock was crowing,
    Oriana:
Winds were blowing, waters flowing,
We heard the steeds to battle going,
    Oriana;
Aloud the hollow bugle blowing,
    Oriana.

In the yew-wood black as night,
    Oriana,
Ere I rode into the fight,
    Oriana,
While blissful tears blinded my sight
By star-shine and by moonlight,
    Oriana,
I to thee my troth did plight,
    Oriana.

She stood upon the castle wall,
    Oriana:
She watch'd my crest among them all,
    Oriana:
She saw me fight, she heard me call,
When forth there stept a foeman tall,
    Oriana,
  Atween me and the castle wall,
    Oriana.

The bitter arrow went aside,
    Oriana:
The false, false arrow went aside,
    Oriana:
The damned arrow glanced aside,
And pierced thy heart, my love, my
  bride,
    Oriana!
Thy heart, my life, my love, my bride,
    Oriana!

Oh! narrow, narrow was the space,
    Oriana.
Loud, loud rung out the bugle's brays,
    Oriana.
Oh! deathful stabs were dealt apace,
The battle deepen'd in its place,
    Oriana;
But I was down upon my face,
    Oriana.

They should have stabb'd me where I
  lay,
    Oriana!
How could I rise and come away,
    Oriana?
How could I look upon the day?
They should have stabb'd me where I
  lay,
    Oriana—
They should have trod me into clay,
    Oriana.

O breaking heart that will not break,
    Oriana!
O pale, pale face so sweet and meek,
    Oriana!
Thou smilest, but thou dost not speak,
And then the tears run down my cheek,
    Oriana:
What wantest thou? whom dost thou
  seek,
    Oriana?

I cry aloud: none hear my cries,
    Oriana.
Thou comest atween me and the skies,
    Oriana.
I feel the tears of blood arise
Up from my heart unto my eyes,
    Oriana.
Within thy heart my arrow lies,
    Oriana.

O cursed hand! O cursed blow!
    Oriana!
O happy thou that liest low,
    Oriana!
All night the silence seems to flow
Beside me in my utter woe,
    Oriana.
A weary, weary way I go,
    Oriana.

When Norland winds pipe down the
  sea,
    Oriana,
I walk, I dare not think of thee,
    Oriana.
Thou liest beneath the greenwood tree,
I dare not die and come to thee,
    Oriana.
I hear the roaring of the sea,
    Oriana.

CIRCUMSTANCE.

Two children in two neighbor villages
Playing mad pranks along the heathy-
  leas;
Two strangers meeting at a festival;
Two lovers whispering by an orchard
  wall;
Two lives bound fast in one with
  golden ease;
Two graves grass-green beside a gray
  church-tower,
Wash'd with still rains and daisy blos-
  somed;
Two children in one hamlet born and
  bred;
So runs the round of life from hour
  to hour.

THE MERMAN.

I.

Who would be
A merman bold,
Sitting alone,
Singing alone
Under the sea,
With a crown of gold,
On a throne?

II.

I would be a merman bold,
I would sit and sing the whole of the
    day;
I would fill the sea-halls with a voice
    of power;
But at night I would roam abroad and
    play
With the mermaids in and out of the
    rocks,
Dressing their hair with the white sea-
    flower;
And holding them back by their flow-
    ing locks
I would kiss them often under the sea,
And kiss them again till they kiss'd
    me
    Laughingly, laughingly;
And then we would wander away, away
To the pale-green sea-groves straight
    and high,
    Chasing each other merrily.

III.

There would be neither moon nor star;
But the wave would make music above
    us afar —
Low thunder and light in the magic
    night —
    Neither moon nor star.
We would call aloud in the dreamy
    dells,
Call to each other and whoop and cry
    All night, merrily, merrily;
They would pelt me with starry span-
    gles and shells,
Laughing and clapping their hands
    between,
    All night, merrily, merrily:
But I would throw to them back in
    mine

Turkis and agate and almondine:
Then leaping out upon them unseen
I would kiss them often under the sea,
And kiss them again till they kiss'd me
    Laughingly, laughingly.
Oh! what a happy life were mine
Under the hollow-hung ocean green!
Soft are the moss-beds under the sea;
We would live merrily, merrily.

THE MERMAID.

I.

Who would be
A mermaid fair,
Singing alone,
Combing her hair
Under the sea,
In a golden curl
With a comb of pearl,
On a throne?

II.

I would be a mermaid fair;
I would sing to myself the whole of
    the day;
With a comb of pearl I would comb
    my hair;
And still as I comb'd I would sing and
    say,
"Who is it loves me? who loves not
    me?"
I would comb my hair till my ringlets
    would fall
    Low adown, low adown,
From under my starry sea-bud crown
    Low adown and around,
And I should look like a fountain of
    gold
    Springing alone
With a shrill inner sound,
    Over the throne
In the midst of the hall;
Till that great sea-snake under the sea
From his coiled sleeps in the central
    deeps
Would slowly trail himself sevenfold
Round the hall where I sate, and look
    in at the gate
With his large calm eyes for the love
    of me.

And all the mermen under the sea
Would feel their immortality
Die in their hearts for the love of me.

III.

But at night I would wander away,
        away,
    I would fling on each side my low-
        flowing locks,
And lightly vault from the throne and
        play
    With the mermen in and out of the
        rocks;
We would run to and fro, and hide
        and seek,
    On the broad sea-wolds in the crim-
        son shells,
    Whose silvery spikes are nighest the
        sea.
But if any came near I would call, and
        shriek,
And adown the steep like a wave I
        would leap
    From the diamond-ledges that jut
        from the dells;
For I would not be kiss'd by all who
        would list,
Of the bold merry mermen under the
        sea;
They would sue me, and woo me, and
        flatter me,
In the purple twilights under the
        sea;
But the king of them all would carry
        me,
Woo me, and win me, and marry
        me,
In the branching jaspers under the
        sea;
Then all the dry pied things that be
In the hueless mosses under the sea
Would curl round my silver feet
        silently,
All looking up for the love of me.
And if I should carol aloud, from aloft
All things that are forked, and horned,
        and soft
Would lean out from the hollow sphere
        of the sea,
All looking down for the love of
        me.

ADELINE.

I.

MYSTERY of mysteries,
    Faintly smiling Adeline,
    Scarce of earth nor all divine,
Nor unhappy, nor at rest,
    But beyond expression fair
    With thy floating flaxen hair;
Thy rose-lips and full blue eyes
    Take the heart from out my
        breast.
Wherefore those dim looks of thine,
    Shadowy, dreaming Adeline?

II.

Whence that aery bloom of thine,
    Like a lily which the sun
Looks thro' in his sad decline,
    And a rose-bush leans upon,
Thou that faintly smilest still,
    As a Naiad in a well,
    Looking at the set of day,
Or a phantom two hours old
    Of a maiden past away,
Ere the placid lips be cold?
Wherefore those faint smiles of
        thine,
    Spiritual Adeline?

III.

What hope or fear or joy is thine?
Who talketh with thee, Adeline?
    For sure thou art not all alone.
        Do beating hearts of salient
            springs
    Keep measure with thine own?
        Hast thou heard the butterflies
    What they say betwixt their
        wings?
    Or in stillest evenings
With what voice the violet woos
To his heart the silver dews?
    Or when little airs arise,
    How the merry bluebell rings
        To the mosses underneath?
        Hast thou look'd upon the breath
Of the lilies at sunrise?
Wherefore that faint smile of thine,
    Shadowy, dreamy Adeline?

IV.

Some honey-converse feeds thy mind,
  Some spirit of a crimson rose
  In love with thee forgets to close
  His curtains, wasting odorous sighs
All night long on darkness blind.
What aileth thee ? whom waitest thou
With thy soften'd, shadow'd brow,
    And those dew-lit eyes of thine,
    Thou faint smiler, Adeline ?

V.

Lovest thou the doleful wind
    When thou gazest at the skies ?
  Doth the low-tongued Orient
    Wander from the side of the
      morn,
    Dripping with Sabæan spice
  On thy pillow, lowly bent
    With melodious airs lovelorn,
  Breathing Light against thy face,
While his locks a-drooping twined
  Round thy neck in subtle ring
Make a carcanet of rays,
    And ye talk together still,
    In the language wherewith Spring
  Letters cowslips on the hill ?
Hence that look and smile of thine,
    Spiritual Adeline.

MARGARET.

I.

O sweet pale Margaret,
  O rare pale Margaret,
What lit your eyes with tearful power,
Like moonlight on a falling shower ?
Who lent you, love, your mortal dower
    Of pensive thought and aspect
      pale,
  Your melancholy sweet and frail
As perfume of the cuckoo-flower ?
From the westward-winding flood,
From the evening-lighted wood,
    From all things outward you have
      won
A tearful grace, as tho' you stood
    Between the rainbow and the sun.
The very smile before you speak,
  That dimples your transparent
    cheek,

  Encircles all the heart, and feedeth
The senses with a still delight
    Of dainty sorrow without sound,
    Like the tender amber round,
  Which the moon about her spread-
    eth,
Moving thro' a fleecy night.

II.

You love, remaining peacefully,
    To hear the murmur of the strife,
    But enter not the toil of life.
Your spirit is the caimed sea,
    Laid by the tumult of the fight.
You are the evening star, alway
    Remaining betwixt dark and
      bright :
Lull'd echoes of laborious day
    Come to you, gleams of mellow
      light
    Float by you on the verge of
      night.

III.

What can it matter, Margaret,
    What songs below the waning
      stars
The lion-heart, Plantagenet,
    Sang looking thro' his prison
      bars ?
    Exquisite Margaret, who can
      tell
The last wild thought of Chatelet,
    Just ere the falling axe did part
    The burning brain from the true
      heart,
    Even in her sight he loved so
      well ?

IV.

A fairy shield your Genius made
    And gave you on your natal day.
Your sorrow, only sorrow's shade,
    Keeps real sorrow far away.
You move not in such solitudes,
    You are not less divine,
But more human in your moods,
    Than your twin-sister, Adeline.
Your hair is darker, and your eyes
    Touch'd with a somewhat darker
      hue,
    And less aerially blue,

But ever-trembling thro' the dew
Of dainty-woful sympathies.

v.

O sweet pale Margaret,
    O rare pale Margaret,
Come down, come down, and hear me
        speak :
Tie up the ringlets on your cheek :
    The sun is just about to set,
The arching limes are tall and shady,
    And faint, rainy lights are seen,
        Moving in the leavy beech.
Rise from the feast of sorrow, lady,
    Where all day long you sit
        between
        Joy and woe, and whisper each.
Or only look across the lawn,
    Look out below your bower-eaves,
Look down, and let your blue eyes
        dawn
    Upon me thro' the jasmine-leaves.

ROSALIND.

i.

MY Rosalind, my Rosalind,
My frolic falcon, with bright eyes,
Whose free delight, from any height
        of rapid flight,
Stoops at all game that wing the skies,
My Rosalind, my Rosalind,
My bright-eyed, wild-eyed falcon
        whither,
Careless both of wind and weather,
Whither fly ye, what game spy ye,
Up or down the streaming wind ?

ii.

The quick lark's closest-caroll'd
        strains,
The shadow rushing up the sea,
The lightning flash atween the rains,
The sunlight driving down the lea,
The leaping stream, the very wind,
That will not stay, upon his way,
To stoop the cowslip to the plains,
Is not so clear and bold and free
As you, my falcon Rosalind.
You care not for another's pains,

Because you are the soul of joy,
Bright metal all without alloy.
Life shoots and glances thro' your
        veins,
And flashes off a thousand ways,
Thro' lips and eyes in subtle rays.
Your hawk-eyes are keen and bright,
Keen with triumph, watching still
To pierce me thro' with pointed light;
But oftentimes they flash and glitter
Like sunshine on a dancing rill,
And your words are seeming-bitter,
Sharp and few, but seeming-bitter
From excess of swift delight.

iii.

Come down, come home, my Rosalind,
My gay young hawk, my Rosalind :
Too long you keep the upper skies ;
Too long you roam and wheel at will;
But we must hood your random eyes,
That care not whom they kill,
And your cheek, whose brilliant hue
Is so sparkling-fresh to view,
Some red heath-flower in the dew,
Touch'd with sunrise. We must bind
And keep you fast, my Rosalind,
Fast, fast, my wild-eyed Rosalind,
And clip your wings, and make you
        love :
When we have lured you from above,
And that delight of frolic flight, by
        day or night,
From North to South,
We'll bind you fast in silken cords
And kiss away the bitter words
From off your rosy mouth.

ELEÄNORE.

i.

THY dark eyes open'd not,
    Nor first reveal'd themselves to
        English air,
    For there is nothing here,
Which, from the outward to the inward
        brought,
Moulded thy baby thought.
Far off from human neighborhood,
    Thou wert born, on a summer
        morn,

A mile beneath the cedar-wood.
Thy bounteous forehead was not
        fann'd
        With breezes from our oaken
            glades,
But thou wert nursed in some delicious
        land
        Of lavish lights, and floating
            shades:
And flattering thy childish thought
        The oriental fairy brought,
            At the moment of thy birth,
From old well-heads of haunted rills,
And the hearts of purple hills,
        And shadow'd coves on a sunny
            shore,
            The choicest wealth of all the
                earth,
        Jewel or shell, or starry ore,
        To deck thy cradle, Eleänore.

II.

Or the yellow-banded bees,
Thro' half-open lattices
Coming in the scented breeze,
        Fed thee, a child, lying alone,
            With whitest honey in fairy gar-
                dens cull'd —
        A glorious child, dreaming alone,
        In silk-soft folds, upon yielding
                down,
With the hum of swarming bees
        Into dreamful slumber lull'd.

III.

Who may minister to thee?
Summer herself should minister
        To thee, with fruitage golden-rinded
        On golden salvers, or it may be,
Youngest Autumn, in a bower
Grape-thicken'd from the light, and
        blinded
        With many a deep-hued bell-like
            flower
Of fragrant trailers, when the air
        Sleepeth over all the heaven,
        And the crag that fronts the Even,
        All along the shadowing shore,
Crimsons over an inland mere,
            Eleänore!

IV.

How many full-sail'd verse express,
        How many measured words adore
            The full-flowing harmony
Of thy swan-like stateliness,
            Eleänore?
        The luxuriant symmetry
Of thy floating gracefulness,
            Eleänore?
        Every turn and glance of thine,
        Every lineament divine,
            Eleänore,
        And the steady sunset glow,
        That stays upon thee? For in thee
        Is nothing sudden, nothing single;
Like two streams of incense free
        From one censer in one shrine,
        Thought and motion mingle,
        Mingle ever. Motions flow
        To one another, even as tho'
        They were modulated so
            To an unheard melody,
        Which lives about thee, and a sweep
        Of richest pauses, evermore
Drawn from each other mellow-deep;
        Who may express thee, Eleänore?

V.

I stand before thee, Eleänore;
        I see thy beauty gradually unfold,
Daily and hourly, more and more.
I muse, as in a trance, the while
        Slowly, as from a cloud of gold,
Comes out thy deep ambrosial smile.
I muse, as in a trance, whene'er
        The languors of thy love-deep eyes
Float on to me. I would I were
        So tranced, so rapt in ecstasies,
To stand apart, and to adore,
Gazing on thee forevermore,
Serene, imperial Eleänore!

VI.

Sometimes, with most intensity
Gazing, I seem to see
Thought folded over thought, smiling
        asleep,
Slowly awaken'd, grow so full and deep
In thy large eyes, that, overpower'd
        quite,

I cannot veil, or droop my sight,
But am as nothing in its light:
As tho' a star, in inmost heaven set,
Ev'n while we gaze on it,
Should slowly round his orb, and
    slowly grow
To a full face, there like a sun remain
Fix'd — then as slowly fade again,
    And draw itself to what it was
        before;
    So full, so deep, so slow,
    Thought seems to come and go
In thy large eyes, imperial Eleänore.

VII.

As thunder-clouds that, hung on high,
    Roof'd the world with doubt and
        fear,
Floating thro' an evening atmosphere,
Grow golden all about the sky;
In thee all passion becomes passion-
    less,
Touch'd by thy spirit's mellowness,
    Losing his fire and active might
    In a silent meditation,
Falling into a still delight,
    And luxury of contemplation:
As waves that up a quiet cove
    Rolling slide, and lying still
        Shadow forth the banks at will:
Or sometimes they swell and move,
    Pressing up against the land,
    With motions of the outer sea:
        And the self-same influence
        Controlleth all the soul and sense
Of Passion gazing upon thee.
His bow-string slacken'd, languid Love,
    Leaning his cheek upon his hand,
    Droops both his wings, regarding
        thee,
        And so would languish evermore,
        Serene, imperial Eleänore.

VIII.

But when I see thee roam, with tresses
    unconfined,
While the amorous, odorous wind
    Breathes low between the sunset
        and the moon;
    Or, in a shadowy saloon,
On silken cushions half reclined;

I watch thy grace; and in its
    place
My heart a charm'd slumber
    keeps,
    While I muse upon thy face;
And a languid fire creeps
    Thro' my veins to all my frame,
Dissolvingly and slowly: soon
    From thy rose-red lips MY name
Floweth; and then, as in a swoon,
    With dinning sound my ears are
        rife,
    My tremulous tongue faltereth,
I lose my color, I lose my breath,
I drink the cup of a costly death,
Brimm'd with delirious draughts of
    warmest life.
    I die with my delight, before
        I hear what I would hear from
            thee;
        Yet tell my name again to me,
    I *would* be dying evermore,
    So dying ever, Eleänore.

————

I.

My life is full of weary days,
    But good things have not kept aloof,
    Nor wander'd into other ways:
    I have not lack'd thy mild reproof,
Nor golden largess of thy praise.

And now shake hands across the brink
    Of that deep grave to which I go:
Shake hands once more: I cannot sink
    So far — far down, but I shall know
    Thy voice, and answer from below.

II.

When in the darkness over me
    The four-handed mole shall scrape,
Plant thou no dusky cypress-tree,
    Nor wreathe thy cap with doleful
        crape,
    But pledge me in the flowing grape.

And when the sappy field and wood
    Grow green beneath the showery
        gray,
And rugged barks begin to bud,

And thro' damp holts new-flush'd
    with may,
Ring sudden scritches of the jay,

Then let wise Nature work her will,
    And on my clay her darnel grow;
Come only, when the days are still,
    And at my headstone whisper low,
    And tell me if the woodbines blow.

EARLY SONNETS.

I.

TO ——.

As when with downcast eyes we muse
    and brood,
And ebb into a former life, or seem
To lapse far back in some confused
    dream
To states of mystical similitude;
If one but speaks or hems or stirs his
    chair,
Ever the wonder waxeth more and
    more,
So that we say, "All this hath been
    before,
All this hath been, I know not when
    or where."
So, friend, when first I look'd upon
    your face,
Our thought gave answer each to each,
    so true —
Opposed mirrors each reflecting each—
That tho' I knew not in what time or
    place,
Methought that I had often met with
    you,
And either lived in either's heart and
    speech.

II.

TO J. M. K.

My hope and heart is with thee — thou
    wilt be
A latter Luther, and a soldier-priest
To scare church-harpies from the
    master's feast;
Our dusted velvets have much need
    of thee :
Thou art no sabbath-drawler of old
    saws,

Distill'd from some worm-canker'd
    homily ;
But spurr'd at heart with fieriest energy
To embattail and to wall about thy
    cause
With iron-worded proof, hating to hark
The humming of the drowsy pulpit-
    drone
Half God's good sabbath, while the
    worn-out clerk
Brow-beats his desk below.   Thou
    from a throne
Mounted in heaven wilt shoot into the
    dark
Arrows of lightnings.   I will stand and
    mark.

III.

MINE be the strength of spirit, full
    and free,
Like some broad river rushing down
    alone,
With the self-same impulse wherewith
    he was thrown
From his loud fount upon the echoing
    lea : —
Which with increasing might doth for-
    ward flee
By town, and tower, and hill, and cape,
    and isle,
And in the middle of the green salt sea
Keeps his blue waters fresh for many
    a mile.
Mine be the power which ever to its
    sway
Will win the wise at once, and by
    degrees
May into uncongenial spirits flow ;
Ev'n as the warm gulf-stream of
    Florida
Floats far away into the Northern seas
The lavish growths of southern Mex-
    ico.

IV.

ALEXANDER.

WARRIOR of God, whose strong right
    arm debased
The throne of Persia, when her Satrap
    bled
At Issus by the Syrian gates, or fled
Beyond the Memmian naphtha-pits,
    disgraced

Forever — thee (thy pathway sand-
    erased)
Gliding with equal crowns two ser-
    pents led
Joyful to that palm-planted fountain-
    fed
Ammonian Oasis in the waste.
There in a silent shade of laurel brown
Apart the Chamian Oracle divine
Shelter'd his unapproached mysteries :
High things were spoken there, un-
    handed down ;
Only they saw thee from the secret
    shrine
Returning with hot cheek and kindled
    eyes.

v.
BUONAPARTE.

HE thought to quell the stubborn
    hearts of oak,
Madman! — to chain with chains, and
    bind with bands
That island queen who sways the floods
    and lands,
From Ind to Ind, but in fair daylight
    woke,
When from her wooden walls, — lit by
    sure hands, —
With thunders, and with lightnings,
    and with smoke, —
Peal after peal, the British battle
    broke,
Lulling the brine against the Coptic
    sands.
We taught him lowlier moods, when
    Elsinore
Heard the war moan along the distant
    sea,
Rocking with shatter'd spars, with
    sudden fires
Flamed over : at Trafalgar yet once
    more
We taught him : late he learned
    humility
Perforce, like those whom Gideon
    school'd with briers.

vi.
POLAND.

How long, O God, shall men be ridden
    down,

And trampled under by the last and
    least
Of men ?   The heart of Poland hath
    not ceased
To quiver, tho' her sacred blood doth
    drown
The fields, and out of every smoulder-
    ing town
Cries to Thee, lest brute Power be in-
    creased,
Till that o'ergrown Barbarian in the
    East
Transgress his ample bound to some
    new crown : —
Cries to Thee, " Lord, how long shall
    these things be ?
How long this icy-hearted Muscovite
Oppress the region ? "   Us, O Just and
    Good,
Forgive, who smiled when she was torn
    in three ;
Us, who stand now, when we should
    aid the right —
A matter to be wept with tears of
    blood !

vii.

CARESS'D or chidden by the slender
    hand,
And singing airy trifles this or that,
Light Hope at Beauty's call would
    perch and stand,
And run thro' every change of sharp
    and flat ;
And Fancy came and at her pillow sat,
When Sleep had bound her in his rosy
    band,
And chased away the still-recurring
    gnat,
And woke her with a lay from fairy
    land.
But now they live with Beauty less
    and less,
For Hope is other Hope and wanders
    far,
Nor cares to lisp in love's delicious
    creeds ;
And Fancy watches in the wilderness,
Poor Fancy sadder than a single
    star,
That sets at twilight in a land of
    reeds.

VIII.

THE form, the form alone is eloquent!
A nobler yearning never broke her
rest
Than but to dance and sing, be gayly
drest,
And win all eyes with all accomplish-
ment:
Yet in the whirling dances as we went,
My fancy made me for a moment blest
To find my heart so near the beauteous
breast
That once had power to rob it of con-
tent.
A moment came the tenderness of
tears,
The phantom of a wish that once could
move,
A ghost of passion that no smiles re-
store —
For ah! the slight coquette, she can-
not love,
And if you kiss'd her feet a thousand
years,
She still would take the praise, and
care no more.

IX.

WAN Sculptor, weepest thou to take
the cast
Of those dead lineaments that near
thee lie?
O sorrowest thou, pale Painter, for the
past,
In painting some dead friend from
memory?
Weep on: beyond his object Love can
last:
His object lives: more cause to weep
have I:
My tears, no tears of love, are flowing
fast,
No tears of love, but tears that Love
can die.
I pledge her not in any cheerful cup,
Nor care to sit beside her where she
sits —
Ah pity — hint it not in human tones,
But breathe it into earth and close it
up

With secret death forever, in the pits
Which some green Christmas crams
with weary bones.

X.

IF I were loved, as I desire to be,
What is there in the great sphere of
the earth,
And range of evil between death and
birth,
That I should fear, — if I were loved
by thee?
All the inner, all the outer world of
pain
Clear Love would pierce and cleave,
if thou wert mine,
As I have heard that, somewhere in
the main,
Fresh-water springs come up through
bitter brine.
'Twere joy, not fear, claspt hand-in-
hand with thee,
To wait for death — mute — careless
of all ills,
Apart upon a mountain, tho' the surge
Of some new deluge from a thousand
hills
Flung leagues of roaring foam into
the gorge
Below us, as far on as eye could see.

XI.

THE BRIDESMAID.

O BRIDESMAID, ere the happy knot
was tied,
Thine eyes so wept that they could
hardly see;
Thy sister smiled and said, "No tears
for me!
A happy bridesmaid makes a happy
bride."
And then, the couple standing side by
side,
Love lighted down between them full
of glee,
And over his left shoulder laugh'd at
thee,
"O happy bridesmaid, make a happy
bride."
And all at once a pleasant truth I
learn'd,

For while the tender service made thee
    weep,
I loved thee for the tear thou couldst
    not hide,
And prest thy hand, and knew the
    press return'd,
And thought, " My life is sick of sin-
    gle sleep :
O happy bridesmaid, make a happy
    bride ! "

———

THE LADY OF SHALOTT.

PART I.

On either side of the river lie
Long fields of barley and of rye,
That clothe the wold and meet the sky ;
And thro' the field the road runs by
    To many-tower'd Camelot ;
And up and down the people go,
Gazing where the lilies blow
Round an island there below
    The island of Shalott.

Willows whiten, aspens quiver,
Little breezes dusk and shiver
Thro' the wave that runs forever
By the island in the river
    Flowing down to Camelot.
Four gray walls, and four gray towers,
Overlook a space of flowers,
And the silent isle embowers
    The Lady of Shalott.

By the margin, willow-veil'd,
Slide the heavy barges trail'd.
By slow horses ; and unhail'd
The shallop flitteth silken-sail'd
    Skimming down to Camelot :
But who hath seen her wave her hand?
Or at the casement seen her stand ?
Or is she known in all the land,
    The Lady of Shalott?

Only reapers, reaping early
In among the bearded barley,
Hear a song that echoes cheerly
From the river winding clearly,
    Down to tower'd Camelot :
And by the moon the reaper weary,

Piling sheaves in uplands airy,
Listening, whispers " 'Tis the fairy
    Lady of Shalott."

PART II.

There she weaves by night and day
A magic web with colors gay.
She has heard a whisper say,
A curse is on her if she stay
    To look down to Camelot.
She knows not what the curse may be
And so she weaveth steadily,
And little other care hath she,
    The Lady of Shalott.

And moving thro' a mirror clear
That hangs before her all the year,
Shadows of the world appear.
There she sees the highway near
    Winding down to Camelot :
There the river eddy whirls,
And there the surly village-churls,
And the red cloaks of market girls,
    Pass onward from Shalott.

Sometimes a troop of damsels glad,
An abbot on an ambling pad,
Sometimes a curly shepherd-lad,
Or long-hair'd page in crimson clad,
    Goes by to tower'd Camelot ;
And sometimes thro' the mirror blue
The knights come riding two and two :
She hath no loyal knight and true,
    The Lady of Shalott.

But in her web she still delights
To weave the mirror's magic sights,
For often thro' the silent nights
A funeral, with plumes and lights
    And music, went to Camelot :
Or when the moon was overhead,
Came two young lovers lately wed ;
" I am half sick of shadows," said
    The Lady of Shalott.

PART III.

A bow-shot from her bower-eaves,
He rode between the barley-sheaves,
The sun came dazzling thro' the leaves
And flamed upon the brazen greaves
    Of bold Sir Lancelot.

A red-cross knight forever kneel'd
To a lady in his shield,
That sparkled on the yellow field,
    Beside remote Shalott.

The gemmy bridle glitter'd free,
Like to some branch of stars we see
Hung in the golden Galaxy.
The bridle bells rang merrily
    As he rode down to Camelot:
And from his blazon'd baldric slung
A mighty silver bugle hung,
And as he rode his armor rung,
    Beside remote Shalott.

All in the blue unclouded weather
Thick-jewell'd shone the saddle-
    leather,
The helmet and the helmet-feather
Burn'd like one burning flame together,
    As he rode down to Camelot.
As often thro' the purple night,
Below the starry clusters bright,
Some bearded meteor, trailing light,
    Moves over still Shalott.

His broad clear brow in sunlight
    glow'd;
On burnish'd hooves his war-horse
    trode;
From underneath his helmet flow'd
His coal-black curls as on he rode,
    As he rode down to Camelot.
From the bank and from the river
He flash'd into the crystal mirror,
"Tirra lirra," by the river
    Sang Sir Lancelot.

She left the web, she left the loom,
She made three paces thro' the room,
She saw the water-lily bloom,
She saw the helmet and the plume,
    She look'd down to Camelot.
Out flew the web and floated wide;
The mirror crack'd from side to side;
"The curse is come upon me," cried
    The Lady of Shalott.

PART IV.

In the stormy east-wind straining,
The pale yellow woods were waning,

The broad stream in his banks com-
    plaining,
Heavily the low sky raining,
    Over tower'd Camelot;
Down she came and found a boat
Beneath a willow left afloat,
And round about the prow she wrote
    The Lady of Shalott.

And down the river's dim expanse
Like some bold seer in a trance,
Seeing all his own mischance —
With a glassy countenance
    Did she look to Camelot.
And at the closing of the day
She loosed the chain, and down she lay;
The broad stream bore her far away,
    The Lady of Shalott.

Lying, robed in snowy white,
That loosely flew to left and right —
The leaves upon her falling light —
Thro' the noises of the night
    She floated down to Camelot:
And as the boat-head wound along
The willowy hills and fields among,
They heard her singing her last song,
    The Lady of Shalott.

Heard a carol, mournful, holy,
Chanted loudly, chanted lowly,
Till her blood was frozen slowly,
And her eyes were darken'd wholly,
    Turn'd to tower'd Camelot.
For ere she reach'd upon the tide
The first house by the water-side,
Singing in her song she died,
    The Lady of Shalott.

Under tower and balcony,
By garden-wall and gallery,
A gleaming shape she floated by,
Dead-pale between the houses high,
    Silent into Camelot.
Out upon the wharfs they came,
Knight and burgher, lord and dame,
And round the prow they read her
    name,
    The Lady of Shalott.

Who is this? and what is here?
And in the lighted palace near

Died the sound of royal cheer;
And they cross'd themselves for fear,
   All the knights at Camelot:
But Lancelot mused a little space;
He said, "She has a lovely face;
God in his mercy lend her grace,
   The Lady of Shalott."

THE TWO VOICES.

A STILL small voice spake unto me,
"Thou art so full of misery,
Were it not better not to be?"

Then to the still small voice I said;
"Let me not cast in endless shade
What is so wonderfully made."

To which the voice did urge reply;
"To-day I saw the dragon-fly
Come from the wells where he did lie.

"An inner impulse rent the veil
Of his old husk: from head to tail
Came out clear plates of sapphire mail.

"He dried his wings: like gauze they
   grew;
Thro' crofts and pastures wet with dew
A living flash of light he flew."

I said, "When first the world began,
Young Nature thro' five cycles ran,
And in the sixth she moulded man.

"She gave him mind, the lordliest
Proportion, and, above the rest,
Dominion in the head and breast."

Thereto the silent voice replied;
"Self-blinded are you by your pride:
Look up thro' night: the world is wide.

"This truth within thy mind rehearse,
That in a boundless universe
Is boundless better, boundless worse.

"Think you this mould of hopes and
   fears
Could find no statelier than his peers
In yonder hundred million spheres?"

It spake, moreover, in my mind:
"Tho' thou wert scatter'd to the wind,
Yet is there plenty of the kind."

Then did my response clearer fall:
"No compound of this earthly ball
Is like another, all in all."

To which he answer'd scoffingly;
"Good soul! suppose I grant it thee,
Who'll weep for thy deficiency?

"Or will one beam be less intense,
When thy peculiar difference
Is cancell'd in the world of sense?"

I would have said, "Thou canst not
   know,"
But my full heart, that work'd below,
Rain'd thro' my sight its overflow.

Again the voice spake unto me:
"Thou art so steep'd in misery,
Surely 'twere better not to be.

"Thine anguish will not let thee sleep,
Nor any train of reason keep:
Thou canst not think, but thou wilt
   weep."

I said, "The years with change ad-
   vance:
If I make dark my countenance,
I shut my life from happier chance.

"Some turn this sickness yet might
   take,
Ev'n yet." But he: "What drug can
   make
A wither'd palsy cease to shake?"

I wept, "Tho' I should die, I know
That all about the thorn will blow
In tufts of rosy-tinted snow;

"And men, thro' novel spheres of
   thought
Still moving after truth long sought,
Will learn new things when I am not."

"Yet," said the secret voice, "some
    time,
Sooner or later, will gray prime
Make thy grass hoar with early rime.

"Not less swift souls that yearn for
    light,
Rapt after heaven's starry flight,
Would sweep the tracts of day and
    night.

"Not less the bee would range her cells,
The furzy prickle fire the dells,
The foxglove cluster dappled bells."

I said that "all the years invent;
Each month is various to present
The world with some development.

"Were this not well, to bide mine hour,
Tho' watching from a ruin'd tower
How grows the day of human power?"

"The highest-mounted mind," he said,
"Still sees the sacred morning spread
The silent summit overhead.

"Will thirty seasons render plain
Those lonely lights that still remain,
Just breaking over land and main?

"Or make that morn, from his cold
    crown
And crystal silence creeping down,
Flood with full daylight glebe and
    town?

"Forerun thy peers, thy time, and let
Thy feet, millenniums hence, be set
In midst of knowledge, dream'd not yet.

"Thou hast not gain'd a real height,
Nor art thou nearer to the light,
Because the scale is infinite.

"'Twere better not to breathe or speak,
Than cry for strength, remaining weak,
And seem to find, but still to seek.

"Moreover, but to seem to find
Asks what thou lackest, thought re-
    sign'd,
A healthy frame, a quiet mind."

I said, "When I am gone away,
'He dared not tarry,' men will say,
Doing dishonor to my clay."

"This is more vile," he made reply,
"To breathe and loathe, to live and
    sigh,
Than once from dread of pain to die.

"Sick art thou — a divided will
Still heaping on the fear of ill
The fear of men, a coward still.

"Do men love thee? Art thou so
    bound
To men, that how thy name may sound
Will vex thee lying underground?

"The memory of the wither'd leaf
In endless time is scarce more brief
Than of the garner'd Autumn-sheaf.

"Go, vexed Spirit, sleep in trust;
The right ear, that is fill'd with dust,
Hears little of the false or just."

"Hard task, to pluck resolve," I cried,
"From emptiness and the waste wide
Of that abyss, or scornful pride!

"Nay — rather yet that I could raise
One hope that warm'd me in the days
While still I yearn'd for human praise.

"When, wide in soul and bold of
    tongue,
Among the tents I paused and sung,
The distant battle flash'd and rung.

"I sung the joyful Pæan clear,
And, sitting, burnish'd without fear
The brand, the buckler, and the spear—

"Waiting to strive a happy strife,
To war with falsehood to the knife,
And not to lose the good of life —

"Some hidden principle to move,
To put together, part and prove,
And mete the bounds of hate and
    love —

" As far as might be, to carve out
Free space for every human doubt,
That the whole mind might orb
    about —

" To search through all I felt or saw,
The springs of life, the depths of awe,
And reach the law within the law :

" At least, not rotting like a weed,
But, having sown some generous seed,
Fruitful of further thought and deed,

" To pass when Life her light with-
    draws,
Not void of righteous self-applause,
Nor in a merely selfish cause —

" In some good cause, not in mine own
To perish, wept for, honor'd, known,
And like a warrior overthrown ;

" Whose eyes are dim with glorious
    tears,
When soil'd with noble dust, he hears
His country's war-song thrill his ears :

" Then dying of a mortal stroke,
What time the foeman's line is broke,
And all the war is rolled in smoke."

" Yea ! " said the voice, " thy dream
    was good,
While thou abodest in the bud.
It was the stirring of the blood.

" If Nature put not forth her power
About the opening of the flower,
Who is it that could live an hour ?

" Then comes the check, the change,
    the fall,
Pain rises up, old pleasures pall.
There is one remedy for all.

" Yet hadst thou, thro' enduring pain,
Link'd month to month with such a
    chain
Of knitted purport, all were vain.

" Thou hadst not between death and
    birth
Dissolved the riddle of the earth.
So were thy labor little-worth.

" That men with knowledge merely
    play'd,
I told thee — hardly nigher made,
Tho' scaling slow from grade to grade ;

" Much less this dreamer, deaf and
    blind,
Named man, may hope some truth to
    find,
That bears relation to the mind.

" For every worm beneath the moon
Draws different threads, and late and
    soon
Spins, toiling out his own cocoon.

" Cry, faint not : either Truth is born
Beyond the polar gleam forlorn,
Or in the gateways of the morn.

" Cry, faint not, climb : the summits
    slope
Beyond the furthest flights of hope,
Wrapt in dense cloud from base to
    cope.

" Sometimes a little corner shines,
As over rainy mist inclines
A gleaming crag with belts of pines.

" I will go forward, sayest thou,
I shall not fail to find her now.
Look up, the fold is on her brow.

" If straight thy track, or if oblique,
Thou know'st not. Shadows thou
    dost strike,
Embracing cloud, Ixion-like ;

" And owning but a little more
Than beasts, abidest lame and poor,
Calling thyself a little lower

" Than angels. Cease to wail and
    brawl !
Why inch by inch to darkness crawl ?
There is one remedy for all."

" O dull, one-sided voice," said I,
" Wilt thou make every thing a lie,
To flatter me that I may die ?

" I know that age to age succeeds,
Blowing a noise of tongues and deeds,
A dust of systems and of creeds.

"I cannot hide that some have striven,
Achieving calm, to whom was given
The joy that mixes man with Heaven:

"Who, rowing hard against the stream,
Saw distant gates of Eden gleam,
And did not dream it was a dream;

"But heard, by secret transport led,
Ev'n in the charnels of the dead,
The murmur of the fountain-head —

"Which did accomplish their desire,
Bore and forebore, and did not tire,
Like Stephen, an unquenched fire.

"He heeded not reviling tones,
Nor sold his heart to idle moans,
Tho' cursed and scorn'd, and bruised
    with stones:

"But looking upward, full of grace,
He pray'd, and from a happy place
God's glory smote him on the face."

The sullen answer slid betwixt:
"Not that the grounds of hope were
    fix'd,
The elements were kindlier mix'd."

I said, " I toil beneath the curse,
But, knowing not the universe,
I fear to slide from bad to worse.

" And that, in seeking to undo,
One riddle, and to find the true,
I knit a hundred others new:

" Or that this anguish fleeting hence,
Unmanacled from bonds of sense,
Be fix'd and froz'n to permanence:

" For I go, weak from suffering here:
Naked I go, and void of cheer:
What is it that I may not fear?"

"Consider well," the voice replied,
"His face, that two hours since hath
    died;
Wilt thou find passion, pain or pride?

"Will he obey when one commands?
Or answer should one press his hands?
He answers not, nor understands.

"His palms are folded on his breast:
There is no other thing express'd
But long disquiet merged in rest.

"His lips are very mild and meek:
Tho' one should smite him on the
    cheek,
And on the mouth, he will not speak.

"His little daughter, whose sweet face
He kiss'd, taking his last embrace,
Becomes dishonor to her race —

"His sons grow up that bear his name,
Some grow to honor, some to shame, —
But he is chill to praise or blame.

"He will not hear the north-wind rave,
Nor, moaning, household shelter crave
From winter rains that beat his grave.

"High up the vapors fold and swim:
About him broods the twilight dim:
The place he knew forgetteth him."

"If all be dark, vague voice," I said,
"These things are wrapt in doubt and
    dread,
Nor canst thou show the dead are dead.

"The sap dries up: the plant declines.
A deeper tale my heart divines.
Know I not Death? the outward signs?

"I found him when my years were few;
A shadow on the graves I knew,
And darkness in the village yew.

"From grave to grave the shadow
    crept:
In her still place the morning wept:
Touch'd by his feet the daisy slept.

" The simple senses crown'd his head:
' Omega! thou art Lord,' they said,
' We find no motion in the dead.'

" Why, if man rot in dreamless ease,
Should that plain fact, as taught by
    these,
Not make him sure that he shall cease ?

" Who forged that other influence,
That heat of inward evidence,
By which he doubts against the sense ?

" He owns the fatal gift of eyes,
That read his spirit blindly wise,
Not simple as a thing that dies.

" Here sits he shaping wings to fly :
His heart forebodes a mystery :
He names the name Eternity.

" That type of Perfect in his mind
In Nature can he nowhere find.
He sows himself on every wind.

" He seems to hear a Heavenly Friend,
And thro' thick veils to apprehend
A labor working to an end.

" The end and the beginning vex
His reason : many things perplex,
With motions, checks, and counter-
    checks.

" He knows a baseness in his blood
At such strange war with something
    good,
He may not do the thing he would.

" Heaven opens inward, chasms yawn,
Vast images in glimmering dawn,
Half shown, are broken and with-
    drawn.

" Ah ! sure within him and without,
Could his dark wisdom find it out,
There must be answer to his doubt.

" But thou canst answer not again.
With thine own weapon art thou slain,
Or thou wilt answer but in vain.

" The doubt would rest, I dare not
    solve.
In the same circle we revolve.
Assurance only breeds resolve."

As when a billow, blown against,
Falls back, the voice with which I
    fenced
A little ceased, but recommenced.

" Where wert thou when thy father
    play'd
In his free field, and pastime made,
A merry boy in sun and shade ?

" A merry boy they call'd him then.
He sat upon the knees of men
In days that never come again.

" Before the little ducts began
To feed thy bones with lime, and ran
Their course, till thou wert also man :

" Who took a wife, who rear'd his race,
Whose wrinkles gather'd on his face,
Whose troubles number with his days :

" A life of nothings, nothing-worth,
From that first nothing ere his birth
To that last nothing under earth ! "

" These words," I said, " are like the
    rest ;
No certain clearness, but at best
A vague suspicion of the breast :

" But if I grant, thou mightst defend
The thesis which thy words intend —
That to begin implies to end ;

" Yet how should I for certain hold
Because my memory is so cold,
That I first was in human mould ?

" I cannot make this matter plain,
But I would shoot, howe'er in vain,
A random arrow from the brain.

" It may be that no life is found,
Which only to one engine bound
Falls off, but cycles always round.

"As old mythologies relate,
Some draught of Lethe might await
The slipping thro' from state to state.

"As here we find in trances, men
Forget the dream that happens then,
Until they fall in trance again.

"So might we, if our state were such
As one before, remember much,
For those two likes might meet and
    touch.

"But if I lapsed from nobler place,
Some legend of a fallen race
Alone might hint of my disgrace;

"Some vague emotion of delight
In gazing up an Alpine height,
Some yearning toward the lamps of
    night;

"Or if thro' lower lives I came —
Tho' all experience past became
Consolidate in mind and frame —

"I might forget my weaker lot;
For is not our first year forgot?
The haunts of memory echo not.

"And men, whose reason long was
    blind,
From cells of madness unconfined,
Oft lose whole years of darker mind.

"Much more, if first I floated free,
As naked essence, must I be
Incompetent of memory:

"For memory dealing but with time,
And he with matter, could she climb
Beyond her own material prime?

"Moreover, something is or seems,
That touches me with mystic gleams,
Like glimpses of forgotten dreams —

"Of something felt, like something
    here;
Of something done, I know not where;
Such as no language may declare."

The still voice laugh'd. "I talk,"
    said he,
"Not with thy dreams. Suffice it thee
Thy pain is a reality."

"But thou," said I, "hast missed thy
    mark,
Who sought'st to wreck thy mortal
    ark,
By making all the horizon dark.

"Why not set forth, if I should do
This rashness, that which might ensue
With this old soul in organs new?

"Whatever crazy sorrow saith,
No life that breathes with human
    breath
Has ever truly long'd for death.

"'Tis life, whereof our nerves are
    scant,
Oh life, not death, for which we pant;
More life, and fuller, that I want."

I ceased, and sat as one forlorn.
Then said the voice, in quiet scorn,
"Behold, it is the Sabbath morn."

And I arose, and I released
The casement, and the light increased
With freshness in the dawning east.

Like soften'd airs that blowing steal,
When meres begin to uncongeal,
The sweet church bells began to peal.

On to God's house the people prest:
Passing the place where each must rest,
Each enter'd like a welcome guest.

One walk'd between his wife and child,
With measured footfall firm and mild,
And now and then he gravely smiled.

The prudent partner of his blood
Lean'd on him, faithful, gentle, good,
Wearing the rose of womanhood.

And in their double love secure,
The little maiden walk'd demure,
Pacing with downward eyelids pure.

These three made unity so sweet,
My frozen heart began to beat,
Remembering its ancient heat.

I blest them, and they wander'd on:
I spoke, but answer came there none:
The dull and bitter voice was gone.

A second voice was at mine ear,
A little whisper silver-clear,
A murmur, "Be of better cheer."

As from some blissful neighborhood,
A notice faintly understood,
"I see the end, and know the good."

A little hint to solace woe,
A hint, a whisper breathing low,
"I may not speak of what I know."

Like an Æolian harp that wakes
No certain air, but overtakes
Far thought with music that it makes:

Such seem'd the whisper at my side:
"What is it thou knowest, sweet
      voice?" I cried.
"A hidden hope," the voice replied:

So heavenly-toned, that in that hour
From out my sullen heart a power
Broke, like the rainbow from the
      shower,

To feel, altho' no tongue can prove,
That every cloud, that spreads above
And veileth love, itself is love.

And forth into the fields I went,
And Nature's living motion lent
The pulse of hope to discontent.

I wonder'd at the bounteous hours,
The slow result of winter showers:
You scarce could see the grass for
      flowers.

I wonder'd while I paced along:
The woods were fill'd so full with song,
There seem'd no room for sense of
      wrong;

And all so variously wrought,
I marvell'd how the mind was brought
To anchor by one gloomy thought;

And wherefore rather I made choice
To commune with that barren voice,
Than him that said, "Rejoice! Re-
      joice!"

THE MILLER'S DAUGHTER.

I SEE the wealthy miller yet,
   His double chin, his portly size,
And who that knew him could forget
   The busy wrinkles round his eyes?
The slow wise smile that, round about
   His dusty forehead dryly curl'd,
Seem'd half-within and half-without,
   And full of dealings with the world?

In yonder chair I see him sit,
   Three fingers round the old silver
      cup—
I see his gray eyes twinkle yet
   At his own jest—gray eyes lit up
With summer lightnings of a soul
   So full of summer warmth, so glad,
So healthy, sound, and clear and
      whole,
   His memory scarce can make me sad.

Yet fill my glass: give me one kiss:
   My own sweet Alice, we must die.
There's somewhat in this world amiss
   Shall be unriddled by and by.
There's somewhat flows to us in life,
   But more is taken quite away.
Pray, Alice, pray, my darling wife,
   That we may die the self-same day.

Have I not found a happy earth?
   I least should breathe a thought of
      pain.
Would God renew me from my birth
   I'd almost live my life again.
So sweet it seems with thee to walk,
   And once again to woo thee mine—
It seems in after-dinner talk
   Across the walnuts and the wine—

To be the long and listless boy
  Late-left an orphan of the squire,
Where this old mansion mounted high
  Looks down upon the village spire:
For even here, where I and you
  Have lived and loved alone so long,
Each morn my sleep was broken thro'
  By some wild skylark's matin song.

And oft I heard the tender dove
  In firry woodlands making moan;
But ere I saw your eyes, my love,
  I had no motion of my own.
For scarce my life with fancy play'd
  Before I dream'd that pleasant
    dream —
Still hither thither idly sway'd
  Like those long mosses in the
    stream.

Or from the bridge I lean'd to hear
  The milldam rushing down with
    noise,
And see the minnows everywhere
  In crystal eddies glance and poise,
The tall flag-flowers when they sprung
  Below the range of stepping-stones,
Or those three chestnuts near, that
    hung
  In masses thick with milky cones.

But, Alice, what an hour was that,
  When after roving in the woods
('Twas April then), I came and sat
  Below the chestnuts, when their
    buds
Were glistening to the breezy blue;
  And on the slope, an absent fool,
I cast me down, nor thought of you,
  But angled in the higher pool.

A love-song I had somewhere read,
  An echo from a measured strain,
Beat time to nothing in my head
  From some odd corner of the brain.
It haunted me, the morning long,
  With weary sameness in the rhymes,
The phantom of a silent song,
  That went and came a thousand
    times.

Then leapt a trout. In lazy mood
  I watch'd the little circles die;
They past into the level flood,
  And there a vision caught my eye;
The reflex of a beauteous form,
  A glowing arm, a gleaming neck,
As when a sunbeam wavers warm
  Within the dark and dimpled beck.

For you remember, you had set,
  That morning, on the casement-edge
A long green box of mignonette,
  And you were leaning from the
    ledge:
And when I raised my eyes, above
  They met with two so full and
    bright—
Such eyes! I swear to you, my love,
  That these have never lost their
    light.

I loved, and love dispell'd the fear
  That I should die an early death:
For love possess'd the atmosphere,
  And fill'd the breast with purer
    breath.
My mother thought, What ails the
    boy?
  For I was alter'd, and began
To move about the house with joy,
  And with the certain step of man.

I loved the brimming wave that swam
  Thro' quiet meadows round the mill,
The sleepy pool above the dam,
  The pool beneath it never still,
The meal-sacks on the whiten'd floor,
  The dark round of the dripping
    wheel,
The very air about the door
  Made misty with the floating meal.

And oft in ramblings on the wold,
  When April nights began to blow,
And April's crescent glimmer'd cold,
  I saw the village lights below;
I knew your taper far away,
  And full at heart of trembling hope,
From off the wold I came, and lay
  Upon the freshly-flower'd slope.

The deep brook groan'd beneath the
 mill;
 And "by that lamp," I thought,
  "she sits!"
The white chalk-quarry from the hill
 Gleam'd to the flying moon by fits.
"O that I were beside her now!
 O will she answer if I call?
O would she give me vow for vow,
 Sweet Alice, if I told her all?"

Sometimes I saw you sit and spin:
 And, in the pauses of the wind,
Sometimes I heard you sing within;
 Sometimes your shadow cross'd the
  blind.
At last you rose and moved the light,
 And the long shadow of the chair
Flitted across into the night,
 And all the casement darken'd there.

But when at last I dared to speak,
 The lanes, you know, were white
  with may,
Your ripe lips moved not, but your
  cheek
 Flush'd like the coming of the day;
And so it was — half-sly, half-shy,
 You would, and would not, little
  one!
Although I pleaded tenderly,
 And you and I were all alone.

And slowly was my mother brought
 To yield consent to my desire:
She wish'd me happy, but she thought
 I might have look'd a little higher;
And I was young — too young to wed:
 "Yet must I love her for your sake;
Go fetch your Alice here," she said:
 Her eyelid quiver'd as she spake.

And down I went to fetch my bride:
 But, Alice, you were ill at ease;
This dress and that by turns you tried,
 Too fearful that you should not
  please.
I loved you better for your fears,
 I knew you could not look but well;
And dews, that would have fall'n in
  tears,
 I kiss'd away before they fell.

I watch'd the little flutterings,
 The doubt my mother would not
  see;
She spoke at large of many things,
 And at the last she spoke of me;
And turning look'd upon your face,
 As near this door you sat apart,
And rose, and, with a silent grace
 Approaching, press'd you heart to
  heart.

Ah, well — but sing the foolish song
 I gave you, Alice, on the day
When, arm in arm, we went along,
 A pensive pair, and you were gay
With bridal flowers — that I may seem,
 As in the nights of old, to lie
Beside the mill-wheel in the stream,
 While those full chestnuts whisper
  by.

> It is the miller's daughter
> And she is grown so dear, so dear,
> That I would be the jewel
> That trembles in her ear:
> For hid in ringlets day and night,
> I'd touch her neck so warm and white.

> And I would be the girdle
> About her dainty dainty waist,
> And her heart would beat against me,
> In sorrow and in rest:
> And I should know if it beat right,
> I'd clasp it round so close and tight.

> And I would be the necklace,
> And all day long to fall and rise
> Upon her balmy bosom,
> With her laughter or her sighs,
> And I would lie so light, so light,
> I scarce should be unclasp'd at night.

A trifle, sweet! which true love spells —
 True love interprets — right alone.
His light upon the letter dwells,
 For all the spirit is his own.
So, if I waste words now, in truth
 You must blame Love. His early
  rage
Had force to make me rhyme in youth,
 And makes me talk too much in age.

And now those vivid hours are gone,
 Like mine own life to me thou art,
Where Past and Present, wound in
  one,

Do make a garland for the heart:
So sing that other song I made,
Half-anger'd with my happy lot,
The day, when in the chestnut shade
I found the blue Forget-me-not.

 Love that hath us in the net
 Can he pass, and we forget?
 Many suns arise and set.
 Many a chance the years beget.
 Love the gift is Love the debt.
  Even so.
 Love is hurt with jar and fret.
 Love is made a vague regret.
 Eyes with idle tears are wet.
 Idle habit links us yet.
 What is love? for we forget:
  Ah, no! no!

Look thro' mine eyes with thine. True
 wife,
 Round my true heart thine arms in-
 twine
My other dearer life in life,
 Look thro' my very soul with thine!
Untouch'd with any shade of years,
 May those kind eyes forever dwell!
They have not shed a many tears,
 Dear eyes, since first I knew them
 well.

Yet tears they shed: they had their
 part
 Of sorrow: for when time was ripe,
The still affection of the heart
 Became an outward breathing type,
That into stillness past again,
 And left a want unknown before;
Although the loss has brought us pain,
 That loss but made us love the more,

With farther lookings on. The kiss,
 The woven arms, seem but to be
Weak symbols of the settled bliss,
 The comfort, I have found in thee:
But that God bless thee, dear — who
 wrought
 Two spirits to one equal mind —
With blessings beyond hope or
 thought,
 With blessings which no words can
 find.

Arise, and let us wander forth,
 To yon old mill across the wolds;

For look, the sunset, south and north,
 Winds all the vale in rosy folds,
And fires your narrow casement glass,
 Touching the sullen pool below:
On the chalk-hill the bearded grass
 Is dry and dewless.   Let us go.

FATIMA.

O Love, Love, Love! O withering
 might!
O sun, that from thy noonday height
Shudderest when I strain my sight,
Throbbing thro' all thy heat and light,
 Lo, falling from my constant mind,
 Lo, parch'd and wither'd, deaf and
 blind,
 I whirl like leaves in roaring wind.

Last night I wasted hateful hours
Below the city's eastern towers:
I thirsted for the brooks, the showers:
I roll'd among the tender flowers:
 I crush'd them on my breast, my
 mouth;
 I look'd athwart the burning drouth
 Of that long desert to the south.

Last night, when some one spoke his
 name,
From my swift blood that went and
 came
A thousand little shafts of flame
Were shiver'd in my narrow frame.
 O Love, O fire! once he drew
 With one long kiss my whole soul
 thro'
 My lips, as sunlight drinketh dew.

Before he mounts the hill, I know
He cometh quickly: from below
Sweet gales, as from deep gardens,
 blow
Before him, striking on my brow.
 In my dry brain my spirit soon,
 Down-deepening from swoon to
 swoon,
 Faints like a dazzled morning moon.

The wind sounds like a silver wire,
And from beyond the noon a fire

Is pour'd upon the hills, and nigher
The skies stoop down in their desire ;
  And, isled in sudden seas of light,
  My heart, pierced thro' with fierce
    delight,
  Bursts into blossom in his sight.

My whole soul waiting silently,
All naked in a sultry sky,
Droops blinded with his shining eye :
I *will* possess him or will die.
  I will grow round him in his place,
  Grow, live, die looking on his face,
  Die, dying clasp'd in his embrace.

ŒNONE.

THERE lies a vale in Ida, lovelier
Than all the valleys of Ionian hills.
The swimming vapor slopes athwart
  the glen,
Puts forth an arm, and creeps from
  pine to pine,
And loiters, slowly drawn. On either
  hand
The lawns and meadow-ledges mid-
  way down
Hang rich in flowers, and far below
  them roars
The long brook falling thro' the
  clov'n ravine
In cataract after cataract to the sea.
Behind the valley topmost Gargarus
Stands up and takes the morning: but
  in front
The gorges, opening wide apart, reveal
Troas and Ilion's column'd citadel,
The crown of Troas.
        Hither came at noon
Mournful Œnone, wandering forlorn
Of Paris, once her playmate on the
  hills.
Her cheek had lost the rose, and round
  her neck
Floated her hair or seem'd to float in
  rest.
She, leaning on a fragment twined
  with vine,
Sang to the stillness, till the mountain-
  shade
Sloped downward to her seat from the
  upper cliff.

"O mother Ida, many-fountain'd
  Ida,
Dear mother Ida, hearken ere I die.
For now the noonday quiet holds the
  hill :
The grasshopper is silent in the grass :
The lizard, with his shadow on the
  stone,
Rests like a shadow, and the winds
  are dead.
The purple flower droops : the golden
  bee
Is lily-cradled : I alone awake.
My eyes are full of tears, my heart of
  love,
My heart is breaking, and my eyes
  are dim,
And I am all aweary of my life.

"O mother Ida, many-fountain'd
  Ida,
Dear mother Ida, hearken ere I die.
Hear me, O Earth, hear me, O Hills,
  O Caves
That house the cold crown'd snake! O
  mountain brooks,
I am the daughter of a River God,
Hear me, for I will speak, and build
  up all
My sorrow with my song, as yonder
  walls
Rose slowly to a music slowly
  breathed,
A cloud that gather'd shape : for it
  may be
That, while I speak of it, a little while
My heart may wander from its deeper
  woe.

"O mother Ida, many-fountain'd
  Ida,
Dear mother Ida, hearken ere I die.
I waited underneath the dawning hills,
Aloft the mountain lawn was dewy-
  dark,
And dewy-dark aloft the mountain
  pine :
Beautiful Paris, evil-hearted Paris,
Leading a jet-black goat white-horn'd,
  white-hooved,
Came up from reedy Simois all alone

" O mother Ida, hearken ere I die.
Far-off the torrent call'd me from the
  cleft:
Far up the solitary morning smote
The streaks of virgin snow. With
  down-dropt eyes
I sat alone: white-breasted like a star
Fronting the dawn he moved; a leop-
  ard skin
Droop'd from his shoulder, but his
  sunny hair
Cluster'd about his temples like a
  God's:
And his cheek brighten'd as the foam-
  bow brightens
When the wind blows the foam, and
  all my heart
Went forth to embrace him coming
  ere he came.

"Dear mother Ida, hearken ere I die.
He smiled, and opening out his milk-
.   white palm
Disclosed a fruit of pure Hesperian
  gold,
That smelt ambrosially, and while I
  look'd
And listen'd, the full-flowing river of
  speech
Came down upon my heart.
      "'My own Œnone,
Beautiful-brow'd Œnone, my own soul,
Behold this fruit, whose gleaming rind
  ingrav'n
"For the most fair," would seem to
  award it thine,
As lovelier than whatever Oread haunt
The knolls of Ida, loveliest in all grace
Of movement, and the charm of mar-
  ried brows.'

" Dear mother Ida, hearken ere I die.
He prest the blossom of his lips to mine,
And added 'This was cast upon the
  board,
When all the full-faced presence of
  the Gods
Ranged in the halls of Peleus ; where-
  upon
Rose feud, with question unto whom
  'twere due :

But light-foot Iris brought it yester-
  eve,
Delivering, that to me, by common
  voice
Elected umpire, Herè comes to-day,
Pallas and Aphroditè, claiming each
This meed of fairest. Thou, within
  the cave
Behind yon whispering tuft of oldest
  pine,
Mayst well behold them unbeheld,
  unheard
Hear all, and see thy Paris judge of
  Gods.'

" Dear mother Ida, hearken ere I die.
It was the deep midnoon: one silvery
  cloud
Had lost his way between the piney
  sides
Of this long glen. Then to the bower
  they came,
Naked they came to that smooth-
  swarded bower,
And at their feet the crocus brake like
  fire,
Violet, amaracus, and asphodel,
Lotos and lilies : and a wind arose,
And overhead the wandering ivy and
  vine,
This way and that, in many a wild
  festoon
Ran riot, garlanding the gnarled
  boughs
With bunch and berry and flower thro'
  and thro'.

" O mother Ida, hearken ere I die.
On the tree-tops a crested peacock lit,
And o'er him flow'd a golden cloud,
  and lean'd
Upon him, slowly dropping fragrant
  dew.
Then first I heard the voice of her, to
  whom
Coming thro' Heaven, like a light that
  grows
Larger and clearer, with one mind the
  Gods
Rise up for reverence. She to Paris
  made

Proffer of royal power, ample rule
Unquestion'd overflowing revenue
Wherewith to embellish state, 'from
    many a vale
And river-sunder'd champaign clothed
    with corn,
Or labor'd mine undrainable of ore.
Honor,' she said, 'and homage, tax
    and toll,
From many an inland town and haven
    large,
Mast-throng'd beneath her shadowing
    citadel
In glassy bays among her tallest
    towers.'

  "O mother Ida, hearken ere I die.
Still she spake on and still she spake
    of power,
'Which in all action is the end of all ;
Power fitted to the season ; wisdom-
    bred
And throned of wisdom — from all
    neighbor crowns
Alliance and Allegiance, till thy hand
Fail from the sceptre-staff. Such
    boon from me,
From me, Heaven's Queen, Paris, to
    thee king-born,
A shepherd all thy life but yet king-
    born,
Should come most welcome, seeing
    men in power
Only, are likest gods, who have attain'd
Rest in a happy place and quiet seats
Above the thunder, with undying bliss
In knowledge of their own supremacy.'

  "Dear mother Ida, hearken ere I die.
She ceased, and Paris held the costly
    fruit
Out at arm's-length, so much the
    thought of power
Flatter'd his spirit ; but Pallas where
    she stood
Somewhat apart, her clear and bared
    limbs
O'erthwarted with the brazen-headed
    spear
Upon her pearly shoulder leaning cold,
The while, above, her full and earnest
    eye

Over her snow-cold breast and angry
    cheek
Kept watch, waiting decision, made
    reply.

  " ' Self-reverence, self-knowledge,
    self-control,
These three alone lead life to sover-
    eign power.
Yet not for power (power of herself
Would come uncall'd for) but to live
    by law,
Acting the law we live by without fear ;
And, because right is right, to follow
    right
Were wisdom in the scorn of conse-
    quence.'

  "Dear mother Ida, hearken ere I die.
Again she said : 'I woo thee not with
    gifts.
Sequel of guerdon could not alter me
To fairer. Judge thou me by what I
    am,
So shalt thou find me fairest.
               Yet, indeed,
If gazing on divinity disrobed
Thy mortal eyes are frail to judge of
    fair,
Unbiass'd by self-profit, oh ! rest thee
    sure
That I shall love thee well and cleave
    to thee,
So that my vigor, wedded to thy blood,
Shall strike within thy pulses, like a
    God's,
To push thee forward thro' a life of
    shocks,
Dangers, and deeds, until endurance
    grow
Sinew'd with action, and the full-grown
    will,
Circled thro' all experiences, pure law,
Commeasure perfect freedom.'
               "Here she ceas'd,
And Paris ponder'd, and I cried, 'O
    Paris,
Give it to Pallas !' but he heard me
    not,
Or hearing would not hear me, woe is
    me !

"O mother Ida, many-fountain'd Ida,
Dear mother Ida, hearken ere I die.
Idalian Aphroditè beautiful,
Fresh as the foam, new-bathed in
    Paphian wells,
With rosy slender fingers backward
    drew
From her warm brows and bosom her
    deep hair
Ambrosial, golden round her lucid
    throat
And shoulder : from the violets her
    light foot
Shone rosy-white, and o'er her rounded
    form
Between the shadows of the vine-
    bunches
Floated the glowing sunlights, as she
    moved.

"Dear mother Ida, hearken ere I die.
She with a subtle smile in her mild
    eyes,
The herald of her triumph, drawing
    nigh
Half-whisper'd in his ear, 'I promise
    thee
The fairest and most loving wife in
    Greece,'
She spoke and laugh'd : I shut my
    sight for fear :
But when I look'd, Paris had raised
    his arm,
And I beheld great Herè's angry eyes,
As she withdrew into the golden cloud,
And I was left alone within the bower ;
And from that time to this I am alone,
And I shall be alone until I die.

"Yet, mother Ida, hearken ere I die.
Fairest — why fairest wife ? am I not
    fair ?
My love hath told me so a thousand
    times.
Methinks I must be fair, for yesterday,
When I past by, a wild and wanton
    pard,
Eyed like the evening star, with play-
    ful tail
Crouch'd fawning in the weed. Most
    loving is she ?

Ah me, my mountain shepherd, that
    my arms
Were wound about thee, and my hot
    lips prest
Close, close to thine in that quick-
    falling dew
Of fruitful kisses, thick as Autumn
    rains
Flash in the pools of whirling Simois.

"O mother, hear me yet before I die.
They came, they cut away my tallest
    pines,
My tall dark pines, that plumed the
    craggy ledge
High over the blue gorge, and all
    between
The snowy peak and snow-white cata-
    ract
Foster'd the callow eaglet— from be-
    neath
Whose thick mysterious boughs in the
    dark morn
The panther's roar came muffled, while
    I sat
Low in the valley. Never, never more
Shall lone Œnone see the morning
    mist
Sweep thro' them ; never see them
    overlaid
With narrow moon-lit slips of silver
    cloud,
Between the loud stream and the trem-
    bling stars.

"O mother, hear me yet before I die.
I wish that somewhere in the ruin'd
    folds,
Among the fragments tumbled from
    the glens,
Or the dry thickets, I could meet with
    her
The Abominable, that uninvited came
Into the fair Peleïan banquet-hall,
And cast the golden fruit upon the
    board,
And bred this change ; that I might
    speak my mind,
And tell her to her face how much I
    hate
Her presence, hated both of Gods and
    men.

" O mother, hear me yet before I die.
Hath he not sworn his love a thousand
   times,
In this green valley, under this green
   hill,
Ev'n on this hand, and sitting on this
   stone ?
Seal'd it with kisses ? water'd it with
   tears ?
O happy tears, and how unlike to
   these !
O happy Heaven, how canst thou see
   my face ?
O happy earth, how canst thou bear
   my weight ?
O death, death, death, thou ever-float-
   ing cloud,
There are enough unhappy on this
   earth,
Pass by the happy souls, that love to
   live :
I pray thee, pass before my light of
   life,
And shadow all my soul that I may
   die.
Thou weighest heavy on the heart
   within,
Weigh heavy on my eyelids : let me
   die.

" O mother, hear me yet before I die.
I will not die alone, for fiery thoughts
Do shape themselves within me, more
   and more,
Whereof I catch the issue. as I hear
Dead sounds at night come from the
   inmost hills,
Like footsteps upon wool. I dimly see
My far-off doubtful purpose. as a
   mother
Conjectures of the features of her
   child
Ere it is born : her child ! — a shudder
   comes
Across me : never child be born of me,
Unblest, to vex me with his father's
   eyes !

" O mother, hear me yet before I die.
Hear me, O earth. I will not die alone,
Lest their shrill happy laughter come
   to me

Walking the cold and starless road of
   Death
Uncomforted, leaving my ancient love
With the Greek woman. I will rise
   and go
Down into Troy, and ere the stars
   come forth
Talk with the wild Cassandra, for she
   says
A fire dances before her, and a sound
Rings ever in her ears of armed men.
What this may be I know not, but I
   know
That, whereso'er I am by night and
   day,
All earth and air seem only burning
   fire."

      ———

THE SISTERS.

We were two daughters of one race :
She was the fairest in the face :
   The wind is blowing in turret and
     tree.
They were together, and she fell ;
Therefore revenge became me well.
   O the Earl was fair to see !

She died : she went to burning flame :
She mix'd her ancient blood with
   shame.
   The wind is howling in turret and
     tree.
Whole weeks and months, and early
   and late,
To win his love I lay in wait :
   O the Earl was fair to see !

I made a feast ; I bade him come ;
I won his love, I brought him home.
   The wind is roaring in turret and
     tree.
And after supper, on a bed,
Upon my lap he laid his head :
   O the Earl was fair to see !

I kiss'd his eyelids into rest :
His ruddy cheek upon my breast.
   The wind is raging in turret and tree
I hated him with the hate of hell.
But I loved his beauty passing well.
   O the Earl was fair to see !

I rose up in the silent night:
I made my dagger sharp and bright.
  The wind is raving in turret and tree.
As half-asleep his breath he drew,
Three times I stabb'd him thro' and
    thro'.
  O the Earl was fair to see!

I curl'd and comb'd his comely head,
He look'd so grand when he was dead.
  The wind is blowing in turret and
    tree.
I wrapt his body in the sheet,
And laid him at his mother's feet.
  O the Earl was fair to see!

————

TO ——.

WITH THE FOLLOWING POEM.

I send you here a sort of allegory,
(For you will understand it) of a soul,
A sinful soul possess'd of many gifts,
A spacious garden full of flowering
    weeds,
A glorious Devil, large in heart and
    brain,
That did love Beauty only, (Beauty
    seen
In all varieties of mould and mind)
And Knowledge for its beauty; or if
    Good,
Good only for its beauty, seeing not
That Beauty, Good, and Knowledge,
    are three sisters
That dote upon each other, friends to
    man,
Living together under the same roof,
And never can be sunder'd without
    tears.
And he that shuts Love out, in turn
    shall be
Shut out from Love, and on her thresh-
    old lie
Howling in outer darkness. Not for
    this
Was common clay ta'en from the com-
    mon earth
Moulded by God, and temper'd with
    the tears
Of angels to the perfect shape of man.

THE PALACE OF ART.

I built my soul a lordly pleasure-
    house,
  Wherein at ease for aye to dwell.
I said, "O Soul, make merry and
    carouse,
  Dear soul, for all is well."

A huge crag-platform, smooth as bur-
    nish'd brass
  I chose. The ranged ramparts
    bright
From level meadow-bases of deep grass
  Suddenly scaled the light.

Thereon I built it firm. Of ledge or
    shelf
  The rock rose clear, or winding stair.
My soul would live alone unto herself
  In her high palace there.

And "while the world runs round and
    round," I said,
  "Reign thou apart, a quiet king,
Still as, while Saturn whirls, his stead-
    fast shade
  Sleeps on his luminous ring."

To which my soul made answer
    readily:
  "Trust me, in bliss I shall abide
In this great mansion that is built for
    me,
  So royal-rich and wide."

    *   *   *   *
    *   *   *   *

Four courts I made, East, West and
    South and North,
  In each a squared lawn, wherefrom
The golden gorge of dragons spouted
    forth
  A flood of fountain-foam.

And round the cool green courts there
    ran a row
  Of cloisters, branch'd like mighty
    woods,
Echoing all night to that sonorous
    flow
  Of spouted fountain-floods.

And round the roofs a gilded gallery
  That lent broad verge to distant
    lands,
Far as the wild swan wings, to where
    the sky
  Dipt down to sea and sands.

From those four jets four currents in
    one swell
  Across the mountain stream'd below
In misty folds, that floating as they
    fell
  Lit up a torrent-bow.

And high on every peak a statue
    seem'd
  To hang on tiptoe, tossing up
A cloud of incense of all odor steam'd
  From out a golden cup.

So that she thought, "And who shall
    gaze upon
  My palace with unblinded eyes,
While this great bow will waver in the
    sun,
  And that sweet incense rise?"

For that sweet incense rose and never
    fail'd,
  And, while day sank or mounted
    higher,
The light aerial gallery, golden-rail'd,
  Burnt like a fringe of fire.

Likewise the deep-set windows, stain'd
    and traced,
  Would seem slow-flaming crimson
    fires
From shadow'd grots of arches inter-
    laced,
  And tipt with frost-like spires.

*   *   *   *
  *   *   *   *

Full of long-sounding corridors it was,
  That over-vaulted grateful gloom,
Thro' which the livelong day my soul
    did pass,
  Well-pleased, from room to room.

Full of great rooms and small the
    palace stood,
  All various, each a perfect whole

From living Nature, fit for every mood
  And change of my still soul.

For some were hung with arras green
    and blue,
  Showing a gaudy summer-morn,
Where with puff'd cheek the belted
    hunter blew
  His wreathed bugle-horn.

One seem'd all dark and red — a tract
    of sand,
  And some one pacing there alone,
Who paced forever in a glimmering
    land,
  Lit with a low large moon.

One show'd an iron coast and angry
    waves.
  You seem'd to hear them climb and
    fall
And roar rock-thwarted under bellow-
    ing caves,
  Beneath the windy wall.

And one, a full-fed river winding slow
  By herds upon an endless plain,
The ragged rims of thunder brooding
    low,
  With shadow-streaks of rain.

And one, the reapers at their sultry
    toil.
  In front they bound the sheaves.
    Behind
Were realms of upland, prodigal in
    oil,
  And hoary to the wind.

And one a foreground black with
    stones and slags,
  Beyond, a line of heights, and higher
All barr'd with long white cloud the
    scornful crags,
  And highest, snow and fire.

And one, an English home — gray
    twilight pour'd
  On dewy pastures, dewy trees,
Softer than sleep — all things in order
    stored,
  A haunt of ancient Peace.

Nor these alone, but every landscape
    fair,
  As fit for every mood of mind,
Or gay, or grave, or sweet, or stern,
    was there
  Not less than truth design'd.

     *   *   *   *
     *   *   *   *

Or the maid-mother by a crucifix,
  In tracts of pasture sunny-warm.
Beneath branch-work of costly sardo-
    nyx
  Sat smiling, babe in arm.

Or in a clear-wall'd city on the sea,
  Near gilded organ-pipes, her hair
Wound with white roses, slept St.
    Cecily;
  An angel look'd at her.

Or thronging all one porch of Paradise
  A group of Houris bow'd to see
The dying Islamite, with hands and
    eyes
  That said, We wait for thee.

Or mythic Uther's deeply-wounded
    son
  In some fair space of sloping greens
Lay, dozing in the vale of Avalon,
  And watch'd by weeping queens.

Or hollowing one hand against his ear,
  To list a foot-fall, ere he saw
The wood-nymph, stay'd the Ausonian
    king to hear
  Of wisdom and of law.

Or over hills with peaky tops engrail'd,
  And many a tract of palm and rice,
The throne of Indian Cama slowly
    sail'd
  A summer fann'd with spice.

Or sweet Europa's mantle blew un-
    clasp'd,
  From off her shoulder backward
    borne:
From one hand droop'd a crocus: one
    hand grasp'd
  The mild bull's golden horn.

Or else flush'd Ganymede, his rosy
    thigh
  Half-buried in the Eagle's down
Sole as a flying star shot thro' the sky
  Above the pillar'd town.

Nor these alone: but every legend fair
  Which the supreme Caucasian mind
Carved out of Nature for itself, was
    there,
  Not less than life, design'd.

     *   *   *   *
     *   *   *   *

Then in the towers I placed great bells
    that swung,
  Moved of themselves, with silver
    sound;
And with choice paintings of wise men
    I hung
  The royal dais round.

For there was Milton like a seraph
    strong,
  Beside him Shakespeare bland and
    mild;
And there the world-worn Dante
    grasp'd his song,
  And somewhat grimly smiled.

And there the Ionian father of the
    rest;
  A million wrinkles carved his skin;
A hundred winters snow'd upon his
    breast,
  From cheek and throat and chin.

Above, the fair hall-ceiling stately-
    set
  Many an arch high up did lift,
And angels rising and descending met
  With interchange of gift.

Below was all mosaic choicely plann'd
  With cycles of the human tale
Of this wide world, the times of every
    land
  So wrought, they will not fail.

The people here, a beast of burden
    slow,
  Toil'd onward, prick'd with goads
    and stings;

Here play'd, a tiger, rolling to and fro
  The heads and crowns of kings;

Here rose, an athlete, strong to break
  or bind
  All force in bonds that might en-
    dure,
And here once more like some sick
  man declined,
  And trusted any cure.

But over these she trod: and those
  great bells
  Began to chime. She took her
    throne:
She sat betwixt the shining Oriels,
  To sing her songs alone.

And thro' the topmost Oriels' colored
  flame
Two godlike faces gazed below;
Plato the wise, and large-brow'd Veru-
  lam,
  The first of those who know.

And all those names, that in their
  motion were
  Full-welling   fountain-heads of
    change,
Betwixt the slender shafts were bla-
  zon'd fair
  In diverse raiment strange:

Thro' which the lights, rose, amber,
  emerald, blue,
  Flush'd in her temples, and her eyes.
And from her lips, as morn from
  Memnon, drew
  Rivers of melodies.

No nightingale delighteth to prolong
  Her low preamble all alone,
More than my soul to hear her echo'd
  song
  Throb thro' the ribbed stone;

Singing and murmuring in her feast-
  ful mirth,
  Joying to feel herself alive,
Lord over Nature, Lord of the visible
  earth,
  Lord of the senses five;

Communing with herself: "All these
  are mine,
  And let the world have peace or
    wars,
'Tis one to me." She — when young
  night divine
  Crown'd dying day with stars,

Making sweet close of his delicious
  toils —
  Lit light in wreaths and anadems,
And pure quintessences of precious
  oils
  In hollow'd moons of gems,

To mimic heaven; and clapt her
  hands and cried,
  " I marvel if my still delight
In this great house so royal-rich, and
  wide,
  Be flatter'd to the height.

" O all things fair to sate my various
  eyes!
  O shapes and hues that please me
    well!
O silent faces of the Great and Wise,
  My Gods, with whom I dwell!

" O God-like isolation which art mine,
  I can but count thee perfect gain,
What time I watch the darkening
  droves of swine
  That range on yonder plain.

" In filthy sloughs they roll a prurient
  skin,
  They graze and wallow, breed and
    sleep;
And oft some brainless devil enters in,
  And drives them to the deep."

Then of the moral instinct would she
  prate
And of the rising from the dead,
As hers by right of full-accomplish'd
  Fate;
  And at the last she said:

" I take possession of man's mind and
  deed.
  I care not what the sects may brawl

I sit as God holding no form of creed,
　　But contemplating all."

　　*　　　*　　　*　　　*
　　*　　　*　　　*　　　*

Full oft the riddle of the painful earth
　　Flash'd thro' her as she sat alone,
Yet not the less held she her solemn
　　　mirth,
　　And intellectual throne.

And so she throve and prosper'd: so
　　　three years
　　She prosper'd: on the fourth she
　　　fell,
Like Herod, when the shout was in
　　　his ears,
　　Struck thro' with pangs of hell.

Lest she should fail and perish utterly,
　　God, before whom ever lie bare
The abysmal deeps of Personality,
　　Plagued her with sore despair.

When she would think, where'er she
　　　turn'd her sight
　　The airy hand confusion wrought,
Wrote, "Mene, mene," and divided
　　　quite
　　The kingdom of her thought.

Deep dread and loathing of her soli-
　　　tude
　　Fell on her, from which mood was
　　　born
Scorn of herself; again, from out that
　　　mood
　　Laughter at her self-scorn.

"What! is not this my place of
　　strength," she said,
　　" My spacious mansion built for me,
Whereof the strong foundation-stones
　　　were laid
　　Since my first memory ? "

But in dark corners of her palace stood
　　Uncertain shapes; and unawares
On white-eyed phantasms weeping
　　tears of blood,
　　And horrible nightmares,

And hollow shades enclosing hearts of
　　　flame,
　　And, with dim fretted foreheads all,
On corpses three-months-old at noon
　　　she came,
　　That stood against the wall.

A spot of dull stagnation, without
　　　light
　　Or power of movement, seem'd my
　　　soul,
'Mid onward-sloping motions infinite
　　Making for one sure goal.

A still salt pool, lock'd in with bars
　　　of sand,
　　Left on the shore; that hears all
　　　night
The plunging seas draw backward
　　　from the land
　　Their moon-led waters white.

A star that with the choral starry
　　　dance
　　Join'd not, but stood, and standing
　　　saw
The hollow orb of moving Circum-
　　　stance
　　Roll'd round by one fix'd law.

Back on herself her serpent pride had
　　　curl'd.
　　"No voice," she shriek'd in that
　　　lone hall,
"No voice breaks thro' the stillness
　　of this world:
　　One deep, deep silence all! "

She, mouldering with the dull earth's
　　　mouldering sod,
　　Inwrapt tenfold in slothful shame,
Lay there exiled from eternal God,
　　Lost to her place and name ;

And death and life she hated equally,
　　And nothing saw, for her despair,
But dreadful time, dreadful eternity,
　　No comfort anywhere ;

Remaining utterly confused with
　　　fears,
　　And ever worse with growing time,

And ever unrelieved by dismal tears,
  And all alone in crime:
Shut up as in a crumbling tomb, girt
    round
  With blackness as a solid wall,
Far off she seem'd to hear the dully
    sound
  Of human footsteps fall.

As in strange lands a traveller walk-
    ing slow,
  In doubt and great perplexity,
A little before moon-rise hears the low
  Moan of an unknown sea;

And knows not if it be thunder, or a
    sound
    Of rocks thrown down, or one deep
      cry
Of great wild beasts; then thinketh,
    "I have found
    A new land, but I die."

She howl'd aloud, "I am on fire within.
  There comes no murmur of reply.
What is it that will take away my sin,
  And save me lest I die?"

So when four years were wholly fin-
    ished,
  She threw her royal robes away.
"Make me a cottage in the vale," she
    said,
    "Where I may mourn and pray.

"Yet pull not down my palace towers,
    that are
  So lightly beautifully built:
Perchance I may return with others
    there
When I have purged my guilt."

LADY CLARA VERE DE VERE.

Lady Clara Vere de Vere,
  Of me you shall not win renown:
You thought to break a country heart
  For pastime, ere you went to town.
At me you smiled, but unbeguiled
  I saw the snare, and I retired:
The daughter of a hundred Earls,
  You are not one to be desired.

Lady Clara Vere de Vere,
  I know you proud to bear your
    name,
Your pride is yet no mate for mine,
  Too proud to care from whence I
    came.
Nor would I break for your sweet sake
  A heart that dotes on truer charms.
A simple maiden in her flower
  Is worth a hundred coats-of-arms.

Lady Clara Vere de Vere,
  Some meeker pupil you must find,
For were you queen of all that is,
  I could not stoop to such a mind.
You sought to prove how I could love;
  And my disdain is my reply.
The lion on your old stone gates
  Is not more cold to you than I.

Lady Clara Vere de Vere,
  You put strange memories in my
    head.
Not thrice your branching limes have
    blown
  Since I beheld young Laurence
    dead.
Oh your sweet eyes, your low replies·
  A great enchantress you may be;
But there was that across his throat
  Which you had hardly cared to see.

Lady Clara Vere de Vere,
  When thus he met his mother's
    view,
She had the passions of her kind,
  She spake some certain truths of
    you.
Indeed I heard one bitter word
  That scarce is fit for you to hear:
Her manners had not that repose
  Which stamps the caste of Vere de
    Vere.

Lady Clara Vere de Vere,
  There stands a spectre in your hall:
The guilt of blood is at your door:
  You changed a wholesome heart to
    gall.
You held your course without remorse,
  To make him trust his modest
    worth,

And, last, you fix'd a vacant stare,
  And slew him with your noble birth.

Trust me, Clara Vere de Vere,
  From yon blue heavens above us
    bent
The gardener Adam and his wife
  Smile at the claims of long descent.
Howe'er it be, it seems to me,
  'Tis only noble to be good.
Kind hearts are more than coronets,
  And simple faith than Norman
    blood.

I know you, Clara Vere de Vere,
  You pine among your halls and
    towers :

The languid light of your proud eyes
  Is wearied of the rolling hours.
In glowing health, with boundless
    wealth,
  But sickening of a vague disease,
You know so ill to deal with time,
  You needs must play such pranks
    as these.

Clara, Clara Vere de Vere,
  If time be heavy on your hands,
Are there no beggars at your gate,
  Nor any poor about your lands ?
Oh ! teach the orphan-boy to read,
  Or teach the orphan-girl to sew,
Pray Heaven for a human heart,
  And let the foolish yeoman go.

THE MAY QUEEN.

You must wake and call me early, call me early, mother dear ;
To-morrow 'ill be the happiest time of all the glad New-year;
Of all the glad New-year, mother, the maddest merriest day ;
For I'm to be Queen o' the May, mother, I'm to be Queen o' the **May.**

There's many a black black eye, they say, but none so bright as mine;
There's Margaret and Mary, there's Kate and Caroline :
But none so fair as little Alice in all the land they say,
So I'm to be Queen o' the May, mother, I'm to be Queen o' the May.

I sleep so sound all night, mother, that I shall never wake,
If you do not call me loud when the day begins to break :
But I must gather knots of flowers, and buds and garlands gay,
For I'm to be Queen o' the May, mother, I'm to be Queen o' the May.

As I came up the valley whom think ye should I see,
But Robin leaning on the bridge beneath the hazel-tree ?
He thought of that sharp look, mother, I gave him yesterday,
But I'm to be Queen o' the May, mother, I'm to be Queen o' the May.

He thought I was a ghost, mother, for I was all in white,
And I ran by him without speaking, like a flash of light.
They call me cruel-hearted, but I care not what they say,
For I'm to be Queen o' the May, mother, I'm to be Queen o' the May.

They say he's dying all for love, but that can never be :
They say his heart is breaking, mother — what is that to me ?
There's many a bolder lad 'ill woo me any summer day,
And I'm to be Queen o' the May, mother, I'm to be Queen o' the May.

Little Effie shall go with me to-morrow to the green,
And you'll be there, too, mother, to see me made the Queen;

For the shepherd lads on every side 'ill come from far away,
And I'm to be Queen o' the May, mother, I'm to be Queen o' the May.

The honeysuckle round the porch has wov'n its wavy bowers,
And by the meadow-trenches blow the faint sweet cuckoo-flowers;
And the wild marsh-marigold shines like fire in swamps and hollows gray,
And I'm to be Queen o' the May, mother, I'm to be Queen o' the May.

The night-winds come and go, mother, upon the meadow-grass,
And the happy stars above them seem to brighten as they pass;
There will not be a drop of rain the whole of the livelong day,
And I'm to be Queen o' the May, mother, I'm to be Queen o' the May.

All the valley, mother, 'ill be fresh and green and still,
And the cowslip and the crowfoot are over all the hill,
And the rivulet in the flowery dale 'ill merrily glance and play,
For I'm to be Queen o' the May, mother, I'm to be Queen o' the May.

So you must wake and call me early, call me early, mother dear
To-morrow 'ill be the happiest time of all the glad New-year:
To-morrow 'ill be of all the year the maddest merriest day,
For I'm to be Queen o' the May, mother, I'm to be Queen o' the May.

NEW–YEAR'S EVE.

IF you're waking call me early, call me early, mother dear,
For I would see the sun rise upon the glad New-year.
It is the last New-year that I shall ever see,
Then you may lay me low i' the mould and think no more of me.

To-night I saw the sun set: he set and left behind
The good old year, the dear old time, and all my peace of mind;
And the New-year's coming up, mother, but I shall never see
The blossom on the blackthorn, the leaf upon the tree.

Last May we made a crown of flowers: we had a merry day;
Beneath the hawthorn on the green they made me Queen of May;
And we danced about the may-pole and in the hazel copse,
Till Charles's Wain came out above the tall white chimney-tops.

There's not a flower on all the hills: the frost is on the pane.
I only wish to live till the snowdrops come again:
I wish the snow would melt and the sun come out on high:
I long to see a flower so before the day I die.

The building rook 'ill caw from the windy tall elm-tree,
And the tufted plover pipe along the fallow lea,
And the swallow 'ill come back again with summer o'er the wave,
But I shall lie alone, mother, within the mouldering grave.

Upon the chancel-casement, and upon that grave of mine,
In the early early morning the summer sun 'ill shine,

Before the red cock crows from the farm upon the hill,
When you are warm-asleep, mother, and all the world is still.

When the flowers come again, mother, beneath the waning light
You'll never see me more in the long gray fields at night;
When from the dry dark wold the summer airs blow cool
On the oat-grass and the sword-grass, and the bulrush in the pool.

You'll bury me, my mother, just beneath the hawthorn shade,
And you'll come sometimes and see me where I am lowly laid.
I shall not forget you, mother, I shall hear you when you pass,
With your feet above my head in the long and pleasant grass.

I have been wild and wayward, but you'll forgive me now;
You'll kiss me, my own mother, and forgive me ere I go;
Nay, nay, you must not weep, nor let your grief be wild,
You should not fret for me, mother, you have another child.

If I can I'll come again, mother, from out my resting-place;
Tho' you'll not see me, mother, I shall look upon your face;
Tho' I cannot speak a word, I shall hearken what you say,
And be often, often with you when you think I'm far away.

Good-night, good-night, when I have said good-night forevermore,
And you see me carried out from the threshold of the door;
Don't let Effie come to see me till my grave be growing green:
She'll be a better child to you than ever I have been.

She'll find my garden-tools upon the granary floor:
Let her take 'em: they are hers: I shall never garden more:
But tell her, when I'm gone, to train the rosebush that I set
About the parlor-window and the box of mignonette.

Good-night, sweet mother: call me before the day is born.
All night I lie awake, but I fall asleep at morn;
But I would see the sun rise upon the glad New-year,
So, if you're waking, call me, call me early, mother dear.

CONCLUSION.

I THOUGHT to pass away before, and yet alive I am;
And in the fields all round I hear the bleating of the lamb.
How sadly, I remember, rose the morning of the year!
To die before the snowdrop came, and now the violet's here.

O sweet is the new violet, that comes beneath the skies,
And sweeter is the young lamb's voice to me that cannot rise,
And sweet is all the land about, and all the flowers that blow,
And sweeter far is death than life to me that long to go.

It seem'd so hard at first, mother, to leave the blessed sun,
And now it seems as hard to stay, and yet His will be done!

But still I think it can't be long before I find release;
And that good man, the clergyman, has told me words of peace.

O blessings on his kindly voice and on his silver hair!
And blessings on his whole life long, until he meet me there!
O blessings on his kindly heart and on his silver head!
A thousand times I blest him, as he knelt beside my bed.

He taught me all the mercy, for he show'd me all the sin.
Now, tho' my lamp was lighted late, there's One will let me in:
Nor would I now be well, mother, again if that could be,
For my desire is but to pass to Him that died for me.

I did not hear the dog howl, mother, or the death-watch beat,
There came a sweeter token when the night and morning meet:
But sit beside my bed, mother, and put your hand in mine,
And Effie on the other side, and I will tell the sign.

All in the wild March-morning I heard the angels call;
It was when the moon was setting, and the dark was over all;
The trees began to whisper, and the wind began to roll,
And in the wild March-morning I heard them call my soul.

For lying broad awake I thought of you and Effie dear;
I saw you sitting in the house, and I no longer here;
With all my strength I pray'd for both, and so I felt resign'd,
And up the valley came a swell of music on the wind.

I thought that it was fancy, and I listen'd in my bed,
And then did something speak to me — I know not what was said;
For great delight and shuddering took hold of all my mind,
And up the valley came again the music on the wind.

But you were sleeping; and I said, "It's not for them: it's mine."
And if it come three times, I thought, I take it for a sign.
And once again it came, and close beside the window-bars,
Then seem'd to go right up to Heaven and die among the stars.

So now I think my time is near. I trust it is. I know
The blessed music went that way my soul will have to go.
And for myself, indeed, I care not if I go to-day.
But, Effie, you must comfort *her* when I am past away.

And say to Robin a kind word, and tell him not to fret;
There's many a worthier than I, would make him happy yet.
If I had lived — I cannot tell — I might have been his wife;
But all these things have ceased to be, with my desire of life.

O look! the sun begins to rise, the heavens are in a glow;
He shines upon a hundred fields, and all of them I know.
And there I move no longer now, and there his light may shine —
Wild flowers in the valley for other hands than mine.

O sweet and strange it seems to me, that ere this day is done
The voice, that now is speaking, may be beyond the sun —
Forever and forever with those just souls and true —
And what is life, that we should moan ? why make we such ado ?

Forever and forever, all in a blessed home —
And there to wait a little while till you and Effie come —
To lie within the light of God, as I lie upon your breast —
And the wicked cease from troubling, and the weary are at rest.

THE LOTOS–EATERS.

"Courage!" he said, and pointed
toward the land,
"This mounting wave will roll us
shoreward soon."
In the afternoon they came unto a
land
In which it seemed always afternoon.
All round the coast the languid air did
swoon,
Breathing like one that hath a weary
dream.
Full-faced above the valley stood the
moon ;
And like a downward smoke, the slender stream
Along the cliff to fall and pause and
fall did seem.

A land of streams ! some, like a downward smoke,
Slow-dropping veils of thinnest lawn,
did go ;
And some thro' wavering lights and
shadows broke,
Rolling a slumbrous sheet of foam
below.
They saw the gleaming river seaward
flow
From the inner land: far off, three
mountain-tops,
Three silent pinnacles of aged snow,
Stood sunset-flush'd ; and, dew'd with
showery drops,
Up-clomb the shadowy pine above the
woven copse.

The charmed sunset linger'd low
adown
In the red West : thro' mountain clefts•
the dale

Was seen far inland, and the yellow
down
Border'd with palm, and many a winding vale
And meadow, set with slender galin-
gale ;
A land where all things always seem'd
the same !
And round about the keel with faces
pale,
Dark faces pale against that rosy flame,
The mild-eyed melancholy Lotos-
eaters came.

Branches they bore of that enchanted
stem,
Laden with flower and fruit, whereof
they gave
To each, but whoso did receive of
them,
And taste, to him the gushing of the
wave
Far far away did seem to mourn and
rave
On alien shores ; and if his fellow
spake,
His voice was thin, as voices from the
grave ;
And deep-asleep he seem'd, yet all
awake,
And music in his ears his beating heart
did make.

They sat them down upon the yellow
sand,
Between the sun and moon upon the
shore ;
And sweet it was to dream of Father-
land,
Of child and wife, and slave ; but
evermore

"In the hollow Lotos-land to live and lie reclined."

Page 60.

Most weary seem'd the sea, weary the
    oar,
Weary the wandering fields of barren
    foam.
Then some one said, " We will return
    no more ; "
And all at once they sang, " Our island
    home
Is far beyond the wave ; we will no
    longer roam."

CHORIC SONG.

I.

THERE is sweet music here that softer
    falls
Than petals from blown roses on the
    grass,
Or night-dews on still waters between
    walls
Of shadowy granite, in a gleaming
    pass ;
Music that gentlier on the spirit lies,
Than tir'd eyelids upon tir'd eyes ;
Music that brings sweet sleep down
    from the blissful skies.
Here are cool mosses deep,
And thro' the moss the ivies creep,
And in the stream the long-leaved
    flowers weep,
And from the craggy ledge the poppy
    hangs in sleep.

II.

Why are we weigh'd upon with heavi-
    ness,
And utterly consumed with sharp dis-
    tress,
While all things else have rest from
    weariness ?
All things have rest : why should we
    toil alone,
We only toil, who are the first of
    things,
And make perpetual moan,
Still from one sorrow to another
    thrown :
Nor ever fold our wings,
And cease from wanderings,
Nor steep our brows in slumber's holy
    balm ;

Nor hearken what the inner spirit
    sings,
" There is no joy but calm ! "
Why should we only toil, the roof and
    crown of things ?

III.

Lo ! in the middle of the wood,
The folded leaf is woo'd from out the
    bud
With winds upon the branch, and
    there
Grows green and broad, and takes no
    care,
Sun-steep'd at noon, and in the moon
Nightly dew-fed ; and turning yellow
Falls, and floats adown the air.
Lo ! sweeten'd with the summer light,
The full-juiced apple, waxing over-
    mellow,
Drops in a silent autumn night.
All its allotted length of days,
The flower ripens in its place,
Ripens and fades, and falls, and hath
    no toil,
Fast-rooted in the fruitful soil.

IV.

Hateful is the dark-blue sky,
Vaulted o'er the dark-blue sea.
Death is the end of life ; ah, why
Should life all labor be ?
Let us alone. Time driveth onward
    fast,
And in a little while our lips are dumb.
Let us alone. What is it that will last?
All things are taken from us, and be-
    come
Portions and parcels of the dreadful
    Past.
Let us alone. What pleasure can we
    have
To war with evil ? Is there any peace
In ever climbing up the climbing
    wave ?
All things have rest, and ripen toward
    the grave
In silence ; ripen, fall and cease :
Give us long rest or death, dark death,
    or dreamful ease.

v.

How sweet it were, hearing the down-
      ward stream,
With half-shut eyes ever to seem
Falling asleep in a half-dream !
To dream and dream, like yonder
      amber light,
Which will not leave the myrrh-bush
      on the height ;
To hear each other's whisper'd speech ;
Eating the Lotos day by day,
To watch the crisping ripples on the
      beach,
And tender curving lines of creamy
      spray ;
To lend our hearts and spirit wholly
To the influence of mild-minded mel-
      ancholy ;
To muse and brood and live again in
      memory,
With those old faces of our infancy
Heap'd over with a mound of grass,
Two handfuls of white dust, shut in
      an urn of brass!

vi.

Dear is the memory of our wedded
      lives,
And dear the last embraces of our
      wives
And their warm tears : but all hath
      suffer'd change :
For surely now our household hearths
      are cold :
Our sons inherit us : our looks are
      strange :
And we should come like ghosts to
      trouble joy.
Or else the island princes over-bold
Have eat our substance, and the min-
      strel sings,
Before them of the ten years' war in
      Troy,
And our great deeds, as half-forgotten
      things.
Is there confusion in the little isle ?
Let what is broken so remain.
The Gods are hard to reconcile :
'Tis hard to settle order once again.
There *is* confusion worse than death,
Trouble on trouble, pain on pain,
Long labor unto aged breath,
Sore task to hearts worn out by many
      wars
And eyes grown dim with gazing on
      the pilot-stars.

vii.

But, propt on beds of amaranth and
      moly,
How sweet (while warm airs lull us,
      blowing lowly)
With half-dropt eyelid still,
Beneath a heaven dark and holy,
To watch the long bright river draw-
      ing slowly
His waters from the purple hill —
To hear the dewy echoes calling
From cave to cave thro' the thick-
      twined vine —
To watch the emerald-color'd water
      falling
Thro' many a wov'n acanthus-wreath
      divine !
Only to hear and see the far-off spar-
      kling brine,
Only to hear were sweet, stretch'd out
      beneath the pine.

viii.

The Lotos blooms below the barren
      peak :
The Lotos blows by every-winding
      creek :
All day the wind breathes low with
      mellower tone :
Thro' every hollow cave and alley lone
Round and round the spicy downs the
      yellow Lotos-dust is blown.
We have had enough of action, and
      of motion we,
Roll'd to starboard, roll'd to larboard,
      when the surge was seething
      free,
Where the wallowing monster spouted
      his foam-fountains in the sea.
Let us swear an oath, and keep it with
      an equal mind,
In the hollow Lotos-land to live and
      lie reclined

On the hills like Gods together, care-
    less of mankind.
For they lie beside their nectar, and
    the bolts are hurl'd
Far below them in the valleys, and
    the clouds are lightly curl'd
Round their golden houses, girdled
    with the gleaming world :
Where they smile in secret, looking
    over wasted lands,
Blight and famine, plague and earth-
    quake, roaring deeps and fiery
    sands,
Clanging fights, and flaming towns,
    and sinking ships, and praying
    hands.
But they smile, they find a music cen-
    tred in a doleful song
Steaming up, a lamentation and an
    ancient tale of wrong,
Like a tale of little meaning tho' the
    words are strong ;
Chanted from an ill-used race of men
    that cleave the soil,
Sow the seed, and reap the harvest
    with enduring toil,
Storing yearly little dues of wheat,
    and wine and oil ;
Till they perish and they suffer —
    some, 'tis whisper'd — down in
    hell
Suffer endless anguish, others in
    Elysian valleys dwell,
Resting weary limbs at last on beds
    of asphodel.
Surely, surely, slumber is more sweet
    than toil, the shore
Than labor in the deep mid-ocean,
    wind and wave and oar ;
Oh rest ye, brother mariners, we will
    not wander more.

A DREAM OF FAIR WOMEN.

I READ, before my eyelids dropt their
    shade,
    " *The Legend of Good Women*," long
    ago
Sung by the morning-star of song,
    who made
    His music heard below ;

Dan Chaucer, the first warbler, whose
    sweet breath
Preluded those melodious bursts that
    fill
The spacious times of great Elizabeth
    With sounds that echo still.

And, for a while, the knowledge of
    his art
    Held me above the subject, as
    strong gales
Hold swollen clouds from raining,
    tho' my heart,
    Brimful of those wild tales,

Charged both mine eyes with tears.
    In every land
    I saw, wherever light illumineth,
Beauty and anguish walking hand in
    hand
    The downward slope to death.

Those far-renowned brides of ancient
    song
    Peopled the hollow dark, like burn-
    ing stars,
And I heard sounds of insult, shame,
    and wrong,
    And trumpets blown for wars ;

And clattering flints batter'd with
    clanging hoofs ;
    And I saw crowds in column'd
    sanctuaries ;
And forms that pass'd at windows
    and on roofs
    Of marble palaces ;

Corpses across the threshold ; heroes
    tall
    Dislodging pinnacle and parapet
Upon the tortoise creeping to the wall ;
    Lances in ambush set ;

And high shrine-doors burst thro' with
    heated blasts
    That run before the fluttering
    tongues of fire ;
White surf wind-scatter'd over sails
    and masts,
    And ever climbing higher

Squadrons and squares of men in
    brazen plates,
  Scaffolds, still sheets of water,
    divers woes,
Ranges of glimmering vaults with
    iron grates,
  And hush'd seraglios.

So shape chased shape as swift as,
    when to land
  Bluster the winds and tides the
    self-same way,
Crisp foam-flakes scud along the
    level sand,
  Torn from the fringe of spray.

I started once, or seem'd to start in
    pain,
  Resolved on noble things, and
    strove to speak,
As when a great thought strikes along
    the brain,
  And flushes all the cheek.

And once my arm was lifted to hew
    down
  A cavalier from off his saddle-bow,
That bore a lady from a leaguer'd
    town;
  And then, I know not how,

All those sharp fancies, by down-
    lapsing thought
  Stream'd onward, lost their edges,
    and did creep
Roll'd on each other, rounded,
    smooth'd, and brought
  Into the gulfs of sleep.

At last methought that I had wan-
    der'd far
  In an old wood: fresh-wash'd in
    coolest dew
The maiden splendors of the morning
    star
  Shook in the steadfast blue.

Enormous elm-tree-boles did stoop
    and lean
  Upon the dusky brushwood under-
    neath

Their broad curved branches, fledged
    with clearest green,
  New from its silken sheath.

The dim red morn had died, her
    journey done,
  And with dead lips smiled at the
    twilight plain,
Half-fall'n across the threshold of
    the sun,
  Never to rise again.

There was no motion in the dumb
    dead air,
  Not any song of bird or sound of
    rill;
Gross darkness of the inner sepulchre
  Is not so deadly still

As that wide forest. Growths of
    jasmine turn'd
  Their humid arms festooning tree
    to tree,
And at the root thro' lush green
    grasses burn'd
  The red anemone.

I knew the flowers, I knew the leaves,
    I knew
  The tearful glimmer of the languid
    dawn
On those long, rank, dark wood-walks
    drench'd in dew,
  Leading from lawn to lawn.

The smell of violets, hidden in the
    green,
  Pour'd back into my empty soul
    and frame
The times when I remember to have
    been
  Joyful and free from blame.

And from within me a clear under-
    tone
  Thrill'd thro' mine ears in that un-
    blissful clime,
"Pass freely thro': the wood is all
    thine own,
  Until the end of time."

At length I saw a lady within call,
  Stiller than chisell'd marble, stand-
    ing there;
A daughter of the gods, divinely tall,
  And most divinely fair.

Her loveliness with shame and with
    surprise
  Froze my swift speech: she turning
    on my face
The star-like sorrows of immortal
    eyes,
  Spoke slowly in her place.

" I had great beauty: ask thou not
    my name:
  No one can be more wise than
    destiny.
Many drew swords and died.
    Where'er I came
  I brought calamity."

" No marvel, sovereign lady: in fair
    field
  Myself for such a face had boldly
    died,"
I answer'd free; and turning I ap-
    peal'd
  To one that stood beside.

But she, with sick and scornful looks
    averse,
  To her full height her stately stat-
    ure draws;
" My youth," she said " was blasted
    with a curse:
  This woman was the cause.

" I was cut off from hope in that sad
    place,
  Which men call'd Aulis in those
    iron years:
My father held his hand upon his face;
  I, blinded with my tears,

" Still strove to speak: my voice was
    thick with sighs
  As in a dream. Dimly I could
    descry
The stern black-bearded kings with
    wolfish eyes,
  Waiting to see me die.

" The high masts flicker'd as they lay
    afloat;
  The crowds, the temples, waver'd,
    and the shore;
The bright death quiver'd at the vic-
    tim's throat;
  Touch'd; and I knew no more."

Whereto the other with a downward
    brow:
  " I would the white cold heavy-
    plunging foam,
Whirl'd by the wind, had roll'd me
    deep below,
  Then when I left my home."

Her slow full words sank thro' the
    silence drear,
  As thunder-drops fall on a sleeping
    sea:
Sudden I heard a voice that cried,
    " Come here,
  That I may look on thee."

I turning saw, throned on a flowery
    rise,
  One sitting on a crimson scarf un-
    roll'd;
A queen, with swarthy cheeks and
    bold black eyes,
  Brow-bound with burning gold.

She, flashing forth a haughty smile,
    began:
  " I govern'd men by change, and
    so I sway'd
All moods. 'Tis long since I have
    seen a man.
  Once, like the moon, I made

" The ever-shifting currents of the
    blood
  According to my humor ebb and
    flow.
I have no men to govern in this wood:
  That makes my only woe.

" Nay — yet it chafes me that I could
    not bend
  One will; nor tame and tutor with
    mine eye

That   dull   cold-blooded   Cæsar.
  Prythee, friend,
    Where is Mark Antony?

"The man, my lover, with whom I
    rode sublime
  On Fortune's neck: we sat as God
    by God:
The Nilus would have risen before his
    time
    And flooded at our nod.

"We drank the Libyan Sun to sleep,
    and lit
  Lamps which out-burn'd Canopus
    O my life
In Egypt! O the dalliance and the wit,
    The flattery and the strife,

"And the wild kiss, when fresh from
    war's alarms,
  My Hercules, my Roman Antony,
My mailed Bacchus leapt into my
    arms,
    Contented there to die!

"And there he died: and when I heard
    my name
  Sigh'd forth with life I would not
    brook my fear
Of the other: with a worm I balk'd
    his fame.
    What else was left? look here!"

(With that she tore her robe apart,
    and half
  The polish'd argent of her breast to
    sight
Laid bare. Thereto she pointed with
    a laugh,
    Showing the aspick's bite.)

"I died a Queen. The Roman soldier
    found
  Me lying dead, my crown about my
    brows,
A name forever!—lying robed and
    crown'd,
    Worthy a Roman spouse."

Her warbling voice, a lyre of widest
    range
  Struck by all passion, did fall down
    and glance
From tone to tone, and glided thro' all
    change
    Of liveliest utterance.

When she made pause I knew not for
    delight:
  Because with sudden motion from
    the ground
She rais'd her piercing orbs, and fill'd
    with light
    The interval of sound.

Still with their fires Love tipt his keen-
    est darts;
  As once they drew into two burning
    rings
All beams of Love, melting the mighty
    hearts
    Of captains and of kings.

Slowly my sense undazzled. Then I
    heard
  A noise of some one coming thro'
    the lawn,
And singing clearer than the crested
    bird
    That claps his wings at dawn.

"The torrent brooks of hallow'd Israel
  From craggy hollows pouring, late
    and soon,
Sound all night long, in falling thro'
    the dell,
    Far-heard beneath the moon.

"The balmy moon of blessed Israel
  Floods all the deep-blue gloom with
    beams divine:
All night the splinter'd crags that wall
    the dell
    With spires of silver shine."

As one that museth where broad sun-
    shine laves
  The lawn by some cathedral, thro'
    the door
Hearing the holy organ rolling waves
    Of sound on roof and floor

Within, and anthem sung, is charm'd
    and tied
  To where he stands,— so stood I,
    when that flow
Of music left the lips of her that died
  To save her father's vow;

The daughter of the warrior Gileadite;
  A maiden pure; as when she went
    along
From Mizpeh's tower'd gate with wel-
    come light,
  With timbrel and with song.

My words leapt forth : "Heaven heads
    the count of crimes
  With that wild oath." She render'd
    answer high :
" Not so, nor once alone; a thousand
    times
  I would be born and die.

" Single I grew, like some green plant,
    whose root
  Creeps to the garden water-pipes
    beneath
Feeding the flower; but ere my flower
    to fruit
  Changed, I was ripe for death.

'My God, my land, my father — these
    did move
  Me from my bliss of life, that Nature
    gave,
Lower'd softly with a threefold cord
    of love
  Down to a silent grave.

' And I went mourning, ' No fair
    Hebrew boy
  Shall smile away my maiden blame
    among
The Hebrew mothers '— emptied of
    all joy,
  Leaving the dance and song,

" Leaving the olive-gardens far below,
  Leaving the promise of my bridal
    bower,
The valleys of grape-loaded vines that
    glow
  Beneath the battled tower.

"The light white cloud swam over us.
    Anon
  We heard the lion roaring from his
    den ;
We saw the large white stars rise one
    by one,
  Or, from the darken'd glen,

" Saw God divide the night with flying
    flame,
  And thunder on the everlasting hills.
I heard Him, for He spake, and grief
    became
  A solemn scorn of ills.

" When the next moon was roll'd into
    the sky,
  Strength came to me that equall'd
    my desire.
How beautiful a thing it was to die
  For God and for my sire !

"It comforts me in this one thought
    to dwell,
  That I subdued me to my father's
    will;
Because the kiss he gave me, ere I
    fell,
  Sweetens the spirit still.

" Moreover it is written that my race
  Hew'd Ammon, hip and thigh, from
    Aroer
On Arnon unto Minneth." Here her
    face
  Glow'd as I look'd at her.

She lock'd her lips : she left me where
    I stood :
  "Glory to God," she sang, and past
    afar,
Thridding the sombre boskage of the
    wood,
  Toward the morning-star.

Losing her carol I stood pensively,
  As one that from a casement leans
    his head,
When midnight bells cease ringing
    suddenly,
  And the old year is dead.

" Alas ! alas ! " a low voice, full of
    care,
  Murmur'd beside me: " Turn and
      look on me :
I am that Rosamond, whom men call
    fair,
  If what I was I be.

" Would I had been some maiden
    coarse and poor !
  O me, that I should ever see the
      light !
Those dragon eyes of anger'd Eleanor
  Do hunt me, day and night."

She ceased in tears, fallen from hope
    and trust :
  To whom the Egyptian : " O, you
      tamely died !
You should have clung to Fulvia's
    waist, and thrust
  The dagger thro' her side."

With that sharp sound the white
    dawn's creeping beams,
  Stol'n to my brain, dissolved the
      mystery
Of folded sleep.   The captain of my
    dreams
  Ruled in the eastern sky.

Morn broaden'd on the borders of
    the dark,
  Ere I saw her, who clasp'd in her
      last trance
Her murder'd father's head, or Joan
    of Arc,
  A light of ancient France ;

Or her who knew that Love can van-
    quish Death,
  Who kneeling, with one arm about
      her king,
Drew forth the poison with her balmy
    breath,
  Sweet as new buds in Spring.

No memory labors longer from the
    deep
  Gold-mines of thought to lift the
      hidden ore

That glimpses, moving up, than I from
    sleep)
  To gather and tell o'er

Each little sound and sight.   With
    what dull pain
  Compass'd, how eagerly I sought to
      strike
Into that wondrous track of dreams
    again !
  But no two dreams are like.

As when a soul laments, which hath
    been blest,
  Desiring what is mingled with past
      years,
In yearnings that can never be exprest
  By signs or groans or tears ;

Because all words, tho' cull'd with
    choicest art,
  Failing to give the bitter of the
      sweet,
Wither beneath the palate, and the
    heart
  Faints, faded by its heat.

_____

THE BLACKBIRD.

O BLACKBIRD ! sing me something
    well :
  While all the neighbors shoot thee
      round,
  I keep smooth plats of fruitful
      ground,
Where thou may'st warble, eat and
    dwell.

The espaliers and the standards all
  Are thine ; the range of lawn and
      park :
  The unnetted black-hearts ripen
      dark,
All thine, against the garden wall.

Yet, tho' I spared thee all the spring
  Thy sole delight is, sitting still,
  With that gold dagger of thy bill
To fret the summer jenneting.

A golden bill ! the silver tongue,
  Cold February loved, is dry :

Plenty corrupts the melody
That made thee famous once, when
    young:

And in the sultry garden-squares,
  Now thy flute notes are changed to
    coarse,
I hear thee not at all, or hoarse
As when a hawker hawks his wares.

Take warning! he that will not sing
  While yon sun prospers in the blue,
  Shall sing for want, ere leaves are
    new,
Caught in the frozen palms of Spring.

THE DEATH OF THE OLD YEAR.

FULL knee-deep lies the winter snow,
  And the winter winds are wearily
    sighing:
Toll ye the church-bell sad and slow,
And tread softly and speak low,
For the old year lies a-dying.
    Old year, you must not die;
    You came to us so readily,
    You lived with us so steadily,
    Old year, you shall not die.

He lieth still: he doth not move:
He will not see the dawn of day.
He hath no other life above.
He gave me a friend, and a true true-
    love,
And the New-year will take 'em away.
    Old year, you must not go;
    So long as you have been with us
    Such joy as you have seen with us,
    Old year, you shall not go.

He froth'd his bumpers to the brim;
A jollier year we shall not see.
But tho' his eyes are waxing dim,
And tho' his foes speak ill of him,
He was a friend to me.
    Old year, you shall not die;
    We did so laugh and cry with you,
    I've half a mind to die with you,
    Old year, if you must die.

He was full of joke and jest,
But all his merry quips are o'er.
To see him die, across the waste
His son and heir doth ride post-haste,
But he'll be dead before.
    Every one for his own.
    The night is starry and cold, my
      friend,
    And the New-year blithe and bold,
      my friend,
    Comes up to take his own.

How hard he breathes! over the snow
I heard just now the crowing cock.
The shadows flicker to and fro:
The cricket chirps: the light burns
    low:
'Tis nearly twelve o'clock.
    Shake hands, before you die.
    Old year, we'll dearly rue for you:
    What is it we can do for you?
    Speak out before you die.

His face is growing sharp and thin.
Alack! our friend is gone.
Close up his eyes: tie up his chin:
Step from the corpse, and let him in
That standeth there alone,
    And waiteth at the door.
    There's a new foot on the floor,
      my friend,
    And a new face at the door, my
      friend,
    A new face at the door.

TO J. S.

THE wind, that beats the mountain,
    blows
  More softly round the open wold,
And gently comes the world to those
    That are cast in gentle mould.

And me this knowledge bolder made,
  Or else I had not dared to flow
In these words toward you, and invade
    Even with a verse your holy woe.

'Tis strange that those we lean on
    most,
  Those in whose laps our limbs
    are nursed,

Fall into shadow, soonest lost :
    Those we love first are taken first.

God gives us love. Something to love
    He lends us; but, when love is
        grown
To ripeness, that on which it throve
    Falls off, and love is left alone.

This is the curse of time. Alas !
    In grief I am not all unlearn'd ;
Once thro' mine own doors Death did
        pass ;
    One went, who never hath re-
        turn'd.

He will not smile — not speak to me
    Once more. Two years his chair
        is seen
Empty before us. That was he
    Without whose life I had not
        been.

Your loss is rarer ; for this star
    Rose with you thro' a little arc
Of heaven, nor having wander'd far
    Shot on the sudden into dark.

I knew your brother : his mute dust
    I honor and his living worth :
A man more pure and bold and just
    Was never born into the earth.

I have not look'd upon you nigh,
    Since that dear soul hath fall'n
        asleep.
Great Nature is more wise than I :
    I will not tell you not to weep.

And tho' mine own eyes fill with dew,
    Drawn from the spirit thro' the
        brain,
I will not even preach to you,
    " Weep, weeping dulls the inward
        pain."

Let Grief be her own mistress still.
    She loveth her own anguish deep
More than much pleasure. Let her
        will
    Be done — to weep or not to weep.

I will not say, " God's ordinance
    Of Death is blown in every wind" ;

For that is not a common chance
    That takes away a noble mind.

His memory long will live alone
    In all our hearts, as mournful light
That broods above the fallen sun,
    And dwells in heaven half the
        night.

Vain solace ! Memory standing near
    Cast down her eyes, and in her
        throat
Her voice seem'd distant, and a tear
    Dropt on the letters as I wrote.

I wrote I know not what. In truth,
    How *should* I soothe you anyway,
Who miss the brother of your youth ?
    Yet something I did wish to say :

For he too was a friend to me :
    Both are my friends, and my true
        breast
Bleedeth for both ; yet it may be
    That only silence suiteth best.

Words weaker than your grief would
        make
    Grief more. 'Twere better I
        should cease
Although myself could almost take
    The place of him that sleeps in
        peace.

Sleep sweetly, tender heart, in peace :
    Sleep, holy spirit, blessed soul,
While the stars burn, the moons in-
        crease,
    And the great ages onward roll.

Sleep till the end, true soul and sweet.
    Nothing comes to thee new or
        strange.
Sleep full of rest from head to feet ;
    Lie still, dry dust, secure of
        change.

ON A MOURNER.

I.

NATURE, so far as in her lies,
    Imitates God, and turns her face
To every land beneath the skies,

Counts nothing that she meets with
   base,
But lives and loves in every place ;

II.

Fills out the homely quickset-screens,
   And makes the purple lilac ripe,
Steps from her airy hill, and greens
   The swamp, where hums the drop-
      ping snipe,
   With moss and braided marish-pipe ;

III.

And on thy heart a finger lays,
   Saying, " Beat quicker, for the time
Is pleasant, and the woods and ways
   Are pleasant, and the beech and
      lime
   Put forth and feel a gladder clime."

IV.

And murmurs of a deeper voice,
   Going before to some far shrine,
Teach that sick heart the stronger
      choice,
   Till all thy life one way incline
   With one wide Will that closes thine.

V.

And when the zoning eve has died
   Where yon dark valleys wind for-
      lorn,
Come Hope and Memory, spouse and
      bride,
   From out the borders of the morn,
   With that fair child betwixt them
      born.

VI.

And when no mortal motion jars
   The blackness round the tombing
      sod,
Thro' silence and the trembling stars
   Comes Faith from tracts no feet
      have trod,
   And Virtue, like a household god

VII.

Promising empire ; such as those
   Once heard at dead of night to greet
Troy's wandering prince, so that he
   rose

With sacrifice, while all the fleet
Had rest by stony hills of Crete.

You ask me, why, tho' ill at ease,
   Within this region I subsist,
   Whose spirits falter in the mist,
And languish for the purple seas.

It is the land that freemen till,
   That sober-suited Freedom chose,
   The land, where girt with friends
      or foes
A man may speak the thing he will ;

A land of settled government,
   A land of just and old renown,
   Where Freedom slowly broadens
      down
From precedent to precedent :

Where faction seldom gathers head,
   But by degrees to fulness wrought,
   The strength of some diffusive
      thought
Hath time and space to work and
      spread.

Should banded unions persecute
   Opinion, and induce a time
   When single thought is civil
      crime,
And individual freedom mute ;

Tho' Power should make from land
      to land
   The name of Britain trebly great—
   Tho' every channel of the State
Should fill and choke with golden
      sand —

Yet waft me from the harbor-mouth,
   Wild wind ! I seek a warmer sky,
   And I will see before I die
The palms and temples of the South.

Of old sat Freedom on the heights,
   The thunders breaking at her feet:
Above her shook the starry lights :
   She heard the torrents meet.

There in her place she did rejoice,
　　Self-gather'd in her prophet-mind,
But fragments of her mighty voice
　　Came rolling on the wind.

Then stept she down thro' town and
　　field
　　To mingle with the human race,
And part by part to men reveal'd
　　The fulness of her face —

Grave mother of majestic works,
　　From her isle-altar gazing down :
Who, God-like, grasps the triple forks,
　　And, King-like, wears the crown ;

Her open eyes desire the truth.
　　The wisdom of a thousand years
Is in them.　May perpetual youth
　　Keep dry their light from tears ;

That her fair form may stand and
　　shine,
　　Make bright our days and light
　　our dreams,
Turning to scorn with lips divine
　　The falsehood of extremes !

————

Love thou thy land, with love far-
　　brought
　　From out the storied Past, and
　　used
Within the Present, but transfused
Thro' future time by power of thought.

True love turn'd round on fixed poles,
　　Love, that endures not sordid ends,
　　For English natures, freemen,
　　friends,
Thy brothers and immortal souls.

But pamper not a hasty time,
　　Nor feed with crude imaginings
　　The herd, wild hearts and feeble
　　wings
That every sophister can lime.

Deliver not the tasks of might
　　To weakness, neither hide the ray

From those, not blind, who wait for
　　day,
Tho' sitting girt with doubtful light.

Make knowledge circle with the
　　winds ;
　　But let her herald, Reverence, fly
　　Before her to whatever sky
Bear seed of men and growth of
　　minds.

Watch what main-currents draw the
　　years :
　　Cut Prejudice against the grain :
　　But gentle words are always gain :
Regard the weakness of thy peers :

Nor toil for title, place, or touch
　　Of pension, neither count on praise :
　　It grows to guerdon after-days :
Nor deal in watch-words overmuch :

Not clinging to some ancient saw ;
　　Nor master'd by some modern term ;
　　Not swift nor slow to change, but
　　firm ;
And in its season bring the law ;

That from Discussion's lip may fall
　　With Life, that, working strongly,
　　binds —
　　Set in all lights by many minds,
To close the interest of all.

For Nature also, cold and warm,
　　And moist and dry, devising long,
　　Thro' many agents making strong,
Matures the individual form.

Meet is it changes should control
　　Our being, lest we rust in ease.
　　We all are changed by still degrees,
All but the basis of the soul.

So let the change which comes be
　　free
　　To ingroove itself with that which
　　flies,
　　And work, a joint of state, that plies
Its office, moved with sympathy.

A saying, hard to shape in act;
 For all the past of Time reveals
 A bridal dawn of thunder-peals,
Wherever Thought hath wedded Fact.

Ev'n now we hear with inward strife
 A motion toiling in the gloom—
 The Spirit of the years to come
Yearning to mix himself with Life.

A slow-develop'd strength awaits
 Completion in a painful school;
 Phantoms of other forms of rule,
New Majesties of mighty States —

The warders of the growing hour,
 But vague in vapor, hard to mark;
 And round them sea and air are
  dark
With great contrivances of Power.

Of many changes, aptly join'd,
 Is bodied forth the second whole.
 Regard gradation, lest the soul
Of Discord race the rising wind;

A wind to puff your idol-fires,
 And heap their ashes on the head;
 To shame the boast so often made,
That we are wiser than our sires.

Oh yet, if Nature's evil star
 Drive men in manhood, as in youth,
 To follow flying steps of Truth
Across the brazen bridge of war —

If New and Old, disastrous feud,
 Must ever shock, like armed foes,
 And this be true, till Time shall
  close,
That Principles are rain'd in blood;

Not yet the wise of heart would cease
 To hold his hope thro' shame and
  guilt,
 But with his hand against the hilt,
Would pace the troubled land, like
  Peace;

Not less, tho' dogs of Faction bay,
 Would serve his kind in deed and
  word,

Certain, if knowledge bring the
  sword,
That knowledge takes the sword
  away —

Would love the gleams of good that
  broke
 From either side, nor veil his eyes:
 And if some dreadful need should
  rise
Would strike, and firmly, and one
  stroke:

To-morrow yet would reap to-day,
 As we bear blossom of the dead;
 Earn well the thrifty months, nor
  wed
Raw Haste, half-sister to Delay.

ENGLAND AND AMERICA
IN 1782.

O THOU, that sendest out the man
 To rule by land and sea,
Strong mother of a Lion-line,
Be proud of those strong sons of thine
 Who wrench'd their rights from
  thee!

What wonder, if in noble heat
 Those men thine arms withstood,
Retaught the lesson thou hadst taught,
And in thy spirit with thee fought —
 Who sprang from English blood!

But Thou rejoice with liberal joy,
 Lift up thy rocky face.
And shatter, when the storms are
  black,
In many a streaming torrent back,
 The seas that shock thy base!

Whatever harmonies of law
 The growing world assume,
Thy work is thine — The single note
From that deep chord which Hampden
  smote
 Will vibrate to the doom.

THE GOOSE.

I KNEW an old wife lean and poor,
  Her rags scarce held together;
There strode a stranger to the door,
  And it was windy weather.

He held a goose upon his arm,
  He utter'd rhyme and reason,
" Here, take the goose, and keep you
    warm,
  It is a stormy season."

She caught the white goose by the leg,
  A goose — 'twas no great matter.
The goose let fall a golden egg
  With cackle and with clatter.

She dropt the goose, and caught the
    pelf,
  And ran to tell her neighbors;
And bless'd herself, and cursed herself,
  And rested from her labors.

And feeding high, and living soft,
  Grew plump and able-bodied;
Until the grave churchwarden doff'd,
  The parson smirk'd and nodded.

So sitting, served by man and maid,
  She felt her heart grow prouder:
But ah! the more the white goose laid
  It clack'd and cackled louder.

It clutter'd here, it chuckled there;
  It stirr'd the old wife's mettle:
She shifted in her elbow-chair,
  And hurl'd the pan and kettle.

" A quinsy choke thy cursed note!"
  Then wax'd her anger stronger.
"Go, take the goose, and wring her
    throat,
  I will not bear it longer."

Then yelp'd the cur, and yawl'd the
    cat;
  Ran Gaffer, stumbled Gammer.
The goose flew this way and flew that,
  And fill'd the house with clamor.

As head and heels upon the floor
  They flounder'd all together,
There strode a stranger to the door,
  And it was windy weather:

He took the goose upon his arm,
  He utter'd words of scorning;
"So keep you cold, or keep you warm,
  It is a stormy morning."

The wild wind rang from park and
    plain,
  And round the attics rumbled,
Till all the tables danced again,
  And half the chimneys tumbled.

The glass blew in, the fire blew out,
  The blast was hard and harder.
Her cap blew off, her gown blew up,
  And a whirlwind clear'd the larder:

And while on all sides breaking loose
  Her household fled the danger,
Quoth she, "The Devil take the goose,
  And God forget the stranger!"

ENGLISH IDYLS AND OTHER POEMS.

———o◦❋◦o———

THE EPIC.

At Francis Allen's on the Christmas-
eve, —
The game of forfeits done — the girls
all kiss'd
Beneath the sacred bush and past
away —
The parson Holmes, the poet Everard
Hall,
The host, and I sat round the wassail-
bowl,
Then half-way ebb'd: and there we
held a talk,
How all the old honor had from
Christmas gone,
Or gone, or dwindled down to some
odd games
In some odd nooks like this; till I,
tired out
With cutting eights that day upon the
pond,
Where, three times slipping from the
outer edge,
I bump'd the ice into three several
stars,
Fell in a doze; and half awake I
heard
The parson taking wide and wider
sweeps,
Now harping on the church-commis-
sioners,
Now hawking at Geology and schism;
Until I woke, and found him settled
down
Upon the general decay of faith
Right thro' the world, "at home was
little left,

And none abroad: there was no
anchor, none,
To hold by." Francis, laughing, clapt
his hand
On Everard's shoulder, with " I hold
by him."
"And I," quoth Everard, "by the
wassail-bowl."
"Why yes," I said, " we knew your
gift that way
At college: but another which you
had,
I mean of verse (for so we held it
then),
What came of that ? " " You know,"
said Frank, " he burnt
His epic, his King Arthur, some twelve
books "—
And then to me demanding why?
"Oh, sir,
He thought that nothing new was said,
or else
Something so said 'twas nothing —
that a truth
Looks freshest in the fashion of the
day:
God knows: he has a mint of reasons:
ask.
It pleased *me* well enough." " Nay,
nay," said Hall,
"Why take the style of those heroic
times ?
For nature brings not back the Mas-
todon,
Nor we those times; and why should
any man
Remodel models ? these twelve books
of mine

Were faint Homeric echoes, nothing-worth,
Mere chaff and draff, much better burnt." " But I,"
Said Francis, " pick'd the eleventh from this hearth
And have it : keep a thing, its use will come.
I hoard it as a sugar-plum for Holmes."
He laugh'd, and I, tho' sleepy, like a horse
That hears the corn-bin open, prick'd my ears ;
For I remember'd Everard's college fame
When we were Freshmen : then at my request
He brought it ; and the poet little urged,
But with some prelude of disparagement,
Read, mouthing out his hollow oes and aes,
Deep-chested music, and to this result.

MORTE D'ARTHUR.

So all day long the noise of battle roll'd
Among the mountains by the winter sea ;
Until King Arthur's table, man by man,
Had fallen in Lyonness about their Lord,
King Arthur : then, because his wound was deep,
The bold Sir Bedivere uplifted him,
Sir Bedivere, the last of all his knights,
And bore him to a chapel nigh the field,
A broken chancel with a broken cross,
That stood on a dark strait of barren land.
On one side lay the Ocean, and on one
Lay a great water, and the moon was full.
Then spake King Arthur to Sir Bedivere :
" The sequel of to-day unsolders all

The goodliest fellowship of famous knights
Whereof this world holds record. Such a sleep
They sleep — the men I loved. I think that we
Shall nevermore, at any future time,
Delight our souls with talk of knightly deeds,
Walking about the gardens and the halls
Of Camelot, as in the days that were.
I perish by this people which I made, —
Tho' Merlin sware that I should come again
To rule once more — but let what will be, be,
I am so deeply smitten thro' the helm
That without help I cannot last till morn.
Thou therefore take my brand Excalibur,
Which was my pride: for thou rememberest how
In those old days, one summer noon, an arm
Rose up from out the bosom of the lake,
Clothed in white samite, mystic, wonderful,
Holding the sword — and how I row'd across
And took it, and have worn it like a king :
And, wheresoever I am sung or told
In aftertime, this also shall be known :
But now delay not: take Excalibur,
And fling him far into the middle mere :
Watch what thou seëst, and lightly bring me word."
To him replied the bold Sir Bedivere :
" It is not meet, Sir King, to leave thee thus,
Aidless, alone, and smitten thro' the helm.
A little thing may harm a wounded man.
Yet I thy hest will all perform at full,

Watch what I see, and lightly bring
thee word."
　So saying, from the ruin'd shrine
he stept
And in the moon athwart the place of
tombs,
Where lay the mighty bones of an-
cient men,
Old knights, and over them the sea-
wind sang
Shrill, chill, with flakes of foam. He,
stepping down
By zig-zag paths, and juts of pointed
rock,
Came on the shining levels of the lake.
　There drew he forth the brand
Excalibur,
And o'er him, drawing it, the winter
moon,
Brightening the skirts of a long cloud,
ran forth
And sparkled keen with frost against
the hilt:
For all the haft twinkled with dia-
mond sparks,
Myriads of topaz-lights, and jacinth-
work
Of subtlest jewelry. He gazed so long
That both his eyes were dazzled, as
he stood,
This way and that dividing the swift
mind,
In act to throw: but at the last it
seem'd
Better to leave Excalibur conceal'd
There in the many-knotted water-flags,
That whistled stiff and dry about the
marge.
So strode he back slow to the wounded
King.
　Then spake King Arthur to Sir
Bedivere:
"Hast thou perform'd my mission
which I gave?
What is it thou hast seen? or what
hast heard?"
　And answer made the bold Sir
Bedivere:
"I heard the ripple washing in the
reeds,
And the wild water lapping on the
crag."

To whom replied King Arthur, faint
and pale:
"Thou hast betray'd thy nature and
thy name,
Not rendering true answer, as be-
seem'd
Thy fealty, nor like a noble knight:
For surer sign had follow'd, either
hand,
Or voice, or else a motion of the mere.
This is a shameful thing for men to
lie.
Yet now, I charge thee, quickly go
again
As thou art lief and dear, and do the
thing
I bade thee, watch, and lightly bring
me word."
　Then went Sir Bedivere the second
time
Across the ridge, and paced beside
the mere,
Counting the dewy pebbles, fix'd in
thought;
But when he saw the wonder of the
hilt,
How curiously and strangely chased,
he smote
His palms together, and he cried aloud,
"And if indeed I cast the brand
away,
Surely a precious thing, one worthy
note,
Should thus be lost for ever from the
earth,
Which might have pleased the eyes
of many men.
What good should follow this, if this
were done?
What harm, undone? deep harm to
disobey,
Seeing obedience is the bond of rule.
Were it well to obey them, if a king
demand
An act unprofitable, against himself?
The King is sick, and knows not what
he does.
What record, or what relic of my lord
Should be to aftertime, but empty
breath
And rumors of a doubt? but were
this kept,

Stored in some treasure-house of
  mighty kings,
Some one might show it at a joust of
  arms,
Saying, 'King Arthur's sword, Excali-
  bur,
Wrought by the lonely maiden of the
  Lake.
Nine years she wrought it, sitting in
  the deeps
Upon the hidden bases of the hills.'
So might some old man speak in the
  aftertime
To all the people, winning reverence.
But now much honor and much fame
  were lost."
    So spake he, clouded with his own
      conceit,
And hid Excalibur the second time,
And so strode back slow to the
  wounded King.
    Then spoke King Arthur, breathing
      heavily:
"What is it thou hast seen? or what
  hast heard?"
    And answer made the bold Sir
      Bedivere:
"I heard the water lapping on the
  crag,
And the long ripple washing in the
  reeds."
    To whom replied King Arthur,
      much in wrath:
"Ah, miserable and unkind, untrue,
Unknightly, traitor-hearted! Woe is
  me!
Authority forgets a dying king,
Laid widow'd of the power in his
  eye
That bow'd the will. I see thee what
  thou art,
For thou, the latest-left of all my
  knights,
In whom should meet the offices of all,
Thou wouldst betray me for the
  precious hilt;
Either from lust of gold, or like a girl
Valuing the giddy pleasure of the eyes.
Yet, for a man may fail in duty twice,
And the third time may prosper, get
  thee hence:
But, if thou spare to fling Excalibur,

I will arise and slay thee with my
  hands."
    Then quickly rose Sir Bedivere, and
      ran,
And, leaping down the ridges lightly,
  plunged
Among the bulrush-beds, and clutch'd
  the sword,
And strongly wheel'd and threw it.
  The great brand
Made lightnings in the splendor of
  the moon,
And flashing round and round, and
  whirl'd in an arch,
Shot like a streamer of the northern
  morn,
Seen where the moving isles of win-
  ter shock
By night, with noises of the northern
  sea.
So flash'd and fell the brand Excalibur:
But ere he dipt the surface, rose an
  arm
Clothed in white samite, mystic, won-
  derful,
And caught him by the hilt, and
  brandish'd him
Three times, and drew him under in
  the mere.
And lightly went the other to the
  King.
    Then spoke King Arthur, drawing
      thicker breath:
"Now see I by thine eyes that this is
  done.
Speak out: what is it thou hast heard,
  or seen?"
    And answer made the bold Sir
      Bedivere:
"Sir King, I closed mine eyelids, lest
  the gems
Should blind my purpose, for I never
  saw,
Nor shall see, here or elsewhere, till I
  die,
Not tho' I live three lives of mortal
  men,
So great a miracle as yonder hilt.
Then with both hands I flung him,
  wheeling him;
But when I look'd again, behold an
  arm,

Clothed in white samite, mystic, wonderful,
That caught him by the hilt, and brandish'd him
Three times, and drew him under in the mere."
And answer made King Arthur, breathing hard:
" My end draws nigh ; 'tis time that I were gone.
Make broad thy shoulders to receive my weight,
And bear me to the margin; yet I fear
My wound hath taken cold, and I shall die."
So saying, from the pavement he half rose,
Slowly, with pain, reclining on his arm,
And looking wistfully with wide blue eyes
As in a picture. Him Sir Bedivere
Remorsefully regarded thro' his tears,
And would have spoken, but he found not words,
Then took with care, and kneeling on one knee,
O'er both his shoulders drew the languid hands,
And rising bore him thro' the place of tombs.
But, as he walk'd, King Arthur panted hard,
Like one that feels a nightmare on his bed
When all the house is mute. So sigh'd the King,
Muttering and murmuring at his ear, " Quick, quick !
I fear it is too late, and I shall die."
But the other swiftly strode from ridge to ridge,
Clothed with his breath, and looking, as he walk'd,
Larger than human on the frozen hills.
He heard the deep behind him, and a cry
Before. His own thought drove him, like a goad.
Dry clash'd his harness in the icy caves

And barren chasms, and all to left and right
The bare black cliff clang'd round him, as he based
His feet on juts of slippery crag that rang
Sharp-smitten with the dint of armed heels —
And on a sudden, lo ! the level lake,
And the long glories of the winter moon.
Then saw they how there hove a dusky barge,
Dark as a funeral scarf from stem to stern,
Beneath them; and descending they were ware
That all the decks were dense with stately forms
Black-stoled, black-hooded, like a dream — by these
Three Queens with crowns of gold — and from them rose
A cry that shiver'd to the tingling stars,
And, as it were one voice an agony
Of lamentation, like a wind, that shrills
All night in a waste land, where no one comes,
Or hath come, since the making of the world.
Then murmur'd Arthur, "Place me in the barge,"
And to the barge they came. There those three Queens
Put forth their hands, and took the King, and wept.
But she, that rose the tallest of them all
And fairest, laid his head upon her lap,
And loosed the shatter'd casque, and chafed his hands,
And call'd him by his name, complaining loud,
And dropping bitter tears against his brow
Striped with dark blood: for all his face was white
And colorless, and like the wither'd moon

Smote by the fresh beam of the springing east;
And all his greaves and cuisses dash'd with drops
Of onset; and the light and lustrous curls —
That made his forehead like a rising sun
High from the daïs-throne — were parch'd with dust;
Or, clotted into points and hanging loose,
Mix'd with the knightly growth that fringed his lips.
So like a shatter'd column lay the King;
Not like that Arthur who, with lance in rest,
From spur to plume a star of tournament,
Shot thro' the lists at Camelot, and charged
Before the eyes of ladies and of kings.
 Then loudly cried the bold Sir Bedivere,
"Ah! my Lord Arthur, whither shall I go?
Where shall I hide my forehead and my eyes?
For now I see the true old times are dead,
When every morning brought a noble chance,
And every chance brought out a noble knight.
Such times have been not since the light that led
The holy Elders with the gift of myrrh.
But now the whole ROUND TABLE is dissolved
Which was an image of the mighty world;
And I, the last, go forth companionless,
And the days darken round me, and the years,
Among new men, strange faces, other minds."
 And slowly answered Arthur from the barge:
"The old order changeth, yielding place to new,

And God fulfils Himself in many ways,
Lest one good custom should corrupt the world.
Comfort thyself: what comfort is in me?
I have lived my life, and that which I have done
May He within Himself make pure! but thou,
If thou shouldst never see my face again,
Pray for my soul. More things are wrought by prayer
Than this world dreams of. Wherefore, let thy voice
Rise like a fountain for me night and day.
For what are men better than sheep or goats
That nourish a blind life within the brain,
If, knowing God, they lift not hands of prayer
Both for themselves and those who call them friend?
For so the whole round earth is every way
Bound by gold chains about the feet of God.
But now farewell. I am going a long way
With these thou seëst — if indeed I go —
(For all my mind is clouded with a doubt)
To the island-valley of Avilion;
Where falls not hail, or rain, or any snow,
Nor ever wind blows loudly; but it lies
Deep-meadow'd, happy, fair with orchard-lawns
And bowery hollows crown'd with summer sea,
Where I will heal me of my grievous wound."
 So said he, and the barge with oar and sail
Moved from the brink, like some full-breasted swan
That, fluting a wild carol ere her death,

Ruffles her pure cold plume, and takes
the flood
With swarthy webs. Long stood Sir
Bedivere
Revolving many memories, till the
hull
Look'd one black dot against the verge
of dawn,
And on the mere the wailing died
away.

HERE ended Hall, and our last light,
that long
Had wink'd and threaten'd darkness,
flared and fell:
At which the Parson, sent to sleep
with sound,
And waked with silence, grunted
"Good!" but we
Sat rapt: it was the tone with which
he read—
Perhaps some modern touches here
and there
Redeem'd it from the charge of noth-
ingness—
Or else we loved the man, and prized
his work;
I know not: but we sitting, as I said,
The cock crew loud; as at that time
of year
The lusty bird takes every hour for
dawn:
Then Francis, muttering, like a man
ill-used,
"There now—that's nothing!" drew
a little back,
And drove his heel into the smoul-
der'd log,
That sent a blast of sparkles up the
flue:
And so to bed; where yet in sleep I
seem'd
To sail with Arthur under looming
shores,
Point after point; till on to dawn,
when dreams
Begin to feel the truth and stir of
day,
To me, methought, who waited with a
crowd,
There came a bark that, blowing forward, bore

King Arthur, like a modern gentle-
man
Of stateliest port; and all the people
cried,
"Arthur is come again: he cannot
die."
Then those that stood upon the hills
behind
Repeated—"Come again, and thrice
as fair;"
And, further inland, voices echoed—
"Come
With all good things, and war shall
be no more."
At this a hundred bells began to peal,
That with the sound I woke, and heard
indeed
The clear church-bells ring in the
Christmas-morn.

THE GARDENER'S DAUGHTER;

OR, THE PICTURES.

THIS morning is the morning of the
day,
When I and Eustace from the city
went
To see the Gardener's Daughter; I
and he,
Brothers in Art; a friendship so com-
plete
Portion'd in halves between us, that
we grew
The fable of the city where we dwelt.
My Eustace might have sat for
Hercules;
So muscular he spread, so broad of
breast.
He, by some law that holds in love,
and draws
The greater to the lesser, long desired
A certain miracle of symmetry,
A miniature of loveliness, all grace
Summ'd up and closed in little;—
Juliet, she
So light of foot, so light of spirit—
oh, she
To me myself, for some three careless
moons,
The summer pilot of an empty heart

Unto the shores of nothing! Know
     you not
Such touches are but embassies of
     love,
To tamper with the feelings, ere he
     found
Empire for life? but Eustace painted
     her,
And said to me, she sitting with us
     then,
" When will *you* paint like this? " and
     I replied,
(My words were half in earnest, half
     in jest,)
" 'Tis not your work, but Love's.
     Love, unperceived,
A more ideal Artist he than all,
Came, drew your pencil from you,
     made those eyes
Darker than darkest pansies, and that
     hair
More black than ashbuds in the front
     of March."
And Juliet answer'd laughing, "Go
     and see
The Gardener's daughter: trust me,
     after that,
You scarce can fail to match his mas-
     terpiece."
And up we rose, and on the spur we
     went.

  Not wholly in the busy world, nor
     quite
Beyond it, blooms the garden that I
     love.
News from the humming city comes
     to it
In sound of funeral or of marriage
     bells;
And, sitting muffled in dark leaves,
     you hear
The windy clanging of the minster
     clock;
Although between it and the garden
     lies
A league of grass, wash'd by a slow
     broad stream,
That, stirr'd with languid pulses of the
     oar,
Waves all its lazy lilies, and creeps on,
Barge-laden, to three arches of a
     bridge

Crown'd with the minster-towers.
                    The fields between
Are dewy-fresh, browsed by deep-
     udder'd kine,
And all about the large lime feathers
     low,
The lime a summer home of murmur-
     ous wings.
  In that still place she, hoarded in
     herself,
Grew, seldom seen; not less among us
     lived
Her fame from lip to lip. Who had
     not heard
Of Rose, the Gardener's daughter?
     Where was he,
So blunt in memory, so old at heart,
At such a distance from his youth in
     grief,
That, having seen, forgot? The com-
     mon mouth,
So gross to express delight, in praise
     of her
Grew oratory. Such a lord is Love,
And Beauty such a mistress of the
     world.
  And if I said that Fancy, led by
     Love,
Would play with flying forms and
     images,
Yet this is also true, that, long before
I look'd upon her, when I heard her
     name
My heart was like a prophet to my
     heart,
And told me I should love. A crowd
     of hopes,
That sought to sow themselves like
     winged seeds,
Born out of everything I heard and
     saw,
Flutter'd about my senses and my soul;
And vague desires, like fitful blasts of
     balm
To one that travels quickly, made the
     air
Of Life delicious, and all kinds of
     thought,
That verged upon them, sweeter than
     the dream
Dream'd by a happy man, when the
     dark East,

Unseen, is brightening to his bridal
   morn.
And sure this orbit of the memory
   folds
For ever in itself the day we went
To see her. All the land in flowery
   squares,
Beneath a broad and equal-blowing
   wind,
Smelt of the coming summer, as one
   large cloud
Drew downward: but all else of
   heaven was pure
Up to the Sun, and May from verge
   to verge,
And May with me from head to heel.
   And now,
As tho' 'twere yesterday, as tho' it
   were
The hour just flown, that morn with
   all its sound,
(For those old Mays had thrice the
   life of these,)
Rings in mine ears. The steer forgot
   to graze,
And, where the hedge-row cuts the
   pathway, stood,
Leaning his horns into the neighbor
   field,
And lowing to his fellows. From the
   woods
Came voices of the well-contented
   doves.
The lark could scarce get out his notes
   for joy,
But shook his song together as he
   near'd
His happy home, the ground. To left
   and right,
The cuckoo told his name to all the
   hills;
The mellow ouzel fluted in the elm;
The redcap whistled; and the night-
   ingale
Sang loud, as tho' he were the bird of
   day.
   And Eustace turn'd, and smiling
   said to me,
"Hear how the bushes echo! by my
   life,
These birds have joyful thoughts.
   Think you they sing

Like poets, from the vanity of song?
Or have they any sense of why they
   sing?
And would they praise the heavens
   for what they have?"
And I made answer, "Were there
   nothing else
For which to praise the heavens but
   only love,
That only love were cause enough for
   praise."
   Lightly he laugh'd, as one that read
   my thought,
And on we went; but ere an hour had
   pass'd,
We reach'd a meadow slanting to the
   North;
Down which a well-worn pathway
   courted us
To one green wicket in a privet hedge;
This, yielding, gave into a grassy
   walk
Thro' crowded lilac-ambush trimly
   pruned;
And one warm gust, full-fed with per-
   fume, blew
Beyond us, as we enter'd in the cool.
The garden stretches southward. In
   the midst
A cedar spread his dark-green layers
   of shade.
The garden-glasses shone, and mo-
   mently
The twinkling laurel scatter'd silver
   lights.
   "Eustace," I said, "this wonder
   keeps the house."
He nodded, but a moment afterwards
He cried, "Look! look!" Before he
   ceased I turn'd,
And, ere a star can wink, beheld her
   there.
   For up the porch there grew an
   Eastern rose,
That, flowering high, the last night's
   gale had caught,
And blown across the walk. One arm
   aloft —
Gown'd in pure white, that fitted to
   the shape —
Holding the bush, to fix it back, she
   stood,

A single stream of all her soft brown
   hair
Pour'd on one side : the shadow of the
   flowers
Stole all the golden gloss, and, wavering
Lovingly lower, trembled on her
   waist —
Ah, happy shade — and still went
   wavering down,
But, ere it touch'd a foot, that might
   have danced
The greensward into greener circles,
   dipt,
And mix'd with shadows of the common ground :
But the full day dwelt on her brows,
   and sunn'd
Her violet eyes, and all her Hebe
   bloom,
And doubled his own warmth against
   her lips,
And on the bounteous wave of such a
   breast
As never pencil drew. Half light,
   half shade,
She stood, a sight to make an old
   man young.
   So rapt, we near'd the house; but
   she, a Rose
In roses, mingled with her fragrant
   toil,
Nor heard us come, nor from her tend-
   ance turn'd
Into the world without; till close at
   hand,
And almost ere I knew mine own in-
   tent,
This murmur broke the stillness of
   that air
Which brooded round about her :
           " Ah, one rose,
One rose, but one, by those fair fingers
   cull'd,
Were worth a hundred kisses press'd
   on lips
Less exquisite than thine."
            She look'd : but all
Suffused with blushes — neither self-
   possess'd
Nor startled, but betwixt this mood
   and that,

Divided in a graceful quiet — paused,
And dropt the branch she held, and
   turning, wound
Her looser hair in braid, and stirr'd
   her lips
For some sweet answer, tho' no answer
   came,
Nor yet refused the rose, but granted it,
And moved away, and left me, statue-
   like,
In act to render thanks.
             I, that whole day,
Saw her no more, altho' I linger'd
   there
Till every daisy slept, and Love's
   white star
Beam'd thro' the thicken'd cedar in
   the dusk.
   So home we went, and all the live-
   long way
With solemn gibe did Eustace banter
   me.
" Now," said he, " will you climb the
   top of Art.
You cannot fail but work in hues to
   dim
The Titianic Flora. Will you match
My Juliet ? you, not you, — the Mas-
   ter, Love,
A more ideal Artist he than all."
   So home I went, but could not sleep
   for joy,
Reading her perfect features in the
   gloom,
Kissing the rose she gave me o'er and
   o'er,
And shaping faithful record of the
   glance
That graced the giving — such a noise
   of life
Swarm'd in the golden present, such
   a voice
Call'd to me from the years to come,
   and such
A length of bright horizon rimm'd the
   dark.
And all that night I heard the watch-
   man peal
The sliding season : all that night I
   heard
The heavy clocks knolling the drowsy
   hours.

The drowsy hours, dispensers of all good,
O'er the mute city stole with folded wings,
Distilling odors on me as they went
To greet their fairer sisters of the East.
  Love at first sight, first-born, and heir to all,
Made this night thus. Henceforward squall nor storm
Could keep me from that Eden where she dwelt.
Light pretexts drew me; sometimes a Dutch love
For tulips; then for roses, moss or musk,
To grace my city rooms; or fruits and cream
Served in the weeping elm; and more and more
A word could bring the color to my cheek;
A thought would fill my eyes with happy dew;
Love trebled life within me, and with each
The year increased.
              The daughters of the year,
One after one, thro' that still garden pass'd;
Each garlanded with her peculiar flower
Danced into light, and died into the shade;
And each in passing touch'd with some new grace
Or seem'd to touch her, so that day by day,
Like one that never can be wholly known,
Her beauty grew; till Autumn brought an hour
For Eustace, when I heard his deep "I will,"
Breathed, like the covenant of a God, to hold
From thence thro' all the worlds: but I rose up
Full of his bliss, and following her dark eyes
Felt earth as air beneath me, till I reach'd

The wicket-gate, and found her standing there.
There sat we down upon a garden mound,
Two mutually enfolded; Love, the third,
Between us, in the circle of his arms
Enwound us both; and over many a range
Of waning lime the gray cathedral towers,
Across a hazy glimmer of the west,
Reveal'd their shining windows: from them clash'd
The bells; we listen'd; with the time we play'd,
We spoke of other things; we coursed about
The subject most at heart, more near and near,
Like doves about a dovecote, wheeling round
The central wish, until we settled there.
  Then, in that time and place, I spoke to her,
Requiring, tho' I knew it was mine own,
Yet for the pleasure that I took to hear,
Requiring at her hand the greatest gift,
A woman's heart, the heart of her I loved;
And in that time and place she answer'd me,
And in the compass of three little words,
More musical than ever came in one,
The silver fragments of a broken voice,
Made me most happy, faltering, "I am thine."
  Shall I cease here? Is this enough to say
That my desire, like all strongest hopes,
By its own energy fulfill'd itself,
Merged in completion? Would you learn at full
How passion rose thro' circumstantial grades
Beyond all grades develop'd? and indeed

I had not staid so long to tell you all,
But while I mused came Memory with
    sad eyes,
Holding the folded annals of my
    youth;
And while I mused, Love with knit
    brows went by,
And with a flying finger swept my lips,
And spake, "Be wise: not easily for-
    given
Are those, who setting wide the doors
    that bar
The secret bridal chambers of the
    heart,
Let in the day." Here, then, my words
    have end.
    Yet might I tell of meetings, of fare-
        wells —
Of that which came between, more
    sweet than each,
In whispers, like the whispers of the
    leaves
That tremble round a nightingale —
    in sighs
Which perfect Joy, perplex'd for ut-
    terance,
Stole from her sister Sorrow. Might
    I not tell
Of difference, reconcilement, pledges
    given,
And vows, where there was never need
    of vows,
And kisses, where the heart on one
    wild leap
Hung tranced from all pulsation, as
    above
The heavens between their fairy fleeces
    pale
Sow'd all their mystic gulfs with fleet-
    ing stars;
Or while the balmy glooming, crescent-
    lit,
Spread the light haze along the river-
    shores,
And in the hollows; or as once we met
Unheedful, tho' beneath a whispering
    rain
Night slid down one long stream of
    sighing wind,
And in her bosom bore the baby, Sleep.
    But this whole hour your eyes have
        been intent

On that veil'd picture — veil'd, for
    what it holds
May not be dwelt on by the common
    day.
This prelude has prepared thee. Raise
    thy soul;
Make thine heart ready with thine
    eyes: the time
Is come to raise the veil.
                    Behold her there,
As I beheld her ere she knew my heart,
My first, last love; the idol of my
    youth,
The darling of my manhood, and, alas!
Now the most blessed memory of mine
    age.

DORA.

With farmer Allan at the farm abode
William and Dora. William was his
    son,
And she his niece. He often look'd
    at them,
And often thought, "I'll make them
    man and wife."
Now Dora felt her uncle's will in all,
And yearn'd towards William; but the
    youth, because
He had been always with her in the
    house,
Thought not of Dora.
                    Then there came a day
When Allan call'd his son, and said,
    "My son:
I married late, but I would wish to see
My grandchild on my knees before I
    die:
And I have set my heart upon a match.
Now therefore look to Dora; she is
    well
To look to; thrifty too beyond her age.
She is my brother's daughter: he and I
Had once hard words, and parted, and
    he died
In foreign lands; but for his sake I
    bred
His daughter Dora: take her for your
    wife;
For I have wish'd this marriage, night
    and day,

"And Dora took the child and went her way
Across the wheat and sat upon a mound."

Page 85.

For many years." But William an-
swer'd short;
" I cannot marry Dora ; by my life,
I will not marry Dora." Then the old
man
Was wroth, and doubled up his hands,
and said:
" You will not, boy! you dare to an-
swer thus !
But in my time a father's word was
law,
And so it shall be now for me. Look
to it ;
Consider, William : take a month to
think,
And let me have an answer to my
wish ;
Or, by the Lord that made me, you
shall pack,
And never more darken my doors
again."
But William answer'd madly ; bit his
lips,
And broke away. The more he look'd
at her
The less he liked her; and his ways
were harsh ;
But Dora bore them meekly. Then
before
The month was out he left his father's
house,
And hired himself to work within the
fields ;
And half in love, half spite, he woo'd
and wed
A laborer's daughter, Mary Morrison.
Then, when the bells were ringing,
Allan call'd
His niece and said: " My girl, I love
you well ;
But if you speak with him that was
my son,
Or change a word with her he calls his
wife,
My home is none of yours. My will
is law."
And Dora promised, being meek. She
thought,
" It cannot be : my uncle's mind will
change !"
    And days went on, and there was
born a boy

To William ; then distresses came on
him ;
And day by day he pass'd his father's
gate,
Heart-broken, and his father help'd
him not.
But Dora stored what little she could
save,
And sent it them by stealth, nor did
they know
Who sent it ; till at last a fever seized
On William, and in harvest time he
died.
    Then Dora went to Mary. Mary sat
And look'd with tears upon her boy,
and thought
Hard things of Dora. Dora came and
said:
" I have obey'd my uncle until now,
And I have sinn'd, for it was all thro'
me
This evil came on William at the first.
But, Mary, for the sake of him that's
gone,
And for your sake, the woman that he
chose,
And for this orphan, I am come to
you :
You know there has not been for these
five years
So full a harvest: let me take the
boy,
And I will set him in my uncle's eye
Among the wheat; that when his heart
is glad
Of the full harvest, he may see the
boy,
And bless him for the sake of him
that's gone."
    And Dora took the child, and went
her way
Across the wheat, and sat upon a
mound
That was unsown, where many poppies
grew.
Far off the farmer came into the field
And spied her not; for none of all his
men
Dare tell him Dora waited with the
child;
And Dora would have risen and gone
to him,

But her heart fail'd her; and the reap-
ers reap'd,
And the sun fell, and all the land was
dark.
But when the morrow came, she rose
and took
The child once more, and sat upon the
mound;
And made a little wreath of all the
flowers
That grew about, and tied it round his
hat
To make him pleasing in her uncle's
eye.
Then when the farmer pass'd into the
field
He spied her, and he left his men at
work,
And came and said: "Where were you
yesterday?
Whose child is that? What are you
doing here?"
So Dora cast her eyes upon the ground,
And answer'd softly, "This is Wil-
liam's child!"
"And did I not," said Allan, "did I
not
Forbid you, Dora?" Dora said again:
"Do with me as you will, but take the
child,
And bless him for the sake of him
that's gone!"
And Allan said, "I see it is a trick
Got up betwixt you and the woman
there.
I must be taught my duty, and by you!
You knew my word was law, and yet
you dared
To slight it. Well — for I will take
the boy;
But go you hence, and never see me
more."
So saying, he took the boy that cried
aloud
And struggled hard. The wreath of
flowers fell
At Dora's feet. She bow'd upon her
hands,
And the boy's cry came to her from the
field,
More and more distant. She bow'd
down her head,

Remembering the day when first she
came,
And all the things that had been. She
bow'd down
And wept in secret; and the reapers
reap'd,
And the sun fell, and all the land was
dark.
Then Dora went to Mary's house,
and stood
Upon the threshold. Mary saw the
boy
Was not with Dora. She broke out
in praise
To God, that help'd her in her widow-
hood.
And Dora said, "My uncle took the
boy;
But, Mary, let me live and work with
you:
He says that he will never see me
more."
Then answer'd Mary, "This shall never
be,
That thou shouldst take my trouble
on thyself:
And, now I think, he shall not have
the boy,
For he will teach him hardness, and
to slight
His mother; therefore thou and I will
go,
And I will have my boy, and bring
him home;
And I will beg of him to take thee
back:
But if he will not take thee back
again,
Then thou and I will live within one
house,
And work for William's child, until
he grows
Of age to help us."
So the women kiss'd
Each other, and set out, and reach'd
the farm.
The door was off the latch: they
peep'd, and saw
The boy set up betwixt his grandsire's
knees,
Who thrust him in the hollows of his
arm,

And clapt him on the hands and on
the cheeks,
Like one that loved him : and the lad
stretch'd out
And babbled for the golden seal, that
hung
From Allan's watch, and sparkled by
the fire.
Then they came in : but when the boy
beheld
His mother, he cried out to come to her :
And Allan set him down, and Mary
said :
   "O Father! — if you let me call
you so —
I never came a-begging for myself,
Or William, or this child ; but now I
come
For Dora : take her back ; she loves
you well.
O Sir, when William died, he died at
peace
With all men ; for I ask'd him, and he
said,
He could not ever rue his marrying
me —
I had been a patient wife : but, Sir,
he said
That he was wrong to cross his father
thus :
'God bless him!' he said, 'and may
he never know
The troubles I have gone thro'!'
Then he turn'd
His face and pass'd — unhappy that I
am!
But now, Sir, let me have my boy, for
you
Will make him hard, and he will learn
to slight
His father's memory ; and take Dora
back,
And let all this be as it was before."
  So Mary said, and Dora hid her face
By Mary. There was silence in the
room ;
And all at once the old man burst in
sobs : —
  "I have been to blame — to blame.
I have killed my son.
I have kill'd him — but I loved him
— my dear son.

May God forgive me ! — I have been
to blame.
Kiss me, my children."
          Then they clung about
The old man's neck, and kiss'd him
many times.
And all the man was broken with re-
morse ;
And all his love came back a hundred-
fold ;
And for three hours he sobb'd o'er
William's child
Thinking of William.
         So those four abode
Within one house together ; and as
years
Went forward, Mary took another
mate ;
But Dora lived unmarried till her
death.

AUDLEY COURT.

"The Bull, the Fleece are cramm'd,
and not a room
For love or money. Let us picnic
there
At Audley Court."
       I spoke, while Audley feast
Humm'd like a hive all round the
narrow quay,
To Francis, with a basket on his arm,
To Francis just alighted from the boat,
And breathing of the sea. "With all
my heart,"
Said Francis. Then we shoulder'd
thro' the swarm,
And rounded by the stillness of the
beach
To where the bay runs up its latest
horn.
  We left the dying ebb that faintly
lipp'd
The flat red granite ; so by many a
sweep
Of meadow smooth from aftermath
we reach'd
The griffin-guarded gates, and pass'd
thro' all
The pillar'd dusk of sounding syca-
mores,

And cross'd the garden to the gardener's lodge,
With all its casements bedded, and its
walls
And chimneys muffled in the leafy
vine.
  There, on a slope of orchard, Francis laid
A damask napkin wrought with horse
and hound,
Brought out a dusky loaf that smelt
of home,
And, half-cut-down, a pasty costly-
made,
Where quail and pigeon, lark and lev-
eret lay,
Like fossils of the rock, with golden
yolks
Imbedded and injellied; last, with
these,
A flask of cider from his father's
vats,
Prime, which I knew; and so we sat
and eat
And talk'd old matters over; who was
dead,
Who married, who was like to be, and
how
The races went, and who would rent
the hall:
Then touch'd upon the game, how
scarce it was
This season; glancing thence, dis-
cuss'd the farm,
The four-field system, and the price of
grain;
And struck upon the corn-laws, where
we split,
And came again together on the king
With heated faces; till he laugh'd
aloud;
And, while the blackbird on the pippin
hung
To hear him, clapt his hand in mine
and sang—
  "Oh! who would fight and march
and countermarch,
Be shot for sixpence in a battle-field,
And shovell'd up into some bloody
trench
Where no one knows? but let me live
my life.

  "Oh! who would cast and balance
at a desk,
Perch'd like a crow upon a three-
legg'd stool,
Till all his juice is dried, and all his
joints
Are full of chalk? but let me live my
life.
  "Who'd serve the state? for if I
carved my name
Upon the cliffs that guard my native
land,
I might as well have traced it in the
sands;
The sea wastes all: but let me live my
life.
  "Oh! who would love? I woo'd a
woman once,
But she was sharper than an eastern
wind,
And all my heart turn'd from her, as
a thorn
Turns from the sea; but let me live
my life."
  He sang his song, and I replied with
mine:
I found it in a volume, all of songs,
Knock'd down to me, when old Sir
Robert's pride,
His books — the more the pity, so I
said —
Came to the hammer here in March —
and this —
I set the words, and added names I
knew.
  "Sleep, Ellen Aubrey, sleep, and
dream of me:
Sleep, Ellen, folded in thy sister's arm,
And sleeping, haply dream her arm is
mine.
  "Sleep, Ellen, folded in Emilia's
arm;
Emilia, fairer than all else but thou,
For thou art fairer than all else that is.
  "Sleep, breathing health and peace
upon her breast:
Sleep, breathing love and trust against
her lip:
I go to-night: I come to-morrow morn.
  "I go, but I return: I would I were
The pilot of the darkness and the
dream.

Sleep, Ellen Aubrey, love, and dream
    of me."
  So sang we each to either, Francis
    Hale,
The farmer's son, who lived across the
    bay,
My friend; and I, that having where-
    withal,
And in the fallow leisure of my life
A rolling stone of here and every-
    where,
Did what I would; but ere the night
    we rose
And saunter'd home beneath a moon,
    that, just
In crescent, dimly rain'd about the
    leaf
Twilights of airy silver, till we reach'd
The limit of the hills; and as we sank
From rock to rock upon the glooming
    quay,
The town was hush'd beneath us:
    lower down
The bay was oily calm; the harbor
    buoy,
Sole star of phosphorescence in the
    calm,
With one green sparkle ever and anon
Dipt by itself, and we were glad at
    heart.

WALKING TO THE MAIL.

John. I'M glad I walk'd. How fresh
    the meadows look
Above the river, and, but a month ago,
The whole hill-side was redder than a
    fox.
Is yon plantation where this byway
    joins
The turnpike?
    James.   Yes.
    John. And when does this come by?
    James. The mail? At one o'clock.
    John.   What is it now?
    James. A quarter to.
    John.   Whose house is that I see?
No, not the County Member's with
    the vane:
Up higher with the yew-tree by it,
    and half

A score of gables.
    James. That? Sir Edward Head's:
But he's abroad: the place is to be
    sold.
    John. Oh, his. He was not broken.
    James.   No, sir, he,
Vex'd with a morbid devil in his
    blood
That veil'd the world with jaundice,
    hid his face
From all men, and commercing with
    himself,
He lost the sense that handles daily
    life —
That keeps us all in order more or
    less —
And sick of home went overseas for
    change.
    John. And whither?
    James. Nay, who knows? he's here
    and there.
But let him go; his devil goes with
    him,
As well as with his tenant, Jocky
    Dawes.
    John. What's that?
    James. You saw the man — on Mon-
    day, was it? —
There by the humpback'd willow;
    half stands up
And bristles; half has fall'n and
    made a bridge;
And there he caught the younker
    tickling trout —
Caught *in flagrante* — what's the Latin
    word? —
Delicto: but his house, for so they
    say,
Was haunted with a jolly ghost, that
    shook
The curtains, whined in lobbies, tapt
    at doors,
And rummaged like a rat: no servant
    stay'd:
The farmer vext packs up his beds
    and chairs,
And all his household stuff; and with
    his boy
Betwixt his knees, his wife upon the
    tilt,
Sets out, and meets a friend who hails
    him, "What!

You're flitting!"   "Yes, we're flitting," says the ghost
(For they had pack'd the thing among
the beds,)
"Oh well," says he, "you flitting with
us too —
Jack, turn the horses' heads and home
again."
    John. He left *his* wife behind; for
so I heard.
    James. He left her, yes. I met my
lady once:
A woman like a butt, and harsh as
crabs.
    John. Oh yet but I remember, ten
years back —
'Tis now at least ten years — and then
she was —
You could not light upon a sweeter
thing:
A body slight and round, and like a
pear
In growing, modest eyes, a hand, a
foot
Lessening in perfect cadence, and a
skin
As clean and white as privet when it
flowers.
    James. Ay, ay, the blossom fades,
and they that loved
At first like dove and dove were cat
and dog.
She was the daughter of a cottager,
Out of her sphere. What betwixt
shame and pride,
New things and old, himself and her,
she sour'd
To what she is: a nature never
kind!
Like men, like manners: like breeds
like, they say:
Kind nature is the best: those manners next
That fit us like a nature second-hand;
Which are indeed the manners of the
great.
    John. But I had heard it was this
bill that past,
And fear of change at home, that
drove him hence.
    James. That was the last drop in
the cup of gall.

I once was near him, when his bailiff
brought
A Chartist pike. You should have
seen him wince
As from a venomous thing: he thought
himself
A mark for all, and shudder'd, lest a
cry
Should break his sleep by night, and
his nice eyes
Should see the raw mechanic's bloody
thumbs
Sweat on his blazon'd chairs, but, sir,
you know
That these two parties still divide the
world —
Of those that want, and those that
have: and still
The same old sore breaks out from
age to age
With much the same result. Now I
myself,
A Tory to the quick, was as a boy
Destructive, when I had not what I
would.
I was at school — a college in the
South:
There lived a flayflint near; we stole
his fruit,
His hens, his eggs; but there was law
for *us*;
We paid in person. He had a sow,
sir. She,
With meditative grunts of much con-
tent,
Lay great with pig, wallowing in sun
and mud.
By night we dragg'd her to the col-
lege tower
From her warm bed, and up the cork-
screw stair
With hand and rope we haled the
groaning sow,
And on the leads we kept her till she
pigg'd.
Large range of prospect had the
mother sow,
And but for daily loss of one she loved
As one by one we took them — but for
this —
As never sow was higher in this
world —

Might have been happy : but what lot
    is pure ?
We took them all, till she was left
    alone
Upon her tower, the Niobe of swine,
And so return'd unfarrow'd to her
    sty.
   John. They found you out ?
   James.   Not they.
   John.   Well — after all —
What know we of the secret of a
    man ?
His nerves were wrong. What ails
    us, who are sound,
That we should mimic this raw fool
    the world,
Which charts us all in its coarse
    blacks or whites,
As ruthless as a baby with a worm,
As cruel as a schoolboy ere he grows
To Pity — more from ignorance than
    will.
    But put your best foot forward, or
    I fear
That we shall miss the mail : and here
    it comes
With five at top : as quaint a four-in-
    hand
As you shall see — three pyebalds and
    a roan.

EDWIN MORRIS;

OR, THE LAKE.

O ME, my pleasant rambles by the lake,
My sweet, wild, fresh three quarters
    of a year,
My one Oasis in the dust and drouth
Of city life ! I was a sketcher then :
See here, my doing : curves of moun-
    tain, bridge,
Boat, island, ruins of a castle, built
When men knew how to build, upon a
    rock
With turrets lichen-gilded like a rock :
And here, new-comers in an ancient
    hold,
New-comers from the Mersey, million-
    aires,
Here lived the Hills — a Tudor-chim-
    nied bulk

Of mellow brickwork on an isle of
    bowers.
    O me, my pleasant rambles by the
    lake
With Edwin Morris and with Edward
    Bull
The curate ; he was fatter than his
    cure.

    But Edwin Morris, he that knew the
    names,
Long learned names of agaric, moss
    and fern,
Who forged a thousand theories of the
    rocks,
Who taught me how to skate, to row,
    to swim,
Who read me rhymes elaborately good,
His own — I call'd him Crichton, for
    he seem'd
All-perfect, finish'd to the finger nail.

    And once I ask'd him of his early
    life,
And his first passion ; and he answer'd
    me ;
And well his words became him : was
    he not
A full-cell'd honeycomb of eloquence
Stored from all flowers ? Poet-like he
    spoke.

    "My love for Nature is as old as I ;
But thirty moons, one honeymoon to
    that,
And three rich sennights more, my love
    for her.
My love for Nature and my love for
    her,
Of different ages, like twin-sisters
    grew,
Twin-sisters differently beautiful.
To some full music rose and sank the
    sun,
And some full music seem'd to move
    and change
With all the varied changes of the
    dark,
And either twilight and the day be-
    tween ;
For daily hope fulfill'd, to rise again

Revolving toward fulfilment, made it
   sweet
To walk, to sit, to sleep, to wake, to
   breathe."

  Or this or something like to this he
   spoke.
Then said the fat-faced curate Edward
   Bull,
  "I take it, God made the woman for
   the man,
And for the good and increase of the
   world.
A pretty face is well, and this is well,
To have a dame indoors, that trims us
   up,
And keeps us tight; but these unreal
   ways
Seem but the theme of writers, and
   indeed
Worn threadbare. Man is made of
   solid stuff.
I say, God made the woman for the
   man,
And for the good and increase of the
   world."

  "Parson," said I, "you pitch the pipe
   too low:
But I have sudden touches, and can
   run
My faith beyond my practice into his:
Tho' if, in dancing after Letty Hill,
I do not hear the bells upon my cap,
I scarce have other music: yet say on.
What should one give to light on such
   a dream?"
I ask'd him half-sardonically.
               "Give?
Give all thou art," he answer'd, and a
   light
Of laughter dimpled in his swarthy
   cheek:
"I would have hid her needle in my
   heart,
To save her little finger from a scratch
No deeper than the skin: my ears
   could hear
Her lightest breath; her least remark
   was worth
The experience of the wise. I went
   and came;

Her voice fled always thro' the summer
   land;
I spoke her name alone. Thrice-happy
   days!
The flower of each, those moments
   when we met,
The crown of all, we met to part no
   more."

  Were not his words delicious, I a
   beast
To take them as I did? but something
   jarr'd;
Whether he spoke too largely; that
   there seem'd
A touch of something false, some self-
   conceit,
Or over-smoothness: howsoe'er it was,
He scarcely hit my humor, and I said:

  "Friend Edwin, do not think your-
   self alone
Of all men happy. Shall not Love to
   me,
As in the Latin song I learnt at school,
Sneeze out a full God-bless-you right
   and left?
But you can talk: yours is a kindly
   vein:
I have, I think, — Heaven knows — as
   much within;
Have, or should have, but for a
   thought or two,
That like a purple beech among the
   greens
Looks out of place: 'tis from no want
   in her:
It is my shyness, or my self-distrust,
Or something of a wayward modern
   mind
Dissecting passion. Time will set me
   right."

  So spoke I knowing not the things
   that were.
Then said the fat-faced curate, Edward
   Bull:
"God made the woman for the use of
   man,
And for the good and increase of the
   world."

And I and Edwin laughed; and now
we paused
About the windings of the marge to
hear
The soft wind blowing over meadowy
holms
And alders, garden-isles; and now we
left
The clerk behind us, I and he, and ran
By ripply shallows of the lisping lake,
Delighted with the freshness and the
sound.

But, when the bracken rusted on
their crags,
My suit had wither'd, nipt to death by
him
That was a God, and is a lawyer's clerk,
The rentroll Cupid of our rainy isles.
'Tis true, we met; one hour I had, no
more:
She sent a note, the seal an *Elle vous
suit,*
The close, " Your Letty, only yours ";
and this
Thrice underscored. The friendly
mist of morn
Clung to the lake. I boated over, ran
My craft aground, and heard with
beating heart
The Sweet-Gale rustle round the shelv-
ing keel;
And out I stept, and up I crept: she
moved,
Like Proserpine in Enna, gathering
flowers:
Then low and sweet I whistled thrice;
and she,
She turn'd, we closed, we kiss'd, swore
faith, I breathed
In some new planet: a silent cousin
stole
Upon us and departed: " Leave," she
cried,
" O leave me!" "Never, dearest,
never: here
I brave the worst: " and while we
stood like fools
Embracing, all at once a score of pugs
And poodles yell'd within, and out
they came
Trustees and Aunts and Uncles.

" What, with him!
Go " (shrill'd the cotton-spinning
chorus); "him!"
I choked. Again they shriek'd the
burthen — "Him!"
Again with hands of wild rejection
"Go! —
Girl, get you in!" She went — and in
one month
They wedded her to sixty thousand
pounds,
To lands in Kent and messuages in
York,
And slight Sir Robert with his watery
smile
And educated whisker. But for me,
They set an ancient creditor to
work:
It seems I broke a close with force
and arms:
There came a mystic token from the
king
To greet the sheriff, needless courtesy!
I read, and fled by night, and flying
turn'd:
Her taper glimmer'd in the lake be-
low:
I turn'd once more, close-button'd to
the storm;
So left the place, left Edwin, nor have
seen
Him since, nor heard of her, nor cared
to hear.

Nor cared to hear? perhaps: yet
long ago
I have pardon'd little Letty; not indeed,
It may be, for her own dear sake but
this,
She seems a part of those fresh days
to me;
For in the dust and drouth of London life
She moves among my visions of the
lake,
While the prime swallow dips his
wing, or then
While the gold-lily blows, and overhead
The light cloud smoulders on the
summer crag.

ST. SIMEON STYLITES.

ALTHO' I be the basest of mankind,
From scalp to sole one slough and
    crust of sin,
Unfit for earth, unfit for heaven,
    scarce meet
For troops of devils, mad with blas-
    phemy,
I will not cease to grasp the hope I
    hold
Of saintdom, and to clamor, mourn
    and sob,
Battering the gates of heaven with
    storms of prayer,
Have mercy, Lord, and take away my
    sin.
    Let this avail, just, dreadful, mighty
        God,
This not be all in vain, that thrice ten
    years,
Thrice multiplied by superhuman
    pangs,
In hungers and in thirsts, fevers and
    cold,
In coughs, aches, stitches, ulcerous
    throes and cramps,
A sign betwixt the meadow and the
    cloud,
Patient on this tall pillar I have borne
Rain, wind, frost, heat, hail, damp,
    and sleet, and snow;
And I had hoped that ere this period
    closed
Thou wouldst have caught me up into
    thy rest,
Denying not these weather-beaten
    limbs
The meed of saints, the white robe
    and the palm.
    O take the meaning, Lord: I do not
        breathe,
Not whisper, any murmur of com-
    plaint.
Pain heap'd ten-hundred-fold to this,
    were still
Less burthen, by ten-hundred-fold, to
    bear,
Than were those lead-like tons of sin,
    that crush'd
My spirit flat before thee.
                    O Lord, Lord,

Thou knowest I bore this better at
    the first,
For I was strong and hale of body
    then;
And tho' my teeth, which now are
    dropt away,
Would chatter with the cold, and all
    my beard
Was tagg'd with icy fringes in the
    moon,
I drown'd the whoopings of the owl
    with sound
Of pious hymns and psalms, and
    sometimes saw
An angel stand and watch me, as I
    sang.
Now am I feeble grown; my end
    draws nigh;
I hope my end draws nigh: half deaf
    I am,
So that I scarce can hear the people
    hum
About the column's base, and almost
    blind,
And scarce can recognize the fields I
    know;
And both my thighs are rotted with
    the dew;
Yet cease I not to clamor and to
    cry,
While my stiff spine can hold my
    weary head,
Till all my limbs drop piecemeal from
    the stone,
Have mercy, mercy: take away my
    sin.
    O Jesus, if thou wilt not save my
        soul,
Who may be saved? who is it may be
    saved?
Who may be made a saint, if I fail
    here?
Show me the man hath suffer'd more
    than I.
For did not all thy martyrs die one
    death?
For either they were stoned, or cruci-
    fied,
Or burn'd in fire, or boil'd in oil, or
    sawn
In twain beneath the ribs; but I die
    here

To-day, and whole years long, a life
    of death
Bear witness, if I could have found a
    way
(And heedfully I sifted all my
    thought)
More slowly-painful to subdue this
    home
Of sin, my flesh, which I despise and
    hate,
I had not stinted practice, O my God.
    For not alone this pillar-punish-
    ment,
Not this alone I bore: but while I
    lived
In the white convent down the valley
    there,
For many weeks about my loins I wore
The robe that haled the buckets from
    the well,
Twisted as tight as I could knot the
    noose;
And spake not of it to a single soul,
Until the ulcer, eating thro' my skin,
Betray'd my secret penance, so that
    all
My brethren marvell'd greatly. More
    than this
I bore, whereof, O God, thou knowest
    all.
    Three winters, that my soul might
    grow to thee,
I lived up there on yonder mountain
    side.
My right leg chain'd into the crag, I
    lay
Pent in a roofless close of ragged
    stones;
Inswathed sometimes in wandering
    mist, and twice
Black'd with thy branding thunder,
    and sometimes
Sucking the damps for drink, and
    eating not,
Except the spare chance-gift of those
    that came
To touch my body and be heal'd, and
    live:
And they say then that I work'd mir-
    acles,
Whereof my fame is loud amongst
    mankind,

Cured lameness, palsies, cancers.
    Thou, O God,
Knowest alone whether this was or no.
Have mercy, mercy! cover all my sin.
    Then, that I might be more alone
    with thee,
Three years I lived upon a pillar,
    high
Six cubits, and three years on one of
    twelve;
And twice three years I crouch'd on
    one that rose
Twenty by measure; last of all, I
    grew
Twice ten long weary weary years to
    this,
That numbers forty cubits from the
    soil.
    I think that I have borne as much
    as this —
Or else I dream — and for so long a
    time,
If I may measure time by yon slow
    light,
And this high dial, which my sorrow
    crowns —
So much — even so.
                And yet I know not well,
For that the evil ones come here, and
    say,
"Fall down, O Simeon: that hast
    suffer'd long
For ages and for ages!" then they
    prate
Of penances I cannot have gone thro',
Perplexing me with lies; and oft I
    fall,
Maybe for months, in such blind
    lethargies
That Heaven, and Earth, and Time
    are choked.
                But yet
Bethink thee, Lord, while thou and
    all the saints
Enjoy themselves in heaven, and men
    on earth
House in the shade of comfortable
    roofs,
Sit with their wives by fires, eat whole-
    some food,
And wear warm clothes, and even
    beasts have stalls,

I, 'tween the spring and downfall of
　　the light,
Bow down one thousand and two hun-
　　dred times,
To Christ, the Virgin Mother, and the
　　saints;
Or in the night, after a little sleep,
I wake: the chill stars sparkle; I am
　　wet
With drenching dews, or stiff with
　　crackling frost.
I wear an undress'd goatskin on my
　　back;
A grazing iron collar grinds my
　　neck;
And in my weak, lean arms I lift the
　　cross,
And strive and wrestle with thee till
　　I die:
O mercy, mercy! wash away my sin.
　　O Lord, thou knowest what a man
　　　I am;
A sinful man, conceived and born in
　　sin:
'Tis their own doing; this is none of
　　mine;
Lay it not to me. Am I to blame for
　　this,
That here come those that worship
　　me? Ha! ha!
They think that I am somewhat.
　　What am I?
The silly people take me for a saint,
And bring me offerings of fruit and
　　flowers:
And I, in truth (thou wilt bear witness
　　here)
Have all in all endured as much, and
　　· more
Than many just and holy men, whose
　　names
Are register'd and calendar'd for
　　saints.
　　Good people, you do ill to kneel to
　　me.
What is it I can have done to merit
　　this?
I am a sinner viler than you all.
It may be I have wrought some mira-
　　cles,
And cured some halt and maim'd; but
　　what of that?

It may be, no one, even among the
　　saints,
May match his pains with mine; but
　　what of that?
Yet do not rise; for you may look on
　　me,
And in your looking you may kneel
　　to God.
Speak! is there any of you halt or
　　maim'd?
I think you know I have some power
　　with Heaven
From my long penance: let him speak
　　his wish.
　　Yes, I can heal him. Power goes
　　forth from me.
They say that they are heal'd. Ah,
　　hark! they shout
"St. Simeon Stylites." Why, if so,
God reaps a harvest in me. O my soul,
God reaps a harvest in thee. If this be,
Can I work miracles and not be saved?
This is not told of any. They were
　　saints.
It cannot be but that I shall be saved;
Yea, crown'd a saint. They shout,
　　"Behold a saint!"
And lower voices saint me from above.
Courage, St. Simeon! This dull chrys-
　　alis
Cracks into shining wings, and hope
　　ere death
Spreads more and more and more, that
　　God hath now
Sponged and made blank of crimeful
　　record all
My mortal archives.
　　　　　　　　　　O my sons, my sons,
I, Simeon of the pillar, by surname
Stylites, among men; I, Simeon,
The watcher on the column till the end;
I, Simeon, whose brain the sunshine
　　bakes;
I, whose bald brows in silent hours
　　become
Unnaturally hoar with rime, do now
From my high nest of penance here
　　proclaim
That Pontius and Iscariot by my side
Show'd like fair seraphs. On the coals
　　I lay,
A vessel full of sin: all hell beneath

Made me boil over. Devils pluck'd
    my sleeve,
Abaddon and Asmodeus caught at me.
I smote them with the cross; they
    swarm'd again.
In bed like monstrous apes they
    crush'd my chest:
They flapp'd my light out as I read: I
    saw
Their faces grow between me and my
    book;
With colt-like whinny and with hog-
    gish whine
They burst my prayer. Yet this way
    was left,
And by this way I 'scaped them.
    Mortify
Your flesh, like me, with scourges
    and with thorns;
Smite, shrink not, spare not. If it
    may be, fast
Whole Lents, and pray. I hardly,
    with slow steps,
With slow, faint steps, and much
    exceeding pain,
Have scrambled past those pits of fire,
    that still
Sing in mine ears. But yield not me
    the praise:
God only through his bounty hath
    thought fit,
Among the powers and princes of this
    world,
To make me an example to mankind,
Which few can reach to. Yet I do
    not say
But that a time may come — yea, even
    now,
Now, now, his footsteps smite the
    threshold stairs
Of life — I say, that time is at the doors
When you may worship me without
    reproach;
For I will leave my relics in your land,
And you may carve a shrine about
    my dust,
And burn a fragrant lamp before my
    bones,
When I am gather'd to the glorious
    saints.
    While I spake then, a sting of
    shrewdest pain

Ran shrivelling thro' me, and a cloud-
    like change,
In passing, with a grosser film made
    thick
These heavy, horny eyes. The end!
    the end!
Surely the end! What's here? a
    shape, a shade,
A flash of light. Is that the angel
    there
That holds a crown? Come, blessed
    brother, come.
I know thy glittering face. I waited
    long;
My brows are ready. What! deny it
    now?
Nay, draw, draw, draw nigh. So I
    clutch it. Christ!
'Tis gone: 'tis here again; the crown!
    the crown!
So now 'tis fitted on and grows to me,
And from it melt the dews of Paradise,
Sweet! sweet! spikenard, and balm,
    and frankincense.
Ah! let me not be fool'd, sweet saints:
    I trust
That I am whole, and clean, and meet
    for Heaven.
    Speak, if there be a priest, a man
    of God,
Among you there, and let him pres-
    ently
Approach, and lean a ladder on the
    shaft,
And climbing up into my airy home,
Deliver me the blessed sacrament;
For by the warning of the Holy Ghost,
I prophesy that I shall die to-night,
A quarter before twelve.
            But thou, O Lord,
Aid all this foolish people; let them
    take
Example, pattern: lead them to thy
    light.

THE TALKING OAK.

ONCE more the gate behind me falls;
    Once more before my face
I see the moulder'd Abbey-walls,
    That stand within the chace.

Beyond the lodge the city lies,
  Beneath its drift of smoke;
And ah! with what delighted eyes
  I turn to yonder oak.

For when my passion first began,
  Ere that, which in me burn'd,
The love, that makes me thrice a man,
  Could hope itself return'd;

To yonder oak within the field
  I spoke without restraint,.
And with a larger faith appeal'd
  Than Papist unto Saint.

For oft I talk'd with him apart,
  And told him of my choice,
Until he plagiarized a heart,
  And answer'd with a voice.

Tho' what he whisper'd under Heaven
  None else could understand;
I found him garrulously given,
  A babbler in the land.

But since I heard him make reply
  Is many a weary hour;
'Twere well to question him, and try
  If yet he keeps the power.

Hail, hidden to the knees in fern,
  Broad Oak of Sumner-chace,
Whose topmost branches can discern
  The roofs of Sumner-place!

Say thou, whereon I carved her name,
  If ever maid or spouse,
As fair as my Olivia, came
  To rest beneath thy boughs. —

" O Walter, I have shelter'd here
  Whatever maiden grace
The good old Summers, year by year
  Made ripe in Sumner-chace:

"Old Summers, when the monk was fat,
  And, issuing shorn and sleek,
Would twist his girdle tight, and pat
  The girls upon the cheek,

" Ere yet, in scorn of Peter's-pence,
  And number'd bead, and shrift,

Bluff Harry broke into the spence
  And turn'd the cowls adrift:

" And I have seen some score of those
  Fresh faces, that would thrive
When his man-minded offset rose
  To chase the deer at five;

"And all that from the town would
    stroll,
  Till that wild wind made work
In which the gloomy brewer's soul
  Went by me, like a stork:

" The slight she-slips of loyal blood,
  And others, passing praise,
Strait-laced, but all-too-full in bud
  For puritanic stays:

" And I have shadow'd many a group
  Of beauties, that were born
In teacup-times of hood and hoop,
  Or while the patch was worn;

"And, leg and arm with love-knots gay,
  About me leap'd and laugh'd
The modish Cupid of the day,
  And shrill'd his tinsel shaft.

" I swear (and else may insects prick
  Each leaf into a gall)
This girl, for whom your heart is sick,
  Is three times worth them all;

"For those and theirs, by Nature's law,
  Have faded long ago;
But in these latter springs I saw
  Your own Olivia blow,

" From when she gamboll'd on the
    greens
  A baby-germ, to when
The maiden blossoms of her teens
  Could number five from ten.

" I swear, by leaf, and wind, and rain,
  (And hear me with thine ears,)
That, tho' I circle in the grain
  Five hundred rings of years —

" Yet, since I first could cast a shade.
  Did never creature pass

So slightly, musically made,
　So light upon the grass :

" For as to fairies, that will flit
　To make the greensward fresh,
I hold them exquisitely knit,
　But far too spare of flesh."

Oh, hide thy knotted knees in fern,
　And overlook the chace ;
And from thy topmost branch discern
　The roofs of Sumner-place.

But thou, whereon I carved her name,
　That oft has heard my vows,
Declare when last Olivia came
　To sport beneath thy boughs.

" O yesterday, you know, the fair
　Was holden at the town ;
Her father left his good arm-chair,
　And rode his hunter down.

" And with him Albert came on his.
　I look'd at him with joy :
As cowslip unto oxlip is,
　So seems she to the boy.

" An hour had past — and, sitting
　　straight
　Within the low-wheel'd chaise,
Her mother trundled to the gate
　Behind the dappled grays.

" But as for her, she stay'd at home,
　And on the roof she went,
And down the way you use to come,
　She look'd with discontent.

" She left the novel half-uncut
　Upon the rosewood shelf ;
She left the new piano shut :
　She could not please herself.

' Then ran she, gamesome as the colt,
　And livelier than a lark
She sent her voice thro' all the holt
　Before her, and the park.

" A light wind chased her on the wing,
　And in the chase grew wild,
As close as might be would he cling
　About the darling child :

" But light as any wind that blows
　So fleetly did she stir,
The flower, she touch'd on, dipt and
　　rose,
　And turn'd to look at her.

" And here she came, and round me
　　play'd,
　And sang to me the whole
Of those three stanzas that you made
　About my 'giant bole ; '

" And in a fit of frolic mirth
　She strove to span my waist :
Alas, I was so broad of girth,
　I could not be embraced.

" I wish'd myself the fair young beech
　That here beside me stands,
That round me, clasping each in each,
　She might have lock'd her hands.

" Yet seem'd the pressure thrice as
　　sweet
　As woodbine's fragile hold,
Or when I feel about my feet
　The berried briony fold."

O muffle round thy knees with fern,
　And shadow Sumner-chace !
Long may thy topmost branch discern
　The roofs of Sumner-place !

But tell me, did she read the name
　I carved with many vows
When last with throbbing heart I came
　To rest beneath thy boughs ?

"O yes, she wander'd round and round
　These knotted knees of mine,
And found, and kiss'd the name she
　　found,
　And sweetly murmur'd thine.

" A teardrop trembled from its source,
　And down my surface crept.
My sense of touch is something coarse,
　But I believe she wept.

" Then flush'd her cheek with rosy
　　light,
　She glanced across the plain ;

But not a creature was in sight:
  She kiss'd me once again.

"Her kisses were so close and kind,
  That, trust me on my word,
Hard wood I am, and wrinkled rind,
  But yet my sap was stirr'd:

"And even into my inmost ring
  A pleasure I discern'd,
Like those blind motions of the Spring,
  That show the year is turn'd.

"Thrice-happy he that may caress
  The ringlet's waving balm —
The cushions of whose touch may press
  The maiden's tender palm.

"I, rooted here among the groves,
  But languidly adjust
My vapid vegetable loves
  With anthers and with dust:

"For ah! my friend, the days were brief
  Whereof the poets talk,
When that, which breathes within the leaf,
  Could slip its bark and walk.

"But could I, as in times foregone,
  From spray, and branch, and stem,
Have suck'd and gather'd into one
  The life that spreads in them,

"She had not found me so remiss;
  But lightly issuing thro',
I would have paid her kiss for kiss,
  With usury thereto."

O flourish high, with leafy towers,
  And overlook the lea,
Pursue thy loves among the bowers
  But leave thou mine to me.

O flourish, hidden deep in fern,
  Old oak, I love thee well;
A thousand thanks for what I learn
  And what remains to tell.

"'Tis little more: the day was warm;
  At last, tired out with play,
She sank her head upon her arm
  And at my feet she lay.

"Her eyelids dropp'd their silken eaves.
  I breathed upon her eyes
Thro' all the summer of my leaves
  A welcome mix'd with sighs.

"I took the swarming sound of life —
  The music from the town —
The murmurs of the drum and fife
  And lull'd them in my own.

"Sometimes I let a sunbeam slip,
  To light her shaded eye;
A second flutter'd round her lip
  Like a golden butterfly;

"A third would glimmer on her neck
  To make the necklace shine;
Another slid, a sunny fleck,
  From head to ankle fine,

"Then close and dark my arms I spread,
  And shadow'd all her rest —
Dropt dews upon her golden head,
  An acorn in her breast.

"But in a pet she started up,
  And pluck'd it out, and drew
My little oakling from the cup,
  And flung him in the dew.

"And yet it was a graceful gift —
  I felt a pang within
As when I see the woodman lift
  His axe to slay my kin.

"I shook him down because he was
  The finest on the tree.
He lies beside thee on the grass.
  O kiss him once for me.

"O kiss him twice and thrice for me,
  That have no lips to kiss,
For never yet was oak on lea
  Shall grow so fair as this."

Step deeper yet in herb and fern,
  Look further thro' the chace,
Spread upward till thy boughs discern
  The front of Sumner-place.

This fruit of thine by Love is blest,
  That but a moment lay
Where fairer fruit of Love may rest
  Some happy future day.

I kiss it twice, I kiss it thrice,
  The warmth it thence shall win
To riper life may magnetize
  The baby-oak within.

But thou, while kingdoms overset,
  Or lapse from hand to hand,
Thy leaf shall never fail, nor yet
  Thine acorn in the land.

May never saw dismember thee,
  Nor wielded axe disjoint,
That art the fairest-spoken tree
  From here to Lizard-point.

O rock upon thy towery-top
  All throats that gurgle sweet!
All starry culmination drop
  Balm-dews to bathe thy feet!

All grass of silky feather grow —
  And while he sinks or swells
The full south-breeze around thee blow
  The sound of minster bells.

The fat earth feed thy branchy root,
  That under deeply strikes!
The northern morning o'er thee shoot,
  High up, in silver spikes!

Nor ever lightning char thy grain,
  But, rolling as in sleep,
Low thunders bring the mellow rain,
  That makes thee broad and deep!

And hear me swear a solemn oath,
  That only by thy side
Will I to Olive plight my troth,
  And gain her for my bride.

And when my marriage morn may fall,
  She, Dryad-like, shall wear
Alternate leaf and acorn-bail
  In wreath about her hair.

And I will work in prose and rhyme,
  And praise thee more in both
Than bard has honor'd beech or lime,
  Or that Thessalian growth,

In which the swarthy ringdove sat,
  And mystic sentence spoke;
And more than England honors that,
  Thy famous brother-oak,

Wherein the younger Charles abode
Till all the paths were dim,
And far below the Roundhead rode,
  And humm'd a surly hymn.

LOVE AND DUTY.

OF love that never found his earthly close,
What sequel? Streaming eyes and breaking hearts?
Or all the same as if he had not been?
  Not so. Shall Error in the round of time
Still father Truth? O shall the braggart shout
For some blind glimpse of freedom work itself
Thro' madness, hated by the wise, to law
System and empire? Sin itself be found
The cloudy porch oft opening on the Sun?
And only he, this wonder, dead, become
Mere highway dust? or year by year alone
Sit brooding in the ruins of a life,
Nightmare of youth, the spectre of himself?
  If this were thus, if this, indeed, were all,
Better the narrow brain, the stony heart,

The staring eye glazed o'er with sap-
    less days,
The long mechanic pacings to and fro,
The set gray life, and apathetic end.
But am I not the nobler thro' thy
    love ?
O three times less unworthy! likewise
    thou
Art more thro' Love, and greater than
    thy years
The Sun will run his orbit, and the
    Moon
Her circle. Wait, and Love himself
    will bring
The drooping flower of knowledge
    changed to fruit
Of wisdom. Wait: my faith is large
    in Time,
And that which shapes it to some per-
    fect end.
    Will some one say, Then why not ill
    for good ?
Why took ye not your pastime? To
    that man
My work shall answer, since I knew
    the right
And did it; for a man is not as God,
But then most Godlike being most a
    man.
— So let me think 'tis well for thee
    and me —
Ill-fated that I am, what lot is mine
Whose foresight preaches peace, my
    heart so slow
To feel it! For how hard it seem'd to
    me,
When eyes, love-languid thro' half
    tears would dwell
One earnest, earnest moment upon
    mine,
Then not to dare to see! when thy low
    voice,
Faltering, would break its syllables, to
    keep
My own full-tuned, — hold passion in
    a leash,
And not leap forth and fall about thy
    neck,
And on thy bosom (deep desired
    relief!)
Rain out the heavy mist of tears, that
    weigh'd

Upon my brain, my senses and my soul!
    For Love himself took part against
    himself
To warn us off, and Duty loved of
    Love —
O this world's curse, — beloved but
    hated — came
Like Death betwixt thy dear embrace
    and mine,
And crying, " Who is this? behold
    thy bride,"
She push'd me from thee.
                    If the sense is hard
To alien ears, I did not speak to these —
No, not to thee, but to thyself in me :
Hard is my doom and thine: thou
    knowest it all.
    Could Love part thus? was it not
    well to speak,
To have spoken once? It could not
    but be well.
The slow sweet hours that bring us all
    things good,
The slow sad hours that bring us all
    things ill,
And all good things from evil, brought
    the night
In which we sat together and alone,
And to the want, that hollow'd all the
    heart,
Gave utterance by the yearning of an
    eye,
That burn'd upon its object thro' such
    tears
As flow but once a life.
                    The trance gave way
To those caresses, when a hundred
    times
In that last kiss, which never was the
    last,   .
Farewell, like endless welcome, lived
    and died.
Then follow'd counsel, comfort, and
    the words
That make a man feel strong in speak-
    ing truth;
Till now the dark was worn, and over-
    head
The lights of sunset and of sunrise
    mix'd
In that brief night; the summer night,
    that paused

Among her stars to hear us; stars
　　that hung
Love-charm'd to listen: all the wheels
　　of Time
Spun round in station, but the end
　　had come.
　O then like those, who clench their
　　nerves to rush
Upon their dissolution, we two rose,
There — closing like an individual
　　life —
In one blind cry of passion and of
　　pain,
Like bitter accusation ev'n to death,
Caught up the whole of love and
　　utter'd it,
And bade adieu for ever.
　　　　　　　　Live — yet live —
Shall sharpest pathos blight us, know-
　　ing all
Life needs for life is possible to
　　will —
Live happy; tend thy flowers; be
　　tended by
My blessing! Should my Shadow
　　cross thy thoughts
Too sadly for their peace, remand it
　　thou
For calmer hours to Memory's dark-
　　est hold,
If not to be forgotten — not at
　　once —
Not all forgotten. Should it cross
　　thy dreams,
O might it come like one that looks
　　content,
With quiet eyes unfaithful to the
　　truth,
And point thee forward to a distant
　　light,
Or seem to lift a burthen from thy
　　heart
And leave thee freër, till thou wake
　　refresh'd
Then when the first low matin-chirp
　　hath grown
Full quire, and morning driv'n her
　　plow of pearl
Far furrowing into light the mounded
　　rack,
Beyond the fair green field and east-
　　ern sea.

THE GOLDEN YEAR.

WELL, you shall have that song which
　　Leonard wrote:
It was last summer on a tour in Wales:
Old James was with me : we that day
　　had been
Up Snowdon ; and I wish'd for Leon-
　　ard there,
And found him in Llanberis: then we
　　crost
Between the lakes, and clamber'd half
　　way up
The counter side ; and that same song
　　of his
He told me ; for I banter'd him, and
　　swore
They said he lived shut up within
　　himself,
A tongue-tied Poet in the feverous
　　days,
That, setting the *how much* before the
　　how,
Cry, like the daughters of the horse-
　　leech, " Give,
Cram us with all," but count not me
　　the herd !
　To which "They call me what they
　　will," he said :
" But I was born too late : the fair new
　　forms,
That float about the threshold of an
　　age,
Like truths of Science waiting to be
　　caught —
Catch me who can, and make the
　　catcher crown'd —
Are taken by the forelock.　Let it be.
But if you care indeed to listen,
　　hear
These measured words, my work of
　　yestermorn.
　" We sleep and wake and sleep, but
　　all things move;
The Sun flies forward to his brother
　　Sun ;
The dark Earth follows wheel'd in her
　　ellipse ;
And human things returning on them-
　　selves
Move onward, leading up the golden
　　year.

" Ah, tho' the times, when some new
    thought can bud,
Are but as poets' seasons when they
    flower,
Yet seas, that daily gain upon the
    shore,
Have ebb and flow conditioning their
    march,
And slow and sure comes up the
    golden year.
   " When wealth no more shall rest
    in mounded heaps
But smit with freër light shall slowly
    melt
In many streams to fatten lower lands,
And light shall spread, and man be
    liker man
Thro' all the season of the golden
    year.
   " Shall eagles not be eagles? wrens
    be wrens?
If all the world were falcons, what of
    that?
The wonder of the eagle were the less,
But he not less the eagle. Happy days
Roll onward, leading up the golden
    year.
   " Fly, happy happy sails, and bear
    the Press;
Fly happy with the mission of the
    Cross;
Knit land to land, and blowing haven-
    ward
With silks, and fruits, and spices, clear
    of toll,
Enrich the markets of the golden year.
   " But we grow old. Ah! when shall
    all men's good
Be each man's rule, and universal
    Peace
Lie like a shaft of light across the land,
And like a lane of beams athwart the
    sea,
Thro' all the circle of the golden
    year?"
    Thus far he flow'd, and ended;
    whereupon
" Ah, folly!" in mimic cadence an-
    swer'd James—
" Ah, folly! for it lies so far away,
Not in our time, nor in our children's
    time,

'Tis like the second world to us that
    live;
'Twere all as one to fix our hopes on
    Heaven
As on this vision of the golden year."
   With that he struck his staff against
    the rocks
And broke it,— James,— you know
    him,— old, but full
Of force and choler, and firm upon his
    feet,
And like an oaken stock in winter
    woods,
O'erflourish'd with the hoary clematis:
Then added, all in heat:
           " What stuff is this!
Old writers push'd the happy season
    back,—
The more fools they,— we forward:
    dreamers both:
You most, that in an age, when every
    hour
Must sweat her sixty minutes to the
    death,
Live on, God love us, as if the seeds-
    man, rapt
Upon the teeming harvest, should not
    plunge
His hand into the bag: but well I
    know
That unto him who works, and feels
    he works,
This same grand year is ever at the
    doors."
   He spoke; and, high above, I heard
    them blast
The steep slate-quarry, and the great
    echo flap
And buffet round the hills, from bluff
    to bluff.

ULYSSES.

It little profits that an idle king,
By this still hearth, among these bar-
    ren crags,
Match'd with an aged wife, I mete and
    dole
Unequal laws unto a savage race,
That hoard, and sleep, and feed, and
    know not me.

I cannot rest from travel : I will drink
Life to the lees : all times I have en-
  joy'd
Greatly, have suffer'd greatly, both
  with those
That loved me, and alone ; on shore,
  and when
Thro' scudding drifts the rainy Hyades
Vext the dim sea: I am become a name;
For always roaming with a hungry
  heart
Much have I seen and known ; cities
  of men
And manners, climates, councils, gov-
  ernments,
Myself not least, but honor'd of them
  all ;
And drunk delight of battle with my
  peers,
Far on the ringing plains of windy
  Troy.
I am a part of all that I have met ;
Yet all experience is an arch where-
  thro'
Gleams that untravell'd world, whose
  margin fades
For ever and for ever when I move.
How dull it is to pause, to make an end,
To rust unburnish'd, not to shine in
  use !
As tho' to breathe were life. Life
  piled on life
Were all too little, and of one to me
Little remains : but every hour is saved
From that eternal silence, something
  more,
A bringer of new things ; and vile it
  were
For some three suns to store and hoard
  myself,
And this gray spirit yearning in desire
To follow knowledge like a sinking
  star,
Beyond the utmost bound of human
  thought.
  This is my son, mine own Telema-
  chus,
To whom I leave the sceptre and the
  isle —
Well-loved of me, discerning to fulfil
This labor, by slow prudence to make
  mild

A rugged people, and thro' soft degrees
Subdue them to the useful and the
  good.
Most blameless is he, centred in the
  sphere
Of common duties, decent not to fail
In offices of tenderness, and pay
Meet adoration to my household gods,
When I am gone.   He works his work,
  I mine.
  There lies the port ; the vessel puffs
  her sail :
There gloom the dark broad seas.   My
  mariners,
Souls that have toil'd, and wrought,
  and thought with me —
That ever with a frolic welcome took
The thunder and the sunshine, and
  opposed
Free hearts, free foreheads — you and
  I are old ;
Old age hath yet his honor and his toil ;
Death closes all : but something ere
  the end,
Some work of noble note, may yet be
  done,
Not unbecoming men that strove with
  Gods.
The lights begin to twinkle from the
  rocks :
The long day wanes : the slow moon
  climbs : the deep
Moans round with many voices.
  Come, my friends,
'Tis not too late to seek a newer world.
Push off, and sitting well in order
  smite
The sounding furrows ; for my pur-
  pose holds
To sail beyond the sunset, and the
  baths
Of all the western stars, until I die.
It may be that the gulfs will wash us
  down :
It may be we shall touch the Happy
  Isles,
And see the great Achilles, whom we
  knew.
Tho' much is taken, much abides ; and
  tho'
We are not now that strength which
  in old days

Moved earth and heaven; that which
we are, we are;
One equal temper of heroic hearts,
Made weak by time and fate, but
strong in will
To strive, to seek, to find, and not to
yield.

TITHONUS.

THE woods decay, the woods decay
and fall,
The vapors weep their burthen to the
ground,
Man comes and tills the field and lies
beneath,
And after many a summer dies the
swan.
Me only cruel immortality
Consumes : I wither slowly in thine
arms,
Here at the quiet limit of the world,
A white-hair'd shadow roaming like a
dream
The ever-silent spaces of the East,
Far-folded mists, and gleaming halls
of morn.

Alas! for this gray shadow, once a
man —
So glorious in his beauty and thy
choice,
Who madest him thy chosen, that he
seem'd
To his great heart none other than a
God!
I ask'd thee, "Give me immortality."
Then didst thou grant mine asking
with a smile,
Like wealthy men who care not how
they give.
But thy strong Hours indignant
work'd their wills,
And beat me down and marr'd and
wasted me,
And tho' they could not end me, left
me maim'd
To dwell in presence of immortal
youth,
Immortal age beside immortal youth,
And all I was, in ashes. Can thy
love,

Thy beauty, make amends, tho' even
now,
Close over us, the silver star, thy
guide,
Shines in those tremulous eyes that
fill with tears
To hear me ? Let me go: take back
thy gift:
Why should a man desire in any way
To vary from the kindly race of men,
Or pass beyond the goal of ordinance
Where all should pause, as is most
meet for all ?

A soft air fans the cloud apart;
there comes
A glimpse of that dark world where
I was born.
Once more the old mysterious glim-
mer steals
From thy pure brows, and from thy
shoulders pure,
And bosom beating with a heart re-
new'd.
Thy cheek begins to redden thro' the
gloom,
Thy sweet eyes brighten slowly close
to mine,
Ere yet they blind the stars, and the
wild team
Which love thee, yearning for thy
yoke, arise,
And shake the darkness from their
loosen'd manes,
And beat the twilight into flakes of
fire.

Lo! ever thus thou growest beautiful
In silence, then before thine answer
given
Departest, and thy tears are on my
cheek.

Why wilt thou ever scare me with
thy tears,
And make me tremble lest a saying
learnt,
In days far-off, on that dark earth, be
true ?
"The Gods themselves cannot recall
their gifts."

Ay me! ay me! with what another heart
In days far-off, and with what other eyes
I used to watch — if I be he that watch'd —
The lucid outline forming round thee; saw
The dim curls kindle into sunny rings;
Changed with thy mystic change, and felt my blood
Glow with the glow that slowly crimson'd all
Thy presence and thy portals, while I lay,
Mouth, forehead, eyelids, growing dewy-warm
With kisses balmier than half-opening buds
Of April, and could hear the lips that kiss'd
Whispering I knew not what of wild and sweet,
Like that strange song I heard Apollo sing,
While Ilion like a mist rose into towers.

Yet hold me not for ever in thine East:
How can my nature longer mix with thine?
Coldly thy rosy shadows bathe me, cold
Are all thy lights, and cold my wrinkled feet
Upon thy glimmering thresholds, when the steam
Floats up from those dim fields about the homes
Of happy men that have the power to die,
And grassy barrows of the happier dead.
Release me, and restore me to the ground;
Thou seëst all things, thou wilt see my grave:
Thou wilt renew thy beauty morn by morn;
I earth in earth forget these empty courts,
And thee returning on thy silver wheels.

LOCKSLEY HALL.

COMRADES, leave me here a little, while as yet 'tis early morn:
Leave me here, and when you want me, sound upon the bugle-horn.

'Tis the place, and all around it, as of old, the curlews call,
Dreary gleams about the moorland flying over Locksley Hall;

Locksley Hall, that in the distance overlooks the sandy tracts,
And the hollow ocean-ridges roaring into cataracts.

Many a night from yonder ivied casement, ere I went to rest,
Did I look on great Orion sloping slowly to the West.

Many a night I saw the Pleiads, rising thro' the mellow shade,
Glitter like a swarm of fire-flies tangled in a silver braid.

Here about the beach I wander'd, nourishing a youth sublime
With the fairy tales of science, and the long result of Time;

When the centuries behind me like a fruitful land reposed;
When I clung to all the present for the promise that it closed.

When I dipt into the future far as human eye could see;
Saw the Vision of the world, and all the wonder that would be. —

In the Spring a fuller crimson comes upon the robin's breast;
In the Spring the wanton lapwing gets himself another crest;

In the Spring a livelier iris changes on the burnish'd dove;
In the Spring a young man's fancy lightly turns to thoughts of love.

Then her cheek was pale and thinner than should be for one so young,
And her eyes on all my motions with a mute observance hung.

And I said, "My cousin Amy, speak, and speak the truth to me,
Trust me, cousin, all the current of my being sets to thee."

On her pallid cheek and forehead came a color and a light,
As I have seen the rosy red flushing in the northern night.

And she turn'd — her bosom shaken with a sudden storm of sighs —
All the spirit deeply dawning in the dark of hazel eyes —

Saying, "I have hid my feelings, fearing they should do me wrong";
Saying, "Dost thou love me, cousin?" weeping, "I have loved thee long."

Love took up the glass of Time, and turn'd it in his glowing hands;
Every moment, lightly shaken, ran itself in golden sands.

Love took up the harp of Life, and smote on all the chords with might;
Smote the chord of Self, that, trembling, pass'd in music out of sight.

Many a morning on the moorland did we hear the copses ring,
And her whisper throng'd my pulses with the fulness of the Spring.

Many an evening by the waters did we watch the stately ships,
And our spirits rush'd together at the touching of the lips.

O my cousin, shallow-hearted!　O my Amy, mine no more!
O the dreary, dreary moorland!　O the barren, barren shore!

Falser than all fancy fathoms, falser than all songs have sung,
Puppet to a father's threat, and servile to a shrewish tongue!

Is it well to wish thee happy? — having known me — to decline
On a range of lower feelings and a narrower heart than mine!

Yet it shall be: thou shalt lower to his level day by day,
What is fine within thee growing coarse to sympathize with clay.

As the husband is, the wife is: thou art mated with a clown,
And the grossness of his nature will have weight to drag thee down.

He will hold thee, when his passion shall have spent its novel force,
Something better than his dog, a little dearer than his horse.

What is this? his eyes are heavy: think not they are glazed with wine.
Go to him: it is thy duty: kiss him: take his hand in thine.

It may be my lord is weary, that his brain is overwrought:
Soothe him with thy finer fancies, touch him with thy lighter thought.

He will answer to the purpose, easy things to understand —
Better thou wert dead before me, tho' I slew thee with my hand!

Better thou and I were lying, hidden from the heart's disgrace,
Roll'd in one another's arms, and silent in a last embrace.

Cursed be the social wants that sin against the strength of youth!
Cursed be the social lies that warp us from the living truth!

Cursed be the sickly forms that err from honest Nature's rule!
Cursed be the gold that gilds the straiten'd forehead of the fool!

Well — 'tis well that I should bluster! — Hadst thou less unworthy
      proved —
Would to God — for I had loved thee more than ever wife was loved.

Am I mad, that I should cherish that which bears but bitter fruit?
I will pluck it from my bosom, tho' my heart be at the root.

Never, tho' my mortal summers to such length of years should come
As the many-winter'd crow that leads the clanging rookery home.

Where is comfort? in division of the records of the mind?
Can I part her from herself, and love her, as I knew her, kind?

I remember one that perish'd: sweetly did she speak and move:
Such a one do I remember, whom to look at was to love.

Can I think of her as dead, and love her for the love she bore?
No — she never loved me truly: love is love for evermore.

Comfort? comfort scorn'd of devils! this is truth the poet sings,
That a sorrow's crown of sorrow is remembering happier things.

Drug thy memories, lest thou learn it, lest thy heart be put to proof,
In the dead unhappy night, and when the rain is on the roof.

Like a dog, he hunts in dreams, and thou art staring at the wall,
Where the dying night-lamp flickers, and the shadows rise and fall.

Then a hand shall pass before thee, pointing to his drunken sleep,
To thy widow'd marriage-pillows to the tears that thou wilt weep.

Thou shalt hear the " Never, never," whisper'd by the phantom years,
And a song from out the distance in the ringing of thine ears;

And an eye shall vex thee, looking ancient kindness on thy pain.
Turn thee, turn thee on thy pillow: get thee to thy rest again.

Nay, but Nature brings thee solace; for a tender voice will cry.
'Tis a purer life than thine; a lip to drain thy trouble dry.

Baby lips will laugh me down: my latest rival brings thee rest.
Baby fingers, waxen touches, press me from the mother's breast.

O, the child too clothes the father with a dearness not his due.
Half is thine and half is his: it will be worthy of the two.

O, I see thee old and formal, fitted to thy petty part,
With a little hoard of maxims preaching down a daughter's heart.

"They were dangerous guides the feelings — she herself was not
      exempt —
Truly, she herself had suffer'd " — Perish in thy self-contempt!

Overlive it — lower yet — be happy! wherefore should I care?
I myself must mix with action, lest I wither by despair.

What is that which I should turn to, lighting upon days like these?
Every door is barr'd with gold, and opens but to golden keys.

Every gate is throng'd with suitors, all the markets overflow.
I have but an angry fancy: what is that which I should do?

I had been content to perish, falling on the foeman's ground,
When the ranks are roll'd in vapor, and the winds are laid with sound.

But the jingling of the guinea helps the hurt that Honor feels,
And the nations do but murmur, snarling at each other's heels.

Can I but relive in sadness?   I will turn that earlier page.
Hide me from thy deep emotion, O thou wondrous Mother-Age!

Make me feel the wild pulsation that I felt before the strife,
When I heard my days before me, and the tumult of my life;

Yearning for the large excitement that the coming years would yield,
Eager-hearted as a boy when first he leaves his father's field,

And at night along the dusky highway near and nearer drawn,
Sees in heaven the light of London flaring like a dreary dawn;

And his spirit leaps within him to be gone before him then,
Underneath the light he looks at, in among the throngs of men:

" Baby fingers, waxen touches, press me from the mother's breast."

Page 110.

Men, my brothers, men the workers, ever reaping something new :
That which they have done but earnest of the things that they shall do:

For I dipt into the future, far as human eye could see,
Saw the Vision of the world, and all the wonder that would be;

Saw the heavens fill with commerce, argosies of magic sails,
Pilots of the purple twilight, dropping down with costly bales ;

Heard the heavens fill with shouting, and there rain'd a ghastly dew
From the nations' airy navies grappling in the central blue;

Far along the world-wide whisper of the south-wind rushing warm,
With the standards of the peoples plunging thro' the thunder-storm ;

Till the war-drum throbb'd no longer, and the battle-flags were furl'd
In the Parliament of man, the Federation of the world.

There the common sense of most shall hold a fretful realm in awe,
And the kindly earth shall slumber, lapt in universal law.

So I triumph'd ere my passion sweeping thro' me left me dry,
Left me with the palsied heart, and left me with the jaundiced eye;

Eye. to which all order festers, all things here are out of joint :
Science moves, but slowly slowly, creeping on from point to point :

Slowly comes a hungry people, as a lion creeping nigher,
Glares at one that nods and winks behind a slowly-dying fire.

Yet I doubt not thro' the ages one increasing purpose runs,
And the thoughts of men are widen'd with the process of the suns.

What is that to him that reaps not harvest of his youthful joys,
Tho' the deep heart of existence beat for ever like a boy's ?

Knowledge comes, but wisdom lingers, and I linger on the shore,
And the individual withers, and the world is more and more.

Knowledge comes, but wisdom lingers, and he bears a laden breast,
Full of sad experience, moving toward the stillness of his rest.

Hark, my merry comrades call me, sounding on the bugle-horn,
They to whom my foolish passion were a target for their scorn:

Shall it not be scorn to me to harp on such a moulder'd string ?
I am shamed thro' all my nature to have loved so slight a thing.

Weakness to be wroth with weakness ! woman's pleasure, woman's pain —
Nature made them blinder motions bounded in a shallower brain:

Woman is the lesser man, and all thy passions, match'd with mine,
Are as moonlight unto sunlight, and as water unto wine —

Here at least, where nature sickens, nothing. Ah, for some retreat
Deep in yonder shining Orient, where my life began to beat;

Where in wild Mahratta-battle fell my father evil-starr'd; —
I was left a trampled orphan, and a selfish uncle's ward.

Or to burst all links of habit — there to wander far away,
On from island unto island at the gateways of the day.

Larger constellations burning, mellow moons and happy skies,
Breadths of tropic shade and palms in cluster, knots of Paradise.

Never comes the trader, never floats an European flag,
Slides the bird o'er lustrous woodland, swings the trailer from the crag;

Droops the heavy-blossom'd bower, hangs the heavy-fruited tree —
Summer isles of Eden lying in dark-purple spheres of sea.

There methinks would be enjoyment more than in this march of mind,
In the steamship, in the railway, in the thoughts that shake mankind.

There the passions cramp'd no longer shall have scope and breathing
　　　　space;
I will take some savage woman, she shall rear my dusky race.

Iron jointed, supple-sinew'd, they shall dive, and they shall run,
Catch the wild goat by the hair, and hurl their lances in the sun;

Whistle back the parrot's call, and leap the rainbows of the brooks,
Not with blinded eyesight poring over miserable books —

Fool, again the dream, the fancy! but I *know* my words are wild,
But I count the gray barbarian lower than the Christian child.

I, to herd with narrow foreheads, vacant of our glorious gains,
Like a beast with lower pleasures, like a beast with lower pains!

Mated with a squalid savage — what to me were sun or clime?
I the heir of all the ages, in the foremost files of time —

I that rather held it better men should perish one by one,
Than that earth should stand at gaze like Joshua's moon in Ajalon!

Not in vain the distance beacons. Forward, forward let us range,
Let the great world spin for ever down the ringing grooves of change.

Thro' the shadow of the globe we sweep into the younger day:
Better fifty years of Europe than a cycle of Cathay.

Mother-Age (for mine I knew not) help me as when life begun :
Rift the hills, and roll the waters, flash the lightnings, weigh the Sun.

O, I see the crescent promise of my spirit hath not set.
Ancient founts of inspiration well thro' all my fancy yet.

Howsoever these things be, a long farewell to Locksley Hall!
Now for me the woods may wither, now for me the roof-tree fall.

Comes a vapor from the margin, blackening over heath and holt,
Cramming all the blast before it, in its breast a thunderbolt.

Let it fall on Locksley Hall, with rain or hail, or fire or snow ;
For the mighty wind arises, roaring seaward, and I go.

GODIVA.

I waited for the train at Coventry ;
*I hung with grooms and porters on the
bridge,*
*To watch the three tall spires ; and there
I shaped*
The city's ancient legend into this : —

Not only we, the latest seed of Time,
New men, that in the flying of a wheel
Cry down the past, not only we, that
prate
Of rights and wrongs, have loved the
people well,
And loathed to see them over-tax'd ;
but she
Did more, and underwent, and over-
came,
The woman of a thousand summers
back,
Godiva, wife to that grim Earl, who
ruled
In Coventry : for when he laid a tax
Upon his town, and all the mothers
brought
Their children, clamoring, "If we pay,
we starve!"
She sought her lord, and found him,
where he strode
About the hall, among his dogs, alone,
His beard a foot before him, and his
hair
A yard behind.   She told him of their
tears,

And pray'd him, "If they pay this tax,
they starve."
Whereat he stared, replying, half-
amazed,
"You would not let your little finger
ache
For such as *these?*" — "But I would
die," said she.
He laugh'd, and swore by Peter and by
Paul :
Then fillip'd at the diamond in her
ear;
"Oh ay, ay, ay, you talk!" — "Alas!"
she said,
"But prove me what it is I would not
do."
And from a heart as rough as Esau's
hand,
He answer'd, "Ride you naked thro'
the town,
And I repeal it"; and nodding, as in
scorn,
He parted, with great strides among
his dogs.
So left alone, the passions of her
mind,
As winds from all the compass shift
and blow,
Made war upon each other for an hour,
Till pity won. She sent a herald forth,
And bade him cry, with sound of
trumpet, all
The hard condition; but that she
would loose

The people : therefore, as they loved
  her well,
From then till noon no foot should
  pace the street,
No eye look down, she passing; but
  that all
Should keep within, door shut, and
  window barr'd.
  Then fled she to her inmost bower,
    and there
Unclasp'd the wedded eagles of her
  belt,
The grim Earl's gift; but ever at a
  breath
She linger'd, looking like a summer
  moon
Half-dipt in cloud : anon she shook
  her head,
And shower'd the rippled ringlets to
  her knee ;
Unclad herself in haste; adown the
  stair
Stole on ; and, like a creeping sun-
  beam, slid
From pillar unto pillar, until she
  reach'd
The gateway ; there she found her
  palfrey trapt
In purple blazon'd with armorial
  gold.
  Then she rode forth, clothed on with
    chastity :
The deep air listen'd round her as she
  rode,
And all the low wind hardly breathed
  for fear.
The little wide-mouth'd heads upon
  the spout
Had cunning eyes to see : the barking
  cur
Made her cheek flame : her palfrey's
  footfall shot
Like horrors thro' her pulses : the
  blind walls
Were full of chinks and holes; and
  overhead
Fantastic gables, crowding, stared :
  but she
Not less thro' all bore up, till, last, she
  saw
The white-flower'd elder-thicket from
  the field

Gleam thro' the Gothic archway in the
  wall.
  Then she rode back, clothed on with
    chastity :
And one low churl, compact of thank-
  less earth,
The fatal byword of all years to come,
Boring a little auger-hole in fear,
Peep'd — but his eyes, before they had
  their will,
Were shrivell'd into darkness in his
  head,
And dropt before him. So the Powers,
  who wait
On noble deeds, cancell'd a sense mis-
  used ;
And she, that knew not, pass'd : and
  all at once,
With twelve great shocks of sound,
  the shameless noon
Was clash'd and hammer'd from a
  hundred towers,
One after one : but even then she
  gain'd
Her bower ; whence reissuing, robed
  and crown'd,
To meet her lord, she took the tax
  away
And built herself an everlasting name.

THE DAY-DREAM.

PROLOGUE.

O Lady Flora, let me speak :
  A pleasant hour has passed away
While, dreaming on your damask
    cheek,
  The dewy sister-eyelids lay.
As by the lattice you reclined,
  I went thro' many wayward moods
To see you dreaming — and, behind,
  A summer crisp with shining woods.
And I too dream'd, until at last
  Across my fancy, brooding warm,
The reflex of a legend past,
  And loosely settled into form.
And would you have the thought I
    had,
  And see the vision that I saw,
Then take the broidery-frame, and add
  A crimson to the quaint Macaw,

And I will tell it. Turn your face,
 Nor look with that too-earnest
  eye —
The rhymes are dazzled from their
  place,
 And order'd words asunder fly.

THE SLEEPING PALACE.

I.

THE varying year with blade and sheaf
 Clothes and reclothes the happy
  plains,
Here rests the sap within the leaf,
 Here stays the blood along the veins.
Faint shadows, vapors lightly curl'd,
 Faint murmurs from the meadows
  come,
Like hints and echoes of the world
 To spirits folded in the womb.

II.

Soft lustre bathes the range of urns
 On every slanting terrace-lawn.
The fountain to his place returns
 Deep in the garden lake withdrawn.
Here droops the banner on the tower,
 On the hall-hearths the festal fires,
The peacock in his laurel bower,
 The parrot in his gilded wires.

III.

Roof-haunting martins warm their
  eggs:
 In these, in those the life is stay'd.
The mantles from the golden pegs
 Droop sleepily: no sound is made,
Not even of a gnat that sings.
 More like a picture seemeth all
Than those old portraits of old kings,
 That watch the sleepers from the
  wall.

IV.

Here sits the Butler with a flask
 Between his knees, half-drain'd; and
  there
The wrinkled steward at his task,
 The maid-of-honor blooming fair;
The page has caught her hand in his:
 Her lips are sever'd as to speak:

His own are pouted to a kiss:
 The blush is fix'd upon her cheek.

V.

Till all the hundred summers pass,
 The beams, that thro' the Oriel shine,
Make prisms in every carven glass,
 And beaker brimm'd with noble
  wine.
Each baron at the banquet sleeps,
 Grave faces gather'd in a ring.
His state the king reposing keeps.
 He must have been a jovial king.

VI.

All round a hedge upshoots, and shows
 At distance like a little wood;
Thorns, ivies, woodbine, mistletoes,
 And grapes with bunches red as
  blood;
All creeping plants, a wall of green
 Close-matted, burr and brake and
  brier,
And glimpsing over these, just seen,
 High up, the topmost palace spire.

VII.

When will the hundred summers die,
 And thought and time be born again,
And newer knowledge, drawing nigh,
 Bring truth that sways the soul of
  men?
Here all things in their place remain,
 As all were order'd, ages since.
Come, Care and Pleasure, Hope and
  Pain,
 And bring the fated fairy Prince.

THE SLEEPING BEAUTY.

I.

YEAR after year unto her feet,
 She lying on her couch alone,
Across the purple coverlet,
 The maiden's jet-black hair has
  grown,
On either side her tranced form
 Forth streaming from a braid of
  pearl:
The slumbrous light is rich and warm,
 And moves not on the rounded curl.

II.

The silk star-broider'd coverlid
  Unto her limbs itself doth mould
Languidly ever; and, amid
  Her full black ringlets downward
    roll'd,
Glows forth each softly-shadow'd arm
  With bracelets of the diamond
    bright:
Her constant beauty doth inform
  Stillness with love, and day with
    light.

III.

She sleeps: her breathings are not
    heard
  In palace chambers far apart.
The fragrant tresses are not stirr'd
  That lie upon her charmed heart.
She sleeps: on either hand upswells
  The gold-fringed pillow lightly
    prest:
She sleeps, nor dreams, but ever dwells
  A perfect form in perfect rest.

THE ARRIVAL.

I.

ALL precious things, discover'd late,
  To those that seek them issue forth;
For love in sequel works with fate,
  And draws the veil from hidden
    worth.
He travels far from other skies —
  His mantle glitters on the rocks —
A fairy Prince, with joyful eyes,
  And lighter-footed than the fox.

II.

The bodies and the bones of those
  That strove in other days to pass,
Are wither'd in the thorny close,
  Or scatter'd blanching on the grass.
He gazes on the silent dead:
  "They perish'd in their daring
    deeds."
This proverb flashes thro' his head,
  "The many fail: the one succeeds."

III.

He comes, scarce knowing what he
    seeks:
  He breaks the hedge: he enters
    there:
The color flies into his cheeks:
  He trusts to light on something fair;
For all his life the charm did talk
  About his path, and hover near
With words of promise in his walk,
  And whisper'd voices at his ear.

IV.

More close and close his footsteps
    wind:
  The Magic Music in his heart
Beats quick and quicker, till he find
  The quiet chamber far apart.
The spirit flutters like a lark,
  He stoops — to kiss her — on his
    knee.
"Love, if thy tresses be so dark,
  How dark those hidden eyes must
    be!"

THE REVIVAL.

I.

A TOUCH, a kiss! the charm was snapt.
  There rose a noise of striking clocks,
And feet that ran, and doors that clapt,
  And barking dogs, and crowing
    cocks;
A fuller light illumined all,
  A breeze thro' all the garden swept,
A sudden hubbub shook the hall,
  And sixty feet the fountain leapt.

II.

The hedge broke in, the banner blew,
  The butler drank, the steward
    scrawl'd,
The fire shot up, the martin flew,
  The parrot scream'd, the peacock
    squall'd,
The maid and page renew'd their strife,
  The palace bang'd, and buzz'd and
    clackt,
And all the long-pent stream of life
  Dash'd downward in a cataract.

III.

And last with these the king awoke,
  And in his chair himself uprear'd,
And yawn'd, and rubb'd his face, and
      spoke,
  "By holy rood, a royal beard!
How say you? we have slept, my lords.
  My beard has grown into my lap."
The barons swore, with many words,
  'Twas but an after-dinner's nap.

IV.

"Pardy," return'd the king, "but still
  My joints are somewhat stiff or so.
My lord, and shall we pass the bill
  I mention'd half an hour ago?"
The chancellor, sedate and vain,
  In courteous words return'd reply:
But dallied with his golden chain,
  And, smiling, put the question by.

THE DEPARTURE.

I.

AND on her lover's arm she leant,
  And round her waist she felt it fold,
And far across the hills they went
  In that new world which is the old:
Across the hills, and far away
  Beyond this utmost purple rim,
And deep into the dying day
  The happy princess follow'd him.

II.

"I'd sleep another hundred years,
  O love, for such another kiss;"
"O wake for ever, love," she hears,
  "O love, 'twas such as this and this."
And o'er them many a sliding star,
  And many a merry wind was borne,
And, stream'd thro' many a golden bar,
  The twilight melted into morn.

III.

"O eyes long laid in happy sleep!"
  "O happy sleep, that lightly fled!"
"O happy kiss, that woke thy sleep!"
  "O love, thy kiss would wake the
      dead!"
And o'er them many a flowing range

Of vapor buoy'd the crescent-bark,
And, rapt thro' many a rosy change
  The twilight died into the dark.

IV.

"A hundred summers! can it be?
  And whither goest thou, tell me
      where?"
"O seek my father's court with me,
  For there are greater wonders
      there."
And o'er the hills, and far away
  Beyond their utmost purple rim,
Beyond the night, across the day,
  Thro' all the world she follow'd him.

MORAL.

I.

So, Lady Flora, take my lay,
  And if you find no moral there,
Go, look in any glass and say,
  What moral is in being fair.
Oh, to what uses shall we put
  The wildweed flower that simply
      blows?
And is there any moral shut
  Within the bosom of the rose?

II.

But any man that walks the mead,
  In bud or blade, or bloom, may find,
According as his humors lead,
  A meaning suited to his mind.
And liberal applications lie
  In Art like Nature, dearest friend;
So 'twere to cramp its use, if I
  Should hook it to some useful end.

L'ENVOI.

I.

YOU shake your head. A random
      string
  Your finer female sense offends.
Well — were it not a pleasant thing
  To fall asleep with all one's friends;
To pass with all our social ties
  To silence from the paths of men;
And every hundred years to rise

And learn the world, and sleep
    again ;
To sleep thro' terms of mighty wars,
    And wake on science grown to more,
On secrets of the brain, the stars,
    As wild as aught of fairy lore ;
And all that else the years will show,
    The Poet-forms of stronger hours,
The vast Republics that may grow,
    The Federations and the Powers ;
Titanic forces taking birth
    In divers seasons, divers climes ;
For we are Ancients of the earth,
    And in the morning of the times.

II.

So sleeping, so aroused from sleep
    Thro' sunny decades new and strange,
Or gay quinquenniads would we reap
    The flower and quintessence of
    change.

III.

Ah, yet would I — and would I might !
    So much your eyes my fancy take —
Be still the first to leap to light
    That I might kiss those eyes awake !
For, am I right, or am I wrong,
    To choose your own you did not
    care ;
You'd have *my* moral from the song,
    And I will take my pleasure there :
And, am I right or am I wrong,
    My fancy, ranging thro' and thro',
To search a meaning for the song,
    Perforce will still revert to you ;
Nor finds a closer truth than this
    All-graceful head, so richly curl'd,
And evermore a costly kiss
    The prelude to some brighter world.

IV.

For since the time when Adam first
    Embraced his Eve in happy hour,
And every bird of Eden burst
    In carol, every bud to flower,
What eyes, like thine, have waken'd
    hopes,
    What lips, like thine, so sweetly
    join'd ?
Where on the double rosebud droops
    The fulness of the pensive mind ;

Which all too dearly self-involved,
    Yet sleeps a dreamless sleep to me ;
A sleep by kisses undissolved,
    That lets thee neither hear nor see :
But break it. In the name of wife,
    And in the rights that name may
    give,
Are clasp'd the moral of thy life,
    And that for which I care to live.

EPILOGUE.

So, Lady Flora, take my lay,
    And, if you find a meaning there,
O whisper to your glass, and say,
    "What wonder, if he thinks me
    fair ? "
What wonder I was all unwise,
    To shape the song for your delight
Like long-tail'd birds of Paradise
    That float thro' Heaven, and cannot
    light ?
Or old-world trains, upheld at court
    By Cupid-boys of blooming hue —
But take it — earnest wed with sport,
    And either sacred unto you.

AMPHION.

My father left a park to me,
    But it is wild and barren,
A garden too with scarce a tree,
    And waster than a warren :
Yet say the neighbors when they call,
    It is not bad but good land,
And in it is the germ of all
    That grows within the woodland.

O had I lived when song was great
    In days of old Amphion,
And ta'en my fiddle to the gate,
    Nor cared for seed or scion !
And had I lived when song was great,
    And legs of trees were limber,
And ta'en my fiddle to the gate,
    And fiddled in the timber !

'Tis said he had a tuneful tongue,
    Such happy intonation,
Wherever he sat down and sung
    He left a small plantation ;

Wherever in a lonely grove
  He set up his forlorn pipes,
The gouty oak began to move,
  And flounder into hornpipes.

The mountain stirr'd its bushy crown,
  And, as tradition teaches,
Young ashes pirouetted down
  Coquetting with young beeches;
And briony-vine and ivy-wreath
  Ran forward to his rhyming,
And from the valleys underneath
  Came little copses climbing.

The linden broke her ranks and rent
  The woodbine wreaths that bind her,
And down the middle, buzz! she went
  With all her bees behind her:
The poplars, in long order due,
  With cypress promenaded,
The shock-head willows two and two
  By rivers gallopaded.

Came wet-shod alder from the wave,
  Came yews, a dismal coterie;
Each pluck'd his one foot from the grave,
  Poussetting with a sloe-tree:
Old elms came breaking from the vine,
  The vine stream'd out to follow,
And, sweating rosin, plump'd the pine
  From many a cloudy hollow.

And wasn't it a sight to see,
  When, ere his song was ended,
Like some great landslip, tree by tree,
  The country-side descended;
And shepherds from the mountain-caves
  Look'd down, half-pleased, half-frighten'd,
As dash'd about the drunken leaves
  The random sunshine lighten'd!

Oh, nature first was fresh to men,
  And wanton without measure;
So youthful and so flexile then,
  You moved her at your pleasure.
Twang out, my fiddle! shake the twigs!

And make her dance attendance;
Blow, flute, and stir the stiff-set sprigs,
  And scirrhous roots and tendons

'Tis vain! in such a brassy age
  I could not move a thistle;
The very sparrows in the hedge
  Scarce answer to my whistle;
Or at the most, when three-parts-sick
  With strumming and with scraping,
A jackass heehaws from the rick,.
  The passive oxen gaping.

But what is that I hear? a sound
  Like sleepy counsel pleading;
O Lord!—'tis in my neighbor's ground,
  The modern Muses reading.
They read Botanic Treatises,
  And Works on Gardening thro' there,
And Methods of transplanting trees
  To look as if they grew there.

The wither'd Misses! how they prose
  O'er books of travell'd seamen,
And show you slips of all that grows
  From England to Van Diemen.
They read in arbors clipt and cut,
  And alleys, faded places,
By squares of tropic summer shut
  And warm'd in crystal cases.

But these, tho' fed with careful dirt,
  Are neither green nor sappy;
Half-conscious of the garden-squirt,
  The spindlings look unhappy.
Better to me the meanest weed
  That blows upon its mountain,
The vilest herb that runs to seed
  Beside its native fountain.

And I must work thro' months of toil
  And years of cultivation,
Upon my proper patch of soil
  To grow my own plantation.
I'll take the showers as they fall,
  I will not vex my bosom:
Enough if at the end of all
  A little garden blossom.

ST. AGNES' EVE.

DEEP on the convent-roof the snows
　　Are sparkling to the moon:
My breath to heaven like vapor goes:
　　May my soul follow soon!
The shadows of the convent-towers
　　Slant down the snowy sward,
Still creeping with the creeping hours
　　That lead me to my Lord:
Make Thou my spirit pure and clear
　　As are the frosty skies,
Or this first snowdrop of the year
　　That in my bosom lies.

As these white robes are soil'd and
　　　dark,
　　To yonder shining ground;
As this pale taper's earthly spark,
　　To yonder argent round;
So shows my soul before the Lamb,
　　My spirit before Thee;
So in mine earthly house I am,
　　To that I hope to be.
Break up the heavens, O Lord! and far,
　　Thro' all yon starlight keen,
Draw me, thy bride, a glittering star,
　　In raiment white and clean.

He lifts me to the golden doors;
　　The flashes come and go;
All heaven bursts her starry floors,
　　And strows her lights below,
And deepens on and up! the gates
　　Roll back, and far within
For me the Heavenly Bridegroom
　　　waits,
　　To make me pure of sin.
The sabbaths of Eternity,
　　One sabbath deep and wide —
A light upon the shining sea —
　　The Bridegroom with his bride!

SIR GALAHAD.

MY good blade carves the casques of
　　　men,
　　My tough lance thrusteth sure,
My strength is as the strength of ten,
　　Because my heart is pure.
The shattering trumpet shrilleth high,
　　The hard brands shiver on the steel,

The splinter'd spear-shafts crack and
　　　fly,
　　The horse and rider reel:
They reel, they roll in clanging lists,
　　And when the tide of combat stands,
Perfume and flowers fall in showers,
　　That lightly rain from ladies' hands.

How sweet are looks that ladies bend
　　On whom their favors fall!
For them I battle till the end,
　　To save from shame and thrall:
But all my heart is drawn above,
　　My knees are bow'd in crypt and
　　　shrine:
I never felt the kiss of love,
　　Nor maiden's hand in mine.
More bounteous aspects on me beam,
　　Me mightier transports move and
　　　thrill;
So keep I fair thro' faith and prayer
　　A virgin heart in work and will.

When down the stormy crescent goes,
　　A light before me swims,
Between dark stems the forest glows,
　　I hear a noise of hymns:
Then by some secret shrine I ride;
　　I hear a voice but none are there;
The stalls are void, the doors are wide,
　　The tapers burning fair.
Fair gleams the snowy altar-cloth,
　　The silver vessels sparkle clean,
The shrill bell rings, the censer swings,
　　And solemn chants resound between.

Sometimes on lonely mountain-meres
　　I find a magic bark;
I leap on board: no helmsman steers:
　　I float till all is dark.
A gentle sound, an awful light!
　　Three angels bear the holy Grail:
With folded feet, in stoles of white,
　　On sleeping wings they sail.
Ah, blessed vision! blood of God!
　　My spirit beats her mortal bars,
As down dark tides the glory slides,
　　And star-like mingles with the stars.

When on my goodly charger borne
　　Thro' dreaming towns I go,

The cock crows ere the Christmas
 morn,
 The streets are dumb with snow.
The tempest crackles on the leads,
 And, ringing, springs from brand
  and mail ;
But o'er the dark a glory spreads,
 And gilds the driving hail.
I leave the plain, I climb the height ;
 No branchy thicket shelter yields ;
But blessed forms in whistling storms
 Fly o'er waste fens and windy fields.

A maiden knight — to me is given
 Such hope, I know not fear ;
I yearn to breathe the airs of heaven
 That often meet me here.
I muse on joy that will not cease,
 Pure spaces clothed in living beams,
Pure lilies of eternal peace,
 Whose odors haunt my dreams ;
And, stricken by an angel's hand,
 This mortal armor that I wear,
This weight and size, this heart and
  eyes,
 Are touch'd, are turn'd to finest air.

The clouds are broken in the sky,
 And thro' the mountain-walls
A rolling organ-harmony
 Swells up, and shakes and falls.
Then move the trees, the copses nod,
 Wings flutter, voices hover clear :
" O just and faithful knight of God !
 Ride on ! the prize is near."
So pass I hostel, hall, and grange ;
 By bridge and ford, by park and
  pale,
All-arm'd I ride, whate'er betide,
 Until I find the holy Grail.

EDWARD GRAY.

Sweet Emma Moreland of yonder
 town
 Met me walking on yonder way,
" And have you lost your heart ? "
 she said ;
 " And are you married yet, Edward
  Gray ? "

Sweet Emma Moreland spoke to me :
 Bitterly weeping I turn'd away :
" Sweet Emma Moreland, love no
  more
 Can touch the heart of Edward
  Gray.

" Ellen Adair she loved me well,
 Against her father's and mother's
  will :
To-day I sat for an hour and wept,
 By Ellen's grave, on the windy hill

" Shy she was, and I thought her cold ;
 Thought her proud, and fled over
  the sea ;
Fill'd I was with folly and spite,
 When Ellen Adair was dying for
  me.

" Cruel, cruel the words I said !
 Cruelly came they back to-day :
' You're too slight and fickle,' I said,
 ' To trouble the heart of Edward
  Gray.'

" There I put my face in the grass —
 Whisper'd, ' Listen to my despair :
I repent me of all I did :
 Speak a little, Ellen Adair ! '

" Then I took a pencil, and wrote
 On the mossy stone, as I lay,
' Here lies the body of Ellen Adair ;
 And here the heart of Edward
  Gray ! '

" Love may come, and love may go,
 And fly, like a bird, from tree to
  tree ;
But I will love no more, no more,
 Till Ellen Adair come back to me

" Bitterly wept I over the stone :
 Bitterly weeping I turn'd away :
There lies the body of Ellen Adair !
 And there the heart of Edward
  Gray ! "

WILL WATERPROOF'S
LYRICAL MONOLOGUE.

MADE AT THE COCK.

O PLUMP head-waiter at The Cock,
  To which I most resort,
How goes the time ? 'Tis five o'clock.
  Go fetch a pint of port:
But let it not be such as that
  You set before chance-comers,
But such whose father-grape grew fat
  On Lusitanian summers.

No vain libation to the Muse,
  But may she still be kind,
And whisper lovely words, and use
  Her influence on the mind,
To make me write my random rhymes,
  Ere they be half-forgotten ;
Nor add and alter, many times,
  Till all be ripe and rotten.

I pledge her, and she comes and dips
  Her laurel in the wine,
And lays it thrice upon my lips,
  These favor'd lips of mine ;
Until the charm have power to make
  New lifeblood warm the bosom,
And barren commonplaces break
  In full and kindly blossom.

I pledge her silent at the board ;
  Her gradual fingers steal
And touch upon the master-chord
  Of all I felt and feel.
Old wishes, ghosts of broken plans,
  And phantom hopes assemble ;
And that child's heart within the man's
  Begins to move and tremble.

Thro' many an hour of summer suns,
  By many pleasant ways,
Against its fountain upward runs
  The current of my days :
I kiss the lips I once have kiss'd ;
  The gas-light wavers dimmer ;
And softly, thro' a vinous mist,
  My college friendships glimmer.

I grow in worth, and wit, and sense,
  Unboding critic-pen,
Or that eternal want of pence,
  Which vexes public men,
Who hold their hands to all, and cry
  For that which all deny them —
Who sweep the crossings, wet or dry,
  And all the world go by them.

Ah yet, tho' all the world forsake,
  Tho' fortune clip my wings,
I will not cramp my heart, nor take
  Half-views of men and things.
Let Whig and Tory stir their blood ;
  There must be stormy weather ;
But for some true result of good
  All parties work together.

Let there be thistles, there are grapes ;
  If old things, there are new ;
Ten thousand broken lights and
      shapes,
  Yet glimpses of the true.
Let raffs be rife in prose and rhyme,
  We lack not rhymes and reasons,
As on this whirligig of Time
  We circle with the seasons.

This earth is rich in man and maid ;
  With fair horizons bound :
This whole wide earth of light and
      shade
  Comes out a perfect round.
High over roaring Temple-bar,
  And set in Heaven's third story,
I look at all things as they are,
  But thro' a kind of glory.

Head-waiter, honor'd by the guest
  Half-mused, or reeling ripe,
The pint, you brought me, was the best
  That ever came from pipe.
But tho' the port surpasses praise,
  My nerves have dealt with stiffer.
Is there some magic in the place ?
  Or do my peptics differ ?

For since I came to live and learn,
  No pint of white or red
Had ever half the power to turn
  This wheel within my head,
Which bears a season'd brain about,
  Unsubject to confusion,
Tho' soak'd and saturate, out and out,
  Thro' every convolution.

" The lily-white doe Lord Ronald had brought
Leapt up from where she lay."
Page 125.

For I am of a numerous house,
  With many kinsmen gay,
Where long and largely we carouse
  As who shall say me nay :
Each month, a birth-day coming on,
  We drink defying trouble,
Or sometimes two would meet in one,
  And then we drank it double ;

Whether the vintage, yet unkept,
  Had relish fiery-new,
Or elbow-deep in sawdust, slept,
  As old as Waterloo ;
Or stow'd, when classic Canning died,
  In musty bins and chambers,
Had cast upon its crusty side
  The gloom of ten Decembers.

The Muse, the jolly Muse, it is !
  She answer'd to my call,
She changes with that mood or this,
  Is all-in-all to all :
She lit the spark within my throat,
  To make my blood run quicker,
Used all her fiery will, and smote
  Her life into the liquor.

And hence this halo lives about
  The waiter's hands, that reach
To each his perfect pint of stout,
  His proper chop to each.
He looks not like the common breed
  That with the napkin dally ;
I think he came like Ganymede,
  From some delightful valley.

The Cock was of a larger egg
  Than modern poultry drop,
Stept forward on a firmer leg,
  And cramm'd a plumper crop ;
Upon an ampler dunghill trod,
  Crow'd lustier late and early,
Sipt wine from silver, praising God,
  And raked in golden barley.

A private life was all his joy,
  Till in a court he saw
A something-pottle-bodied boy
  That knuckled at the taw :
He stoop'd and clutch'd him, fair and
  good,

Flew over roof and casement :
His brothers of the weather stood
  Stock-still for sheer amazement.

But he, by farmstead, thorpe and spire,
  And follow'd with acclaims,
A sign to many a staring shire
  Came crowing over Thames.
Right down by smoky Paul's they bore,
  Till, where the street grows straiter,
One fix'd for ever at the door,
  And one became head-waiter.

———

But whither would my fancy go ?
  How out of place she makes
The violet of a legend blow
  Among the chops and steaks !
'Tis but a steward of the can,
  One shade more plump than com-
  mon ;
As just and mere a serving-man
  As any born of woman.

I ranged too high : what draws me
  down
  Into the common day ?
Is it the weight of that half-crown,
  Which I shall have to pay ?
For, something duller than at first,
  Nor wholly comfortable,
I sit, my empty glass reversed,
  And thrumming on the table :

Half fearful that, with self at strife,
  I take myself to task ;
Lest of the fulness of my life
  I leave an empty flask :
For I had hope, by something rare
  To prove myself a poet :
But, while I plan and plan, my hair
  Is gray before I know it.

So fares it since the years began,
  Till they be gather'd up ;
The truth, that flies the flowing can,
  Will haunt the vacant cup :
And others' follies teach us not,
  Nor much their wisdom teaches ;
And most, of sterling worth, is what
  Our own experience preaches.

Ah, let the rusty theme alone!
  We know not what we know.
But for my pleasant hour, 'tis gone;
  'Tis gone, and let it go.
'Tis gone: a thousand such have slipt
  Away from my embraces,
And fall'n into the dusty crypt
  Of darken'd forms and faces.

Go, therefore, thou! thy betters went
  Long since, and came no more;
With peals of genial clamor sent
  From many a tavern-door,
With twisted quirks and happy hits,
  From misty men of letters;
The tavern-hours of mighty wits —
  Thine elders and thy betters.

Hours, when the Poet's words and
    looks
  Had yet their native glow:
Nor yet the fear of little books
  Had made him talk for show;
But, all his vast heart sherris-warm'd,
  He flash'd his random speeches,
Ere days, that deal in ana, swarm'd
  His literary leeches.

So mix for ever with the past,
  Like all good things on earth!
For should I prize thee, couldst thou
    last,
  At half thy real worth?
I hold it good, good things should
    pass:
  With time I will not quarrel:
It is but yonder empty glass
  That makes me maudlin-moral.

Head-waiter of the chop-house here,
  To which I most resort,
I too must part: I hold thee dear
  For this good pint of port.
For this, thou shalt from all things
    suck
  Marrow of mirth and laughter;
And wheresoe'er thou move, good luck
  Shall fling her old shoe after.

But thou wilt never move from hence,
  The sphere thy fate allots:
Thy latter days increased with pence

Go down among the pots:
Thou battenest by the greasy gleam
  In haunts of hungry sinners,
Old boxes, larded with the steam
  Of thirty thousand dinners.

We fret, we fume, would shift our
    skins,
  Would quarrel with our lot;
Thy care is, under polish'd tins,
  To serve the hot-and-hot;
To come and go, and come again,
  Returning like the pewit,
And watch'd by silent gentlemen,
  That trifle with the cruet.

Live long, ere from thy topmost head
  The thick-set hazel dies;
Long, ere the hateful crow shall tread
  The corners of thine eyes:
Live long, nor feel in head or chest
  Our changeful equinoxes,
Till mellow Death, like some late
    guest,
  Shall call thee from the boxes.

But when he calls, and thou shalt
    cease
  To pace the gritted floor,
And, laying down an unctuous lease
  Of life, shalt earn no more;
No carved cross-bones, the types of
    Death,
  Shall show thee past to Heaven:
But carved cross-pipes, and, under-
    neath,
  A pint-pot neatly graven.

―――――

LADY CLARE.

IT was the time when lilies blow
  And clouds are highest up in air,
Lord Ronald brought a lily-white doe
  To give his cousin, Lady Clare.

I trow they did not part in scorn:
  Lovers long-betroth'd were they:
They too will wed the morrow morn:
  God's blessing on the day!

" He does not love me for my birth,
    Nor for my lands so broad and fair;
He loves me for my own true worth,
    And that is well," said Lady Clare.

In there came old Alice the nurse,
    Said, " Who was this that went from
        thee ? "
" It was my cousin," said Lady Clare,
    " To-morrow he weds with me."

" O God be thank'd ! " said Alice the
        nurse,
    " That all comes round so just and
        fair :
Lord Ronald is heir of all your lands,
    And you are *not* the Lady Clare."

" Are ye out of your mind, my nurse,
        my nurse ? "
    Said Lady Clare, " that ye speak so
        wild ? "
" As God's above," said Alice the
        nurse,
    " I speak the truth . you are my
        child.

" The old Earl's daughter died at my
        breast ;
    I speak the truth, as I live by bread !
I buried her like my own sweet child,
    And put my child in her stead."

" Falsely, falsely have ye done,
    O mother," she said, " if this be true,
To keep the best man under the sun
    So many years from his due."

" Nay now, my child," said Alice the
        nurse,
    " But keep the secret for your life,
And all you have will be Lord
        Ronald's,
    When you are man and wife."

" If I'm a beggar born," she said,
    " I will speak out, for I dare not lie.
Pull off, pull off, the brooch of gold,
    And fling the diamond necklace by."

" Nay now, my child," said Alice the
        nurse,
    " But keep the secret all ye can."
She said, " Not so : but I will know
    If there be any faith in man."

" Nay now, what faith ? " said Alice
        the nurse,
    " The man will cleave unto his
        right."
" And he shall have it," the lady
        replied,
    " Tho' I should die to-night."

" Yet give one kiss to your mother
        dear !
    Alas, my child, I sinn'd for thee."
" O mother, mother, mother," she said,
    " So strange it seems to me.

" Yet here's a kiss for my mother dear.
    My mother dear, if this be so,
And lay your hand upon my head,
    And bless me, mother, ere I go."

She clad herself in a russet gown,
    She was no longer Lady Clare :
She went by dale, and she went by
        down,
    With a single rose in her air.

The lily-white doe Lord Ronald had
        brought
    Leapt up from where she lay,
Dropt her head in the maiden's hand,
    And follow'd her all the way.

Down stept Lord Ronald from his
        tower :
    " O Lady Clare, you shame your
        worth !
Why come you drest like a village
        maid,
    That are the flower of the earth ? "

" If I come drest like a village maid,
    I am but as my fortunes are :
I am a beggar born," she said,
    " And not the Lady Clare."

"Play me no tricks," said Lord Ro-
  nald,
  "For I am yours in word and in
    deed.
Play me no tricks," said Lord Ronald,
  "Your riddle is hard to read."

O and proudly stood she up!
  Her heart within her did not fail:
She look'd into Lord Ronald's eyes,
  And told him all her nurse's tale.

He laugh'd a laugh of merry scorn:
  He turn'd and kiss'd her where she
    stood:
"If you are not the heiress born,
  And I," said he, "the next in
    blood —

"If you are not the heiress born,
  And I," said he, "the lawful heir,
We two will wed to-morrow morn,
  And you shall still be Lady Clare."

THE CAPTAIN.

A LEGEND OF THE NAVY.

HE that only rules by terror
  Doeth grievous wrong.
Deep as Hell I count his error.
  Let him hear my song.
Brave the Captain was: the seamen
  Made a gallant crew,
Gallant sons of English freemen,
  Sailors bold and true.
But they hated his oppression,
  Stern he was and rash;
So for every light transgression
  Doom'd them to the lash.
Day by day more harsh and cruel
  Seem'd the Captain's mood.
Secret wrath like smother'd fuel
  Burnt in each man's blood.
Yet he hoped to purchase glory,
  Hoped to make the name
Of his vessel great in story,
  Wheresoe'er he came.
So they past by capes and islands,
  Many a harbor-mouth,
Sailing under palmy highlands
  Far within the South.
On a day when they were going

O'er the lone expanse,
In the north, her canvas flowing,
  Rose a ship of France.
Then the Captain's color heighten'd,
  Joyful came his speech:
But a cloudy gladness lighten'd
  In the eyes of each.
"Chase," he said: the ship flew for
    ward,
  And the wind did blow;
Stately, lightly, went she Norward,
  Till she near'd the foe.
Then they look'd at him they hated,
  Had what they desired:
Mute with folded arms they waited —
  Not a gun was fired.
But they heard the foeman's thunder
  Roaring out their doom;
All the air was torn in sunder,
  Crashing went the boom,
Spars were splinter'd, decks were shat-
    ter'd,
  Bullets fell like rain;
Over mast and deck were scatter'd
  Blood and brains of men.
Spars were splinter'd; decks were
    broken:
  Every mother's son —
Down they dropt — no word was
    spoken —
  Each beside his gun.
On the decks as they were lying,
  Were their faces grim.
In their blood, as they lay dying,
  Did they smile on him.
Those, in whom he had reliance
  For his noble name,
With one smile of still defiance
  Sold him unto shame.
Shame and wrath his heart con-
    founded,
  Pale he turn'd and red,
Till himself was deadly wounded
  Falling on the dead.
Dismal error! fearful slaughter!
  Years have wander'd by,
Side by side beneath the water
  Crew and Captain lie;
There the sunlit ocean tosses
  O'er them mouldering,
And the lonely seabird crosses
  With one waft of the wing.

THE LORD OF BURLEIGH.

In her ear he whispers gayly,
  "If my heart by signs can tell,
Maiden, I have watch'd thee daily,
  And I think thou lov'st me well."
She replies, in accents fainter,
  "There is none I love like thee."
He is but a landscape-painter,
  And a village maiden she.
He to lips, that fondly falter,
  Presses his without reproof :
Leads her to the village altar,
  And they leave her father's roof.
" I can make no marriage present :
  Little can I give my wife.
Love will make our cottage pleasant,
  And I love thee more than life."
They by parks and lodges going
  See the lordly castles stand :
Summer woods, about them blowing,
  Made a murmur in the land.
From deep thought himself he rouses,
  Says to her that loves him well,
" Let us see these handsome houses
  Where the wealthy nobles dwell."
So she goes by him attended,
  Hears him lovingly converse,
Sees whatever fair and splendid
  Lay betwixt his home and hers ;
Parks with oak and chestnut shady,
  Parks and order'd gardens great,
Ancient homes of lord and lady,
  Built for pleasure and for state.
All he shows her makes him dearer :
  Evermore she seems to gaze
On that cottage growing nearer,
  Where they twain will spend their
    days.
O but she will love him truly !
  He shall have a cheerful home ;
She will order all things duly,
  When beneath his roof they come.
Thus her heart rejoices greatly,
  Till a gateway she discerns
With armorial bearings stately,
  And beneath the gate she turns ;
Sees a mansion more majestic
  Than all those she saw before :
Many a gallant gay domestic
  Bows before him at the door.
And they speak in gentle murmur,
  When they answer to his call,

While he treads with footsteps firmer,
  Leading on from hall to hall.
And, while now she wonders blindly,
  Nor the meaning can divine,
Proudly turns he round and kindly,
  " All of this is mine and thine."
Here he lives in state and bounty,
  Lord of Burleigh, fair and free,
Not a lord in all the county
  Is so great a lord as he.
All at once the color flushes
  Her sweet face from brow to chin :
As it were with shame she blushes,
  And her spirit changed within.
Then her countenance all over
  Pale again as death did prove :
But he clasp'd her like a lover,
  And he cheer'd her soul with love.
So she strove against her weakness,
  Tho' at times her spirit sank :
Shaped her heart with woman's meek-
    ness
  To all duties of her rank :
And a gentle consort made he,
  And her gentle mind was such
That she grew a noble lady,
  And the people loved her much.
But a trouble weigh'd upon her,
  And perplex'd her, night and morn,
With the burthen of an honor
  Unto which she was not born.
Faint she grew, and ever fainter,
  And she murmur'd, "Oh, that he
Were once more that landscape-
    painter,
  Which did win my heart from me !"
So she droop'd and droop'd before him,
  Fading slowly from his side :
Three fair children first she bore him,
  Then before her time she died.
Weeping, weeping late and early,
  Walking up and pacing down,
Deeply mourn'd the Lord of Burleigh,
  Burleigh-house by Stamford-town.
And he came to look upon her,
  And he look'd at her and said,
" Bring the dress and put it on her,
  That she wore when she was wed."
Then her people, softly treading,
  Bore to earth her body, drest
In the dress that she was wed in,
  That her spirit might have rest.

THE VOYAGE.

I.

We left behind the painted buoy
   That tosses at the harbor-mouth;
And madly danced our hearts with joy,
   As fast we fleeted to the South:
How fresh was every sight and sound
   On open main or winding shore!
We knew the merry world was round,
   And we might sail for evermore.

II.

Warm broke the breeze against the
   brow,
   Dry sang the tackle, sang the sail:
The Lady's-head upon the prow
   Caught the shrill salt, and sheer'd
     the gale.
The broad seas swell'd to meet the
   keel,
   And swept behind; so quick the run,
We felt the good ship shake and reel,
   We seem'd to sail into the Sun!

III.

How oft we saw the Sun retire,
   And burn the threshold of the night,
Fall from his Ocean-lane of fire,
   And sleep beneath his pillar'd light!
How oft the purple-skirted robe
   Of twilight slowly downward drawn,
As thro' the slumber of the globe
   Again we dash'd into the dawn!

IV.

New stars all night above the brim
   Of waters lighten'd into view;
They climb'd as quickly, for the rim
   Changed every moment as we flew.
Far ran the naked moon across
   The houseless ocean's heaving field,
Or flying shone, the silver boss
   Of her own halo's dusky shield;

V.

The peaky islet shifted shapes,
   High towns on hills were dimly seen,
We past long lines of Northern capes
   And dewy Northern meadows green.
We came to warmer waves, and deep
Across the boundless east we drove,
   Where those long swells of breaker
     sweep
   The nutmeg rocks and isles of clove.

VI.

By peaks that flamed, or, all in shade,
   Gloom'd the low coast and quivering
     brine
With ashy rains, that spreading made
   Fantastic plume or sable pine;
By sands and steaming flats, and floods
   Of mighty mouth, we scudded fast,
And hills and scarlet-mingled woods
   Glow'd for a moment as we past.

VII.

O hundred shores of happy climes,
   How swiftly stream'd ye by the
     bark!
At times the whole sea burn'd, at times
   With wakes of fire we tore the dark;
At times a carven craft would shoot
   From havens hid in fairy bowers,
With naked limbs and flowers and
     fruit,
   But we nor paused for fruit nor
     flowers.

VIII.

For one fair Vision ever fled
   Down the waste waters day and
     night,
And still we follow'd where she led,
   In hope to gain upon her flight.
Her face was evermore unseen,
   And fixt upon the far sea-line;
But each man murmur'd, "O my
     Queen,
I follow till I make thee mine."

IX.

And now we lost her, now she gleam'd
   Like Fancy made of golden air,
Now nearer to the prow she seem'd
   Like Virtue firm, like Knowledge
     fair,
Now high on waves that idly burst
   Like Heavenly Hope she crown'd
     the sea,
And now, the bloodless point reversed,
   She bore the blade of Liberty.

x.

And only one among us — him
  We pleased not — he was seldom
    pleased:
He saw not far: his eyes were dim:
  But ours he swore were all diseased.
" A ship of fools," he shriek'd in spite,
  " A ship of fools," he sneer'd and
    wept.
And overboard one stormy night
  He cast his body, and on we swept.

xi.

And never sail of ours was furl'd,
  Nor anchor dropt at eve or morn;
We lov'd the glories of the world,
  But laws of nature were our scorn.
For blasts would rise and rave and
    cease,
  But whence were those that drove
    the sail
Across the whirlwind's heart of peace,
  And to and thro' the counter gale?

xii.

Again to colder climes we came,
  For still we follow'd where she led:
Now mate is blind and captain lame,
  And half the crew are sick or dead,
But, blind or lame or sick or sound,
  We follow that which flies before:
We know the merry world is round,
  And we may sail for evermore.

SIR LAUNCELOT AND
QUEEN GUINEVERE.

A FRAGMENT.

Like souls that balance joy and pain,
With tears and smiles from heaven
    again
The maiden Spring upon the plain
Came in a sun-lit fall of rain.
  In crystal vapor everywhere
Blue isles of heaven laugh'd between,
And far, in forest-deeps unseen,
The topmost elm-tree gather'd green
  From draughts of balmy air.

Sometimes the linnet piped his song:
Sometimes the throstle whistled
    strong:
Sometimes the sparhawk, wheel'd
    along,
Hush'd all the groves from fear of
    wrong:
  By grassy capes with fuller sound
In curves the yellowing river ran,
And drooping chestnut-buds began
To spread into the perfect fan,
  Above the teeming ground.

Then, in the boyhood of the year,
Sir Launcelot and Queen Guinevere
Rode thro' the coverts of the deer,
With blissful treble ringing clear.
  She seem'd a part of joyous
    Spring:
A gown of grass-green silk she wore,
Buckled with golden clasps before;
A light-green tuft of plumes she bore
  Closed in a golden ring.

Now on some twisted ivy-net,
Now by some tinkling rivulet,
In mosses mixt with violet
Her cream-white mule his pastern set:
  And fleeter now she skimm'd the
    plains
Than she whose elfin prancer springs
By night to eery warblings,
When all the glimmering moorland
    rings
  With jingling bridle-reins.

As she fled fast thro' sun and shade,
The happy winds upon her play'd,
Blowing the ringlet from the braid:
She look'd so lovely, as she sway'd
  The rein with dainty finger-tips,
A man had given all other bliss,
And all his wordly worth for this,
To waste his whole heart in one kiss
  Upon her perfect lips.

A FAREWELL.

Flow down, cold rivulet, to the sea,
  Thy tribute wave deliver:
No more by thee my steps shall be,
  For ever and for ever.

Flow, softly flow, by lawn and lea,
  A rivulet then a river:
No where by thee my steps shall be,
  For ever and for ever.

But here will sigh thine alder tree,
  And here thine aspen shiver;
And here by thee will hum the bee,
  For ever and for ever.

A thousand suns will stream on thee,
  A thousand moons will quiver;
But not by thee my steps shall be,
  For ever and for ever.

THE BEGGAR MAID.

HER arms across her breast she laid;
  She was more fair than words can
    say:
Bare-footed came the beggar maid
  Before the king Cophetua.
In robe and crown the king stept down,
  To meet and greet her on her way;
" It is no wonder," said the lords,
  " She is more beautiful than day."

As shines the moon in clouded skies,
  She in her poor attire was seen:
One praised her ankles, one her eyes,
  One her dark hair and lovesome
    mien.
So sweet a face, such angel grace,
  In all that land had never been:
Cophetua sware a royal oath:
  " This beggar maid shall be my
    queen ! "

THE EAGLE.

FRAGMENT.

HE clasps the crag with crooked
  hands ;
Close to the sun in lonely lands,
Ring'd with the azure world, he stands.

The wrinkled sea beneath him crawls ;
He watches from his mountain walls,
And like a thunderbolt he falls.

MOVE eastward, happy earth, and leave
  Yon orange sunset waning slow :
From fringes of the faded eve,
  O, happy planet, eastward go ;
Till over thy dark shoulder glow
  Thy silver sister-world, and rise
To glass herself in dewy eyes
  That watch me from the glen below.

Ah, bear me with thee, smoothly borne,
  Dip forward under starry light,
And move me to my marriage-morn,
  And round again to happy night.

COME not, when I am dead,
  To drop thy foolish tears upon my
    grave,
To trample round my fallen head,
  And vex the unhappy dust thou
    wouldst not save.
There let the wind sweep and the
  plover cry ;
    But thou, go by.

Child, if it were thine error or thy
  crime
I care no longer, being all unblest:
Wed whom thou wilt, but I am sick
  of Time,
  And I desire to rest.
Pass on, weak heart, and leave me
  where I lie :
    Go by, go by.

THE LETTERS.

I.

STILL on the tower stood the vane,
  A black yew gloom'd the stagnant
    air,
I peer'd athwart the chancel pane
  And saw the altar cold and bare.
A clog of lead was round my feet,
  A band of pain across my brow ;
" Cold altar, Heaven and earth shall
  meet
  Before you hear my marriage vow."

II.

I turn'd and humm'd a bitter song
  That mock'd the wholesome human
    heart,

And then we met in wrath and wrong,
  We met, but only meant to part.
Full cold my greeting was and dry ;
   She faintly smiled, she hardly
     moved ;
I saw with half-unconscious eye
  She wore the colors I approved.

III.

She took the little ivory chest,
  With half a sigh she turn'd the key,
Then raised her head with lips com-
    prest,
  And gave my letters back to me.
And gave the trinkets and the rings,
  My gifts, when gifts of mine could
    please ;
As looks a father on the things
  Of his dead son, I look'd on these.

IV.

She told me all her friends had said ;
  I raged against the public liar ;
She talk'd as if her love were dead,
  But in my words were seeds of fire.
" No more of love ; your sex is known :
  I never will be twice deceived.
Henceforth I trust the man alone.
  The woman cannot be believed.

V.

" Thro' slander, meanest spawn of
    Hell —
  And women's slander is the worst,
And you, whom once I lov'd so well,
  Thro' you, my life will be accurst."
I spoke with heart, and heat and force,
  I shook her breast with vague
    alarms —
Like torrents from a mountain source
  We rush'd into each other's arms.

VI.

We parted : sweetly gleam'd the stars,
  And sweet the vapor-braided blue,
Low breezes fann'd the belfry bars,
  As homeward by the church I drew.
The very graves appear'd to smile,
  So fresh they rose in shadow'd
    swells ;
" Dark porch," I said, " and silent
    aisle,
  There comes a sound of marriage
    bells.

THE VISION OF SIN.

I.

I HAD a vision when the night was late :
A youth came riding toward a palace-
    gate.
He rode a horse with wings, that would
    have flown,
But that his heavy rider kept him
    down.
And from the palace came a child of
    sin,
And took him by the curls, and led
    him in,
Where sat a company with heated
    eyes,
Expecting when a fountain should
    arise :
A sleepy light upon their brows and
    lips —
As when the sun, a crescent of eclipse,
Dreams over lake and lawn, and isles
    and capes —
Suffused them, sitting, lying, languid
    shapes,
By heaps of gourds, and skins of wine,
    and piles of grapes.

II.

Then methought I heard a mellow
    sound,
Gathering up from all the lower
    ground ;
Narrowing in to where they sat assem-
    bled
Low voluptuous music winding trem-
    bled,
Wov'n in circles : they that heard it
    sigh'd,
Panted hand-in-hand with faces pale,
Swung themselves, and in low tones
    replied ;
Till the fountain spouted, showering
    wide
Sleet of diamond-drift and pearly hail ;
Then the music touch'd the gates and
    died,
Rose again from where it seem'd to
    fail,
Storm'd in orbs of song, a growing
    gale ;

Till thronging in and in, to where they
　　waited,
As 'twere a hundred-throated nightin-
　　gale,
The strong tempestuous treble throbb'd
　　and palpitated;
Ran into its giddiest whirl of sound,
Caught the sparkles, and in circles,
Purple gauzes, golden hazes, liquid
　　mazes,
Flung the torrent rainbow round:
Then they started from their places,
Moved with violence, changed in hue,
Caught each other with wild grimaces,
Half-invisible to the view,
Wheeling with precipitate paces
To the melody, till they flew,
Hair, and eyes, and limbs, and faces,
Twisted hard in fierce embraces,
Like to Furies, like to Graces,
Dash'd together in blinding dew:
Till, kill'd with some luxurious agony,
The nerve-dissolving melody
Flutter'd headlong from the sky.

III.

And then I look'd up toward a moun-
　　tain-tract,
That girt the region with high cliff and
　　lawn:
I saw that every morning, far with-
　　drawn
Beyond the darkness and the cataract,
God made Himself an awful rose of
　　dawn,
Unheeded: and detaching, fold by fold,
From those still heights, and, slowly
　　drawing near,
A vapor heavy, hueless, formless, cold,
Came floating on for many a month
　　and year,
Unheeded: and I thought I would
　　have spoken,
And warn'd that madman ere it grew
　　too late:
But, as in dreams, I could not. Mine
　　was broken,
When that cold vapor touch'd the
　　palace gate,
And link'd again. I saw within my
　　head

A gray and gap-tooth'd man as lean
　　as death,
Who slowly rode across a wither'd
　　heath,
And lighted at a ruin'd inn, and said:

IV.

"Wrinkled ostler, grim and thin!
　　Here is custom come your way;
Take my brute, and lead him in,
　　Stuff his ribs with mouldy hay.

"Bitter barmaid, waning fast!
　　See that sheets are on my bed;
What! the flower of life is past:
　　It is long before you wed.

"Slip-shod waiter, lank and sour,
　　At the Dragon on the heath!
Let us have a quiet hour,
　　Let us hob-and-nob with Death.

"I am old, but let me drink;
　　Bring me spices, bring me wine;
I remember, when I think,
　　That my youth was half divine.

"Wine is good for shrivell'd lips,
　　When a blanket wraps the day,
When the rotten woodland drips,
　　And the leaf is stamp'd in clay.

"Sit thee down, and have no shame,
　　Cheek by jowl, and knee by knee:
What care I for any name?
　　What for order or degree?

"Let me screw thee up a peg:
　　Let me loose thy tongue with wine:
Callest thou that thing a leg?
　　Which is thinnest? thine or mine?

"Thou shalt not be saved by works:
　　Thou hast been a sinner too:
Ruin'd trunks on wither'd forks,
　　Empty scarecrows, I and you!

"Fill the cup, and fill the can:
　　Have a rouse before the morn:
Every moment dies a man,
　　Every moment one is born.

"We are men of ruin'd blood;
   Therefore comes it we are wise.
Fish are we that love the mud,
   Rising to no fancy-flies.

"Name and fame! to fly sublime
   Thro' the courts, the camps, the schools,
Is to be the ball of Time,
   Bandied by the hands of fools.

"Friendship!— to be two in one —
   Let the canting liar pack!
Well I know, when I am gone,
   How she mouths behind my back.

"Virtue!— to be good and just —
   Every heart, when sifted well,
Is a clot of warmer dust,
   Mix'd with cunning sparks of hell.

"O! we two as well can look
   Whited thought and cleanly life
As the priest, above his book
   Leering at his neighbor's wife.

"Fill the cup, and fill the can:
   Have a rouse before the morn:
Every moment dies a man,
   Every moment one is born.

"Drink, and let the parties rave:
   They are fill'd with idle spleen;
Rising, falling, like a wave,
   For they know not what they mean

"He that roars for liberty
   Faster binds a tyrant's power;
And the tyrant's cruel glee
   Forces on the freer hour.

"Fill the can, and fill the cup:
   All the windy ways of men
Are but dust that rises up,
   And is lightly laid again.

"Greet her with applausive breath,
   Freedom, gayly doth she tread;
In her right a civic wreath,
   In her left a human head.

"No, I love not what is new;
   She is of an ancient house:

And I think we know the hue
   Of that cap upon her brows.

"Let her go! her thirst she slakes
   Where the bloody conduit runs,
Then her sweetest meal she makes
   On the first-born of her sons.

"Drink to lofty hopes that cool —
   Visions of a perfect State:
Drink we, last, the public fool,
   Frantic love and frantic hate.

"Chant me now some wicked stave,
   Till thy drooping courage rise,
And the glow-worm of the grave
   Glimmer in thy rheumy eyes.

"Fear not thou to loose thy tongue;
   Set thy hoary fancies free;
What is loathsome to the young
   Savors well to thee and me.

"Change, reverting to the years,
   When thy nerves could understand
What there is in loving tears,
   And the warmth of hand in hand.

"Tell me tales of thy first love —
   April hopes, the fools of chance;
Till the graves begin to move,
   And the dead begin to dance.

"Fill the can, and fill the cup:
   All the windy ways of men
Are but dust that rises up,
   And is lightly laid again.

"Trooping from their mouldy dens
   The chap-fallen circle spreads:
Welcome, fellow-citizens,
   Hollow hearts and empty heads!

"You are bones, and what of that?
   Every face, however full,
Padded round with flesh and fat,
   Is but modell'd on a skull.

"Death is king, and Vivat Rex!
   Tread a measure on the stones,
Madam — if I know your sex,
   From the fashion of your bones.

"No, I cannot praise the fire
In your eye — nor yet your lip:
All the more do I admire
Joints of cunning workmanship.

"Lo! God's likeness — the ground-
plan —
Neither modell'd, glazed, nor
framed:
Buss me, thou rough sketch of man,
Far too naked to be shamed!

"Drink to Fortune, drink to Chance,
While we keep a little breath!
Drink to heavy Ignorance!
Hob-and-nob with brother Death!

"Thou art mazed, the night is long,
And the longer night is near:
What! I am not all as wrong
As a bitter jest is dear.

"Youthful hopes, by scores, to all,
When the locks are crisp and curl'd;
Unto me my maudlin gall
And my mockeries of the world.

"Fill the cup and fill the can:
Mingle madness, mingle scorn!
Dregs of life, and lees of man:
Yet we will not die forlorn."

v.

The voice grew faint: there came a
further change:
Once more uprose the mystic mountain-
range:
Below were men and horses pierced
with worms,
And slowly quickening into lower
forms;
By shards and scurf of salt, and scum
of dross,
Old plash of rains, and refuse patch'd
with moss.
Then some one spake: "Behold! it
was a crime
Of sense avenged by sense that wore
with time."
Another said: "The crime of sense
became

The crime of malice, and is equal
blame."
And one: "He had not wholly
quench'd his power;
A little grain of conscience made him
sour."
At last I heard a voice upon the slope
Cry to the summit, "Is there any
hope?"
To which an answer peal'd from that
high land,
But in a tongue no man could understand;
And on the glimmering limit far withdrawn
God made Himself an awful rose of
dawn.

———

TO ——,

AFTER READING A LIFE AND LETTERS.

"Cursed be he that moves my bones."
Shakespeare's Epitaph.

You might have won the Poet's name,
If such be worth the winning now,
And gain'd a laurel for your brow
Of sounder leaf than I can claim;

But you have made the wiser choice,
A life that moves to gracious ends
Thro' troops of unrecording friends,
A deedful life, a silent voice:

And you have miss'd the irreverent
doom
Of those that wear the Poet's crown:
Hereafter, neither knave nor clown
Shall hold their orgies at your tomb.

For now the Poet cannot die,
Nor leave his music as of old,
But round him ere he scarce be cold
Begins the scandal and the cry:

"Proclaim the faults he would not
show:
Break lock and seal: betray the
trust:
Keep nothing sacred: tis but just
The many-headed beast should know."

"Break, break, break,
On thy cold gray stones, O Sea!"
Page 135

Ah shameless! for he did but sing
  A song that pleased us from its
    worth;
  No public life was his on earth,
No blazon'd statesman he, nor king.

He gave the people of his best:
  His worst he kept, his best he gave.
  My Shakespeare's curse on clown
    and knave
Who will not let his ashes rest!

Who make it seem more sweet to be
  The little life of bank and brier,
  The bird that pipes his lone desire
And dies unheard within his tree,

Than he that warbles long and loud
  And drops at Glory's temple-gates,
  For whom the carrion vulture waits
To tear his heart before the crowd!

TO E. L., ON HIS TRAVELS IN GREECE.

ILLYRIAN woodlands, echoing falls
  Of water, sheets of summer glass,
  The long divine Peneïan pass,
The vast Akrokeraunian walls,

Tomohrit, Athos, all things fair,
  With such a pencil, such a pen,
  You shadow forth to distant men,
I read and felt that I was there:

And trust me while I turn'd the page,
  And track'd you still on classic
    ground,
  I grew in gladness till I found
My spirits in the golden age.

For me the torrent ever pour'd
  And glisten'd — here and there alone
  The broad-limb'd Gods at random
    thrown
By fountain-urns; — and Naiads oar'd

A glimmering shoulder under gloom
  Of cavern pillars; on the swell
  The silver lily heaved and fell;
And many a slope was rich in bloom

From him that on the mountain lea
  By dancing rivulets fed his flocks
  To him who sat upon the rocks,
And fluted to the morning sea.

BREAK, break, break,
  On thy cold gray stones, O Sea!
And I would that my tongue could
    utter
  The thoughts that arise in me.

O well for the fisherman's boy,
  That he shouts with his sister at
    play!
O well for the sailor lad,
  That he sings in his boat on the bay!

And the stately ships go on
  To their haven under the hill;
But O for the touch of a vanish'd
    hand,
  And the sound of a voice that is
    still!

Break, break, break,
  At the foot of thy crags, O Sea!
But the tender grace of a day that is
    dead
  Will never come back to me.

THE POET'S SONG.

THE rain had fallen, the Poet arose,
  He pass'd by the town and out of
    the street,
A light wind blew from the gates of
    the sun,
  And waves of shadow went over the
    wheat,
And he sat him down in a lonely place,

And chanted a melody loud and
    sweet,
That made the wild-swan pause in her
    cloud,
And the lark drop down at his feet.

The swallow stopt as he hunted the
    bee,
    The snake slipt under a spray,
The wild hawk stood with the down
    on his beak,
    And stared, with his foot on the
      prey,
And the nightingale thought, " I have
    sung many songs,
    But never a one so gay,
For he sings of what the world will be
When the years have died away."

THE BROOK.

Here, by this brook, we parted; I to
    the East
And he for Italy — too late — too late :
One whom the strong sons of the
    world despise;
For lucky rhymes to him were scrip
    and share,
And mellow metres more than cent
    for cent;
Nor could he understand how money
    breeds,
Thought it a dead thing; yet himself
    could make
The thing that is not as the thing
    that is.
O had he lived! In our schoolbooks
    we say,
Of those that held their heads above
    the crowd,
They flourish'd then or then; but life
    in him
Could scarce be said to flourish, only
    touch'd
On such a time as goes before the leaf,
When all the wood stands in a mist
    of green,
And nothing perfect : yet the brook
    he loved,
For which, in branding summers of
    Bengal,

Or ev'n the sweet half-English Neil
    gherry air
I panted, seems, as I re-listen to it,
Prattling the primrose fancies of the
    boy,
To me that loved him; for "O brook,"
    he says,
"O babbling brook," says Edmund in
    his rhyme,
"Whence come you?" and the brook
    why not? replies.

    I come from haunts of coot and hern
      I make a sudden sally,
    And sparkle out among the fern,
      To bicker down a valley.

    By thirty hills I hurry down,
      Or slip between the ridges,
    By twenty thorps, a little town,
      And half a hundred bridges.

    Till last by Philip's farm I flow
      To join the brimming river,
    For men may come and men may go,
      But I go on for ever.

"Poor lad, he died at Florence, quite
    worn out,
Travelling to Naples.   There is Darn-
    ley bridge,
It has more ivy; there the river; and
    there
Stands Philip's farm where brook and
    river meet.

    I chatter over stony ways,
      In little sharps and trebles,
    I bubble into eddying bays,
      I babble on the pebbles.

    With many a curve my banks I fret
      By many a field and fallow,
    And many a fairy foreland set
      With willow-weed and mallow.

    I chatter, chatter, as I flow
      To join the brimming river,
    For men may come and men may go,
      But I go on for ever.

"But Philip chatter'd more than
    brook or bird;
Old Philip; all about the fields you
    caught
His weary daylong chirping, like the
    dry
High-elbow'd grigs that leap in sum-
    mer grass.

"And sparkle out among the fern,
To bicker down a valley."

Page 136.

I wind about, and in and out,
  With here a blossom sailing,
And here and there a lusty trout,
  And here and there a grayling,

And here and there a foamy flake
  Upon me, as I travel
With many a silvery waterbreak
  Above the golden gravel,

And draw them all along, and flow
  To join the brimming river,
For men may come and men may go,
  But I go on for ever.

"O darling Katie Willows, his one
  child!
A maiden of our century, yet most
  meek;
A daughter of our meadows, yet not
  coarse;
Straight, but as lissome as a hazel
  wand;
Her eyes a bashful azure, and her hair
In gloss and hue the chestnut, when
  the shell
Divides threefold to show the fruit
  within.

"Sweet Katie, once I did her a good
  turn,
Her and her far-off cousin and be-
  trothed,
James Willows, of one name and
  heart with her.
For here I came, twenty years back —
  the week
Before I parted with poor Edmund,
  crost
By that old bridge which, half in
  ruins then,
Still makes a hoary eyebrow for the
  gleam
Beyond it, where the waters marry —
  crost,
Whistling a random bar of Bonny
  Doon,
And push'd at Philip's garden-gate.
  The gate,
Half-parted from a weak and scolding
  hinge,
Stuck; and he clamor'd from a case-
  ment, 'Run'
To Katie somewhere in the walks
  below,

'Run, Katie!' Katie never ran: she
  moved
To meet me, winding under woodbine
  bowers,
A little flutter'd, with her eyelids
  down,
Fresh apple-blossom, blushing for a
  boon.

"What was it? less of sentiment
  than sense
Had Katie; not illiterate; nor of those
Who dabbling in the fount of fictive
  tears,
And nursed by mealy-mouth'd philan-
  thropies,
Divorce the Feeling from her mate
  the Deed.

"She told me. She and James had
  quarrell'd. Why?
What cause of quarrel? None, she
  said, no cause;
James had no cause: but when I prest
  the cause,
I learnt that James had flickering
  jealousies
Which anger'd her. Who anger'd
  James? I said.
But Katie snatch'd her eyes at once
  from mine,
And sketching with her slender pointed
  foot
Some figure like a wizard pentagram
On garden gravel, let my query pass
Unclaim'd, in flushing silence, till I
  ask'd
If James were coming. 'Coming
  every day,'
She answer'd, 'ever longing to explain,
But evermore her father came across
With some long-winded tale, and broke
  him short;
And James departed vext with him
  and her.'
How could I help her? 'Would I—
  was it wrong?'
(Claspt hands and that petitionary
  grace
Of sweet seventeen subdued me ere
  she spoke)

'O would I take her father for one
    hour,
For one half-hour, and let him talk to
    me!'
And even while she spoke, I saw where
    James
Made toward us, like a wader in the
    surf,
Beyond the brook, waist-deep in
    meadow-sweet.

"O Katie, what I suffer'd for your
    sake!
For in I went, and call'd old Philip out
To show the farm: full willingly he
    rose:
He led me thro' the short sweet-
    smelling lanes
Of his wheat-suburb, babbling as he
    went.
He praised his land, his horses, his
    machines;
He praised his ploughs, his cows, his
    hogs, his dogs;
He praised his hens, his geese, his
    guinea-hens;
His pigeons, who in session on their
    roofs
Approved him, bowing at their own
    deserts:
Then from the plaintive mother's teat
    he took
Her blind and shuddering puppies,
    naming each,
And naming those, his friends, for
    whom they were:
Then crost the common into Darnley
    chase
To show Sir Arthur's deer. In copse
    and fern
Twinkled the innumerable ear and tail.
Then, seated on a serpent-rooted beech,
He pointed out a pasturing colt, and
    said:
'That was the four-year-old I sold the
    Squire.'
And there he told a long long-winded
    tale
Of how the Squire had seen the colt
    at grass,
And how it was the thing his daughter
    wish'd,

And how he sent the bailiff to the
    farm
To learn the price, and what the price
    he ask'd,
And how the bailiff swore that he was
    mad,
But he stood firm; and so the matter
    hung;
He gave them line: and five days after
    that
He met the bailiff at the Golden Fleece,
Who then and there had offer'd some-
    thing more,
But he stood firm; and so the matter
    hung;
He knew the man; the colt would fetch
    its price;
He gave them line: and how by chance
    at last
(It might be May or April, he forgot,
The last of April or the first of May)
He found the bailiff riding by the
    farm,
And, talking from the point, he drew
    him in,
And there he mellow'd all his heart
    with ale,
Until they closed a bargain, hand in
    hand.

"Then, while I breathed in sight of
    haven, he,
Poor fellow, could he help it? recom-
    menced,
And ran thro' all the coltish chronicle,
Wild Will, Black Bess, Tantivy,
    Tallyho,
Reform, White Rose, Bellerophon, the
    Jilt,
Arbaces, and Phenomenon, and the
    rest,
Till, not to die a listener, I arose,
And with me Philip, talking still; and
    so
We turn'd our foreheads from the fall-
    ing sun,
And following our own shadows thrice
    as long
As when they follow'd us from Philip's
    door,
Arrived, and found the sun of sweet
    content

Re-risen in Katie's eyes, and all things
    well.

> I steal by lawns and grassy plots,
>   I slide by hazel covers;
> I move the sweet forget-me-nots
>   That grow for happy lovers.

> I slip, I slide, I gloom, I glance,
>   Among my skimming swallows;
> I make the netted sunbeam dance
>   Against my sandy shallows.

> I murmur under moon and stars
>   In brambly wildernesses;
> I linger by my shingly bars;
>   I loiter round my cresses;

> And out again I curve and flow
>   To join the brimming river,
> For men may come and men may go,
>   But I go on for ever.

Yes, men may come and go; and these
    are gone,
All gone. My dearest brother, Ed-
    mund, sleeps,
Not by the well-known stream and
    rustic spire,
But unfamiliar Arno, and the dome
Of Brunelleschi; sleeps in peace: and
    he,
Poor Philip, of all his lavish waste of
    words
Remains the lean P. W. on his tomb:
I scraped the lichen from it: Katie
    walks
By the long wash of Australasian seas
Far off, and holds her head to other
    stars,
And breathes in converse seasons. All
    are gone."

    So Lawrence Aylmer, seated on a
    stile
In the long hedge, and rolling in his
    mind
Old waifs of rhyme, and bowing o'er
    the brook
A tonsured head in middle age forlorn,
Mused, and was mute. On a sudden
    a low breath
Of tender air made tremble in the
    hedge

The fragile bindweed-bells and briony
    rings;
And he look'd up. There stood a
    maiden near,
Waiting to pass. In much amaze he
    stared
On eyes a bashful azure, and on hair
In gloss and hue the chestnut, when
    the shell
Divides threefold to show the fruit
    within:
Then, wondering, ask'd her " Are you
    from the farm ? "
" Yes," answer'd she. " Pray stay a
    little: pardon me;
What do they call you ? " " Katie."
    " That were strange.
What surname ? " " Willows." "No!"
    " That is my name."
" Indeed ! " and here he look'd so self-
    perplext,
That Katie laugh'd, and laughing
    blush'd, till he
Laugh'd also, but as one before he
    wakes,
Who feels a glimmering strangeness
    in his dream.
Then looking at her; " Too happy,
    fresh and fair,
Too fresh and fair in our sad world's
    best bloom,
To be the ghost of one who bore your
    name
About these meadows, twenty years
    ago."

    " Have you not heard ? " said Katie,
    " we came back.
We bought the farm we tenanted be-
    fore.
Am I so like her ? so they said on
    board.
Sir, if you knew her in her English
    days,
My mother, as it seems you did, the
    days
That most she loves to talk of, come
    with me.
My brother James is in the harvest-
    field:
But she — you will be welcome — O,
    come in ! "

AYLMER'S FIELD.

1793.

DUST are our frames; and, gilded dust,
    our pride
Looks only for a moment whole and
    sound;
Like that long-buried body of the king,
Found lying with his urns and orna-
    ments,
Which at a touch of light, an air of
    heaven,
Slipt into ashes, and was found no
    more.

Here is a story which in rougher
    shape
Came from a grizzled cripple, whom
    I saw
Sunning himself in a waste field
    alone —
Old, and a mine of memories — who
    had served,
Long since, a bygone Rector of the
    place,
And been himself a part of what he
    told.

SIR AYLMER AYLMER, that al-
    mighty man,
The county God — in whose capacious
    hall,
Hung with a hundred shields, the
    family tree
Sprang from the midriff of a prostrate
    king —
Whose blazing wyvern weathercock'd
    the spire,
Stood from his walls and wing'd his
    entry-gates
And swang besides on many a windy
    sign —
Whose eyes from under a pyramidal
    head
Saw from his windows nothing save
    his own —
What lovelier of his own had he than
    her,
His only child, his Edith, whom he
    loved
As heiress and not heir regretfully?
But "he that marries her marries her
    name"

This fiat somewhat soothed himself
    and wife,
His wife a faded beauty of the
    Baths,
Insipid as the Queen upon a card;
Her all of thought and bearing hardly
    more
Than his own shadow in a sickly sun.

A land of hops and poppy-mingled
    corn,
Little about it stirring save a brook!
A sleepy land, where under the same
    wheel
The same old rut would deepen year
    by year;
Where almost all the village had one
    name;
Where Aylmer followed Aylmer at
    the Hall
And Averill Averill at the Rectory
Thrice over; so that Rectory and
    Hall,
Bound in an immemorial intimacy,
Were open to each other; tho' to
    dream
That Love could bind them closer well
    had made
The hoar hair of the Baronet bristle
    up
With horror, worse than had he heard
    his priest
Preach an inverted scripture, sons of
    men
Daughters of God; so sleepy was the
    land.

And might not Averill, had he will'd
    it so,
Somewhere beneath his own low range
    of roofs,
Have also set his many-shielded tree?
There was an Aylmer-Averill mar-
    riage once.
When the red rose was redder than
    itself,
And York's white rose as red as Lan-
    caster's,
With wounded peace which each had
    prick'd to death.
"Not proven" Averill said, or laugh-
    ingly

"Some other race of Averills"—prov'n
or no,
What cared he? what, if other or the
same?
He lean'd not on his fathers but him-
self.
But Leolin, his brother, living oft
With Averill, and a year or two before
Call'd to the bar, but ever call'd away
By one low voice to one dear neigh-
borhood,
Would often, in his walks with Edith,
claim
A distant kinship to the gracious blood
That shook the heart of Edith hearing
him.

Sanguine he was: a but less vivid hue
Than of that islet in the chestnut-
bloom
Flamed in his cheek; and eager eyes,
that still
Took joyful note of all things joyful,
beam'd,
Beneath a manelike mass of rolling
gold,
Their best and brightest, when they
dwelt on hers,
Edith, whose pensive beauty, perfect
else,
But subject to the season or the mood,
Shone like a mystic star between the
less
And greater glory varying to and fro,
We know not wherefore; bounteously
made,
And yet so finely, that a troublous
touch
Thinn'd, or would seem to thin her in
a day,
A joyous to dilate, as toward the light.
And these had been together from the
first.
Leolin's first nurse was, five years
after, hers:
So much the boy foreran: but when
his date
Doubled her own, for want of play-
mates, he
(Since Averill was a decade and a half
His elder, and their parents under-
ground)

Had tost his ball and flown his kite,
and roll'd
His hoop to pleasure Edith, with her
dipt
Against the rush of the air in the
prone swing,
Made blossom-ball or daisy-chain, ar-
ranged
Her garden, sow'd her name and kept
it green
In living letters, told her fairy-tales,
Show'd her the fairy footings on the
grass,
The little dells of cowslip, fairy palms,
The petty marestail forest, fairy
pines,
Or from the tiny pitted target blew
What look'd a flight of fairy arrows
aim'd
All at one mark, all hitting: make-
believes
For Edith and himself: or else he
forged,
But that was later, boyish histories
Of battle, bold adventure, dungeon,
wreck,
Flights, terrors, sudden rescues, and
true love
Crown'd after trial; sketches rude and
faint,
But where a passion yet unborn per-
haps
Lay hidden as the music of the moon
Sleeps in the plain eggs of the nightin-
gale.
And thus together, save for college-
times
Or Temple-eaten terms, a couple, fair
As ever painter painted, poet sang,
Or Heaven in lavish bounty moulded,
grew.
And more and more, the maiden
woman-grown,
He wasted hours with Averill; there,
when first
The tented winter-field was broken up
Into that phalanx of the summer
spears
That soon should wear the garland;
there again
When burr and bine were gather'd:
lastly there

At Christmas; ever welcome at the
      Hall,
On whose dull sameness his full tide
      of youth
Broke with a phosphorescence charm-
      ing even
My lady; and the Baronet yet had
      laid
No bar between them: dull and self-
      involved,
Tall and erect, but bending from his
      height
With half-allowing smiles for all the
      world,
And mighty courteous in the main —
      his pride
Lay deeper than to wear it as his
      ring —
He, like an Aylmer in his Aylmerism,
Would care no more for Leolin's walk-
      ing with her
Than for his old Newfoundland's, when
      they ran
To loose him at the stables, for he
      rose
Two footed at the limit of his chain,
Roaring to make a third: and how
      should Love,
Whom the cross-lightnings of four
      chance-met eyes
Flash into fiery life from nothing,
      follow
Such dear familiarities of dawn?
Seldom, but when he does, Master of
      all.

So these young hearts not knowing
      that they loved,
Not she at least, nor conscious of a
      bar
Between them, nor by plight or broken
      ring
Bound, but an immemorial intimacy,
Wander'd at will, and oft accompanied
By Averill: his, a brother's love, that
      hung
With wings of brooding shelter o'er
      her peace,
Might have been other, save for
      Leolin's —
Who knows? but so they wander'd,
      hour by hour

Gather'd the blossom that rebloom'd,
      and drank
The magic cup that filled itself anew.

A whisper half reveal'd her to her-
      self.
For out beyond her lodges, where the
      brook
Vocal, with here and there a silence,
      ran
By sallowy rims, arose the laborers'
      homes,
A frequent haunt of Edith, on low
      knolls
That dimpling died into each other,
      huts
At random scatter'd, each a nest in
      bloom.
Her art, her hand, her counsel all had
      wrought
About them: here was one that, sum-
      mer-blanch'd,
Was parcel-bearded with the trav-
      eller's joy
In Autumn, parcel ivy-clad; and here
The warm-blue breathings of a hidden
      hearth
Broke from a bower of vine and
      honeysuckle:
One look'd all rosetree, and another
      wore
A close-set robe of jasmine sown
      with stars:
This had a rosy sea of gillyflowers
About it; this, a milky-way on earth,
Like visions in the Northern dreamer's
      heavens,
A lily-avenue climbing to the doors;
One, almost to the martin-haunted
      eaves
A summer burial deep in hollyhocks;
Each, its own charm; and Edith's
      everywhere;
And Edith ever visitant with him,
He but less loved than Edith, of her
      poor:
For she — so lowly-lovely and so
      loving,
Queenly responsive when the loyal
      hand
Rose from the clay it work'd in as she
      past,

Not sowing hedgerow texts and pass-
    ing by,
Nor dealing goodly counsel from a
    height
That makes the lowest hate it, but a
    voice
Of comfort and an open hand of help,
A splendid presence flattering the
    poor roofs
Revered as theirs, but kindlier than
    themselves
To ailing wife or wailing infancy
Or old bedridden palsy, — was adored;
He, loved for her and for himself.
    A grasp
Having the warmth and muscle of
    the heart,
A childly way with children, and a
    laugh
Ringing like proven golden coinage
    true,
Were no false passport to that easy
    realm,
Where once with Leolin at her side
    the girl,
Nursing a child, and turning to the
    warmth
The tender pink five-beaded baby-
    soles,
Heard the good mother softly whis-
    per " Bless,
God bless 'em: marriages are made
    in Heaven."

    A flash of semi-jealousy clear'd it
    to her.
My lady's Indian kinsman unan-
    nounced
With half a score of swarthy faces
    came.
His own, tho' keen and bold and sol-
    dierly,
Sear'd by the close ecliptic, was not
    fair;
Fairer his talk, a tongue that ruled
    the hour,
Tho' seeming boastful: so when first
    he dash'd
Into the chronicle of a deedful day,
Sir Aylmer half forgot his lazy smile
Of patron " Good! my lady's kins-
    man! good!"

My lady with her fingers interlock'd,
And rotatory thumbs on silken knees,
Call'd all her vital spirits into each ear
To listen: unawares they flitted off,
Busying themselves about the flow-
    erage
That stood from out a stiff brocade
    in which,
The meteor of a splendid season, she,
Once with this kinsman, ah so long ago,
Stept thro' the stately minuet of those
    days:
But Edith's eager fancy hurried with
    him
Snatch'd thro' the perilous passes of
    his life:
Till Leolin ever watchful of her eye,
Hated him with a momentary hate.
Wife-hunting, as the rumor ran, was
    he:
I know not, for he spoke not, only
    shower'd
His oriental gifts on everyone
And most on Edith: like a storm he
    came,
And shook the house, and like a
    storm he went.

    Among the gifts he left her (possibly
He flow'd and ebb'd uncertain, to
    return
When others had been tested) there
    was one,
A dagger, in rich sheath with jewels
    on it
Sprinkled about in gold that branch'd
    itself
Fine as ice-ferns on January panes
Made by a breath. I know not
    whence at first,
Nor of what race, the work; but as he
    told
The story, storming a hill-fort of
    thieves
He got it; for their captain after fight,
His comrades having fought their
    last below,
Was climbing up the valley; at whom
    he shot:
Down from the beetling crag to which
    he clung
Tumbled the tawny rascal at his feet,

This dagger with him, which when
  now admired
By Edith whom his pleasure was to
  please,
At once the costly Sahib yielded to
  her.

And Leolin, coming after he was
  gone,
Tost over all her presents petulantly:
And when she show'd the wealthy
  scabbard, saying
"Look what a lovely piece of work-
  manship!"
Slight was his anwser "Well — I care
  not for it":
Then playing with the blade he
  prick'd his hand,
"A gracious gift to give a lady, this!"
"But would it be more gracious"
  ask'd the girl
"Were I to give this gift of his to one
That is no lady?" "Gracious? No"
  said he.
"Me? — but I cared not for it. O
  pardon me,
I seem to be ungraciousness itself."
"Take it" she added sweetly, "tho'
  his gift;
For I am more ungracious ev'n than
  you,
I care not for it either"; and he said
"Why then I love it": but Sir Aylmer
  past,
And neither loved nor liked the thing
  he heard.

The next day came a neighbor.
  Blues and reds
They talk'd of: blues were sure of it,
  he thought:
Then of the latest fox — where started
  — kill'd
In such a bottom: "Peter had the
  brush,
My Peter, first": and did Sir Aylmer
  know
That great pock-pitten fellow had
  been caught?
Then made his pleasure echo, hand to
  hand,

And rolling as it were the substance
  of it
Between his palms a moment up and
  down —
"The birds were warm, the birds were
  warm upon him;
We have him now" and had Sir
  Aylmer heard —
Nay, but he must — the land was
  ringing of it —
This blacksmith border-marriage —
  one they knew —
Raw from the nursery — who could
  trust a child?
That cursed France with her égalities!
And did Sir Aylmer (deferentially
With nearing chair and lower'd ac-
  cent) think —
For people talk'd — that it was wholly
  wise
To let that handsome fellow Averill
  walk
So freely with his daughter? people
  talk'd —
The boy might get a notion into
  him;
The girl might be entangled ere she
  knew.
Sir Aylmer Aylmer slowly stiffening
  spoke:
"The girl and boy, Sir, know their
  differences!"
"Good," said his friend, "but watch!"
  and he, "Enough,
More than enough, Sir! I can guard
  my own."
They parted, and Sir Aylmer Aylmer
  watch'd.

Pale, for on her the thunders of the
  house
Had fallen first, was Edith that same
  night;
Pale as the Jephtha's daughter, a
  rough piece
Of early rigid color, under which
Withdrawing by the counter door to
  that
Which Leolin open'd, she cast back
  upon him
A piteous glance, and vanish'd. He,
  as one

Caught in a burst of unexpected storm,
And pelted with outrageous epithets,
Turning beheld the Powers of the House
On either side the hearth, indignant; her,
Cooling her false cheek with a feather-fan,
Him, glaring, by his own stale devil spurr'd,
And, like a beast hard-ridden, breathing hard.
" Ungenerous, dishonorable, base,
Presumptuous! trusted as he was with her,
The sole succeeder to their wealth, their lands,
The last remaining pillar of their house,
The one transmitter of their ancient name,
Their child." "Our child!" "Our heiress!" "Ours!" for still,
Like echoes from beyond a hollow, came
Her sicklier iteration. Last he said,
" Boy, mark me! for your fortunes are to make.
I swear you shall not make them out of mine.
Now inasmuch as you have practised on her,
Perplext her, made her half forget herself,
Swerve from her duty to herself and us —
Things in an Aylmer deem'd impossible,
Far as we track ourselves — I say that this —
Else I withdraw favor and countenance
From you and yours for ever — shall you do.
Sir, when you see her — but you shall not see her —
No, you shall write, and not to her, but me:
And you shall say that having spoken with me,

And after look'd into yourself, you find
That you meant nothing — as indeed you know
That you meant nothing. Such a match as this !
Impossible, prodigious!" These were words,
As meted by his measure of himself,
Arguing boundless forbearance: after which,
And Leolin's horror-stricken answer, " I
So foul a traitor to myself and her,
Never oh never," for about as long
As the wind-hover hangs in balance, paused
Sir Aylmer reddening from the storm within,
Then broke all bonds of courtesy, and crying
" Boy, should I find you by my doors again,
My men shall lash you from them like a dog;
Hence!" with a sudden execration drove
The footstool from before him, and arose;
So, stammering " scoundrel" out of teeth that ground
As in a dreadful dream, while Leolin still
Retreated half-aghast, the fierce old man
Follow'd, and under his own lintel stood
Storming with lifted hands, a hoary face
Meet for the reverence of the hearth, but now,
Beneath a pale and unimpassion'd moon,
Vext with unworthy madness, and deform'd.

Slowly and conscious of the rageful eye
That watch'd him, till he heard the ponderous door
Close, crashing with long echoes thro' the land,

Went Leolin; then, his passions all
  in flood
And masters of his motion, furiously
Down thro' the bright lawns to his
  brother's ran,
And foam'd away his heart at Aver-
  ill's ear:
Whom Averill solaced as he might,
  amazed:
The man was his, had been his fath-
  er's, friend:
He must have seen, himself had seen
  it long;
He must have known, himself had
  known: besides,
He never yet had set his daughter
  forth
Here in the woman-markets of the
  west,
Where our Caucasians let themselves
  be sold.
Some one, he thought, had slander'd
  Leolin to him.
"Brother, for I have loved you more
  as son
Than brother, let me tell you: I my-
  self —
What is their pretty saying? jilted,
  is it?
Jilted I was: I say it for your peace.
Pain'd, and, as bearing in myself the
  shame
The woman should have borne, humili-
  ated,
I lived for years a stunted sunless life;
Till after our good parents past away
Watching your growth, I seem'd again
  to grow.
Leolin, I almost sin in envying you:
The very whitest lamb in all my fold
Loves you: I know her: the worst
  thought she has
Is whiter even than her pretty hand:
She must prove true: for, brother,
  where two fight
The strongest wins, and truth and love
  are strength,
And you are happy: let her parents
  be."

But Leolin cried out the more upon
  them —

Insolent, brainless, heartless! heiress,
  wealth,
Their wealth, their heiress! wealth
  enough was theirs
For twenty matches. Were he lord
  of this,
Why twenty boys and girls should
  marry on it,
And forty blest ones bless him, and
  himself
Be wealthy still, ay wealthier. He
  believed
This filthy marriage-hindering Mam-
  mon made
The harlot of the cities: nature crost
Was mother of the foul adulteries
That saturate soul with body. Name,
  too! name,
Their ancient name! they *might* be
  proud; its worth
Was being Edith's. Ah how pale she
  had look'd
Darling, to-night! they must have
  rated her
Beyond all tolerance. These old
  pheasant-lords,
These partridge-breeders of a thou-
  sand years,
Who had mildew'd in their thousands,
  doing nothing
Since Egbert — why, the greater their
  disgrace!
Fall back upon a name! rest, rot in
  that!
Not *keep* it noble, make it nobler?
  fools,
With such a vantage-ground for nobleness!
He had known a man, a quintessence
  of man,
The life of all — who madly loved —
  and he,
Thwarted by one of these old father-
  fools,
Had rioted his life out, and made an
  end.
He would not do it! her sweet face
  and faith
Held him from that: but he had powers, he knew it:
Back would he to his studies, make a
  name,

Name, fortune too: the world should
	ring of him
To shame these mouldy Aylmers in
	their graves:
Chancellor, or what is greatest would
	he be —
"O brother, I am grieved to learn
	your grief —
Give me my fling, and let me say my
	say."

At which, like one that sees his own
	excess,
And easily forgives it as his own,
He laugh'd; and then was mute; but
	presently
Wept like a storm: and honest Averill
	seeing
How low his brother's mood had fallen,
	fetch'd
His richest beeswing from a binn re-
	served
For banquets, praised the waning red,
	and told
The vintage — when *this* Aylmer came
	of age —
Then drank and past it; till at length
	the two,
Tho' Leolin flamed and fell again,
	agreed
That much allowance must be made
	for men.
After an angry dream this kindlier
	glow
Faded with morning, but his purpose
	held.

Yet once by night again the lovers
	met,
A perilous meeting under the tall pines
That darken'd all the northward of
	her Hall.
Him, to her meek and modest bosom
	prest
In agony, she promised that no force,
Persuasion, no, nor death could alter
	her:
He, passionately hopefuller, would go,
Labor for his own Edith, and return
In such a sunlight of prosperity
He should not be rejected. "Write to
	me!

They loved me, and because I love
	their child
They hate me: there is war between
	us, dear,
Which breaks all bonds but ours; we
	must remain
Sacred to one another." So they
	talk'd,
Poor children, for their comfort: the
	wind blew;
The rain of heaven, and their own
	bitter tears,
Tears, and the careless rain of heaven,
	mixt
Upon their faces, as they kiss'd each
	other
In darkness, and above them roar'd
	the pine.

So Leolin went; and as we task our-
	selves
To learn a language known but smat-
	teringly
In phrases here and there at random,
	toil'd
Mastering the lawless science of our
	law,
That codeless myriad of precedent,
That wilderness of single instances,
Thro' which a few, by wit or fortune
	led,
May beat a pathway out to wealth and
	fame.
The jests, that flash'd about the plead-
	er's room,
Lightning of the hour, the pun, the
	scurrilous tale, —
Old scandals buried now seven decades
	deep
In other scandals that have lived and
	died,
And left the living scandal that shall
	die —
Were dead to him already; bent as he
	was
To make disproof of scorn, and strong
	in hopes,
And prodigal of all brain-labor he,
Charier of sleep, and wine, and exer-
	cise,
Except when for a breathing-while at
	eve,

Some niggard fraction of an hour, he
    ran
Beside the river-bank : and then indeed
Harder the times were, and the hands
    of power
Were bloodier, and the according
    hearts of men
Seem'd harder too ; but the soft river-
    breeze,
Which fann'd the gardens of that rival
    rose
Yet fragrant in a heart remembering
His former talks with Edith, on him
    breathed
Far purelier in his rushings to and fro,
After his books, to flush his blood with
    air,
Then to his books again. My lady's
    cousin,
Half-sickening of his pension'd after-
    noon,
Drove in upon the student once or
    twice,
Ran a Malayan amuck against the
    times,
Had golden hopes for France and all
    mankind,
Answer'd all queries touching those at
    home
With a heaved shoulder and a saucy
    smile,
And fain had haled him out into the
    world,
And air'd him there : his nearer friend
    would say
" Screw not the chord too sharply lest
    it snap."
Then left alone he pluck'd her dagger
    forth
From where his worldless heart had
    kept it warm,
Kissing his vows upon it like a knight.
And wrinkled benchers often talk'd of
    him
Approvingly, and prophesied his rise :
For heart, I think, help'd head : her
    letters too,
Tho' far between, and coming fitfully
Like broken music, written as she
    found
Or made occasion, being strictly
    watch'd,

Charm'd him thro' every labyrinth till
    he saw
An end, a hope, a light breaking upon
    him.

But they that cast her spirit into
    flesh,
Her worldly-wise begetters, plagued
    themselves
To sell her, those good parents, for her
    good.
Whatever eldest-born of rank or
    wealth
Might lie within their compass, him
    they lured
Into their net made pleasant by the
    baits
Of gold and beauty, wooing him to woo.
So month by month the noise about
    their doors,
And distant blaze of those dull ban-
    quets, made
The nightly wirer of their innocent
    hare
Falter before he took it. All in vain.
Sullen, defiant, pitying, wroth, return'd
Leolin's rejected rivals from their suit
So often, that the folly taking wings
Slipt o'er those lazy limits down the
    wind
With rumor, and became in other fields
A mockery to the yeomen over ale,
And laughter to their lords : but those
    at home,
As hunters round a hunted creature
    draw,
The cordon close and closer toward
    the death,
Narrow'd her goings out and comings
    in ;
Forbade her first the house of Averill,
Then closed her access to the wealthier
    farms,
Last from her own home-circle of the
    poor
They barr'd her : yet she bore it : yet
    her cheek
Kept color : wondrous ! but, O mystery !
What amulet drew her down to that
    old oak,
So old, that twenty years before, a
    part

Falling had let appear the brand of John —
Once grovelike, each huge arm a tree, but now
The broken base of a black tower, a cave
Of touchwood, with a single flourishing spray.
There the manorial lord too curiously
Raking in that millennial touchwood-dust
Found for himself a bitter treasure-trove;
Burst his own wyvern on the seal, and read
Writhing a letter from his child, for which
Came at the moment Leolin's emissary,
A crippled lad, and coming turn'd to fly,
But scared with threats of jail and halter gave
To him that fluster'd his poor parish wits
The letter which he brought, and swore besides
To play their go-between as heretofore
Nor let them know themselves betray'd; and then,
Soul-stricken at their kindness to him, went
Hating his own lean heart and miserable.

Thenceforward oft from out a despot dream
The father panting woke, and oft, as dawn
Aroused the black republic on his elms,
Sweeping the frothfly from the fescue brush'd
Thro' the dim meadow toward his treasure-trove,
Seized it, took home, and to my lady, — who made
A downward crescent of her minion mouth,
Listless in all despondence, — read; and tore,
As if the living passion symbol'd there
Were living nerves to feel the rent; and burnt,

Now chafing at his own great self defied,
Now striking on huge stumbling-blocks of scorn
In babyisms, and dear diminutives
Scatter'd all over the vocabulary
Of such a love as like a chidden child,
After much wailing, hush'd itself at last
Hopeless of answer: then tho' Averill wrote
And bade him with good heart sustain himself —
All would be well — the lover heeded not,
But passionately restless came and went,
And rustling once at night about the place,
There by a keeper shot at, slightly hurt,
Raging return'd: nor was it well for her
Kept to the garden now, and grove of pines,
Watch'd even there; and one was set to watch
The watcher, and Sir Aylmer watch'd them all,
Yet bitterer from his readings: once indeed,
Warm'd with his wines, or taking pride in her,
She look'd so sweet, he kiss'd her tenderly
Not knowing what possess'd him: that one kiss
Was Leolin's one strong rival upon earth;
Seconded, for my lady follow'd suit,
Seem'd hope's returning rose: and then ensued
A Martin's summer of his faded love,
Or ordeal by kindness; after this
He seldom crost his child without a sneer;
The mother flow'd in shallower acrimonies:
Never one kindly smile, one kindly word:
So that the gentle creature shut from all
Her charitable use, and face to face

With twenty months of silence, slowly
　　lost
Nor greatly cared to lose, her hold on
　　life.
Last, some low fever ranging round
　　to spy
The weakness of a people or a house,
Like flies that haunt a wound, or deer,
　　or men,
Or almost all that is, hurting the
　　hurt —
Save Christ as we believe him — found
　　the girl
And flung her down upon a couch of
　　fire,
Where careless of the household faces
　　near,
And crying upon the name of Leolin,
She, and with her the race of Aylmer,
　　past.

　　Star to star vibrates light: may
　　　　soul to soul
Strike thro' a finer element of her
　　own?
So, — from afar, — touch as at once?
　　or why
That night, that moment, when she
　　named his name,
Did the keen shriek "Yes love, yes,
　　Edith, yes,"
Shrill, till the comrade of his cham-
　　bers woke,
And came upon him half-arisen from
　　sleep,
With a weird bright eye, sweating and
　　trembling,
His hair as it were crackling into
　　flames,
His body half flung forward in pursuit,
And his long arms stretch'd as to grasp
　　a flyer:
Nor knew he wherefore he had made
　　the cry;
And being much befool'd and idioted
By the rough amity of the other, sank
As into sleep again.　The second day,
My lady's Indian kinsman rushing in,
A breaker of the bitter news from
　　home,
Found a dead man, a letter edged with
　　death

Beside him, and the dagger which him-
　　self
Gave Edith, redden'd with no bandit's
　　blood:
"From Edith" was engraven on the
　　blade.

　　Then Averill went and gazed upon
　　　　his death.
And when he came again, his flock
　　believed —
Beholding how the years which are
　　not Time's
Had blasted him — that many thou-
　　sand days
Were clipt by horror from his term
　　of life.
Yet the sad mother, for the second
　　death
Scarce touch'd her thro' that nearness
　　of the first,
And being used to find her pastor
　　texts,
Sent to the harrow'd brother, praying
　　him
To speak before the people of her
　　child,
And fixt the Sabbath.　Darkly that
　　day rose:
Autumn's mock sunshine of the faded
　　woods
Was all the life of it; for hard on
　　these,
A breathless burthen of low-folded
　　heavens
Stifled and chill'd at once; but every
　　roof
Sent out a listener: many too had
　　known
Edith among the hamlets round, and
　　since
The parents' harshness and the hap-
　　less loves
And double death were widely mur-
　　mur'd, left
Their own gray tower, or plain-faced
　　tabernacle,
To hear him; all in mourning these,
　　and those
With blots of it about them, ribbon,
　　glove

Or kerchief; while the church, — one night, except
For greenish glimmerings thro' the lancets, — made
Still paler the pale head of him, who tower'd
Above them, with his hopes in either grave.

Long o'er his bent brows linger'd Averill,
His face magnetic to the hand from which
Livid he pluck'd it forth, and labor'd thro'
His brief prayer-prelude, gave the verse " Behold,
Your house is left unto you desolate!"
But lapsed into so long a pause again
As half amazed half frighted all his flock:
Then from his height and loneliness of grief
Bore down in flood, and dash'd his angry heart
Against the desolations of the world.

Never since our bad earth became one sea,
Which rolling o'er the palaces of the proud,
And all but those who knew the living God —
Eight that were left to make a purer world —
When since had flood, fire, earthquake, thunder, wrought
Such waste and havoc as the idolatries,
Which from the low light of mortality
Shot up their shadows to the Heaven of Heavens,
And worshipt their own darkness as the Highest?
" Gash thyself, priest, and honor thy brute Baäl,
And to thy worst self sacrifice thyself,
For with thy worst self hast thou clothed thy God.
Then came a Lord in no wise like to Baäl.

The babe shall lead the lion.   Surely now
The wilderness shall blossom as the rose.
Crown thyself, worm, and worship thine own lusts! —
No coarse and blockish God of acreage
Stands at thy gate for thee to grovel to —
Thy God is far diffused in noble groves
And princely halls, and farms, and flowing lawns,
And heaps of living gold that daily grow,
And title-scrolls and gorgeous heraldries.
In such a shape dost thou behold thy God.
Thou wilt not gash thy flesh for *him;* for thine
Fares richly, in fine linen, not a hair
Ruffled upon the scarfskin, even while
The deathless ruler of thy dying house
Is wounded to the death that cannot die;
And tho' thou numberest with the followers
Of One who cried, ' Leave all and follow me.'
Thee therefore with His light about thy feet,
Thee with His message ringing in thine ears,
Thee shall thy brother man, the Lord from Heaven,
Born of a village girl, carpenter's son,
Wonderful, Prince of peace, the Mighty God,
Count the more base idolater of the two;
Crueller: as not passing thro' the fire
Bodies, but souls — thy children's — thro' the smoke.
The blight of low desires — darkening thine own
To thine own likeness; or if one of these,
Thy better born unhappily from thee,
Should, as by miracle, grow straight and fair —
Friends, I was bid to speak of such a one

By those who most have cause to sor-
   row for her —
Fairer than Rachel by the palmy well,
Fairer than Ruth among the fields of
   corn,
Fair as the angel that said 'Hail!'
   she seem'd,
Who entering fill'd the house with
   sudden light.
For so mine own was brighten'd:
   where indeed
The roof so lowly but that beam of
   Heaven
Dawn'd sometime thro' the doorway? whose the babe
Too ragged to be fondled on her lap,
Warm'd at her bosom? The poor
   child of shame
The common care whom no one cared
   for, leapt
To greet her, wasting his forgotten
   heart,
As with the mother he had never
   known,
In gambols; for her fresh and inno-
   cent eyes
Had such a star of morning in their
   blue,
That all neglected places of the field
Broke into nature's music when they
   saw her.
Low was her voice, but won mysteri-
   ous way
Thro' the seal'd ear to which a louder
   one
Was all but silence — free of alms
   her hand —
The hand that robed your cottage-
   walls with flowers
Has often toil'd to clothe your little
   ones;
How often placed upon the sick man's
   brow
Cool'd it, or laid his feverous pillow
   smooth!
Had you one sorrow and she shared
   it not?
One burthen and she would not lighten
   it?
One spiritual doubt she did not soothe?
Or when some heat of difference
   sparkled out,

How sweetly would she glide between
   your wraths,
And steal you from each other! for
   she walk'd
Wearing the light yoke of that Lord
   of love,
Who still'd the rolling wave of
   Galilee!
And one — of him I was not bid to
   speak —
Was always with her, whom you also
   knew.
Him too you loved, for he was worthy
   love.
And these had been together from the
   first;
They might have been together till
   the last.
Friends, this frail bark of ours, when
   sorely tried,
May wreck itself without the pilot's
   guilt,
Without the captain's knowledge:
   hope with me.
Whose shame is that, if he went
   hence with shame?
Nor mine the fault, if losing both of
   these
I cry to vacant chairs and widow'd
   walls,
'My house is left unto me desolate.'"

While thus he spoke, his hearers
   wept; but some,
Sons of the glebe, with other frowns
   than those
That knit themselves for summer
   shadow, scowl'd
At their great lord. He, when it
   seem'd he saw
No pale sheet-lightnings from afar,
   but fork'd
Of the near storm, and aiming at his
   head,
Sat anger-charm'd from sorrow, sol-
   dier-like,
Erect: but when the preacher's cadence flow'd
Softening thro' all the gentle attributes
Of his lost child, the wife, who watch'd
   his face,

Paled at a sudden twitch of his iron
mouth;
And "O pray God that he hold up"
she thought
"Or surely I shall shame myself and
him."

"Nor yours the blame—for who
beside your hearths
Can take her place—if echoing me
you cry
'Our house is left unto us desolate'?
But thou, O thou that killest, hadst
thou known,
O thou that stonest, hadst thou under-
stood
The things belonging to thy peace
and ours!
Is there no prophet but the voice that
calls
Doom upon kings, or in the waste
'Repent'?
Is not our own child on the narrow
way,
Who down to those that saunter in
the broad
Cries 'Come up hither,' as a prophet
to us?
Is there no stoning save with flint
and rock?
Yes, as the dead we weep for testify—
No desolation but by sword and fire?
Yes, as your moanings witness, and
myself
Am lonelier, darker, earthlier for my
loss.
Give me your prayers, for he is past
your prayers,
Not past the living fount of pity in
Heaven.
But I that thought myself long-suffer-
ing, meek,
Exceeding 'poor in spirit'—how the
words
Have twisted back upon themselves,
and mean
Vileness, we are grown so proud—I
wish'd my voice
A rushing tempest of the wrath of God
To blow these sacrifices thro' the
world—
Sent like the twelve-divided concubine

To inflame the tribes: but there—
out yonder—earth
Lightens from her own central Hell
—O there
The red fruit of an old idolatry—
The heads of chiefs and princes fall
so fast,
They cling together in the ghastly
sack—
The land all shambles—naked mar
riages
Flash from the bridge, and ever-mur-
der'd France,
By shores that darken with the gath-
ering wolf,
Runs in a river of blood to the sick sea.
Is this a time to madden madness then?
Was this a time for these to flaunt
their pride?
May Pharaoh's darkness, folds as
dense as those
Which hid the Holiest from the peo-
ple's eyes
Ere the great death, shroud this great
sin from all!
Doubtless our narrow world must
canvass it:
O rather pray for those and pity them,
Who, thro' their own desire accom-
plish'd, bring
Their own gray hairs with sorrow to
the grave—
Who broke the bond which they
desired to break,
Which else had link'd their race with
times to come—
Who wove coarse webs to snare her
purity,
Grossly contriving their dear daugh-
ter's good—
Poor souls, and knew not what they
did, but sat
Ignorant, devising their own daugh-
ter's death!
May not that earthly chastisement
suffice?
Have not our love and reverence left
them bare?
Will not another take their heritage?
Will there be children's laughter in
their hall
For ever and for ever, or one stone

Left on another, or is it a light thing
That I, their guest, their host, their
    ancient friend,
I made by these the last of all my
    race,
Must cry to these the last of theirs, as
    cried
Christ ere His agony to those that
    swore
Not by the temple but the gold, and
    made
Their own traditions God, and slew
    the Lord,
And left their memories a world's
    curse — 'Behold,
Your house is left unto you deso-
    late'?"

Ended he had not, but she brook'd
    no more:
Long since her heart had beat remorse-
    lessly,
Her crampt-up sorrow pain'd her, and
    a sense
Of meanness in her unresisting life.
Then their eyes vext her; for on en-
    tering
He had cast the curtains of their seat
    aside —
Black velvet of the costliest — she
    herself
Had seen to that: fain had she closed
    them now,
Yet dared not stir to do it, only near'd
Her husband inch by inch, but when
    she laid,
Wifelike, her hand in one of his, he
    veil'd
His face with the other, and at once,
    as falls
A creeper when the prop is broken,
    fell
The woman shrieking at his feet, and
    swoon'd.
Then her own people bore along the
    nave
Her pendent hands, and narrow mea-
    gre face
Seam'd with the shallow cares of fifty
    years:
And her the Lord of all the landscape
    round

Ev'n to its last horizon, and of all
Who peer'd at him so keenly, follow'd
    out
Tall and erect, but in the middle aisle
Reel'd, as a footsore ox in crowded
    ways
Stumbling across the market to his
    death,
Unpitied; for he groped as blind, and
    seem'd
Always about to fall, grasping the
    pews
And oaken finials till he touch'd the
    door;
Yet to the lychgate, where his chariot
    stood,
Strode from the porch, tall and erect
    again.

But nevermore did either pass the
    gate
Save under pall with bearers. In one
    month,
Thro' weary and yet ever wearier
    hours,
The childless mother went to seek her
    child;
And when he felt the silence of his
    house
About him, and the change and not
    the change,
And those fixt eyes of painted ances-
    tors
Staring for ever from their gilded
    walls
On him their last descendant, his own
    head
Began to droop, to fall; the man be-
    came
Imbecile; his one word was "deso-
    late";
Dead for two years before his death
    was he;
But when the second Christmas came,
    escaped
His keepers, and the silence which he
    felt,
To find a deeper in the narrow
    gloom
By wife and child; nor wanted at his
    end
The dark retinue reverencing death

At golden thresholds; nor from tender hearts,
And those who sorrow'd o'er a vanish'd race,
Pity, the violet on the tyrant's grave.
Then the great Hall was wholly broken down,
And the broad woodland parcell'd into farms;
And where the two contrived their daughter's good,
Lies the hawk's cast, the mole has made his run,
The hedgehog underneath the plantain bores,
The rabbit fondles his own harmless face,
The slow-worm creeps, and the thin weasel there
Follows the mouse, and all is open field.

SEA DREAMS.

A CITY clerk, but gently born and bred;
His wife, an unknown artist's orphan child —
One babe was theirs, a Margaret, three years old:
They, thinking that her clear germander eye
Droopt in the giant-factoried city-gloom,
Came, with a month's leave given them, to the sea:
For which his gains were dock'd, however small:
Small were his gains, and hard his work; besides,
Their slender household fortunes (for the man
Had risk'd his little) like the little thrift,
Trembled in perilous places o'er a deep:
And oft, when sitting all alone, his face
Would darken, as he cursed his credulousness,
And that one unctuous mouth which lured him, rogue,

To buy strange shares in some Peruvian mine.
Now seaward-bound for health they gain'd a coast,
All sand and cliff and deep-inrunning cave,
At close of day; slept, woke, and went the next,
The Sabbath, pious variers from the church,
To chapel; where a heated pulpiteer,
Not preaching simple Christ to simple men,
Announced the coming doom, and fulminated
Against the scarlet woman and her creed;
For sideways up he swung his arms, and shriek'd
"Thus, thus with violence," ev'n as if he held
The Apocalyptic millstone, and himself
Were that great Angel; "Thus with violence
Shall Babylon be cast into the sea;
Then comes the close." The gentle-hearted wife
Sat shuddering at the ruin of a world;
He at his own: but when the wordy storm
Had ended, forth they came and paced the shore,
Ran in and out the long sea-framing caves,
Drank the large air, and saw, but scarce believed
(The sootflake of so many a summer still
Clung to their fancies) that they saw, the sea.
So now on sand they walk'd, and now on cliff,
Lingering about the thymy promontories,
Till all the sails were darken'd in the west,
And rosed in the east: then homeward and to bed:
Where she, who kept a tender Christian hope,
Haunting a holy text, and still to that

Returning, as the bird returns, at
    night,
"Let not the sun go down upon your
    wrath,"
Said, "Love, forgive him:" but he
    did not speak;
And silenced by that silence lay the
    wife,
Remembering her dear Lord who died
    for all,
And musing on the little lives of men,
And how they mar this little by their
    feuds.

But while the two were sleeping, a
    full tide
Rose with ground-swell, which, on the
    foremost rocks
Touching, upjetted in spirts of wild
    sea-smoke,
And scaled in sheets of wasteful foam,
    and fell
In vast sea-cataracts — ever and anon
Dead claps of thunder from within
    the cliffs
Heard thro' the living roar. At this
    the babe,
Their Margaret cradled near them,
    wail'd and woke
The mother, and the father suddenly
    cried,
"A wreck, a wreck!" then turn'd, and
    groaning said,

"Forgive! How many will say, 'for-
    give,' and find
A sort of absolution in the sound
To hate a little longer! No; the sin
That neither God nor man can well
    forgive,
Hypocrisy, I saw it in him at once.
Is it so true that second thoughts are
    best?
Not first, and third, which are a riper
    first?
Too ripe, too late! they come too late
    for use.
Ah love, there surely lives in man and
    beast
Something divine to warn them of
    their foes:

And such a sense, when first I fronted
    him,
Said, 'Trust him not;' but after,
    when I came
To know him more, I lost it, knew him
    less;
Fought with what seem'd my own
    uncharity;
Sat at his table; drank his costly wines;
Made more and more allowance for
    his talk;
Went further, fool! and trusted him
    with all,
All my poor scrapings from a dozen
    years
Of dust and deskwork: there is no
    such mine,
None; but a gulf of ruin, swallowing
    gold,
Not making. Ruin'd! ruin'd! the
    sea roars
Ruin: a fearful night!"

                    "Not fearful; fair,"
Said the good wife, "if every star in
    heaven
Can make it fair: you do but hear
    the tide.
Had you ill dreams?"

        "O yes," he said, "I dream'd
Of such a tide swelling toward the land,
And I from out the boundless outer
    deep
Swept with it to the shore, and enter'd
    one
Of those dark caves that run beneath
    the cliffs.
I thought the motion of the boundless
    deep
Bore thro' the cave, and I was heaved
    upon it
In darkness: then I saw one lovely star
Larger and larger. 'What a world,'
    I thought,
'To live in!' but in moving on I found
Only the landward exit of the cave,
Bright with the sun upon the stream
    beyond:
And near the light a giant woman sat,
All over earthy, like a piece of earth,
A pickaxe in her hand: then out I slipt

Into a land all sun and blossom, trees
As high as heaven, and every bird
    that sings :
And here the night-light flickering in
    my eyes
Awoke me."

  "That was then your dream," she
    said,
" Not sad, but sweet."

      " So sweet, I lay," said he,
" And mused upon it, drifting up the
    stream
In fancy, till I slept again, and pieced
The broken vision; for I dream'd that
    still
The motion of the great deep bore
    me on,
And that the woman walk'd upon
    the brink :
I wonder'd at her strength, and ask'd
    her of it :
' It came,' she said, ' by working in
    the mines : '
O then to ask her of my shares, I
    thought ;
And ask'd ; but not a word ; she shook
    her head.
And then the motion of the current
    ceased,
And there was rolling thunder; and
    we reach'd
A mountain, like a wall of burs and
    thorns ;
But she with her strong feet up the
    hill
Trod out a path : I follow'd ; and at
    top
She pointed seaward : there a fleet of
    glass,
That seem'd a fleet of jewels under me,
Sailing along before a gloomy cloud
That not one moment ceased to thun-
    der, past
In sunshine : right across its track
    there lay,
Down in the water, a long reef of gold,
Or what seem'd gold : and I was glad
    at first
To think that in our often-ransack'd
    world

Still so much gold was left; and then
    I fear'd
Lest the gay navy there should splin-
    ter on it,
And fearing waved my arm to warn
    them off ;
An idle signal, for the brittle fleet
(I thought I could have died to save
    it) near'd,
Touch'd, clink'd, and clash'd, and
    vanish'd, and I woke,
I heard the clash so clearly. Now I
    see
My dream was Life ; the woman hon-
    est Work ;
And my poor venture but a fleet of
    glass
Wreck'd on a reef of visionary gold."

  " Nay," said the kindly wife to com-
    fort him,
" You raised your arm, you tumbled
    down and broke
The glass with little Margaret's medi-
    cine in it ;
And, breaking that, you made and
    broke your dream :
A trifle makes a dream, a trifle breaks."

  " No trifle," groan'd the husband;
    "yesterday
I met him suddenly in the street, and
    ask'd
That which I ask'd the woman in my
    dream.
Like her, he shook his head. ' Show
    me the books ! '
He dodged me with a long and loose
    account.
' The books, the books ! ' but he, he
    could not wait,
Bound on a matter he of life and
    death :
When the great Books (see Daniel
    seven and ten)
Were open'd, I should find he meant
    me well ;
And then began to bloat himself, and
    ooze
All over with the fat affectionate smile
That makes the widow lean. ' My
    dearest friend,

Have faith, have faith! We live by
   faith,' said he;
' And all things work together for the
   good
Of those ' — it makes me sick to quote
   him — last
Gript my hand hard, and with God-
   bless-you went.
I stood like one that had received a
   blow:
I found a hard friend in his loose ac-
   counts,
A loose one in the hard grip of his
   hand,
A curse in his God-bless-you : then my
   eyes
Pursued him down the street, and far
   away,
Among the honest shoulders of the
   crowd,
Read rascal in the motions of his back,
And scoundrel in the supple-sliding
   knee."

"Was he so bound, poor soul?"
   said the good wife;
" So are we all : but do not call him,
   love,
Before you prove him, rogue, and
   proved, forgive.
His gain is loss; for he that wrongs
   his friend
Wrongs himself more, and ever bears
   about
A silent court of justice in his breast,
Himself the judge and jury, and himself
The prisoner at the bar, ever condemn'd:
And that drags down his life: then
   comes what comes
Hereafter : and he meant, he said he
   meant,
Perhaps he meant, or partly meant,
   you well."

" ' With all his conscience and one
   eye askew ' —
Love, let me quote these lines, that
   you may learn
A man is likewise counsel for himself,

Too often, in that silent court of
   yours —
' With all his conscience and one eye
   askew,
So false, he partly took himself for
   true ;
Whose pious talk, when most his
   heart was dry,
Made wet the crafty crowsfoot round
   his eye ;
Who, never naming God except for
   gain,
So never took that useful name in
   vain,
Made Him his catspaw and the Cross
   his tool,
And Christ the bait to trap his dupe
   and fool;
Nor deeds of gift, but gifts of grace
   he forged,
And snake-like slimed his victim ere
   he gorged ;
And oft at Bible meetings, o'er the
   rest
Arising, did his holy oily best,
Dropping the too rough H in Hell
   and Heaven,
To spread the Word by which him-
   self had thriven.'
How like you this old satire ? "

                           "Nay," she said,
"I loathe it: he had never kindly
   heart,
Nor ever cared to better his own kind,
Who first wrote satire, with no pity
   in it.
But will you hear *my* dream, for I
   had one
That altogether went to music ? Still
It awed me."

      Then she told it, having dream'd
Of that same coast.

      — But round the North, a light,
A belt, it seem'd, of luminous vapor,
   lay,
And ever in it a low musical note
Swell'd up and died; and, as it
   swell'd, a ridge

Of breaker issued from the belt, and
    still
Grew with the growing note, and when
    the note
Had reach'd a thunderous fullness,
    on those cliffs
Broke, mixt with awful light (the
    same as that
Living within the belt) whereby she
    saw
That all those lines of cliffs were
    cliffs no more,
But huge cathedral fronts of every
    age,
Grave, florid, stern, as far as eye
    could see,
One after one: and then the great
    ridge drew,
Lessening to the lessening music,
    back,
And past into the belt and swell'd
    again
Slowly to music : ever when it broke
The statues, king or saint, or founder
    fell;
Then from the gaps and chasms of
    ruin left
Came men and women in dark clusters
    round,
Some crying, "Set them up ! they shall
    not fall!"
And others, "Let them lie, for they
    have fall'n."
And still they strove and wrangled:
    and she grieved
In her strange dream, she knew not
    why, to find
Their wildest wailings never out of
    tune
With that sweet note; and ever as
    their shrieks
Ran highest up the gamut, that great
    wave
Returning, while none mark'd it, on
    the crowd
Broke, mixt with awful light, and
    show'd their eyes
Glaring, with passionate looks, and
    swept away
The men of flesh and blood, and men
    of stone,
To the waste deeps together.

           "Then I fixt
My wistful eyes on two fair images,
Both crown'd with stars and high
    among the stars, —
The Virgin Mother standing with her
    child
High up on one of those dark min-
    ster-fronts —
Till she began to totter, and the child
Clung to the mother, and sent out a
    cry
Which mixt with little Margaret's,
    and I woke,
And my dream awed me: — well —
    but what are dreams ?
Yours came but from the breaking of
    a glass,
And mine but from the crying of a
    child."

   "Child ? No!" said he, "but this
    tide's roar, and his,
Our Boanerges with his threats of
    doom,
And loud-lung'd Antibabylonianisms
(Altho' I grant but little music there)
Went both to make your dream : but
    if there were
A music harmonizing our wild cries,
Sphere-music such as that you
    dream'd about,
Why, that would make our passions
    far too like
The discords dear to the musician
    No —
One shriek of hate would jar all the
    hymns of heaven :
True Devils with no ear, they howl
    in tune
With nothing but the Devil !"

          "'True' indeed!
One out of our town, but later by an
    hour
Here than ourselves, spoke with me
    on the shore ;
While you were running down the
    sands, and made
The dimpled flounce of the sea-furbe-
    low flap,
Good man, to please the child. She
    brought strange news.

Why were you silent when I spoke
    to-night?
I had set my heart on your forgiving
    him
Before you knew. We *must* forgive
    the dead."

    "Dead! who is dead?"

      "The man your eye pursued.
A little after you had parted with
    him,
He suddenly dropt dead of heart-
    disease."

"Dead? he? of heart-disease? what
    heart had he
To die of? dead?"

      "Ah, dearest, if there be
A devil in man, there is an angel too,
And if he did that wrong you charge
    him with,
His angel broke his heart. But your
    rough voice
(You spoke so loud) has roused the
    child again.
Sleep, little birdie, sleep! will she not
    sleep
Without her 'little birdie'? well then,
    sleep,
And I will sing you, 'birdie.'"

      Saying this,
The woman half turn'd round from
    him she loved,
Left him one hand, and reaching
    thro' the night
Her other, found (for it was close
    beside)
And half-embraced the basket cradle-
    head
With one soft arm, which, like the
    pliant bough
That moving moves the nest and
    nestling, sway'd
The cradle, while she sang this baby
    song.

    What does little birdie say
    In her nest at peep of day?
    Let me fly, says little birdie,

    Mother, let me fly away.
    Birdie, rest a little longer,
    Till the little wings are stronger.
    So she rests a little longer,
    Then she flies away.

    What does little baby say,
    In her bed at peep of day?
    Baby says, like little birdie,
    Let me rise and fly away.
    Baby, sleep a little longer,
    Till the little limbs are stronger.
    If she sleeps a little longer,
    Baby too shall fly away.

"She sleeps: let us too, let all evil,
    sleep.
He also sleeps—another sleep than
    ours.
He can do no more wrong: forgive
    him, dear,
And I shall sleep the sounder!"

      Then the man,
"His deeds yet live, the worst is yet
    to come.
Yet let your sleep for this one night
    be sound:
I do forgive him!"

      "Thanks, my love," she said,
"Your own will be the sweeter," and
    they slept.

LUCRETIUS.

LUCILIA, wedded to Lucretius, found
Her master cold; for when the morn-
    ing flush
Of passion and the first embrace had
    died
Between them, tho' he lov'd her none
    the less,
Yet often when the woman heard his
    foot
Return from pacings in the field, and
    ran
To greet him with a kiss, the master
    took
Small notice, or austerely, for—his
    mind

Half buried in some weightier argument,
Or fancy, borne perhaps upon the rise
And long roll of the Hexameter — he
  past
To turn and ponder those three hundred scrolls
Left by the Teacher, whom he held
  divine.
She brook'd it not; but wrathful, petulant,
Dreaming some rival, sought and
  found a witch
Who brew'd the philtre which had
  power, they said,
To lead an errant passion home again.
And this, at times, she mingled with
  his drink,
And this destroy'd him; for the wicked
  broth
Confused the chemic labor of the
  blood,
And tickling the brute brain within
  the man's
Made havoc among those tender cells,
  and check'd
His power to shape: he loathed himself; and once
After a tempest woke upon a morn
That mock'd him with returning calm,
  and cried:

  "Storm in the night! for thrice I
    heard the rain
Rushing; and once the flash of a
  thunderbolt —
Methought I never saw so fierce a
  fork —
Struck out the streaming mountainside, and show'd
A riotous confluence of watercourses
Blanching and billowing in a hollow
  of it,
Where all but yester-eve was dusty-
  dry.

  "Storm, and what dreams, ye holy
    Gods, what dreams!
For thrice I waken'd after dreams.
  Perchance
We do but recollect the dreams that
  come

Just ere the waking: terrible! for it
  seem'd
A void was made in Nature; all her
  bonds
Crack'd; and I saw the flaring atom-
  streams
And torrents of her myriad universe,
Ruining along the illimitable inane,
Fly on to clash together again, and
  make
Another and another frame of things
For ever: that was mine, my dream, I
  knew it —
Of and belonging to me, as the dog
With inward yelp and restless forefoot
  plies
His function of the woodland: but the
  next!
I thought that all the blood by Sylla
  shed
Came driving rainlike down again on
  earth,
And where it dash'd the reddening
  meadow, sprang
No dragon warriors from Cadmean
  teeth,
For these I thought my dream would
  show to me,
But girls, Hetairai, curious in their art,
Hired animalisms, vile as those that
  made
The mulberry-faced Dictator's orgies
  worse
Than aught they fable of the quiet
  Gods.
And hands they mixt, and yell'd and
  round me drove
In narrowing circles till I yell'd again
Half-suffocated, and sprang up, and
  saw —
Was it the first beam of my latest
  day?

  "Then, then, from utter gloom stood
    out the breasts,
The breasts of Helen, and hoveringly
  a sword
Now over and now under, now direct,
Pointed itself to pierce, but sank down
  shamed
At all that beauty; and as I stared, a
  fire,

The fire that left a roofless Ilion,
Shot out of them, and scorch'd me
    that I woke.

  " Is this thy vengeance, holy Venus,
    thine,
Because I would not one of thine own
    doves,
Not ev'n a rose, were offer'd to thee ?
    thine,
Forgetful how my rich procemion
    makes
Thy glory fly along the Italian field,
In lays that will outlast thy Deity ?

  " Deity ? nay, thy worshippers. My
    tongue
Trips, or I speak profanely. Which of
    these
Angers thee most, or angers thee at
    all ?
Not if thou be'st of those who, far
    aloof
From envy, hate and pity, and spite
    and scorn,
Live the great life which all our great-
    est fain
Would follow, center'd in eternal calm.

  " Nay, if thou canst, O Goddess, like
    ourselves
Touch, and be touch'd, then would I
    cry to thee
To kiss thy Mavors, roll thy tender
    arms
Round him, and keep him from the
    lust of blood
That makes a steaming slaughter-
    house of Rome.

  " Ay, but I meant not thee ; I meant
    not her,
Whom all the pines of Ida shook to
    see
Slide from that quiet heaven of hers,
    and tempt
The Trojan, while his neat-herds were
    abroad ;
Nor her that o'er her wounded hunter
    wept
Her Deity false in human-amorous
    tears ;

Nor whom her beardless apple-arbiter
Decided fairest. Rather, O ye Gods,
Poet-like, as the great Sicilian called
Calliope to grace his golden verse —
Ay, and this Kypris also — did I take
That popular name of thine to shadow
    forth
The all-generating powers and genial
    heat
Of Nature, when she strikes thro' the
    thick blood
Of cattle, and light is large, and lambs
    are glad
Nosing the mother's udder, and the
    bird
Makes his heart voice amid the blaze
    of flowers :
Which things appear the work of
    mighty Gods.

  " The Gods ! and if I go, *my* work is
    left
Unfinish'd — *if* I go. The Gods, who
    haunt
The lucid interspace of world and
    world,
Where never creeps a cloud, or moves
    a wind,
Nor ever falls the least white star of
    snow,
Nor ever lowest roll of thunder moans,
Nor sound of human sorrow mounts to
    mar
Their sacred everlasting calm ! and
    such,
Not all so fine, nor so divine a calm,
Not such, nor all unlike it, man may
    gain
Letting his own life go. The Gods,
    the Gods !
If all be atoms, how then should the
    Gods
Being atomic not be dissoluble,
Not follow the great law ? My master
    held
That Gods there are, for all men so
    believe.
I prest my footsteps into his, and
    meant
Surely to lead my Memmius in a train
Of flowery clauses onward to the proof
That Gods there are, and deathless.

Meant ?   I meant ?
I have forgotten what I meant: my
  mind
Stumbles, and all my faculties are
  lamed.

" Look where another of our Gods,
  the Sun,
Apollo, Delius, or of older use
All-seeing Hyperion — what you
  will —
Has mounted yonder; since he never
  sware,
Except his wrath were wreak'd on
  wretched man,
That he would only shine among the
  dead
Hereafter; tales! for never yet on
  earth
Could dead flesh creep, or bits of roast-
  ing ox
Moan round the spit — nor knows he
  what he sees ;
King of the East altho' he seem, and
  girt
With song and flame and fragrance,
  slowly lifts
His golden feet on those empurpled
  stairs
That climb into the windy halls of
  heaven :
And here he glances on an eye new-
  born,
And gets for greeting but a wail of
  pain ;
And here he stays upon a freezing
  orb
That fain would gaze upon him to the
  last ;
And here upon a yellow eyelid fall'n
And closed by those who mourn a
  friend in vain,
Not thankful that his troubles are no
  more.
And me, altho' his fire is on my face
Blinding, he sees not, nor at all can
  tell
Whether I mean this day to end my-
  self,
Or lend an ear to Plato where he says,
That men like soldiers may not quit
  the post

Allotted by the Gods : but he that
  holds
The Gods are careless, wherefore need
  he care
Greatly for them, nor rather plunge
  at once,
Being troubled, wholly out of sight,
  and sink
Past earthquake — ay, and gout and
  stone, that break
Body toward death, and palsy, death-
  in-life,
And wretched age — and worst disease
  of all,
These prodigies of myriad naked-
  nesses,
And twisted shapes of lust, unspeak-
  able,
Abominable, strangers at my hearth
Not welcome, harpies miring every
  dish,
The phantom husks of something
  foully done,
And fleeting thro' the boundless uni-
  verse,
And blasting the long quiet of my
  breast
With animal heat and dire insanity?

" How should the mind, except it
  loved them, clasp
These idols to herself ? or do they fly
Now thinner, and now thicker, like
  the flakes
In a fall of snow, and so press in, per-
  force
Of multitude, as crowds that in an
  hour
Of civic tumult jam the doors, and
  bear
The keepers down, and throng, their
  rags and they
The basest, far into that council-hall
Where sit the best and stateliest of
  the land ?

" Can I not fling this horror off me
  again,
Seeing with how great ease Nature
  can smile,
Balmier and nobler from her bath of
  storm,

At random ravage? and how easily
The mountain there has cast his
   cloudy slough,
Now towering o'er him in serenest air,
A mountain o'er a mountain,—ay,
   and within
All hollow as the hopes and fears of
   men?

   "But who was he, that in the gar-
   den snared
Picus and Faunus, rustic Gods? a tale
To laugh at—more to laugh at in
   myself—
Nor look! what is it? there? yon
   arbutus
Totters; a noiseless riot underneath
Strikes through the wood, sets all the
   tops quivering—
The mountain quickens into Nymph
   and Faun;
And here an Oread—how the sun
   delights
To glance and shift about her slippery
   sides,
And rosy knees and supple rounded-
   ness,
And budded bosom-peaks—who this
   way runs
Before the rest—A satyr, a satyr, see,
Follows; but him I proved impossible;
Twy-natured is no nature: yet he
   draws
Nearer and nearer, and I scan him
   now
Beastlier than any phantom of his
   kind
That ever butted his rough brother-
   brute
For lust or lusty blood or provender:
I hate, abhor, spit, sicken at him; and
   she
Loathes him as well; such a precipi-
   tate heel,
Fledged as it were with Mercury's
   ankle-wing,
Whirls her to me: but will she fling
   herself,
Shameless upon me? Catch her,
   goat-foot: nay,
Hide, hide them, million-myrtled
   wilderness,

And cavern-shadowing laurels, hide!
   do I wish—
What?—that the bush were leafless?
   or to whelm
All of them in one massacre? O ye
   Gods,
I know you careless, yet, behold, to
   you
From childly wont and ancient use I
   call—
I thought I lived securely as your-
   selves—
No lewdness, narrowing envy, monkey-
   spite,
No madness of ambition, avarice,
   none:
No larger feast than under plane or
   pine
With neighbors laid along the grass,
   to take
Only such cups as left us friendly-
   warm,
Affirming each his own philosophy—
Nothing to mar the sober majesties
Of settled, sweet, Epicurean life.
But now it seems some unseen mon-
   ster lays
His vast and filthy hands upon my
   will,
Wrenching it backward into his; and
   spoils
My bliss in being; and it was not
   great;
For save when shutting reasons up in
   rhythm,
Or Heliconian honey in living words,
To make a truth less harsh, I often
   grew
Tired of so much within our little life,
Or of so little in our little life—
Poor little life that toddles half an
   hour
Crown'd with a flower or two, and
   there an end—
And since the nobler pleasure seems
   to fade,
Why should I, beastlike as I find my-
   self,
Not manlike end myself?—our privi-
   lege—
What beast has heart to do it? And
   what man,

What Roman would be dragg'd in triumph thus ?
Not I; not he, who bears one name with her
Whose death-blow struck the dateless doom of kings,
When, brooking not the Tarquin in her veins,
She made her blood in sight of Collatine
And all his peers, flushing the guiltless air,
Spout from the maiden fountain in her heart.
And from it sprang the Commonwealth, which breaks
As I am breaking now !

     " And therefore now
Let her, that is the womb and tomb of all,
Great Nature, take, and forcing far apart
Those blind beginnings that have made me man,
Dash them anew together at her will
Thro' all her cycles — into man once more,
Or beast or bird or fish, or opulent flower :
But till this cosmic order everywhere
Shatter'd into one earthquake in one day
Cracks all to pieces, — and that hour perhaps
Is not so far when momentary man
Shall seem no more a something to himself,
But he, his hopes and hates, his homes and fanes,
And even his bones long laid within the grave,
The very sides of the grave itself shall pass,
Vanishing, atom and void, atom and void,
Into the unseen for ever, — till that hour,
My golden work in which I told a truth
That stays the rolling Ixionian wheel,
And numbs the Fury's ringlet-snake, and plucks

The mortal soul from out immortal hell,
Shall stand : ay, surely : then it fails at last
And perishes as I must ; for O Thou,
Passionless bride, divine Tranquillity,
Yearn'd after by the wisest of the wise,
Who fail to find thee, being as thou art
Without one pleasure and without one pain,
Howbeit I know thou surely must be mine
Or soon or late, yet out of season, thus
I woo thee roughly, for thou carest not
How roughly men may woo thee so they win —
Thus — thus : the soul flies out and dies in the air."

  With that he drove the knife into his side :
She heard him raging, heard him fall ; ran in,
Beat breast, tore hair, cried out upon herself
As having fail'd in duty to him, shriek'd
That she but meant to win him back, fell on him,
Clasp'd, kiss'd him, wail'd : he answer'd, " Care not thou !
Thy duty ? What is duty ? Fare thee well ! "

ODE ON THE DEATH OF THE DUKE OF WELLINGTON.

PUBLISHED IN 1852.

I.

BURY the Great Duke
  With an empire's lamentation,
Let us bury the Great Duke
  To the noise of the mourning of a mighty nation,
Mourning when their leaders fall,
Warriors carry the warrior's pall,
And sorrow darkens hamlet and hall.

II.

Where shall we lay the man whom
   we deplore ?
Here, in streaming London's central
   roar.
Let the sound of those he wrought for,
And the feet of those he fought for,
Echo round his bones for evermore.

III.

Lead out the pageant : sad and slow,
As fits an universal woe,
Let the long long procession go,
And let the sorrowing crowd about it
   grow,
And let the mournful martial music
   blow ;
The last great Englishman is low.

IV.

Mourn, for to us he seems the last,
Remembering all his greatness in the
   Past.
No more in soldier fashion will he
   greet
With lifted hand the gazer in the
   street.
O friends, our chief state-oracle is
   mute :
Mourn for the man of long-enduring
   blood,
The statesman-warrior, moderate, res-
   olute,
Whole in himself, a common good.
Mourn for the man of amplest influ-
   ence,
Yet clearest of ambitious crime,
Our greatest yet with least pretence,
Great in council and great in war,
Foremost captain of his time,
Rich in saving common-sense,
And, as the greatest only are,
In his simplicity sublime.
O good gray head which all men knew,
O voice from which their omens all
   men drew,
O iron nerve to true occasion true,
O fall'n at length that tower of
   strength
Which stood four-square to all the
   winds that blew !

Such was he whom we deplore.
The long self-sacrifice of life is o'er.
The great World-victor's victor will
   be seen no more.

V.

All is over and done :
Render thanks to the **Giver,**
England, for thy son.
Let the bell be toll'd.
Render thanks to the Giver,
And render him to the mould.
Under the cross of gold
That shines over city and river,
There he shall rest for ever
Among the wise and the bold.
Let the bell be toll'd :
And a reverent people behold
The towering car, the sable steeds :
Bright let it be with its blazon'd
   deeds,
Dark in its funeral fold.
Let the bell be toll'd :
And a deeper knell in the heart be
   knoll'd ;
And the sound of the sorrowing an-
   them roll'd
Thro' the dome of the golden cross ;
And the volleying cannon thunder his
   loss ;
He knew their voices of old.
For many a time in many a clime
His captain's-ear has heard them
   boom
Bellowing victory, bellowing doom :
When he with those deep voices
   wrought,
Guarding realms and kings from
   shame ;
With those deep voices our dead cap-
   tain taught
The tyrant, and asserts his claim
In that dread sound to the great name
Which he has worn so pure of blame,
In praise and in dispraise the same,
A man of well-attemper'd frame.
O civic muse, to such a name,
To such a name for ages long,
To such a name,
Preserve a broad approach of fame,
And ever-echoing avenues of song.

VI.

Who is he that cometh, like an honor'd guest,
With banner and with music, with soldier and with priest,
With a nation weeping, and breaking on my rest?
Mighty Seaman, this is he
Was great by land as thou by sea.
Thine island loves thee well, thou famous man,
The greatest sailor since our world began.
Now, to the roll of muffled drums,
To thee the greatest soldier comes;
For this is he
Was great by land as thou by sea;
His foes were thine; he kept us free;
O give him welcome, this is he
Worthy of our gorgeous rites,
And worthy to be laid by thee;
For this is England's greatest son,
He that gain'd a hundred fights,
Nor ever lost an English gun:
This is he that far away
Against the myriads of Assaye
Clash'd with his fiery few and won;
And underneath another sun,
Warring on a later day,
Round affrighted Lisbon drew
The treble works, the vast designs
Of his labor'd rampart-lines,
Where he greatly stood at bay,
Whence he issued forth anew,
And ever great and greater grew,
Beating from the wasted vines
Back to France her banded swarms,
Back to France with countless blows,
Till o'er the hills her eagles flew
Beyond the Pyrenean pines,
Follow'd up in valley and glen
With blare of bugle, clamor of men,
Roll of cannon and clash of arms,
And England pouring on her foes.
Such a war had such a close.
Again their ravening eagle rose
In anger, wheel'd on Europe-shadowing wings,
And barking for the thrones of kings;
Till one that sought but Duty's iron crown
On that loud Sabbath shook the spoiler down;
A day of onsets of despair!
Dash'd on every rocky square
Their surging charges foam'd themselves away;
Last, the Prussian trumpet blew;
Thro' the long-tormented air
Heaven flash'd a sudden jubilant ray,
And down we swept and charged and overthrew.
So great a soldier taught us there,
What long-enduring hearts could do
In that world earthquake, Waterloo!
Mighty Seaman, tender and true,
And pure as he from taint of craven guile,
O saviour of the silver-coasted isle,
O shaker of the Baltic and the Nile,
If aught of things that here befall
Touch a spirit among things divine,
If love of country move thee there at all,
Be glad, because his bones are laid by thine!
And thro' the centuries let a people's voice
In full acclaim,
A people's voice,
The proof and echo of all human fame,
A people's voice, when they rejoice
At civic revel and pomp and game,
Attest their great commander's claim
With honor, honor, honor, honor to him,
Eternal honor to his name.

VII.

A people's voice! we are a people yet.
Tho' all men else their nobler dreams forget,
Confused by brainless mobs and lawless Powers;
Thank Him who isled us here, and roughly set
His Briton in blown seas and storming showers,
We have a voice, with which to pay the debt
Of boundless love and reverence and regret

To those great men who fought, and
  kept it ours.
And keep it ours, O God, from brute
  control;
O Statesmen, guard us, guard the eye,
  the soul
Of Europe, keep our noble England
  whole,
And save the one true seed of free-
  dom sown
Betwixt a people and their ancient
  throne,
That sober freedom out of which
  there springs
Our loyal passion for our temperate
  kings;
For, saving that, ye help to save man-
  kind
Till public wrong be crumbled into
  dust,
And drill the raw world for the march
  of mind,
Till crowds at length be sane and
  crowns be just.
But wink no more in slothful over-
  trust.
Remember him who led your hosts;
He bade you guard the sacred coasts.
Your cannons moulder on the seaward
  wall;
His voice is silent in your council-hall
For ever; and whatever tempests lour
For ever silent; even if they broke
In thunder, silent; yet remember all
He spoke among you, and the Man
  who spoke;
Who never sold the truth to serve the
  hour,
Nor palter'd with Eternal God for
  power;
Who let the turbid streams of rumor
  flow
Thro' either babbling world of high
  and low;
Whose life was work, whose language
  rife
With rugged maxims hewn from life;
Who never spoke against a foe;
Whose eighty winters freeze with one
  rebuke
All great self-seekers trampling on
  the right:

Truth-teller was our England's Alfred
  named;
Truth-lover was our English Duke;
Whatever record leap to light
He never shall be shamed.

VIII.

Lo, the leader in these glorious wars
Now to glorious burial slowly borne,
Follow'd by the brave of other lands,
He, on whom from both her open
  hands
Lavish Honor shower'd all her stars,
And affluent Fortune emptied all her
  horn.
Yea, let all good things await
Him who cares not to be great,
But as he saves or serves the state.
Not once or twice in our rough island-
  story,
The path of duty was the way to glory:
He that walks it, only thirsting
For the right, and learns to deaden
Love of self, before his journey closes,
He shall find the stubborn thistle
  bursting
Into glossy purples, which outredden
All voluptuous garden-roses.
Not once or twice in our fair island-
  story,
The path of duty was the way to glory:
He, that ever following her commands,
On with toil of heart and knees and
  hands,
Thro' the long gorge to the far light
  has won
His path upward, and prevail'd,
Shall find the toppling crags of Duty
  scaled
Are close upon the shining table-
  lands
To which our God Himself is moon
  and sun.
Such was he: his work is done.
But while the races of mankind en-
  dure,
Let his great example stand
Colossal, seen of every land,
And keep the soldier firm, the states-
  man pure:
Till in all lands and thro' all human
  story

The path of duty be the way to glory:
And let the land whose hearts he
    saved from shame
For many and many an age proclaim
At civic revel and pomp and game,
And when the long-illumined cities
    flame,
Their ever-loyal iron leader's fame,
With honor, honor, honor, honor to
    him,
Eternal honor to his name.

IX.

Peace, his triumph will be sung
By some yet unmoulded tongue
Far on in summers that we shall not
    see:
Peace, it is a day of pain
For one about whose patriarchal knee
Late the little children clung:
O peace, it is a day of pain
For one, upon whose hand and heart
    and brain
Once the weight and fate of Europe
    hung.
Ours the pain, be his the gain!
More than is of man's degree
Must be with us, watching here
At this, our great solemnity.
Whom we see not we revere;
We revere, and we refrain
From talk of battles loud and vain,
And brawling memories all too free
For such a wise humility
As befits a solemn fane:
We revere, and while we hear
The tides of Music's golden sea
Setting toward eternity,
Uplifted high in heart and hope are
    we,
Until we doubt not that for one so
    true
There must be other nobler work to
    do
Than when he fought at Waterloo,
And Victor he must ever be.
For tho' the Giant Ages heave the
    hill
And break the shore, and evermore
Make and break, and work their will;
Tho' world on world in myriad myriads
    roll

Round us, each with different powers,
And other forms of life than ours,
What know we greater than the soul?
On God and Godlike men we build our
    trust.
Hush, the Dead March wails in the
    people's ears:
The dark crowd moves, and there are
    sobs and tears:
The black earth yawns: the mortal
    disappears;
Ashes to ashes, dust to dust;
He is gone who seem'd so great. —
Gone; but nothing can bereave him
Of the force he made his own
Being here, and we believe him
Something far advanced in State,
And that he wears a truer crown
Than any wreath that man can weave
    him.
Speak no more of his renown,
Lay your earthly fancies down,
And in the vast cathedral leave him.
God accept him, Christ receive him.

THE THIRD OF FEBRUARY,
1852.

MY Lords, we heard you speak: you
    told us all
    That England's honest censure went
        too far;
That our free press should cease to
    brawl,
    Not sting the fiery Frenchman into
        war.
It was our ancient privilege, my Lords,
To fling whate'er we felt, not fearing,
    into words.

We love not this French God, the
    child of Hell,
    Wild War, who breaks the converse
        of the wise;
But though we love kind Peace so
    well,
    We dare not ev'n by silence sanction
        lies.
It might be safe our censures to with-
    draw;
And yet, my Lords, not well: there is
    a higher law.

As long as we remain, we must speak free,
  Tho' all the storm of Europe on us break ;
No little German state are we,
  But the one voice in Europe : we *must* speak ;
That if to-night our greatness were struck dead,
There might be left some record of the things we said.

If you be fearful, then must we be bold.
  Our Britain cannot salve a tyrant o'er.
Better the waste Atlantic roll'd
On her and us and ours for evermore.
What ! have we fought for Freedom from our prime,
At last to dodge and palter with a public crime ?

Shall we fear *him* ? our own we never fear'd.
  From our first Charles by force we wrung our claims.
Prick'd by the Papal spur, we rear'd,
  We flung the burden of the second James.
I say, we *never* feared ! and as for these,
We broke them on the land, we drove them on the seas.

And you, my Lords, you make the people muse
  In doubt if you be of our Barons' breed —
Were those your sires who fought at Lewes ?
  Is this the manly strain of Runny-mede ?
O fall'n nobility, that, overawed,
Would lisp in honey'd whispers of this monstrous fraud !

We feel, at least, that silence here were sin,
  Not ours the fault if we have feeble hosts —
If easy patrons of their kin

Have left the last free race with naked coasts !
They knew the precious things they had to guard :
For us, we will not spare the tyrant one hard word.

Tho' niggard throats of Manchester may bawl,
  What England was, shall her true sons forget ?
We are not cotton-spinners all,
  But some love England and her honor yet.
And these in our Thermopylæ shall stand,
And hold against the world this honor of the land.

THE CHARGE OF THE LIGHT BRIGADE.

I.

HALF a league, half a league,
  Half a league onward,
All in the valley of Death
  Rode the six hundred.
" Forward, the Light Brigade !
Charge for the guns," he said :
Into the valley of Death
  Rode the six hundred.

II.

" Forward, the Light Brigade ! "
Was there a man dismay'd ?
Not tho' the soldier knew
  Some one had blunder'd :
Theirs not to make reply,
Theirs not to reason why,
Theirs but to do and die :
Into the valley of Death
  Rode the six hundred.

III.

Cannon to right of them,
Cannon to left of them,
Cannon in front of them
  Volley'd and thunder'd ;
Storm'd at with shot and shell,
Boldly they rode and well,

THE GRANDMOTHER. — Page 173.

Into the jaws of Death,
Into the mouth of Hell
 Rode the six hundred.

IV.

Flash'd all their sabres bare,
Flash'd as they turn'd in air
Sabring the gunners there,
Charging an army, while
 All the world wonder'd :
Plunged in the battery-smoke
Right thro' the line they broke;
Cossack and Russian
Reel'd from the sabre-stroke
 Shatter'd and sunder'd.
Then they rode back, but not,
 Not the six hundred.

V.

Cannon to right of them,
Cannon to left of them,
Cannon behind them
 Volley'd and thunder'd;
Storm'd at with shot and shell,
While horse and hero fell,
They that had fought so well
Came thro' the jaws of Death,
Back from the mouth of Hell,
All that was left of them,
 Left of six hundred.

VI.

When can their glory fade?
O the wild charge they made!
 All the world wonder'd.
Honor the charge they made!
Honor the Light Brigade,
 Noble six hundred!

ODE SUNG AT THE OPENING
OF THE INTERNATIONAL
EXHIBITION.

I.

UPLIFT a thousand voices full and
 sweet,
 In this wide hall with earth's inven-
 tion stored,
And praise the invisible universal
 Lord,

Who lets once more in peace the nations meet,
 Where Science, Art, and Labor
 have outpour'd
Their myriad horns of plenty at our
 feet.

II.

O silent father of our Kings to be
Mourn'd in this golden hour of jubilee,
For this, for all, we weep our thanks
 to thee !

III.

The world-compelling plan was
 thine, —
And, lo ! the long laborious miles
Of Palace ; lo ! the giant aisles,
Rich in model and design ;
Harvest-tool and husbandry,
Loom and wheel and enginery,
Secrets of the sullen mine,
Steel and gold, and corn and wine,
Fabric rough, or fairy-fine,
Sunny tokens of the Line,
Polar marvels, and a feast
Of wonder, out of West and East,
And shapes and hues of Art divine !
All of beauty, all of use,
That one fair planet can produce,
 Brought from under every star,
Blown from over every main,
And mixt, as life is mixt with pain,
 The works of peace with works of
 war.

IV.

 Is the goal so far away ?
 Far, how far no tongue can say,
 Let us dream our dream to-day.

V.

O ye, the wise who think, the wise who
 reign,
From growing commerce loose her
 latest chain,
And let the fair white-wing'd peace-
 maker fly
To happy havens under all the sky,
And mix the seasons and the golden
 hours ;
Till each man find his own in all
 men's good,

And all men work in noble brotherhood,
Breaking their mailed fleets and
armed towers,
And ruling by obeying Nature's
powers,
And gathering all the fruits of earth
and crown'd with all her flowers.

A WELCOME TO ALEXANDRA.
MARCH 7, 1863.

SEA-KINGS' daughter from over the
sea,   Alexandra!
Saxon and Norman and Dane are we,
But all of us Danes in our welcome
of thee,   Alexandra!
Welcome her, thunders of fort and of
fleet!
Welcome her, thundering cheer of the
street!
Welcome her, all things youthful and
sweet,
Scatter the blossom under her feet!
Break, happy land, into earlier flow-
ers!
Make music, O bird, in the new-budded
bowers!
Blazon your mottoes of blessing and
prayer!
Welcome her, welcome her, all that is
ours!
Warble, O bugle, and trumpet, blare!
Flags, flutter out upon turrets and
towers!
Flames, on the windy headland flare!
Utter your jubilee, steeple and spire!
Clash, ye bells, in the merry March
air!
Flash, ye cities, in rivers of fire!
Rush to the roof, sudden rocket, and
higher
Melt into stars for the land's desire!
Roll and rejoice, jubilant voice,
Roll as a ground-swell dash'd on the
strand,
Roar as the sea when he welcomes the
land,
And welcome her, welcome the land's
desire,

The sea-kings' daughter as happy as
fair,
Blissful bride of a blissful heir,
Bride of the heir of the kings of the
sea —
O joy to the people and joy to the
throne,
Come to us, love us and make us your
own:
For Saxon or Dane or Norman we,
Teuton or Celt, or whatever we be,
We are each all Dane in our welcome
of thee,   Alexandra!

A WELCOME TO HER ROYAL HIGHNESS MARIE ALEX- ANDROVNA, DUCHESS OF EDINBURGH.
MARCH 7, 1874.
I.

THE Son of him with whom we strove
for power—
Whose will is lord thro' all his
world-domain —
Who made the serf a man, and burst
his chain —
Has given our Prince his own imperial
Flower,
Alexandrovna.
And welcome, Russian flower, a
people's pride,
To Britain, when her flowers begin
to blow!
From love to love, from home to
home you go,
From mother unto mother, stately
bride,
Marie Alexandrovna!

II.
The golden news along the steppes is
blown,
And at thy name the Tartar tents
are stirr'd;
Elburz and all the Caucasus have
heard;
And all the sultry palms of India
known,
Alexandrovna.

The voices of our universal sea
  On capes of Afric as on cliffs of
    Kent,
  The Maoris and that Isle of Conti-
    nent,
And loyal pines of Canada murmur
  thee,
            Marie Alexandrovna!

III.

Fair empires branching, both, in lusty
  life! —
  Yet Harold's England fell to Nor-
    man swords;
  Yet thine own land has bow'd to
    Tartar hordes
Since English Harold gave its throne
  a wife,
            Alexandrovna!
For thrones and peoples are as waifs
  that swing,
  And float or fall, in endless ebb and
    flow;
  But who love best have best the
    grace to know
That Love by right divine is deathless
  king,
            Marie Alexandrovna!

IV.

And Love has led thee to the stranger
  land,

Where men are bold and strongly
  say their say; —
  See, empire upon empire smiles to-
    day,
As thou with thy young lover hand in
  hand,
            Alexandrovna!
So now thy fuller life is in the west,
  Whose hand at home was gracious
    to thy poor:
  Thy name was blest within the nar-
    row door;
Here also, Marie, shall thy name be
  blest,
            Marie Alexandrovna!

V.

Shall fears and jealous hatreds flame
  again?
  Or at thy coming, Princess, every-
    where,
  The blue heaven break, and some
    diviner air
Breathe thro' the world and change
  the hearts of men,
            Alexandrovna!
But hearts that change not, love that
  cannot cease,
  And peace be yours, the peace of
    soul in soul!
  And howsoever this wild world may
    roll,
Between your people's truth and man-
  ful peace,
        Alfred — Alexandrovna!

THE GRANDMOTHER.

I.

AND Willy, my eldest-born, is gone, you say, little Anne?
Ruddy and white, and strong on his legs, he looks like a man.
And Willy's wife has written: she never was over-wise,
Never the wife for Willy: he wouldn't take my advice.

II.

For, Annie, you see, her father was not the man to save,
Hadn't a head to manage, and drank himself into his grave.
Pretty enough, very pretty! but I was against it for one.
Eh! — but he wouldn't hear me — and Willy, you say, is gone.

III.

Willy, my beauty, my eldest-born, the flower of the flock;
Never a man could fling him: for Willy stood like a rock.
" Here's a leg for a babe of a week!" says doctor; and he would be bound,
There was not his like that year in twenty parishes round.

IV.

Strong of his hands, and strong on his legs, but still of his tongue!
I ought to have gone before him: I wonder he went so young.
I cannot cry for him, Annie: I have not long to stay;
Perhaps I shall see him the sooner, for he lived far away.

V.

Why do you look at me, Annie? you think I am hard and cold;
But all my children have gone before me, I am so old:
I cannot weep for Willy, nor can I weep for the rest;
Only at your age, Annie, I could have wept with the best.

VI.

For I remember a quarrel I had with your father, my dear,
All for a slanderous story, that cost me many a tear.
I mean your grandfather, Annie: it cost me a world of woe,
Seventy years ago, my darling, seventy years ago.

VII.

For Jenny, my cousin, had come to the place, and I knew right well
That Jenny had tript in her time: I knew, but I would not tell.
And she to be coming and slandering me, the base little liar!
But the tongue is a fire as you know, my dear, the tongue is a fire.

VIII.

And the parson made it his text that week, and he said likewise,
That a lie which is half a truth is ever the blackest of lies,
That a lie which is all a lie may be met and fought with outright,
But a lie which is part a truth is a harder matter to fight.

IX.

And Willy had not been down to the farm for a week and a day;
And all things look'd half-dead, tho' it was the middle of May.
Jenny, to slander me, who knew what Jenny had been!
But soiling another, Annie, will never make one's self clean.

X.

And I cried myself well-nigh blind, and all of an evening late
I climb'd to the top of the garth, and stood by the road at the gate.
The moon like a rick on fire was rising over the dale,
And whit, whit, whit, in the bush beside me chirrupt the nightingale.

XI.

All of a sudden he stopt: there past by the gate of the farm,
Willy, — he didn't see me, — and Jenny hung on his arm.
Out into the road I started, and spoke I scarce knew how;
Ah, there's no fool like the old one — it makes me angry now.

XII.

Willy stood up like a man, and look'd the thing that he meant;
Jenny, the viper, made me a mocking curtsey and went.
And I said, "Let us part: in a hundred years it'll all be the same.
You cannot love me at all, if you love not my good name."

XIII.

And he turn'd, and I saw his eyes all wet, in the sweet moonshine:
"Sweetheart, I love you so well that your good name is mine.
And what do I care for Jane, let her speak of you well or ill;
But marry me out of hand: we two shall be happy still."

XIV.

"Marry you, Willy!" said I, "but I needs must speak my mind,
And I fear you'll listen to tales, be jealous and hard and unkind."
But he turn'd and claspt me in his arms, and answer'd, "No, love, no;"
Seventy years ago, my darling, seventy years ago.

XV.

So Willy and I were wedded : I wore a lilac gown;
And the ringers rang with a will, and he gave the ringers a crown.
But the first that ever I bare was dead before he was born,
Shadow and shine is life, little Annie, flower and thorn.

XVI.

That was the first time, too, that ever I thought of death.
There lay the sweet little body that never had drawn a breath.
I had not wept, little Anne, not since I had been a wife;
But I wept like a child that day, for the babe had fought for his life.

XVII.

His dear little face was troubled, as if with anger or pain:
I look'd at the still little body — his trouble had all been in vain.
For Willy I cannot weep, I shall see him another morn:
But I wept like a child for the child that was dead before he was born.

XVIII.

But he cheer'd me, my good man, for he seldom said me nay:
Kind, like a man, was he; like a man, too, would have his way:
Never jealous — not he: we had many a happy year;
And he died, and I could not weep — my own time seem'd so near.

XIX.

But I wish'd it had been God's will that I, too, then could have died:
I began to be tired a little, and fain had slept at his side.
And that was ten years back, or more, if I don't forget:
But as to the children, Annie, they're all about me yet.

XX.

Pattering over the boards, my Annie who left me at two,
Patter she goes, my own little Annie, an Annie like you:
Pattering over the boards, she comes and goes at her will,
While Harry is in the five-acre and Charlie ploughing the hill.

XXI.

And Harry and Charlie, I hear them too — they sing to their team:
Often they come to the door in a pleasant kind of a dream.
They come and sit by my chair, they hover about my bed —
I am not always certain if they be alive or dead.

XXII.

And yet I know for a truth, there's none of them left alive;
For Harry went at sixty, your father at sixty-five:
And Willy, my eldest-born, at nigh threescore and ten;
I knew them all as babies, and now they're elderly men.

XXIII.

For mine is a time of peace, it is not often I grieve;
I am oftener sitting at home in my father's farm at eve:
And the neighbors come and laugh and gossip, and so do I;
I find myself often laughing at things that have long gone by.

XXIV.

To be sure the preacher says, our sins should make us sad:
But mine is a time of peace, and there is Grace to be had;
And God, not man, is the Judge of us all when life shall cease
And in this Book, little Annie, the message is one of Peace.

XXV.

And age is a time of peace, so it be free from pain,
And happy has been my life; but I would not live it again.
I seem to be tired a little, that's all, and long for rest;
Only at your age, Annie, I could have wept with the best.

XXVI.

So Willy has gone, my beauty, my eldest-born, my flower;
But how can I weep for Willy, he has but gone for an hour, —
Gone for a minute, my son, from this room into the next;
I, too, shall go in a minute.   What time have I to be vext?

XXVII.

And Willy's wife has written, she never was over-wise.
Get me my glasses, Annie : thank God that I keep my eyes.
There is but a trifle left you, when I shall have past away.
But stay with the old woman now : you cannot have long to stay.

NORTHERN FARMER.

OLD STYLE.

I.

WHEER 'asta beän saw long and meä liggin' 'ere aloän ?
Noorse ? thoort nowt o' a noorse : whoy, Doctor's abeän an' agoän :
Says that I moänt 'a naw moor aäle : but I beänt a fool :
Git ma my aäle, fur I beänt a-gooin' to breäk my rule.

II.

Doctors, they knaws nowt, fur a says what's nawways true :
Naw soort o' koind o' use to saäy the things that a do.
I've 'ed my point o' aäle ivry noight sin' I beän 'ere,
An' I've 'ed my quart ivry market-noight for foorty year.

III.

Parson's a beän loikewoise, an' a sittin' ere o' my bed.
"The amoighty's a taäkin o' you to 'issén, my friend," a said,
An' a towd ma my sins, an's toithe were due, an' I gied it in hond ;
I done moy duty boy 'um, as I 'a done boy the lond.

IV.

Larn'd a ma' beä.   I reckons I 'annot sa mooch to larn.
But a cast oop, thot a did, 'boot Bessy Marris's barne.
Thaw a knaws I hallus voäted wi' Squoire an' choorch an' staäte,
An' i' the woost o' toimes I wur niver agin the raäte.

V.

An' I hallus coom'd to's choorch afoor moy Sally wur deäd,
An' 'eerd 'um a bummin' awaäy loike a buzzard-clock[1] ower my 'eäd,
An' I niver knaw'd whot a meän'd but I thowt a 'ad summut to saäy,
An' I thowt a said whot a owt to 'a said an' I coom'd awaäy.

VI.

Bessy Marris's barne ! tha knaws she laäid it to meä.
Mowt a bean, mayhap, for she wur a bad un, sheä.
'Siver, I kep 'um, I kep 'um, my lass, tha mun understond ;
I done moy duty boy 'um as I 'a done boy the lond.

[1] Cockchafer.

VII.

But Parson a cooms an' a goos, an' a says it eäsy an' freeä
"The amoighty's a taäkin o' you to 'issén, my friend," says 'eä.
I weänt saäy men be loiars, thaw summum said it in 'aäste :
But 'e reäds wonn sarmin a weeük, an' I 'a stubb'd Thurnaby waäste

VIII.

D'ya moind the waäste, my lass ? naw, naw, tha was not born then;
Theer wur a boggle in it, I often 'eerd 'um mysen ;
Moäst loike a butter-bump,[1] fur I 'eerd 'um aboot an' aboot,
But I stubb'd 'um oop wi' the lot, an' raäved an' rembled 'um oot.

IX.

Keäper's it wur ; fo' they fun 'um theer a-laäid of 'is faäce
Doon i' the woild 'enemies [2] afoor I coom'd to the plaäce.
Noäks or Thimbleby — toäner 'ed shot 'um as deäd as a naäil.
Noäks wur 'ang'd for it oop at 'soize — but git ma my aäle.

X.

Dubbut loook at the waäste : theer warn't not feeäd for a cow ;
Nowt at all but bracken an' fuzz, an' loook at it now —
Warnt worth nowt a haäcre, an' now theer's lots o' feeäd,
Fourscoor yows upon it an' some on it doon i' seeäd.

XI.

Nobbut a bit on it's left, an' I meän'd to 'a stubb'd it at fall,
Done it ta-year I meän'd, an' runn'd plow thruff it an' all,
If godamoighty an' parson 'ud nobbut let me aloän,
Meä, wi' haäte oonderd haäcre o' Squoire's an' lond o' my oän.

XII.

Do godamoighty knaw what a's doing a-taäkin' o' meä ?
I beänt wonn as saws 'ere a beän an' yonder a peä ;
An' Squoire 'ull be sa mad an' all — a' dear a' dear !
And I 'a managed for Squoire coom Michaelmas thutty year.

XIII.

A mowt 'a taäen owd Joänes, as 'ant nor a 'aäpoth o' sense,
Or a mowt 'a taäen young Robins — a niver mended a fence :
But godamoighty a moost taäke meä an' taäke ma now
Wi' aäf the cows to cauve an' Thurnaby hoälms to plow !

XIV.

Loook 'ow quoloty smoiles when they seeäs ma a passin' boy,
Says to thessén naw doubt "what a man a beä sewer-loy !"
Fur they knaws what I beän to Squoire sin fust a coom'd to the 'All ;
I done moy duty by Squoire an' I done moy duty boy hall.

[1] Bittern.   [2] Anemones.

"Nowt at all but bracken an' fuzz, — an' loook at it now!"

Page 178.

xv.

Squoire's i' Lunnon, an' summun I reckons 'ull 'a to wroite,
For whoä's to howd the lond ater meä thot muddles ma quoit;
Sartin-sewer I beä, thot a weänt niver give it to Joänes,
Naw, nor a moänt to Robins — a niver rembles the stoäns.

xvl

But summun 'ull come ater meä mayhap wi' 'is kittle o' steäm
Huzzin' an' maäzin' the blessed feälds wi' the Divil's oän teäm.
Sin' I mun doy I mun doy, thaw loife they says is sweet,
But sin' I mun doy I mun doy, for I couldn abeär to see it.

xvii.

What atta stannin' theer fur, an' doesn bring ma the aäle ?
Doctor's a 'toättler, lass, an a's hallus i' the owd taäle ;
I weänt breäk rules fur Doctor, a knaws naw moor nor a floy ;
Git ma my aäle I tell tha, an' if I mun doy I mun doy.

NORTHERN FARMER.

NEW STYLE.

I.

Dosn't thou 'ear my 'erse's legs, as they canters awaäy ?
Proputty, proputty, proputty — that's what I 'ears 'em saäy.
Proputty, proputty, proputty — Sam, thou's an ass for thy paaïns:
Theer's moor sense i' one o' 'is legs nor in all thy braaïns.

II.

Woä — theer's a craw to pluck wi' tha, Sam: yon's parson's 'ouse —
Dosn't thou knaw that a man mun be eäther a man or a mouse ?
Time to think on it then; for thou'll be twenty to weeäk.[1]
Proputty, proputty — woä then woä — let ma 'ear mysén speäk.

III.

Me an' thy muther, Sammy, 'as beän a-talkin' o' thee;
Thou's beän talkin' to muther, an' she beän a te..in' it me.
Thou'll not marry for munny — thou's sweet upo' parson's lass —
Noä — thou'll marry for luvv — an' we boäth on us thinks tha an ass.

IV.

Seeä'd her todaäy goä by — Saäint's daäy — they was ringing the bells.
She's a beauty thou thinks — an' soä is scoors o' gells,
Them as 'as munny an' all — wot's a beauty ? — the flower as blaws.
But proputty, proputty sticks, an' proputty, proputty graws.

[1] This week.

v.

Do'ant be stunt :[1] taäke time : I knaws what maäkes tha sa mad.
Warn't I craäzed fur the lasses mysén when I wur a lad ?
But I knaw'd a Quaäker feller as often 'as towd ma this:
"Doänt thou marry for munny, but goä wheer munny is!"

vi.

An' I went wheer munny war : an' thy muther coom to 'and,
Wi' lots o' munny laaïd by, an' a nicetish bit o' land.
Maäybe she warn't a beauty — I niver giv it a thowt —
But warn't she as good to cuddle an' kiss as a lass as 'ant nowt ?

vii.

Parson's lass 'ant nowt, an' she weänt 'a nowt when 'e's deäd,
Mun be a guvness, lad, or summut, and addle [2] her breäd :
Why ? fur 'e's nobbut a curate, an' weänt niver git naw 'igher ;
An' 'e maäde the bed as 'e ligs on afoor 'e coom'd to the shire.

viii.

An thin 'e coom'd to the parish wi' lots o' Varsity debt,
Stook to his taaïl they did, an' 'e 'ant got shut on 'em yet.
An' 'e ligs on 'is back i' the grip, wi' noän to lend 'im a shove,
Woorse nor a far-welter'd [3] yowe : fur, Sammy, 'e married fur luvv.

ix.

Luvv ? what's luvv ? thou can luvv thy lass an' 'er munny too,
Maakin' 'em goä togither as they've good right to do.
Could'n I luvv thy muther by cause o' 'er munny laaïd by ?
Naäy — fur I luvv'd 'er a vast sight moor fur it : reäson why.

x.

Ay an' thy muther says thou wants to marry the lass,
Cooms of a gentleman burn : an' we boäth on us thinks tha an ass.
Woä then, proputty, wiltha ? — an ass as near as mays nowt[4] —
Woä then. wiltha ? dangtha ! — the bees is as fell as owt.[5]

xi.

Breäk me a bit o' the esh for his 'eäd, lad, out o' the fence !
Gentleman burn ! what's gentleman burn ? is it shillins an' pence ?
Proputty, proputty's ivrything 'ere, an', Sammy, I'm blest
If it isn't the saäme oop yonder, fur them as 'as it's the best.

xii.

Tis'n them as 'as munny as breäks into 'ouses an' steäls,
Them as 'as coäts to their backs an' taäkes their regular meäls.
Noä, but it's them as niver knaws wheer a meäl's to be 'ad.
Taäke my word for it, Sammy, the poor in a loomp is bad.

---

[1] Obstinate.   [2] Earn.
[3] Or fow-welter'd, — said of a sheep lying on its back in the furrow.
[4] Makes nothing.   [5] The flies are as fierce as anything.

XIII.

Them or thir feythers, tha sees, mun 'a beän a laäzy lot,
Fur work mun 'a gone to the gittin' whiniver munny was got.
Feyther 'ad ammost nowt; leastways 'is munny was 'id.
But 'e tued an' moil'd 'issén deäd, an 'e died a good un, 'e did.

XIV.

Loook thou theer wheer Wrigglesby beck cooms out by the 'ill
Feyther run oop to the farm, an' I runs oop to the mill;
An' I'll run oop to the brig, an' that thou'll live to see;
And if thou marries a good un I'll leäve the land to thee.

XV.

Thim's my noätions, Sammy, wheerby I means to stick;
But if thou marries a bad un, I'll leave the land to Dick. —
Coom oop, proputty, proputty — that's what I 'ears 'im saäy —
Proputty, proputty, proputty — canter an' canter awaäy

THE DAISY.

WRITTEN AT EDINBURGH.

O LOVE, what hours were thine and
        mine,
In lands of palm and southern pine;
    In lands of palm, of orange-blossom,
Of olive, aloe, and maize and vine.

What Roman strength Turbìa show'd
In ruin, by the mountain road;
    How like a gem, beneath, the city
Of little Monaco, basking, glow'd.

How richly down the rocky dell
The torrent vineyard streaming fell
    To meet the sun and sunny waters,
That only heaved with a summer swell.

What slender campanili grew
By bays, the peacock's neck in hue;
    Where, here and there, on sandy
        beaches
A milky-bell'd amaryllis blew.

How young Columbus seem'd to rove,
Yet present in his natal grove,
    Now watching high on mountain
        cornice,
And steering, now, from a purple cove,

Now pacing mute by ocean's rim;
Till, in a narrow street and dim,
    I stay'd the wheels at Cogoletto,
And drank, and loyally drank to him.

Nor knew we well what pleased us most,
Not the clipt palm of which they boast;
    But distant color, happy hamlet,
A moulder'd citadel on the coast,

Or tower, or high hill-convent, seen
A light amid its olives green;
    Or olive-hoary cape in ocean;
Or rosy blossom in hot ravine,

Where oleanders flush'd the bed
Of silent torrents, gravel-spread;
    And, crossing, oft we saw the glisten
Of ice, far up on a mountain head.

We loved that hall, tho' white and cold,
Those niched shapes of noble mould,
    A princely people's awful princes,
The grave, severe Genovese of old.

At Florence too what golden hours,
In those long galleries, were ours;
    What drives about the fresh Cascinè,
Or walks in Boboli's ducal bowers.

In bright vignettes, and each com-
plete,
Of tower or duomo, sunny-sweet,
    Or palace, how the city glitter'd,
Thro' cypress avenues, at our feet.

But when we crost the Lombard plain
Remember what a plague of rain ;
    Of rain at Reggio, rain at Parma ;
At Lodi, rain, Piacenza, rain.

And stern and sad (so rare the smiles
Of sunlight) look'd the Lombard piles ;
    Porch-pillars on the lion resting,
And sombre, old, colonnaded aisles.

O Milan, O the chanting quires,
The giant windows' blazon'd fires,
    The height, the space, the gloom,
        the glory !
A mount of marble, a hundred spires !

I climb'd the roofs at break of day ;
Sun-smitten Alps before me lay.
    I stood among the silent statues,
And statued pinnacles, mute as they.

How faintly-flush'd, how phantom-fair,
Was Monte Rosa, hanging there
    A thousand shadowy-pencill'd val-
        leys
And snowy dells in a golden air.

Remember how we came at last
To Como ; shower and storm and blast
    Had blown the lake beyond his limit,
And all was flooded ; and how we past

From Como, when the light was gray,
And in my head, for half the day,
    The rich Virgilian rustic measure
Of Lari Maxume, all the way,

Like ballad-burthen music, kept,
As on The Lariano crept
    To that fair port below the castle
Of Queen Theodolind, where we slept ;

Or hardly slept, but watch'd awake
A cypress in the moonlight shake,
    The moonlight touching o'er a
        terrace
One tall Agavè above the lake.

What more ? we took our last adieu,
And up the snowy Splugen drew,
    But ere we reach'd the highest
        summit
I pluck'd a daisy, I gave it you.

It told of England then to me,
And now it tells of Italy.
    O love, we two shall go no longer
To lands of summer across the sea ;

So dear a life your arms enfold
Whose crying is a cry for gold :
    Yet here to-night in this dark city,
When ill and weary, alone and cold,

I found, tho' crush'd to hard and dry,
This nursling of another sky
    Still in the little book you lent me,
And where you tenderly laid it by :

And I forgot the clouded Forth,
The gloom that saddens Heaven and
        Earth,
    The bitter east, the misty summer
And gray metropolis of the North.

Perchance, to lull the throbs of pain,
Perchance, to charm a vacant brain,
    Perchance, to dream you still be-
        side me,
My fancy fled to the South again.

* * *

TO THE REV. F. D. MAURICE.
JANUARY, 1854.

COME, when no graver cares employ,
Godfather, come and see your boy :
    Your presence will be sun in winter,
Making the little one leap for joy.

For, being of that honest few,
Who give the Fiend himself his due,
    Should eighty-thousand college-
        councils
Thunder " Anathema," friend, at you ;

Should all our churchmen foam in spite
At you, so careful of the right,
    Yet one lay-hearth would give you
        welcome
(Take it and come) to the Isle of
        Wight ;

Where, far from noise and smoke of
    town,
I watch the twilight falling brown
  All round a careless-order'd garden
Close to the ridge of a noble down.

You'll have no scandal while you dine,
But honest talk and wholesome wine,
  And only hear the magpie gossip
Garrulous under a roof of pine :

For groves of pine on either hand,
To break the blast of winter, stand ;
  And further on, the hoary Channel
Tumbles a billow on chalk and sand ;

Where, if below the milky steep
Some ship of battle slowly creep,
  And on thro' zones of light and
    shadow
Glimmer away to the lonely deep,

We might discuss the Northern sin
Which made a selfish war begin ;
  Dispute the claims, arrange the
    chances ;
Emperor, Ottoman, which shall win :

Or whether war's avenging rod
Shall lash all Europe into blood ;
  Till you should turn to dearer
    matters,
Dear to the man that is dear to God ;

How best to help the slender store,
How mend the dwellings, of the poor ;
  How gain in life, as life advances,
Valor and charity more and more.

Come, Maurice, come : the lawn as yet
Is hoar with rime, or spongy-wet ;
  But when the wreath of March has
    blossom'd,
Crocus, anemone, violet,

Or later, pay one visit here,
For those are few we hold as dear ;
  Nor pay but one, but come for
    many,
Many and many a happy year.

WILL.

I.

O WELL for him whose will is strong !
He suffers, but he will not suffer long ;
He suffers, but he cannot suffer
    wrong :
For him nor moves the loud world's
    random mock,
Nor all Calamity's hugest waves con-
    found,
Who seems a promontory of rock,
That, compass'd round with turbulent
    sound,
In middle ocean meets the surging
    shock,
Tempest-buffeted, citadel-crown'd.

II.

But ill for him who, bettering not
    with time,
Corrupts the strength of heaven-
    descended Will,
And ever weaker grows thro' acted
    crime,
Or seeming-genial venial fault,
Recurring and suggesting still !
He seems as one whose footsteps
    halt,
Toiling in immeasurable sand,
And o'er a weary sultry land,
Far beneath a blazing vault,
Sown in a wrinkle in the monstrous
    hill,
The city sparkles like a grain of salt.

IN THE VALLEY OF
CAUTERETZ.

ALL along the valley, stream that
    flashest white,
Deepening thy voice with the deepen-
    ing of the night,
All along the valley, where thy waters
    flow,
I walk'd with one I loved two and
    thirty years ago.
All along the valley, while I walk'd
    to-day,

The two and thirty years were a mist
    that rolls away ;
For all along the valley, down thy
    rocky bed,
Thy living voice to me was as the
    voice of the dead,
And all along the valley, by rock and
    cave and tree,
The voice of the dead was a living
    voice to me.

IN THE GARDEN AT SWAINSTON.

NIGHTINGALES warbled without,
    Within was weeping for thee :
Shadows of three dead men
    Walk'd in the walks with me,
    Shadows of three dead men and
        thou wast one of the three.

Nightingales sang in his woods :
    The Master was far away :
Nightingales warbled and sang
    Of a passion that lasts but a day ;
Still in the house in his coffin the
    Prince of courtesy lay.

Two dead men have I known
    In courtesy like to thee :
Two dead men have I loved
    With a love that ever will be :
Three dead men have I loved, and
    thou art last of the three.

THE FLOWER.

ONCE in a golden hour
    I cast to earth a seed.
Up there came a flower,
    The people said, a weed.

To and fro they went
    Thro' my garden-bower,
And muttering discontent
    Cursed me and my flower.

Then it grew so tall
    It wore a crown of light,
But thieves from o'er the wall
    Stole the seed by night.

Sow'd it far and wide
    By every town and tower,
Till all the people cried,
    "Splendid is the flower."

Read my little fable :
    He that runs may read.
Most can raise the flowers now,
    For all have got the seed.

And some are pretty enough,
    And some are poor indeed ;
And now again the people
    Call it but a weed.

REQUIESCAT.

FAIR is her cottage in its place,
    Where yon broad water sweetly,
        slowly glides.
It sees itself from thatch to base
    Dream in the sliding tides.

And fairer she, but ah how soon to
    die !
    Her quiet dream of life this hour
        may cease.
Her peaceful being slowly passes by
    To some more perfect peace.

THE SAILOR BOY.

HE rose at dawn and, fired with hope,
    Shot o'er the seething harbor-bar,
And reach'd the ship and caught the
    rope,
    And whistled to the morning star.

And while he whistled long and loud
    He heard a fierce mermaiden cry,
"O boy, tho' thou art young and
    proud,
    I see the place where thou wilt lie.

"The sands and yeasty surges mix
    In caves about the dreary bay,
And on thy ribs the limpet sticks,
    And in thy heart the scrawl shall
        play."

"Fool," he answer'd, "death is sure
  To those that stay and those that
    roam,
But I will nevermore endure
  To sit with empty hands at home.

"My mother clings about my neck,
  My sisters crying, 'Stay for shame;'
My father raves of death and wreck,
  They are all to blame, they are all
    to blame.

"God help me! save I take my part
  Of danger on the roaring sea,
A devil rises in my heart,
  Far worse than any death to me."

THE ISLET.

"WHITHER, O whither, love, shall we
  go,
For a score of sweet little summers or
  so?"
The sweet little wife of the singer said,
On the day that follow'd the day she
  was wed,
"Whither, O whither, love, shall we
  go?"
And the singer shaking his curly head
Turn'd as he sat, and struck the keys
There at his right with a sudden crash,
Singing, "And shall it be over the seas
With a crew that is neither rude nor
  rash,
But a bevy of Eroses apple-cheek'd,
In a shallop of crystal ivory-beak'd,
With a satin sail of a ruby glow,
To a sweet little Eden on earth that I
  know,
A mountain islet pointed and peak'd;
Waves on a diamond shingle dash,
Cataract brooks to the ocean run,
Fairily-delicate palaces shine
Mixt with myrtle and clad with vine,
And overstream'd and silvery-streak'd
With many a rivulet high against the
  Sun
The facets of the glorious mountain
  flash
Above the valleys of palm and pine."

"Thither, O thither, love, let us go."

"No, no, no!
For in all that exquisite isle, my dear,
There is but one bird with a musical
  throat,
And his compass is but of a single
  note,
That it makes one weary to hear."

"Mock me not! mock me not! love,
  let us go."

"No, love, no.
For the bud ever breaks into bloom
  on the tree,
And a storm never wakes on the lonely
  sea,
And a worm is there in the lonely
  wood,
That pierces the liver and blackens
  the blood;
And makes it a sorrow to be."

CHILD–SONGS.

I.

THE CITY CHILD.

DAINTY little maiden, whither would
  you wander?
  Whither from this pretty home, the
    home where mother dwells?
"Far and far away," said the dainty
  little maiden,
"All among the gardens, auriculas,
  anemones,
  Roses and lilies and Canterbury-
    bells."

Dainty little maiden, whither would
  you wander?
  Whither from this pretty house,
    this city-house of ours?
"Far and far away," said the dainty
  little maiden,
"All among the meadows, the clover
  and the clematis,
  Daisies and kingcups and honey-
    suckle-flowers."

II.

MINNIE AND WINNIE.

MINNIE and Winnie
　Slept in a shell.
Sleep, little ladies!
　And they slept well.

Pink was the shell within.
　Silver without;
Sounds of the great sea
　Wander'd about.

Sleep, little ladies!
　Wake not soon!
Echo on echo
　Dies to the moon.

Two bright stars
　Peep'd into the shell.
"What are they dreaming of?
　Who can tell?"

Started a green linnet
　Out of the croft;
Wake, little ladies,
　The sun is aloft!

THE SPITEFUL LETTER.

HERE, it is here, the close of the year,
　And with it a spiteful letter.
My name in song has done him much
　　wrong,
　For himself has done much better.

O little bard, is your lot so hard,
　If men neglect your pages?
I think not much of yours or of mine,
　I hear the roll of the ages.

Rhymes and rhymes in the range of
　　the times!
　Are mine for the moment stronger?
Yet hate me not, but abide your lot,
　I last but a moment longer.

This faded leaf, our names are as
　　brief;
　What room is left for a hater?

Yet the yellow leaf hates the greener
　　leaf,
　For it hangs one moment later.

Greater than I — is that your cry?
　And men will live to see it.
Well — if it be so — so it is, you know;
　And if it be so, so be it.

Brief, brief is a summer leaf,
　But this is the time of hollies.
O hollies and ivies and evergreens,
　How I hate the spites and the
　　follies!

LITERARY SQUABBLES.

AH God! the petty fools of rhyme
　That shriek and sweat in pigmy wars
Before the stony face of Time,
　And look'd at by the silent stars:

Who hate each other for a song,
　And do their little best to bite
And pinch their brethren in the throng,
　And scratch the very dead for spite:

And strain to make an inch of room
　For their sweet selves, and cannot
　　hear
The sullen Lethe rolling doom
　On them and theirs and all things
　　here:

When one small touch of Charity
　Could lift them nearer God-like state
Than if the crowned Orb should cry
　Like those who cried Diana great:

And I too, talk, and lose the touch
　I talk of.　Surely, after all,
The noblest answer unto such
　Is perfect stillness when they brawl.

THE VICTIM.

I.

A PLAGUE upon the people fell,
　A famine after laid them low,
Then thorpe and byre arose in fire,

For on them brake the sudden foe;
So thick they died the people cried,
"The Gods are moved against the
land."
The Priest in horror about his altar
To Thor and Odin lifted a hand:
"Help us from famine
And plague and strife!
What would you have of us?
Human life?
Were it our nearest,
Were it our dearest,
(Answer, O answer)
We give you his life."

II.

But still the foeman spoil'd and burn'd,
And cattle died, and deer in wood,
And bird in air, and fishes turn'd
And whiten'd all the rolling flood;
And dead men lay all over the way,
Or down in a furrow scathed with
flame:
And ever and aye the Priesthood
moan'd,
Till at last it seem'd that an answer
came.
"The King is happy
In child and wife;
Take you his dearest,
Give us a life."

III.

The Priest went out by heath and hill;
The King was hunting in the wild;
They found the mother sitting still;
She cast her arms about the child.
The child was only eight summers old,
His beauty still with his years in-
creased,
His face was ruddy, his hair was gold,
He seem'd a victim due to the priest.
The Priest beheld him,
And cried with joy,
"The Gods have answer'd:
We give them the boy."

IV.

The King return'd from out the wild,
He bore but little game in hand;

The mother said, "They have taken
the child
To spill his blood and heal the
land:
The land is sick, the people diseased,
And blight and famine on all the
lea:
The holy Gods, they must be appeased,
So I pray you tell the truth to me.
They have taken our son,
They will have his life.
Is *he* your dearest?
Or I, the wife?'"

V.

The King bent low, with hand on
brow,
He stay'd his arms upon his knee:
"O wife, what use to answer now?
For now the Priest has judged for
me."
The King was shaken with holy
fear;
"The Gods," he said, "would have
chosen well;
Yet both are near, and both are dear,
And which the dearest I cannot tell!"
But the Priest was happy,
His victim won:
"We have his dearest,
His only son!"

VI.

The rites prepared, the victim bared,
The knife uprising toward the
blow
To the altar-stone she sprang alone,
"Me, not my darling, no!"
He caught her away with a sudden
cry;
Suddenly from him brake his wife,
And shrieking "*I* am his dearest, I—
I am his dearest!" rush'd on the
knife.
And the Priest was happy,
"O, Father Odin,
We give you a life.
Which was his nearest?
Who was his dearest?
The Gods have answer'd;
We give them the wife!"

WAGES.

GLORY of warrior, glory of orator, glory of song,
  Paid with a voice flying by to be lost on an endless sea —
Glory of Virtue, to fight, to struggle, to right the wrong —
  Nay, but she aim'd not at glory, no lover of glory she:
Give her the glory of going on, and still to be.

The wages of sin is death: if the wages of Virtue be dust,
  Would she have heart to endure for the life of the worm and the fly?
She desires no isles of the blest, no quiet seats of the just,
  To rest in a golden grove, or to bask in a summer sky:
Give her the wages of going on, and not to die.

THE HIGHER PANTHEISM.

THE sun, the moon, the stars, the seas, the hills and the plains —
Are not these, O Soul, the Vision of Him who reigns?

Is not the Vision He? tho' He be not that which He seems?
Dreams are true while they last, and do we not live in dreams?

Earth, these solid stars, this weight of body and limb,
Are they not sign and symbol of thy division from Him?

Dark is the world to thee: thyself art the reason why;
For is He not all but thou, that hast power to feel "I am I"?

Glory about thee, without thee; and thou fulfillest thy doom
Making Him broken gleams, and a stifled splendor and gloom.

Speak to Him thou for He hears, and Spirit with Spirit can meet —
Closer is He than breathing, and nearer than hands and feet.

God is law, say the wise; O Soul, and let us rejoice,
For if He thunder by law the thunder is yet His voice.

Law is God, say some: no God at all, says the fool;
For all we have power to see is a straight staff bent in a pool;

And the ear of man cannot hear, and the eye of man cannot see;
But if we could see and hear, this Vision — were it not He?

THE VOICE AND THE PEAK.

I.

THE voice and the Peak
  Far over summit and lawn,
The lone glow and long roar
  Green-rushing from the rosy thrones
    of dawn!

II.

All night have I heard the voice
  Rave over the rocky bar,
But thou wert silent in heaven,
  Above thee glided the star.

III.

Hast thou no voice, O Peak,
   That standest high above all?
" I am the voice of the Peak,
   I roar and rave for I fall.

IV.

" A thousand voices go
   To North, South, East, and West;
They leave the heights and are
      troubled,
   And moan and sink to their rest.

V.

" The fields are fair beside them,
   The chestnut towers in his bloom;
But they — they feel the desire of the
      deep —
   Fall, and follow their doom.

VI.

" The deep has power on the height,
   And the height has power on the
      deep;
They are raised for ever and ever,
   And sink again into sleep."

VII.

Not raised for ever and ever,
   But when their cycle is o'er,
The valley, the voice, the peak, the
      star
   Pass, and are found no more.

VIII.

The Peak is high and flush'd
   At his highest with sunrise fire;
The Peak is high, and the stars are
      high,
   And the thought of a man is higher.

IX.

A deep below the deep,
   And a height beyond the height!
Our hearing is not hearing,
   And our seeing is not sight.

X.

The voice and the Peak
   Far into heaven withdrawn,
The lone glow and long roar
   Green-rushing from the rosy thrones
      of dawn!

————

FLOWER in the crannied wall,
I pluck you out of the crannies,
I hold you here, root and all, in my
      hand,
Little flower — but *if* I could under-
      stand
What you are, root and all, and all in
      all,
I should know what God and man is.

————

A DEDICATION.

DEAR, near and true — no truer Time
      himself
Can prove you, tho' he make you ever-
      more
Dearer and nearer, as the rapid of
      life
Shoots to the fall — take this and pray
      that he
Who wrote it, honoring your sweet
      faith in him,
May trust himself; and after praise
      and scorn,
As one who feels the immeasurable
      world,
Attain the wise indifference of the
      wise;
And after Autumn past — if left to
      pass
His autumn into seeming-leafless
      days —
Draw toward the long frost and long-
      est night,
Wearing his wisdom lightly, like the
      fruit
Which in our winter woodland looks
      a flower.[1]

[1] The fruit of the Spindle-tree (*Euony-
mus Europæus*).

EXPERIMENTS.

BOÄDICEA.

WHILE about the shore of Mona those Neronian legionaries
Burnt and broke the grove and altar of the Druid and Druidess,
Far in the East Boädicéa, standing loftily charioted,
Ma'd and maddening all that heard her in her fierce volubility,
Girt by half the tribes of Britain, near the colony Cámodúne,
Yell'd and shriek'd between her daughters o'er a wild confederacy.

"They that scorn the tribes and call us Britain's barbarous populaces,
Did they hear me, would they listen, did they pity me supplicating?
Shall I heed them in their anguish? shall I brook to be supplicated?
Hear Icenian, Catieuchlanian, hear Coritanian, Trinobant!
Must their ever-ravening eagle's beak and talon annihilate us?
Tear the noble heart of Britain, leave it gorily quivering?
Bark an answer, Britain's raven! bark and blacken innumerable,
Blacken round the Roman carrion, make the carcase a skeleton,
Kite and kestrel, wolf and wolfkin, from the wilderness, wallow in it,
Till the face of Bel be brighten'd, Taranis be propitiated.
Lo their colony half-defended! low their colony, Cámodúne!
There the horde of Roman robbers mock at a barbarous adversary.
There the hive of Roman liars worship a gluttonous emperor-idiot.
Such is Rome, and this her deity: hear it, Spirit of Cássivëlaún!

"Hear it, Gods! the Gods have heard it, O Icenian, O Coritanian!
Doubt not ye the Gods have answer'd, Catieuchlanian, Trinobant.
These have told us all their anger in miraculous utterances,
Thunder, a flying fire in heaven, a murmur heard aërially,
Phantom sound of blows descending, moan of an enemy massacred,
Phantom wail of women and children, multitudinous agonies.
Bloodily flow'd the Tamesa rolling phantom bodies of horses and men;
Then a phantom colony smoulder'd on the refluent estuary;
Lastly yonder yester-even, suddenly giddily tottering—
There was one who watch'd and told me—down their statue of Victory fell.
Lo their precious Roman bantling, lo the colony Cámodúne,
Shall we teach it a Roman lesson? shall we care to be pitiful?
Shall we deal with it as an infant? shall we dandle it amorously?

"Hear Icenian, Catieuchlanian, hear Coritanian, Trinobant!
While I roved about the forest, long and bitterly meditating,
There I heard them in the darkness, at the mystical ceremony,
Loosely robed in flying raiment, sang the terrible prophetesses,
'Fear not, isle of blowing woodland, isle of silvery parapets!
Tho' the Roman eagle shadow thee, tho' the gathering enemy narrow thee,
Thou shalt wax and he shall dwindle, thou shalt be the mighty one yet!

Thine the liberty, thine the glory, thine the deeds to be celebrated,
Thine the myriad-rolling ocean, light and shadow illimitable,
Thine the lands of lasting summer, many-blossoming Paradises,
Thine the North and thine the South and thine the battle-thunder of God.'
So they chanted: how shall Britain light upon auguries happier?
So they chanted in the darkness, and there cometh a victory now.

" Hear Icenian, Catieuchlanian, hear Coritanian, Trinobant!
Me the wife of rich Prasútagus, me the lover of liberty,
Me they seized and me they tortured, me they lash'd and humiliated,
Me the sport of ribald Veterans, mine of ruffian violators!
See they sit, they hide their faces, miserable in ignominy!
Wherefore in me burns an anger, not by blood to be satiated.
Lo the palaces and the temple, lo the colony Cámulodúne!
There they ruled, and thence they wasted all the flourishing territory,
Thither at their will they haled the yellow-ringleted Britoness —
Bloodily, bloodily fall the battle-axe, unexhausted, inexorable.
Shout Icenian, Catieuchlanian, shout Coritanian, Trinobant,
Till the victim hear within and yearn to hurry precipitously
Like the leaf in a roaring whirlwind, like the smoke in a hurricane whirl'd.
Lo the colony, there they rioted in the city of Cúnobelíne!
There they drank in cups of emerald, there at tables of ebony lay,
Rolling on their purple couches in their tender effeminacy.
There they dwelt and there they rioted; there — there — they dwell no more.
Burst the gates, and burn the palaces, break the works of the statuary,
Take the hoary Roman head and shatter it, hold it abominable,
Cut the Roman boy to pieces in his lust and voluptuousness,
Lash the maiden into swooning, me they lash'd and humiliated,
Chop the breasts from off the mother, dash the brains of the little one out,
Up my Britons, on my chariot, on my chargers, trample them under us."

So the Queen Boädicéa, standing loftily charioted,
Brandishing in her hand a dart and rolling glances lioness-like,
Yell'd and shriek'd between her daughters in her fierce volubility.
Till her people all around the royal chariot agitated,
Madly dash'd the darts together, writhing barbarous lineaments,
Made the noise of frosty woodlands, when they shiver in January,
Roar'd as when the roaring breakers boom and blanch on the precipices,
Yell'd as when the winds of winter tear an oak on a promontory.
So the silent colony hearing her tumultuous adversaries
Clash the darts and on the buckler beat with rapid unanimous hand,
Thought on all her evil tyrannies, all her pitiless avarice,
Till she felt the heart within her fall and flutter tremulously,
Then her pulses at the clamoring of her enemy fainted away.
Out of evil evil flourishes, out of tyranny tyranny buds.
Ran the land with Roman slaughter, multitudinous agonies.
Perish'd many a maid and matron, many a valorous legionary,
Fell the colony, city, and citadel, London, Verulam, Cámulodúne.

IN QUANTITY.

ON TRANSLATIONS OF HOMER.

Hexameters and Pentameters.

THESE lame hexameters the strong-wing'd music of Homer!
　No — but a most burlesque barbarous experiment.
When was a harsher sound ever heard, ye Muses, in England?
　When did a frog coarser croak upon our Helicon?
Hexameters no worse than daring Germany gave us,
　Barbarous experiment, barbarous hexameters.

MILTON.

Alcaics.

O MIGHTY-MOUTH'D inventor of harmonies,
O skill'd to sing of Time or Eternity,
　God-gifted organ-voice of England,
　　Milton, a name to resound for ages;
Whose Titan angels, Gabriel, Abdiel,
Starr'd from Jehovah's gorgeous armories,
　Tower, as the deep-domed empyrëan
　　Rings to the roar of an angel onset —
Me rather all that bowery loneliness,
The brooks of Eden mazily murmuring,
　And bloom profuse and cedar arches
　　Charm, as a wanderer out in ocean,
Where some refulgent sunset of India
Streams o'er a rich ambrosial ocean isle,
　And crimson-hued the stately palm-woods
　　Whisper in odorous heights of even.

Hendecasyllabics.

O YOU chorus of indolent reviewers,
Irresponsible, indolent reviewers,
Look, I come to the test, a tiny poem
All composed in a metre of Catullus,
All in quantity, careful of my motion,
Like the skater on ice that hardly bears him,
Lest I fall unawares before the people,
Waking laughter in indolent reviewers.
Should I flounder awhile without a tumble
Thro' this metrification of Catullus,
They should speak to me not without a welcome,
All that chorus of indolent reviewers.
Hard, hard, hard is it, only not to tumble,
So fantastical is the dainty metre.
Wherefore slight me not wholly, nor believe me
Too presumptuous, indolent reviewers,
O blatant Magazines, regard me rather —
Since I blush to belaud myself a moment —
As some rare little rose, a piece of inmost
Horticultural art, or half coquette-like
Maiden, not to be greeted unbenignly.

SPECIMEN OF A TRANSLATION OF THE ILIAD IN BLANK VERSE.

So Hector spake; the Trojans roar'd applause;
Then loosed their sweating horses from the yoke,
And each beside his chariot bound his own;
And oxen from the city, and goodly sheep

In haste they drove, and honey-hearted wine
And bread from out the houses brought, and heap'd
Their firewood, and the winds from off the plain
Roll'd the rich vapor far into the heaven.
And these all night upon the bridge[1] of war
Sat glorying; many a fire before them blazed:
As when in heaven the stars about the moon
Look beautiful, when all the winds are laid,
And every height comes out, and jutting peak

1 Or ridge.

And valley, and the immeasurable heavens
Break open to their highest, and all the stars
Shine, and the Shepherd gladdens in his heart:
So many a fire between the ships and stream
Of Xanthus blazed before the towers of Troy,
A thousand on the plain; and close by each
Sat fifty in the blaze of burning fire;
And eating hoary grain and pulse the steeds,
Fixt by their cars, waited the golden dawn.   *Iliad* VIII. 542–561.

THE WINDOW;

OR, THE SONG OF THE WRENS.

Four years ago Mr. Sullivan requested me to write a little song-cycle, German fashion, for him to exercise his art upon. He had been very successful in setting such old songs as " Orpheus with his lute," and I drest up for him, partly in the old style, a puppet, whose almost only merit is, perhaps, that it can dance to Mr. Sullivan's instrument. I am sorry that my four-year-old puppet should have to dance at all in the dark shadow of these days; but the music is now completed, and I am bound by my promise.

A. TENNYSON.
December, 1870.

THE WINDOW.

ON THE HILL.

THE lights and shadows fly!
Yonder it brightens and darkens down on the plain.
A jewel, a jewel dear to a lover's eye!
Oh is it the brook, or a pool, or her window pane,
  When the winds are up in the morning?

Clouds that are racing above,
And winds and lights and shadows that cannot be still,
  All running on one way to the home of my love,
You are all running on, and I stand on the slope of the hill,
  And the winds are up in the morning!

Follow, follow the chase!
And my thoughts are as quick and as quick, ever on, on, on.
O lights, are you flying over her sweet little face?
And my heart is there before you are come, and gone,
  When the winds are up in the morning!

Follow them down the slope!
And I follow them down to the window-pane of my dear,
  And it brightens and darkens and brightens like my hope,
And it darkens and brightens and darkens like my fear,
  And the winds are up in the morning.

AT THE WINDOW.

Vine, vine and eglantine,
Clasp her window, trail and twine!
Rose, rose and clematis,
Trail and twine and clasp and kiss,
Kiss, kiss; and make her a bower
    All of flowers, and drop me a flower,
      Drop me a flower.

Vine, vine and eglantine,
Cannot a flower, a flower, be mine?
Rose, rose and clematis,
Drop me a flower, a flower, to kiss,
Kiss, kiss — and out of her bower
    All of flowers, a flower, a flower,
      Dropt, a flower.

GONE.

Gone!
Gone, till the end of the year,
Gone, and the light gone with her, and
    left me in shadow here!
      Gone — flitted away,
Taken the stars from the night and
    the sun from the day!
Gone, and a cloud in my heart, and a
    storm in the air!
Flown to the east or the west, flitted
    I know not where!
Down in the south is a flash and a
    groan: she is there! she is
    there!

WINTER.

The frost is here,
And fuel is dear,
And woods are sear,
And fires burn clear,
And frost is here
And has bitten the heel of the going
    year.

Bite, frost, bite!
You roll up away from the light
The blue wood-louse, and the plump
    dormouse,
And the bees are still'd, and the flies
    are kill'd,
And you bite far into the heart of the
    house,
But not into mine.

Bite, frost, bite!
The woods are all the searer,
The fuel is all the dearer,
The fires are all the clearer,
My spring is all the nearer,
You have bitten into the heart of the
    earth,
But not into mine.

SPRING.

Birds' love and birds' song
    Flying here and there,
Birds' song and birds' love,
    And you with gold for hair!
Birds' song and birds' love,
    Passing with the weather,
Men's song and men's love,
    To love once and for ever.

Men's love and birds' love,
    And women's love and men's!
And you my wren with a crown of
    gold,
    You my queen of the wrens!
You the queen of the wrens —
    We'll be birds of a feather,
I'll be King of the Queen of the
    wrens,
    And all in a nest together.

THE LETTER.

Where is another sweet as my sweet,
    Fine of the fine, and shy of the shy?
Fine little hands, fine little feet —
    Dewy blue eye.
Shall I write to her? shall I go?
    Ask her to marry me by and by?
Somebody said that she'd say no;
    Somebody knows that she'll say ay!

Ay or no, if ask'd to her face?
    Ay or no, from shy of the shy?
Go, little letter, apace, apace,
    Fly;
Fly to the light in the valley below —
    Tell my wish to her dewy blue eye:
Somebody said that she'd say no;
    Somebody knows that she'll say ay!

NO ANSWER.

The mist and the rain, the mist and
    the rain!

Is it ay or no ? is it ay or no ?
And never a glimpse of her window
    pane !
  And I may die but the grass will
    grow,
And the grass will grow when I am
    gone,
And the wet west wind and the world
    will go on.
Ay is the song of the wedded spheres,
  No is trouble and cloud and storm,
Ay is life for a hundred years,
  No will push me down to the worm,
And when I am there and dead and
    gone,
The wet west wind and the world will
    go on.

The wind and the wet, the wind and
    the wet !
  Wet west wind how you blow, you
    blow !
And never a line from my lady yet !
  Is it ay or no ? is it ay or no ?
Blow then, blow, and when I am gone,
The wet west wind and the world may
    go on.

NO ANSWER.

Winds are loud and you are dumb,
Take my love, for love will come,
  Love will come but once a life.
Winds are loud and winds will pass !
Spring is here with leaf and grass :
  Take my love and be my wife.
After-loves of maids and men
Are but dainties drest again :
Love me now, you'll love me then :
  Love can love but once a life.

THE ANSWER.

Two little hands that meet,
Claspt on her seal, my sweet !
Must I take you and break you,
Two little hands that meet ?
I must take you, and break you,
And loving hands must part —
Take, take — break, break —
Break — you may break my heart.
  Faint heart never won —
  Break, break, and all's done.

AY.

Be merry, all birds, to-day,
  Be merry on earth as you never
    were merry before,
Be merry in heaven, O larks, and far
    away,
  And merry for ever and ever, and
    one day more.
      Why ?
For it's easy to find a rhyme.
Look, look, how he flits,
  The fire-crown'd king of the wrens,
    from out of the pine !
Look how they tumble the blossom,
    the mad little tits !
  " Cuck-oo ! Cuck-oo ! " was ever a
    May so fine ?
      Why ?
For it's easy to find a rhyme.
O merry the linnet and dove,
  And swallow and sparrow and
    throstle, and have your desire !
O merry my heart, you have gotten
    the wings of love,
  And flit like the king of the wrens
    with a crown of fire.
      Why ?
For its ay ay, ay ay.

WHEN.

Sun comes, moon comes,
  Time slips away.
Sun sets, moon sets,
  Love, fix a day.

" A year hence, a year hence."
  " We shall both be gray."
" A month hence, a month hence."
  " Far, far away."

" A week hence, a week hence."
  " Ah, the long delay."
" Wait a little, wait a little,
  You shall fix a day."

" To-morrow, love, to-morrow,
  And that's an age away."
Blaze upon her window, sun,
  And honor all the day.

MARRIAGE MORNING.

Light, so low upon earth,
  You send a flash to the sun.
Here is the golden close of love,
  All my wooing is done.
Oh, the woods and the meadows,
  Woods where we hid from the wet,
Stiles where we stay'd to be kind,
  Meadows in which we met!

Light, so low in the vale
  You flash and lighten afar,
For this is the golden morning of love,
  And you are his morning star.
Flash, I am coming, I come,
  By meadow and stile and wood,
Oh, lighten into my eyes and my heart,
  Into my heart and my blood!

Heart, are you great enough
  For a love that never tires?
O heart, are you great enough for love?
  I have heard of thorns and briers.
Over the thorns and briers,
  Over the meadows and stiles,
Over the world to the end of it
  Flash for a million miles.

IDYLS OF THE KING.

—◦◦◦◦◦—

DEDICATION.

THESE to His Memory — since he held
   them dear,
Perchance as finding there uncon-
   sciously
Some image of himself — I dedicate,
I dedicate, I consecrate with tears —
These Idylls.

       And indeed He seems to me
Scarce other than my king's ideal
   knight,
" Who reverenced his conscience as
   his king;
Whose glory was, redressing human
   wrong;
Who spake no slander, no, nor listen'd
   to it;
Who loved one only and who clave to
   her — "
Her — over all whose realms to their
   last isle,
Commingled with the gloom of im-
   minent war,
The shadow of His loss drew like
   eclipse,
Darkening the world. We have lost
   him : he is gone :
We know him now: all narrow jeal-
   ousies
Are silent; and we see him as he
   moved,
How modest, kindly, all-accomplish'd,
   wise,
With what sublime repression of himself,
And in what limits, and how tenderly ;

Not swaying to this faction or to that ;
Not making his high place the lawless
   perch
Of wing'd ambitions, nor a vantage-
   ground
For pleasure ; but thro' all this tract
   of years
Wearing the white flower of a blame-
   less life,
Before a thousand peering littlenesses,
In that fierce light which beats upon
   a throne,
And blackens every blot: for where
   is he,
Who dares foreshadow for an only son
A lovelier life, a more unstain'd, than
   his ?
Or how should England dreaming of
   his sons
Hope more for these than some in-
   heritance
Of such a life, a heart, a mind as thine,
Thou noble Father of her Kings to be,
Laborious for her people and her
   poor —
Voice in the rich dawn of an ampler
   day —
Far-sighted summoner of War and
   Waste
To fruitful strifes and rivalries of
   peace —
Sweet nature gilded by the gracious
   gleam
Of letters, dear to Science, dear to Art,
Dear to thy land and ours, a Prince
   indeed,
Beyond all titles, and a household
   name,

Hereafter, thro' all times, Albert the
    Good.

Break not, O woman's-heart, but
    still endure;
Break not, for thou art Royal, but
    endure,
Remembering all the beauty of that
    star
Which shone so close beside Thee that
    ye made
One light together, but has past and
    leaves
The Crown a lonely splendor.

             May all love,
His love, unseen but felt, o'ershadow
    Thee,
The love of all Thy sons encompass
    Thee,
The love of all Thy daughters cherish
    Thee,
The love of all Thy people comfort
    Thee,
Till God's love set Thee at his side
    again!

THE COMING OF ARTHUR.

Leodogran, the King of Cameliard,
Had one fair daughter, and none other
    child;
And she was fairest of all flesh on
    earth,
Guinevere, and in her his one delight.

For many a petty king ere Arthur
    came
Ruled in this isle, and ever waging
    war
Each upon other, wasted all the land;
And still from time to time the
    heathen host
Swarm'd overseas, and harried what
    was left.
And so there grew great tracts of wil-
    derness,
Wherein the beast was ever more and
    more,
But man was less and less, till Arthur
    came.

For first Aurelius lived and fought
    and died,
And after him King Uther fought and
    died,
But either fail'd to make the kingdom
    one.
And after these King Arthur for a
    space,
And thro' the puissance of his Table
    Round,
Drew all their petty princedoms under
    him,
Their king and head, and made a realm,
    and reign'd.

And thus the land of Cameliard
    was waste,
Thick with wet woods, and many a
    beast therein,
And none or few to scare or chase the
    beast;
So that wild dog, and wolf and boar
    and bear
Came night and day, and rooted in
    the fields,
And wallow'd in the gardens of the
    King.
And ever and anon the wolf would
    steal
The children and devour, but now and
    then,
Her own brood lost or dead, lent her
    fierce teat
To human sucklings; and the children,
    housed
In her foul den, there at their meat
    would growl,
And mock their foster-mother on four
    feet,
Till, straighten'd, they grew up to
    wolf-like men,
Worse than the wolves. And King
    Leodogran
Groan'd for the Roman legions here
    again,
And Cæsar's eagle: then his brother
    king,
Urien, assail'd him: last a heathen
    horde,
Reddening the sun with smoke and
    earth with blood,

"and Guinevere
Stood by the castle walls to watch him pass."

Page 199.

And on the spike that split the
  mother's heart
Spitting the child, brake on him, till,
  amazed,
He knew not whither he should turn
  for aid.

  But — for he heard of Arthur newly
    crown'd,
Tho' not without an uproar made by
  those
Who cried, "He is not Uther's son"
  — the King
Sent to him, saying, "Arise, and help
  us thou!
For here between the man and beast
  we die."

  And Arthur yet had done no deed
    of arms,
But heard the call, and came: and
  Guinevere
Stood by the castle walls to watch him
  pass;
But since he neither wore on helm or
  shield
The golden symbol of his kinglihood,
But rode a simple knight among his
  knights,
And many of these in richer arms
  than he,
She saw him not, or mark'd not, if she
  saw,
One among many, tho' his face was
  bare.
But Arthur, looking downward as he
  past,
Felt the light of her eyes into his life
Smite on the sudden, yet rode on, and
  pitch'd
His tents beside the forest.   Then he
  drave
The heathen; after, slew the beast,
  and fell'd
The forest, letting in the sun, and
  made
Broad pathways for the hunter and
  the knight
And so return'd.

    For while he linger'd there,
A doubt that ever smoulder'd in the
  hearts

Of those great Lords and Barons of
  his realm
Flash'd forth and into war: for most
  of these,
Colleaguing with a score of petty
  kings,
Made head against him, crying, "Who
  is he
That he should rule us? who hath
  proven him
King Uther's son? for lo! we look at
  him,
And find nor face nor bearing, limbs
  nor voice,
Are like to those of Uther whom we
  knew.
This is the son of Gorloïs, not the
  King;
This is the son of Anton, not the
  King."

  And Arthur, passing thence to
    battle, felt
Travail, and throes and agonies of the
  life,
Desiring to be join'd with Guinevere;
And thinking as he rode, "Her father
  said
That there between the man and beast
  they die.
Shall I not lift her from this land of
  beasts
Up to my throne, and side by side
  with me?
What happiness to reign a lonely
  king,
Vext — O ye stars that shudder over
  me,
O earth that soundest hollow under
  me,
Vext with waste dreams? for saving
  I be join'd
To her that is the fairest under heaven,
I seem as nothing in the mighty world,
And cannot will my will, nor work my
  work
Wholly, nor make myself in mine own
  realm
Victor and lord.   But were I join'd
  with her,
Then might we live together as one
  life,

And reigning with one will in everything
Have power in this dark land to
lighten it,
And power on this dead world to
make it live."

Thereafter — as he speaks who tells
the tale —
When Arthur reach'd a field-of-battle
bright
With pitch'd pavilions of his foe, the
world
Was all so clear about him, that he
saw
The smallest rock far on the faintest
hill,
And even in high day the morning
star.
So when the King had set his banner
broad,
At once from either side, with trumpet-
blast,
And shouts, and clarions shrilling unto
blood,
The long-lanced battle let their horses
run.
And now the Barons and the kings
prevail'd,
And now the King, as here and there
that war
Went swaying; but the Powers who
walk the world
Made lightnings and great thunders
over him,
And dazed all eyes, till Arthur by
main might,
And mightier of his hands with every
blow,
And leading all his knighthood threw
the kings
Carádos, Urien, Cradlemont of Wales,
Claudias, and Clariance of Northum-
berland,
The King Brandagoras of Latangor,
With Anguisant of Erin, Morganore,
And Lot of Orkney. Then, before a
voice
As dreadful as the shout of one who
sees
To one who sins, and deems himself
alone

And all the world asleep, they swerved
and brake
Flying, and Arthur call'd to stay the
brands
That hack'd among the flyers, " Ho!
they yield ! "
So like a painted battle the war stood
Silenced, the living quiet as the dead,
And in the heart of Arthur joy was
lord.
He laugh'd upon his warrior whom
he loved
And honor'd most. " Thou dost not
doubt me King,
So well thine arm hath wrought for
me to-day."
" Sir and my liege," he cried, " the
fire of God
Descends upon thee in the battle-field :
I know thee for my King ! " Whereat
the two,
For each had warded either in the
fight,
Sware on the field of death a deathless
love.
And Arthur said, " Man's word is God
in man :
Let chance what will, I trust thee to
the death."

Then quickly from the foughten
field he sent
Ulfius, and Brastias, and Bedivere,
His new-made knights, to King Leodogran,
Saying, " If I in aught have served
thee well,
Give me thy daughter Guinevere to
wife."

Whom when he heard, Leodogran
in heart
Debating — " How should I that am a
king,
However much he holp me at my
need,
Give my one daughter saving to a
king,
And a king's son ? " — lifted his voice,
and call'd
A hoary man, his chamberlain, to
whom

He trusted all things, and of him
  required
His counsel: "Knowest thou aught of
  Arthur's birth?"

Then spake the hoary chamberlain
  and said,
"Sir King, there be but two old men
  that know:
And each is twice as old as I; and one
Is Merlin, the wise man that ever
  served
King Uther thro' his magic art; and
  one
Is Merlin's master (so they call him)
  Bleys,
Who taught him magic; but the
  scholar ran
Before the master, and so far, that
  Bleys
Laid magic by, and sat him down, and
  wrote
All things and whatsoever Merlin did
In one great annal-book, where after
  years
Will learn the secret of our Arthur's
  birth."

To whom the King Leodogran
  replied,
"O friend, had I been holpen half as
  well
By this King Arthur as by thee to-
  day,
Then beast and man had had their
  share of me:
But summon here before us yet once
  more
Ulfius, and Brastias, and Bedivere."

Then, when they came before him,
  the King said,
"I have seen the cuckoo chased by
  lesser fowl,
And reason in the chase: but wherefore now
Do these your lords stir up the heat
  of war,
Some calling Arthur born of Gorloïs,
Others of Anton? Tell me, ye yourselves,

Hold ye this Arthur for King Uther's
  son?"

And Ulfius and Brastius answer'd,
  "Ay."
Then Bedivere, the first of all his
  knights
Knighted by Arthur at his crowning,
  spake—
For bold in heart and act and word
  was he,
Whenever slander breathed against
  the King—

"Sir, there be many rumors on this
  head:
For there be those who hate him in
  their hearts,
Call him baseborn, and since his ways
  are sweet,
And theirs are bestial, hold him less
  than man:
And there be those who deem him
  more than man,
And dream he dropt from heaven: but
  my belief
In all this matter—so ye care to
  learn—
Sir, for ye know that in King Uther's
  time
The prince and warrior Gorloïs, he
  that held
Tintagil castle by the Cornish sea,
Was wedded with a winsome wife,
  Ygerne:
And daughters had she borne him,—
  one whereof,
Lot's wife, the Queen of Orkney,
  Bellicent,
Hath ever like a loyal sister cleaved
To Arthur,—but a son she had not
  borne.
And Uther cast upon her eyes of love:
But she, a stainless wife to Gorloïs,
So loathed the bright dishonor of his
  love,
That Gorloïs and King Uther went to
  war:
And overthrown was Gorloïs and slain.
Then Uther in his wrath and heat
  besieged

Ygerne within Tintagil, where her men,

Seeing the mighty swarm about their walls,

Left her and fled, and Uther enter'd in,

And there was none to call to but himself.

So, compass'd by the power of the King,

Enforced she was to wed him in her tears,

And with a shameful swiftness: afterward,

Not many moons, King Uther died himself,

Moaning and wailing for an heir to rule

After him, lest the realm should go to wrack.

And that same night, the night of the new year,

By reason of the bitterness and grief

That vext his mother, all before his time

Was Arthur born, and all as soon as born

Deliver'd at a secret postern-gate

To Merlin, to be holden far apart

Until his hour should come; because the lords

Of that fierce day were as the lords of this,

Wild beasts, and surely would have torn the child

Piecemeal among them, had they known; for each

But sought to rule for his own self and hand,

And many hated Uther for the sake

Of Gorloïs. Wherefore Merlin took the child,

And gave him to Sir Anton, an old knight

And ancient friend of Uther; and his wife

Nursed the young prince, and rear'd him with her own;

And no man knew. And ever since the lords

Have foughten like wild beasts among themselves,

So that the realm has gone to wrack: but now,

This year, when Merlin (for his hour had come)

Brought Arthur forth, and set him in the hall,

Proclaiming, 'Here is Uther's heir, your king,'

A hundred voices cried, 'Away with him!

No king of ours! a son of Gorloïs he,

Or else the child of Anton, and no king,

Or else baseborn.' Yet Merlin thro' his craft,

And while the people clamor'd for a king,

Had Arthur crown'd; but after, the great lords

Banded, and so brake out in open war."

Then while the King debated with himself

If Arthur were the child of shamefulness,

Or born the son of Gorloïs, after death,

Or Uther's son, and born before his time,

Or whether there were truth in anything

Said by these three, there came to Cameliard,

With Gawain and young Modred, her two sons,

Lot's wife, the Queen of Orkney, Bellicent;

Whom as he could, not as he would, the King

Made feast for, saying, as they sat at meat,

"A doubtful throne is ice on summer seas.

Ye come from Arthur's court. Victor his men

Report him! Yea, but ye — think ye this king —

So many those that hate him, and so strong,

So few his knights, however brave
  they be —
Hath body enow to hold his foemen
  down ? "

  " O King," she cried, " and I will
    tell thee : few,
Few, but all brave, all of one mind
  with him ;
For I was near him when the savage
  yells
Of Uther's peerage died, and Arthur
  sat
Crown'd on the daïs, and his warriors
  cried,
' Be thou the king, and we will work
  thy will
Who love thee.' Then the King in
  low deep tones,
And simple words of great authority,
Bound them by so strait vows to his
  own self,
That when they rose, knighted from
  kneeling,
Were pale as at the passing of a ghost,
Some flush'd, and others dazed, as one
  who wakes
Half-blinded at the coming of a light.

  " But when he spake and cheer'd
    his Table Round
With large divine and comfortable
  words
Beyond my tongue to tell thee — I
  beheld
From eye to eye thro' all their Order
  flash
A momentary likeness of the King :
And ere it left their faces, thro' the
  cross
And those around it and the Crucified,
Down from the casement over Arthur,
  smote
Flame-color, vert and azure, in three
  rays,
One falling upon each of three fair
  queens,
Who stood in silence near his throne,
  the friends
Of Arthur, gazing on him, tall, with
  bright

Sweet faces, who will help him at his
  need.

  " And there I saw mage Merlin,
    whose vast wit
And hundred winters are but as the
  hands
Of loyal vassals toiling for their liege.

  " And near him stood the Lady of
    the Lake,
Who knows a subtler magic than his
  own —
Clothed in white samite, mystic, won-
  derful.
She gave the King his huge cross-
  hilted sword,
Whereby to drive the heathen out : a
  mist
Of incense curl'd about her, and her
  face
Wellnigh was hidden in the minster
  gloom ;
But there was heard among the holy
  hymns
A voice as of the waters, for she dwells
Down in a deep, calm, whatsoever
  storms
May shake the world, and when the
  surface rolls,
Hath power to walk the waters like
  our Lord.

  " There likewise I beheld Excalibur
Before him at his crowning borne, the
  sword
That rose from out the bosom of the
  lake,
And Arthur row'd across and took it
  — rich
With jewels, elfin Urim, on the hilt,
Bewildering heart and eye — the blade
  so bright
That men are blinded by it — on one
  side,
Graven in the oldest tongue of all this
  world,
' Take me,' but turn the blade and ye
  shall see,
And written in the speech ye speak
  yourself,

'Cast me away!' And sad was
Arthur's face
Taking it, but old Merlin counsell'd
him,
'Take thou and strike! the time to
cast away
Is yet far-off.' So this great brand
the king
Took, and by this will beat his foemen
down."

Thereat Leodogram rejoiced, but
thought
To sift his doubtings to the last, and
ask'd,
Fixing full eyes of question on her
face,
"The swallow and the swift are near
akin,
But thou art closer to this noble prince,
Being his own dear sister;" and she
said,
"Daughter of Gorloïs and Ygerne am
I;"
"And therefore Arthur's sister?"
ask'd the King.
She answer'd, "These be secret things,"
and sign'd
To those two sons to pass and let
them be.
And Gawain went, and breaking into
song
Sprang out, and follow'd by his flying
hair
Ran like a colt, and leapt at all he
saw:
But Modred laid his ear beside the
doors,
And there half-heard; the same that
afterward
Struck for the throne, and striking
found his doom.

And then the Queen made answer,
"What know I?
For dark my mother was in eyes and
hair,
And dark in hair and eyes am I; and
dark
Was Gorloïs, yea and dark was Uther
too,

Wellnigh to blackness; but this King
is fair
Beyond the race of Britons and of men.
Moreover, always in my mind I hear
A cry from out the dawning of my life,
A mother weeping, and I hear her say,
'O that ye had some brother, pretty
one,
To guard thee on the rough ways of
the world.'"

"Ay," said the King, "and hear ye
such a cry?
But when did Arthur chance upon
thee first?"

"O King!" she cried, "and I will
tell thee true:
He found me first when yet a little
maid:
Beaten I had been for a little fault
Whereof I was not guilty; and out I
ran
And flung myself down on a bank of
heath,
And hated this fair world and all
therein,
And wept, and wish'd that I were
dead; and he —
I know not whether of himself he
came,
Or brought by Merlin, who, they say,
can walk
Unseen at pleasure — he was at my
side
And spake sweet words, and comforted
my heart,
And dried my tears, being a child with
me.
And many a time he came, and evermore
As I grew greater grew with me; and
sad*
At times he seem'd, and sad with him
was I,
Stern too at times, and then I loved
him not,
But sweet again, and then I loved him
well.
And now of late I see him less and
less,

But those first days had golden hours
for me,
For then I surely thought he would
be king.

"But let me tell thee now another
tale:
For Bleys, our Merlin's master, as
they say,
Died but of late, and sent his cry to
me,
To hear him speak before he left his
life.
Shrunk like a fairy changeling lay
the mage;
And when I enter'd told me that him-
self
And Merlin ever served about the
King,
Uther, before he died; and on the
night
When Uther in Tintagil past away
Moaning and wailing for an heir, the
two
Left the still King, and passing forth
to breathe,
Then from the castle gateway by the
chasm
Descending thro' the dismal night—
a night
In which the bounds of heaven and
earth were lost—
Beheld, so high upon the dreary
deeps
It seem'd in heaven, a ship, the shape
thereof
A dragon wing'd, and all from stem
to stern
Bright with a shining people on the
decks,
And gone as soon as seen. And then
the two
Dropt to the cove, and watch'd the
great sea fall,
Wave after wave, each mightier than
the last,
Till last, a ninth one, gathering half
the deep
And full of voices, slowly rose and
plunged
Roaring, and all the wave was in a
flame:

And down the wave and in the flame
was borne
A naked babe, and rode to Merlin's
feet,
Who stoopt and caught the babe, and
cried 'The King!
Here is an heir for Uther!' And the
fringe
Of that great breaker, sweeping up
the strand,
Lash'd at the wizard as he spake the
word,
And all at once all round him rose in
fire,
So that the child and he were clothed
in fire.
And presently thereafter follow'd
calm,
Free sky and stars: 'And this same
child,' he said,
'Is he who reigns; nor could I part
in peace
Till this were told.' And saying this
the seer
Went thro' the strait and dreadful
pass of death,
Not ever to be question'd any more
Save on the further side; but when I
met
Merlin, and ask'd him if these things
were truth—
The shining dragon and the naked
child
Descending in the glory of the seas—
He laugh'd as is his wont, and an-
swer'd me
In riddling triplets of old time, and
said:

   "'Rain, rain, and sun! a rainbow
   in the sky!
A young man will be wiser by and by;
An old man's wit may wander ere he
   die.
   Rain, rain, and sun! a rainbow on
   the lea!
And truth is this to me, and that to
thee;
And truth or clothed or naked let it
be.
   Rain, sun, and rain! and the free
   blossom blows:

Sun, rain, and sun! and where is he
    who knows ?
From the great deep to the great deep
    he goes.'

    "So Merlin riddling anger'd me;
        but thou
Fear not to give this King thine only
    child,
Guinevere: so great bards of him will
    sing
Hereafter; and dark sayings from of
    old
Ranging and ringing thro' the minds
    of men,
And echo'd by old folk beside their
    fires
For comfort after their wage-work is
    done,
Speak of the King; and Merlin in our
    time
Hath spoken also, not in jest, and
    sworn
Tho' men may wound him that he will
    not die,
But pass, again to come ; and then or
    now
Utterly smite the heathen underfoot,
Till these and all men hail him for
    their king."

    She spake and King Leodogran
        rejoiced,
But musing "Shall I answer yea or
    nay ?"
Doubted, and drowsed, nodded, and
    slept, and saw,
Dreaming, a slope of land that ever
    grew,
Field after field, up to a height, the
    peak
Haze-hidden, and thereon a phantom
    king,
Now looming, and now lost; and on
    the slope
The sword rose, the hind fell, the herd
    was driven,
Fire glimpsed ; and all the land from
    roof and rick,
In drifts of smoke before a rolling
    wind,

Stream'd to the peak, and mingled
    with the haze
And made it thicker; while the phan-
    tom king
Sent out at times a voice; and here
    or there
Stood one who pointed toward the
    voice, the rest
Slew on and burnt, crying, " No king
    of ours,
No son of Uther, and no king of ours ; "
Till with a wink his dream was
    changed, the haze
Descended, and the solid earth be-
    came
As nothing, but the King stood out
    in heaven,
Crown'd. And Leodogran awoke, and
    sent
Ulfius, and Brastias and Bedivere,
Back to the court of Arthur answer-
    ing yea.

    Then Arthur charged his warrior
        whom he loved
And honor'd most, Sir Lancelot, to
    ride forth
And bring the Queen ; — and watch'd
    him from the gates :
And Lancelot past away among the
    flowers,
(For then was latter April) and
    return'd
Among the flowers, in May, with
    Guinevere.
To whom arrived, by Dubric the high
    saint,
Chief of the church in Britain, and
    before
The stateliest of her altar-shrines, the
    King
That morn was married, while in stain-
    less white,
The fair beginners of a nobler time,
And glorying in their vows and him,
    his knights
Stood round him, and rejoicing in his
    joy.
Far shone the fields of May thro'
    open door,
The sacred altar blossom'd white with
    May,

The Sun of May descended on their King,
They gazed on all earth's beauty in their Queen,
Roll'd incense, and there past along the hymns
A voice as of the waters, while the two
Sware at the shrine of Christ a deathless love:
And Arthur said, "Behold, thy doom is mine.
Let chance what will, I love thee to the death!"
To whom the Queen replied with drooping eyes,
"King and my lord, I love thee to the death!"
And holy Dubric spread his hands and spake,
"Reign ye, and live and love, and make the world
Other, and may thy Queen be one with thee,
And all this Order of thy Table Round
Fulfil the boundless purpose of their King!"

So Dubric said; but when they left the shrine
Great Lords from Rome before the portal stood,
In scornful stillness gazing as they past;
Then while they paced a city all on fire
With sun and cloth of gold, the trumpets blew,
And Arthur's knighthood sang before the King:—

"Blow trumpet, for the world is white with May;
Blow trumpet, the long night hath roll'd away!
Blow thro' the living world—'Let the King reign.'

"Shall Rome or Heathen rule in Arthur's realm?
Flash brand and lance, fall battleaxe upon helm,
Fall battleaxe, and flash brand! Let the King reign.

"Strike for the King and live! his knights have heard
That God hath told the King a secret word.
Fall battleaxe, and flash brand! Let the King reign.

"Blow trumpet! he will lift us from the dust.
Blow trumpet! live the strength and die the lust!
Clang battleaxe, and clash brand! Let the King reign.

"Strike for the King and die! and if thou diest,
The King is King, and ever wills the highest.
Clang battleaxe, and clash brand! Let the King reign.

"Blow, for our Sun is mighty in his May!
Blow, for our Sun is mightier day by day!
Clang battleaxe, and clash brand! Let the King reign.

"The King will follow Christ, and we the King
In whom high God hath breathed a secret thing.
Fall battleaxe, and flash brand! Let the King reign."

So sang the knighthood, moving to their hall.
There at the banquet those great Lords from Rome,
The slowly-fading mistress of the world,
Strode in, and claim'd their tribute as of yore.
But Arthur spake, "Behold, for these have sworn
To wage my wars, and worship me their King;
The old order changeth, yielding place to new;

And we that fight for our fair father
Christ,
Seeing that ye be grown too weak and
old
To drive the heathen from your
Roman wall,
No tribute will we pay ": so those
great lords
Drew back in wrath, and Arthur
strove with Rome.

And Arthur and his knighthood for
a space
Were all one will, and thro' that
strength the King
Drew in the petty princedoms under
him,
Fought, and in twelve great battles
overcame
The heathen hordes, and made a realm
and reign'd.

THE ROUND TABLE.

GARETH AND LYNETTE.

THE last tall son of Lot and Bellicent,
And tallest, Gareth, in a showerful
spring
Stared at the spate. A slender-shafted
Pine
Lost footing, fell, and so was whirl'd
away.
"How he went down," said Gareth,
"as a false knight
Or evil king before my lance if lance
Were mine to use — O senseless cata-
ract,
Bearing all down in thy precipitancy —
And yet thou art but swollen with
cold snows
And mine is living blood: thou dost
His will,
The Maker's, and not knowest, and I
that know,
Have strength and wit, in my good
mother's hall
Linger with vacillating obedience,
Prison'd, and kept and coax'd and
whistled to —
Since the good mother holds me still
a child!
Good mother is bad mother unto me!
A worse were better; yet no worse
would I.

Heaven yield her for it, but in me put
force
To weary her ears with one continuous
prayer,
Until she let me fly discaged to
sweep
In ever-highering eagle-circles up
To the great Sun of Glory, and thence
swoop
Down upon all things base, and dash
them dead,
A knight of Arthur, working out his
will,
To cleanse the world. Why, Gawain,
when he came
With Modred hither in the summer-
time,
Ask'd me to tilt with him, the proven
knight.
Modred for want of worthier was the
judge.
Then I so shook him in the saddle, he
said,
'Thou hast half prevail'd against me,'
said so — he —
Tho' Modred biting his thin lips was
mute,
For he is alway sullen: what care I ? "

And Gareth went, and hovering
round her chair

Gareth & Lynette

Ask'd, "Mother, tho' ye count me still
 the child,
Sweet mother, do ye love the child?"
 She laugh'd,
"Thou art but a wild-goose to ques-
 tion it."
"Then, mother, an ye love the child,"
 he said,
"Being a goose and rather tame than
 wild,
Hear the child's story." "Yea, my
 well-beloved,
An 'twere but of goose and golden
 eggs."

 And Gareth answer'd her with kind-
 ling eyes,
"Nay, nay, good mother, but this egg
 of mine
Was finer gold than any goose can
 lay;
For this an Eagle, a royal Eagle, laid
Almost beyond eye-reach, on such a
 palm
As glitters gilded in thy Book of
 Hours.
And there was ever haunting round
 the palm
A lusty youth, but poor, who often
 saw
The splendor sparkling from aloft,
 and thought
'An I could climb and lay my hand
 .upon it,
Then were I wealthier than a leash of
 kings,'
But ever when he reach'd a hand to
 climb,
One, that had loved him from his
 childhood, caught
And stay'd him, 'Climb not lest thou
 break thy neck,
I charge thee by my love,' and so the
 boy,
Sweet mother, neither clomb, nor
 brake his neck,
But brake his very heart in pining
 for it,
And past away."

  To whom the mother said,
"True love, sweet son, had risk'd himself and climb'd,

And handed down the golden treasure
 to him."

 And Gareth answer'd her with kindling eyes,
"Gold? said I gold? — ay then, why
 he, or she,
Or whoso'er it was, or half the world
Had ventured — *had* the thing I spake
 of been
Mere gold — but this was all of that
 true steel,
Whereof they forged the brand Excalibur,
And lightnings play'd about it in the
 storm,
And all the little fowl were flurried
 at it,
And there were cries and clashings in
 the nest,
That sent him from his senses: let me
 go."

 Then Bellicent bemoan'd herself
 and said,
"Hast thou no pity upon my loneli-
 ness?
Lo, where thy father Lot beside the
 hearth
Lies like a log, and all but smoulder'd
 out!
For ever since when traitor to the
 King
He fought against him in the Barons'
 war,
And Arthur gave him back his terri-
 tory,
His age hath slowly droopt, and now
 lies there
A yet-warm corpse, and yet unburia-
 ble,
No more; nor sees, nor hears, nor
 speaks, nor knows.
And both thy brethren are in Arthur's
 hall,
Albeit neither loved with that full
 love
I feel for thee, nor worthy such a
 love:
Stay therefore thou; red berries charm
 the bird,
And thee, mine innocent, the jousts,
 the wars,

Who never knewest finger-ache, nor
    pang
Of wrench'd or broken limb — an often
    chance
In those brain-stunning shocks, and
    tourney-falls,
Frights to my heart; but stay: follow
    the deer
By these tall firs and our fast-falling
    burns ;
So make thy manhood mightier day
    by day;
Sweet is the chase: and I will seek
    thee out
Some comfortable bride and fair, to
    grace
Thy climbing life, and cherish my
    prone year,
Till falling into Lot's forgetfulness
I know not thee, myself, nor any-
    thing.
Stay, my best son! ye are yet more
    boy than man."

    Then Gareth, "An ye hold me yet
    for child,
Hear yet once more the story of the
    child.
For, mother, there was once a King,
    like ours.
The prince his heir, when tall and
    marriageable,
Ask'd for a bride; and thereupon the
    King
Set two before him. One was fair,
    strong, arm'd —
But to be won by force — and many
    men
Desired her ; one, good lack, no man
    desired.
And these were the conditions of the
    King :
That save he won the first by force,
    he needs
Must wed that other, whom no man
    desired,
A red-faced bride who knew herself
    so vile,
That evermore she long'd to hide her-
    self,
Nor fronted man or woman, eye to
    eye —

Yea — some she cleaved to, but they
    died of her.
And one — they call'd her Fame; and
    one, — O Mother,
How can ye keep me tether'd to you
    — Shame !
Man am I grown, a man's work must
    I do.
Follow the deer ? follow the Christ,
    the King,
Live pure, speak true, right wrong,
    follow the King —
Else, wherefore born ? "

        To whom the mother said,
"Sweet son, for there be many who
    deem him not,
Or will not deem him, wholly proven
    King —
Albeit in mine own heart I knew him
    King,
When I was frequent with him in my
    youth,
And heard him Kingly speak, and
    doubted him
No more than he, himself; but felt
    him mine,
Of closest kin to me : yet — wilt thou
    leave
Thine easeful biding here, and risk
    thine all,
Life, limbs, for one that is not proven
    King ?
Stay, till the cloud that settles round
    his birth
Hath lifted but a little. Stay, sweet
    son."

    And Gareth answer'd quickly, " Not
    an hour,
So that ye yield me — I will walk thro'
    fire,
Mother, to gain it — your full leave to
    go.
Not proven, who swept the dust of
    ruin'd Rome
From off the threshold of the realm,
    and crush'd
The Idolaters, and made the people
    free ?
Who should be King save him who
    makes us free ? "

So when the Queen, who long had
    sought in vain
To break him from the intent to which
    he grew,
Found her son's will unwaveringly
    one,
She answer'd craftily, " Will ye walk
    thro' fire ?
Who walks thro' fire will hardly heed
    the smoke.
Ay, go then, an ye must: only one
    proof,
Before thou ask the King to make thee
    knight,
Of thine obedience and thy love to
    me,
Thy mother, — I demand."

            And Gareth cried,
" A hard one, or a hundred, so I go.
Nay — quick ! the proof to prove me
    to the quick ! "

    But slowly spake the mother look-
    ing at him,
" Prince, thou shalt go disguised to
    Arthur's hall,
And hire thyself to serve for meats
    and drinks
Among the scullions and the kitchen-
    knaves,
And those that hand the dish across
    the bar.
Nor shalt thou tell thy name to any-
    one.
And thou shalt serve a twelvemonth
    and a day."

    For so the Queen believed that when
    her son
Beheld his only way to glory lead
Low down thro' villain kitchen-vas-
    salage,
Her own true Gareth was too princely-
    proud
To pass thereby ; so should he rest
    with her,
Closed in her castle from the sound of
    arms.

    Silent awhile was Gareth, then
    replied,

" The thrall in person may be free in
    soul,
And I shall see the jousts. Thy son
    am I,
And since thou art my mother, must
    obey.
I therefore yield me freely to thy will ;
For hence will I, disguised, and hire
    myself
To serve with scullions and with
    kitchen-knaves ;
Nor tell my name to any — no, not the
    King."

    Gareth awhile linger'd. The
    mother's eye
Full of the wistful fear that he would
    go,
And turning toward him wheresoe'er
    he turn'd,
Perplext his outward purpose, till an
    hour,
When waken'd by the wind which with
    full voice
Swept bellowing thro' the darkness on
    to dawn,
He rose, and out of slumber calling
    two
That still had tended on him from his
    birth,
Before the wakeful mother heard him,
    went.

    The three were clad like tillers of
    the soil.
Southward they set their faces. The
    birds made
Melody on branch, and melody in mid
    air.
The damp hill-slopes were quicken'd
    into green,
And the live green had kindled into
    flowers,
For it was past the time of Easterday.

    So, when their feet were planted on
    the plain
That broaden'd toward the base of
    Camelot,
Far off they saw the silver-misty morn
Rolling her smoke about the Royal
    mount,

That rose between the forest and the field.

At times the summit of the high city flash'd;

At times the spires and turrets half-way down

Prick'd thro' the mist; at times the great gate shone

Only, that open'd on the field below:

Anon, the whole fair city had disappear'd.

Then those who went with Gareth were amazed,

One crying, "Let us go no further, lord.

Here is a city of Enchanters, built

By fairy kings." The second echo'd him,

"Lord, we have heard from our wise man at home

To Northward, that this King is not the King,

But only changeling out of Fairy-land,

Who drave the heathen hence by sorcery

And Merlin's glamour." Then the first again,

"Lord, there is no such city anywhere,

But all a vision."

Gareth answer'd them

With laughter, swearing he had glamour enow

In his own blood, his princedom, youth and hopes,

To plunge old Merlin in the Arabian sea;

So push'd them all unwilling toward the gate.

And there was no gate like it under heaven.

For barefoot on the keystone, which was lined

And rippled like an ever-fleeting wave,

The Lady of the Lake stood: all her dress

Wept from her sides as water flowing away;

But like the cross her great and goodly arms

Stretch'd under all the cornice and upheld:

And drops of water fell from either hand;

And down from one a sword was hung, from one

A censer, either worn with wind and storm;

And o'er her breast floated the sacred fish;

And in the space to left of her, and right,

Were Arthur's wars in weird devices done,

New things and old co-twisted, as if Time

Were nothing, so inverately, that men

Were giddy gazing there; and over all

High on the top were those three Queens, the friends

Of Arthur, who should help him at his need.

Then those with Gareth for so long a space

Stared at the figures, that at last it seem'd

The dragon-boughts and elvish emblemings

Began to move, seethe, twine and curl: they call'd

To Gareth, "Lord, the gateway is alive."

And Gareth likewise on them fixt his eyes

So long, that ev'n to him they seem'd to move.

Out of the city a blast of music peal'd.

Back from the gate started the three, to whom

From out thereunder came an ancient man,

Long-bearded, saying, "Who be ye, my sons?"

Then Gareth, "We be tillers of the soil,

Who leaving share in furrow come to see

The glories of our King: but these,
  my men,
(Your city moved so weirdly in the
  mist)
Doubt if the King be King at all, or
  come
From Fairyland; and whether this
  be built
By magic, and by fairy Kings and
  Queens;
Or whether there be any city at all,
Or all a vision: and this music now
Hath scared them both, but tell thou
  these the truth."

Then that old Seer made answer
  playing on him
And saying, "Son, I have seen the
  good ship sail
Keel upward and mast downward in
  the heavens,
And solid turrets topsy-turvy in air:
And here is truth; but an it please
  thee not,
Take thou the truth as thou hast told
  it me.
For truly as thou sayest, a Fairy King
And Fairy Queens have built the city,
  son;
They came from out a sacred mountain-
  cleft
Toward the sunrise, each with harp
  in hand,
And built it to the music of their harps.
And as thou sayest it is enchanted,
  son,
For there is nothing in it as it seems
Saving the King; tho' some there be
  that hold
The King a shadow, and the city real:
Yet take thou heed of him, for, so
  thou pass
Beneath this archway, then wilt thou
  become
A thrall to his enchantments, for the
  King
Will bind thee by such vows, as is a
  shame
A man should not be bound by, yet
  the which
No man can keep; but, so thou dread
  to swear,

Pass not beneath this gateway, but
  abide
Without, among the cattle of the field.
For an ye heard a music, like enow
They are building still, seeing the city
  is built
To music, therefore never built at all,
And therefore built for ever.

                    Gareth spake
Anger'd, "Old Master, reverence thine
  own beard
That looks as white as utter truth,
  and seems
Wellnigh as long as thou art statured
  tall!
Why mockest thou the stranger that
  hath been
To thee fair-spoken?"

                    But the Seer replied,
"Know ye not then the Riddling of
  the Bards?
'Confusion, and illusion, and relation,
Elusion, and occasion, and evasion'?
I mock thee not but as thou mockest
  me,
And all that see thee, for thou art not
  who
Thou seemest, but I know thee who
  thou art.
And now thou goest up to mock the
  King,
Who cannot brook the shadow of any
  lie."

Unmockingly the mocker ending
  here
Turn'd to the right, and past along
  the plain;
Whom Gareth looking after said, "My
  men,
Our one white lie sits like a little ghost
Here on the threshold of our enter-
  prise.
Let love be blamed for it, nor she, nor
  I:
Well, we will make amends."

                    With all good cheer
He spake and laugh'd, then enter'd
  with his twain

Camelot, a city of shadowy palaces
And stately, rich in emblem and the
    work
Of ancient kings who did their days in
    stone;
Which Merlin's hand, the Mage at
    Arthur's court,
Knowing all arts, had touch'd, and
    everywhere
At Arthur's ordinance, tipt with lessen-
    ing peak
And pinnacle, and had made it spire
    to heaven.
And ever and anon a knight would pass
Outward, or inward to the hall: his
    arms
Clash'd; and the sound was good to
    Gareth's ear.
And out of bower and casement shyly
    glanced
Eyes of pure women, wholesome stars
    of love;
And all about a healthful people stept
As in the presence of a gracious king.

Then into hall Gareth ascending
    heard
A voice, the voice of Arthur, and be-
    held
Far over heads in that long-vaulted
    hall
The splendor of the presence of the
    King
Throned, and delivering doom — and
    look'd no more —
But felt his young heart hammering
    in his ears,
And thought, "For this half-shadow
    of a lie
The truthful King will doom me when
    I speak."
Yet pressing on, tho' all in fear to find
Sir Gawain or Sir Modred, saw nor one
Nor other, but in all the listening eyes
Of those tall knights, that ranged
    about the throne,
Clear honor shining like the dewy star
Of dawn, and faith in their great King,
    with pure
Affection, and the light of victory,
And glory gain'd, and evermore to
    gain.

Then came a widow crying to the
    King,
"A boon, Sir King! Thy father,
    Uther, reft
From my dead lord a field with vio-
    lence:
For howsoe'er at first he proffer'd gold,
Yet, for the field was pleasant in our
    eyes,
We yielded not; and then he reft us
    of it
Perforce, and left us neither gold nor
    field."

Said Arthur, "Whether would ye?
    gold or field?"
To whom the woman weeping, "Nay,
    my lord,
The field was pleasant in my hus-
    band's eye."

And Arthur, "Have thy pleasant
    field again,
And thrice the gold for Uther's use
    thereof,
According to the years. No boon is
    here,
But justice, so thy say be proven
    true.
Accursed, who from the wrongs his
    father did
Would shape himself a right!"

                        And while she past,
Came yet another widow crying to
    him,
"A boon, Sir King! Thine enemy,
    King, am I.
With thine own hand thou slewest my
    dear lord,
A knight of Uther in the Barons' war,
When Lot and many another rose and
    fought
Against thee, saying thou wert basely
    born.
I held with these, and loathe to ask
    thee aught.
Yet lo! my husband's brother had my
    son
Thrall'd in his castle, and hath starved
    him dead;
And standeth seized of that inheritance

Which thou that slewest the sire hast
    left the son.
So tho' I scarce can ask it thee for
    hate,
Grant me some knight to do the battle
    for me,
Kill the foul thief, and wreak me for
    my son."

Then strode a good knight forward,
    crying to him,
"A boon, Sir King! I am her kins-
    man, I.
Give me to right her wrong, and slay
    the man."

Then came Sir Kay, the seneschal,
    and cried,
"A boon, Sir King! ev'n that thou
    grant her none,
This railer, that hath mock'd thee in
    full hall —
None; or the wholesome boon of gyve
    and gag."

But Arthur, "We sit King, to help
    the wrong'd
Thro' all our realm. The woman loves
    her lord.
Peace to thee, woman, with thy loves
    and hates!
The kings of old had doom'd thee to
    the flames,
Aurelius Emrys would have scourged
    thee dead,
And Uther slit thy tongue: but get
    thee hence —
Lest that rough humor of the kings of
    old
Return upon me! Thou that art her
    kin,
Go likewise; lay him low and slay
    him not,
But bring him here, that I may judge
    the right,
According to the justice of the King:
Then, be he guilty, by that deathless
    King
Who lived and died for men, the man
    shall die."

Then came in hall the messenger of
    Mark,

A name of evil savor in the land,
The Cornish king. In either hand he
    bore
What dazzled all, and shone far-off as
    shines
A field of charlock in the sudden sun
Between two showers, a cloth of palest
    gold,
Which down he laid before the throne,
    and knelt,
Delivering, that his lord, the vassal
    king,
Was ev'n upon his way to Camelot;
For having heard that Arthur of his
    grace
Had made his goodly cousin, Tristram,
    knight,
And, for himself was of the greater
    state,
Being a king, he trusted his liege-lord
Would yield him this large honor all
    the more;
So pray'd him well to accept this cloth
    of gold,
In token of true heart and feälty.

Then Arthur cried to rend the cloth,
    to rend
In pieces, and so cast it on the
    hearth.
An oak-tree smoulder'd there. "The
    goodly knight!
What! shall the shield of Mark stand
    among these?"
For, midway down the side of that long
    hall
A stately pile, — whereof along the
    front,
Some blazon'd, some but carven, and
    some blank,
There ran a treble range of stony
    shields, —
Rose, and high-arching overbrow'd the
    hearth.
And under every shield a knight was
    named:
For this was Arthur's custom in his
    hall;
When some good knight had done one
    noble deed,
His arms were carven only; but if
    twain

His arms were blazon'd also; but if none
The shield was blank and bare without a sign
Saving the name beneath ; and Gareth saw
The shield of Gawain blazon'd rich and bright,
And Modred's blank as death; and Arthur cried
To rend the cloth and cast it on the hearth.

"More like are we to reave him of his crown
Than make him knight because men call him king.
The kings we found, ye know we stay'd their hands
From war among themselves, but left them kings ;
Of whom were any bounteous, merciful,
Truth-speaking, brave, good livers, them we enroll'd
Among us, and they sit within our hall.
But Mark hath tarnish'd the great name of king,
As Mark would sully the low state of churl :
And, seeing he hath sent us cloth of gold,
Return, and meet, and hold him from our eyes,
Lest we should lap him up in cloth of lead,
Silenced for ever — craven — a man of plots,
Craft, poisonous counsels, wayside ambushings —
No fault of thine: let Kay the seneschal
Look to thy wants, and send thee satisfied —
Accursed, who strikes nor lets the hand be seen !"

And many another suppliant crying came
With noise of ravage wrought by beast and man,
And evermore a knight would ride away.

Last, Gareth leaning both hands heavily
Down on the shoulders of the twain, his men,
Approach'd between them toward the King, and ask'd,
"A boon, Sir King (his voice was all ashamed),
For see ye not how weak and hunger-worn
I seem — leaning on these ? grant me to serve
For meat and drink among thy kitchen-knaves
A twelvemonth and a day, nor seek my name.
Hereafter I will fight."

To him the King,
"A goodly youth and worth a goodlier boon !
But so thou wilt no goodlier, then must Kay,
The master of the meats and drinks, be thine."

He rose and past ; then Kay, a man of mien
Wan-sallow as the plant that feels itself
Root-bitten by white lichen,

"Lo ye now !
This fellow hath broken from some Abbey, where,
God wot, he had not beef and brewis enow,
However that might chance ! but an he work,
Like any pigeon will I cram his crop,
And sleeker shall he shine than any hog."

Then Lancelot standing near, "Sir Seneschal,
Sleuth-hound thou knowest, and gray, and all the hounds ;
A horse thou knowest, a man thou dost not know :

Broad brows and fair, a fluent hair
    and fine,
High nose, a nostril large and fine,
    and hands
Large, fair and fine! — some young
    lad's mystery —
But, or from sheepcot or king's hall,
    the boy
Is noble-natured. Treat him with all
    grace,
Lest he should come to shame thy
    judging of him."

    Then Kay, " What murmurest thou
    of mystery ?
Think ye this fellow will poison the
    King's dish ?
Nay, for he spake too fool-like :
    mystery!
Tut, an the lad were noble, he had
    ask'd
For horse and armor : fair and fine,
    forsooth !
Sir Fine-face, Sir Fair-hands ? but see
    thou to it
That thine own fineness, Lancelot,
    some fine day
Undo thee not — and leave my man
    to me."

    So Gareth all for glory underwent
The sooty yoke of kitchen-vassalage ;
Ate with young lads his portion by
    the door,
And couch'd at night with grimy
    kitchen-knaves.
And Lancelot ever spake him pleas-
    antly,
But Kay the seneschal who loved him
    not
Would hustle and harry him, and
    labor him
Beyond his comrade of the hearth,
    and set
To turn the broach, draw water, or
    hew wood,
Or grosser tasks ; and Gareth bow'd
    himself
With all obedience to the King, and
    wrought
All kind of service with a noble
    ease

That graced the lowliest act in doing
    it.
And when the thralls had talk among
    themselves,
And one would praise the love that
    linkt the King
And Lancelot — how the King had
    saved his life
In battle twice, and Lancelot once the
    King's —
For Lancelot was the first in Tourna-
    ment,
But Arthur mightiest on the battle-
    field —
Gareth was glad. Or if some other
    told,
How once the wandering forester at
    dawn,
Far over the blue tarns and hazy
    seas,
On Caer-Eryri's highest found the
    King,
A naked babe, of whom the Prophet
    spake,
" He passes to the Isle Avilion,
He passes and is heal'd and cannot
    die " —
Gareth was glad. But if their talk
    were foul,
Then would he whistle rapid as any
    lark,
Or carol some old roundelay, and so
    loud
That first they mock'd, but, after,
    reverenced him.
Or Gareth telling some prodigious tale
Of knights, who sliced a red life-bub-
    bling way
Thro' twenty folds of twisted dragon,
    held
All in a gap-mouth'd circle his good
    mates
Lying or sitting round him, idle hands,
Charm'd ; till Sir Kay, the seneschal,
    would come
Blustering upon them, like a sudden
    wind
Among dead leaves, and drive them
    all apart.
Or when the thralls had sport among
    themselves,
So there were any trial of mastery,

He, by two yards in casting bar or
   stone
Was counted best; and if there
   chanced a joust,
So that Sir Kay nodded him leave to
   go,
Would hurry thither, and when he
   saw the knights
Clash like the coming and retiring
   wave,
And the spear spring, and good horse
   reel, the boy
Was half beyond himself for ecstasy.

So for a month he wrought among
   the thralls ;
But in the weeks that follow'd, the
   good Queen,
Repentant of the word she made him
   swear,
And saddening in her childless castle,
   sent,
Between the in-crescent and de-cres-
   cent moon,
Arms for her son, and loosed him from
   his vow.

This, Gareth hearing from a squire
   of Lot
With whom he used to play at tourney
   once,
When both were children, and in
   lonely haunts
Would scratch a ragged oval on the
   sand,
And each at either dash from either
   end —
Shame never made girl redder than
   Gareth joy.
He laugh'd ; he sprang. "Out of the
   smoke, at once
I leap from Satan's foot to Peter's
   knee —
These news be mine, none other's —
   nay, the King's —
Descend into the city :" whereon he
   sought
The King alone, and found, and told
   him all.

"I have stagger'd thy strong Gawain in a tilt

For pastime ; yea, he said it : joust
   can I.
Make me thy knight — in secret! let
   my name
Be hidd'n, and give me the first quest,
   I spring
Like flame from ashes."

Here the King's calm eye
Fell on, and check'd, and made him
   flush, and bow
Lowly, to kiss his hand, who answer'd
   him,
"Son, the good mother let me know
   thee here,
And sent her wish that I would yield
   thee thine.
Make thee my knight ? my knights
   are sworn to vows
Of utter hardihood, utter gentleness,
And, loving, utter faithfulness in love,
And uttermost obedience to the King."

Then Gareth, lightly springing from
   his knees,
"My King, for hardihood I can prom-
   ise thee.
For uttermost obedience make de-
   mand
Of whom ye gave me to, the Seneschal,
No mellow master of the meats and
   drinks !
And as for love, God wot, I love not
   yet,
But love I shall, God willing."

And the King —
"Make thee my knight in secret ? yea,
   but he,
Our noblest brother, and our truest
   man,
And one with me in all, he needs
   must know."

"Let Lancelot know, my King, let
   Lancelot know,
Thy noblest and thy truest!"

And the King —
"But wherefore would ye men should
   wonder at you ?

Nay, rather for the sake of me, their
King,
And the deed's sake my knighthood
do the deed,
Than to be noised of."

　　　　　Merrily Gareth ask'd,
" Have I not earn'd my cake in baking
of it ?
Let be my name until I make my
name !
My deeds will speak : it is but for a
day."
So with a kindly hand on Gareth's
arm
Smiled the great King, and half-
unwillingly
Loving his lusty youthhood yielded
to him.
Then, after summoning Lancelot
privily,
" I have given him the first quest : he
is not proven.
Look therefore when he calls for this
in hall,
Thou get to horse and follow him far
away.
Cover the lions on thy shield, and see
Far as thou mayest, he be nor ta'en
nor slain."

　　Then that same day there past into
the hall
A damsel of high lineage, and a brow
May-blossom, and a cheek of apple-
blossom,
Hawk-eyes ; and lightly was her slen-
der nose
Tip-tilted like the petal of a flower ;
She into hall past with her page and
cried,

　　" O King, for thou hast driven the
foe without,
See to the foe within ! bridge, ford,
beset
By bandits, everyone that owns a
tower
The Lord for half a league. Why sit
ye there ?
Rest would I not, Sir King, an I were
king,

Till ev'n the lonest hold were all as
free
From cursed bloodshed, as thine altar-
cloth
From that best blood it is a sin to
spill."

　　" Comfort thyself," said Arthur, " I
nor mine
Rest : so my knighthood keep the
vows they swore,
The wastest moorland of our realm
shall be
Safe, damsel, as the centre of this hall.
What is thy name ? thy need ? "

　　　　　" My name ? " she said—
" Lynette my name ; noble ; my need,
a knight
To combat for my sister, Lyonors,
A lady of high lineage, of great lands,
And comely, yea, and comelier than
myself.
She lives in Castle Perilous : a river
Runs in three loops about her living-
place ;
And o'er it are three passings, and
three knights
Defend the passings, brethren, and a
fourth
And of that four the mightiest, holds
her stay'd
In her own castle, and so besieges her
To break her will, and make her wed
with him :
And but delays his purport till thou
send
To do the battle with him, thy chief
man
Sir Lancelot whom he trusts to over-
throw,
Then wed, with glory : but she will
not wed
Save whom she loveth, or a holy life.
Now therefore have I come for
Lancelot."

　　Then Arthur mindful of Sir Gareth
ask'd,
" Damsel, ye know this Order lives to
crush

All wrongers of the Realm. But say,
　　these four,
Who be they ?　What the fashion of
　　the men ? ”

　　“ They be of foolish fashion, O Sir
　　　King,
The fashion of that old knight-
　　errantry
Who ride abroad and do but what
　　they will;
Courteous or bestial from the moment,
　　such
As have nor law nor king; and three
　　of these
Proud in their fantasy call themselves
　　the Day,
Morning-Star, and Noon-Sun, and
　　Evening-Star,
Being strong fools ; and never a whit
　　more wise
The fourth who alway rideth arm'd
　　in black,
A huge man-beast of boundless sav-
　　agery.
He names himself the Night, and
　　oftener Death,
And wears a helmet mounted with a
　　skull,
And bears a skeleton figured on his
　　arms,
To show that who may slay or scape
　　the three
Slain by himself shall enter endless
　　night.
And all these four be fools, but mighty
　　men,
And therefore am I come for Lance-
　　lot.”

　　Hereat Sir Gareth call'd from where
　　he rose,
A head with kindling eyes above the
　　throng,
“ A boon, Sir King — this quest ! ”
　　then — for he mark'd
Kay near him groaning like a wounded
　　bull —
“ Yea, King, thou knowest thy kitchen-
　　knave am I,
And mighty thro' thy meats and drinks
　　am I.

And I can topple over a hundred such.
Thy promise, King,” and Arthur glanc-
　　ing at him,
Brought down a momentary brow.
　　“ Rough, sudden,
And pardonable, worthy to be knight—
Go, therefore,” and all hearers were
　　amazed.

　　But on the damsel's forehead shame,
　　pride, wrath
Slew the May-white : she lifted either
　　arm,
“ Fie on thee, King !　I ask'd for thy
　　chief knight,
And thou hast given me but a kitchen-
　　knave.”
Then ere a man in hall could stay her,
　　turn'd,
Fled down the lane of access to the
　　King,
Took horse, descended the slope street,
　　and past
The weird white gate, and paused with-
　　out, beside
The field of tourney, murmuring
　　“ kitchen-knave.”

　　Now two great entries open'd from
　　the hall,
At one end one, that gave upon a
　　range
Of level pavement where the King
　　would pace
At sunrise, gazing over plain and
　　wood ;
And down from this a lordly stairway
　　sloped
Till lost in blowing trees and tops of
　　towers ;
And out by this main doorway past
　　the King.
But one was counter to the hearth,
　　and rose
High that the highest-crested helm
　　could ride
Therethro' nor graze : and by this entry
　　fled
The damsel in her wrath, and on to
　　this
Sir Gareth strode, and saw without
　　the door

King Arthur's gift, the worth of half
    a town,
A warhorse of the best, and near it
    stood
The two that out of north had fol-
    low'd him:
This bare a maiden shield, a casque;
    that held
The horse, the spear; whereat Sir
    Gareth loosed
A cloak that dropt from collar-bone
    to heel,
A cloth of roughest web, and cast it
    down,
And from it like a fuel-smother'd fire,
That lookt half-dead, brake bright, and
    flash'd as those
Dull-coated things, that making slide
    apart
Their dusk wing-cases, all beneath
    there burns
A jewell'd harness, ere they pass and
    fly.
So Gareth ere he parted flash'd in
    arms.
Then as he donn'd the helm, and took
    the shield
And mounted horse and graspt a
    spear, of grain
Storm-strengthen'd on a windy site,
    and tipt
With trenchant steel, around him
    slowly prest
The people, while from out of kitchen
    came
The thralls in throng, and seeing who
    had work'd
Lustier than any, and whom they could
    but love,
Mounted in arms, threw up their caps
    and cried,
"God bless the King, and all his
    fellowship!"
And on thro' lanes of shouting Gareth
    rode
Down the slope street, and past with-
    out the gate.

    So Gareth past with joy; but as the
    cur
Pluckt from the cur he fights with,
    ere his cause

Be cool'd by fighting, follows, being
    named,
His owner, but remembers all, and
    growls
Remembering, so Sir Kay beside the
    door
Mutter'd in scorn of Gareth whom he
    used
To harry and hustle.

            "Bound upon a quest
With horse and arms — the King hath
    past his time —
My scullion knave! Thralls to your
    work again,
For an your fire be low ye kindle
    mine!
Will there be dawn in West and eve
    in East?
Begone! — my knave! — belike and
    like enow
Some old head-blow not heeded in his
    youth
So shook his wits they wander in his
    prime —
Crazed! how the villain lifted up his
    voice,
Nor shamed to bawl himself a kitchen-
    knave.
Tut: he was tame and meek enow with
    me,
Till peacock'd up with Lancelot's
    noticing.
Well — I will after my loud knave,
    and learn
Whether he know me for his master
    yet.
Out of the smoke he came, and so my
    lance
Hold, by God's grace, he shall into
    the mire —
Thence, if the King awaken from his
    craze,
Into the smoke again."

            But Lancelot said,
"Kay, wherefore wilt thou go against
    the King,
For that did never he whereon ye rail,
But ever meekly served the King in
    thee?
Abide: take counsel; for this lad is
    great

And lusty, and knowing both of lance
        and sword."
"Tut, tell not me," said Kay, "ye are
        overfine
To mar stout knaves with foolish
        courtesies : "
Then mounted, on thro' silent faces
        rode
Down the slope city, and out beyond
        the gate.

But by the field of tourney linger-
        ing yet
Mutter'd the damsel, "Wherefore did
        the King
Scorn me ? for, were Sir Lancelot
        lackt, at least
He might have yielded to me one of
        those
Who tilt for lady's love and glory
        here,
Rather than — O sweet heaven! O
        fie upon him —
His kitchen-knave."

        To whom Sir Gareth drew
(And there were none but few goodlier
        than he)
Shining in arms, "Damsel, the quest
        is mine.
Lead, and I follow." She thereat, as
        one
That smells a foul-flesh'd agaric in the
        holt,
And deems it carrion of some wood-
        land thing,
Or shrew, or weasel, nipt her slender
        nose
With petulant thumb and finger,
        shrilling, "Hence!
Avoid, thou smellest all of kitchen-
        grease.
And look who comes behind," for
        there was Kay.
"Knowest thou not me ? thy master ?
        I am Kay.
We lack thee by the hearth."

        And Gareth to him,
"Master no more! too well I know
        thee, ay —

The most ungentle knight in Arthur's
        hall."
"Have at thee then," said Kay: they
        shock'd, and Kay
Fell shoulder-slipt, and Gareth cried
        again,
"Lead, and I follow," and fast away
        she fled.

But after sod and shingle ceased to
        fly
Behind her, and the heart of her good
        horse
Was nigh to burst with violence of the
        beat,
Perforce she stay'd, and overtaken
        spoke.

"What doest thou, scullion, in my
        fellowship ?
Deem'st thou that I accept thee aught
        the more
Or love thee better, that by some
        device
Full cowardly, or by mere unhappi-
        ness,
Thou hast overthrown and slain thy
        master — thou! —
Dish-washer and broach-turner, loon!
        — to me
Thou smellest all of kitchen as be-
        fore."

"Damsel," Sir Gareth answer'd
        gently, "say
Whate'er ye will, but whatsoe'er ye
        say,
I leave not till I finish this fair quest,
Or die therefore."

        "Ay, wilt thou finish it ?
Sweet lord, how like a noble knight he
        talks !
The listening rogue hath caught the
        manner of it.
But, knave, anon thou shalt be met
        with, knave,
And then by such a one that thou for
        all
The kitchen brewis that was ever supt
Shalt not once dare to look him in the
        face."

" I shall assay," said Gareth with a
  smile
That madden'd her, and away she
  flash'd again
Down the long avenues of a boundless
  wood,
And Gareth following was again be-
  knaved.

" Sir Kitchen-knave, I have miss'd
  the only way
Where Arthur's men are set along the
  wood ;
The wood is nigh as full of thieves as
  leaves :
If both be slain, I am rid of thee; but
  yet,
Sir Scullion, canst thou use that spit
  of thine ?
Fight, an thou canst : I have miss'd
  the only way."

So till the dusk that follow'd even-
  song
Rode on the two, reviler and reviled ;
Then after one long slope was
  mounted, saw,
Bowl-shaped, thro' tops of many thou-
  sand pines
A gloomy-gladed hollow slowly sink
To westward — in the deeps whereof
  a mere,
Round as the red eye of an Eagle-
  owl,
Under the half-dead sunset glared ;
  and shouts
Ascended, and there brake a serving-
  man
Flying from out the black wood, and
  crying,
" They have bound my lord to cast
  him in the mere."
Then Gareth, " Bound am I to right
  the wrong'd,
But straitlier bound am I to bide with
  thee."
And when the damsel spake contempt-
  uously,
" Lead, and I follow," Gareth cried
  again,
" Follow, I lead ! " so down among the
  pines

He plunged ; and there, blackshadow'd
  nigh the mere,
And mid-thigh-deep in bulrushes and
  reed,
Saw six tall men haling a seventh
  along,
A stone about his neck to drown him
  in it.
Three with good blows he quieted, but
  three
Fled thro' the pines ; and Gareth loosed
  the stone
From off his neck, then in the mere
  beside
Tumbled it ; oilily bubbled up the
  mere.
Last, Gareth loosed his bonds and on
  free feet
Set him, a stalwart Baron, Arthur's
  friend.

" Well that ye came, or else these
  caitiff rogues
Had wreak'd themselves on me ; good
  cause is theirs
To hate me, for my wont hath ever
  been
To catch my thief, and then like vermin here
Drown him, and with a stone about
  his neck ;
And under this wan water many of
  them
Lie rotting, but at night let go the
  stone,
And rise, and flickering in a grimly
  light
Dance on the mere. Good now, ye
  have saved a life
Worth somewhat as the cleanser of
  this wood.
And fain would I reward thee worshipfully.
What guerdon will ye ? "

                    Gareth sharply spake,
" None ! for the deed's sake have I
  done the deed,
In uttermost obedience to the King.
But wilt thou yield this damsel har-
  borage ? "

Whereat the Baron saying, "I well
     believe
You be of Arthur's Table," a light
     laugh
Broke from Lynette, "Ay, truly of a
     truth,
And in a sort, being Arthur's kitchen-
     knave! —
But deem not I accept thee aught the
     more,
Scullion, for running sharply with thy
     spit
Down on a rout of craven foresters.
A thresher with his flail had scatter'd
     them.
Nay — for thou smellest of the kitchen
     still.
But an this lord will yield us harbor-
     age,
Well."

     So she spake. A league beyond
     the wood,
All in a full-fair manor and a rich,
His towers where that day a feast had
     been
Held in high wall, and many a viand
     left,
And many a costly cate, received the
     three.
And there they placed a peacock in
     his pride
Before the damsel, and the Baron
     set
Gareth beside her, but at once she
     rose.

     "Meseems, that here is much dis-
     courtesy,
Setting this knave, Lord Baron, at my
     side.
Hear me — this morn I stood in
     Arthur's hall,
And pray'd the King would grant me
     Lancelot
To fight the brotherhood of Day and
     Night —
The last a monster unsubduable
Of any save of him for whom I
     call'd —
Suddenly bawls this frontless kitchen-
     knave,

'The quest is mine; thy kitchen-
     knave am I,
And mighty thro' thy meats and
     drinks am I.'
Then Arthur all at once gone mad
     replies,
'Go therefore,' and so gives the quest
     to him —
Him — here — a villain fitter to stick
     swine
Than ride abroad redressing women's
     wrong,
Or sit beside a noble gentlewoman."

     Then   half-ashamed   and   part-
     amazed, the lord
Now look'd at one and now at other,
     left
The damsel by the peacock in his
     pride,
And, seating Gareth at another board,
Sat down beside him, ate and then
     began.

     "Friend, whether thou be kitchen-
     knave, or not,
Or whether it be the maiden's fantasy,
And whether she be mad, or else the
     King,
Or both or neither, or thyself be mad,
I ask not: but thou strikest a strong
     stroke,
For strong thou art and goodly there-
     withal,
And saver of my life; and therefore
     now,
For here be mighty men to joust with,
     weigh
Whether thou wilt not with thy dam-
     sel back
To crave again Sir Lancelot of the
     King.
Thy pardon; I but speak for thine
     avail,
The saver of my life."

               And Gareth said,
"Full pardon, but I follow up the
     quest,
Despite of Day and Night and Death
     and Hell."

So when, next morn, the lord whose life he saved
Had, some brief space, convey'd them on their way
And left them with God-speed, Sir Gareth spake,
"Lead, and I follow." Haughtily she replied,

" I fly no more : I allow thee for an hour.
Lion and stoat have isled together, knave,
In time of flood. Nay, furthermore, methinks
Some ruth is mine for thee. Back wilt thou, fool ?
For hard by here is one will overthrow
And slay thee : then will I to court again,
And shame the King for only yielding me
My champion from the ashes of his hearth."

To whom Sir Gareth answer'd courteously,
" Say thou thy say, and I will do my deed.
Allow me for mine hour, and thou wilt find
My fortunes all as fair as hers who lay
Among the ashes and wedded the King's son."

Then to the shore of one of those long loops
Wherethro' the serpent river coil'd, they came.
Rough-thicketed were the banks and steep; the stream
Full, narrow; this a bridge of single arc
Took at a leap; and on the further side
Arose a silk pavilion, gay with gold
In streaks and rays, and all Lent-lily in hue,
Save that the dome was purple, and above,
Crimson, a slender banneret fluttering.

And therebefore the lawless warrior paced
Unarm'd, and calling, "Damsel, is this he,
The champion thou hast brought from Arthur's hall ?
For whom we let thee pass." " Nay, nay," she said,
"Sir Morning-Star. The King in utter scorn
Of thee and thy much folly hath sent thee here
His kitchen-knave : and look thou to thyself :
See that he fall not on thee suddenly,
And slay thee unarm'd : he is not knight but knave."

Then at his call, "O daughters of the Dawn,
And servants of the Morning-Star, approach,
Arm me," from out the silken curtain-folds
Bare-footed and bare-headed three fair girls
In gilt and rosy raiment came : their feet
In dewy grasses glisten'd; and the hair
All over glanced with dewdrop or with gem
Like sparkles in the stone Avanturine.
These arm'd him in blue arms, and gave a shield
Blue also, and thereon the morning star.
And Gareth silent gazed upon the knight,
Who stood a moment ere his horse was brought,
Glorying; and in the stream beneath him, shone
Immingled with Heaven's azure waveringly,
The gay pavilion and the naked feet,
His arms, the rosy raiment, and the star.

Then she that watch'd him, "Wherefore stare ye so ?

Thou shakest in thy fear : there yet is
    time :
Flee down the valley before he get to
    horse.
Who will cry shame ?   Thou art not
    knight but knave."

  Said Gareth, "Damsel, whether
    knave or knight,
Far liefer had I fight a score of times
Than hear thee so missay me and re-
    vile.
Fair words were best for him who
    fights for thee ;
But truly foul are better, for they
    send
That strength of anger thro' mine
    arms, I know
That I shall overthrow him."

                    And he that bore
The star, being mounted, cried from
    o'er the bridge,
"A kitchen-knave, and sent in scorn
    of me !
Such fight not I, but answer scorn
    with scorn.
For this were shame to do him further
    wrong
Than set him on his feet, and take his
    horse
And arms, and so return him to the
    King.
Come, therefore, leave thy lady lightly,
    knave.
Avoid : for it beseemeth not a knave
To ride with such a lady."

                    "Dog, thou liest.
I spring from loftier lineage than
    thine own."
He spake, and all at fiery speed the
    two
Shock'd on the central bridge, and
    either spear
Bent but not brake, and either knight
    at once,
Hurl'd as a stone from out of a cata-
    pult
Beyond his horse's crupper and the
    bridge,

Fell, as if dead ; but quickly rose and
    drew,
And Gareth lash'd so fiercely with his
    brand
He drave his enemy backward down
    the bridge,
The damsel crying, "Well-stricken,
    kitchen-knave ! "
Till Gareth's shield was cloven ; but
    one stroke
Laid him that clove it grovelling on
    the ground.

  Then cried the fall'n, "Take not my
    life : I yield."
And Gareth, "So this damsel ask it
    of me
Good — I accord it easily as a grace."
She reddening, "Insolent scullion : I
    of thee ?
I bound to thee for any favor ask'd ! "
"Then shall he die."   And Gareth
    there unlaced
His helmet as to slay him, but she
    shriek'd,
"Be not so hardy, scullion, as to
    slay
One nobler than thyself."   "Damsel,
    thy charge
Is an abounding pleasure to me.
    Knight,
Thy life is thine at her command.
    Arise
And quickly pass to Arthur's hall,
    and say
His kitchen-knave hath sent thee.
    See thou crave
His pardon for thy breaking of his
    laws.
Myself, when I return, will plead for
    thee.
Thy shield is mine — farewell ; and,
    damsel, thou,
Lead, and I follow."

                    And fast away she fled.
Then when he came upon her, spake,
    "Methought,
Knave, when I watch'd thee striking
    on the bridge
The savor of thy kitchen came upon
    me

A little faintlier: but the wind hath
   changed:
I scent it twenty-fold." And then she
   sang,
"'O morning star' (not that tall felon
   there
Whom thou by sorcery or unhappiness
Or some device, hast foully overthrown),
'O morning star that smilest in the
   blue,
O star, my morning dream hath
   proven true,
Smile sweetly, thou! my love hath
   smiled on me.'

"But thou begone, take counsel,
   and away,
For hard by here is one that guards a
   ford —
The second brother in their fool's
   parable —
Will pay thee all thy wages, and to
   boot.
Care not for shame: thou art not
   knight but knave."

To whom Sir Gareth answer'd,
   laughingly,
"Parables? Hear a parable of the
   knave.
When I was kitchen-knave among the
   rest
Fierce was the hearth, and one of my
   co-mates
Own'd a rough dog, to whom he cast
   his coat,
'Guard it,' and there was none to
   meddle with it.
And such a coat art thou, and thee
   the King
Gave me to guard, and such a dog
   am I,
To worry, and not to flee — and —
   knight or knave —
The knave that doth thee service as
   full knight
Is all as good, meseems, as any knight
Toward thy sister's freeing."

        "Ay, Sir Knave!
Ay, knave, because thou strikest as a
   knight,

Being but knave, I hate thee all the
   more."

"Fair damsel, you should worship
   me the more,
That, being but knave, I throw thine
   enemies."

"Ay, ay," she said, "but thou shalt
   meet thy match."

So when they touch'd the second
   river-loop,
Huge on a huge red horse, and all in
   mail
Burnish'd to blinding, shone the Noon-
   day Sun
Beyond a raging shallow. As if the
   flower,
That blows a globe of after arrowlets,
Ten thousand-fold had grown, flash'd
   the fierce shield,
All sun; and Gareth's eyes had flying
   blots
Before them when he turn'd from
   watching him.
He from beyond the roaring shallow
   roar'd,
"What doest thou, brother, in my
   marches here?"
And she athwart the shallow shrill'd
   again,
"Here is a kitchen-knave from
   Arthur's hall
Hath overthrown thy brother, and
   hath his arms."
"Ugh!" cried the Sun, and vizoring
   up a red
And cipher face of rounded foolish-
   ness,
Push'd horse across the foamings of
   the ford,
Whom Gareth met midstream: no
   room was there
For lance or tourney-skill: four
   strokes they struck
With sword, and these were mighty;
   the new knight
Had fear he might be shamed; but as
   the Sun
Heaved up a ponderous arm to strike
   the fifth,

The hoof of his horse slipt in the
    stream, the stream
Descended, and the Sun was wash'd
    away.

    Then Gareth laid his lance athwart
        the ford ;
So drew him home ; but he that fought
    no more,
As being all bone-batter'd on the rock,
Yielded ; and Gareth sent him to the
    King.
" Myself when I return will plead for
    thee."
" Lead, and I follow." Quietly she
    led.
" Hath not the good wind, damsel,
    changed again ? "
" Nay, not a point : nor art thou victor
    here.
There lies a ridge of slate across the
    ford ;
His horse thereon stumbled — ay, for
    I saw it.

    " ' O Sun ' (not this strong fool
        whom thou, Sir Knave,
Hast overthrown thro' mere unhappi-
    ness),
' O Sun, that wakenest all to bliss or
    pain,
O moon, that layest all to sleep again,
Shine sweetly : twice my love hath
    smiled on me.'

    " What knowest thou of lovesong
        or of love ?
Nay, nay, God wot, so thou wert nobly
    born,
Thou hast a pleasant presence. Yea,
    perchance, —

    " ' O dewy flowers that open to the
        sun,
O dewy flowers that close when day is
    done,
Blow sweetly : twice my love hath
    smiled on me.'

    " What knowest thou of flowers,
        except, belike,

To garnish meats with ? hath not our
    good King
Who lent me thee, the flower of
    kitchendom,
A foolish love for flowers ? what stick
    ye round
The pasty ? wherewithal deck the
    boar's head ?
Flowers ? nay, the boar hath rose-
    maries and bay.

    " ' O birds, that warble to the morn-
        ing sky,
O birds that warble as the day goes
    by,
Sing sweetly : twice my love hath
    smiled on me.'

    " What knowest thou of birds, lark,
        mavis, merle,
Linnet ? what dream ye when they
    utter forth
May-music growing with the growing
    light,
Their sweet sun-worship ? these be for
    the snare
(So runs thy fancy) these be for the
    spit,
Larding and basting. See thou have
    not now
Larded thy last, except thou turn and
    fly.
There stands the third fool of their
    allegory."

    For there beyond a bridge of treble
        bow,
All in a rose-red from the west, and
    all
Naked it seem'd, and glowing in the
    broad
Deep-dimpled current underneath, the
    knight,
That named himself the Star of
    Evening, stood.

    And Gareth, " Wherefore waits the
        madman there
Naked in open dayshine ? "   " Nay,"
    she cried,
" Not naked, only wrapt in harden'd
    skins

That fit him like his own; and so ye
  cleave
His armor off him, these will turn the
  blade."

Then the third brother shouted o'er
  the bridge,
"O brother-star, why shine ye here so
  low?
Thy ward is higher up: but have ye
  slain
The damsel's champion?" and the
  damsel cried,

"No star of thine, but shot from
  Arthur's heaven
With all disaster unto thine and thee!
For both thy younger brethren have
  gone down
Before this youth; and so wilt thou,
  Sir Star;
Art thou not old?"

  "Old, damsel, old and hard,
Old, with the might and breath of
  twenty boys."
Said Gareth, "Old, and over-bold in
  brag!
But that same strength which threw
  the Morning Star
Can throw the Evening."

        Then that other blew
A hard and deadly note upon the horn.
"Approach and arm me!" With slow
  steps from out
An old storm-beaten, russet, many-
  stain'd
Pavilion, forth a grizzled damsel
  came,
And arm'd him in old arms, and
  brought a helm
With but a drying evergreen for crest,
And gave a shield whereon the Star of
  Even
Half-tarnish'd and half-bright, his
  emblem, shone.
But when it glitter'd o'er the saddle-
  bow,
They madly hurl'd together on the
  bridge;

And Gareth overthrew him, lighted,
  drew,
There met him drawn, and overthrew
  him again,
But up like fire he started: and as
  oft
As Gareth brought him grovelling on
  his knees,
So many a time he vaulted up again;
Till Gareth panted hard, and his great
  heart,
Foredooming all his trouble was in
  vain,
Labor'd within him, for he seem'd as
  one
That all in later, sadder age begins
To war against ill uses of a life,
But these from all his life arise, and
  cry,
"Thou hast made us lords, and canst
  not put us down!"
He half despairs; so Gareth seem'd to
  strike
Vainly, the damsel clamoring all the
  while,
"Well done, knave-knight, well
  stricken, O good knight-
  knave—
O knave, as noble as any of all the
  knights—
Shame me not, shame me not. I have
  prophesied—
Strike, thou art worthy of the Table
  Round—
His arms are old, he trusts the hard-
  en'd skin—
Strike—strike—the wind will never
  change again."
And Gareth hearing ever stronglier
  smote,
And hew'd great pieces of his armor
  off him,
But lash'd in vain against the harden'd
  skin,
And could not wholly bring him
  under, more
Than loud Southwesterns, rolling
  ridge on ridge,
The buoy that rides at sea, and dips
  and springs
For ever; till at length Sir Gareth's
  brand

Clash'd his, and brake it utterly to the
  hilt.
"I have thee now;" but forth that
  other sprang,
And, all unknightlike, writhed his
  wiry arms
Around him, till he felt, despite his
  mail,
Strangled, but straining ev'n his uttermost
Cast, and so hurl'd him headlong o'er
  the bridge
Down to the river, sink or swim, and
  cried,
"Lead, and I follow."

          But the damsel said,
"I lead no longer; ride thou at my
  side;
Thou art the kingliest of all kitchen-
  knaves.

   "'O trefoil, sparkling on the rainy
  plain,
O rainbow with three colors after rain,
Shine sweetly: thrice my love hath
  smiled on me.'

   "Sir, — and, good faith, I fain had
  added — Knight,
But that I heard thee call thyself a
  knave, —
Shamed am I that I so rebuked,
  reviled,
Missaid thee; noble I am; and
  thought the King
Scorn'd me and mine; and now thy
  pardon, friend,
For thou hast ever answer'd courteously,
And wholly bold thou art, and meek
  withal
As any of Arthur's best, but, being
  knave,
Hast mazed my wit: I marvel what
  thou art.

   "Damsel," he said, "you be not all
  to blame,
Saving that you mistrusted our good
  King

Would handle scorn, or yield you,
  asking, one
Not fit to cope your quest.   You said
  your say;
Mine answer was my deed.   Good
  sooth! I hold
He scarce is knight, yea but half-man,
  nor meet
To fight for gentle damsel, he, who
  lets
His heart be stirr'd with any foolish
  heat
At any gentle damsel's waywardness.
Shamed? care not! thy foul sayings
  fought for me:
And seeing now thy words are fair,
  methinks
There rides no knight, not Lancelot,
  his great self,
Hath force to quell me."

          Nigh upon that hour
When the lone hern forgets his mel-
  ancholy,
Lets down his other leg, and stretch-
  ing, dreams
Of goodly supper in the distant pool,
Then turn'd the noble damsel smiling
  at him,
And told him of a cavern hard at
  hand,
Where bread and baken meats and
  good red wine
Of Southland, which the Lady Lyo-
  nors
Had sent her coming champion, waited
  him.

   Anon they past a narrow comb
  wherein
Were slabs of rock with figures,
  knights on horse
Sculptured, and deckt in slowly-wan-
  ing hues.
"Sir Knave, my knight, a hermit once
  was here,
Whose holy hand hath fashion'd on
  the rock
The war of Time against the soul of
  man.
And yon four fools have suck'd their
  allegory

From these damp walls, and taken
but the form.
Know ye not these?" and Gareth
lookt and read —
In letters like to those the vexillary
Hath left crag-carven o'er the stream-
ing Gelt —
"Phosphorus," then "Meridies" —
"Hesperus" —
"Nox" — "Mors," beneath five fig-
ures, armed men,
Slab after slab, their faces forward
all,
And running down the Soul, a Shape
that fled
With broken wings, torn raiment and
loose hair,
For help and shelter to the hermit's
cave.
"Follow the faces, and we find it.
Look,
Who comes behind?"

For one — delay'd at first
Thro' helping back the dislocated Kay
To Camelot, then by what thereafter
chanced,
The damsel's headlong error thro' the
wood —
Sir Lancelot, having swum the river-
loops —
His blue shield-lions cover'd — softly
drew
Behind the twain, and when he saw
the star
Gleam, on Sir Gareth's turning to
him, cried,
"Stay, felon-knight, I avenge me for
my friend."
And Gareth crying prick'd against the
cry ;
But when they closed — in a moment
— at one touch
Of that skill'd spear, the wonder of
the world —
Went sliding down so easily, and fell,
That when he found the grass within
his hands
He laugh'd ; the laughter jarr'd upon
Lynette :
Harshly she ask'd him, "Shamed and
overthrown,

And tumbled back into the kitchen-
knave,
Why laugh ye? that ye blew your
boast in vain?"
"Nay, noble damsel, but that I, the
son
Of old King Lot and good Queen Bel-
licent,
And victor of the bridges and the ford,
And knight of Arthur, here lie thrown
by whom
I know not, all thro' mere unhappi-
ness —
Device and sorcery and unhappi-
ness —
Out, sword ; we are thrown !" And
Lancelot answer'd, "Prince,
O Gareth — thro' the mere unhappi-
ness
Of one who came to help thee, not to
harm,
Lancelot, and all as glad to find thee
whole,
As on the day when Arthur knighted
him."

Then Gareth, "Thou — Lancelot !
— thine the hand
That threw me? An some chance to
mar the boast
Thy brethren of thee make — which
could not chance —
Had sent thee down before a lesser
spear,
Shamed had I been, and sad — O
Lancelot — thou !"

Whereat the maiden, petulant,
"Lancelot,
Why came ye not, when call'd? and
wherefore now
Come ye, not call'd? I gloried in my
knave,
Who being still rebuked, would answer
still
Courteous as any knight — but now,
if knight,
The marvel dies, and leaves me fool'd
and trick'd,
And only wondering wherefore play'd
upon :

And doubtful whether I and mine be
  scorn'd.
Where should be truth if not in
  Arthur's hall,
In Arthur's presence?   Knight,
  knave, prince and fool,
I hate thee and for ever."

                    And Lancelot said,
" Blessed be thou, Sir Gareth! knight
  art thou
To the King's best wish. O damsel,
  be you wise
To call him shamed, who is but over-
  thrown?
Thrown have I been, nor once, but
  many a time.
Victor from vanquish'd issues at the
  last,
And overthrower from being over-
  thrown.
With sword we have not striven; and
  thy good horse
And thou are weary; yet not less I
  felt
Thy manhood thro' that wearied lance
  of thine.
Well hast thou done; for all the
  stream is freed,
And thou hast wreak'd his justice on
  his foes,
And when reviled, hast answer'd
  graciously,
And makest merry when overthrown.
  Prince, Knight,
Hail, Knight and Prince, and of our
  Table Round!"

And then when turning to Lynette
  he told
The tale of Gareth, petulantly she
  said,
" Ay well — ay well — for worse than
  being fool'd
Of others, is to fool one's self. A
  cave,
Sir Lancelot, is hard by, with meats
  and drinks
And forage for the horse, and flint for
  fire.

But all about it flies a honeysuckle.
Seek, till we find."   And when they
  sought and found,
Sir Gareth drank and ate, and all his
  life
Past into sleep ; on whom the maiden
  gazed.
" Sound sleep be thine! sound cause
  to sleep hast thou.
Wake lusty! seem I not as tender to
  him
As any mother?   Ay, but such a one
As all day long hath rated at her
  child,
And vext his day, but blesses him
  asleep —
Good lord, how sweetly smells the
  honeysuckle
In the hush'd night, as if the world
  were one
Of utter peace, and love, and gentleness !
O Lancelot, Lancelot " — and she
  clapt her hands —
" Full merry am I to find my goodly
  knave
Is knight and noble.   See now, sworn
  have I,
Else yon black felon had not let me
  pass,
To bring thee back to do the battle
  with him.
Thus an thou goest, he will fight thee
  first ;
Who doubts thee victor?   so will my
  knight-knave
Miss the full flower of this accom-
  plishment."

                    Said Lancelot, " Peradventure he,
  you name,
May know my shield. Let Gareth,
  an he will,
Change his for mine, and take my
  charger, fresh,
Not to be spurr'd, loving the battle as
  well
As he that rides him."   " Lancelot-
  like," she said,
" Courteous in this, Lord Lancelot, as
  in all."

And Gareth, wakening, fiercely clutch'd the shield;
" Ramp ye lance-splintering lions, on whom all spears
Are rotten sticks! ye seem agape to roar!
Yea, ramp and roar at leaving of your lord! —
Care not, good beasts, so well I care for you.
O noble Lancelot, from my hold on these
Streams virtue — fire — thro' one that will not shame
Even the shadow of Lancelot under shield.
Hence: let us go."

            Silent the silent field
They traversed. Arthur's harp tho' summer-wan,
In counter motion to the clouds, allured
The glance of Gareth dreaming on his liege.
A star shot: "Lo," said Gareth, " the foe falls ! "
An owl whoopt: "Hark the victor pealing there ! "
Suddenly she that rode upon his left
Clung to the shield that Lancelot lent him, crying,
" Yield, yield him this again: 'tis he must fight:
I curse the tongue that all thro' yesterday
Reviled thee, and hath wrought on Lancelot now
To lend thee horse and shield: wonders ye have done ;
Miracles ye cannot: here is glory enow
In having flung the three : I see thee maim'd,
Mangled : I swear thou canst not fling the fourth."

" And wherefore, damsel ? tell me all ye know.
You cannot scare me ; nor rough face, or voice,
Brute bulk of limb, or boundless savagery
Appal me from the quest."

            " Nay, Prince," she cried,
"God wot, I never look'd upon the face,
Seeing he never rides abroad by day ;
But watch'd him have I like a phantom pass
Chilling the night : nor have I heard the voice.
Always he made his mouthpiece of a page
Who came and went, and still reported him
As closing in himself the strength of ten,
And when his anger tare him, massacring
Man, woman, lad and girl — yea, the soft babe !
Some hold that he hath swallow'd infant flesh,
Monster ! O Prince, I went for Lancelot first,
The quest is Lancelot's : give him back the shield."

Said Gareth laughing, " An he fight for this,
Belike he wins it as the better man :
Thus — and not else ! "

            But Lancelot on him urged
All the devisings of their chivalry
When one might meet a mightier than himself ;
How best to manage horse, lance, sword and shield,
And so fill up the gap where force might fail
With skill and fineness. Instant were his words.

Then Gareth, "Here be rules. I know but one —
To dash against mine enemy and to win.
Yet have I watch'd thee victor in the joust,
And seen thy way."   " Heaven help thee," sigh'd Lynette.

Then for a space, and under cloud
  that grew
To thunder-gloom palling all stars,
  they rode
In converse till she made her palfrey
  halt,
Lifted an arm, and softly whisper'd,
  "There."
And all the three were silent seeing,
  pitch'd
Beside the Castle Perilous on flat field,
A huge pavilion like a mountain peak
Sunder the glooming crimson on the
  marge,
Black, with black banner, and a long
  black horn
Beside it hanging; which Sir Gareth
  graspt,
And so, before the two could hinder
  him,
Bent all his heart and breath thro' all
  the horn.
Echo'd the walls; a light twinkled;
  anon
Came lights and lights, and once again
  he blew;
Whereon were hollow tramplings up
  and down
And muffled voices heard, and shadows
  past;
Till high above him, circled with her
  maids,
The Lady Lyonors at a window stood,
Beautiful among lights, and waving to
  him
White hands, and courtesy; but when
  the Prince
Three times had blown — after long
  hush —
  at last —
The huge pavilion slowly yielded up,
Thro' those black foldings, that which
  housed therein.
High on a nightblack horse, in night-
  black arms,
With white breast-bone, and barren
  ribs of Death,
And crown'd with fleshless laughter —
  some ten steps —
In the half-light — thro' the dim dawn
  — advanced
The monster, and then paused, and
  spake no word.

But Gareth spake and all indig-
  nantly,
"Fool, for thou hast, men say, the
  strength of ten,
Canst thou not trust the limbs thy
  God hath given,
But must, to make the terror of thee
  more,
Trick thyself out in ghastly imageries
Of that which Life hath done with,
  and the clod,
Less dull than thou, will hide with
  mantling flowers
As if for pity?" But he spake no
  word;
Which set the horror higher: a maiden
  swoon'd;
The Lady Lyonors wrung her hands
  and wept,
As doom'd to be the bride of Night
  and Death;
Sir Gareth's head prickled beneath his
  helm;
And ev'n Sir Lancelot thro' his warm
  blood felt
Ice strike, and all that mark'd him
  were aghast.

At once Sir Lancelot's charger
  fiercely neigh'd,
And Death's dark war-horse bounded
  forward with him.
Then those that did not blink the
  terror, saw
That Death was cast to ground, and
  slowly rose.
But with one stroke Sir Gareth split
  the skull.
Half fell to right and half to left and
  lay.
Then with a stronger buffet he clove
  the helm
As throughly as the skull; and out
  from this
Issued the bright face of a blooming
  boy
Fresh as a flower new-born, and crying,
  "Knight,
Slay me not: my three brethren bade
  me do it,
To make a horror all about the
  house,

And stay the world from Lady Lyon-
    ors.
They never dream'd the passes would
    be past."
Answer'd Sir Gareth graciously to one
Not many a moon his younger, " My
    fair child,
What madness made thee challenge
    the chief knight
Of Arthur's hall?" "Fair Sir, they
    bade me do it.
They hate the King, and Lancelot, the
    King's friend,
They hoped to slay him somewhere
    on the stream,
They never dream'd the passes could
    be past."

Then sprang the happier day from
    underground;
And Lady Lyonors and her house,
    with dance
And revel and song, made merry over
    Death,
As being after all their foolish fears
And horrors only proven a blooming
    boy.
So large mirth lived and Gareth won
    the quest.

And he that told the tale in older
    times
Says that Sir Gareth wedded Lyonors,
But he, that told it later, says Lynette.

GERAINT AND ENID.

I.

THE brave Geraint, a knight of
    Arthur's court,
A tributary prince of Devon, one
Of that great Order of the Table
    Round,
Had married Enid, Yniol's only child,
And loved her, as he loved the light
    of Heaven.
And as the light of Heaven varies, now
At sunrise, now at sunset, now by
    night
With moon and trembling stars, so
    loved Geraint

To make her beauty vary day by day,
In crimsons and in purples and in
    gems.
And Enid, but to please her husband's
    eye,
Who first had found and loved her in
    a state
Of broken fortunes, daily fronted
    him
In some fresh splendor; and the Queen
    herself,
Grateful to Prince Geraint for service
    done,
Loved her, and often with her own
    white hands
Array'd and deck'd her, as the love-
    liest,
Next after her own self, in all the
    court.
And Enid loved the Queen, and with
    true heart
Adored her, as the stateliest and the
    best
And loveliest of all women upon earth.
And seeing them. so tender and so
    close,
Long in their common love rejoiced
    Geraint.
But when a rumor rose about the
    Queen,
Touching her guilty love for Lancelot,
Tho' yet there lived no proof, nor yet
    was heard
The world's loud whisper breaking
    into storm,
Not less Geraint believed it; and there
    fell
A horror on him, lest his gentle wife,
Thro' that great tenderness for Guin-
    evere,
Had suffer'd, or should suffer any
    taint
In nature: wherefore going to the
    King,
He made this pretext, that his prince-
    dom lay
Close on the borders of a territory,
Wherein were bandit earls, and caitiff
    knights,
Assassins, and all flyers from the hand
Of Justice, and whatever loathes a
    law :

And therefore, till the King himself
  should please
To cleanse this common sewer of all
  his realm,
He craved a fair permission to depart,
And there defend his marches; and
  the King
Mused for a little on his plea, but, last,
Allowing it, the Prince and Enid rode,
And fifty knights rode with them, to
  the shores
Of Severn, and they past to their own
  land;
Where, thinking, that if ever yet was
  wife
True to her lord, mine shall be so to me,
He compass'd her with sweet observ-
  ances
And worship, never leaving her, and
  grew
Forgetful of his promise to the King,
Forgetful of the falcon and the hunt,
Forgetful of the tilt and tournament,
Forgetful of his glory and his name,
Forgetful of his princedom and its
  cares.
And this forgetfulness was hateful to
  her.
And by and by the people, when they
  met
In twos and threes, or fuller com-
  panies,
Began to scoff and jeer and babble of
  him
As of a prince whose manhood was all
  gone,
And molten down in mere uxorious-
  ness.
And this she gather'd from the peo-
  ple's eyes:
This too the women who attired her
  head,
To please her, dwelling on his bound-
  less love,
Told Enid, and they sadden'd her the
  more:
And day by day she thought to tell
  Geraint,
But could not out of bashful delicacy;
While he that watch'd her sadden, was
  the more
Suspicious that her nature had a taint.

At last, it chanced that on a summer
  morn
(They sleeping each by either) the
  new sun
Beat thro' the blindless casement of
  the room,
And heated the strong warrior in his
  dreams;
Who, moving, cast the coverlet
  aside,
And bared the knotted column of his
  throat,
The massive square of his heroic
  breast,
And arms on which the standing
  muscle sloped,
As slopes a wild brook o'er a little
  stone,
Running too vehemently to break
  upon it.
And Enid woke and sat beside the
  couch,
Admiring him, and thought within
  herself,
Was ever man so grandly made as
  he?
Then, like a shadow, past the people's
  talk
And accusation of uxoriousness
Across her mind, and bowing over
  him,
Low to her own heart piteously she
  said:

"O noble breast and all-puissant
  arms,
Am I the cause, I the poor cause that
  men
Reproach you, saying all your force
  is gone?
I *am* the cause, because I dare not
  speak
And tell him what I think and what
  they say.
And yet I hate that he should linger
  here;
I cannot love my lord and not his
  name.
Far liefer had I gird his harness on
  him,
And ride with him to battle and stand
  by,

And watch his mightful hand striking
  great blows
At caitiffs and at wrongers of the
  world.
Far better were I laid in the dark
  earth,
Not hearing any more his noble voice,
Not to be folded more in these dear
  arms,
And darken'd from the high light in
  his eyes,
Than that my lord thro' me should
  suffer shame.
Am I so bold, and could I so stand
  by,
And see my dear lord wounded in the
  strife,
Or maybe pierced to death before
  mine eyes,
And yet not dare to tell him what I
  think,
And how men slur him, saying all his
  force
Is melted into mere effeminacy ?
O me, I fear that I am no true wife."

Half inwardly, half audibly she
  spoke,
And the strong passion in her made
  her weep
True tears upon his broad and naked
  breast,
And these awoke him, and by great
  mischance
He heard but fragments of her later
  words,
And that she fear'd she was not a true
  wife.
And then he thought, " In spite of all
  my care,
For all my pains, poor man, for all
  my pains,
She is not faithful to me, and I see her
Weeping for some gay knight in
  Arthur's hall."
Then tho' he loved and reverenced
  her too much
To dream she could be guilty of foul
  act,
Right thro' his manful breast darted
  the pang

That makes a man, in the sweet face
  of her
Whom he loves most, lonely and mis-
  erable.
At this he hurl'd his huge limbs out
  of bed,
And shook his drowsy squire awake
  and cried,
" My charger and her palfrey ; " then
  to her,
" I will ride forth into the wilderness ;
For tho' it seems my spurs are yet to
  win,
I have not fall'n so low as some would
  wish.
And thou, put on thy worst and mean-
  est dress
And ride with me." And Enid ask'd,
  amazed,
" If Enid errs, let Enid learn her
  fault."
But he, " I charge thee, ask not, but
  obey."
Then she bethought her of a faded
  silk,
A faded mantle and a faded veil,
And moving toward a cedarn cabinet,
Wherein she kept them folded rever-
  ently
With sprigs of summer laid between
  the folds,
She took them, and array'd herself
  therein,
Remembering when first he came on
  her
Drest in that dress, and how he loved
  her in it,
And all her foolish fears about the
  dress,
And all his journey to her, as himself
Had told her, and their coming to the
  court.

For Arthur on the Whitsuntide
  before
Held court at old Caerleon upon Usk.
There on a day, he sitting high in
  hall,
Before him came a forester of Dean,
Wet from the woods, with notice of a
  hart

Taller than all his fellows, milky-
  white,
First seen that day : these things he
  told the King.
Then the good King gave order to let
  blow
His horns for hunting on the morrow
  morn.
And when the Queen petition'd for his
  leave
To see the hunt, allow'd it easily.
So with the morning all the court were
  gone.
But Guinevere lay late into the morn,
Lost in sweet dreams, and dreaming
  of her love
For Lancelot, and forgetful of the
  hunt ;
But rose at last, a single maiden with
  her,
Took horse, and forded Usk, and
  gain'd the wood ;
There, on a little knoll beside it,
  stay'd
Waiting to hear the hounds ; but
  heard instead
A sudden sound of hoofs, for Prince
  Geraint,
Late also, wearing neither hunting-
  dress
Nor weapon, save a golden-hilted
  brand,
Came quickly flashing thro' the shal-
  low ford
Behind them, and so gallop'd up the
  knoll.
A purple scarf, at either end whereof
There swung an apple of the purest
  gold,
Sway'd round about him, as he gal-
  lop'd up
To join them, glancing like a dragon-
  fly
In summer suit and silks of holiday.
Low bow'd the tributary Prince, and
  she,
Sweetly and statelily, and with all
  grace
Of womanhood and queenhood,
  answer'd him :
"Late, late, Sir Prince," she said,
  "later than we!"

"Yea, noble Queen," he answer'd,
  "and so late
That I but come like you to see the
  hunt,
Not join it." "Therefore wait with
  me," she said ;
"For on this little knoll, if anywhere,
There is good chance that we shall
  hear the hounds :
Here often they break covert at our
  feet."

  And while they listen'd for the dis-
    tant hunt,
And chiefly for the baying of Cavall,
King Arthur's hound of deepest
  mouth, there rode
Full slowly by a knight, lady, and
  dwarf ;
Whereof the dwarf lagg'd latest, and
  the knight
Had vizor up, and show'd a youthful
  face,
Imperious, and of haughtiest linea-
  ments.
And Guinevere, not mindful of his
  face
In the King's hall, desired his name,
  and sent
Her maiden to demand it of the
  dwarf ;
Who being vicious, old and irritable,
And doubling all his master's vice of
  pride,
Made answer sharply that she should
  not know.
"Then will I ask it of himself," she
  said.
"Nay, by my faith, thou shalt not,"
  cried the dwarf ;
"Thou art not worthy ev'n to speak
  of him ;"
And when she put her horse toward
  the knight,
Struck at her with his whip, and she
  return'd
Indignant to the Queen ; whereat
  Geraint
Exclaiming, "Surely I will learn the
  name,"
Made sharply to the dwarf, and ask'd
  it of him,

Who answer'd as before; and when
    the Prince
Had put his horse in motion toward
    the knight,
Struck at him with his whip, and cut
    his cheek.
The Prince's blood spirted upon the
    scarf,
Dyeing it; and his quick, instinctive
    hand
Caught at the hilt, as to abolish him:
But he, from his exceeding manful-
    ness
And pure nobility of temperament,
Wroth to be wroth at such a worm,
    refrain'd
From ev'n a word, and so returning
    said:

"I will avenge this insult, noble
    Queen,
Done in your maiden's person to your-
    self:
And I will track this vermin to their
    earths:
For tho' I ride unarm'd, I do not doubt
To find, at some place I shall come at,
    arms
On loan, or else for pledge; and, being
    found,
Then will I fight him, and will break
    his pride,
And on the third day will again be
    here,
So that I be not fall'n in fight. Fare-
    well."

"Farewell, fair Prince," answer'd
    the stately Queen.
"Be prosperous in this journey, as in
    all;
And may you light on all things that
    you love,
And live to wed with her whom first
    you love:
But ere you wed with any, bring your
    bride,
And I, were she the daughter of a
    king,
Yea, tho' she were a beggar from the
    hedge,
Will clothe her for her bridals like
    the sun."

And Prince Geraint, now thinking
    that he heard
The noble hart at bay, now the far
    horn,
A little vext at losing of the hunt,
A little at the vile occasion, rode,
By ups and downs, thro' many a grassy
    glade
And valley, with fixt eye following
    the three.
At last they issued from the world of
    wood,
And climb'd upon a fair and even
    ridge,
And show'd themselves against the
    sky, and sank.
And thither came Geraint, and under
    neath
Beheld the long street of a little town
In a long valley, on one side
    whereof,
White from the mason's hand, a for-
    tress rose;
And on one side a castle in decay,
Beyond a bridge that spann'd a dry
    ravine:
And out of town and valley came a
    noise
As of a broad brook o'er a shingly bed
Brawling, or like a clamor of the rooks
At distance, ere they settle for the
    night.

And onward to the fortress rode the
    three,
And enter'd, and were lost behind the
    walls.
"So," thought Geraint, "I have
    track'd him to his earth."
And down the long street riding
    wearily,
Found every hostel full, and every-
    where
Was hammer laid to hoof, and the
    hot hiss
And bustling whistle of the youth
    who scour'd
His master's armor; and of such a
    one
He ask'd, "What means the tumult
    in the town?"

Who told him, scouring still, " The
  sparrow-hawk ! "
Then riding close behind an ancient
  churl,
Who, smitten by the dusty sloping
  beam,
Went sweating underneath a sack of
  corn,
Ask'd yet once more what meant the
  hubbub here ?
Who answer'd gruffly, " Ugh ! the
  sparrow-hawk."
Then riding further past an armorer's,
Who, with back turn'd, and bow'd
  above his work,
Sat riveting a helmet on his knee,
He put the self-same query, but the
  man
Not turning round, nor looking at
  him, said :
" Friend, he that labors for the spar-
  row-hawk
Has little time for idle questioners."
Whereat Geraint flash'd into sudden
  spleen :
" A thousand pips eat up your spar-
  row-hawk !
Tits, wrens, and all wing'd nothings
  peck him dead !
Ye think the rustic cackle of your
  bourg
The murmur of the world ! What is
  it to me ?
O wretched set of sparrows, one and
  all,
Who pipe of nothing but of sparrow-
  hawks !
Speak, if ye be not like the rest,
  hawk-mad,
Where can I get me harborage for
  the night ?
And arms, arms, arms to fight my
  enemy ? Speak ! "
Whereat the armorer turning all
  amazed
And seeing one so gay in purple silks,
Came forward with the helmet yet in
  hand
And answer'd, " Pardon me, O stran-
  ger knight ;
We hold a tourney here to-morrow
  morn,

And there is scantly time for half the
  work.
Arms ? truth ! I know not : all are
  wanted here.
Harborage ? truth, good truth, I know
  not, save,
It may be, at Earl Yniol's, o'er the
  bridge
Yonder." He spoke and fell to work
  again.

Then rode Geraint, a little spleen-
  ful yet,
Across the bridge that spann'd the
  dry ravine.
There musing sat the hoary-headed
  Earl,
(His dress a suit of fray'd magnifi-
  cence,
Once fit for feasts of ceremony) and
  said :
" Whither, fair son ? " to whom Ger-
  aint replied,
" O friend, I seek a harborage for the
  night."
Then Yniol, " Enter therefore and
  partake
The slender entertainment of a house
Once rich, now poor, but ever open-
  door'd."
" Thanks, venerable friend," replied
  Geraint ;
" So that you do not serve me spar-
  row-hawks
For supper, I will enter, I will eat
With all the passion of a twelve
  hours' fast."
Then sigh'd and smiled the hoary-
  headed Earl,
And answer'd, " Graver cause than
  yours is mine
To curse this hedgerow thief, the
  sparrow-hawk :
But in, go in ; for save yourself de-
  sire it,
We will not touch upon him ev'n in
  jest."

Then rode Geraint into the castle
  court,
His charger trampling many a prickly
  star

Of sprouted thistle on the broken
  stones.
He look'd and saw that all was
  ruinous.
Here stood a shatter'd archway
  plumed with fern;
And here had fall'n a great part of
  a tower,
Whole, like a crag that tumbles from
  the cliff,
And like a crag was gay with wilding
  flowers:
And high above a piece of turret stair,
Worn by the feet that now were
  silent, wound
Bare to the sun, and monstrous ivy-
  stems
Claspt the gray walls with hairy-
  fibred arms,
And suck'd the joining of the stones,
  and look'd
A knot, beneath, of snakes, aloft, a
  grove.

And while he waited in the castle
  court,
The voice of Enid, Yniol's daughter,
  rang
Clear thro' the open casement of the
  hall,
Singing; and as the sweet voice of a
  bird,
Heard by the lander in a lonely isle,
Moves him to think what kind of bird
  it is
That sings so delicately clear, and
  make
Conjecture of the plumage and the
  form;
So the sweet voice of Enid moved
  Geraint;
And made him like a man abroad at
  morn
When first the liquid note beloved of
  men
Comes flying over many a windy wave
To Britain, and in April suddenly
Breaks from a coppice gemm'd with
  green and red,
And he suspends his converse with a
  friend,
Or it may be the labor of his hands,

To think or say, " There is the nightingale";
So fared it with Geraint, who thought
  and said,
" Here, by God's grace, is the one
  voice for me."

It chanced the song that Enid sang
  was one
Of Fortune and her wheel, and Enid
  sang:

" Turn, Fortune, turn thy wheel
  and lower the proud;
Turn thy wild wheel thro' sunshine,
  storm, and cloud;
Thy wheel and thee we neither love
  nor hate.

" Turn, Fortune, turn thy wheel
  with smile or frown;
With that wild wheel we go not up or
  down;
Our hoard is little, but our hearts are
  great.

" Smile and we smile, the lords of
  many lands;
Frown and we smile, the lords of our
  own hands;
For man is man and master of his
  fate.

" Turn, turn thy wheel above the
  staring crowd;
Thy wheel and thou are shadows in
  the cloud;
Thy wheel and thee we neither love
  nor hate."

" Hark, by the bird's song ye may
  learn the nest,"
Said Yniol; " enter quickly." Entering then,
Right o'er a mount of newly-fallen
  stones,
The dusky-rafter'd many-cobweb'd
  hall,
He found an ancient dame in dim
  brocade;
And near her, like a blossom vermeil-
  white,

That lightly breaks a faded flower-
sheath,
Moved the fair Enid, all in faded
silk,
Her daughter.   In a moment thought
Geraint,
"Here by God's rood is the one maid
for me."
But none spake word except the hoary
Earl:
"Enid, the good knight's horse stands
in the court;
Take him to stall, and give him corn,
and then
Go to the town and buy us flesh and
wine;
And we will make us merry as we
may.
Our hoard is little, but our hearts are
great."

He spake: the Prince, as Enid past
him, fain
To follow, strode a stride, but Yniol
caught
His purple scarf, and held, and said,
"Forbear!
Rest! the good house, tho' ruin'd, O
my son,
Endures not that her guest should
serve himself."
And reverencing the custom of the
house
Geraint, from utter courtesy, forbore.

So Enid took his charger to the
stall;
And after went her way across the
bridge,
And reach'd the town, and while the
Prince and Earl
Yet spoke together, came again with
one,
A youth, that following with a costrel
bore
The means of goodly welcome, flesh
and wine.
And Enid brought sweet cakes to
make them cheer,
And in her veil unfolded, manchet
bread.

And then, because their hall must also
serve
For kitchen, boil'd the flesh, and
spread the board,
And stood behind, and waited on the
three.
And seeing her so sweet and service-
able,
Geraint had longing in him evermore
To stoop and kiss the tender little
thumb,
That crost the trencher as she laid it
down:
But after all had eaten, then Geraint,
For now the wine made summer in his
veins,
Let his eye rove in following, or rest
On Enid at her lowly handmaid-work,
Now here, now there, about the dusky
hall;
Then suddenly addrest the hoary
Earl:

"Fair Host and Earl, I pray your
courtesy;
This sparrow-hawk, what is he? tell
me of him.
His name? but no, good faith, I will
not have it:
For if he be the knight whom late I
saw
Ride into that new fortress by your
town,
White from the mason's hand, then
have I sworn
From his own lips to have it — I am
Geraint
Of Devon — for this morning when the
Queen
Sent her own maiden to demand the
name,
His dwarf, a vicious under-shapen
thing,
Struck at her with his whip, and she
return'd
Indignant to the Queen; and then I
swore
That I would track this caitiff to his
hold,
And fight and break his pride, and
have it of him.

And all unarm'd I rode, and thought
to find
Arms in your town, where all the men
are mad;
They take the rustic murmur of their
bourg
For the great wave that echoes round
the world;
They would not hear me speak: but
if ye know
Where I can light on arms, or if your-
self
Should have them, tell me, seeing I
have sworn
That I will break his pride and learn
his name,
Avenging this great insult done the
Queen."

Then cried Earl Yniol, "Art thou
he indeed,
Geraint, a name far-sounded among
men
For noble deeds? and truly I, when
first
I saw you moving by me on the
bridge,
Felt ye were somewhat, yea, and by
your state
And presence might have guess'd you
one of those
That eat in Arthur's hall at Camelot.
Nor speak I now from foolish flat-
tery;
For this dear child hath often heard
me praise
Your feats of arms, and often when I
paused
Hath ask'd again, and ever loved to
hear;
So grateful is the noise of noble deeds
To noble hearts who see but acts of
wrong:
O never yet had woman such a pair
Of suitors as this maiden; first Lim-
ours,
A creature wholly given to brawls and
wine,
Drunk even when he woo'd; and be
he dead
I know not, but he passed to the wild
land.

The second was your foe, the sparrow-
hawk,
My curse, my nephew — I will not let
his name
Slip from my lips if I can help it —
he,
When I that knew him fierce and tur-
bulent
Refused her to him, then his pride
awoke;
And since the proud man often is the
mean,
He sow'd a slander in the common ear,
Affirming that his father left him
gold,
And in my charge, which was not ren-
der'd to him;
Bribed with large promises the men
who served
About my person, the more easily
Because my means were somewhat
broken into
Thro' open doors and hospitality;
Raised my own town against me in
the night
Before my Enid's birthday, sack'd my
house;
From mine own earldom foully ousted
me;
Built that new fort to overawe my
friends,
For truly there are those who love me
yet;
And keeps me in this ruinous castle
here,
Where doubtless he would put me
soon to death,
But that his pride too much despises
me:
And I myself sometimes despise my-
self;
For I have let men be, and have their
way;
Am much too gentle, have not used
my power:
Nor know I whether I be very base
Or very manful, whether very wise
Or very foolish; only this I know,
That whatsoever evil happen to me,
I seem to suffer nothing heart or
limb,
But can endure it all most patiently.'

"Well said, true heart," replied
  Geraint, "but arms,
That if the sparrow-hawk, this
  nephew, fight
In next day's tourney I may break
  his pride."

And Yniol answer'd, "Arms, indeed,
  but old
And rusty, old and rusty, Prince
  Geraint,
Are mine, and therefore at thine ask-
  ing, thine.
But in this tournament can no man
  tilt,
Except the lady he loves best be
  there.
Two forks are fixt into the meadow
  ground,
And over these is placed a silver
  wand,
And over that a golden sparrow-hawk,
The prize of beauty for the fairest
  there.
And this, what knight soever be in
  field
Lays claim to for the lady at his
  side,
And tilts with my good nephew there-
  upon,
Who being apt at arms and big of
  bone
Has ever won it for the lady with
  him,
And toppling over all antagonism
Has earn'd himself the name of spar-
  row-hawk.
But thou, that hast no lady, canst not
  fight."

To whom Geraint with eyes all
  bright replied,
Leaning a little toward him, "Thy
  leave!
Let *me* lay lance in rest, O noble host,
For this dear child, because I never
  saw,
Tho' having seen all beauties of our
  time,
Nor can see elsewhere, anything so
  fair.
And if I fall her name will yet remain

Untarnish'd as before; but if I live,
So aid me Heaven when at mine uttermost,
As I will make her truly my true
  wife."

Then, howsoever patient, Yniol's
  heart
Danced in his bosom, seeing better
  days.
And looking round he saw not Enid
  there,
(Who hearing her own name had
  stol'n away)
But that old dame, to whom full tenderly
And fondling all her hand in his he
  said,
"Mother, a maiden is a tender thing,
And best by her that bore her understood.
Go thou to rest, but ere thou go to
  rest
Tell her, and prove her heart toward
  the Prince."

So spake the kindly-hearted Earl,
  and she
With frequent smile and nod depart-
  ing found,
Half disarray'd as to her rest, the girl;
Whom first she kiss'd on either cheek,
  and then
On either shining shoulder laid a hand,
And kept her off and gazed upon her
  face,
And told her all their converse in the
  hall,
Proving her heart: but never light and
  shade
Coursed one another more on open
  ground
Beneath a troubled heaven, than red
  and pale
Across the face of Enid hearing her;
While slowly falling as a scale that
  falls,
When weight is added only grain by
  grain,
Sank her sweet head upon her gentle
  breast;

Nor did she lift an eye nor speak a
  word,
Rapt in the fear and in the wonder of
  it;
So moving without answer to her rest
She found no rest, and ever fail'd to
  draw
The quiet night into her blood, but
  lay
Contemplating her own unworthiness;
And when the pale and bloodless east
  began
To quicken to the sun, arose, and
  raised
Her mother too, and hand in hand
  they moved
Down to the meadow where the jousts
  were held,
And waited there for Yniol and
  Geraint.

  And thither came the twain, and
    when Geraint
Beheld her first in field, awaiting him,
He felt, were she the prize of bodily
  force,
Himself beyond the rest pushing could
  move
The chair of Idris. Yniol's rusted
  arms
Were on his princely person, but thro'
  these
Princelike his bearing shone; and
  errant knights
And ladies came, and by and by the
  town
Flow'd in, and settling circled all the
  lists.
And there they fixt the forks into the
  ground,
And over these they placed the silver
  wand,
And over that the golden sparrow-
  hawk.
Then Yniol's nephew, after trumpet
  blown,
Spake to the lady with him and proclaim'd,
"Advance and take as fairest of the
  fair,
For I these two years past have won
  it for thee,

The prize of beauty." Loudly spake
  the Prince,
"Forbear: there is a worthier," and
  the knight
With some surprise and thrice as much
  disdain
Turn'd, and beheld the four, and all
  his face
Glow'd like the heart of a great fire
  at Yule,
So burnt he was with passion, crying
  out,
"Do battle for it then," no more; and
  thrice
They clash'd together, and thrice they
  brake their spears.
Then each, dishorsed and drawing,
  lash'd at each
So often and with such blows, that all
  the crowd
Wonder'd, and now and then from
  distant walls
There came a clapping as of phantom
  hands.
So twice they fought, and twice they
  breathed, and still
The dew of their great labor, and the
  blood
Of their strong bodies, flowing, drain'd
  their force.
But either's force was match'd till
  Yniol's cry,
"Remember that great insult done the
  Queen,"
Increased Geraint's, who heaved his
  blade aloft,
And crack'd the helmet thro', and bit
  the bone,
And fell'd him, and set foot upon his
  breast,
And said, "Thy name?" To whom
  the fallen man
Made answer, groaning, "Edyrn, son
  of Nudd!
Ashamed am I that I should tell it
  thee.
My pride is broken: men have seen
  my fall."
"Then, Edyrn, son of Nudd," replied
  Geraint,
"These two things shalt thou do, or
  else thou diest.

First, thou thyself, with damsel and
with dwarf,
Shalt ride to Arthur's court, and com-
ing there,
Crave pardon for that insult done the
Queen,
And shalt abide her judgment on it;
next,
Thou shalt give back their earldom to
thy kin.
These two things shalt thou do, or
thou shalt die."
And Edyrn answer'd, " These things
will I do,
For I have never yet been overthrown,
And thou hast overthrown me, and my
pride
Is broken down, for Enid sees my
fall!"
And rising up, he rode to Arthur's
court,
And there the Queen forgave him
easily.
And being young, he changed and
came to loathe
His crime of traitor, slowly drew him-
self
Bright from his old dark life, and fell
at last
In the great battle fighting for the
King.

But when the third day from the
hunting-morn
Made a low splendor in the world, and
wings
Moved in her ivy, Enid, for she
lay
With her fair head in the dim-yellow
light,
Among the dancing shadows of the
birds,
Woke and bethought her of her
promise given
No later than last eve to Prince
Geraint —
So bent he seem'd on going the third
day,
He would not leave her, till her prom-
ise given —
To ride with him this morning to the
court,

And there be made known to the
stately Queen,
And there be wedded with all cere-
mony.
At this she cast her eyes upon her
dress,
And thought it never yet had look'd
so mean.
For as a leaf in mid-November is
To what it was in mid-October, seem'd
The dress that now she look'd on to
the dress
She look'd on ere the coming of
Geraint.
And still she look'd, and still the
terror grew
Of that strange bright and dreadful
thing, a court,
All staring at her in her faded silk :
And softly to her own sweet heart she
said :

" This noble prince who won our
earldom back,
So splendid in his acts and his attire,
Sweet heaven, how much I shall dis-
credit him !
Would he could tarry with us here
awhile,
But being so beholden to the Prince,
It were but little grace in any of us,
Bent as he seem'd on going this third
day,
To seek a second favor at his hands.
Yet if he could but tarry a day or two,
Myself would work eye dim, and finger
lame,
Far liefer than so much discredit him."

And Enid fell in longing for a dress
All branch'd and flower'd with gold,
a costly gift
Of her good mother, given her on the
night
Before her birth day, three sad years
ago,
That night of fire, when Edyrn sack'd
their house,
And scatter'd all they had to all the
winds :
For while the mother show'd it, and
the two

Were turning and admiring it, the work
To both appear'd so costly, rose a cry
That Edyrn's men were on them, and they fled
With little save the jewels they had on,
Which being sold and sold had bought them bread :
And Edyrn's men had caught them in their flight,
And placed them in this ruin; and she wish'd
The Prince had found her in her ancient home ;
Then let her fancy flit across the past,
And roam the goodly places that she knew;
And last bethought her how she used to watch,
Near that old home, a pool of golden carp ;
And one was patch'd and blurr'd and lustreless
Among his burnish'd brethren of the pool;
And half asleep she made comparison
Of that and these to her own faded self
And the gay court, and fell asleep again;
And dreamt herself was such a faded form
Among her burnish'd sisters of the pool;
But this was in the garden of a king;
And tho' she lay dark in the pool, she knew
That all was bright ; that all about were birds
Of sunny plume in gilded trellis-work ;
That all the turf was rich in plots that look'd
Each like a garnet or a turkis in it ;
And lords and ladies of the high court went
In silver tissue talking things of state ;
And children of the King in cloth of gold
Glanced at the doors or gambol'd down the walks ;
And while she thought " They will not see me," came

A stately queen whose name was Guinevere,
And all the children in their cloth of gold
Ran to her, crying, " If we have fish at all
Let them be gold; and charge the gardeners now
To pick the faded creature from the pool,
And cast it on the mixen that it die."
And therewithal one came and seized on her,
And Enid started waking, with her heart
All overshadow'd by the foolish dream,
And lo ! it was her mother grasping her
To get her well awake; and in her hand
A suit of bright apparel, which she laid
Flat on the couch, and spoke exultingly :

" See here, my child, how fresh the colors look,
How fast they hold like colors of a shell
That keeps the wear and polish of the wave.
Why not? It never yet was worn, I trow :
Look on it, child, and tell me if ye know it."

And Enid look'd, but all confused at first,
Could scarce divide it from her foolish dream :
Then suddenly she knew it and rejoiced,
And answer'd, " Yea, I know it; your good gift,
So sadly lost on that unhappy night;
Your own good gift !" " Yea, surely," said the dame,
" And gladly given again this happy morn.
For when the jousts were ended yesterday,

Went Yniol thro' the town, and every-
　　where
He found the sack and plunder of our
　　house
All scatter'd thro' the houses of the
　　town;
And gave command that all which
　　once was ours
Should now be ours again: and yes-
　　ter-eve,
While ye were talking sweetly with
　　your Prince,
Came one with this and laid it in my
　　hand,
For love or fear, or seeking favor of
　　us,
Because we have our earldom back
　　again.
And yester-eve I would not tell you
　　of it,
But kept it for a sweet surprise at
　　morn.
Yea, truly is it not a sweet surprise?
For I myself unwillingly have worn
My faded suit, as you, my child, have
　　yours,
And howsoever patient, Yniol his.
Ah, dear, he took me from a goodly
　　house,
With store of rich apparel, sumptuous
　　fare,
And page, and maid, and squire, and
　　seneschal,
And pastime both of hawk and hound,
　　and all
That appertains to noble maintenance.
Yea, and he brought me to a goodly
　　house;
But since our fortune swerved from
　　sun to shade,
And all thro' that young traitor, cruel
　　need
Constrain'd us, but a better time has
　　come;
So clothe yourself in this, that better
　　fits
Our mended fortunes and a Prince's
　　bride:
For tho' ye won the prize of fairest
　　fair,
And tho' I heard him call you fairest
　　fair,

Let never maiden think, however fair,
She is not fairer in new clothes than
　　old.
And should some great court-lady
　　say, the Prince
Hath pick'd a ragged-robin from the
　　hedge,
And like a madman brought her
　　to the court,
Then were ye shamed, and, worse,
　　might shame the Prince
To whom we are beholden; but I
　　know,
When my dear child is set forth at
　　her best,
That neither court nor country, tho'
　　they sought
Thro' all the provinces like those of
　　old
That lighted on Queen Esther, has
　　her match."

　　Here ceased the kindly mother out
　　of breath;
And Enid listen'd brightening as she
　　lay;
Then, as the white and glittering star
　　of morn
Parts from a bank of snow, and by
　　and by
Slips into golden cloud, the maiden
　　rose,
And left her maiden couch, and robed
　　herself,
Help'd by the mother's careful hand
　　and eye,
Without a mirror, in the gorgeous
　　gown;
Who, after, turn'd her daughter round,
　　and said,
She never yet had seen her half so
　　fair;
And call'd her like that maiden in the
　　tale,
Whom Gwydion made by glamour out
　　of flowers,
And sweeter than the bride of Cas-
　　sivelaun,
Flur, for whose love the Roman
　　Cæsar first
Invaded Britain, "But we beat him
　　back,

As this great Prince invaded us, and
    we,
Not beat him back, but welcomed him
    with joy.
And I can scarcely ride with you to
    court,
For old am I, and rough the ways and
    wild;
But Yniol goes, and I full oft shall
    dream
I see my princess as I see her now,
Clothed with my gift, and gay among
    the gay."

But while the women thus rejoiced,
    Geraint
Woke where he slept in the high hall,
    and call'd
For Enid, and when Yniol made report
Of that good mother making Enid
    gay
In such apparel as might well beseem
His princess, or indeed the stately
    Queen,
He answer'd: "Earl, entreat her by
    my love,
Albeit I give no reason but my wish,
That she ride with me in her faded
    silk."
Yniol with that hard message went;
    it fell
Like flaws in summer laying lusty
    corn:
For Enid, all abash'd she knew not
    why,
Dared not to glance at her good
    mother's face,
But silently, in all obedience,
Her mother silent too, nor helping her,
Laid from her limbs the costly-broid-
    er'd gift,
And robed them in her ancient suit
    again,
And so descended. Never man re-
    joiced
More than Geraint to greet her thus
    attired;
And glancing all at once as keenly at
    her
As careful robins eye the delver's toil,
Made her cheek burn and either eye-
    lid fall,

But rested with her sweet face satis-
    fied;
Then seeing cloud upon the mother's
    brow,
Her by both hands he caught, and
    sweetly said,

  "O my new mother, be not wroth
    or grieved
At thy new son, for my petition to
    her.
When late I left Caerleon, our great
    Queen,
In words whose echo lasts, they were
    so sweet,
Made promise, that whatever bride I
    brought,
Herself would clothe her like the sun
    in Heaven.
Thereafter, when I reach'd this ruin'd
    hall,
Beholding one so bright in dark estate,
I vow'd that could I gain her, our fair
    Queen,
No hand but hers, should make your
    Enid burst
Sunlike from cloud — and likewise
    thought perhaps,
That service done so graciously would
    bind
The two together; fain I would the
    two
Should love each other: how can
    Enid find
A nobler friend? Another thought
    was mine;
I came among you here so suddenly,
That tho' her gentle presence at the
    lists
Might well have served for proof that
    I was loved,
I doubted whether daughter's tender-
    ness,
Or easy nature, might not let itself
Be moulded by your wishes for her
    weal;
Or whether some false sense in her
    own self
Of my contrasting brightness, over-
    bore
Her fancy dwelling in this dusky
    hall;

And such a sense might make her
    long for court
And all its perilous glories: and I
    thought,
That could I someway prove such
    force in her
Link'd with such love for me, that at
    a word
(No reason given her) she could cast
    aside
A splendor dear to women, new to
    her,
And therefore dearer; or if not so
    new,
Yet therefore tenfold dearer by the
    power
Of intermitted usage; then I felt
That I could rest, a rock in ebbs and
    flows,
Fixt on her faith. Now, therefore, I
    do rest,
A prophet certain of my prophecy,
That never shadow of mistrust can
    cross
Between us. Grant me pardon for
    my thoughts:
And for my strange petition I will
    make
Amends hereafter by some gaudy-day,
When your fair child shall wear your
    costly gift
Beside your own warm hearth, with,
    on her knees,
Who knows? another gift of the high
    God,
Which, maybe, shall have learn'd to
    lisp you thanks."

He spoke: the mother smiled, but
    half in tears,
Then brought a mantle down and
    wrapt her in it,
And claspt and kiss'd her, and they
    rode away.

Now thrice that morning Guinevere
    had climb'd
The giant tower, from whose high
    crest, they say,
Men saw the goodly hills of Somerset,
And white sails flying on the yellow
    sea;

But not to goodly hill or yellow sea
Look'd the fair Queen, but up the
    vale of Usk,
By the flat meadow, till she saw them
    come;
And then descending met them at the
    gates,
Embraced her with all welcome as a
    friend,
And did her honor as the Prince's
    bride,
And clothed her for her bridals like
    the sun;
And all that week was old Caerleon
    gay,
For by the hands of Dubric, the high
    saint,
They twain were wedded with all
    ceremony.

And this was on the last year's
    Whitsuntide.
But Enid ever kept the faded silk,
Remembering how first he came on
    her,
Drest in that dress, and how he loved
    her in it,
And all her foolish fears about the
    dress,
And all his journey toward her, as
    himself
Had told her, and their coming to the
    court.

And now this morning when he said
    to her,
"Put on your worst and meanest
    dress," she found
And took it, and array'd herself
    therein.

II.

O purblind race of miserable men,
How many among us at this very hour
Do forge a life-long trouble for our-
    selves,
By taking true for false, or false for
    true;
Here, thro' the feeble twilight of this
    world

Groping, how many, until we pass and
     reach
That other, where we see as we are
     seen !

  So fared it with Geraint, who issu-
     ing forth
That morning, when they both had
     got to horse,
Perhaps because he loved her passion-
     ately,
And felt that tempest brooding round
     his heart,
Which, if he spoke at all, would break
     perforce
Upon a head so dear in thunder, said :
" Not at my side. I charge thee ride
     before,
Ever a good way on before ; and this
I charge thee, on thy duty as a wife,
Whatever happens, not to speak to
     me,
No, not a word !" and Enid was
     aghast ;
And forth they rode, but scarce three
     paces on,
When crying out, " Effeminate as I
     am,
I will not fight my way with gilded
     arms,
All shall be iron ; " he loosed a mighty
     purse,
Hung at his belt, and hurl'd it toward
     the squire.
So the last sight that Enid had of
     home
Was all the marble threshold flashing,
     strown
With gold and scatter'd coinage, and
     the squire
Chafing his shoulder : then he cried
     again,
" To the wilds !" and Enid leading
     down the tracks
Thro' which he bade her lead him on,
     they past
The marches, and by bandit-haunted
     holds,
Gray swamps and pools, waste places
     of the hern,
And wildernesses, perilous paths, they
     rode :

Round was their pace at first, but
     slacken'd soon :
A stranger meeting them had surely
     thought
They rode so slowly and they look'd
     so pale,
That each had suffer'd some exceed-
     ing wrong.
For he was ever saying to himself,
" O I that wasted time to tend upon
     her,
To compass her with sweet obser-
     vances,
To dress her beautifully and keep her
     true " —
And there he broke the sentence in
     his heart
Abruptly, as a man upon his tongue
May break it, when his passion mas-
     ters him.
And she was ever praying the sweet
     heavens
To save her dear lord whole from any
     wound.
And ever in her mind she cast
     about
For that unnoticed failing in herself,
Which made him look so cloudy and
     so cold ;
Till the great plover's human whistle
     amazed
Her heart, and glancing round the
     waste she fear'd
In every wavering brake an ambus-
     cade.
Then thought again, " If there be such
     in me,
I might amend it by the grace of
     Heaven,
If he would only speak and tell me of
     it."

  But when the fourth part of the day
     was gone,
Then Enid was aware of three tall
     knights
On horseback, wholly arm'd, behind a
     rock
In shadow, waiting for them, caitiffs
     all ;
And heard one crying to his fellow,
     " Look,

Here comes a laggard hanging down
　　his head,
Who seems no bolder than a beaten
　　hound;
Come, we will slay him and will have
　　his horse
And armor, and his damsel shall be
　　ours."

　　Then Enid ponder'd in her heart,
　　　and said:
" I will go back a little to my lord,
And I will tell him all their caitiff
　　talk;
For, be he wroth even to slaying me,
Far liefer by his dear hand had I die,
Than that my lord should suffer loss
　　or shame."

　　Then she went back some paces of
　　　return,
Met his full frown timidly firm, and
　　said;
" My lord, I saw three bandits by the
　　rock
Waiting to fall on you, and heard
　　them boast
That they would slay you, and possess
　　your horse
And armor, and your damsel should
　　be theirs."

　　He made a wrathful answer: " Did
　　　I wish
Your warning or your silence? one
　　command
I laid upon you, not to speak to me,
And thus ye keep it! Well then, look
　　— for now,
Whether ye wish me victory or defeat,
Long for my life, or hunger for my
　　death,
Yourself shall see my vigor is not
　　lost."

　　Then Enid waited pale and sorrow-
　　　ful,
And down upon him bare the bandit
　　three.
And at the midmost charging, Prince
　　Geraint

Drave the long spear a cubit thro' his
　　breast
And out beyond; and then against his
　　brace
Of comrades, each of whom had
　　broken on him
A lance that splinter'd like an icicle,
Swung from his brand a windy buffet
　　out
Once, twice, to right, to left, and
　　stunn'd the twain
Or slew them, and dismounting like a
　　man
That skins the wild beast after slaying
　　him,
Stript from the three dead wolves of
　　woman born
The three gay suits of armor which
　　they wore,
And let the bodies lie, but bound the
　　suits
Of armor on their horses, each on each,
And tied the bridle-reins of all the
　　three
Together, and said to her, "Drive
　　them on
Before you;" and she drove them
　　thro' the waste.

　　He follow'd nearer: ruth began to
　　　work
Against his anger in him, while he
　　watch'd
The being he loved best in all the
　　world,
With difficulty in mild obedience
Driving them on: he fain had spoken
　　to her,
And loosed in words of sudden fire the
　　wrath
And smoulder'd wrong that burnt him
　　all within;
But evermore it seem'd an easier thing
At once without remorse to strike her
　　dead,
Than to cry "Halt," and to her own
　　bright face
Accuse her of the least immodesty:
And thus tongue-tied, it made him
　　wroth the more
That she *could* speak whom his own
　　ear had heard

Call herself false : and suffering thus
    he made
Minutes an age : but in scarce longer
    time
Than at Caerleon the full-tided Usk,
Before he turn to fall seaward again,
Pauses, did Enid, keeping watch, be-
    hold
In the first shallow shade of a deep
    wood,
Before a gloom of stubborn-shafted
    oaks,
Three other horsemen waiting, wholly
    arm'd,
Whereof one seem'd far larger than
    her lord,
And shook her pulses, crying, " Look,
    a prize !
Three horses and three goodly suits
    of arms,
And all in charge of whom ? a girl :
    set on."
" Nay," said the second, "yonder
    comes a knight."
The third, " A craven; how he hangs
    his head."
The giant answer'd merrily, "Yea, but
    one ?
Wait here, and when he passes fall
    upon him."

And Enid ponder'd in her heart and
    said,
"I will abide the coming of my lord,
And I will tell him all their villany.
My lord is weary with the fight before,
And they will fall upon him unawares.
I needs must disobey him for his
    good ;
How should I dare obey him to his
    harm ?
Needs must I speak, and tho' he kill
    me for it,
I save a life dearer to me than mine."

And she abode his coming, and said
    to him
With timid firmness, "Have I leave
    to speak ? "
He said, "Ye take it, speaking," and
    she spoke.

"There lurk three villains yonder
    in the wood,
And each of them is wholly arm'd,
    and one
Is larger-limb'd than you are, and they
    say
That they will fall upon you while ye
    pass."

To which he flung a wrathful an-
    swer back :
" And if there were an hundred in the
    wood,
And every man were larger-limb'd
    than I,
And all at once should sally out upon
    me,
I swear it would not ruffle me so much
As you that not obey me. Stand
    aside,
And if I fall, cleave to the better
    man."

And Enid stood aside to wait the
    event,
Not dare to watch the combat, only
    breathe
Short fits of prayer, at every stroke a
    breath.
And he, she dreaded most, bare down
    upon him.
Aim'd at the helm, his lance err'd; but
    Geraint's,
A little in the late encounter strain'd,
Struck thro' the bulky bandit's corse-
    let home,
And then brake short, and down his
    enemy roll'd,
And there lay still; as he that tells
    the tale
Saw once a great piece of a promon-
    tory,
That had a sapling growing on it, slide
From the long shore-cliff's windy walls
    to the beach,
And there lie still, and yet the sapling
    grew :
So lay the man transfixt. His craven
    pair
Of comrades making slowlier at the
    Prince,

When now they saw their bulwark
  fallen, stood,
On whom the victor, to confound them
  more,
Spurr'd with his terrible war-cry; for
  as one,
That listens near a torrent mountain-
  brook,
All thro' the crash of the near cataract
  hears
The drumming thunder of the huger
  fall
At distance, were the soldiers wont to
  hear
His voice in battle, and be kindled by
  it,
And foemen scared, like that false
  pair who turn'd
Flying, but, overtaken, died the death
Themselves had wrought on many an
  innocent.

Thereon   Geraint,   dismounting,
  pick'd the lance
That pleased him best, and drew from
  those dead wolves
Their three gay suits of armor, each
  from each,
And bound them on their horses, each
  on each,
And tied the bridle-reins of all the
  three
Together, and said to her, "Drive
  them on
Before you," and she drove them thro'
  the wood.

He follow'd nearer still: the pain
  she had
To keep them in the wild ways of the
  wood,
Two sets of three laden with jingling
  arms,
Together, served a little to disedge
The sharpness of that pain about her
  heart:
And they themselves, like creatures
  gently born
But into bad hands fall'n, and now so
  long
By bandits groom'd, prick'd their light
  ears, and felt

Her low firm voice and tender government.

So thro' the green gloom of the wood
  they past,
And issuing under open heavens be-
  held
A little town with towers, upon a rock,
And close beneath, a meadow gemlike
  chased
In the brown wild, and mowers mow-
  ing in it:
And down a rocky pathway from the
  place
There came a fair-hair'd youth, that
  in his hand
Bare victual for the mowers: and
  Geraint
Had ruth again on Enid looking pale
Then, moving downward to the
  meadow ground,
He, when the fair-hair'd youth came
  by him, said,
"Friend, let her eat; the damsel is so
  faint."
"Yea, willingly," replied the youth;
  "and thou,
My lord, eat also, tho' the fare is
  coarse,
And only meet for mowers;" then set
  down
His basket, and dismounting on the
  sward
They let the horses graze, and ate
  themselves.
And Enid took a little delicately,
Less having stomach for it than desire
To close with her lord's pleasure; but
  Geraint
Ate all the mowers' victual unawares,
And when he found all empty, was
  amazed;
And, "Boy," said he, "I have eaten
  all, but take
A horse and arms for guerdon; choose
  the best."
He, reddening in extremity of delight,
"My lord, you overpay me fifty-fold."
"Ye will be all the wealthier," cried
  the Prince.
"I take it as free gift, then," said the
  boy,

"Not guerdon; for myself can easily,
While your good damsel rests, return, and fetch
Fresh victual for these mowers of our Earl;
For these are his, and all the field is his,
And I myself am his; and I will tell him
How great a man thou art: he loves to know
When men of mark are in his territory:
And he will have thee to his palace here,
And serve thee costlier than with mowers' fare."

Then said Geraint, "I wish no better fare:
I never ate with angrier appetite
Than when I left your mowers dinnerless.
And into no Earl's palace will I go.
I know, God knows, too much of palaces!
And if he want me, let him come to me.
But hire us some fair chamber for the night,
And stalling for the horses, and return
With victual for these men, and let us know."

"Yea, my kind lord," said the glad youth, and went,
Held his head high, and thought himself a knight,
And up the rocky pathway disappear'd,
Leading the horse, and they were left alone.

But when the Prince had brought his errant eyes
Home from the rock, sideways he let them glance
At Enid, where she droopt: his own false doom,
That shadow of mistrust should never cross

Betwixt them, came upon him, and he sigh'd;
Then with another humorous ruth remark'd
The lusty mowers laboring dinnerless,
And watch'd the sun blaze on the turning scythe,
And after nodded sleepily in the heat.

But she, remembering her old ruin'd hall,
And all the windy clamor of the daws
About her hollow turret, pluck'd the grass
There growing longest by the meadow's edge,
And into many a listless annulet,
Now over, now beneath her marriage ring,
Wove and unwove it, till the boy return'd
And told them of a chamber, and they went;
Where, after saying to her, "If ye will,
Call for the woman of the house," to which
She answer'd, "Thanks, my lord;" the two remain'd
Apart by all the chamber's width, and mute
As creatures voiceless thro' the fault of birth,
Or two wild men supporters of a shield,
Painted, who stare at open space, nor glance
The one at other, parted by the shield.

On a sudden, many a voice along the street,
And heel against the pavement echoing, burst
Their drowse; and either started while the door,
Push'd from without, drave backward to the wall,
And midmost of a rout of roisterers,
Femininely fair and dissolutely pale,
Her suitor in old years before Geraint,
Enter'd, the wild lord of the place,
Limours.

He moving up with pliant courtliness,
Greeted Geraint full face, but stealthily,
In the mid-warmth of welcome and graspt hand,
Found Enid with the corner of his eye,
And knew her sitting sad and solitary.
Then cried Geraint for wine and goodly cheer
To feed the sudden guest, and sumptuously
According to his fashion, bade the host
Call in what men soever were his friends,
And feast with these in honor of their Earl;
"And care not for the cost; the cost is mine."

And wine and food were brought, and Earl Limours
Drank till he jested with all ease, and told
Free tales, and took the word and play'd upon it,
And made it of two colors; for his talk,
When wine and free companions kindled him,
Was wont to glance and sparkle like a gem
Of fifty facets; thus he moved the Prince
To laughter and his comrades to applause.
Then, when the Prince was merry, ask'd Limours,
"Your leave, my lord, to cross the room, and speak
To your good damsel there who sits apart,
And seems so lonely?" "My free leave," he said;
"Get her to speak: she doth not speak to me."
Then rose Limours, and looking at his feet,
Like him who tries the bridge he fears may fail,

Crost and came near, lifted adoring eyes,
Bow'd at her side and utter'd whisperingly:

"Enid, the pilot star of my lone life,
Enid, my early and my only love,
Enid, the loss of whom hath turn'd me wild—
What chance is this? how is it I see you here?
Ye are in my power at last, are in my power.
Yet fear me not: I call mine own self wild,
But keep a touch of sweet civility
Here in the heart of waste and wilderness.
I thought, but that your father came between,
In former days you saw me favorably.
And if it were so do not keep it back:
Make me a little happier: let me know it:
Owe you me nothing for a life half-lost?
Yea, yea, the whole dear debt of all you are.
And, Enid, you and he, I see with joy,
Ye sit apart, you do not speak to him,
You come with no attendance, page or maid,
To serve you—doth he love you as of old?
For, call it lovers' quarrels, yet I know
Tho' men may bicker with the things they love,
They would not make them laughable in all eyes,
Not while they loved them; and your wretched dress,
A wretched insult on you, dumbly speaks
Your story, that this man loves you no more.
Your beauty is no beauty to him now:
A common chance—right well I know it—pall'd—
For I know men: nor will ye win him back,
For the man's love once gone never returns.

But here is one who loves you as of old;
With more exceeding passion than of
    old:
Good, speak the word: my followers
    ring him round:
He sits unarm'd; I hold a finger up;
They understand: nay; I do not mean
    blood:
Nor need ye look so scared at what I
    say:
My malice is no deeper than a moat,
No stronger than a wall: there is the
    keep;
He shall not cross us more; speak but
    the word:
Or speak it not; but then by Him that
    made me
The one true lover whom you ever
    own'd,
I will make use of all the power I have.
O pardon me! the madness of that
    hour,
When first I parted from thee, moves
    me yet."

    At this the tender sound of his own
        voice
And sweet self-pity, or the fancy of it
Made his eye moist; but Enid fear'd
    his eyes,
Moist as they were, wine-heated from
    the feast;
And answer'd with such craft as
    women use,
Guilty or guiltless, to stave off a
    chance
That breaks upon them perilously,
    and said:

    "Earl, if you love me as in former
        years,
And do not practise on me, come with
    morn,
And snatch me from him as by
    violence;
Leave me to-night: I am weary to the
    death."

    Low at leave-taking, with his bran-
        dish'd plume
Brushing his instep, bow'd the all-
    amorous Earl,

And the stout Prince bade him a loud
    good-night.
He moving homeward babbled to his
    men,
How Enid never loved a man but him,
Nor cared a broken egg-shell for her
    lord.

    But Enid left alone with Prince
        Geraint,
Debating his command of silence
    given,
And that she now perforce must vio-
    late it,
Held commune with herself, and while
    she held
He fell asleep, and Enid had no heart
To wake him, but hung o'er him,
    wholly pleased
To find him yet unwounded after fight,
And hear him breathing low and
    equally.
Anon she rose, and stepping lightly,
    heap'd
The pieces of his armor in one place,
All to be there against a sudden need;
Then dozed awhile herself, but over-
    toil'd
By that day's grief and travel, ever-
    more
Seem'd catching at a rootless thorn,
    and then
Went slipping down horrible prec-
    ipices,
And strongly striking out her limbs
    awoke;
Then thought she heard the wild Earl
    at the door,
With all his rout of random followers,
Sound on a dreadful trumpet, sum-
    moning her;
Which was the red cock shouting to
    the light,
As the gray dawn stole o'er the dewy
    world,
And glimmer'd on his armor in the
    room.
And once again she rose to look at it,
But touch'd it unawares: jangling,
    the casque
Fell, and he started up and stared at
    her.

Then breaking his command of silence
    given,
She told him all that Earl Limours
    had said,
Except the passage that he loved her
    not;
Nor left untold the craft herself had
    used;
But ended with apology so sweet,
Low-spoken, and of so few words, and
    seem'd
So justified by that necessity,
That tho' he thought "was it for him
    she wept
In Devon?" he but gave a wrathful
    groan,
Saying, "Your sweet faces make good
    fellows fools
And traitors. Call the host and bid
    him bring
Charger and palfrey." So she glided
    out
Among the heavy breathings of the
    house,
And like a household Spirit at the
    walls
Beat, till she woke the sleepers, and
    return'd:
Then tending her rough lord, tho' all
    unask'd,
In silence, did him service as a squire;
Till issuing arm'd he found the host
    and cried,
"Thy reckoning, friend?" and ere he
    learnt it, "Take
Five horses and their armors"; and
    the host
Suddenly honest, answer'd in amaze,
"My lord, I scarce have spent the
    worth of one!"
"Ye will be all the wealthier," said
    the Prince,
And then to Enid, "Forward! and
    to-day
I charge you, Enid, more especially,
What thing soever ye may hear, or see,
Or fancy (tho' I count it of small use
To charge you) that ye speak not but
    obey."

    And Enid answer'd, "Yea, my lord,
        I know

Your wish, and would obey; but rid-
    ing first,
I hear the violent threats you do not
    hear,
I see the danger which you cannot see:
Then not to give you warning, that
    seems hard;
Almost beyond me: yet I would
    obey."

    "Yea so," said he, "do it: be not
        too wise;
Seeing that ye are wedded to a man,
Not all mismated with a yawning
    clown,
But one with arms to guard his head
    and yours,
With eyes to find you out however
    far,
And ears to hear you even in his
    dreams."

    With that he turn'd and look'd as
        keenly at her
As careful robins eye the delver's
    toil;
And that within her, which a wanton
    fool,
Or hasty judger would have call'd her
    guilt,
Made her cheek burn and either eye-
    lid fall.
And Geraint look'd and was not satis-
    fied.

    Then forward by a way which,
        beaten broad,
Led from the territory of false
    Limours
To the waste earldom of another earl,
Doorm, whom his shaking vassals
    call'd the Bull,
Went Enid with her sullen follower
    on.
Once she look'd back, and when she
    saw him ride
More near by many a rood than yes-
    termorn,
It wellnigh made her cheerful; till
    Geraint
Waving an angry hand as who should
    say

"Ye watch me," sadden'd all her heart
again.
But while the sun yet beat a dewy
blade,
The sound of many a heavily-gallop-
ing hoof
Smote on her ear, and turning round
she saw
Dust, and the points of lances bicker
in it.
Then not to disobey her lord's behest,
And yet to give him warning, for he
rode
As if he heard not, moving back she
held
Her finger up, and pointed to the dust.
At which the warrior in his obstinacy,
Because she kept the letter of his
word,
Was in a manner pleased, and turning,
stood.
And in the moment after, wild
Limours,
Borne on a black horse, like a thun-
der-cloud
Whose skirts are loosen'd by the
breaking storm,
Half ridden off with by the thing he
rode,
And all in passion uttering a dry
shriek,
Dash'd on Geraint, who closed with
him, and bore
Down by the length of lance and arm
beyond
The crupper, and so left him stunn'd
or dead,
And overthrew the next that follow'd
him,
And blindly rush'd on all the rout
behind.
But at the flash and motion of the
man
They vanish'd panic-stricken, like a
shoal
Of darting fish, that on a summer
morn
Adown the crystal dykes at Camelot
Come slipping o'er their shadows on
the sand,
But if a man who stands upon the
brink

But lift a shining hand against the
sun,
There is not left the twinkle of a fin
Betwixt the cressy islets white in
flower;
So, scared but at the motion of the
man,
Fled all the boon companions of the
Earl,
And left him lying in the public way;
So vanish friendships only made in
wine.

Then like a stormy sunlight smiled
Geraint,
Who saw the chargers of the two that
fell
Start from their fallen lords, and
wildly fly,
Mixt with the flyers. "Horse and
man," he said,
"All of one mind and all right-honest
friends!
Not a hoof left: and I methinks till
now
Was honest — paid with horses and
with arms;
I cannot steal or plunder, no nor beg:
And so what say ye, shall we strip
him there
Your lover? has your palfrey heart
enough
To bear his armor? shall we fast, or
dine?
No? — then do thou, being right hon-
est, pray
That we may meet the horsemen of
Earl Doorm,
I too would still be honest." Thus
he said:
And sadly gazing on her bridle-reins,
And answering not a word, she led the
way.

But as a man to whom a dreadful
loss
Falls in a far land and he knows it
not,
But coming back he learns it, and the
loss
So pains him that he sickens nigh to
death;

So fared it with Geraint, who being
  prick'd
In combat with the follower of
  Limours,
Bled underneath his armor secretly,
And so rode on, nor told his gentle
  wife
What ail'd him, hardly knowing it
  himself,
Till his eye darken'd and his helmet
  wagg'd ;
And at a sudden swerving of the road,
Tho' happily down on a bank of grass,
The Prince, without a word, from his
  horse fell.

And Enid heard the clashing of his
  fall,
Suddenly came, and at his side all
  pale
Dismounting, loosed the fastenings of
  his arms,
Nor let her true hand falter, nor blue
  eye
Moisten, till she had lighted on his
  wound,
And tearing off her veil of faded silk
Had bared her forehead to the blister-
  ing sun,
And swathed the hurt that drain'd her
  dear lord's life.
Then after all was done that hand
  could do,
She rested, and her desolation came
Upon her, and she wept beside the
  way.

And many past, but none regarded
  her,
For in that realm of lawless turbu-
  lence,
A woman weeping for her murder'd
  mate
Was cared as much for as a summer
  shower :
One took him for a victim of Earl
  Doorm,
Nor dared to waste a perilous pity on
  him :
Another hurrying past, a man-at-arms,
Rode on a mission to the bandit Earl ;

Half whistling and half singing a
  coarse song,
He drove the dust against her veilless
  eyes :
Another, flying from the wrath of
  Doorm
Before an ever-fancied arrow, made
The long way smoke beneath him in
  his fear ;
At which her palfrey whinnying lifted
  heel
And scour'd into the coppices and was
  lost,
While the great charger stood, grieved
  like a man.

But at the point of noon the huge
  Earl Doorm,
Broad-faced with under-fringe of rus-
  set beard,
Bound on a foray, rolling eyes of
  prey,
Came riding with a hundred lances
  up ;
But ere he came, like one that hails a
  ship,
Cried out with a big voice, " What, is
  he dead ? "
" No, no, not dead ! " she answer'd in
  all haste.
" Would some of your kind people
  take him up,
And bear him hence out of this cruel
  sun ?
Most sure am I, quite sure, he is not
  dead."

Then said Earl Doorm : " Well, if
  he be not dead,
Why wail ye for him thus ? ye seem a
  child.
And be he dead, I count you for a
  fool ;
Your wailing will not quicken him :
  dead or not,
Ye mar a comely face with idiot tears.
Yet, since the face *is* comely — some
  of you,
Here, take him up, and bear him to
  our hall :
An if he live, we will have him of our
  band ;

And if he die, why earth has earth
　enough
To hide him.　See ye take the charger
　too,
A noble one."

　　　He spake, and past away,
But left two brawny spearmen, who
　advanced,
Each growling like a dog, when his
　good bone
Seems to be pluck'd at by the village
　boys
Who love to vex him eating, and he
　fears
To lose his bone, and lays his foot
　upon it,
Gnawing and growling: so the ruffians
　growl'd,
Fearing to lose, and all for a dead
　man,
Their chance of booty from the morn-
　ing's raid,
Yet raised and laid him on a litter-
　bier,
Such as they brought upon their forays
　out
For those that might be wounded; laid
　him on it
All in the hollow of his shield, and
　took
And bore him to the naked hall of
　Doorm,
(His gentle charger following him
　unled)
And cast him and the bier in which
　he lay
Down on an oaken settle in the
　hall,
And then departed, hot in haste to
　join
Their luckier mates, but growling as
　before,
And cursing their lost time, and the
　dead man,
And their own Earl, and their own
　souls, and her.
They might as well have blest her:
　she was deaf
To blessing or to cursing save from
　one.

So for long hours sat Enid by her
　lord,
There in the naked hall, propping his
　head,
And chafing his pale hands, and call-
　ing to him.
Till at the last he waken'd from his
　swoon,
And found his own dear bride prop-
　ping his head,
And chafing his faint hands, and
　calling to him ;
And felt the warm tears falling on his
　face ;
And said to his own heart, " She weeps
　for me " :
And yet lay still, and feign'd himself
　as dead,
That he might prove her to the utter-
　most,
And say to his own heart, " She weeps
　for me."

But in the falling afternoon return'd
The huge Earl Doorm with plunder
　to the hall.
His lusty spearmen follow'd him with
　noise :
Each hurling down a heap of things
　that rang
Against the pavement, cast his lance
　aside,
And doff'd his helm: and then there
　flutter'd in,
Half-bold, half-frighted, with dilated
　eyes,
A tribe of women, dress'd in many
　hues,
And mingled with the spearmen : and
　Earl Doorm
Struck with a knife's haft hard
　against the board,
And call'd for flesh and wine to feed
　his spears.
And men brought in whole hogs and
　quarter beeves,
And all the hall was dim with steam
　of flesh :
And none spake word, but all sat
　down at once,
And ate with tumult in the naked
　hall,

Feeding like horses when you hear
    them feed;
Till Enid shrank far back into herself,
To shun the wild ways of the lawless
    tribe.
But when Earl Doorm had eaten all
    he would,
He roll'd his eyes about the hall, and
    found
A damsel drooping in a corner of it.
Then he remember'd her, and how she
    wept;
And out of her there came a power
    upon him;
And rising on the sudden he said,
    "Eat!
I never yet beheld a thing so pale.
God's curse, it makes me mad to see
    you weep.
Eat! Look yourself. Good luck had
    your good man,
For were I dead who is it would
    weep for me?
Sweet lady, never since I first drew
    breath
Have I beheld a lily like yourself.
And so there lived some color in your
    cheek,
There is not one among my gentle-
    women
Were fit to wear your slipper for a
    glove.
But listen to me, and by me be
    ruled,
And I will do the thing I have not
    done,
For ye shall share my earldom with
    me, girl,
And we will live like two birds in one
    nest,
And I will fetch you forage from all
    fields,
For I compel all creatures to my will."

He spoke: the brawny spearman
    let his cheek
Bulge with the unswallow'd piece, and
    turning stared;
While some, whose souls the old ser-
    pent long had drawn
Down, as the worm draws in the
    wither'd leaf

And makes it earth, hiss'd each at
    other's ear
What shall not be recorded — women
    they,
Women, or what had been those
    gracious things,
But now desired the humbling of their
    best,
Yea, would have help'd him to it: and
    all at once
They hated her, who took no thought
    of them,
But answer'd in low voice, her meek
    head yet
Drooping, "I pray you of your cour-
    tesy,
He being as he is, to let me be."

She spake so low he hardly heard
    her speak,
But like a mighty patron, satisfied
With what himself had done so gra-
    ciously,
Assumed that she had thank'd him,
    adding, "Yea,
Eat and be glad, for I account you
    mine."

She answer'd meekly, "How should
    I be glad
Henceforth in all the world at any-
    thing,
Until my lord arise and look upon
    me?"

Here the huge Earl cried out upon
    her talk,
As all but empty heart and weariness
And sickly nothing; suddenly seized
    on her,
And bare her by main violence to the
    board,
And thrust the dish before her, cry-
    ing, "Eat."

"No, no," said Enid, vext, "I will
    not eat
Till yonder man upon the bier arise,
And eat with me." "Drink, then,"
    he answer'd. "Here!"
(And fill'd a horn with wine and held
    it to her,)

"Lo! I, myself, when flush'd with
    fight, or hot,
God's curse, with anger — often I
    myself,
Before I well have drunken, scarce
    can eat:
Drink therefore and the wine will
    change your will."

"Not so," she cried, "By Heaven, I
    will not drink
Till my dear lord arise and bid me do
    it,
And drink with me; and if he rise no
    more,
I will not look at wine until I die."

At this he turn'd all red and paced
    his hall,
Now gnaw'd his under, now his upper
    lip,
And coming up close to her, said at
    last:
"Girl, for I see ye scorn my courte-
    sies,
Take warning: yonder man is surely
    dead;
And I compel all creatures to my
    will.
Not eat nor drink? And wherefore
    wail for one,
Who put your beauty to this flout and
    scorn
By dressing it in rags? Amazed am
    I,
Beholding how ye butt against my
    wish,
That I forbear you thus: cross me
    no more.
At least put off to please me this poor
    gown,
This silken rag, this beggar-woman's
    weed:
I love that beauty should go beauti-
    fully:
For see ye not my gentlewomen here,
How gay, how suited to the house of
    one
Who loves that beauty should go
    beautifully?
Rise therefore; robe yourself in this:
    obey."

He spoke, and one among his gen-
    tle women
Display'd a splendid silk of foreign
    loom,
Where like a shoaling sea the lovely
    blue
Play'd into green, and thicker down
    the front
With jewels than the sward with
    drops of dew,
When all night long a cloud clings
    to the hill,
And with the dawn ascending lets the
    day
Strike where it clung: so thickly
    shone the gems.

But Enid answer'd, harder to be
    moved
Than hardest tyrants in their day of
    power,
With life-long injuries burning un-
    avenged,
And now their hour has come; and
    Enid said:

"In this poor gown my dear lord
    found me first,
And loved me serving in my father's
    hall:
In this poor gown I rode with him to
    court,
And there the Queen array'd me like
    the sun:
In this poor gown he bade me clothe
    myself,
When now we rode upon this fatal
    quest
Of honor, where no honor can be
    gain'd:
And this poor gown I will not cast
    aside
Until himself arise a living man,
And bid me cast it. I have griefs
    enough:
Pray you be gentle, pray you let me
    be:
I never loved, can never love but him:
Yea, God, I pray you of your gentle-
    ness,
He being as he is, to let me be."

Then strode the brute Earl up and
    down his hall,
And took his russet beard between his
    teeth ;
Last, coming up quite close, and in his
    mood
Crying, " I count it of no more avail,
Dame, to be gentle than ungentle with
    you ;
Take my salute," unknightly with flat
    hand,
However lightly, smote her on the
    cheek.

Then Enid, in her utter helplessness,
And since she thought, " He had not
    dared to do it,
Except he surely knew my lord was
    dead,
Sent forth a sudden sharp and bitter
    cry,
As of a wild thing taken in the trap,
Which sees the trapper coming thro'
    the wood.

This heard Geraint, and grasping at
    his sword,
(It lay beside him in the hollow
    shield),
Made but a single bound, and with a
    sweep of it
Shore thro' the swarthy neck, and like
    a ball
The russet-bearded head roll'd on the
    floor.
So died Earl Doorm by him he counted
    dead.
And all the men and women in the
    hall
Rose when they saw the dead man
    rise, and fled
Yelling as from a spectre, and the two
Were left alone together, and he said :

" Enid, I have used you worse than
    that dead man ;
Done you more wrong : we both have
    undergone
That trouble which has left me thrice
    your own :
Henceforward I will rather die than
    doubt.

And here I lay this penance on my-
    self,
Not, tho' mine own ears heard you
    yestermorn —
You thought me sleeping, but I heard
    you say,
I heard you say, that you were no true
    wife :
I swear I will not ask your meaning
    in it :
I do believe yourself against yourself,
And will henceforward rather die than
    doubt."

And Enid could not say one tender
    word,
She felt so blunt and stupid at the
    heart :
She only pray'd him, " Fly, they will
    return
And slay you ; fly, your charger is
    without,
My palfrey lost."   " Then, Enid, shall
    you ride
Behind me."   " Yea," said Enid, " let
    us go."
And moving out they found the stately
    horse,
Who now no more a vassal to the
    thief,
But free to stretch his limbs in lawful
    fight,
Neigh'd with all gladness as they
    came, and stoop'd
With a low whinny toward the pair :
    and she
Kiss'd the white star upon his noble
    front,
Glad also ; then Geraint upon the
    horse
Mounted, and reach'd a hand, and on
    his foot
She set her own and climb'd ; he turn'd
    his face
And kiss'd her climbing, and she cast
    her arms
About him, and at once they rode
    away.

And never yet, since high in Para-
    dise
O'er the four rivers the first roses blew,

Came purer pleasure unto mortal kind
Than lived thro' her, who in that per-
ilous hour
Put hand to hand beneath her hus-
band's heart,
And felt him hers again : she did not
weep,
But o'er her meek eyes came a happy
mist
Like that which kept the heart of
Eden green
Before the useful trouble of the rain :
Yet not so misty were her meek blue
eyes
As not to see before them on the path,
Right in the gateway of the bandit
hold,
A knight of Arthur's court, who laid
his lance
In rest, and made as if to fall upon
him.
Then, fearing for his hurt and loss of
blood,
She, with her mind all full of what
had chanced,
Shriek'd to the stranger "Slay not a
dead man !"
"The voice of Enid," said the knight ;
but she,
Beholding it was Edyrn son of Nudd,
Was moved so much the more, and
shriek'd again,
"O cousin, slay not him who gave you
life."
And Edyrn moving frankly forward
spake :
"My lord Geraint, I greet you with
all love ;
I took you for a bandit knight of
Doorm ;
And fear not, Enid, I should fall upon
him,
Who love you, Prince, with something
of the love
Wherewith we love the Heaven that
chastens us.
For once, when I was up so high in
pride
That I was half-way down the slope
to Hell,
By overthrowing me you threw me
higher.

Now, made a knight of Arthur's Table
Round,
And since I knew this Earl, when I
myself
Was half a bandit in my lawless hour,
I come the mouthpiece of our King to
Doorm
(The King is close behind me) bidding
him
Disband himself, and scatter all his
powers,
Submit, and hear the judgment of the
King."

"He hears the judgment of the King
of kings,"
Cried the wan Prince ; "and lo, the
powers of Doorm
Are scatter'd," and he pointed to the
field,
Where, huddled here and there on
mound and knoll,
Were men and women staring and
aghast,
While some yet fled ; and then he
plainlier told
How the huge Earl lay slain within
his hall.
But when the knight besought him,
"Follow me,
Prince, to the camp, and in the King's
own ear
Speak what has chanced ; ye surely
have endured
Strange chances here alone ;" that
other flush'd,
And hung his head, and halted in
reply,
Fearing the mild face of the blameless
King,
And after madness acted question
ask'd :
Till Edyrn crying, "If ye will not go
To Arthur, then will Arthur come to
you."
"Enough," he said, "I follow," and
they went.
But Enid in their going had two fears,
One from the bandit scatter'd in the
field,
And one from Edyrn. Every now
and then,

When Edyrn rein'd his charger at
　her side,
She shrank a little.　In a hollow land,
From which old fires have broken,
　men may fear
Fresh fire and ruin.　He, perceiving,
　said:

"Fair and dear cousin, you that
　most had cause
To fear me, fear no longer, I am
　changed.
Yourself were first the blameless
　cause to make
My nature's prideful sparkle in the
　blood
Break into furious flame; being re-
　pulsed
By Yniol and yourself, I schemed and
　wrought
Until I overturn'd him; then set up
(With one main purpose ever at my
　heart)
My haughty jousts, and took a para-
　mour;
Did her mock-honor as the fairest
　fair,
And, toppling over all antagonism,
So wax'd in pride, that I believed
　myself
Unconquerable, for I was wellnigh
　mad:
And, but for my main purpose in
　these jousts,
I should have slain your father, seized
　yourself.
I lived in hope that sometime you
　would come
To these my lists with him whom best
　you loved;
And there, poor cousin, with your
　meek blue eyes,
The truest eyes that ever answer'd
　Heaven,
Behold me overturn and trample on
　him.
Then, had you cried, or knelt, or
　pray'd to me,
I should not less have kill'd him.
　And you came, —
But once you came, — and with your
　own true eyes

Beheld the man you loved (I speak as
　one
Speaks of a service done him) over-
　throw
My proud self, and my purpose three
　years old,
And set his foot upon me, and give
　me life.
There was I broken down; there was
　I saved:
Tho' thence I rode all-shamed, hating
　the life
He gave me, meaning to be rid of it.
And all the penance the Queen laid
　upon me
Was but to rest awhile within her
　court;
Where first as sullen as a beast new-
　caged,
And waiting to be treated like a
　wolf,
Because I knew my deeds were known,
　I found,
Instead of scornful pity or pure scorn,
Such fine reserve and noble reticence,
Manners so kind, yet stately, such a
　grace
Of tenderest courtesy, that I began
To glance behind me at my former
　life,
And find that it had been the wolf's
　indeed:
And oft I talk'd with Dubric, the high
　saint,
Who, with mild heat of holy oratory,
Subdued me somewhat to that gentle-
　ness,
Which, when it weds with manhood,
　makes a man.
And you were often there about the
　Queen,
But saw me not, or mark'd not if you
　saw;
Nor did I care or dare to speak with
　you,
But kept myself aloof till I was
　changed;
And fear not, cousin; I am changed
　indeed."

He spoke, and Enid easily believed,
Like simple noble natures, credulous

Of what they long for, good in friend or foe,
There most in those who most have done them ill.
And when they reach'd the camp the King himself
Advanced to greet them, and beholding her
Tho' pale, yet happy, ask'd her not a word,
But went apart with Edyrn, whom he held
In converse for a little, and return'd,
And, gravely smiling, lifted her from horse,
And kiss'd her with all pureness, brother-like,
And show'd an empty tent allotted her,
And glancing for a minute, till he saw her
Pass into it turn'd to the Prince, and said:

"Prince, when of late ye pray'd me for my leave
To move to your own land, and there defend
Your marches, I was prick'd with some reproof,
As one that let foul wrong stagnate and be,
By having look'd too much thro' alien eyes,
And wrought too long with delegated hands,
Not used mine own: but now behold me come
To cleanse this common sewer of all my realm,
With Edyrn and with others: have ye look'd
At Edyrn? have ye seen how nobly changed?
This work of his is great and wonderful.
His very face with change of heart is changed,
The world will not believe a man repents:
And this wise world of ours is mainly right.

Full seldom doth a man repent, or use
Both grace and will to pick the vicious quitch
Of blood and custom wholly out of him,
And make all clean, and plant himself afresh.
Edyrn has done it, weeding all his heart
As I will weed this land before I go.
I, therefore, made him of our Table Round,
Not rashly, but have proved him everyway
One of our noblest, our most valorous,
Sanest and most obedient: and indeed
This work of Edyrn wrought upon himself
After a life of violence, seems to me
A thousand-fold more great and wonderful
Than if some knight of mine, risking his life,
My subject with my subjects under him,
Should make an onslaught single on a realm
Of robbers, tho' he slew them one by one,
And were himself nigh wounded to the death."

So spake the King; low bow'd the Prince, and felt
His work was neither great nor wonderful,
And past to Enid's tent; and thither came
The King's own leech to look into his hurt;
And Enid tended on him there; and there
Her constant motion round him, and the breath
Of her sweet tendance hovering over him,
Fill'd all the genial courses of his blood
With deeper and with ever deeper love,
As the south-west that blowing Bala lake

Fills all the sacred Dee. So past the days.

But while Geraint lay healing of
    his hurt,
The blameless King went forth and
    cast his eyes
On each of all whom Uther left in
    charge
Long since, to guard the justice of the
    King :
He look'd and found them wanting ;
    and as now
Men weed the white horse on the
    Berkshire hills
To keep him bright and clean as here-
    tofore,
He rooted out the slothful officer
Or guilty, which for bribe had wink'd
    at wrong,
And in their chairs set up a stronger
    race
With hearts and hands, and sent a
    thousand men
To till the wastes, and moving every-
    where
Clear'd the dark places and let in the
    law,
And broke the bandit holds and
    cleansed the land.

Then, when Geraint was whole
    again, they past
With Arthur to Caerleon upon Usk.
There the great Queen once more em-
    braced her friend,
And clothed her in apparel like the
    day.
And tho' Geraint could never take
    again
That comfort from their converse
    which he took
Before the Queen's fair name was
    breathed upon,
He rested well content that all was
    well.
Thence after tarrying for a space they
    rode,
And fifty knights rode with them to
    the shores
Of Severn, and they past to their own
    land.

And there he kept the justice of the
    King
So vigorously yet mildly, that all
    hearts
Applauded, and the spiteful whisper
    died :
And being ever foremost in the chase,
And victor at the tilt and tournament,
They call'd him the great Prince and
    man of men.
But Enid, whom the ladies loved to
    call
Enid the Fair, a grateful people
    named
Enid the Good ; and in their halls
    arose
The cry of children, Enids and
    Geraints
Of times to be ; nor did he doubt her
    more,
But rested in her feälty, till he
    crown'd
A happy life with a fair death, and
    fell
Against the heathen of the Northern
    Sea
In battle, fighting for the blameless
    King.

MERLIN AND VIVIEN.

A STORM was coming, but the winds
    were still,
And in the wild woods of Broceliande,
Before an oak, so hollow, huge and
    old
It look'd a tower of ruin'd masonwork,
At Merlin's feet the wily Vivien lay.

Whence came she ? One that bare
    in bitter grudge
The scorn of Arthur and his Table,
    Mark
The Cornish King, had heard a wan-
    dering voice,
A minstrel of Caerleon by strong storm
Blown into shelter at Tintagil, say
That out of naked knightlike purity
Sir Lancelot worshipt no unmarried
    girl

But the great Queen herself, fought
in her name,
Sware by her — vows like theirs, that
high in heaven
Love most, but neither marry, nor are
given
In marriage, angels of our Lord's report.

He ceased, and then — for Vivien
sweetly said
(She sat beside the banquet nearest
Mark),
"And is the fair example follow'd,
Sir,
In Arthur's household?" — answer'd
innocently:

"Ay, by some few — ay, truly —
youths that hold
It more beseems the perfect virgin
knight
To worship woman as true wife be-
yond
All hopes of gaining, than as maiden
girl.
They place their pride in Lancelot and
the Queen.
So passionate for an utter purity
Beyond the limit of their bond, are
these,
For Arthur bound them not to single-
ness.
Brave hearts and clean! and yet —
God guide them — young."

Then Mark was half in heart to
hurl his cup
Straight at the speaker, but forbore:
he rose
To leave the hall, and, Vivien following him,
Turn'd to her: "Here are snakes
within the grass;
And you methinks, O Vivien, save ye
fear
The monkish manhood, and the mask
of pure
Worn by this court, can stir them till
they sting."

And Vivien answer'd, smiling scorn-
fully,
"Why fear? because that foster'd at
thy court
I savor of thy — virtues? fear them?
no.
As Love, if Love be perfect, casts out
fear,
So Hate, if Hate be perfect, casts out
fear.
My father died in battle against the
King,
My mother on his corpse in open field;
She bore me there, for born from
death was I
Among the dead and sown upon the
wind —
And then on thee! and shown the
truth betimes,
That old true filth, and bottom of the
well,
Where Truth is hidden.   Gracious
lessons thine
And maxims of the mud!   'This
Arthur pure!
Great Nature thro' the flesh herself
hath made
Gives him the lie!   There is no being
pure,
My cherub; saith not Holy Writ the
same?' —
If I were Arthur, I would have thy
blood.
Thy blessing, stainless King!   I bring
thee back,
When I have ferreted out their bur-
rowings,
The hearts of all this Order in mine
hand —
Ay — so that fate and craft and folly
close,
Perchance, one curl of Arthur's
golden beard.
To me this narrow grizzled fork of
thine
Is cleaner-fashion'd — Well, I loved
thee first,
That warps the wit."

Loud laugh'd the graceless Mark.
But Vivien into Camelot stealing,
lodged

Low in the city, and on a festal day
When Guinevere was crossing the
  great hall
Cast herself down, knelt to the Queen,
  and wail'd.

  "Why kneel ye there ?   What evil
  have ye wrought ?
Rise !" and the damsel bidden rise
  arose
And stood with folded hands and
  downward eyes
Of glancing corner, and all meekly
  said,
"None wrought, but suffer'd much,
  an orphan maid !
My father died in battle for thy King,
My mother on his corpse — in open
  field,
The sad sea-sounding wastes of Lyon-
  esse —
Poor wretch — no friend ! — and now
  by Mark the King
For that small charm of feature mine,
  pursued —
If any such be mine — I fly to thee.
Save, save me thou — Woman of
  women — thine
The wreath of beauty, thine the crown
  of power,
Be thine the balm of pity, O Heaven's
  own white
Earth-angel, stainless bride of stain-
  less King —
Help, for he follows ! take me to thy-
  self !
O yield me shelter for mine innocency
Among thy maidens ! "

              Here her slow sweet eyes
Fear-tremulous, but humbly hopeful,
  rose
Fixt on her hearer's, while the Queen
  who stood
All glittering like May sunshine on
  May leaves
In green and gold, and plumed with
  green replied,
"Peace, child ! of overpraise and over-
  blame
We choose the last.   Our noble
  Arthur, him

Ye scarce can overpraise, will hear
  and know.
Nay — we believe all evil of thy
  Mark —
Well, we shall test thee farther; but
  this hour
We ride a-hawking with Sir Lancelot.
He hath given us a fair falcon which
  he train'd ;
We go to prove it.   Bide ye here the
  while."

  She past; and Vivien murmur'd
  after " Go !
I bide the while."   Then thro' the
  portal-arch
Peering askance, and muttering
  broken-wise,
As one that labors with an evil dream,
Beheld the Queen and Lancelot get to
  horse.

  "Is that the Lancelot ? goodly —
  ay, but gaunt :
Courteous — amends for gauntness —
  takes her hand —
That glance of theirs, but for the
  street, had been
A clinging kiss — how hand lingers
  in hand !
Let go at last ! — they ride away —
  to hawk
For waterfowl.   Royaller game is
  mine.
For such a supersensual sensual bond
As that gray cricket chirpt of at our
  hearth —
Touch flax with flame — a glance will
  serve — the liars !
Ah little rat that borest in the dyke
Thy hole by night to let the boundless
  deep
Down upon far-off cities while they
  dance —
Or dream — of thee they dream'd not
  — nor of me
These — ay, but each of either : ride
  and dream
The mortal dream that never yet was
  mine —
Ride, ride and dream until ye wake —
  to me !

Then, narrow court and lubber King,
    farewell!
For Lancelot will be gracious to the
    rat,
And our wise Queen, if knowing that
    I know,
Will hate, loathe, fear — but honor
    me the more."

    Yet while they rode together down
        the plain,
Their talk was all of training, terms
    of art,
Diet and seeling, jesses, leash and lure.
" She is too noble " he said " to check
    at pies,
Nor will she rake : there is no base-
    ness in her."
Here when the Queen demanded as by
    chance
" Know ye the stranger woman ? "
        " Let her be,"
Said Lancelot and unhooded casting
    off
The goodly falcon free ; she tower'd ;
    her bells,
Tone under tone, shrill'd ; and they
    lifted up
Their eager faces, wondering at the
    strength,
Boldness and royal knighthood of the
    bird
Who pounced her quarry and slew it.
    Many a time
As once — of old — among the flowers
    — they rode.

    But Vivien half-forgotten of the
        Queen
Among her damsels broidering sat,
    heard, watch'd
And whisper'd : thro' the peaceful
    court she crept
And whisper'd : then as Arthur in the
    highest
Leaven'd the world, so Vivien in the
    lowest,
Arriving at a time of golden rest,
And sowing one ill hint from ear to
    ear,
While all the heathen lay at Arthur's
    feet,

And no quest came, but all was joust
    and play,
Leaven'd his hall. They heard and
    let her be.

    Thereafter as an enemy that has left
Death in the living waters, and with-
    drawn,
The wily Vivien stole from Arthur's
    court.

    She hated all the knights, and heard
        in thought
Their lavish comment when her name
    was named.
For once, when Arthur walking all
    alone,
Vext at a rumor issued from herself
Of some corruption crept among his
    knights,
Had met her, Vivien, being greeted
    fair,
Would fain have wrought upon his
    cloudy mood
With reverent eyes mock-loyal,
    shaken voice,
And flutter'd adoration, and at last
With dark sweet hints of some who
    prized him more
Than who should prize him most ; at
    which the King
Had gazed upon her blankly and gone
    by :
But one had watch'd, and had not held
    his peace :
It made the laughter of an afternoon
That Vivien should attempt the
    blameless King.
And after that, she set herself to gain
Him, the most famous man of all
    those times,
Merlin, who knew the range of all
    their arts,
Had built the King his havens, ships,
    and halls,
Was also Bard, and knew the starry
    heavens ;
The people call'd him Wizard ; whom
    at first
She play'd about with slight and
    sprightly talk,

And vivid smiles, and faintly-venom'd
  points
Of slander, glancing here and grazing
  there;
And yielding to his kindlier moods,
  the Seer
Would watch her at her petulance,
  and play,
Ev'n when they seem'd unloveable,
  and laugh
As those that watch a kitten; thus he
  grew
Tolerant of what he half disdain'd,
  and she,
Perceiving that she was but half disdain'd,
Began to break her sports with graver
  fits,
Turn red or pale, would often when
  they met
Sigh fully, or all-silent gaze upon him
With such a fixt devotion, that the old
  man,
Tho' doubtful, felt the flattery, and at
  times
Would flatter his own wish in age for
  love,
And half believe her true: for thus at
  times
He waver'd; but that other clung to
  him,
Fixt in her will, and so the seasons
  went.

  Then fell on Merlin a great melan-
    choly;
He walk'd with dreams and darkness,
  and he found
A doom that ever poised itself to fall,
An ever-moaning battle in the mist,
World-war of dying flesh against the
  life,
Death in all life and lying in all love,
The meanest having power upon the
  highest,
And the high purpose broken by the
  worm.

  So leaving Arthur's court he gain'd
    the beach;
There found a little boat, and stept
  into it;

And Vivien follow'd, but he mark'd
  her not.
She took the helm and he the sail,
  the boat
Drave with a sudden wind across the
  deeps,
And touching Breton sands, they dis-
  embark'd.
And then she follow'd Merlin all the
  way,
Ev'n to the wild woods of Broceliande.
For Merlin once had told her of a
  charm,
The which if any wrought on anyone
With woven paces and with waving
  arms,
The man so wrought on ever seem'd
  to lie
Closed in the four walls of a hollow
  tower,
From which was no escape for ever-
  more;
And none could find that man for
  evermore,
Nor could he see but him who wrought
  the charm
Coming and going, and he lay as dead
And lost to life and use and name
  and fame.
And Vivien ever sought to work the
  charm
Upon the great Enchanter of the
  Time,
As fancying that her glory would be
  great
According to his greatness whom she
  quench'd.

  There lay she all her length and
    kiss'd his feet,
As if in deepest reverence and in love.
A twist of gold was round her hair; a
  robe
Of samite without price, that more
  exprest
Than hid her, clung about her lissome
  limbs,
In color like the satin-shining palm
On sallows in the windy gleams of
  March:
And while she kiss'd them, crying,
  "Trample me,

Dear feet, that I have follow'd thro'
   the world,
And I will pay you worship ; tread
   me down
And I will kiss you for it ;" he was
   mute :
So dark a forethought roll'd about his
   brain,
As on a dull day in an Ocean cave
The blind wave feeling round his long
   sea-hall
In silence : wherefore, when she lifted
   up
A face of sad appeal, and spake and
   said,
"O Merlin, do ye love me ?" and
   again,
"O Merlin, do ye love me ?" and once
   more,
"Great Master, do ye love me ?" he
   was mute.
And lissome Vivien, holding by his
   heel,
Writhed toward him, slided up his
   knee and sat,
Behind his ankle twined her hollow
   feet
Together, curved an arm about his
   neck,
Clung like a snake ; and letting her
   left hand
Droop from his mighty shoulder, as a
   leaf,
Made with her right a comb of pearl
   to part
The lists of such a beard as youth gone
   out
Had left in ashes : then he spoke and
   said,
Not looking at her, " Who are wise in
   love
Love most, say least," and Vivien
   answer'd quick,
" I saw the little elf-god eyeless once
In Arthur's arras hall at Camelot :
But neither eyes nor tongue — O
   stupid child !
Yet you are wise who say it ; let me
   think
Silence is wisdom : I am silent then,
And ask no kiss ;" then adding all at
   once,

" And lo, I clothe myself with wis-
   dom," drew
The vast and shaggy mantle of his
   beard
Across her neck and bosom to her
   knee,
And call'd herself a gilded summer fly
Caught in a great old tyrant spider's
   web,
Who meant to eat her up in that wild
   wood
Without one word. So Vivien call'd
   herself,
But rather seem'd a lovely baleful star
Veil'd in gray vapor ; till he sadly
   smiled :
" To what request for what strange
   boon," he said,
" Are these your pretty tricks and
   fooleries,
O Vivien, the preamble ? yet my
   thanks,
For these have broken up my melan-
   choly."

   And Vivien answer'd smiling sau-
   cily,
" What, O my Master, have ye found
   your voice ?
I bid the stranger welcome. Thanks
   at last !
But yesterday you never open'd lip,
Except indeed to drink : no cup had
   we :
In mine own lady palms I cull'd the
   spring
That gather'd trickling dropwise from
   the cleft,
And made a pretty cup of both my
   hands
And offer'd you it kneeling : then you
   drank
And knew no more, nor gave me one
   poor word ;
O no more thanks than might a goat
   have given
With no more sign of reverence than
   a beard.
And when we halted at that other
   well,
And I was faint to swooning, and you
   lay

Foot-gilt with all the blossom-dust of
   those
Deep meadows we had traversed, did
   you know
That Vivien bathed your feet before
   her own?
And yet no thanks: and all thro' this
   wild wood
And all this morning when I fondled
   you:
Boon, ay, there was a boon, one not
   so strange —
How had I wrong'd you? surely ye
   are wise,
But such a silence is more wise than
   kind."

And Merlin lock'd his hand in hers
   and said:
"O did ye never lie upon the shore,
And watch the curl'd white of the
   coming wave
Glass'd in the slippery sand before it
   breaks?
Ev'n such a wave, but not so pleasur-
   able,
Dark in the glass of some presageful
   mood,
Had I for three days seen, ready to
   fall.
And then I rose and fled from Arthur's
   court
To break the mood. You follow'd me
   unask'd;
And when I look'd, and saw you following still,
My mind involved yourself the nearest
   thing
In that mind-mist: for shall I tell you
   truth?
You seem'd that wave about to break
   upon me
And sweep me from my hold upon the
   world,
My use and name and fame. Your
   pardon, child.
Your pretty sports have brighten'd all
   again.
And ask your boon, for boon I owe
   you thrice,
Once for wrong done you by confusion,
   next

For thanks it seems till now neglected,
   last
For these your dainty gambols:
   wherefore ask;
And take this boon so strange and not
   so strange."

And Vivien answer'd smiling mourn-
   fully:
"O not so strange as my long asking
   it,
Not yet so strange as you yourself are
   strange,
Nor half so strange as that dark mood
   of yours.
I ever fear'd ye were not wholly
   mine;
And see, yourself have own'd ye did
   me wrong.
The people call you prophet: let it
   be:
But not of those that can expound
   themselves.
Take Vivien for expounder; she will
   call
That three-days-long presageful gloom
   of yours
No presage, but the same mistrustful
   mood
That makes you seem less noble than
   yourself,
Whenever I have ask'd this very
   boon,
Now ask'd again: for see you not,
   dear love,
That such a mood as that, which
   lately gloom'd
Your fancy when ye saw me following you,
Must make me fear still more you are
   not mine,
Must make me yearn still more to
   prove you mine,
And make me wish still more to learn
   this charm
Of woven paces and of waving hands,
As proof of trust. O Merlin, teach it
   me.
The charm so taught will charm us
   both to rest.
For, grant me some slight power upon
   your fate,

I, feeling that you felt me worthy
trust,
Should rest and let you rest, knowing
you mine.
And therefore be as great as ye are
named,
Not muffled round with selfish reti-
cence.
How hard you look and how deny-
ingly!
O, if you think this wickedness in me,
That I should prove it on you una-
wares,
That makes me passing wrathful; then
our bond
Had best be loosed for ever: but
think or not,
By Heaven that hears I tell you the
clean truth,
As clean as blood of babes, as white
as milk;
O Merlin, may this earth, if ever I,
If these unwitty wandering wits of
mine,
Ev'n in the jumbled rubbish of a
dream,
Have tript on such conjectural treach-
ery —
May this hard earth cleave to the
Nadir hell
Down, down, and close again, and nip
me flat,
If I be such a traitress. Yield my
boon,
Till which I scarce can yield you all
I am;
And grant my re-reiterated wish,
The great proof of your love: because
I think,
However wise, ye hardly know me
yet."

And Merlin loosed his hand from
hers and said,
" I never was less wise, however wise,
Too curious Vivien, tho' you talk of
trust,
Than when I told you first of such a
charm.
Yea, if ye talk of trust I tell you this,
Too much I trusted when I told you
that,

And stirr'd this vice in you which
ruin'd man
Thro' woman the first hour; for
howsoe'er
In children a great curiousness be
well,
Who have to learn themselves and all
the world,
In you, that are no child, for still I
find
Your face is practised when I spell
the lines,
I call it, — well, I will not call it vice:
But since you name yourself the
summer fly,
I well could wish a cobweb for the
gnat,
That settles, beaten back, and beaten
back
Settles, till one could yield for weariness:
But since I will not yield to give you
power
Upon my life and use and name and
fame,
Why will ye never ask some other
boon?
Yea, by God's rood, I trusted you too
much."

And Vivien, like the tenderest-
hearted maid
That ever bided tryst at village stile,
Made answer, either eyelid wet with
tears:
" Nay, Master, be not wrathful with
your maid;
Caress her: let her feel herself for-
given
Who feels no heart to ask another
boon.
I think ye hardly know the tender
rhyme
Of 'trust me not at all or all in all.'
I heard the great Sir Lancelot sing it
once,
And it shall answer for me. Listen
to it.

' In Love, if Love be Love, if Love
be ours,

Faith and unfaith can ne'er be equal
    powers :
Unfaith in aught is want of faith in
    all.

    ' It is the little rift within the lute,
That by and by will make the music
    mute,
And ever widening slowly silence all.

    ' The little rift within the lover's
    lute
Or little pitted speck in garner'd fruit,
That rotting inward slowly moulders
    all.

    ' It is not worth the keeping : let it
    go :
But shall it ? answer, darling, answer,
    no.
And trust me not at all or all in all.'

O Master, do ye love my tender
    rhyme ? "

And Merlin look'd and half believed
    her true,
So tender was her voice, so fair her
    face,
So sweetly gleam'd her eyes behind
    her tears
Like sunlight on the plain behind a
    shower :
And yet he answer'd half indignantly :

    " Far other was the song that once
    I heard
By this huge oak, sung nearly where
    we sit :
For here we met, some ten or twelve
    of us,
To chase a creature that was current
    then
In these wild woods, the hart with
    golden horns.
It was the time when first the ques-
    tion rose
About the founding of a Table Round,
That was to be, for love of God and
    men
And noble deeds, the flower of all the
    world.

And each incited each to noble deeds.
And while we waited, one, the young-
    est of us,
We could not keep him silent, out he
    flash'd,
And into such a song, such fire for
    fame,
Such trumpet-blowings in it, coming
    down
To such a stern and iron-clashing
    close,
That when he stopt we long'd to hurl
    together,
And should have done it ; but the
    beauteous beast
Scared by the noise upstarted at our
    feet,
And like a silver shadow slipt away
Thro' the dim land ; and all day long
    we rode
Thro' the dim land against a rushing
    wind,
That glorious roundel echoing in our
    ears,
And chased the flashes of his golden
    horns
Until they vanish'd by the fairy well
That laughs at iron — as our warriors
    did —
Where children cast their pins and
    nails, and cry,
' Laugh, little well ! ' but touch it with
    a sword,
It buzzes fiercely round the point ; and
    there
We lost him : such a noble song was
    that.
But, Vivien, when you sang me that
    sweet rhyme,
I felt as tho' you knew this cursed
    charm,
Were proving it on me, and that I
    lay
And felt them slowly ebbing, name
    and fame."

    And Vivien answer'd smiling
    mournfully :
" O mine have ebb'd away for ever-
    more,
And all thro' following you to this
    wild wood,

Because I saw you sad, to comfort
    you.
Lo now, what hearts have men! they
    never mount
As high as woman in her selfless
    mood.
And touching fame, howe'er ye scorn
    my song,
Take one verse more — the lady
    speaks it — this :

    " ' My name, once mine, now thine,
    is closelier mine,
For fame, could fame be mine, that
    fame were thine,
And shame, could shame be thine,
    that shame were mine.
So trust me not at all or all in all.'

    "Says she not well? and there is
    more — this rhyme
Is like the fair pearl-necklace of the
    Queen,
That burst in dancing, and the pearls
    were spilt;
Some lost, some stolen, some as relics
    kept.
But nevermore the same two sister
    pearls
Ran down the silken thread to kiss
    each other
On her white neck — so is it with this
    rhyme :
It lives dispersedly in many hands,
And every minstrel sings it differ-
    ently;
Yet is there one true line, the pearl of
    pearls :
' Man dreams of Fame while woman
    wakes to love.'
Yea! Love, tho' Love were of the
    grossest, carves
A portion from the solid present, eats
And uses, careless of the rest; but
    Fame,
The Fame that follows death is noth-
    ing to us;
And what is Fame in life but half-
    disfame,
And counterchanged with darkness?
    ye yourself

Know well that Envy calls you Devil's
    son,
And since ye seem the Master of all
    Art,
They fain would make you Master of
    all vice."

    And Merlin lock'd his hand in hers
    and said,
" I once was looking for a magic weed,
And found a fair young squire who
    sat alone,
Had carved himself a knightly shield
    of wood,
And then was painting on it fancied
    arms,
Azure, an Eagle rising or, the Sun
In dexter chief; the scroll ' I follow
    fame.'
And speaking not, but leaning over
    him,
I took his brush and blotted out the
    bird,
And made a Gardener putting in
    graff,
With this for motto, ' Rather use than
    fame.'
You should have seen him blush; but
    afterwards
He made a stalwart knight. O Vivien,
For you, methinks you think you love
    me well;
For me, I love you somewhat; rest :
    and Love
Should have some rest and pleasure
    in himself,
Not ever be too curious for a boon,
Too prurient for a proof against the
    grain
Of him ye say ye love : but Fame with
    men,
Being but ampler means to serve
    mankind,
Should have small rest or pleasure in
    herself,
But work as vassal to the larger love,
That dwarfs the petty love of one to
    one.
Use gave me Fame at first, and Fame
    again
Increasing gave me use. Lo, there
    my boon!

What other ? for men sought to prove
   me vile,
Because I fain had given them greater
   wits :
And then did Envy call me Devil's
   son :
The sick weak beast seeking to help
   herself
By striking at her better miss'd, and
   brought
Her own claw back, and wounded her
   own heart.
Sweet were the days when I was all
   unknown,
But when my name was lifted up, the
   storm
Brake on the mountain and I cared
   not for it.
Right well know I that Fame is half-
   disfame,
Yet needs must work my work. That
   other fame,
To one at least, who hath not children,
   vague,
The cackle of the unborn about the
   grave,
I cared not for it : a single misty star,
Which is the second in a line of stars
That seem a sword beneath a belt of
   three,
I never gazed upon it but I dreamt
Of some vast charm concluded in that
   star
To make fame nothing. Wherefore,
   if I fear,
Giving you power upon me thro' this
   charm,
That you might play me falsely, hav-
   ing power,
However well ye think ye love me now
(As sons of kings loving in pupilage
Have turn'd to tyrants when they
   came to power)
I rather dread the loss of use than
   fame ;
If you — and not so much from
   wickedness,
As some wild turn of anger, or a mood
Of overstrain'd affection, it may be,
To keep me all to your own self, — or
   else
A sudden spurt of woman's jealousy,—

Should try this charm on whom ye say
   ye love."

And Vivien answer'd smiling as in
   wrath :
" Have I not sworn ? I am not trusted.
   Good !
Well, hide it, hide it ; I shall find it
   out ;
And being found take heed of Vivien.
A woman and not trusted, doubtless I
Might feel some sudden turn of anger
   born
Of your misfaith ; and your fine
   epithet
Is accurate too, for this full love of
   mine
Without the full heart back may
   merit well
Your term of overstrain'd. So used
   as I,
My daily wonder is, I love at all.
And as to woman's jealousy, O why
   not ?
O to what end, except a jealous one,
And one to make me jealous if I love,
Was this fair charm invented by your-
   self ?
I well believe that all about this world
Ye cage a buxom captive here and
   there,
Closed in the four walls of a hollow
   tower
From which is no escape for ever-
   more."

Then the great Master merrily answer'd her :
" Full many a love in loving youth
   was mine ;
I needed then no charm to keep them
   mine
But youth and love ; and that full
   heart of yours
Whereof ye prattle, may now assure
   you mine ;
So live uncharm'd. For those who
   wrought it first,
The wrist is parted from the hand
   that waved,
The feet unmortised from their ankle-
   bones

Who paced it, ages back: but will ye
   hear
The legend as in guerdon for your
   rhyme?

   "There lived a king in the most
      Eastern East,
Less old than I, yet older, for my
   blood
Hath earnest in it of far springs to be.
A tawny pirate anchor'd in his port,
Whose bark had plunder'd twenty
   nameless isles;
And passing one, at the high peep of
   dawn,
He saw two cities in a thousand boats
All fighting for a woman on the sea.
And pushing his black craft among
   them all,
He lightly scatter'd theirs and brought
   her off,
With loss of half his people arrow-
   slain;
A maid so smooth, so white, so won-
   derful,
They said a light came from her when
   she moved:
And since the pirate would not yield
   her up,
The King impaled him for his piracy;
Then made her Queen: but those isle-
   nurtured eyes
Waged such unwilling tho' successful
   war
On all the youth, they sicken'd; coun-
   cils thinn'd,
And armies waned, for magnet-like
   she drew
The rustiest iron of old fighters'
   hearts;
And beasts themselves would worship;
   camels knelt
Unbidden, and the brutes of mountain
   back
That carry kings in castles, bow'd
   black knees
Of homage, ringing with their serpent
   hands,
To make her smile, her golden ankle-
   bells.
What wonder, being jealous, that he
   sent

His horns of proclamation out thro'
   all
The hundred under-kingdoms that he
   sway'd
To find a wizard who might teach the
   King
Some charm, which being wrought
   upon the Queen
Might keep her all his own: to such a
   one
He promised more than ever king has
   given,
A league of mountain full of golden
   mines,
A province with a hundred miles of
   coast,
A palace and a princess, all for
   him:
But on all those who tried and fail'd,
   the King
Pronounced a dismal sentence, mean-
   ing by it
To keep the list low and pretenders
   back,
Or like a king, not to be trifled with —
Their heads should moulder on the
   city gates.
And many tried and fail'd, because
   the charm
Of nature in her overbore their own:
And many a wizard brow bleach'd on
   the walls:
And many weeks a troop of carrion
   crows
Hung like a cloud above the gateway
   towers."

   And Vivien breaking in upon him,
      said:
"I sit and gather honey; yet, me-
   thinks,
Thy tongue has tript a little: ask thy-
   self.
The lady never made *unwilling* war
With those fine eyes: she had her
   pleasure in it,
And made her good man jealous with
   good cause.
And lived there neither dame nor
   damsel then
Wroth at a lover's loss? were all as
   tame,

I mean, as noble, as their Queen was
    fair ?
Not one to flirt a venom at her eyes,
Or pinch a murderous dust into her
    drink,
Or make her paler with a poison'd
    rose ?
Well, those were not our days : but
    did they find
A wizard ?   Tell me, was he like to
    thee ? "

    She ceased, and made her lithe arm
    round his neck
Tighten, and then drew back, and let
    her eyes
Speak for her, glowing on him, like a
    bride's
On her new lord, her own, the first of
    men.

    He answer'd laughing, "Nay, not
    like to me.
At last they found — his foragers for
    charms —
A little glassy-headed hairless man,
Who lived alone in a great wild on
    grass ;
Read but one book, and ever reading
    grew
So grated down and filed away with
    thought,
So lean his eyes were monstrous ;
    while the skin
Clung but to crate and basket, ribs
    and spine.
And since he kept his mind on one
    sole aim,
Nor ever touch'd fierce wine, nor tasted
    flesh,
Nor own'd a sensual wish, to him the
    wall
That sunders ghosts and shadow-cast-
    ing men
Became a crystal, and he saw them
    thro' it,
And heard their voices talk behind
    the wall,
And learnt their elemental secrets,
    powers
And forces ; often o'er the sun's bright
    eye

Drew the vast eyelid of an inky cloud,
And lash'd it at the base with slanting
    storm ;
Or in the noon of mist and driving
    rain,
When the lake whiten'd and the pine-
    wood roar'd,
And the cairn'd mountain was a
    shadow, sunn'd
The world to peace again : here was
    the man.
And so by force they dragg'd him to
    the King.
And then he taught the King to
    charm the Queen
In such-wise, that no man could see
    her more,
Nor saw she save the King, who
    wrought the charm,
Coming and going, and she lay as
    dead,
And lost all use of life : but when the
    King
Made proffer of the league of golden
    mines,
The province with a hundred miles of
    coast,
The palace and the princess, that old
    man
Went back to his old wild, and lived
    on grass,
And vanish'd, and his book came
    down to me."

    And Vivien answer'd smiling sau-
    cily :
"Ye have the book : the charm is
    written in it :
Good : take my counsel : let me know
    it at once :
For keep it like a puzzle chest in
    chest,
With each chest lock'd and padlock'd
    thirty-fold,
And whelm all this beneath as vast a
    mound
As after furious battle turfs the
    slain
On some wild down above the windy
    deep,
I yet should strike upon a sudden
    means

To dig, pick, open, find and read the charm:
Then, if I tried it, who should blame me then ? "

And smiling as a master smiles at one
That is not of his school, nor any school
But that where blind and naked Ignorance
Delivers brawling judgments, unashamed,
On all things all day long, he answer'd her:

"Thou read the book, my pretty Vivien!
O ay, it is but twenty pages long,
But every page having an ample marge,
And every marge enclosing in the midst
A square of text that looks a little blot,
The text no larger than the limbs of fleas ;
And every square of text an awful charm,
Writ in a language that has long gone by.
So long, that mountains have arisen since
With cities on their flanks — thou read the book!
And every margin scribbled, crost, and cramm'd
With comment, densest condensation, hard
To mind and eye ; but the long sleepless nights
Of my long life have made it easy to me.
And none can read the text, not even I ;
And none can read the comment but myself ;
And in the comment did I find the charm.
O, the results are simple; a mere child
Might use it to the harm of any one,

And never could undo it: ask no more:
For tho' you should not prove it upon me,
But keep that oath ye sware, ye might, perchance,
Assay it on some one of the Table Round,
And all because ye dream they babble of you."

And Vivien, frowning in true anger, said :
" What dare the full-fed liars say of me ?
They ride abroad redressing human wrongs !
They sit with knife in meat and wine in horn !
They bound to holy vows of chastity !
Were I not woman, I could tell a tale.
But you are man, you well can understand
The shame that cannot be explain'd for shame.
Not one of all the drove should touch me: swine ! "

Then answer'd Merlin careless of her words :
" You breathe but accusation vast and vague,
Spleen-born, I think, and proofless. If ye know,
Set up the charge ye know, to stand or fall ! "

And Vivien answer'd frowning wrathfully :
" O ay, what say ye to Sir Valence, him
Whose kinsman left him watcher o'er his wife
And two fair babes, and went to distant lands ;
Was one year gone, and on returning found
Not two but three ? there lay the reckling, one
But one hour old ! What said the happy sire ?

A seven-months' babe had been a
    truer gift.
Those twelve sweet moons confused
    his fatherhood."

    Then answer'd Merlin, "Nay, I
    know the tale.
Sir Valence wedded with an outland
    dame :
Some cause had kept him sunder'd
    from his wife :
One child they had : it lived with her :
    she died :
His kinsman travelling on his own
    affair
Was charged by Valence to bring
    home the child.
He brought, not found it therefore :
    take the truth."

    "O ay," said Vivien, "overtrue a
    tale.
What say ye then to sweet Sir Sag-
    ramore,
That ardent man ? 'to pluck the
    flower in season,'
So says the song, 'I trow it is no
    treason.'
O Master, shall we call him overquick
To crop his own sweet rose before the
    hour ?"

    And Merlin answer'd, "Overquick
    art thou
To catch a loathly plume fall'n from
    the wing
Of that foul bird of rapine whose
    whole prey
Is man's good name : he never wrong'd
    his bride.
I know the tale. An angry gust of
    wind
Puff'd out his torch among the myriad-
    room'd
And many-corridor'd complexities
Of Arthur's palace : then he found a
    door,
And darkling felt the sculptured
    ornament
That wreathen round it made it seem
    his own ;

And wearied out made for the couch
    and slept,
A stainless man beside a stainless
    maid ;
And either slept, nor knew of other
    there ;
Till the high dawn piercing the royal
    rose
In Arthur's casement glimmer'd
    chastely down,
Blushing upon them blushing, and at
    once
He rose without a word and parted
    from her :
But when the thing was blazed about
    the court,
The brute world howling forced them
    into bonds,
And as it chanced they are happy,
    being pure."

    "O ay," said Vivien, "that were
    likely too.
What say ye then to fair Sir Percivale
And of the horrid foulness that he
    wrought,
The saintly youth, the spotless lamb
    of Christ,
Or some black wether of St. Satan's
    fold.
What, in the precincts of the chapel-
    yard,
Among the knightly brasses of the
    graves,
And by the cold Hic Jacets of the
    dead !"

    And Merlin answer'd careless of her
    charge,
"A sober man is Percivale and pure ;
But once in life was fluster'd with new
    wine,
Then paced for coolness in the chapel-
    yard ;
Where one of Satan's shepherdesses
    caught
And meant to stamp him with her
    master's mark ;
And that he sinn'd is not believable ;
For, look upon his face ! — but if he
    sinn'd,

The sin that practice burns into the
 blood,
And not the one dark hour which
 brings remorse,
Will brand us, after, of whose fold we
 be:
Or else were he, the holy king, whose
 hymns
Are chanted in the minster, worse
 than all.
But is your spleen froth'd out, or have
 ye more ? "

And Vivien answer'd frowning yet
 in wrath :
" O ay ; what say ye to Sir Lancelot,
 friend
Traitor or true ? that commerce with
 the Queen,
I ask you, is it clamor'd by the child,
Or whisper'd in the corner ? do ye
 know it? "

To which he answer'd sadly, " Yea,
 I know it.
Sir Lancelot went ambassador, at
 first,
To fetch her, and she watch'd him
 from her walls.
A rumor runs, she took him for the
 King,
So fixt her fancy on him : let them be.
But have ye no one word of loyal
 praise
For Arthur, blameless King and stain-
 less man ? "

She answer'd with a low and chuck-
 ling laugh :
" Man ! is he man at all, who knows
 and winks ?
Sees what his fair bride is and does,
 and winks ?
By which the good King means to
 blind himself,
And blinds himself and all the Table
 Round
To all the foulness that they work.
 Myself
Could call him (were it not for
 womanhood)

The pretty, popular name such manhood earns,
Could call him the main cause of all
 their crime ;
Yea, were he not crown'd King,
 coward, and fool."

Then Merlin to his own heart,
 loathing, said :
" O true and tender ! O my liege and
 King !
O selfless man and stainless gentle-
 man,
Who wouldst against thine own eye-
 witness fain
Have all men true and leal, all women
 pure ;
How, in the mouths of base inter-
 preters,
From over-fineness not intelligible
To things with every sense as false
 and foul
As the poach'd filth that floods the
 middle street,
Is thy white blamelessness accounted
 blame ! "

But Vivien, deeming Merlin overborne
By instance, recommenced, and let
 her tongue
Rage like a fire among the noblest
 names,
Polluting, and imputing her whole
 self,
Defaming and defacing, till she left
Not even Lancelot brave, nor Galahad
 clean.

Her words had issue other than she
 will'd.
He dragg'd his eyebrow bushes down,
 and made
A snowy penthouse for his hollow
 eyes,
And mutter'd in himself, " Tell *her* the
 charm !
So, if she had it, would she rail on me
To snare the next, and if she have it
 not
So will she rail. What did the wanton say ?

' Not mount as high;' we scarce can
  sink as low:
For men at most differ as Heaven and
  earth,
But women, worst and best, as Heaven
  and Hell.
I know the Table Round, my friends
  of old;
All brave, and many generous, and
  some chaste.
She cloaks the scar of some repulse
  with lies;
I well believe she tempted them and
  fail'd,
Being so bitter: for fine plots may
  fail,
Tho' harlots paint their talk as well
  as face
With colors of the heart that are not
  theirs.
I will not let her know: nine tithes of
  times
Face-flatterer and backbiter are the
  same.
And they, sweet soul, that most impute a crime
Are pronest to it, and impute themselves,
Wanting the mental range; or low
  desire
Not to feel lowest makes them level
  all;
Yea, they would pare the mountain
  to the plain,
To leave an equal baseness; and in
  this
Are harlots like the crowd, that if
  they find
Some stain or blemish in a name of
  note,
Not grieving that their greatest are so
  small,
Inflate themselves with some insane
  delight,
And judge all nature from her feet of
  clay,
Without the will to lift their eyes, and
  see
Her godlike head crown'd with spiritual fire,
And touching other worlds. I am
  weary of her."

He spoke in words part heard, in
  whispers part,
Half-suffocated in the hoary fell
And many-winter'd fleece of throat
  and chin.
But Vivien, gathering somewhat of
  his mood,
And hearing "harlot" mutter'd twice
  or thrice,
Leapt from her session on his lap, and
  stood
Stiff as a viper frozen; loathsome
  sight,
How from the rosy lips of life and
  love,
Flash'd the bare-grinning skeleton of
  death!
White was her cheek; sharp breaths
  of anger puff'd
Her fairy nostril out; her hand half-
  clench'd
Went faltering sideways downward to
  her belt,
And feeling; had she found a dagger
  there
(For in a wink the false love turns
  to hate)
She would have stabb'd him; but she
  found it not:
His eye was calm, and suddenly she
  took
To bitter weeping like a beaten child,
A long, long weeping, not consolable.
Then her false voice made way, broken
  with sobs:

  "O crueller than was ever told in
    tale,
Or sung in song! O vainly lavish'd
    love!
O cruel, there was nothing wild or
    strange,
Or seeming shameful — for what
    shame in love,
So love be true, and not as yours is —
    nothing
Poor Vivien had not done to win his
    trust
Who call'd her what he call'd her —
    all her crime,
All — all — the wish to prove him
    wholly hers."

She mused a little, and then clapt
    her hands
Together with a wailing shriek, and
    said:
"Stabb'd through the heart's affec-
    tions to the heart!
Seethed like the kid in its own mother's
    milk!
Kill'd with a word worse than a life
    of blows!
I thought that he was gentle, being
    great:
O God, that I had loved a smaller man!
I should have found in him a greater
    heart.
O, I, that flattering my true passion,
    saw
The knights, the court, the King, dark
    in your light,
Who loved to make men darker than
    they are,
Because of that high pleasure which
    I had
To seat you sole upon my pedestal
Of worship — I am answer'd, and
    henceforth
The course of life that seem'd so
    flowery to me
With you for guide and master, only
    you,
Becomes the sea-cliff pathway broken
    short,
And ending in a ruin — nothing left,
But into some low cave to crawl, and
    there,
If the wolf spare me, weep my life
    away,
Kill'd with inutterable unkindliness."

She paused, she turn'd away, she
    hung her head,
The snake of gold slid from her hair,
    the braid
Slipt and uncoil'd itself, she wept
    afresh,
And the dark wood grew darker
    toward the storm
In silence, while his anger slowly died
Within him, till he let his wisdom go
For ease of heart, and half believed
    her true:
Call'd her to shelter in the hollow oak,

"Come from the storm," and having
    no reply,
Gazed at the heaving shoulder, and
    the face
Hand-hidden, as for utmost grief or
    shame;
Then thrice essay'd, by tenderest-
    touching terms,
To sleek her ruffled peace of mind, in
    vain.
At last she let herself be conquer'd by
    him,
And as the cageling newly flown re-
    turns,
The seeming-injured, simple-hearted
    thing
Came to her old perch back, and set-
    tled there.
There while she sat, half-falling from
    his knees,
Half-nestled at his heart, and since he
    saw
The slow tear creep from her closed
    eye-lid yet,
About her, more in kindness than in
    love,
The gentle wizard cast a shielding
    arm.
But she dislink'd herself at once and
    rose,
Her arms upon her breast across, and
    stood,
A virtuous gentlewoman deeply
    wrong'd,
Upright and flush'd before him: then
    she said:

"There must be now no passages of
    love
Betwixt us twain henceforward ever-
    more;
Since, if I be what I am grossly call'd,
What should be granted which your
    own gross heart
Would reckon worth the taking? I
    will go.
In truth, but one thing now — better
    have died
Thrice than have ask'd it once — could
    make me stay —
That proof of trust — so often ask'd
    in vain!

How justly, after that vile term of
    yours,
I find with grief ! I might believe you
    then,
Who knows ? once more.   Lo ! what
    was once to me
Mere matter of the fancy, now hath
    grown
The vast necessity of heart and life.
Farewell ; think gently of me, for I
    fear
My fate or folly, passing gayer youth
For one so old, must be to love thee
    still.
But ere I leave thee let me swear once
    more
That if I schemed against thy peace
    in this,
May yon just heaven, that darkens
    o'er me, send
One flash, that, missing all things else,
    may make
My scheming brain a cinder, if I
    lie."

    Scarce had she ceased, when out of
        heaven a bolt
(For now the storm was close above
    them) struck,
Furrowing a giant oak, and javelining
With darted spikes and splinters of
    the wood
The dark earth round.   He raised his
    eyes and saw
The tree that shone white-listed thro'
    the gloom.
But Vivien, fearing heaven had heard
    her oath,
And dazzled by the livid-flickering
    fork,
And deafen'd with the stammering
    cracks and claps
That follow'd, flying back and crying
    out,
"O Merlin, tho' you do not love me,
    save,
Yet save me !" clung to him and
    hugg'd him close ;
And call'd him dear protector in her
    fright,
Nor yet forgot her practice in her
    fright,

But wrought upon his mood and
    hugg'd him close.
The pale blood of the wizard at her
    touch
Took gayer colors, like an opal
    warm'd.
She blamed herself for telling hearsay
    tales :
She shook from fear, and for her faul
    she wept
Of petulancy ; she call'd him lord and
    liege,
Her seer, her bard, her silver star of
    eve,
Her God, her Merlin, the one passion-
    ate love
Of her whole life ; and ever overhead
Bellow'd the tempest, and the rotten
    branch
Snapt in the rushing of the river-rain
Above them ; and in change of glare
    and gloom
Her eyes and neck glittering went and
    came ;
Till now the storm, its burst of passion
    spent,
Moaning and calling out of other
    lands,
Had left the ravaged woodland yet
    once more
To peace ; and what should not have
    been had been,
For Merlin, overtalk'd and overworn,
Had yielded, told her all the charm,
    and slept.

    Then, in one moment, she put forth
        the charm
Of woven paces and of waving hands,
And in the hollow oak he lay as dead,
And lost to life and use and name and
    fame.

    Then crying "I have made his glory
        mine,"
And shrieking out "O fool !" the har-
    lot leapt
Adown the forest, and the thicket
    closed
Behind her, and the forest echo'd
    "fool."

LANCELOT AND ELAINE.

ELAINE the fair, Elaine the loveable,
Elaine, the lily maid of Astolat,
High in her chamber up a tower to
the east
Guarded the sacred shield of Lance-
lot;
Which first she placed where morn-
ing's earliest ray
Might strike it, and awake her with
the gleam;
Then fearing rust or soilure fashion'd
for it
A case of silk, and braided thereupon
All the devices blazon'd on the shield
In their own tinct, and added, of her
wit,
A border fantasy of branch and flower,
And yellow-throated nestling in the
nest.
Nor rested thus content, but day by
day,
Leaving her household and good
father, climb'd
That eastern tower, and entering
barr'd her door,
Stript off the case, and read the naked
shield,
Now guess'd a hidden meaning in his
arms,
Now made a pretty history to herself
Of every dint a sword had beaten in
it,
And every scratch a lance had made
upon it,
Conjecturing when and where: this
cut is fresh;
That ten years back; this dealt him
at Caerlyle;
That at Caerleon; this at Camelot:
And ah God's mercy, what a stroke
was there!
And here a thrust that might have
kill'd, but God
Broke the strong lance, and roll'd his
enemy down,
And saved him: so she lived in fan-
tasy.

How came the lily maid by that
good shield

Of Lancelot, she that knew not ev'n
his name?
He left it with her, when he rode to
tilt
For the great diamond in the diamond
jousts,
Which Arthur had ordain'd, and by
that name
Had named them, since a diamond
was the prize.

For Arthur, long before they
crown'd him King,
Roving the trackless realms of Lyonnesse,
Had found a glen, gray boulder and
black tarn.
A horror lived about the tarn, and
clave
Like its own mists to all the mountain
side:
For here two brothers, one a king,
had met
And fought together; but their names
were lost;
And each had slain his brother at a
blow;
And down they fell and made the glen
abhorr'd:
And there they lay till all their bones
were bleach'd,
And lichen'd into color with the crags:
And he, that once was king, had on a
crown
Of diamonds, one in front, and four
aside.
And Arthur came, and laboring up the
pass,
All in a misty moonshine, unawares
Had trodden that crown'd skeleton,
and the skull
Brake from the nape, and from the
skull the crown
Roll'd into light, and turning on its
rims
Fled like a glittering rivulet to the
tarn:
And down the shingly scaur he
plunged, and caught,
And set it on his head, and in his heart
Heard murmurs, "Lo, thou likewise
shalt be King."

Thereafter, when a King, he had the gems
Pluck'd from the crown, and show'd them to his knights,
Saying "These jewels, whereupon I chanced
Divinely, are the kingdom's, not the King's —
For public use : henceforward let there be,
Once every year, a joust for one of these :
For so by nine years' proof we needs must learn
Which is our mightiest, and ourselves shall grow
In use of arms and manhood, till we drive
The heathen, who, some say, shall rule the land
Hereafter, which God hinder." Thus he spoke :
And eight years past, eight jousts had been, and still
Had Lancelot won the diamond of the year,
With purpose to present them to the Queen,
When all were won; but meaning all at once
To snare her royal fancy with a boon
Worth half her realm, had never spoken word.

Now for the central diamond and the last
And largest, Arthur, holding then his court
Hard on the river nigh the place which now
Is this world's hugest, let proclaim a joust
At Camelot, and when the time drew nigh
Spake (for she had been sick) to Guinevere,
"Are you so sick, my Queen, you cannot move
To these fair jousts ? " " Yea, lord," she said, "ye know it."
"Then will ye miss," he answer'd, "the great deeds

Of Lancelot, and his prowess in the lists,
A sight ye love to look on." And the Queen
Lifted her eyes, and they dwelt languidly
On Lancelot, where he stood beside the King.
He thinking that he read her meaning there,
"Stay with me, I am sick; my love is more
Than many diamonds," yielded; and a heart
Love-loyal to the least wish of the Queen
(However much he yearn'd to make complete
The tale of diamonds for his destined boon)
Urged him to speak against the truth, and say,
"Sir King, mine ancient wound is hardly whole,
And lets me from the saddle ; " and the King
Glanced first at him, then her, and went his way.
No sooner gone than suddenly she began :

"To blame, my lord Sir Lancelot, much to blame!
Why go ye not to these fair jousts ? the knights
Are half of them our enemies, and the crowd
Will murmur, 'Lo the shameless ones, who take
Their pastime now the trustful King is gone ! ' "
Then Lancelot vext at having lied in vain :
"Are ye so wise ? ye were not once so wise,
My Queen, that summer, when ye loved me first.
Then of the crowd ye took no more account
Than of the myriad cricket of the mead,

When its own voice clings to each
  blade of grass,
And every voice is nothing. As to
  knights,
Them surely can I silence with all
  ease.
But now my loyal worship is allow'd
Of all men: many a bard, without
  offence,
Has link'd our names together in his
  lay,
Lancelot, the flower of bravery,
  Guinevere,
The pearl of beauty : and our knights
  at feast
Have pledged us in this union, while
  the King
Would listen smiling. How then ? is
  there more ?
Has Arthur spoken aught ? or would
  yourself,
Now weary of my service and devoir,
Henceforth be truer to your faultless
  lord ? ."

  She broke into a little scornful
  laugh:
" Arthur, my lord, Arthur, the fault-
  less King,
That passionate perfection, my good
  lord —
But who can gaze upon the Sun in
  heaven ?
He never spake word of reproach to
  me,
He never had a glimpse of mine un-
  truth,
He cares not for me : only here to-day
There gleam'd a vague suspicion in his.
  eyes :
Some meddling rogue has tamper'd
  with him — else
Rapt in this fancy of his Table Round,
And swearing men to vows impossible,
To make them like himself: but,
  friend, to me
He is all fault who hath no fault at
  all :
For who loves me must have a touch
  of earth ;
The low sun makes the color: I am
  yours,

Not Arthur's, as ye know, save by
  the bond.
And therefore hear my words : go to
  the jousts :
The tiny-trumpeting gnat can break
  our dream
When sweetest ; and the vermin
  voices here
May buzz so loud — we scorn them,
  but they sting."

  Then answer'd Lancelot, the chief
  of knights :
" And with what face, after my pre-
  text made,
Shall I appear, O Queen, at Camelot,
  I
Before a King who honors his own
  work,
As if it were his God's ? "

            " Yea," said the Queen,
" A moral child without the craft to
  rule,
Else had he not lost me : but listen to
  me,
If I must find you wit : we hear it
  said
That men go down before your spear
  at a touch,
But knowing you are Lancelot ; your
  great name,
This conquers: hide it therefore ; go
  unknown :
Win ! by this kiss you will : and our
  true King
Will then allow your pretext, O my
  knight,
As all for glory ; for to speak him
  true,
Ye know right well, how meek soe'er
  he seem,
No keener hunter after glory breathes.
He loves it in his knights more than
  himself :
They prove to him his work : win and
  return."

  Then got Sir Lancelot suddenly to
  horse,
Wroth at himself. Not willing to be
  known,

He left the barren-beaten thorough-
   fare,
Chose the green path that show'd the
   rarer foot,
And there among the solitary downs,
Full often lost in fancy, lost his
   way;
Till as he traced a faintly-shadow'd
   track,
That all in loops and links among the
   dales
Ran to the Castle of Astolat, he saw
Fired from the west, far on a hill, the
   towers.
Thither he made, and blew the gate-
   way horn.
Then came an old, dumb, myriad-
   wrinkled man,
Who let him into lodging and dis-
   arm'd.
And Lancelot marvell'd at the word-
   less man;
And issuing found the lord of Astolat
With two strong sons, Sir Torre and
   Sir Lavaine,
Moving to meet him in the castle
   court;
And close behind them stept the lily
   maid
Elaine, his daughter: mother of the
   house
There was not: some light jest
   among them rose
With laughter dying down as the
   great knight
Approach'd them: then the Lord of
   Astolat:
"Whence comest thou, my guest, and
   by what name
Livest between the lips? for by thy
   state
And presence I might guess thee
   chief of those,
After the King, who eat in Arthur's
   halls.
Him have I seen: the rest, his Table
   Round,
Known as they are, to me they are
   unknown."

Then answer'd Lancelot, the chief
   of knights:

"Known am I, and of Arthur's hall,
   and known,
What I by mere mischance have
   brought, my shield.
But since I go to joust as one unknown
At Camelot for the diamond, ask me
   not,
Hereafter ye shall know me — and
   the shield —
I pray you lend me one, if such you
   have,
Blank, or at least with some device
   not mine."

Then said the Lord of Astolat,
   "Here is Torre's:
Hurt in his first tilt was my son, Sir
   Torre.
And so, God wot, his shield is blank
   enough.
His ye can have." Then added plain
   Sir Torre,
"Yea, since I cannot use it, ye may
   have it."
Here laugh'd the father saying, "Fie,
   Sir Churl,
Is that an answer for a noble knight?
Allow him! but Lavaine, my younger
   here,
He is so full of lustihood, he will ride,
Joust for it, and win, and bring it in
   an hour,
And set it in this damsel's golden
   hair,
To make her thrice as wilful as be-
   fore."

"Nay, father, nay good father,
   shame me not
Before this noble knight," said young
   Lavaine,
"For nothing. Surely I but play'd
   on Torre:
He seem'd so sullen, vext he could
   not go:
A jest, no more! for, knight, the
   maiden dreamt
That some one put this diamond in
   her hand,
And that it was too slippery to be
   held,

And slipt and fell into some pool or
stream,
The castle-well, belike; and then I
said
That *if* I went and *if* I fought and
won it
(But all was jest and joke among ourselves)
Then must she keep it safelier. All
was jest.
But, father, give me leave, an if he
will,
To ride to Camelot with this noble
knight:
Win shall I not, but do my best to
win:
Young as I am, yet would I do my
best."

"So ye will grace me," answer'd
Lancelot,
Smiling a moment, "with your fellow-
ship
O'er these waste downs whereon I
lost myself,
Then were I glad of you as guide and
friend:
And you shall win this diamond, —
as I hear
It is a fair large diamond, — if ye
may,
And yield it to this maiden, if ye
will."
"A fair large diamond," added plain
Sir Torre,
"Such be for queens, and not for sim-
ple maids."
Then she, who held her eyes upon the
ground,
Elaine, and heard her name so tost
about,
Flush'd slightly at the slight dispar-
agement
Before the stranger knight, who, look-
ing at her,
Full courtly, yet not falsely, thus
return'd:
"If what is fair be but for what is
fair,
And only queens are to be counted so,
Rash were my judgment then, who
deem this maid

Might wear as fair a jewel as is on
earth,
Not violating the bond of like to like."

He spoke and ceased: the lily maid
Elaine,
Won by the mellow voice before she
look'd,
Lifted her eyes, and read his linea-
ments.
The great and guilty love he bare the
Queen,
In battle with the love he bare his
lord,
Had marr'd his face, and mark'd it
ere his time.
Another sinning on such heights with
one,
The flower of all the west and all the
world,
Had been the sleeker for it: but in
him
His mood was often like a fiend, and
rose
And drove him into wastes and soli-
tudes
For agony, who was yet a living soul.
Marr'd as he was, he seem'd the good-
liest man
That ever among ladies ate in hall,
And noblest, when she lifted up her
eyes.
However marr'd, of more than twice
her years,
Seam'd with an ancient swordcut on
the cheek,
And bruised and bronzed, she lifted up
her eyes
And loved him, with that love which
was her doom.

Then the great knight, the darling
of the court,
Loved of the loveliest, into that rude
hall
Stept with all grace, and not with half
disdain
Hid under grace, as in a smaller time,
But kindly man moving among his
kind:
Whom they with meats and vintage
of their best

And talk and minstrel melody enter-
     tain'd.
And much they ask'd of court and
     Table Round,
And ever well and readily answer'd
     he :
But Lancelot, when they glanced at
     Guinevere,
Suddenly speaking of the wordless
     man,
Heard from the Baron that, ten years
     before,
The heathen caught and reft him of
     his tongue.
" He learnt and warn'd me of their
     fierce design
Against my house, and him they
     caught and maim'd ;
But I, my sons, and little daughter
     fled
From bonds or death, and dwelt among
     the woods
By the great river in a boatman's
     hut.
Dull days were those, till our good
     Arthur broke
The Pagan yet once more on Badon
     hill."

     "O there, great lord, doubtless,"
     Lavaine said, rapt
By all the sweet and sudden passion
     of youth
Toward greatness in its elder, " you
     have fought.
O tell us — for we live apart — you
     know
Of Arthur's glorious wars."   And
     Lancelot spoke
And answer'd him at full, as having
     been
With Arthur in the fight which all
     day long
Rang by the white mouth of the vio-
     lent Glem ;
And in the four loud battles by the
     shore
Of Duglas ; that on Bassa ; then the
     war
That thunder'd in and out the gloomy
     skirts
Of Celidon the forest ; and again

By castle Gurnion, where the glorious
     King
Had on his cuirass worn our Lady's
     Head,
Carved of one emerald center'd in a
     sun
Of silver rays, that lighten'd as he
     breathed ;
And at Caerleon had he helped his
     lord,
When the strong neighings of the wild
     white Horse
Set every gilded parapet shuddering ;
And up in Agned-Cathregonion too,
And down the waste sand-shores of
     Trath Treroit,
Where many a heathen fell ; " and on
     the mount
Of Badon I myself beheld the King
Charge at the head of all his Table
     Round,
And all his legions crying Christ and
     him,
And break them ; and I saw him, after,
     stand
High on a heap of slain, from spur to
     plume
Red as the rising sun with heathen
     blood,
And seeing me, with a great voice he
     cried,
' They are broken, they are broken ! '
     for the King,
However mild he seems at home, nor
     cares
For triumph in our mimic wars, the
     jousts —
For if his own knight cast him down,
     he laughs
Saying, his knights are better men
     than he —
Yet in this heathen war the fire of
     God
Fills him : I never saw his like : there
     lives
No greater leader."

                    While he utter'd this,
Low to her own heart said the lily
     maid,
" Save your great self, fair lord ; "
     and when he fell

From talk of war to traits of pleas-
antry —
Being mirthful he, but in a stately
kind —
She still took note that when the
living smile
Died from his lips, across him came
a cloud
Of melancholy severe, from which
again,
Whenever in her hovering to and
fro
The lily maid had striven to make him
cheer,
There brake a sudden-beaming ten-
derness
Of manners and of nature : and she
thought
That all was nature, all, perchance,
for her.
And all night long his face before her
lived,
As when a painter, poring on a face,
Divinely thro' all hindrance finds the
man
Behind it, and so paints him that his
face,
The shape and color of a mind and
life,
Lives for his children, ever at its best
And fullest ; so the face before her
lived,
Dark-splendid, speaking in the silence,
full
Of noble things, and held her from
her sleep.
Till rathe she rose, half-cheated in the
thought
She needs must bid farewell to sweet
Lavaine.
First as in fear, step after step, she
stole
Down the long tower-stairs, hesitat-
ing :
Anon, she heard Sir Lancelot cry in
the court,
"This shield, my friend, where is it ? "
and Lavaine
Past inward, as she came from out
the tower.
There to his proud horse Lancelot
turn'd, and smooth'd

The glossy shoulder, humming to
himself.
Half-envious of the flattering hand,
she drew
Nearer and stood. He look'd, and
more amazed
Than if seven men had set upon him,
saw
The maiden standing in the dewy
light.
He had not dream'd she was so beau-
tiful.
Then came on him a sort of sacred
fear,
For silent, tho' he greeted her, she
stood
Rapt on his face as if it were a God's.
Suddenly flash'd on her a wild desire,
That he should wear her favor at the
tilt.
She braved a riotous heart in asking
for it.
"Fair lord, whose name I know not —
noble it is,
I well believe, the noblest — will you
wear
My favor at this tourney ? "   "Nay,"
said he,
"Fair lady, since I never yet have
worn
Favor of any lady in the lists.
Such is my wont, as those, who know
me, know."
"Yea, so," she answer'd ; "then in
wearing mine
Needs must be lesser likelihood, noble
lord,
That those who know should know
you."   And he turn'd
Her counsel up and down within his
mind,
And found it true, and answer'd
"True, my child.
Well, I will wear it : fetch it out to
me :
What is it ? " and she told him "A red
sleeve
Broider'd with pearls," and brought
it : then he bound
Her token on his helmet, with a smile
Saying, "I never yet have done so
much

For any maiden living," and the blood
Sprang to her face and fill'd her with
    delight;
But left her all the paler, when
    Lavaine
Returning brought the yet-unblazon'd
    shield,
His brother's; which he gave to
    Lancelot,
Who parted with his own to fair
    Elaine:
"Do me this grace, my child, to have
    my shield
In keeping till I come." "A grace to
    me,"
She answer'd, "twice to-day. I am
    your squire!"
Whereat Lavaine said, laughing,
    "Lily maid,
For fear our people call you lily maid
In earnest, let me bring your color
    back;
Once, twice, and thrice: now get you
    hence to bed:"
So kiss'd her, and Sir Lancelot his
    own hand,
And thus they moved away: she
    stay'd a minute,
Then made a sudden step to the gate,
    and there —
Her bright hair blown about the
    serious face
Yet rosy-kindled with her brother's
    kiss —
Paused by the gateway, standing near
    the shield
In silence, while she watch'd their
    arms far-off
Sparkle, until they dipt below the
    downs.
Then to her tower she climb'd, and
    took the shield,
There kept it, and so lived in fantasy.

Meanwhile the new companions
    past away
Far o'er the long backs of the bushless
    downs,
To where Sir Lancelot knew there
    lived a knight
Not far from Camelot, now for forty
    years

A hermit, who had pray'd, labor'd and
    pray'd,
And ever laboring had scoop'd him-
    self
In the white rock a chapel and a hall
On massive columns, like a shorecliff
    cave,
And cells and chambers: all were fair
    and dry;
The green light from the meadows
    underneath
Struck up and lived along the milky
    roofs;
And in the meadows tremulous aspen-
    trees
And poplars made a noise of falling
    showers.
And thither wending there that night
    they bode.

But when the next day broke from
    underground,
And shot red fire and shadows thro'
    the cave,
They rose, heard mass, broke fast, and
    rode away:
Then Lancelot saying, "Hear, but
    hold my name
Hidden, you ride with Lancelot of the
    Lake."
Abash'd Lavaine, whose instant rev-
    erence,
Dearer to true young hearts than their
    own praise,
But left him leave to stammer, "Is it
    indeed?"
And after muttering "The great
    Lancelot,"
At last he got his breath and answer'd,
    "One,
One have I seen — that other, our
    liege lord,
The dread Pendragon, Britain's King
    of kings,
Of whom the people talk mysteriously,
He will be there — then were I stricken
    blind
That minute, I might say that I had
    seen."

So spake Lavaine, and when they
    reach'd the lists

By Camelot in the meadow, let his
  eyes
Run thro' the peopled gallery which
  half round
Lay like a rainbow fall'n upon the
  grass,
Until they found the clear-faced King,
  who sat
Robed in red samite, easily to be
  known,
Since to his crown the golden dragon
  clung,
And down his robe the dragon writhed
  in gold,
And from the carven-work behind
  him crept
Two dragons gilded, sloping down to
  make
Arms for his chair, while all the rest
  of them
Thro' knots and loops and folds innumerable
Fled ever thro' the woodwork, till they
  found
The new design wherein they lost
  themselves,
Yet with all ease, so tender was the
  work :
And, in the costly canopy o'er him
  set,
Blazed the last diamond of the nameless king.

  Then Lancelot answer'd young
    Lavaine and said,
" Me you call great : mine is the
  firmer seat,
The truer lance : but there is many a
  youth
Now crescent, who will come to all I
  am
And overcome it ; and in me there
  dwells
No greatness, save it be some far-off
  touch
Of greatness to know well I am not
  great :
There is the man." And Lavaine
  gaped upon him
As on a thing miraculous, and anon
The trumpets blew ; and then did
  either side,

They that assail'd, and they that held
  the lists,
Set lance in rest, strike spur, suddenly
  move,
Meet in the midst, and there so
  furiously
Shock, that a man far-off might well
  perceive,
If any man that day were left afield,
The hard earth shake, and a low thun-
  der of arms.
And Lancelot bode a little, till he saw
Which were the weaker ; then he
  hurl'd into it
Against the stronger : little need to
  speak
Of Lancelot in his glory ! King, duke,
  earl,
Count, baron — whom he smote, he
  overthrew.

  But in the field were Lancelot's
    kith and kin,
Ranged with the Table Round that
  held the lists,
Strong men, and wrathful that a
  stranger knight
Should do and almost overdo the
  deeds
Of Lancelot ; and one said to the
  other, " Lo !
What is he ? I do not mean the force
  alone —
The grace and versatility of the man !
Is it not Lancelot ? " " When has
  Lancelot worn
Favor of any lady in the lists ?
Not such his wont, as we, that know
  him, know."
" How then ? who then ? " a fury
  seized them all,
A fiery family passion for the name
Of Lancelot, and a glory one with
  theirs.
They couch'd their spears and prick'd
  their steeds, and thus,
Their plumes driv'n backward by the
  wind they made
In moving, all together down upon
  him
Bare, as a wild wave in the wide
  North-sea,

Green-glimmering toward the summit,
  bears, with all
Its stormy crests that smoke against
  the skies,
Down on a bark, and overbears the
  bark,
And him that helms it, so they overbore
Sir Lancelot and his charger, and a
  spear
Down-glancing lamed the charger, and
  a spear
Prick'd sharply his own cuirass, and
  the head
Pierced thro' his side, and there snapt,
  and remain'd.

Then Sir Lavaine did well and wor-
  shipfully;
He bore a knight of old repute to the
  earth,
And brought his horse to Lancelot
  where he lay.
He up the side, sweating with agony,
  got,
But thought to do while he might yet
  endure,
And being lustily holpen by the rest,
His party, — tho' it seem'd half-
  miracle
To those he fought with, — drave his
  kith and kin,
And all the Table Round that held
  the lists,
Back to the barrier; then the trum-
  pets blew
Proclaiming his the prize, who wore
  the sleeve
Of scarlet, and the pearls; and all the
  knights,
His party, cried "Advance and take
  thy prize
The diamond;" but he answer'd,
  "Diamond me
No diamonds! for God's love, a little
  air!
Prize me no prizes, for my prize is
  death!
Hence will I, and I charge you, follow
  me not."

He spoke, and vanish'd suddenly
  from the field

With young Lavaine into the poplar
  grove.
There from his charger down he slid,
  and sat,
Gasping to Sir Lavaine, "Draw the
  lance-head:"
"Ah my sweet lord Sir Lancelot," said
  Lavaine,
"I dread me, if I draw it, you will
  die."
But he, "I die already with it: draw —
Draw," — and Lavaine drew, and Sir
  Lancelot gave
A marvellous great shriek and ghastly
  groan,
And half his blood burst forth, and
  down he sank
For the pure pain, and wholly swoon'd
  away.
Then came the hermit out and bare
  him in,
There stanch'd his wound; and there,
  in daily doubt
Whether to live or die, for many a
  week
Hid from the wide world's rumor by
  the grove
Of poplars with their noise of falling
  showers,
And ever-tremulous aspen-trees, he
  lay.

But on that day when Lancelot fled
  the lists,
His party, knights of utmost North
  and West,
Lords of waste marches, kings of desolate isles,
Came round their great Pendragon,
  saying to him,
"Lo, Sire, our knight, thro' whom we
  won the day,
Hath gone sore wounded, and hath
  left his prize
Untaken, crying that his prize is
  death."
"Heaven hinder," said the King, "that
  such an one,
So great a knight as we have seen
  to-day —
He seem'd to me another Lancelot —

Yea, twenty times I thought him Lancelot—
He must not pass uncared for. Wherefore, rise,
O Gawain, and ride forth and find the knight.
Wounded and wearied needs must he be near.
I charge you that you get at once to horse.
And, knights and kings, there breathes not one of you
Will deem this prize of ours is rashly given:
His prowess was too wondrous. We will do him
No customary honor: since the knight
Came not to us, of us to claim the prize,
Ourselves will send it after. Rise and take
This diamond, and deliver it, and return,
And bring us where he is, and how he fares,
And cease not from your quest until ye find."

So saying, from the carven flower above,
To which it made a restless heart, he took,
And gave, the diamond: then from where he sat
At Arthur's right, with smiling face arose,
With smiling face and frowning heart, a Prince
In the mid might and flourish of his May,
Gawain, surnamed The Courteous, fair and strong,
And after Lancelot, Tristram, and Geraint
And Gareth, a good knight, but therewithal
Sir Modred's brother, and the child of Lot,
Nor often loyal to his word, and now
Wroth that the King's command to sally forth

In quest of whom he knew not, made him leave
The banquet, and concourse of knights and kings.

So all in wrath he got to horse and went;
While Arthur to the banquet, dark in mood,
Past, thinking "Is it Lancelot who hath come
Despite the wound he spake of, all for gain
Of glory, and hath added wound to wound,
And ridd'n away to die?" So fear'd the King,
And, after two days' tarriance there, return'd.
Then when he saw the Queen, embracing ask'd,
"Love, are you yet so sick?" "Nay, lord," she said.
"And where is Lancelot?" Then the Queen amazed,
"Was he not with you? won he not your prize?"
"Nay, but one like him." "Why that like was he."
And when the King demanded how she knew,
Said, "Lord, no sooner had ye parted from us,
Than Lancelot told me of a common talk
That men went down before his spear at a touch,
But knowing he was Lancelot; his great name
Conquer'd; and therefore would he hide his name
From all men, ev'n the King, and to this end
Had made the pretext of a hindering wound,
That he might joust unknown of all, and learn
If his old prowess were in aught decay'd;
And added, 'Our true Arthur, when he learns,

Will well allow my pretext, as for gain
Of purer glory.'"

   Then replied the King:
" Far lovelier in our Lancelot had it
 been,
In lieu of idly dallying with the truth,
To have trusted me as he hath trusted
 thee.
Surely his King and most familiar
 friend
Might well have kept his secret. True,
 indeed,
Albeit I know my knights fantastical,
So fine a fear in our large Lancelot
Must needs have moved my laughter:
 now remains
But little cause for laughter: his own
 kin —
Ill news, my Queen, for all who love
 him, this! —
His kith and kin, not knowing, set
 upon him;
So that he went sore wounded from
 the field:
Yet good news too: for goodly hopes
 are mine
That Lancelot is no more a lonely
 heart.
He wore, against his wont, upon his
 helm
A sleeve of scarlet, broider'd with
 great pearls,
Some gentle maiden's gift."

   " Yea, lord," she said,
"Thy hopes are mine," and saying
 that, she choked,
And sharply turn'd about to hide her
 face,
Past to her chamber, and there flung
 herself
Down on the great King's couch, and
 writhed upon it,
And clench'd her fingers till they bit
 the palm,
And shriek'd out "Traitor" to the
 unhearing wall,
Then flash'd into wild tears, and rose
 again,
And moved about her palace, proud
 and pale.

Gawain the while thro' all the region
 round
Rode with his diamond, wearied of
 the quest,
Touch'd at all points, except the poplar grove,
And came at last, tho' late, to Astolat
Whom glittering in enamell'd arms
 the maid
Glanced at, and cried, " What news
 from Camelot, lord?
What of the knight with the red
 sleeve? " " He won."
" I knew it," she said. " But parted
 from the jousts
Hurt in the side," whereat she caught
 her breath;
Thro' her own side she felt the sharp
 lance go;
Thereon she smote her hand: wellnigh
 she swoon'd:
And, while he gazed wonderingly at
 her, came
The Lord of Astolat out, to whom
 the Prince
Reported who he was, and on what
 quest
Sent, that he bore the prize and could
 not find
The victor, but had ridd'n a random
 round
To seek him, and had wearied of the
 search.
To whom the Lord of Astolat, "Bide
 with us,
And ride no more at random, noble
 Prince!
Here was the knight, and here he left
 a shield;
This will he send or come for: fur-
 thermore
Our son is with him; we shall hear
 anon,
Needs must we hear." To this the
 courteous Prince
Accorded with his wonted courtesy,
Courtesy with a touch of traitor
 in it,
And stay'd; and cast his eyes on fair
 Elaine:
Where could be found face daintier?
 then her shape

From forehead down to foot, perfect
— again
From foot to forehead exquisitely
turn'd :
" Well — if I bide, lo ! this wild flower
for me ! "
And oft they met among the garden
yews,
And there he set himself to play upon
her
With sallying wit, free flashes from a
height
Above her, graces of the court, and
songs,
Sighs, and slow smiles, and golden
eloquence
And amorous adulation, till the
maid
Rebell'd against it, saying to him,
" Prince,
O loyal nephew of our noble King,
Why ask you not to see the shield he
left,
Whence you might learn his name ?
Why slight your King,
And lose the quest he sent you on,
and prove
No surer than our falcon yesterday,
Who lost the hern we slipt her at,
and went
To all the winds ? "   " Nay, by mine
head," said he,
" I lose it, as we lose the lark in
heaven,
O damsel, in the light of your blue
eyes ;
But an ye will it let me see the
shield."
And when the shield was brought, and
Gawain saw
Sir Lancelot's azure lions, crown'd
with gold,
Ramp in the field, he smote his thigh,
and mock'd :
" Right was the King ! our Lancelot !
that true man ! "
" And right was I," she answer'd
merrily, " I,
Who dream'd my knight the greatest
knight of all."
" And if *I* dream'd," said Gawain,
" that you love

This greatest knight, your pardon ! lo,
ye know it !
Speak therefore : shall I waste myself
in vain ? "
Full simple was her answer, " What
know I ?
My brethren have been all my fellow-
ship ;
And I, when often they have talk'd
of love,
Wish'd it had been my mother, for
they talk'd,
Meseem'd, of what they knew not ; so
myself —
I know not if I know what true love is,
But if I know, then, if I love not him,
I know there is none other I can
love."
" Yea, by God's death," said he, " ye
love him well,
But would not, knew ye what all
others know,
And whom he loves."   " So be it,"
cried Elaine,
And lifted her fair face and moved
away :
But he pursued her, calling, " Stay a
little !
One golden minute's grace ! he wore
your sleeve :
Would he break faith with one I may
not name ?
Must our true man change like a leaf
at last ?
Nay — like enow : why then, far be it
from me
To cross our mighty Lancelot in his
loves !
And, damsel, for I deem you know
full well
Where your great knight is hidden,
let me leave
My quest with you ; the diamond also ;
here !
For if you love, it will be sweet to
give it ;
And if he love, it will be sweet to have
it
From your own hand ; and whether
he love or not,
A diamond is a diamond.   Fare you
well

A thousand times!—a thousand times
　　farewell!
Yet, if he love, and his love hold, we
　　two
May meet at court hereafter: there,
　　I think,
So ye will learn the courtesies of the
　　court,
We two shall know each other."

　　　　　　　　　　　　Then he gave,
And slightly kiss'd the hand to which
　　he gave,
The diamond, and all wearied of the
　　quest
Leapt on his horse, and carolling as he
　　went,
A true-love ballad, lightly rode away.

　　Thence to the court he past; there
　　　told the King
What the King knew, "Sir Lancelot
　　is the knight."
And added, "Sire, my liege, so much
　　I learnt;
But fail'd to find him, tho' I rode all
　　round
The region: but I lighted on the maid
Whose sleeve he wore; she loves him;
　　and to her,
Deeming our courtesy is the truest
　　law,
I gave the diamond: she will render it;
For by mine head she knows his hid-
　　ing-place."

　　The seldom-frowning King frown'd,
　　　and replied,
"Too courteous truly! ye shall go no
　　more
On quest of mine, seeing that ye for-
　　get
Obedience is the courtesy due to
　　kings."

　　He spake and parted. Wroth, but
　　　all in awe,
For twenty strokes of the blood, with-
　　out a word,
Linger'd that other, staring after him;
Then shook his hair, strode off, and
　　buzz'd abroad
About the maid of Astolat, and her
　　love.

All ears were prick'd at once, all
　　tongues were loosed:
"The maid of Astolat loves Sir Lance-
　　lot,
Sir Lancelot loves the maid of Asto-
　　lat."
Some read the King's face, some the
　　Queen's, and all
Had marvel what the maid might be,
　　but most
Predoom'd her as unworthy. One old
　　dame
Came suddenly on the Queen with the
　　sharp news.
She, that had heard the noise of it
　　before,
But sorrowing Lancelot should have
　　stoop'd so low,
Marr'd her friend's aim with pale
　　tranquillity.
So ran the tale like fire about the
　　court,
Fire in dry stubble a nine-days' won-
　　der flared:
Till ev'n the knights at banquet twice
　　or thrice
Forgot to drink to Lancelot and the
　　Queen,
And pledging Lancelot and the lily
　　maid
Smiled at each other, while the Queen,
　　who sat
With lips severely placid, felt the
　　knot
Climb in her throat, and with her feet
　　unseen
Crush'd the wild passion out against
　　the floor
Beneath the banquet, where the meats
　　became
As wormwood, and she hated all who
　　pledged.

　　But far away the maid in Astolat,
Her guiltless rival, she that ever
　　kept
The one-day-seen Sir Lancelot in her
　　heart,
Crept to her father, while he mused
　　alone,
Sat on his knee, stroked his gray
　　face and said,

" Father, you call me wilful, and the fault

Is yours who let me have my will, and now,

Sweet father, will you let me lose my wits ? "

" Nay," said he, " surely." " Wherefore, let me hence,"

She answer'd, " and find out our dear Lavaine."

" Ye will not lose your wits for dear Lavaine :

Bide," answer'd he : " we needs must hear anon

Of him, and of that other." " Ay," she said,

" And of that other, for I needs must hence

And find that other, wheresoe'er he be,

And with mine own hand give his diamond to him,

Lest I be found as faithless in the quest

As yon proud Prince who left the quest to me.

Sweet father, I behold him in my dreams

Gaunt as it were the skeleton of himself,

Death - pale, for lack of gentle maiden's aid.

The gentler-born the maiden, the more bound,

My father, to be sweet and serviceable

To noble knights in sickness, as ye know

When these have worn their tokens : let me hence

I pray you." Then her father nodding said,

" Ay, ay, the diamond : wit ye well, my child,

Right fain were I to learn this knight were whole,

Being our greatest : yea, and you must give it —

And sure I think this fruit is hung too high

For any mouth to gape for save a queen's —

Nay, I mean nothing : so then, get you gone,

Being so very wilful you must go."

Lightly, her suit allow'd, she slipt away,

And while she made her ready for her ride,

Her father's latest word humm'd in her ear,

" Being so very wilful you must go,"

And changed itself and echo'd in her heart,

" Being so very wilful you must die."

But she was happy enough and shook it off,

As we shake off the bee that buzzes at us ;

And in her heart she answer'd it and said,

" What matter, so I help him back to life ? "

Then far away with good Sir Torre for guide

Rode o'er the long backs of the bushless downs

To Camelot, and before the city-gates

Came on her brother with a happy face

Making a roan horse caper and curvet

For pleasure all about a field of flowers ;

Whom when she saw, " Lavaine," she cried, " Lavaine,

How fares my lord Sir Lancelot ? " He amazed,

" Torre and Elaine ! why here ? Sir Lancelot !

How know ye my lord's name is Lancelot ? "

But when the maid had told him all her tale,

Then turn'd Sir Torre, and being in his moods

Left them, and under the strange-statued gate,

Where Arthur's wars were render'd mystically,

Past up the still rich city to his kin,

His own far blood, which dwelt at Camelot ;

And her, Lavaine across the poplar grove
Led to the caves : there first she saw the casque
Of Lancelot on the wall : her scarlet sleeve,
Tho' carved and cut, and half the pearls away,
Stream'd from it still ; and in her heart she laugh'd,
Because he had not loosed it from his helm,
But meant once more perchance to tourney in it.
And when they gain'd the cell wherein he slept,
His battle-writhen arms and mighty hands
Lay naked on the wolfskin, and a dream
Of dragging down his enemy made them move.
Then she that saw him lying unsleek, unshorn,
Gaunt as it were the skeleton of himself,
Utter'd a little tender dolorous cry.
The sound not wonted in a place so still
Woke the sick knight, and while he roll'd his eyes
Yet blank from sleep, she started to him, saying,
" Your prize the diamond sent you by the King : "
His eyes glisten'd : she fancied " Is it for me ? "
And when the maid had told him all the tale
Of King and Prince, the diamond sent, the quest
Assign'd to her not worthy of it, she knelt
Full lowly by the corners of his bed,
And laid the diamond in his open hand.
Her face was near, and as we kiss the child
That does the task assign'd, he kiss'd her face.
At once she slipt like water to the floor.

" Alas," he said, " your ride hath wearied you.
Rest must you have." " No rest for me," she said ;
" Nay, for near you, fair lord, I am at rest."
What might she mean by that ? his large black eyes,
Yet larger thro' his leanness, dwelt upon her,
Till all her heart's sad secret blazed itself
In the heart's colors on her simple face ;
And Lancelot look'd and was perplext in mind,
And being weak in body said no more ;
But did not love the color ; woman's love,
Save one, he not regarded, and so turn'd
Sighing, and feign'd a sleep until he slept.

Then rose Elaine and glided thro' the fields,
And past beneath the weirdly-sculptured gates
Far up the dim rich city to her kin ;
There bode the night : but woke with dawn, and past
Down thro' the dim rich city to the the fields,
Thence to the cave : so day by day she past
In either twilight ghost-like to and fro
Gliding, and every day she tended him,
And likewise many a night : and Lancelot
Would, tho' he call'd his wound a little hurt
Whereof he should be quickly whole, at times
Brain-feverous in his heat and agony, seem
Uncourteous, even he : but the meek maid
Sweetly forbore him ever, being to him
Meeker than any child to a rough nurse,

Milder than any mother to a sick child,
And never woman yet, since man's
    first fall,
Did kindlier unto man, but her deep
    love
Upbore her; till the hermit, skill'd in
    all
The simples and the science of that
    time,
Told him that her fine care had saved
    his life.
And the sick man forgot her simple
    blush,
Would call her friend and sister,
    sweet Elaine,
Would listen for her coming and
    regret
Her parting step, and held her ten-
    derly,
And loved her with all love except
    the love
Of man and woman when they love
    their best,
Closest and sweetest, and had died the
    death
In any knightly fashion for her sake.
And peradventure had he seen her
    first
She might have made this and that
    other world
Another world for the sick man; but
    now
The shackles of an old love straiten'd
    him,
His honor rooted in dishonor stood,
And faith unfaithful kept him falsely
    true.

Yet the great knight in his mid-sick-
    ness made
Full many a holy vow and pure re-
    solve.
These, as but born of sickness, could
    not live:
For when the blood ran lustier in him
    again,
Full often the bright image of one
    face,
Making a treacherous quiet in his
    heart,
Dispersed his resolution like a
    cloud.

Then if the maiden, while that ghostly
    grace
Beam'd on his fancy, spoke, he
    answer'd not,
Or short and coldly, and she knew
    right well
What the rough sickness meant, but
    what this meant
She knew not, and the sorrow dimm'd
    her sight,
And drave her ere her time across the
    fields
Far into the rich city, where alone
She murmur'd, "Vain, in vain: it
    cannot be.
He will not love me: how then? must
    I die?"
Then as a little helpless innocent bird,
That has but one plain passage of few
    notes,
Will sing the simple passage o'er and
    o'er
For all an April morning, till the ear
Wearies to hear it, so the simple maid
Went half the night repeating, "Must
    I die?"
And now to right she turn'd, and now
    to left,
And found no ease in turning or in
    rest;
And "Him or death," she mutter'd,
    "death or him,"
Again and like a burthen, "Him or
    death."

But when Sir Lancelot's deadly hurt
    was whole,
To Astolat returning rode the three.
There morn by morn, arraying her
    sweet self
In that wherein she deem'd she look'd
    her best,
She came before Sir Lancelot, for she
    thought
"If I be loved, these are my festal
    robes,
If not, the victim's flowers before he
    fall."
And Lancelot ever prest upon the
    maid
That she should ask some goodly gift
    of him

For her own self or hers; "and do not
   shun
To speak the wish most near to your
   true heart;
Such service have ye done me, that I
   make
My will of yours, and Prince and Lord
   am I
In mine own land, and what I will I
   can."
Then like a ghost she lifted up her
   face,
But like a ghost without the power to
   speak.
And Lancelot saw that she withheld
   her wish,
And bode among them yet a little
   space
Till he should learn it; and one morn
   it chanced
He found her in among the garden
   yews,
And said, "Delay no longer, speak
   your wish,
Seeing I go to-day": then out she
   brake:
"Going? and we shall never see you
   more.
And I must die for want of one bold
   word."
"Speak: that I live to hear," he said,
   "is yours."
Then suddenly and passionately she
   spoke:
"I have gone mad. I love you: let
   me die."
"Ah, sister," answer'd Lancelot,
   "what is this?"
And innocently extending her white
   arms,
"Your love," she said, "your love —
   to be your wife."
And Lancelot answer'd, "Had I chosen
   to wed,
I had been wedded earlier, sweet
   Elaine:
But now there never will be wife of
   mine."
"No, no," she cried, "I care not to be
   wife,
But to be with you still, to see your
   face,

To serve you, and to follow you thro'
   the world."
And Lancelot answer'd, "Nay, the
   world, the world,
All ear and eye, with such a stupid
   heart
To interpret ear and eye, and such a
   tongue
To blare its own interpretation — nay,
Full ill then should I quit your
   brother's love,
And your good father's kindness."
   And she said,
"Not to be with you, not to see your
   face —
Alas for me then, my good days are
   done."
"Nay, noble maid," he answer'd, "ten
   times nay!
This is not love: but love's first flash
   in youth,
Most common: yea, I know it of mine
   own self:
And you yourself will smile at your
   own self
Hereafter, when you yield your flower
   of life
To one more fitly yours, not thrice
   your age:
And then will I, for true you are and
   sweet
Beyond mine old belief in woman-
   hood,
More specially should your good
   knight be poor,
Endow you with broad land and territory
Even to the half my realm beyond
   the seas,
So that would make you happy:
   furthermore,
Ev'n to the death, as tho' ye were my
   blood,
In all your quarrels will I be your
   knight.
This will I do, dear damsel, for your
   sake,
And more than this I cannot."

                    While he spoke
She neither blush'd nor shook, but
   deathly-pale

Stood grasping what was nearest, then replied:
"Of all this will I nothing;" and so fell,
And thus they bore her swooning to her tower.

Then spake, to whom thro' those black walls of yew
Their talk had pierced, her father:
"Ay, a flash,
I fear me, that will strike my blossom dead.
Too courteous are ye, fair Lord Lancelot.
I pray you, use some rough discourtesy
To blunt or break her passion."

Lancelot said,
"That were against me: what I can I will;"
And there that day remain'd, and toward even
Sent for his shield: full meekly rose the maid,
Stript off the case, and gave the naked shield;
Then, when she heard his horse upon the stones,
Unclasping flung the casement back, and look'd
Down on his helm, from which her sleeve had gone.
And Lancelot knew the little clinking sound;
And she by tact of love was well aware
That Lancelot knew that she was looking at him.
And yet he glanced not up, nor waved his hand,
Nor bade farewell, but sadly rode away.
This was the one discourtesy that he used.

So in her tower alone the maiden sat:
His very shield was gone; only the case,
Her own poor work, her empty labor, left.

But still she heard him, still his picture form'd
And grew between her and the pictured wall.
Then came her father, saying in low tones,
"Have comfort," whom she greeted quietly.
Then came her brethren saying, "Peace to thee,
Sweet sister," whom she answer'd with all calm.
But when they left her to herself again,
Death, like a friend's voice from a distant field
Approaching thro' the darkness, call'd; the owls
Wailing had power upon her, and she mixt
Her fancies with the sallow-rifted glooms
Of evening, and the moanings of the wind.

And in those days she made a little song,
And call'd her song "The Song of Love and Death,"
And sang it: sweetly could she make and sing.

"Sweet is true love tho' given in vain, in vain;
And sweet is death who puts an end to pain:
I know not which is sweeter, no, not I.

"Love, art thou sweet? then bitter death must be:
Love, thou art bitter; sweet is death to me.
O Love, if death be sweeter, let me die.

"Sweet love, that seems not made to fade away,
Sweet death, that seems to make us loveless clay,
I know not which is sweeter, no, not I.

" I fain would follow love, if that
  could be ;
I needs must follow death, who calls
  for me ;
Call and I follow, I follow ! let me
  die."

High with the last line scaled her
  voice, and this,
All in a fiery dawning wild with wind
That shook the tower, the brothers
  heard, and thought
With shuddering, " Hark the Phantom of the house
That ever shrieks before a death,"
  and call'd
The father, and all three in hurry and
  fear
Ran to her, and lo ! the blood-red light
  of dawn
Flared on her face, she shrilling, "Let
  me die !"

As when we dwell upon a word we
  know,
Repeating, till the word we know so
  well
Becomes a wonder, and we know not
  why,
So dwelt the father on her face, and
  thought
" Is this Elaine ? " till back the maiden
  fell,
Then gave a languid hand to each,
  and lay,
Speaking a still good-morrow with her
  eyes.
At last she said, " Sweet brothers, yes-
  ter-night
I seem'd a curious little maid again,
As happy as when we dwelt among
  the woods,
And when ye used to take me with
  the flood
Up the great river in the boatman's
  boat.
Only ye would not pass beyond the
  cape
That has the poplar on it : there ye
  fixt
Your limit, oft returning with the
  tide,

And yet I cried because ye would not
  pass
Beyond it, and far up the shining
  flood
Until we found the palace of the
  King.
And yet ye would not : but this night
  I dream'd
That I was all alone upon the flood,
And then I said, ' Now shall I have
  my will : '
And there I woke, but still the wish
  remain'd.
So let me hence that I may pass at
  last
Beyond the poplar and far up the
  flood,
Until I find the palace of the King.
There will I enter in among them all,
And no man there will dare to mock
  at me ;
But there the fine Gawain will wonder
  at me,
And there the great Sir Lancelot muse
  at me ;
Gawain, who bade a thousand fare-
  wells to me,
Lancelot, who coldly went, nor bade
  me one :
And there the King will know me and
  my love,
And there the Queen herself will pity
  me,
And all the gentle court will welcome
  me,
And after my long voyage I shall
  rest ! "

" Peace," said her father, " O my
  child, ye seem
Light-headed, for what force is yours
  to go
So far, being sick ? and wherefore
  would ye look
On this proud fellow again, who
  scorns us all ? "

Then the rough Torre began to
  heave and move,
And bluster into stormy sobs and
  say,

"I never loved him: an I meet with
   him,
I care not howsoever great he be,
Then will I strike at him and strike
   him down.
Give me good fortune, I will strike
   him dead,
For this discomfort he hath done the
   house."

   To whom the gentle sister made
   reply,
"Fret not yourself, dear brother, nor
   be wroth,
Seeing it is no more Sir Lancelot's
   fault
Not to love me, than it is mine to
   love
Him of all men who seems to me the
   highest."

   "Highest?" the father answer'd,
   echoing "highest?"
(He meant to break the passion in
   her) "nay,
Daughter, I know not what you call
   the highest;
But this I know, for all the people
   know it,
He loves the Queen, and in an open
   shame:
And she returns his love in open
   shame;
If this be high, what is it to be low?"

   Then spake the lily maid of Asto-
   lat:
"Sweet father, all too faint and sick
   am I
For anger: these are slanders: never
   yet
Was noble man but made ignoble talk.
He makes no friend who never made
   a foe.
But now it is my glory to have loved
One peerless, without stain: so let me
   pass,
My father, howsoe'er I seem to you,
Not all unhappy, having loved God's
   best
And greatest, tho' my love had no
   return:

Yet, seeing you desire your child to
   live,
Thanks, but you work against your
   own desire;
For if I could believe the things you
   say
I should but die the sooner; wherefore
   cease,
Sweet father, and bid call the ghostly
   man
Hither, and let me shrive me clean,
   and die."

   So when the ghostly man had come
   and gone,
She with a face, bright as for sin forgiven,
Besought Lavaine to write as she
   devised
A letter, word for word; and when he
   ask'd
"Is it for Lancelot, is it for my dear
   lord?
Then will I bear it gladly;" she re-
   plied,
"For Lancelot and the Queen and all
   the world,
But I myself must bear it." Then he
   wrote
The letter she devised; which being
   writ
And folded, "O sweet father, tender
   and true,
Deny me not," she said — "ye never
   yet
Denied my fancies — this, however
   strange,
My latest: lay the letter in my
   hand
A little ere I die, and close the hand
Upon it; I shall guard it even in
   death.
And when the heat is gone from out
   my heart,
Then take the little bed on which I
   died
For Lancelot's love, and deck it like
   the Queen's
For richness, and me also like the
   Queen
In all I have of rich, and lay me on
   it.

And let there be prepared a chariot-
    bier
To take me to the river, and a barge
Be ready on the river, clothed in black.
I go in state to court, to meet the
    Queen.
There surely I shall speak for mine
    own self,
And none of you can speak for me
    so well.
And therefore let our dumb old man
    alone
Go with me, he can steer and row,
    and he
Will guide me to that palace, to the
    doors."

    She ceased : her father promised ;
        whereupon
She grew so cheerful that they deem'd
    her death
Was rather in the fantasy than the
    blood.
But ten slow mornings past, and on
    the eleventh
Her father laid the letter in her hand,
And closed the hand upon it, and she
    died.
So that day there was dole in Astolat.

    But when the next sun brake from
        underground,
Then, those two brethren slowly with
    bent brows
Accompanying, the sad chariot-bier
Past like a shadow thro' the field,
    that shone
Full-summer, to that stream whereon
    the barge,
Pall'd all its length in blackest samite,
    lay.
There sat the lifelong creature of the
    house,
Loyal, the dumb old servitor, on deck,
Winking his eyes, and twisted all his
    face.
So those two brethren from the chariot
    took
And on the black decks laid her in
    her bed,
Set in her hand a lily, o'er her hung

The silken case with braided blazon-
    ings,
And kiss'd her quiet brows, and saying
    to her
" Sister, farewell for ever," and again
" Farewell, sweet sister," parted all in
    tears.
Then rose the dumb old servitor, and
    the dead,
Oar'd by the dumb, went upward with
    the flood —
In her right hand the lily, in her left
The letter — all her bright hair stream-
    ing down —
And all the coverlid was cloth of gold
Drawn to her waist, and she herself
    in white
All but her face, and that clear-fea-
    tured face
Was lovely, for she did not seem as
    dead,
But fast asleep, and lay as tho' she
    smiled.

    That day Sir Lancelot at the palace
        craved
Audience of Guinevere, to give at last
The price of half a realm, his costly
    gift,
Hard-won and hardly won with bruise
    and blow,
With deaths of others, and almost his
    own,
The nine-years-fought-for diamonds :
    for he saw
One of her house, and sent him to the
    Queen
Bearing his wish, whereto the Queen
    agreed
With such and so unmoved a majesty
She might have seem'd her statue, but
    that he,
Low-drooping till he wellnigh kiss'd
    her feet
For loyal awe, saw with a sidelong
    eye
The shadow of some piece of pointed
    lace,
In the Queen's shadow, vibrate on the
    walls,
And parted, laughing in his courtly
    heart.

All in an oriel on the summer side,
Vine-clad, of Arthur's palace toward
the stream,
They met, and Lancelot kneeling
utter'd, "Queen,
Lady, my liege, in whom I have my
joy,
Take, what I had not won except for
you,
These jewels, and make me happy,
making them
An armlet for the roundest arm on
earth,
Or necklace for a neck to which the
swan's
Is tawnier than her cygnet's: these
are words:
Your beauty is your beauty, and I
sin
In speaking, yet O grant my worship
of it
Words, as we grant grief tears. Such
sin in words
Perchance, we both can pardon: but,
my Queen,
I hear of rumors flying thro' your
court.
Our bond, as not the bond of man and
wife,
Should have in it an absoluter trust
To make up that defect: let rumors
be:
When did not rumors fly? these, as I
trust
That you trust me in your own nobleness,
I may not well believe that you believe."

While thus he spoke, half turn'd
away, the Queen
Brake from the vast oriel-embowering
vine
Leaf after leaf, and tore, and cast
them off,
Till all the place whereon she stood
was green;
Then, when he ceased, in one cold
passive hand
Received at once and laid aside the
gems
There on a table near her, and replied:

"It may be, I am quicker of belief
Than you believe me, Lancelot of the
Lake.
Our bond is not the bond of man and
wife.
This good is in it, whatsoe'er of ill,
It can be broken easier. I for you
This many a year have done despite
and wrong
To one whom ever in my heart of
hearts
I did acknowledge nobler. What are
these?
Diamonds for me! they had been
thrice their worth
Being your gift, had you not lost your
own.
To loyal hearts the value of all
gifts
Must vary as the giver's. Not for
me!
For her! for your new fancy. Only
this
Grant me, I pray you: have your joys
apart.
I doubt not that however changed,
you keep
So much of what is graceful: and
myself
Would shun to break those bounds of
courtesy
In which as Arthur's Queen I move
and rule:
So cannot speak my mind. An end
to this!
A strange one! yet I take it with
Amen.
So pray you, add my diamonds to her
pearls;
Deck her with these; tell her, she
shines me down:
An armlet for an arm to which the
Queen's
Is haggard, or a necklace for a neck
O as much fairer — as a faith once fair
Was richer than these diamonds —
hers not mine —
Nay, by the mother of our Lord him-
self,
Or hers or mine, mine now to work
my will —
She shall not have them."

Saying which she seized,
And, thro' the casement standing wide
    for heat,
Flung them, and down they flash'd,
    and smote the stream.
Then from the smitten surface flash'd,
    as it were,
Diamonds to meet them, and they past
    away.
Then while Sir Lancelot leant, in half
    disdain
At love, life, all things, on the window
    ledge,
Close underneath his eyes, and right
    across
Where these had fallen, slowly past
    the barge
Whereon the lily maid of Astolat
Lay smiling, like a star in blackest
    night.

But the wild Queen, who saw not,
    burst away
To weep and wail in secret; and the
    barge,
On to the palace-doorway sliding,
    paused.
There two stood arm'd, and kept the
    door; to whom,
All up the marble stair, tier over
    tier,
Were added mouths that gaped, and
    eyes that ask'd
"What is it?" but that oarsman's
    haggard face,
As hard and still as is the face that
    men
Shape to their fancy's eye from broken
    rocks
On some cliff-side, appall'd them, and
    they said,
"He is enchanted, cannot speak —
    and she,
Look how she sleeps — the Fairy
    Queen, so fair!
Yea, but how pale! what are they?
    flesh and blood?
Or come to take the King to Fairy-
    land?
For some do hold our Arthur cannot
    die,
But that he passes into Fairyland."

While thus they babbled of the
    King, the King
Came girt with knights : then turn'd
    the tongueless man
From the half-face to the full eye,
    and rose
And pointed to the damsel, and the
    doors.
So Arthur bade the meek Sir Percivale
And pure Sir Galahad to uplift the
    maid;
And reverently they bore her into
    hall.
Then came the fine Gawain and won-
    der'd at her,
And Lancelot later came and mused
    at her,
And last the Queen herself, and pitied
    her:
But Arthur spied the letter in her
    hand,
Stoopt, took, brake seal, and read it;
    this was all:

    "Most noble lord, Sir Lancelot of
        the Lake,
I, sometime call'd the maid of Astolat,
Come, for you left me taking no fare-
    well,
Hither, to take my last farewell of
    you.
I loved you, and my love had no
    return,
And therefore my true love has been
    my death.
And therefore to our Lady Guinevere,
And to all other ladies, I make moan.
Pray for my soul, and yield me burial.
Pray for my soul thou too, Sir Lan-
    celot,
As thou art a knight peerless."

                    Thus he read;
And ever in the reading, lords and
    dames
Wept, looking often from his face who
    read
To hers which lay so silent, and at
    times,
So touch'd were they, half-thinking
    that her lips,

Who had devised the letter, moved again.

Then freely spoke Sir Lancelot to them all:
" My lord liege Arthur, and all ye that hear,
Know that for this most gentle maiden's death
Right heavy am I; for good she was and true,
But loved me with a love beyond all love
In women, whomsoever I have known.
Yet to be loved makes not to love again;
Not at my years, however it hold in youth.
I swear by truth and knighthood that I gave
No cause, not willingly, for such a love:
To this I call my friends in testimony,
Her brethren, and her father, who himself
Besought me to be plain and blunt, and use,
To break her passion, some discourtesy
Against my nature: what I could, I did.
I left her and I bade her no farewell;
Tho', had I dreamt the damsel would have died,
I might have put my wits to some rough use,
And help'd her from herself."

Then said the Queen
(Sea was her wrath, yet working after storm)
" Ye might at least have done her so much grace,
Fair lord, as would have help'd her from her death."
He raised his head, their eyes met and hers fell,
He adding,
" Queen, she would not be content
Save that I wedded her, which could not be.
Then might she follow me thro' the world, she ask'd·

It could not be.   I told her that her love
Was but the flash of youth, would darken down
To rise hereafter in a stiller flame
Toward one more worthy of her — then would I,
More specially were he, she wedded, poor,
Estate them with large land and territory
In mine own realm beyond the narrow seas,
To keep them in all joyance: more than this
I could not; this she would not, and she died."

He pausing, Arthur answer'd, " O my knight,
It will be to thy worship, as my knight,
And mine, as head of all our Table Round,
To see that she be buried worshipfully."

So toward that shrine which then in all the realm
Was richest, Arthur leading, slowly went
The marshall'd Order of their Table Round,
And Lancelot sad beyond his wont, to see,
The maiden buried, not as one unknown,
Nor meanly, but with gorgeous obsequies,
And mass, and rolling music, like a queen.
And when the knights had laid her comely head
Low in the dust of half-forgotten kings,
Then Arthur spake among them, " Let her tomb
Be costly, and her image thereupon,
And let the shield of Lancelot at her feet
Be carven, and her lily in her hand.

And let the story of her dolorous
  voyage
For all true hearts be blazon'd on her
  tomb
In letters gold and azure!" which was
  wrought
Thereafter; but when now the lords
  and dames
And people, from the high door
  streaming, brake
Disorderly, as homeward each, the
  Queen,
Who mark'd Sir Láncelot where he
  moved apart,
Drew near, and sigh'd in passing,
  "Lancelot,
Forgive me; mine was jealousy in
  love."
He answer'd with his eyes upon the
  ground,
"That is love's curse; pass on, my
  Queen, forgiven."
But Arthur, who beheld his cloudy
  brows,
Approach'd him, and with full affec-
  tion said,

"Lancelot, my Lancelot, thou in
  whom I have
Most joy and most affiance, for I
  know
What thou hast been in battle by my
  side,
And many a time have watch'd thee
  at the tilt
Strike down the lusty and long practised knight,
And let the younger and unskill'd
  go by
To win his honor and to make his
  name,
And loved thy courtesies and thee, a
  man
Made to be loved; but now I would
  to God,
Seeing the homeless trouble in thine
  eyes,
Thou couldst have loved this maiden,
  shaped, it seems,
By God for thee alone, and from her
  face,

If one may judge the living by the
  dead,
Delicately pure and marvellously fair,
Who might have brought thee, now a
  lonely man
Wifeless and heirless, noble issue, sons
Born to the glory of thy name and
  fame,
My knight, the great Sir Lancelot of
  the Lake."

Then answer'd Lancelot, "Fair she
  was, my King,
Pure, as you ever wish your knights
  to be.
To doubt her fairness were to want an
  eye,
To doubt her pureness were to want a
  heart —
Yea, to be loved, if what is worthy love
Could bind him, but free love will not
  be bound."

"Free love, so bound, were freëst,"
  said the King.
"Let love be free; free love is for
  the best:
And, after heaven, on our dull side of
  death,
What should be best, if not so pure a
  love
Clothed in so pure a loveliness? yet
  thee
She fail'd to bind, tho' being, as I
  think,
Unbound as yet, and gentle, as I
  know."

And Lancelot answer'd nothing, but
  he went,
And at the inrunning of a little brook
Sat by the river in a cove, and
  watch'd
The high reed wave, and lifted up his
  eyes
And saw the barge that brought her
  moving down,
Far-off, a blot upon the stream, and
  said
Low in himself, "Ah simple heart and
  sweet,

Ye loved me, damsel, surely with a love
Far tenderer than my Queen's. Pray for thy soul?
Ay, that will I. Farewell too — now at last —
Farewell, fair lily. 'Jealousy in love?'
Not rather dead love's harsh heir, jealous pride?
Queen, if I grant the jealousy as of love,
May not your crescent fear for name and fame
Speak, as it waxes, of a love that wanes?
Why did the King dwell on my name to me?
Mine own name shames me, seeming a reproach,
Lancelot, whom the Lady of the Lake
Caught from his mother's arms — the wondrous one
Who passes thro' the vision of the night —
She chanted snatches of mysterious hymns
Heard on the winding waters, eve and morn
She kiss'd me saying, 'Thou art fair, my child,
As a king's son,' and often in her arms
She bare me, pacing on the dusky mere.
Would she had drown'd me in it, where'er it be!
For what am I? what profits me my name
Of greatest knight? I fought for it, and have it:
Pleasure to have it, none; to lose it, pain;
Now grown a part of me: but what use in it?
To make men worse by making my sin known?
Or sin seem less, the sinner seeming great?
Alas for Arthur's greatest knight, a man
Not after Arthur's heart! I needs must break

These bonds that so defame me: not without
She wills it: would I, if she will'd it? nay,
Who knows? but if I would not, then may God,
I pray him, send a sudden Angel down
To seize me by the hair and bear me far,
And fling me deep in that forgotten mere,
Among the tumbled fragments of the hills."

So groan'd Sir Lancelot in remorseful pain,
Not knowing he should die a holy man.

THE HOLY GRAIL.

FROM noiseful arms, and acts of prowess done
In tournament or tilt, Sir Percivale,
Whom Arthur and his knighthood call'd The Pure,
Had pass'd into the silent life of prayer,
Praise, fast, and alms; and leaving for the cowl
The helmet in an abbey far away
From Camelot, there, and not long after, died.

And one, a fellow-monk among the rest,
Ambrosius, loved him much beyond the rest,
And honor'd him, and wrought into his heart
A way by love that waken'd love within,
To answer that which came: and as they sat
Beneath a world-old yew-tree, darkening half
The cloisters, on a gustful April morn
That puff'd the swaying branches into smoke
Above them, ere the summer when he died,

The monk Ambrosius question'd
    Percivale:

  "O brother, I have seen this yew-
    tree smoke,
Spring after spring, for half a hun-
    dred years:
For never have I known the world
    without,
Nor ever stray'd beyond the pale: but
    thee,
When first thou camest — such a
    courtesy
Spake thro' the limbs and in the
    voice —
    I knew
For one of those who eat in Arthur's
    hall;
For good ye are and bad, and like to
    coins,
Some true, some light, but every one
    of you
Stamp'd with the image of the King;
    and now
Tell me, what drove thee from the
    Table Round,
My brother? was it earthly passion
    crost?"

  "Nay," said the knight; "for no
    such passion mine
But the sweet vision of the Holy
    Grail
Drove me from all vainglories, rival-
    ries,
And earthly heats that spring and
    sparkle out
Among us in the jousts, while women
    watch
Who wins, who falls; and waste the
    spiritual strength
Within us, better offer'd up to
    Heaven."

  To whom the monk: "The Holy
    Grail! — I trust
We are green in Heaven's eyes; but
    here too much
We moulder — as to things without I
    mean —
Yet one of your own knights, a guest
    of ours,

Told us of this in our refectory,
But spake with such a sadness and so
    low
We heard not half of what he said.
    What is it?
The phantom of a cup that comes
    and goes?"

  "Nay, monk! what phantom?"
    answer'd Percivale.
"The cup, the cup itself, from which
    our Lord
Drank at the last sad supper with his
    own.
This, from the blessed land of Aro-
    mat —
After the day of darkness, when the
    dead
Went wandering o'er Moriah — the
    good saint
Arimathæan Joseph, journeying
    brought
To Glastonbury, where the winter
    thorn
Blossoms at Christmas, mindful of
    our Lord.
And there awhile it bode; and if a
    man
Could touch or see it, he was heal'd
    at once,
By faith, of all his ills. But then the
    times
Grew to such evil that the holy cup
Was caught away to Heaven, and
    disappear'd."

  To whom the monk: "From our
    old books I know
That Joseph came of old to Glaston-
    bury,
And there the heathen Prince, Arvi-
    ragus,
Gave him an isle of marsh whereon to
    build;
And there he built with wattles from
    the marsh
A little lonely church in days of yore,
For so they say, these books of ours,
    but seem
Mute of this miracle, far as I have read.
But who first saw the holy thing to-
    day?"

"A woman," answer'd Percivale,
"a nun,
And one no further off in blood from
me
Than sister; and if ever holy maid
With knees of adoration wore the
stone,
A holy maid; tho' never maiden
glow'd,
But that was in her earlier maiden-
hood,
With such a fervent flame of human
love,
Which being rudely blunted, glanced
and shot
Only to holy things; to prayer and
praise
She gave herself, to fast and alms.
And yet,
Nun as she was, the scandal of the
Court,
Sin against Arthur and the Table
Round,
And the strange sound of an adulter-
ous race,
Across the iron grating of her cell
Beat, and she pray'd and fasted all
the more.

"And he to whom she told her sins,
or what
Her all but utter whiteness held for
sin,
A man wellnigh a hundred winters old,
Spake often with her of the Holy Grail,
A legend handed down thro' five or six,
And each of these a hundred winters
old,
From our Lord's time. And when
King Arthur made
His Table Round, and all men's hearts
became
Clean for a season, surely he had
thought
That now the Holy Grail would come
again;
But sin broke out. Ah, Christ, that it
would come,
And heal the world of all their wicked-
ness!
'O Father!' ask'd the maiden, 'might
it come

To me by prayer and fasting?' 'Nay,'
said he,
'I know not, for thy heart is pure as
snow.'
And so she pray'd and fasted, till the
sun
Shone, and the wind blew, thro' her,
and I thought
She might have risen and floated when
I saw her.

"For on a day she sent to speak
with me.
And when she came to speak, behold
her eyes
Beyond my knowing of them, beauti-
ful,
Beyond all knowing of them, won-
derful,
Beautiful in the light of holiness.
And 'O my brother Percivale,' she
said,
'Sweet brother, I have seen the Holy
Grail:
For, waked at dead of night, I heard
a sound
As of a silver horn from o'er the hills
Blown, and I thought, "It is not
Arthur's use
To hunt by moonlight;" and the slen-
der sound
As from a distance beyond distance
grew
Coming upon me — O never harp nor
horn,
Nor aught we blow with breath, or
touch with hand,
Was like that music as it came; and
then
Stream'd thro' my cell a cold and
silver beam,
And down the long beam stole the
Holy Grail,
Rose-red with beatings in it, as if
alive,
Till all the white walls of my cell were
dyed
With rosy colors leaping on the wall;
And then the music faded, and the
Grail
Past, and the beam decay'd, and from
the walls

The rosy quiverings died into the night.
So now the Holy Thing is here again
Among us, brother, fast thou too and pray,
And tell thy brother knights to fast and pray,
That so perchance the vision may be seen
By thee and those, and all the world be heal'd.'

"Then leaving the pale nun, I spake of this
To all men; and myself fasted and pray'd
Always, and many among us many a week
Fasted and pray'd even to the uttermost,
Expectant of the wonder that would be.

"And one there was among us, ever moved
Among us in white armor, Galahad.
'God make thee good as thou art beautiful,'
Said Arthur, when he dubb'd him knight; and none,
In so young youth, was ever made a knight
Till Galahad; and this Galahad, when he heard
My sister's vision, fill'd me with amaze;
His eyes became so like her own, they seem'd
Hers, and himself her brother more than I.

"Sister or brother none had he; but some
Call'd him a son of Lancelot, and some said
Begotten by enchantment—chatterers they,
Life birds of passage piping up and down,
That gape for flies — we know not whence they come;
For when was Lancelot wanderingly lewd?

"But she, the wan sweet maiden, shore away
Clean from her forehead all that wealth of hair
Which made a silken mat-work for her feet;
And out of this she plaited broad and long
A strong sword-belt, and wove with silver thread
And crimson in the belt a strange device,
A crimson grail within a silver beam;
And saw the bright boy-knight, and bound it on him,
Saying, 'My knight, my love, my knight of heaven,
O thou, my love, whose love is one with mine,
I, maiden, round thee, maiden, bind my belt.
Go forth, for thou shalt see what I have seen,
And break thro' all, till one will crown thee king
Far in the spiritual city:' and as she spake
She sent her deathless passion in her eyes
Thro' him, and made him hers, and laid her mind
On him, and he believed in her belief.

"Then came a year of miracle: O brother,
In our great hall there stood a vacant chair,
Fashion'd by Merlin ere he past away,
And carven with strange figures; and in and out
The figures, like a serpent, ran a scroll
Of letters in a tongue no man could read.
And Merlin call'd it 'The Siege perilous.'
Perilous for good and ill; 'for there,' he said,
'No man could sit but he should lose himself:'
And once by misadventure Merlin sat
In his own chair, and so was lost; but he,

Galahad, when he heard of Merlin's
doom,
Cried, 'If I lose myself, I save myself!'

"Then on a summer night it came
to pass,
While the great banquet lay along the
hall,
That Galahad would sit down in Merlin's chair.

"And all at once, as there we sat,
we heard
A cracking and a riving of the roofs,
And rending, and a blast, and over-
head
Thunder, and in the thunder was a cry.
And in the blast there smote along the
hall
A beam of light seven times more
clear than day:
And down the long beam stole the
Holy Grail
All over cover'd with a luminous cloud,
And none might see who bare it, and
it past.
But every knight beheld his fellow's
face
As in a glory, and all the knights arose,
And staring each at other like dumb
men
Stood, till I found a voice and sware
a vow.

"I sware a vow before them all,
that I,
Because I had not seen the Grail, would
ride
A twelvemonth and a day in quest of
it,
Until I found and saw it, as the nun
My sister saw it; and Galahad sware
the vow,
And good Sir Bors, our Lancelot's
cousin, sware,
And Lancelot sware, and many among
the knights,
And Gawain sware, and louder than
the rest."

Then spake the monk Ambrosius,
asking him,

"What said the King? Did Arthur
take the vow?"

"Nay, for my lord," said Percivale,
"the King,
Was not in hall: for early that same
day,
Scaped thro' a cavern from a bandit
hold,
An outraged maiden sprang into the
hall
Crying on help: for all her shining
hair
Was smear'd with earth, and either
milky arm
Red-rent with hooks of bramble, and
all she wore
Torn as a sail that leaves the rope is
torn
In tempest: so the King arose and
went
To smoke the scandalous hive of those
wild bees
That made such honey in his realm.
Howbeit
Some little of this marvel he too saw,
Returning o'er the plain that then
began
To darken under Camelot; whence the
King
Look'd up, calling aloud, 'Lo, there!
the roofs
Of our great hall are roll'd in thunder-
smoke!
Pray Heaven, they be not smitten by
the bolt.'
For dear to Arthur was that hall of
ours,
As having there so oft with all his
knights
Feasted, and as the stateliest under
heaven.

"O brother, had you known our
mighty hall,
Which Merlin built for Arthur long
ago!
For all the sacred mount of Camelot,
And all the dim rich city, roof by
roof,
Tower after tower, spire beyond spire,

By grove, and garden-lawn, and rush-
    ing brook,
Climbs to the mighty hall that Merlin
    built.
And four great zones of sculpture, set
    betwixt
With many a mystic symbol, gird the
    hall:
And in the lowest beasts are slaying
    men,
And in the second men are slaying
    beasts,
And on the third are warriors, perfect
    men,
And on the fourth are men with grow-
    ing wings,
And over all one statue in the mould
Of Arthur, made by Merlin, with a
    crown,
And peak'd wings pointed to the
    Northern Star.
And eastward fronts the statue, and
    the crown
And both the wings are made of gold,
    and flame
At sunrise till the people in far
    fields,
Wasted so often by the heathen
    hordes,
Behold it, crying, 'We have still a
    King.'

    "And, brother, had you known our
        hall within,
Broader and higher than any in all
    the lands!
Where twelve great windows blazon
    Arthur's wars,
And all the light that falls upon the
    board
Streams thro' the twelve great battles
    of our King.
Nay, one there is, and at the eastern
    end,
Wealthy with wandering lines of
    mount and mere,
Where Arthur finds the brand Excali-
    bur.
And also one to the west, and counter
    to it,
And blank: and who shall blazon it?
    when and how? —

O there, perchance, when all our wars
    are done,
The brand Excalibur will be cast
    away.

    "So to this hall full quickly rode
        the King,
In horror lest the work by Merlin
    wrought,
Dreamlike, should on the sudden van-
    ish, wrapt
In unremorseful folds of rolling fire.
And in he rode, and up I glanced, and
    saw
The golden dragon sparkling over all:
And many of those who burnt the
    hold, their arms
Hack'd, and their foreheads grimed
    with smoke, and sear'd,
Follow'd, and in among bright faces,
    ours,
Full of the vision, prest: and then the
    King
Spake to me, being nearest, 'Perci-
    vale,'
(Because the hall was all in tumult —
    some
Vowing, and some protesting), 'what
    is this?'

    "O brother, when I told him what
        had chanced,
My sister's vision, and the rest, his
    face
Darken'd, as I have seen it more than
    once,
When some brave deed seem'd to be
    done in vain,
Darken; and 'Woe is me, my knights,'
    he cried,
'Had I been here, ye had not sworn
    the vow.'
Bold was mine answer, 'Had thyself
    been here,
My King, thou wouldst have sworn.'
'Yea, yea,' said he,
'Art thou so bold and hast not seen
    the Grail?'

    "'Nay, lord, I heard the sound, I
        saw the light,

But since I did not see the Holy
    Thing,
I sware a vow to follow it till I saw.'

    " Then when he ask'd us, knight by
      knight, if any
Had seen it, all their answers were as
    one :
'Nay, lord, and therefore have we
    sworn our vows.'

    " ' Lo now,' said Arthur, ' have ye
      seen a cloud ?
What go ye into the wilderness to
    see ? '

    " Then Galahad on the sudden, and
      in a voice
Shrilling along the hall to Arthur,
    call'd,
'But I, Sir Arthur, saw the Holy
    Grail,
I saw the Holy Grail and heard a cry —
    " O Galahad, and O Galahad, follow
    me." '

    " ' Ah, Galahad, Galahad,' said the
      King, ' for such
As thou art is the vision, not for
    these.
Thy holy nun and thou have seen a
    sign —
Holier is none, my Percivale, than
    she —
A sign to maim this Order which I
    made.
But ye, that follow but the leader's
    bell '
(Brother, the King was hard upon his
    knights)
'Taliessin is our fullest throat of song,
And one hath sung and all the dumb
    will sing.
Lancelot is Lancelot, and hath over-
    borne
Five knights at once, and every
    younger knight,
Unproven, holds himself as Lancelot,
Till overborne by one, he learns — and
    ye,
What are ye ? Galahads ? — no, nor
    Percivales '

(For thus it pleased the King to range
    me close
After Sir Galahad) ; 'nay,' said he,
    ' but men
With strength and will to right the
    wrong'd, of power
To lay the sudden heads of violence
    flat,
Knights that in twelve great battles
    splash'd and dyed
The strong White Horse in his own
    heathen blood —
But one hath seen, and all the blind
    will see.
Go, since your vows are sacred, being
    made :
Yet — for ye know the cries of all my
    realm
Pass thro' this hall — how often, O my
    knights,
Your places being vacant at my
    side,
This chance of noble deeds will come
    and go
Unchallenged, while ye follow wan-
    dering fires
Lost in the quagmire ! Many of you,
    yea most,
Return no more : ye think I show my-
    self
Too dark a prophet : come now, let
    us meet
The morrow morn once more in one
    full field
Of gracious pastime, that once more
    the King,
Before ye leave him for this Quest,
    may count
The yet-unbroken strength of all his
    knights,
Rejoicing in that Order which he
    made.'

    " So when the sun broke next from
      under ground,
All the great table of our Arthur
    closed
And clash'd in such a tourney and so
    full,
So many lances broken — never yet
Had Camelot seen the like, since
    Arthur came ;

And I myself and Galahad, for a
strength
Was in us from the vision, overthrew
So many knights that all the people
cried,
And almost burst the barriers in their
heat,
Shouting, ' Sir Galahad and Sir Percivale !'

"But when the next day brake
from under ground —
O brother, had you known our Came-
lot,
Built by old kings, age after age, so
old
The King himself had fears that it
would fall,
So strange, and rich, and dim; for
where the roofs
Totter'd toward each other in the
sky,
Met foreheads all along the street of
those
Who watch'd us pass ; and lower, and
where the long
Rich galleries, lady-laden, weigh'd the
necks
Of dragons clinging to the crazy walls,
Thicker than drops from thunder,
showers of flowers
Fell as we past; and men and boys
astride
On wyvern, lion, dragon, griffin, swan,
At all the corners, named us each by
name,
Calling ' God speed !' but in the ways
below
The knights and ladies wept, and rich
and poor
Wept, and the King himself could
hardly speak
For grief, and all in middle street the
Queen,
Who rode by Lancelot, wail'd and
shriek'd aloud,
'This madness has come on us for our
sins.'
So to the Gate of the three Queens we
came,
Where Arthur's wars are render'd
mystically,

And thence departed every one his
way.

" And I was lifted up in heart, and
thought
Of all my late-shown prowess in the
lists,
How my strong lance had beaten down
the knights,
So many and famous names ; and
never yet
Had heaven appear'd so blue, nor
earth so green,
For all my blood danced in me, and I
knew
That I should light upon the Holy
Grail.

"Thereafter, the dark warning of
our King,
That most of us would follow wander-
ing fires,
Came like a driving gloom across my
mind.
Then every evil word I had spoken
once,
And every evil thought I had thought
of old,
And every evil deed I ever did,
Awoke and cried, ' This Quest is not
for thee.'
And lifting up mine eyes, I found my-
self
Alone, and in a land of sand and
thorns,
And I was thirsty even unto death ;
And I, too, cried, ' This Quest is not
for thee.'

" And on I rode, and when I thought
my thirst
Would slay me, saw deep lawns, and
then a brook,
With one sharp rapid, where the crisping white
Play'd ever back upon the sloping
wave,
And took both ear and eye ; and o'er
the brook
Were apple-trees, and apples by the
brook

Fallen, and on the lawns. 'I will rest
   here,'
I said, 'I am not worthy of the Quest;'
But even while I drank the brook, and
   ate
The goodly apples, all these things at
   once
Fell into dust, and I was left alone,
And thirsting, in a land of sand and
   thorns.

   "And then behold a woman at a
   door
Spinning; and fair the house whereby
   she sat,
And kind the woman's eyes and inno-
   cent,
And all her bearing gracious; and she
   rose
Opening her arms to meet me, as who
   should say,
'Rest here;' but when I touch'd her,
   lo! she, too,
Fell into dust and nothing, and the
   house
Became no better than a broken shed.
And in it a dead babe; and also this
Fell into dust, and I was left alone.

   "And on I rode, and greater was
   my thirst.
Then flash'd a yellow gleam across
   the world,
And where it smote the plowshare in
   the field,
The plowman left his plowing, and
   fell down
Before it; where it glitter'd on her
   pail,
The milkmaid left her milking, and
   fell down
Before it, and I knew not why, but
   thought
'The sun is rising,' tho' the sun had
   risen.
Then was I ware of one that on me
   moved
In golden armor with a crown of gold
About a casque all jewels; and his
   horse
In golden armor jewell'd everywhere:

And on the splendor came, flashing
   me blind;
And seem'd to me the Lord of all the
   world,
Being so huge. But when I thought
   he meant
To crush me, moving on me, lo! he,
   too,
Open'd his arms to embrace me as he
   came,
And up I went and touch'd him, and
   he, too,
Fell into dust, and I was left alone
And wearying in a land of sand and
   thorns.

   "And I rode on and found a mighty
   hill,
And on the top, a city wall'd: the
   spires
Prick'd with incredible pinnacles into
   heaven.
And by the gateway stirr'd a crowd;
   and these
Cried to me climbing, 'Welcome, Per-
   civale!
Thou mightiest and thou purest
   among men!'
And glad was I and clomb, but found
   at top
No man, nor any voice. And thence
   I past
Far thro' a ruinous city, and I saw
That man had once dwelt there; but
   there I found
Only one man of an exceeding age.
'Where is that goodly company,' said I,
'That so cried out upon me?' and he
   had
Scarce any voice to answer, and yet
   gasp'd,
'Whence and what art thou?' and
   even as he spoke
Fell into dust, and disappear'd, and I
Was left alone once more, and cried
   in grief,
'Lo, if I find the Holy Grail itself
And touch it, it will crumble into
   dust.'

   "And thence I dropt into a lowly
   vale,

Low as the hill was high, and where the vale
Was lowest, found a chapel, and thereby
A holy hermit in a hermitage,
To whom I told my phantoms, and he said:

"'O son, thou hast not true humility,
The highest virtue, mother of them all;
For when the Lord of all things made Himself
Naked of glory for His mortal change,
"Take thou my robe," she said, "for all is thine,"
And all her form shone forth with sudden light
So that the angels were amazed, and she
Follow'd Him down, and like a flying star
Led on the gray-hair'd wisdom of the east;
But her thou hast not known: for what is this
Thou thoughtest of thy prowess and thy sins?
Thou hast not lost thyself to save thyself
As Galahad.' When the hermit made an end,
In silver armor suddenly Galahad shone
Before us, and against the chapel door
Laid lance, and enter'd, and we knelt in prayer.
And there the hermit slaked my burning thirst,
And at the sacring of the mass I saw
The holy elements alone; but he,
'Saw ye no more? I, Galahad, saw the Grail,
The Holy Grail, descend upon the shrine:
I saw the fiery face as of a child
That smote itself into the bread, and went;
And hither am I come; and never yet
Hath what thy sister taught me first to see,
This Holy Thing, fail'd from my side, nor come

Cover'd, but moving with me night and day,
Fainter by day, but always in the night
Blood-red, and sliding down the blacken'd marsh
Blood-red, and on the naked mountain top
Blood-red, and in the sleeping mere below
Blood-red. And in the strength of this I rode,
Shattering all evil customs everywhere,
And past thro' Pagan realms, and made them mine,
And clash'd with Pagan hordes, and bore them down,
And broke thro' all, and in the strength of this
Come victor. But my time is hard at hand,
And hence I go; and one will crown me king
Far in the spiritual city; and come thou, too,
For thou shalt see the vision when I go.'

"While thus he spake, his eye, dwelling on mine,
Drew me, with power upon me, till I grew
One with him, to believe as he believed.
Then, when the day began to wane, we went.

"There rose a hill that none but man could climb,
Scarr'd with a hundred wintry watercourses —
Storm at the top, and when we gain'd it, storm
Round us and death; for every moment glanced
His silver arms and gloom'd: so quick and thick
The lightnings here and there to left and right
Struck, till the dry old trunks about us, dead,

Yea, rotten with a hundred years of
death,
Sprang into fire : and at the base we
found
On either hand, as far as eye could see,
A great black swamp and of an evil
smell,
Part black, part whiten'd with the
bones of men,
Not to be crost, save that some ancient
king
Had built a way, where, link'd with
many a bridge,
A thousand piers ran into the great
Sea.
And Galahad fled along them bridge
by bridge,
And every bridge as quickly as he
crost
Sprang into fire and vanish'd, tho' I
yearn'd
To follow; and thrice above him all
the heavens
Open'd and blazed with thunder such
as seem'd
Shoutings of all the sons of God: and
first
At once I saw him far on the great
Sea,
In silver-shining armor starry-clear ;
And o'er his head the Holy Vessel
hung
Clothed in white samite or a luminous
cloud.
And with exceeding swiftness ran the
boat,
If boat it were — I saw not whence it
came.
And when the heavens open'd and
blazed again
Roaring, I saw him like a silver star —
And had he set the sail, or had the
boat
Become a living creature clad with
wings ?
And o'er his head the Holy Vessel
hung
Redder than any rose, a joy to me,
For now I knew the veil had been
withdrawn.
Then in a moment when they blazed
again

Opening, I saw the least of little stars
Down on the waste, and straight
beyond the star
I saw the spiritual city and all her
spires
And gateways in a glory like one
pearl —
No larger, tho' the goal of all the
saints —
Strike from the sea ; and from the
star there shot
A rose-red sparkle to the city, and
there
Dwelt, and I know it was the Holy
Grail,
Which never eyes on earth again
shall see.
Then fell the floods of heaven drown-
ing the deep.
And how my feet recrost the death-
ful ridge
No memory in me lives ; but that I
touch'd
The chapel-doors at dawn I know;
and thence
Taking my war-horse from the holy
man,
Glad that no phantom vext me more,
return'd
To whence I came, the gate of Arthur's
wars."

" O brother," ask'd Ambrosius, —
"for in sooth
These ancient books — and they would
win thee — teem,
Only I find not there this Holy Grail,
With miracles and marvels like to
these,
Not all unlike ; which oftentime I read,
Who read but on my breviary with
ease,
Till my head swims ; and then go forth
and pass
Down to the little thorpe that lies so
close,
And almost plaster'd like a martin's
nest
To these old walls — and mingle with
our folk ;
And knowing every honest face of
theirs

As well as ever shepherd knew his
   sheep,
And every homely secret in their
   hearts,
Delight myself with gossip and old
   wives,
And ills and aches, and teethings,
   lyings-in,
And mirthful sayings, children of the
   place,
That have no meaning half a league
   away :
Or lulling random squabbles when
   they rise,
Chafferings and chatterings at the
   market-cross,
Rejoice, small man, in this small world
   of mine,
Yea, even in their hens and in their
   eggs —
O brother, saving this Sir Galahad,
Came ye on none but phantoms in
   your quest,
No man, no woman ? "

        Then Sir Percivale :
" All men, to one so bound by such a
   vow,
And women were as phantoms. O,
   my brother,
Why wilt thou shame me to confess
   to thee
How far I falter'd from my quest and
   vow ?
For after I had lain so many nights,
A bedmate of the snail and eft and
   snake,
In grass and burdock, I was changed
   to wan
And meagre, and the vision had not
   come ;
And then I chanced upon a goodly
   town
With one great dwelling in the middle
   of it ;
Thither I made, and there was I dis-
   arm'd
By maidens each as fair as any flower :
But when they led me into hall, be-
   hold,
The Princess of that castle was the
   one,

Brother, and that one only, who had
   ever
Made my heart leap ; for when I
   moved of old
A slender page about her father's hall,
And she a slender maiden, all my
   heart
Went after her with longing : yet we
   twain
Had never kiss'd a kiss, or vow'd a
   vow.
And now I came upon her once again,
And one had wedded her, and he was
   dead,
And all his land and wealth and state
   were hers.
And while I tarried, every day she
   set
A banquet richer than the day before
By me ; for all her longing and her
   will
Was toward me as of old ; till one
   fair morn,
I walking to and fro beside a stream
That flash'd across her orchard under-
   neath
Her castle-walls, she stole upon my
   walk,
And calling me the greatest of all
   knights,
Embraced me, and so kiss'd me the
   first time,
And gave herself and all her wealth
   to me.
Then I remember'd Arthur's warning
   word,
That most of us would follow wan-
   dering fires,
And the Quest faded in my heart.
   Anon,
The heads of all her people drew to
   me,
With supplication both of knees and
   tongue :
' We have heard of thee : thou art
   our greatest knight,
Our Lady says it, and we well believe :
Wed thou our Lady, and rule over us,
And thou shalt be as Arthur in our
   land.'
O me, my brother ! but one night my
   vow

Burnt me within, so that I rose and
        fled,
But wail'd and wept, and hated mine
        own self,
And ev'n the Holy Quest, and all but
        her;
Then after I was join'd with Galahad
Cared not for her, nor anything upon
        earth."

  Then said the monk, "Poor men,
        when yule is cold,
Must be content to sit by little fires.
And this am I, so that ye care for me
Ever so little; yea, and blest be
        Heaven
That brought thee here to this poor
        house of ours
Where all the brethren are so hard,
        to warm
My cold heart with a friend: but O
        the pity
To find thine own first love once
        more — to hold,
Hold her a wealthy bride within thine
        arms,
Or all but hold, and then — cast her
        aside,
Foregoing all her sweetness, like a
        weed.
For we that want the warmth of
        double life,
We that are plagued with dreams of
        something sweet
Beyond all sweetness in a life so
        rich, —
Ah, blessed Lord, I speak too earthly-
        wise,
Seeing I never stray'd beyond the cell,
But live like an old badger in his
        earth,
With earth about him everywhere,
        despite
All fast and penance. Saw ye none
        beside,
None of your knights ? "

        " Yea so," said Percivale:
" One night my pathway swerving
        east, I saw
The pelican on the casque of our Sir
        Bors

All in the middle of the rising moon:
And toward him spurr'd, and hail'd
        him, and he me,
And each made joy of either; then
        he ask'd,
' Where is he ? hast thou seen him —
        Lancelot ? — Once.'
Said good Sir Bors, ' he dash'd across
        me — mad,
And maddening what he rode: and
        when I cried,
" Ridest thou then so hotly on a quest
So holy," Lancelot shouted, " Stay
        me not !
I have been the sluggard, and I ride
        apace,
For now there is a lion in the way."
So vanish'd.'

        " Then Sir Bors had ridden on
Softly, and sorrowing for our Lan-
        celot,
Because his former madness, once the
        talk
And scandal of our table, had re-
        turn'd:
For Lancelot's kith and kin so wor-
        ship him
That ill to him is ill to them; to Bors
Beyond the rest: he well had been
        content
Not to have seen, so Lancelot might
        have seen,
The Holy Cup of healing; and, indeed,
Being so clouded with his grief and
        love,
Small heart was his after the Holy
        Quest:
If God would send the vision, well:
        if not,
The Quest and he were in the hands
        of Heaven.

        " And then, with small adventure
        met, Sir Bors
Rode to the loneliest tract of all the
        realm,
And found a people there among
        their crags,
Our race and blood, a remnant that
        were left

Paynim amid their circles, and the stones
They pitch up straight to heaven: and their wise men
Were strong in that old magic which can trace
The wandering of the stars, and scoff'd at him
And this high Quest as at a simple thing:
Told him he follow'd — almost Arthur's words —
A mocking fire: 'what other fire than he,
Whereby the blood beats, and the blossom blows,
And the sea rolls, and all the world is warm'd?'
And when his answer chafed them, the rough crowd,
Hearing he had a difference with their priests,
Seized him, and bound and plunged him into a cell
Of great piled stones; and lying bounden there
In darkness thro' innumerable hours
He heard the hollow-ringing heavens sweep
Over him till by miracle — what else? —
Heavy as it was, a great stone slipt and fell,
Such as no wind could move: and thro' the gap
Glimmer'd the streaming scud: then came a night
Still as the day was loud; and thro' the gap
The seven clear stars of Arthur's Table Round —
For, brother, so one night, because they roll
Thro' such a round in heaven, we named the stars,
Rejoicing in ourselves and in our King —
And these, like bright eyes of familiar friends,
In on him shone: 'And then to me, to me,'

Said good Sir Bors, 'beyond all hopes of mine,
Who scarce had pray'd or ask'd it for myself —
Across the seven clear stars — O grace to me —
In color like the fingers of a hand
Before a burning taper, the sweet Grail
Glided and past, and close upon it peal'd
A sharp quick thunder.' Afterwards, a maid,
Who kept our holy faith among her kin
In secret, entering, loosed and let him go."

To whom the monk: "And I remember now
That pelican on the casque: Sir Bors it was
Who spake so low and sadly at our board;
And mighty reverent at our grace was he:
A square-set man and honest; and his eyes,
An out-door sign of all the warmth within,
Smiled with his lips — a smile beneath a cloud,
But heaven had meant it for a sunny one:
Ay, ay, Sir Bors, who else? But when ye reach'd
The city, found ye all your knights return'd,
Or was there sooth in Arthur's prophecy,
Tell me, and what said each, and what the King?"

Then answer'd Percivale: "And that can I,
Brother, and truly; since the living words
Of so great men as Lancelot and our King
Pass not from door to door and out again,
But sit within the house. O, when we reach'd

The city, our horses stumbling as
    they trode
On heaps of ruin, hornless unicorns,
Crack'd basilisks, and splinter'd cock-
    atrices,
And shatter'd talbots, which had left
    the stones
Raw, that they fell from, brought us
    to the hall.

  " And there sat Arthur on the daïs-
    throne,
And those that had gone out upon the
    Quest,
Wasted and worn, and but a tithe of
    them,
And those that had not, stood before
    the King,
Who, when he saw me, rose, and bade
    me hail,
Saying, ' A welfare in thine eye re-
    proves
Our fear of some disastrous chance
    for thee
On hill, or plain, at sea, or flooding
    ford.
So fierce a gale made havoc here of
    late
Among the strange devices of our
    kings;
Yea, shook this newer, stronger hall
    of ours,
And from the statue Merlin moulded
    for us
Half-wrench'd a golden wing; but
    now — the Quest,
This vision — hast thou seen the Holy
    Cup,
That Joseph brought of old to Glas-
    tonbury ? "

  " So when I told him all thyself
    hast heard,
Ambrosius, and my fresh but fixt re-
    solve
To pass away into the quiet life,
He answer'd not, but, sharply turn-
    ing, ask'd
Of Gawain, ' Gawain, was this Quest
    for thee ? '

  " ' Nay, lord,' said Gawain, ' not for
    such as I.
Therefore I communed with a saintly
    man,
Who made me sure the Quest was not
    for me;
For I was much awearied of the
    Quest:
But found a silk pavilion in a field,
And merry maidens in it; and then
    this gale
Tore my pavilion from the tenting-
    pin,
And blew my merry maidens all
    about
With all discomfort; yea, and but for
    this,
My twelvemonth and a day were
    pleasant to me.'

  " He ceased; and Arthur turn'd to
    whom at first
He saw not, for Sir Bors, on entering,
    push'd
Athwart the throng to Lancelot,
    caught his hand,
Held it, and there, half-hidden by him,
    stood,
Until the King espied him, saying to
    him,
' Hail, Bors ! if ever loyal man and
    true
Could see it, thou hast seen the Grail;'
    and Bors,
' Ask me not, for I may not speak of
    it :
I saw it;' and the tears were in his
    eyes.

  " Then there remain'd but Lance-
    lot, for the rest
Spake but of sundry perils in the
    storm;
Perhaps, like him of Cana in Holy
    Writ,
Our Arthur kept his best until the
    last;
' Thou, too, my Lancelot,' ask'd the
    King, ' my friend,
Our mightiest, hath this Quest avail'd
    for thee ? '

"'Our mightiest!' answer'd Lance-
lot, with a groan;
'O King!'— and when he paused,
   methought I spied
A dying fire of madness in his eyes —
'O King, my friend, if friend of thine
   I be,
Happier are those that welter in their
   sin,
Swine in the mud, that cannot see for
   slime,
Slime of the ditch: but in me lived a
   sin
So strange, of such a kind, that all of
   pure,
Noble, and knightly in me twined
   and clung
Round that one sin, until the whole-
   some flower
And poisonous grew together, each as
   each,
Not to be pluck'd asunder; and when
   thy knights
Sware, I sware with them only in the
   hope
That could I touch or see the Holy
   Grail
They might be pluck'd asunder. Then
   I spake
To one most holy saint, who wept and
   said,
That save they could be pluck'd
   asunder, all
My quest were but in vain; to whom
   I vow'd
That I would work according as he
   will'd.
And forth I went, and while I yearn'd
   and strove
To tear the twain asunder in my
   heart,
My madness came upon me as of old,
And whipt me into waste fields far
   away;
There was I beaten down by little
   men,
Mean knights, to whom the moving
   of my sword
And shadow of my spear had been
   enow
To scare them from me once; and
   then I came

All in my folly to the naked shore,
Wide flats, where nothing but coarse
   grasses grew;
But such a blast, my King, began to
   blow,
So loud a blast along the shore and
   sea,
Ye could not hear the waters for the
   blast,
Tho' heapt in mounds and ridges all
   the sea
Drove like a cataract, and all the sand
Swept like a river, and the clouded
   heavens
Were shaken with the motion and the
   sound.
And blackening in the sea-foam
   sway'd a boat,
Half-swallow'd in it, anchor'd with a
   chain;
And in my madness to myself I said,
"I will embark and I will lose myself,
And in the great sea wash away my
   sin."
I burst the chain, I sprang into the
   boat.
Seven days I drove along the dreary
   deep,
And with me drove the moon and all
   the stars;
And the wind fell, and on the seventh
   night
I heard the shingle grinding in the
   surge,
And felt the boat shock earth, and
   looking up,
Behold, the enchanted towers of Car-
   bonek,
A castle like a rock upon a rock,
With chasm-like portals open to the
   sea,
And steps that met the breaker! there
   was none
Stood near it but a lion on each side
That kept the entry, and the moon
   was full.
Then from the boat I leapt, and up
   the stairs.
There drew my sword. With sudden-
   flaring manes
Those two great beasts rose upright
   like a man,

Each gript a shoulder, and I stood
between;
And, when I would have smitten
them, heard a voice,
"Doubt not, go forward; if thou
doubt, the beasts
Will tear thee piecemeal." Then with
violence
The sword was dash'd from out my
hand, and fell.
And up into the sounding hall I past;
But nothing in the sounding hall I
saw,
No bench nor table, painting on the
wall
Or shield of knight; only the rounded
moon
Thro' the tall oriel on the rolling sea.
But always in the quiet house I heard,
Clear as a lark, high o'er me as a lark,
A sweet voice singing in the topmost
tower
To the eastward: up I climb'd a thou-
sand steps
With pain: as in a dream I seem'd to
climb
For ever: at the last I reach'd a door,
A light was in the crannies, and I
heard,
"Glory and joy and honor to our
Lord
And to the Holy Vessel of the Grail."
Then in my madness I essay'd the
door;
It gave; and thro' a stormy glare, a
heat
As from a seventimes-heated furnace,
I,
Blasted and burnt, and blinded as I
was,
With such a fierceness that I swoon'd
away —
O, yet methought I saw the Holy
Grail,
All pall'd in crimson samite, and
around
Great angels, awful shapes, and wings
and eyes.
And but for all my madness and my
sin,
And then my swooning, I had sworn
I saw

That which I saw; but what I saw
was veil'd
And cover'd; and this Quest was not
for me.'

"So speaking, and here ceasing,
Lancelot left
The hall long silent, till Sir Gawain
— nay,
Brother, I need not tell thee foolish
words, —
A reckless and irreverent knight was
he,
Now bolden'd by the silence of his
King, —
Well, I tell thee: 'O King, my
liege,' he said,
'Hath Gawain fail'd in any quest of
thine?
When have I stinted stroke in fough-
ten field?
But as for thine, my good friend
Percivale,
Thy holy nun and thou have driven
men mad,
Yea, made our mightiest madder than
our least.
But by mine eyes and by mine ears I
swear,
I will be deafer than the blue-eyed
cat,
And thrice as blind as any noonday
owl,
To holy virgins in their ecstasies,
Henceforward."

" ' Deafer,' said the blameless
King,
' Gawain, and blinder unto holy
things
Hope not to make thyself by idle
vows,
Being too blind to have desire to see.
But if indeed there came a sign from
heaven,
Blessed are Bors, Lancelot and Per-
civale,
For these have seen according to
their sight.
For every fiery prophet in old times,
And all the sacred madness of the
bard,

When God make music thro' them,
    could but speak
His music by the framework and the
    chord ;
And as ye saw it ye have spoken
    truth.

    " ' Nay — but thou errest, Lancelot :
    never yet
Could all of true and noble in knight
    and man
Twine round one sin, whatever it
    might be,
With such a closeness, but apart there
    grew,
Save that he were the swine thou
    spakest of,
Some root of knighthood and pure
    nobleness ;
Whereto see thou, that it may bear
    its flower.

    " ' And spake I not too truly, O my
    knights ?
Was I too dark a prophet when I said
To those who went upon the Holy
    Quest,
That most of them would follow
    wandering fires,
Lost in the quagmire ? — lost to me
    and gone,
And left me gazing at a barren board,
And a lean Order — scarce return'd a
    tithe —
And out of those to whom the vision
    came
My greatest hardly will believe he
    saw ;
Another hath beheld it afar off,
And leaving human wrongs to right
    themselves,
Cares but to pass into the silent life.
And one hath had the vision face to
    face,
And now his chair desires him here
    in vain,
However they may crown him other-
    where.

    " ' And some among you held, that
    if the King
Had seen the sight he would have
    sworn the vow :

Not easily, seeing that the King must
    guard
That which he rules, and is but as the
    hind
To whom a space of land is given to
    plow,
Who may not wander from the allot-
    ted field
Before his work be done ; but, being
    done,
Let visions of the night or of the
    day
Come, as they will; and many a time
    they come,
Until this earth he walks on seems
    not earth,
This light that strikes his eyeball is
    not light,
This air that smites his forehead is
    not air
But vision — yea, his very hand and
    foot —
In moments when he feels he cannot
    die,
And knows himself no vision to him-
    self,
Nor the high God a vision, nor that
    One
Who rose again : ye have seen what
    ye have seen.'

    " So spake the King : I knew not all.
    he meant."

PELLEAS AND ETTARRE.

KING ARTHUR made new knights to
    fill the gap
Left by the Holy Quest ; and as he
    sat
In the hall at old Caerleon, the high
    doors
Were softly sunder'd, and thro' these
    a youth,
Pelleas, and the sweet smell of the
    fields
Past, and the sunshine came along
    with him.

    " Make me thy knight, because I
    know, Sir King,

All that belongs to knighthood, and I
  love."
Such was his cry : for having heard
  the King
Had let proclaim a tournament — the
  prize
A golden circlet and a knightly sword,
Full fain had Pelleas for his lady
  won
The golden circlet, for himself the
  sword :
And there were those who knew him
  near the King,
And promised for him : and Arthur
  made him knight.

And this new knight, Sir Pelleas of
  the isles —
But lately come to his inheritance,
And lord of many a barren isle was
  he —
Riding at noon, a day or twain before,
Across the forest call'd of Dean, to
  find
Caerleon and the King, had felt the
  sun
Beat like a strong knight on his
  helm, and reel'd
Almost to falling from his horse ; but
  saw
Near him a mound of even-sloping
  side,
Whereon a hundred stately beeches
  grew,
And here and there great hollies under
  them ;
But for a mile all round was open
  space,
And fern and heath : and slowly Pel-
  leas drew
To that dim day, then binding his
  good horse
To a tree, cast himself down ; and as
  he lay
At random looking over the brown
  earth
Thro' that green-glooming twilight of
  the grove,
It seem'd to Pelleas that the fern
  without
Burnt as a living fire of emeralds,

So that his eyes were dazzled looking
  at it.
Then o'er it crost the dimness of a
  cloud
Floating, and once the shadow of a
  bird
Flying, and then a fawn ; and his
  eyes closed.
And since he loved all maidens, but
  no maid
In special, half-awake he whisper'd,
  " Where ?
O where ? I love thee, tho' I know
  thee not.
For fair thou art ·and pure as Guine-
  vere,
And I will make thee with my spear
  and sword
As famous — O my Queen my Guine-
  vere,
For I will be thine Arthur when we
  meet."

  Suddenly waken'd with a sound of
  talk
And laughter at the limit of the wood,
And glancing thro' the hoary boles,
  he saw
Strange as to some old prophet might
  have seem'd
A vision hovering on a sea of fire,
Damsels in divers colors like the cloud
Of sunset and sunrise, and all of them
On horses, and the horses richly trapt
Breast-high in that bright line of
  bracken stood :
And all the damsels talk'd confusedly,
And one was pointing this way, and
  one that,
Because the way was lost.

          And Pelleas rose,
And loosed his horse, and led him to
  the light.
There she that seem'd the chief among
  them said,
" In happy time behold our pilot-star !
Youth, we are damsels-errant, and we
  ride,
Arm'd as ye see, to tilt against the
  knights

There at Caerleon, but have lost our
　　way :
To right ? to left ? straight forward ?
　　back again ?
Which ? tell us quickly."

　　　　And Pelleas gazing thought,
" Is Guinevere herself so beautiful ? "
For large her violet eyes look'd, and
　　her bloom
A rosy dawn kindled in stainless
　　heavens,
And round her limbs, mature in
　　womanhood ;
And slender was her hand and small
　　her shape ;
And but for those large eyes, the haunts
　　of scorn,
She might have seem'd a toy to trifle
　　with,
And pass and care no more. But
　　while he gazed
The beauty of her flesh abash'd the
　　boy,
As tho' it were the beauty of her soul :
For as the base man, judging of the
　　good,
Puts his own baseness in him by
　　default
Of will and nature, so did Pelleas lend
All the young beauty of his own soul
　　to hers,
Believing her ; and when she spake
　　to him,
Stammer'd, and could not make her a
　　reply.
For out of the waste islands had he
　　come,
Where saving his own sisters he had
　　known
Scarce any but the women of his isles,
Rough wives, that laugh'd and
　　scream'd against the gulls,
Makers of nets, and living from the
　　sea.

　　Then with a slow smile turn'd the
　　lady round
And look'd upon her people ; and as
　　when
A stone is flung into some sleeping
　　tarn,

The circle widens till it lip the marge,
Spread the slow smile thro' all her
　　company.
Three knights were thereamong ; and
　　they too smiled,
Scorning him ; for the lady was
　　Ettarre,
And she was a great lady in her land.

　　Again she said, " O wild and of the
　　woods,
Knowest thou not the fashion of our
　　speech ?
Or have the Heavens but given thee
　　a fair face,
Lacking a tongue ? "

　　　　　　" O damsel," answer'd he,
" I woke from dreams ; and coming
　　out of gloom
Was dazzled by the sudden light, and
　　crave
Pardon : but will ye to Caerleon ?　I
Go likewise : shall I lead you to the
　　King ? "

　　" Lead then," she said ; and thro'
　　the woods they went.
And while they rode, the meaning in
　　his eyes,
His tenderness of manner, and chaste
　　awe,
His broken utterances and bashful-
　　ness,
Were all a burthen to her, and in her
　　heart
She mutter'd, " I have lighted on a
　　fool,
Raw, yet so stale ! " But since her
　　mind was bent
On hearing, after trumpet blown, her
　　name
And title, " Queen of Beauty," in the
　　lists
Cried — and beholding him so strong,
　　she thought
That peradventure he will fight for
　　me,
And win the circlet : therefore flatter'd
　　him,
Being so gracious, that he wellnigh
　　deem'd

His wish by hers was echo'd; and her
   knights
And all her damsels too were gracious
   to him,
For she was a great lady.

             And when they reach'd
Caerleon, ere they past to lodging,
   she,
Taking his hand, "O the strong hand,"
   she said,
"See! look at mine! but wilt thou
   fight for me,
And win me this fine circlet, Pelleas,
That I may love thee ? "

             Then his helpless heart
Leapt, and he cried, "Ay! wilt thou
   if I win ? "
"Ay, that will I," she answer'd, and
   she laugh'd,
And straitly nipt the hand, and flung
   it from her;
Then glanced askew at those three
   knights of hers,
Till all her ladies laugh'd along with
   her.

"O happy world," thought Pelleas,
   "all, meseems,
Are happy; I the happiest of them
   all."
Nor slept that night for pleasure in
   his blood,
And green wood-ways, and eyes among
   the leaves;
Then being on the morrow knighted,
   sware
To love one only. And as he came
   away,
The men who met him rounded on
   their heels
And wonder'd after him, because his
   face
Shone like the countenance of a priest
   of old
Against the flame about a sacrifice
Kindled by fire from heaven : so glad
   was he.

Then Arthur made vast banquets,
   and strange knights

From the four winds came in: and
   each one sat,
Tho' served with choice from air, land,
   stream, and sea,
Oft in mid-banquet measuring with
   his eyes
His neighbor's make and might: and
   Pelleas look'd
Noble among the noble, for he dream'd
His lady loved him, and he knew him-
   self
Loved of the King : and him his new-
   made knight
Worshipt, whose lightest whisper
   moved him more
Than all the ranged reasons of the
   world.

Then blush'd and brake the morn-
   ing of the jousts,
And this was call'd "The Tournament
   of Youth : "
For Arthur, loving his young knight,
   withheld
His older and his mightier from the
   lists,
That Pelleas might obtain his lady's
   love,
According to her promise, and remain
Lord of the tourney. And Arthur
   had the jousts
Down in the flat field by the shore of
   Usk
Holden : the gilded parapets were
   crown'd
With faces, and the great tower fill'd
   with eyes
Up to the summit, and the trumpets
   blew.
There all day long Sir Pelleas kept
   the field
With honor: so by that strong hand
   of his
The sword and golden circlet were
   achieved.

Then rang the shout his lady loved :
   the heat
Of pride and glory fired her face; her
   eye
Sparkled; she caught the circlet from
   his lance,

And there before the people crown'd
    herself :
So for the last time she was gracious
    to him.

    Then at Caerleon for a space — her
        look
Bright for all others, cloudier on her
    knight —
Linger'd Ettarre : and seeing Pelleas
    droop,
Said Guinevere, " We marvel at thee
    much,
O damsel, wearing this unsunny face
To him who won thee glory !" And
    she said,
" Had ye not held your Lancelot in
    your bower,
My Queen, he had not won." Where-
    at the Queen,
As one whose foot is bitten by an ant,
Glanced down upon her, turn'd and
    went her way.

    But after, when her damsels, and
    herself,
And those three knights all set their
    faces home,
Sir Pelleas follow'd. She that saw
    him cried,
"Damsels — and yet I should be
    shamed to say it —
I cannot bide Sir Baby. Keep him back
Among yourselves. Would rather
    that we had
Some rough old knight who knew the
    worldly way,
Albeit grizzlier than a bear, to ride
And jest with : take him to you, keep
    him off,
And pamper him with papmeat, if ye
    will,
Old milky fables of the wolf and sheep,
Such as the wholesome mothers tell
    their boys.
Nay, should ye try him with a merry
    one
To find his mettle, good : and if he fly
    us,
Small matter! let him." This her
    damsels heard,

And mindful of her small and cruel
    hand,
They, closing round him thro' the
    journey home,
Acted her hest, and always from her
    side
Restrain'd him with all manner of
    device,
So that he could not come to speech
    with her.
And when she gain'd her castle, up-
    sprang the bridge,
Down rang the grate of iron thro' the
    groove,
And he was left alone in open field.

    "These be the ways of ladies,"
    Pelleas thought,
" To those who love them, trials of
    our faith.
Yea, let her prove me to the uttermost,
For loyal to the uttermost am I."
So made his moan ; and, darkness
    falling, sought
A priory not far off, there lodged, but
    rose
With morning every day, and, moist
    or dry,
Full-arm'd upon his charger all day
    long
Sat by the walls, and no one open'd to
    him.

    And this persistence turn'd her
    scorn to wrath.
Then calling her three knights, she
    charged them, " Out!
And drive him from the walls." And
    out they came,
But Pelleas overthrew them as they
    dash'd
Against him one by one ; and these
    return'd,
But still he kept his watch beneath
    the wall.

    Thereon her wrath became a hate ;
    and once,
A week beyond, while walking on the
    walls
With her three knights, she pointed
    downward, " Look,

He haunts me — I cannot breathe —
    besieges me;
Down! strike him! put my hate into
    your strokes,
And drive him from my walls." And
    down they went,
And Pelleas overthrew them one by
    one;
And from the tower above him cried
    Ettarre,
"Bind him, and bring him in."

          He heard her voice;
Then let the strong hand, which had
    overthrown
Her minion-knights, by those he over-
    threw
Be bounden straight, and so they
    brought him in.

Then when he came before Ettarre,
    the sight
Of her rich beauty made him at one
    glance
More bondsman in his heart than in
    his bonds.
Yet with good cheer he spake, "Be-
    hold me, Lady,
A prisoner, and the vassal of thy will;
And if thou keep me in thy donjon here,
Content am I so that I see thy face
But once a day: for I have sworn my
    vows,
And thou hast given thy promise, and
    I know
That all these pains are trials of my
    faith,
And that thyself, when thou hast seen
    me strain'd
And sifted to the utmost, wilt at length
Yield me thy love and know me for
    thy knight."

Then she began to rail so bitterly,
With all her damsels, he was stricken
    mute;
But when she mock'd his vows and
    the great King,
Lighted on words: "For pity of thine
    own self,
Peace, Lady, peace: is he not thine
    and mine?"

"Thou fool," she said, "I never heard
    his voice
But long'd to break away. Unbind
    him now,
And thrust him out of doors; for save
    he be
Fool to the midmost marrow of his
    bones,
He will return no more." And those,
    her three,
Laugh'd, and unbound, and thrust him
    from the gate.

And after this, a week beyond, again
She call'd them, saying, "There he
    watches yet,
There like a dog before his master's
    door!
Kick'd, he returns: do ye not hate
    him, ye?
Ye know yourselves: how can ye bide
    at peace,
Affronted with his fulsome innocence?
Are ye but creatures of the board and
    bed,
No men to strike? Fall on him all at
    once,
And if ye slay him I reck not: if ye fail,
Give ye the slave mine order to be
    bound,
Bind him as heretofore, and bring him
    in:
It may be ye shall slay him in his
    bonds."

She spake; and at her will they
    couch'd their spears,
Three against one: and Gawain pass-
    ing by,
Bound upon solitary adventure, saw
Low down beneath the shadow of
    those towers
A villany, three to one: and thro' his
    heart
The fire of honor and all noble deeds
Flash'd, and he call'd, "I strike upon
    thy side —
The caitiffs!" "Nay," said Pelleas,
    "but forbear;
He needs no aid who doth his lady's
    will."

So Gawain, looking at the villany
   done,
Forebore, but in his heat and eagerness
Trembled and quiver'd, as the dog,
   withheld
A moment from the vermin that he
   sees
Before him, shivers, ere he springs
   and kills.

And Pelleas overthrew them, one to
   three;
And they rose up, and bound, and
   brought him in.
Then first her anger, leaving Pelleas,
   burn'd
Full on her knights in many an evil
   name
Of craven, weakling, and thrice-beaten
   hound:
"Yet, take him, ye that scarce are fit
   to touch,
Far less to bind, your victor, and
   thrust him out,
And let who will release him from his
   bonds.
And if he comes again"—there she
   brake short;
And Pelleas answer'd, "Lady, for indeed
I loved you and I deem'd you beautiful,
I cannot brook to see your beauty
   marr'd
Thro' evil spite: and if ye love me not,
I cannot bear to dream you so forsworn:
I had liefer ye were worthy of my
   love,
Than to be loved again of you—farewell;
And tho' ye kill my hope, not yet my
   love,
Vex not yourself: ye will not see me
   more."

While thus he spake, she gazed
   upon the man
Of princely bearing, tho' in bonds,
   and thought,
"Why have I push'd him from me?
   this man loves,

If love there be: yet him I loved not.
   Why?
I deem'd him fool? yea, so? or that
   in him
A something—was it nobler than my-
   self?—
Seem'd my reproach? He is not of
   my kind.
He could not love me, did he know me
   well.
Nay, let him go—and quickly." And
   her knights
Laugh'd not, but thrust him bounden
   out of door.

Forth sprang Gawain, and loosed
   him from his bonds,
And flung them o'er the walls; and
   afterward,
Shaking his hands, as from a lazar's
   rag,
"Faith of my body," he said, "and
   art thou not—
Yea thou art he, whom late our Arthur
   made
Knight of his table; yea and he that
   won
The circlet? wherefore hast thou so
   defamed
Thy brotherhood in me and all the
   rest,
As let these caitiffs on thee work their
   will?"

And Pelleas answer'd, "O, their
   wills are hers
For whom I won the circlet; and
   mine, hers,
Thus to be bounden, so to see her
   face,
Marr'd tho' it be with spite and mockery now,
Other than when I found her in the
   woods;
And tho' she hath me bounden but in
   spite,
And all to flout me, when they bring
   me in,
Let me be bounden, I shall see her
   face;
Else must I die thro' mine unhappiness."

And Gawain answer'd kindly tho'
in scorn,
"Why, let my lady bind me if she
will,
And let my lady beat me if she will:
But an she send her delegate to thrall
These fighting hands of mine — Christ
kill me then
But I will slice him handless by the
wrist,
And let my lady sear the stump for
him,
Howl as he may. But hold me for
your friend :
Come, ye know nothing : here I pledge
my troth,
Yea, by the honor of the Table Round,
I will be leal to thee and work thy
work,
And tame thy jailing princess to
thine hand.
Lend me thine horse and arms, and I
will say
That I have slain thee. She will let
me in
To hear the manner of thy fight and
fall ;
Then, when I come within her coun-
sels, then
From prime to vespers will I chant
thy praise
As prowest knight and truest lover,
more
Than any have sung thee living, till
she long
To have thee back in lusty life again,
Not to be bound, save by white bonds
and warm,
Dearer than freedom. Wherefore now
thy horse
And armor : let me go : be comforted :
Give me three days to melt her fancy,
and hope
The third night hence will bring thee
news of gold."

Then Pelleas lent his horse and all
his arms,
Saving the goodly sword, his prize,
and took
Gawain's, and said, " Betray me not,
but help —

Art thou not he whom men call light-
of-love ? "

" Ay," said Gawain, " for women be
so light."
Then bounded forward to the castle
walls,
And raised a bugle hanging from his
neck,
And winded it, and that so musically
That all the old echoes hidden in the
wall
Rang out like hollow woods at hunt-
ing-tide.

Up ran a score of damsels to the
tower ;
" Avaunt," they cried, " our lady loves
thee not."
But Gawain lifting up his vizor said,
" Gawain am I, Gawain of Arthur's
court,
And I have slain this Pelleas whom
ye hate:
Behold his horse and armor. Open
gates,
And I will make you merry."

And down they ran,
Her damsels, crying to their lady,
" Lo !
Pelleas is dead — he told us — he that
hath
His horse and armor : will ye let him
in ?
He slew him ! Gawain, Gawain of the
court,
Sir Gawain — there he waits below the
wall,
Blowing his bugle as who should say
him nay."

And so, leave given, straight on
thro' open door
Rode Gawain, whom she greeted courteously.
" Dead, is it so ? " she ask'd. " Ay,
ay," said he,
" And oft in dying cried upon your
name."
" Pity on him," she answer'd, " a good
knight,

But never let me bide one hour at
    peace."
" Ay," thought Gawain, " and you be
    fair enow :
But I to your dead man have given
    my troth,
That whom ye loathe, him will I make
    you love."

    So those three days, aimless about
      the land,
Lost in a doubt, Pelleas wandering
Waited, until the third night brought
    a moon
With promise of large light on woods
    and ways.

    Hot was the night and silent ; but a
      sound
Of Gawain ever coming, and this
    lay —
Which Pelleas had heard sung before
    the Queen,
And seen her sadden listening — vext
    his heart,
And marr'd his rest — " A worm
    within the rose."

    " A rose, but one, none other rose
      had I,
A rose, one rose, and this was won-
    drous fair,
One rose, a rose that gladden'd earth
    and sky,
One rose, my rose, that sweeten'd all
    mine air —
I cared not for the thorns ; the thorns
    were there.

    " One rose, a rose to gather by and
      by,
One rose, a rose, to gather and to
    wear,
No rose but one — what other rose
    had I ?
One rose, my rose ; a rose that will
    not die, —
He dies who loves it, — if the worm
    be there."

    This tender rhyme, and evermore
    the doubt,

" Why lingers Gawain with his golden
    news ? "
So shook him that he could not rest,
    but rode
Ere midnight to her walls, and bound
    his horse
Hard by the gates.   Wide open were
    the gates,
And no watch kept; and in thro'
    these he past,
And heard but his own steps, and his
    own heart
Beating, for nothing moved but his
    own self,
And his own shadow.   Then he crost
    the court,
And spied not any light in hall or
    bower,
But saw the postern portal also wide
Yawning ; and up a slope of garden, all
Of roses white and red, and brambles
    mixt
And overgrowing them, went on, and
    found,
Here too, all hush'd below the mellow
    moon,
Save that one rivulet from a tiny cave
Came lightening downward, and so
    spilt itself
Among the roses, and was lost again.

    Then was he ware of three pavil-
    ions rear'd
Above the bushes, gilden-peakt : in one,
Red after revel, droned her lurdane
    knights
Slumbering, and their three squires
    across their feet :
In one, their malice on the placid lip
Froz'n by sweet sleep, four of her
    damsels lay :
And in the third, the circlet of the
    jousts
Bound on her brow, were Gawain and
    Ettarre.

    Back, as a hand that pushes thro
    the leaf
To find a nest and feels a snake, he
    drew :
Back, as a coward slinks from what
    he fears

To cope with, or a traitor proven, or
    hound
Beaten, did Pelleas in an utter shame
Creep with his shadow thro' the court
    again,
Fingering at his sword-handle until he
    stood
There on the castle-bridge once more,
    and thought,
" I will go back, and slay them where
    they lie."

    And so went back, and seeing them
    yet in sleep
Said, " Ye, that so dishallow the holy
    sleep,
Your sleep is death," and drew the
    sword, and thought,
" What ! slay a sleeping knight? the
    King hath bound
And sworn me to this brotherhood ; "
    again,
" Alas that ever a knight should be
    so false."
Then turn'd, and so return'd, and
    groaning laid
The naked sword athwart their naked
    throats,
There left it, and them sleeping ; and
    she lay,
The circlet of the tourney round her
    brows,
And the sword of the tourney across her
    throat.

    And forth he past, and mounting
    on his horse
Stared at his towers that, larger than
    themselves
In their own darkness, throng'd into
    the moon.
Then crush'd the saddle with his
    thighs, and clench'd
His hands, and madden'd with himself
    and moan'd :

    " Would they have risen against
    me in their blood
At the last day ? I might have an-
    swer'd them
Even before high God. O towers so
    strong,

Huge, solid, would that even while I
    gaze
The crack of earthquake shivering to
    your base
Split you, and Hell burst up your
    harlot roofs
Bellowing, and charr'd you thro' and
    thro' within,
Black as the harlot's heart — hollow
    as a skull !
Let the fierce east scream thro' your
    eyelet-holes,
And whirl the dust of harlots round
    and round
In dung and nettles ! hiss, snake — I
    saw him there —
Let the fox bark, let the wolf yell.
    Who yells
Here in the still sweet summer night,
    but I —
I, the poor Pelleas whom she call'd
    her fool ?
Fool, beast — he, she, or I ? myself
    most fool ;
Beast too, as lacking human wit —
    disgraced,
Dishonor'd all for trial of true love —
Love ? — we be all alike : only the
    King
Hath made us fools and liars. O
    noble vows !
O great and sane and simple race of
    brutes
That own no lust because they have
    no law !
For why should I have loved her to
    my shame ?
I loathe her, as I loved her to my
    shame.
I never loved her, I but lusted for her —
Away — "

    He dash'd the rowel into his
    horse,
And bounded forth and vanish'd thro'
    the night.

    Then she, that felt the cold touch
    on her throat,
Awaking knew the sword, and turn'd
    herself

To Gawain: "Liar, for thou hast not slain
This Pelleas! here he stood, and might have slain
Me and thyself." And he that tells the tale
Says that her ever-veering fancy turn'd
To Pelleas, as the one true knight on earth,
And only lover; and thro' her love her life
Wasted and pined, desiring him in vain.

But he by wild and way, for half the night,
And over hard and soft, striking the sod
From out the soft, the spark from off the hard,
Rode till the star above the wakening sun,
Beside that tower where Percivale was cowl'd,
Glanced from the rosy forehead of the dawn.
For so the words were flash'd into his heart
He knew not whence or wherefore: "O sweet star,
Pure on the virgin forehead of the dawn!"
And there he would have wept, but felt his eyes
Harder and drier than a fountain bed
In summer: thither came the village girls
And linger'd talking, and they come no more
Till the sweet heavens have fill'd it from the heights
Again with living waters in the change
Of seasons: hard his eyes; harder his heart
Seem'd; but so weary were his limbs, that he,
Gasping, "Of Arthur's hall am I, but here,
Here let me rest and die," cast himself down,
And gulf'd his griefs in inmost sleep; so lay,

Till shaken by a dream, that Gawain fired
The hall of Merlin, and the morning star
Reel'd in the smoke, brake into flame, and fell.

He woke, and being ware of some one nigh,
Sent hands upon him, as to tear him, crying,
"False! and I held thee pure as Guinevere."

But Percivale stood near him and replied
"Am I but false as Guinevere is pure?
Or art thou mazed with dreams? or being one
Of our free-spoken Table hast not heard
That Lancelot"—there he check'd himself and paused.

Then fared it with Sir Pelleas as with one
Who gets a wound in battle, and the sword
That made it plunges thro' the wound again,
And pricks it deeper: and he shrank and wail'd,
"Is the Queen false?" and Percivale was mute.
"Have any of our Round Table held their vows?"
And Percivale made answer not a word.
"Is the King true?" "The King!" said Percivale.
"Why then let men couple at once with wolves.
What! art thou mad?

But Pelleas, leaping up,
Ran thro' the doors and vaulted on his horse
And fled: small pity upon his horse had he,
Or on himself, or any, and when he met

A cripple, one that held a hand for
alms —
Hunch'd as he was, and like an old
dwarf-elm
That turns its back on the salt blast,
the boy
Paused not, but overrode him, shouting, "False,
And false with Gawain!" and so left
him bruised
And batter'd, and fled on, and hill
and wood
Went ever streaming by him till the
gloom,
That follows on the turning of the
world,
Darken'd the common path: he
twitch'd the reins,
And made his beast that better knew
it, swerve
Now off it and now on; but when he
saw
High up in heaven the hall that Merlin built,
Blackening against the dead-green
stripes of even,
"Black nest of rats," he groan'd, "ye
build too high."

Not long thereafter from the city
gates
Issued Sir Lancelot riding airily,
Warm with a gracious parting from
the Queen,
Peace at his heart, and gazing at a
star
And marvelling what it was: on
whom the boy,
Across the silent seeded meadow-
grass
Borne, clash'd: and Lancelot, saying,
"What name hast thou
That ridest here so blindly and so
hard?"
"I have no name," he shouted, "a
scourge am I,
To lash the treasons of the Table
Round."
"Yea, but thy name?" "I have
many names," he cried:
"I am wrath and shame and hate
and evil fame,

And like a poisonous wind I pass to
blast
And blaze the crime of Lancelot and
the Queen."
"First over me," said Lancelot, "shalt
thou pass."
"Fight therefore," yell'd the other,
and either knight
Drew back a space, and when they
closed, at once
The weary steed of Pelleas floundering flung
His rider, who call'd out from the
dark field,
"Thou art false as Hell: slay me: I
have no sword."
Then Lancelot, "Yea, between thy
lips — and sharp;
But here will I disedge it by thy
death."
"Slay then," he shriek'd, "my will is
to be slain,"
And Lancelot, with his heel upon the
fall'n,
Rolling his eyes, a moment stood,
then spake:
"Rise, weakling; I am Lancelot; say
thy say."

And Lancelot slowly rode his war-
horse back
To Camelot, and Sir Pelleas in brief
while
Caught his unbroken limbs from the
dark field,
And follow'd to the city. It chanced
that both
Brake into hall together, worn and
pale.
There with her knights and dames
was Guinevere.
Full wonderingly she gazed on Lance-
lot
So soon return'd, and then on Pelleas,
him
Who had not greeted her, but cast
himself
Down on a bench, hard-breathing.
"Have ye fought?"
She ask'd of Lancelot. "Ay, my
Queen," he said.

"And thou hast overthrown him?"
  "Ay, my Queen."
Then she, turning to Pelleas, "O
    young knight,
Hath the great heart of knighthood
    in thee fail'd
So far thou canst not bide, unfro-
    wardly,
A fall from him?" Then, for he
    answer'd not,
"Or hast thou other griefs? If I,
    the Queen,
May help them, loose thy tongue, and
    let me know."
But Pelleas lifted up an eye so fierce
She quail'd; and he, hissing "I have
    no sword,"
Sprang from the door into the dark.
    The Queen
Look'd hard upon her lover, he on
    her;
And each foresaw the dolorous day
    to be:
And all talk died, as in a grove all
    song
Beneath the shadow of some bird of
    prey;
Then a long silence came upon the
    hall,
And Modred thought, "The time is
    hard at hand."

THE LAST TOURNAMENT.

DAGONET, the fool, whom Gawain in
    his mood
Had made mock-knight of Arthur's
    Table Round,
At Camelot, high above the yellow-
    ing woods,
Danced like a wither'd leaf before the
    hall.
And toward him from the hall, with
    harp in hand,
And from the crown thereof a car-
    canet
Of ruby swaying to and fro, the prize
Of Tristram in the jousts of yesterday,
Came Tristram, saying, "Why skip
    ye so, Sir Fool?"

For Arthur and Sir Lancelot riding
    once
Far down beneath a winding wall of
    rock
Heard a child wail. A stump of oak
    half dead,
From roots like some black coil of
    carven snakes,
Clutch'd at the crag, and started thro'
    mid air
Bearing an eagle's nest: and thro'
    the tree
Rush'd ever a rainy wind, and thro'
    the wind
Pierced ever a child's cry: and crag
    and tree
Scaling, Sir Lancelot from the peril-
    ous nest,
This ruby necklace thrice around her
    neck,
And all unscarr'd from beak or talon,
    brought
A maiden babe; which Arthur pity-
    ing took,
Then gave it to his Queen to rear:
    the Queen
But coldly acquiescing, in her white
    arms
Received, and after loved it tenderly,
And named it Nestling; so forgot
    herself
A moment, and her cares; till that
    young life
Being smitten in mid heaven with
    mortal cold
Past from her; and in time the carcanet
Vext her with plaintive memories of
    the child:
So she, delivering it to Arthur, said
"Take thou the jewels of this dead
    innocence,
And make them, an thou wilt, a tour-
    ney-prize."

To whom the King, "Peace to thine
    eagle-borne
Dead nestling, and this honor after
    death,
Following thy will! but, O my Queen,
    I muse
Why ye not wear on arm, or neck, or
    zone

Those diamonds that I rescued from
the tarn,
And Lancelot won, methought, for
thee to wear."

"Would rather you had let them
fall," she cried,
"Plunge and be lost — ill-fated as
they were,
A bitterness to me! — ye look amazed,
Not knowing they were lost as soon
as given —
Slid from my hands, when I was lean-
ing out
Above the river — that unhappy child
Past in her barge : but rosier luck
will go
With these rich jewels, seeing that
they came
Not from the skeleton of a brother-
slayer,
But the sweet body of a maiden babe.
Perchance — who knows ? — the pur-
est of thy knights
May win them for the purest of my
maids."

She ended, and the cry of a great
jousts
With trumpet-blowings ran on all the
ways
From Camelot in among the faded
fields
To furthest towers ; and everywhere
the knights
Arm'd for a day of glory before the
King.

But on the hither side of that loud
morn
Into the hall stagger'd, his visage
ribb'd
From ear to ear with dogwhip-weals,
his nose
Bridge-broken, one eye out, and one
hand off,
And one with shatter'd fingers dan-
gling lame,
A churl, to whom indignantly the
King.

"My churl, for whom Christ died,
what evil beast
Hath drawn his claws athwart thy
face ? or fiend ?
Man was it who marr'd heaven's
image in thee thus ? "

Then, sputtering thro' the hedge of
splinter'd teeth,
Yet strangers to the tongue, and with
blunt stump
Pitch-blacken'd sawing the air, said
the maim'd churl,

"He took them and he drave them
to his tower —
Some hold he was a table-knight of
thine —
A hundred goodly ones — the Red
Knight, he —
Lord, I was tending swine, and the
Red Knight
Brake in upon me and drave them to
his tower ;
And when I call'd upon thy name as
one
That doest right by gentle and by
churl,
Maim'd me and maul'd, and would
outright have slain,
Save that he sware me to a message,
saying,
'Tell thou the King and all his liars,
that I
Have founded my Round Table in
the North,
And whatsoever his own knights have
sworn
My knights have sworn the counter
to it — and say
My tower is full of harlots, like his
court,
But mine are worthier, seeing they
profess
To be none other than themselves —
and say
My knights are all adulterers like his
own,
But mine are truer, seeing they profess
To be none other ; and say his hour is
come,

The heathen are upon him, his long
    lance
Broken, and his Excalibur a straw.' "

Then Arthur turned to Kay the
    seneschal,
"Take thou my churl, and tend him
    curiously
Like a king's heir, till all his hurts be
    whole.
The heathen — but that ever-climbing
    wave,
Hurl'd back again so often in empty
    foam,
Hath lain for years at rest — and
    renegades,
Thieves, bandits, leavings of confu-
    sion, whom
The wholesome realm is purged of
    otherwhere,
Friends, thro' your manhood and your
    fëalty, — now
Make their last head like Satan in
    the North.
My younger knights, new-made, in
    whom your flower
Waits to be solid fruit of golden
    deeds,
Move with me toward their quelling,
    which achieved,
The loneliest ways are safe from
    shore to shore.
But thou, Sir Lancelot, sitting in my
    place
Enchair'd to-morrow, arbitrate the
    field;
For wherefore shouldst thou care to
    mingle with it,
Only to yield my Queen her own
    again?
Speak, Lancelot, thou art silent: is it
    well? "

Thereto Sir Lancelot answer'd, "It
    is well:
Yet better if the King abide, and
    leave
The leading of his younger knights
    to me.
Else, for the King has will'd it, it is
    well."

Then Arthur rose and Lancelot fol-
    low'd him,
And while they stood without the
    doors, the King
Turn'd to him saying, " Is it then so
    well?
Or mine the blame that oft I seem as he
Of whom was written, 'A sound is in
    his ears' ?
The foot that loiters, bidden go, — the
    glance
That only seems half-loyal to com-
    mand, —
A manner somewhat fall'n from rev-
    erence —
Or have I dream'd the bearing of our
    knights
Tells of a manhood ever less and
    lower?
Or whence the fear lest this my
    realm, uprear'd,
By noble deeds at one with noble vows,
From flat confusion and brute vio-
    lences,
Reel back into the beast, and be no
    more? "

He spoke, and taking all his younger
    knights,
Down the slope city rode, and sharply
    turn'd
North by the gate.   In her high bower
    the Queen,
Working a tapestry, lifted up her
    head,
Watch'd her lord pass, and knew not
    that she sigh'd.
Then ran across her memory the
    strange rhyme
Of bygone Merlin, " Where is he who
    knows?
From the great deep to the great
    deep he goes."

But when the morning of a tourna-
    ment,
By these in earnest those in mockery
    call'd
The Tournament of the Dead Inno-
    cence,
Brake with a wet wind blowing, Lan-
    celot,

Round whose sick head all night, like
  birds of prey,
The words of Arthur flying shriek'd,
  arose,
And down a streetway hung with folds
  of pure
White samite, and by fountains running wine,
Where children sat in white with cups
  of gold,
Moved to the lists, and there, with slow
  sad steps
Ascending, fill'd his double-dragon'd
  chair.

He glanced and saw the stately galleries,
Dame, damsel, each thro' worship of
  their Queen
White-robed in honor of the stainless
  child,
And some with scatter'd jewels, like
  a bank
Of maiden snow mingled with sparks
  of fire.
He look'd but once, and vail'd his
  eyes again.

The sudden trumpet sounded as in
  a dream
To ears but half-awaked, then one low
  roll
Of Autumn thunder, and the jousts
  began:
And ever the wind blew, and yellowing leaf
And gloom and gleam, and shower
  and shorn plume
Went down it. Sighing weariedly, as
  one
Who sits and gazes on a faded fire,
When all the goodlier guests are past
  away,
Sat their great umpire, looking o'er
  the lists.
He saw the laws that ruled the
  tournament
Broken, but spake not; once, a knight
  cast down
Before his throne of arbitration
  cursed

The dead babe and the follies of the
  King;
And once the laces of a helmet crack'd,
And show'd him, like a vermin in its
  hole,
Modred, a narrow face: anon he heard
The voice that billow'd round the
  barriers roar
An ocean-sounding welcome to one
  knight,
But newly-enter'd, taller than the rest,
And armor'd all in forest green,
  whereon
There tript a hundred tiny silver deer,
And wearing but a holly-spray for
  crest,
With ever-scattering berries, and on
  shield
A spear, a harp, a bugle — Tristram
  — late
From overseas in Brittany return'd,
And marriage with a princess of that
  realm,
Isolt the White — Sir Tristram of the
  Woods —
Whom Lancelot knew, had held some-
  time with pain
His own against him, and now yearn'd
  to shake
The burden off his heart in one full
  shock
With Tristram ev'n to death: his
  strong hands gript
And dinted the gilt dragons right and
  left,
Until he groan'd for wrath — so many
  of those,
That ware their ladies' colors on the
  casque,
Drew from before Sir Tristram to the
  bounds,
And there with gibes and flickering
  mockeries
Stood, while he mutter'd, "Craven
  crests! O shame!
What faith have these in whom they
  sware to love?
The glory of our Round Table is no
  more."

So Tristram won, and Lancelot
  gave, the gems,

Not speaking other word than " Hast
　　thou won ?
Art thou the purest, brother ?　See,
　　the hand
Wherewith thou takest this, is red ! "
　　to whom
Tristram, half plagued by Lancelot's
　　languorous mood,
Made answer, " Ay, but wherefore toss
　　me this
Like a dry bone cast to some hungry
　　hound ?
Let be thy fair Queen's fantasy.
　　Strength of heart
And might of limb, but mainly use
　　and skill,
Are winners in this pastime of our
　　King.
My hand — belike the lance hath dript
　　upon it —
No blood of mine, I trow ; but O chief
　　knight,
Right arm of Arthur in the battlefield,
Great brother, thou nor I have made
　　the world ;
Be happy in thy fair Queen as I in
　　mine."

And Tristram round the gallery
　　made his horse
Caracole ; then bow'd his homage,
　　bluntly saying,
" Fair damsels, each to him who wor-
　　ships each
Sole Queen of Beauty and of love,
　　behold
This day my Queen of Beauty is not
　　here."
And most of these were mute, some
　　anger'd, one,
Murmuring, " All courtesy is dead,"
　　and one,
" The glory of our Round Table is no
　　more."

Then fell thick rain, plume droopt
　　and mantle clung,
And pettish cries awoke, and the wan
　　day
Went glooming down in wet and
　　weariness :

But under her black brows a swarthy
　　one
Laugh'd shrilly, crying, " Praise the
　　patient saints,
Our one white day of Innocence hath
　　past,
Tho' somewhat draggled at the skirt.
　　So be it.
The snowdrop only, flowering thro' the
　　year,
Would make the world as blank as
　　Winter-tide.
Come — let us gladden their sad eyes,
　　our Queen's
And Lancelot's at this night's solemnity
With all the kindlier colors of the
　　field."

So dame and damsel glitter'd at the
　　feast
Variously gay : for he that tells the
　　tale
Liken'd them, saying, as when an hour
　　of cold
Falls on the mountain in midsummer
　　snows,
And all the purple slopes of mountain
　　flowers
Pass under white, till the warm hour
　　returns
With veer of wind, and all are flowers
　　again ;
So dame and damsel cast the simple
　　white,
And glowing in all colors, the live
　　grass,
Rose-campion, bluebell, kingcup, pop-
　　py, glanced
About the revels, and with mirth so
　　loud
Beyond all use, that, half-amazed,
　　the Queen,
And wroth at Tristram and the law-
　　less jousts,
Brake up their sports, then slowly to
　　her bower
Parted, and in her bosom pain was lord.

And little Dagonet on the morrow
　　morn,
High over all the yellowing Autumn-
　　tide,

Danced like a wither'd leaf before the hall.
Then Tristram saying, " Why skip ye so, Sir Fool ? "
Wheel'd round on either heel, Dagonet replied,
" Belike for lack of wiser company ;
Or being fool, and seeing too much wit
Makes the world rotten, why, belike I skip
To know myself the wisest knight of all."
" Ay, fool," said Tristram, but 'tis eating dry
To dance without a catch, a roundelay
To dance to." Then he twangled on his harp,
And while he twangled little Dagonet stood
Quiet as any water-sodden log
Stay'd in the wandering warble of a brook ;
But when the twangling ended, skipt again ;
And being ask'd, " Why skip ye not, Sir Fool ? "
Made answer, " I had liefer twenty years
Skip to the broken music of my brains
Than any broken music thou canst make."
Then Tristram, waiting for the quip to come,
" Good now, what music have I broken, fool ? "
And little Dagonet, skipping, "Arthur, the King's ;
For when thou playest that air with Queen Isolt,
Thou makest broken music with thy bride,
Her daintier namesake down in Brittany —
And so thou breakest Arthur's music too."
" Save for that broken music in thy brains,
Sir Fool," said Tristram, " I would break thy head.
Fool, I came late, the heathen wars were o'er,

The life had flown, we sware but by the shell —
I am but a fool to reason with a fool —
Come, thou art crabb'd and sour : but lean me down,
Sir Dagonet, one of thy long asses' ears,
And harken if my music be not true.

" ' Free love — free field — we love but while we may :
The woods are hush'd, their music is no more :
The leaf is dead, the yearning past away :
New leaf, new life — the days of frost are o'er :
New life, new love, to suit the newer day :
New loves are sweet as those that went before :
Free love — free field — we love but while we may.'

" Ye might have moved slow-measure to my tune,
Not stood stockstill. I made it in the woods,
And heard it ring as true as tested gold."

But Dagonet with one foot poised in his hand,
" Friend, did ye mark that fountain yesterday
Made to run wine ? — but this had run itself
All out like a long life to a sour end —
And them that round it sat with golden cups
To hand the wine to whosoever came —
The twelve small damosels white as Innocence,
In honor of poor Innocence the babe,
Who left the gems which Innocence the Queen
Lent to the King, and Innocence the King
Gave for a prize — and one of those white slips

Handed her cup and piped, the pretty
     one,
'Drink, drink, Sir Fool,' and there-
     upon I drank,
Spat—pish—the cup was gold, the
     draught was mud."

And Tristram, "Was it muddier than
     thy gibes?
Is all the laughter gone dead out of
     thee?—
Not marking how the knighthood
     mock thee, fool—
'Fear God: honor the King—his
     one true knight—
Sole follower of the vows'—for here
     be they
Who knew thee swine enow before I
     came,
Smuttier than blasted grain: but
     when the King
Had made thee fool, thy vanity so
     shot up
It frighted all free fool from out
     thy heart;
Which left thee less than fool, and less
     than swine,
A naked aught—yet swine I hold
     thee still,
For I have flung thee pearls and find
     thee swine."

And little Dagonet mincing with his
     feet,
"Knight, an ye fling those rubies
     round my neck
In lieu of hers, I'll hold thou hast
     some touch
Of music, since I care not for thy
     pearls.
Swine? I have wallow'd, I have
     wash'd—the world
Is flesh and shadow—I have had my
     day.
The dirty nurse, Experience, in her
     kind
Hath foul'd me—an I wallow'd, then
     I wash'd—
I have had my day and my philoso-
     phies—
And thank the Lord I am King Ar-
     thur's fool.

Swine, say ye? swine, goats, asses,
     rams and geese
Troop'd round a Paynim harper once,
     who thrumm'd
On such a wire as musically as thou
Some such fine song—but never a
     king's fool."

And Tristram, "Then were swine,
     goats, asses, geese
The wiser fools, seeing thy Paynim
     bard
Had such a mastery of his mystery
That he could harp his wife up out
     of hell."

Then Dagonet, turning on the ball
     of his foot,
"And whither harp'st thou thine?
     down! and thyself
Down! and two more: a helpful harp-
     er thou,
That harpest downward! Dost thou
     know the star
We call the harp of Arthur up in
     heaven?"

And Tristram, "Ay, Sir Fool, for
     when our King
Was victor wellnigh day by day, the
     knights,
Glorying in each new glory, set his
     name
High on hills, and in the signs of
     heaven."

And Dagonet answer'd, "Ay, and
     when the land
Was freed, and the Queen false, ye
     set yourself
To babble about him, all to show your
     wit—
And whether he were King by cour-
     tesy,
Or King by right—and so went harp-
     ing down
The black king's highway, got so far,
     and grew
So witty that ye play'd at ducks and
     drakes
With Arthur's vows on the great lake
     of fire.

Tuwhoo! do ye see it? do ye see the
   star?

"Nay, fool," said Tristram, "not in
   open day."
And Dagonet, "Nay, nor will: I see
   it and hear.
It makes a silent music up in heaven,
And I, and Arthur and the angels
   hear,
And then we skip." "Lo, fool," he
   said, "ye talk
Fool's treason: is the King thy brother
   fool?"
Then little Dagonet clapt his hands
   and shrill'd,
"Ay, ay, my brother fool, the king of
   fools!
Conceits himself as God that he can
   make
Figs out of thistles, silk from bristles,
   milk
From burning spurge, honey from hor-
   net-combs,
And men from beasts — Long live the
   king of fools!"

And down the city Dagonet danced
   away;
But thro' the slowly-mellowing ave-
   nues
And solitary passes of the wood
Rode Tristram toward Lyonnesse and
   the west.
Before him fled the face of Queen Isolt
With ruby-circled neck, but evermore
Past, as a rustle or twitter in the wood
Made dull his inner, keen his outer eye
For all that walk'd, or crept, or
   perch'd, or flew.
Anon the face, as, when a gust hath
   blown,
Unruffling waters re-collect the shape
Of one that in them sees himself, re-
   turn'd;
But at the slot or fewmets of a deer,
Or ev'n a fall'n feather, vanish'd again.

So on for all that day from lawn to
   lawn
Thro' many a league-long bower he
   rode. At length

A lodge of intertwisted beechen-
   boughs
Furze-cramm'd, and bracken-rooft, the
   which himself
Built for a summer day with Queen
   Isolt
Against a shower, dark in the golden
   grove
Appearing, sent his fancy back to
   where
She lived a moon in that low lodge
   with him:
Till Mark her lord had past, the Corn-
   ish King,
With six or seven, when Tristram was
   away,
And snatch'd her thence; yet dread-
   ing worse than shame
Her warrior Tristram, spake not any
   word,
But bode his hour, devising wretched-
   ness.

And now that desert lodge to Tris-
   tram lookt
So sweet, that halting, in he past, and
   sank
Down on a drift of foliage random
   blown;
But could not rest for musing how to
   smoothe
And sleek his marriage over to the
   Queen.
Perchance in lone Tintagil far from
   all
The tonguesters of the court she had
   not heard.
But then what folly had sent him over-
   seas
After she left him lonely here? a
   name?
Was it the name of one in Brittany,
Isolt, the daughter of the King?
   "Isolt
Of the white hands" they call'd her:
   the sweet name
Allured him first, and then the maid
   herself,
Who served him well with those white
   hands of hers,
And loved him well, until himself had
   thought

He loved her also, wedded easily,
But left her all as easily and return'd.
The black-blue Irish hair and Irish eyes
Had drawn him home — what marvel? then he laid
His brows upon the drifted leaf and dream'd.

He seem'd to pace the strand of Brittany
Between Isolt of Britain and his bride,
And show'd them both the ruby-chain, and both
Began to struggle for it, till his Queen
Graspt it so hard, that all her hand was red.
Then cried the Breton, "Look, her hand is red!
These be no rubies, this is frozen blood,
And melts within her hand — her hand is hot
With ill desires, but this I gave thee, look,
Is all as cool and white as any flower."
Follow'd a rush of eagle's wings, and then
A whimpering of the spirit of the child,
Because the twain had spoiled her carcanet.

He dream'd; but Arthur with a hundred spears
Rode far, till o'er the illimitable reed,
And many a glancing plash and sallowy isle,
The wide-wing'd sunset of the misty marsh
Glared on a huge machicolated tower
That stood with open doors, whereout was roll'd
A roar of riot, as from men secure
Amid their marshes, ruffians at their ease
Among their harlot-brides, an evil song.
"Lo there," said one of Arthur's youth, for there,

High on a grim dead tree before the tower,
A goodly brother of the Table Round
Swung by the neck: and on the boughs a shield
Showing a shower of blood in a field noir,
And there beside a horn, inflamed the knights
At that dishonor done the gilded spur,
Till each would clash the shield, and blow the horn.
But Arthur waved them back. Alone he rode.
Then at the dry harsh roar of the great horn,
That sent the face of all the marsh aloft
An ever upward-rushing storm and cloud
Of shriek and plume, the Red Knight heard, and all,
Even to tipmost lance and topmost helm,
In blood-red armor sallying, howl'd to the King,

"The teeth of Hell flay bare and gnash thee flat! —
Lo! art thou not that eunuch-hearted King
Who fain had clipt free manhood from the world —
The woman-worshipper? Yea, God's curse, and I!
Slain was the brother of my paramour
By a knight of thine, and I that heard her whine
And snivel, being eunuch-hearted too,
Sware by the scorpion-worm that twists in hell,
And stings itself to everlasting death,
To hang whatever knight of thine I fought
And tumbled. Art thou King? — Look to thy life!"

He ended: Arthur knew the voice; the face
Wellnigh was helmet-hidden, and the name

Went wandering somewhere darkling
    in his mind.
And Arthur deign'd not use of word
    or sword,
But let the drunkard, as he stretch'd
    from horse
To strike him, overbalancing his
    bulk,
Down from the causeway heavily to
    the swamp
Fall, as the crest of some slow-arching
    wave,
Heard in dead night along that table-
    shore,
Drops flat, and after the great waters
    break
Whitening for half a league, and thin
    themselves,
Far over sands marbled with moon
    and cloud,
From less and less to nothing; thus
    he fell
Head-heavy; then the knights, who
    watch'd him, roar'd
And shouted and leapt down upon the
    fall'n ;
There trampled out his face from
    being known,
And sank his head in mire, and slimed
    themselves :
Nor heard the King for their own
    cries, but sprang
Thro' open doors, and swording right
    and left
Men, women, on their sodden faces,
    hurl'd
The tables over and the wines, and
    slew
Till all the rafters rang with woman-
    yells,
And all the pavement stream'd with
    massacre :
Then, yell with yell echoing, they
    fired the tower,
Which half that autumn night, like
    the live North,
Red-pulsing up thro' Alioth and
    Alcor,
Made all above it, and a hundred
    meres
About it, as the water Moab
    saw

Come round by the East, and out be-
    yond them flush'd
The long low dune, and lazy-plunging
    sea.

So all the ways were safe from
    shore to shore,
But in the heart of Arthur pain was
    lord.

Then, out of Tristram waking, the
    red dream
Fled with a shout, and that low lodge
    return'd,
Mid-forest, and the wind among the
    boughs.
He whistled his good warhorse left to
    graze
Among the forest greens, vaulted
    upon him,
And rode beneath an ever-showering
    leaf,
Till one lone woman, weeping near a
    cross,
Stay'd him. "Why weep ye?"
    "Lord," she said, "my man
Hath left me or is dead;" whereon he
    thought —
"What, if she hate me now? I
    would not this.
"What, if she loves me still? I
    would not that.
I know not what I would"—but said
    to her,
"Yet weep not thou, lest, if thy mate
    return,
He find thy favor changed and love
    thee not" —
Then pressing day by day thro'
    Lyonnesse
Last in a rocky hollow, belling, heard
The hounds of Mark, and felt the
    goodly hounds
Yelp at his heart, but turning, past
    and gain'd
Tintagil, half in sea, and high on
    land,
A crown of towers.

        Down in a casement sat,
A low sea-sunset glorying round her
    hair

And glossy-throated grace, Isolt the
　　Queen.
And when she heard the feet of Tris-
　　tram grind
The spiring stone that scaled about
　　her tower,
Flush'd, started, met him at the doors,
　　and there
Belted his body with her white em-
　　brace,
Crying aloud, "Not Mark — not
　　Mark, my soul !
The footstep flutter'd me at first : not
　　he :
Catlike thro' his own castle steals my
　　Mark,
But warrior-wise thou stridest thro'
　　his halls
Who hates thee, as I him — ev'n to
　　the death.
My soul, I felt my hatred for my
　　Mark
Quicken within me, and knew that
　　thou wert nigh."
To whom Sir Tristram smiling, "I am
　　here.
Let be thy Mark, seeing he is not
　　thine."

　　And drawing somewhat backward
　　she replied,
"Can he be wrong'd who is not ev'n
　　his own,
But save for dread of thee had beaten
　　me,
Scratch'd, bitten, blinded, marr'd me
　　somehow — Mark ?
What rights are his that dare not
　　strike for them ?
Not lift a hand — not, tho' he found
　　me thus !
But hearken ! have ye met him ?
　　hence he went
To-day for three days' hunting — as
　　he said —
And so returns belike within an hour.
Mark's way, my soul ! — but eat not
　　thou with Mark,
Because he hates thee even more than
　　fears ;
Nor drink : and when thou passest
　　any wood

Close vizor, lest an arrow from the
　　bush
Should leave me all alone with Mark
　　and hell.
My God, the measure of my hate for
　　Mark
Is as the measure of my love for
　　thee."

　　So, pluck'd one way by hate and
　　one by love,
Drain'd of her force, again she sat,
　　and spake
To Tristram, as he knelt before her,
　　saying,
"O hunter, and O blower of the horn,
Harper, and thou hast been a rover
　　too,
For, ere I mated with my shambling
　　king,
Ye twain had fallen out about the
　　bride
Of one — his name is out of me — the
　　prize,
If prize she were — (what marvel —
　　she could see) —
Thine, friend ; and ever since my
　　craven seeks
To wreck thee villanously : but, O
　　Sir Knight,
What dame or damsel have ye kneel'd
　　to last ? "

　　And Tristram, "Last to my Queen
　　Paramount,
Here now to my Queen Paramount of
　　love
And loveliness — ay, lovelier than
　　when first
Her light feet fell on our rough Ly-
　　onnesse,
Sailing from Ireland."

　　　　　　　・　　　Softly laugh'd Isolt ;
"Flatter me not, for hath not our great
　　Queen
My dole of beauty trebled ? " and he
　　said,
"Her beauty is her beauty, and thine
　　thine,
And thine is more to me — soft, gra-
　　cious, kind —

Save when thy Mark is kindled on
  thy lips
Most gracious ; but she, haughty, ev'n
  to him,
Lancelot; for I have seen him wan enow
To make one doubt if ever the great
  Queen
Have yielded him her love."

                        To whom Isolt,
" Ah then, false hunter and false harper, thou
Who brakest thro' the scruple of my
  bond,
Calling me thy white hind, and saying to me
That Guinevere had sinn'd against
  the highest,
And I — misyoked with such a want
  of man —
That I could hardly sin against the
  lowest."

He answer'd, " O my soul, be comforted !
If this be sweet, to sin in leading-
  strings,
If here be comfort, and if ours be sin,
Crown'd warrant had we for the
  crowning sin
That made us happy : but how ye
  greet me — fear
And fault and doubt — no word of
  that fond tale —
Thy deep heart-yearnings, thy sweet
  memories
Of Tristram in that year he was
  away."

And, saddening on the sudden, spake
  Isolt,
" I had forgotten all in my strong joy
To see thee — yearnings ? — ay ! for,
  hour by hour,
Here in the never-ended afternoon,
O sweeter than all memories of thee,
Deeper than any yearnings after thee
Seem'd those far-rolling, westward-
  smiling seas,
Watch'd from this tower. Isolt of
  Britain dash'd
Before Isolt of Brittany on the strand,

Would that have chill'd her bride-
  kiss ? Wedded her ?
Fought in her father's battles ?
  wounded there ?
The King was all fulfill'd with grate-
  fulness,
And she, my namesake of the hands,
  that heal'd
Thy hurt and heart with unguent and
  caress —
Well — can I wish her any huger
  wrong
Than having known thee ? her too
  hast thou left
To pine and waste in those sweet
  memories.
O were I not my Mark's, by whom all
  men
Are noble, I should hate thee more
  than love."

And Tristram, fondling her light
  hands, replied,
" Grace, Queen, for being loved : she
  loved me well.
Did I love her ? the name at least I
  loved.
Isolt ? — I fought his battles, for Isolt !
The night was dark ; the true star set.
  Isolt !
The name was ruler of the dark ——
  Isolt ?
Care not for her ! patient, and prayer-
  ful, meek,
Pale-blooded, she will yield herself to
  God."

And Isolt answer'd, " Yea, and why
  not I ?
Mine is the larger need, who am not
  meek,
Pale-blooded, prayerful. Let me tell
  thee now.
Here one black, mute midsummer
  night I sat,
Lonely, but musing on thee, wondering where,
Murmuring a light song I had heard
  thee sing,
And once or twice I spake thy name
  aloud.

Then flash'd a levin-brand; and near
  me stood,
In fuming sulphur blue and green, a
  fiend —
Mark's way to steal behind one in the
  dark —
For there was Mark: 'He has wedded
  her,' he said,
Not said, but hiss'd it: then this crown
  of towers
So shook to such a roar of all the
  sky,
That here in utter dark I swoon'd
  away,
And woke again in utter dark, and
  cried,
'I will flee hence and give myself to
  God' —
And thou wert lying in thy new
  leman's arms."

  Then Tristram, ever dallying with
    her hand,
" May God be with thee, sweet, when
    old and gray,
And past desire!" a saying that
    anger'd her.
" 'May God be with thee, sweet, when
    thou art old,
And sweet no more to me!' I need
    Him now.
For when had Lancelot utter'd aught
    so gross
Ev'n to the swineherd's malkin in the
    mast ?
The greater man, the greater courtesy.
Far other was the Tristram, Arthur's
    knight!
But thou, thro' ever harrying thy
    wild beasts —
Save that to touch a harp, tilt with a
    lance
Becomes thee well — art grown wild
    beast thyself.
How darest thou, if lover, push me
    even
In fancy from thy side, and set me
    far
In the gray distance, half a life away,
Her to be loved no more ? Unsay it,
    unswear!
Flatter me rather, seeing me so weak,

Broken with Mark and hate and soli-
    tude,
Thy marriage and mine own, that I
    should suck
Lies like sweet wines: lie to me: I
    believe.
Will ye not lie ? not swear, as there
    ye kneel,
And solemnly as when ye sware to
    him,
The man of men, our King—My
    God, the power
Was once in vows when men believed
    the King!
They lied not then, who sware, and
    thro' their vows
The King prevailing made his realm:
    —I say,
Swear to me thou wilt love me ev'n
    when old,
Gray-hair'd, and past desire, and in
    despair."

  Then Tristram, pacing moodily up
    and down,
"Vows! did you keep the vow you
    made to Mark
More than I mine ? Lied, say ye ?
    Nay, but learnt,
The vow that binds too strictly snaps
    itself —
My knighthood taught me this — ay,
    being snapt —
We run more counter to the soul
    thereof
Than had we never sworn. I swear
    no more.
I swore to the great King, and am
    forsworn.
For once — ev'n to the height — I
    honor'd him.
' Man, is he man at all ?' methought,
    when first
I rode from our rough Lyonnesse, and
    beheld
That victor of the Pagan throned in
    hall —
His hair, a sun that ray'd from off a
    brow
Like hillsnow high in heaven, the
    steel-blue eyes,

The golden beard that clothed his
    lips with light —
Moreover, that weird legend of his
    birth,
With Merlin's mystic babble about
    his end
Amazed me; then, his foot was on a
    stool
Shaped as a dragon; he seem'd to me
    no man,
But Michaël trampling Satan; so I
    sware,
Being amazed: but this went by —
    The vows!
O ay — the wholesome madness of
    an hour —
They served their use, their time; for
    every knight
Believed himself a greater than him-
    self,
And every follower eyed him as a God;
Till he, being lifted up beyond him-
    self,
Did mightier deeds than elsewise he
    had done,
And so the realm was made; but
    then their vows —
First mainly thro' that sullying of
    our Queen —
Began to gall the knighthood, asking
    whence
Had Arthur right to bind them to
    himself?
Dropt down from heaven? wash'd
    up from out the deep?
They fail'd to trace him thro' the
    flesh and blood
Of our old kings: whence then? a
    doubtful lord
To bind them by inviolable vows,
Which flesh and blood perforce would
    violate:
For feel this arm of mine — the tide
    within
Red with free chase and heather-
    scented air,
Pulsing full man; can Arthur make
    me pure
As any maiden child? lock up my
    tongue
From uttering freely what I freely
    hear?

Bind me to one? The wide world
    laughs at it.
And worldling of the world am I, and
    know
The ptarmigan that whitens ere his
    hour
Woos his own end; we are not angels
    here
Nor shall be: vows — I am woodman
    of the woods,
And hear the garnet-headed yaffingale
Mock them: my soul, we love but
    while we may;
And therefore is my love so large for
    thee,
Seeing it is not bounded save by
    love."

Here ending, he moved toward her,
    and she said,
"Good: an I turn'd away my love for
    thee
To some one thrice as courteous as
    thyself —
For courtesy wins women all as well
As valor may, but he that closes both
Is perfect, he is Lancelot — taller in-
    deed,
Rosier and comelier, thou — but say I
    loved
This knightliest of all knights, and
    cast thee back
Thine own small saw, 'We love but
    while we may,'
Well then, what answer?'

            He that while she spake,
Mindful of what he brought to adorn
    her with,
The jewels, had let one finger lightly
    touch
The warm white apple of her throat,
    replied,
"Press this a little closer, sweet,
    until —
Come, I am hunger'd and half-an-
    ger'd — meat,
Wine, wine — and I will love thee to
    the death,
And out beyond into the dream to
    come."

So then, when both were brought
  to full accord,
She rose, and set before him all he
  will'd;
And after these had comforted the
  blood
With meats and wines, and satiated
  their hearts —
Now talking of their woodland paradise,
The deer, the dews, the fern, the
  founts, the lawns;
Now mocking at the much ungainli-
  ness,
And craven shifts, and long crane
  legs of Mark —
Then Tristram laughing caught the
  harp, and sang:

"Ay, ay, O ay — the winds that
  bend the brier!
A star in heaven, a star within the
  mere!
Ay, ay, O ay — a star was my desire,
And one was far apart, and one was
  near:
Ay, ay, O ay — the winds that bow
  the grass!
And one was water and one star was
  fire,
And one will ever shine and one will
  pass.
Ay, ay, O ay — the winds that move
  the mere."

Then in the light's last glimmer
  Tristram show'd
And swung the ruby carcanet. She
  cried,
"The collar of some Order, which
  our King
Hath newly founded, all for thee, my
  soul,
For thee, to yield thee grace beyond
  thy peers."

"Not so, my Queen," he said, "but
  the red fruit
Grown on a magic oak-tree in mid-
  heaven,
And won by Tristram as a tourney-
  prize,

And hither brought by Tristram for
  his last
Love-offering and peace-offering unto
  thee."

He spoke, he turn'd, then, flinging
  round her neck,
Claspt it, and cried "Thine Order, O
  my Queen!"
But, while he bow'd to kiss the jewell'd throat,
Out of the dark, just as the lips had
  touch'd,
Behind him rose a shadow and a
  shriek —
"Mark's way," said Mark, and clove
  him thro' the brain.

That night came Arthur home, and
  while he climb'd,
All in a death-dumb autumn-drip-
  ping gloom,
The stairway to the hall, and look'd
  and saw
The great Queen's bower was dark, —
  about his feet
A voice clung sobbing till he question'd it,
"What art thou?" and the voice
  about his feet
Sent up an answer, sobbing, "I am
  thy fool,
And I shall never make thee smile
  again."

GUINEVERE.

QUEEN GUINEVERE had fled the court,
  and sat
There in the holy house at Almesbury
Weeping, none with her save a little
  maid,
A novice: one low light betwixt them
  burn'd
Blurr'd by the creeping mist, for all
  abroad,
Beneath a moon unseen albeit at full,
The white mist, like a face-cloth to
  the face,
Clung to the dead earth, and the land
  was still.

For hither had she fled, her cause
  of flight
Sir Modred; he that like a subtle
  beast
Lay couchant with his eyes upon the
  throne,
Ready to spring, waiting a chance:
  for this
He chill'd the popular praises of the
  King
With silent smiles of slow disparage-
  ment;
And tamper'd with the Lords of the
  White Horse,
Heathen, the brood by Hengist left;
  and sought
To make disruption in the Table Round
Of Arthur, and to splinter it into feuds
Serving his traitorous end; and all
  his aims
Were sharpen'd by strong hate for
  Lancelot.

For thus it chanced one morn when
  all the court,
Green-suited, but with plumes that
  mock'd the may,
Had been, their wont, a-maying and
  return'd,
That Modred still in green, all ear
  and eye,
Climb'd to the high top of the garden-
  wall
To spy some secret scandal if he might,
And saw the Queen who sat betwixt
  her best
Enid, and lissome Vivien, of her court
The wiliest and the worst; and more
  than this
He saw not, for Sir Lancelot passing
  by
Spied where he crouch'd, and as the
  gardener's hand
Picks from the colewort a green cater-
  pillar,
So from the high wall and the flower-
  ing grove
Of grasses Lancelot pluck'd him by
  the heel,
And cast him as a worm upon the way;
But when he knew the Prince tho'
  marr'd with dust,

He, reverencing king's blood in a bad
  man,
Made such excuses as he might, and
  these
Full knightly without scorn; for in
  those days
No knight of Arthur's noblest dealt
  in scorn;
But, if a man were halt or hunch'd,
  in him
By those whom God had made full-
  limb'd and tall,
Scorn was allow'd as part of his defect,
And he was answer'd softly by the King
And all his Table. So Sir Lancelot
  holp
To raise the Prince, who rising twice
  or thrice
Full sharply smote his knees, and
  smiled, and went:
But, ever after, the small violence done
Rankled in him and ruffled all his heart,
As the sharp wind that ruffles all day
  long
A little bitter pool about a stone
On the bare coast.

    But when Sir Lancelot told
This matter to the Queen, at first she
  laugh'd
Lightly, to think of Modred's dusty fall,
Then shudder'd, as the village wife
  who cries
" I shudder, some one steps across my
  grave;"
Then laugh'd again, but faintlier, for
  indeed
She half-foresaw that he, the subtle
  beast,
Would track her guilt until he found,
  and hers
Would be for evermore a name of scorn.
Henceforward rarely could she front
  in hall,
Or elsewhere, Modred's narrow foxy
  face,
Heart-hiding smile, and gray persis-
  tent eye:
Henceforward too, the Powers that
  tend the soul,
To help it from the death that cannot
  die,

And save it even in extremes, began
To vex and plague her. Many a time
    for hours,
Beside the placid breathings of the
    King,
In the dead night, grim faces came
    and went
Before her, or a vague spiritual fear —
Like to some doubtful noise of creak-
    ing doors,
Heard by the watcher in a haunted
    house,
That keeps the rust of murder on the
    walls —
Held her awake: or if she slept, she
    dream'd
An awful dream; for then she seem'd
    to stand
On some vast plain before a setting
    sun,
And from the sun there swiftly made
    at her
A ghastly something, and its shadow
    flew
Before it, till it touch'd her, and she
    turn'd —
When lo! her own, that broadening
    from her feet,
And blackening, swallow'd all the
    land, and in it
Far cities burnt, and with a cry she
    woke.
And all this trouble did not pass but
    grew;
Till ev'n the clear face of the guileless
    King,
And trustful courtesies of household
    life,
Became her bane; and at the last she
    said,
" O Lancelot, get thee hence to thine
    own land,
For if thou tarry we shall meet again,
And if we meet again, some evil chance
Will make the smouldering scandal
    break and blaze
Before the people, and our lord the
    King."
And Lancelot ever promised, but re-
    main'd,
And still they met and met. Again
    she said,

" O Lancelot, if thou love me get thee
    hence."
And then they were agreed upon a
    night
(When the good King should not be
    there) to meet
And part for ever. Passion-pale they
    met
And greeted: hands in hands, and eye
    to eye,
Low on the border of her couch they
    sat
Stammering and staring: it was their
    last hour,
A madness of farewells. And Modred
    brought
His creatures to the basement of the
    tower
For testimony; and crying with full
    voice
" Traitor, come out, ye are trapt at
    last," aroused
Lancelot, who rushing outward lionlike
Leapt on him, and hurl'd him head-
    long, and he fell
Stunn'd, and his creatures took and
    bare him off,
And all was still: then she, " The end
    is come,
And I am shamed for ever;" and he
    said,
" Mine be the shame; mine was the
    sin: but rise,
And fly to my strong castle overseas:
There will I hide thee, till my life
    shall end,
There hold thee with my life against
    the world."
She answer'd, "Lancelot, wilt thou
    hold me so?
Nay, friend, for we have taken our
    farewells.
Would God that thou couldst hide me
    from myself!
Mine is the shame, for I was wife, and
    thou
Unwedded: yet rise now, and let us fly,
For I will draw me into sanctuary,
And bide my doom." So Lancelot
    got her horse,
Set her thereon, and mounted on his
    own,

And then they rode to the divided way,
There kiss'd, and parted weeping : for
he past,
Love-loyal to the least wish of the
Queen,
Back to his land ; but she to Almes-
bury
Fled all night long by glimmering
waste and weald,
And heard the spirits of the waste
and weald
Moan as she fled, or thought she heard
them moan :
And in herself she moan'd "Too late,
too late !"
Till in the cold wind that foreruns the
morn,
A blot in heaven, the Raven, flying
high,
Croak'd, and she thought, "He spies
a field of death ;
For now the Heathen of the Northern
Sea,
Lured by the crimes and frailties of
the court,
Begin to slay the folk, and spoil the
land."

And when she came to Almesbury
she spake
There to the nuns, and said, "Mine
enemies
Pursue me, but, O peaceful Sisterhood,
Receive, and yield me sanctuary, nor
ask
Her name to whom ye yield it, till her
time
To tell you :" and her beauty, grace
and power,
Wrought as a charm upon them, and
they spared
To ask it.

So the stately Queen abode
For many a week, unknown, among
the nuns ;
Nor with them mix'd, nor told her
name, nor sought,
Wrapt in her grief, for housel or for
shrift,
But communed only with the little
maid,

Who pleased her with a babbling
heedlessness
Which often lured her from herself ;
but now,
This night, a rumor wildly blown
about
Came, that Sir Modred had usurp'd
the realm,
And leagued him with the heathen,
while the King
Was waging war on Lancelot : then
she thought,
"With what a hate the people and
the King
Must hate me," and bow'd down upon
her hands
Silent, until the little maid, who
brook'd
No silence, brake it, uttering "Late !
so late !
What hour, I wonder, now ?" and when
she drew
No answer, by and by began to hum
An air the nuns had taught her ;
"Late, so late !"
Which when she heard, the Queen
look'd up, and said,
"O maiden, if indeed ye list to sing,
Sing, and unbind my heart that I may
weep."
Whereat full willingly sang the little
maid.

"Late, late, so late ! and dark the
night and chill !
Late, late, so late ! but we can enter
still.
Too late, too late ! ye cannot enter
now.

"No light had we : for that we do
repent ;
And learning this, the bridegroom
will relent.
Too late, too late ! ye cannot enter
now.

"No light : so late ! and dark
and chill the night !
O let us in, that we may find the light !
Too late, too late : ye cannot enter
now.

" Have we not heard the bridegroom
　　is so sweet ?
O let us in, tho' late, to kiss his feet !
No, no, too late ! ye cannot enter
　　now."

So sang the novice, while full pas-
　　sionately,
Her head upon her hands, remember-
　　ing
Her thought when first she came,
　　wept the sad Queen.
Then said the little novice prattling
　　to her,

" O pray you, noble lady, weep no
　　more ;
But let my words, the words of one
　　so small,
Who knowing nothing knows but to
　　obey,
And if I do not there is penance giv-
　　en —
Comfort your sorrows; for they do
　　not flow
From evil done ; right sure I am of
　　that,
Who see your tender grace and state-
　　liness.
But weigh your sorrows with our lord
　　the King's,
And weighing find them less ; for
　　gone is he
To wage grim war against Sir Lance-
　　lot there,
Round that strong castle where he
　　holds the Queen ;
And Modred whom he left in charge
　　of all,
The traitor — Ah sweet lady, the
　　King's grief
For his own self, and his own Queen,
　　and realm,
Must needs be thrice as great as any
　　of ours.
For me, I thank the saints, I am not
　　great.
For if there ever come a grief to me
I cry my cry in silence, and have done.
None knows it, and my tears have
　　brought me good :
But even were the griefs of little ones

As great as those of great ones, yet
　　this grief
Is added to the griefs the great must
　　bear,
That howsoever much they may desire
Silence, they cannot weep behind a
　　cloud :
As even here they talk at Almesbury
About the good King and his wicked
　　Queen,
And were I such a King with such a
　　Queen,
Well might I wish to veil her wicked-
　　ness,
But were I such a King, it could not
　　be."

Then to her own sad heart mutter'd
　　the Queen,
" Will the child kill me with her inno-
　　cent talk ? "
But openly she answer'd, " Must not I,
If this false traitor have displaced his
　　lord,
Grieve with the common grief of all
　　the realm ? "

" Yea," said the maid, " this is all
　　woman's grief,
That *she* is woman, whose disloyal life
Hath wrought confusion in the Table
　　Round
Which good King Arthur founded,
　　years ago,
With signs and miracles and wonders,
　　there
At Camelot, ere the coming of the
　　Queen."

Then thought the Queen within her-
　　self again,
" Will the child kill me with her fool-
　　ish prate ? "
But openly she spake and said to her,
" O little maid, shut in by nunnery
　　walls,
What canst thou know of Kings and
　　Tables Round,
Or what of signs and wonders, but the
　　signs
And simple miracles of thy nunnery ?"

To whom the little novice garru-
lously,
" Yea, but I know : the land was full
of signs
And wonders ere the coming of the
Queen.
So said my father, and himself was
knight
Of the great Table — at the founding
of it ;
And rode thereto from Lyonnesse,
and he said
That as he rode, an hour or maybe
twain
After the sunset, down the coast, he
heard
Strange music, and he paused, and
turning — there,
All down the lonely coast of Lyonnesse,
Each with a beacon-star upon his head,
And with a wild sea-light about his feet,
He saw them — headland after head-
land flame
Far on into the rich heart of the west :
And in the light the white mermaiden
swam,
And strong man-breasted things stood
from the sea,
And sent a deep sea-voice thro' all the
land,
To which the little elves of chasm and
cleft
Made answer, sounding like a distant
horn.
So said my father — yea, and further-
more,
Next morning, while he past the dim-
lit woods,
Himself beheld three spirits mad with
joy
Come dashing down on a tall wayside
flower,
That shook beneath them, as the thistle shakes
When three gray linnets wrangle for
the seed :
And still at evenings on before his
horse
The flickering fairy-circle wheel'd and
broke
Flying, and link'd again, and wheel'd
and broke

Flying, for all the land was full of life.
And when at last he came to Camelot,
A wreath of airy dancers hand-in-hand
Swung round the lighted lantern of
the hall ;
And in the hall itself was such a feast
As never man had dream'd ; for every
knight
Had whatsoever meat he long'd for
served
By hands unseen ; and even as he said
Down in the cellars merry bloated
things
Shoulder'd the spigot, straddling on
the butts
While the wine ran : so glad were
spirits and men
Before the coming of the sinful
Queen."

Then spake the Queen and somewhat bitterly,
" Were they so glad ? ill prophets
were they all,
Spirits and men : could none of them
foresee,
Not even thy wise father with his signs
And wonders, what has fall'n upon
the realm ? "

To whom the novice garrulously
again,
" Yea, one, a bard ; of whom my father
said,
Full many a noble war-song had he
sung,
Ev'n in the presence of an enemy's
fleet,
Between the steep cliff and the coming wave ;
And many a mystic lay of life and
death
Had chanted on the smoky mountain-
tops,
When round him bent the spirits of
the hills
With all their dewy hair blown back
like flame :
So said my father — and that night
the bard
Sang Arthur's glorious wars, and
sang the King

As wellnigh more than man, and rail'd
  at those
Who call'd him the false son of Gor-
  loïs:
For there was no man knew from
  whence he came;
But after tempest, when the long
  wave broke
All down the thundering shores of
  Bude and Bos,
There came a day as still as heaven,
  and then
They found a naked child upon the
  sands
Of dark Tintagil by the Cornish sea;
And that was Arthur; and they fos-
  ter'd him
Till he by miracle was approven King:
And that his grave should be a mystery
From all men, like his birth; and
  could he find
A woman in her womanhood as great
As he was in his manhood, then, he
  sang,
The twain together well might change
  the world.
But even in the middle of his song
He falter'd, and his hand fell from the
  harp,
And pale he turn'd, and reel'd, and
  would have fall'n,
But that they stay'd him up; nor
  would he tell
His vision; but what doubt that he
  foresaw
This evil work of Lancelot and the
  Queen?"

Then thought the Queen, "Lo!
  they have set her on,
Our simple-seeming Abbess and her
  nuns,
To play upon me," and bow'd her
  head nor spake.
Whereat the novice crying, with
  clasp'd hands,
Shame on her own garrulity garru-
  lously,
Said the good nuns would check her
  gadding tongue
Full often, "and, sweet lady, if I seem
To vex an ear too sad to listen to me,

Unmannerly, with prattling and the
  tales
Which my good father told me, check
  me too
Nor let me shame my father's memory, one
Of noblest manners, tho' himself
  would say
Sir Lancelot had the noblest; and he
  died,
Kill'd in a tilt, come next, five summers back,
And left me; but of others who remain,
And of the two first-famed for
  courtesy—
And pray you check me if I ask
  amiss—
But pray you, which had noblest,
  while you moved
Among them, Lancelot or our lord
  the King?"

Then the pale Queen look'd up and
  answer'd her,
"Sir Lancelot, as became a noble
  knight,
Was gracious to all ladies, and the
  same
In open battle or the tilting-field
Forbore his own advantage, and the
  King
In open battle or the tilting-field
Forbore his own advantage, and these
  two
Were the most nobly-manner'd men
  of all;
For manners are not idle, but the fruit
Of loyal nature, and of noble mind."

"Yea," said the maid, "be manners
  such fair fruit?
Then Lancelot's needs must be a thousand-fold
Less noble, being, as all rumor runs,
The most disloyal friend in all the
  world."

To which a mournful answer made
  the Queen:
"O closed about by narrowing nun-
  nery-walls,

What knowest thou of the world, and
    all its lights
And shadows, all the wealth and all
    the woe?
If ever Lancelot, that most noble
    knight,
Were for one hour less noble than
    himself,
Pray for him that he scape the doom
    of fire,
And weep for her who drew him to
    his doom."

"Yea," said the little novice, "I
    pray for both;
But I should all as soon believe that
    his,
Sir Lancelot's, were as noble as the
    King's,
As I could think, sweet lady, yours
    would be
Such as they are, were you the sinful
    Queen."

So she, like many another babbler,
    hurt
Whom she would soothe, and harm'd
    where she would heal;
For here a sudden flush of wrathful
    heat
Fired all the pale face of the Queen,
    who cried,
"Such as thou art be never maiden
    more
For ever! thou their tool, set on to
    plague
And play upon, and harry me, petty spy
And traitress." When that storm of
    anger brake
From Guinevere, aghast the maiden
    rose,
White as her veil, and stood before
    the Queen
As tremulously as foam upon the
    beach
Stands in a wind, ready to break and
    fly,
And when the Queen had added "Get
    thee hence,"
Fled frighted. Then that other left
    alone

Sigh'd, and began to gather heart
    again,
Saying in herself, "The simple, fear-
    ful child
Meant nothing, but my own too-fear-
    ful guilt,
Simpler than any child, betrays itself.
But help me, heaven, for surely I
    repent.
For what is true repentance but in
    thought —
Not ev'n in inmost thought to think
    again
The sins that made the past so pleasant
    to us:
And I have sworn never to see him
    more,
To see him more."

              And ev'n in saying this,
Her memory from old habit of the
    mind
Went slipping back upon the golden
    days
In which she saw him first, when
    Lancelot came,
Reputed the best knight and goodliest
    man,
Ambassador, to lead her to his lord
Arthur, and led her forth, and far
    ahead
Of his and her retinue moving, they,
Rapt in sweet talk or lively, all on
    love
And sport and tilts and pleasure,
    (for the time
Was maytime, and as yet no sin was
    dream'd,)
Rode under groves that look'd a para-
    dise
Of blossom, over sheets of hyacinth
That seem'd the heavens upbreaking
    thro' the earth,
And on from hill to hill, and every day
Beheld at noon in some delicious
    dale
The silk pavilions of King Arthur
    raised
For brief repast or afternoon repose
By couriers gone before; and on again,
Till yet once more ere set of sun they
    saw

The Dragon of the great Pendragon-
ship,
That crown'd the state pavilion of the
King,
Blaze by the rushing brook or silent
well.

But when the Queen immersed in
such a trance,
And moving thro' the past uncon-
sciously,
Came to that point where first she
saw the King
Ride toward her from the city, sigh'd
to find
Her journey done, glanced at him,
thought him cold,
High, self-contain'd, and passionless,
not like him,
"Not like my Lancelot " — while she
brooded thus
And grew half-guilty in her thoughts
again,
There rode an armed warrior to the
doors.
A murmuring whisper thro' the nun-
nery ran,
Then on a sudden a cry "The King."
She sat
Stiff-stricken, listening; but when
armed feet
Thro' the long gallery from the outer
doors
Rang coming, prone from off her seat
she fell,
And grovell'd with her face against
the floor:
There with her milkwhite arms and
shadowy hair
She made her face a darkness from
the King:
And in the darkness heard his armed
feet
Pause by her; then came silence, then
a voice,
Monotonous and hollow like a Ghost's
Denouncing judgment, but tho'
changed, the King's:

" Liest thou here so low, the child
of one

I honor'd, happy, dead before thy
shame ?
Well is it that no child is born of
thee.
The children born of thee are sword
and fire,
Red ruin, and the breaking up of
laws,
The craft of kindred and the Godless
hosts
Of heathen swarming o'er the Northern
Sea ;
Whom I, while yet Sir Lancelot, my
right arm
The mightiest of my knights, abode
with me,
Have everywhere about this land of
Christ
In twelve great battles ruining over-
thrown.
And knowest thou now from whence
I come — from him,
From waging bitter war with him:
and he,
That did not shun to smite me in
worse way,
Had yet that grace of courtesy in him
left,
He spared to lift his hand against the
King
Who made him knight: but many a
knight was slain;
And many more, and all his kith and
kin
Clave to him, and abode in his own
land.
And many more when Modred raised
revolt,
Forgetful of their troth and fealty,
clave
To Modred, and a remnant stays with
me.
And of this remnant will I leave a
part,
True men who love me still, for whom
I live,
To guard thee in the wild hour coming
on,
Lest but a hair of this low head be
harm'd.
Fear not: thou shalt be guarded till
my death.

Howbeit I know, if ancient prophecies
Have err'd not, that I march to meet
  my doom.
Thou hast not made my life so sweet
  to me,
That I the King should greatly care
  to live;
For thou hast spoilt the purpose of
  my life.
Bear with me for the last time while
  I show,
Ev'n for thy sake, the sin which thou
  hast sinn'd.
For when the Roman left us, and
  their law
Relax'd its hold upon us, and the
  ways
Were fill'd with rapine, here and there
  a deed
Of prowess done redress'd a random
  wrong.
But I was first of all the kings who
  drew
The knighthood-errant of this realm
  and all
The realms together under me, their
  Head,
In that fair Order of my Table Round,
A glorious company, the flower of
  men,
To serve as model for the mighty
  world,
And be the fair beginning of a time.
I made them lay their hands in mine
  and swear
To reverence the King, as if he were
Their conscience, and their conscience
  as their King,
To break the heathen and uphold the
  Christ,
To ride abroad redressing human
  wrongs,
To speak no slander, no, nor listen to
  it,
To honor his own word as if his God's,
To lead sweet lives in purest chastity,
To love one maiden only, cleave to
  her,
And worship her by years of noble
  deeds,
Until they won her; for indeed I
  knew

Of no more subtle master under
  heaven
Than is the maiden passion for a
  maid,
Not only to keep down the base in
  man,
But teach high thought, and amiable
  words
And courtliness, and the desire of
  fame,
And love of truth, and all that makes
  a man.
And all this throve before I wedded
  thee,
Believing, ' lo mine helpmate, one to
  feel
My purpose and rejoicing in my
  joy.'
Then came thy shameful sin with
  Lancelot;
Then came the sin of Tristram and
  Isolt;
Then others, following these my
  mightiest knights,
And drawing foul ensample from fair
  names,
Sinn'd also, till the loathsome opposite
Of all my heart had destined did ob-
  tain,
And all thro' thee! so that this life of
  mine
I guard as God's high gift from scathe
  and wrong,
Not greatly care to lose; but rather
  think
How sad it were for Arthur, should he
  live,
To sit once more within his lonely
  hall,
And miss the wonted number of my
  knights,
And miss to hear high talk of noble
  deeds
As in the golden days before thy sin.
For which of us, who might be left,
  could speak
Of the pure heart, nor seem to glance
  at thee?
And in thy bowers of Camelot or of
  Usk
Thy shadow still would glide from
  room to room,

And I should evermore be vext with thee
In hanging robe or vacant orna-
ment,
Or ghostly footfall echoing on the
stair.
For think not, tho' thou wouldst not
love thy lord,
Thy lord has wholly lost his love for
thee.
I am not made of so slight elements.
Yet must I leave thee, woman, to thy
shame.
I hold that man the worst of public
foes
Who either for his own or children's
sake,
To save his blood from scandal, lets
the wife
Whom he knows false, abide and rule
the house:
For being thro' his cowardice allow'd
Her station, taken everywhere for
pure,
She like a new disease, unknown to
men,
Creeps, no precaution used, among the
crowd,
Makes wicked lightnings of her eyes,
and saps
The fealty of our friends, and stirs the
pulse
With devil's leaps, and poisons half
the young.
Worst of the worst were that man he
that reigns!
Better the King's waste hearth and
aching heart
Than thou reseated in thy place of
light,
The mockery of my people, and their
bane."

He paused, and in the pause she
crept an inch
Nearer, and laid her hands about his
feet.
Far off a solitary trumpet blew.
Then waiting by the doors the war-
horse neigh'd
As at a friend's voice, and he spake
again:

" Yet think not that I come to urge
thy crimes,
I did not come to curse thee, Guinevere,
I, whose vast pity almost makes me
die
To see thee, laying there thy golden
head,
My pride in happier summers, at my
feet.
The wrath which forced my thoughts
on the fierce law,
The doom of treason and the flaming
death,
(When first I learnt thee hidden here)
is past.
The pang — which while I weigh'd thy
heart with one
Too wholly true to dream untruth in
thee,
Made my tears burn — is also past —
in part.
And all is past, the sin is sinn'd, and I,
Lo! I forgive thee, as Eternal God
Forgives: do thou for thine own soul
the rest.
But how to take last leave of all I
loved?
O golden hair, with which I used to
play
Not knowing! O imperial-moulded
form,
And beauty such as never woman
wore,
Until it came a kingdom's curse with
thee —
I cannot touch thy lips, they are not
mine,
But Lancelot's: nay, they never were
the King's.
I cannot take thy hand; that too is
flesh,
And in the flesh thou hast sinn'd;
and mine own flesh,
Here looking down on thine polluted,
cries
'I loathe thee:' yet not less, O Guinevere,
For I was ever virgin save for thee,
My love thro' flesh hath wrought into
my life
So far, that my doom is, I love thee
still.

" He paused ; and in the pause she crept an inch
Nearer, and laid her hands about his feet."

Page 366.

Let no man dream but that I love thee
    still.
Perchance, and so thou purify thy
    soul,
And so thou lean on our fair father
    Christ,
Hereafter in that world where all are
    pure
We two may meet before high God,
    and thou
Wilt spring to me, and claim me thine,
    and know
I am thine husband — not a smaller
    soul,
Nor Lancelot, nor another. Leave me
    that,
I charge thee, my last hope. Now
    must I hence.
Thro' the thick night I hear the trum-
    pet blow :
They summon me their King to lead
    mine hosts
Far down to that great battle in the
    west,
Where I must strike against the man
    they call
My sister's son — no kin of mine, who
    leagues
With Lords of the White Horse,
    heathen, and knights,
Traitors — and strike him dead, and
    meet myself
Death, or I know not what mysterious
    doom.
And thou remaining here wilt learn
    the event;
But hither shall I never come again,
Never lie by thy side; see thee no
    more —
Farewell ! ''

And while she grovell'd at his feet,
She felt the King's breath wander o'er
    her neck,
And in the darkness o'er her fallen
    head,
Perceived the waving of his hands
    that blest.

Then, listening till those armed
    steps were gone,

Rose the pale Queen, and in her an-
    guish found
The casement : "peradventure," so
    she thought,
" If I might see his face, and not be
    seen."
And lo, he sat on horseback at the door!
And near him the sad nuns with each
    a light
Stood, and he gave them charge about
    the Queen,
To guard and foster her for evermore.
And while he spake to these his helm
    was lower'd,
To which for crest the golden dragon
    clung
Of Britain; so she did not see the face,
Which then was as an angel's, but she
    saw,
Wet with the mists and smitten by the
    lights,
The Dragon of the great Pendragon-
    ship
Blaze, making all the night a steam
    of fire.
And even then he turn'd; and more
    and more
The moony vapor rolling round the
    King,
Who seem'd the phantom of a Giant
    in it,
Enwound him fold by fold, and made
    him gray
And grayer, till himself became as mist
Before her, moving ghostlike to his
    doom.

Then she stretch'd out her arms and
    cried aloud
" Oh Arthur ! " there her voice brake
    suddenly,
Then — as a stream that spouting from
    a cliff
Fails in mid air, but gathering at the
    base
Re-makes itself, and flashes down the
    vale —
Went on in passionate utterance :

           " Gone — my lord!
Gone thro' my sin to slay and to be
    slain !

And he forgave me, and I could not
  speak.
Farewell?   I should have answer'd
  his farewell.
His mercy choked me.   Gone, my lord
  the King,
My own true lord! how dare I call
  him mine?
The shadow of another cleaves to me,
And makes me one pollution: he, the
  King,
Call'd me polluted: shall I kill my-
  self?
What help in that?   I cannot kill my
  sin,
If soul be soul; nor can I kill my
  shame;
No, nor by living can I live it down.
The days will grow to weeks, the weeks
  to months,
The months will add themselves and
  make the years,
The years will roll into the centuries,
And mine will ever be a name of scorn.
I must not dwell on that defeat of
  fame.
Let the world be; that is but of the
  world
What else? what hope? I think there
  was a hope,
Except he mock'd me when he spake
  of hope;
His hope he call'd it; but he never
  mocks,
For mockery is the fume of little
  hearts.
And blessed be the King, who hath
  forgiven
My wickedness to him, and left me
  hope
That in mine own heart I can live
  down sin
And be his mate hereafter in the
  heavens
Before high God.   Ah great and gentle lord,
Who wast, as is the conscience of a
  saint
Among his warring senses, to thy
  knights —
To whom my false voluptuous pride,
  that took

Full easily all impressions from below,
Would not look up, or half-despised
  the height
To which I would not or I could not
  climb —
I thought I could not breathe in that
  fine air
That pure severity of perfect light —
I wanted warmth and color which I
  found
In Lancelot — now I see thee what
  thou art,
Thou art the highest and most human
  too,
Not Lancelot, nor another.   Is there
  none
Will tell the King I love him tho' so
  late?
Now — ere he goes to the great Bat-
  tle? none:
Myself must tell him in that purer
  life,
But now it were too daring.   Ah my
  God,
What might I not have made of thy
  fair world,
Had I but loved thy highest creature
  here?
It was my duty to have loved the
  highest:
It surely was my profit had I
  known:
It would have been my pleasure had
  I seen.
We needs must love the highest when
  we see it,
Not Lancelot, nor another."

                            Here her hand
Grasp'd, made her vail her eyes: she
  look'd and saw
The novice, weeping, suppliant, and
  said to her,
"Yea, little maid, for am I not forgiven?"
Then glancing up beheld the holy
  nuns
All round her, weeping; and her heart
  was loosed
Within her, and she wept with these
  and said,

"Ye know me then, that wicked one, who broke
The vast design and purpose of the King.
O shut me round with narrowing nunnery walls,
Meek maidens, from the voices crying ' shame.'
I must not scorn myself : he loves me still.
Let no one dream but that he loves me still.
So let me, if you do not shudder at me,
Nor shun to call me sister, dwell with you;
Wear black and white, and be a nun like you,
Fast with your fasts, not feasting with your feasts ;
Grieve with your griefs, not grieving at your joys,
But not rejoicing; mingle with your rites ;
Pray and be pray'd for; lie before your shrines ;
Do each low office of your holy house ;
Walk your dim cloister, and distribute dole
To poor sick people, richer in His eyes

Who ransom'd us, and haler too than I;
And treat their loathsome hurts and heal mine own ;
And so wear out in almsdeed and in prayer
The sombre close of that voluptuous day,
Which wrought the ruin of my lord the King."

She said: they took her to themselves ; and she
Still hoping, fearing "is it yet too late ? "
Dwelt with them, till in time their Abbess died.
Then she, for her good deeds and her pure life,
And for the power of ministration in her,
And likewise for the high rank she had borne,
Was chosen Abbess, there, an Abbess, lived
For three brief years, and there, an Abbess, past
To where beyond these voices there is peace.

End of " The Round Table."

THE PASSING OF ARTHUR.

THAT story which the bold Sir Bedivere,
First made and latest left of all the knights,
Told, when the man was no more than a voice
In the white winter of his age, to those
With whom he dwelt, new faces, other minds.

For on their march to westward, Bedivere,
Who slowly paced among the slumbering host,
Heard in his tent the moanings of the King:

" I found Him in the shining of the stars,
I mark'd Him in the flowering of His fields,
But in His ways with men I find Him not.
I waged His wars, and now I pass and die.
O me ! for why is all around us here
As if some lesser god had made the world,
But had not force to shape it as he would,
Till the High God behold it from beyond,
And enter it, and make it beautiful ?

Or else as if the world were wholly
fair,
But that these eyes of men are dense
and dim,
And have not power to see it as it is:
Perchance, because we see not to the
close ; —
For I, being simple, thought to work
His will,
And have but stricken with the sword
in vain ;
And all whereon I lean'd in wife and
friend
Is traitor to my peace, and all my
realm
Reels back into the beast, and is no
more.
My God, thou hast forgotten me in
my death :
Nay — God my Christ — I pass but
shall not die."

Then, ere that last weird battle in
the west,
There came on Arthur sleeping, Gawain kill'd
In Lancelot's war, the ghost of Gawain
blown
Along a wandering wind, and past his
ear
Went shrilling, "Hollow, hollow all
delight!
Hail, King! to-morrow thou shalt pass
away.
Farewell! there is an isle of rest for
thee.
And I am blown along a wandering
wind,
And hollow, hollow, hollow all delight."
And fainter onward, like wild birds
that change
Their season in the night and wail
their way
From cloud to cloud, down the long
wind the dream
Shrill'd ; but in going mingled with
dim cries
Far in the moonlit haze among the
hills,
As of some lonely city sack'd by
night,

When all is lost, and wife and child
with wail
Pass to new lords ; and Arthur woke
and call'd,
"Who spake ? A dream. O light
upon the wind,
Thine, Gawain, was the voice — are
these dim cries
Thine ? or doth all that haunts the
waste and wild
Mourn, knowing it will go along with
me ? "

This heard the bold Sir Bedivere
and spake :
"O me, my King, let pass whatever
will,
Elves, and the harmless glamour of
the field ;
But in their stead thy name and glory
cling
To all high places like a golden cloud
For ever : but as yet thou shalt not
pass.
Light was Gawain in life, and light in
death
Is Gawain, for the ghost is as the
man ;
And care not thou for dreams from
him, but rise —
I hear the steps of Modred in the
west,
And with him many of thy people,
and knights
Once thine, whom thou hast loved,
but grosser grown
Than heathen, spitting at their vows
and thee.
Right well in heart they know thee
for the King.
Arise, go forth and conquer as of old."

Then spake King Arthur to Sir
Bedivere :
"Far other is this battle in the west
Whereto we move, than when we
strove in youth,
And brake the petty kings, and fought
with Rome,
Or thrust the heathen from the Roman
wall,

And shook him thro' the north. Ill
  doom is mine
To war against my people and my
  knights.
The king who fights his people fights
  himself.
And they my knights, who loved me
  once, the stroke
That strikes them dead is as my death
  to me.
Yet let us hence, and find or feel a
  way
Thro' this blind haze, which ever
  since I saw
One lying in the dust at Almesbury,
Hath folded in the passes of the
  world."

Then rose the King and moved his
  host by night,
And ever push'd Sir Modred, league
  by league,
Back to the sunset bound of Lyon-
  nesse —
A land of old upheaven from the abyss
By fire, to sink into the abyss again;
Where fragments of forgotten peoples
  dwelt,
And the long mountains ended in a
  coast
Of ever-shifting sand, and far away
The phantom circle of a moaning sea.
There the pursuer could pursue no
  more,
And he that fled no further fly the
  King;
And there, that day when the great
  light of heaven
Burn'd at his lowest in the rolling
  year,
On the waste sand by the waste sea
  they closed.
Nor ever yet had Arthur fought a
  fight
Like this last, dim, weird battle of the
  west.
A deathwhite mist slept over sand and
  sea:
Whereof the chill, to him who breathed
  it, drew
Down with his blood, till all his heart
  was cold

With formless fear; and ev'n on
  Arthur fell
Confusion, since he saw not whom he
  fought.
For friend and foe were shadows in
  the mist,
And friend slew friend not knowing
  whom he slew;
And some had visions out of golden
  youth,
And some beheld the faces of old
  ghosts
Look in upon the battle; and in the
  mist
Was many a noble deed, many a base,
And chance and craft and strength in
  single fights,
And ever and anon with host to
  host
Shocks, and the splintering spear, the
  hard mail hewn,
Shield-breakings, and the clash of
  brands, the crash
Of battle-axes on shatter'd helms, and
  shrieks
After the Christ, of those who falling
  down
Look'd up for heaven, and only saw
  the mist;
And shouts of heathen and the traitor
  knights,
Oaths, insult, filth, and monstrous
  blasphemies,
Sweat, writhings, anguish, laboring of
  the lungs
In that close mist, and cryings for the
  light,
Moans of the dying, and voices of the
  dead.

Last, as by some one deathbed after
  wail
Of suffering, silence follows, or thro'
  death
Or deathlike swoon, thus over all that
  shore,
Save for some whisper of the seething
  seas,
A dead hush fell; but when the dolorous day
Grew drearier toward twilight falling,
  came

A bitter wind, clear from the North, and blew
The mist aside, and with that wind the tide
Rose, and the pale King glanced across the field
Of battle: but no man was moving there;
Nor any cry of Christian heard thereon,
Nor yet of heathen; only the wan wave
Brake in among dead faces, to and fro
Swaying the helpless hands, and up and down
Tumbling the hollow helmets of the fallen,
And shiver'd brands that once had fought with Rome,
And rolling far along the gloomy shores
The voice of days of old and days to be.

Then spake King Arthur to Sir Bedivere,
And whiter than the mist that all day long
Had held the field of battle was the King:

"Hearest thou this great voice that shakes the world,
And wastes the narrow realm whereon we move,
And beats upon the faces of the dead,
My dead, as tho' they had not died for me? —
O Bedivere, for on my heart hath fall'n
Confusion, till I know not what I am,
Nor whence I am, nor whether I be King.
Behold, I seem but King among the dead."

Then spake the bold Sir Bedivere: "My King,
King everywhere! and so the dead have kings,
There also will I worship thee as King.

Yet still thy life is whole, and still I live
Who love thee; but who hates thee, he that brought
The heathen back among us, yonder stands,
Modred, unharm'd, the traitor of thine house."

Then spake the King: "My house hath been my doom.
But call not thou this traitor of my house
Who hath but dwelt beneath one roof with me.
My house are rather they who sware my vows,
Yea, even while they brake them, own'd me King.
And well for thee, saying in my dark hour,
When all the purport of my throne hath fail'd,
That quick or dead thou holdest me for King.
King am I, whatsoever be their cry;
And one last act of kinghood shalt thou see
Yet, ere I pass." And uttering this the King
Made at the man: then Modred smote his liege
Hard on that helm which many a heathen sword
Had beaten thin; while Arthur at one blow,
Striking the last stroke with Excalibur,
Slew him, and all but slain himself, he fell.

So all day long the noise of battle roll'd
Among the mountains by the winter sea;
Until King Arthur's Table, man by man,
Had fall'n in Lyonnesse about their lord,
King Arthur. Then, because his wound was deep,
The bold Sir Bedivere uplifted him,

And bore him to a chapel nigh the
    field,
A broken chancel with a broken cross,
That stood on a dark strait of barren
    land :
On one side lay the Ocean, and on one
Lay a great water, and the moon was
    full.

    Then spake King Arthur to Sir
        Bedivere :
" The sequel of to-day unsolders all
The goodliest fellowship of famous
    knights
Whereof this world holds record. Such a sleep
They sleep — the men I loved. I
    think that we
Shall never more, at any future time,
Delight our souls with talk of knight-
    ly deeds,
Walking about the gardens and the
    halls
Of Camelot, as in the days that were.
I perish by this people which I made,—
Tho' Merlin sware that I should come
    again
To rule once more ; but, let what will
    be, be,
I am so deeply smitten thro' the helm
That without help I cannot last till
    morn.
Thou therefore take my brand Excal-
    libur,
Which was my pride : for thou re-
    memberest how
In those old days, one summer noon,
    an arm
Rose up from out the bosom of the
    lake,
Clothed in white samite, mystic, won-
    derful,
Holding the sword — and how I row'd
    across
And took it, and have worn it, like a
    king ;
And, wheresoever I am sung or
    told
In aftertime, this also shall be known :
But now delay not : take Excalibur,
And fling him far into the middle
    mere :

Watch what thou seëst, and lightly
    bring me word."

    To him replied the bold Sir Bedi-
        vere :
" It is not meet, Sir King, to leave thee
    thus,
Aidless, alone, and smitten thro'
    the helm —
A little thing may harm a wounded
    man ;
Yet I thy hest will all perform at full,
Watch what I see, and lightly bring
    thee word."

    So saying, from the ruin'd shrine
    he stept,
And in the moon athwart the place of
    tombs,
Where lay the mighty bones of an-
    cient men,
Old knights, and over them the sea-
    wind sang
Shrill, chill, with flakes of foam. He,
    stepping down
By zigzag paths, and juts of pointed
    rock,
Came on the shining levels of the
    lake.

    There drew he forth the brand Ex-
    calibur,
And o'er him, drawing it, the winter
    moon,
Brightening the skirts of a long cloud,
    ran forth
And sparkled keen with frost against
    the hilt :
For all the haft twinkled with dia-
    mond sparks,
Myriads of topaz-lights, and jacinth-
    work
Of subtlest jewelry. He gazed so
    long
That both his eyes were dazzled as he
    stood,
This way and that dividing the swift
    mind,
In act to throw : but at the last it
    seem'd
Better to leave Excalibur conceal'd
There in the many-knotted waterflags,

That whistled stiff and dry about the
marge.
So strode he back slow to the wounded King.

Then spake King Arthur to Sir Bedivere:
"Hast thou perform'd my mission
which I gave?
What is it thou hast seen? or what
hast heard?"

And answer made the bold Sir Bedivere:
"I heard the ripple washing in the
reeds,
And the wild water lapping on the
crag."

To whom replied King Arthur, faint
and pale:
"Thou hast betray'd thy nature and
thy name,
Not rendering true answer, as be-
seem'd
Thy fëalty, nor like a noble knight:
For surer sign had follow'd, either
hand,
Or voice, or else a motion of the mere.
This is a shameful thing for men to lie.
Yet now, I charge thee, quickly go
again,
As thou art lief and dear, and do the
thing
I bade thee, watch, and lightly bring
me word."

Then went Sir Bedivere the second
time
Across the ridge, and paced beside
the mere,
Counting the dewy pebbles, fix'd in
thought;
But when he saw the wonder of the
hilt,
How curiously and strangely chased,
he smote
His palms together, and he cried
aloud:

"And if indeed I cast the brand
away,

Surely a precious thing, one worthy
note,
Should thus be lost for ever from the
earth,
Which might have pleased the eyes
of many men.
What good should follow this, if this
were done?
What harm, undone? Deep harm to
disobey,
Seeing obedience is the bond of rule.
Were it well to obey then, if a king
demand
An act unprofitable, against himself?
The King is sick, and knows not what
he does.
What record, or what relic of my lord
Should be to aftertime, but empty
breath
And rumors of a doubt? But were
this kept,
Stored in some treasure-house of
mighty kings,
Some one might show it at a joust of
arms,
Saying, 'King Arthur's sword, Excali-
bur,
Wrought by the lonely maiden of the
Lake.
Nine years she wrought it, sitting in
the deeps
Upon the hidden bases of the hills.'
So might some old man speak in the
aftertime
To all the people, winning reverence.
But now much honor and much fame
were lost."

So spake he, clouded with his own
conceit,
And hid Excalibur the second time,
And so strode back slow to the wounded King.

Then spoke King Arthur, breathing heavily:
"What is it thou hast seen? or what
hast heard?"

And answer made the bold Sir Bedivere:

"I heard the water lapping on the crag,
And the long ripple washing in the
    reeds."

To whom replied King Arthur,
    much in wrath:
"Ah, miserable and unkind, untrue,
Unknightly, traitor-hearted! Woe is
    me!
Authority forgets a dying king,
Laid widow'd of the power in his eye
That bowed the will. I see thee what
    thou art,
For thou, the latest-left of all my
    knights,
In whom should meet the offices of all,
Thou wouldst betray me for the pre-
    cious hilt;
Either from lust of gold, or like a girl
Valuing the giddy pleasure of the
    eyes.
Yet, for a man may fail in duty twice,
And the third time may prosper, get
    thee hence:
But, if thou spare to fling Excalibur,
I will arise and slay thee with my
    hands."

Then quickly rose Sir Bedivere,
    and ran,
And, leaping down the ridges lightly,
    plunged
Among the bulrush beds, and clutch'd
    the sword,
And strongly wheel'd and threw it.
    The great brand
Made lightnings in the splendor of
    the moon,
And flashing round and round, and
    whirl'd in an arch,
Shot like a streamer of the northern
    morn,
Seen where the moving isles of win-
    ter shock
By night, with noises of the Northern
    Sea.
So flash'd and fell the brand Ex-
    calibur:
But ere he dipt the surface, rose an
    arm
Clothed in white samite, mystic, won-
    derful,

And caught him by the hilt, and
    brandish'd him
Three times, and drew him under in
    the mere.
And lightly went the other to the
    King.

Then spoke King Arthur, drawing
    thicker breath:
"Now see I by thine eyes that this is
    done.
Speak out: what is it thou hast heard,
    or seen?"

And answer made the bold Sir Bed-
    ivere:
"Sir King, I closed mine eyelids, lest
    the gems
Should blind my purpose, for I never
    saw,
Nor shall see, here or elsewhere, till
    I die,
Not tho' I live three lives of mortal
    men,
So great a miracle as yonder hilt.
Then with both hands I flung him,
    wheeling him;
But when I look'd again, behold an
    arm,
Clothed in white samite, mystic, won-
    derful,
That caught him by the hilt, and
    brandish'd him
Three times, and drew him under in
    the mere."

And answer made King Arthur,
    breathing hard:
"My end draws nigh; 'tis time that
    I were gone.
Make broad thy shoulders to receive
    my weight,
And bear me to the margin; yet I
    fear
My wound hath taken cold, and I
    shall die."

So saying, from the pavement he
    half rose,
Slowly, with pain, reclining on his
    arm,

And looking wistfully with wide blue
    eyes
As in a picture. Him Sir Bedivere
Remorsefully regarded thro' his tears,
And would have spoken, but he found
    not words ;
Then took with care, and kneeling on
    one knee,
O'er both his shoulders drew the lan-
    guid hands,
And rising bore him thro' the place
    of tombs.

  But, as he walk'd, King Arthur
    panted hard,
Like one that feels a nightmare on
    his bed
When all the house is mute. So
    sigh'd the King,
Muttering and murmuring at his ear,
    " Quick, quick !
I fear it is too late, and I shall die."
But the other swiftly strode from
    ridge to ridge,
Clothed with his breath, and looking,
    as he walk'd,
Larger than human on the frozen
    hills.
He heard the deep behind him, and a
    cry
Before. His own thought drove him
    like a goad.
Dry clash'd his harness in the icy
    caves
And barren chasms, and all to left
    and right
The bare black cliff clang'd round
    him, as he based
His feet on juts of slippery crag that
    rang
Sharp-smitten with the dint of armed
    heels —
And on a sudden, lo ! the level lake,
And the long glories of the winter
    moon.

  Then saw they how there hove a
    dusky barge,
Dark as a funeral scarf from stem to
    stern,
Beneath them ; and descending they
    were ware

That all the decks were dense with
    stately forms,
Black-stoled, black-hooded, like a
    dream — by these
Three Queens with crowns of gold :
    and from them rose
A cry that shiver'd to the tingling
    stars,
And, as it were one voice, an agony
Of lamentation, like a wind that
    shrills
All night in a waste land, where no
    one comes,
Or hath come, since the making of
    the world.

  Then murmur'd Arthur, "Place me
    in the barge."
So to the barge they came. There
    those three Queens
Put forth their hands, and took the
    King, and wept.
But she, that rose the tallest of them
    all
And fairest, laid his head upon her
    lap,
And loosed the shatter'd casque, and
    chafed his hands,
And call'd him by his name, complain-
    ing loud,
And dropping bitter tears against a
    brow
Striped with dark blood : for all his
    face was white
And colorless, and like the wither'd
    moon
Smote by the fresh beam of the
    springing east ;
And all his greaves and cuisses dash'd
    with drops
Of onset ; and the light and lustrous
    curls —
That made his forehead like a rising
    sun
High from the daïs-throne — were
    parch'd with dust ,
Or, clotted into points and hanging
    loose,
Mix'd with the knightly growth that
    fringed his lips.
So like a shatter'd column lay the
    King ;

Not like that Arthur who, with lance
in rest,
From spur to plume a star of tournament,
Shot thro' the lists at Camelot, and
charged
Before the eyes of ladies and of kings.

Then loudly cried the bold Sir
Bedivere :
" Ah ! my Lord Arthur, whither shall
I go ?
Where shall I hide my forehead and
my eyes ?
For now I see the true old times are dead,
When every morning brought a noble
chance,
And every chance brought out a noble
knight.
Such times have been not since the
light that led
The holy Elders with the gift of
myrrh.
But now the whole Round Table is
dissolved
Which was an image of the mighty
world,
And I, the last, go forth companion-
less,
And the days darken round me, and
the years,
Among new men, strange faces, other
minds."

And slowly answer'd Arthur from
the barge :
" The old order changeth, yielding
place to new,
And God fulfils himself in many ways,
Lest one good custom should corrupt
the world.
Comfort thyself : what comfort is in me ?
I have lived my life, and that which
I have done
May He within himself make pure !
but thou,
If thou shouldst never see my face
again,
Pray for my soul. More things are
wrought by prayer
Than this world dreams of. Where-
fore, let thy voice

Rise like a fountain for me night and
day.
For what are men better than sheep
or goats
That nourish a blind life within the
brain,
If, knowing God, they lift not hands
of prayer
Both for themselves and those who
call them friend ?
For so the whole round earth is every
way
Bound by gold chains about the feet
of God.
But now farewell. I am going a long
way
With these thou seëst — if indeed I go
(For all my mind is clouded with a
doubt) —
To the island-valley of Avilion ;
Where falls not hail, or rain, or any
snow,
Nor ever wind blows loudly ; but it
lies
Deep-meadow'd, happy, fair with or-
chard lawns
And bowery hollows crown'd with
summer sea,
Where I will heal me of my grievous
wound."

So said he, and the barge with oar
and sail
Moved from the brink, like some full-
breasted swan
That, fluting a wild carol ere her death,
Ruffles her pure cold plume, and takes
the flood
With swarthy webs. Long stood Sir
Bedivere
Revolving many memories, till the hull
Look'd one black dot against the verge
of dawn,
And on the mere the wailing died away.

But when that moan had past for
evermore,
The stillness of the dead world's win-
ter dawn
Amazed him, and he groan'd, " The
King is gone."

And therewithal came on him the weird
rhyme,
"From the great deep to the great
deep he goes."

Whereat he slowly turn'd and slowly
clomb
The last hard footstep of that iron
crag;
Thence mark'd the black hull moving
yet, and cried,
"He passes to be King among the
dead,
And after healing of his grievous
wound
He comes again; but — if he come no
more —
O me, be yon dark Queens in yon
black boat,
Who shriek'd and wail'd, the three
whereat we gazed
On that high day, when, clothed with
living light,
They stood before his throne in silence, friends

Of Arthur, who should help him at his
need?"

Then from the dawn it seem'd there
came, but faint
As from beyond the limit of the world,
Like the last echo born of a great cry,
Sounds, as if some fair city were one
voice
Around a king returning from his wars.

Thereat once more he moved about,
and clomb
Ev'n to the highest he could climb,
and saw,
Straining his eyes beneath an arch of
hand,
Or thought he saw, the speck that
bare the King,
Down that long water opening on the
deep
Somewhere far off, pass on and on,
and go
From less to less and vanish into light.
And the new sun rose bringing the new
year.

TO THE QUEEN.

O LOYAL to the royal in thyself,
And loyal to thy land, as this to
thee ——
Bear witness, that rememberable day,
When, pale as yet, and fever-worn, the
Prince
Who scarce had pluck'd his flickering
life again
From halfway down the shadow of
the grave,
Past with thee thro' thy people and
their love,
And London roll'd one tide of joy
thro' all
Her trebled millions, and loud leagues
of man
And welcome! witness, too, the silent
cry,
The prayer of many a race and creed,
and clime —
Thunderless lightnings striking under
sea

From sunset and sunrise of all thy
realm,
And that true North, whereof we lately
heard
A strain to shame us "keep you to
yourselves;
So loyal is too costly! friends — your
love
Is but a burthen: loose the bond, and
go."
Is this the tone of empire? here the
faith
That made us rulers? this, indeed,
her voice
And meaning, whom the roar of Hou-
goumont
Left mightiest of all peoples under
heaven?
What shock has fool'd her since, that
she should speak
So feebly? wealthier — wealthier —
hour by hour!

The voice of Britain, or a sinking land,
Some third-rate isle half-lost among
her seas?
There rang her voice, when the full
city peal'd
Thee and thy Prince! The loyal to
their crown
Are loyal to their own far sons, who
love
Our ocean-empire with her boundless
homes
For ever-broadening England, and her
throne
In our vast Orient, and one isle, one
isle,
That knows not her own greatness: if
she knows
And dreads it we are fall'n.—— But
thou, my Queen,
Not for itself, but thro' thy living love
For one to whom I made it o'er his
grave
Sacred, accept this old imperfect tale,
New-old, and shadowing Sense at war
with Soul
Rather than that gray king, whose
name, a ghost,
Streams like a cloud, man-shaped,
from mountain peak,
And cleaves to cairn and cromlech
still; or him
Of Geoffrey's book, or him of Malle-
or's, one
Touch'd by the adulterous finger of a
time
That hover'd between war and wan-
tonness,
And crownings and dethronements:
take withal

Thy poet's blessing, and his trust that
Heaven
Will blow the tempest in the distance
back
From thine and ours: for some are
scared, who mark,
Or wisely or unwisely, signs of storm,
Waverings of every vane with every
wind,
And wordy trucklings to the transient
hour,
And fierce or careless looseners of the
faith,
And Softness breeding scorn of simple
life,
Or Cowardice, the child of lust for gold,
Or Labor, with a groan and not a voice,
Or Art with poisonous honey stol'n
from France,
And that which knows, but careful for
itself,
And that which knows not, ruling that
which knows
To its own harm: the goal of this
great world
Lies beyond sight: yet — if our slowly-
grown
And crown'd Republic's crowning
common-sense,
That saved her many times, not fail —
their fears
Are morning shadows huger than the
shapes
That cast them, not those gloomier
which forego
The darkness of that battle in the
West,
Where all of high and holy dies
away.

THE PRINCESS;

A MEDLEY.

PROLOGUE.

Sir Walter Vivian all a summer's day
Gave his broad lawns until the set of
  sun
Up to the people: thither flock'd at
  noon
His tenants, wife and child, and
  thither half
The neighboring borough with their
  Institute
Of which he was the patron. I was
  there
From college, visiting the son, — the
  son
A Walter too, — with others of our
  set,
Five others: we were seven at Vivian-
  place.

And me that morning Walter
  show'd the house,
Greek, set with busts: from vases in
  the hall
Flowers of all heavens, and lovelier
  than their names,
Grew side by side; and on the pave-
  ment lay
Carved stones of the Abbey-ruin in the
  park,
Huge Ammonites, and the first bones
  of Time;
And on the tables every clime and
  age
Jumbled together; celts and calumets,
Claymore and snowshoe, toys in lava,
  fans
Of sandal, amber, ancient rosaries,

Laborious orient ivory sphere in
  sphere,
The cursed Malayan crease, and
  battle-clubs
From the isles of palm: and higher on
  the walls,
Betwixt the monstrous horns of elk
  and deer,
His own forefathers' arms and armor
  hung.

And "this" he said "was Hugh's at
  Agincourt;
And that was old Sir Ralph's at As-
  calon:
A good knight he! we keep a chronicle
With all about him"—which he
  brought, and I
Dived in a hoard of tales that dealt
  with knights,
Half-legend, half-historic, counts and
  kings
Who laid about them at their wills
  and died;
And mixt with these, a lady, one that
  arm'd
Her own fair head, and sallying thro'
  the gate,
Had beat her foes with slaughter from
  her walls.

"O miracle of women," said the
  book,
"O noble heart who, being strait-
  besieged
By this wild king to force her to his
  wish,
Nor bent, nor broke, nor shunn'd a
  soldier's death,

But now when all was lost or seem'd
    as lost —
Her stature more than mortal in the
    burst
Of sunrise, her arm lifted, eyes on
    fire —
Brake with a blast of trumpets from
    the gate,
And, falling on them like a thunder-
    bolt,
She trampled some beneath her
    horses' heels,
And some were whelm'd with missiles
    of the wall,
And some were push'd with lances
    from the rock,
And part were drown'd within the
    whirling brook:
O miracle of noble womanhood!"

So sang the gallant glorious chroni-
    cle;
And, I all rapt in this, "Come out,"
    he said,
"To the Abbey: there is Aunt Eliza-
    beth
And sister Lilia with the rest." We
    went
(I kept the book and had my finger
    in it)
Down thro' the park: strange was the
    sight to me;
For all the sloping pasture murmur'd,
    sown
With happy faces and with holiday.
There moved the multitude, a thou-
    sand heads:
The patient leaders of their Institute
Taught them with facts. One rear'd
    a font of stone
And drew, from butts of water on the
    slope,
The fountain of the moment, playing,
    now
A twisted snake, and now a rain of
    pearls,
Or steep-up spout whereon the gilded
    ball
Danced like a wisp: and somewhat
    lower down
A man with knobs and wires and vials
    fired

A cannon: Echo answer'd in her sleep
From hollow fields: and here were
    telescopes
For azure views; and there a group
    of girls
In circle waited, whom the electric
    shock
Dislink'd with shrieks and laughter:
    round the lake
A little clock-work steamer paddling
    plied
And shook the lilies: perch'd about
    the knolls
A dozen angry models jetted steam:
A petty railway ran: a fire-balloon
Rose gem-like up before the dusky
    groves
And dropt a fairy parachute and
    past:
And there thro' twenty posts of tele-
    graph
They flash'd a saucy message to and
    fro
Between the mimic stations; so that
    sport
Went hand in hand with Science;
    otherwhere
Pure sport: a herd of boys with
    clamor bowl'd
And stump'd the wicket; babies roll'd
    about
Like tumbled fruit in grass; and men
    and maids
Arranged a country dance, and flew
    thro' light
And shadow, while the twangling
    violin
Struck up with Soldier-laddie, and
    overhead
The broad ambrosial aisles of lofty
    lime
Made noise with bees and breeze from
    end to end.

Strange was the sight and smacking
    of the time;
And long we gazed, but satiated at
    length
Came to the ruins. High-arch'd and
    ivy-claspt,
Of finest Gothic lighter than a
    fire,

Thro' one wide chasm of time and
    frost they gave
The park, the crowd, the house; but
    all within
The sward was trim as any garden
    lawn:
And here we lit on Aunt Elizabeth,
And Lilia with the rest, and lady
    friends
From neighbor seats: and there was
    Ralph himself,
A broken statue propt against the wall,
As gay as any. Lilia, wild with sport,
Half child half woman as she was,
    had wound
A scarf of orange round the stony
    helm,
And robed the shoulders in a rosy silk,
That made the old warrior from his
    ivied nook
Glow like a sunbeam: near his tomb
    a feast
Shone, silver-set; about it lay the
    guests,
And there we join'd them: then the
    maiden Aunt
Took this fair day for text, and from
    it preach'd
An universal culture for the crowd,
And all things great; but we, un-
    worthier, told
Of college: he had climb'd across the
    spikes,
And he had squeezed himself betwixt
    the bars,
And he had breath'd the Proctor's
    dogs; and one
Discuss'd his tutor, rough to common
    men,
But honeying at the whisper of a lord;
And one the Master, as a rogue in
    grain
Veneer'd with sanctimonious theory.

But while they talk'd, above their
    heads I saw
The feudal warrior lady-clad; which
    brought
My book to mind: and opening this I
    read
Of old Sir Ralph a page or two that
    rang

With tilt and tourney; then the tale
    of her
That drove her foes with slaughter
    from her walls,
And much I praised her nobleness,
    and "Where,"
Ask'd Walter, patting Lilia's head
    (she lay
Beside him) "lives there such a
    woman now?"

Quick answer'd Lilia "There are
    thousands now
Such women, but convention beats
    them down:
It is but bringing up; no more than
    that:
You men have done it: how I hate
    you all!
Ah, were I something great! I wish I
    were
Some mighty poetess, I would shame
    you then,
That love to keep us children! O I
    wish
That I were some great princess, I
    would build
Far off from men a college like a
    man's,
And I would teach them all that men
    are taught;
We are twice as quick!" And here
    she shook aside
The hand that play'd the patron with
    her curls.

And one said smiling "Pretty were
    the sight
If our old halls could change their
    sex, and flaunt
With prudes for proctors, dowagers
    for deans,
And sweet girl-graduates in their
    golden hair.
I think they should not wear our rusty
    gowns,
But move as rich as Emperor-moths,
    or Ralph
Who shines so in the corner; yet I
    fear,
If there were many Lilias in the brood,

However deep you might embower the
  nest,
Some boy would spy it."
          At this upon the sward
She tapt her tiny silken-sandal'd foot:
"That's your light way; but I would
  make it death
For any male thing but to peep at us."

Petulant she spoke, and at herself
  she laugh'd;
A rosebud set with little wilful thorns,
And sweet as English air could make
  her, she:
But Walter hail'd a score of names
  upon her,
And "petty Ogress," and "ungrateful
  Puss,"
And swore he long'd at college,
  only long'd,
All else was well, for she-society.
They boated and they cricketed; they
  talk'd
At wine, in clubs, of art, of politics;
They lost their weeks; they vext the
  souls of deans;
They rode; they betted; made a hun-
  dred friends,
And caught the blossom of the flying
  terms,
But miss'd the mignonette of Vivian-
  place,
The little hearth-flower Lilia. Thus
  he spoke,
Part banter, part affection.
          "True," she said,
"We doubt not that. O yes, you
  miss'd us much.
I'll stake my ruby ring upon it you
  did."

She held it out; and as a parrot
  turns
Up thro' gilt wires a crafty loving eye,
And takes a lady's finger with all care,
And bites it for true heart and not for
  harm,
So he with Lilia's. Daintily she
  shriek'd
And wrung it. "Doubt my word
  again!" he said.

"Come, listen! here is proof that you
  were miss'd:
We seven stay'd at Christmas up to
  read;
And there we took one tutor as to
  read:
The hard-grain'd Muses of the cube
  and square
Were out of season: never man, I
  think,
So moulder'd in a sinecure as
  he:
For while our cloisters echo'd frosty
  feet,
And our long walks were stript as bare
  as brooms,
We did but talk you over, pledge you
  all
In wassail; often, like as many girls —
Sick for the hollies and the yews of
  home —
As many little trifling Lilias — play'd
Charades and riddles as at Christmas
  here,
And *what's my thought* and *when* and
  where and *how*,
And often told a tale from mouth to
  mouth
As here at Christmas."
          She remember'd that:
A pleasant game, she thought: she
  liked it more
Than magic music, forfeits, all the
  rest.
But these — what kind of tales did
  men tell me,
She wonder'd by themselves?
          A half-disdain
Perch'd on the pouted blossom of her
  lips:
And Walter nodded at me; " *He*
  began,
The rest would follow, each in turn;
  and so
We forged a sevenfold story. Kind?
  what kind?
Chimeras, crotchets, Christmas sole-
  cisms,
Seven-headed monsters only made to
  kill
Time by the fire in winter."
          'Kill him now,

The tyrant! kill him in the summer
    too,"
Said Lilia; "Why not now?" the
    maiden Aunt.
"Why not a summer's as a winter's
    tale?
A tale for summer as befits the time,
And something it should be to suit the
    place,
Heroic, for a hero lies beneath,
Grave, solemn!"
      Walter warp'd his mouth at this
To something so mock-solemn, that I
    laugh'd
And Lilia woke with sudden-shrilling
    mirth
An echo like a ghostly woodpecker,
Hid in the ruins; till the maiden
    Aunt
(A little sense of wrong had touch'd
    her face
With color) turn'd to me with "As
    you will;
Heroic if you will, or what you will,
Or be yourself your hero if you will."

"Take Lilia, then, for heroine"
    clamor'd he,
"And make her some great Princess,
    six feet high,
Grand, epic, homicidal; and be you
The Prince to win her!"

"Then follow me, the Prince,"
I answer'd, "each be hero in his turn!
Seven and yet one, like shadows in a
    dream. —
Heroic seems our Princess as re-
    quired —
But something made to suit with Time
    and place,
A Gothic ruin and a Grecian house,
A talk of college and of ladies' rights,
A feudal knight in silken masquerade,
And, yonder, shrieks and strange ex-
    periments
For which the good Sir Ralph had
    burnt them all —
This *were* a medley! we should have
    him back
Who told the 'Winter's tale' to do it
    for us.

No matter   we will say whatever
    comes.
And let the ladies sing us, if they will,
From time to time, some ballad or a
    song
To give us breathing-space."
              So I began,
And the rest follow'd. and the women
    sang
Between the rougher voices of the
    men,
Like linnets in the pauses of the wind:
And here I give the story and the
    songs.

I.

A prince I was, blue-eyed, and fair in
    face,
Of temper amorous, as the first of
    May,
With lengths of yellow ringlet, like a
    girl,
For on my cradle shone the Northern
    star

There lived an ancient legend in
    our house.
Some sorcerer, whom a far-off grand-
    sire burnt
Because he cast no shadow, had fore-
    told,
Dying, that none of all our blood
    should know
The shadow from the substance, and
    that one
Should come to fight with shadows
    and to fall.
For so, my mother said, the story ran.
And, truly, waking dreams were, more
    or less,
An old and strange affection of the
    house.
Myself too had weird seizures, Heaven
    knows what:
On a sudden in the midst of men and
    day,
And while I walk'd and talk'd as here-
    tofore,
I seem'd to move among a world of
    ghosts,
And feel myself the shadow of a
    dream.

Our great court-Galen poised his gilt-
   head cane,
And paw'd his beard, and mutter'd
   "catalepsy."
My mother pitying made a thousand
   prayers;
My mother was as mild as any saint,
Half-canonized by all that look'd on
   her,
So gracious was her tact and tender-
   ness:
But my good father thought a king a
   king;
He cared not for the affection of the
   house;
He held his sceptre like a pedant's
   wand
To lash offence, and with long arms
   and hands
Reach'd out, and pick'd offenders
   from the mass
For judgment.
    Now it chanced that I had been,
While life was yet in bud and blade,
   betroth'd
To one, a neighboring Princess: she
   to me
Was proxy-wedded with a bootless calf
At eight years old; and still from
   time to time
Came murmurs of her beauty from
   the South,
And of her brethren, youths of puis-
   sance;
And still I wore her picture by my
   heart,
And one dark tress; and all around
   them both
Sweet thoughts would swarm as bees
   about their queen.

   But when the days drew nigh that
   I should wed,
My father sent ambassadors with
   furs
And jewels, gifts, to fetch her: these
   brought back
A present, a great labor of the loom;
And therewithal an answer vague as
   wind:
Besides, they saw the king; he took
   the gifts;

He said there was a compact; that
   was true:
But then she had a will; was he to
   blame?
And maiden fancies; loved to live
   alone
Among her women; certain, would
   not wed.

   That morning in the presence room
   I stood
With Cyril and with Florian, my two
   friends:
The first, a gentleman of broken means
(His father's fault) but given to starts
   and bursts
Of revel; and the last, my other heart,
And almost my half-self, for still we
   moved
Together, twinn'd as horse's ear and
   eye.

   Now, while they spake, I saw my
   father's face
Grow long and troubled like a rising
   moon,
Inflamed with wrath: he started on
   his feet,
Tore the king's letter, snow'd it down,
   and rent
The wonder of the loom thro' warp
   and woof
From skirt to skirt; and at the last
   he sware
That he would send a hundred thousand men,
And bring her in a whirlwind: then
   he chew'd
The thrice-turn'd cud of wrath, and
   cook'd his spleen,
Communing with his captains of the
   war.

   At last I spoke. " My father, let me
   go.
It cannot be but some gross error lies
In this report, this answer of a king,
Whom all men rate as kind and hos-
   pitable:
Or, maybe, I myself, my bride once
   seen,
Whate'er my grief to find her less
   than fame,

May rue the bargain made." And
    Florian said:
" I have a sister at the foreign court,
Who moves about the Princess; she,
    you know,
Who wedded with a nobleman from
    thence:
He, dying lately, left her, as I hear,
The lady of three castles in that land:
Thro' her this matter might be sifted
    clean."
And Cyril whisper'd: "Take me with
    you too."
Then laughing "what, if these weird
    seizures come
Upon you in those lands, and no one
    near
To point you out the shadow from the
    truth!
Take me: I'll serve you better in a
    strait;
I grate on rusty hinges here:" but
    "No!"
Roar'd the rough king, "you shall not;
    we ourself
Will crush her pretty maiden fancies
    dead
In iron gauntlets: break the council
    up."

But when the council broke, I rose
    and past
Thro' the wild woods that hung about
    the town;
Found a still place, and pluck'd her
    likeness out;
Laid it on flowers, and watch'd it
    lying bathed
In the green gleam of dewy-tassell'd
    trees:
What were those fancies? wherefore
    break her troth?
Proud look'd the lips: but while I
    meditated
A wind arose and rush'd upon the
    South,
And shook the songs, the whispers,
    and the shrieks
Of the wild woods together; and a
    Voice
Went with it, "Follow, follow, thou
    shalt win."

Then, ere the silver sickle of that
    month
Became her golden shield, I stole from
    court
With Cyril and with Florian, unper-
    ceived,
Cat-footed thro' the town and half in
    dread
To hear my father's clamor at our
    backs
With Ho! from some bay-window
    shake the night;
But all was quiet: from the bastion'd
    walls
Like threaded spiders, one by one, we
    dropt,
And flying reach'd the frontier: then
    we crost
To a livelier land; and so by tilth
    and grange,
And vines, and blowing bosks of wil-
    derness,
We gain'd the mother-city thick with
    towers,
And in the imperial palace found the
    king.

His name was Gama; crack'd and
    small his voice,
But bland the smile that like a wrin-
    kling wind
On glassy water drove his cheek in
    lines;
A little dry old man, without a star,
Not like a king: three days he feasted
    us,
And on the fourth I spake of why we
    came,
And my betroth'd. "You do us,
    Prince," he said,
Airing a snowy hand and signet
    gem,
" All honor. We remember love our-
    selves
In our sweet youth: there did a com-
    pact pass
Long summers back, a kind of cere-
    mony —
I think the year in which our olives
    fail'd.
I would you had her, prince, with all
    my heart,

With my full heart: but there were
   widows here,
Two widows, Lady Psyche, Lady
   Blanche;
They fed her theories, in and out of
   place
Maintaining that with equal hus-
   bandry
The woman were an equal to the man.
They harp'd on this; with this our
   banquets rang;
Our dances broke and buzz'd in knots
   of talk;
Nothing but this; my very ears were hot
To hear them: knowledge, so my
   daughter held,
Was all in all: they had but been, she
   thought,
As children; they must lose the child,
   assume
The woman: then, Sir, awful odes she
   wrote,
Too awful, sure, for what they treated
   of,
But all she is and does is awful;
   odes
About this losing of the child; and
   rhymes
And dismal lyrics, prophesying change
Beyond all reason: these the women
   sang;
And they that know such things — I
   sought but peace;
No critic I — would call them master-
   pieces:
They master'd *me*. At last she begg'd
   a boon,
A certain summer-palace which I
   have
Hard by your father's frontier: I said
   no,
Yet being an easy man, gave it: and
   there,
All wild to found an University
For maidens, on the spur she fled;
   and more
We know not, — only this: they see
   no men,
Not ev'n her brother Arac, nor the twins
Her brethren, tho' they love her, look
   upon her
As on a kind of paragon; and I

(Pardon me saying it) were much loth
   to breed
Dispute betwixt myself and mine: but
   since
(And I confess with right) you think
   me bound
In some sort, I can give you letters to
   her;
And yet, to speak the truth, I rate
   your chance
Almost as naked nothing."

                Thus the king;
And I, tho' nettled that he seem'd to
   slur
With garrulous ease and oily courte-
   sies
Our formal compact, yet, not less (all
   frets
But chafing me on fire to find my
   bride)
Went forth again with both my
   friends. We rode
Many a long league back to the North.
   At last
From hills, that look'd across a land
   of hope,
We dropt with evening on a rustic
   town
Set in a gleaming river's crescent-
   curve,
Close at the boundary of the liberties;
There, enter'd an old hostel, call'd
   mine host
To council, plied him with his richest
   wines,
And show'd the late-writ letters of
   the king.

He with a long low sibilation, stared
As blank as death in marble; then ex-
   claim'd
Averring it was clear against all rules
For any man to go: but as his brain
Began to mellow, "If the king," he
   said,
" Had given us letters, was he bound
   to speak ?
The king would bear him out;" and
   at the last —
The summer of the vine in all his
   veins —

" No doubt that we might make it worth his while.
She once had passed that way; he heard her speak;
She scared him; life ! he never saw the like;
She look'd as grand as doomsday and as grave :
And he, he reverenced his liege-lady there;
He always made a point to post with mares;
His daughter and his housemaid were the boys:
The land, he understood, for miles about
Was till'd by women; all the swine were sows,
And all the dogs "—
      But while he jested thus,
A thought flash'd thro' me which I clothed in act,
Remembering how we three presented Maid
Or Nymph, or Goddess, at high tide of feast,
In masque or pageant at my father's court.
We sent mine host to purchase female gear;
He brought it, and himself, a sight to shake
The midriff of despair with laughter, holp
To lace us up, till, each, in maiden plumes
We rustled : him we gave a costly bribe
To guerdon silence, mounted our good steeds,
And boldly ventured on the liberties.

    We follow'd up the river as we rode,
And rode till midnight when the college lights
Began to glitter firefly-like in copse
And linden alley : then we past an arch,
Whereon a woman-statue rose with wings

From four wing'd horses dark against the stars;
And some inscription ran along the front,
But deep in shadow : further on we gain'd
A little street half garden and half house;
But scarce could hear each other speak for noise
Of clocks and chimes, like silver hammers falling
On silver anvils, and the splash and stir
Of fountains spouted up and showering down
In meshes of the jasmine and the rose :
And all about us peal'd the nightingale,
Rapt in her song, and careless of the snare.

    There stood a bust of Pallas for a sign,
By two sphere lamps blazon'd like Heaven and Earth
With constellation and with continent,
Above an entry : riding in, we call'd;
A plump-arm'd Ostleress and a stable wench
Came running at the call, and help'd us down.
Then stept a buxon hostess forth, and sail'd,
Full-blown, before us into rooms which gave
Upon a pillar'd porch, the bases lost
In laurel : her we ask'd of that and this,
And who were tutors. " Lady Blanche," she said,
" And Lady Psyche." " Which was prettiest,
Best-natured ? " " Lady Psyche." " Hers are we,"
One voice, we cried; and I sat down and wrote,
In such a hand as when a field of corn
Bows all its ears before the roaring East;

"Three ladies of the Northern empire
    pray
Your Highness would enroll them with
    your own,
As Lady Psyche's pupils."
             This I seal'd :
The seal was Cupid bent above a scroll,
And o'er his head Uranian Venus hung,
And rais'd the blinding bandage from
    his eyes :
I gave the letter to be sent with dawn ;
And then to bed, where half in doze I
    seem'd
To float about a glimmering night,
    and watch
A full sea glazed with muffled moon-
    light, swell
On some dark shore just seen that it
    was rich.

II.

As thro' the land at eve we went,
   And pluck'd the ripen'd ears,
We fell out, my wife and I,
O we fell out I know not why,
   And kiss'd again with tears.
And blessings on the falling out
   That all the more endears,
When we fall out with those we love
   And kiss again with tears!
For when we came where lies the child
   We lost in other years,
There above the little grave,
O there above the little grave,
   We kiss'd again with tears.

At break of day the College Portress
    came :
She brought us Academic silks, in hue
The lilac, with a silken hood to each,
And zoned with gold ; and now when
    these were on,
And we as rich as moths from dusk
    cocoons,
She, courtesying her obeisance, let us
    know
The Princess Ida waited : out we paced,
I first, and following thro' the porch
    that sang
All round with laurel, issued in a court
Compact of lucid marbles, boss'd with
    lengths
Of classic frieze, with ample awnings
    gay
Betwixt the pillars, and with great
    urns of flowers.

The Muses and the Graces, group'd in
    threes,
Enring'd a billowing fountain in the
    midst ;
And here and there on lattice edges
    lay
Or book or lute ; but hastily we past,
And up a flight of stairs into the hall.

There at a board by tome and paper
    sat,
With two tame leopards couch'd be-
    side her throne
All beauty compass'd in a female form,
The Princess ; liker to the inhabitant
Of some clear planet close upon the
    Sun,
Than our man's earth ; such eyes were
    in her head,
And so much grace and power, breath-
    ing down
From over her arch'd brows, with
    every turn
Lived thro' her to the tips of her long
    hands,
And to her feet.   She rose her height,
    and said :

"We give you welcome : not with-
    out redound
Of use and glory to yourselves ye
    come,
The first-fruits of the stranger : after-
    time,
And that full voice which circles round
    the grave,
Will rank you nobly, mingled up with
    me.
What ! are the ladies of your land so
    tall ? "
"We of the court " said Cyril. "From
    the court "
She answer'd, "then ye know the
    Prince ? " and he :
"The climax of his age ! as tho' there
    were
One rose in all the world, your High-
    ness that,
He worships your ideal : " she replied :
" We scarcely thought in our own hall
    to hear

This barren verbiage, current among men,
Light coin, the tinsel clink of compliment.
Your flight from out your bookless wilds would seem
As arguing love of knowledge and of power ;
Your language proves you still the child. Indeed,
We dream not of him : when we set our hand
To this great work, we purposed with ourself
Never to wed. You likewise will do well,
Ladies, in entering here, to cast and fling
The tricks, which make us toys of men, that so,
Some future time, if so indeed you will,
You may with those self-styled our lords ally
Your fortunes, justlier balanced, scale with scale."

At those high words, we conscious of ourselves,
Perused the matting; then an officer
Rose up, and read the statutes, such as these :
Not for three years to correspond with home ;
Not for three years to cross the liberties ;
Not for three years to speak with any men ;
And many more, which hastily subscribed,
We enter'd on the boards : and " Now," she cried,
" Ye are green wood, see ye warp not. Look, our hall !
Our statues ! -- not of those that men desire,
Sleek Odalisques, or oracles of mode,
Nor stunted squaws of West or East ; but she
That taught the Sabine how to rule, and she
The foundress of the Babylonian wall,
The Carian Artemisia strong in war,

The Rhodope, that built the pyramid,
Clelia, Cornelia, with the Palmyrene
That fought Aurelian, and the Roman brows
Of Agrippina. Dwell with these, and lose
Convention, since to look on noble forms
Makes noble thro' the sensuous organism
That which is higher. O lift your natures up :
Embrace our aims : work out your freedom. Girls,
Knowledge is now no more a fountain seal'd :
Drink deep, until the habits of the slave,
The sins of emptiness, gossip and spite
And slander, die. Better not be at all
Than not be noble. Leave us : you may go :
To-day the Lady Psyche will harangue
The fresh arrivals of the week before;
For they press in from all the provinces,
And fill the hive."
            She spoke, and bowing waved
Dismissal : back again we crost the court
To Lady Psyche's : as we enter'd in,
There sat along the forms, like morning doves
That sun their milky bosoms on the thatch,
A patient range of pupils ; she herself
Erect behind a desk of satin-wood,
A quick brunette, well-moulded, falcon-eyed,
And on the hither side, or so she look'd,
Of twenty summers. At her left, a child,
In shining draperies, headed like a star,
Her maiden babe, a double April old,
Aglaïa slept. We sat : the Lady glanced :
Then Florian, but no livelier than the dame

That whisper'd "Asses' ears," among
   the sedge,
"My sister." "Comely, too, by all
   that's fair,"
Said Cyril. "O hush, hush!" and she
   began.

   "This world was once a fluid haze
      of light,
Till toward the centre set the starry
   tides,
And eddied into suns, that wheeling
   cast
The planets: then the monster, then
   the man;
Tattoo'd or woaded, winter-clad in
   skins,
Raw from the prime, and crushing
   down his mate;
As yet we find in barbarous isles, and
   here
Among the lowest."
                Thereupon she took
A bird's-eye view of all the ungracious
   past;
Glanced at the legendary Amazon
As emblematic of a nobler age;
Appraised the Lycian custom, spoke
   of those
That lay at wine with Lar and Lucu-
   mo;
Ran down the Persian, Grecian, Ro-
   man lines
Of empire, and the woman's state in
   each,
How far from just; till warming with
   her theme
She fulmined out her scorn of laws
   Salique
And little-footed China, touch'd on
   Mahomet
With much contempt, and came to
   chivalry:
When some respect, however slight,
   was paid
To woman, superstition all awry:
However then commenced the dawn:
   a beam
Had slanted forward, falling in a
   land
Of promise; fruit would follow. Deep,
   indeed,

Their debt of thanks to her who first
   had dared
To leap the rotten pales of prejudice,
Disyoke their necks from custom, and
   assert
None lordlier than themselves but
   that which made
Woman and man. She had founded;
   they must build.
Here might they learn whatever men
   were taught:
Let them not fear: some said their
   heads were less:
Some men's were small; not they the
   least of men;
For often fineness compensated size:
Besides the brain was like the hand,
   and grew
With using; thence the man's, if more
   was more;
He took advantage of his strength to
   be
First in the field: some ages had been
   lost;
But woman ripen'd earlier, and her
   life
Was longer; and albeit their glorious
   names
Were fewer, scatter'd stars, yet since
   in truth
The highest is the measure of the man,
And not the Kaffir, Hottentot, Malay,
Nor those horn-handed breakers of
   the glebe,
But Homer, Plato, Verulam; even so
With woman: and in arts of govern-
   ment
Elizabeth and others; arts of war
The peasant Joan and others; arts of
   grace
Sappho and others vied with any man;
And, last not least, she who had left
   her place,
And bow'd her state to them, that they
   might grow
To use and power on this Oasis, lapt
In the arms of leisure, sacred from
   the blight
Of ancient influence and scorn.
                           At last
She rose upon a wind of prophecy
Dilating on the future; "everywhere

Two heads in council, two beside the
  hearth,
Two in the tangled business of the
  world,
Two in the liberal offices of life,
Two plummets dropt for one to sound
  the abyss   .
Of science, and the secrets of the
  mind:
Musician, painter, sculptor, critic,
  more :
And everywhere the broad and bounteous Earth
Should bear a double growth of those
  rare souls,
Poets, whose thoughts enrich the
  blood of the world."

  She ended here, and beckon'd us:
  the rest
Parted; and, glowing full-faced wel-
  come, she
Began to address us, and was moving
  on
In gratulation, till as when a boat
Tacks, and the slacken'd sail flaps,
  all her voice
Faltering and fluttering in her throat,
  she cried
" My brother!" "Well, my sister."
  " O," she said,
" What do you here? and in this
  dress? and these?
Why who are these? a wolf within
  the fold!
A pack of wolves! the Lord be gra-
  cious to me!
A plot, a plot, a plot, to ruin all!"
" No plot, no plot," he answer'd.
  " Wretched boy,
How saw you not the inscription on
  the gate,
LET NO MAN ENTER IN ON PAIN OF
  DEATH ? "
" And if I had," he answer'd, "who
  could think
The softer Adams of your Academe,
O sister, Sirens tho' they be, were
  such
As chanted on the blanching bones of
  men ? "

" But you will find it otherwise " she
  said.
" You jest: ill jesting with edge-tools!
  my vow
Binds me to speak, and O that iron
  will,
That axelike edge unturnable, our
  Head,
The Princess." " Well then, Psyche,
  take my life,
And nail me like a weasel on a grange
For warning: bury me beside the
  gate,
And cut this epitaph above my bones;
Here lies a brother by a sister slain,
All for the common good of womankind."
" Let me die too," said Cyril, " having
  seen
And heard the Lady Psyche."
                    I struck in:
" Albeit so mask'd, Madam, I love the
  truth;
Receive it; and in me behold the
  Prince
Your countryman, affianced years ago
To the Lady Ida: here, for here she
  was,
And thus (what other way was left) I
  came."
" O Sir, O Prince, I have no country;
  none;
If any, this; but none. Whate'er I
  was
Disrooted, what I am is grafted here.
Affianced, Sir? love-whispers may
  not breathe
Within this vestal limit, and how
  should I,
Who am not mine, say, live: the
  thunder-bolt
Hangs silent; but prepare: I speak;
  it falls."
" Yet pause," I said : "for that in-
  scription there,
I think no more of deadly lurks therein,
Than in a clapper clapping in a garth,
To scare the fowl from fruit: if more
  there be,
If more and acted on, what follows?
  war;
Your own work marr'd: for this your
  Academe,

Whichever side be Victor, in the hal-
loo
Will topple to the trumpet down, and
pass
With all fair theories only made to
gild
A stormless summer." "Let the
Princess judge
Of that" she said: "farewell, Sir —
and to you.
I shudder at the sequel, but I go."

"Are you that Lady Psyche," I re-
join'd,
"The fifth in line from that old Flo-
rian,
Yet hangs his portrait in my father's
hall
(The gaunt old Baron with his beetle
brow
Sun-shaded in the heat of dusty fights)
As he bestrode my Grandsire, when he
fell,
And all else fled: we point to it, and
we say,
The loyal warmth of Florian is not
cold,
But branches current yet in kindred
veins."
"Are you that Psyche," Florian add-
ed: "she
With whom I sang about the morning
hills,
Flung ball, flew kite, and raced the
purple fly,
And snared the squirrel of the glen?
are you
That Psyche, wont to bind my throb-
bing brow,
To smoothe my pillow, mix the foam-
ing draught
Of fever, tell me pleasant tales, and
read
My sickness down to happy dreams?
are you
That brother-sister Psyche, both in
one?
You were that Psyche, but what are
you now?"
"You are that Psyche," Cyril said,
"for whom
I would be that for ever which I seem,

Woman, if I might sit beside your feet,
And glean your scatter'd sapience."
                                   Then once more,
"Are you that Lady Psyche," I began,
"That on her bridal morn before she
past
From all her old companions, when
the king
Kiss'd her pale cheek, declared that
ancient ties
Would still be dear beyond the south-
ern hills;
That were there any of our people
there
In want or peril, there was one to hear
And help them? look! for such are
these and I."
"Are you that Psyche," Florian ask'd,
"to whom,
In gentler days, your arrow-wounded
fawn
Came flying while you sat beside the
well?
The creature laid his muzzle on your
lap,
And sobb'd, and you sobb'd with it,
and the blood
Was sprinkled on your kirtle, and you
wept.
That was fawn's blood, not brother's,
yet you wept.
O by the bright head of my little
niece,
You were that Psyche, and what are
you now?"
"You are that Psyche," Cyril said
again,
"The mother of the sweetest little
maid,
That ever crow'd for kisses."
                                   "Out upon it!"
She answer'd, "peace! and why should
I not play
The Spartan Mother with emotion, be
The Lucius Junius Brutus of my kind?
Him you call great: he for the com-
mon weal,
The fading politics of mortal Rome,
As I might slay this child, if good
need were,
Slew both his sons: and I, shall I, on
whom

The secular emancipation turns
Of half this world, be swerved from
    right to save
A prince, a brother? a little will I
    yield.
Best so, perchance, for us, and well
    for you.
O hard, when love and duty clash! I
    fear
My conscience will not count me fleck-
    less; yet —
Hear my conditions: promise (other-
    wise
You perish) as you came, to slip away
To-day, to-morrow, soon: it shall be
    said,
These women were too barbarous,
    would not learn;
They fled, who might have shamed
    us: promise, all."

What could we else, we promised
    each; and she,
Like some wild creature newly-caged,
    commenced
A to-and-fro, so pacing till she paused
By Florian; holding out her lily
    arms
Took both his hands, and smiling
    faintly said:
"I knew you at the first: tho' you
    have grown
You scarce have alter'd: I am sad and
    glad
To see you, Florian. *I* give thee to
    death,
My brother! it was duty spoke, not I.
My needful seeming harshness, pardon
    it.
Our mother, is she well?"
            With that she kiss'd
His forehead, then, a moment after,
    clung
About him, and betwixt them blos-
    som'd up
From out a common vein of memory
Sweet household talk, and phrases of
    the hearth,
And far allusion, till the gracious
    dews
Began to glisten and to fall: and
    while

They stood, so rapt, we gazing, came
    a voice,
"I brought a message here from Lady
    Blanche."
Back started she, and turning round
    we saw
The Lady Blanche's daughter where
    she stood,
Melissa, with her hand upon the lock,
A rosy blonde, and in a college gown,
That clad her like an April daffodilly
(Her mother's color) with her lips
    apart,
And all her thoughts as fair within
    her eyes,
As bottom agates seen to wave and
    float
In crystal currents of clear morning
    seas.

So stood that same fair creature at
    the door.
Then Lady Psyche, "Ah — Melissa —
    you!
You heard us?" and Melissa, "O
    pardon me
I heard, I could not help it, did not
    wish:
But, dearest Lady, pray you fear me
    not,
Nor think I bear that heart within my
    breast,
To give three gallant gentlemen to
    death."
"I trust you," said the other, "for
    we two
Were always friends, none closer, elm
    and vine:
But yet your mother's jealous tem-
    perament —
Let not your prudence, dearest,
    drowse, or prove
The Danaïd of a leaky vase, for fear
This whole foundation ruin, and I lose
My honor, these their lives." "Ah,
    fear me not"
Replied Melissa; "no — I would not
    tell,
No, not for all Aspasia's cleverness,
No, not to answer, Madam, all those
    hard things
That Sheba came to ask of Solomon."

"Be it so" the other, "that we still
    may lead
The new light up, and culminate in
    peace,
For Solomon may come to Sheba yet."
Said Cyril, "Madam, he the wisest
    man
Feasted the woman wisest then, in
    halls
Of Lebanonian cedar: nor should you
(Tho' Madam *you* should answer, *we*
    would ask)
Less welcome find among us, if you
    came
Among us, debtors for our lives to you,
Myself for something more." He said
    not what,
But "Thanks," she answer'd "Go:
    we have been too long
Together: keep your hoods about the
    face;
They do so that affect abstraction
    here.
Speak little; mix not with the rest;
    and hold
Your promise: all, I trust, may yet
    be well."

We turn'd to go, but Cyril took the
    child,
And held her round the knees against
    his waist,
And blew the swoll'n cheek of a
    trumpeter,
While Psyche watch'd them, smiling,
    and the child
Push'd her flat hand against his face
    and laugh'd;
And thus our conference closed.
            And then we stroll'd
For half the day thro' stately theatres
Bench'd crescent-wise. In each we
    sat, we heard
The grave Professor. On the lecture
    slate
The circle rounded under female
    hands
With flawless demonstration: follow'd
    then
A classic lecture, rich in sentiment,
With scraps of thundrous Epic lilted
    out

By violet-hooded Doctors, elegies
And quoted odes, and jewels five-
    words-long
That on the stretch'd forefinger of all
    Time
Sparkle for ever: then we dipt in all
That treats of whatsoever is, the state,
The total chronicles of man, the mind,
The morals, something of the frame,
    the rock,
The star, the bird, the fish, the shell,
    the flower,
Electric, chemic laws, and all the rest,
And whatsoever can be taught and
    known;
Till like three horses that have broken
    fence,
And glutted all night long breast-
    deep in corn,
We issued gorged with knowledge,
    and I spoke:
"Why, Sirs, they do all this as well
    as we."
"They hunt old trails," said Cyril,
    "very well;
But when did woman ever yet in-
    vent?"
"Ungracious!" answer'd Florian;
    "have you learnt
No more from Psyche's lecture, you
    that talk'd
The trash that made me sick, and
    almost sad?"
"O trash," he said, "but with a ker-
    nel in it.
Should I not call her wise, who made
    me wise?
And learnt? I learnt more from her
    in a flash,
Than if my brainpan were an empty
    hull,
And every Muse tumbled a science in.
A thousand hearts lie fallow in these
    halls,
And round these halls a thousand
    baby loves
Fly twanging headless arrows at the
    hearts,
Whence follows many a vacant pang;
    but O
With me, Sir, enter'd in the bigger
    boy,

The Head of all the golden-shafted firm,
The long-limb'd lad that had a Psyche too ;
He cleft me thro' the stomacher ; and now
What think you of it, Florian ? do I chase
The substance or the shadow ? will it hold ?
I have no sorcerer's malison on me,
No ghostly hauntings like his Highness. I
Flatter myself that always everywhere
I know the substance when I see it. Well,
Are castles shadows ? Three of them ? Is she
The sweet proprietress a shadow ? If not,
Shall those three castles patch my tatter'd coat ?
For dear are those three castles to my wants,
And dear is sister Psyche to my heart,
And two dear things are one of double worth,
And much I might have said, but that my zone
Unmann'd me : then the Doctors ! O to hear
The Doctors ! O to watch the thirsty plants
Imbibing ! once or twice I thought to roar,
To break my chain, to shake my mane : but thou,
Modulate me, Soul of mincing mimicry !
Make liquid treble of that bassoon, my throat ;
Abase those eyes that ever loved to meet
Star-sisters answering under crescent brows ;
Abate the stride, which speaks of man, and loose
A flying charm of blushes o'er this cheek,
Where they like swallows coming out of time

Will wonder why they came : but hark the bell
For dinner, let us go !"
                And in we stream'd
Among the columns, pacing staid and still
By twos and threes, till all from end to end
With beauties every shade of brown and fair
In colors gayer than the morning mist,
The long hall glitter'd like a bed of flowers.
How might a man not wander from his wits
Pierced thro' with eyes, but that I kept mine own
Intent on her, who rapt in glorious dreams,
The second-sight of some Astræan age,
Sat compass'd with professors : they, the while,
Discuss'd a doubt and tost it to and fro :
A clamor thicken'd, mixt with inmost terms
Of art and science : Lady Blanche alone
Of faded form and haughtiest lineaments,
With all her autumn tresses falsely brown,
Shot sidelong daggers at us, a tiger-cat
In act to spring.
                At last a solemn grace
Concluded, and we sought the gardens : there
One walk'd reciting by herself, and one
In this hand held a volume as to read,
And smoothed a petted peacock down with that :
Some to a low song oar'd a shallop by,
Or under arches of the marble bridge
Hung, shadow'd from the heat : some hid and sought
In the orange thickets : others tost a ball
Above the fountain-jets, and back again
With laughter : others lay about the lawns,

Of the older sort, and murmur'd that
   their May
Was passing : what was learning unto
   them ?
They wish'd to marry; they could
   rule a house ;
Men hated learned women: but we
   three
Sat muffled like the Fates; and often
   came
Melissa hitting all we saw with shafts
Of gentle satire, kin to charity,
That harm'd not : then day droopt;
   the chapel bells
Call'd us: we left the walks; we mixt
   with those
Six hundred maidens clad in purest
   white,
Before two streams of light from wall
   to wall,
While the great organ almost burst
   his pipes,
Groaning for power, and rolling thro'
   the court
A long melodious thunder to the sound
Of solemn psalms, and silver litanies,
The work of Ida, to call down from
   Heaven
A blessing on her labors for the world.

III.

Sweet and low, sweet and low,
   Wind of the western sea,
Low, low, breathe and blow,
   Wind of the western sea!
Over the rolling waters go,
Come from the dying moon, and blow,
   Blow him again to me;
While my little one, while my pretty one,
   sleeps.

Sleep and rest, sleep and rest,
   Father will come to thee soon;
Rest, rest, on mother's breast,
   Father will come to thee soon;
Father will come to his babe in the nest,
Silver sails all out of the west
   Under the silver moon :
Sleep, my little one, sleep, my pretty one,
   sleep.

Morn in the white wake of the morning star
Came furrowing all the orient into
   gold.

We rose, and each by other drest with
   care
Descended to the court that lay three
   parts
In shadow, but the Muses' heads were
   touch'd
Above the darkness from their native
   East.

There while we stood beside the fount,
   and watch'd
Or seem'd to watch the dancing bub-
   ble, approach'd
Melissa, tinged with wan from lack of
   sleep,
Or grief, and glowing round her dewy
   eyes
The circled Iris of a night of tears;
"And fly," she cried, "O fly, while
   yet you may!
My mother knows:" and when I
   ask'd her "how,"
"My fault," she wept, "my fault! and
   yet not mine;
Yet mine in part. O hear me, pardon
   me.
My mother, 'tis her wont from night
   to night
To rail at Lady Psyche and her side.
She says the Princess should have
   been the Head,
Herself and Lady Psyche the two
   arms;
And so it was agreed when first they
   came;
But Lady Psyche was the right hand
   now,
And she the left, or not, or seldom
   used;
Hers more than half the students, all
   the love.
And so last night she fell to canvass
   you :
Her countrywomen ! she did not envy
   her.
' Who ever saw such wild barbarians ?
Girls ? — more like men ! ' and at these
   words the snake,
My secret, seem'd to stir within my
   breast;
And oh, Sirs, could I help it, but my
   cheek

Began to burn and burn, and her lynx
  eye
To fix and make me hotter, till she
  laugh'd:
'O marvellously modest maiden, you!
Men! girls, like men! why, if they
  had been men
You need not set your thoughts in
  rubric thus
For wholesale comment.' Pardon, I
  am shamed
That I must needs repeat for my
  excuse
What looks so little graceful: 'men'
  (for still
My mother went revolving on the
  word)
'And so they are, — very like men
  indeed —
And with that woman closeted for
  hours!'
Then came these dreadful words out
  one by one,
'Why — these — *are* — men:' I shudder'd: 'and you know it.'
'O ask me nothing,' I said: 'And
  she knows too,
And she conceals it.' So my mother
  clutch'd
The truth at once, but with no word
  from me;
And now thus early risen she goes to
  inform
The Princess: Lady Psyche will be
  crush'd;
But you may yet be saved, and therefore fly:
But heal me with your pardon ere you
  go."

"What pardon, sweet Melissa, for a
  blush?"
Said Cyril: "Pale one, blush again:
  than wear
Those lilies, better blush our lives
  away.
Yet let us breathe for one hour more
  in Heaven"
He added, "lest some classic Angel
  speak
In scorn of us, 'They mounted, Gany-
  medes,

To tumble, Vulcans, on the second
  morn.'
But I will melt this marble into wax
To yield us farther furlough:" and he
  went.

Melissa shook her doubtful curls,
  and thought
He scarce would prosper. "Tell us,"
  Florian ask'd,
"How grew this feud betwixt the
  right and left."
"O long ago," she said, "betwixt these
  two
Division smoulders hidden; 'tis my
  mother,
Too jealous, often fretful as the wind
Pent in a crevice: much I bear with
  her:
I never knew my father, but she says
(God help her) she was wedded to a
  fool;
And still she rail'd against the state
  of things.
She had the care of Lady Ida's youth,
And from the Queen's decease she
  brought her up.
But when your sister came she won
  the heart
Of Ida: they were still together, grew
(For so they said themselves) inoscu-
  lated;
Consonant chords that shiver to one
  note;
One mind in all things: yet my mother
  still
Affirms your Psyche thieved her the-
  ories,
And angled with them for her pupil's
  love:
She calls her plagiarist; I know not
  what:
But I must go: I dare not tarry," and
  light,
As flies the shadow of a bird, she fled.

Then murmur'd Florian gazing after
  her,
"An open-hearted maiden, true and
  pure.
If I could love, why this were she
  how pretty

Her blushing was, and how she blush'd
　　again,
As if to close with Cyril's random
　　wish:
Not like your Princess cramm'd with
　　erring pride,
Nor like poor Psyche whom she drags
　　in tow."

"The crane," I said, "may chatter
　　of the crane,
The dove may murmur of the dove,
　　but I
An eagle clang an eagle to the sphere.
My princess, O my princess! true she
　　errs,
But in her own grand way: being her-
　　self
Three times more noble than three
　　score of men,
She sees herself in every woman else,
And so she wears her error like a
　　crown
To blind the truth and me: for her,
　　and her,
Hebes are they to hand ambrosia, mix
The nectar; but — ah she — whene'er
　　she moves
The Samian Herè rises and she speaks
A Memnon smitten with the morning
　　Sun."

So saying from the court we paced,
　　and gain'd
The terrace ranged along the North-
　　ern front,
And leaning there on those balusters,
　　high
Above the empurpled champaign,
　　drank the gale
That blown about the foliage under-
　　neath,
And sated with the innumerable rose,
Beat balm upon our eyelids. Hither
　　came
Cyril, and yawning "O hard task,"
　　he cried;
"No fighting shadows here! I forced
　　a way
Thro' solid opposition crabb'd and
　　gnarl'd.

Better to clear prime forests, heave
　　and thump
A league of street in summer solstice
　　down,
Than hammer at this reverend gentle-
　　woman.
I knock'd and, bidden, enter'd; found
　　her there
At point to move, and settled in her
　　eyes
The green malignant light of coming
　　storm.
Sir, I was courteous, every phrase
　　well-oil'd,
As man's could be; yet maiden-meek
　　I pray'd
Concealment: she demanded who we
　　were,
And why we came? I fabled nothing
　　fair,
But, your example pilot, told her all.
Up went the hush'd amaze of hand
　　and eye.
But when I dwelt upon your old affi-
　　ance,
She answer'd sharply that I talk'd
　　astray.
I urged the fierce inscription on the
　　gate,
And our three lives. True — we had
　　limed ourselves
With open eyes, and we must take
　　the chance.
But such extremes, I told her, well
　　might harm
The woman's cause. 'Not more than
　　now,' she said,
'So puddled as it is with favoritism.'
I tried the mother's heart. Shame
　　might befall
Melissa, knowing, saying not she
　　knew:
Her answer was 'Leave me to deal
　　with that.'
I spoke of war to come and many
　　deaths,
And she replied, her duty was to
　　speak,
And duty duty, clear of consequences.
I grew discouraged, Sir; but since I
　　knew
No rock so hard but that a little wave

May beat admission in a thousand
years,
I recommenced; 'Decide not ere you
pause.
I find you here but in the second place,
Some say the third — the authentic
foundress you.
I offer boldly: we will seat you highest:
Wink at our advent: help my prince
to gain
His rightful bride, and here I promise
you
Some palace in our land, where you
shall reign
The head and heart of all our fair she-
world,
And your great name flow on with
broadening time
For ever.' Well, she balanced this a
little,
And told me she would answer us to-
day,
Meantime be mute: thus much, nor
more I gain'd."

He ceasing, came a message from
the Head.
" That afternoon the Princess rode to
take
The dip of certain strata to the North.
Would we go with her ? we should find
the land
Worth seeing; and the river made a
fall
Out yonder:" then she pointed on to
where
A double hill ran up his furrowy forks
Beyond the thick-leaved platans of
the vale.

Agreed to, this, the day fled on thro'
all
Its range of duties to the appointed
hour.
Then summon'd to the porch we went.
She stood
Among her maidens, higher by the
head,
Her back against a pillar, her foot on
one

Of those tame leopards. Kittenlike
he roll'd
And paw'd about her sandal. I drew
near;
I gazed. On a sudden my strange
seizure came
Upon me, the weird vision of our
house:
The Princess Ida seem'd a hollow
show,
Her gay-furr'd cats a painted fantasy,
Her college and her maidens, empty
masks,
And I myself the shadow of a dream,
For all things were and were not. Yet
I felt
My heart beat thick with passion and
with awe;
Then from my breast the involuntary
sigh
Brake, as she smote me with the light
of eyes
That lent my knee desire to kneel, and
shook
My pulses, till to horse we got, and so
Went forth in long retinue following
up
The river as it narrow'd to the hills.

I rode beside her and to me she
said:
" O friend, we trust that you esteem'd
us not
Too harsh to your companion yestermorn;
Unwillingly we spake." "No — not
to her,"
I answer'd, "but to one of whom we
spake
Your Highness might have seem'd the
thing you say."
"Again ?" she cried, "are you am-
bassadresses
From him to me ? we give you, being
strange,
A license: speak, and let the topic
die."

I stammer'd that I knew him —
could have wish'd —
"Our king expects — was there no
precontract ?

There is no truer-hearted — ah, you
    seem
All he prefigured, and he could not see
The bird of passage flying south but
    long'd
To follow: surely, if your Highness
    keep
Your purport, you will shock him ev'n
    to death,
Or baser courses, children of despair."

"Poor boy," she said, "can he not
    read — no books?
Quoit, tennis, ball — no games? nor
    deals in that
Which men delight in, martial exer-
    cise?
To nurse a blind ideal like a girl,
Methinks he seems no better than a
    girl;
As girls were once, as we ourself have
    been:
We had our dreams; perhaps he mixt
    with them:
We touch on our dead self, nor shun
    to do it,
Being other — since we learnt our
    meaning here,
To lift the woman's fall'n divinity
Upon an even pedestal with man."

She paused, and added with a
    haughtier smile
"And as to precontracts, we move, my
    friend,
At no man's beck, but know ourself
    and thee,
O Vashti, noble Vashti! Summon'd
    out
She kept her state, and left the
    drunken king
To brawl at Shushan underneath the
    palms."

"Alas your Highness breathes full
    East," I said,
"On that which leans to you. I know
    the Prince,
I prize his truth: and then how vast
    a work
To assail this gray preeminence of
    man!

You grant me license; might I use it?
    think;
Ere half be done perchance your life
    may fail;
Then comes the feebler heiress of your
    plan,
And takes and ruins all; and thus
    your pains
May only make that footprint upon
    sand
Which old-recurring waves of preju-
    dice
Resmooth to nothing: might I dread
    that you,
With only Fame for spouse and your
    great deeds
For issue, yet may live in vain, and
    miss,
Meanwhile, what every woman counts
    her due,
Love, children, happiness?"
           And she exclaim'd,
"Peace, you young savage of the
    Northern wild!
What! tho' your Prince's love were
    like a God's,
Have we not made ourself the sacri-
    fice?
You are bold indeed: we are not
    talk'd to thus:
Yet will we say for children, would
    they grew
Like field-flowers everywhere! we like
    them well:
But children die; and let me tell you,
    girl,
Howe'er you babble, great deeds can-
    not die;
They with the sun and moon renew
    their light
For ever, blessing those that look on
    them.
Children — that men may pluck them
    from our hearts,
Kill us with pity, break us with our-
    selves —
O — children — there is nothing upon
    earth
More miserable than she that has a
    son
And sees him err: nor would we work
    for fame;

Tho' she perhaps might reap the ap-
plause of Great,
Who learns the one ΠΟΥ ΣΤΩ whence
after-hands
May move the world, tho' she herself
effect
But little : wherefore up and act, nor
shrink
For fear our solid aim be dissipated
By frail successors. Would, indeed,
we had been,
In lieu of many mortal flies, a race
Of giants living, each, a thousand
years,
That we might see our own work out,
and watch
The sandy footprint harden into
stone."

I answer'd nothing, doubtful in
myself
If that strange Poet-princess with her
grand
Imaginations might at all be won.
And she broke out interpreting my
thoughts:

"No doubt we seem a kind of
monster to you ;
We are used to that : for women, up
till this
Cramp'd under worse than South-sea
isle taboo,
Dwarfs of the gynæceum, fail so far
In high desire, they know not, cannot
guess
How much their welfare is a passion
to us.
If we could give them surer, quicker
proof —
Oh if our end were less achievable
By slow approaches, than by single
act
Of immolation, any phase of death,
We were as prompt to spring against
the pikes,
Or down the fiery gulf as talk of it,
To compass our dear sisters' lib-
erties."

She bow'd as if to vail a noble
tear ;

And up we came to where the river
sloped
To plunge in cataract, shattering on
black blocks
A breadth of thunder. O'er it shook
the woods,
And danced the color, and, below,
stuck out
The bones of some vast bulk that
lived and roar'd
Before man was. She gazed awhile
and said,
"As these rude bones to us, are we to
her
That will be." "Dare we dream of
that," I ask'd,
"Which wrought us, as the workman
and his work,
That practice betters ? " "How," she
cried, "you love
The metaphysics! read and earn
our prize,
A golden brooch : beneath an emerald
plane
Sits Diotima, teaching him that died
Of hemlock ; our device ; wrought to
the life ;
She rapt upon her subject, he on her :
For there are schools for all." "And
yet " I said
"Methinks I have not found among
them all
One anatomic." "Nay, we thought
of that,"
She answer'd, "but it pleased us not :
in truth
We shudder but to dream our maids
should ape
Those monstrous males that carve
the living hound,
And cram him with the fragments of
the grave,
Or in the dark dissolving human
heart,
And holy secrets of this microcosm,
Dabbling a shameless hand with
shameful jest,
Encarnalize their spirits: yet we
know
Knowledge is knowledge, and this
matter hangs :
Howbeit ourself, foreseeing casualty,

Nor willing men should come among
us, learnt,
For many weary moons before we
came,
This craft of healing. Were you
sick, ourself
Would tend upon you. To your
question now,
Which touches on the workman and
his work.
Let there be light and there was
light : 'tis so :
For was, and is, and will be, are but
is ;
And all creation is one act at once,
The birth of light : but we that are
not all,
As parts, can see but parts, now this,
now that,
And live, perforce, from thought to
thought, and make
One act a phantom of succession :
thus
Our weakness somehow shapes the
shadow, Time ;
But in the shadow will we work, and
mould
The woman to the fuller day."

She spake
With kindled eyes : we rode a league
beyond,
And, o'er a bridge of pinewood cross-
ing, came
On flowery levels underneath the crag,
Full of all beauty. "O how sweet"
I said
(For I was half-oblivious of my mask)
"To linger here with one that loved
us." "Yea,"
She answer'd, "or with fair philoso-
phies
That lift the fancy ; for indeed these
fields
Are lovely, lovelier not the Elysian
lawns,
Where paced the Demigods of old,
and saw
The soft white vapor streak the
crowned towers
Built to the Sun :" then, turning to
her maids,

"Pitch our pavilion here upon the
sward ;
Lay out the viands." At the word,
they raised
A tent of satin, elaborately wrought
With fair Corinna's triumph ; here
she stood,
Engirt with many a florid maiden-
cheek,
The woman conqueror ; woman-con-
quer'd there
The bearded Victor of ten-thousand
hymns,
And all the men mourn'd at his side :
but we
Set forth to climb ; then, climbing,
Cyril kept
With Psyche, with Melissa Florian, I
With mine affianced. Many a little
hand
Glanced like a touch of sunshine on
the rocks,
Many a light foot shone like a jewel
set
In the dark crag : and then we turn'd,
we wound
About the cliffs, the copses, out and in,
Hammering and clinking, chattering
stony names
Of shale and hornblende, rag and
trap and tuff,
Amygdaloid and trachyte, till the Sun
Grew broader toward his death and
fell, and all
The rosy heights came out above the
lawns.

IV.

The splendor falls on castle walls
   And snowy summits old in story :
The long light shakes across the lakes,
   And the wild cataract leaps in glory.
Blow, bugle, blow, set the wild echoes flying,
Blow, bugle ; answer, echoes, dying, dying,
   dying.

O hark, O hear ! how thin and clear,
   And thinner, clearer, farther going !
O sweet and far from cliff and scar
   The horns of Elfland faintly blowing !
Blow, let us hear the purple glens replying :
Blow, bugle ; answer, echoes, dying, dying,
   dying.

O love, they die in yon rich sky,
   They faint on hill or field or river :
Our echoes roll from soul to soul,

And grow for ever and for ever.
Blow, bugle, blow, set the wild echoes flying,
And answer, echoes, answer, dying, dying,
    dying.

"There sinks the nebulous star we
    call the Sun,
If that hypothesis of theirs be sound."
Said Ida; "let us down and rest;"
    and we
Down from the lean and wrinkled
    precipices,
By every coppice-feather'd chasm and
    cleft,
Dropt thro' the ambrosial gloom to
    where below
No bigger than a glow-worm shone
    the tent
Lamp-lit from the inner. Once she
    lean'd on me,
Descending; once or twice she lent
    her hand,
And blissful palpitations in the blood,
Stirring a sudden transport rose and
    fell.

But when we planted level feet,
    and dipt
Beneath the satin dome and enter'd in,
There leaning deep in broider'd down
    we sank
Our elbows: on a tripod in the midst
A fragrant flame rose, and before us
    glow'd
Fruit, blossom, viand, amber wine,
    and gold.

Then she, "Let some one sing to
    us: lightlier move
The minutes fledged with music:"
    and a maid,
Of those beside her, smote her harp,
    and sang.

"Tears, idle tears, I know not what they
    mean,
Tears from the depth of some divine despair
Rise in the heart, and gather to the eyes,
In looking on the happy Autumn-fields,
And thinking of the days that are no more.

"Fresh as the first beam glittering on a sail,
That brings our friends up from the under-
    world,
Sad as the last which reddens over one

That sinks with all we love below the verge;
So sad, so fresh, the days that are no more.

"Ah, sad and strange as in dark summer
    dawns
The earliest pipe of half-awaken'd birds
To dying ears, when unto dying eyes
The casement slowly grows a glimmering
    square;
So sad, so strange, the days that are no more.

"Dear as remember'd kisses after death,
And sweet as those by hopeless fancy feign'd
On lips that are for others; deep as love,
Deep as first love, and wild with all regret;
O Death in Life, the days that are no more."

She ended with such passion that
    the tear,
She sang of, shook and fell, an erring
    pearl
Lost in her bosom: but with some
    disdain
Answer'd the Princess, "If indeed
    there haunt
About the moulder'd lodges of the Past
So sweet a voice and vague, fatal to
    men,
Well needs it we should cram our ears
    with wool
And so pace by: but thine are fancies
    hatch'd
In silken-folded idleness; nor is it
Wiser to weep a true occasion lost,
But trim our sails, and let old bygones
    be,
While down the streams that float us
    each and all
To the issue, goes, like glittering
    bergs of ice,
Throne after throne, and molten on
    the waste
Becomes a cloud: for all things serve
    their time
Toward that great year of equal
    mights and rights,
Nor would I fight with iron laws, in
    the end
Found golden: let the past be past;
    let be
Their cancell'd Babels: tho' the rough
    kex break
The starr'd mosaic, and the beard-
    blown goat
Hang on the shaft, and the wild fig-
    tree split

Their monstrous idols, care not while
    we hear
A trumpet in the distance pealing news
Of better, and Hope, a poising eagle,
    burns
Above the unrisen morrow:" then to
    me;
"Know you no song of your own land,"
    she said,
" Not such as moans about the retro-
    spect,
But deals with the other distance and
    the hues
Of promise; not a death's-head at the
    wine."

    Then I remember'd one myself had
    made,
What time I watch'd the swallow
    winging south
From mine own land, part made long
    since, and part
Now while I sang, and maidenlike as
    far
As I could ape their treble, did I sing.

    " O Swallow, Swallow, flying, flying South,
Fly to her, and fall upon her gilded eaves,
And tell her, tell her, what I tell to thee.

    "O tell her, Swallow, thou that knowest
    each,
That bright and fierce and fickle is the South,
And dark and true and tender is the North.

    "O Swallow, Swallow, if I could follow,
    and light
Upon her lattice, I would pipe and trill,
And cheep and twitter twenty million loves.

    " O were I thou that she might take me in,
And lay me on her bosom, and her heart
Would rock the snowy cradle till I died.

    " Why lingereth she to clothe her heart
    with love,
Delaying as the tender ash delays
To clothe herself, when all the woods are
    green ?

    " O tell her, Swallow, that thy brood is
    flown:
Say to her, I do but wanton in the South,
But in the North long since my nest is made.

    "O tell her, brief is life but love is long,
And brief the sun of summer in the North,
And brief the moon of beauty in the South.

    " O Swallow, flying from the golden woods,
Fly to her, and pipe and woo her, and make
    her mine,
And tell her, tell her, that I follow thee."

    I ceased, and all the ladies, each at
    each,
Like the Ithacensian suitors in old
    time,
Stared with great eyes, and laugh'd
    with alien lips,
And knew not what they meant; for
    still my voice
Rang false: but smiling "Not for
    thee," she said,
" O Bulbul, any rose of Gulistan
Shall burst her veil: marsh-divers,
    rather, maid,
Shall croak thee sister, or the meadow-
    crake
Grate her harsh kindred in the grass:
    and this
A mere love-poem! O for such, my
    friend,
We hold them slight: they mind us of
    the time
When we made bricks in Egypt.
    Knaves are men,
That lute and flute fantastic tender-
    ness,
And dress the victim to the offering up.
And paint the gates of Hell with Par-
    adise,
And play the slave to gain the tyranny.
Poor soul! I had a maid of honor once;
She wept her true eyes blind for such
    a one,
A rogue of canzonets and serenades.
I loved her. Peace be with her. She
    is dead.
So they blaspheme the muse! But
    great is song
Used to great ends: ourself have often
    tried
Valkyrian hymns, or into rhythm
    have dash'd
The passion of the prophetess; for song
Is duer unto freedom, force and growth
Of spirit than to junketing and love.
Love is it ? Would this same mock-
    love, and this
Mock-Hymen were laid up like winter
    bats,

Till all men grew to rate us at our
 worth,
Not vassals to be beat, nor pretty babes
To be dandled, no, but living wills,
 and sphered
Whole in ourselves and owed to none.
 Enough!
But now to leaven play with profit,
 you,
Know you no song, the true growth of
 your soil,
That gives the manners of your coun-
 try-women?

She spoke and turn'd her sumptu-
 ous head with eyes
Of shining expectation fixt on mine.
Then while I dragg'd my brains for
 such a song,
Cyril, with whom the bell-mouth'd
 glass had wrought,
Or master'd by the sense of sport, be-
 gan
To troll a careless, careless tavern-
 catch
Of Moll and Meg, and strange experi-
 ences
Unmeet for ladies. Florian nodded
 at him,
I frowning; Psyche flush'd and wann'd
 and shook;
The lilylike Melissa droop'd her brows;
"Forbear," the Princess cried; "For-
 bear, Sir," I;
And heated thro' and thro' with wrath
 and love,
I smote him on the breast; he started
 up;
There rose a shriek as of a city sack'd;
Melissa clamor'd "Flee the death;"
"To horse,"
Said Ida; "home! to horse!" and
 fled, as flies
A troop of snowy doves athwart the
 dusk,
When some one batters at the dove-
 cote-doors,
Disorderly the women. Alone I stood
With Florian, cursing Cyril, vext at
 heart,
In the pavilion: there like parting
 hopes

I heard them passing from me: hoof
 by hoof,
And every hoof a knell to my desires,
Clang'd on the bridge; and then an-
 other shriek,
"The Head, the Head, the Princess, O
 the Head!"
For blind with rage she miss'd the
 plank, and roll'd
In the river. Out I sprang from glow
 to gloom:
There whirl'd her white robe like a
 blossom'd branch
Rapt to the horrible fall: a glance I
 gave,
No more; but woman-vested as I was
Plunged; and the flood drew; yet I
 caught her; then
Oaring one arm, and bearing in my
 left
The weight of all the hopes of half
 the world,
Strove to buffet to land in vain. A tree
Was half-disrooted from his place and
 stoop'd
To drench his dark locks in the gur-
 gling wave
Mid-channel. Right on this we drove
 and caught,
And grasping down the boughs I
 gain'd the shore.

There stood her maidens glimmer-
 ingly group'd
In the hollow bank. One reaching
 forward drew
My burthen from mine arms; they
 cried "she lives:"
They bore her back into the tent: but
 I,
So much a kind of shame within me
 wrought,
Not yet endured to meet her opening
 eyes,
Nor found my friends; but push'd
 alone on foot
(For since her horse was lost I left
 her mine)
Across the woods, and less from
 Indian craft
Than beelike instinct hiveward, found
 at length

The garden portals. Two great
statues, Art
And Science, Caryatids lifted up
A weight of emblem, and betwixt were
valves
Of open-work in which the hunter
rued
His rash intrusion, manlike, but his
brows
Had sprouted, and the branches thereupon
Spread out at top, and grimly spiked
the gates.

A little space was left between the
horns,
Thro' which I clamber'd o'er at top
with pain,
Dropt on the sward, and up the linden
walks,
And, tost on thoughts that changed
from hue to hue,
Now poring on the glowworm, now
the star,
I paced the terrace, till the Bear had
wheel'd
Thro' a great arc his seven slow suns.

A step
Of lightest echo, then a loftier form
Than female, moving thro' the uncer-
tain gloom,
Disturb'd me with the doubt "if this
were she,"
But it was Florian. "Hist O Hist,"
he said,
"They seek us: out so late is out of
rules.
Moreover 'seize the strangers' is the
cry.
How came you here?" I told him:
"I" said he,
"Last of the train, a moral leper, I,
To whom none spake, half-sick at
heart, return'd.
Arriving all confused among the rest
With hooded brows I crept into the
hall,
And, couch'd behind a Judith, under-
neath
The head of Holofernes peep'd and saw.
Girl after girl was call'd to trial: each

Disclaim'd all knowledge of us: last
of all,
Melissa: trust me, Sir, I pitied her.
She, question'd if she knew us men,
at first
Was silent; closer prest, denied it
not:
And then, demanded if her mother
knew,
Or Psyche, she affirm'd not, or denied:
From whence the Royal mind, familiar with her,
Easily gather'd either guilt. She
sent
For Psyche, but she was not there;
she call'd
For Psyche's child to cast it from
the doors;
She sent for Blanche to accuse her
face to face;
And I slipt out: but whither will you
now?
And where are Psyche, Cyril? both
are fled:
What, if together? that were not so
well.
Would rather we had never come! I
dread
His wildness, and the chances of the
dark."

"And yet," I said, "you wrong him
more than I
That struck him: this is proper to the
clown,
Tho' smock'd, or furr'd and purpled,
still the clown,
To harm the thing that trusts him,
and to shame
That which he says he loves: for
Cyril, howe'er
He deal in frolic, as to-night — the
song
Might have been worse and sinn'd in
grosser lips
Beyond all pardon — as it is, I hold
These flashes on the surface are not
he.
He has a solid base of temperament:
But as the waterlily starts and slides
Upon the level in little puffs of wind,

Tho' anchor'd to the bottom, such is
he."

Scarce had I ceased when from a
    tamarisk near
Two Proctors leapt upon us, crying,
    " Names : "
He, standing still, was clutch'd ; but
    I began
To thrid the musky-circled mazes,
    wind
And double in and out the boles, and
    race
By all the fountains : fleet I was of
    foot :
Before me shower'd the rose in flakes ;
    behind
I heard the puff'd pursuer ; at mine
    ear
Bubbled the nightingale and heeded
    not,
And secret laughter tickled all my
    soul.
At last I hook'd my ankle in a vine,
That claspt the feet of a Mnemosyne,
And falling on my face was caught
    and known.

They haled us to the Princess
    where she sat
High in the hall : above her droop'd
    a lamp,
And made the single jewel on her
    brow
Burn like the mystic fire on a mast-
    head,
Prophet of storm : a handmaid on
    each side
Bow'd toward her, combing out her
    long black hair
Damp from the river ; and close be-
    hind her stood
Eight daughters of the plough,
    stronger than men,
Huge women blowzed with health,
    and wind, and rain,
And labor. Each was like a Druid
    rock ;
Or like a spire of land that stands
    apart
Cleft from the main, and wail'd about
    with mews.

Then, as we came, the crowd divid-
    ing clove
An advent to the throne : and there-
    beside,
Half-naked as if caught at once from
    bed
And tumbled on the purple footcloth,
    lay
The lily-shining child ; and on the
    left,
Bow'd on her palms and folded up
    from wrong,
Her round white shoulder shaken with
    her sobs,
Melissa knelt ; but Lady Blanche
    erect
Stood up and spake, an affluent
    orator.

" It was not thus, O Princess, in old
    days :
You prized my counsel, lived upon
    my lips :
I led you then to all the Castalies ;
I fed you with the milk of every
    Muse ;
I loved you like this kneeler, and you
    me
Your second mother : those were
    gracious times.
Then came your new friend : you
    began to change —
I saw it and grieved — to slacken and
    to cool ;
Till taken with her seeming openness
You turn'd your warmer currents all
    to her,
To me you froze : this was my meed
    for all.
Yet I bore up in part from ancient
    love,
And partly that I hoped to win you
    back,
And partly conscious of my own
    deserts,
And partly that you were my civil
    head,
And chiefly you were born for some-
    thing great,
In which I might your fellow-worker
    be,

When time should serve; and thus a
　　noble scheme
Grew up from seed we two long since
　　had sown;
In us true growth, in her a Jonah's
　　gourd,
Up in one night and due to sudden
　　sun:
We took this palace; but even from
　　the first
You stood in your own light and
　　darken'd mine.
What student came but that you
　　planed her path
To Lady Psyche, younger, not so wise,
A foreigner, and I your country-
　　woman,
I your old friend and tried, she new
　　in all?
But still her lists were swell'd and
　　mine were lean;
Yet I bore up in hope she would be
　　known:
Then came these wolves: *they* knew
　　her: *they* endured,
Long-closeted with her the yester-
　　morn,
To tell her what they were, and she
　　to hear:
And me none told: not less to an eye
　　like mine
A lidless watcher of the public weal,
Last night, their mask was patent,
　　and my foot
Was to you: but I thought again: I
　　fear'd
To meet a cold 'We thank you, we
　　shall hear of it
From Lady Psyche:' you had gone
　　to her,
She told, perforce; and winning easy
　　grace,
No doubt, for slight delay, remain'd
　　among us
In our young nursery still unknown,
　　the stem
Less grain than touchwood, while my
　　honest heat
Were all miscounted as malignant
　　haste
To push my rival out of place and
　　power.

But public use required she should be
　　known;
And since my oath was ta'en for
　　public use,
I broke the letter of it to keep the
　　sense.
I spoke not then at first, but watch'd
　　them well,
Saw that they kept apart, no mischief
　　done;
And yet this day (tho' you should
　　hate me for it)
I came to tell you; found that you
　　had gone,
Ridd'n to the hills, she likewise: now,
　　I thought,
That surely she will speak; if not,
　　then I:
Did she? These monsters blazon'd
　　what they were,
According to the coarseness of their
　　kind,
For thus I hear; and known at last
　　(my work)
And full of cowardice and guilty
　　shame,
I grant in her some sense of shame,
　　she flies;
And I remain on whom to wreak
　　your rage,
I, that have lent my life to build up
　　yours,
I that have wasted here health, wealth,
　　and time,
And talent, I — you know it — I will
　　not boast:
Dismiss me, and I prophesy your plan,
Divorced from my experience, will be
　　chaff
For every gust of chance, and men
　　will say
We did not know the real light, but
　　chased
The wisp that flickers where no foot
　　can tread."

　　She ceased: the Princess answer'd
　　coldly, " Good :
Your oath is broken: we dismiss you:
　　go.
For this lost lamb (she pointed to the
　　child)

Our mind is changed: we take it to
    ourself."

Thereat the Lady stretch'd a vul-
    ture throat,
And shot from crooked lips a haggard
    smile.
"The plan was mine. I built the
    nest" she said
"To hatch the cuckoo. Rise!" and
    stoop'd to updrag
Melissa: she, half on her mother propt,
Half-drooping from her, turn'd her
    face, and cast
A liquid look on Ida, full of prayer,
Which melted Florian's fancy as she
    hung,
A Niobëan daughter, one arm out,
Appealing to the bolts of Heaven;
    and while
We gazed upon her came a little stir
About the doors, and on a sudden
    rush'd
Among us, out of breath, as one pur-
    sued,
A woman-post in flying raiment. Fear
Stared in her eyes, and chalk'd her
    face, and wing'd
Her transit to the throne, whereby she
    fell
Delivering seal'd dispatches which
    the Head
Took half-amazed, and in her lion's
    mood
Tore open, silent we with blind surmise
Regarding, while she read, till over
    brow
And cheek and bosom brake the
    wrathful bloom
As of some fire against a stormy
    cloud,
When the wild peasant rights him-
    self, the rick
Flames, and his anger reddens in the
    heavens;
For anger most it seem'd, while now
    her breast,
Beaten with some great passion at
    her heart,
Palpitated, her hand shook, and we
    heard

In the dead hush the papers that she
    held
Rustle: at once the lost lamb at her
    feet
Sent out a bitter bleating for its dam;
The plaintive cry jarr'd on her ire;
    she crush'd
The scrolls together, made a sudden
    turn
As if to speak, but, utterance failing
    her,
She whirl'd them on to me, as who
    should say
"Read," and I read — two letters —
    one her sire's.

"Fair daughter, when we sent the
    Prince your way
We knew not your ungracious laws,
    which learnt,
We, conscious of what temper you
    are built,
Came all in haste to hinder wrong,
    but fell
Into his father's hands, who has this
    night,
You lying close upon his territory,
Slipt round and in the dark invested
    you,
And here he keeps me hostage for his
    son."

The second was my father's running
    thus:
"You have our son: touch not a hair
    of his head:
Render him up unscathed: give him
    your hand:
Cleave to your contract: tho' indeed
    we hear
You hold the woman is the better man;
A rampant heresy, such as if it spread
Would make all women kick against
    their Lords
Thro' all the world, and which might
    well deserve
That we this night should pluck your
    palace down;
And we will do it, unless you send us
    back
Our son, on the instant, whole,"

So far I read;
And then stood up and spoke impetuously.

　"O not to pry and peer on your
reserve,
But led by golden wishes, and a hope
The child of regal compact, did I
break
Your precinct; not a scorner of your
sex
But venerator, zealous it should be
All that it might be: hear me, for I
bear,
Tho' man, yet human, whatsoe'er
your wrongs,
From the flaxen curl to the gray lock
a life
Less mine than yours: my nurse
would tell me of you;
I babbled for you, as babies for the
moon,
Vague brightness; when a boy, you
stoop'd to me
From all high places, lived in all fair
lights,
Came in long breezes rapt from in-
most south
And blown to inmost north; at eve
and dawn
With Ida, Ida, Ida, rang the woods;
The leader wildswan in among the
stars
Would clang it, and lapt in wreaths
of glowworm light
The mellow breaker murmur'd Ida.
Now,
Because I would have reach'd you,
had you been
Sphered up with Cassiopëia, or the
enthroned
Persephonè in Hades, now at length,
Those winters of abeyance all worn out,
A man I came to see you: but, indeed,
Not in this frequence can I lend full
tongue,
O noble Ida, to those thoughts that
wait
On you, their centre: let me say but
this,
That many a famous man and woman,
town

And landskip, have I heard of, after
seen
The dwarfs of presage: tho' when
known, there grew
Another kind of beauty in detail
Made them worth knowing; but in
you I found
My boyish dream involved and daz-
zled down
And master'd, while that after-beauty
makes
Such head from act to act, from hour
to hour,
Within me, that except you slay me
here,
According to your bitter statute-book,
I cannot cease to follow you, as they say
The seal does music; who desire you
more.
Than growing boys their manhood;
dying lips,
With many thousand matters left to
do,
The breath of life; O more than poor
men wealth,
Than sick men health — yours, yours,
not mine — but half
Without you; with you, whole; and
of those halves
You worthiest; and howe'er you block
and bar
Your heart with system out from mine,
I hold
That it becomes no man to nurse
despair,
But in the teeth of clench'd antago-
nisms
To follow up the worthiest till he die:
Yet that I came not all unauthorized
Behold your father's letter."

　　　　　　　　　　On one knee
Kneeling, I gave it, which she caught,
and dash'd
Unopen'd at her feet: a tide of fierce
Invective seem'd to wait behind her
lips,
As waits a river level with the dam
Ready to burst and flood the world
with foam:
And so she would have spoken, but
there rose

A hubbub in the court of half the
    maids
Gather'd together: from the illumined
    hall
Long lanes of splendor slanted o'er a
    press
Of snowy shoulders, thick as herded
    ewes,
And rainbow robes, and gems and
    gemlike eyes,
And gold and golden heads; they to
    and fro
Fluctuated, as flowers in storm, some
    red, some pale,
All open-mouth'd, all gazing to the
    light,
Some crying there was an army in the
    land,
And some that men were in the very
    walls,
And some they cared not; till a
    clamor grew
As of a new-world Babel, woman-
    built,
And worse-confounded: high above
    them stood
The placid marble Muses, looking
    peace.

Not peace she look'd, the Head:
    but rising up
Robed in the long night of her deep
    hair, so
To the open window moved, remaining
    there
Fixt like a beacon-tower above the
    waves
Of tempest, when the crimson-rolling
    eye
Glares ruin, and the wild birds on the
    light
Dash themselves dead. She stretch'd
    her arms and call'd
Across the tumult and the tumult fell.

"What fear ye, brawlers? am not
    I your Head?
On me, me, me, the storm first breaks:
    I dare
All these male thunderbolts: what is
    it ye fear?

Peace! there are those to avenge us
    and they come:
If not, —myself were like enough, O
    girls,
To unfurl the maiden banner of our
    rights,
And clad in iron burst the ranks of
    war,
Or, falling, protomartyr of our cause,
Die: yet I blame you not so much for
    fear;
Six thousand years of fear have made
    you that
From which I would redeem you: but
    for those
That stir this hubbub — you and you
    — I know
Your faces there in the crowd — to-
    morrow morn
We hold a great convention: then
    shall they
That love their voices more than duty,
    learn
With whom they deal, dismiss'd in
    shame to live
No wiser than their mothers, house-
    hold stuff,
Live chattels, mincers of each other's
    fame,
Full of weak poison, turnspits for the
    clown,
The drunkard's football, laughing-
    stocks of Time,
Whose brains are in their hands and
    in their heels,
But fit to flaunt, to dress, to dance, to
    thrum,
To tramp, to scream, to burnish, and
    to scour,
For ever slaves at home and fools
    abroad."

She, ending, waved her hands:
    thereat the crowd
Muttering, dissolved: then with a
    smile, that look'd
A stroke of cruel sunshine on the
    cliff,
When all the glens are drown'd in
    azure gloom
Of thunder-shower, she floated to us
    and said:

"You have done well and like a
    gentleman,
And like a prince : you have our
    thanks for all :
And you look well too in your woman's
    dress :
Well have you done and like a gentle-
    man.
You saved our life : we owe you bitter
    thanks :
Better have died and spilt our bones
    in the flood —
Then men had said — but now — What
    hinders me
To take such bloody vengeance on you
    both ? —
Yet since our father — Wasps in our
    good hive,
You would-be quenchers of the light
    to be,
Barbarians, grosser than your native
    bears —
O would I had his sceptre for one
    hour !
You that have dared to break our
    bound, and gull'd
Our servants, wrong'd and lied and
    thwarted us —
I wed with thee ! *I* bound by precontract
Your bride, your bondslave ! not tho'
    all the gold
That veins the world were pack'd to
    make your crown,
And every spoken tongue should lord
    you. Sir,
Your falsehood and yourself are hate-
    ful to us :
I trample on your offers and on you :
Begone : we will not look upon you
    more.
Here, push them out at gates."
                    In wrath she spake.
Then those eight mighty daughters of
    the plough
Bent their broad faces toward us and
    address'd
Their motion : twice I sought to plead
    my cause,
But on my shoulder hung their heavy
    hands,
The weight of destiny : so from her
    face

They push'd us, down the steps, and
    thro' the court,
And with grim laughter thrust us out
    at gates.

We cross'd the street and gain'd a
    petty mound
Beyond it, whence we saw the lights
    and heard
The voices murmuring.   While I
    listen'd, came
On a sudden the weird seizure and the
    doubt :
I seem'd to move among a world of
    ghosts ;
The Princess with her monstrous
    woman-guard,
The jest and earnest working side by
    side,
The cataract and the tumult and the
    kings
Were shadows ; and the long fantas-
    tic night
With all its doings had and had not
    been,
And all things were and were not.
                    This went by
As strangely as it came, and on my
    spirits
Settled a gentle cloud of melancholy ;
Not long ; I shook it off ; for spite of
    doubts
And sudden ghostly shadowings I was
    one
To whom the touch of all mischance
    but came
As night to him that sitting on a hill
Sees the midsummer, midnight, Nor-
    way sun
Set into sunrise ; then we moved away.

Thy voice is heard thro' rolling drums,
    That beat to battle where he stands ;
Thy face across his fancy comes,
    And gives the battle to his hands :
A moment, while the trumpets blow,
    He sees his brood about thy knee ;
The next, like fire he meets the foe,
    And strikes him dead for thine and thee.

So Lilia sang : we thought her half-
    possess'd,
She struck such warbling fury thro'
    the words ;

And, after, feigning pique at what she
    call'd
The raillery, or grotesque, or false
    sublime —
Like one that wishes at a dance to
    change
The music — clapt her hands and
    cried for war,
Or some grand fight to kill and make
    an end :
And he that next inherited the tale
Half turning to the broken statue, said,
"Sir Ralph has got your colors : if I
    prove
Your knight, and fight your battle,
    what for me ? "
It chanced, her empty glove upon the
    tomb
Lay by her like a model of her hand.
She took it and she flung it. "Fight,"
    she said,
"And make us all we would be, great
    and good."
He knightlike in his cap instead of
    casque,
A cap of Tyrol borrow'd from the hall,
Arranged the favor, and assumed the
    Prince.

v.

Now, scarce three paces measured
    from the mound,
We stumbled on a stationary voice,
And "Stand, who goes ? " "Two
    from the palace " I.
" The second two : they wait," he said,
    "pass on ;
His Highness wakes : " and one, that
    clash'd in arms,
By glimmering lanes and walls of
    canvass led
Threading the soldier-city, till we
    heard
The drowsy folds of our great ensign
    shake
From blazon'd lions o'er the imperial
    tent
Whispers of war.
        Entering, the sudden light
Dazed me half-blind : I stood and
    seem'd to hear,

As in a poplar grove when a light
    wind wakes
A lisping of the innumerous leaf and
    dies,
Each hissing in his neighbor's ear ;
    and then
A strangled titter, out of which there
    brake
On all sides, clamoring etiquette to
    death,
Unmeasured mirth ; while now the two
    old kings
Began to wag their baldness up and
    down,
The fresh young captains flash'd their
    glittering teeth,
The huge bush-bearded Barons heaved
    and blew,
And slain with laughter roll'd the
    gilded Squire.

    At length my Sire, his rough cheek
    wet with tears,
Panted from weary sides " King, you
    are free !
We did but keep you surety for our
    son,
If this be he, — or a draggled mawkin,
    thou,
That tends her bristled grunters in
    the sludge : "
For I was drench'd with ooze, and
    torn with briers,
More crumpled than a poppy from the
    sheath,
And all one rag, disprinced from head
    to heel.
Then some one sent beneath his
    vaulted palm
A whisper'd jest to some one near
    him, " Look,
He has been among his shadows."
    " Satan take
The old women and their shadows !
    (thus the King
Roar'd) make yourself a man to fight
    with men.
Go : Cyril told us all."
        As boys that slink
From ferule and the trespass-chiding
    eye,
Away we stole, and transient in a trice

From what was left of faded woman-
slough
To sheathing splendors and the golden
scale
Of harness, issued in the sun, that
now
Leapt from the dewy shoulders of the
Earth,
And hit the Northern hills.   Here
Cyril met us.
A little shy at first, but by and by
We twain, with mutual pardon ask'd
and given
For stroke and song, resolder'd peace,
whereon
Follow'd his tale.   Amazed he fled
away
Thro' the dark land, and later in the
night
Had came on Psyche weeping: "then
we fell
Into your father's hand, and there she
lies,
But will not speak, nor stir."
                    He show'd a tent
A stone-shot off: we enter'd in, and
there
Among piled arms and rough ac-
coutrements,
Pitiful sight, wrapp'd in a soldier's
cloak,
Like some sweet sculpture draped
from head to foot,
And push'd by rude hands from its
pedestal,
All her fair length upon the ground
she lay:
And at her head a follower of the
camp,
A charr'd and wrinkled piece of womanhood,
Sat watching like a watcher by the
dead.

Then Florian knelt, and "Come"
he whisper'd to her,
"Lift up your head, sweet sister: lie
not thus.
What have you done but right? you
could not slay
Me, nor your prince: look up: be
comforted:

Sweet is it to have done the thing one
ought,
When fallen in darker ways." And
likewise I:
"Be comforted: have I not lost her
too,
In whose least act abides the nameless
charm
That none has else for me?" She
heard, she moved,
She moan'd, a folded voice; and up
she sat,
And raised the cloak from brows as
pale and smooth
As those that mourn half-shrouded
over death
In deathless marble. "Her," she
said, "my friend—
Parted from her—betray'd her cause
and mine—
Where shall I breathe? why kept ye
not your faith?
O base and bad! what comfort? none
for me!"
To whom remorseful Cyril, "Yet I pray
Take comfort: live, dear lady, for your
child!"
At which she lifted up her voice and
cried.

"Ah me, my babe, my blossom, ah,
my child,
My one sweet child, whom I shall see
no more!
For now will cruel Ida keep her back;
And either she will die from want of
care,
Or sicken with ill-usage, when they say
The child is hers—for every little
fault,
The child is hers; and they will beat
my girl
Remembering her mother: O my
flower!
Or they will take her, they will make
her hard,
And she will pass me by in after-life
With some cold reverence worse than
were she dead.
Ill mother that I was to leave her there,
To lag behind, scared by the cry
they made,

The horror of the shame among them all :
But I will go and sit beside the doors,
And make a wild petition night and day,
Until they hate to hear me like a wind
Wailing for ever, till they open to me,
And lay my little blossom at my feet,
My babe, my sweet Aglaïa, my one child :
And I will take her up and go my way,
And satisfy my soul with kissing her :
Ah ! what might that man not deserve of me
Who gave me back my child ? " " Be comforted,"
Said Cyril, " you shall have it : " but again
She veil'd her brows, and prone she sank, and so
Like tender things that being caught feign death,
Spoke not, nor stirr'd.
　　　　　By this a murmur ran
Thro' all the camp and inward raced the scouts
With rumor of Prince Arac hard at hand.
We left her by the woman, and without
Found the gray kings at parle : and " Look you " cried
My father " that our compact be fulfill'd :
You have spoilt this child ; she laughs at you and man :
She wrongs herself, her sex, and me, and him :
But red-faced war has rods of steel and fire ;
She yields, or war."
　　　　　Then Gama turn'd to me :
" We fear, indeed, you spent a stormy time
With our strange girl : and yet they say that still
You love her. Give us, then, your mind at large :
How say you, war or not ? "
　　　　　" Not war, if possible,
O king," I said, " lest from the abuse of war,

The desecrated shrine, the trampled year,
The smouldering homestead, and the household flower
Torn from the lintel — all the common wrong —
A smoke go up thro' which I loom to her
Three times a monster : now she lightens scorn
At him that mars her plan, but then would hate
(And every voice she talk'd with ratify it,
And every face she look'd on justify it)
The general foe. More soluble is this knot,
By gentleness than war. I want her love.
What were I nigher this altho' we dash'd
Your cities into shards with catapults,
She would not love ; — or brought her chain'd, a slave,
The lifting of whose eyelash is my lord,
Not ever would she love ; but brooding turn
The book of scorn, till all my flitting chance
Were caught within the record of her wrongs,
And crush'd to death : and rather, Sire, than this
I would the old God of war himself were dead,
Forgotten, rusting on his iron hills,
Rotting on some wild shore with ribs of wreck,
Or like an old-world mammoth bulk'd in ice,
Not to be molten out."
　　　　　And roughly spake
My father, " Tut, you know them not, the girls.
Boy, when I hear you prate I almost think
That idiot legend credible. Look you, Sir !
Man is the hunter ; woman is his game :
The sleek and shining creatures of the chase,

We hunt them for the beauty of their
    skins;
They love us for it, and we ride them
    down.
Wheedling and siding with them!
    Out! for shame!
Boy, there's no rose that's half so dear
    to them
As he that does the thing they dare
    not do,
Breathing and sounding beauteous
    battle, comes
With the air of the trumpet round
    him, and leaps in
Among the women, snares them by
    the score
Flatter'd and fluster'd, wins, tho'
    dash'd with death
He reddens what he kisses: thus I won
Your mother, a good mother, a good
    wife,
Worth winning; but this firebrand—
    gentleness
To such as her! if Cyril spake her true,
To catch a dragon in a cherry net,
To trip a tigress with a gossamer,
Were wisdom to it."
                "Yea but Sire," I cried,
"Wild natures need wise curbs.   The
    soldier?   No:
What dares not Ida do that she should
    prize
The soldier?   I beheld her, when she
    rose
The yesternight, and storming in ex-
    tremes,
Stood for her cause, and flung defiance
    down
Gagelike to man, and had not shunn'd
    the death,
No, not the soldier's: yet I hold her,
    king,
True woman: but you clash them all
    in one,
That have as many differences as we.
The violet varies from the lily as far
As oak from elm: one loves the sol-
    dier, one
The silken priest of peace, one this,
    one that,
And some unworthily; their sinless
    faith,

A maiden moon that sparkles on a sty,
Glorifying clown and satyr; whence
    they need
More breadth of culture: is not Ida
    right?
They worth it?   truer to the law with-
    in?
Severer in the logic of a life?
Twice as magnetic to sweet influences
Of earth and heaven?   and she of
    whom you speak,
My mother, looks as whole as some
    serene
Creation minted in the golden moods
Of sovereign artists; not a thought,
    a touch,
But pure as lines of green that streak
    the white
Of the first snowdrop's inner leaves;
    I say,
Not like the piebald miscellany, man,
Bursts of great heart and slips in
    sensual mire,
But whole and one: and take them
    all-in-all,
Were we ourselves but half as good,
    as kind,
As truthful, much that Ida claims as
    right
Had ne'er been mooted, but as frankly
    theirs
As dues of Nature.   To our point:
    not war:
Lest I lose all."
        "Nay, nay, you spake but sense,"
Said Gama.   "We remember love
    ourself
In our sweet youth; we did not rate
    him then
This red-hot iron to be shaped with
    blows.
You talk almost like Ida: *she* can talk;
And there is something in it as you
    say:
But you talk kindlier: we esteem you
    for it. —
He seems a gracious and a gallant
    Prince,
I would he had our daughter: for the
    rest,
Our own detention, why, the causes
    weigh'd,

Fatherly fears — you used us cour-
teously —
We would do much to gratify your
Prince —
We pardon it; and for your ingress
here
Upon the skirt and fringe of our fair
land,
You did but come as goblins in the
night,
Nor in the furrow broke the plough-
man's head,
Nor burnt the grange, nor buss'd the
milking-maid,
Nor robb'd the farmer of his bowl of
cream:
But let your Prince (our royal word
upon it,
He comes back safe) ride with us to
our lines,
And speak with Arac: Arac's word
is thrice
As ours with Ida: something may be
done —
I know not what — and ours shall see
us friends.
You, likewise, our late guests, if so
you will,
Follow us: who knows? we four may
build some plan
Foursquare to opposition."
        Here he reach'd
White hands of farewell to my sire,
who growl'd
An answer which, half-muffled in his
beard,
Let so much out as gave us leave to
go.

Then rode we with the old king
across the lawns
Beneath huge trees, a thousand rings
of Spring
In every bole, a song on every spray
Of birds that piped their Valentines,
and woke
Desire in me to infuse my tale of
love
In the old king's ears, who promised
help, and oozed
All o'er with honey'd answer as we
rode

And blossom-fragrant slipt the heavy
dews
Gather'd by night and peace, with
each light air
On our mail'd heads: but other
thoughts than Peace
Burnt in us, when we saw the em-
battled squares,
And squadrons of the Prince, tramp-
ling the flowers
With clamor: for among them rose a
cry
As if to greet the king; they made a
halt;
The horses yell'd; they clash'd their
arms; the drum
Beat; merrily-blowing shrill'd the
martial fife;
And in the blast and bray of the long
horn
And serpent-throated bugle, undulated
The banner: anon to meet us lightly
pranced
Three captains out; nor ever had I
seen
Such thews of men: the midmost and
the highest
Was Arac: all about his motion
clung
The shadow of his sister, as the beam
Of the East, that play'd upon them,
made them glance
Like those three stars of the airy
Giant's zone,
That glitter burnish'd by the frosty
dark;
And as the fiery Sirius alters hue,
And bickers into red and emerald,
shone
Their morions, wash'd with morning,
as they came.

And I that prated peace, when first
I heard
War-music, felt the blind wildbeast of
of force,
Whose home is in the sinews of a
man,
Stir in me as to strike: then took the
king
His three broad sons; with now a
wandering hand

And now a pointed finger, told them all :
A common light of smiles at our dis-
    guise
Broke from their lips, and, ere the
    windy jest
Had labor'd down within his ample
    lungs,
The genial giant, Arac, roll'd himself
Thrice in the saddle, then burst out in
    words.

"Our land invaded, 'sdeath! and he
    himself
Your captive, yet my father wills not
    war :
And, 'sdeath! myself, what care I,
    war or no ?
But then this question of your troth
    remains :
And there's a downright honest mean-
    ing in her ;
She flies too high, she flies too high !
    and yet
She ask'd but space and fairplay for
    her scheme ;
She prest and prest it on me — I my-
    self,
What know I of these things ? but,
    life and soul !
I thought her half-right talking of her
    wrongs ;
I say she flies too high, 'sdeath ! what
    of that ?
I take her for the flower of woman-
    kind,
And so I often told her, right or wrong,
And, Prince, she can be sweet to those
    she loves,
And, right or wrong, I care not : this
    is all,
I stand upon her side : she made me
    swear it —
'Sdeath — and with solemn rites by
    candlelight —
Swear by St. something — I forget
    her name —
Her that talk'd down the fifty wisest
    men ;
She was a princess too ; and so I
    swore.
Come, this is all ; she will not : waive
    your claim

If not, the foughten field, what else,
    at once
Decides it, 'sdeath ! against my
    father's will."

I lagg'd in answer loth to render up
My precontract, and loth by brainless
    war
To cleave the rift of difference deeper
    yet ;
Till one of those two brothers, half
    aside
And fingering at the hair about his
    lip,
To prick us on to combat "Like to
    like !
The woman's garment hid the
    woman's heart."
A taunt that clench'd his purpose
    like a blow !
For fiery-short was Cyril's counter-
    scoff,
And sharp I answer'd, touch'd upon
    the point
Where idle boys are cowards to their
    shame,
"Decide it here : why not ? we are
    three to three."

Then spake the third "But three to
    three ? no more ?
No more, and in our noble sister's
    cause ?
More, more, for honor : every captain
    waits
Hungry for honor, angry for his king.
More, more, some fifty on a side, that
    each
May breathe himself, and quick ! by
    overthrow
Of these or those, the question set-
    tled die."

"Yea," answer'd I, "for this wild
    wreath of air,
This flake of rainbow flying on the
    highest
Foam of men's deeds — this honor, if
    ye will.
It needs must be for honor if at all :
Since, what decision ? if we fail, we
    fail,

And if we win, we fail: she would not
keep
Her compact." " 'Sdeath! but we
will send to her,"
Said Arac, "worthy reasons why she
should
Bide by this issue: let our missive thro',
And you shall have her answer by
the word."

"Boys!" shriek'd the old king, but
vainlier than a hen
To her false daughters in the pool;
for none
Regarded; neither seem'd there more
to say:
Back rode we to my father's camp,
and found
He thrice had sent a herald to the
gates,
To learn if Ida yet would cede our
claim,
Or by denial flush her babbling wells
With her own people's life: three
times he went:
The first, he blew and blew, but none
appear'd:
He batter'd at the doors; none came:
the next,
An awful voice within had warn'd
him thence:
The third, and those eight daughters
of the plough
Came sallying thro' the gates, and
caught his hair,
And so belabor'd him on rib and
cheek
They made him wild: not less one
glance he caught
Thro' open doors of Ida station'd
there
Unshaken, clinging to her purpose,
firm
Tho' compass'd by two armies and
the noise
Of arms; and standing like a stately
Pine
Set in a cataract on an island-crag,
When storm is on the heights, and
right and left
Suck'd from the dark heart of the
long hills roll

The torrents, dash'd to the vale: and
yet her will
Bred will in me to overcome it or fall.

But when I told the king that I
was pledged
To fight in tourney for my bride, he
clash'd
His iron palms together with a cry;
Himself would tilt it out among the
lads:
But overborne by all his bearded
lords
With reasons drawn from age and
state, perforce
He yielded, wroth and red, with fierce
demur:
And many a bold knight started up in
heat,
And sware to combat for my claim
till death.

All on this side the palace ran the
field
Flat to the garden-wall: and likewise
here,
Above the garden's glowing blossom-
belts,
A column'd entry shone and marble
stairs,
And great bronze valves, emboss'd
with Tomyris
And what she did to Cyrus after fight,
But now fast barr'd: so here upon
the flat
All that long morn the lists were
hammer'd up,
And all that morn the heralds to and
fro,
With message and defiance, went and
came;
Last, Ida's answer, in royal hand,
But shaken here and there, and rol-
ling words
Oration-like. I kiss'd it and I read.

"O brother, you have known the
pangs we felt,
What heats of indignation when we
heard
Of those that iron-cramp'd their
women's feet;

Of lands in which at the altar the
poor bride
Gives her harsh groom for bridal-gift
a scourge;
Of living hearts that crack within the
fire
Where smoulder their dead despots;
and of those, —
Mothers, — that, all prophetic pity,
fling
Their pretty maids in the running
flood, and swoops
The vulture, beak and talon, at the
heart
Made for all noble motion: and I saw
That equal baseness lived in sleeker
times
With smoother men: the old leaven
leaven'd all:
Millions of throats would bawl for
civil rights,
No woman named: therefore I set
my face
Against all men, and lived but for
mine own.
Far off from men I built a fold for
them:
I stored it full of rich memorial:
I fenced it round with gallant insti-
tutes,
And biting laws to scare the beasts
of prey
And prosper'd; till a rout of saucy
boys
Brake on us at our books, and marr'd
our peace,
Mask'd like our maids, blustering I
know not what
Of insolence and love, some pretext
held
Of baby troth, invalid, since my
will
Seal'd not the bond — the striplings!
— for their sport! —
I tamed my leopards: shall I not
tame these?
Or you? or I? for since you think me
touch'd
In honor — what, I would not aught
of false —
Is not our cause pure? and whereas I
know

Your prowess, Arac, and what
mother's blood
You draw from, fight; you failing, I
abide
What end soever: fail you will not.
Still
Take not his life: he risk'd it for my
own;
His mother lives: yet whatsoe'er you
do,
Fight and fight well; strike and strike
home. O dear
Brothers, the woman's Angel guards
you, you
The sole men to be mingled with our
cause,
The sole men we shall prize in the
aftertime,
Your very armor hallow'd, and your
statues
Rear'd, sung to, when, this gad-fly
brush'd aside,
We plant a solid foot into the Time,
And mould a generation strong to
move
With claim on claim from right to
right, till she
Whose name is yoked with children's,
know herself;
And Knowledge in our own land
make her free,
And, ever following those two crowned
twins,
Commerce and conquest, shower the
fiery grain
Of freedom broadcast over all that
orbs
Between the Northern and the Southern
morn."

Then came a postscript dash'd
across the rest.
"See that there be no traitors in your
camp:
We seem a nest of traitors — none to
trust
Since our arms fail'd — this Egypt-
plague of men!
Almost our maids were better at their
homes,
Than thus man-girled here: indeed I
think

Our chiefest comfort is the little child
Of one unworthy mother; which she
    left:
She shall not have it back: the child
    shall grow
To prize the authentic mother of her
    mind.
I took it for an hour in mine own bed
This morning: there the tender orphan
    hands
Felt at my heart, and seem'd to charm
    from thence
The wrath I nursed against the world :
    farewell."

    I ceased; he said, "Stubborn, but
    she may sit
Upon a king's right hand in thunder-
    storms,
And breed up warriors! See now, tho'
    yourself
Be dazzled by the wildfire Love to
    sloughs
That swallow common sense, the
    spindling king,
This Gama swamp'd in lazy tolerance.
When the man wants weight, the
    woman takes it up,
And topples down the scales; but this
    is fixt
As are the roots of earth and base of
    all ;
Man for the field and woman for the
    hearth:
Man for the sword and for the needle
    she :
Man with the head and woman with
    heart:
Man to command and woman to
    obey ;
All else confusion. Look you! the
    gray mare
Is ill to live with, when her whinny
    shrills
From tile to scullery, and her small
    goodman
Shrinks in his arm-chair while the
    fires of Hell
Mix with his hearth: but you — she's
    yet a colt —
Take, break her: strongly groom'd and
    straitly curb'd

She might not rank with those detest-
    able
That let the bantling scald at home,
    and brawl
Their rights or wrongs like potherbs
    in the street.
They say she's comely; there's the
    fairer chance :
I like her none the less for rating at
    her !
Besides, the woman wed is not as we,
But suffers change of frame. A lusty
    brace
Of twins may weed her of her folly.
    Boy,
The bearing and training of a child
Is woman's wisdom."

              Thus the hard old king :
I took my leave, for it was nearly
    noon :
I pored upon her letter which I held,
And on the little clause "take not his
    life : "
I mused on that wild morning in the
    woods,
And on the "Follow, follow, thou shalt
    win : "
I thought on all the wrathful king had
    said,
And how the strange betrothment
    was to end :
Then I remember'd that burnt sor-
    cerer's curse
That one should fight with shadows
    and should fall;
And like a flash the weird affection
    came :
King, camp and college turn'd to hol-
    low shows ;
I seem'd to move in old memorial tilts,
And doing battle with forgotten
    ghosts,
To dream myself the shadow of a
    dream :
And ere I woke it was the point of
    noon,
The lists were ready. Empanoplied
    and plumed
We enter'd in, and waited, fifty there
Opposed to fifty, till the trumpet
    blared

At the barrier like a wild horn in a
    land
Of echoes, and a moment, and once
    more
The trumpet, and again: at which the
    storm
Of galloping hoofs bare on the ridge
    of spears
And riders front to front, until they
    closed
In conflict with the crash of shivering
    points,
And thunder. Yet it seem'd a dream,
    I dream'd
Of fighting. On his haunches rose
    the steed,
And into fiery splinters leapt the
    lance,
And out of stricken helmets sprang
    the fire.
Part sat like rocks: part reel'd but
    kept their seats:
Part roll'd on the earth and rose
    again and drew:
Part stumbled mixt with floundering
    horses. Down
From those two bulks at Arac's side,
    and down
From Arac's arm, as from a giant's
    flail,
The large blows rain'd, as here and
    everywhere
He rode the mellay, lord of the ring-
    ing lists,
And all the plain, — brand, mace, and
    shaft, and shield —
Shock'd, like an iron-clanging anvil
    bang'd
With hammers; till I thought, can
    this be he
From Gama's dwarfish loins? if this
    be so,
The mother makes us most — and in
    my dream
I glanced aside, and saw the palace-
    front
Alive with fluttering scarfs and ladies'
    eyes,
And highest, among the statues,
    statue-like,
Between a cymbal'd Miriam and a
    Jael,

With Psyche's babe, was Ida watch-
    ing us,
A single band of gold about her hair,
Like a Saint's glory up in heaven: but
    she
No saint — inexorable — no tender-
    ness —
Too hard, too cruel: yet she sees me
    fight,
Yea, let her see me fall! with that I
    drave
Among the thickest and bore down a
    Prince,
And Cyril, one. Yea, let me make
    my dream
All that I would. But that large-
    moulded man,
His visage all agrin as at a wake,
Made at me thro' the press, and, stag-
    gering back
With stroke on stroke the horse and
    horseman, came
As comes a pillar of electric cloud,
Flaying the roofs and sucking up the
    drains,
And shadowing down the champaign
    till it strikes
On a wood, and takes, and breaks, and
    cracks, and splits,
And twists the grain with such a roar
    that Earth
Reels, and the herdsmen cry; for
    everything
Gave way before him: only Florian, he
That loved me closer than his own
    right eye,
Thrust in between; but Arac rode
    him down:
And Cyril seeing it, push'd against
    the Prince,
With Psyche's color round his helmet,
    tough,
Strong, supple, sinew-corded, apt at
    arms;
But tougher, heavier, stronger, he that
    smote
And threw him: last I spurr'd; I felt
    my veins
Stretch with fierce heat; a moment
    hand to hand,
And sword to sword, and horse to
    horse we hung,

Till I struck out and shouted; the blade glanced,
I did but shear a feather, and dream and truth
Flow'd from me; darkness closed me; and I fell.

VI.

Home they brought her warrior dead:
  She nor swoon'd, nor utter'd cry:
All her maidens, watching, said,
  "She must weep or she will die."

Then they praised him, soft and low,
  Call'd him worthy to be loved,
Truest friend and noblest foe;
  Yet she neither spoke nor moved.

Stole a maiden from her place,
  Lightly to the warrior stept
Took the face-cloth from the face;
  Yet she neither moved nor wept.

Rose a nurse of ninety years,
  Set his child upon her knee—
Like summer tempest came her tears—
  "Sweet my child, I live for thee."

My dream had never died or lived again.
As in some mystic middle state I lay;
Seeing I saw not, hearing not I heard:
Tho', if I saw not, yet they told me all
So often that I speak as having seen.

For so it seem'd, or so they said to me,
That all things grew more tragic and more strange;
That when our side was vanquish'd and my cause
For ever lost, there went up a great cry,
The Prince is slain. My father heard and ran
In on the lists, and there unlaced my casque
And grovell'd on my body, and after him
Came Psyche, sorrowing for Aglaïa.

But high upon the palace Ida stood
With Psyche's babe in arm: there on the roofs
Like that great dame of Lapidoth she sang.

"Our enemies have fall'n, have fall'n: the seed,
The little seed they laugh'd at in the dark,
Has risen and cleft the soil, and grown a bulk
Of spanless girth, that lays on every side
A thousand arms and rushes to the Sun.

"Our enemies have fall'n, have fall'n: they came,
The leaves were wet with women's tears: they heard
A noise of songs they would not understand:
They mark'd it with the red cross to the fall,
And would have strown it, and are fall'n themselves.

"Our enemies have fall'n, have fall'n: they came,
The woodmen with their axes: lo the tree!
But we will make it faggots for the hearth,
And shape it plank and beam for roof and floor,
And boats and bridges for the use of men.

"Our enemies have fall'n, have fall'n: they struck;
With their own blows they hurt themselves, nor knew
There dwelt an iron nature in the grain:
The glittering axe was broken in their arms,
Their arms were shatter'd to the shoulder blade.

"Our enemies have fall'n, but this shall grow
A night of Summer from the heat, a breadth
Of Autumn, dropping fruits of power: and roll'd
With music in the growing breeze of Time,
The tops shall strike from star to star, the fangs
Shall move the stony bases of the world.

"And now, O maids, behold our sanctuary
Is violate, our laws broken: fear we not
To break them more in their behoof, whose arms
Champion'd our cause and won it with a day
Blanch'd in our annals, and perpetual feast,
When dames and heroines of the golden year
Shall strip a hundred hollows bare of Spring,
To rain an April of ovation round
Their statues, borne aloft, the three: but come,
We will be liberal, since our rights are won.

Let them not lie in the tents with
    coarse mankind,
Ill nurses ; but descend, and proffer
    these
The brethren of our blood and cause,
    that there
Lie bruised and maim'd, the tender
    ministries
Of female hands and hospitality."

    She spoke, and with the babe yet
      in her arms,
Descending, burst the great bronze
    valves, and led
A hundred maids in train across the
    Park.
Some cowl'd, and some bare-headed,
    on they came,
Their feet in flowers, her loveliest :
    by them went
The enamor'd air sighing, and on
    their curls
From the high tree the blossom waver-
    ing fell,
And over them the tremulous isles of
    light
Slided, they moving under shade : but
    Blanche
At distance follow'd : so they came :
    anon
Thro' open field into the lists they
    wound
Timorously ; and as the leader of the
    herd
That holds a stately fretwork to the
    Sun,
And follow'd up by a hundred airy
    does,
Steps with a tender foot, light as on
    air,
The lovely, lordly creature floated
    on
To where her wounded brethren lay ;
    there stay'd ;
Knelt on one knee, — the child on one,
    — and prest
Their hands, and call'd them dear
    deliverers,
And happy warriors, and immortal
    names,
And said "You shall not lie in the
    tents but here,

And nursed by those for whom you
    fought, and served
With female hands and hospitality."

    Then, whether moved by this, or
      was it chance,
She past my way. Up started from
    my side
The old lion, glaring with his whelp-
    less eye,
Silent ; but when she saw me lying
    stark,
Dishelm'd and mute, and motionlessly
    pale,
Cold ev'n to her, she sigh'd ; and when
    she saw
The haggard father's face and rev-
    erend beard
Of grisly twine, all dabbled with the
    blood
Of his own son, shudder'd, a twitch of
    pain
Tortured her mouth, and o'er her
    forehead past
A shadow, and her hue changed, and
    she said :
" He saved my life : my brother slew
    him for it."
No more : at which the king in bitter
    scorn
Drew from my neck the painting and
    the tress,
And held them up : she saw them,
    and a day
Rose from the distance on her memory,
When the good Queen, her mother,
    shore the tress
With kisses, ere the days of Lady
    Blanche :
And then once more she look'd at my
    pale face :
Till understanding all the foolish
    work
Of fancy, and the bitter close of all,
Her iron will was broken in her
    mind ;
Her noble heart was molten in her
    breast ;
She bow'd, she set the child on the
    earth ; she laid
A feeling finger on my brows, and
    presently

'O Sire," she said, "he lives: he is not dead:
O let me have him with my brethren here
In our own palace: we will tend on him
Like one of these: if so, by any means,
To lighten this great clog of thanks, that make
Our progress falter to the woman's goal."

She said: but at the happy word "he lives"
My father stoop'd, re-father'd o'er my wounds.
So those two foes above my fallen life,
With brow to brow like night and evening mixt
Their dark and gray, while Psyche ever stole
A little nearer, till the babe that by us,
Half-lapt in glowing gauze and golden brede,
Lay like a new-fall'n meteor on the grass,
Uncared for, spied its mother and began
A blind and babbling laughter, and to dance
Its body, and reach its fatling innocent arms
And lazy lingering fingers. She the appeal
Brook'd not, but clamoring out "Mine — mine — not yours,
It is not yours, but mine: give me the child"
Ceased all on tremble: piteous was the cry:
So stood the unhappy mother open-mouth'd,
And turn'd each face her way: wan was her cheek
With hollow watch, her blooming mantle torn,
Red grief and mother's hunger in her eye,
And down dead-heavy sank her curls, and half

The sacred mother's bosom, panting, burst
The laces toward her babe; but she nor cared
Nor knew it, clamoring on, till Ida heard,
Look'd up, and rising slowly from me, stood
Erect and silent, striking with her glance
The mother, me, the child; but he that lay
Beside us, Cyril, batter'd as he was,
Trail'd himself up on one knee: then he drew
Her robe to meet his lips, and down she look'd
At the arm'd man sideways, pitying as it seem'd,
Or self-involved; but when she learnt his face,
Remembering his ill-omen'd song, arose
Once more thro' all her height, and o'er him grew
Tall as a figure lengthen'd on the sand
When the tide ebbs in sunshine, and he said:

"O fair and strong and terrible! Lioness
That with your long locks play the Lion's mane!
But Love and Nature, these are two more terrible
And stronger. See, your foot is on our necks,
We vanquish'd, you the Victor of your will.
What would you more? give her the child! remain
Orb'd in your isolation: he is dead,
Or all as dead: henceforth we let you be:
Win you the hearts of women; and beware
Lest, where you seek the common love of these,
The common hate with the revolving wheel
Should drag you down, and some great Nemesis

Break from a darken'd future, crown'd
    with fire,
And tread you out for ever: but how-
    soe'er
Fix'd in yourself, never in your own
    arms
To hold your own, deny not hers to
    her,
Give her the child! O if, I say, you
    keep
One pulse that beats true woman, if
    you loved
The breast that fed or arm that dan-
    dled you,
Or own one port of sense not flint to
    prayer,
Give her the child! or if you scorn
    to lay it,
Yourself, in hands so lately claspt
    with yours,
Or speak to her, your dearest, her
    one fault
The tenderness, not yours, that could
    not kill,
Give *me* it: *I* will give it her."
                 He said:
At first her eye with slow dilation
    roll'd
Dry flame, she listening; after sank
    and sank
And, into mournful twilight mellow-
    ing, dwelt
Full on the child; she took it:
    "Pretty bud!
Lily of the vale! half open'd bell of
    the woods!
Sole comfort of my dark hour, when
    a world
Of traitorous friend and broken sys-
    tem made
No purple in the distance, mystery,
Pledge of a love not to be mine,
    farewell;
These men are hard upon us as of old,
We two must part: and yet how fain
    was I
To dream thy cause embraced in
    mine, to think
I might be something to thee, when I
    felt
Thy helpless warmth about my barren
    breast

In the dead prime: but may thy
    mother prove
As true to thee as false, false, false to
    me!
And, if thou needs must bear the
    yoke, I wish it
Gentle as freedom" — here she kiss'd
    it: then —
"All good go with thee! take it, Sir,"
    and so
Laid the soft babe in his hard-mailed
    hands,
Who turn'd half-round to Psyche as
    she sprang
To meet it, with an eye that swum in
    thanks;
Then felt it sound and whole from
    head to foot,
And hugg'd and never hugg'd it close
    enough,
And in her hunger mouth'd and mum-
    bled it,
And hid her bosom with it; after that
Put on more calm and added suppli-
    antly:

"We two were friends: I go to
    mine own land
For ever: find some other: as for me
I scarce am fit for your great plans:
    yet speak to me,
Say one soft word and let me part
    forgiven."

But Ida spoke not, rapt upon the
    child.
Then Arac. "Ida —'sdeath! you
    blame the man;
You wrong yourselves — the woman
    is so hard
Upon the woman. Come, a grace to
    me!
I am your warrior. I and mine have
    fought
Your battle: kiss her; take her hand,
    she weeps:
'Sdeath! I would sooner fight thrice
    o'er than see it."

But Ida spoke not, gazing on the
    ground,

And reddening in the furrows of his
   chin,
And moved beyond his custom, Gama
   said :

"I've heard that there is iron in the
   blood,
And I believe it. Not one word ? not
   one ?
Whence drew you this steel temper ?
   not from me,
Not from your mother, now a saint
   with saints.
She said you had a heart — I heard
   her say it —
'Our Ida has a heart' — just ere she
   died —
'But see that some one with authority
Be near her still' and I — I sought
   for one —
All people said she had authority —
The Lady Blanche : much profit !
   Not one word ;
No ! tho' your father sues : see how
   you stand
Stiff as Lot's wife, and all the good
   knights maim'd,
I trust that there is no one hurt to
   death,
For your wild whim : and was it then
   for this,
Was it for this we gave our palace up,
Where we withdrew from summer
   heats and state,
And had our wine and chess beneath
   the planes,
And many a pleasant hour with her
   that's gone,
Ere you were born to vex us ? Is it
   kind ?
Speak to her I say : is this not she of
   whom,
When first she came, all flush'd you
   said to me
Now had you got a friend of your
   own age,
Now could you share your thought ;
   now should men see
Two women faster welded in one
   love
Than pairs of wedlock ; she you
   walk'd with, she

You talk'd with, whole nights long, up
   in the tower,
Of sine and arc, spheroïd and azimuth,
And right ascension, Heaven knows
   what ; and now
A word, but one, one little kindly
   word,
Not one to spare her : out upon you,
   flint !
You love nor her, nor me, nor any ;
   nay,
You shame your mother's judgment
   too. Not one ?
You will not ? well — no heart have
   you, or such
As fancies like the vermin in a nut
Have fretted all to dust and bitter-
   ness."
So said the small king moved beyond
   his wont.

But Ida stood nor spoke, drain'd of
   her force
By many a varying influence and so
   long.
Down thro' her limbs a drooping languor wept :
Her head a little bent ; and on her
   mouth
A doubtful smile dwelt like a clouded
   moon
In a still water : then brake out my
   sire,
Lifting his grim head from my
   wounds. "O you,
Woman, whom we thought woman
   even now,
And were half fool'd to let you tend
   our son,
Because he might have wish'd it —
   but we see
The accomplice of your madness un
   forgiven,
And think that you might mix his
   draught with death,
When your skies change again : the
   rougher hand
Is safer : on to the tents : take up the
   Prince."

He rose, and while each ear was
   prick'd to attend

A tempest, thro' the cloud that dimm'd her broke
A genial warmth and light once more, and shone
Thro' glittering drops on her sad friend.

     " Come hither,
O Psyche," she cried out, "embrace me, come
Quick while I melt; make reconcilement sure
With one that cannot keep her mind an hour:
Come to the hollow heart they slander so!
Kiss and be friends, like children being chid!
I seem no more: *I* want forgiveness too:
I should have had to do with none but maids,
That have no links with men. Ah false but dear,
Dear traitor, too much loved, why? — why? — Yet see,
Before these kings we embrace you yet once more
With all forgiveness, all oblivion,
And trust, not love, you less.

     And now, O sire,
Grant me your son, to nurse, to wait upon him,
Like mine own brother. For my debt to him,
This nightmare weight of gratitude, I know it;
Taunt me no more: yourself and yours shall have
Free adit; we will scatter all our maids
Till happier times each to her proper hearth:
What use to keep them here — now? grant my prayer.
Help, father, brother, help; speak to the king:
Thaw this male nature to some touch of that
Which kills me with myself, and drags me down
From my fixt height to mob me up with all

The soft and milky rabble of womankind,
Poor weakling ev'n as they are."

     Passionate tears
Follow'd: the king replied not: Cyril said:
" Your brother, Lady — Florian, — ask for him
Of your great head — for he is wounded too —
That you may tend upon him with the prince."
" Ay so," said Ida with a bitter smile,
" Our laws are broken: let him enter too."
Then Violet, she that sang the mournful song,
And had a cousin tumbled on the plain,
Petition'd too for him. " Ay so," she said,
"I stagger in the stream: I cannot keep
My heart an eddy from the brawling hour:
We break our laws with ease, but let it be."
" Ay so?" said Blanche: " Amazed am I to hear
Your Highness: but your Highness breaks with ease
The law your Highness did not make: 'twas I.
I had been wedded wife, I knew mankind,
And block'd them out; but these men came to woo
Your Highness — verily I think to win."

  So she, and turn'd askance a wintry eye:
But Ida with a voice, that like a bell
Toll'd by an earthquake in a trembling tower,
Rang ruin, answer'd full of grief and scorn.

  " Fling our doors wide! all, all, not one, but all,
Not only he, but by my mother's soul,
Whatever man lies wounded, friend or foe,

Shall enter, if he will. Let our girls
    flit,
Till the storm die ! but had you stood
    by us,
The roar that breaks the Pharos from
    his base
Had left us rock. She fain would
    sting us too,
But shall not. Pass, and mingle with
    your likes.
We brook no further insult but are
    gone."

    She turn'd; the very nape of her
    white neck
Was rosed with indignation : but the
    Prince
Her brother came; the king her father
    charm'd
Her wounded soul with words: nor
    did mine own
Refuse her proffer, lastly gave his
    hand.

    Then us they lifted up, dead
    weights, and bare
Straight to the doors: to them the
    doors gave way
Groaning, and in the Vestal entry
    shriek'd
The virgin marble under iron heels:
And on they moved and gain'd the
    hall, and there
Rested . but great the crush was, and
    each base,
To left and right, of those tall columns
    drown'd
In silken fluctuation and the swarm
Of female whisperers : at the further
    end
Was Ida by the throne, the two great
    cats
Close by her, like supporters on a
    shield,
Bow-back'd with fear: but in the cen-
    tre stood
The common men with rolling eyes;
    amazed
They glared upon the women, and
    aghast
The women stared at these, all silent,
    save

When armor clash'd or jingled,
    while the day,
Descending, struck athwart the hall,
    and shot
A flying splendor out of brass and
    steel,
That o'er the statues leapt from head
    to head,
Now fired an angry Pallas on the
    helm,
Now set a wrathful Dian's moon on
    flame,
And now and then an echo started
    up,
And shuddering fled from room to
    room, and died
Of fright in far apartments.
                Then the voice
Of Ida sounded, issuing ordinance :
And me they bore up the broad stairs,
    and thro'
The long-laid galleries past a hundred
    doors
To one deep chamber shut from
    sound, and due
To languid limbs and sickness ; left
    me in it;
And others otherwhere they laid; and
    all
That afternoon a sound arose of hoof
And chariot, many a maiden passing
    home
Till happier times ; but some were left
    of those
Held sagest, and the great lords out
    and in,
From those two hosts that lay beside
    the walls,
Walked at their will, and everything
    was chang'd.

VII.

Ask me no more: the moon may draw the
    sea;
  The cloud may stoop from heaven and
    take the shape
    With fold to fold, of mountain or of cape;
But O too fond, when have I answer'd thee?
          Ask me no more.

Ask me no more: what answer should I
    give?
  I love not hollow cheek or faded eye:
  Yet, O my friend, I will not have thee die !
Ask me no more, lest I should bid thee live;
          Ask me no more.

Ask me no more: thy fate and mine are
seal'd:
  I strove against the stream and all in vain:
  Let the great river take me to the main:
No more, dear love, for at a touch I yield;
       Ask me no more.

So was their sanctuary violated,
So their fair college turn'd to hos-
    pital;
At first with all confusion: by and
  by
Sweet order lived again with other
  laws:
A kindlier influence reign'd; and
  everywhere
Low voices with the ministering hand
Hung round the sick: the maidens
  came, they talk'd,
They sang, they read: till she not fair
  began
To gather light, and she that was, be-
  came
Her former beauty treble; and to and
  fro
With books, with flowers, with Angel
  offices,
Like creatures native unto gracious
  act,
And in their own clear element, they
  moved.

But sadness on the soul of Ida fell,
And hatred of her weakness, blent
  with shame.
Old studies fail'd; seldom she spoke:
  but oft
Clomb to the roofs, and gazed alone
  for hours
On that disastrous leaguer, swarms of
  men
Darkening her female field: void was
  her use,
And she as one that climbs a peak to
  gaze
O'er land and main, and sees a great
  black cloud
Drag inward from the deeps, a wall
  of night,
Blot out the slope of sea from verge
  to shore,
And suck the blinding splendor from
  the sand,

And quenching lake by lake and tarn
  by tarn
Expunge the world: so fared she gazing there;
So blacken'd all her world in secret,
  blank
And waste it seem'd and vain; till
  down she came,
And found fair peace once more among
  the sick.

And twilight dawn'd; and morn by
  morn the lark
Shot up and shrill'd in flickering gyres,
  but I
Lay silent in the muffled cage of life:
And twilight gloom'd; and broader-
  grown the bowers
Drew the great night into themselves,
  and Heaven,
Star after star, arose and fell; but I,
Deeper than those weird doubts could
  reach me, lay
Quite sunder'd from the moving Uni-
  verse,
Nor knew what eye was on me, nor
  the hand
That nursed me, more than infants in
  their sleep.

But Psyche tended Florian: with
  her oft,
Melissa came; for Blanche had gone,
  but left
Her child among us, willing she should
  keep
Court-favor · here and there the small
  bright head,
A light of healing, glanced about the
  couch,
Or thro' the parted silks the tender face
Peep'd, shining in upon the wounded
  man
With blush and smile, a medicine in
  themselves
To wile the length from languorous
  hours, and draw
The sting from pain; nor seem'd it
  strange that soon
He rose up whole, and those fair
  charities

Join'd at her side; nor stranger seem'd
  that hearts
So gentle, so employ'd, should close
  in love,
Than when two dewdrops on the petal
  shake
To the same sweet air, and tremble
  deeper down,
And slip at once all-fragrant into one.

Less prosperously the second suit
  obtain'd
At first with Psyche. Not tho' Blanche
  had sworn
That after that dark night among the
  fields
She needs must wed him for her own
  good name;
Not tho' he built upon the babe restored;
Nor tho' she liked him, yielded she,
  but fear'd
To incense the Head once more; till
  on a day
When Cyril pleaded, Ida came behind
Seen but of Psyche: on her foot she
  hung
A moment, and she heard, at which
  her face
A little flush'd, and she past on; but
  each
Assumed from thence a half-consent
  involved
In stillness, plighted troth, and were
  at peace.

Nor only these: Love in the sacred
  halls
Held carnival at will, and flying struck
With showers of random sweet on
  maid and man.
Nor did her father cease to press my
  claim,
Nor did mine own now reconciled; nor
  yet
Did those twin brothers, risen again
  and whole;
Nor Arac, satiate with his victory.

But I lay still, and with me oft she
  sat:

Then came a change; for sometimes
  I would catch
Her hand in wild delirium, gripe it hard,
And fling it like a viper off, and shriek
"You are not Ida;" clasp it once again,
And call her Ida, tho' I know her not,
And call her sweet, as if in irony,
And call her hard and cold which
  seem'd a truth:
And still she fear'd that I should lose
  my mind,
And often she believed that I should
  die:
Till out of long frustration of her care,
And pensive tendance in the all-weary
  noons,
And watches in the dead, the dark,
  when clocks
Throbb'd thunder thro' the palace
  floors, or call'd
On flying Time from all their silver
  tongues —
And out of memories of her kindlier
  days,
And sidelong glances at my father's
  grief,
And at the happy lovers heart in
  heart —
And out of hauntings of my spoken
  love,
And lonely listenings to my mutter'd
  dream,
And often feeling of the helpless
  hands,
And wordless broodings on the wasted
  cheek —
From all a closer interest flourish'd up,
Tenderness touch by touch, and last,
  to these,
Love, like an Alpine harebell hung
  with tears
By some cold morning glacier; frail
  at first
And feeble, all unconscious of itself,
But such as gather'd color day by day.

Last I woke sane, but well-nigh close
  to death
For weakness: it was evening: silent
  light
Slept on the painted walls, wherein
  were wrought

Two grand designs; for on one side
   arose
The women up in wild revolt, and
   storm'd
At the Oppian law. Titanic shapes,
   they cramm'd
The forum, and half-crush'd among
   the rest
A dwarf-like Cato cower'd. On the
   other side
Hortensia spoke against the tax; be-
   hind,
A train of dames: by axe and eagle
   sat,
With all their foreheads drawn in
   Roman scowls,
And half the wolf's-milk curdled in
   their veins,
The fierce triumvirs; and before them
   paused
Hortensia pleading: angry was her
   face.

I saw the forms: I knew not where
   I was:
They did but look like hollow shows;
   nor more
Sweet Ida: palm to palm she sat: the
   dew
Dwelt in her eyes, and softer all her
   shape
And rounder seem'd: I moved: I
   sigh'd: a touch
Came round my wrist, and tears upon
   my hand:
Then all for languor and self-pity ran
Mine down my face, and with what
   life I had,
And like a flower that cannot all un-
   fold,
So drench'd it is with tempest, to the
   sun,
Yet, as it may, turns toward him, I on
   her
Fixt my faint eyes, and utter'd whisperingly:

"If you be, what I think you, some
   sweet dream,
I would but ask you to fulfil yourself:
But if you be that Ida whom I knew,

I ask you nothing: only, if a dream,
Sweet dream, be perfect. I shall die
   to-night.
Stoop down and seem to kiss me ere I
   die."

I could no more, but lay like one in
   trance,
That hears his burial talk'd of by his
   friends,
And cannot speak, nor move, nor
   make one sign,
But lies and dreads his doom. She
   turn'd; she paused;
She stoop'd; and out of languor leapt
   a cry;
Leapt fiery Passion from the brinks of
   death;
And I believed that in the living world
My spirit closed with Ida's at the lips;
Till back I fell, and from mine arms
   she rose
Glowing all over noble shame; and all
Her falser self slipt from her like a
   robe,
And left her woman, lovelier in her
   mood
Than in her mould that other, when
   she came
From barren deeps to conquer all
   with love;
And down the streaming crystal
   dropt; and she
Far-fleeted by the purple island-sides,
Naked, a double light in air and wave,
To meet her Graces, where they
   deck'd her out
For worship without end; nor end of
   mine,
Stateliest, for thee! but mute she
   glided forth,
Nor glanced behind her, and I sank
   and slept,
Fill'd thro' and thro' with Love, a
   happy sleep.

Deep in the night I woke: she, near
   me, held
A volume of the Poets of her land:
There to herself, all in low tones, she
   read.

"Now sleeps the crimson petal, now the
    white;
Nor waves the cypress in the palace walk;
Nor winks the gold fin in the porphyry font:
The fire-fly wakens: waken thou with me.

Now droops the milkwhite peacock like a
    ghost,
And like a ghost she glimmers on to me.

Now lies the earth all Danaë to the stars,
And all thy heart lies open unto me.

Now slides the silent meteor on, and leaves
A shining furrow, as thy thoughts in me.

Now folds the lily all her sweetness up,
And slips into the bosom of the lake:
So fold thyself, my dearest, thou, and slip
Into my bosom and be lost in me."

I heard her turn the page; she
    found a small
Sweet Idyl, and once more, as low,
    she read:

" Come down, O maid, from yonder moun-
    tain height:
What pleasure lives in height (the shepherd
    sang)
In height and cold, the splendor of the hills?
But cease to move so near the Heavens, and
    cease
To glide a sunbeam by the blasted Pine,
To sit a star upon the sparkling spire;
And come, for Love is of the valley, come,
For Love is of the valley, come thou down
And find him; by the happy threshold, he,
Or hand in hand with Plenty in the maize,
Or red with spirted purple of the vats,
Or foxlike in the vine; nor cares to walk
With Death and Morning on the silver horns,
Nor wilt thou snare him in the white ravine,
Nor find him dropt upon the firths of ice,
That huddling slant in furrow-cloven falls
To roll the torrent out of dusky doors:
But follow; let the torrent dance thee down
To find him in the valley; let the wild
Lean-headed Eagles yelp alone, and leave
The monstrous ledges there to slope, and
    spill
Their thousand wreaths of dangling water-
    smoke,
That like a broken purpose waste in air:
So waste not thou; but come; for all the vales
Await thee; azure pillars of the hearth
Arise to thee; the children call, and I
Thy shepherd pipe, and sweet is every sound,
Sweeter thy voice, but every sound is sweet;
Myriads of rivulets hurrying thro' the lawn,
The moan of doves in immemorial elms,
And murmuring of innumerable bees."

So she low-toned; while with shut
    eyes I lay

Listening; then look'd.   Pale was the
    perfect face;
The bosom with long sighs labor'd;
    and meek
Seem'd the full lips, and mild the
    luminous eyes,
And the voice trembled and the hand.
    She said
Brokenly, that she knew it, she had
    fail'd
In sweet humility; had fail'd in all;
That all her labor was but as a block
Left in the quarry; but she still were
    loth,
She still were loth to yield herself to
    one
That wholly scorn'd to help their
    equal rights
Against the sons of men, and barbar-
    ous laws.
She pray'd me not to judge their
    cause from her
That wrong'd it, sought far less for
    truth than power
In knowledge: something wild within
    her breast,
A greater than all knowledge, beat
    her down.
And she had nursed me there from
    week to week:
Much had she learnt in little time.
    In part
It was ill counsel had misled the girl
To vex true hearts: yet was she but a
    girl—
" Ah fool, and made myself a Queen
    of farce !
When comes another such ? never, I
    think,
Till the Sun drop, dead, from the
    signs."
                                                Her voice
Choked, and her forehead sank upon
    her hands,
And her great heart thro' all the
    faultful Past
Went sorrowing in a pause I dared
    not break;
Till notice of a change in the dark
    world
Was lispt about the acacias, and a
    bird,

That early woke to feed her little ones,
Sent from a dewy breast a cry for
    light :
She moved, and at her feet the volume
    fell.

"Blame not thyself too much," I
    said, " nor blame
Too much the sons of men and bar-
    barous laws ;
These were the rough ways of the
    world till now.
Henceforth thou hast a helper, me,
    that know
The woman's cause is man's : they
    rise or sink
Together, dwarf'd or godlike, bond or
    free :
For she that out of Lethe scales with
    man
The shining steps of Nature, shares
    with man
His nights, his days, moves with him
    to one goal,
Stays all the fair young planet in her
    hands —
If she be small, slight-natured, miser-
    able,
How shall men grow ? but work no
    more alone !
Our place is much : as far as in us lies
We two will serve them both in aid-
    ing her —
Will clear away the parasitic forms
That seem to keep her up but drag
    her down —
Will leave her space to burgeon out
    of all
Within her — let her make herself
    her own
To give or keep, to live and learn and
    be
All that not harms distinctive woman-
    hood.
For woman is not undevelopt man,
But diverse : could we make her as
    the man,
Sweet Love were slain : his dearest
    bond is this,
Not like to like, but like in difference.
Yet in the long years liker must they
    grow ;

The man be more of woman, she of
    man ;
He gain in sweetness and in moral
    height,
Nor lose the wrestling thews that
    throw the world ;
She mental breadth, nor fail in child-
    ward care,
Nor lose the childlike in the larger
    mind ;
Till at the last she set herself to man,
Like perfect music unto noble words ;
And so these twain, upon the skirts of
    Time,
Sit side by side, full-summ'd in all
    their powers,
Dispensing harvest, sowing the To-be,
Self-reverent each and reverencing
    each,
Distinct in individualities,
But like each other ev'n as those who
    love.
Then comes the statelier Eden back
    to men :
Then reign the world's great bridals,
    chaste and calm :
Then springs the crowning race of
    human-kind.
May these things be ! "
                Sighing she spoke " I fear
They will not."
        " Dear, but let us type them now
In our own lives, and this proud
    watchword rest
Of equal ; seeing either sex alone
Is half itself, and in true marriage lies
Nor equal, nor unequal : each fulfils
Defect in each, and always thought
    in thought,
Purpose in purpose, will in will, they
    grow,
The single pure and perfect animal,
The two-cell'd heart beating, with one
    full stroke,
Life."
    And again sighing she spoke : " A
    dream
That once was mine ! what woman
    taught you this ? "

    " Alone," I said, " from earlier than
    I know,

Immersed in rich foreshadowings of
   the world,
I loved the woman : he, that doth not,
   lives
A drowning life, besotted in sweet
   self,
Or pines in sad experience worse than
   death,
Or keeps his wing'd affections clipt
   with crime :
Yet was there one thro' whom I loved
   her, one
Not learned, save in gracious household ways,
Not perfect, nay, but full of tender
   wants,
No Angel, but a dearer being, all
   dipt
In Angel instincts, breathing Para-
   dise,
Interpreter between the Gods and
   men,
Who look'd all native to her place,
   and yet
On tiptoe seem'd to touch upon a
   sphere
Too gross to tread, and all male
   minds perforce
Sway'd to her from their orbits as
   they moved,
And girdled her with music. Happy
   he
With such a mother ! faith in woman-
   kind
Beats with his blood, and trust in all
   things high
Comes easy to him, and tho' he trip
   and fall
He shall not blind his soul with clay."
                 " But I,"
Said Ida, tremulously, " so all un-
   like —
It seems you love to cheat yourself
   with words :
This mother is your model. I have
   heard
Of your strange doubts : they well
   might be : I seem
A mockery to my own self. Never,
   Prince ;
You cannot love me."
         " Nay but thee," I said

" From yearlong poring on thy pictured eyes,
Ere seen I loved, and loved thee seen,
   and saw
Thee woman thro' the crust of iron
   moods
That mask'd thee from men's reverence up, and forced
Sweet love on pranks of saucy boyhood : now,
Giv'n back to life, to life indeed, thro'
   thee,
Indeed I love : the new day comes, the
   light
Dearer for night, as dearer thou for
   faults
Lived over : lift thine eyes ; my doubts
   are dead,
My haunting sense of hollow shows :
   the change,
This truthful change in thee has kill'd
   it. Dear,
Look up, and let thy nature strike on
   mine,
Like yonder morning on the blind
   half-world ;
Approach and fear not ; breathe upon
   my brows ;
In that fine air I tremble, all the past
Melts mist-like into this bright hour,
   and this
Is morn to more, and all the rich to-
   come
Reels, as the golden Autumn wood-
   land reels
Athwart the smoke of burning weeds.
   Forgive me,
I waste my heart in signs : let be. My
   bride,
My wife, my life. O we will walk this
   world,
Yoked in all exercise of noble end,
And so thro' those dark gates across
   the wild
That no man knows. Indeed I love
   thee : come,
Yield thyself up : my hopes and thine
   are one :
Accomplish thou my manhood and
   thyself ;
Lay thy sweet hands in mine and
   trust to me."

CONCLUSION.

So closed our tale, of which I give
    you all
The random scheme as wildly as it
    rose:
The words are mostly mine; for when
    we ceased
There came a minute's pause, and
    Walter said,
"I wish she had not yielded!" then to
    me,
"What, if you drest it up poetically!"
So pray'd the men, the women: I gave
    assent:
Yet how to bind the scatter'd scheme
    of seven
Together in one sheaf? What style
    could suit?
The men required that I should give
    throughout
The sort of mock-heroic gigantesque,
With which we banter'd little Lilia
    first:
The women — and perhaps they felt
    their power,
For something in the ballads which
    they sang,
Or in their silent influence as they sat,
Had ever seem'd to wrestle with bur-
    lesque,
And drove us, last, to quite a solemn
    close —
They hated banter, wish'd for some-
    thing real,
A gallant fight, a noble princess —
    why
Not make her true-heroic — true-
    sublime?
Or all, they said, as earnest as the
    close?
Which yet with such a framework
    scarce could be.
Then rose a little feud betwixt the
    two,
Betwixt the mockers and the realists:
And I, betwixt them both, to please
    them both,
And yet to give the story as it rose,
I moved as in a strange diagonal,
And maybe neither pleased myself
    nor them.

But Lilia pleased me, for she took
    no part
In our dispute: the sequel of the tale
Had touch'd her; and she sat, she
    pluck'd the grass,
She flung it from her, thinking: last,
    she fixt
A showery glance upon her aunt, and
    said,
"You — tell us what we are" who
    might have told,
For she was cramm'd with theories
    out of books,
But that there rose a shout: the gates
    were closed
At sunset, and the crowd were swarm-
    ing now,
To take their leave, about the garden
    rails.

So I and some went out to these:
    we climb'd
The slope to Vivian-place, and turn-
    ing saw
The happy valleys, half in light, and
    half
Far-shadowing from the west, a land
    of peace;
Gray halls alone among their massive
    groves;
Trim hamlets; here and there a rustic
    tower
Half-lost in belts of hop and breadths
    of wheat;
The shimmering glimpses of a stream;
    the seas;
A red sail, or a white; and far be-
    yond,
Imagined more than seen, the skirts
    of France.

"Look there, a garden!" said my
    college friend,
The Tory member's elder son, "and
    there!
God bless the narrow sea which keeps
    her off,
And keeps our Britain, whole within
    herself,
A nation yet, the rulers and the
    ruled —
Some sense of duty, something of a
    faith,

Some reverence for the laws ourselves
   have made,
Some patient force to change them
   when we will,
Some civic manhood firm against the
   crowd —
But yonder, whiff! there comes a sud-
   den heat,
The gravest citizen seems to lose his
   head,
The king is scared, the soldier will
   not fight,
The little boys begin to shoot and
   stab,
A kingdom topples over with a shriek
Like an old woman, and down rolls
   the world
In mock heroics stranger than our
   own;
Revolts, republics, revolutions, most
No graver than a schoolboys' barring
   out;
Too comic for the solemn things they
   are,
Too solemn for the comic touches in
   them,
Like our wild Princess with as wise
   a dream
As some of theirs — God bless the
   narrow seas!
I wish they were a whole Atlantic
   broad."

"Have patience," I replied, "ourselves are full
Of social wrong; and maybe wildest
   dreams
Are but the needful preludes of the
   truth:
For me, the genial day, the happy
   crowd,
The sport half-science, fill me with a
   faith,
This fine old world of ours is but a
   child
Yet in the go-cart. Patience! Give
   it time
To learn its limbs: there is a hand
   that guides."

In such discourse we gain'd the
   garden rails,

And there we saw Sir Walter where
   he stood,
Before a tower of crimson holly-oaks,
Among six boys, head under head,
   and look'd
No little lily-handed Baronet he,
A great broad-shoulder'd genial Eng-
   lishman,
A lord of fat prize-oxen and of sheep,
A raiser of huge melons and of pine,
A patron of some thirty charities,
A pamphleteer on guano and on
   grain,
A quarter-sessions chairman, abler
   none;
Fair-hair'd and redder than a windy
   morn;
Now shaking hands with him, now
   him, of those
That stood the nearest — now ad-
   dress'd to speech —
Who spoke few words and pithy, such
   as closed
Welcome, farewell, and welcome for
   the year
To follow: a shout rose again, and
   made
The long line of the approaching
   rookery swerve
From the broad elms, and shook the
   branches of the deer
From slope to slope thro' distant ferns,
   and rang
Beyond the bourn of sunset; O, a
   shout
More joyful than the city-roar that
   hails
Premier or king! Why should not
   these great Sirs
Give up their parks some dozen times
   a year
To let the people breathe? So thrice
   they cried,
I likewise, and in groups they stream'd
   away.

But we went back to the Abbey,
   and sat on,
So much the gathering darkness
   charm'd: we sat
But spoke not, rapt in nameless
   reverie,

Perchance upon the future man: the walls
Blacken'd about us, bats wheel'd, and owls whoop'd,
And gradually the powers of the night,
That range above the region of the wind,
Deepening the courts of twilight broke them up

Thro' all the silent spaces of the worlds,
Beyond all thought into the Heaven of Heavens.

Last little Lilia, rising quietly,
Disrobed the glimmering statue of Sir Ralph
From those rich silks, and home well-pleased we went.

MAUD; A MONODRAMA.

PART I.

I.

I.

I HATE the dreadful hollow behind the little wood,
Its lips in the field above are dabbled with blood-red heath,
The red-ribb'd ledges drip with a silent horror of blood,
And Echo there, whatever is ask'd her, answers " Death."

II.

For there in the ghastly pit long since a body was found,
His who had given me life — O father! O God! was it well? —
Mangled, and flatten'd, and crush'd, and dinted into the ground:
There yet lies the rock that fell with him when he fell.

III.

Did he fling himself down? who knows? for a vast speculation had fail'd,
And ever he mutter'd and madden'd, and ever wann'd with despair,
And out he walk'd when the wind like a broken worldling wail'd,
And the flying gold of the ruin'd woodlands drove thro' the air.

IV.

I remember the time, for the roots of my hair were stirr'd
By a shuffled step, by a dead weight trail'd, by a whisper'd fright,
And my pulses closed their gates with a shock on my heart as I heard
The shrill-edged shriek of a mother divide the shuddering night.

V.

Villany somewhere! whose? One says, we are villains all.
Not he: his honest fame should at least by me be maintained:
But that old man, now lord of the broad estate and the Hall,
Dropt off gorged from a scheme that had left us flaccid and drain'd.

VI.

Why do they prate of the blessings of Peace? we have made them a curse,
Pickpockets, each hand lusting for all that is not its own;
And lust of gain, in the spirit of Cain, is it better or worse
Than the heart of the citizen hissing in war on his own hearthstone?

VII.

But these are the days of advance, the works of the men of mind,
When who but a fool would have faith in a tradesman's ware or his word ?
Is it peace or war ?   Civil war, as I think, and that of a kind
The viler, as underhand, not openly bearing the sword.

VIII.

Sooner or later I too may passively take the print
Of the golden age — why not ?   I have neither hope nor trust;
May make my heart as a millstone, set my face as a flint,
Cheat and be cheated, and die : who knows ? we are ashes and dust.

IX.

Peace sitting under her olive, and slurring the days gone by,
When the poor are hovell'd and hustled together, each sex, like swine,
When only the ledger lives, and when only not all men lie ;
Peace in her vineyard — yes ! — but a company forges the wine.

X.

And the vitriol madness flushes up in the ruffian's head,
Till the filthy by-lane rings to the yell of the trampled wife,
And chalk and alum and plaster are sold to the poor for bread,
And the spirit of murder works in the very means of life,

XI.

And Sleep must lie down arm'd, for the villanous centre-bits
Grind on the wakeful ear in the hush of the moonless nights,
While another is cheating the sick of a few last gasps, as he sits
To pestle a poison'd poison behind his crimson lights.

XII.

When a Mammonite mother kills her babe for a burial fee,
And Timour-Mammon grins on a pile of children's bones,
Is it peace or war ? better, war ! loud war by land and by sea,
War with a thousand battles, and shaking a hundred thrones.

XIII.

For I trust if an enemy's fleet came yonder round by the hill,
And the rushing battle-bolt sang from the three-decker out of the foam,
That the smooth-faced snubnosed rogue would leap from his counter and till,
And strike, if he could, were it but with his cheating yardwand, home. ——

XIV.

What ! am I raging alone as my father raged in his mood ?
Must *I* too creep to the hollow and dash myself down and die
Rather than hold by the law that I made, nevermore to brood
On a horror of shatter'd limbs and a wretched swindler's lie ?

xv.

Would there be sorrow for *me?* there was *love* in the passionate shriek,
Love for the silent thing that had made false haste to the grave —
Wrapt in a cloak, as I saw him, and thought he would rise and speak
And rave at the lie and the liar, ah God, as he used to rave.

xvi.

I am sick of the Hall and the hill, I am sick of the moor and the main.
Why should I stay? can a sweeter chance ever come to me here?
O, having the nerves of motion as well as the nerves of pain,
Were it not wise if I fled from the place and the pit and the fear?

xvii.

Workmen up at the Hall! — they are coming back from abroad;
The dark old place will be gilt by the touch of a millionaire:
I have heard, I know not whence, of the singular beauty of Maud;
I play'd with the girl when a child; she promised then to be fair.

xviii.

Maud with her venturous climbings and tumbles and childish escapes,
Maud the delight of the village, the ringing joy of the Hall,
Maud with her sweet purse-mouth when my father dangled the grapes,
Maud the beloved of my mother, the moon-faced darling of all, —

xix.

What is she now? My dreams are bad. She may bring me a curse.
No, there is fatter game on the moor; she will let me alone.
Thanks, for the fiend best knows whether woman or man be the worse.
I will bury myself in myself, and the Devil may pipe to his own.

II.

Long have I sigh'd for a calm: God grant I may find it at last!
It will never be broken by Maud, she has neither savor nor salt,
But a cold and clear-cut face, as I found when her carriage past,
Perfectly beautiful: let it be granted her: where is the fault?
All that I saw (for her eyes were downcast, not to be seen)
Faultily faultless, icily regular, splendidly null,
Dead perfection, no more; nothing more, if it had not been
For a chance of travel, a paleness, an hour's defect of the rose,
Or an underlip, you may call it a little too ripe, too full,
Or the least little delicate aquiline curve in a sensitive nose,
From which I escaped heart-free, with the least little touch of spleen.

III.

Cold and clear-cut face, why come you so cruelly meek,
Breaking a slumber in which all spleenful folly was drown'd,
Pale with the golden beam of an eyelash dead on the cheek,
Passionless, pale, cold face, star-sweet on a gloom profound;
Womanlike, taking revenge too deep for a transient wrong
Done but in thought to your beauty, and ever as pale as before

Growing and fading and growing upon me without a sound,
Luminous, gemlike, ghostlike, deathlike, half the night long
Growing and fading and growing, till I could bear it no more,
But arose, and all by myself in my own dark garden ground,
Listening now to the tide in its broad-flung shipwrecking roar,
Now to the scream of a madden'd beach dragg'd down by the wave,
Walk'd in a wintry wind by a ghastly glimmer, and found
The shining daffodil dead, and Orion low in his grave.

IV.

I.

A million emeralds break from the ruby-budded lime
In the little grove where I sit — ah, wherefore cannot I be
Like things of the season gay, like the bountiful season bland,
When the far-off sail is blown by the breeze of a softer clime,
Half-lost in the liquid azure bloom of a crescent of sea,
The silent sapphire-spangled marriage ring of the land?

II.

Below me, there, is the village, and looks how quiet and small!
And yet bubbles o'er like a city, with gossip, scandal, and spite;
And Jack on his ale-house bench has as many lies as a Czar;
And here on the landward side, by a red rock, glimmers the Hall;
And up in the high Hall-garden I see her pass like a light;
But sorrow seize me if ever that light be my leading star!

III.

When have I bow'd to her father, the wrinkled head of the race?
I met her to-day with her brother, but not to her brother I bow'd:
I bow'd to his lady-sister as she rode by on the moor;
But the fire of a foolish pride flash'd over her beautiful face.
O child, you wrong your beauty, believe it, in being so proud;
Your father has wealth well-gotten, and I am nameless and poor.

IV.

I keep but a man and a maid, ever ready to slander and steal;
I know it, and smile a hard-set smile, like a stoic, or like
A wiser epicurean, and let the world have its way:
For nature is one with rapine, a harm no preacher can heal;
The Mayfly is torn by the swallow, the sparrow spear'd by the shrike,
And the whole little wood where I sit is a world of plunder and prey.

V.

We are puppets, Man in his pride, and Beauty fair in her flower;
Do we move ourselves, or are we moved by an unseen hand at a game
That pushes us off from the board, and others ever succeed?
Ah yet, we cannot be kind to each other here for an hour;
We whisper, and hint, and chuckle, and grin at a brother's shame;
However we brave it out, we men are a little breed.

VI.

A monstrous eft was of old the Lord and Master of Earth,
For him did his high sun flame, and his river billowing ran,
And he felt himself in his force to be Nature's crowning race.
As nine months go to the shaping an infant ripe for his birth,
So many a million of ages have gone to the making of man:
He now is first, but is he the last ? is he not too base ?

VII

The man of science himself is fonder of glory, and vain,
An eye well-practised in nature, a spirit bounded and poor;
The passionate heart of the poet is whirl'd into folly and vice.
I would not marvel at either, but keep a temperate brain;
For not to desire or admire, if a man could learn it, were more
Than to walk all day like the sultan of old in a garden of spice.

VIII.

For the drift of the Maker is dark, an Isis hid by the veil.
Who knows the ways of the world, how God will bring them about ?
Our planet is one, the suns are many, the world is wide.
Shall I weep if a Poland fall ? shall I shriek if a Hungary fail ?
Or an infant civilization be ruled with rod or with knout ?
I have not made the world, and He that made it will guide.

IX.

Be mine a philosopher's life in the quiet woodland ways,
Where if I cannot be gay let a passionless peace be my lot,
Far-off from the clamor of liars belied in the hubbub of lies;
From the long-neck'd geese of the world that are ever hissing dispraise
Because their natures are little, and, whether he heed it or not,
Where each man walks with his head in a cloud of poisonous flies.

X.

And most of all would I flee from the cruel madness of love,
The honey of poison-flowers and all the measureless ill.
Ah Maud, you milk-white fawn, you are all unmeet for a wife.
Your mother is mute in her grave as her image in marble above;
Your father is ever in London, you wander about at your will;
You have but fed on the roses and lain in the lilies of life.

V.

I.

A voice by the cedar tree
In the meadow under the Hall!
She is singing an air that is known to
me,
A passionate ballad gallant and gay,
A martial song like a trumpet's call!
Singing alone in the morning of life,

In the happy morning of life and of May,
Singing of men that in battle array,
Ready in heart and ready in hand,
March with banner and bugle and fife
To the death, for their native land.

II.

Maud with her exquisite face,
And wild voice pealing up to the
sunny sky,

And feet like sunny gems on an English green,
Maud in the light of her youth and her grace,
Singing of Death, and of Honor that cannot die,
Till I well could weep for a time so sordid and mean,
And myself so languid and base.

III.

Silence, beautiful voice!
Be still, for you only trouble the mind
With a joy in which I cannot rejoice,
A glory I shall not find.
Still! I will hear you no more,
For your sweetness hardly leaves me a choice
But to move to the meadow and fall before
Her feet on the meadow grass, and adore,
Not her, who is neither courtly nor kind,
Not her, not her, but a voice.

VI.

I.

Morning arises stormy and pale,
No sun, but a wannish glare
In fold upon fold of hueless cloud,
And the budded peaks of the wood are bow'd
Caught and cuff'd by the gale:
I had fancied it would be fair.

II.

Whom but Maud should I meet
Last night, when the sunset burn'd
On the blossom'd gable-ends
At the head of the village street,
Whom but Maud should I meet?
And she touch'd my hand with a smile so sweet,
She made me divine amends
For a courtesy not return'd.

III.

And thus a delicate spark
Of glowing and growing light
Thro' the livelong hours of the dark

Kept itself warm in the heart of my dreams,
Ready to burst in a color'd flame;
Till at last when the morning came
In a cloud, it faded, and seems
But an ashen-gray delight.

IV.

What if with her sunny hair,
And smile as sunny as cold,
She meant to weave me a snare
Of some coquettish deceit,
Cleopatra-like as of old
To entangle me when we met,
To have her lion roll in a silken net
And fawn at a victor's feet.

V.

Ah, what shall I be at fifty
Should Nature keep me alive,
If I find the world so bitter
When I am but twenty-five?
Yet, if she were not a cheat,
If Maud were all that she seem'd,
And her smile were all that I dream'd,
Then the world were not so bitter
But a smile could make it sweet.

VI.

What if tho' her eye seem'd full
Of a kind intent to me,
What if that dandy-despot, he,
That jewell'd mass of millinery,
That oil'd and curl'd Assyrian Bull
Smelling of musk and of insolence,
Her brother, from whom I keep aloof,
Who wants the finer politic sense
To mask, tho' but in his own behoof,
With a glassy smile his brutal scorn —
What if he had told her yestermorn
How prettily for his own sweet sake
A face of tenderness might be feign'd,
And a moist mirage in desert eyes,
That so, when the rotten hustings shake
In another month to his brazen lies,
A wretched vote may be gain'd.

VII.

For a raven ever croaks, at my side,
Keep watch and ward, keep watch and ward,

Or thou wilt prove their tool.
Yea, too, myself from myself I guard,
For often a man's own angry pride
Is cap and bells for a fool.

VIII.

Perhaps the smile and tender tone
Came out of her pitying womanhood,
For am I not, am I not, here alone
So many a summer since she died,
My mother, who was so gentle and
    good?
Living alone in an empty house,
Here half-hid in the gleaming wood,
Where I hear the dead at midday
    moan,
And the shrieking rush of the wainscot
    mouse,
And my own sad name in corners
    cried,
When the shiver of dancing leaves is
    thrown
About its echoing chambers wide,
Till a morbid hate and horror have
    grown
Of a world in which I have hardly
    mixt,
And a morbid eating lichen fixt
On a heart half-turn'd to stone.

IX.

O heart of stone, are you flesh, and
    caught
By that you swore to withstand?
For what was it else within me wrought
But, I fear, the new strong wine of
    love,
That made my tongue so stammer and
    trip
When I saw the treasured splendor,
    her hand,
Come sliding out of her sacred glove,
And the sunlight broke from her lip?

X.

I have play'd with her when a child;
She remembers it now we meet.
Ah well, well, well, I *may* be beguiled
By some coquettish deceit.
Yet, if she were not a cheat,

If Maud were all that she seem'd,
And her smile had all that I dream'd,
Then the world were not so bitter
But a smile could make it sweet.

VII.

I.

Did I hear it half in a doze
    Long since, I know not where?
Did I dream it an hour ago,
    When asleep in this arm-chair?

II.

Men were drinking together,
    Drinking and talking of me;
" Well, if it prove a girl, the boy
    Will have plenty: so let it be."

III.

Is it an echo of something
    Read with a boy's delight,
Viziers nodding together
    In some Arabian night?

IV.

Strange, that I hear two men,
    Somewhere, talking of me;
" Well, if it prove a girl, my boy
    Will have plenty; so let it be."

VIII.

She came to the village church,
And sat by a pillar alone;
An angel watching an urn
Wept over her, carved in stone;
And once, but once, she lifted her
    eyes,
And suddenly, sweetly, strangely
    blush'd
To find they were met by my own;
And suddenly, sweetly, my heart beat
    stronger
And thicker, until I heard no longer
The snowy-banded, dilettante,
Delicate-handed priest intone;
And thought, is it pride, and mused
    and sigh'd
" No surely, now it cannot be pride."

IX.

I was walking a mile,
More than a mile from the shore,
The sun look'd out with a smile
Betwixt the cloud and the moor,
And riding at set of day
Over the dark moor land,
Rapidly riding far away,
She waved to me with her hand.
There were two at her side,
Something flash'd in the sun,
Down by the hill I saw them ride,
In a moment they were gone:
Like a sudden spark
Struck vainly in the night,
Then returns the dark
With no more hope of light.

X.

I.

Sick, am I sick of a jealous dread?
Was not one of the two at her side
This new-made lord, whose splendor
  plucks
The slavish hat from the villager's
  head?
Whose old grandfather has lately died,
Gone to a blacker pit, for whom
Grimy nakedness dragging his trucks
And laying his trams in a poison'd
  gloom
Wrought, till he crept from a gutted
  mine
Master of half a servile shire,
And left his coal all turn'd into gold
To a grandson, first of his noble line,
Rich in the grace all women desire,
Strong in the power that all men
  adore,
And simper and set their voices lower,
And soften as if to a girl, and hold
Awe-stricken breaths at a work divine,
Seeing his gewgaw castle shine,
New as his title, built last year,
There amid perky larches and pine,
And over the sullen-purple moor
(Look at it) pricking a cockney ear.

II.

What, has he found my jewel out?
For one of the two that rode at her
  side

Bound for the Hall, I am sure was he:
Bound for the Hall, and I think for a
  bride.
Blithe would her brother's acceptance
  be.
Maud could be gracious too, no doubt
To a lord, a captain, a padded shape,
A bought commission, a waxen face,
A rabbit mouth that is ever agape —
Bought? what is it he cannot buy?
And therefore splenetic, personal,
  base,
A wounded thing with a rancorous cry,
At war with myself and a wretched
  race,
Sick, sick to the heart of life, am I.

III.

Last week came one to the county
  town,
To preach our poor little army down,
And play the game of the despot kings,
Tho' the state has done it and thrice
  as well:
This broad-brimm'd hawker of holy
  things,
Whose ear is cramm'd with his cotton,
  and rings
Even in dreams to the chink of his
  pence,
This huckster put down war! can he
  tell
Whether war be a cause or a conse-
  quence?
Put down the passions that make
  earth Hell!
Down with ambition, avarice, pride,
Jealousy, down! cut off from the mind
The bitter springs of anger and fear;
Down too, down at your own fireside,
With the evil tongue and the evil ear,
For each is at war with mankind.

IV.

I wish I could hear again
The chivalrous battle-song
That she warbled alone in her joy!
I might persuade myself then
She would not do herself this great
  wrong,
To take a wanton dissolute boy
For a man and leader of men.

V.

Ah God, for a man with heart, head,
    hand,
Like some of the simple great ones
    gone
For ever and ever by,
One still strong man in a blatant land,
Whatever they call him, what care I,
Aristocrat, democrat, autocrat — one
Who can rule and dare not lie.

VI.

And ah for a man to arise in me,
That the man I am may cease to be!

XI.

I.

O let the solid ground
    Not fail beneath my feet
Before my life has found
    What some have found so sweet;
Then let come what come may,
What matter if I go mad,
I shall have had my day.

II.

Let the sweet heavens endure,
    Not close and darken above me
Before I am quite quite sure
    That there is one to love me;
Then let come what come may
To a life that has been so sad,
I shall have had my day.

XII.

I.

Birds in the high Hall-garden
    When twilight was falling,
Maud, Maud, Maud, Maud,
    They were crying and calling.

II.

Where was Maud? in our wood;
    And I, who else, was with her,
Gathering woodland lilies,
    Myriads blow together.

III.

Birds in our wood sang
    Ringing thro' the valleys,
Maud is here, here, here
    In among the lilies.

IV.

I kiss'd her slender hand,
    She took the kiss sedately;
Maud is not seventeen,
    But she is tall and stately.

V.

I to cry out on pride
    Who have won her favor!
O Maud were sure of Heaven
    If lowliness could save her.

VI.

I know the way she went
    Home with her maiden posy,
For her feet have touch'd the meadows
    And left the daisies rosy.

VII.

Birds in the high Hall-garden
    Were crying and calling to her,
Where is Maud, Maud, Maud?
    One is come to woo her.

VIII.

Look, a horse at the door,
    And little King Charley snarling,
Go back, my lord, across the moor,
    You are not her darling.

XIII.

I.

Scorn'd, to be scorn'd by one that I
    scorn,
Is that a matter to make me fret?
That a calamity hard to be borne?
Well, he may live to hate me yet.
Fool that I am to be vext with his pride!
I past him, I was crossing his lands;
He stood on the path a little aside;
His face, as I grant, in spite of spite,
Has a broad-blown comeliness, red
    and white,
And six feet two, as I think, he stands;
But his essences turn'd the live air sick,
And barbarous opulence jewel-thick
Sunn'd itself on his breast and his
    hands.

II.

Who shall call me ungentle, unfair,
I long'd so heartily then and there
To give him the grasp of fellowship;

But while I past he was humming an
    air,
Stopt, and then with a riding whip
Leisurely tapping a glossy boot,
And curving a contumelious lip,
Gorgonized me from head to foot
    With a stony British stare.

III.

Why sits he here in his father's chair?
That old man never comes to his place:
Shall I believe him ashamed to be
    seen?
For only once, in the village street,
Last year, I caught a glimpse of his
    face,
A gray old wolf and a lean.
Scarcely, now, would I call him a
    cheat;
For then, perhaps, as a child of deceit,
She might by a true descent be untrue;
And Maud is as true as Maud is sweet:
Tho' I fancy her sweetness only due
To the sweeter blood by the other side;
Her mother has been a thing complete,
However she came to be so allied.
And fair without, faithful within,
Maud to him is nothing akin:
Some peculiar mystic grace
Made her only the child of her mother,
And heap'd the whole inherited sin
On that huge scapegoat of the race,
All, all upon the brother.

IV.

Peace, angry spirit, and let him be!
Has not his sister smiled on me?

XIV.

I.

Maud has a garden of roses
And lilies fair on a lawn;
There she walks in her state
And tends upon bed and bower,
And thither I climb'd at dawn
And stood by her garden-gate;
A lion ramps at the top,
He is claspt by a passion-flower.

II.

Maud's own little oak-room
(Which Maud, like a precious stone
Set in the heart of the carven gloom,
Lights with herself, when alone
She sits by her music and books
And her brother lingers late
With a roystering company) looks
Upon Maud's own garden-gate:
And I thought as I stood, if a hand,
    as white
As ocean-foam in the moon, were laid
On the hasp of the window, and my
    Delight
Had a sudden desire, like a glorious
    ghost, to glide,
Like a beam of the seventh Heaven,
    down to my side,
There were but a step to be made.

III.

The fancy flatter'd my mind,
And again seem'd overbold;
Now I thought that she cared for me,
Now I thought she was kind
Only because she was cold.

IV.

I heard no sound where I stood
But the rivulet on from the lawn
Running down to my own dark wood;
Or the voice of the long sea-wave as
    it swell'd
Now and then in the dim-gray dawn,
But I look'd, and round, all round the
    house I beheld
The death-white curtain drawn;
Felt a horror over me creep,
Prickle my skin and catch my breath,
Knew that the death-white curtain
    meant but sleep,
Yet I shudder'd and thought like a
    fool of the sleep of death.

XV.

So dark a mind within me dwells,
    And I make myself such evil cheer,
That if *I* be dear to some one else,
    Then some one else may have much
        to fear;
But if *I* be dear to some one else,
    Then I should be to myself more
        dear.

Shall I not take care of all that I think,
Yea ev'n of wretched meat and drink,
If I be dear,
If I be dear to some one else.

XVI.

I.

This lump of earth has left his estate
The lighter by the loss of his weight ;
And so that he find what he went to
    seek,
And fulsome Pleasure clog him, and
    drown
His heart in the gross mud-honey of
    town,
He may stay for a year who has gone
    for a week :
But this is the day when I must speak,
And I see my Oread coming down,
O this is the day !
O beautiful creature, what am I
That I dare to look her way ;
Think I may hold dominion sweet,
Lord of the pulse that is lord of her
    breast,
And dream of her beauty with tender
    dread,
From the delicate Arab arch of her
    feet
To the grace that, bright and light as
    the crest
Of a peacock, sits on her shining head,
And she knows it not : O, if she knew it,
To know her beauty might half undo it.
I know it the one bright thing to save
My yet young life in the wilds of Time,
Perhaps from madness, perhaps from
    crime,
Perhaps from a selfish grave.

II.

What, if she be fasten'd to this fool
    lord,
Dare I bid her abide by her word ?
Should I love her so well if she
Had given her word to a thing so low ?
Shall I love her as well if she
Can break her word were it even for
    me ?
I trust that it is not so.

III.

Catch not my breath, O clamorous
    heart,
Let not my tongue be a thrall to my
    eye,
For I must tell her before we part,
I must tell her, or die.

XVII.

Go not, happy day,
    From the shining fields,
Go not, happy day,
    Till the maiden yields.
Rosy is the West,
    Rosy is the South,
Roses are her cheeks,
    And a rose her mouth
When the happy Yes
    Falters from her lips,
Pass and blush the news
    Over glowing ships ;
Over blowing seas,
    Over seas at rest,
Pass the happy news,
    Blush it thro' the West ;
Till the red man dance
    By his red cedar-tree,
And the red man's babe
    Leap, beyond the sea.
Blush from West to East,
    Blush from East to West,
Till the West is East,
    Blush it thro' the West.
Rosy is the West,
    Rosy is the South,
Roses are her cheeks,
    And a rose her mouth.

XVIII.

I.

I have led her home, my love, my
    only friend.
There is none like her, none.
And never yet so warmly ran my
    blood
And sweetly, on and on
Calming itself to the long-wish'd-for
    end,
Full to the banks, close on the prom-
    ised good.

II.

None like her, none.
Just now the dry-tongued laurels'
    pattering talk
Seem'd her light foot along the
    garden walk,
And shook my heart to think she
    comes once more;
But even then I heard her close the
    door,
The gates of Heaven are closed, and
    she is gone.

III.

There is none like her, none.
Nor will be when our summers have
    deceased.
O, art thou sighing for Lebanon
In the long breeze that streams to thy
    delicious East,
Sighing for Lebanon,
Dark cedar, tho' thy limbs have here
    increased,
Upon a pastoral slope as fair,
And looking to the South, and fed
With honey'd rain and delicate air,
And haunted by the starry head
Of her whose gentle will has changed
    my fate,
And made my life a perfumed altar-
    flame;
And over whom thy darkness must
    have spread
With such delight as theirs of old,
    thy great
Forefathers of the thornless garden,
    there
Shadowing the snow-limb'd Eve from
    whom she came.

IV.

Here will I lie, while these long
    branches sway,
And you fair stars that crown a
    happy day
Go in and out as if at merry play,
Who am no more so all forlorn,
As when it seem'd far better to be
    born
To labor and the mattock-harden'd
    hand,

Than nursed at ease and brought to
    understand
A sad astrology, the boundless plan
That makes you tyrants in your iron
    skies,
Innumerable, pitiless, passionless eyes,
Cold fires, yet with power to burn and
    brand
His nothingness into man.

V.

But now shine on, and what care I,
Who in this stormy gulf have found a
    pearl
The countercharm of space and hol-
    low sky,
And do accept my madness, and would
    die
To save from some slight shame one
    simple girl.

VI.

Would die; for sullen-seeming Death
    may give
More life to Love than is or ever was
In our low world, where yet 'tis sweet
    to live.
Let no one ask me how it came to
    pass;
It seems that I am happy, that to me
A livelier emerald twinkles in the
    grass,
A purer sapphire melts into the sea.

VII.

Not die; but live a life of truest
    breath,
And teach true life to fight with
    mortal wrongs.
O, why should Love, like men in
    drinking-songs,
Spice his fair banquet with the dust
    of death?
Make answer, Maud my bliss,
Maud made my Maud by that long
    loving kiss,
Life of my life, wilt thou not answer
    this?
"The dusky strand of Death inwoven
    here
With dear Love's tie, makes Love
    himself more dear."

VIII.

Is that enchanted moan only the swell
Of the long waves that roll in yonder bay?
And hark the clock within, the silver knell
Of twelve sweet hours that past in bridal white,
And died to live, long as my pulses play;
But now by this my love has closed her sight
And given false death her hand, and stol'n away
To dreamful wastes where footless fancies dwell
Among the fragments of the golden day.
May nothing there her maiden grace affright!
Dear heart, I feel with thee the drowsy spell.
My bride to be, my evermore delight,
My own heart's heart, my ownest own, farewell;
It is but for a little space I go:
And ye meanwhile far over moor and fell
Beat to the noiseless music of the night!
Has our whole earth gone nearer to the glow
Of your soft splendors that you look so bright?
I have climb'd nearer out of lonely Hell.
Beat, happy stars, timing with things below,
Beat with my heart more blest than heart can tell,
Blest, but for some dark undercurrent woe
That seems to draw — but it shall not be so:
Let all be well, be well.

XIX.

I.

Her brother is coming back to-night,
Breaking up my dream of delight.

II.

My dream? do I dream of bliss?
I have walk'd awake with Truth.
O when did a morning shine
So rich in atonement as this
For my dark-dawning youth,
Darken'd watching a mother decline
And that dead man at her heart and mine:
For who was left to watch her but I?
Yet so did I let my freshness die.

III.

I trust that I did not talk
To gentle Maud in our walk
(For often in lonely wanderings
I have cursed him even to lifeless things)
But I trust that I did not talk,
Not touch on her father's sin:
I am sure I did but speak
Of my mother's faded cheek
When it slowly grew so thin,
That I felt she was slowly dying
Vext with lawyers and harass'd with debt:
For how often I caught her with eyes all wet,
Shaking her head at her son and sighing
A world of trouble within!

IV.

And Maud too, Maud was moved
To speak of the mother she loved
As one scarce less forlorn,
Dying abroad and it seems apart
From him who had ceased to share her heart,
And ever mourning over the feud,
The household Fury sprinkled with blood
By which our houses are torn:
How strange was what she said,
When only Maud and the brother
Hung over her dying bed —
That Maud's dark father and mine
Had bound us one to the other,
Betrothed us over their wine,
On the day when Maud was born;
Seal'd her mine from her first sweet breath.

Mine, mine by a right, from birth till
death.
Mine, mine — our fathers have sworn.

v.

But the true blood spilt had in it a
heat
To dissolve the precious seal on a
bond,
That, if left uncancell'd, had been so
sweet:
And none of us thought of a some-
thing beyond,
A desire that awoke in the heart of
the child,
As it were a duty done to the tomb,
To be friends for her sake, to be re-
conciled;
And I was cursing them and my
doom,
And letting a dangerous thought run
wild
While often abroad in the fragrant
gloom
Of foreign churches — I see her
there,
Bright English lily, breathing a
prayer
To be friends, to be reconciled!

vi.

But then what a flint is he!
Abroad, at Florence, at Rome,
I find whenever she touch'd on me
This brother had laugh'd her down,
And at last, when each came home,
He had darken'd into a frown,
Chid her, and forbid her to speak
To me, her friend of the years be-
fore;
And this was what had redden'd her
cheek
When I bow'd to her on the moor.

vii.

Yet Maud, altho' not blind
To the faults of his heart and mind,
I see she cannot but love him,
And says he is rough but kind,
And wishes me to approve him,
And tells me, when she lay

Sick once, with a fear of worse,
Then he left his wine and horses and
play,
Sat with her, read to her, night and
day,
And tended her like a nurse.

viii.

Kind? but the deathbed desire
Spurn'd by this heir of the liar —
Rough but kind? yet I know
He has plotted against me in this,
That he plots against me still.
Kind to Maud? that were not amiss.
Well, rough but kind; why let it be
so:
For shall not Maud have her will?

ix.

For, Maud, so tender and true,
As long as my life endures
I feel I shall owe you a debt,
That I never can hope to pay;
And if ever I should forget
That I owe this debt to you
And for your sweet sake to yours;
O then, what then shall I say? —
If ever I *should* forget,
May God make me more wretched
Than ever I have been yet!

x.

So now I have sworn to bury
All this dead body of hate,
I feel so free and so clear
By the loss of that dead weight,
That I should grow light-headed, I
fear,
Fantastically merry;
But that her brother comes, like a
blight
On my fresh hope, to the Hall to-
night.

XX.

i.

Strange, that I felt so gay,
Strange, that *I* tried to-day
To beguile her melancholy;
The Sultan, as we name him,—

She did not wish to blame him —
But he vext her and perplext her
With his worldly talk and folly:
Was it gentle to reprove her
For stealing out of view
From a little lazy lover
Who but claims her as his due ?
Or for chilling his caresses
By the coldness of her manners,
Nay, the plainness of her dresses ?
Now I know her but in two,
Nor can pronounce upon it
If one should ask me whether
The habit, hat, and feather,
Or the frock and gipsy bonnet
Be the neater and completer;
For nothing can be sweeter
Than maiden Maud in either.

II.

But to-morrow, if we live,
Our ponderous squire will give
A grand political dinner
To half the squirelings near ;
And Maud will wear her jewels,
And the bird of prey will hover,
And the titmouse hope to win her
With his chirrup at her ear.

III.

A grand political dinner
To the men of many acres,
A gathering of the Tory,
A dinner and then a dance
For the maids and marriage-makers,
And every eye but mine will glance
At Maud in all her glory.

IV.

For I am not invited,
But, with the Sultan's pardon,
I am all as well delighted,
For I know her own rose-garden,
And mean to linger in it
Till the dancing will be over ;
And then, oh then, come out to me
For a minute, but for a minute,
Come out to your own true lover,
That your true lover may see
Your glory also, and render
All homage to his own darling,
Queen Maud in all her splendor.

XXI.

Rivulet crossing my ground,
And bringing me down from the
    Hall
This garden-rose that I found,
Forgetful of Maud and me,
And lost in trouble and moving round
Here at the head of a tinkling fall,
And trying to pass to the sea ;
O Rivulet, born at the Hall,
My Maud has sent it by thee
(If I read her sweet will right)
On a blushing mission to me,
Saying in odor and color, " Ah, be
Among the roses to-night."

XXII.

I.

Come into the garden, Maud,
    For the black bat, night, has flown,
Come into the garden, Maud,
    I am here at the gate alone ;
And the woodbine spices are wafted
        abroad,
    And the musk of the rose is blown.

II.

For a breeze of morning moves,
    And the planet of Love is on high,
Beginning to faint in the light that
        she loves
    On a bed of daffodil sky,
To faint in the light of the sun she
        loves,
    To faint in his light, and to die.

III.

All night have the roses heard
    The flute, violin, bassoon ;
All night has the casement jessamine
        stirr'd
    To the dancers dancing in tune ;
Till a silence fell with the waking
        bird,
    And a hush with the setting moon.

IV.

I said to the lily, " There is but one
    With whom she has heart to be gay.
When will the dancers leave her
        alone ?

"She is coming, my own, my sweet!"

Page 455.

She is weary of dance and play."
Now half to the setting moon are gone,
  And half to the rising day ;
Low on the sand and loud on the
    stone
  The last wheel echoes away.

v.

I said to the rose, "The brief night
    goes
  In babble and revel and wine.
O young lord-lover, what sighs are
    those,
  For one that will never be thine ?
But mine, but mine," so I sware to
    the rose,
"For ever and ever, mine."

vi.

And the soul of the rose went into
    my blood,
  As the music clash'd in the hall ;
And long by the garden lake I stood,
  For I heard your rivulet fall
From the lake to the meadow and on
    to the wood,
  Our wood, that is dearer than all ;

vii.

From the meadow your walks have
    left so sweet
  That whenever a March-wind sighs
He sets the jewel-print of your feet
  In violets blue as your eyes,
To the woody hollows in which we
    meet
And the valleys of Paradise.

viii.

The slender acacia would not shake
  One long milk-bloom on the tree ;
The white lake-blossom fell into the
    lake
  As the pimpernel dozed on the lea ;
But the rose was awake all night for
    your sake,
  Knowing your promise to me ;
The lilies and roses were all awake,
  They sigh'd for the dawn and thee.

ix.

Queen rose of the rosebud garden of
    girls,
  Come hither, the dances are done,
In gloss of satin and glimmer of
    pearls,
  Queen lily and rose in one ;
Shine out, little head, sunning over
    with curls,
  To the flowers, and be their sun.

x.

There has fallen a splendid tear
  From the passion-flower at the gate.
She is coming, my dove, my dear ;
  She is coming, my life, my fate ;
The red rose cries, "She is near, she
    is near ; "
  And the white rose weeps, "She is
    late ; "
The larkspur listens, "I hear, I hear ; "
  And the lily whispers, "I wait."

xi.

She is coming, my own, my sweet ;
  Were it ever so airy a tread,
My heart would hear her and beat,
  Were it earth in an earthy bed ;
My dust would hear her and beat,
  Had I lain for a century dead ;
Would start and tremble under her
    feet,
  And blossom in purple and red.

PART II.
I.
i.

"THE fault was mine, the fault was
    mine " —
Why am I sitting here so stunn'd and
    still,
Plucking the harmless wild-flower on
    the hill ? —
It is this guilty hand ! —
And there rises ever a passionate cry
From underneath in the darkening
    land —
What is it, that has been done ?
O dawn of Eden bright over earth
    and sky,
The fires of Hell brake out of thy
    rising sun,
The fires of Hell and of Hate ;
For she, sweet soul, had hardly spoken
    a word,

When her brother ran in his rage to
the gate,
He came with the babe-faced lord ;
Heap'd on her terms of disgrace,
And while she wept, and I strove to
be cool,
He fiercely gave me the lie,
Till I with as fierce an anger spoke,
And he struck me, madman, over the
face,
Struck me before the languid fool,
Who was gaping and grinning by :
Struck for himself an evil stroke ;
Wrought for his house an irredeem-
able woe ;
For front to front in an hour we stood,
And a million horrible bellowing
echoes broke
From the red-ribb'd hollow behind
the wood,
And thunder'd up into Heaven the
Christless code,
That must have life for a blow.
Ever and ever afresh they seem'd to
grow.
Was it he lay there with a fading eye ?
" The fault was mine," he whisper'd,
" fly ! "
Then glided out of the joyous wood
The ghastly Wraith of one that I
know ;
And there rang on a sudden a pas-
sionate cry,
A cry for a brother's blood :
It will ring in my heart and my ears,
till I die, till I die.

II.

Is it gone ? my pulses beat —
What was it ? a lying trick of the
brain ?
Yet I thought I saw her stand,
A shadow there at my feet,
High over the shadowy land.
It is gone ; and the heavens fall in a
gentle rain,
When they should burst and drown
with deluging storms
The feeble vassals of wine and anger
and lust,
The little hearts that know not how
to forgive :

Arise, my God, and strike, for we hold
Thee just,
Strike dead the whole weak race of
venomous worms,
That sting each other here in the dust ;
We are not worthy to live.

II.

I.

See what a lovely shell,
Small and pure as a pearl,
Lying close to my foot,
Frail, but a work divine,
Made so fairily well
With delicate spire and whorl,
How exquisitely minute,
A miracle of design !

II.

What is it ? a learned man
Could give it a clumsy name.
Let him name it who can,
The beauty would be the same.

III.

The tiny cell is forlorn,
Void of the little living will
That made it stir on the shore.
Did he stand at the diamond door
Of his house in a rainbow frill ?
Did he push, when he was uncurl'd,
A golden foot or a fairy horn
Thro' his dim water-world ?

IV.

Slight, to be crush'd with a tap
Of my finger-nail on the sand,
Small, but a work divine,
Frail, but of force to withstand,
Year upon year, the shock
Of cataract seas that snap
The three decker's oaken spine
Athwart the ledges of rock,
Here on the Breton strand !

V.

Breton, not Briton ; here
Like a shipwreck'd man on a coast
Of ancient fable and fear —

Plagued with a flitting to and fro,
A disease, a hard mechanic ghost
That never came from on high
Nor ever arose from below,
But only moves with the moving eye,
Flying along the land and the main —
Why should it look like Maud?
Am I to be overawed
By what I cannot but know
Is a juggle born of the brain?

VI.

Back from the Breton coast,
Sick of a nameless fear,
Back to the dark sea-line
Looking, thinking of all I have lost;
An old song vexes my ear;
But that of Lamech is mine.

VII.

For years, a measureless ill,
For years, for ever, to part —
But she, she would love me still;
And as long, O God, as she
Have a grain of love for me,
So long, no doubt, no doubt,
Shall I nurse in my dark heart,
However weary, a spark of will
Not to be trampled out.

VIII.

Strange, that the mind, when fraught
With a passion so intense
One would think that it well
Might drown all life in the eye, —
That it should, by being so over-
    wrought,
Suddenly strike on a sharper sense
For a shell, or a flower, little things
Which else would have been past by!
And now I remember, I,
When he lay dying there,
I noticed one of his many rings
(For he had many, poor worm) and
    thought
It is his mother's hair.

IX.

Who knows if he be dead?
Whether I need have fled?
Am I guilty of blood?

However this may be,
Comfort her, comfort her, all things
    good,
While I am over the sea!
Let me and my passionate love go by,
But speak to her all things holy and
    high,
Whatever happen to me!
Me and my harmful love go by;
But come to her waking, find her
    asleep,
Powers of the height, Powers of the
    deep,
And comfort her tho' I die.

III.

Courage, poor heart of stone!
I will not ask thee why
Thou canst not understand
That thou art left for ever alone:
Courage, poor stupid heart of stone. —
Or if I ask thee why,
Care not thou to reply:
She is but dead, and the time is at
    hand
When thou shalt more than die.

IV.

I.

O that 'twere possible
After long grief and pain
To find the arms of my true love
Round me once again!

II.

When I was wont to meet her
In the silent woody places
By the home that gave me birth,
We stood tranced in long embraces
Mixt with kisses sweeter sweeter
Than anything on earth.

III.

A shadow flits before me,
Not thou, but like to thee:
Ah Christ, that it were possible
For one short hour to see
The souls we loved, that they might
    tell us
What and where they be.

IV.

It leads me forth at evening,
It lightly winds and steals
In a cold white robe before me,
When all my spirit reels
At the shouts, the leagues of lights,
And the roaring of the wheels.

V.

Half the night I waste in sighs,
Half in dreams I sorrow after
The delight of early skies;
In a wakeful doze I sorrow
For the hand, the lips, the eyes,
For the meeting of the morrow,
The delight of happy laughter,
The delight of low replies.

VI.

'Tis a morning pure and sweet,
And a dewy splendor falls
On the little flower that clings
To the turrets and the walls;
'Tis a morning pure and sweet,
And the light and shadow fleet;
She is walking in the meadow,
And the woodland echo rings;
In a moment we shall meet;
She is singing in the meadow
And the rivulet at her feet
Ripples on in light and shadow
To the ballad that she sings.

VII.

Do I hear her sing as of old,
My bird with the shining head,
My own dove with the tender eye?
But there rings on a sudden a passionate cry,
There is some one dying or dead,
And a sullen thunder is roll'd;
For a tumult shakes the city,
And I wake, my dream is fled;
In the shuddering dawn, behold,
Without knowledge, without pity,
By the curtains of my bed
That abiding phantom cold.

VIII.

Get thee hence, nor come again,
Mix not memory with doubt,
Pass, thou deathlike type of pain,
Pass and cease to move about!
'Tis the blot upon the brain
That *will* show itself without.

IX.

Then I rise, the eavedrops fall,
And the yellow vapors choke
The great city sounding wide;
The day comes, a dull red ball
Wrapt in drifts of lurid smoke
On the misty river-tide.

X.

Thro' the hubbub of the market
I steal, a wasted frame,
It crosses here, it crosses there,
Thro' all that crowd confused and loud,
The shadow still the same;
And on my heavy eyelids
My anguish hangs like shame.

XI.

Alas for her that met me,
That heard me softly call,
Came glimmering thro' the laurels
At the quiet evenfall,
In the garden by the turrets
Of the old manorial hall.

XII.

Would the happy spirit descend,
From the realms of light and song,
In the chamber or the street,
As she looks among the blest,
Should I fear to greet my friend
Or to say "Forgive the wrong,"
Or to ask her, "Take me, sweet,
To the regions of thy rest"?

XIII.

But the broad light glares and beats,
And the shadow flits and fleets
And will not let me be;
And I loathe the squares and streets
And the faces that one meets,
Hearts with no love for me:
Always I long to creep

Into some still cavern deep,
There to weep, and weep, and weep
My whole soul out to thee.

V.

I.

Dead, long dead,
Long dead!
And my heart is a handful of dust,
And the wheels go over my head,
And my bones are shaken with pain,
For into a shallow grave they are
    thrust,
Only a yard beneath the street,
And the hoofs of the horses beat,
    beat,
The hoofs of the horses beat,
Beat into my scalp and my brain,
With never an end to the stream of
    passing feet,
Driving, hurrying, marrying, burying,
Clamor and rumble, and ringing and
    clatter,
And here beneath it is all as bad,
For I thought the dead had peace, but
    it is not so;
To have no peace in the grave, is that
    not sad?
But up and down and to and fro,
Ever about me the dead men go;
And then to hear a dead man chatter
Is enough to drive one mad.

II.

Wretchedest age, since Time began,
They cannot even bury a man;
And tho' we paid our tithes in the
    days that are gone,
Not a bell was rung, not a prayer was
    read;
It is that which makes us loud in the
    world of the dead;
There is none that does his work, not
    one;
A touch of their office might have
    sufficed,
But the churchmen fain would kill
    their church,
As the churches have kill'd their
    Christ.

III.

See, there is one of us sobbing,
No limit to his distress;
And another, a lord of all things,
    praying
To his own great self, as I guess;
And another, a statesman there, be-
    traying
His party-secret, fool, to the press;
And yonder a vile physician, blabbing
The case of his patient — all for
    what?
To tickle the maggot born in an
    empty head,
And wheedle a world that loves him
    not,
For it is but a world of the dead.

IV.

Nothing but idiot gabble!
For the prophecy given of old
And then not understood,
Has come to pass as foretold;
Not let any man think for the public
    good,
But babble, merely for babble.
For I never whisper'd a private affair
Within the hearing of cat or mouse,
No, not to myself in the closet alone,
But I heard it shouted at once from
    the top of the house;
Everything came to be known.
Who told *him* we were there?

V.

Not that gray old wolf, for he came
    not back
From the wilderness, full of wolves,
    where he used to lie;
He has gather'd the bones for his
    o'ergrown whelp to crack;
Crack them now for yourself, and
    howl, and die.

VI.

Prophet, curse me the blabbing lip,
And curse me the British vermin, the
    rat;
I know not whether he came in the
    Hanover ship,

But I know that he lies and listens
    mute
In an ancient mansion's crannies and
    holes :
Arsenic, arsenic, sure, would do it,
Except that now we poison our babes,
    poor souls !
It is all used up for that.

VII.

Tell him now : she is standing here at
    my head ;
Not beautiful now, not even kind ;
He may take her now ; for she never
    speaks her mind,
But is ever the one thing silent here.
She is not *of* us, as I divine ;
She comes from another stiller world
    of the dead,
Stiller, not fairer than mine.

VIII.

But I know where a garden grows,
Fairer than aught in the world be-
    side,
All made up of the lily and rose
That blow by night, when the season
    is good,
To the sound of dancing music and
    flutes :
It is only flowers, they had no fruits,
And I almost fear they are not roses,
    but blood ;
For the keeper was one, so full of
    pride,
He linkt a dead man there to a spec-
    tral bride ;
For he, if he had not been a Sultan of
    brutes,
Would he have that hole in his side ?

IX.

But what will the old man say ?
He laid a cruel snare in a pit
To catch a friend of mine one stormy
    day ;
Yet now I could even weep to think
    of it ;
For what will the old man say
When he comes to the second corpse
    in the pit ?

X.

Friend, to be struck by the public
    foe,
Then to strike him and lay him low,
That were a public merit, far,
Whatever the Quaker holds, from
    sin ;
But the red life spilt for a private
    blow —
I swear to you, lawful and lawless
    war
Are scarcely even akin.

XI.

O me, why have they not buried me
    deep enough ?
Is it kind to have made me a grave so
    rough,
Me, that was never a quiet sleeper ?
Maybe still I am but half-dead ;
Then I cannot be wholly dumb ;
I will cry to the steps above my head
And somebody, surely, some kind
    heart will come
To bury me, bury me
Deeper, ever so little deeper.

PART III.

VI.

I.

My life has crept so long on a broken wing
Thro' cells of madness, haunts of horror and fear,
That I come to be grateful at last for a little thing:
My mood is changed, for it fell at a time of year
When the face of night is fair on the dewy downs,

And the shining daffodil dies, and the Charioteer
And starry Gemini hang like glorious crowns
Over Orion's grave low down in the west,
That like a silent lightning under the stars
She seem'd to divide in a dream from a band of the blest,
And spoke of a hope for the world in the coming wars —
" And in that hope, dear soul, let trouble have rest,
Knowing I tarry for thee," and pointed to Mars
As he glow'd like a ruddy shield on the Lion's breast.

II.

And it was but a dream, yet it yielded a dear delight
To have look'd, tho' but in a dream, upon eyes so fair,
That had been in a weary world my one thing bright;
And it was but a dream, yet it lighten'd my despair
When I thought that a war would arise in defence of the right,
That an iron tyranny now should bend or cease,
The glory of manhood stand on his ancient height,
Nor Britain's one sole God be the millionaire :
No more shall commerce be all in all, and Peace
Pipe on her pastoral hillock a languid note,
And watch her harvest ripen, her herd increase,
Nor the cannon-bullet rust on a slothful shore,
And the cobweb woven across the cannon's throat
Shall shake its threaded tears in the wind no more.

III.

And as months ran on and rumor of battle grew,
"It is time, it is time, O passionate heart," said I
(For I cleaved to a cause that I felt to be pure and true),
"It is time, O passionate heart and morbid eye,
That old hysterical mock-disease should die."
And I stood on a giant deck and mix'd my breath
With a loyal people shouting a battle cry,
Till I saw the dreary phantom arise and fly
Far into the North, and battle, and seas of death.

IV.

Let it go or stay, so I wake to the higher aims
Of a land that has lost for a little her lust of gold,
And love of a peace that was full of wrongs and shames,
Horrible, hateful, monstrous, not to be told ;
And hail once more to the banner of battle unroll'd !
Tho' many a light shall darken, and many shall weep
For those that are crush'd in the clash of jarring claims,
Yet God's just wrath shall be wreak'd on a giant liar ;
And many a darkness into the light shall leap,
And shine in the sudden making of splendid names,
And noble thought be freër under the sun,
And the heart of a people beat with one desire ;

For the peace, that I deem'd no peace, is over and done,
And now by the side of the Black and the Baltic deep,
And deathful-grinning mouths of the fortress, flames
The blood-red blossom of war with a heart of fire.

v.

Let it flame or fade, and the war roll down like a wind,
We have proved we have hearts in a cause, we are noble still,
And myself have awaked, as it seems, to the better mind;
It is better to fight for the good than to rail at the ill;
I have felt with my native land, I am one with my kind,
I embrace the purpose of God, and the doom assign'd.

ENOCH ARDEN

AND OTHER POEMS.

———∘∘꙳∘∘———

ENOCH ARDEN.

Long lines of cliff breaking have left
    a chasm;
And in the chasm are foam and yel-
    low sands;
Beyond, red roofs about a narrow
    wharf
In cluster; then a moulder'd church;
    and higher
A long street climbs to one tall-tower'd
    mill;
And high in heaven behind it a gray
    down
With Danish barrows; and a hazel-
    wood,
By autumn nutters haunted, flourishes
Green in a cuplike hollow of the
    down.

Here on this beach a hundred years
    ago,
Three children of three houses, Annie
    Lee,
The prettiest little damsel in the port,
And Philip Ray the miller's only son,
And Enoch Arden, a rough sailor's lad
Made orphan by a winter shipwreck,
    play'd
Among the waste and lumber of the
    shore,
Hard coils of cordage, swarthy fish-
    ing-nets,
Anchors of rusty-fluke, and boats up-
    drawn;

And built their castles of dissolving
    sand
To watch them overflow'd, or follow-
    ing up
And flying the white breaker, daily
    left
The little footprint daily wash'd away.

A narrow cave ran in beneath the
    cliff:
In this the children play'd at keeping
    house.
Enoch was host one day, Philip the
    next,
While Annie still was mistress; but
    at times
Enoch would hold possession for a
    week:
"This is my house and this my little
    wife."
"Mine too" said Philip "turn and
    turn about":
When, if they quarrell'd, Enoch
    stronger-made
Was master: then would Philip, his
    blue eyes
All flooded with the helpless wrath of
    tears,
Shriek out "I hate you, Enoch," and
    at this
The little wife would weep for com-
    pany,
And pray them not to quarrel for he
    sake,
And say she would be little wife to
    both.

But when the dawn of rosy child-
hood past,
And the new warmth of life's ascend-
ing sun
Was felt by either, either fixt his
heart
On that one girl; and Enoch spoke
his love,
But Philip loved in silence; and the
girl
Seem'd kinder unto Philip than to
him;
But she loved Enoch; tho' she knew
it not,
And would if ask'd deny it. Enoch
set
A purpose evermore before his eyes,
To hoard all savings to the uttermost,
To purchase his own boat, and make
a home
For Annie: and so prosper'd that at
last
A luckier or a bolder fisherman,
A carefuller in peril, did not breathe
For leagues along that breaker-beaten
coast
Than Enoch. Likewise had he served
a year
On board a merchantman, and made
himself
Full sailor; and he thrice had pluck'd
a life
From the dread sweep of the down-
streaming seas:
And all men look'd upon him favora-
bly:
And ere he touch'd his one-and-
twentieth May,
He purchased his own boat, and made
a home
For Annie, neat and nestlike, halfway
up
The narrow street that clamber'd
toward the mill.

Then, on a golden autumn eventide,
The younger people making holiday,
With bag and sack and basket, great
and small,
Went nutting to the hazels. Philip
stay'd

(His father lying sick and needing
him)
An hour behind; but as he climb'd
the hill,
Just where the prone edge of the
wood began
To feather toward the hollow, saw the
pair,
Enoch and Annie, sitting hand-in-
hand,
His large gray eyes and weather-
beaten face
All-kindled by a still and sacred fire,
That burn'd as on an altar. Philip
look'd,
And in their eyes and faces read his
doom;
Then, as their faces drew together,
groan'd,
And slipt aside, and like a wounded
life
Crept down into the hollows of the
wood;
There, while the rest were loud in
merrymaking,
Had his dark hour unseen, and rose
and past
Bearing a lifelong hunger in his heart.

So these were wed, and merrily
rang the bells,
And merrily ran the years, seven
happy years,
Seven happy years of health and
competence,
And mutual love and honorable toil;
With children; first a daughter. In
him woke,
With his first babe's first cry, the
noble wish
To save all earnings to the uttermost,
And give his child a better bringing-up
Than his had been, or hers; a wish
renew'd,
When two years after came a boy to be
The rosy idol of her solitudes,
While Enoch was abroad on wrathful
seas,
Or often journeying landward; for in
truth
Enoch's white horse, and Enoch's
ocean-spoil

In ocean-smelling osier, and his face,
Rough-redden'd with a thousand win-
    ter gales,
Not only to the market-cross were
    known,
But in the leafy lanes behind the
    down,
Far as the portal-warding lion-whelp,
And peacock-yewtree of the lonely
    Hall,
Whose Friday fare was Enoch's min-
    istering.

    Then came a change, as all things
        human change.
Ten miles to northward of the narrow
    port
Open'd a larger haven: thither used
Enoch at times to go by land or
    sea;
And once when there, and clambering
    on a mast
In harbor, by mischance he slipt and
    fell:
A limb was broken when they lifted
    him;
And while he lay recovering there,
    his wife
Bore him another son, a sickly one:
Another hand crept too across his
    trade
Taking her bread and theirs: and on
    him fell,
Altho' a grave and staid God-fearing
    man,
Yet lying thus inactive, doubt and
    gloom.
He seem'd, as in a nightmare of the
    night,
To see his children leading evermore
Low miserable lives of hand-to-mouth,
And her, he loved, a beggar: then he
    pray'd
" Save them from this, whatever
    comes to me."
And while he pray'd, the master of
    that ship
Enoch had served in, hearing his mis-
    chance,
Came, for he knew the man and
    valued him,
Reporting of his vessel China-bound,

And wanting yet a boatswain. Would
    he go?
There yet were many weeks before she
    sail'd,
Sail'd from this port. Would Enoch
    have the place?
And Enoch all at once assented to it,
Rejoicing at that answer to his prayer.

    So now that shadow of mischance
        appear'd
No graver than as when some little
    cloud
Cuts off the fiery highway of the sun,
And isles a light in the offing: yet the
    wife —
When he was gone — the children —
    what to do?
Then Enoch lay long-pondering on his
    plans;
To sell the boat — and yet he loved
    her well —
How many a rough sea had he weath-
    er'd in her!
He knew her, as a horseman knows his
    horse —
And yet to sell her — then with what
    she brought
Buy goods and stores — set Annie forth
    in trade
With all that seamen needed or their
    wives —
So might she keep the house while he
    was gone.
Should he not trade himself out yon-
    der? go
This voyage more than once? yea twice
    or thrice —
As oft as needed — last, returning rich,
Become the master of a larger craft,
With fuller profits lead an easier life,
Have all his pretty young ones edu-
    cated,
And pass his days in peace among his
    own.

    Thus Enoch in his heart determined
        all:
Then moving homeward came on Annie
    pale,
Nursing the sickly babe, her latest-born.
Forward she started with a happy cry,

And laid the feeble infant in his arms;
Whom Enoch took, and handled all his
 limbs,
Appraised his weight and fondled
 fatherlike,
But had no heart to break his purposes
To Annie, till the morrow, when he
 spoke.

Then first since Enoch's golden ring
 had girt
Her finger, Annie fought against his
 will:
Yet not with brawling opposition she,
But manifold entreaties, many a tear,
Many a sad kiss by day by night re-
 new'd
(Sure that all evil would come out of
 it)
Besought him, supplicating, if he cared
For her or his dear children, not to go.
He not for his own self caring but her,
Her and her children, let her plead in
 vain;
So grieving held his will, and bore it
 thro'.

For Enoch parted with his old sea-
 friend,
Bought Annie goods and stores, and
 set his hand
To fit their little streetward sitting-
 room
With shelf and corner for the goods
 and stores.
So all day long till Enoch's last at
 home,
Shaking their pretty cabin, hammer
 and axe,
Auger and saw, while Annie seem'd to
 hear
Her own death-scaffold raising, shrill'd
 and rang,
Till this was ended, and his careful
 hand, —
The space was narrow, — having order'd all
Almost as neat and close as Nature
 packs
Her blossom or her seedling, paused;
 and he,

Who needs would work for Annie to
 the last,
Ascending tired, heavily slept till morn.

And Enoch faced this morning of
 farewell
Brightly and boldly.   All his Annie's
 fears,
Save, as his Annie's, were a laughter
 to him.
Yet Enoch as a brave God-fearing man
Bow'd himself down, and in that mys-
 tery
Where God-in-man is one with man-
 in-God,
Pray'd for a blessing on his wife and
 babes
Whatever came to him: and then he
 said
"Annie, this voyage by the grace of
 God
Will bring fair weather yet to all of us.
Keep a clean hearth and a clear fire for
 me,
For I'll be back, my girl, before you
 know it."
Then lightly rocking baby's cradle
 "and he,
This pretty, puny, weakly little one, —
Nay — for I love him all the better for
 it —
God bless him, he shall sit upon my
 knees
And I will tell him tales of foreign
 parts,
And make him merry, when I come
 home again.
Come, Annie, come, cheer up before I
 go."

Him running on thus hopefully she
 heard,
And almost hoped herself; but when
 he turn'd
The current of his talk to graver things
In sailor fashion roughly sermonizing
On providence and trust in Heaven,
 she heard,
Heard and not heard him; as the vil-
 lage girl,
Who sets her pitcher underneath the
 spring,

Musing on him that used to fill it for
      her,
Hears and not hears, and lets it over-
      flow.

    At length she spoke " O Enoch, you
      are wise;
And yet for all your wisdom well
      know I
That I shall look upon your face no
      more."

    " Well then," said Enoch, " I shall
      look on yours.
Annie, the ship I sail in passes here
(He named the day) get you a seaman's
      glass,
Spy out my face, and laugh at all your
      fears."

    But when the last of those last mo-
      ments came,
" Annie, my girl, cheer up, be com-
      forted,
Look to the babes, and till I come
      again
Keep everything shipshape, for I must
      go.
And fear no more for me; or if you
      fear
Cast all your cares on God; that an-
      chor holds.
Is He not yonder in those uttermost
Parts of the morning? if I flee to these
Can I go from Him? and the sea is His,
The sea is His: He made it."

                        Enoch rose,
Cast his strong arms about his droop-
      ing wife,
And kiss'd his wonder-stricken little
      ones;
But for the third, the sickly one, who
      slept
After a night of feverous wakefulness,
When Annie would have raised him
      Enoch said
" Wake him not; let him sleep; how
      should the child
Remember this? " and kiss'd him in
      his cot.
But Annie from her baby's forehead
      clipt

A tiny curl, and gave it: this he kept
Thro' all his future; but now hastily
      caught
His bundle, waved his hand, and went
      his way.

    She, when the day that Enoch
      mention'd, came,
Borrow'd a glass, but all in vain:
      perhaps
She could not fix the glass to suit her
      eye;
Perhaps her eye was dim, hand trem-
      ulous;
She saw him not: and while he stood
      on deck
Waving, the moment and the vessel
      past.

    Ev'n to the last dip of the vanishing
      sail
She watch'd it, and departed weeping
      for him;
Then, tho' she mourn'd his absence as
      his grave,
Set her sad will no less to chime with
      his,
But throve not in her trade, not being
      bred
To barter, nor compensating the want
By shrewdness, neither capable of lies,
Nor asking overmuch and taking less,
And still foreboding "what would
      Enoch say? "
For more than once, in days of diffi-
      culty
And pressure, had she sold her wares
      for less
Than what she gave in buying what
      she sold:
She fail'd and sadden'd knowing it;
      and thus,
Expectant of that news which never
      came,
Gain'd for her own a scanty suste-
      nance,
And lived a life of silent melancholy.

    Now the third child was sickly-born
      and grew
Yet sicklier, tho' the mother cared for
      it

With all a mother's care: neverthe-
less,
Whether her business often call'd her
from it,
Or thro' the want of what it needed
most,
Or means to pay the voice who best
could tell
What most it needed — howsoe'er it
was,
After a lingering, — ere she was
aware, —
Like the caged bird escaping suddenly,
The little innocent soul flitted away.

In that same week when Annie
buried it,
Philip's true heart, which hunger'd for
her peace
(Since Enoch left he had not look'd
upon her),
Smote him, as having kept aloof so
long.
"Surely," said Philip, "I may see her
now,
May be some little comfort"; there-
fore went,
Past thro' the solitary room in front,
Paused for a moment at an inner door,
Then struck it thrice, and, no one
opening,
Enter'd; but Annie, seated with her
grief,
Fresh from the burial of her little one,
Cared not to look on any human face,
But turn'd her own toward the wall
and wept.
Then Philip standing up said falter-
ingly
"Annie, I came to ask a favor of you."

He spoke; the passion in her moan'd
reply
"Favor from one so sad and so forlorn
As I am!" half abash'd him; yet
unask'd,
His bashfulness and tenderness at war,
He set himself beside her, saying to
her:

"I came to speak to you of what he
wish'd,

Enoch, your husband: I have ever
said
You chose the best among us — a
strong man:
For where he fixt his heart he set his
hand
To do the thing he will'd, and bore it
thro'.
And wherefore did he go this weary
way,
And leave you lonely? not to see the
world —
For pleasure? — nay, but for the
wherewithal
To give his babes a better bringing-up
Than his had been, or yours: that was
his wish.
And if he come again, vext will he be
To find the precious morning hours
were lost.
And it would vex him even in his
grave,
If he could know his babes were run-
ning wild
Like colts about the waste. So, Annie,
now —
Have we not known each other all our
lives?
I do beseech you by the love you
bear
Him and his children not to say me
nay —
For, if you will, when Enoch comes
again
Why then he shall repay me — if you
will,
Annie — for I am rich and well-to-do.
Now let me put the boy and girl to
school:
This is the favor that I came to ask."

Then Annie with her brows against
the wall
Answer'd "I cannot look you in the
face;
I seem so foolish and so broken down.
When you came in my sorrow broke
me down;
And now I think your kindness breaks
me down;
But Enoch lives; that is borne in on
me:

He will repay you : money can be
  repaid ;
Not kindness such as yours."

                    And Philip ask'd
"Then you will let me, Annie ? "

                    There she turn'd,
She rose, and fixt her swimming eyes
  upon him,
And dwelt a moment on his kindly
  face,
Then calling down a blessing on his
  head
Caught at his hand, and wrung it pas-
  sionately,
And past into the little garth beyond.
So lifted up in spirit he moved away.

  Then Philip put the boy and girl to
  school,
And bought them needful books, and
  everyway,
Like one who does his duty by his own,
Made himself theirs ; and tho' for
  Annie's sake,
Fearing the lazy gossip of the port,
He oft denied his heart his dearest
  wish,
And seldom crost her threshold, yet
  he sent
Gifts by the children, garden-herbs
  and fruit,
The late and early roses from his wall,
Or conies from the down, and now and
  then,
With some pretext of fineness in the
  meal
To save the offence of charitable, flour
From his tall mill that whistled on the
  waste.

  But Philip did not fathom Annie's
  mind :
Scarce could the woman when he came
  upon her,
Out of full heart and boundless gratitude
Light on a broken word to thank him
  with.
But Philip was her children's all-in-
  all ;

From distant corners of the street they
  ran
To greet his hearty welcome heartily ;
Lords of his house and of his mill were
  they ;
Worried his passive ear with petty
  wrongs
Or pleasures, hung upon him, play'd
  with him
And call'd him Father Philip. Philip
  gain'd
As Enoch lost ; for Enoch seem'd to
  them
Uncertain as a vision or a dream,
Faint as a figure seen in early dawn
Down at the far end of an avenue,
Going we know not where : and so ten
  years,
Since Enoch left his hearth and native
  land,
Fled forward, and no news of Enoch
  came.

  It chanced one evening Annie's children long'd
To go with others, nutting to the wood,
And Annie would go with them ; then
  they begg'd
For Father Philip (as they call'd him)
  too :
Him, like the working bee in blossom-
  dust,
Blanch'd with his mill, they found ;
  and saying to him
"Come with us Father Philip" he
  denied ;
But when the children pluck'd at him
  to go,
He laugh'd, and yielded readily to
  their wish,
For was not Annie with them ? and
  they went.

  But after scaling half the weary
  down,
Just where the prone edge of the wood
  began
To feather toward the hollow, all her
  force
Fail'd her ; and sighing, " Let me rest "
  she said :
So Philip rested with her well-content :

While all the younger ones with jubilant cries
Broke from their elders, and tumul-
  tuously
Down thro' the whitening hazels made
  a plunge
To the bottom, and dispersed, and
  bent or broke
The lithe reluctant boughs to tear
  away
Their tawny clusters, crying to each
  other
And calling, here and there, about the
  wood.

But Philip sitting at her side forgot
Her presence, and remember'd one
  dark hour
Here in this wood, when like a wounded
  life
He crept into the shadow: at last he
  said,
Lifting his honest forehead, "Listen,
  Annie,
How merry they are down yonder in
  the wood.
Tired, Annie?" for she did not speak
  a word.
"Tired?" but her face had fall'n upon
  her hands;
At which, as with a kind of anger in
  him,
"The ship was lost," he said, "the
  ship was lost!
No more of that! why should you kill
  yourself
And make them orphans quite?" And
  Annie said
"I thought not of it: but — I know
  not why —
Their voices make me feel so solitary."

Then Philip coming somewhat closer
  spoke.
"Annie, there is a thing upon my
  mind,
And it has been upon my mind so long,
That tho' I know not when it first
  came there,
I know that it will out at last. O
  Annie,

It is beyond all hope, against all
  chance,
That he who left you ten long years
  ago
Should still be living; well then —
  let me speak ·
I grieve to see you poor and wanting
  help:
I cannot help you as I wish to do
Unless — they say that women are so
  quick —
Perhaps you know what I would have
  you know —
I wish you for my wife. I fain would
  prove
A father to your children: I do
  think
They love me as a father: I am sure
That I love them as if they were mine
  own;
And I believe, if you were fast my
  wife,
That after all these sad uncertain
  years,
We might be still as happy as God
  grants
To any of his creatures. Think upon
  it:
For I am well-to-do — no kin, no care,
No burthen, save my care for you and
  yours:
And we have known each other all our
  lives,
And I have loved you longer than you
  know."

Then answer'd Annie; tenderly she
  spoke:
"You have been as God's good angel
  in our house.
God bless you for it, God reward you
  for it,
Philip, with something happier than
  myself.
Can one love twice? can you be ever
  loved
As Enoch was? what is it that you
  ask?"
"I am content" he answer'd "to be
  loved
A little after Enoch." "O" she
  cried,

Scared as it were, "dear Philip, wait
    a while :
If Enoch comes — but Enoch will not
    come —
Yet wait a year, a year is not so long:
Surely I shall be wiser in a year :
O wait a little!" Philip sadly said
"Annie, as I have waited all my life
I well may wait a little." "Nay" she
    cried
"I am bound: you have my promise
    — in a year:
Will you not bide your year as I bide
    mine ? "
And Philip answer'd " I will bide my
    year."

Here both were mute, till Philip
    glancing up
Beheld the dead flame of the fallen
    day
Pass from the Danish barrow over-
    head ;
Then fearing night and chill for
    Annie, rose
And sent his voice beneath him thro'
    the wood.
Up came the children laden with their
    spoil ;
Then all descended to the port, and
    there
At Annie's door he paused and gave
    his hand,
Saying gently " Annie, when I spoke
    to you,
That was your hour of weakness. I
    was wrong,
I am always bound to you, but you
    are free."
Then Annie weeping answer'd "I am
    bound."

She spoke ; and in one moment as
    it were,
While yet she went about her house-
    hold ways,
Ev'n as she dwelt upon his latest
    words,
That he had loved her longer than she
    knew,
That autumn into autumn flash'd
    again,

And there he stood once more before
    her face,
Claiming her promise. "Is it a year ?"
    she ask'd.
" Yes, if the nuts " he said " be ripe
    again :
Come out and see." But she — she
    put him off —
So much to look to — such a change
    —a month —
Give her a month — she knew that
    she was bound —
A month — no more. Then Philip
    with his eyes
Full of that lifelong hunger, and his
    voice
Shaking a little like a drunkard's hand,
" Take your own time, Annie, take
    your own time."
And Annie could have wept for pity
    of him ;
And yet she held him on delayingly
With many a scarce-believable excuse,
Trying his truth and his long-suffer-
    ance,
Till half-another year had slipt away.

By this the lazy gossips of the port,
Abhorrent of a calculation crost,
Began to chafe as at a personal wrong.
Some thought that Philip did but
    trifle with her ;
Some that she but held off to draw
    him on ;
And others laugh'd at her and Philip
    too,
As simple folk that knew not their
    own minds,
And one, in whom all evil fancies clung
Like serpent eggs together, laughingly
Would hint at worse in either. Her
    own son
Was silent, tho' he often look'd his
    wish ;
But evermore the daughter prest upon
    her
To wed the man so dear to all of them
And lift the household out of poverty ;
And Philip's rosy face contracting
    grew
Careworn and wan ; and all these
    things fell on her

Sharp as reproach.

> At last one night it chanced
That Annie could not sleep, but earnestly
Pray'd for a sign "my Enoch is he
     gone ? "
Then compass'd round by the blind
     wall of night
Brook'd not the expectant terror of
     her heart,
Started from bed, and struck herself
     a light,
Then desperately seized the holy Book,
Suddenly set it wide to find a sign,
Suddenly put her finger on the text,
" Under the palm-tree." That was
     nothing to her :
No meaning there : she closed the
     Book and slept :
When lo ! her Enoch sitting on a
     height,
Under a palm-tree, over him the
     Sun :
" He is gone," she thought, " he is
     happy, he is singing
Hosanna in the highest : yonder shines
The Sun of Righteousness, and these
     be palms
Whereof the happy people strowing
     cried
' Hosanna in the highest ! ' " Here
     she woke,
Resolved, sent for him and said wildly
     to him
" There is no reason why we should
     not wed."
" Then for God's sake," he answer'd,
     " both our sakes,
So you will wed me, let it be at once."

> So these were wed and merrily rang
     the bells,
Merrily rang the bells and they were
     wed.
But never merrily beat Annie's heart.
A footstep seem'd to fall beside her
     path,
She knew not whence ; a whisper on
     her ear,
She knew not what ; nor loved she to
     be left

Alone at home, nor ventured out
     alone.
What ail'd her then, that ere she
     enter'd, often
Her hand dwelt lingeringly on the
     latch,
Fearing to enter : Philip thought he
     knew :
Such doubts and fears were common
     to her state,
Being with child : but when her child
     was born,
Then her new child was as herself
     renew'd,
Then the new mother came about her
     heart,
Then her good Philip was her all-in-all,
And that mysterious instinct wholly
     died.

> And where was Enoch ? prosperously sail'd
The ship " Good Fortune," tho' at
     setting forth
The Biscay, roughly ridging eastward,
     shook
And almost overwhelm'd her, yet
     unvext
She slipt across the summer of the
     world,
Then after a long tumble about the
     Cape
And frequent interchange of foul and
     fair,
She passing thro' the summer world
     again,
The breath of heaven came continually
And sent her sweetly by the golden
     isles,
Till silent in her oriental haven.

> There Enoch traded for himself,
     and bought
Quaint monsters for the market of
     those times,
A gilded dragon, also, for the babes.

> Less lucky her home-voyage : at
     first indeed
Thro' many a fair sea-circle, day by
     day,

" There often as he watched or seemed to watch,
  So still, the golden lizard on him paused."

Page 474.

Scarce-rocking, her full-busted figure-
head
Stared o'er the ripple feathering from
her bows :
Then follow'd calms, and then winds
variable,
Then baffling, a long course of them;
and last
Storm, such as drove her under moon-
less heavens
Till hard upon the cry of "breakers"
came
The crash of ruin, and the loss of all
But Enoch and two others. Half the
night,
Buoy'd upon floating tackle and
broken spars,
These drifted, stranding on an isle at
morn
Rich, but the loneliest in a lonely sea.

No want was there of human suste-
nance,
Soft fruitage, mighty nuts, and nour-
ishing roots ;
Nor save for pity was it hard to take
The helpless life so wild that it was
tame.
There in a seaward-gazing mountain-
gorge
They built, and thatch'd with leaves
of palm, a hut,
Half hut, half native cavern. So the
three,
Set in this Eden of all plenteousness,
Dwelt with eternal summer, ill-
content.

For one, the youngest, hardly more
than boy,
Hurt in that night of sudden ruin and
wreck,
Lay lingering out a five-years' death-
in-life.
They could not leave him. After he
was gone,
The two remaining found a fallen
stem ;
And Enoch's comrade, careless of
himself,
Fire-hollowing this in Indian fashion,
fell

Sun-stricken, and that other lived
alone.
In those two deaths he read God's
warning "wait."

The mountain wooded to the peak,
the lawns
And winding glades high up like ways
to Heaven,
The slender coco's drooping crown of
plumes,
The lightning flash of insect and of
bird,
The lustre of the long convolvuluses
That coil'd around the stately stems,
and ran
Ev'n to the limit of the land, the glows
And glories of the broad belt of the
world,
All these he saw; but what he fain
had seen
He could not see, the kindly human
face,
Nor ever hear a kindly voice, but heard
The myriad shriek of wheeling ocean-
fowl,
The league-long roller thundering on
the reef,
The moving whisper of huge trees
that branch'd
And blossom'd in the zenith, or the
sweep
Of some precipitous rivulet to the
wave,
As down the shore he ranged, or all
day long
Sat often in the seaward-gazing gorge,
A shipwreck'd sailor, waiting for a
sail :
No sail from day to day, but every day
The sunrise broken into scarlet shafts
Among the palms and ferns and
precipices ;
The blaze upon the waters to the east ;
The blaze upon his island overhead ;
The blaze upon the waters to the west ;
Then the great stars that globed
themselves in Heaven,
The hollower-bellowing ocean, and
again
The scarlet shafts of sunrise — but no
sail.

There often as he watch'd or seem'd
  to watch,
So still, the golden lizard on him
  paused,
A phantom made of many phantoms
  moved
Before him haunting him, or he him-
  self
Moved haunting people, things and
  places, known
Far in a darker isle beyond the line;
The babes, their babble, Annie, the
  small house,
The climbing street, the mill, the
  leafy lanes,
The peacock-yewtree and the lonely
  Hall,
The horse he drove, the boat he sold,
  the chill
November dawns and dewy-glooming
  downs,
The gentle shower, the smell of dying
  leaves,
And the low moan of leaden-color'd
  seas.

Once likewise, in the ringing of his
  ears,
Tho' faintly, merrily — far and far
  away —
He heard the pealing of his parish
  bells;
Then, tho' he knew not wherefore,
  started up
Shuddering, and when the beauteous
  hateful isle
Return'd upon him, had not his poor
  heart
Spoken with That, which being everywhere
Lets none, who speaks with Him, seem
  all alone,
Surely the man had died of solitude.

Thus over Enoch's early-silvering
  head
The sunny and rainy seasons came
  and went
Year after year. His hopes to see
  his own,
And pace the sacred old familiar
  fields,

Not yet had perish'd, when his lonely
  doom
Came suddenly to an end. Another
  ship
(She wanted water) blown by baffling
  winds,
Like the Good Fortune, from her
  destined course,
Stay'd by this isle, not knowing where
  she lay:
For since the mate had seen at early
  dawn
Across a break on the mist-wreathen
  isle
The silent water slipping from the
  hills,
They sent a crew that landing burst
  away
In search of stream or fount, and
  fill'd the shores
With clamor. Downward from his
  mountain gorge
Stept the long-hair'd, long-bearded
  solitary,
Brown, looking hardly human,
  strangely clad,
Muttering and mumbling, idiotlike it
  seem'd,
With inarticulate rage, and making
  signs
They knew not what: and yet he led
  the way
To where the rivulets of sweet water
  ran;
And ever as he mingled with the crew,
And heard them talking, his long-
  bounden tongue
Was loosen'd, till he made them
  understand;
Whom, when their casks were fill'd
  they took aboard:
And there the tale he utter'd brokenly,
Scarce-credited at first but more and
  more,
Amazed and melted all who listen'd
  to it:
And clothes they gave him and free
  passage home;
But oft he work'd among the rest and
  shook
His isolation from him. None of
  these

Came from his country, or could an-
swer him,
If question'd, aught of what he cared
to know.
And dull the voyage was with long
delays,
The vessel scarce sea-worthy; but
evermore
His fancy fled before the lazy wind
Returning, till beneath a clouded
moon
He like a lover down thro' all his
blood
Drew in the dewy meadowy morning-
breath
Of England, blown across her ghostly
wall:
And that same morning officers and
men
Levied a kindly tax upon themselves,
Pitying the lonely man, and gave him
it:
Then moving up the coast they landed
him,
Ev'n in that harbor whence he sail'd
before.

There Enoch spoke no word to any
one,
But homeward — home — what home?
had he a home?
His home, he walk'd. Bright was that
afternoon,
Sunny but chill; till drawn thro' either
chasm,
Where either haven open'd on the
deeps,
Roll'd a sea-haze and whelm'd the
world in gray;
Cut off the length of highway on before,
And left but narrow breadth to left
and right
Of wither'd holt or tilth or pasturage.
On the nigh-naked tree the robin
piped
Disconsolate, and thro' the dripping
haze
The dead weight of the dead leaf bore
it down:
Thicker the drizzle grew, deeper the
gloom;

Last, as it seem'd, a great mist-blotted
light
Flared on him, and he came upon the
place.

Then down the long street having
slowly stolen,
His heart foreshadowing all calamity,
His eyes upon the stones, he reach'd
the home
Where Annie lived and loved him, and
his babes
In those far-off seven happy years were
born;
But finding neither light nor murmur
there
(A bill of sale gleam'd thro' the drizzle)
crept
Still downward thinking "dead or
dead to me!"

Down to the pool and narrow wharf
he went,
Seeking a tavern which of old he knew,
A front of timber-crost antiquity,
So propt, worm eaten, ruinously old,
He thought it must have gone; but he
was gone
Who kept it; and his widow Miriam
Lane,
With daily-dwindling profits held the
house;
A haunt of brawling seamen once, but
now
Stiller, with yet a bed for wandering
men.
There Enoch rested silent many days.

But Miriam Lane was good and
garrulous,
Nor let him be, but often breaking in,
Told him, with other annals of the
port,
Not knowing — Enoch was so brown,
so bow'd,
So broken — all the story of his house.
His baby's death, her growing poverty,
How Philip put her little ones to
school,
And kept them in it, his long wooing
her,

Her slow consent, and marriage, and
    the birth
Of Philip's child : and o'er his coun-
    tenance
No shadow past, nor motion : any one,
Regarding, well had deem'd he felt
    the tale
Less than the teller : only when she
    closed
"Enoch, poor man, was cast away and
    lost"
He, shaking his gray head pathetically,
Repeated muttering "cast away and
    lost ";
Again in deeper inward whispers
    "lost ! "

But Enoch yearn'd to see her face
    again ;
"If I might look on her sweet face
    again
And know that she is happy." So the
    thought
Haunted and harass'd him, and drove
    him forth,
At evening when the dull November
    day
Was growing duller twilight, to the
    hill.
There he sat down gazing on all below ;
There did a thousand memories roll
    upon him,
Unspeakable for sadness. By and by
The ruddy square of comfortable light,
Far-blazing from the rear of Philip's
    house,
Allured him, as the beacon-blaze al-
    lures
The bird of passage, till he madly
    strikes
Against it, and beats out his weary
    life.

For Philip's dwelling fronted on the
    street,
The latest house to landward ; but be-
    hind,
With one small gate that open'd on
    the waste,
Flourish'd a little garden square and
    wall'd :

And in it throve an ancient evergreen.
A yewtree, and all round it ran a walk
Of shingle, and a walk divided it :
But Enoch shunn'd the middle walk
    and stole
Up by the wall, behind the yew ; and
    thence
That which he better might have
    shunn'd, if griefs
Like his have worse or better, Enoch
    saw.

For cups and silver on the burnish'd
    board
Sparkled and shone ; so genial was the
    hearth :
And on the right hand of the hearth
    he saw
Philip, the slighted suitor of old times,
Stout, rosy, with his babe across his
    knees ;
And o'er her second father stoopt a
    girl,
A later but a loftier Annie Lee,
Fair-hair'd and tall, and from her
    lifted hand
Dangled a length of ribbon and a ring
To tempt the babe, who rear'd his
    creasy arms,
Caught at and ever miss'd it, and they
    laugh'd ;
And on the left hand of the hearth he
    saw
The mother glancing often toward her
    babe,
But turning now and then to speak
    with him,
Her son, who stood beside her tall and
    strong,
And saying that which pleased him,
    for he smiled.

Now when the dead man come to life
    beheld
His wife his wife no more, and saw the
    babe
Hers, yet not his, upon the father's
    knee,
And all the warmth, the peace, the
    happiness,
And his own children tall and beauti-
    ful,

And him, that other, reigning in his
place,
Lord of his rights and of his children's
love, —
Then he, tho' Miriam Lane had told
him all,
Because things seen are mightier than
things heard,
Stagger'd and shook, holding the
branch, and fear'd
To send abroad a shrill and terrible
cry,
Which in one moment, like the blast
of doom,
Would shatter all the happiness of the
hearth.

He therefore turning softly like a
thief,
Lest the harsh shingle should grate
underfoot,
And feeling all along the garden-wall,
Lest he should swoon and tumble and
be found,
Crept to the gate, and open'd it, and
closed,
As lightly as a sick man's chamber-
door,
Behind him, and came out upon the
waste.

And there he would have knelt, but
that his knees
Were feeble, so that falling prone he
dug
His fingers into the wet earth, and
pray'd.

"Too hard to bear! why did they
take me thence?
O God Almighty, blessed Saviour,
Thou
That didst uphold me on my lonely
isle,
Uphold me, Father, in my loneliness
A little longer! aid me, give me
strength
Not to tell her, never to let her know.
Help me not to break in upon her
peace.
My children too! must I not speak to
these?

They know me not. I should betray
myself.
Never: No father's kiss for me — the
girl
So like her mother, and the boy, my
son."

There speech and thought and na-
ture fail'd a little,
And he lay tranced; but when he rose
and paced
Back toward his solitary home again,
All down the long and narrow street
he went
Beating it in upon his weary brain,
As tho' it were the burthen of a song,
"Not to tell her, never to let her
know."

He was not all unhappy. His resolve
Upbore him, and firm faith, and ever-
more
Prayer from a living source within the
will,
And beating up thro' all the bitter
world,
Like fountains of sweet water in the
sea,
Kept him a living soul. "This miller's wife"
He said to Miriam "that you spoke
about,
Has she no fear that her first husband
lives?"
"Ay, ay, poor soul" said Miriam,
"fear enow!
If you could tell her you had seen him
dead,
Why, that would be her comfort;"
and he thought
"After the Lord has call'd me she
shall know,
I wait His time," and Enoch set himself,
Scorning an alms, to work whereby
to live.
Almost to all things could he turn his
hand.
Cooper he was and carpenter, and
wrought
To make the boatmen fishing-nets, or
help'd

At lading and unlading the tall barks,
That brought the stinted commerce
    of those days;
Thus earn'd a scanty living for him-
    self:
Yet since he did but labor for himself,
Work without hope, there was not life
    in it
Whereby the man could live; and as
    the year
Roll'd itself round again to meet the
    day
When Enoch had return'd, a languor
    came
Upon him, gentle sickness, gradually
Weakening the man, till he could do
    no more,
But kept the house, his chair, and last
    his bed.
And Enoch bore his weakness cheer-
    fully.
For sure no gladlier does the stranded
    wreck
See thro' the gray skirts of a lifting
    squall
The boat that bears the hope of life
    approach
To save the life despair'd of, than he
    saw
Death dawning on him, and the close
    of all.

For thro' that dawning gleam'd a
    kindlier hope
On Enoch thinking "after I am
    gone,
Then may she learn I lov'd her to the
    last."
He call'd aloud for Miriam Lane and
    said
"Woman, I have a secret—only swear,
Before I tell you—swear upon the
    book
Not to reveal it, till you see me dead."
"Dead," clamor'd the good woman,
    "hear him talk!
I warrant, man, that we shall bring
    you round."
"Swear" added Enoch sternly "on
    the book."
And on the book, half-frighted, Miriam
    swore.

Then Enoch rolling his gray eyes upon
    her,
"Did you know Enoch Arden of this
    town?"
"Know him?" she said "I knew him
    far away.
Ay, ay, I mind him coming down the
    street;
Held his head high, and cared for no
    man, he."
Slowly and sadly Enoch answer'd
    her;
"His head is low, and no man cares
    for him.
I think I have not three days more to
    live;
I am the man." At which the woman
    gave
A half-incredulous, half-hysterical
    cry.
"You Arden, you! nay,—sure he was
    a foot
Higher than you be." Enoch said
    again
"My God has bow'd me down to what
    I am;
My grief and solitude have broken
    me;
Nevertheless, know you that I am he
Who married—but that name has
    twice been changed—
I married her who married Philip
    Ray.
Sit, listen." Then he told her of his
    voyage,
His wreck, his lonely life, his coming
    back,
His gazing in on Annie, his resolve,
And how he kept it. As the woman
    heard,
Fast flow'd the current of her easy
    tears,
While in her heart she yearn'd inces-
    santly
To rush abroad all round the little
    haven,
Proclaiming Enoch Arden and his
    woes;
But awed and promise-bounden she
    forbore,
Saying only "See your bairns before
    you go!

Eh, let me fetch 'em, Arden," and arose
Eager to bring them down, for Enoch hung
A moment on her words, but then replied:

"Woman, disturb me not now at the last,
But let me hold my purpose till I die.
Sit down again; mark me and understand,
While I have power to speak. I charge you now,
When you shall see her, tell her that I died
Blessing her, praying for her, loving her;
Save for the bar between us, loving her
As when she laid her head beside my own.
And tell my daughter Annie, whom I saw
So like her mother, that my latest breath
Was spent in blessing her and praying for her.
And tell my son that I died blessing him.
And say to Philip that I blest him too;
He never meant us any thing but good.
But if my children care to see me dead,
Who hardly knew me living, let them come,
I am their father; but she must not come,
For my dead face would vex her afterlife.
And now there is but one of all my blood

Who will embrace me in the world-to-be:
This hair is his: she cut it off and gave it,
And I have borne it with me all these years.
And thought to bear it with me to my grave;
But now my mind is changed, for I shall see him,
My babe in bliss: wherefore when I am gone,
Take, give her this, for it may comfort her:
It will moreover be a token to her,
That I am he."

He ceased; and Miriam Lane
Made such a voluble answer promising all,
That once again he roll'd his eyes upon her
Repeating all he wish'd, and once again
She promised.

Then the third night after this,
While Enoch slumber'd motionless and pale,
And Miriam watch'd and dozed at intervals,
There came so loud a calling of the sea,
That all the houses in the haven rang.
He woke, he rose, he spread his arms abroad
Crying with a loud voice "A sail! a sail!
I am saved;" and so fell back and spoke no more.

So past the strong heroic soul away.
And when they buried him the little port
Had seldom seen a costlier funeral.

IN MEMORIAM A. H. H.

OBIIT MDCCCXXXIII.

STRONG Son of God, immortal Love,
　　Whom we, that have not seen thy
　　　　face,
　　By faith, and faith alone, embrace,
Believing where we cannot prove;

Thine are these orbs of light and
　　shade;
　　Thou madest Life in man and
　　　　brute;
　　Thou madest Death; and lo, thy
　　　　foot
Is on the skull which thou hast made.

Thou wilt not leave us in the dust:
　　Thou madest man, he knows not
　　　　why,
　　He thinks he was not made to die;
And thou hast made him: thou art
　　just.

Thou seemest human and divine,
　　The highest, holiest manhood,
　　　　thou:
　　Our wills are ours, we know not
　　　　how;
Our wills are ours, to make them
　　thine.

Our little systems have their day,
　　They have their day and cease
　　　　to be:
　　They are but broken lights of
　　　　thee,
And thou, O Lord, art more than they.

We have but faith: we cannot know;
　　For knowledge is of things we see;
　　And yet we trust it comes from
　　　　thee,
A beam in darkness: let it grow.

Let knowledge grow from more to
　　more,
　　But more of reverence in us
　　　　dwell;

That mind and soul, according
　　well,
May make one music as before,

But vaster. We are fools and slight;
　　We mock thee when we do not
　　　　fear:
　　But help thy foolish ones to bear;
Help thy vain worlds to bear thy light.

Forgive what seem'd my sin in me;
　　What seem'd my worth since I
　　　　began;
　　For merit lives from man to man,
And not from man, O Lord, to thee.

Forgive my grief for one removed,
　　Thy creature, whom I found so
　　　　fair.
　　I trust he lives in thee, and there
I find him worthier to be loved.

Forgive these wild and wandering
　　cries,
　　Confusions of a wasted youth;
　　Forgive them where they fail in
　　　　truth,
And in thy wisdom make me wise.
　　　　　　　　　　　　　　　　1849.

I.

I HELD it truth, with him who sings
　　To one clear harp in divers tones,
　　That men may rise on stepping-
　　　　stones
Of their dead selves to higher things.

But who shall so forecast the years
　　And find in loss a gain to match?
　　Or reach a hand thro' time to
　　　　catch
The far-off interest of tears?

Let Love clasp Grief lest both be
　　drown'd,

Let darkness keep her raven
    gloss :
Ah, sweeter to be drunk with loss,
To dance with death, to beat the
    ground,

Than that the victor Hours should
    scorn
    The long result of love, and
      boast,
    "Behold the man that loved and
      lost,
But all he was is overworn."

II.

Old Yew, which graspest at the stones
    That name the under-lying dead,
    Thy fibres net the dreamless head,
Thy roots are wrapt about the bones.

The seasons bring the flower again,
    And bring the firstling to the
      flock ;
    And in the dusk of thee, the
      clock
Beats out the little lives of men.

O not for thee the glow, the bloom,
    Who changest not in any gale,
    Nor branding summer suns avail
To touch thy thousand years of
      gloom :

And gazing on thee, sullen tree,
    Sick for thy stubborn hardihood,
    I seem to fail from out my blood
And grow incorporate into thee.

III.

O Sorrow, cruel fellowship,
    O Priestess in the vaults of Death,
    O sweet and bitter in a breath,
What whispers from thy lying lip ?

"The stars," she whispers, "blindly
    run ;
    A web is wov'n across the sky ;
    From out waste places comes a
      cry,
And murmurs from the dying sun :

"And all the phantom, Nature,
    stands —
    With all the music in her tone,
    A hollow echo of my own, —
A hollow form with empty hands."

And shall I take a thing so blind,
    Embrace her as my natural good ;
    Or crush her, like a vice of blood,
Upon the threshold of the mind ?

IV.

To Sleep I give my powers away ;
    My will is bondsman to the dark ;
    I sit within a helmless bark,
And with my heart I muse and say:

O heart, how fares it with thee now,
    That thou should'st fail from thy
      desire,
    Who scarcely darest to inquire,
"What is it makes me beat so low ? "

Something it is which thou hast lost,
    Some pleasure from thine early
      years.
    Break, thou deep vase of chilling
      tears,
That grief hath shaken into frost !

Such clouds of nameless trouble cross
    All night below the darken'd
      eyes ;
    With morning wakes the will, and
      cries,
"Thou shalt not be the fool of loss."

V.

I sometimes hold it half a sin
    To put in words the grief I feel ;
    For words, like Nature, half re-
      veal
And half conceal the Soul within.

But, for the unquiet heart and brain,
    A use in measured language lies ;
    The sad mechanic exercise,
Like dull narcotics, numbing pain.

In words, like weeds, I'll wrap me o'er,
    Like coarsest clothes against the
      cold :

But that large grief which these
    enfold
Is given in outline and no more.

VI.

One writes, that " Other friends re-
    main,"
    That " Loss is common to the
    race " —
And common is the commonplace,
And vacant chaff well meant for grain.

That loss is common would not make
    My own less bitter, rather more :
    Too common ! Never morning
    wore
To evening, but some heart did break.

O father, wheresoe'er thou be,
    Who pledgest now thy gallant son;
    A shot, ere half thy draught be
    done,
Hath still'd the life that beat from thee.

O mother, praying God will save
    Thy sailor, — while thy head is
    bow'd
    His   heavy-shotted   hammock-
    shroud
Drops in his vast and wandering grave.

Ye know no more than I who wrought
    At that last hour to please him
    well ;
    Who mused on all I had to tell,
And   something   written,   something
    thought ;

Expecting still his advent home ;
    And ever met him on his way
    With wishes, thinking, " here to-
    day,"
Or " here to-morrow will he come."

O somewhere, meek, unconscious dove,
    That sittest ranging golden hair;
    And glad to find thyself so fair,
Poor child, that waitest for thy love !

For now her father's chimney glows
    In expectation of a guest ;

And thinking " this will please
    him best,"
She takes a riband or a rose ;

For he will see them on to-night;
    And with the thought her color
    burns ;
    And, having left the glass, she
    turns
Once more to set a ringlet right;

And, even when she turn'd, the curse
    Had fallen, and her future Lord
    Was drown'd in passing thro' the
    ford,
Or kill'd in falling from his horse.

O what to her shall be the end ?
    And what to me remains of good ?
    To her, perpetual maidenhood,
And unto me no second friend.

VII.

Dark house, by which once more I
    stand
    Here in the long unlovely street,
    Doors, where my heart was used
    to beat
So quickly, waiting for a hand,

A hand that can be clasp'd no more —
    Behold me, for I cannot sleep,
    And like a guilty thing I creep
At earliest morning to the door.

He is not here ; but far away
    The noise of life begins again,
    And ghastly thro' the drizzling
    rain
On the bald street breaks the blank
    day.

VIII.

A happy lover who has come
    To look on her that loves him well,
    Who 'lights and rings the gate-
    way bell,
And learns her gone and far from
    home ;

He saddens, all the magic light

Dies off at once from bower and
    hall,
And all the place is dark, and all
The chambers emptied of delight:

So find I every pleasant spot
    In which we two were wont to
      meet,
    The field, the chamber and the
      street,
For all is dark where thou art not.

Yet as that other, wandering there
    In those deserted walks, may find
    A flower beat with rain and wind,
Which once she foster'd up with care;

So seems it in my deep regret,
    O my forsaken heart, with thee
    And this poor flower of poesy
Which little cared for fades not yet.

But since it pleased a vanish'd eye,
    I go to plant it on his tomb,
    That if it can it there may bloom,
Or dying, there at least may die.

IX.

Fair ship, that from the Italian shore
    Sailest the placid ocean-plains
    With my lost Arthur's loved re-
      mains,
Spread thy full wings, and waft him
    o'er.

So draw him home to those that mourn
    In vain; a favorable speed
    Ruffle thy mirror'd mast, and lead
Thro' prosperous floods his holy urn.

All night no ruder air perplex
    Thy sliding keel, till Phosphor,
      bright
    As our pure love, thro' early light
Shall glimmer on the dewy decks.

Sphere all your lights around, above;
    Sleep, gentle heavens, before the
      prow;
    Sleep, gentle winds, as he sleeps
      now,
My friend, the brother of my love;

My Arthur, whom I shall not see
    Till all my widow'd race be run;
    Dear as the mother to the son,
More than my brothers are to me.

X.

I hear the noise about thy keel;
    I hear the bell struck in the night:
    I see the cabin-window bright;
I see the sailor at the wheel.

Thou bring'st the sailor to his wife,
    And travell'd men from foreign
      lands;
    And letters unto trembling hands;
And, thy dark freight, a vanish'd life.

So bring him: we have idle dreams:
    This look of quiet flatters thus
    Our home-bred fancies: O to us,
The fools of habit, sweeter seems

To rest beneath the clover sod,
    That takes the sunshine and the
      rains,
    Or where the kneeling hamlet
      drains
The chalice of the grapes of God;

Than if with thee the roaring wells
    Should gulf him fathom-deep in
      brine;
    And hands so often clasp'd in
      mine,
Should toss with tangle and with shells.

XI.

Calm is the morn without a sound,
    Calm as to suit a calmer grief,
    And only thro' the faded leaf
The chestnut pattering to the ground:

Calm and deep peace on this high wold,
    And on these dews that drench
      the furze,
    And all the silvery gossamers
That twinkle into green and gold:

Calm and still light on yon great plain
    That sweeps with all its autumn
      bowers,

And crowded farms and lessening
    towers,
To mingle with the bounding main :

Calm and deep peace in this wide air,
    These leaves that redden to the
        fall;
    And in my heart, if calm at all,
If any calm, a calm despair :

Calm on the seas, and silver sleep,
    And waves that sway themselves
        in rest,
    And dead calm in that noble
        breast
Which heaves but with the heaving
    deep.

XII.

Lo, as a dove when up she springs
    To bear thro' Heaven a tale of woe,
    Some dolorous message knit below
The wild pulsation of her wings;

Like her I go ; I cannot stay ;
    I leave this mortal ark behind,
    A weight of nerves without a mind,
And leave the cliffs, and haste away

O'er ocean-mirrors rounded large,
    And reach the glow of southern
        skies,
    And see the sails at distance rise,
And linger weeping on the marge,

And saying; "Comes he thus, my
    friend ?
    Is this the end of all my care ? "
    And circle moaning in the air :
" Is this the end ? Is this the end ? "

And forward dart again, and play
    About the prow, and back return
    To where the body sits, and learn
That I have been an hour away.

XIII.

Tears of the widower, when he sees
    A late-lost form that sleep reveals,
    And moves his doubtful arms,
        and feels
Her place is empty, fall like these ;

Which weep a loss for ever new,
    A void where heart on heart re-
        posed ;
    And, where warm hands have
        prest and closed,
Silence, till I be silent too.

Which weep the comrade of my
    choice,
    An awful thought, a life re-
        moved,
    The human-hearted man I loved,
A Spirit, not a breathing voice.

Come Time, and teach me, many
    years,
    I do not suffer in a dream :
    For now so strange do these
        things seem,
Mine eyes have leisure for their
    tears ;

My fancies time to rise on wing,
    And glance about the approach-
        ing sails,
    As tho' they brought but mer-
        chants' bales,
And not the burthen that they bring.

XIV.

If one should bring me this report,
    That thou hadst touch'd the land
        to-day,
    And I went down unto the quay,
And found thee lying in the port ;

And standing, muffled round with
    woe,
    Should see thy passengers in
        rank
    Come stepping lightly down the
        plank,
And beckoning unto those they know ;

And if along with these should come
    The man I held as half-divine ;
    Should strike a sudden hand in
        mine,
And ask a thousand things of home ;

And I should tell him all my pain,
 And how my life had droop'd of
  late,
 And he should sorrow o'er my
  state
And marvel what possess'd my brain;

And I perceived no touch of change,
 No hint of death in all his frame,
 But found him all in all the
  same,
I should not feel it to be strange.

xv.

To-night the winds begin to rise
 And roar from yonder dropping
  day:
 The last red leaf is whirl'd away,
The rooks are blown about the skies;

The forest crack'd, the waters curl'd,
 The cattle huddled on the lea;
 And wildly dash'd on tower and
  tree
The sunbeam strikes along the world:

And but for fancies, which aver
 That all thy motions gently pass
 Athwart a plane of molten glass,
I scarce could brook the strain and
  stir

That makes the barren branches
  loud;
 And but for fear it is not so,
 The wild unrest that lives in woe
Would dote and pore on yonder cloud

That rises upward always higher,
 And onward drags a laboring
  breast,
 And topples round the dreary
  west,
A looming bastion fringed with fire.

xvi.

What words are these have fall'n
  from me?
 Can calm despair and wild unrest
 Be tenants of a single breast,
Or sorrow such a changeling be?

Or doth she only seem to take
 The touch of change in calm or
  storm;
 But knows no more of transient
  form
In her deep self, than some dead lake

That holds the shadow of a lark
 Hung in the shadow of a heaven?
 Or has the shock, so harshly
  given,
Confused me like the unhappy bark

That strikes by night a craggy shelf,
 And staggers blindly ere she
  sink?
 And stunn'd me from my power
  to think
And all my knowledge of myself;

And made me that delirious man
 Whose fancy fuses old and new,
 And flashes into false and true,
And mingles all without a plan?

xvii.

Thou comest, much wept for: such a
  breeze
 Compell'd thy canvas, and my
  prayer
 Was as the whisper of an air
To breathe thee over lonely seas.

For I in spirit saw thee move
 Thro' circles of the bounding
  sky,
 Week after week: the days go
  by:
Come quick, thou bringest all I love.

Henceforth, wherever thou may'st
  roam,
 My blessing, like a line of light,
 Is on the waters day and night,
And like a beacon guards thee home.

So may whatever tempest mars
 Mid-ocean, spare thee, sacred
  bark;
 And balmy drops in summer
  dark
Slide from the bosom of the stars.

So kind an office hath been done,
  Such precious relics brought by
   thee ;
  The dust of him I shall not see
Till all my widow'd race be run.

XVIII.

'Tis well ; 'tis something ; we may
   stand
  Where he in English earth is laid,
  And from his ashes may be made
The violet of his native land.

'Tis little ; but it looks in truth
  As if the quiet bones were blest
  Among familiar names to rest
And in the places of his youth.

Come then, pure hands, and bear the
   head
  That sleeps or wears the mask of
   sleep,
  And come, whatever loves to
   weep,
And hear the ritual of the dead.

Ah yet, ev'n yet, if this might be,
  I, falling on his faithful heart,
  Would breathing thro' his lips
   impart
The life that almost dies in me ;

That dies not, but endures with pain,
  And slowly forms the firmer
   mind,
  Treasuring the look it cannot
   find,
The words that are not heard again.

XIX.

The Danube to the Severn gave
  The darken'd heart that beat no
   more ;
  They laid him by the pleasant
   shore,
And in the hearing of the wave.

There twice a day the Severn fills ;
  The salt sea-water passes by,
  And hushes half the babbling
   Wye,
And makes a silence in the hills.

The Wye is hush'd nor moved along,
  And hush'd my deepest grief of
   all,
  When fill'd with tears that can-
   not fall,
I brim with sorrow drowning song.

The tide flows down, the wave again
  Is vocal in its wooded walls ;
  My deeper anguish also falls,
And I can speak a little then.

XX.

The lesser griefs that may be said,
  That breathe a thousand tender
   vows,
  Are but as servants in a house
Where lies the master newly dead ;

Who speak their feeling as it is,
  And weep the fulness from the
   mind :
  " It will be hard," they say, " to
   find
Another service such as this."

My lighter moods are like to these,
  That out of words a comfort
   win ;
  But there are other griefs within,
And tears that at their fountain
   freeze ;

For by the hearth the children sit
  Cold in that atmosphere of
   Death,
  And scarce endure to draw the
   breath,
Or like to noiseless phantoms flit :

But open converse is there none,
  So much the vital spirits sink
  To see the vacant chair, and
   think,
" How good ! how kind ! and he is
   gone."

XXI.

I sing to him that rests below,
  And, since the grasses round me
   wave,

I take the grasses of the grave,
And make them pipes whereon to
blow.

The traveller hears me now and then,
And sometimes harshly will he
speak:
"This fellow would make weak-
ness weak,
And melt the waxen hearts of men."

Another answers, "Let him be,
He loves to make parade of pain,
That with his piping he may gain
The praise that comes to constancy."

A third is wroth: "Is this an hour
For private sorrow's barren song,
When more and more the people
throng
The chairs and thrones of civil power?

"A time to sicken and to swoon,
When Science reaches forth her
arms
To feel from world to world, and
charms
Her secret from the latest moon?"

Behold, ye speak an idle thing:
Ye never knew the sacred dust:
I do but sing because I must,
And pipe but as the linnets sing:

And one is glad; her note is gay,
For now her little ones have
ranged;
And one is sad; her note is
changed,
Because her brood is stol'n away.

XXII.

The path by which we twain did go,
Which led by tracts that pleased
us well,
Thro' four sweet years arose and
fell,
From flower to flower, from snow to
snow:

And we with singing cheer'd the way,
And, crown'd with all the season
lent,
From April on to April went,
And glad at heart from May to May:

But where the path we walk'd began
To slant the fifth autumnal slope,
As we descended following Hope,
There sat the Shadow fear'd of man;

Who broke our fair companionship,
And spread his mantle dark and
cold,
And wrapt thee formless in the
fold,
And dull'd the murmur on thy lip,

And bore thee where I could not see
Nor follow, tho' I walk in haste,
And think, that somewhere in the
waste
The Shadow sits and waits for me.

XXIII.

Now, sometimes in my sorrow shut,
Or breaking into song by fits,
Alone, alone, to where he sits,
The Shadow cloak'd from head to foot,

Who keeps the keys of all the creeds,
I wander, often falling lame,
And looking back to whence I
came,
Or on to where the pathway leads;

And crying, How changed from where
it ran
Thro' lands where not a leaf was
dumb;
But all the lavish hills would hum
The murmur of a happy Pan:

When each by turns was guide to each,
And Fancy light from Fancy
caught,
And Thought leapt out to wed
with Thought
Ere Thought could wed itself with
Speech;

And all we met was fair and good,
    And all was good that Time could
      bring,
    And all the secret of the Spring
Moved in the chambers of the blood;

And many an old philosophy
    On Argive heights divinely sang,
    And round us all the thicket rang
To many a flute of Arcady.

XXIV.

And was the day of my delight
    As pure and perfect as I say ?
    The very source and fount of Day
Is dash'd with wandering isles of
    night.

If all was good and fair we met,
    This earth had been the Paradise
    It never look'd to human eyes
Since our first Sun arose and set.

And is it that the haze of grief
    Makes former gladness loom so
      great ?
    The lowness of the present state,
That sets the past in this relief ?

Or that the past will always win
    A glory from its being far;
    And orb into the perfect star
We saw not, when we moved therein ?

XXV.

I know that this was life, — the track
    Whereon with equal feet we
      fared ;
    And then, as now, the day pre-
      pared
The daily burden for the back.

But this it was that made me move
    As light as carrier-birds in air ;
    I loved the weight I had to bear,
Because it needed help of Love :

Nor could I weary, heart or limb,
    When mighty Love would cleave
      in twain
    The lading of a single pain,
And part it, giving half to him.

XXVI.

Still onward winds the dreary way ;
    I with it ; for I long to prove
    No lapse of moons can canker
      Love,
Whatever fickle tongues may say.

And if that eye which watches guilt
    And goodness, and hath power
      to see
    Within the green the moulder'd
      tree,
And towers fall'n as soon as built —

Oh, if indeed that eye foresee
    Or see (in Him is no before)
    In more of life true life no more
And Love the indifference to be,

Then might I find, ere yet the morn
    Breaks hither over Indian seas,
    That shadow waiting with the
      keys,
To shroud me from my proper scorn.

XXVII.

I envy not in any moods
    The captive void of noble rage,
    The linnet born within the cage,
That never knew the summer woods :

I envy not the beast that takes
    His license in the field of time,
    Unfetter'd by the sense of crime,
To whom a conscience never wakes ;

Nor, what may count itself as blest,
    The heart that never plighted
      troth
    But stagnates in the weeds of
      sloth;
Nor any want-begotten rest.

I hold it true, what'er befall ;
    I feel it, when I sorrow most ;
    'Tis better to have loved and lost
Than never to have loved at all.

XXVIII.

The time draws near the birth of
    Christ :
    The moon is hid ; the night is still;

The Christmas bells from hill to
hill
Answer each other ir the mist.

Four voices of four hamlets round,
   From far and near, on mead and
    moor,
   Swell out and fail, as if a door
Were shut between me and the sound:

Each voice four changes on the wind,
   That now dilate, and now de-
    crease,
   Peace and goodwill, goodwill and
    peace,
Peace and goodwill, to all mankind.

This year I slept and woke with pain,
   I almost wish'd no more to wake,
   And that my hold on life would
    break
Before I heard those bells again:

But they my troubled spirit rule,
   For they controll'd me when a boy;
   They bring me sorrow touch'd
    with joy,
The merry merry bells of Yule.

XXIX.

With such compelling cause to grieve
   As daily vexes household peace,
   And chains regret to his decease,
How dare we keep our Christmas-eve;

Which brings no more a welcome
    guest
   To enrich the threshold of the
    night
   With shower'd largess of delight
In dance and song and game and jest?

Yet go, and while the holly boughs
   Entwine the cold baptismal font,
   Make one wreath more for Use
    and Wont,
That guard the portals of the house;

Old sisters of a day gone by,
   Gray nurses, loving nothing new;
   Why should they miss their
    yearly due
Before their time? They too will
    die.

XXX.

With trembling fingers did we weave
   The holly round the Christmas
    hearth;
   A rainy cloud possess'd the earth.
And sadly fell our Christmas-eve.

At our old pastimes in the hall
   We gambol'd, making vain pre-
    tence
   Of gladness, with an awful sense
Of one mute Shadow watching all.

We paused: the winds were in the
    beech:
   We heard them sweep the winter
    land;
   And in a circle hand-in-hand
Sat silent, looking each at each.

Then echo-like our voices rang;
   We sung, tho' every eye was dim,
   A merry song we sang with him
Last year: impetuously we sang:

We ceased: a gentler feeling crept
   Upon us: surely rest is meet:
   "They rest," we said, "their sleep
    is sweet,"
And silence follow'd, and we wept.

Our voices took a higher range;
   Once more we sang: "They do
    not die
   Nor lose their mortal sympathy,
Nor change to us, although they
    change;

"Rapt from the fickle and the frail
   With gather'd power, yet the
    same,
   Pierces the keen seraphic flame
From orb to orb, from veil to veil."

Rise, happy morn, rise, holy morn,
   Draw forth the cheerful day from
    night:
   O Father, touch the east, and
    light
The light that shone when Hope was
    born.

XXXI.

When Lazarus left his charnel-cave,
  And home to Mary's house re-
    turn'd,
  Was this demanded—if he yearn'd
To hear her weeping by his grave?

"Where wert thou, brother, those
    four days?"
  There lives no record of reply,
  Which telling what it is to die
Had surely added praise to praise.

From every house the neighbors met,
  The streets were fill'd with joyful
    sound,
  A solemn gladness even crown'd
The purple brows of Olivet.

Behold a man raised up by Christ!
  The rest remaineth unreveal'd;
  He told it not; or something
    seal'd
The lips of that Evangelist.

XXXII.

Her eyes are homes of silent prayer,
  Nor other thought her mind ad-
    mits
  But, he was dead, and there he
    sits,
And he that brought him back is
    there.

Then one deep love doth supersede
  All other, when her ardent gaze
  Roves from the living brother's
    face,
And rests upon the Life indeed.

All subtle thought, all curious fears,
  Borne down by gladness so com-
    plete,
  She bows, she bathes the
    Saviour's feet
With costly spikenard and with tears.

Thrice blest whose lives are faithful
    prayers,
  Whose loves in higher love en-
    dure;

What souls possess themselves so
    pure,
Or is their blessedness like theirs?

XXXIII.

O thou that after toil and storm
  Mayst seem to have reach'd a
    purer air,
  Whose faith has centre every-
    where,
Nor cares to fix itself to form,

Leave thou thy sister when she prays,
  Her early Heaven, her happy
    views;
  Nor thou with shadow'd hint con-
    fuse
A life that leads melodious days.

Her faith thro' form is pure as thine,
  Her hands are quicker unto good:
  Oh, sacred be the flesh and blood
To which she links a truth divine!

See thou, that countest reason ripe
  In holding by the law within,
  Thou fail not in a world of sin,
And ev'n for want of such a type.

XXXIV.

My own dim life should teach me
    this,
  That life shall live for evermore,
  Else earth is darkness at the core,
And dust and ashes all that is;

This round of green, this orb of flame,
  Fantastic beauty; such as lurks
  In some wild Poet, when he works
Without a conscience or an aim.

What then were God to such as I?
  'Twere hardly worth my while to
    choose
  Of things all mortal, or to use
A little patience ere I die;

'Twere best at once to sink to peace,
  Like birds the charming serpent
    draws,

To drop head-foremost in the jaws
Of vacant darkness and to cease.

XXXV.

Yet if some voice that man could trust
Should murmur from the narrow house,
"The cheeks drop in; the body bows;
Man dies: nor is there hope in dust:"

Might I not say? "Yet even here,
But for one hour, O Love, I strive
To keep so sweet a thing alive:"
But I should turn mine ears and hear

The moanings of the homeless sea,
The sound of streams that swift or slow
Draw down Æonian hills, and sow
The dust of continents to be;

And Love would answer with a sigh,
"The sound of that forgetful shore
Will change my sweetness more and more,
Half-dead to know that I shall die."

O me, what profits it to put
An idle case? If Death were seen
At first as Death, Love had not been,
Or been in narrowest working shut,

Mere fellowship of sluggish moods,
Or in his coarsest Satyr-shape
Had bruised the herb and crush'd the grape,
And bask'd and batten'd in the woods.

XXXVI.

Tho' truths in manhood darkly join,
Deep-seated in our mystic frame,
We yield all blessing to the name
Of Him that made them current coin;

For Wisdom dealt with mortal powers,
Where truth in closest words shall fail,
When truth embodied in a tale
Shall enter in at lowly doors.

And so the Word had breath, and wrought
With human hands the creed of creeds
In loveliness of perfect deeds,
More strong than all poetic thought;

Which he may read that binds the sheaf,
Or builds the house, or digs the grave,
And those wild eyes that watch the wave
In roarings round the coral reef.

XXXVII.

Urania speaks with darken'd brow:
"Thou pratest here where thou art least;
This faith has many a purer priest,
And many an abler voice than thou.

"Go down beside thy native rill,
On thy Parnassus set thy feet,
And hear thy laurel whisper sweet
About the ledges of the hill."

And my Melpomene replies,
A touch of shame upon her cheek:
"I am not worthy ev'n to speak
Of thy prevailing mysteries;

"For I am but an earthly Muse,
And owning but a little art
To lull with song an aching heart,
And render human love his dues;

"But brooding on the dear one dead,
And all he said of things divine,
(And dear to me as sacred wine
To dying lips is all he said),

"I murmur'd, as I came along,
Of comfort clasp'd in truth reveal'd;
And loiter'd in the master's field,
And darken'd sanctities with song."

XXXVIII.

With weary steps I loiter on,
    Tho' always under alter'd skies
    The purple from the distance dies,
My prospect and horizon gone.

No joy the blowing season gives,
    The herald melodies of spring,
    But in the songs I love to sing
A doubtful gleam of solace lives.

If any care for what is here
    Survive in spirits render'd free,
    Then are these songs I sing of
      thee
Not all ungrateful to thine ear.

XXXIX.

Old warder of these buried bones,
    And answering now my random
      stroke
    With fruitful cloud and living
      smoke,
Dark yew, that graspest at the stones

And dippest toward the dreamless
      head,
    To thee too comes the golden hour
    When flower is feeling after
      flower;
But Sorrow — fixt upon the dead,

And darkening the dark graves of
      men, —
    What whisper'd from her lying
      lips?
    Thy gloom is kindled at the tips,
And passes into gloom again.

XL.

Could we forget the widow'd hour
    And look on Spirits breathed
      away,
    As on a maiden in the day
When first she wears her orange-
      flower!

When crown'd with blessing she doth
      rise
    To take her latest leave of home,

And hopes and light regrets that
      come
Make April of her tender eyes;

And doubtful joys the father move,
    And tears are on the mother's
      face,
    As parting with a long embrace
She enters other realms of love;

Her office there to rear, to teach,
    Becoming as is meet and fit
    A link among the days, to knit
The generations each with each;

And, doubtless, unto thee is given
    A life that bears immortal fruit
    In those great offices that suit
The full-grown energies of heaven.

Ay me, the difference I discern!
    How often shall her old fireside
    Be cheer'd with tidings of the
      bride,
How often she herself return,

And tell them all they would have
      told,
    And bring her babe, and make
      her boast,
    Till even those that miss'd her
      most
Shall count new things as dear as old:

But thou and I have shaken hands,
    Till growing winters lay me low;
    My paths are in the fields I know,
And thine in undiscover'd lands.

XLI.

Thy spirit ere our fatal loss
    Did ever rise from high to higher;
    As mounts the heavenward altar-
      fire,
As flies the lighter thro' the gross.

But thou art turn'd to something
      strange,
    And I have lost the links that
      bound

Thy changes; here upon the ground,
No more partaker of thy change.

Deep folly! yet that this could be—
    That I could wing my will with might
    To leap the grades of life and light,
And flash at once, my friend, to thee.

For tho' my nature rarely yields
    To that vague fear implied in death;
    Nor shudders at the gulfs beneath,
The howlings from forgotten fields;

Yet oft when sundown skirts the moor
    An inner trouble I behold,
    A spectral doubt which makes me cold,
That I shall be thy mate no more,

Tho' following with an upward mind
    The wonders that have come to thee,
    Thro' all the secular to-be,
But evermore a life behind.

XLII.

I vex my heart with fancies dim:
    He still outstript me in the race;
    It was but unity of place
That made me dream I rank'd with him.

And so may Place retain us still,
    And he the much-beloved again,
    A lord of large experience, train
To riper growth the mind and will:

And what delights can equal those
    That stir the spirit's inner deeps,
    When one that loves but knows not, reaps
A truth from one that loves and knows?

XLIII.

If Sleep and Death be truly one,
    And every spirit's folded bloom

Thro' all its intervital gloom
In some long trance should slumber on;

Unconscious of the sliding hour,
    Bare of the body, might it last,
    And silent traces of the past
Be all the color of the flower:

So then were nothing lost to man;
    So that still garden of the souls
    In many a figured leaf enrolls
The total world since life began;

And love will last as pure and whole
    As when he loved me here in Time,
    And at the spiritual prime
Rewaken with the dawning soul.

XLIV.

How fares it with the happy dead?
    For here the man is more and more;
    But he forgets the days before
God shut the doorways of his head.

The days have vanish'd, tone and tint,
    And yet perhaps the hoarding sense
    Gives out at times (he knows not whence)
A little flash, a mystic hint;

And in the long harmonious years
    (If Death so taste Lethean springs),
    May some dim touch of earthly things
Surprise thee ranging with thy peers.

If such a dreamy touch should fall,
    O turn thee round, resolve the doubt;
    My guardian angel will speak out
In that high place, and tell thee all.

XLV.

The baby new to earth and sky,
    What time his tender palm is prest
    Against the circle of the breast,
Has never thought that "this is I:"

But as he grows he gathers much,
    And learns the use of " I," and
      " me,"
    And finds " I am not what I see,
And other than the things I touch."

So rounds he to a separate mind
    From whence clear memory may
      begin,
    As thro' the frame that binds him
      in
His isolation grows defined.

This use may lie in blood and breath,
    Which else were fruitless of their
      due,
    Had man to learn himself anew
Beyond the second birth of Death.

XLVI.

We ranging down this lower track,
    The path we came by, thorn and
      flower,
    Is shadow'd by the growing hour,
Lest life should fail in looking back.

So be it: there no shade can last
    In that deep dawn behind the
      tomb,
    But clear from marge to marge
      shall bloom
The eternal landscape of the past;

A lifelong tract of time reveal'd;
    The fruitful hours of still increase;
    Days order'd in a wealthy peace,
And those five years its richest field.

O Love, thy province were not large,
    A bounded field, nor stretching
      far;
    Look also, Love, a brooding star,
A rosy warmth from marge to marge.

XLVII.

That each, who seems a separate
    whole,
    Should move his rounds, and fus-
      ing all
    The skirts of self again, should
      fall
Remerging in the general Soul,

Is faith as vague as all unsweet:
    Eternal form shall still divide
    The eternal soul from all beside;
And I shall know him when we meet:

And we shall sit at endless feast,
    Enjoying each the other's good:
    What vaster dream can hit the
      mood
Of Love on earth ?   He seeks at least

Upon the last and sharpest height,
    Before the spirits fade away,
    Some landing-place, to clasp and
      say,
" Farewell !   We lose ourselves in
    light."

XLVIII.

If these brief lays, of Sorrow born,
    Were taken to be such as closed
    Grave doubts and answers here
      proposed,
Then these were such as men might
    scorn:

Her care is not to part and prove;
    She takes, when harsher moods
      remit,
    What slender shade of doubt may
      flit,
And makes it vassal unto love:

And hence, indeed, she sports with
    words,
    But better serves a wholesome
      law,
    And holds it sin and shame to
      draw
The deepest measure from the chords:

Nor dare she trust a larger lay,
    But rather loosens from the lip
    Short swallow-flights of song, that
      dip
Their wings in tears, and skim away.

XLIX.

From art, from nature, from the
    schools,
    Let random influences glance,

Like light in many a shiver'd lance
That breaks about the dappled pools:

The lightest wave of thought shall lisp,
    The   fancy's   tenderest   eddy
        wreathe,
    The slightest air of song shall
        breathe
To make the sullen surface crisp.

And look thy look, and go thy way,
    But blame not thou the winds that
        make
    The seeming-wanton ripple break,
The tender-pencil'd shadow play.

Beneath all fancied hopes and fears
    Ay me, the sorrow deepens down,
    Whose muffled motions blindly
        drown
The bases of my life in tears.

L.

Be near me when my light is low,
    When the blood creeps, and the
        nerves prick
    And tingle ; and the heart is sick,
And all the wheels of Being slow.

Be near me when the sensuous frame
    Is rack'd with pangs that conquer
        trust ;
    And Time, a maniac scattering
        dust,
And Life, a Fury slinging flame.

Be near me when my faith is dry,
    And men the flies of latter spring,
    That lay their eggs, and sting
        and sing
And weave their petty cells and die.

Be near me when I fade away,
    To point the term of human strife,
    And on the low dark verge of life
The twilight of eternal day.

LI.

Lo we indeed desire the dead
    Should still be near us at our side ?

Is there no baseness we would
    hide ?
No inner vileness that we dread ?

Shall he for whose applause I strove,
    I had such reverence for his
        blame,
    See with clear eye some hidden
        shame
And I be lessen'd in his love ?

I wrong the grave with fears untrue .
    Shall love be blamed for want of
        faith ?
    There must be wisdom with great
        Death :
The dead shall look me thro' and thro'.

Be near us when we climb or fall :
    Ye watch, like God, the rolling
        hours
    With larger other eyes than ours,
To make allowance for us all.

LII

I cannot love thee as I ought,
    For love reflects the thing be-
        loved ;
    My words are only words, and
        moved
Upon the topmost froth of thought.

" Yet blame not thou my plaintive
    song,"
    The Spirit of true love replied ;
    " Thou canst not move me from
        thy side,
Nor human frailty do me wrong.

" What keeps a spirit wholly true
    To that ideal which he bears ?
    What record ? not the sinless
        years
That breathed beneath the Syrian
    blue :

" So fret not, like an idle girl,
    That life is dash'd with flecks of
        sin.
    Abide : thy wealth is gather'd in,
When Time hath sunder'd shell from
    pearl."

LIII.

How many a father have I seen,
    A sober man, among his boys,
    Whose youth was full of foolish
        noise,
Who wears his manhood hale and
    green :

And dare we to this fancy give,
    That had the wild oat not been
        sown,
    The soil, left barren, scarce had
        grown
The grain by which a man may live ?

Or, if we held the doctrine sound
    For life outliving heats of youth,
    Yet who would preach it as a
        truth
To those that eddy round and round ?

Hold thou the good : define it well :
    For fear divine Philosophy
    Should push beyond her mark,
        and be
Procuress to the Lords of Hell.

LIV.

Oh yet we trust that somehow good
    Will be the final goal of ill,
    To pangs of nature, sins of will,
Defects of doubt, and taints of blood ;

That nothing walks with aimless feet ;
    That not one life shall be de-
        stroy'd,
    Or cast as rubbish to the void,
When God hath made the pile com-
        plete ;

That not a worm is cloven in vain ;
    That not a moth with vain desire
    Is shrivell'd in a fruitless fire,
Or but subserves another's gain.

Behold, we know not anything ;
    I can but trust that good shall
        fall
    At last — far off — at last, to all,
And every winter change to spring.

So runs my dream : but what am I ?
    An infant crying in the night :
    An infant crying for the light :
And with no language but a cry.

LV.

The wish, that of the living whole
    No life may fail beyond the grave,
    Derives it not from what we have
The likest God within the soul ?

Are God and Nature then at strife,
    That Nature lends such evil
        dreams ?
    So careful of the type she seems,
So careless of the single life ;

That I, considering everywhere
    Her secret meaning in her deeds,
    And finding that of fifty seeds
She often brings but one to bear,

I falter where I firmly trod,
    And falling with my weight of
        cares
    Upon the great world's altar-stairs
That slope thro' darkness up to God,

I stretch lame hands of faith, and
        grope,
    And gather dust and chaff, and
        call
    To what I feel is Lord of all,
And faintly trust the larger hope.

LVI.

"So careful of the type ? " but no.
    From scarped cliff and quarried
        stone
    She cries, " A thousand types are
        gone :
I care for nothing, all shall go.

" Thou makest thine appeal to me :
    I bring to life, I bring to death .
    The spirit does but mean the
        breath :
I know no more." And he, shall he,

Man, her last work, who seem'd so
    fair,

Such splendid purpose in his eyes,
Who roil'd the psalm to wintry
    skies,
Who built him fanes of fruitless
    prayer,

Who trusted God was love indeed
    And love Creation's final law —
    Tho' Nature, red in tooth and
        claw
With ravine, shriek'd against his
    creed —

Who loved, who suffer'd countless ills,
    Who battled for the True, the
        Just,
    Be blown about the desert dust,
Or seal'd within the iron hills ?

No more ?   A monster then, a dream,
    A discord.   Dragons of the
        prime,
    That tare each other in their
        slime,
Were mellow music match'd with him.

O life as futile, then, as frail !
    O for thy voice to soothe and
        bless !
    What hope of answer, or redress ?
Behind the veil, behind the veil.

LVII.

Peace ; come away : the song of woe
    Is after all an earthly song :
    Peace ; come away : we do him
        wrong
To sing so wildly : let us go.

Come ; let us go : your cheeks are
        pale ;
    But half my life I leave behind :
    Methinks my friend is richly
        shrined ;
But I shall pass ; my work will fail.

Yet in these ears, till hearing dies,
    One set slow bell will seem to toll
    The passing of the sweetest soul
That ever look'd with human eyes.

I hear it now, and o'er and o'er,
    Eternal greetings to the dead ;
    And " Ave, Ave, Ave," said,
" Adieu, adieu " for evermore.

LVIII.

In those sad words I took farewell :
    Like echoes in sepulchral halls,
    As drop by drop the water falls
In vaults and catacombs, they fell ;

And, falling, idly broke the peace
    Of hearts that beat from day to
        day,
    Half-conscious of their dying
        clay,
And those cold crypts where they
    shall cease.

The high Muse answer'd : " Wherefore
        grieve
    Thy brethren with a fruitless
        tear ?
    Abide a little longer here,
And thou shalt take a nobler leave."

LIX.

O Sorrow, wilt thou live with me
    No casual mistress, but a wife,
    My bosom-friend and half of
        life ;
As I confess it needs must be ;

O Sorrow, wilt thou rule my blood,
    Be sometimes lovely like a bride,
    And put thy harsher moods aside,
If thou wilt have me wise and good.

My centred passion cannot move,
    Nor will it lessen from to-day ;
    But I'll have leave at times to
        play
As with the creature of my love ;

And set thee forth, for thou art mine,
    With so much hope for years to
        come,
    That, howsoe'er I know thee, some
Could hardly tell what name were
    thine.

LX.

He past ; a soul of nobler tone :
    My spirit loved and loves him yet,
    Like some poor girl whose heart is set
On one whose rank exceeds her own.

He mixing with his proper sphere,
    She finds the baseness of her lot,
    Half jealous of she knows not what,
And envying all that meet him there.

The little village looks forlorn ;
    She sighs amid her narrow days,
    Moving about the household ways,
In that dark house where she was born.

The foolish neighbors come and go,
    And tease her till the day draws by :
    At night she weeps, " How vain am I !
How should he love a thing so low ? "

LXI.

If, in thy second state sublime,
    Thy ransom'd reason change replies
    With all the circle of the wise,
The perfect flower of human time ;

And if thou cast thine eyes below,
    How dimly character'd and slight,
    How dwarf'd a growth of cold and night,
How blanch'd with darkness must I grow !

Yet turn thee to the doubtful shore,
    Where thy first form was made a man ;
    I loved thee, Spirit, and love, nor can
The soul of Shakspeare love thee more.

LXII.

Tho' if an eye that's downward cast
    Could make thee somewhat blench or fail,
    Then be my love an idle tale,
And fading legend of the past ;

And thou, as one that once declined,
    When he was little more than boy,
    On some unworthy heart with joy,
But lives to wed an equal mind ;

And breathes a novel world, the while
    His other passion wholly dies,
    Or in the light of deeper eyes
Is matter for a flying smile.

LXIII.

Yet pity for a horse o'er-driven,
    And love in which my hound has part,
    Can hang no weight upon my heart
In its assumptions up to heaven ;

And I am so much more than these,
    As thou, perchance, art more than I,
    And yet I spare them sympathy,
And I would set their pains at ease.

So mayst thou watch me where I weep,
    As, unto vaster motions bound,
    The circuits of thine orbit round
A higher height, a deeper deep.

LXIV.

Dost thou look back on what hath been,
    As some divinely gifted man,
    Whose life in low estate began
And on a simple village green ;

Who breaks his birth's invidious bar,
    And grasps the skirts of happy chance,
    And breasts the blows of circumstance,
And grapples with his evil star ;

Who makes by force his merit known
  And lives to clutch the golden
    keys,
  To mould a mighty state's decrees,
And shape the whisper of the throne;

And moving up from high to higher,
  Becomes on Fortune's crowning
    slope
  The pillar of a people's hope,
The centre of a world's desire;

Yet feels, as in a pensive dream,
  When all his active powers are
    still,
  A distant dearness in the hill,
A secret sweetness in the stream,

The limit of his narrower fate,
  While yet beside its vocal springs
  He play'd at counsellors and kings,
With one that was his earliest mate;

Who ploughs with pain his native lea
  And reaps the labor of his hands,
  Or in the furrow musing stands,
" Does my old friend remember me ? "

LXV.

Sweet soul, do with me as thou wilt;
  I lull a fancy trouble-tost
  With " Love's too precious to be
    lost,
A little grain shall not be spilt."

And in that solace can I sing,
  Till out of painful phases wrought
  There flutters up a happy thought,
Self-balanced on a lightsome wing:

Since we deserved the name of friends,
  And thine effect so lives in me,
  A part of mine may live in thee
And move thee on to noble ends.

LXVI.

You thought my heart too far diseased;
  You wonder when my fancies play
  To find me gay among the gay,
Like one with any trifle pleased.

The shade by which my life was crost,
  Which makes a desert in the mind,
  Has made me kindly with my kind,
And like to him whose sight is lost;

Whose feet are guided thro' the land,
  Whose jest among his friends is
    free,
  Who takes the children on his
    knee,
And winds their curls about his hand:

He plays with threads, he beats his
    chair
  For pastime, dreaming of the sky,
  His inner day can never die,
His night of loss is always there.

LXVII.

When on my bed the moonlight falls,
  I know that in thy place of rest
  By that broad water of the west,
There comes a glory on the walls:

Thy marble bright in dark appears,
  As slowly steals a silver flame
  Along the letters of thy name,
And o'er the number of thy years·

The mystic glory swims away;
  From off my bed the moonlight
    dies;
  And closing eaves of wearied eyes
I sleep till dusk is dipt in gray:

And then I know the mist is drawn
  A lucid veil from coast to coast,
  And in the dark church like a
    ghost
Thy tablet glimmers to the dawn.

LXVIII.

When in the down I sink my head,
  Sleep, Death's twin-brother, times
    my breath;
  Sleep, Death's twin-brother, knows
    not Death,
Nor can I dream of thee as dead:

I walk as ere I walk'd forlorn,
  When all our path was fresh with
    dew,

And all the bugle breezes blew
Reveillée to the breaking morn.

But what is this?   I turn about,
   I find a trouble in thine eye,
   Which makes me sad I know not
     why,
Nor can my dream resolve the doubt:

But ere the lark hath left the lea
   I wake, and I discern the truth;
   It is the trouble of my youth
That foolish sleep transfers to thee.

LXIX.

I dream'd there would be Spring no
     more,
   That Nature's ancient power was
     lost:
   The streets were black with smoke
     and frost,
They chatter'd trifles at the door:

I wander'd from the noisy town,
   I found a wood with thorny
     boughs:
   I took the thorns to bind my
     brows,
I wore them like a civic crown:

I met with scoffs, I met with scorns
   From youth and babe and hoary
     hairs:
   They call'd me in the public
     squares
The fool that wears a crown of thorns.

They call'd me fool, they call'd me
     child:
   I found an angel of the night;
   The voice was low, the look was
     bright;
He look'd upon my crown and smiled:

He reach'd the glory of a hand,
   That seem'd to touch it into leaf:
   The voice was not the voice of
     grief,
The words were hard to understand.

LXX.

I cannot see the features right,
   When on the gloom I strive to
     paint
   The face I know; the hues are
     faint
And mix with hollow masks of night;

Cloud-towers by ghostly masons
     wrought,
   A gulf that ever shuts and gapes,
   A hand that points, and palled
     shapes
In shadowy thoroughfares of thought;

And crowds that stream from yawn-
     ing doors,
   And shoals of pucker'd faces
     drive;
   Dark bulks that tumble half alive,
And lazy lengths on boundless shores;

Till all at once beyond the will
   I hear a wizard music roll,
   And thro' a lattice on the soul
Looks thy fair face and makes it still.

LXXI.

Sleep, kinsman thou to death and
     trance
   And madness, thou hast forged
     at last
   A night-long Present of the Past
In which we went thro' summer
     France.

Hadst thou such credit with the soul?
   Then bring an opiate trebly
     strong,
   Drug down the blindfold sense of
     wrong
That so my pleasure may be whole;

While now we talk as once we talk'd
   Of men and minds, the dust of
     change,
   The days that grow to something
     strange,
In walking as of old we walk'd

Beside the river's wooded reach,
    The fortress, and the mountain
        ridge,
    The cataract flashing from the
        bridge,
The breaker breaking on the beach.

LXXII.

Risest thou thus, dim dawn, again,
    And howlest, issuing out of night,
    With blasts that blow the poplar
        white,
And lash with storm the streaming
    pane?

Day, when my crown'd estate begun
    To pine in that reverse of doom,
    Which sicken'd every living
        bloom,
And blurr'd the splendor of the sun;

Who usherest in the dolorous hour
    With thy quick tears that make
        the rose
    Pull sideways, and the daisy close
Her crimson fringes to the shower;

Who might'st have heaved a windless
    flame
    Up the deep East, or, whispering,
        play'd
    A chequer-work of beam and
        shade
Along the hills, yet look'd the same.

As wan, as chill, as wild as now;
    Day, mark'd as with some hideous
        crime,
    When the dark hand struck down
        thro' time,
And cancell'd nature's best: but thou,

Lift as thou may'st thy burthen'd
    brows
    Thro' clouds that drench the
        morning star,
    And whirl the ungarner'd sheaf
        afar,
And sow the sky with flying boughs,

And up thy vault with roaring sound
    Climb thy thick noon, disastrous
        day;
    Touch thy dull goal of joyless
        gray,
And hide thy shame beneath the
    ground.

LXXIII.

So many worlds, so much to do,
    So little done, such things to be,
    How know I what had need of
        thee,
For thou wert strong as thou wert true?

The fame is quench'd that I foresaw,
    The head hath miss'd an earthly
        wreath:
    I curse not nature, no, nor death;
For nothing is that errs from law.

We pass; the path that each man trod
    Is dim, or will be dim, with weeds:
    What fame is left for human deeds
In endless age? It rests with God.

O hollow wraith of dying fame,
    Fade wholly, while the soul
        exults,
    And self-infolds the large results
Of force that would have forged a
    name.

LXXIV.

As sometimes in a dead man's face,
    To those that watch it more and
        more,
    A likeness, hardly seen before,
Comes out — to some one of his race:

So, dearest, now thy brows are cold,
    I see thee what thou art, and
        know
    Thy likeness to the wise below,
Thy kindred with the great of old.

But there is more than I can see,
    And what I see I leave unsaid,
    Nor speak it, knowing Death has
        made
His darkness beautiful with thee.

LXXV.

I leave thy praises unexpress'd
    In verse that brings myself relief,
    And by the measure of my grief
I leave thy greatness to be guess'd;

What practice howsoe'er expert
    In fitting aptest words to things,
    Or voice the richest-toned that
        sings,
Hath power to give thee as thou wert?

I care not in these fading days
    To raise a cry that lasts not long,
    And round thee with the breeze
        of song
To stir a little dust of praise.

Thy leaf has perish'd in the green,
    And, while we breathe beneath the
        sun,
    The world which credits what is
        done
Is cold to all that might have been.

So here shall silence guard thy fame;
    But somewhere, out of human
        view,
    Whate'er thy hands are set to do
Is wrought with tumult of acclaim.

LXXVI.

Take wings of fancy, and ascend,
    And in a moment set thy face
    Where all the starry heavens of
        space
Are sharpen'd to a needle's end;

Take wings of foresight; lighten thro'
    The secular abyss to come,
    And lo, thy deepest lays are dumb
Before the mouldering of a yew;

And if the matin songs, that woke
    The darkness of our planet, last,
    Thine own shall wither in the vast,
Ere half the lifetime of an oak.

Ere these have clothed their branchy
        bowers
    With fifty Mays, thy songs are
        vain;

And what are they when these
        remain
The ruin'd shells of hollow towers?

LXXVII.

What hope is here for modern rhyme
    To him, who turns a musing eye
    On songs, and deeds, and lives,
        that lie
Foreshorten'd in the tract of time?

These mortal lullabies of pain
    May bind a book, may line a box,
    May serve to curl a maiden's
        locks;
Or when a thousand moons shall wane

A man upon a stall may find,
    And, passing, turn the page that
        tells
    A grief, then changed to some-
        thing else,
Sung by a long-forgotten mind.

But what of that? My darken'd ways
    Shall ring with music all the same;
    To breathe my loss is more than
        fame,
To utter love more sweet than praise.

LXXVIII.

Again at Christmas did we weave
    The holly round the Christmas
        hearth;
    The silent snow possess'd the
        earth,
And calmly fell our Christmas-eve:

The yule-clog sparkled keen with frost,
    No wing of wind the region swept,
    But over all things brooding slept
The quiet sense of something lost.

As in the winters left behind,
    Again our ancient games had
        place,
    The mimic picture's breathing
        grace,
And dance and song and hoodman-
        blind.

Who show'd a token of distress ?
    No single tear, no mark of pain :
    O sorrow, then can sorrow wane ?
O grief, can grief be changed to less ?

O last regret, regret can die !
    No — mixt with all this mystic
        frame,
    Her deep relations are the same,
But with long use her tears are dry.

LXXIX.

" More than my brothers are to me,"—
    Let this not vex thee, noble heart !
    I know thee of what force thou
        art
To hold the costliest love in fee.

But thou and I are one in kind,
    As moulded like in Nature's mint;
    And hill and wood and field did
        print
The same sweet forms in either mind.

For us the same cold streamlet curl'd
    Thro' all his eddying coves ; the
        same
    All winds that roam the twilight
        came
In whispers of the beauteous world.

At one dear knee we proffer'd vows,
    One lesson from one book we
        learn'd,
    Ere childhood's flaxen ringlet
        turn'd
To black and brown on kindred brows.

And so my wealth resembles thine,
    But he was rich where I was poor,
    And he supplied my want the more
As his unlikeness fitted mine.

LXXX.

If any vague desire should rise,
    That holy Death ere Arthur died
    Had moved me kindly from his
        side,
And dropt the dust on tearless eyes ;

Then fancy shapes, as fancy can,
    The grief my loss in him had
        wrought,
    A grief as deep as life or thought,
But stay'd in peace with God and man.

I make a picture in the brain ;
    I hear the sentence that he speaks;
    He bears the burthen of the weeks
But turns his burthen into gain.

His credit thus shall set me free;
    And, influence-rich to soothe and
        save,
    Unused example from the grave
Reach out dead hands to comfort me.

LXXXI.

Could I have said while he was here,
    " My love shall now no further
        range ;
    There cannot come a mellower
        change,
For now is love mature in ear."

Love, then, had hope of richer store :
    What end is here to my com-
        plaint ?
    This haunting whisper makes me
        faint,
" More years had made me love thee
        more."

But Death returns an answer sweet :
    " My sudden frost was sudden
        gain,
    And gave all ripeness to the grain,
It might have drawn from after-heat."

LXXXII.

I wage not any feud with Death
    For changes wrought on form and
        face ;
    No lower life that earth's embrace
May breed with him, can fright my
    faith.

Eternal process moving on,
    From state to state the **spirit**
        walks ;

And these are but the shatter'd
 stalks,
Or ruin'd chrysalis of one.

Nor blame I Death, because he bare
 The use of virtue out of earth :
  I know transplanted human worth
Will bloom to profit, otherwhere.

For this alone on Death I wreak
 The wrath that garners in my
  heart;
 He put our lives so far apart
We cannot hear each other speak.

LXXXIII.

Dip down upon the northern shore,
 O sweet new-year delaying long ;
  Thou doest expectant nature
  wrong ;
Delaying long, delay no more.

What stays thee from the clouded
 noons,
 Thy sweetness from its proper
  place ?
 Can trouble live with April days,
Or sadness in the summer moons ?

Bring orchis, bring the foxglove spire,
 The little speedwell's darling blue,
  Deep tulips dash'd with fiery dew,
Laburnums, dropping-wells of fire.

O thou, new-year, delaying long,
 Delayest the sorrow in my blood,
  That longs to burst a frozen bud
And flood a fresher throat with song.

LXXXIV.

When I contemplate all alone
 The life that had been thine below,
  And fix my thoughts on all the
  glow
To which thy crescent would have
 grown ;

I see thee sitting crown'd with good,
 A central warmth diffusing bliss
  In glance and smile, and clasp
  and kiss,
On all the branches of thy blood ;

Thy blood, my friend, and partly mine;
 For now the day was drawing on,
  When thou should'st link thy life
  with one
Of mine own house, and boys of thine

Had babbled "Uncle" on my knee :
 But that remorseless iron hour
  Made cypress of her orange flower,
Despair of Hope, and earth of thee.

I seem to meet their least desire,
 To clap their cheeks, to call them
  mine.
 I see their unborn faces shine
Beside the never-lighted fire.

I see myself an honor'd guest,
 Thy partner in the flowery walk
  Of letters, genial table-talk,
Or deep dispute, and graceful jest ;

While now thy prosperous labor fills
 The lips of men with honest praise,
  And sun by sun the happy days
Descend below the golden hills

With promise of a morn as fair ;
 And all the train of bounteous
  hours
 Conduct by paths of growing
  powers,
To reverence and the silver hair ;

Till slowly worn her earthly robe,
 Her lavish mission richly
  wrought,
 Leaving great legacies of thought,
Thy spirit should fail from off the
 globe ;

What time mine own might also flee,
 As link'd with thine in love and
  fate,
 And, hovering o'er the dolorous
  strait
To the other shore, involved in thee,

Arrive at last the blessed goal,
 And He that died in Holy Land
  Would reach us out the shining
  hand,
And take us as a single soul.

What reed was that on which I leant?
    Ah, backward fancy, wherefore
      wake
    The old bitterness again, and
      break
The low beginnings of content.

LXXXV.

This truth came borne with bier and
      pall,
    I felt it, when I sorrow'd most,
    'Tis better to have loved and lost,
Than never to have loved at all ——

O true in word, and tried in deed,
    Demanding, so to bring relief
    To this which is our common
      grief,
What kind of life is that I lead;

And whether trust in things above
    Be dimm'd of sorrow, or sustain'd;
    And whether love for him have
      drain'd
My capabilities of love;

Your words have virtue such as draws
    A faithful answer from the
      breast,
    Thro' light reproaches, half ex-
      prest,
And loyal unto kindly laws.

My blood an even tenor kept,
    Till on mine ear this message
      falls,
    That in Vienna's fatal walls
God's finger touch'd him, and he slept.

The great Intelligences fair
    That range above our mortal
      state,
    In circle round the blessed gate,
Received and gave him welcome
      there;

And led him thro' the blissful climes,
    And show'd him in the fountain
      fresh
    All knowledge that the sons of
      flesh
Shall gather in the cycled times.

But I remain'd, whose hopes were dim,
    Whose life, whose thoughts were
      little worth,
    To wander on a darken'd earth,
Where all things round me breathed
      of him.

O friendship, equal-poised control,
    O heart, with kindliest motion
      warm,
    O sacred essence, other form,
O solemn ghost, O crowned soul!

Yet none could better know than I,
    How much of act at human hands
    The sense of human will demands
By which we dare to live or die.

Whatever way my days decline,
    I felt and feel, tho' left alone,
    His being working in mine own,
The footsteps of his life in mine;

A life that all the Muses deck'd
    With gifts of grace, that might
      express
    All-comprehensive tenderness,
All-subtilizing intellect:

And so my passion hath not swerved
    To works of weakness, but I find
    An image comforting the mind,
And in my grief a strength reserved.

Likewise the imaginative woe,
    That loved to handle spiritual
      strife,
    Diffused the shock thro' all my
      life,
But in the present broke the blow.

My pulses therefore beat again
    For other friends that once I met,
    Nor can it suit me to forget
The mighty hopes that make us men.

I woo your love: I count it crime
    To mourn for any overmuch;
    I, the divided half of such
A friendship as had master'd Time;

Which masters Time indeed, and is
    Eternal, separate from fears:
      The all-assuming months and
        years
Can take no part away from this:

But Summer on the steaming floods,
    And Spring that swells the nar-
      row brooks,
    And Autumn, with a noise of
      rooks,
That gather in the waning woods,

And every pulse of wind and wave
    Recalls, in change of light or
      gloom,
    My old affection of the tomb,
And my prime passion in the grave:

My old affection of the tomb,
    A part of stillness, yearns to
      speak:
    "Arise, and get thee forth and
      seek
A friendship for the years to come.

"I watch thee from the quiet shore;
    Thy spirit up to mine can reach;
    But in dear words of human
      speech
We two communicate no more."

And I, "Can clouds of nature stain
    The starry clearness of the free?
    How is it? Canst thou feel for
      me
Some painless sympathy with pain?"

And lightly does the whisper fall;
    "'Tis hard for thee to fathom
      this;
    I triumph in conclusive bliss,
And that serene result of all."

So hold I commerce with the dead;
    Or so methinks the dead would
      say;
    Or so shall grief with symbols
      play
And pining life be fancy-fed.

Now looking to some settled end,
    That these things pass, and I shall
      prove
    A meeting somewhere, love with
      love,
I crave your pardon, O my friend;

If not so fresh, with love as true,
    I, clasping brother-hands, aver
    I could not, if I would, transfer
The whole I felt for him to you.

For which be they that hold apart
    The promise of the golden hours?
    First love, first friendship, equal
      powers,
That marry with the virgin heart.

Still mine, that cannot but deplore,
    That beats within a lonely place,
    That yet remembers his embrace,
But at his footstep leaps no more,

My heart, tho' widow'd, may not rest
    Quite in the love of what is gone,
    But seeks to beat in time with one
That warms another living breast.

Ah, take the imperfect gift I bring,
    Knowing the primrose yet is dear,
    The primrose of the later year,
As not unlike to that of Spring.

LXXXVI.

Sweet after showers, ambrosial air,
    That rollest from the gorgeous
      gloom
    Of evening over brake and bloom
And meadow, slowly breathing bare

The round of space, and rapt below
    Thro' all the dewy-tassell'd wood,
    And shadowing down the horned
      flood
In ripples, fan my brows and blow

The fever from my cheek, and sigh
    The full new life that feeds thy
      breath
    Throughout my frame, till Doubt
      and Death,
Ill brethren, let the fancy fly

From belt to belt of crimson seas
    On leagues of odor streaming far,
    To where in yonder orient star
A hundred spirits whisper " Peace."

LXXXVII.

I past beside the reverend walls
    In which of old I wore the gown;
    I roved at random thro' the town,
And saw the tumult of the halls ;

And heard once more in college fanes
    The storm their high-built organs
      make,
    And thunder-music, rolling, shake
The prophet blazon'd on the panes ;

And caught once more the distant
    shout,
    The measured pulse of racing
      oars
    Among the willows ; paced the
      shores
And many a bridge, and all about

The same gray flats again, and felt
    The same, but not the same ; and
      last
    Up that long walk of limes I past
To see the rooms in which he dwelt.

Another name was on the door :
    I linger'd ; all within was noise
    Of songs, and clapping hands,
      and boys
That crash'd the glass and beat the
    floor ;

Where once we held debate, a band
    Of youthful friends, on mind and
      art,
    And labor, and the changing mart,
And all the framework of the land ;

When one would aim an arrow fair,
    But send it slackly from the
      string ;
    And one would pierce an outer
      ring,
And one an inner, here and there ;

And last the master-bowman, he,
    Would cleave the mark. A wil-
      ling ear
    We lent him. Who, but hung to
      hear
The rapt oration flowing free

From point to point, with power and
    grace
    And music in the bounds of law,
    To those conclusions when we
      saw
The God within him light his face,

And seem to lift the form, and glow
    In azure orbits heavenly-wise ;
    And over those ethereal eyes
The bar of Michael Angelo.

LXXXVIII.

Wild bird, whose warble, liquid sweet,
    Rings Eden thro' the budded
      quicks,
    O tell me where the senses mix,
O tell me where the passions meet,

Whence radiate · fierce extremes em-
    ploy
    Thy spirits in the darkening leaf,
    And in the midmost heart of
      grief
Thy passion clasps a secret joy .

And I — my harp would prelude
    woe —
    I cannot all command the strings ;
    The glory of the sum of things
Will flash along the chords and go.

LXXXIX.

Witch-elms that counterchange the
    floor
    Of this flat lawn with dusk and
      bright ;
    And thou, with all thy breadth
      and height
Of foliage, towering sycamore ;

How often, hither wandering down,
    My Arthur found your shadows
      fair,

And shook to all the liberal air
The dust and din and steam of town:

He brought an eye for all he saw;
    He mixt in all our simple sports;
    They pleased him, fresh from
        brawling courts
And dusty purlieus of the law.

O joy to him in this retreat,
    Immantled in ambrosial dark,
    To drink the cooler air, and mark
The landscape winking thro' the heat:

O sound to rout the brood of cares,
    The sweep of scythe in morning
        dew,
    The gust that round the garden
        flew,
And tumbled half the mellowing
    pears!

O bliss, when all in circle drawn
    About him, heart and ear were fed
    To hear him, as he lay and read
The Tuscan poets on the lawn:

Or in the all-golden afternoon
    A guest, or happy sister, sung,
    Or here she brought the harp and
        flung
A ballad to the brightening moon:

Nor less it pleased in livelier moods,
    Beyond the bounding hill to stray,
    And break the lifelong summer
        day
With banquet in the distant woods;

Whereat we glanced from theme to
    theme,
    Discuss'd the books to love or
        hate,
    Or touch'd the changes of the
        state,
Or threaded some Socratic dream;

But if I praised the busy town,
    He loved to rail against it still,
    For "ground in yonder social
        mill
We rub each other's angles down,

"And merge" he said "in form and
    gloss
    The picturesque of man and
        man."
    We talk'd: the stream beneath
        us ran,
The wine-flask lying couch'd in moss,

Or cool'd within the glooming wave;
    And last, returning from afar,
    Before the crimson-circled star
Had fall'n into her father's grave,

And brushing ankle-deep in flowers,
    We heard behind the woodbine
        veil
    The milk that bubbled in the pail,
And buzzings of the honied hours.

xc.

He tasted love with half his mind,
    Nor ever drank the inviolate
        spring
    Where nighest heaven, who first
        could fling
This bitter seed among mankind;

That could the dead, whose dying
    eyes
    Were closed with wail, resume
        their life,
    They would but find in child and
        wife
An iron welcome when they rise:

'Twas well, indeed, when warm with
    wine,
    To pledge them with a kindly
        tear,
    To talk them o'er, to wish them
        here,
To count their memories half divine;

But if they came who past away,
    Behold their brides in other
        hands;
    The hard heir strides about their
        lands,
And will not yield them for a day.

Yea, tho' their sons were none of
    these,

Not less the yet-loved sire would
    make
Confusion worse than death, and
    shake
The pillars of domestic peace.

Ah dear, but come thou back to me:
    Whatever change the years have
        wrought,
    I find not yet one lonely thought
That cries against my wish for thee.

XCI.

When rosy plumelets tuft the larch,
    And rarely pipes the mounted
        thrush;
    Or underneath the barren bush
Flits by the sea-blue bird of March;

Come, wear the form by which I
    know
    Thy spirit in time among thy
        peers;
    The hope of unaccomplish'd years
Be large and lucid round thy brow.

When summer's hourly-mellowing
    change
    May breathe, with many roses
        sweet,
    Upon the thousand waves of
        wheat,
That ripple round the lonely grange;

Come: not in watches of the night,
    But where the sunbeam broodeth
        warm,
    Come, beauteous in thine after
        form,
And like a finer light in light.

XCII.

If any vision should reveal
    Thy likeness, I might count it
        vain
    As but the canker of the brain;
Yea, tho' it spake and made appeal

To chances where our lots were cast
    Together in the days behind,
    I might but say, I hear a wind
Of memory murmuring the past.

Yea, tho' it spake and bared to view
    A fact within the coming year;
    And tho' the months, revolving
        near,
Should prove the phantom-warning
    true,

They might not seem thy prophecies,
    But spiritual presentiments,
    And such refraction of events
As often rises ere they rise.

XCIII.

I shall not see thee. Dare I say
    No spirit ever brake the band
    That stays him from the native
        land
Where first he walk'd when claspt in
    clay?

No visual shade of some one lost,
    But he, the Spirit himself, may
        come
    Where all the nerve of sense is
        numb;
Spirit to Spirit, Ghost to Ghost.

O, therefore from thy sightless range
    With gods in unconjectured bliss,
    O, from the distance of the abyss
Of tenfold-complicated change,

Descend, and touch, and enter; hear
    The wish too strong for words to
        name;
    That in this blindness of the
        frame
My Ghost may feel that thine is near.

XCIV.

How pure at heart and sound in head,
    With what divine affections bold
    Should be the man whose thought
        would hold
An hour's communion with the dead.

In vain shalt thou, or any, call
    The spirits from their golden day,
    Except, like them, thou too canst
        say,
My spirit is at peace with all.

They haunt the silence of the breast,
 Imaginations calm and fair,
 The memory like a cloudless air,
The conscience as a sea at rest:

But when the heart is full of din,
 And doubt beside the portal waits,
 They can but listen at the gates,
And hear the household jar within.

XCV.

By night we linger'd on the lawn,
 For underfoot the herb was dry;
 And genial warmth; and o'er the sky
The silvery haze of summer drawn;

And calm that let the tapers burn
 Unwavering: not a cricket chirr'd:
 The brook alone far-off was heard,
And on the board the fluttering urn:

And bats went round in fragrant skies,
 And wheel'd or lit the filmy shapes
 That haunt the dusk, with ermine capes
And woolly breasts and beaded eyes;

While now we sang old songs that peal'd
 From knoll to knoll, where, couch'd at ease,
 The white kine glimmer'd, and the trees
Laid their dark arms about the field.

But when those others, one by one,
 Withdrew themselves from me and night,
 And in the house light after light
Went out, and I was all alone,

A hunger seized my heart; I read
 Of that glad year which once had been,
 In those fall'n leaves which kept their green,
The noble letters of the dead:

And strangely on the silence broke
 The silent-speaking words, and strange
 Was love's dumb cry defying change
To test his worth; and strangely spoke

The faith, the vigor, bold to dwell
 On doubts that drive the coward back,
 And keen thro' wordy snares to track
Suggestion to her inmost cell.

So word by word, and line by line,
 The dead man touch'd me from the past,
 And all at once it seem'd at last
The living soul was flash'd on mine,

And mine in this was wound, and whirl'd
 About empyreal heights of thought,
 And came on that which is, and caught
The deep pulsations of the world,

Æonian music measuring out
 The steps of Time — the shocks of Chance —
 The blows of Death. At length my trance
Was cancell'd, stricken thro' with doubt.

Vague words! but ah, how hard to frame
 In matter-moulded forms of speech,
 Or ev'n for intellect to reach
Thro' memory that which I became:

Till now the doubtful dusk reveal'd
 The knolls once more where, couch'd at ease,
 The white kine glimmer'd, and the trees
Laid their dark arms about the field:

And suck'd from out the distant gloom
 A breeze began to tremble o'er
 The large leaves of the sycamore,
And fluctuate all the still perfume,

And gathering freshlier overhead,
    Rock'd the full-foliaged elms,
      and swung
    The heavy-folded rose, and flung
The lilies to and fro, and said

"The dawn, the dawn," and died
    away ;
    And East and West, without a
      breath,
    Mixt their dim lights, like life
      and death,
To broaden into boundless day.

XCVI.

You say, but with no touch of scorn,
    Sweet-hearted, you, whose light-
     blue eyes
    Are tender over drowning flies,
You tell me, doubt is Devil-born.

I know not : one indeed I knew
    In many a subtle question versed,
    Who touch'd a jarring lyre at first,
But ever strove to make it true :

Perplext in faith, but pure in deeds,
    At last he beat his music out.
    There lives more faith in honest
     doubt,
Believe me, than in half the creeds.

He fought his doubts and gather'd
    strength,
    He would not make his judgment
     blind,
    He faced the spectres of the mind
And laid them : thus he came at length

To find a stronger faith his own ;
    And Power was with him in the
     night,
    Which makes the darkness and
     the light,
And dwells not in the light alone,

But in the darkness and the cloud,
    As over Sinaï's peaks of old,
    While Israel made their gods of
     gold,
Altho' the trumpet blew so loud.

XCVII.

My love has talk'd with rocks and
    trees ;
    He finds on misty mountain-
     ground
    His own vast shadow glory-
     crown'd ;
He sees himself in all he sees.

Two partners of a married life —
    I look'd on these and thought of
     thee
    In vastness and in mystery,
And of my spirit as of a wife.

These two — they dwelt with eye on
    eye,
    Their hearts of old have beat in
     tune,
    Their meetings made December
     June,
Their every parting was to die.

Their love has never past away ;
    The days she never can forget
    Are earnest that he loves her yet,
Whate'er the faithless people say.

Her life is lone, he sits apart,
    He loves her yet, she will not weep,
    Tho' rapt in matters dark and
     deep
He seems to slight her simple heart.

He thrids the labyrinth of the mind,
    He reads the secret of the star,
    He seems so near and yet so far,
He looks so cold : she thinks him kind.

She keeps the gift of years before,
    A wither'd violet is her bliss :
    She knows not what his great-
     ness is,
For that, for all, she loves him more.

For him she plays, to him she sings
    Of early faith and plighted vows ;
    She knows but matters of the
     house,
And he, he knows a thousand things

Her faith is fixt and cannot move,
 She darkly feels him great and
  wise,
 She dwells on him with faithful
  eyes,
"I cannot understand : I love."

XCVIII.

You leave us : you will see the Rhine,
 And those fair hills I sail'd below,
 When I was there with him ; and
  go
By summer belts of wheat and vine

To where he breathed his latest breath,
 That City. All her splendor
  seems
 No livelier than the wisp that
  gleams
On Lethe in the eyes of Death.

Let her great Danube rolling fair
 Enwind her isles, unmark'd of
  me :
 I have not seen, I will not see
Vienna ; rather dream that there,

A treble darkness, Evil haunts
 The birth, the bridal ; friend from
  friend
 Is oftener parted, fathers bend
Above more graves, a thousand wants

Gnarr at the heels of men, and prey
 By each cold hearth, and sad-
  ness flings
 Her shadow on the blaze of
  kings :
And yet myself have heard him say,

That not in any mother town
 With statelier progress to and
  fro
 The double tides of chariots flow
By park and suburb under brown

Of lustier leaves ; nor more content,
 He told me, lives in any crowd,
 When all is gay with lamps, and
  loud
With sport and song, in booth and
  tent,

Imperial halls, or open plain ;
 And wheels the circled dance, and
  breaks
 The rocket molten into flakes
Of crimson or in emerald rain.

XCIX.

Risest thou thus, dim dawn, again,
 So loud with voices of the birds,
 So thick with lowings of the
  herds,
Day, when I lost the flower of men ;

Who tremblest thro' thy darkling red
 On yon swoll'n brook that bubbles
  fast
 By meadows breathing of the
  past,
And woodlands holy to the dead ;

Who murmurest in the foliaged eaves
 A song that slights the coming
  care,
 And Autumn laying here and
  there
A fiery finger on the leaves ;

Who wakenest with thy balmy breath
 To myriads on the genial earth,
 Memories of bridal, or of birth,
And unto myriads more, of death.

O wheresoever those may be,
 Betwixt the slumber of the poles,
 To-day they count as kindred
  souls ;
They know me not, but mourn with
  me.

C.

I climb the hill : from end to end
 Of all the landscape underneath,
 I find no place that does not
  breathe
Some gracious memory of my friend ;

No gray old grange, or lonely fold,
 Or low morass and whispering
  reed,
 Or simple stile from mead to
  mead,
Or sheepwalk up the windy wold ;

Nor hoary knoll of ash and haw
  That hears the latest linnet trill,
  Nor quarry trench'd along the
    hill
And haunted by the wrangling daw;

Nor runlet tinkling from the rock;
  Nor pastoral rivulet that swerves
  To left and right thro' meadowy
    curves,
That feed the mothers of the flock;

But each has pleased a kindred eye,
  And each reflects a kindlier day;
  And, leaving these, to pass away,
I think once more he seems to die.

CI.

Unwatch'd, the garden bough shall
    sway,
  The tender blossom flutter down,
  Unloved, that beech will gather
    brown,
This maple burn itself away;

Unloved, the sun-flower, shining fair,
  Ray round with flames her disk
    of seed,
  And many a rose-carnation feed
With summer spice the humming air;

Unloved, by many a sandy bar,
  The brook shall babble down the
    plain,
  At noon or when the lesser wain
Is twisting round the polar star;

Uncared for, gird the windy grove,
  And flood the haunts of hern and
    crake;
  Or into silver arrows break
The sailing moon in creek and cove;

Till from the garden and the wild
  A fresh association blow,
  And year by year the landscape
    grow
Familiar to the stranger's child;

As year by year the laborer tills
  His wonted glebe, or lops the
    glades;

And year by year our memory
    fades
From all the circle of the hills.

CII.

We leave the well-beloved place
  Where first we gazed upon the
    sky;
  The roofs, that heard our earliest
    cry,
Will shelter one of stranger race.

We go, but ere we go from home,
  As down the garden-walks т
    move,
  Two spirits of a diverse love
Contend for loving masterdom.

One whispers, "Here thy boyhood
    sung
  Long since its matin song, and
    heard
  The low love-language of the bird
In native hazels tassel-hung."

The other answers, "Yea, but here
  Thy feet have stray'd in after
    hours
  With thy lost friend among the
    bowers,
And this hath made them trebly
    dear."

These two have striven half the day,
  And each prefers his separate
    claim,
  Poor rivals in a losing game,
That will not yield each other way.

I turn to go: my feet are set
  To leave the pleasant fields and
    farms;
  They mix in one another's arms
To one pure image of regret.

CIII.

On that last night before we went
  From out the doors where ı was
    bred,
  I dream'd a vision of the dead,
Which left my after-morn content.

Methought I dwelt within a hall,
    And maidens with me: distant
        hills
    From hidden summits fed with
        rills
A river sliding by the wall.

The hall with harp and carol rang.
    They sang of what is wise and
        good
    And graceful. In the centre
        stood
A statue veil'd, to which they sang;

And which, tho' veil'd, was known to
      me,
    The shape of him I loved, and
        love
    For ever: then flew in a dove
And brought a summons from the
      sea:

And when they learnt that I must go
    They wept and wail'd, but led the
        way
    To where a little shallop lay
At anchor in the flood below;

And on by many a level mead,
    And shadowing bluff that made
        the banks,
    We glided winding under ranks
Of iris, and the golden reed;

And still as vaster grew the shore
    And roll'd the floods in grander
        space,
    The maidens gather'd strength
        and grace
And presence, lordlier than before;

And I myself, who sat apart
    And watch'd them, wax'd in every
        limb;
    I felt the thews of Anakim,
The pulses of a Titan's heart;

As one would sing the death of war,
    And one would chant the history
        Of that great race, which is to
        be,
And one the shaping of a star;

Until the forward-creeping tides
    Began to foam, and we to draw
    From deep to deep, to where we
        saw
A great ship lift her shining sides.

The man we loved was there on deck,
    But thrice as large as man he bent
    To greet us. Up the side I went,
And fell in silence on his neck:

Whereat those maidens with one mind
    Bewail'd their lot; I did them
        wrong:
    " We served thee here," they said,
      " so long,
And wilt thou leave us now behind?"

So rapt I was, they could not win
    An answer from my lips, but he
    Replying, " Enter likewise ye
And go with us:" they enter'd in.

And while the wind began to sweep
    A music out of sheet and shroud,
    We steer'd her toward a crimson
        cloud
That landlike slept along the deep.

CIV.

The time draws near the birth of
      Christ;
    The moon is hid; the night is still;
    A single church below the hill
Is pealing, folded in the mist.

A single peal of bells below,
    That wakens at this hour of rest
    A single murmur in the breast,
That these are not the bells I know.

Like strangers' voices here they sound,
    In lands where not a memory
        strays,
    Nor landmark breathes of other
        days,
But all is new unhallow'd ground.

CV.

To-night ungather'd let us leave
    This laurel, let this holly stand:
    We live within the stranger's land,
And strangely falls our Christmas-eve.

Our father's dust is left alone
　　And silent under other snows :
　　There in due time the woodbine
　　　　blows,
The violet comes, but we are gone.

No more shall wayward grief abuse
　　The genial hour with mask and
　　　　mime ;
　　For change of place, like growth
　　　　of time,
Has broke the bond of dying use.

Let cares that petty shadows cast,
　　By which our lives are chiefly
　　　　proved,
　　A little spare the night I loved,
And hold it solemn to the past.

But let no footstep beat the floor,
　　Nor bowl of wassail mantle warm ;
　　For who would keep an ancient
　　　　form
Thro' which the spirit breathes no
　　　　more ?

Be neither song, nor game, nor feast ;
　　Nor harp be touch'd, nor flute be
　　　　blown ;
　　No dance, no motion, save alone
What lightens in the lucid east

Of rising worlds by yonder wood.
　　Long sleeps the summer in the
　　　　seed ;
　　Run out your measured arcs, and
　　　　lead
The closing cycle rich in good.

CVI.

Ring out, wild bells, to the wild sky,
　　The flying cloud, the frosty light :
　　The year is dying in the night ;
Ring out, wild bells, and let him die.

Ring out the old, ring in the new,
　　Ring, happy bells, across the
　　　　snow :
　　The year is going, let him go ;
Ring out the false, ring in the true.

Ring out the grief that saps the mind,
　　For those that here we see no
　　　　more ;
　　Ring out the feud of rich and
　　　　poor,
Ring in redress to all mankind.

Ring out a slowly dying cause,
　　And ancient forms of party strife ;
　　Ring in the nobler modes of life,
With sweeter manners, purer laws.

Ring out the want, the care, the sin,
　　The faithless coldness of the
　　　　times ;
　　Ring out, ring out my mournful
　　　　rhymes,
But ring the fuller minstrel in.

Ring out false pride in place and
　　　　blood,
　　The civic slander and the spite ;
　　Ring in the love of truth and right,
Ring in the common love of good.

Ring out old shapes of foul disease ;
　　Ring out the narrowing lust of
　　　　gold ;
　　Ring out the thousand wars of old,
Ring in the thousand years of peace.

Ring in the valiant man and free,
　　The larger heart, the kindlier
　　　　hand ;
　　Ring out the darkness of the land,
Ring in the Christ that is to be.

CVII.

It is the day when he was born,
　　A bitter day that early sank
　　Behind a purple-frosty bank
Of vapor, leaving night forlorn.

The time admits not flowers or leaves
　　To deck the banquet. Fiercely
　　　　flies
　　The blast of North and East, and
　　　　ice
Makes daggers at the sharpen'd eaves,

And bristles all the brakes and thorns
　　To yon hard crescent, as she hangs

Above the wood which grides and
    clangs
Its leafless ribs and iron horns

Together, in the drifts that pass
    To darken on the rolling brine
    That breaks the coast. But fetch
        the wine,
Arrange the board and brim the glass;

Bring in great logs and let them lie,
    To make a solid core of heat;
    Be cheerful-minded, talk and treat
Of all things ev'n as he were by;

We keep the day. With festal cheer,
    With books and music, surely we
    Will drink to him, whate'er he be,
And sing the songs he loved to hear.

CVIII.

I will not shut me from my kind,
    And, lest I stiffen into stone,
    I will not eat my heart alone,
Nor feed with sighs a passing wind:

What profit lies in barren faith,
    And vacant yearning, tho' with
        might
    To scale the heaven's highest
        height,
Or dive below the wells of Death?

What find I in the highest place,
    But mine own phantom chanting
        hymns?
    And on the depths of death there
        swims
The reflex of a human face.

I'll rather take what fruit may be
    Of sorrow under human skies:
    'Tis held that sorrow makes us
        wise,
Whatever wisdom sleep with thee.

CIX.

Heart-affluence in discursive talk
    From household fountains never
        dry;
    The critic clearness of an eye,
That saw thro' all the Muses' walk;

Seraphic intellect and force
    To seize and throw the doubts of
        man;
    Impassion'd logic, which outran
The hearer in its fiery course;

High nature amorous of the good,
    But touch'd with no ascetic
        gloom;
    And passion pure in snowy bloom
Thro' all the years of April blood;

A love of freedom rarely felt,
    Of freedom in her regal seat
    Of England; not the schoolboy
        heat,
The blind hysterics of the Celt;

And manhood fused with female grace
    In such a sort, the child would
        twine
    A trustful hand, unask'd, in thine,
And find his comfort in thy face;

All these have been, and thee mine
        eyes
    Have look'd on: if they look'd
        in vain,
    My shame is greater who remain,
Nor let thy wisdom make me wise.

CX.

Thy converse drew us with delight,
    The men of rathe and riper years:
    The feeble soul, a haunt of fears,
Forgot his weakness in thy sight.

On thee the loyal-hearted hung,
    The proud was half disarm'd of
        pride,
    Nor cared the serpent at thy side
To flicker with his double tongue.

The stern were mild when thou wert by,
    The flippant put himself to school
    And heard thee, and the brazen
        fool
Was soften'd, and he knew not why;

While I, thy nearest, sat apart,
    And felt thy triumph was as mine:

And loved them more, that they
    were thine,
The graceful tact, the Christian art;

Nor mine the sweetness or the skill,
    But mine the love that will not
        tire,
    And, born of love, the vague
        desire
That spurs an imitative will.

CXI.

The churl in spirit, up or down
    Along the scale of ranks, thro' all,
    To him who grasps a golden ball,
By blood a king, at heart a clown;

The churl in spirit, howe'er he veil
    His want in forms for fashion's
        sake,
    Will let his coltish nature break
At seasons thro' the gilded pale:

For who can always act? but he,
    To whom a thousand memories
        call,
    Not being less but more than all
The gentleness he seem'd to be,

Best seem'd the thing he was, and
    join'd
    Each office of the social hour
    To noble manners, as the flower
And native growth of noble mind;

Nor ever narrowness or spite,
    Or villain fancy fleeting by,
    Drew in the expression of an eye,
Where God and Nature met in light;

And thus he bore without abuse
    The grand old name of gentleman,
    Defamed by every charlatan,
And soil'd with all ignoble use.

CXII.

High wisdom holds my wisdom less,
    That I, who gaze with temperate
        eyes
    On glorious insufficiencies,
Set light by narrower perfectness.

But thou, that fillest all the room
    Of all my love, art reason why
    I seem to cast a careless eye
On souls, the lesser lords of doom.

For what wert thou? some novel
    power
    Sprang up for ever at a touch,
    And hope could never hope too
        much,
In watching thee from hour to hour,

Large elements in order brought,
    And tracts of calm from tempest
        made,
    And world-wide fluctuation sway'd
In vassal tides that follow'd thought.

CXIII.

'Tis held that sorrow makes us wise;
    Yet how much wisdom sleeps
        with thee
    Which not alone had guided me,
But served the seasons that may rise;

For can I doubt, who knew thee keen
    In intellect, with force and skill
    To strive, to fashion, to fulfil —
I doubt not what thou wouldst have
        been:

A life in civic action warm,
    A soul on highest mission sent,
    A potent voice of Parliament,
A pillar steadfast in the storm,

Should licensed boldness gather force,
    Becoming, when the time has
        birth,
    A lever to uplift the earth
And roll it in another course,

With thousand shocks that come and
    go,
    With agonies, with energies,
    With overthrowings, and with
        cries,
And undulations to and fro.

CXIV.

Who loves not Knowledge? Who
    shall rail

Against her beauty ?　May she
　　mix
　　With men and prosper !　Who
　　shall fix
Her pillars ?　Let her work prevail.

But on her forehead sits a fire :
　　She sets her forward countenance
　　And leaps into the future chance,
Submitting all things to desire.

Half-grown as yet, a child, and vain —
　　She cannot fight the fear of death.
　　What is she, cut from love and
　　faith,
But some wild Pallas from the brain

Of Demons ?　fiery-hot to burst
　　All barriers in her onward race
　　For power.　Let her know her
　　place ;
She is the second, not the first.

A higher hand must make her mild,
　　If all be not in vain ; and guide
　　Her footsteps, moving side by side
With wisdom, like the younger child :

For she is earthly of the mind,
　　But Wisdom heavenly of the soul.
　　O, friend, who camest to thy goal
So early, leaving me behind,

I would the great world grew like thee,
　　Who grewest not alone in power
　　And knowledge, but by year and
　　hour
In reverence and in charity.

CXV.

Now fades the last long streak of snow,
　　Now burgeons every maze of
　　quick
　　About the flowering squares, and
　　thick
By ashen roots the violets blow.

Now rings the woodland loud and long,
　　The distance takes a lovelier hue,
　　And drown'd in yonder living blue
The lark becomes a sightless song.

Now dance the lights on lawn and lea,
　　The flocks are whiter down the
　　vale,
　　And milkier every milky sail
On winding stream or distant sea ;

Where now the seamew pipes, or dives
　　In yonder greening gleam, and fly
　　The happy birds, that change
　　their sky
To build and brood ; that live their
　　lives

From land to land ; and in my breast
　　Spring wakens too ; and my re-
　　gret
　　Becomes an April violet,
And buds and blossoms like the rest.

CXVI.

Is it, then, regret for buried time
　　That keenlier in sweet April
　　wakes,
　　And meets the year, and gives
　　and takes
The colors of the crescent prime ?

Not all : the songs, the stirring air,
　　The life re-orient out of dust,
　　Cry thro' the sense to hearten
　　trust
In that which made the world so fair.

Not all regret : the face will shine
　　Upon me, while I muse alone ;
　　And that dear voice, I once have
　　known,
Still speak to me of me and mine :

Yet less of sorrow lives in me
　　For days of happy commune
　　dead ;
　　Less yearning for the friendship
　　fled,
Than some strong bond which is to be.

CXVII.

O days and hours, your work is this
　　To hold me from my proper place,
　　A little while from his embrace,
For fuller gain of after bliss :

That out of distance might ensue
   Desire of nearness doubly sweet;
   And unto meeting when we meet,
Delight a hundredfold accrue,

For every grain of sand that runs,
   And every span of shade that
      steals,
   And every kiss of toothed wheels,
And all the courses of the suns.

CXVIII.

Contemplate all this work of Time,
   The giant laboring in his youth;
   Nor dream of human love and
      truth,
As dying Nature's earth and lime;

But trust that those we call the dead
   Are breathers of an ampler day
   For ever nobler ends. They say,
The solid earth whereon we tread

In tracts of fluent heat began,
   And grew to seeming-random
      forms,
   The seeming prey of cyclic
      storms,
Till at the last arose the man;

Who throve and branch'd from clime
    to clime,
   The herald of a higher race,
   And of himself in higher place,
If so he type this work of time

Within himself, from more to more;
   Or, crown'd with attributes of woe
   Like glories, move his course,
      and show
That life is not as idle ore,

But iron dug from central gloom,
   And heated hot with burning
      fears,
   And dipt in baths of hissing tears,
And batter'd with the shocks of doom

To shape and use. Arise and fly
   The reeling Faun, the sensual
      feast;

Move upward, working out the
    beast,
And let the ape and tiger die.

CXIX.

Doors, where my heart was used to
    beat
   So quickly, not as one that weeps
   I come once more; the city sleeps;
I smell the meadow in the street;

I hear a chirp of birds; I see
   Betwixt the black fronts long-
      withdrawn
   A light-blue lane of early dawn,
And think of early days and thee,

And bless thee, for thy lips are bland,
   And bright the friendship of
      thine eye;
   And in my thoughts with scarce
      a sigh
I take the pressure of thine hand.

CXX.

I trust I have not wasted breath:
   I think we are not wholly brain,
   Magnetic mockeries; not in vain,
Like Paul with beasts, I fought with
    Death;

Not only cunning casts in clay:
   Let Science prove we are, and
      then
   What matters Science unto men,
At least to me? I would not stay.

Let him, the wiser man who springs
   Hereafter, up from childhood
      shape
   His action like the greater ape,
But I was *born* to other things.

CXXI.

Sad Hesper o'er the buried sun
   And ready, thou, to die with him.
   Thou watchest all things ever
      dim
And dimmer, and a glory done:

The team is loosen'd from the wain,
    The boat is drawn upon the shore;
    Thou listenest to the closing door,
And life is darken'd in the brain.

Bright Phosphor, fresher for the night,
    By thee the world's great work is
      heard
    Beginning, and the wakeful bird;
Behind thee comes the greater light:

The market boat is on the stream,
    And voices hail it from the
      brink;
    Thou hear'st the village hammer
      clink,
And see'st the moving of the team.

Sweet Hesper-Phosphor, double name
    For what is one, the first, the last,
    Thou, like my present and my
      past,
Thy place is changed; thou art the
    same.

CXXII.

Oh, wast thou with me, dearest, then,
    While I rose up against my doom,
    And yearn'd to burst the folded
      gloom,
To bare the eternal Heavens again,

To feel once more, in placid awe,
    The strong imagination roll
    A sphere of stars about my soul,
In all her motion one with law;

If thou wert with me, and the grave
    Divide us not, be with me now,
    And enter in at breast and brow,
Till all my blood, a fuller wave,

Be quicken'd with a livelier breath,
    And like an inconsiderate boy,
    As in the former flash of joy,
I slip the thoughts of life and death;

And all the breeze of Fancy blows,
    And every dew-drop paints a bow,
    The wizard lightnings deeply
      glow,
And every thought breaks out a rose.

CXXIII.

There rolls the deep where grew the
    tree.
    O earth, what changes hast thou
      seen!
    There where the long street roars,
      hath been
The stillness of the central sea.

The hills are shadows, and they flow
    From form to form, and nothing
      stands;
    They melt like mist, the solid lands,
Like clouds they shape themselves
    and go.

But in my spirit will I dwell,
    And dream my dream, and hold
      it true;
    For tho' my lips may breathe adieu,
I cannot think the thing farewell.

CXXIV.

That which we dare invoke to bless;
    Our dearest faith; our ghastliest
      doubt;
    He, They, One, All; within, with-
      out;
The Power in darkness whom we
    guess;

I found Him not in world or sun,
    Or eagle's wing, or insect's eye;
    Nor thro' the questions men may
      try,
The petty cobwebs we have spun:

If e'er when faith had fall'n asleep,
    I heard a voice "believe no more"
    And heard an ever-breaking shore
That tumbled in the Godless deep;

A warmth within the breast would
    melt
    The freezing reason's colder part,
    And like a man in wrath the
      heart
Stood up and answer'd "I have felt."

No, like a child in doubt and fear:
    But that blind clamor made me
      wise;

Then was I as a child that cries,
But, crying, knows his father near;

And what I am beheld again
    What is, and no man understands;
    And out of darkness came the
        hands
That reach thro' nature, moulding
    men.

CXXXV.

Whatever I have said or sung,
    Some bitter notes my harp would
        give,
    Yea, tho' there often seem'd to
        live
A contradiction on the tongue,

Yet Hope had never lost her youth;
    She did but look through dimmer
        eyes;
    Or Love but play'd with gracious
        lies,
Because he felt so fix'd in truth:

And if the song were full of care,
    He breathed the spirit of the song;
    And if the words were sweet and
        strong
He set his royal signet there;

Abiding with me till I sail
    To seek thee on the mystic deeps,
    And this electric force, that keeps
A thousand pulses dancing, fail.

CXXXVI.

Love is and was my Lord and King,
    And in his presence I attend
    To hear the tidings of my friend,
Which every hour his couriers bring.

Love is and was my King and Lord,
    And will be, tho' as yet I keep
    Within his court on earth, and
        sleep
Encompass'd by his faithful guard,

And hear at times a sentinel
    Who moves about from place to
        place,

And whispers to the worlds of
        space,
In the deep night, that all is well.

CXXXVII.

And all is well, tho' faith and form
    Be sunder'd in the night of fear;
    Well roars the storm to those that
        hear
A deeper voice across the storm,

Proclaiming social truth shall spread,
    And justice, ev'n tho' thrice again
    The red fool-fury of the Seine
Should pile her barricades with dead.

But ill for him that wears a crown,
    And him, the lazar, in his rags:
    They' tremble, the sustaining
        crags;
The spires of ice are toppled down,

And molten up, and roar in flood;
    The fortress crashes from on high,
    The brute earth lightens to the
        sky,
And the great Æon sinks in blood,

And compass'd by the fires of Hell;
    While thou, dear spirit, happy
        star,
    O'erlook'st the tumult from afar,
And smilest, knowing all is well.

CXXXVIII.

The love that rose on stronger wings,
    Unpalsied when he met with
        Death,
    Is comrade of the lesser faith
That sees the course of human things.

No doubt vast eddies in the flood
    Of onward time shall yet be made,
    And throned races may degrade;
Yet O ye mysteries of good,

Wild Hours that fly with Hope and
        Fear,
    If all your office had to do
    With old results that look like
        new;
If this were all your mission here,

To draw, to sheathe a useless sword,
　　To fool the crowd with glorious
　　　　lies,
　　　　To cleave a creed in sects and
　　　　　cries,
To change the bearing of a word,

To shift an arbitrary power,
　　To cramp the student at his desk,
　　To make old bareness picturesque
And tuft with grass a feudal tower;

Why then my scorn might well descend
　　On you and yours.　I see in part
　　That all, as in some piece of art,
Is toil coöperant to an end.

CXXIX.

Dear friend, far off, my lost desire,
　　So far, so near in woe and weal;
　　O loved the most, when most I feel
There is a lower and a higher;

Known and unknown; human, divine;
　　Sweet human hand and lips and
　　　eye;
　　Dear heavenly friend that canst
　　　not die,
Mine, mine, for ever, ever mine;

Strange friend, past, present, and to be;
　　Loved deeplier, darklier under-
　　　stood;
　　Behold, I dream a dream of good,
And mingle all the world with thee.

CXXX.

Thy voice is on the rolling air;
　　I hear thee where the waters run;
　　Thou standest in the rising sun,
And in the setting thou art fair.

What art thou then?　I cannot guess;
　　But tho' I seem in star and flower
　　To feel thee some diffusive power,
I do not therefore love thee less:

My love involves the love before;
　　My love is vaster passion now;
　　Tho' mix'd with God and Nature
　　　thou,
I seem to love thee more and more.

Far off thou art, but ever nigh,
　　I have thee still, and I rejoice;
　　I prosper, circled with thy voice;
I shall not lose thee tho' I die.

CXXXI.

O living will that shalt endure
　　When all that seems shall suffer
　　　shock,
　　Rise in the spiritual rock,
Flow thro' our deeds and make them
　　pure,

That we may lift from out of dust
　　A voice as unto him that hears,
　　A cry above the conquer'd years
To one that with us works, and trust,

With faith that comes of self-control,
　　The truths that never can be
　　　proved
　　Until we close with all we loved,
And all we flow from, soul in soul.

———

O true and tried, so well and long,
　　Demand not thou a marriage lay;
　　In that it is thy marriage day
Is music more than any song.

Nor have I felt so much of bliss
　　Since first he told me that he
　　　loved
　　A daughter of our house; nor
　　　proved
Since that dark day a day like this;

Tho' I since then have number'd o'er
　　Some thrice three years: they went
　　　and came,
　　Remade the blood and changed
　　　the fame,
And yet is love not less, but more;

No longer caring to embalm
　　In dying songs a dead regret,
　　But like a statue solid-set,
And moulded in colossal calm.

Regret is dead, but love is more
　　Than in the summers that are
　　　flown,

For I myself with these have
    grown
To something greater than before;

Which makes appear the songs I
    made
    As echoes out of weaker times,
    As half but idle brawling rhymes,
The sport of random sun and shade.

But where is she, the bridal flower,
    That must be made a wife ere
        noon ?
    She enters, glowing like the moon
Of Eden on its bridal bower:

On me she bends her blissful eyes
    And then on thee; they meet thy
        look
    And brighten like the star that
        shook
Betwixt the palms of paradise.

O when her life was yet in bud,
    He too foretold the perfect rose.
    For thee she grew, for thee she
        grows
For ever, and as fair as good.

And thou art worthy; full of power;
    As gentle; liberal-minded, great.
    Consistent; wearing all that
        weight
Of learning lightly like a flower.

But now set out: the noon is near,
    And I must give away the bride;
    She fears not, or with thee
        beside
And me behind her, will not fear.

For I that danced her on my knee,
    That watch'd her on her nurse's
        arm,
    That shielded all her life from
        harm
At last must part with her to thee;

Now waiting to be made a wife,
    Her feet, my darling, on the dead;
    Their pensive tablets round her
        head,
And the most living words of life

Breathed in her ear. The ring is on,
    The "wilt thou" answer'd, and
        again
    The "wilt thou" ask'd, till out of
        twain
Her sweet "I will" has made you one.

Now sign your names, which shall be
    read,
    Mute symbols of a joyful morn,
    By village eyes as yet unborn;
The names are sign'd, and overhead

Begins the clash and clang that tells
    The joy to every wandering
        breeze;
    The blind wall rocks, and on the
        trees
The dead leaf trembles to the bells.

O happy hour, and happier hours
    Await them. Many a merry face
    Salutes them — maidens of the
        place,
That pelt us in the porch with flowers.

O happy hour, behold the bride
    With him to whom her hand I
        gave.
    They leave the porch, they pass
        the grave
That has to-day its sunny side.

To-day the grave is bright for me,
    For them the light of life in-
        creased,
    Who stay to share the morning
        feast,
Who rest to-night beside the sea.

Let all my genial spirits advance
    To meet and greet a whiter sun;
    My drooping memory will not
        shun
The foaming grape of eastern France.

It circles round, and fancy plays,
    And hearts are warm'd and faces
        bloom,
    As drinking health to bride and
        groom
We wish them store of happy days.

Nor count me all to blame if I
    Conjecture of a stiller guest,
    Perchance, perchance, among the
      rest,
And, tho' in silence, wishing joy.

But they must go, the time draws on,
    And those white-favor'd horses
      wait;
    They rise, but linger; it is late;
Farewell, we kiss, and they are gone.

A shade falls on us like the dark
    From little cloudlets on the grass,
    But sweeps away as out we pass
To range the woods, to roam the park,

Discussing how their courtship grew,
    And talk of others that are wed,
    And how she look'd, and what he
      said,
And back we come at fall of dew.

Again the feast, the speech, the glee,
    The shade of passing thought,
      the wealth
    Of words and wit, the double
      health,
The crowning cup, the three-times-
      three,

And last the dance; — till I retire:
    Dumb is that tower which spake
      so loud,
    And high in heaven the stream-
      ing cloud,
And on the downs a rising fire:

And rise, O moon, from yonder down,
    Till over down and over dale
    All night the shining vapor sail
And pass the silent-lighted town,

The white-faced halls, the glancing
    rills,

    And catch at every mountain
      head,
    And o'er the friths that branch
      and spread
Their sleeping silver thro' the hills;

And touch with shade the bridal doors,
    With tender gloom the roof, the
      wall;
    And breaking let the splendor fall
To spangle all the happy shores

By which they rest, and ocean sounds,
    And, star and system rolling past,
    A soul shall draw from out the
      vast
And strike his being into bounds,

And, moved thro' life of lower phase,
    Result in man, be born and think,
    And act and love, a closer link
Betwixt us and the crowning race

Of those that, eye to eye, shall look
    On knowledge; under whose com-
      mand
    Is Earth and Earth's, and in their
      hand
Is Nature like an open book;

No longer half-akin to brute,
    For all we thought and loved and
      did,
    And hoped, and suffer'd, is but
      seed
Of what in them is flower and fruit;

Whereof the man, that with me trod
    This planet, was a noble type
    Appearing ere the times were ripe,
That friend of mine who lives in God,

That God, which ever lives and loves,
    One God, one law, one element,
    And one far-off divine event,
To which the whole creation moves.

THE LOVER'S TALE.

—o○◦◦◦──

THE original Preface to "The Lover's Tale" states that it was composed in my nineteenth year. Two only of the three parts then written were printed, when, feeling the imperfection of the poem, I withdrew it from the press. One of my friends however who, boylike, admired the boy's work, distributed among our common associates of that hour some copies of these two parts, without my knowledge, without the omissions and amendments which I had in contemplation, and marred by the many misprints of the compositor. Seeing that these two parts have of late been mercilessly pirated, and that what I had deemed scarce worthy to live is not allowed to die, may I not be pardoned if I suffer the whole poem at last to come into the light—accompanied with a reprint of the sequel—a work of my mature life —"The Golden Supper"?
May, 1879.

ARGUMENT.

JULIAN, whose cousin and foster-sister, Camilla, has been wedded to his friend and rival, Lionel, endeavors to narrate the story of his own love for her, and the strange sequel. He speaks (in Parts II. and III.) of having been haunted by visions and the sound of bells, tolling for a funeral, and at last ringing for a marriage; but he breaks away, overcome, as he approaches the Event, and a witness to it completes the tale.

I.

HERE far away, seen from the topmost cliff,
Filling with purple gloom the vacancies
Between the tufted hills, the sloping seas
Hung in mid-heaven, and half-way down rare sails,
White as white clouds, floated from sky to sky.
Oh! pleasant breast of waters, quiet bay,
Like to a quiet mind in the loud world,
Where the chafed breakers of the outer sea
Sank powerless, as anger falls aside
And withers on the breast of peaceful love;
Thou didst receive the growth of pines that fledged
The hills that watch'd thee, as Love watcheth Love,
In thine own essence, and delight thyself
To make it wholly thine on sunny days.
Keep thou thy name of "Lover's Bay." See, sirs,
Even now the Goddess of the Past, that takes
The heart, and sometimes touches but one string
That quivers, and is silent, and sometimes
Sweeps suddenly all its half-moulder'd chords
To some old melody, begins to play
That air which pleased her first. I feel thy breath;
I come, great Mistress of the ear and eye:
Thy breath is of the pinewood; and tho' years
Have hollow'd out a deep and stormy strait
Betwixt the native land of Love and me,
Breathe but a little on me, and the sail
Will draw me to the rising of the sun,

The lucid chambers of the morning
        star,
And East of Life.

        Permit me, friend, I prythee,
To pass my hand across my brows,
        and muse
On those dear hills, that never more
        will meet
The sight that throbs and aches be-
        neath my touch,
As tho' there beat a heart in either
        eye;
For when the outer lights are darken'd
        thus,
The memory's vision hath a keener
        edge.
It grows upon me now — the semi-
        circle
Of dark-blue waters and the narrow
        fringe
Of curving beach — its wreaths of
        dripping green —
Its pale pink shells — the summer-
        house aloft
That open'd on the pines with doors
        of glass,
A mountain nest — the pleasure-boat
        that rock'd,
Light-green with its own shadow, keel
        to keel,
Upon the dappled dimplings of the
        wave,
That blanch'd upon its side.

        O Love, O Hope!
They come, they crowd upon me all
        at once —
Moved from the cloud of unforgotten
        things,
That sometimes on the horizon of the
        mind
Lies folded, often sweeps athwart in
        storm —
Flash upon flash they lighten thro' me
        — days
Of dewy dawning and the amber
        eves
When thou and I, Camilla, thou and
        I
Were borne about the bay or safely
        moor'd

Beneath a low-brow'd cavern, where
        the tide
Plash'd, sapping its worn ribs; and all
        without
The slowly-ridging rollers on the
        cliffs
Clash'd, calling to each other, and
        thro' the arch
Down those loud waters, like a setting
        star,
Mixt with the gorgeous west the light-
        house shone,
And silver-smiling Venus ere she fell
Would often loiter in her balmy
        blue,
To crown it with herself.

        Here, too, my love
Waver'd at anchor with me, when day
        hung
From his mid-dome in Heaven's airy
        halls;
Gleams of the water-circles as they
        broke,
Flicker'd like doubtful smiles about
        her lips,
Quiver'd a flying glory on her hair,
Leapt like a passing thought across
        her eyes;
And mine with one that will not pass,
        till earth
And heaven pass too, dwelt on my
        heaven, a face
Most starry-fair, but kindled from
        within
As 'twere with dawn. She was dark-
        hair'd, dark-eyed:
Oh, such dark eyes! a single glance
        of them
Will govern a whole life from birth
        to death,
Careless of all things else, led on
        with light
In trances and in visions: look at
        them,
You lose yourself in utter ignorance;
You cannot find their depth; for they
        go back,
And farther back, and still withdraw
        themselves
Quite into the deep soul, that ever
        more

Fresh springing from her fountains in
the brain,
Still pouring thro', floods with redun-
dant life
Her narrow portals.

Trust me, long ago
I should have died, if it were possible
To die in gazing on that perfectness
Which I do bear within me: I had
died,
But from my farthest lapse, my latest
ebb,
Thine image, like a charm of light
and strength
Upon the waters, push'd me back
again
On these deserted sands of barren
life.
Tho' from the deep vault where the
heart of Hope
Fell into dust, and crumbled in the
dark—
Forgetting how to render beautiful
Her countenance with quick and
healthful blood—
Thou didst not sway me upward; could
I perish
While thou, a meteor of the sepul-
chre,
Didst swathe thyself all round Hope's
quiet urn
For ever? He, that saith it, hath
o'er-stept
The slippery footing of his narrow
wit,
And fall'n away from judgment.
Thou art light,
To which my spirit leaneth all her
flowers,
And length of days, and immortality
Of thought, and freshness ever self-
renew'd.
For Time and Grief abode too long
with Life,
And, like all other friends i' the world,
at last
They grew aweary of her fellowship:
So Time and Grief did beckon unto
Death,
And Death drew nigh and beat the
doors of Life;

But thou didst sit alone in the inner
house,
A wakeful portress, and didst parle
with Death,—
"This is a charmed dwelling which I
old;"
So Death gave back, and would no
further come.
Yet is my life nor in the present time,
Nor in the present place. To me
alone,
Push'd from his chair of regal heri-
tage,
The Present is the vassal of the Past:
So that, in that I *have* lived, do I live,
And cannot die, and am, in having
been—
A portion of the pleasant yesterday,
Thrust forward on to-day and out of
place;
A body journeying onward, sick with
toil,
The weight as if of age upon my
limbs,
The grasp of hopeless grief about my
heart,
And all the senses weaken'd, save in
that,
Which long ago they had glean'd and
garner'd up
Into the granaries of memory—
The clear brow, bulwark of the
precious brain,
Chink'd as you see, and seam'd—and
all the while
The light soul twines and mingles
with the growths
Of vigorous early days, attracted,
won,
Married, made one with, molten into
all
The beautiful in Past of act or place,
And like the all-enduring camel,
driven
Far from the diamond fountain by the
palms,
Who toils across the middle moonlit
nights,
Or when the white heats of the blind-
ing noons
Beat from the concave sand; yet in
him keeps

A draught of that sweet fountain that
　　he loves,
To stay his feet from falling, and his
　　spirit
From bitterness of death.

　　　　　　Ye ask me, friends,
When I began to love. How should
　　I tell you?
Or from the after-fulness of my heart,
Flow back again unto my slender
　　spring
And first of love, tho' every turn and
　　depth
Between is clearer in my life than all
Its present flow. Ye know not what
　　ye ask.
How should the broad and open flower
　　tell
What sort of bud it was, when, prest
　　together
In its green sheath, close-lapt in silken
　　folds,
It seem'd to keep its sweetness to it-
　　self,
Yet was not the less sweet for that it
　　seem'd?
For young Life knows not when young
　　Life was born,
But takes it all for granted: neither
　　Love,
Warm in the heart, his cradle, can
　　remember
Love in the womb, but resteth satis-
　　fied,
Looking on her that brought him to
　　the light:
Or as men know not when they fall
　　asleep
Into delicious dreams, our other life,
So know I not when I began to love.
This is my sum of knowledge — that
　　my love
Grew with myself — say rather, was
　　my growth,
My inward sap, the hold I have on
　　earth,
My outward circling air wherewith I
　　breathe,
Which yet upholds my life, and ever-
　　more
Is to me daily life and daily death;

For how should I have lived and not
　　have loved?
Can ye take off the sweetness from
　　the flower,
The color and the sweetness from the
　　rose,
And place them by themselves; or set
　　apart
Their motions and their brightness
　　from the stars,
And then point out the flower or the
　　star?
Or build a wall betwixt my life and love,
And tell me where I am? 'Tis even
　　thus:
In that I live I love; because I love
I live: whate'er is fountain to the one
Is fountain to the other; and whene'er
Our God unknits the riddle of the
　　one,
There is no shade or fold of mystery
Swathing the other.

　　　　　　Many, many years,
(For they seem many and my most of
　　life,
And well I could have linger'd in that
　　porch,
So unproportion'd to the dwelling-
　　place,)
In the Maydews of childhood, opposite
The flush and dawn of youth, we lived
　　together,
Apart, alone together on those hills.

Before he saw my day my father
　　died,
And he was happy that he saw it not;
But I and the first daisy on his grave
From the same clay came into light
　　at once.
As Love and I do number equal years,
So she, my love, is of an age with me.
How like each other was the birth of
　　each!
On the same morning, almost the same
　　hour,
Under the selfsame aspect of the stars,
(Oh falsehood of all starcraft!) we
　　were born.
How like each other was the birth of
　　each!

The sister of my mother — she that bore
Camilla close beneath her beating heart,
Which to the imprison'd spirit of the child,
With its true-touched pulses in the flow
And hourly visitation of the blood,
Sent notes of preparation manifold,
And mellow'd echoes of the outer world —
My mother's sister, mother of my love,
Who had a twofold claim upon my heart,
One twofold mightier than the other was,
In giving so much beauty to the world,
And so much wealth as God had charged her with —
Loathing to put it from herself for ever,
Left her own life with it; and dying thus,
Crown'd with her highest act the placid face
And breathless body of her good deeds past.

So were we born, so orphan'd. She was motherless
And I without a father. So from each
Of those two pillars which from earth uphold
Our childhood, one had fallen away, and all
The careful burthen of our tender years
Trembled upon the other. He that gave
Her life, to me delightedly fulfill'd
All lovingkindnesses, all offices
Of watchful care and trembling tenderness.
He waked for both: he pray'd for both: he slept
Dreaming of both: nor was his love the less
Because it was divided, and shot forth

Boughs on each side, laden with wholesome shade,
Wherein we nested sleeping or awake,
And sang aloud the matin-song of life.

She was my foster-sister: on one arm
The flaxen ringlets of our infancies
Wander'd, the while we rested: one soft lap
Pillow'd us both: a common light of eyes
Was on us as we lay: our baby lips,
Kissing one bosom, ever drew from thence
The stream of life, one stream, one life, one blood,
One sustenance, which, still as thought grew large,
Still larger moulding all the house of thought,
Made all our tastes and fancies like, perhaps —
All — all but one; and strange to me, and sweet,
Sweet thro' strange years to know that whatsoe'er
Our general mother meant for me alone,
Our mutual mother dealt to both of us:
So what was earliest mine in earliest life,
I shared with her in whom myself remains.
As was our childhood, so our infancy,
They tell me, was a very miracle
Of fellow-feeling and communion.
They tell me that we would not be alone, —
We cried when we were parted; when I wept,
Her smile lit up the rainbow on my tears,
Stay'd on the cloud of sorrow; that we loved
The sound of one-another's voices more
Than the gray cuckoo loves his name, and learn'd
To lisp in tune together; that we slept

In the same cradle always, face to face.
Heart beating time to heart, lip press-
    ing lip,
Folding each other, breathing on each
    other,
Dreaming together (dreaming of each
    other
They should have added), till the
    morning light
Sloped thro' the pines, upon the dewy
    pane
Falling, unseal'd our eyelids, and we
    woke
To gaze upon each other. If this be
    true,
At thought of which my whole soul
    languishes
And faints, and hath no pulse, no
    breath — as tho'
A man in some still garden should in-
    fuse
Rich atar in the bosom of the rose,
Till, drunk with its own wine, and
    overfull
Of sweetness, and in smelling of itself,
It fall on its own thorns — if this be
    true —
And that way my wish leads me ever-
    more
Still to believe it — 'tis so sweet a
    thought,
Why in the utter stillness of the
    soul
Doth question'd memory answer not,
    nor tell
Of this our earliest, our closest-drawn,
Most loveliest, earthly-heavenliest har-
    mony ?
  O blossom'd portal of the lonely
    house,
Green prelude, April promise, glad
    new year
Of Being, which with earliest violets
And lavish carol of clear-throated larks
Fill'd all the March of life ! — I will
    not speak of thee.
These have not seen thee, these can
    never know thee,
They cannot understand me. Pass
    we then
A term of eighteen years. Ye would
    but laugh,

If I should tell you how I hoard in
    thought
The faded rhymes and scraps of an-
    cient crones,
Gray relics of the nurseries of the
    world,
Which are as gems set in my memory,
Because she learnt them with me; or
    what use
To know her father left us just before
The daffodil was blown ? or how we
    found
The dead man cast upon the shore ?
    All this
Seems to the quiet daylight of your
    minds
But cloud and smoke, and in the dark
    of mine
Is traced with flame. Move with me
    to the event.

  There came a glorious morning,
    such a one
As dawns but once a season. Mercury
On such a morning would have flung
    himself
From cloud to cloud, and swum with
    balanced wings
To some tall mountain: when I said
    to her,
"A day for Gods to stoop," she an-
    swered. "Ay,
And men to soar:" for as that other
    gazed,
Shading his eyes till all the fiery cloud,
The prophet and the chariot and the
    steeds,
Suck'd into oneness like a little star
Were drunk into the inmost blue, we
    stood,
When first we came from out the
    pines at noon,
With hands for eaves, uplooking and
    almost
Waiting to see some blessed shape in
    heaven,
So bathed we were in brilliance.
    Never yet
Before or after have I known the
    spring
Pour with such sudden deluges of
    light

Into the middle summer; for that day
Love, rising, shook his wings, and
    charged the winds
With spiced May-sweets from bound
    to bound, and blew
Fresh fire into the sun, and from
    within
Burst thro' the heated buds, and sent
    his soul
Into the songs of birds, and touch'd
    far-off
His mountain-altars, his high hills,
    with flame
Milder and purer.

    Thro' the rocks we wound:
The great pine shook with lonely
    sounds of joy
That came on the sea-wind. As
    mountain streams
Our blood ran free: the sunshine
    seem'd to brood
More warmly on the heart than on
    the brow.
We often paused, and, looking back,
    we saw
The clefts and openings in the moun-
    tains fill'd
With the blue valley and the glisten-
    ing brooks,
And all the low dark groves, a land
    of love!
A land of promise, a land of memory,
A land of promise flowing with the
    milk
And honey of delicious memories!
And down to sea, and far as eye could
    ken,
Each way from verge to verge a Holy
    Land,
Still growing holier as you near'd the
    bay,
For there the Temple stood.

      When we had reach'd
The grassy platform on some hill, I
    stoop'd,
I gather'd the wild herbs, and for her
    brows
And mine made garlands of the self-
    same flower,
Which she took smiling, and with my
    work thus

Crown'd her clear forehead. Once or
    twice she told me
(For I remember all things) to let grow
The flowers that run poison in their
    veins.
She said, "The evil flourish in the
    world."
Then playfully she gave herself the
    lie —
"Nothing in nature is unbeautiful;
So, brother, pluck and spare not."
    So I wove
Ev'n the dull-blooded poppy-stem,
    "whose flower,
Hued with the scarlet of a fierce sun-
    rise,
Like to the wild youth of an evil prince,
Is without sweetness, but who crowns
    himself
Above the naked poisons of his heart
In his old age." A graceful thought
    of hers
Grav'n on my fancy! And oh, how
    like a nymph,
A stately mountain nymph she look'd!
    how native
Unto the hills she trod on! While I
    gazed
My coronal slowly disentwined itself
And fell between us both; tho' while
    I gazed
My spirit leap'd as with those thrills
    of bliss
That strike across the soul in prayer,
    and show us
That we are surely heard. Methought
    a light
Burst from the garland I had wov'n,
    and stood
A solid glory on her bright black hair;
A light methought broke from her
    dark, dark eyes,
And shot itself into the singing winds;
A mystic light flash'd ev'n from her
    white robe
As from a glass in the sun, and fell
    about
My footsteps on the mountains.

      Last we came
To what our people call "The Hill of
    Woe."

A bridge is there, that, look'd at from
  beneath
Seems but a cobweb filament to link
The yawning of an earthquake-cloven
  chasm.
And thence one night, when all the
  winds were loud,
A woful man (for so the story went)
Had thrust his wife and child and
  dash'd himself
Into the dizzy depth below. Below,
Fierce in the strength of far descent,
  a stream
Flies with a shatter'd foam along the
  chasm.

The path was perilous, loosely strown
  with crags:
We mounted slowly; yet to both
  there came
The joy of life in steepness overcome,
And victories of ascent, and looking
  down
On all that had look'd down on us;
  and joy
In breathing nearer heaven; and joy
  to me,
High over all the azure-circled earth,
To breath with her as if in heaven it-
  self;
And more than joy that I to her be-
  came
Her guardian and her angel, raising her
Still higher, past all peril, until she saw
Beneath her feet the region far away,
Beyond the nearest mountain's bosky
  brows,
Arise in open prospect—heath and hill,
And hollow lined and wooded to the
  lips,
And deep-down walls of battlemented
  rock
Gilded with broom, or shatter'd into
  spires,
And glory of broad waters interfused,
Whence rose as it were breath and
  steam of gold,
And over all the great wood rioting
And climbing, streak'd or starr'd at
  intervals
With falling brook or blossom'd bush
  — and last,

Framing the mighty landscape to the
  west,
A purple range of mountain-cones,
  between
Whose interspaces gush'd in blinding
  bursts
The incorporate blaze of sun and sea.

　　　　　　　　　　At length
Descending from the point and stand-
  ing both,
There on the tremulous bridge, that
  from beneath
Had seem'd a gossamer filament up in
  air,
We paused amid the splendor. All
  the west
And ev'n unto the middle south was
  ribb'd
And barr'd with bloom on bloom.
  The sun below,
Held for a space 'twixt cloud and
  wave, shower'd down
Rays of a mighty circle, weaving over
That various wilderness a tissue of
  light
Unparallel'd. On the other side, the
  moon,
Half-melted into thin blue air, stood
  still,
And pale and fibrous as a wither'd
  leaf,
Not yet endured in presence of His eyes
To indue his lustre; most unloverlike,
Since in his absence full of light and
  joy,
And giving light to others. But this
  most,
Next to her presence whom I loved
  so well,
Spoke loudly even into my inmost
  heart
As to my outward hearing: the loud
  stream,
Forth issuing from his portals in the
  crag
(A visible link unto the home of my
  heart),
Ran amber toward the west, and nigh
  the sea
Parting my own loved mountains was
  received,

Shorn of its strength, into the sympathy
Of that small bay, which out to open
main
Glow'd intermingling close beneath
the sun.
Spirit of Love! that little hour was
bound
Shut in from Time, and dedicate to
thee :
Thy fires from heaven had touch'd it,
and the earth
They fell on became hallow'd evermore.

We turn'd : our eyes met : hers
were bright, and mine
Were dim with floating tears, that shot
the sunset
In lightnings round me ; and my name
was borne
Upon her breath. Henceforth my
name has been
A hallow'd memory like the names of
old,
A center'd, glory-circled memory,
And a peculiar treasure, brooking
not
Exchange or currency : and in that
hour
A hope flow'd round me, like a golden
mist
Charm'd amid eddies of melodious airs,
A moment, ere the onward whirlwind
shatter it,
Waver'd and floated — which was less
than Hope,
Because it lack'd the power of perfect
Hope ;
But which was more and higher than
all Hope,
Because all other Hope had lower aim ;
Even that this name to which her
gracious lips
Did lend such gentle utterance, this
one name,
In some obscure hereafter, might in-
wreathe
(How lovelier, nobler then !) her life,
her love,
With my life, love, soul, spirit, and
heart and strength.

"Brother," she said, "let this be
call'd henceforth
The Hill of Hope ; " and I replied,
"O sister,
My will is one with thine ; the Hill of
Hope."
Nevertheless, we did not change the
name.

I did not speak : I could not speak
my love.
Love lieth deep : Love dwells not in
lip-depths.
Love wraps his wings on either side
the heart,
Constraining it with kisses close and
warm,
Absorbing all the incense of sweet
thoughts
So that they pass not to the shrine of
sound.
Else had the life of that delighted hour
Drunk in the largeness of the utter-
ance
Of Love ; but how should Earthly
measure mete
The Heavenly-unmeasured or unlimit-
ed Love,
Who scarce can tune his high majestic
sense
Unto the thundersong that wheels the
spheres,
Scarce living in the Æolian harmony,
And flowing odor of the spacious air,
Scarce housed within the circle of this
Earth,
Be cabin'd up in words and syllables,
Which pass with that which breathes
them ? Sooner Earth
Might go round Heaven, and the strait
girth of Time
Inswathe the fulness of Eternity,
Than language grasp the infinite of
Love.

O day which did enwomb that happy
hour,
Thou art blessed in the years, divinest
day !
O Genius of that hour which dost uphold
Thy coronal of glory like a God,

Amid thy melancholy mates far-seen,
Who walk before thee, ever turning
　　round
To gaze upon thee till their eyes are
　　dim
With dwelling on the light and depth
　　of thine,
Thy name is ever worshipp'd among
　　hours!
Had I died then, I had not seem'd to
　　die,
For bliss stood round me like the light
　　of Heaven, —
Had I died then, I had not known the
　　death;
Yea had the Power from whose right
　　hand the light
Of Life issueth, and from whose left
　　hand floweth
The Shadow of Death, perennial efflu-
　　ences,
Whereof to all that draw the whole-
　　some air,
Somewhile the one must overflow the
　　other;
Then had he stemm'd my day with
　　night, and driven
My current to the fountain whence it
　　sprang, —
Even his own abiding excellence —
On me, methinks, that shock of gloom
　　had fall'n
Unfelt, and in this glory I had merged
The other, like the sun I gazed
　　upon,
Which seeming for the moment due
　　to death,
And dipping his head low beneath the
　　verge,
Yet bearing round about him his own
　　day,
In confidence of unabated strength,
Steppeth from Heaven to Heaven,
　　from light to light,
And holdeth his undimmed forehead
　　far
Into a clearer zenith, pure of cloud.

We trod the shadow of the down-
　　ward hill;
We past from light to dark. On the
　　other side

Is scoop'd a cavern and a mountain
　　hall,
Which none have fathom'd. If you
　　go far in
(The country people rumor) you may
　　hear
The moaning of the woman and the
　　child,
Shut in the secret chambers of the
　　rock.
I too have heard a sound — perchance
　　of streams
Running far on within its inmost
　　halls,
The home of darkness; but the cav-
　　ern-mouth,
Half overtrailed with a wanton weed,
Gives birth to a brawling brook, that
　　passing lightly
Adown a natural stair of tangled roots,
Is presently received in a sweet grave
Of eglantines, a place of burial
Far lovelier than its cradle; for un-
　　seen,
But taken with the sweetness of the
　　place,
It makes a constant bubbling melody
That drowns the nearer echoes. Low-
　　er down
Spreads out a little lake, that, flood-
　　ing, leaves
Low banks of yellow sand; and from
　　the woods
That belt it rise three dark, tall cy-
　　presses, —
Three cypresses, symbols of mortal
　　woe,
That men plant over graves.

　　　　　　　　Hither we came,
And sitting down upon the golden
　　moss,
Held converse sweet and low — low
　　converse sweet,
In which our voices bore least part.
　　The wind
Told a lovetale beside us, how he woo'd
The waters, and the waters answering
　　lisp'd
To kisses of the wind, that, sick with
　　love,
Fainted at intervals, and grew again

To utterance of passion. Ye cannot
  shape
Fancy so fair as is this memory.
Methought all excellence that ever was
Had drawn herself from many thou-
  sand years,
And all the separate Edens of this
  earth,
To centre in this place and time. I
  listen'd,
And her words stole with most pre-
  vailing sweetness
Into my heart, as thronging fancies
  come
To boys and girls when summer days
  are new,
And soul and heart and body are all
  at ease :
What marvel my Camilla told me all ?
It was so happy an hour, so sweet a
  place,
And I was as the brother of her blood,
And by that name I moved upon her
  breath ;
Dear name, which had too much of
  nearness in it
And heralded the distance of this time!
At first her voice was very sweet and
  low,
As if she were afraid of utterance ;
But in the onward current of her
  speech,
(As echoes of the hollow-banked
  brooks
Are fashion'd by the channel which
  they keep),
Her words did of their meaning bor-
  row sound,
Her cheek did catch the color of her
  words.
I heard and trembled, yet I could but
  hear ;
My heart paused — my raised eyelids
  would not fall,
But still I kept my eyes upon the sky.
I seem'd the only part of Time stood
  still,
And saw the motion cf all other things;
While her words, syllable by syllable,
Like water, drop by drop, upon my ear
Fell; and I wish'd, yet wish'd her not
  to speak ;

But she spake on, for I did name no
  wish,
What marvel my Camilla told me all
Her maiden dignities of Hope and
  Love —
"Perchance," she said, "return'd."
  Even then the stars
Did tremble in their stations as I gazed;
But she spake on, for I did name no
  wish,
No wish — no hope. Hope was not
  wholly dead,
But breathing hard at the approach
  of Death, —
Camilla, my Camilla, who was mine
No longer in the dearest sense of mine —
For all the secret of her inmost heart,
And all the maiden empire of her
  mind,
Lay like a map before me, and I saw
There, where I hoped myself to reign
  as king,
There, where that day I crown'd my-
  self as king,
There in my realm and even on my
  throne,
Another ! then it seem'd as tho' a link
Of some tight chain within my inmost
  frame
Was riven in twain: that life I heeded
  not
Flow'd from me, and the darkness of
  the grave,
The darkness of the grave and utter
  night,
Did swallow up my vision ; at her feet,
Even the feet of her I loved, I fell,
Smit with exceeding sorrow unto
  Death.

Then had the earth beneath me
  yawing cloven
With such a sound as when an iceberg
  splits
From cope to base — had Heaven from
  all her doors,
With all her golden thresholds clashing, roll'd
Her heaviest thunder — I had lain as
  dead,
Mute, blind and motionless as then I
  lay ;

Dead, for henceforth there was no life
    for me!
Mute, for henceforth what use were
    words to me!
Blind, for the day was as the night to
    me!
The night to me was kinder than the
    day;
The night in pity took away my day,
Because my grief as yet was newly
    born
Of eyes too weak to look upon the
    light;
And thro' the hasty notice of the ear
Frail Life was startled from the ten-
    der love
Of him she brooded over. Would I
    had lain
Until the plaited ivy-tress had wound
Round my worn limbs, and the wild
    brier had driven
Its knotted thorns thro' my unpain-
    ing brows,
Leaning its roses on my faded eyes.
The wind had blown above me, and
    the rain
Had fall'n upon me, and the gilded
    snake
Had nestled in this bosom-throne of
    Love,
But I had been at rest for evermore.

Long time entrancement held me.
    All too soon
Life (like a wanton too-officious friend,
Who will not *hear* denial, vain and
    rude
With proffer of unwish'd-for services)
Entering all the avenues of sense
Past thro' into his citadel, the brain,
With hated warmth of apprehensive-
    ness.
And first the chillness of the sprinkled
    brook
Smote on my brows, and then I seem'd
    to hear
Its murmur, as the drowning seaman
    hears,
Who with his head below the surface
    dropt
Listens the muffled booming indistinct
Of the confused floods, and dimly knows

His head shall rise no more: and then
    came in
The white light of the weary moon
    above,
Diffused and molten into flaky cloud.
Was my sight drunk that it did shape
    to me
Him who should own that name? Were
    it not well
If so be that the echo of that name
Ringing within the fancy had updrawn
A fashion and a phantasm of the
    form
It should attach to? Phantom! —
    had the ghastliest
That ever lusted for a body, sucking
The foul steam of the grave to thicken
    by it,
There in the shuddering moonlight
    brought its face
And what it has for eyes as close to
    mine
As he did — better that than his, than
    he
The-friend, the neighbor, Lionel, the
    beloved,
The loved, the lover, the happy Lionel,
The low-voiced, tender-spirited Lionel,
All joy, to whom my agony was a joy.
O how her choice did leap forth from
    his eyes!
O how her love did clothe itself in
    smiles
About his lips! and — not one mo-
    ment's grace —
Then when the effect weigh'd seas
    upon my head
To come my way! to twit me with the
    cause!

Was not the land as free thro' all
    her ways
To him as me? Was not his wont to
    walk
Between the going light and growing
    night?
Had I not learnt my loss before he
    came?
Could that be more because he came
    my way?
Why should he not come my way if
    he would?

And yet to-night, to-night — when all
  my wealth
Flash'd from me in a moment and I
  fell
Beggar'd for ever — why *should* he
  come my way
Robed in those robes of light I must
  not wear,
With that great crown of beams about
  his brows —
Come like an angel to a damned soul,
To tell him of the bliss he had with
  God —
Come like a careless and a greedy
  heir
That scarce can wait the reading of
  the will
Before he takes possession ?   Was
  mine a mood
To be invaded rudely, and not rather
A sacred, secret unapproached woe,
Unspeakable ?   I was shut up with
  Grief ;
She took the body of my past delight,
Narded and swathed and balm'd it
  for herself,
And laid it in a sepulchre of rock
Never to rise again.   I was led mute
Into her temple like a sacrifice ;
I was the High Priest in her holiest
  place,
Not to be loudly broken in upon.

Oh friend, thoughts deep and heavy
  as these well-nigh
O'erbore the limits of my brain : but he
Bent o'er me, and my neck his arm
  upstay'd.
I thought it was an adder's fold, and
  once
I strove to disengage myself, but
  fail'd,
Being so feeble : she bent above me,
  too ;
Wan was her cheek ; for whatsoe'er
  of blight
Lives in the dewy touch of pity had
  made
The red rose there a pale one — and
  her eyes —
I saw the moonlight glitter on their
  tears —

And some few drops of that distress-
  ful rain
Fell on my face, and her long ringlets
  moved,
Drooping and beaten by the breeze,
  and brush'd
My fallen forehead in their to and
  fro,
For in the sudden anguish of her heart
Loosed from their simple thrall they
  had flow'd abroad,
And floated on and parted round her
  neck,
Mantling her form halfway.   She,
  when I woke,
Something she ask'd, I know not what,
  and ask'd,
Unanswer'd, since I spake not ; for
  the sound
Of that dear voice so musically low,
And now first heard with any sense
  of pain,
As it had taken life away before,
Choked all the syllables, that strove
  to rise
From my full heart.

                    The blissful lover, too,
From his great hoard of happiness
  distill'd
Some drops of solace ; like a vain
  rich man,
That, having always prosper'd in the
  world,
Folding his hands, deals comfortable
  words
To hearts wounded for ever ; yet, in
  truth,
Fair speech was his and delicate of
  phrase,
Falling in whispers on the sense, address'd
More to the inward than the outward
  ear,
As rain of the midsummer midnight
  soft,
Scarce-heard, recalling fragrance and
  the green
Of the dead spring : but mine was
  wholly dead,
No bud, no leaf, no flower, no fruit
  for me.

Yet who had done, or who had suffer'd
　　wrong ?
And why was I to darken their pure
　　love,
If, as I found, they two did love each
　　other,
Because my own was darken'd ? Why
　　was I
To cross between their happy star and
　　them ?
To stand a shadow by their shining
　　doors,
And vex them with my darkness ?
　　Did I love her ?
Ye know that I did love her ; to this
　　present
My full-orb'd love has waned not.
　　Did I love her,
And could I look upon her tearful
　　eyes ?
What had *she* done to weep ? Why
　　should *she* weep ?
O innocent of spirit — let my heart
Break rather — whom the gentlest
　　airs of Heaven
Should kiss with an unwonted gentle-
　　ness.
Her love did murder mine ? What
　　then ? She deem'd
I wore a brother's mind : she call'd
　　me brother :
She told me all her love : she shall
　　not weep.

The brightness of a burning thought,
　　awhile
In battle with the glooms of my dark
　　will,
Moonlike emerged, and to itself lit up
There on the depth of an unfathom'd
　　woe
Reflex of action. Starting up at once,
As from a dismal dream of my own
　　death,
I, for I loved her, lost my love in
　　Love ;
I, for I loved her, graspt the hand she
　　lov'd,
And laid it in her own, and sent my
　　cry
Thro' the blank night to Him who
　　loving made

The happy and the unhappy love,
　　that He
Would hold the hand of blessing over
　　them,
Lionel, the happy, and her, and her,
　　his bride !
Let them so love that men and boys
　　may say,
"Lo ! how they love each other !" till
　　their love
Shall ripen to a proverb, unto all
Known, when their faces are forgot in
　　the land —
One golden dream of love, from which
　　may death
Awake them with heaven's music in a
　　life
More living to some happier happi-
　　ness,
Swallowing its precedent in victory.
And as for me, Camilla, as for me, —
The dew of tears is an unwholesome
　　dew,
They will but sicken the sick plant
　　the more.
Deem that I love thee but as brothers
　　do,
So shalt thou love me still as sisters
　　do ;
Or if thou dream aught farther,
　　dream but how
I could have loved thee, had there
　　been none else
To love as lovers, loved again by
　　thee.

Or this, or somewhat like to this, I
　　spake,
When I beheld her weep so rue-
　　fully ;
For sure my love should ne'er indue
　　the front
And mask of Hate, who lives on
　　others' moans.
Shall Love pledge Hatred in her bit-
　　ter draughts,
And batten on her poisons ? Love
　　forbid !
Love passeth not the threshold of cold
　　Hate,
And Hate is strange beneath the roof
　　of Love.

O Love, if thou be'st Love, dry up
these tears
Shed for the love of Love ; for tho'
mine image,
The subject of thy power, be cold in
her,
Yet, like cold snow, it /melteth in the
source
Of these sad tears, and feeds their
downward flow.
So Love, arraign'd to judgment and
to death,
Received unto himself a part of
blame,
Being guiltless, as an innocent prisoner,
Who, when the woful sentence hath
been past,
And all the clearness of his fame hath
gone
Beneath the shadow of the curse of
man,
First falls asleep in swoon, wherefrom
awaked,
And looking round upon his tearful
friends,
Forthwith and in his agony con-
ceives
A shameful sense as of a cleaving
crime —
For whence without some guilt should
such grief be ?

So died that hour, and fell into the
abysm
Of forms outworn, but not to me outworn,
Who never hail'd another — was there
one ?
There might be one — one other, worth
the life
That made it sensible. So that hour
died
Like odor rapt into the winged
wind
Borne into alien lands and far away.

There be some hearts so airily built,
that they,
They — when their love is wreck'd —
if Love can wreck —
On that sharp ridge of utmost doom
ride highly

Above the perilous seas of Change
and Chance ;
Nay, more, hold out the lights of
cheerfulness ;
As the tall ship, that many a dreary
year
Knit to some dismal sandbank far at
sea,
All thro' the livelong hours of utter
dark,
Showers slanting light upon the dolor-
ous wave.
For me — what light, what gleam on
those black ways
Where Love could walk with banish d
Hope no more ?

It was ill-done to part you, Sisters
fair ;
Love's arms were wreath'd about the
neck of Hope,
And Hope kiss'd Love, and Love
drew in her breath
In that close kiss, and drank her
whisper'd tales.
They said that Love would die when
Hope was gone,
And Love mourn'd long, and sorrow'd
after Hope ;
At last she sought out Memory, and
they trod
The same old paths where Love had
walk'd with Hope,
And Memory fed the soul of Love
with tears.

II.

FROM that time forth I would not see
her more ;
But many a weary moons I lived
alone —
Alone, and in the heart of the great
forest.
Sometimes upon the hills beside the
sea
All day I watch'd the floating isles of
shade,
And sometimes on the shore, upon the
sands
Insensibly I drew her name, until
The meaning of the letters shot into

My brain; anon the wanton billow
    wash'd
Them over, till they faded like my
    love.
The hollow caverns heard me — the
    black brooks
Of the midforest heard me — the soft
    winds,
Laden with thistledown and seeds of
    flowers,
Paused in their course to hear me, for
    my voice
Was all of thee: the merry linnet
    knew me,
The squirrel knew me, and the dragon-
    fly
Shot by me like a flash of purple fire.
The rough brier tore my bleeding
    palms; the hemlock,
Brow-high, did strike my forehead as
    I past;
Yet trod I not the wildflower in my
    path,
Nor bruised the wildbird's egg.

                        Was this the end?
Why grew we then together in one
    plot?
Why fed we from one fountain? drew
    one sun?
Why were our mothers' branches of
    one stem?
Why were we one in all things, save
    in that
Where to have been one had been the
    cope and crown
Of all I hoped and fear'd? — if that
    same nearness
Were father to this distance, and that
    one
Vauntcourier to the *double*? if Affec-
    tion
Living slew Love, and Sympathy
    hew'd out
The bosom-sepulchre of Sympathy?

  Chiefly I sought the cavern and the
    hill
Where last we roam'd together, for the
    sound
Of the loud stream was pleasant, and
    the wind

Came wooingly with woodbine smells.
    Sometimes
All day I sat within the cavern-mouth,
Fixing my eyes on those three cypress-
    cones
That spired above the wood; and with
    mad hand
Tearing the bright leaves of the ivy-
    screen,
I cast them in the noisy brook be-
    neath,
And watch'd them till they vanish'd
    from my sight
Beneath the bower of wreathed eglan-
    tines:
And all the fragments of the living
    rock
(Huge blocks, which some old trem-
    bling of the world
Had loosen'd from the mountain, till
    they fell
Half-digging their own graves) these
    in my agony
Did I make bare of all the golden
    moss,
Wherewith the dashing runnel in the
    spring
Had liveried them all over. In my
    brain
The spirit seem'd to flag from thought
    to thought,
As moonlight wandering thro' a mist:
    my blood
Crept like marsh drains thro' all my
    languid limbs;
The motions of my heart seem'd far
    within me,
Unfrequent, low, as tho' it told its
    pulses;
And yet it shook me, that my frame
    would shudder,
As if 'twere drawn asunder by the rack.
But over the deep graves of Hope and
    Fear,
And all the broken palaces of the
    Past,
Brooded one master-passion evermore,
Like to a low-hung and a fiery sky
Above some fair metropolis, earth-
    shock'd, —
Hung round with ragged rims and
    burning folds, —

Embathing all with wild and woful
    hues,
Great hills of ruins, and collapsed
    masses
Of thundershaken columns indistinct,
And fused together in the tyrannous
    light —
Ruins, the ruin of all my life and me!

Sometimes I thought Camilla was
    no more,
Some one had told me she was dead,
    and ask'd
If I would see her burial: then I seem'd
To rise, and through the forest-shadow
    borne
With more than mortal swiftness, I
    ran down
The steepy sea-bank, till I came upon
The rear of a procession, curving round
The silver-sheeted bay: in front of
    which
Six stately virgins, all in white, upbear
A broad earth-sweeping pall of whitest
    lawn,
Wreathed round the bier with gar-
    lands: in the distance,
From out the yellow woods upon the
    hill
Look'd forth the summit and the pin-
    nacles
Of a gray steeple — thence at intervals
A low bell tolling. All the pageantry,
Save those six virgins which upheld
    the bier,
Were stoled from head to foot in flow-
    ing black;
One walk'd abreast with me, and veil'd
    his brow,
And he was loud in weeping and in
    praise
Of her we follow'd: a strong sympathy
Shook all my soul: I flung myself
    upon him
In tears and cries: I told him all my
    love,
How I had loved her from the first;
    whereat
He shrank and howl'd, and from his
    brow drew back
His hand to push me from him; and
    the face,

The very face and form of Lionel
Flash'd thro' my eyes into my inner-
    most brain,
And at his feet I seem'd to faint and
    fall,
To fall and die away. I could not rise
Albeit I strove to follow. They past
    on,
The lordly Phantasms! in their float-
    ing folds
They past and were no more: but I
    had fallen
Prone by the dashing runnel on the
    grass.

Alway the inaudible invisible
    thought,
Artificer and subject, lord and slave,
Shaped by the audible and visible,
Moulded the audible and visible;
All crisped sounds of wave and leaf
    and wind,
Flatter'd the fancy of my fading brain;
The cloud-pavilion'd element, the
    wood,
The mountain, the three cypresses, the
    cave,
Storm, sunset, glows and glories of
    the moon
Below black firs, when silent-creeping
    winds
Laid the long night in silver streaks
    and bars,
Were wrought into the tissue of my
    dream:
The moanings in the forest, the loud
    brook,
Cries of the partridge like a rusty key
Turn'd in a lock, owl-whoop and dor-
    hawk-whirr
Awoke me not, but were a part of
    sleep,
And voices in the distance calling to me
And in my vision bidding me dream on,
Like sounds without the twilight realm
    of dreams,
Which wander round the bases of the
    hills,
And murmur at the low-dropt eaves
    of sleep,
Half-entering the portals. Oftentimes
The vision had fair prelude, in the end

Opening on darkness, stately vesti-
    bules
To caves and shows of Death : wheth-
    er the mind,
With some revenge — even to itself
    unknown, —
Made strange division of its suffering
With her, whom to have suffering
    view'd had been
Extremest pain ; or that the clear-eyed
    Spirit,
Being blunted in the Present, grew at
    length
Prophetical and prescient of whate'er
The Future had in store : or that
    which most
Enchains belief, the sorrow of my
    spirit
Was of so wide a compass it took in
All I had loved, and my dull agony,
Ideally to her transferr'd, became
Anguish intolerable.

          The day waned ;
Alone I sat with her : about my
    brow
Her warm breath floated in the utter-
    ance
Of silver-chorded tones : her lips
    were sunder'd
With smiles of tranquil bliss, which
    broke in light
Like morning from her eyes — her
    eloquent eyes,
(As I have seen them many a hundred
    times)
Fill'd all with pure clear fire, thro'
    mine down rain'd
Their spirit-searching splendors. As
    a vision
Unto a haggard prisoner, iron-stay'd
In damp and dismal dungeons under-
    ground,
Confined on points of faith, when
    strength is shock'd
With torment, and expectancy of
    worse
Upon the morrow, thro' the ragged
    walls,
All unawares before his half-shut eyes,
Comes in upon him in the dead of
    night,

And with the excess of sweetness and
    of awe,
Makes the heart tremble, and the
    sight run over
Upon his steely gyves ; so those fair
    eyes
Shone on my darkness, forms which
    ever stood
Within the magic cirque of memory,
Invisible but deathless, waiting still
The edict of the will to reassume
The semblance of those rare realities
Of which they were the mirrors. Now
    the light
Which was their life, burst through
    the cloud of thought
Keen, irrepressible.

          It was a room
Within the summer-house of which I
    spake,
Hung round with paintings of the sea,
    and one
A vessel in mid-ocean, her heaved
    prow
Clambering, the mast bent and the
    ravin wind
In her sail roaring. From the outer
    day,
Betwixt the close-set ivies came a
    broad
And solid beam of isolated light,
Crowded with driving atomies, and
    fell
Slanting upon that picture, from prime
    youth
Well-known well-loved. She drew it
    long ago
Forthgazing on the waste and open
    sea,
One morning when the upblown bil-
    low ran
Shoreward beneath red clouds, and I
    had pour'd
Into the shadowing pencil's naked
    forms
Color and life : it was a bond and seal
Of friendship, spoken of with tearful
    smiles ;
A monument of childhood and of
    love ;
The poesy of childhood ; my lost love

Symbol'd in storm. We gazed on it
    together
In mute and glad remembrance, and
    each heart
Grew closer to the other, and the eye
Was riveted and charm-bound, gazing
    like
The Indian on a still-eyed snake, low-
    couch'd —
A beauty which is death; when all at
    once
That painted vessel, as with inner
    life,
Began to heave upon that painted
    sea ;
An earthquake, my loud heart-beats,
    made the ground
Reel under us, and all at once, soul,
    life
And breath and motion, past and
    flow'd away
To those unreal billows : round and
    round
A whirlwind caught and bore us ;
    mighty gyres
Rapid and vast, of hissing spray wind-
    driven
Far thro' the dizzy dark. Aloud she
    shriek'd ;
My heart was cloven with pain; I
    wound my arms
About her : we whirl'd giddily; the
    wind
Sung ; but I clasp'd her without fear :
    her weight
Shrank in my grasp, and over my dim
    eyes,
And parted lips which drank her
    breath, down-hung
The jaws of Death : I, groaning, from
    me flung
Her empty phantom : all the sway and
    whirl
Of the storm dropt to windless calm,
    and I
Down welter'd thro' the dark ever and
    ever.

III.

I CAME one day and sat among the
    stones

Strewn in the entry of the moaning
    cave ;
A morning air, sweet after rain, ran
    over
The rippling levels of the lake, and
    blew
Coolness and moisture and all smells
    of bud
And foliage from the dark and. drip-
    ping woods
Upon my fever'd brows that shook
    and throbb'd
From temple unto temple. To what
    height
The day had grown I know not. Then
    came on me
The hollow tolling of the bell, and all
The vision of the bier. As heretofore
I walk'd behind with one who veil'd
    his brow.
Methought by slow degrees the sullen
    bell
Toll'd quicker, and the breakers on the
    shore
Sloped into louder surf : those that
    went with me,
And those that held the bier before
    my face,
Moved with one spirit round about
    the bay,
Trod swifter steps ; and while I walk'd
    with these
In marvel at that gradual change, I
    thought
Four bells instead of one began to
    ring,
Four merry bells, four merry marriage-
    bells,
In clanging cadence jangling peal on
    peal —
A long loud clash of rapid marriage-
    bells.
Then those who led the van, and those
    in rear,
Rush'd into dance, and like wild Bac-
    chanals
Fled onward to the steeple in the
    woods :
I, too, was borne along and felt the
    blast
Beat on my heated eyelids : all at
    once

The front rank made a sudden halt;
the bells
Lapsed into frightful stillness; the
surge fell
From thunder into whispers; those six
maids
With shrieks and ringing laughter on
the sand
Threw down the bier; the woods upon
the hill
Waved with a sudden gust that sweep-
ing down
Took the edges of the pall, and blew
it far
Until it hung, a little silver cloud
Over the sounding seas: I turn'd: my
heart
Shrank in me, like a snowflake in the
hand,
Waiting to see the settled countenance
Of her I loved, adorn'd with fading
flowers.
But she from out her death-like
chrysalis,
She from her bier, as into fresher
life,
My sister, and my cousin, and my
love,
Leapt lightly clad in bridal white —
her hair
Studded with one rich Provence rose
— a light
Of smiling welcome round her lips —
her eyes
And cheeks as bright as when she
climb'd the hill.
One hand she reach'd to those that
came behind,
And while I mused nor yet endured
to take
So rich a prize, the man who stood
with me
Stept gaily forward, throwing down
his robes,
And claspt her hand in his: again the
bells
Jangled and clang'd: again the stormy
surf
Crash'd in the shingle: and the whirling rout
Led by those two rush'd into dance,
and fled

Wind-footed to the steeple in the
woods,
Till they were swallow'd in the leafy
bowers,
And I stood sole beside the vacant
bier.

There, there, my latest vision — then
the event!

IV.

THE GOLDEN SUPPER.[1]

(Another speaks.)

HE flies the event: he leaves the event
to me:
Poor Julian — how he rush'd away;
the bells,
Those marriage-bells, echoing in ear
and heart —
But cast a parting glance at me, you
saw,
As who should say "Continue." Well
he had
One golden hour — of triumph shall I
say?
Solace at least — before he left his
home.

Would you had seen him in that
hour of his!
He moved thro' all of it majesti-
cally —
Restrain'd himself quite to the close —
but now —

Whether they *were* his lady's mar-
riage bells,
Or prophets of them in his fantasy,
I never ask'd: but Lionel and the girl
Were wedded, and our Julian came
again
Back to his mother's house among the
pines.
But these, their gloom, the mountains
and the Bay,
The whole land weigh'd him down as
Ætna does
The Giant of Mythology: he would
go,

[1] This poem is founded upon a story in
Boccaccio. See Introduction, p. 647.

Would leave the land for ever, and
    had gone
Surely, but for a whisper, " Go not
    yet,"
Some warning — sent divinely — as it
    seem'd
By that which follow'd — but of this
    I deem
As of the visions that he told — the
    event
Glanced back upon them in his after
    life,
And partly made them — tho' he knew
    it not.

    And thus he stay'd and would not
      look at her —
No not for months : but, when the
    eleventh moon
After their marriage lit the lover's Bay,
Heard yet once more the tolling bell,
    and said,
Would you could toll me out of life,
    but found —
All softly as his mother broke it to
    him —
A crueller reason than a crazy ear,
For that low knell tolling his lady
    dead —
Dead — and had lain three days with-
    out a pulse :
All that look'd on her had pronounced
    her dead.
And so they bore her (for in Julian's
    land
They never nail a dumb head up in
    elm),
Bore her free-faced to the free airs of
    heaven,
And laid her in the vault of her own
    kin.

    What did he then ? not die: he is
      here and hale —
Not plunge headforemost from the
    mountain there,
And leave the name of Lover's Leap :
    not he :
He knew the meaning of the whisper
    now,
Thought that he knew it. " This, I
    stay'd for this ;

O love, I have not seen you for so
    long.
Now, now, will I go down into the
    grave,
I will be all alone with all I love,
And kiss her on the lips. She is his
    no more :
The dead returns to me, and I go down
To kiss the dead."

             The fancy stirr'd him so
He rose and went, and entering the
    dim vault,
And, making there a sudden light, be-
    held
All round about him that which all
    will be.
The light was but a flash, and went
    again.
Then at the far end of the vault he saw
His lady with the moonlight on her
    face ;
Her breast as in a shadow-prison, bars
Of black and bands of silver, which
    the moon
Struck from an open grating overhead
High in the wall, and all the rest of
    her
Drown'd in the gloom and horror of
    the vault.

    " It was my wish," he said, " to pass,
    to sleep,
To rest, to be with her — till the great
    day
Peal'd on us with that music which
    rights all,
And raised us hand in hand." And
    kneeling there
Down in the dreadful dust that once
    was man,
Dust, as he said, that once was loving
    hearts,
Hearts that had beat with such a love
    as mine —
Not such as mine, no, nor for such as
    her —
He softly put his arm about her neck
And kiss'd her more than once, till
    helpless death
And silence made him bold — nay, but
    I wrong him,

He reverenced his dear lady even in
    death;
But, placing his true hand upon her
    heart,
"O, you warm heart," he moan'd,
    "not even death
Can chill you all at once:" then start-
    ing, thought
His dreams had come again. "Do I
    wake or sleep?
Or am I made immortal, or my love
Mortal once more?" It beat — the
    heart — it beat:
Faint — but it beat: at which his own
    began
To pulse with such a vehemence that
    it drown'd
The feebler motion underneath his
    hand.
But when at last his doubts were sat-
    isfied,
He raised her softly from the sepul-
    chre,
And, wrapping her all over with the
    cloak
He came in, and now striding fast, and
    now
Sitting awhile to rest, but evermore
Holding his golden burthen in his
    arms,
So bore her thro' the solitary land
Back to the mother's house where she
    was born.

    There the good mother's kindly min-
    istering,
With half a night's appliances, recall'd
Her fluttering life: she rais'd an eye
    that ask'd
"Where?" till the things familiar to
    her youth
Had made a silent answer: then she
    spoke
"Here! and how came I here?" and
    learning it
(They told her somewhat rashly as I
    think)
At once began to wander and to wail,
"Ay, but you know that you must give
    me back:
Send! bid him come;" but Lionel
    was away —

Stung by his loss had vanish'd, none
    knew where.
"He casts me out," she wept, "and
    goes" — a wail
That seeming something, yet was noth-
    ing, born
Not from believing mind, but shatter'd
    nerve,
Yet haunting Julian, as her own re-
    proof
At some precipitance in her burial.
Then, when her own true spirit had
    return'd,
"Oh yes, and you," she said, "and
    none but you?
For you have given me life and love
    again,
And none but you yourself shall tell
    him of it,
And you shall give me back when he
    returns."
"Stay then a little," answer'd Julian,
    "here,
And keep yourself, none knowing, to
    yourself;
And I will do your will. I may not
    stay,
No, not an hour; but send me notice
    of him
When he returns, and then will I re-
    turn,
And I will make a solemn offering of
    you
To him you love." And faintly she
    replied,
"And I will do *your* will, and none
    shall know."

    Not know? with such a secret to be
    known.
But all their house was old and loved
    them both,
And all the house had known the loves
    of both;
Had died almost to serve them any
    way,
And all the land was waste and soli-
    tary:
And then he rode away; but after this,
An hour or two, Camilla's travail came
Upon her, and that day a boy was born,
Heir of his face and land, to Lionel.

And thus our lonely lover rode away,
And pausing at a hostel in a marsh,
There fever seized upon him : myself
    was then
Travelling that land, and meant to
    rest an hour ;
And sitting down to such a base repast,
It makes me angry yet to speak of it —
I heard a groaning overhead, and
    climb'd
The moulder'd stairs (for everything
    was vile)
And in a loft, with none to wait on
    him,
Found, as it seem'd, a skeleton alone,
Raving of dead men's dust and beat-
    ing hearts.

A dismal hostel in a dismal land,
A flat malarial world of reed and rush !
But there from fever and my care of
    him
Sprang up a friendship that may help
    us yet.
For while we roam'd along the dreary
    coast,
And waited for her message, piece by
    piece
I learnt the drearier story of his life ;
And, tho' he loved and honor'd Lionel,
Found that the sudden wail his lady
    made
Dwelt in his fancy : did he know her
    worth,
Her beauty even ? should he not be
    taught,
Ev'n by the price that others set upon it,
The value of that jewel he had to
    guard ?

Suddenly came her notice and we
    past,
I with our lover to his native Bay.

This love is of the brain, the mind,
    the soul :
That makes the sequel pure ; tho'
    some of us
Beginning at the sequel know no more.
Not such am I : and yet I say the bird
That will not hear my call, however
    sweet,

But if my neighbor whistle answers
    him —
What matter ? there are others in the
    wood.
Yet when I saw her (and I thought him
    crazed,
Tho' not with such a craziness as needs
A cell and keeper), those dark eyes
    of hers —
Oh ! such dark eyes ! and not her eyes
    alone,
But all from these to where she touch'd
    on earth,
For such a craziness as Julian's look'd
No less than one divine apology.

So sweetly and so modestly she came
To greet us, her young hero in her
    arms !
" Kiss him," she said.   " You gave me
    life again.
He, but for you, had never seen it once.
His other father you ! Kiss him, and
    then
Forgive him, if his name be Julian too."

Talk of lost hopes and broken heart !
    his own
Sent such a flame into his face, I
    knew
Some sudden vivid pleasure hit him
    there.

But he was all the more resolved to
    go,
And sent at once to Lionel, praying
    him
By that great love they both had
    borne the dead,
To come and revel for one hour with
    him
Before he left the land for evermore ;
And then to friends — they were not
    many — who lived
Scatteringly about that lonely land
    of his,
And bade them to a banquet of fare-
    wells.

And Julian made a solemn feast : I
    never
Sat at a costlier ; for all round his hall

From column on to column, as in a
  wood,
Not such as here — an equatorial one,
Great garlands swung and blossom'd;
  and beneath,
Heirlooms, and ancient miracles of
  Art,
Chalice and salver, wines that, Heaven
  knows when,
Had suck'd the fire of some forgotten
  sun,
And kept it thro' a hundred years of
  gloom,
Yet glowing in a heart of ruby — cups
Where nymph and god ran ever round
  in gold —
Others of glass as costly — some with
  gems
Movable and resettable at will,
And trebling all the rest in value —
  Ah heavens!
Why need I tell you all ? — suffice to
  say
That whatsoever such a house as his,
And his was old, has in it rare or fair
Was brought before the guest : and
  they, the guests,
Wonder'd at some strange light in
  Julian's eyes
(I told you that he had his golden
  hour),
And such a feast, ill-suited as it seem'd
To such a time, to Lionel's loss and his
And that resolved self-exile from a
  land
He never would revisit, such a feast
So rich, so strange, and stranger ev'n
  than rich,
But rich as for the nuptials of a king.

And stranger yet, at one end of the
  hall
Two great funereal curtains, looping
  down,
Parted a little ere they met the floor,
About a picture of his lady, taken
Some years before, and falling hid the
  frame.
And just above the parting was a
  lamp:
So the sweet figure folded round with
  night

Seem'd stepping out of darkness with
  a smile.

Well then — our solemn feast — we
  ate and drank,
And might — the wines being of such
  nobleness —
Have jested also, but for Julian's eyes,
And something weird and wild about
  it all :
What was it ? for our lover seldom
  spoke,
Scarce touch'd the meats ; but ever
  and anon
A priceless goblet with a priceless wine
Arising, show'd he drank beyond his
  use ;
And when the feast was near an end,
  he said :

  "There is a custom in the Orient,
    friends —
I read of it in Persia — when a man
Will honor those who feast with him,
  he brings
And shows them whatsoever he ac-
  counts
Of all his treasures the most beautiful,
Gold, jewels, arms, whatever it may be.
This custom —— "

              Pausing here a moment, all
The guests broke in upon him with
  meeting hands
And cries about the banquet — " Beautiful!
Who could desire more beauty at a
  feast ? "

The lover answer'd, " There is more
  than one
Here sitting who desires it.   Laud me
  not
Before my time, but hear me to the
  close.
This custom steps yet further when
  the guest
Is loved and honor'd to the uttermost.
For after he hath shown him gems or
  gold,
He brings and sets before him in rich
  guise

That which is thrice as beautiful as
   these,
The beauty that is dearest to his
   heart —
'O my heart's lord, would I could
   show you,' he says,
'Ev'n my heart too.' And I propose
   to-night
To show you what is dearest to my
   heart,
And my heart too.

    " But solve me first a doubt.
I knew a man, nor many years ago;
He had a faithful servant, one who
   loved
His master more than all on earth
   beside.
He falling sick, and seeming close on
   death,
His master would not wait until he
   died,
But bade his menials bear him from
   the door,
And leave him in the public way to
   die.
I knew another, not so long ago,
Who found the dying servant, took
   him home,
And fed, and cherish'd him, and saved
   his life.
I ask you now, should this first master
   claim
His service, whom does it belong to ?
   him
Who thrust him out, or him who saved
   his life ? "

   This question, so flung down before
   the guests,
And balanced either way by each, at
   length
When some were doubtful how the
   law would hold,
Was handed over by consent of all
To one who had not spoken, Lionel.

   Fair speech was his, and delicate of
   phrase.
And he beginning languidly — his loss
Weigh'd on him yet — but warming
   as he went,

Glanced at the point of law, to pass
   it by,
Affirming that as long as either lived,
By all the laws of love and grateful-
   ness,
The service of the one so saved was
   due
All to the saver — adding, with a
   smile,
The first for many weeks — a semi-
   smile
As at a strong conclusion — "body
   and soul
And life and limbs, all his to work his
   will."

   Then Julian made a secret sign to
   me
To bring Camilla down before them
   all.
And crossing her own picture as she
   came,
And looking as much lovelier as herself
Is lovelier than all others — on her
   head
A diamond circlet, and from under
   this ,
A veil, that seemed no more than
   gilded air,
Flying by each fine ear, an Eastern
   gauze
With seeds of gold — so, with that
   grace of hers,
Slow-moving as a wave against the
   wind,
That flings a mist behind it in the
   sun —
And bearing high in arms the mighty
   babe,
The younger Julian, who himself was
   crown'd
With roses, none so rosy as himself —
And over all her babe and her the
   jewels
Of many generations of his house
Sparkled and flash'd, for he had
   decked them out
As for a solemn sacrifice of love —
So she came in : — I am long in telling
   it,
I never yet beheld a thing so strange,

Sad, sweet, and strange together —
    floated in —
While all the guests in mute amaze-
    ment rose —
And slowly pacing to the middle
    hall,
Before the board, there paused and
    stood, her breast
Hard-heaving, and her eyes upon her
    feet,
Not daring yet to glance at Lionel.
But him she carried, him nor lights
    nor feast
Dazed or amazed, nor eyes of men;
    who cared
Only to use his own, and staring wide
And hungering for the gilt and
    jewell'd world
About him, look'd, as he is like to
    prove,
When Julian goes, the lord of all he
    saw.

    "My guests," said Julian: "you
        are honor'd now
Ev'n to the uttermost: in her behold
Of all my treasures the most beau-
    tiful,
Of all things upon earth the dearest to
    me."
Then waving us a sign to seat our-
    selves,
Led his dear lady to a chair of state.
And I, by Lionel sitting, saw his face
Fire, and dead ashes and all fire again
Thrice in a second, felt him tremble
    too,
And heard him muttering, "So like,
    so like;
She never had a sister. I knew none.
Some cousin of his and hers — O God,
    so like!"
And then he suddenly ask'd her if
    she were.
She shook, and cast her eyes down,
    and was dumb.
And then some other question'd if she
    came
From foreign lands, and still she did
    not speak.
Another, if the boy were hers: but
    she

To all their queries answer'd not a
    word,
Which made the amazement more,
    till one of them
Said, shuddering, "Her spectre!"
    But his friend
Replied, in half a whisper, "Not at
    least
The spectre that will speak if spoken
    to.
Terrible pity, if one so beautiful
Prove, as I almost dread to find her,
    dumb!"

    But Julian, sitting by her, answer'd
        all:
"She is but dumb, because in her you
    see
That faithful servant whom we spoke
    about,
Obedient to her second master now;
Which will not last. I have here to-
    night a guest
So bound to me by common love and
    loss —
What! shall I bind him more? in his
    behalf,
Shall I exceed the Persian, giving
    him
That which of all things is the dearest
    to me,
Not only showing? and he himself
    pronounced
That my rich gift is wholly mine to
    give.

    "Now all be dumb, and promise all
        of you
Not to break in on what I say by
    word
Or whisper, while I show you all my
    heart."
And then began the story of his love
As here to-day, but not so wordily —
The passionate moment would not
    suffer that —
Past thro' his visions to the burial;
    thence
Down to this last strange hour in his
    own hall;
And then rose up, and with him all
    his guests

Once more as by enchantment; all
    but he,
Lionel, who fain had risen, but fell
    again,
And sat as if in chains — to whom he
    said :

    "Take my free gift, my cousin, for
    your wife;
And were it only for the giver's sake,
And tho' she seem so like the one you
    lost,
Yet cast her not away so suddenly,
Lest there be none left here to bring
    her back :
I leave this land for ever." Here he
    ceased.

    Then taking his dear lady by one
    hand,
And bearing   one arm the noble
    babe,
He slowly brought them both to
    Lionel.
And there the widower husband and
    dead wife
Rush'd each at each with a cry, that
    rather seem'd

For some new death than for a life
    renew'd;
Whereat the very babe began to wail;
At once they turn'd, and caught and
    brought him in
To their charm'd circle, and, half kill-
    ing him
With kisses, round him closed and
    claspt again.
But Lionel, when at last he freed him-
    self
From wife and child, and lifted up a
    face
All over glowing with the sun of
    life,
And love, and boundless thanks —
    the sight of this
So frighted our good friend, that turn-
    ing to me
And saying, "It is over: let us
    go" —
There were our horses ready at the
    doors —
We bade them no farewell, but mount-
    ing these
He past for ever from his native land;
And I with him, my Julian, back to
    mine.

BALLADS AND OTHER POEMS.

TO

ALFRED TENNYSON,

MY GRANDSON.

GOLDEN-HAIR'D Ally whose name is one with mine,
Crazy with laughter and babble and earth's new wine,
Now that the flower of a year and a half is thine,
O little blossom, O mine, and mine of mine,
Glorious poet who never hast written a line,
Laugh, for the name at the head of my verse is thine.
May'st thou never be wrong'd by the name that is mine!

THE FIRST QUARREL.

(IN THE ISLE OF WIGHT.)

I.

"WAIT a little," you say, "you are
sure it'll all come right,"
But the boy was born i' trouble, an'
looks so wan an' so white:
Wait! an' once I ha' waited — I hadn't
to wait for long.
Now I wait, wait, wait for Harry. —
No, no, you are doing me
wrong!
Harry and I were married: the boy
can hold up his head,
The boy was born in wedlock, but
after my man was dead;
I ha' work'd for him fifteen years, an'
I work an' I wait to the end.
I am all alone in the world, an' you
are my only friend.

II.

Doctor, if *you* can wait, I'll tell you
the tale o' my life.
When Harry an' I were children, he
call'd me his own little wife;
I was happy when I was with him, an'
sorry when he was away,
An' when we play'd together, I loved
him better than play;
He workt me the daisy chain — he
made me the cowslip ball,
He fought the boys that were rude,
an' I loved him better than all.
Passionate girl tho' I was, an' often at
home in disgrace,
I never could quarrel with Harry — I
had but to look in his face.

III.

There was a farmer in Dorset of
Harry's kin, that had need
Of a good stout lad at his farm; he
sent, an' the father agreed;
So Harry was bound to the Dorsetshire
farm for years an' for years.
I walked with him down to the quay,
poor lad, an' we parted in tears.
The boat was beginning to move, we
heard them a-ringing the bell,
"I'll never love any but you, God
bless you, my own little Nell."

IV.

I was a child, an' he was a child, an'
he came to harm;

There was a girl, a hussy, that workt
    with him up at the farm,
One had deceived her an' left her
    alone with her sin an'her shame,
And so she was wicked with Harry; the
    girl was the most to blame.

v.

And years went over till I that was
    little had grown so tall,
The men would say of the maids, " Our
    Nelly's the flower of 'em all."
I didn't take heed o' *them*, but I taught
    myself all I could
To make a good wife for Harry, when
    Harry came home for good.

vi.

Often I seem'd unhappy, and often as
    happy too,
For I heard it abroad in the fields " I'll
    never love any but you ";
" I'll never love any but you" the
    morning song of the lark,
"I'll never love any but you" the night-
    ingale's hymn in the dark.

vii.

And Harry came home at last, but he
    look'd at me sidelong and shy,
Vext me a bit, till he told me that so
    many years had gone by,
I had grown so handsome and tall —
    that I might ha' forgot him
    somehow —
For he thought — there were other
    lads — he was fear'd to look
    at me now.

viii.

Hard was the frost in the field, we were
    married o' Christmas day,
Married among the red berries, an' all
    as merry as May —
Those were the pleasant times, my
    house an' my man were my
    pride,
We seem'd like ships i' the Channel
    a-sailing with wind an' tide.

ix.

But work was scant in the Isle, tho'
    he tried the villages round,
So Harry went over the Solent to see
    if work could be found ;
An' he wrote, " I ha' six weeks' work,
    little wife, so far as I know ;
I'll come for an hour to-morrow, an'
    kiss you before I go."

x.

So I set to righting the house, for
    wasn't he coming that day ?
An' I hit on an old deal-box that was
    push'd in a corner away,
It was full of old odds an' ends, an' a
    letter along wi' the rest,
I had better ha' put my naked hand
    in a hornets' nest.

xi.

" Sweetheart " — this was the letter —
    this was the letter I read —
" You promised to find me work near
    you, an' I wish I was dead —
Didn't you kiss me an' promise ? you
    haven't done it, my lad,
An' I almost died o' your going away,
    an' I wish that I had."

xii.

I too wish that I had — in the pleasant
    times that had past,
Before I quarrell'd with Harry — *my*
    quarrel — the first an' the last.

xiii.

For Harry came in, an' I flung him
    the letter that drove me wild,
An' he told it me all at once, as simple
    as any child,
" What can it matter, my lass, what I
    did wi' my single life ?
I ha' been as true to you as ever a
    man to his wife ;
An' *she* wasn't one o' the worst."
    " Then," I said, " I'm none o' the
    best."
An' he smiled at me, " Ain't you, my
    love ? Come, come, little wife,
    let it rest !

The man isn't like the woman, no
　　need to make such a stir."
But he anger'd me all the more, an' I
　　said "You were keeping with her,
When I was a-loving you all along an'
　　the same as before."
An' he didn't speak for a while, an'
　　he anger'd me more and more.
Then he patted my hand in his gentle
　　way, "Let bygones be!"
"Bygones! you kept yours hush'd," I
　　said, "when you married me!
By-gones ma' be come-agains; an' *she*
　　— in her shame an' her sin —
You'll have her to nurse my child, if
　　I die o' my lying in!
You'll make her its second mother! I
　　hate her — an' I hate you!"
Ah, Harry, my man, you had better
　　ha' beaten me black an' blue
Than ha' spoken as kind as you did,
　　when I were so crazy wi' spite,
"Wait a little, my lass, I am sure it 'ill
　　all come right."

XIV.

An' he took three turns in the rain,
　　an' I watch'd him, an' when he
　　came in
I felt that my heart was hard, he was
　　all wet thro' to the skin,
An' I never said "off wi' the wet," I
　　never said "on wi' the dry,"
So I knew my heart was hard, when
　　he came to bid me goodbye.
"You said that you hated me, Ellen,
　　but that isn't true, you know;
I am going to leave you a bit — you'll
　　kiss me before I go?"

XV.

"Going! you're going to her — kiss
　　her — if you will," I said, —
I was near my time wi' the boy, I must
　　ha' been light i' my head —
"I had sooner be cursed than kiss'd!"
　　— I didn't know well what I
　　meant,
But I turn'd my face from *him*, an' he
　　turn'd *his* face an' he went.

XVI.

And then he sent me a letter, "I've
　　gotten my work to do;
You wouldn't kiss me, my lass, an' I
　　never loved any but you;
I am sorry for all the quarrel an' sorry
　　for what she wrote,
I ha' six weeks' work in Jersey an' go
　　to-night by the boat."

XVII.

An' the wind began to rise, an' I
　　thought of him out at sea,
An' I felt I had been to blame; he
　　was always kind to me.
"Wait a little, my lass, I am sure it
　　'ill all come right" —
An' the boat went down that night —
　　the boat went down that night.

RIZPAH.

17—.

I.

WAILING, wailing, wailing, the wind
　　over land and sea —
And Willy's voice in the wind, "O
　　mother, come out to me."
Why should he call me to-night, when
　　he knows that I cannot go?
For the downs are as bright as day, and
　　the full moon stares at the snow.

II.

We should be seen, my dear; they
　　would spy us out of the town.
The loud black nights for us, and the
　　storm rushing over the down,
When I cannot see my own hand, but
　　am led by the creak of the chain,
And grovel and grope for my son till I
　　find myself drenched with the
　　rain.

III.

Anything fallen again? nay — what
　　was there left to fall?
I have taken them home, I have num-
　　ber'd the bones, I have hidden
　　them all.

What am I saying ? and what are *you* ?
do you come as a spy ?
Falls ? what falls ? who knows ? As
the tree falls so must it lie.

IV.

Who let her in? how long has she been?
you — what have you heard ?
Why did you sit so quiet ? you never
have spoken a word.
O — to pray with me — yes — a lady
— none of their spies —
But the night has crept into my heart,
and begun to darken my eyes.

V.

Ah — you, that have lived so soft,
what should *you* know of the
night,
The blast and the burning shame and
the bitter frost and the fright ?
I have done it, while you were asleep —
you were only made for the day.
I have gather'd my baby together —
and now you may go your way.

VI.

Nay — for it's kind of you, Madam, to
sit by an old dying wife.
But say nothing hard of my boy, I
have only an hour of life.
I kiss'd my boy in the prison, before
he went out to die.
"They dared me to do it," he said,
and he never has told me a lie.
I whipt him for robbing an orchard
once when he was but a child —
"The farmer dared me to do it," he
said ; he was always so wild —
And idle — and couldn't be idle — my
Willy — he never could rest.
The King should have made him a
soldier, he would have been
one of his best.

VII.

But he lived with a lot of wild mates,
and they never would let him
be good ;
They swore that he dare not rob the
mail, and he swore that he
would :

And he took no life, but he took one
purse, and when all was done
He flung it among his fellows — I'll
none of it, said my son.

VIII.

I came into court to the Judge and the
lawyers. I told them my tale,
God's own truth — but they kill'd him,
they kill'd him for robbing the
mail.
They hang'd him in chains for a show
— we had always borne a good
name —
To be hang'd for a thief — and then
put away — isn't that enough
shame ?
Dust to dust — low down — let us hide !
but they set him so high
That all the ships of the world could
stare at him, passing by.
God 'ill pardon the hell-black raven
and horrible fowls of the air,
But not the black heart of the lawyer
who kill'd him and hang'd him
there.

IX.

And the jailer forced me away. I had
bid him my last goodbye ;
They had fasten'd the door of his cell.
"O mother!" I heard him cry.
I couldn't get back tho' I tried, he had
something further to say,
And now I never shall know it. The
jailer forced me away.

X.

Then since I couldn't but hear that
cry of my boy that was dead,
They seized me and shut me up : they
fasten'd me down on my bed.
"Mother, O mother!" — he call'd in the
dark to me year after year —
They beat me for that, they beat me
— you know that I couldn't but
hear ;
And then at the last they found I had
grown so stupid and still
They let me abroad again — but the
creatures had worked their will.

XI.

Flesh of my flesh was gone, but bone
of my bone was left —
I stole them all from the lawyers —
and you, will you call it a
theft ? —
My baby, the bones that had suck'd
me, the bones that had laughed
and had cried —
Theirs ? O no! they are mine — not
theirs — they had moved in my
side.

XII.

Do you think I was scared by the
bones ? I kiss'd 'em, I buried
'em all —
I can't dig deep, I am old — in the
night by the churchyard wall.
My Willy 'ill rise up whole when the
trumpet of judgment 'ill sound,
But I charge you never to say that I
laid him in holy ground.

XIII.

They would scratch him up — they
would hang him again on the
cursed tree.
Sin ? O yes — we are sinners, I know
— let all that be,
And read me a Bible verse of the
Lord's good will toward men —
"Full of compassion and mercy, the
Lord " — let me hear it again;
"Full of compassion and mercy —
long-suffering." Yes, O yes !
For the lawyer is born but to murder
— the Saviour lives but to bless.
He'll never put on the black cap except
for the worst of the worst,
And the first may be last — I have
heard it in church — and the
last may be first.
Suffering — O long-suffering — yes, as
the Lord must know,
Year after year in the mist and the
wind and the shower and the
snow.

XIV.

Heard, have you ? what ? they have
told you he never repented his
sin.
How do they know it ? are *they* his
mother ? are *you* of his kin ?
Heard! have you ever heard, when
the storm on the downs began,
The wind that 'ill wail like a child and
the sea that 'ill moan like a
man ?

XV.

Election, Election and Reprobation —
it's all very well.
But I go to-night to my boy, and I
shall not find him in Hell.
For I cared so much for my boy that
the Lord has look'd into my
care,
And He means me I'm sure to be happy
with Willy, I know not where.

XVI.

And if *he* be lost — but to save *my* soul,
that is all your desire :
Do you think that I care for *my* soul
if my boy be gone to the fire ?
I have been with God in the dark — go,
go, you may leave me alone —
You never have borne a child — you
are just as hard as a stone.

XVII.

Madam, I beg your pardon ! I think
that you mean to be kind,
But I cannot hear what you say for my
Willy's voice in the wind —
The snow and the sky so bright — he
used but to call in the dark,
And he calls to me now from the
church and not from the gibbet
— for hark !
Nay — you can hear it yourself — it is
coming — shaking the walls —
Willy — the moon's in a cloud ——
Good night. I am going. He
calls.

THE NORTHERN COBBLER.

I.

Waäit till our Sally cooms in, fur
  thou mun a' sights [1] to tell.
Eh, but I be maäin glad to seeä tha sa
  'arty an' well.
" Cast awaäy an a disolut land wi' a
  vartical soon [2] ! "
Strange fur to goä fur to think what
  saäilors a' seeän an' a' doon ;
" Summat to drink — sa' 'ot ? " I 'a
  nowt but Adam's wine :
What's the 'eät o' this little 'ill-side to
  the 'eät o' the line ?

II.

" What's i' tha bottle a-stanning
  theer ? " I'll tell tha. Gin.
But if thou wants thy grog, tha mun
  goä fur it down to the inn.
Naay — fur I be maän-glad, but thaw
  tha was iver sa dry,
Thou gits naw gin fro' the bottle theer,
  an' I'll tell tha why.

III.

Meä an' thy sister was married, when
  wur it ? back-end o' June,
Ten year sin', and wa 'greed as well
  as a fiddle i' tune :
I could fettle and clump owd booöts
  and shoes wi' the best on 'em all,
As fur as fro' Thursby thurn hup to
  Harmsby and Hutterby Hall.
We was busy as beeäs i' the bloom an'
  as 'appy as 'art could think,
An' then the babby wur burn, and
  then I taäkes to the drink.

---

[1] The vowels *aï*, pronounced separately
though in the closest conjunction, best render
the sound of the long *i* and *y* in this dialect.
But since such words as *craïin'*, *daïin'*, *whaï*,
aï (I), etc., look awkward except in a page
of express phonetics, I have thought it better
to leave the simple *i* and *y*, and trust that my
readers will give them the broader pronunci-
ation.

[2] The *oo* short, as in " wood."

IV.

An' I weänt gaäinsaäy it, my lad, thaw
  I be hafe shaämed on it now,
We could sing a good song at the
  Plow, we could sing a good song
  at the Plow ;
Thaw once of a frosty night I slither'd
  an' hurted my huck,[1]
An' I coom'd neck-an-crop soomtimes
  slaäpe down i' the squad an'
  the muck :
An' once I fowt wi' the Taäilor — not
  hafe ov a man, my lad —
Fur he scrawm'd an' scratted my faäce
  like a cat, an' it maäde 'er sa
  mad
That Sally she turn'd a tongue-bang-
  er, [2] an' raäted ma, ' Sottin' thy
  braäins
Guzzlin' an' soäkin' an' smoäkin' an'
  hawmin' [3] about i' the laänes,
Soä sow-droonk that tha doesn not
  touch thy 'at to the Squire ; '
An' I looök'd cock-eyed at my noäse
  an' I seeäd 'im a-gitten' o' fire ;
But sin' I wur hallus i' liquor an' hallus as droonk as a king,
Foälks' coostom flitted awaäy like a
  kite wi' a brokken string.

V.

An' Sally she wesh'd foälks' cloäths
  to keep the wolf fro' the door,
Eh but the moor she riled me, she
  druv me to drink the moor,
Fur I fun', when 'er back wur turn'd,
  wheer Sally's owd stockin' wur
  'id,
An' I grabb'd the munny she maäde,
  and I weär'd it o' liquor, I did.

VI.

An' one night I cooms 'oäm like a
  bull gotten loose at a faäir,
An' she wur a-waäitin' fo'mma, an'
  cryin' and teärin' 'er 'aäir,
An' I tummled athurt the craädle an'
  sweär'd as I'd break ivry stick

---

[1] Hip.   [2] Scold.   [3] Lounging.

O' furnitur 'ere i' the 'ouse, an' I gied
  our Sally a kick,
An' I mash'd the taäbles an' chairs,
  an' she an' the babby beäl'd,[1]
Fur I knaw'd naw moor what I did
  nor a mortal beäst o' the feäld.

VII.

An' when I waäked i' the murnin' I
  seeäd that our Sally went
  laämed
Cos' o' the kick as I gied 'er, an' I wur
  dreädful ashaämed ;
An' Sally wur sloomy[2] an' draggle
  taäil'd in an owd turn gown,
An' the babby's faäce wurn't wesh'd
  and the 'ole 'ouse hupside down.

VIII.

An' then I minded our Sally sa pratty
  an' neät an' sweeät,
Straät as a pole an' cleän as a flower
  fro' 'eäd to feeät :
An' then I minded the fust kiss I gied
  'er by Thursby thurn ;
Theer wur a lark a-singin' 'is best of
  a Sunday at murn,
Couldn't see 'im, we 'eärd 'im a-
  mountin' oop 'igher an' 'igher,
An' then 'e turn'd to the sun, an' 'e
  shined like a sparkle o' fire.
" Doesn't tha see 'im," she axes, " fur
  I can see 'im ? " an' I
Seeäd nobbut the smile o' the sun as
  danced in 'er pratty blue eye ;
An' I says " I mun gie tha a kiss," an'
  Sally says " Noä, thou moänt,"
But I gied 'er a kiss, an' then anoother,
  an' Sally says " doänt ! "

IX.

An' when we coom'd into Meeätin', at
  fust she wur all in a tew,
But, arter, we sing'd the 'ymn togither
  like birds on a beugh ;
An' Muggins 'e preäch'd o' Hell-fire
  an' the loove o' God fur men,
An then upo' coomin' awaäy Sally
  gied me a kiss ov 'ersen.

---

[1] Bellowed, cried out.
[2] Sluggish, out of spirits.

X.

Heer wur a fall fro' a kiss to a kick
  like Saätan as fell
Down out o' heaven i' Hell-fire — thaw
  theer's naw drinkin' i' Hell ;
Meä fur to kick our Sally as kep the
  wolf fro' the door,
All along o' the drink, fur I loov'd 'er
  as well as afoor.

XI.

Sa like a graät num-cumpus I blubber'd awaäy o' the bed —
" Weänt niver do it naw moor ; "
  an' Sally looökt up an' she said,
" I'll upowd it[1] tha weänt ; thou'rt
  like the rest o' the men,
Thou'll goä sniffin' about the tap till
  tha does it agëan.
Theer's thy hennemy, man, an' I
  knaws, as knaws tha sa well,
That, if tha seeäs 'im an' smells 'im
  tha'll foller 'im slick into Hell."

XII.

" Naäy," says I, " fur I weänt goä
  sniffin' about the tap."
" Weänt tha ? " she says, an' mysen I
  thowt i' mysen " mayhap."
" Noä : " an' I started awaäy like a
  shot, an' down to the Hinn,
An' I browt what tha seeäs stannin'
  theer, yon big black bottle o'
  gin.

XIII.

" That caps owt,"[2] says Sally, an' saw
  she begins to cry,
But I puts it inter 'er 'ands 'an I says
  to 'er, " Sally," says I,
" Stan' 'im theer i' the naäme o' the
  Lord an' the power ov 'is
  Graäce,
Stan' 'im theer, fur I'll looök my
  hennemy straït i' the faäce,
Stan' 'im theer i' the winder, an' let
  ma looök at 'im then,
'E seeäms naw moor nor watter, an'
  'e's the Divil's oän sen."

---

[1] I'll uphold it.
[2] That's beyond everything.

XIV.

An' I wur down i' tha mouth, couldn't
    do naw work an' all,
Nasty an' snaggy an' shaäky, an'
    poonch'd my 'and wi' the hawl,
But she wur a power o' coomfut, an'
    sattled 'ersen o' my knee,
An' coäxd an' coodled me oop till
    ageän I feel'd mysen free.

XV.

An' Sally she tell'd it about, an' foälk
    stood a-gawmin'[1] in,
As thaw it wur summat bewitch'd
    istead of a quart o' gin;
An' some on 'em said it wur watter —
    an' I wur chousin' the wife,
Fur I couldn't 'owd 'ands off gin, wur
    it nobbut to saäve my life;
An' blacksmith 'e strips me the thick
    ov 'is airm, an' 'e shaws it to me,
"Feëal thou this! thou can't graw
    this upo' watter!" says he.
An' Doctor 'e calls o' Sunday an' just
    as candles was lit,
"Thou moänt do it," he says, "tha
    mun breäk 'im off bit by bit."
"Thou'rt but a Methody-man," says
    Parson, and laäys down 'is 'at,
An' 'e points to the bottle o' gin, "but
    I respecks tha fur that;"
An' Squire, his oän very sen, walks
    down fro' the 'All to see,
An' 'e spanks 'is 'and into mine, "fur
    I respecks tha," says 'e;
An' coostom ageän draw'd in like a
    wind fro' far an' wide,
And browt me the booöts to be cob-
    bled fro' hafe the coontryside.

XVI.

An' theer 'e stans an' theer 'e shall
    stan to my dying daäy;
I 'a gotten to loov 'im ageän in
    anoother kind of a waäy,
Proud on 'im, like, my lad, an' I
    keeäps 'im cleän an' bright,
Loovs 'im, an' roobs 'im, an' doosts
    'im, an' puts 'im back i' the light.

[1] Staring vacantly.

XVII.

Wouldn't a pint a' sarved as well as a
    quart? Naw doubt:
But I liked a bigger feller to fight wi'
    an' fowt it out.
Fine an' meller 'e mun be by this, if I
    cared to taäste,
But I moänt, my lad, and I weänt, fur
    I'd feäl mysen cleän dis-
    graäced.

XVIII.

An' once I said to the Missis, "My
    lass, when I cooms to die,
Smash the bottle to smithers, the
    Divil's in 'im," said I.
But arter I chaänged my mind, an' if
    Sally be left aloän,
I'll hev 'im a-buried wi'mma an' taäke
    'im afoor the Throän.

XIX.

Coom thou 'eer — yon laädy a-steppin'
    along the streeät,
Doesn't tha knaw 'er — sa pratty, an'
    feät, an' neät, an' sweeät?
Look at the cloäths on 'er back,
    thebbe ammost spick-span-new,
An' Tommy's faäce be as fresh as a
    codlin wesh'd i' the dew.

XX.

'Ere be our Sally an' Tommy, an' we
    be a-goin to dine,
Baäcon an' taätes, an' a beslings-pud-
    din'[1] an' Adam's wine;
But if tha wants ony grog tha mun
    goä fur it down to the Hinn,
Fur I weänt shed a drop on 'is blood,
    noä, not fur Sally's oän kin.

THE REVENGE.

A BALLAD OF THE FLEET.

I.

At Flores in the Azores Sir Richard
    Grenville lay,
And a pinnace, like a flutter'd bird,
    came flying from far away:

[1] A pudding made with the first milk of
the cow after calving.

"Spanish ships of war at sea! we
    have sighted fifty-three!"
Then sware Lord Thomas Howard:
    " 'Fore God I am no coward;
But I cannot meet them here, for my
    ships are out of gear,
And the half my men are sick. I
    must fly, but follow quick.
We are six ships of the line; can we
    fight with fifty-three?"

II.

Then spake Sir Richard Grenville: " I
    know you are no coward;
You fly them for a moment to fight
    with them again.
But I've ninety men and more that
    are lying sick ashore.
I should count myself the coward if I
    left them, my Lord Howard,
To these Inquisition dogs and the
    devildoms of Spain."

III.

So Lord Howard past away with five
    ships of war that day,
Till he melted like a cloud in the
    silent summer heaven;
But Sir Richard bore in hand all his
    sick men from the land
Very carefully and slow,
Men of Bideford in Devon,
And we laid them on the ballast down
    below;
For we brought them all aboard,
And they blest him in their pain, that
    they were not left to Spain,
To the thumbscrew and the stake, for
    the glory of the Lord.

IV.

He had only a hundred seamen to
    work the ship and to fight,
And he sailed away from Flores till
    the Spaniard came in sight,
With his huge sea-castles heaving
    upon the weather bow.
"Shall we fight or shall we fly?
Good Sir Richard, tell us now,
For to fight is but to die!

There'll be little of us left by the
    time this sun be set."
And Sir Richard said again: " We be
    all good English men.
Let us bang these dogs of Seville, the
    children of the devil,
For I never turn'd my back upon
    Don or devil yet."

V.

Sir Richard spoke and he laugh'd, and
    we roar'd a hurrah, and so
The little Revenge ran on sheer into
    the heart of the foe,
With her hundred fighters on deck,
    and her ninety sick below;
For half of their fleet to the right
    and half to the left were seen,
And the little Revenge ran on thro'
    the long sea-lane between.

VI.

Thousands of their soldiers look'd
    down from their decks and
    laugh'd,
Thousands of their seamen made
    mock at the mad little craft
Running on and on, till delay'd
By their mountain-like San Philip
    that, of fifteen hundred tons,
And up-shadowing high above us with
    her yawning tiers of guns,
Took the breath from our sails, and
    we stay'd.

VII.

And while now the great San Philip
    hung above us like a cloud
Whence the thunderbolt will fall
Long and loud,
Four galleons drew away
From the Spanish fleet that day,
And two upon the larboard and two
    upon the starboard lay,
And the battle-thunder broke from
    them all.

VIII.

But anon the great San Philip, she be-
    thought herself and went
Having that within her womb that
    had left her ill content;

And the rest they came aboard us, and
    they fought us hand to hand,
For a dozen times they came with
    their pikes and musqueteers,
And a dozen times we shook 'em off
    as a dog that shakes his ears
When he leaps from the water to the
    land.

IX.

And the sun went down, and the stars
    came out far over the summer
    sea,
But never a moment ceased the fight
    of the one and the fifty-three.
Ship after ship, the whole night long,
    their high-built galleons came,
Ship after ship, the whole night long,
    with her battle-thunder and
    flame;
Ship after ship, the whole night long,
    drew back with her dead and her
    shame.
For some were sunk and many were
    shatter'd, and so could fight us
    no more —
God of battles, was ever a battle like
    this in the world before?

X.

For he said " Fight on ! fight on ! "
Tho' his vessel was all but a wreck;
And it chanced that, when half of the
    short summer night was gone,
With a grisly wound to be drest he
    had left the deck,
But a bullet struck him that was
    dressing it suddenly dead,
And himself he was wounded again in
    the side and the head,
And he said " Fight on ! fight on ! "

XI.

And the night went down, and the sun
    smiled out far over the summer
    sea,
And the Spanish fleet with broken
    sides lay round us all in a ring;
But they dared not touch us again,
    for they fear'd that we still
    could sting,

So they watch'd what the end would be.
And we had not fought them in vain,
But in perilous plight were we,
Seeing forty of our poor hundred **were**
    slain,
And half of the rest of us maim'd for
    life
In the crash of the cannonades and
    the desperate strife;
And the sick men down in the hold
    were most of them stark and
    cold,
And the pikes were all broken or bent,
    and the powder was all of it
    spent;
And the masts and the rigging were
    lying over the side;
But Sir Richard cried in his English
    pride,
" We have fought such a fight for a
    day and a night
As may never be fought again!
We have won great glory, my men!
And a day less or more
At sea or ashore,
We die — does it matter when?
Sink me the ship, Master Gunner —
    sink her, split her in twain!
Fall into the hands of God, not into
    the hands of Spain ! "

XII.

And the gunner said " Ay, ay," but
    the seamen made reply :
" We have children, we have wives,
And the Lord hath spared our lives.
We will make the Spaniard promise,
    if we yield, to let us go;
We shall live to fight again and to
    strike another blow."
And the lion there lay dying, and they
    yielded to the foe.

XIII.

And the stately Spanish men to their
    flagship bore him then,
Where they laid him by the mast, old
    Sir Richard caught at last,
And they praised him to his face with
    their courtly foreign grace;
But he rose upon their decks, and he
    cried:

" I have fought for Queen and Faith
  like a valiant man and true ;
I have only done my duty as a man is
  bound to do :
With a joyful spirit I Sir Richard
  Grenville die ! "
And he fell upon their decks, and he
  died.

XIV.

And they stared at the dead that had
  been so valiant and true,
And had holden the power and glory
  of Spain so cheap
That he dared her with one little ship
  and his English few ;
Was he devil or man ?   He was devil
  for aught they knew,
But they sank his body with honor
  down into the deep,
And they mann'd the Revenge with a
  swarthier alien crew,
And away she sail'd with her loss and
  long'd for her own ;
When a wind from the lands they had
  ruin'd awoke from sleep,
And the water began to heave and the
  weather to moan,
And or ever that evening ended a
  great gale blew,
And a wave like the wave that is
  raised by an earthquake grew,
Till it smote on their hulls and their
  sails and their masts and their
  flags,
And the whole sea plunged and fell on
  the shot-shatter'd navy of Spain,
And the little Revenge herself went
  down by the island crags
To be lost evermore in the main.

THE SISTERS.

THEY have left the doors ajar ; and
  by their clash,
And prelude on the keys, I know the
  song,
Their favorite — which I call " The
  Tables Turned."
Evelyn begins it " O diviner Air."

EVELYN.

O diviner Air,
Thro' the heat, the drowth, the dust,
  the glare,
Far from out the west in shadowing
  showers,
Over all the meadow baked and bare,
Making fresh and fair
All the bowers and the flowers,
Fainting flowers, faded bowers,
Over all this weary world of ours,
Breathe, diviner Air !

A sweet voice that — you scarce could
  better that.
Now follows Edith echoing Evelyn.

EDITH.

O diviner light,
Thro' the cloud that roofs our noon
  with night,
Thro' the blotting mist, the blinding
  showers,
Far from out a sky for ever bright,
Over all the woodland's flooded bowers,
Over all the meadow's drowning flow-
  ers,
Over all this ruin'd world of ours,
Break, diviner light !

Marvellously like, their voices — and
  themselves !
Tho' one is somewhat deeper than the
  other,
As one is somewhat graver than the
  other —
Edith than Evelyn.   Your good Uncle,
  whom
You count the father of your fortune,
  longs
For this alliance : let me ask you then,
Which voice most takes you ? for I
  do not doubt
Being a watchful parent, you are
  taken
With one or other : tho' sometimes I
  fear
You may be flickering, fluttering in a
  doubt
Between the two — which must not be
  — which might

Be death to one : they both are beau-
tiful :
Evelyn is gayer, wittier, prettier, says
The common voice, if one may trust
it : she ?
No ! but the paler and the graver,
Edith.
Woo her and gain her then : no
wavering, boy !
The graver is perhaps the one for you
Who jest and laugh so easily and so
well.
For love will go by contrast, as by
likes.

No sisters ever prized each other
more.
Not so : their mother and her sister
loved
More passionately still.
But that my best
And oldest friend, your Uncle, wishes
it,
And that I know you worthy every-
way
To be my son, I might, perchance, be
loath
To part them, or part from them : and
yet one
Should marry, or all the broad lands
in your view
From this bay window — which our
house has held
Three hundred years — will pass col-
laterally.

My father with a child on either
knee,
A hand upon the head of either child,
Smoothing their locks, as golden as
his own
Were silver, "get them wedded"
would he say.
And once my prattling Edith ask'd
him "why ? "
Ay, why ? said he, " for why should I
go lame ? "
Then told them of his wars, and of
his wound.
For see — this wine — the grape from
whence it flow'd
Was blackening on the slopes of
Portugal,

When that brave soldier, down the
terrible ridge
Plunged in the last fierce charge at
Waterloo,
And caught the laming bullet. He
left me this,
Which yet retains a memory of its
youth,
As I of mine, and my first passion.
Come !
Here's to your happy union with my
child !

Yet must you change your name :
no fault of mine !
You say that you can do it as willingly
As birds make ready for their bridal-
time
By change of feather : for all that,
my boy,
Some birds are sick and sullen when
they moult.
An old and worthy name ! but mine
that stirr'd
Among our civil wars and earlier too
Among the Roses, the more venerable.
I care not for a name — no fault of
mine.
Once more — a happier marriage than
my own !

You see yon Lombard poplar on the
plain.
The highway running by it leaves a
breadth
Of sward to left and right, where, long
ago,
One bright May morning in a world
of song,
I lay at leisure, watching overhead
The aërial poplar wave, an amber
spire.

I dozed ; I woke. An open landau-
let
Whirl'd by, which, after it had past
me, show'd
Turning my way, the loveliest face
on earth.
The face of one there sitting opposite,
On whom I brought a strange unhap-
piness,
That time I did not see.

Love at first sight
May seem — with goodly rhyme and
 reason for it —
Possible — at first glimpse, and for a
 face
Gone in a moment — strange. Yet
 once, when first
I came on lake Llanberris in the dark,
A moonless night with storm — one
 lightning-fork
Flash'd out the lake; and tho' I
 loiter'd there
The full day after, yet in retrospect
That less than momentary thunder-
 sketch
Of lake and mountain conquers all
 the day.

The Sun himself has limn'd the face
 for me.
Not quite so quickly, no, nor half as
 well.
For look you here — the shadows are
 too deep,
And like the critic's blurring comment
 make
The veriest beauties of the work
 appear
The darkest faults: the sweet eyes
 frown: the lips
Seem but a gash. My sole memorial
Of Edith — no, the other, — both
 indeed.

So that bright face was flash'd thro'
 sense and soul
And by the poplar vanish'd — to be
 found
Long after, as it seem'd, beneath the
 tall
Tree-bowers, and those long-sweeping
 beechen boughs
Of our New Forest. I was there
 alone:
The phantom of the whirling landau-
 let
For ever past me by: when one quick
 peal
Of laughter drew me thro' the glimmering glades
Down to the snowlike sparkle of a
 cloth

On fern and foxglove. Lo, the face
 again,
My Rosalind in this Arden — Edith
 — all
One bloom of youth, health, beauty,
 happiness,
And moved to merriment at a passing
 jest.

There one of those about her know-
 ing me
Call'd me to join them; so with these
 I spent
What seem'd my crowning hour, my
 day of days.

I woo'd her then, nor unsuccess-
 fully,
The worse for her, for me! was I con-
 tent?
Ay — no, not quite; for now and then
 I thought
Laziness, vague love-longings, the
 bright May,
Had made a heated haze to magnify
The charm of Edith — that a man's
 ideal
Is high in Heaven, and lodged with
 Plato's God,
Not findable here — content, and not
 content,
In some such fashion as a man may
 be
That having had the portrait of his
 friend
Drawn by an artist, looks at it, and
 says,
"Good! very like! not altogether he."

As yet I had not bound myself by
 words,
Only, believing I loved Edith, made
Edith love *me*. Then came the day
 when I,
Flattering myself that all my doubts
 were fools
Born of the fool this Age that doubts
 of all —
Not I that day of Edith's love or
 mine —
Had braced my purpose to declare
 myself:

I stood upon the stairs of Paradise.
The golden gates would open at a
    word.
I spoke it — told her of my passion,
    seen
And lost and found again, had got so
    far,
Had caught her hand, her eyelids
    fell — I heard
Wheels, and a noise of welcome at
    the doors —
On a sudden after two Italian years
Had set the blossom of her health
    again,
The younger sister, Evelyn, enter'd
    — there,
There was the face, and altogether
    she.
The mother fell about the daughter's
    neck,
The sisters closed in one another's
    arms,
Their people throng'd about them
    from the hall,
And in the thick of question and
    reply
I fled the house, driven by one angel
    face,
And all the Furies.

                    I was bound to her;
I could not free myself in honor —
    bound
Not by the sounded letter of the word,
But counterpressures of the yielded
    hand
That timorously and faintly echoed
    mine,
Quick blushes, the sweet dwelling of
    her eyes
Upon me when she thought I did not
    see —
Were these not bonds? nay, nay, but
    could I wed her
Loving the other? do her that great
    wrong?
Had I not dream'd I loved her yester-
    morn?
Had I not known where Love, at first
    a fear,
Grew after marriage to full height
    and form?

Yet after marriage, that mock-sister
    there —
Brother-in-law — the fiery nearness of
    it —
Unlawful and disloyal brotherhood —
What end but darkness could ensue
    from this
For all the three? So Love and Honor
    jarr'd
Tho' Love and Honor join'd to raise
    the full
High-tide of doubt that sway'd me up
    and down
Advancing nor retreating.

                    Edith wrote:
"My mother bids me ask" (I did not
    tell you —
A widow with less guile than many a
    child.
God help the wrinkled children that
    are Christ's
As well as the plump cheek — she
    wrought us harm,
Poor soul, not knowing) "are you
    ill?" (so ran
The letter) "you have not been here
    of late.
You will not find me here. At last I
    go
On that long-promised visit to the
    North.
I told your wayside story to my
    mother
And Evelyn. She remembers you.
    Farewell.
Pray come and see my mother. Al-
    most blind
With ever-growing cataract, yet she
    thinks
She sees you when she hears. Again
    farewell."

    Cold words from one I had hoped to
        warm so far
That I could stamp my image on her
    heart!
"Pray come and see my mother, and
    farewell."
Cold, but as welcome as free airs of
    heaven
After a dungeon's closeness. Selfish,
    strange!

What dwarfs are men! my strangled
    vanity
Utter'd a stifled cry — to have vext
    myself
And all in vain for her — cold heart
    or none —
No bride for me. Yet so my path
    was clear
To win the sister.
           Whom I woo'd and won.
For Evelyn knew not of my former
    suit,
Because the simple mother work'd upon
By Edith pray'd me not to whisper of it.
And Edith would be bridesmaid on
    the day.
    But on that day, not being all at
    ease,
I from the altar glancing back upon
    her,
Before the first "I will" was utter'd,
    saw
The bridesmaid pale, statuelike, pas-
    sionless —
"No harm, no harm" I turn'd again,
    and placed
My ring upon the finger of my bride.

So, when we parted, Edith spoke
    no word,
She wept no tear, but round my
    Evelyn clung
In utter silence for so long, I thought
"What, will she never set her sister
    free?"

We left her, happy each in each,
    and then,
As tho' the happiness of each in each
Were not enough, must fain have tor-
    rents, lakes,
Hills, the great things of Nature and
    the fair,
To lift us as it were from common-
    place,
And help us to our joy. Better have
    sent
Our Edith thro' the glories of the
    earth,
To change with her horizon, if true
    Love
Were not his own imperial all-in-all.

Far off we went. My God, I would
    not live
Save that I think this gross hard-
    seeming world
Is our misshaping vision of the Powers
Behind the world, that make our griefs
    our gains.

    For on the dark night of our mar-
    riage-day
The great Tragedian, that had
    quench'd herself
In that assumption of the bridesmaid
    — she
That loved me — our true Edith —
    her brain broke
With over-acting, till she rose and
    fled
Beneath a pitiless rush of Autumn
    rain
To the deaf church — to be let in —
    to pray
Before *that* altar — so I think; and
    there
They found her beating the hard Pro-
    testant doors.
She died and she was buried ere we
    knew.

    I learnt it first. I had to speak.
    At once
The bright quick smile of Evelyn,
    that had sunn'd
The morning of our marriage, past
    away:
And on our home-return the daily
    want
Of Edith in the house, the garden,
    still
Haunted us like her ghost; and by
    and by,
Either from that necessity for talk
Which lives with blindness, or plain
    innocence
Of nature, or desire that her lost
    child
Should earn from both the praise of
    heroism,
The mother broke her promise to the
    dead,
And told the living daughter with
    what love

Edith had welcomed my brief wooing
    of her,
And all her sweet self-sacrifice and
    death.

Henceforth that mystic bond be-
    twixt the twins —
Did I not tell you they were twins?
    — prevail'd
So far that no caress could win my
    wife
Back to that passionate answer of full
    heart
I had from her at first. Not that her
    love,
Tho' scarce as great as Edith's power
    of love,
Had lessen'd, but the mother's gar-
    rulous wail
For ever woke the unhappy Past
    again,
Till that dead bridesmaid, meant to
    be my bride,
Put forth cold hands between us, and
    I fear'd
The very fountains of her life were
    chill'd;
So took her thence, and brought her
    here, and here
She bore a child, whom reverently we
    call'd
Edith; and in the second year was
    born
A second — this I named from her
    own self,
Evelyn; then two weeks — no more
    — she joined,
In and beyond the grave, that one
    she loved.

Now in this quiet of declining life,
Thro' dreams by night and trances of
    the day,
The sisters glide about me hand in
    hand,
Both beautiful alike, nor can I tell
One from the other, no, nor care to tell
One from the other, only know they
    come,
They smile upon me, till, remembering
    all
The love they both have borne me,
    and the love

I bore them both — divided as I am
From either by the stillness of the
    grave —
I know not which of these I love the
    best.

But *you* love Edith; and her own
    true eyes
Are traitors to her; our quick Ev-
    elyn —
The merrier, prettier, wittier, as they
    talk,
And not without good reason, my
    good son —
Is yet untouch'd: and I that hold
    them both
Dearest of all things — well, I am not
    sure —
But if there lie a preference either way,
And in the rich vocabulary of Love
" Most dearest " be a true superla-
    tive —
I think *I* likewise love your Edith
    most.

THE VILLAGE WIFE; OR, THE ENTAIL. [1]

I.

'OUSE-KEEPER sent tha my lass, fur
    New Squire coom'd last night.
Butter an' heggs — yis — yis. I'll
    goä wi' tha back: all right;
Butter I warrants be prime, an' I war-
    rants the heggs be as well,
Hafe a pint o' milk runs out when ya
    breäks the shell.

II.

Sit thysen down fur a bit: hev a glass
    o' cowslip wine!
I liked the owd Squire an' 'is gells as
    thaw they was gells o' mine,
Fur then we was all es one, the Squire
    an' 'is darters an' me,
Hall but Miss Annie, the heldest, I
    niver not took to she:
But Nelly, the last o' the cletch [2] I
    liked 'er the fust on 'em all,

[1] See note to " Northern Cobbler."

[2] A brood of chickens.

Fur hoffens we talkt o' my darter es
    died o' the fever at fall :
An' I thowt 'twur the will o' the Lord,
    but Miss Annie she said it wur
    draäins,
Fur she hedn't naw coomfut in 'er, an'
    arn'd naw thanks fur 'er paäins.
Eh ! thebbe all wi' the Lord my childer,
    I han't gotten none !
Sa new Squire's coom'd wi' 'is taäil in
    'is 'and, an' owd Squire's gone.

III.

Fur 'staäte be i' taäil, my lass : tha
    dosn' knaw what that be ?
But I knaws the law, I does, for the
    lawyer ha towd it me.
" When theer's naw 'eäd to a 'Ouse by
    the fault o' that ere maäle —
The gells they counts fur nowt, and
    the next un he taäkes the taäil."

IV.

What be the next un like ? can tha
    tell ony harm on 'im lass ?
Naay sit down — naw 'urry — sa
    cowd ! — hev another glass !
Straänge an' cowd fur the time ! we
    may happen a fall o' snaw —
Not es I cares fur to hear ony harm,
    but I likes to knaw.
An' I 'oaps es 'e beänt boooklarn'd :
    but 'e dosn' not coom fro' the
    shere ;
We' anew o' that wi' the Squire, an'
    we haätes boooklarnin' ere.

V.

Fur Squire wur a Varsity scholard, an'
    niver lookt arter the land —
Whoäts or turmuts or taätes — e' 'ed
    hallus a booök i' 'is 'and,
Hallus aloän wi' 'is booöks, thaw nigh
    upo' seventy year.
An' booöks, what's booöks ? thou
    knaws thebbe neyther 'ere nor
    theer.

VI.

An' the gells, they hadn't naw taäils,
    an' the lawyer he towd it me

That 'is taäil were soä tied up es he
    couldn't cut down a tree !
" Drat the trees," says I, to be sewer I
    haätes 'em, my lass,
Fur we puts the muck o' the land an'
    they sucks the muck fro' the
    grass.

VII.

An' Squire wur hallus a-smilin', an'
    gied to the tramps goin' by —
An' all o' the wust i' the parish — wi'
    hoffens a drop in 'is eye.
An' ivry darter o' Squire's hed her
    awn ridin-erse to 'ersen,
An' they rampaged about wi' their
    grooms, an' was 'untin' arter
    the men,
An' hallus a-dallackt [1] an' dizen'd out,
    an' a-buyin' new cloäthes,
While 'e sit like a graät glimmer-
    gowk [2] wi' 'is glasses athurt 'is
    noäse,
An' 'is noäse sa grufted wi' snuff as it
    couldn't be scroob'd awaäy,
Fur atween 'is reädin' an' writin' 'e
    snifft up a box in a daäy,
An' 'e niver runn'd arter the fox, nor
    arter the birds wi' 'is gun,
An' 'e niver not shot one 'are, but 'e
    leäved it to Charlie 'is son,
An' 'e niver not fish'd 'is awn ponds,
    but Charlie 'e cotch'd the pike,
For 'e warn't not burn to the land, an'
    'e didn't take kind to it like ;
But I eärs es 'e'd gie fur a howry [3] owd
    book thutty pound an' moor,
An' 'e'd wrote an owd book, his awn
    sen, sa I knaw'd es 'e'd coom
    to be poor ;
An' 'e gied — I be fear'd to tell tha 'ow
    much — fur an owd scratted
    stoän,
An' 'e digg'd up a loomp i' the land
    an' 'e got a brown pot an' a
    boän,
An' 'e bowt owd money, es wouldn't
    goä, wi' good gowd o' the
    Queen,

---

[1] Overdressed in gay colors.   [2] Owl.
[3] Filthy.

An' 'e bowt little statutes all-naäkt
    an' which was a shaame to be
    seen ;
But 'e niver looökt ower a bill, nor 'e
    niver not seed to owt,
An' 'e niver knawd nowt but booöks,
    an' booöks, as thou knaws,
    beänt nowt.

VIII.

But owd Squire's laädy es long es she
    lived she kep 'em all clear,
Thaw es long es she lived I never hed
    none of 'er darters 'ere ;
But arter she died we was all es one,
    the childer an' me,
An' sarvints runn'd in an' out, an'
    offens we hed 'em to tea.
Lawk ! 'ow I laugh'd when the lasses
    'ud talk o' their Missis's waäys,
An' the Missisis talk'd o' the lasses. —
    I'll tell tha some o' these daäys.
Hoänly Miss Annie were saw stuck
    oop, like 'er mother afoor —
'Er an' 'er blessed darter — they niver
    derken'd my door.

IX.

An' Squire 'e smiled an' 'e smiled till
    'e'd gotten a fright at last,
An' 'e calls fur 'is son, fur the 'turney's
    letters they foller'd sa fast ;
But Squire wur afear'd o' 'is son,
    an' 'e says to 'im, meek as a
    mouse,
" Lad, thou mun cut off thy taäil, or
    the gells 'ull goä to the 'Ouse,
Fur I finds es I be that i' debt, es I
    'oäps es thou'll 'elp me a bit,
An' if thou'll 'gree to cut off thy taäil
    I may saäve mysen yit."

X.

But Charlie 'e sets back 'is ears, 'an 'e
    sweärs, an' 'e says to im " Noä.
I've gotten the 'staäte by the taäil an'
    be dang'd if I iver let goä !
Coom ! coom ! feyther," 'e says, " why
    shouldn't thy booöks be sowd ?
I hears es soom o' thy booöks mebbe
    worth their weight i' gowd."

XI.

Heäps an' heäps o' booöks, I ha' see'd
    'em, belong'd to the Squire,
But the lasses 'ed teärd out leaves i'
    the middle to kindle the fire ;
Sa moäst on 'is owd big booöks fetch'd
    nigh to nowt at the saäle,
And Squire were at Charlie ageän to
    git 'im to cut off 'is taäil.

XII.

Ya wouldn't find Charlie's likes — 'e
    were that outdacious at oäm,
Not thaw ya went fur to raäke out Hell
    wi' a small-tooth coämb —
Droonk wi' the Quoloty's wine, an'
    droonk wi' the farmer's aäle,
Mad wi' the lasses an' all — an' 'e
    wouldn't cut off the taäil.

XIII.

Thou's coom'd oop by the beck ; and
    a thurn be a-grawin' theer,
I niver ha seed it sa white wi' the
    Maäy es I see'd it to-year —
Theerabouts Charlie joompt — and it
    gied me a scare tother night,
Fur I thowt it wur Charlie's ghoäst i'
    the derk, fur it looökt sa white.
" Billy," says 'e, " hev a joomp ! " —
    thaw the banks o' the beck be
    sa high,
Fur he ca'd 'is 'erse Billy-rough-un,
    thaw niver a hair wur awry ;
But Billy fell bakkuds o' Charlie, an'
    Charlie 'e brok 'is neck,
Sa theer wur a hend o' the taäil, fur
    'e lost 'is taäil i' the beck.

XIV.

Sa 'is taäil wur lost an' 'is booöks wur
    gone an' 'is boy wur deäd,
An' Squire 'e smiled an' 'e smiled, but
    'e niver not lift oop 'is 'eäd :
Hallus a soft un Squire ! an' 'e smiled,
    fur 'e hedn't naw friend,
Sa feyther an' son was buried togither,
    an' this wur the hend.

XV.

An' Parson as hesn't the call, nor the
    mooney, but hes the pride,

'E reäds of a sewer an' sartan 'oäp o'
  the tother side;
But I beänt that sewer es the Lord,
  howsiver they praäy'd an'
  praäy'd,
Lets them inter 'eaven eäsy es leäves
  their debts to be paäid.
Siver the mou'ds rattled down upo'
  poor owd Squire i' the wood,
An' I cried along wi' the gells, fur
  they weant niver coom to naw
  good.

XVI.

Fur Molly the long un she walkt
  awaäy wi' a hofficer lad,
An' nawbody 'eard on 'er sin, sa o'
  coorse she be gone to the bad!
An' Lucy wur laäme o' one leg, sweet-
  'arts she niver 'ed none—
Straänge an' unheppen[1] Miss Lucy!
  we naämed her "Dot an' gaw
  one!"
An' Hetty wur weak i' the hattics,
  wi'out ony harm i' the legs,
An' the fever 'ed baäked Jinny's 'ead
  as bald as one o' them heggs,
An' Nelly wur up fro' the craädle as
  big i' the mouth as a cow,
An' saw she mun hammergrate,[2] lass,
  or she weänt git a maäte onyhow!
An' es for Miss Annie es call'd me
  afoor my awn foälks to my
  faäce
"A hignorant village wife as 'ud hev
  to be larn'd her awn plaäce,"
Hes for Miss Hannie the heldest hes
  now be a grawin sa howd,
I knaws that mooch o' sheä, es it beänt
  not fit to be towd!

XVII.

Sa I didn't not taäke it kindly ov owd
  Miss Annie to saäy
Es I should be talkin ageän 'em, es
  soon es they went awaäy,
Fur, lawks! 'ow I cried when they
  went, an' our Nelly she gied me
  'er 'and,

Fur I'd ha done owt for the Squire an'
  'is gells es belong'd to the land;
Booöks, es I said afoor, thebbe ney-
  ther 'ere nor theer!
But I sarved 'em wi' butter an' heggs
  fur huppuds o' twenty year.

XVIII.

An' they hallus paäid what I hax'd,
  sa I hallus deal'd wi' the Hall,
An' they knaw'd what butter wur, an'
  they knaw'd what a hegg wur
  an' all;
Hugger-mugger they lived, but they
  wasn't that eäsy to pleäse,
Till I gied 'em Hinjian curn, an' they
  laäid big heggs es tha seeas;
An' I niver puts saäme[1] i' *my* butter,
  they does it at Willis's farm,
Taäste another drop o' the wine—
  tweänt do tha na harm.

XIX.

Sa new Squire's coom'd wi' 'is taäil in
  'is 'and, an' owd Squire's gone;
I heard 'im a roomlin' by, but arter
  my nightcap wur on;
Sa I han't clapt eyes on 'im yit, fur he
  coom'd last night sa laäte—
Pluksh!!![2] the hens i' the peäs! why
  didn't tha hesp tha gaäte?

IN THE CHILDREN'S
HOSPITAL.

EMMIE.

I.

Our doctor had call'd in another, I
  never had seen him before,
But he sent a chill to my heart when
  I saw him come in at the door,
Fresh from the surgery-schools of
  France and of other lands—
Harsh red hair, big voice, big chest,
  big merciless hands!
Wonderful cures he had done, O yes,
  but they said too of him

---

[1] Ungainly, awkward.   [2] Emigrate.

[1] Lard.

[2] A cry accompanied by a clapping of hands
to scare trespassing fowl.

He was happier using the knife than
in trying to save the limb,
And that I can well believe, for he
look'd so coarse and so red,
I could think he was one of those who
would break their jests on the
dead,
And mangle the living dog that had
loved him and fawn'd at his
knee —
Drench'd with the hellish oorali — that
ever such things should be!

II.

Here was a boy — I am sure that some
of our children would die
But for the voice of Love, and the
smile, and the comforting eye —
Here was a boy in the ward, every
bone seem'd out of its place —
Caught in a mill and crush'd — it was
all but a hopeless case:
And he handled him gently enough;
but his voice and his face were
not kind,
And it was but a hopeless case, he
had seen it and made up his
mind,
And he said to me roughly "The lad
will need little more of your
care."
" All the more need," I told him, " to
seek the Lord Jesus in prayer ;
They are all his children here, and I
pray for them all as my own :"
But he turn'd to me, " Ay, good woman,
can prayer set a broken bone?"
Then he mutter'd half to himself, but
I know that I heard him say
" All very well — but the good Lord
Jesus has had his day."

III.

Had? has it come? It has only
dawn'd. It will come by and
by.
O how could I serve in the wards if the
hope of the world were a lie?
How could I bear with the sights and
the loathsome smells of disease
But that He said "Ye do it to me,
when ye do it to these"?

IV.

So he went. And we past to this
ward where the younger children are laid :
Here is the cot of our orphan, our darling, our meek little maid ;
Empty you see just now! We have
lost her who loved her so
much —
Patient of pain tho' as quick as a sensitive plant to the touch ;
Hers was the prettiest prattle, it often
moved me to tears,
Hers was the gratefullest heart I have
found in a child of her years —
Nay you remember our Emmie ; you
used to send her the flowers ;
How she would smile at 'em, play
with 'em, talk to 'em hours
after hours!
They that can wander at will where the
works of the Lord are reveal'd
Little guess what joy can be got from
a cowslip out of the fields ;
Flowers to these "spirits in prison"
are all they can know of the
spring,
They freshen and sweeten the wards
like the waft of an Angel's
wing ;
And she lay with a flower in one hand
and her thin hands crost on her
breast —
Wan, but as pretty as heart can desire, and we thought her at rest,
Quietly sleeping — so quiet, our doctor said " Poor little dear,
Nurse, I must do it to-morrow ; she'll
never live thro' it, I fear."

V.

I walk'd with our kindly old doctor as
far as the head of the stair,
Then I return'd to the ward ; the child
didn't see I was there.

VI.

Never since I was nurse, had I been
so grieved and so vext !
Emmie had heard him. Softly she
call'd from her cot to the next,

" He says I shall never live thro' it, O
    Annie, what shall I do ? "
Annie consider'd. "If I," said the
    wise little Annie, " was you,
I should cry to the dear Lord Jesus to
    help me, for, Emmie, you see,
It's all in the picture there; ' Little
    children should come to me.' "
(Meaning the print that you gave us,
    I find that it always can please
Our children, the dear Lord Jesus
    with children about his knees.)
" Yes, and I will," said Emmie, " but
    then if I call to the Lord,
How should he know that it's me ?
    such a lot of beds in the ward ! "
That was a puzzle for Annie. Again
    she consider'd and said :
"Emmie, you put out your arms, and
    you leave 'em outside on the
    bed —
The Lord has so *much* to see to ! but,
    Emmie, you tell it him plain,
It's the little girl with her arms lying
    out on the counterpane."

VII.

I had sat three nights by the child —
    I could not watch her for four —
My brain had begun to reel — I felt I
    could do it no more.
That was my sleeping-night, but I
    thought that it never would
    pass.
There was a thunderclap once, and a
    clatter of hail on the glass,
And there was a phantom cry that I
    heard as I tost about,
The motherless bleat of a lamb in the
    storm and the darkness with-
    out;
My sleep was broken beside with
    dreams of the dreadful knife
And fears for our delicate Emmie who
    scarce would escape with her
    life ;
Then in the gray of the morning it
    seem'd she stood by me and
    smiled,
And the doctor came at his hour, and
    we went to see to the child.

VIII.

He had brought his ghastly tools : we
    believed her asleep again —
Her dear, long, lean, little arms lying
    out on the counterpane ;
Say that His day is done ! Ah why
    should we care what they say ?
The Lord of the children had heard
    her, and Emmie had past away

DEDICATORY POEM TO THE PRINCESS ALICE.

DEAD PRINCESS, living Power, if that,
    which lived
True life, live on — and if the fatal
    kiss,
Born of true life and love, divorce
    thee not
From earthly love and life — if what
    we call
The spirit flash not all at once from
    out
This shadow into Substance — then
    perhaps
The mellow'd murmur of the people's
    praise
From thine own State, and all our
    breadth of realm,
Where Love and Longing dress thy
    deeds in light,
Ascends to thee; and this March
    morn that sees
Thy Soldier-brother's bridal orange-
    bloom
Break thro' the yews and cypress of
    thy grave,
And thine Imperial mother smile
    again,
May send one ray to thee ! and who
    can tell —
Thou — England's England-loving
    daughter — thou
Dying so English thou wouldst have
    her flag
Borne on thy coffin — where is he can
    swear
But that some broken gleam from our
    poor earth
May touch thee, while remembering
    thee, I lay

At thy pale feet this ballad of the deeds
Of England, and her banner in the East?

THE DEFENCE OF LUCKNOW.

I.

BANNER of England, not for a season,
    O banner of Britain, hast thou
Floated in conquering battle or flapt
    to the battle-cry!
Never with mightier glory than when
    we had rear'd thee on high
Flying at top of the roofs in the
    ghastly siege of Lucknow —
Shot thro' the staff or the halyard,
    but ever we raised thee anew,
And ever upon the topmost roof our
    banner of England blew.

II.

Frail were the works that defended
    the hold that we held with our
    lives —
Women and children among us, God
    help them, our children and
    wives!
Hold it we might — and for fifteen
    days or for twenty at most.
"Never surrender, I charge you, but
    every man die at his post!"
Voice of the dead whom we loved,
    our Lawrence the best of the
    brave:
Cold were his brows when we kiss'd
    him — we laid him that night
    in his grave.
"Every man die at his post!" and
    there hail'd on our houses and
    halls
Death from their rifle-bullets, and
    death from their cannon-balls,
Death in our innermost chamber, and
    death at our slight barricade,
Death while we stood with the mus-
    ket, and death while we stoopt
    to the spade,
Death to the dying, and wounds to
    the wounded, for often there
    fell,

Striking the hospital wall, crashing
    thro' it, their shot and their
    shell,
Death — for their spies were among
    us, their marksmen were told
    of our best,
So that the brute bullet broke thro'
    the brain that could think for
    the rest;
Bullets would sing by our foreheads,
    and bullets would rain at our
    feet —
Fire from ten thousand at once of the
    rebels that girdled us round —
Death at the glimpse of a finger from
    over the breadth of a street,
Death from the heights of the mosque
    and the palace, and death in
    ground!
Mine? yes, a mine! Countermine!
    down, down! and creep thro'
    the hole!
Keep the revolver in hand! you can
    hear him — the murderous mole!
Quiet, ah! quiet — wait till the point
    of the pickaxe be thro'!
Click with the pick, coming nearer
    and nearer again than before —
Now let it speak, and you fire, and the
    dark pioneer is no more;
And ever upon the topmost roof our
    banner of England blew!

III.

Ay, but the foe sprung his mine many
    times, and it chanced on a day
Soon as the blast of that underground
    thunderclap echo'd away,
Dark thro' the smoke and the sulphur
    like so many fiends in their
    hell —
Cannon-shot, musket-shot, volley on
    volley, and yell upon yell —
Fiercely on all the defences our myr-
    iad enemy fell.
What have they done? where is it?
    Out yonder. Guard the Redan!
Storm at the Water-gate! storm at the
    Bailey-gate! storm, and it ran
Surging and swaying all round us, as
    ocean on every side

Plunges and heaves at a bank that is
    daily drown'd by the tide —
So many thousands that if they be bold
    enough, who shall escape?
Kill or be kill'd, live or die, they shall
    know we are soldiers and men!
Ready! take aim at their leaders —
    their masses are gapp'd with
    our grape —
Backward they reel like the wave, like
    the wave flinging forward again,
Flying and foil'd at the last by the
    handful they could not subdue;
And ever upon the topmost roof our
    banner of England blew.

IV.

Handful of men as we were, we were
    English in heart and in limb,
Strong with the strength of the race
    to command, to obey, to endure,
Each of us fought as if hope for the
    garrison hung but on him;
Still — could we watch at all points?
    we were every day fewer and
    fewer.
There was a whisper among us, but
    only a whisper that past:
"Children and wives — if the tigers
    leap into the fold unawares —
Every man die at his post — and the
    foe may outlive us at last —
Better to fall by the hands that they
    love, than to fall into theirs!"
Roar upon roar in a moment two
    mines by the enemy sprung
Clove into perilous chasms our walls
    and our poor palisades.
Rifleman, true is your heart, but be
    sure that your hand be as true!
Sharp is the fire of assault, better aimed
    are your flank fusillades —
Twice do we hurl them to earth from
    the ladders to which they had
    clung,
Twice from the ditch where they shel-
    ter we drive them with hand-
    grenades;
And ever upon the topmost roof our
    banner of England blew.

V.

Then on another wild morning another
    wild earthquake out-tore
Clean from our lines of defence ten or
    twelve good paces or more.
Rifleman, high on the roof, hidden
    there from the light of the
    sun —
One has leapt up on the beach, crying
    out: "Follow me, follow me!"—
Mark him — he falls! then another,
    and *him* too, and down goes he.
Had they been bold enough then, who
    can tell but the traitors had
    won?
Boardings and rafters and doors — an
    embrasure! make way for the
    gun!
Now double-charge it with grape! It
    is charged and we fire, and they
    run.
Praise to our Indian brothers, and let
    the dark face have his due!
Thanks to the kindly dark faces who
    fought with us, faithful and few,
Fought with the bravest among us,
    and drove them, and smote
    them, and slew,
That ever upon the topmost roof our
    banner in India blew.

VI.

Men will forget what we suffer and
    not what we do. We can fight!
But to be soldier all day and be senti-
    nel all thro' the night —
Ever the mine and assault, our sallies,
    their lying alarms,
Bugles and drums in the darkness, and
    shoutings and soundings to
    arms,
Ever the labor of fifty that had to be
    done by five,
Ever the marvel among us that one
    should be left alive,
Ever the day with its traitorous death
    from the loopholes around,
Ever the night with its coffinless
    corpse to be laid in the ground,
Heat like the mouth of a hell, or a
    deluge of cataract skies,

Stench of old offal decaying, and infinite torment of flies,
Thoughts of the breezes of May blowing over an English field,
Cholera, scurvy, and fever, the wound
that *would* not be heal'd,
Lopping away of the limb by the pit-
iful-pitiless knife, —
Torture and trouble in vain, — for it
never could save us a life.
Valor of delicate women who tended
the hospital bed,
Horror of women in travail among
the dying and dead,
Grief for our perishing children, and
never a moment for grief,
Toil and ineffable weariness, faltering
hopes of relief,
Havelock baffled, or beaten, or butcher'd for all that we knew —
Then day and night, day and night,
coming down on the still-shat-
ter'd walls
Millions of musket-bullets, and thousands of cannon-balls —
But ever upon the topmost roof our
banner of England blew.

VII.

Hark cannonade, fusillade! is it true
what was told by the scout,
Outram and Havelock breaking their
way through the fell mutineers?
Surely the pibroch of Europe is ring-
ing again in our ears!
All on a sudden the garrison utter a
jubilant shout,
Havelock's glorious Highlanders an-
swer with conquering cheers,
Sick from the hospital echo them,
women and children come out,
Blessing the wholesome white faces
of Havelock's good fusileers,
Kissing the war-harden'd hand of the
Highlander wet with their tears!
Dance to the pibroch! — saved! we are
saved! — is it you? is it you?
Saved by the valor of Havelock, saved
by the blessing of Heaven!
"Hold it for fifteen days!" we have
held it for eighty-seven!

And ever aloft on the palace roof the
old banner of England blew.

SIR JOHN OLDCASTLE, LORD COBHAM.

(IN WALES.)

MY friend should meet me somewhere
hereabout
To take me to that hiding in the hills.

I have broke their cage, no gilded
one, I trow —
I read no more the prisoner's mute wail
Scribbled or carved upon the pitiless
stone;
I find hard rocks, hard life, hard cheer,
or none,
For I am emptier than a friar's brains;
But God is with me in this wilderness,
These wet black passes and foam-
churning chasms —
And God's free air, and hope of bet-
ter things.

I would I knew their speech; not
now to glean,
Not now — I hope to do it — some
scatter'd ears,
Some ears for Christ in this wild field
of Wales —
But, bread, merely for bread. This
tongue that wagg'd
They said with such heretical arro-
gance
Against the proud archbishop Arun-
del —
So much God's cause was fluent in it
— is here
But as a Latin Bible to the crowd;
"Bara!" — what use? The Shepherd,
when I speak,
Vailing a sudden eyelid with his hard
"Dim Saesneg" passes, wroth at
things of old —
No fault of mine. Had he God's word
in Welsh
He might be kindlier: happily come
the day!

Not least art thou, thou little Bethle-
hem

In Judah, for in thee the Lord was born;
Nor thou in Britain, little Lutterworth,
Least, for in thee the word was born
    again.

Heaven-sweet Evangel, ever-living
    word,
Who whilome spakest to the South in
    Greek
About the soft Mediterranean shores,
And then in Latin to the Latin crowd,
As good need was — thou hast come
    to talk our isle.
Hereafter thou, fulfilling Pentecost,
Must learn to use the tongues of all
    the world.
Yet art thou thine own witness that
    thou bringest
Not peace, a sword, a fire.
            What did he say,
My frighted Wiclif-preacher whom I
    crost
In flying hither ? that one night a
    crowd
Throng'd the waste field about the
    city gates:
The king was on them suddenly with
    a host.
Why there ? they came to hear their
    preacher. Then
Some cried on Cobham, on the good
    Lord Cobham ;
Ay, for they love me ! but the king —
    nor voice
Nor finger raised against him — took
    and hang'd,
Took, hang'd and burnt — how many
    — thirty-nine —
Call'd it rebellion — hang'd, poor
    friends, as rebels
And burn'd alive as heretics ! for
    your Priest
Labels — to take the king along with
    him —
All heresy, treason : but to call men
    traitors
May make men traitors.
            Rose of Lancaster,
Red in thy birth, redder with house-
    hold war,
Now reddest with the blood of holy
    men,

Redder to be, red rose of Lancaster —
If somewhere in the North, as Rumor
    sang
Fluttering the hawks of this crown-
    lusting line —
By firth and loch thy silver sister
    grow,[1]
That were my rose, there my allegi-
    ance due.
Self-starved, they say — nay, mur-
    der'd, doubtless dead.
So to this king I cleaved : my friend
    was he,
Once my fast friend : I would have
    given my life
To help his own from scathe, a thou-
    sand lives
To save his soul. He might have
    come to learn
Our Wiclif's learning: but the worldly
    Priests
Who fear the king's hard common-
    sense should find
What rotten piles uphold their mason-
    work,
Urge him to foreign war. O had he
    will'd
I might have stricken a lusty stroke
    for him,
But he would not; far liever led my
    friend
Back to the pure and universal
    church,
But he would not: whether that heir-
    less flaw
In his throne's title make him feel so
    frail,
He leans on Antichrist; or that his
    mind,
So quick, so capable in soldiership,
In matters of the faith, alas the while !
More worth than all the kingdoms of
    this world,
Runs in the rut, a coward to the
    Priest.

Burnt — good Sir Roger Acton, my
    dear friend !
Burnt too, my faithful preacher,
    Beverley !

[1] Richard II.

Lord give thou power to thy two wit-
    nesses!
Lest the false faith make merry over
    them!
Two — nay but thirty-nine have risen
    and stand,
Dark with the smoke of human sacri-
    fice,
Before thy light, and cry continually—
Cry — against whom?
        Him, who should bear the sword
Of Justice — what! the kingly, kindly
    boy;
Who took the world so easily hereto-
    fore,
My boon companion, tavern-fellow —
    him
Who gibed and japed — in many a
    merry tale
That shook our sides — at Pardoners,
    Summoners,
Friars, absolution-sellers, monkeries
And nunneries, when the wild hour
    and the wine
Had set the wits aflame.
              Harry of Monmouth,
Or Amurath of the East?
             Better to sink
Thy fleurs-de-lys in slime again, and
    fling
Thy royalty back into the riotous fits
Of wine and harlotry — thy shame,
    and mine,
Thy comrade — than to persecute the
    Lord,
And play the Saul that never will be
    Paul.

Burnt, burnt! and while this mitred
    Arundel
Dooms our unlicensed preacher to
    the flame,
The mitre-sanction'd harlot draws his
    clerks
Into the suburb — their hard celibacy,
Sworn to be veriest ice of pureness,
    molten
Into adulterous living, or such crimes
As holy Paul — a shame to speak of
    them —
Among the heathen —
             Sanctuary granted

To bandit, thief, assassin—yea to him
Who hacks his mother's throat —
    denied to him,
Who finds the Saviour in his mother
    tongue.
The Gospel, the Priest's pearl, flung
    down to swine —
The swine, lay-men, lay-women, who
    will come,
God willing, to outlearn the filthy friar.
Ah rather, Lord, than that thy
    Gospel, meant
To course and range thro' all the
    world, should be
Tether'd to these dead pillars of the
    Church —
Rather than so, if thou wilt have
    it so,
Burst vein, snap sinew, and crack
    heart, and life
Pass in the fire of Babylon! but how
    long,
O Lord, how long!
        My friend should meet me here.
Here is the copse, the fountain and—
    a Cross!
To thee, dead wood, I bow not head
    nor knees.
Rather to thee, green boscage, work
    of God,
Black holly, and white-flower'd way-
    faring-tree!
Rather to thee, thou living water,
    drawn
By this good Wiclif mountain down
    from heaven,
And speaking clearly in thy native
    tongue —
No Latin — He that thirsteth, come
    and drink!

Eh! how I anger'd Arundel asking
    me
To worship Holy Cross! I spread
    mine arms,
God's work, I said, a cross of flesh
    and blood
And holier. That was heresy. (My
    good friend
By this time should be with me.)
    "Images?"
"Bury them as God's truer images

Are daily buried." "Heresy. —
Penance ?" "Fast,
Hairshirt and scourge — nay, let a
man repent,
Do penance in his heart, God hears
him." "Heresy —
Not shriven, not saved ?" "What
profits an ill Priest
Between me and my God ? I would
not spurn
Good counsel of good friends, but
shrive myself
No, not to an Apostle." "Heresy."
(My friend is long in coming.) "Pil-
grimages ?"
Drink, bagpipes, revelling, devil's-
dances, vice.
The poor man's money gone to fat the
friar.
Who reads of begging saints in Scrip-
ture ?" — "Heresy" —
(Hath he been here — not found me
— gone again ?
Have I mislearnt our place of meet-
ing ?) "Bread —
Bread left after the blessing ?" how
they stared,
That was their main test-question —
glared at me !
"He veil'd himself in flesh, and now
He veils
His flesh in bread, body and bread
together."
Then rose the howl of all the cassock'd
wolves,
"No bread, no bread. God's body !"
Archbishop, Bishop,
Priors, Canons, Friars, bellringers,
Parish-clerks —
"No bread, no bread !" — "Authority
of the Church,
Power of the keys !" — Then I, God
help me, I
So mock'd, so spurn'd, so baited two
whole days —
I lost myself and fell from evenness,
And rail'd at all the Popes, that ever
since
Sylvester shed the venom of world-
wealth
Into the church, had only prov'n
themselves

Poisoners, murderers. Well — God
pardon all —
Me, them, and all the world — yea,
that proud Priest,
That mock-meek mouth of utter Anti-
christ,
That traitor to King Richard and the
truth,
Who rose and doom'd me to the fire.
                                    Amen !
Nay, I can burn, so that the Lord of
life
Be by me in my death.
                    Those three ! the fourth
Was like the Son of God ! Not burnt
were they.
On *them* the smell of burning had not
past.
That was a miracle to convert the king.
These Pharisees, this Caiaphas-Arundel
What miracle could turn ? *He* here
again,
He thwarting their traditions of Him-
self,
He would be found a heretic to Him-
self,
And doom'd to burn alive.
                    So, caught, I burn.
Burn ? heathen men have borne as
much as this,
For freedom, or the sake of those they
loved,
Or some less cause, some cause far
less than mine ;
For every other cause is less than
mine.
The moth will singe her wings, and
singed return,
Her love of light quenching her fear
of pain —
How now, my soul, we do not heed the
fire ?
Faint - hearted ? tut ! — faint - stom -
ach'd ! faint as I am,
God willing, I will burn for Him.
                                    Who comes ?
A thousand marks are set upon my
head.
Friend ? — foe perhaps — a tussle for
it then !
Nay, but my friend. Thou art so well
disguised,

I knew thee not. Hast thou brought
    bread with thee ?
I have not broken bread for fifty hours.
None ? I am damn'd already by the
    Priest
For holding there was bread where
    bread was none —
No bread. My friends await me yon-
    der ? Yes.
Lead on then. *Up* the mountain ?
    Is it far ?
Not far. Climb first and reach me
    down thy hand.
I am not like to die for lack of bread,
For I must live to testify by fire.[1]

___

COLUMBUS.

CHAINS, my good lord: in your raised
    brows I read
Some wonder at our chamber orna-
    ments.
We brought this iron from our isles
    of gold.

Does the king know you deign to
    visit him
Whom once he rose from off his
    throne to greet
Before his people, like his brother
    king ?
I saw your face that morning in the
    crowd.

At Barcelona — tho' you were not
    then
So bearded. Yes. The city deck'd
    herself
To meet me, roar'd my name; the
    king, the queen
Bade me be seated, speak, and tell
    them all
The story of my voyage, and while I
    spoke
The crowd's roar fell as at the " Peace,
    be still ! "
And when I ceased to speak, the king,
    the queen,
Sank from their thrones, and melted
    into tears,

And knelt, and lifted hand and heart
    and voice
In praise to God who led me thro' the
    waste.
And then the great " Laudamus " rose
    to heaven.

Chains for the Admiral of the
    Ocean ! chains
For him who gave a new heaven, a
    new earth,
As holy John had prophesied of me,
Gave glory and more empire to the
    kings
Of Spain than all their battles ! chains
    for him
Who push'd his prows into the setting
    sun,
And made West East, and sail'd the
    Dragon's mouth,
And came upon the Mountain of the
    World,
And saw the rivers roll from Paradise !

Chains ! we are Admirals of the
    Ocean, we,
We and our sons for ever. Ferdinand
Hath sign'd it and our Holy Catholic
    queen —
Of the Ocean — of the Indies — Ad-
    mirals we —
Our title, which we never mean to
    yield,
Our guerdon not alone for what we
    did,
But our amends for all we might have
    done —
The vast occasion of our stronger
    life —
Eighteen long years of waste, seven in
    your Spain,
Lost, showing courts and kings a truth
    the babe
Will suck in with his milk hereafter
    — earth
A sphere.

Were *you* at Salamanca ? No.
We fronted there the learning of all
    Spain,
All their cosmogonies, their astrono-
    mies :

Guess-work *they* guess'd it, but the golden guess
Is morning-star to the full round of truth.
No guess-work! I was certain of my goal;
Some thought it heresy, but that would not hold.
King David call'd the heavens a hide, a tent
Spread over earth, and so this earth was flat:
Some cited old Lactantius: could it be
That trees grew downward, rain fell upward, men
Walk'd like the fly on ceilings? and besides,
The great Augustine wrote that none could breathe
Within the zone of heat; so might there be
Two Adams, two mankinds, and that was clean
Against God's word: thus was I beaten back,
And chiefly to my sorrow by the Church,
And thought to turn my face from Spain, appeal
Once more to France or England; but our Queen
Recall'd me, for at last their Highnesses
Were half-assured this earth might be a sphere.

All glory to the all-blessed Trinity,
All glory to the mother of our Lord,
And Holy Church, from whom I never swerved
Not even by one hair's-breadth of heresy,
I have accomplish'd what I came to do.

Not yet — not all — last night a dream — I sail'd
On my first voyage, harass'd by the frights
Of my first crew, their curses and their groans.
The great flame-banner borne by Tene-riffe,

The compass, like an old friend false at last
In our most need, appall'd them, and the wind
Still westward, and the weedy seas — at length
The landbird, and the branch with berries on it,
The carven staff — and last the light, the light
On Guanahani! but I changed the name;
San Salvador I call'd it; and the light
Grew as I gazed, and brought out a broad sky
Of dawning over — not those alien palms,
The marvel of that fair new nature — not
That Indian isle, but our most ancient East
Moriah with Jerusalem; and I saw
The glory of the Lord flash up, and beat
Thro' all the homely town from jasper, sapphire,
Chalcedony, emerald, sardonyx, sardius,
Chrysolite, beryl, topaz, chrysoprase,
Jacynth, and amethyst — and those twelve gates,
Pearl — and I woke, and thought — death — I shall die —
I am written in the Lamb's own Book of Life
To walk within the glory of the Lord
Sunless and moonless, utter light — but no!
The Lord had sent this bright, strange dream to me
To mind me of the secret vow I made
When Spain was waging war against the Moor —
I strove myself with Spain against the Moor.
There came two voices from the Sepulchre,
Two friars crying that if Spain should oust
The Moslem from her limit, he, the fierce

Soldan of Egypt, would break down
    and raze
The blessed tomb of Christ; whereon
    I vow'd
That, if our Princes harken'd to my
    prayer,
Whatever wealth I brought from that
    new world
Should, in this old, be consecrate to
    lead
A new crusade against the Saracen,
And free the Holy Sepulchre from
    thrall.

    Gold? I had brought your Princes
    gold enough
If left alone! Being but a Genovese,
I am handled worse than had I been a
    Moor,
And breach'd the belting wall of
    Cambalu,
And given the Great Khan's palaces
    to the Moor,
Or clutch'd the sacred crown of Pres-
    ter John,
And cast it to the Moor: but *had* I
    brought
From Solomon's now-recover'd Ophir
    all
The gold that Solomon's navies car-
    ried home,
Would that have gilded *me?* Blue
    blood of Spain,
Tho' quartering your own royal arms
    of Spain,
I have not: blue blood and black blood
    of Spain,
The noble and the convict of Cas-
    tile,
Howl'd me from Hispaniola: for you
    know
The flies at home, that ever swarm
    about
And cloud the highest heads, and
    murmur down
Truth in the distance — these out-
    buzz'd me so
That even our prudent king, our right-
    eous queen —
I pray'd them being so calumniated
They would commission one of weight
    and worth

To judge between my slander'd self
    and me —
Fonseca my main enemy at their court,
They send me out *his* tool, Bovadilla,
    one
As ignorant and impolitic as a beast —
Blockish irreverence, brainless greed
    — who sack'd
My dwelling, seized upon my papers,
    loosed
My captives, feed the rebels of the
    crown,
Sold the crown-farms for all but noth-
    ing, gave
All but free leave for all to work the
    mines,
Drove me and my good brothers home
    in chains,
And gathering ruthless gold — a sin-
    gle piece
Weigh'd nigh four thousand Castil-
    lanos — so
They tell me — weigh'd him down
    into the abysm —
The hurricane of the latitude on him
    fell,
The seas of our discovering over-roll
Him and his gold; the frailer caravel,
With what was mine, came happily to
    the shore.
There was a glimmering of God's hand.

                And God
Hath more than glimmer'd on me. O
    my lord,
I swear to you I heard his voice be-
    tween
The thunders in the black Veragua
    nights,
" O soul of little faith, slow to believe!
Have I not been about thee from thy
    birth?
Given thee the keys of the great
    Ocean-sea?
Set thee in light till time shall be no
    more?
Is it I who have deceived thee or the
    world?
Endure! thou hast done so well for
    men, that men
Cry out against thee: was it otherwise
With mine own Son? "

And more than once in days
Of doubt and cloud and storm, when
     drowning hope
Sank all but out of sight, I heard his
     voice,
"Be not cast down. I lead thee by
     the hand,
Fear not." And I shall hear his
     voice again —
I know that he has led me all my life,
I am not yet too old to work his will —
His voice again.

          Still for all that, my lord,
I lying here bedridden and alone,
Cast off, put by, scouted by court and
     king —
The first discoverer starves — his fol-
     lowers, all
Flower into fortune — our world's way
     — and I,
Without a roof that I can call mine
     own,
With scarce a coin to buy a meal
     withal,
And seeing what a door for scoundrel
     scum
I open'd to the West, thro' which the
     lust,
Villany, violence, avarice, of your
     Spain
Pour'd in on all those happy naked
     isles —
Their kindly native princes slain or
     slaved,
Their wives and children Spanish con-
     cubines,
Their innocent hospitalities quench'd
     in blood,
Some dead of hunger, some beneath
     the scourge,
Some over-labor'd, some by their own
     hands, —
Yea, the dear mothers, crazing Nature,
     kill
Their babies at the breast for hate of
     Spain —
Ah God, the harmless people whom
     we found
In Hispaniola's island-Paradise!
Who took us for the very Gods from
     Heaven,

And we have sent them very fiends
     from Hell;
And I myself, myself not blameless, I
Could sometimes wish I had never led
     the way.

     Only the ghost of our great Catholic
          Queen
Smiles on me, saying, "Be thou com-
     forted!
This creedless people will be brought
     to Christ
And own the holy governance of
     Rome."

     But who could dream that we, who
          bore the Cross
Thither, were excommunicated there,
For curbing crimes that scandalized
     the Cross,
By him, the Catalonian Minorite,
Rome's Vicar in our Indies? who be-
     lieve
These hard memorials of our truth to
     Spain
Clung closer to us for a longer term
Than any friend of ours at Court?
     and yet
Pardon — too harsh, unjust. I am
     rack'd with pains.

     You see that I have hung them by
          my bed,
And I will have them buried in my
     grave.

     Sir, in that flight of ages which are
          God's
Own voice to justify the dead — per-
     chance
Spain once the most chivalric race on
     earth,
Spain then the mightiest, wealthiest
     realm on earth,
So made by me, may seek to unbury
     me,
To lay me in some shrine of this old
     Spain,
Or in that vaster Spain I leave to
     Spain.
Then some one standing by my grave
     will say,

" Behold the bones of Christopher
   Colòn " —
" Ay, but the chains, what do *they*
   mean — the chains ? " —
I sorrow for that kindly child of Spain
Who then will have to answer, " These
   same chains
Bound these same bones back thro'
   the Atlantic sea,
Which he unchain'd for all the world
   to come."

  O Queen of Heaven who seest the
   souls in Hell
And purgatory, I suffer all as much
As they do — for the moment. Stay,
   my son
Is here anon : my son will speak for
   me
Ablier than I can in these spasms that
   grind
Bone against bone. You will not.
   One last word.

  You move about the Court, I pray
   you tell
King Ferdinand who plays with me,
   that one,
Whose life has been no play with him
   and his
Hidalgos — shipwrecks, famines, fe-
   vers, fights,
Mutinies, treacheries — wink'd at, and
   condoned —
That I am loyal to him till the death,
And ready — tho' our Holy Catholic
   Queen,
Who fain had pledged her jewels on
   my first voyage,
Whose hope was mine to spread the
   Catholic faith,
Who wept with me when I return'd
   in chains,
Who sits beside the blessed Virgin
   now,
To whom I send my prayer by night
   and day —
She is gone — but you will tell the
   King, that I,
Rack'd as I am with gout, and
   wrench'd with pains
Gain'd in the service of His Highness,
   yet

Am ready to sail forth on one last
   voyage,
And readier, if the King would hear,
   to lead
One last crusade against the Saracen,
And save the Holy Sepulchre from
   thrall.

  Going ? I am old and slighted : you
   have dared
Somewhat perhaps in coming ? my
   poor thanks !
I am but an alien and a Genovese.

THE VOYAGE OF MAELDUNE.

(FOUNDED ON AN IRISH LEGEND.
A.D. 700.)

I.

I was the chief of the race — he had
   stricken my father dead —
But I gather'd my fellows together, I
   swore I would strike off his
   head.
Each one of them look'd like a king,
   and was noble in birth as in
   worth,
And each of them boasted he sprang
   from the oldest race upon earth.
Each was as brave in the fight as the
   bravest hero of song,
And each of them liefer had died than
   have done one another a wrong.
He lived on an isle in the ocean — we
   sail'd on a Friday morn —
He that had slain my father the day
   before I was born.

II.

And we came to the isle in the ocean,
   and there on the shore was he.
But a sudden blast blew us out and
   away thro' a boundless sea.

III.

And we came to the Silent Isle that
   we never had touch'd at before,
Where a silent ocean always broke on
   a silent shore,

And the brooks glitter'd on in the light
    without sound, and the long
    waterfalls
Pour'd in a thunderless plunge to the
    base of the mountain walls,
And the poplar and cypress unshaken
    by storm flourish'd up beyond
    sight,
And the pine shot aloft from the crag
    to an unbelievable height,
And high in the heaven above it there
    flicker'd a songless lark,
And the cock couldn't crow, and the
    bull couldn't low, and the dog
    couldn't bark.
And round it we went, and thro' it, but
    never a murmur, a breath —
It was all of it fair as life, it was all
    of it quiet as death,
And we hated the beautiful Isle, for
    whenever we strove to speak
Our voices were thinner and fainter
    than any flittermouse-shriek ;
And the men that were mighty of
    tongue and could raise such
    a battle-cry
That a hundred who heard it would
    rush on a thousand lances and
    die —
O they to be dumb'd by the charm !
    — so fluster'd with anger were
    they
They almost fell on each other ; but
    after we sail'd away.

IV.

And we came to the Isle of Shouting,
    we landed, a score of wild birds
Cried from the topmost summit with
    human voices and words ;
Once in an hour they cried, and when-
    ever their voices peal'd
The steer fell down at the plow and
    the harvest died from the field,
And the men dropt dead in the valleys
    and half of the cattle went lame,
And the roof sank in on the hearth,
    and the dwelling broke into
    flame ;
And the shouting of these wild birds
    ran into the hearts of my crew,

Till they shouted along with the shout-
    ing and seized one another and
    slew ;
But I drew them the one from the
    other ; I saw that we could not
    stay,
And we left the dead to the birds and
    we sail'd with our wounded
    away.

V.

And we came to the Isle of Flowers :
    their breath met us out on the
    seas,
For the Spring and the middle Sum-
    mer sat each on the lap of the
    breeze ;
And the red passion-flower to the
    cliffs, and the dark-blue cle-
    matis, clung,
And starr'd with a myriad blossom
    the long convolvulus hung ;
And the topmost spire of the moun-
    tain was lilies in lieu of snow,
And the lilies like glaciers winded
    down, running out below
Thro' the fire of the tulip and poppy,
    the blaze of gorse, and the
    blush
Of millions of roses that sprang with-
    out leaf or a thorn from the
    bush ;
And the whole isle-side flashing down
    from the peak without ever a
    tree
Swept like a torrent of gems from the
    sky to the blue of the sea ;
And we roll'd upon capes of crocus
    and vaunted our kith and our
    kin,
And we wallow'd in beds of lilies,
    and chanted the triumph of
    Finn,
Till each like a golden image was
    pollen'd from head to feet
And each was as dry as a cricket,
    with thirst in the middle-day
    heat.
Blossom and blossom, and promise of
    blossom, but never a fruit !
And we hated the Flowering Isle, as
    we hated the isle that was mute,

And we tore up the flowers by the
    million and flung them in bight
    and bay,
And we left but a naked rock, and in
    anger we sail'd away.

VI.

And we came to the Isle of Fruits :
    all round from the cliffs and
    the capes,
Purple or amber, dangled a hundred
    fathom of grapes,
And the warm melon lay like a little
    sun on the tawny sand,
And the fig ran up from the beach
    and rioted over the land,
And the mountain arose like a jew-
    ell'd throne thro' the fragrant
    air,
Glowing with all-color'd plums and
    with golden masses of pear,
And the crimson and scarlet of berries
    that flamed upon bine and vine,
But in every berry and fruit was the
    poisonous pleasure of wine ;
And the peak of the mountain was
    apples, the hugest that ever
    were seen,
And they prest, as they grew, on each
    other, with hardly a leaflet be-
    tween,
And all of them redder than rosiest
    health or than utterest shame,
And setting, when Even descended,
    the very sunset aflame ;
And we stay'd three days, and we
    gorged and we madden'd, till
    every one drew
His sword on his fellow to slay him,
    and ever they struck and they
    slew ;
And myself, I had eaten but sparely,
    and fought till I sunder'd the
    fray,
Then I bade them remember my
    father's death, and we sail'd
    away.

VII.

And we came to the Isle of Fire : we
    were lured by the light from
    afar,

For the peak sent up one league of
    fire to the Northern Star :
Lured by the glare and the blare, but
    scarcely could stand upright,
For the whole isle shudder'd and
    shook like a man in a mortal
    affright :
We were giddy besides with the fruits
    we had gorged, and so crazed
    that at last
There were some leap'd into the fire ;
    and away we sail'd, and we
    past
Over that undersea isle, where the
    water is clearer than air :
Down we look'd : what a garden ! O
    bliss, what a Paradise there !
Towers of a happier time, low down
    in a rainbow deep
Silent palaces, quiet fields of eternal
    sleep !
And three of the gentlest and best of
    my people, whate'er I could
    say,
Plunged head down in the sea, and
    the Paradise trembled away.

VIII.

And we came to the Bounteous Isle,
    where the heavens lean low on
    the land,
And ever at dawn from the cloud
    glitter'd o'er us a sunbright
    hand,
Then it open'd and dropt at the side
    of each man, as he rose from
    his rest,
Bread enough for his need till the
    laborless day dipt under the
    West ;
And we wander'd about it and thro'
    it. O never was time so
    good !
And we sang of the triumphs of
    Finn, and the boast of our
    ancient blood,
And we gazed at the wandering wave
    as we sat by the gurgle of
    springs,
And we chanted the songs of the
    Bards and the glories of fairy
    kings ;

But at length we began to be weary,
 to sigh, and to stretch and
 yawn,
Till we hated the Bounteous Isle and
 the sunbright hand of the
 dawn,
For there was not an enemy near, but
 the whole green Isle was our
 own,
And we took to playing at ball, and
 we took to throwing the stone,
And we took to playing at battle, but
 that was a perilous play,
For the passion of the battle was in
 us, we slew and we sail'd
 away.

IX.

And we came to the Isle of Witches
 and heard their musical cry —
" Come to us, O come, come " in the
 stormy red of a sky
Dashing the fires and the shadows of
 dawn on the beautiful shapes,
For a wild witch naked as heaven
 stood on each of the loftiest
 capes,
And a hundred ranged on the rock
 like white sea-birds in a row,
And a hundred gamboll'd and pranced
 on the wrecks in the sand below,
And a hundred splash'd from the
 ledges, and bosom'd the burst
 of the spray,
But I knew we should fall on each
 other, and hastily sail'd away.

X.

And we came in an evil time to the
 Isle of the Double Towers,
One was of smooth-cut stone, one
 carved all over with flowers,
But an earthquake always moved in
 the hollows under the dells,
And they shock'd on each other and
 butted each other with clashing
 of bells,
And the daws flew out of the Towers
 and jangled and wrangled in
 vain,
And the clash and boom of the bells
 rang into the heart and the brain,

Till the passion of battle was on us,
 and all took sides with the
 Towers,
There were some for the clean-cut
 stone, there were more for the
 carven flowers,
And the wrathful thunder of God
 peal'd over us all the day,
For the one half slew the other and
 after we sail'd away.

XI.

And we came to the Isle of a Saint
 who had sail'd with St. Brendan
 of yore,
He had lived ever since on the Isle
 and his winters were fifteen score,
And his voice was low as from other
 worlds, and his eyes were
 sweet,
And his white hair sank to his heels
 and his white beard fell to his
 feet,
And he spake to me, " O Maeldune,
 let be this purpose of thine !
Remember the words of the Lord
 when he told us ' Vengeance is
 mine ! '
His fathers have slain thy fathers
 in war or in single strife,
Thy fathers have slain his fathers,
 each taken a life for a life,
Thy father had slain his father, how
 long shall the murder last ?
Go back to the Isle of Finn and suffer
 the Past to be Past."
And we kiss'd the fringe of his beard
 and we pray'd as we heard him
 pray,
And the Holy man he assoil'd us, and
 sadly we sail'd away.

XII.

And we came to the Isle we were blown
 from, and there on the shore
 was he,
The man that had slain my father. I
 saw him and let him be.
O weary was I of the travel, the
 trouble, the strife and the sin,
When I landed again, with a tithe of
 my men, on the Isle of Finn.

DE PROFUNDIS:

THE TWO GREETINGS.

I.

Out of the deep, my child, out of the
  deep,
Where all that was to be, in all that
  was,
Whirl'd for a million æons thro' the
  vast
Waste dawn of multitudinous-eddy-
  ing light —
Out of the deep, my child, out of the
  deep,
Thro' all this changing world of
  changeless law,
And every phase of ever-heightening
  life,
And nine long months of antenatal
  gloom,
With this last moon, this crescent —
  her dark orb
Touch'd with earth's light — thou
  comest, darling boy;
Our own; a babe in lineament and
  limb
Perfect, and prophet of the perfect
  man;
Whose face and form are hers and
  mine in one,
Indissolubly married like our love;
Live, and be happy in thyself, and
  serve
This mortal race thy kin so well, that
  men
May bless thee as we bless thee, O
  young life
Breaking with laughter from the dark;
  and may
The fated channel where thy motion
  lives
Be prosperously shaped, and sway thy
  course
Along the years of haste and random
  youth
Unshatter'd; then full-current thro'
  full man;
And last in kindly curves, with gen-
  tlest fall,
By quiet fields, a slowly-dying power,

To that last deep where we and thou
  are still.

II.

i.

Out of the deep, my child, out of the
  deep,
From that great deep, before our
  world begins,
Whereon the Spirit of God moves as
  he will —
Out of the deep, my child, out of the
  deep,
From that true world within the world
  we see,
Whereof our world is but the bounding shore —
Out of the deep, Spirit, out of the deep,
With this ninth moon, that sends the
  hidden sun
Down yon dark sea, thou comest,
  darling boy.

ii.

For in the world, which is not ours,
  They said
" Let us make man " and that which
  should be man,
From that one light no man can look
  upon,
Drew to this shore lit by the suns and
  moons
And all the shadows. O dear Spirit
  half-lost
In thine own shadow and this fleshly
  sign
That thou art thou — who wailest
  being born
And banish'd into mystery, and the
  pain
Of this divisible-indivisible world
Among the numerable-innumerable
Sun, sun, and sun, thro' finite-infinite
  space
In finite-infinite Time — our mortal
  veil
And shatter'd phantom of that infinite
  One,
Who made thee unconceivably Thy-
  self
Out of His whole World-self and all
  in all —

Live thou! and of the grain and husk, the grape
And ivyberry, choose; and still depart
From death to death thro' life and life, and find
Nearer and ever nearer Him, who wrought
Not Matter, nor the finite-infinite,
But this main-miracle, that thou art thou,
With power on thine own act and on the world.

THE HUMAN CRY.

I.

HALLOWED be Thy name — Halleluiah!—
    Infinite Ideality!
    Immeasurable Reality!
    Infinite Personality!
Hallowed be Thy name — Halleluiah!

II.

We feel we are nothing — for all is Thou and in Thee;
We feel we are something — *that* also has come from Thee;
We know we are nothing — but Thou wilt help us to be.
Hallowed be Thy name — Halleluiah!

PREFATORY SONNET

TO THE " NINETEENTH CENTURY."

THOSE that of late had fleeted far and fast
To touch all shores, now leaving to the skill
Of others their old craft seaworthy still,
Have charter'd this; where, mindful of the past,
Our true co-mates regather round the mast;
Of diverse tongue, but with a common will
Here, in this roaring moon of daffodil
And crocus, to put forth and brave the blast;
For some, descending from the sacred peak

Of hoar high-templed Faith, have leagued again
Their lot with ours to rove the world about;
And some are wilder comrades, sworn to seek
If any golden harbor be for men
In seas of Death and sunless gulfs of Doubt.

TO THE REV. W. H. BROOKFIELD.

BROOKS, for they call'd you so that knew you best,
Old Brooks, who loved so well to mouth my rhymes,
How oft we two have heard St. Mary's chimes!
How oft the Cantab supper, host and guest,
Would echo helpless laughter to your jest!
How oft with him we paced that walk of lines,
Him, the lost light of those dawn-golden times,
Who loved you well! Now both are gone to rest.
You man of humorous-melancholy mark,
Dead of some inward agony — is it so?
Our kindlier, trustier Jaques, past away!
I cannot laud this life, it looks so dark:
Σκιᾶς ὄναρ — dream of a shadow, go —
God bless you. I shall join you in a day.

MONTENEGRO.

THEY rose to where their sovran eagle sails,
They kept their faith, their freedom, on the height,
Chaste, frugal, savage, arm'd by day and night
Against the Turk; whose inroad nowhere scales
Their headlong passes, but his footstep fails,

And red with blood the Crescent reels
   from fight
Before their dauntless hundreds, in
   prone flight
By thousands down the crags and
   thro' the vales.
O smallest among peoples! rough
   rock-throne
Of Freedom! warriors beating back
   the swarm
Of Turkish Islam for five hundred
   years,
Great Tsernogora! never since thine
   own
Black ridges drew the cloud and brake
   the storm
Has breathed a race of mightier
   mountaineers.

TO VICTOR HUGO.

VICTOR in Drama, Victor in Romance,
Cloud-weaver of phantasmal hopes
   and fears,

French of the French, and Lord of
   human tears;
Child-lover; Bard whose fame-lit
   laurels glance
Darkening the wreaths of all that
   would advance,
Beyond our strait, their claim to be
   thy peers;
Weird Titan by thy winter weight of
   years
As yet unbroken, Stormy voice of
   France!
Who dost not love our England — so
   they say;
I know not — England, France, all
   man to be
Will make one people ere man's race
   be run:
And I, desiring that diviner day,
Yield thee full thanks for thy full
   courtesy
To younger England in the boy my
   son.

TRANSLATIONS, ETC.

BATTLE OF BRUNANBURH.

Constantinus, King of the Scots, after
having sworn allegiance to Athelstan, allied
himself with the Danes of Ireland under
Anlaf, and invading England, was defeated
by Athelstan and his brother Edmund with
great slaughter at Brunanburh in the year
937.

I.

[1]ATHELSTAN King,
  Lord among Earls,
Bracelet-bestower and
  Baron of Barons,
He with his brother,
  Edmund Atheling,
Gaining a lifelong
  Glory in battle,

[1] I have more or less availed myself of my
son's prose translation of this poem in the
Contemporary Review (November 1876).

Slew with the sword-edge
There by Brunanburh,
Brake the shield-wall,
Hew'd the linden-wood,[1]
Hack'd the battleshield,
Sons of Edward with hammer'd brands.

II.

Theirs was a greatness
  Got from their Grandsires —
Theirs that so often in
  Strife with their enemies
Struck for their hoards and their
  hearths and their homes.

III.

Bow'd the spoiler,
Bent the Scotsman,

[1] Shields of lindenwood.

Fell the shipcrews
Doom'd to the death.
All the field with blood of the fighters
Flow'd, from when first the great
Sun-star of morningtide,
Lamp of the Lord God
Lord everlasting,
Glode over earth till the glorious
creature
Sank to his setting.

IV.

There lay many a man
Marr'd by the javelin,
Men of the Northland
Shot over shield.
There was the Scotsman
Weary of war.

V.

We the West-Saxons,
Long as the daylight
Lasted, in companies
Troubled the track of the host that
we hated,
Grimly with swords that were sharp
from the grindstone,
Fiercely we hack'd at the flyers before
us.

VI.

Mighty the Mercian,
Hard was his hand-play,
Sparing not any of
Those that with Anlaf,
Warriors over the
Weltering waters
Borne in the bark's-bosom,
Drew to this island :
Doom'd to the death.

VII.

Five young kings put asleep by the
sword-stroke,
Seven strong Earls of the army of
Anlaf
Fell on the war-field, numberless
numbers,
Shipmen and Scotsmen.

VIII.

Then the Norse leader,
Dire was his need of it,
Few were his following,

Fled to his warship :
Fleeted his vessel to sea with the king
in it,
Saving his life on the fallow flood.

IX.

Also the crafty one,
Constantinus,
Crept to his North again,
Hoar-headed hero !

X.

Slender warrant had
He to be proud of
The welcome of war-knives —
He that was reft of his
Folk and his friends that had
Fallen in conflict,
Leaving his son too
Lost in the carnage,
Mangled to morsels,
A youngster in war !

XI.

Slender reason had
He to be glad of
The clash of the war-glaive —
Traitor and trickster
And spurner of treaties —
He nor had Anlaf
With armies so broken
A reason for bragging
That they had the better
In perils of battle
On places of slaughter —
The struggle of standards,
The rush of the javelins,
The crash of the charges,[1]
The wielding of weapons —
The play that they play'd with
The children of Edward.

XII.

Then with their nail'd prows
Parted the Norsemen, a
Blood-redden'd relic of
Javelins over
The jarring breaker, the deep-
sea billow,
Shaping their way toward Dy-
flen [2] again,
Shamed in their souls.

[1] Lit. " the gathering of men."   [2] Dublin.

XIII.

Also the brethren,
King and Atheling,
Each in his glory,
Went to his own in his own West-
Saxonland,
Glad of the war.

XIV.

Many a carcase they left to be carrion,
Many a livid one, many a sallow-
skin —
Left for the white-tail'd eagle to tear
it, and
Left for the horny-nibb'd raven to
rend it, and
Gave to the garbaging war-hawk to
gorge it, and
That gray beast, the wolf of the weald.

XV.

Never had huger
Slaughter of heroes
Slain by the sword-edge —
Such as old writers
Have writ of in histories —
Hapt in this isle, since
Up from the East hither
Saxon and Angle from
Over the broad billow
Broke into Britain with
Haughty war-workers who
Harried the Welshman, when
Earls that were lured by the
Hunger of glory gat
Hold of the land.

ACHILLES OVER THE
TRENCH.

ILIAD, xviii. 202.

So saying, light-foot Iris pass'd away.
Then rose Achilles dear to Zeus; and
round
The warrior's puissant shoulders Pallas
flung
Her fringed ægis, and around his
head
The glorious goddess wreath'd a
golden cloud,
And from it lighted an all-shining
flame.
As when a smoke from a city goes to
heaven
Far off from out an island girt by
foes,
All day the men contend in grievous
war
From their own city, but with set of
sun
Their fires flame thickly, and aloft the
glare
Flies streaming, if perchance the
neighbors round
May see, and sail to help them in the
war;
So from his head the splendor went
to heaven.
From wall to dyke he stept, he stood,
nor join'd
The Achæans — honoring his wise
mother's word —
There standing, shouted, and Pallas
far away
Call'd; and a boundless panic shook
the foe.
For like the clear voice when a trum-
pet shrills,
Blown by the fierce beleaguerers of a
town,
So rang the clear voice of Æakidês;
And when the brazen cry of Æakidês
Was heard among the Trojans, all
their hearts
Were troubled, and the full-maned
horses whirl'd
The chariots backward, knowing griefs
at hand;
And sheer-astounded were the chari-
oteers
To see the dread, unweariable fire
That always o'er the great Peleion's
head
Burn'd, for the bright-eyed goddess
made it burn.
Thrice from the dyke he sent his
mighty shout,
Thrice backward reel'd the Trojans
and allies;
And there and then twelve of their
noblest died
Among their spears and chariots.

TO PRINCESS FREDERICA
ON HER MARRIAGE.

O you that were eyes and light to the
    King till he past away
    From the darkness of life —
He saw not his daughter — he blest
    her: the blind King sees you
    to-day,
    He blesses the wife.

SIR JOHN FRANKLIN.
ON THE CENOTAPH IN WESTMINSTER ABBEY.

Not here! the white North has thy
    bones; and thou,
    Heroic sailor-soul,
Art passing on thine happier voyage
    now
    Toward no earthly pole.

TO DANTE.
(WRITTEN AT REQUEST OF THE FLORENTINES.)

King, that hast reign'd six hundred years, and grown
In power, and ever growest, since thine own
Fair Florence honoring thy nativity,
Thy Florence now the crown of Italy,
Hath sought the tribute of a verse from me,
I, wearing but the garland of a day,
Cast at thy feet one flower that fades away.

TIRESIAS AND OTHER POEMS.

—○○✦○○—

TO MY GOOD FRIEND

ROBERT BROWNING,

WHOSE GENIUS AND GENIALITY

WILL BEST APPRECIATE WHAT MAY BE BEST,

AND MAKE MOST ALLOWANCE FOR WHAT MAY BE WORST,

THIS VOLUME

IS AFFECTIONATELY DEDICATED.

TO E. FITZGERALD.

OLD FITZ, who from your suburb
    grange,
  Where once I tarried for a while,
Glance at the wheeling Orb of change,
  And greet it with a kindly smile;
Whom yet I see as there you sit
  Beneath your sheltering garden-
    tree,
And watch your doves about you flit,
  And plant on shoulder, hand and
    knee,
Or on your head their rosy feet,
  As if they knew your diet spares
Whatever moved in that full sheet
  Let down to Peter at his prayers;
Who live on milk and meal and
    grass;
  And once for ten long weeks I tried
Your table of Pythagoras,
  And seem'd at first 'a thing en-
    skied'
(As Shakespeare has it) airy-light
  To float above the ways of men,
Then fell from that half-spiritual
    height
  Chill'd, till I tasted flesh again

One night when earth was winter-
    black,
  And all the heavens flash'd in frost;
And on me, half-asleep, came back
  That wholesome heat the blood had
    lost,
And set me climbing icy capes
  And glaciers, over which there
    roll'd
To meet me long-arm'd vines with
    grapes
  Of Eshcol hugeness; for the cold
Without, and warmth within me,
    wrought
  To mould the dream; but none can
    say
That Lenten fare makes Lenten
    thought,
  Who reads your golden Eastern
    lay,
Than which I know no version done
  In English more divinely well;
A planet equal to the sun
  Which cast it, that large infidel
Your Omar; and your Omar drew
  Full-handed plaudits from our best
In modern letters, and from two,
  Old friends outvaluing all the rest,

Two voices heard on earth no more;
  But we old friends are still alive,
And I am nearing seventy-four,
  While you have touch'd at seventy-
    five,
And so I send a birthday line
  Of greeting; and my son, who dipt
In some forgotten book of mine
  With sallow scraps of manuscript,
And dating many a year ago,
  Has hit on this, which you will take,
My Fitz, and welcome, as I know
  Less for its own than for the sake
Of one recalling gracious times,
  When, in our younger London days,
You found some merit in my rhymes,
  And I more pleasure in your praise.

TIRESIAS.

I wish I were as in the years of old,
While yet the blessed daylight made
  itself
Ruddy thro' both the roofs of sight,
  and woke
These eyes, now dull, but then so
  keen to seek
The meanings ambush'd under all
  they saw,
The flight of birds, the flame of sac-
  rifice,
What omens may foreshadow fate to
  man
And woman, and the secret of the Gods.
  My son, the Gods, despite of human
    prayer,
Are slower to forgive than human
  kings.
The great God, Arês, burns in anger
  still
Against the guiltless heirs of him
  from Tyre,
Our Cadmus, out of whom thou art,
  who found
Beside the springs of Dircê, smote,
  and still'd
Thro' all its folds the multitudinous
  beast,
The dragon, which our trembling
  fathers call'd
The God's own son.

        A tale, that told to me,
When but thine age, by age as win-
  ter-white
As mine is now, amazed, but made
  me yearn
For larger glimpses of that more
  than man
Which rolls the heavens, and lifts,
  and lays the deep,
Yet loves and hates with mortal hates
  and loves,
And moves unseen among the ways
  of men.
  Then, in my wanderings all the
  lands that lie
Subjected to the Heliconian ridge
Have heard this footstep fall, altho'
  my wont
Was more to scale the highest of the
  heights
With some strange hope to see the
  nearer God.
  One naked peak — the sister of the
  sun
Would climb from out the dark, and
  linger there
To silver all the valleys with her
  shafts —
There once, but long ago, five-fold
  thy term
Of years, I lay; the winds were dead
  for heat;
The noonday crag made the hand
  burn; and sick
For shadow — not one bush was near
  — I rose
Following a torrent till its myriad falls
Found silence in the hollows under-
  neath.
  There in a secret olive-glade I saw
Pallas Athene climbing from the
  bath
In anger; yet one glittering foot dis-
  turb'd
The lucid well; one snowy knee was
  prest
Against the margin flowers; a dread-
  ful light
Came from her golden hair, her gold-
  en helm
And all her golden armor on the
  grass,

And from her virgin breast, and virgin eyes
Remaining fixt on mine, till mine
grew dark
For ever, and I heard a voice that
said
'Henceforth be blind, for thou hast
seen too much,
And speak the truth that no man may
believe.'
   Son, in the hidden world of sight,
that lives
Behind this darkness, I behold her
still,
Beyond all work of those who carve
the stone,
Beyond all dreams of Godlike woman-
hood,
Ineffable beauty, out of whom, at a
glance,
And as it were, perforce, upon me
flash'd
The power of prophesying — but to
me
No power — so chain'd and coupled
with the curse
Of blindness and their unbelief, who
heard
And heard not, when I spake of fam-
ine, plague,
Shrine-shattering earthquake, fire,
flood, thunderbolt,
And angers of the Gods for evil
done
And expiation lack'd — no power on
Fate,
Theirs, or mine own! for when the
crowd would roar
For blood, for war, whose issue was
their doom,
To cast wise words among the multi-
tude
Was flinging fruit to lions; nor, in
hours
Of civil outbreak, when I knew the
twain
Would each waste each, and bring on
both the yoke
Of stronger states, was mine the voice
to curb
The madness of our cities and their
kings.

Who ever turn'd upon his heel to
hear
My warning that the tyranny of one
Was prelude to the tyranny of all?
My counsel that the tyranny of all
Led backward to the tyranny of one?
   This power hath work'd no good to
aught that lives,
And these blind hands were useless in
their wars.
O therefore that the unfulfill'd desire,
The grief for ever born from griefs
to be,
The boundless yearning of the Proph-
et's heart —
Could *that* stand forth, and like a
statue, rear'd
To some great citizen, win all praise
from all
Who past it, saying, 'That was he!'
                                   In vain!
Virtue must shape itself in deed, and
those
Whom weakness or necessity have
cramp'd
Within themselves, immerging, each,
his urn
In his own well, draw solace as he
may.
   Menaceus, thou hast eyes, and I
can hear
Too plainly what full tides of onset
sap
Our seven high gates, and what a
weight of war
Rides on those ringing axles! jingle
of bits,
Shouts, arrows, tramp of the horn-
footed horse
That grind the glebe to powder!
Stony showers
Of that ear-stunning hail of Arês
crash
Along the sounding walls. Above,
below,
Shock after shock, the song-built
towers and gates
Reel, bruised and butted with the
shuddering
War-thunder of iron rams; and from
within
The city comes a murmur void of joy,

Lest she be taken captive — maidens,
wives,
And mothers with their babblers of
the dawn,
And oldest age in shadow from the
night,
Falling about their shrines before
their Gods,
And wailing ' Save us.'
　　　　　　And they wail to thee!
These eyeless eyes, that cannot see
thine own,
See this, that only in thy virtue lies
The saving of our Thebes; for, yes-
ternight,
To me, the great God Arês, whose
one bliss
Is war, and human sacrifice — himself
Blood-red from battle, spear and
helmet tipt
With stormy light as on a mast at
sea,
Stood out before a darkness, crying
' Thebes,
Thy Thebes shall fall and perish, for
I loathe
The seed of Cadmus — yet if one of
these
By his own hand — if one of these ——'
　　　　　　My son,
No sound is breathed so potent to
coerce,
And to conciliate, as their names who
dare
For that sweet motherland which gave
them birth
Nobly to do, nobly to die.　Their
names,
Graven on memorial columns, are a
song
Heard in the future; few, but more
than wall
And rampart, their examples reach a
hand
Far thro' all years, and everywhere
they meet
And kindle generous purpose, and the
strength
To mould it into action pure as theirs.
　Fairer thy fate than mine, if life's
best end
Be to end well! and thou refusing this,

Unvenerable will thy memory be
While men shall move the lips : but
if thou dare —
Thou, one of these, the race of Cad-
mus — then
No stone is fitted in yon marble girth
Whose echo shall not tongue thy
glorious doom,
Nor in this pavement but shall ring
thy name
To every hoof that clangs it, and the
springs
Of Dircê laving yonder battle-plain,
Heard from the roofs by night, will
murmur thee
To thine own Thebes, while Thebes
thro' thee shall stand
Firm-based with all her Gods.
　　　　　　The Dragon's cave
Half hid, they tell me, now in flowing
vines —
Where once he dwelt and whence he
roll'd himself
At dead of night — thou knowest, and
that smooth rock
Before it, altar-fashion'd, where of late
The woman-breasted Sphinx, with
wings drawn back,
Folded her lion paws, and look'd to
Thebes.
There blanch the bones of him she
slew, and these
Mixt with her own, because the fierce
beast found
A wiser than herself, and dash'd her-
self
Dead in her rage : but thou art wise
enough,
Tho' young, to love thy wiser, blunt
the curse
Of Pallas, hear, and tho' I speak the
truth
Believe I speak it, let thine own hand
strike
Thy youthful pulses into rest and
quench
The red God's anger, fearing not to
plunge
Thy torch of life in darkness, rather
— thou
Rejoicing that the sun, the moon, the
stars

Send no such light upon the ways of men
As one great deed.
      Thither, my son, and there
Thou, that hast never known the embrace of love,
Offer thy maiden life.
      This useless hand!
I felt one warm tear fall upon it. Gone!
He will achieve his greatness.
      But for me,
I would that I were gather'd to my rest,
And mingled with the famous kings of old,
On whom about their ocean-islands flash
The faces of the Gods — the wise man's word,
Here trampled by the populace underfoot,
There crown'd with worship — and these eyes will find
The men I knew, and watch the chariot whirl
About the goal again, and hunters race
The shadowy lion, and the warrior-kings,
In height and prowess more than human, strive
Again for glory, while the golden lyre
Is ever sounding in heroic ears
Heroic hymns, and every way the vales
Wind, clouded with the grateful incense-fume
Of those who mix all odor to the Gods
On one far height in one far-shining fire.

' One height and one far-shining fire'
And while I fancied that my friend
For this brief idyll would require
A less diffuse and opulent end,
And would defend his judgment well,
If I should deem it over nice —
The tolling of his funeral bell
Broke on my Pagan Paradise,
And mixt the dream of classic times,
And all the phantoms of the dream,
With present grief, and made the rhymes,
That miss'd his living welcome, seem
Like would-be guests an hour too late,
Who down the highway moving on
With easy laughter find the gate
Is bolted, and the master gone.
Gone into darkness, that full light
Of friendship ! past, in sleep, away
By night, into the deeper night!
The deeper night ? A clearer day
Than our poor twilight dawn on earth —
If night, what barren toil to be !
What life, so maim'd by night, were worth
Our living out ? Not mine to me
Remembering all the golden hours
Now silent, and so many dead,
And him the last ; and laying flowers,
This wreath, above his honor'd head,
And praying that, when I from hence
Shall fade with him into the unknown,
My close of earth's experience
May prove as peaceful as his own.

THE WRECK.

I.

HIDE me, Mother! my Fathers belong'd to the church of old,
I am driven by storm and sin and death to the ancient fold,
I cling to the Catholic Cross once more, to the Faith that saves,
My brain is full of the crash of wrecks, and the roar of waves,
My life itself is a wreck, I have sullied a noble name,
I am flung from the rushing tide of the world as a waif of shame,

I am roused by the wail of a child, and awake to a livid light,
And a ghastlier face than ever has haunted a grave by night,
I would hide from the storm without, I would flee from the storm within,
I would make my life one prayer for a soul that died in his sin,
I was the tempter, Mother, and mine was the deeper fall;
I will sit at your feet, I will hide my face, I will tell you all.

II.

He that they gave me to, Mother, a heedless and innocent bride —
I never have wrong'd his heart, I have only wounded his pride —
Spain in his blood and the Jew —— dark-visaged, stately and tall —
A princelier-looking man never stept thro' a Prince's hall.
And who, when his anger was kindled, would venture to give him the nay ?
And a man men fear is a man to be loved by the women they say.
And I could have loved him too, if the blossom can doat on the blight,
Or the young green leaf rejoice in the frost that sears it at night;
He would open the books that I prized, and toss them away with a yawn,
Repell'd by the magnet of Art to the which my nature was drawn,
The word of the Poet by whom the deeps of the world are stirr'd,
The music that robes it in language beneath and beyond the word !
My Shelley would fall from my hands when he cast a contemptuous glance
From where he was poring over his Tables of Trade and Finance;
My hands, when I heard him coming would drop from the chords or the keys,
But ever I fail'd to please him, however I strove to please —
All day long far-off in the cloud of the city, and there
Lost, head and heart, in the chances of dividend, consol, and share —
And at home if I sought for a kindly caress, being woman and weak,
His formal kiss fell chill as a flake of snow on the cheek :
And so, when I bore him a girl, when I held it aloft in my joy,
He look'd at it coldly, and said to me " Pity it isn't a boy."
The one thing given me, to love and to live for, glanced at in scorn !
The child that I felt I could die for — as if she were basely born !
I had lived a wild-flower life, I was planted now in a tomb;
The daisy will shut to the shadow, I closed my heart to the gloom;
I threw myself all abroad — I would play my part with the young
By the low foot-lights of the world — and I caught the wreath that was flung

III.

Mother, I have not — however their tongues may have babbled of me —
Sinn'd thro' an animal vileness, for all but a dwarf was he,
And all but a hunchback too ; and I look'd at him, first, askance
With pity — not he the knight for an amorous girl's romance !
Tho' wealthy enough to have bask'd in the light of a dowerless smile,
Having lands at home and abroad in a rich West-Indian isle;
But I came on him once at a ball, the heart of a listening crowd —
Why, what a brow was there ! he was seated — speaking aloud
To women, the flower of the time, and men at the helm of state —
Flowing with easy greatness and touching on all things great,
Science, philosophy, song — till I felt myself ready to weep
For I knew not what, when I heard that voice, — as mellow and deep

As a psalm by a mighty master and peal'd from an organ, — roll
Rising and falling — for, Mother, the voice was the voice of the soul;
And the sun of the soul made day in the dark of his wonderful eyes.
Here was the hand that would help me, would heal me — the heart that was
    wise!
And he, poor man, when he learnt that I hated the ring I wore,
He helpt me with death, and he heal'd me with sorrow forevermore.

IV.

For I broke the bond. That day my nurse had brought me the child.
The small sweet face was flush'd, but it coo'd to the Mother and smiled.
"Anything ailing," I ask'd her, "with baby?" She shook her head,
And the Motherless Mother kiss'd it, and turn'd in her haste and fled.

V.

Low warm winds had gently breathed us away from the land —
Ten long sweet summer days upon deck, sitting hand in hand —
When he clothed a naked mind with the wisdom and wealth of his own,
And I bow'd myself down as a slave to his intellectual throne,
When he coin'd into English gold some treasure of classical song,
When he flouted a statesman's error, or flamed at a public wrong,
When he rose as it were on the wings of an eagle beyond me, and past
Over the range and the change of the world from the first to the last,
When he spoke of his tropical home in the canes by the purple tide,
And the high star-crowns of his palms on the deep-wooded mountain-side,
And cliffs all robed in lianas that dropt to the brink of his bay,
And trees like the towers of a minster, the sons of a winterless day.
"Paradise there!" so he said, but I seem'd in Paradise then
With the first great love I had felt for the first and greatest of men,
Ten long days of summer and sin — if it must be so —
But days of a larger light than I ever again shall know —
Days that will glimmer, I fear, thro' life to my latest breath;
"No frost there," so he said, "as in truest Love no Death."

VI.

Mother, one morning a bird with a warble plaintively sweet
Perch'd on the shrouds, and then fell fluttering down at my feet;
I took it, he made it a cage, we fondled it, Stephen and I,
But it died, and I thought of the child for a moment, I scarce know why.

VII.

But if sin be sin, not inherited fate, as many will say,
My sin to my desolate little one found me at sea on a day,
When her orphan wail came borne in the shriek of a growing wind,
And a voice rang out in the thunders of Ocean and Heaven "Thou hast sinn'd."
And down in the cabin were we, for the towering crest of the tides
Plunged on the vessel and swept in a cataract off from her sides,
And ever the great storm grew with a howl and a hoot of the blast
In the rigging, voices of hell — then came the crash of the mast.

" The wages of sin is death," and then I began to weep,
" I am the Jonah, the crew should cast me into the deep,
For ah God, what a heart was mine to forsake her even for you."
" Never the heart among women," he said, " more tender and true."
" The heart! not a mother's heart, when I left my darling alone."
" Comfort yourself, for the heart of the father will care for his own."
" The heart of the father will spurn her," I cried, " for the sin of the wife,
The cloud of the mother's shame will enfold her and darken her life."
Then his pale face twitch'd ; " O Stephen, I love you, I love you, and yet " —
As I lean'd away from his arms — " would God, we had never met ! "
And he spoke not — only the storm ; till after a little, I yearn'd
For his voice again, and he call'd to me " Kiss me ! " and there — as I turn'd —
" The heart, the heart ! " I kiss'd him, I clung to the sinking form,
And the storm went roaring above us, and he — was out of the storm.

VIII.

And then, then, Mother, the ship stagger'd under a thunderous shock,
That shook us asunder, as if she had struck and crash'd on a rock ;
For a huge sea smote every soul from the decks of The Falcon but one ;
All of them, all but the man that was lash'd to the helm had gone ;
And I fell — and the storm and the days went by, but I knew no more —
Lost myself — lay like the dead by the dead on the cabin floor,
Dead to the death beside me, and lost to the loss that was mine,
With a dim dream, now and then, of a hand giving bread and wine,
Till I woke from the trance, and the ship stood still, and the skies were blue,
But the face I had known, O Mother, was not the face that I knew.

IX.

The strange misfeaturing mask that I saw so amazed me, that I
Stumbled on deck, half mad.   I would fling myself over and die !
But one — he was waving a flag — the one man left on the wreck —
" Woman " — he graspt at my arm — " stay there " — I crouch'd on the deck —
" We are sinking, and yet there's hope : look yonder," he cried, " a sail "
In a tone so rough that I broke into passionate tears, and the wail
Of a beaten babe, till I saw that a boat was nearing us — then
All on a sudden I thought, I shall look on the child again.

X.

They lower'd me down the side, and there in the boat I lay
With sad eyes fixt on the lost sea-home, as we glided away,
And I sigh'd, as the low dark hull dipt under the smiling main,
" Had I stayed with *him*, I had now — with *him* — been out of my pain."

XI.

They took us aboard : the crew were gentle, the captain kind ;
But *I* was the lonely slave of an often-wandering mind ;
For whenever a rougher gust might tumble a stormier wave,
" O Stephen," I moan'd, " I am coming to thee in thine Ocean-**grave.**"
And again, when a balmier breeze curl'd over a peacefuller sea,
I found myself moaning again " O child, I am coming to thee."

XII.

The broad white brow of the Isle — that bay with the color'd sand —
Rich was the rose of sunset there, as we drew to the land;
All so quiet the ripple would hardly blanch into spray
At the feet of the cliff; and I pray'd — "my child" — for I still could pray —
"May her life be as blissfully calm, be never gloom'd by the curse
Of a sin, not hers!"
                    Was it well with the child?
                                    I wrote to the nurse
Who had borne my flower on her hireling heart; and an answer came
Not from the nurse — nor yet to the wife — to her maiden name!
I shook as I open'd the letter — I knew that hand too well, —
And from it a scrap, clipt out of the "deaths" in a paper, fell.
"Ten long sweet summer days" of fever, and want of care!
And gone — that day of the storm — O Mother, she came to me there.

DESPAIR.

A man and his wife having lost faith in a God, and hope of a life to come, and being utterly miserable in this, resolve to end themselves by drowning. The woman is drowned, but the man rescued by a minister of the sect he had abandoned.

I.

Is it you, that preach'd in the chapel there looking over the sand?
Follow'd us too that night, and dogg'd us, and drew me to land?

II.

What did I feel that night? You are curious. How should I tell?
Does it matter so much what I felt? You rescued me — yet — was it well
That you came unwish'd for, uncall'd, between me and the deep and my doom,
Three days since, three more dark days of the Godless gloom
Of a life without sun, without health, without hope, without any delight
In anything here upon earth? but ah God, that night, that night
When the rolling eyes of the light-house there on the fatal neck
Of land running out into rock — they had saved many hundreds from wreck —
Glared on our way toward death, I remember I thought, as we past,
Does it matter how many they saved? we are all of us wreck'd at last —
"Do you fear," and there came thro' the roar of the breaker a whisper, a breath,
"Fear? am I not with you? I am frighted at life not death."

III.

And the suns of the limitless Universe sparkled and shone in the sky,
Flashing with fires as of God, but we knew that their light was a lie —
Bright as with deathless hope — but, however they sparkled and shone,
The dark little worlds running round them were worlds of woe like our own —
No soul in the heaven above, no soul on the earth below,
A fiery scroll written over with lamentation and woe.

IV.

See, we were nursed in the drear night-fold of your fatalist creed,
And we turn'd to the growing dawn, we had hoped for a dawn indeed,
When the light of a Sun that was coming would scatter the ghosts of the Past,
And the cramping creeds that had madden'd the peoples would vanish at last,
And we broke away from the Christ, our human brother and friend,
For He spoke, or it seem'd that He spoke, of a Hell without help, without end.

V.

Hoped for a dawn and it came, but the promise had faded away;
We had past from a cheerless night to the glare of a drearier day;
He is only a cloud and a smoke who was once a pillar of fire,
The guess of a worm in the dust and the shadow of its desire —
Of a worm as it writhes in a world of the weak trodden down by the strong,
Of a dying worm in a world, all massacre, murder, and wrong.

VI.

O we poor orphans of nothing — alone on that lonely shore —
Born of the brainless Nature who knew not that which she bore!
Trusting no longer that earthly flower would be heavenly fruit —
Come from the brute, poor souls — no souls — and to die with the brute ——

VII.

Nay, but I am not claiming your pity: I know you of old —
Small pity for those that have ranged from the narrow warmth of your fold,
Where you bawl'd the dark side of your faith and a God of eternal rage,
Till you flung us back on ourselves, and the human heart, and the Age.

VIII.

But pity — the Pagan held it a vice — was in her and in me,
Helpless, taking the place of the pitying God that should be!
Pity for all that aches in the grasp of an idiot power,
And pity for our own selves on an earth that bore not a flower;
Pity for all that suffers on land or in air or the deep,
And pity for our own selves till we long'd for eternal sleep.

IX.

" Lightly step over the sands! the waters — you hear them call!
Life with its anguish, and horrors, and errors — away with it all! "
And she laid her hand in my own — she was always loyal and sweet —
Till the points of the foam in the dusk came playing about our feet.
There was a strong sea-current would sweep us out to the main.
" Ah God " tho' I felt as I spoke I was taking the name in vain —
" Ah God " and we turn'd to each other, we kiss'd, we embraced she and I.
Knowing the Love we were used to believe everlasting would die:

We had read their know-nothing books and we lean'd to the darker side —
Ah God, should we find Him, perhaps, perhaps, if we died, if we died;
We never had found Him on earth, this earth is a fatherless Hell —
"Dear Love, forever and ever, forever and ever farewell,"
Never cry so desolate, not since the world began,
Never a kiss so sad, no, not since the coming of man!

x.

But the blind wave cast me ashore, and you saved me, a valueless life.
Not a grain of gratitude mine! You have parted the man from the wife.
I am left alone on the land, she is all alone in the sea;
If a curse meant ought, I would curse you for not having let me be.

xi.

Visions of youth — for my brain was drunk with the water, it seems;
I had past into perfect quiet at length out of pleasant dreams,
And the transient trouble of drowning — what was it when match'd with the pains
Of the hellish heat of a wretched life rushing back thro' the veins?

xii.

Why should I live? one son had forged on his father and fled,
And if I believed in a God, I would thank him, the other is dead,
And there was a baby-girl, that had never look'd on the light:
Happiest she of us all, for she past from the night to the night.

xiii.

But the crime, if a crime, of her eldest-born, her glory, her boast,
Struck hard at the tender heart of the mother, and broke it almost;
Tho' glory and shame dying out forever in endless time,
Does it matter so much whether crown'd for a virtue, or hang'd for a crime?

xiv.

And ruin'd by *him*, by *him*, I stood there, naked, amazed
In a world of arrogant opulence, fear'd myself turning crazed,
And I would not be mock'd in a madhouse! and she, the delicate wife,
With a grief that could only be cured, if cured, by the surgeon's knife, —

xv.

Why should we bear with an hour of torture, a moment of pain,
If every man die forever, if all his griefs are in vain,
And the homeless planet at length will be wheel'd thro' the silence of space,
Motherless evermore of an ever-vanishing race,
When the worm shall have writhed its last, and its last brother-worm will have fled
From the dead fossil skull that is left in the rocks of an earth that is dead?

XVI.

Have I crazed myself over their horrible infidel writings? O yes,
For these are the new dark ages, you see, of the popular press,
When the bat comes out of his cave, and the owls are whooping at noon,
And Doubt is the lord of this dunghill and crows to the sun and the moon,
Till the Sun and the Moon of our science are both of them turn'd into blood,
And Hope will have broken her heart, running after a shadow of good;
For their knowing and know-nothing books are scatter'd from hand to hand —
We have knelt in your know-all chapel too looking over the sand.

XVII.

What! I should call on that Infinite Love that has served us so well?
Infinite cruelty rather that made everlasting Hell,
Made us, foreknew us, foredoom'd us, and does what he will with his own;
Better our dead brute mother who never has heard us groan!

XVIII.

Hell? if the souls of men were immortal, as men have been told,
The lecher would cleave to his lusts, and the miser would yearn for his gold,
And so there were Hell forever! but were there a God as you say,
His Love would have power over Hell till it utterly vanish'd away.

XIX.

Ah yet — I have had some glimmer, at times, in my gloomiest woe,
Of a God behind all — after all — the great God for aught that I know;
But the God of Love and of Hell together — they cannot be thought,
If there be such a God, may the Great God curse him and bring him to nought!

XX.

Blasphemy! whose is the fault? is it mine? for why would you save
A madman to vex you with wretched words, who is best in his grave?
Blasphemy! ay, why not, being damn'd beyond hope of grace?
O would I were yonder with her, and away from your faith and your face!
Blasphemy! true! I have scared you pale with my scandalous talk,
But the blasphemy to *my* mind lies all in the way that you walk.

XXI.

Hence! she is gone! can I stay? can I breathe divorced from the Past?
You needs must have good lynx-eyes if I do not escape you at last.
Our orthodox coroner doubtless will find it a felode-se,
And the stake and the cross-road, fool, if you will, does it matter to me?

THE ANCIENT SAGE.

A THOUSAND summers ere the time of Christ
From out his ancient city came a Seer
Whom one that loved, and honor'd him, and yet
Was no disciple, richly garb'd, but worn
From wasteful living, follow'd — in his hand
A scroll of verse — till that old man before
A cavern whence an affluent fountain pour'd
From darkness into daylight, turn'd and spoke.

This wealth of waters might but seem to draw
From yon dark cave, but, son, the source is higher,
Yon summit half-a-league in air — and higher,
The cloud that hides it — higher still, the heavens
Whereby the cloud was moulded, and whereout
The cloud descended. Force is from the heights.
I am wearied of our city, son, and go
To spend my one last year among the hills.
What hast thou there ? Some death-song for the Ghouls
To make their banquet relish ? let me read.

How far thro' all the bloom and brake
   That nightingale is heard !
What power but the bird's could make
   This music in the bird?
How summer-bright are yonder skies,
   And earth as fair in hue !
And yet what sign of aught that lies
   Behind the green and blue?
But man to-day is fancy's fool
   As man hath ever been.
The nameless Power, or Powers, that rule
   Were never heard or seen.

If thou would'st hear the Nameless, and wilt dive
Into the Temple-cave of thine own self,
There, brooding by the central altar, thou
May'st haply learn the Nameless hath a voice,
By which thou wilt abide, if thou be wise,
As if thou knewest, tho' thou canst not know ;
For Knowledge is the swallow on the lake
That sees and stirs the surface-shadow there
But never yet hath dipt into the abysm,
The Abysm of all Abysms, beneath, within
The blue of sky and sea, the green of earth,
And in the million-millionth of a grain
Which cleft and cleft again fore more,
And ever vanishing, never vanishes,
To me, my son, more mystic than myself,
Or even than the Nameless is to me.
   And when thou sendest thy free soul thro' heaven,
Nor understandest bound nor boundlessness,
Thou seest the Nameless of the hundred names.
   And if the Nameless should withdraw from all
Thy frailty counts most real, all thy world
Might vanish like thy shadow in the dark.

And since — from when this earth began —
   The Nameless never came
Among us, never spake with man,
   And never named the Name —

Thou canst not prove the Nameless, O my son,
Nor canst thou prove the world thou movest in,
Thou canst not prove that thou art body alone,
Nor canst thou prove that thou art spirit alone
Nor canst thou prove that thou art both in one :

Thou canst not prove thou art im-
    mortal, no
Nor yet that thou art mortal — nay
    my son,
Thou canst not prove that I, who
    speak with thee,
Am not thyself in converse with thyself,
For nothing worthy proving can be
    proven,
Nor yet disproven : wherefore thou
    be wise,
Cleave ever to the sunnier side of
    doubt,
And cling to Faith beyond the forms
    of Faith !
She reels not in the storm of warring
    words,
She brightens at the clash of "Yes"
    and "No,"
She sees the Best that glimmers thro'
    the Worst,
She feels the Sun is hid but for a
    night,
She spies the summer thro' the winter
    bud,
She tastes the fruit before the blos-
    som falls,
She hears the lark within the songless
    egg,
She finds the fountain where they
    wail'd " Mirage ! "

    What Power? aught akin to Mind,
      The mind in me and you?
    Or power as of the Gods gone blind
      Who see not what they do?

But some in yonder city hold, my son,
That none but Gods could build this
    house of ours,
So beautiful, vast, various, so beyond
All work of man, yet, like all work of
    man,
A beauty with defect ———— till That
    which knows,
And is not known, but felt thro' what
    we feel
Within ourselves is highest, shall
    descend
On this half-deed, and shape it at the
    last
According to the Highest in the
    Highest.

    What Power but the Years that make
      And break the vase of clay,
    And stir the sleeping earth, and wake
      The bloom that fades away ?
    What rulers but the Days and Hours
      That cancel weal with woe,
    And wind the front of youth with flowers,
      And cap our age with snow?

The days and hours are ever glanc-
    ing by,
And seem to flicker past thro' sun
    and shade,
Or short, or long, as Pleasure leads,
    or Pain ;
But with the Nameless is nor Day nor
    Hour ;
Tho' we, thin minds, who creep from
    thought to thought
Break into "Thens" and "Whens"
    the Eternal Now :
This double seeming of the single
    world ! —
My words are like the babblings in a
    dream
Of nightmare, when the babblings
    break the dream.
But thou be wise in this dream-world
    of ours,
Nor take thy dial for thy deity,
But make the passing shadow serve
    thy will.

    The years that made the stripling wise
      Undo their work again,
    And leave him, blind of heart and eyes,
      The last and least of men ;
    Who clings to earth, and once would dare
      Hell-heat or Arctic cold,
    And now one breath of cooler air
      Would loose him from his hold ;
    His winter chills him to the root,
      He withers marrow and mind ;
    The kernel of the shrivell'd fruit
      Is jutting thro' the rind ;
    The tiger spasms tear his chest,
      The palsy wags his head ;
    The wife, the sons, who love him best
      Would fain that he were dead ;
    The griefs by which he once was wrung
      Were never worth the while —

Who knows ? or whether this earth-
    narrow life
Be yet but yolk, and forming in the
    shell ?

    The shaft of scorn that once had stung
    But wakes a dotard smile.

The placid gleam of sunset after
    storm!

    The statesman's brain that sway'd the past
      Is feebler than his knees;
    The passive sailor wrecks at last
      In ever-silent seas;
    The warrior hath forgot his arms,
      The Learned all his lore;
    The changing market frets or charms
      The merchant's hope no more;
    The prophet's beacon burn'd in vain,
      And now is lost in cloud;
    The plowman passes, bent with pain,
      To mix with what he plow'd;
    The poet whom his Age would quote
      As heir of endless fame—
    He knows not ev'n the book he wrote,
      Not even his own name.
    For man has overlived his day,
      And, darkening in the light,
    Scarce feels the senses break away
      To mix with ancient Night.

The shell must break before the bird
    can fly.

    The years that when my Youth began
      Had set the lily and rose
    By all my ways where'er they ran,
      Have ended mortal foes;
    My rose of love forever gone,
      My lily of truth and trust—
    They made her lily and rose in one,
      And changed her into dust.
    O rosetree planted in my grief,
      And growing, on her tomb,
    Her dust is greening in your leaf,
      Her blood is in your bloom.
    O slender lily waving there,
      And laughing back the light,
    In vain you tell me " Earth is fair "
      When all is dark as night.

My son, the world is dark with griefs
    and graves,
So dark that men cry out against the
    Heavens.
Who knows but that the darkness is
    in man ?
The doors of Night may be the gates
    of Light;
For wert thou born or blind or deaf,
    and then
Suddenly heal'd, how would'st thou
    glory in all
The splendors and the voices of the
    world !
And we, the poor earth's dying race,
    and yet

No phantoms, watching from a phan-
    tom shore
Await the last and largest sense to
    make
The phantom walls of this illusion
    fade,
And show us that the world is wholly
    fair.

    But vain the tears for darken'd years
      As laughter over wine,
    And vain the laughter as the tears,
      O brother, mine or thine,
    For all that laugh, and all that weep,
      And all that breathe are one
    Slight ripple on the boundless deep
      That moves, and all is gone.

But that one ripple on the boundless
    deep
Feels that the deep is boundless, and
    itself
Forever changing form, but evermore
One with the boundless motion of the
    deep.

    Yet wine and laughter friends ! and set
      The lamps alight, and call
    For golden music, and forget
      The darkness of the pall.

If utter darkness closed the day,
    my son ——
But earth's dark forehead flings
    athwart the heavens
Her shadow crown'd with stars — and
    yonder — out
To northward — some that never set,
    but pass
From sight and night to lose them-
    selves in day.
I hate the black negation of the bier,
And wish the dead, as happier than
    ourselves
And higher, having climb'd one step
    beyond
Our village miseries, might be borne
    in white
To burial or to burning, hymn'd from
    hence
With songs in praise of death, and
    crown'd with flowers !

    O worms and maggots of to-day
    Without their hope of wings!

But louder than thy rhyme the silent
      Word
Of that world-prophet in the heart of
      man.

Tho' some have gleams or so they say
      Of more than mortal things.

To-day ? but what of yesterday ? for
      oft
On me, when boy, there came what
      then I call'd,
Who knew no books and no philoso-
      phies,
In my boy-phrase "The Passion of
      the Past."
The first gray streak of earliest sum-
      mer-dawn,
The last long stripe of waning crim-
      son gloom,
As if the late and early were but one —
A height, a broken grange, a grove, a
      flower
Had murmurs "Lost and gone and
      lost and gone !"
A breath, a whisper — some divine
      farewell —
Desolate sweetness — far and far
      away —
What had he loved, what had he lost,
      the boy ?
I know not and I speak of what has
      been.
      And more, my son ! for more than
      once when I
Sat all alone, revolving in myself
The word that is the symbol of myself,
The mortal limit of the Self was
      loosed,
And past into the Nameless, as a cloud
Melts into Heaven. I touch'd my
      limbs, the limbs
Were strange not mine — and yet no
      shade of doubt,
But utter clearness, and thro' loss of
      Self
The gain of such large life as match'd
      with ours
Were Sun to spark — unshadowable
      in words,
Themselves but shadows of a shadow-
      world.

And idle gleams will come and go,
      But still the clouds remain;

The clouds themselves are children of
      the Sun.

And Night and Shadow rule below
      When only Day should reign.

And Day and Night are children of
      the Sun,
And idle gleams to thee are light to me,
Some say, the Light was father of the
      Night,
And some, the Night was father of
      the Light.
No night no day ! — I touch thy world
      again —
No ill no good ! such counter-terms,
      my son,
Are border-races, holding, each its
      own
By endless war : but night enough is
      there
In yon dark city : get thee back : and
      since
The key to that weird casket, which
      for thee
But holds a skull, is neither thine nor
      mine,
But in the hand of what is more than
      man,
Or in man's hand when man is more
      than man,
Let be thy wail and help thy fellow
      men,
And make thy gold thy vassal not thy
      king,
And fling free alms into the beggar's
      bowl,
And send the day into the darken'd
      heart;
Nor list for guerdon in the voice of
      men,
A dying echo from a falling wall;
Nor care — for Hunger hath the Evil
      eye —
To vex the noon with fiery gems, or
      fold
Thy presence in the silk of sumptu-
      ous looms;
Nor roll thy viands on a luscious
      tongue,

Nor drown thyself with flies in honied
wine;
Nor thou be rageful, like a handled
bee,
And lose thy life by usage of thy
sting;
Nor harm an adder thro' the lust for
harm,
Nor make a snail's horn shrink for
wantonness;
And more — think well! Do-well
will follow thought,
And in the fatal sequence of this
world
An evil thought may soil thy chil-
dren's blood;
But curb the beast would cast thee in
the mire,
And leave the hot swamp of voluptu-
ousness
A cloud between the Nameless and
thyself,
And lay thine uphill shoulder to the
wheel,
And climb the Mount of Blessing,
whence, if thou
Look higher, then — perchance — thou
mayest — beyond
A hundred ever-rising mountain
lines,
And past the range of Night and
Shadow — see
The high-heaven dawn of more than
mortal day
Strike on the Mount of Vision!
So, farewell.

THE FLIGHT.

I.

ARE you sleeping? have you forgotten? do not sleep, my sister dear!
How *can* you sleep? the morning brings the day I hate and fear;
The cock has crow'd already once, he crows before his time;
Awake! the creeping glimmer steals, the hills are white with rime.

II.

Ah, clasp me in your arms, sister, ah, fold me to your breast!
Ah, let me weep my fill once more, and cry myself to rest!
To rest? to rest and wake no more were better rest for me,
Than to waken every morning to that face I loathe to see:

III.

I envied your sweet slumber, all night so calm you lay,
The night was calm, the morn is calm, and like another day;
But I could wish yon moaning sea would rise and burst the shore,
And such a whirlwind blow these woods, as never blew before.

IV.

For, one by one, the stars went down across the gleaming pane,
And project after project rose, and all of them were vain;
The blackthorn-blossom fades and falls and leaves the bitter sloe,
The hope I catch at vanishes and youth is turn'd to woe.

V.

Come, speak a little comfort! all night I pray'd with tears,
And yet no comfort came to me, and now the morn appears,
When he will tear me from your side, who bought me for his slave :
This father pays his debt with me, and weds me to my grave.

VI.

What father, this or mine, was he, who, on that summer day
When I had fall'n from off the crag we clamber'd up in play,
Found, fear'd me dead, and groan'd, and took and kiss'd me, and again
He kiss'd me; and I loved him then; he *was* my father then.

VII.

No father now, the tyrant vassal of a tyrant vice!
The Godless Jephtha vows his child . . . to one cast of the dice.
These ancient woods, this Hall at last will go — perhaps have gone,
Except his own meek daughter yield her life, heart, soul to one —

VIII.

To one who knows I scorn him. O the formal mocking bow,
The cruel smile, the courtly phrase that masks his malice now —
But often in the sidelong eyes a gleam of all things ill —
It is not Love but Hate that weds a bride against her will;

IX.

Hate, that would pluck from this true breast the locket that I wear,
The precious crystal into which I braided Edwin's hair!
The love that keeps this heart alive beats on it night and day —
One golden curl, his golden gift, before he past away.

X.

He left us weeping in the woods; his boat was on the sand;
How slowly down the rocks he went, how loth to quit the land!
And all my life was darken'd, as I saw the white sail run,
And darken, up that lane of light into the setting sun.

XI.

How often have we watch'd the sun fade from us thro' the West,
And follow Edwin to those isles, those islands of the Blest!
Is *he* not there? would I were there, the friend, the bride, the wife,
With him, where summer never dies, with Love, the Sun of life!

XII.

O would I were in Edwin's arms — once more — to feel his breath
Upon my cheek — on Edwin's ship, with Edwin, ev'n in death,
Tho' all about the shuddering wreck the death-white sea should rave,
Or if lip were laid to lip on the pillows of the wave.

XIII.

Shall I take *him?* I kneel with *him?* I swear and swear forsworn
To love him most, whom most I loathe, to honor whom I scorn?
The Fiend would yell, the grave would yawn, my mother's ghost would
    rise —
To lie, to lie — in God's own house — the blackest of all lies!

XIV.

Why — rather than that hand in mine, tho' every pulse would freeze,
I'd sooner fold an icy corpse dead of some foul disease :
Wed him ? I will not wed him, let them spurn me from the doors,
And I will wander till I die about the barren moors.

XV.

The dear, mad bride who stabb'd her bridegroom on her bridal night —
If mad, then I am mad, but sane, if she were in the right.
My father's madness makes me mad — but words are only words !
I am not mad, not yet, not quite — There ! listen how the birds

XVI.

Begin to warble yonder in the budding orchard trees !
The lark has past from earth to Heaven upon the morning breeze.
How gladly, were I one of those, how early would I wake !
And yet the sorrow that I bear is sorrow for *his* sake.

XVII.

They love their mates, to whom they sing ; or else their songs, that meet
The morning with such music, would never be so sweet !
And tho' these fathers will not hear, the blessed Heavens are just,
And Love is fire, and burns the feet would trample it to dust.

XVIII.

A door was open'd in the house — who ? who ? my father sleeps !
A stealthy foot upon the stair ! he — some one — this way creeps !
If he ? yes, he . . . lurks, listens, fears his victim may have fled —
He ! where is some sharp-pointed thing ? he comes, and finds me dead.

XIX.

Not he, not yet ! and time to act — but how my temples burn !
And idle fancies flutter me, I know not where to turn ;
Speak to me, sister ; counsel me ; this marriage must not be.
You only know the love that makes the world a world to me !

xx.

Our gentle mother, had *she* lived — but we were left alone:
That other left us to ourselves; he cared not for his own;
So all the summer long we roam'd in these wild woods of ours,
My Edwin loved to call us then " His two wild woodland flowers."

xxi.

Wild flowers blowing side by side in God's free light and air,
Wild flowers of the secret woods, when Edwin found us there,
Wild woods in which we roved with him, and heard his passionate vow,
Wild woods in which we rove no more, if we be parted now!

xxii.

You will not leave me thus in grief to wander forth forlorn;
We never changed a bitter word, not one since we were born;
Our dying mother join'd our hands; she knew this father well;
She bad us love, like souls in Heaven, and now I fly from Hell,

xxiii.

And you with me; and we shall light upon some lonely shore,
Some lodge within the waste sea-dunes, and hear the waters roar,
And see the ships from out the West go dipping thro' the foam,
And sunshine on that sail at last which brings our Edwin home.

xxiv.

But look, the morning grows apace, and lights the old church-tower,
And lights the clock! the hand points five — O me — it strikes the hour —
I bide no more, I meet my fate, whatever ills betide!
Arise, my own true sister, come forth! the world is wide.

xxv.

And yet my heart is ill at ease, my eyes are dim with dew,
I seem to see a new-dug grave up yonder by the yew!
If we should never more return, but wander hand in hand
With breaking hearts, without a friend, and in a distant land.

xxvi.

O sweet, they tell me that the world is hard, and harsh of mind,
But can it be so hard, so harsh, as those that should be kind?
That matters not: let come what will; at last the end is sure,
And every heart that loves with truth is equal to endure.

TOMORROW.

I.

Her, that yer Honor was spakin' to?   Whin, yer Honor? last year —
Standin' here be the bridge, when last yer Honor was here?
An' yer Honor ye gev her the top of the mornin', "Tomorra" says she.
What did they call her, yer Honor?   They call'd her Molly Magee.
An' yer Honor's the thrue ould blood that always manes to be kind,
But there's rason in all things, yer Honor, for Molly was out of her mind.

II.

Shure, an' meself remimbers wan night comin' down be the sthrame,
An' it seems to me now like a bit of yisther-day in a dhrame —
Here where yer Honor seen her — there was but a slip of a moon,
But I hard thim — Molly Magee wid her batchelor, Danny O'Roon —
"You've been takin' a dhrop o' the crathur" an' Danny says "Troth, an' I been
Dhrinkin' yer health wid Shamus O'Shea at Katty's shebeen;[1]
But I must be lavin' ye soon."   "Ochone are ye goin' away?"
"Goin' to cut the Sassenach whate" he says "over the say" —
"An' whin will ye meet me agin?" an' I hard him "Molly asthore,
I'll meet you agin tomorra," says he, "be the chapel-door."
"An' whin are ye goin' to lave me?"   "O' Monday mornin'" says he;
"An' shure thin ye'll meet me tomorra?"   "Tomorra, tomorra, Machree!"
Thin Molly's ould mother, yer Honor, that had no likin' for Dan,
Call'd from her cabin an' tould her to come away from the man,
An' Molly Magee kem flyin' acrass me, as light as a lark,
An' Dan stood there for a minute, an' thin wint into the dark.
But wirrah! the storm that night — the tundher, an' rain that fell,
An' the sthrames runnin' down at the back o' the glin 'ud 'a dhrownded Hell.

III.

But airth was at pace nixt mornin', an' Hiven in its glory smiled,
As the Holy Mother o' Glory that smiles at her sleepin' child —
Ethen — she stept an the chapel-green, an' she turn'd herself roun'
Wid a diamond dhrop in her eye, for Danny was not to be foun',
An' many's the time that I watch'd her at mass lettin' down the tear,
For the Divil a Danny was there, yer Honor, for forty year.

IV.

Och, Molly Magee, wid the red o' the rose an' the white o' the May,
An' yer hair as black as the night, an' yer eyes as bright as the day!
Achora, yer laste little whishper was sweet as the lilt of a bird!
Acushla, ye set me heart batin' to music wid ivery word!
An' sorra the Queen wid her sceptre in sich an illigant han',
An' the fall of yer foot in the dance was as light as snow an the lan',

---

[1] Grog-shop.

An' the sun kem out of a cloud whiniver ye walkt in the shtreet,
An' Shamus O'Shea was yer shadda, an' laid himself undher yer feet,
An' I loved ye meself wid a heart and a half, me darlin', and he
'Ud 'a shot his own sowl dead for a kiss of ye, Molly Magee.

v.

But shure we wor betther frinds whin I crack'd his skull for her sake,
An' he ped me back wid the best he could give at ould Donovan's wake —
For the boys wor about her agin whin Dan didn't come to the fore,
An' Shamus along wid the rest, but she put thim all to the door.
An', afther, I thried her meself av the bird 'ud come to me call,
But Molly, begorrah, 'ud listhen to naither at all, at all.

vi.

An' her nabors an' frinds 'ud consowl an' condowl wid her, airly and late,
"Your Danny," they says, "niver crasst over say to the Sassenach whate;
He's gone to the States, aroon, an' he's married another wife,
An' ye'll niver set eyes an the face of the thraithur agin in life!
An' to dhrame of a married man, death alive, is a mortial sin."
But Molly says " I'd his hand-promise, an' shure he'll meet me agin."

vii.

An' afther her paärints had inter'd glory, an' both in wan day,
She began to spake to herself, the crathur, an' whishper, an' say
"Tomorra, Tomorra!" an' Father Molowny he tuk her in han',
" Molly, you're manin'," he says, "me dear, av I undherstan',
That ye'll meet your paärints agin an' yer Danny O'Roon afore God
Wid his blessed Marthyrs an' Saints; " an' she gev him a frindly nod,
"Tomorra, Tomorra," she says, an' she didn't intind to desave,
But her wits wor dead, an' her hair was white as the snow an a grave.

viii.

Arrah now, here last month they wor diggin' the bog, an' they foun'
Dhrownded in black bog-wather a corp lyin' undher groun'.

ix.

Yer Honor's own agint, he says to me wanst, at Katty's shebeen,
"The Divil take all the black lan', for a blessin' 'ud come wid the green!"
An' where 'ud the poor man, thin, cut his bit o' turf for the fire ?
But och ! bad scran to the bogs whin they swallies the man intire !
An' sorra the bog that's in Hiven wid all the light an' the glow,
An' there's hate enough, shure, widout *thim* in the Divil's kitchen below.

x.

Thim ould blind nagers in Agypt, I hard his Riverence say,
Could keep their haithen kings in the flesh for the Jidgemint day,
An', faix, be the piper o' Moses, they kep the cat an' the dog,
But it 'ud 'a been aisier work av they lived be an Irish bog.

XI.

How-an-iver they laid this body they foun' an the grass
Be the chapel-door, an' the people 'ud see it that wint into mass —
But a frish gineration had riz, an' most of the ould was few,
An' I didn't know him meself, an' nōne of the parish knew.

XII.

But Molly kem limpin' up wid her stick, she was lamed iv a knee,
Thin a slip of a gossoon call'd, "Div ye know him, Molly Magee?"
An' she stood up strait as the Queen of the world — she lifted her head —
"He said he would meet me tomorra!" an' dhropt down dead an the dead.

XIII.

Och, Molly, we thought, machree, ye would start back agin into life,
Whin we laid yez, aich be aich, at yer wake like husban' an' wife.
Sorra the dhry eye thin but was wet for the frinds that was gone!
Sorra the silent throat but we hard it cryin' "Ochone!"
An' Shamus O'Shea that has now ten childer, hansome an' tall,
Him an' his childer wor keenin' as if he had lost thim all.

XIV.

Thin his Riverence buried thim both in wan grave be the dead boor-tree,[1]
The young man Danny O'Roon wid his ould woman, Molly Magee.

XV.

May all the flowers o' Jeroosilim blossom an' spring from the grass,
Imbrashin' an' kissin' aich other — as ye did — over yer Crass!
An' the lark fly out o' the flowers wid his song to the Sun an' the Moon,
An' tell thim in Hiven about Molly Magee an' her Danny O'Roon,
Till Holy St. Pether gets up wid his kays an' opens the gate!
An' shure, be the Crass, that's betther nor cuttin' the Sassenach whate
To be there wid the Blessed Mother, an' Saints an' Marthyrs galore,
An' singin' yer "Aves" an' "Pathers" foriver an' ivermore.

XVI.

An' now that I tould yer Honor whativer I hard an' seen,
Yer Honor 'ill give me a thrifle to dhrink yer health in potheen.

THE SPINSTER'S SWEET-ARTS.

I.

MILK for my sweet-arts, Bess! fur it mun be the time about now
When Molly cooms in fro' the far-end close wi' her paäils fro' the cow.
Eh! tha be new to the plaäce — thou'rt gaäpin' — doesn't tha see
I calls 'em arter the fellers es once was sweet upo' me?

---

[1] Elder-tree.

II.

Naäy to be sewer it be past 'er time. What maäkes 'er sa laäte?
Goä to the laäne at the back, an' looök thruf Maddison's gaäte!

III.

Sweet-arts! Molly belike may 'a lighted to-night upo' one.
Sweet-arts! thanks to the Lord that I niver not listen'd to noän!
So I sits i' my oän armchair wi' my oän kettle theere o' the hob,
An' Tommy the fust, an' Tommy the second, an' Steevie an' Rob.

IV.

Rob, coom oop 'ere o' my knee. Thou sees that i' spite o' the men
I 'a kep' thruf thick an' thin my two 'oonderd a-year to mysen;
Yis! thaw tha call'd me es pretty es ony lass i' the Shere,
An' thou be es pretty a Tabby, but Robby I seed thruf ya theere.

V.

Feyther 'ud saäy I wur ugly as sin, an' I beänt not vaäin,
But I niver wur downright hugly, thaw soom 'ud 'a thowt ma plaäin,
An' I wasn't sa plaäin i' pink ribbons, ye said I wur pretty i' pinks,
An' I liked to 'ear it I did, but I beänt sich a fool as ye thinks;
Ye was stroäkin ma down wi' the 'air, as I be a-stroäkin o' you,
But whiniver I looök'd i' the glass I wur sewer that it couldn't be true;
Niver wur pretty, not I, but ye knaw'd it wur pleasant to 'ear,
Thaw it warn't not me es wur pretty, but my two 'oonderd a-year.

VI.

D'ya mind the murnin' when we was a-walkin' togither, an' stood
By the claäy'd-oop pond, that the foälk be sa scared at, i' Gigglesby wood,
Wheer the poor wench drowndid hersen, black Sal, es 'ed been disgraäced?
An' I feel'd thy arm es I stood wur a-creeäpin about my waäist;
An' me es wur allus afear'd of a man's gittin' ower fond,
I sidled awaäy an' awaäy till I plumpt foot fust i' the pond;
And, Robby, I niver 'a liked tha sa well, as I did that daäy,
Fur tha joompt in thysen, an' tha hoickt my feet wi' a flop fro' the claäy.
Ay, stick oop thy back, an' set oop thy taäil, tha may gie ma a kiss,
Fur I walk'd wi' tha all the way hoam an' wur niver sa nigh saäyin' Yis.
But wa boäth was i' sich a clat we was shaämed to cross Gigglesby Greeän,
Fur a cat may looök at a king thou knaws but the cat mun be cleän.
Sa we boäth on us kep out o' sight o' the winders o' Gigglesby Hinn —
Naäy, but the claws o' tha! quiet! they pricks cleän thruf to the skin —
An' wa boäth slinkt 'oäm by the brokken shed i' the laäne at the back,
Wheer the poodle runn'd at tha' once, an' thou runn'd oop o' the thack;
An' tha squeedg'd my 'and i' the shed, fur theere we was forced to 'ide,
Fur I seed that Steevie wur coomin', and one o' the Tommies beside.

VII.

Theere now, what art'a mewin at, Steevie? for owt I can tell —
Robby wur fust to be sewer, or I mowt 'a liked tha as well.

VIII.

But, Robby, I thowt o' tha all the while I wur chaängin' my gown,
An' I thowt shall I chaänge my staäte ? but, O Lord, upo' coomin' down —
My bran-new carpet es fresh es a midder o' flowers i' Maäy —
Why 'edn't tha wiped thy shoes ? it wur clatted all ower wi' claäy.
An' I could 'a cried ammost, fur I seed that it couldn't be,
An' Robby I gied tha a raätin that sattled thy coortin o' me.
An' Molly an' me was agreed, as we was a-cleänin' the floor,
That a man be a durty thing an' a trouble an' plague wi' indoor.
But I rued it arter a bit, fur I stuck to tha more na the rest,
But I couldn't 'a lived wi' a man an' I knaws it be all fur the best.

IX.

Naäy — let ma stroäk tha down till I maäkes tha as smooth as silk,
But if I 'ed married tha, Robby, thou'd not 'a been worth thy milk,
Thou'd niver 'a cotch'd ony mice but 'a left me the work to do,
And 'a taäen to the bottle beside, so es all that I 'ears be true ;
But I loovs tha to maäke thysen 'appy, an' soa purr awaäy, my dear,
Thou 'ed wellnigh purr'd ma awaäy fro' my oän two 'oonderd a-year.

X.

Sweärin agean, you Toms, as ye used to do twelve years sin' !
Ye niver 'eärd Steevie sweär 'cep' it wur at a dog coomin' in.
An' boath o' ye mun be fools to be hallus a-shawin' your claws,
Fur I niver cared nothink for neither — an' one o' ye deäd ye knaws !
Coom giv hoäver then, weant ye ? I warrant ye soom fine daäy —
Theere, lig down — I shall hev to gie one or tother awaäy.
Can't ye taäke pattern by Steevie ? ye shant hev a drop fro' the paäil.
Steevie be right good manners bang thruf to the tip o' the taäil.

XI.

Robby, git down wi'tha, wilt tha ? let Steevie coom oop o' my knee.
Steevie, my lad, thou 'ed very nigh been the Steevie fur me !
Robby wur fust to be sewer, 'e wur burn an' bred i' the 'ouse,
But thou be es 'ansom a tabby as iver patted a mouse.

XII.

An' I beänt not vaäin, but I knaws I 'ed led tha a quieter life
Nor her wi' the hepitaph yonder ! " A faäithful an' loovin' wife ! "
An' 'cos o' thy farm by the beck, an' thy windmill oop o' the croft,
Tha thowt tha would marry ma, did tha ? but that wur a bit ower soft,
Thaw thou was es soäber as daäy, wi' a niced red faäce, an' es cleän
Es a shillin' fresh fro' the mint wi' a bran-new 'eäd o' the Queeän,
An' thy farmin' es cleän es thysen, fur, Steevie, tha kep' it sa neät
That I niver not spied sa much as a poppy along wi' the wheät,
An' the wool of a thistle a-flyin' an' seeädin' tha haäted to see ;
'Twur as bad as a battle-twig [1] 'ere i' my oän blue chaumber to me.
Ay, roob thy whiskers ageän ma, fur I could 'a taäen to tha well,
But fur thy bairns, poor Steevie, a bouncin' boy an' a gell.

[1] Earwig.

XIII.

An' thou was es fond o' thy bairns es I be mysen o' my cats,
But I niver not wish'd fur childer, I hevn't naw likin' fur brats;
Pretty anew when ya dresses 'em oop, an' they goäs fur a walk,
Or sits wi' their 'ands afoor 'em, an' doesn't not 'inder the talk!
But their bottles o' pap, an' their mucky bibs, an' the clats an' the clouts,
An' their mashin' their toys to pieäces an' maäkin' ma deäf wi' their shouts,
An' hallus a-joompin' about ma as if they was set upo' springs,
An' a haxin' ma hawkard questions, an' saäyin' ondecent things,
An' a-callin' ma " hugly " mayhap to my faäce, or a teärin' my gown —
Dear! dear! dear! I mun part them Tommies — Steevie git down.

XIV.

Ye be wuss nor the men-tommies, you.   I tell'd ya, na moor o' that!
Tom, lig theere o' the cushion, an' tother Tom 'ere o' the mat.

XV.

Theere! I ha' master'd *them!*   Hed I married the Tommies — O Lord,
To loove an' obaäy the Tommies!   I couldn't 'a stuck by my word.
To be horder'd about, an' waäked, when Molly 'd put out the light,
By a man coomin' in wi' a hiccup at ony hour o' the night!
An' the taäble staäin'd wi' 'is aäle, an' the mud o' 'is boots o' the stairs,
An' the stink o' 'is pipe i' the 'ouse, an' the mark o' 'is 'eäd o' the chairs!
An' noän o' my four sweet-arts 'ud 'a let me 'a hed my oän waäy,
Sa I likes 'em best wi' taäils when they 'evn't a word to saäy.

XVI.

An' I sits i' my oän little parlor, an' sarved by my oän little lass,
Wi' my oän little garden outside, an' my oän bed o' sparrow-grass,
An' my oän door-poorch wi' the woodbine an' jessmine a-dressin' it greeän,
An' my oän fine Jackman i' purple a roäbin' the 'ouse like a Queeän.

XVII.

An' the little gells bobs to ma hoffens es I be abroad i' the laänes,
When I goäs to coomfut the poor es be down wi' their haäches an' their paäins :
An' a haäf-pot o' jam, or a mossel o' meät when it beänt too dear,
They maäkes ma a graäter Laädy nor 'er i' the mansion theer,
Hes 'es hallus to hax of a man how much to spare or to spend;
An' a spinster I be an' I will be, if soä pleäse God, to the hend.

XVIII.

Mew! mew! — Bess wi' the milk! what ha' maäde our Molly sa laäte?
It should 'a been 'ere by seven, an' theere — it be strikin' height —
" Cushie wur craäzed fur 'er cauf " well — I 'eärd 'er a maäkin' 'er moän,
An' I thowt to mysen " thank God that I hevn't naw cauf o' my oän."
Theere !

    Set it down !

                Now Robby !

                        You Tommies shall waäit to-night
Till Robby an' Steevie 'es 'ed their lap — an' it sarves ye right.

BALIN AND BALAN.[1]

PELLAM the King, who held and lost
  with Lot
In that first war, and had his realm
  restored
But render'd tributary, fail'd of late
To send his tribute; wherefore Ar-
  thur call'd
His treasurer, one of many years, and
  spake,
"Go thou with him and him and
  bring it to us,
Lest we should set one truer on his
  throne.
Man's word is God in man."
                 His Baron said
"We go but harken: there be two
  strange knights
Who sit near Camelot at a fountain-
  side,
A mile beneath the forest, challeng-
  ing
And overthrowing every knight who
  comes.
Wilt thou I undertake them as we
  pass,
And send them to thee?"
            Arthur laugh'd upon him.
"Old friend, too old to be so young,
  depart,
Delay not thou for ought, but let
  them sit,
Until they find a lustier than them-
  selves."
  So these departed. Early, one fair
  dawn,
The light-wing'd spirit of his youth
  return'd
On Arthur's heart; he arm'd himself
  and went,
So coming to the fountain-side beheld
Balin and Balan sitting statuelike,
Brethren, to right and left the spring,
  that down,
From underneath a plume of lady-fern,
Sang, and the sand danced at the bot-
  tom of it.
And on the right of Balin Balin's
  horse

---

[1] An introduction to "Merlin and Vivien."

Was fast beside an alder, on the left
Of Balan Balan's near a poplartree.
"Fair Sirs," said Arthur, "wherefore
  sit ye here?"
Balin and Balan answer'd "For the
  sake
Of glory; we be mightier men than
  all
In Arthur's court; that also have we
  proved;
For whatsoever knight against us
  came
Or I or he have easily overthrown."
"I too," said Arthur, "am of Arthur's
  hall,
But rather proven in his Paynim
  wars
Than famous jousts; but see, or
  proven or not,
Whether me likewise ye can over-
  throw."
And Arthur lightly smote the breth-
  ren down,
And lightly so return'd, and no man
  knew.
  Then Balin rose, and Balan, and
  beside
The carolling water set themselves
  again,
And spake no word until the shadow
  turn'd;
When from the fringe of coppice
  round them burst
A spangled pursuivant, and crying
  "Sirs,
Rise, follow! ye be sent for by the
  King,"
They follow'd; whom when Arthur
  seeing ask'd
"Tell me your names; why sat ye
  by the well?"
Balin the stillness of a minute broke
Saying "An unmelodious name to
  thee,
Balin, 'the Savage'—that addition
  thine—
My brother and my better, this man
  here,
Balan. I smote upon the naked
  skull
A thrall of thine in open hall, my
  hand

Was gauntleted, half slew him; for
    I heard
He had spoken evil of me; thy just
    wrath
Sent me a three-years' exile from
    thine eyes.
I have not lived my life delight-
    somely:
For I that did that violence to thy
    thrall,
Had often wrought some fury on my-
    self,
Saving for Balan: those three king-
    less years
Have past — were wormwood-bitter
    to me. King,
Methought that if we sat beside the
    well,
And hurl'd to ground what knight
    soever spurr'd
Against us, thou would'st take me
    gladlier back,
And make, as ten-times worthier to
    be thine
Than twenty Balins, Balan knight.
    I have said.
Not so — not all. A man of thine
    to-day
Abash'd us both, and brake my boast.
    Thy will ? "
Said Arthur " Thou hast ever spoken
    truth;
Thy too fierce manhood would not
    let thee lie.
Rise, my true knight. As children
    learn, be thou
Wiser for falling! walk with me,
    and move
To music with thine Order and the
    King.
Thy chair, a grief to all the brethren,
    stands
Vacant, but thou retake it, mine
    again ! "
    Thereafter, when Sir Balin enter'd
    hall,
The Lost one Found was greeted as
    in Heaven
With joy that blazed itself in wood-
    land wealth
Of leaf, and gayest garlandage of
    flowers,

Along the walls and down the board;
    they sat,
And cup clash'd cup; they drank
    and some one sang,
Sweet-voiced, a song of welcome,
    whereupon
Their common shout in chorus,
    mounting, made
Those banners of twelve battles over-
    head
Stir, as they stirr'd of old, when Ar-
    thur's host
Proclaim'd him Victor, and the day
    was won.
    Then Balan added to their Order
    lived
A wealthier life than heretofore with
    these
And Balin, till their embassage re-
    turn'd.
    " Sir King " they brought report
    " we hardly found,
So bush'd about it is with gloom, the
    hall
Of him to whom ye sent us, Pellam,
    once
A Christless foe of thine as ever
    dash'd
Horse against horse; but seeing that
    thy realm
Hath prosper'd in the name of Christ,
    the King
Took, as in rival heat, to holy things;
And finds himself descended from the
    Saint
Arimathæan Joseph; him who first
Brought the great faith to Britain
    over seas;
He boasts his life as purer than thine
    own;
Eats scarce enow to keep his pulse
    abeat;
Hath push'd aside his faithful wife,
    nor lets
Or dame or damsel enter at his
    gates
Lest he should be polluted. This
    gray King
Show'd us a shrine wherein were won-
    ders — yea —
Rich arks with priceless bones of
    martyrdom,

Thorns of the crown and shivers of
the cross,
And therewithal (for thus he told us)
brought
By holy Joseph hither, that same spear
Wherewith the Roman pierced the
side of Christ.
He much amazed us; after, when we
sought
The tribute, answer'd 'I have quite
foregone
All matters of this world: Garlon,
mine heir
Of him demand it,' which this Garlon gave
With much ado, railing at thine and
thee.

But when we left, in those deep
woods we found
A knight of thine spear-stricken from
behind,
Dead, whom we buried; more than
one of us
Cried out on Garlon, but a woodman
there
Reported of some demon in the woods
Was once a man, who driven by evil
tongues
From all his fellows, lived alone, and
came
To learn black magic, and to hate his
kind
With such a hate, that when he died,
his soul
Became a Fiend, which, as the man
in life
Was wounded by blind tongues he saw
not whence,
Strikes from behind. This woodman
show'd the cave
From which he sallies, and wherein
he dwelt.
We saw the hoof-print of a horse, no
more."
Then Arthur, " Let who goes before
me, see
He do not fall behind me: foully
slain
And villainously! who will hunt for
me
This demon of the woods?" Said
Balan, "I"!

So claim'd the quest and rode away,
but first,
Embracing Balin, " Good, my brother,
hear !
Let not thy moods prevail, when I am
gone
Who used to lay them! hold them
outer fiends,
Who leap at thee to tear thee; shake
them aside,
Dreams ruling when wit sleeps! yea,
but to dream
That any of these would wrong thee,
wrongs thyself.
Witness their flowery welcome. Bound
are they
To speak no evil. Truly save for
fears,
My fears for thee, so rich a fellowship
Would make me wholly blest: thou
one of them,
Be one indeed: consider them, and all
Their bearing in their common bond
of love,
No more of hatred than in Heaven
itself,
No more of jealousy than in Paradise."

So Balan warn'd, and went; Balin
remain'd:
Who — for but three brief moons had
glanced away
From being knighted till he smote the
thrall,
And faded from the presence into
years
Of exile — now would strictlier set
himself
To learn what Arthur meant by courtesy,
Manhood, and knighthood; wherefore
hover'd round
Lancelot, but when he mark'd his
high sweet smile
In passing, and a transitory word
Made knight or churl or child or damsel seem
From being smiled at happier in
themselves —
Sigh'd, as a boy lame-born beneath a
height,

That glooms his valley, sighs to see
    the peak
Sun-flush'd, or touch at night the
    northern star;
For one from out his village lately
    climb'd
And brought report of azure lands
    and fair,
Far seen to left and right; and he
    himself
Hath hardly scaled with help a hun-
    dred feet
Up from the base: so Balin marvel-
    ling oft
How far beyond him Lancelot seem'd
    to move,
Groan'd, and at times would mutter,
    " These be gifts,
Born with the blood, not learnable,
    divine,
Beyond *my* reach. Well had I
    foughten — well —
In those fierce wars, struck hard —
    and had I crown'd
With my slain self the heaps of whom
    I slew —
So — better ! — But this worship of
    the Queen,
That honor too wherein she holds him
    — this,
This was the sunshine that hath given
    the man
A growth, a name that branches o'er
    the rest,
And strength against all odds, and
    what the King
So prizes — overprizes — gentleness.
Her likewise would I worship an I
    might.
I never can be close with her, as he
That brought her hither. Shall I
    pray the King
To let me bear some token of his
    Queen
Whereon to gaze, remembering her
    — forget
My heats and violences ? live afresh ?
What, if the Queen disdain'd to grant
    it ! nay
Being so stately-gentle,would she make
My darkness blackness ? and with
    how sweet grace

She greeted my return ! Bold will I
    be —
Some goodly cognizance of Guinevere,
In lieu of this rough beast upon my
    shield,
Langued gules, and tooth'd with grin-
    ning savagery."
    And Arthur, when Sir Balin sought
    him, said
" What wilt thou bear ? " Balin was
    bold, and ask'd
To bear her own crown-royal upon
    shield,
Whereat she smiled and turn'd her to
    the King,
Who answer'd " Thou shalt put the
    crown to use.
The crown is but the shadow of the
    King,
And this a shadow's shadow, let him
    have it,
So this will help him of his vio-
    lences ! "
" No shadow" said Sir Balin "O my
    Queen,
But light to me ! no shadow, O my King
But golden earnest of a gentler life ! "
    So Balin bare the crown, and all
    the knights
Approved him, and the Queen, and
    all the world
Made music, and he felt his being
    move
In music with his Order, and the
    King.
    The nightingale, full-toned in mid-
    dle May,
Hath ever and anon a note so thin
It seems another voice in other
    groves;
Thus, after some quick burst of sud-
    den wrath,
The music in him seem'd to change,
    and grow
Faint and far-off.
            And once he saw the thrall
His passion half had gauntleted to
    death,
That causer of his banishment and
    shame,
Smile at him, as he deem'd, presump-
    tuously:

His arm half rose to strike again, but
  fell:
The memory of that cognizance on
  shield
Weighted it down, but in himself he
  moan'd:
  "Too high this mount of Camelot
  for me:
These high-set courtesies are not for
  me.
Shall I not rather prove the worse
  for these?
Fierier and stormier from restraining,
  break
Into some madness ev'n before the
  Queen?"
  Thus, as a hearth lit in a mountain
  home,
And glancing on the window, when
  the gloom
Of twilight deepens round it, seems a
  flame
That rages in the woodland far below,
So when his moods were darken'd,
  court and King
And all the kindly warmth of Ar-
  thur's hall
Shadow'd an angry distance: yet he
  strove
To learn the graces of their Table,
  fought
Hard with himself, and seem'd at
  length in peace.
  Then chanced, one morning, that
  Sir Balin sat
Close-bower'd in that garden nigh the
  hall.
A walk of roses ran from door to
  door;
A walk of lilies crost it to the bower:
And down that range of roses the
  great Queen
Came with slow steps, the morning
  on her face;
And all in shadow from the counter
  door
Sir Lancelot as to meet her, then at
  once,
As if he saw not, glanced aside, and
  paced
The long white walk of lilies toward
  the bower.

Follow'd the Queen; Sir Balin heard
  her "Prince,
Art thou so little loyal to thy Queen,
As pass without good morrow to thy
  Queen?"
To whom Sir Lancelot with his eyes
  on earth,
"Fain would I still be loyal to the
  Queen."
"Yea so" she said "but so to pass
  me by—
So loyal scarce is loyal to thyself,
Whom all men rate the king of cour-
  tesy.
Let be: ye stand, fair lord, as in a
  dream."
  Then Lancelot with his hand among
  the flowers
"Yea—for a dream. Last night me-
  thought I saw
That maiden Saint who stands with
  lily in hand
In yonder shrine. All round her
  prest the dark,
And all the light upon her silver
  face
Flow'd from the spiritual lily that
  she held.
Lo! these her emblems drew mine
  eyes—away:
For see, how perfect-pure! As light
  a flush
As hardly tints the blossom of the
  quince
Would mar their charm of stainless
  maidenhood."
  "Sweeter to me" she said "this
  garden rose
Deep-hued and many-folded! sweeter
  still
The wild-wood hyacinth and the
  bloom of May.
Prince, we have ridd'n before among
  the flowers
In those fair days—not all as cool as
  these,
Tho' season-earlier. Art thou sad?
  or sick?
Our noble King will send thee his
  own leech—
Sick? or for any matter anger'd at
  me?"

Then Lancelot lifted his large eyes;
    they dwelt
Deep-tranced on hers, and could not
    fall: her hue
Changed at his gaze: so turning side
    by side
They past, and Balin started from
    his bower.
    "Queen? subject? but I see not
    what I see.
Damsel and lover? hear not what I
    hear.
My father hath begotten me in his
    wrath.
I suffer from the things before me,
    know,
Learn nothing; am not worthy to be
    knight;
A churl, a clown!" and in him gloom
    on gloom
Deepen'd: he sharply caught his
    lance and shield,
Nor stay'd to crave permission of the
    king,
But, mad for strange adventure,
    dash'd away.
    He took the selfsame track as Ba-
    lan, saw
The fountain where they sat together,
    sigh'd
" Was I not better there with him?"
    and rode
The skyless woods, but under open
    blue
Came on the hoarhead woodman at a
    bough
Wearily hewing, " Churl, thine axe!"
    he cried,
Descended, and disjointed it at a
    blow:
To whom the woodman utter'd won-
    deringly
" Lord, thou couldst lay the Devil of
    these woods
If arm of flesh could lay him." Ba-
    lin cried
" Him, or the viler devil who plays
    his part,
To lay that devil would lay the Devil
    in me."
" Nay " said the churl, " our devil is a
    truth,

I saw the flash of him but yestereven.
And some *do* say that our Sir Garlon
    too
Hath learn'd black magic, and to ride
    unseen.
Look to the cave." But Balin
    answer'd him
"Old fabler, these be fancies of the
    churl,
Look to thy woodcraft," and so leav-
    ing him,
Now with slack rein and careless of
    himself,
Now with dug spur and raving at
    himself,
Now with droopt brow down the long
    glades he rode;
So mark'd not on his right a cavern-
    chasm
Yawn over darkness, where, not far
    within
The whole day died, but, dying,
    gleam'd on rocks
Roof-pendent, sharp; and others from
    the floor,
Tusklike, arising, made that mouth
    of night
Whereout the Demon issued up from
    Hell.
He mark'd not this, but blind and
    deaf to all
Save that chain'd rage, which ever
    yelpt within,
Past eastward from the falling sun.
    At once
He felt the hollow-beaten mosses
    thud
And tremble, and then the shadow of
    a spear,
Shot from behind him, ran along the
    ground.
Sideways he started from the path,
    and saw,
With pointed lance as if to pierce, a
    shape,
A light of armor by him flash, and pass
And vanish in the woods; and fol-
    low'd this,
But all so blind in rage that una-
    wares
He burst his lance against a forest
    bough,

Dishorsed himself, and rose again, and fled
Far, till the castle of a King, the hall
Of Pellam, lichen-bearded, grayly draped
With streaming grass, appear'd, low-built but strong;
The ruinous donjon as a knoll of moss,
The battlement overtopt with ivytods,
A home of bats, in every tower an owl.
    Then spake the men of Pellam crying " Lord,
Why wear ye this crown-royal upon shield ? "
Said Balin " For the fairest and the best
Of ladies living gave me this to bear."
So stall'd his horse, and strode across the court,
But found the greetings both of knight and King
Faint in the low dark hall of banquet: leaves
Laid their green faces flat against the panes,
Sprays grated, and the canker'd boughs without
Whined in the wood; for all was hush'd within,
Till when at feast Sir Garlon likewise ask'd
" Why wear ye that crown-royal ?"
                Balin said
" The Queen we worship, Lancelot, I, and all,
As fairest, best and purest, granted me
To bear it!" Such a sound (for Arthur's knights
Were hated strangers in the hall) as makes
The white swan-mother, sitting, when she hears
A strange knee rustle thro' her secret reeds,
Made Garlon, hissing; then he sourly smiled.
" Fairest I grant her: I have seen; but best,

Best, purest ? *thou* from Arthur's hall, and yet
So simple ! hast thou eyes, or if, are these
So far besotted that they fail to see
This fair wife-worship cloaks a secret shame ?
Truly, ye men of Arthur be but babes."
    A goblet on the board by Balin, boss'd
With holy Joseph's legend, on his right
Stood, all of massiest bronze : one side had sea
And ship and sail and angels blowing on it :
And one was rough with pole and scaffoldage
Of that low church he built at Glastonbury.
This Balin graspt, but while in act to hurl,
Thro' memory of that token on the shield
Relax'd his hold: " I will be gentle " he thought
" And passing gentle" caught his hand away,
Then fiercely to Sir Garlon " eyes have I
That saw to-day the shadow of a spear,
Shot from behind me, run along the ground;
Eyes too that long have watch'd how Lancelot draws
From homage to the best and purest, might,
Name, manhood, and a grace, but scantly thine,
Who, sitting in thine own hall, canst endure
To mouth so huge a foulness — to thy guest,
Me, me of Arthur's Table. Felon talk !
Let be ! no more ! "
            But not the less by night
The scorn of Garlon, poisoning all his rest,
Stung him in dreams. At length, and dim thro' leaves

Blinkt the white morn, sprays grated, and old boughs
Whined in the wood. He rose, descended, met
The scorner in the castle court, and fain,
For hate and loathing, would have past him by;
But when Sir Garlon utter'd mockingwise;
" What, wear ye still that same crownscandalous ? "
His countenance blacken'd, and his forehead veins
Bloated, and branch'd; and tearing out of sheath
The brand, Sir Balin with a fiery " Ha !
So thou be shadow, here I make thee ghost,"
Hard upon helm smote him, and the blade flew
Splintering in six, and clinkt upon the stones.
Then Garlon, reeling slowly backward, fell,
And Balin by the banneret of his helm
Dragg'd him, and struck, but from the castle a cry
Sounded across the court, and — men-at-arms,
A score with pointed lances, making at him —
He dash'd the pummel at the foremost face,
Beneath a low door dipt, and made his feet
Wings thro' a glimmering gallery, till he mark'd
The portal of King Pellam's chapel wide
And inward to the wall; he stept behind;
Thence in a moment heard them pass like wolves
Howling; but while he stared about the shrine,
In which he scarce could spy the Christ for Saints,
Beheld before a golden altar lie
The longest lance his eyes had ever seen,

Point-painted red; and seizing thereupon
Push'd thro' an open casement down, lean'd on it,
Leapt in a semicircle, and lit on earth;
Then hand at ear, and harkening from what side
The blindfold rummage buried in the walls
Might echo, ran the counter path, and found
His charger, mounted on him and away.
An arrow whizz'd to the right, one to the left,
One overhead; and Pellam's feeble cry
" Stay, stay him ! he defileth heavenly things
With earthly uses " — made him quickly dive
Beneath the boughs, and race thro' many a mile
Of dense and open, till his goodly horse,
Arising wearily at a fallen oak,
Stumbled headlong, and cast him face to ground.
  Half-wroth he had not ended, but all glad,
Knightlike, to find his charger yet unlamed,
Sir Balin drew the shield from off his neck,
Stared at the priceless cognizance, and thought
" I have shamed thee so that now thou shamest me,
Thee will I bear no more," high on a branch
Hung it, and turn'd aside into the woods,
And there in gloom cast himself all along,
Moaning " My violences, my violences ! "
  But now the wholesome music of the wood
Was dumb'd by one from out the hall of Mark,
A damsel-errant, warbling, as she rode

The woodland alleys, Vivien, with
  her Squire.
  "The fire of Heaven has kill'd the
    barren cold,
And kindled all the plain and all the
  wold.
The new leaf ever pushes off the old.
The fire of Heaven is not the flame
  of Hell.
  Old priest, who mumble worship in
    your quire —
Old monk and nun, ye scorn the
    world's desire,
Yet in your frosty cells ye feel the
  fire!
The fire of Heaven is not the flame
  of Hell.
  The fire of Heaven is on the dusty
    ways.
The wayside blossoms open to the
  blaze.
The whole wood-world is one full
  peal of praise.
The fire of Heaven is not the flame
  of Hell.
  The fire of Heaven is lord of all
    things good,
And starve not thou this fire within
  thy blood,
But follow Vivien thro' the fiery
  flood!
The fire of Heaven is not the flame of
  Hell!"
  Then turning to her Squire "This
    fire of Heaven,
This old sun-worship, boy, will rise
  again,
And beat the cross to earth, and break
  the King
And all his Table."
            Then they reach'd a glade,
Where under one long lane of cloud-
  less air
Before another wood, the royal crown
Sparkled, and swaying upon a restless
  elm
Drew the vague glance of Vivien, and
  her Squire;
Amazed were these; "Lo there" she
  cried — "a crown —
Borne by some high lord-prince of
  Arthur's hall,

And there a horse! the rider? where
  is he?
See, yonder lies one dead within the
  wood.
Not dead; he stirs! — but sleeping.
  I will speak.
Hail, royal knight, we break on thy
  sweet rest,
Not, doubtless, all unearn'd by noble
  deeds.
But bounden art thou, if from
  Arthur's hall,
To help the weak. Behold, I fly from
  shame,
A lustful King, who sought to win my
  love
Thro' evil ways: the knight, with
  whom I rode,
Hath suffer'd misadventure, and my
  squire
Hath in him small defence; but thou,
  Sir Prince,
Wilt surely guide me to the warrior
  King,
Arthur the blameless, pure as any
  maid,
To get me shelter for my maiden-
  hood.
I charge thee by that crown upon thy
  shield,
And by the great Queen's name, arise
  and hence."
  And Balin rose, "Thither no more!
    nor Prince
Nor knight am I, but one that hath
  defamed
The cognizance she gave me: here I
  dwell
Savage among the savage woods,
  here die —
Die: let the wolves' black maws en-
  sepulchre
Their brother beast, whose anger was
  his lord.
O me, that such a name as Guine-
  vere's,
Which our high Lancelot hath so
  lifted up,
And been thereby uplifted, should
  thro' me,
My violence, and my villainy, come
  to shame."

Thereat she suddenly laugh'd and shrill, anon
Sigh'd all as suddenly. Said Balin to her
" Is this thy courtesy — to mock me, ha ?
Hence, for I will not with thee."
Again she sigh'd
" Pardon, sweet lord ! we maidens often laugh
When sick at heart, when rather we should weep.
I knew thee wrong'd. I brake upon thy rest,
And now full loth am I to break thy dream,
But thou art man, and canst abide a truth,
Tho' bitter. Hither, boy — and mark me well.
Dost thou remember at Caerleon once —
A year ago — nay, then I love thee not —
Ay, thou rememberest well — one summer dawn —
By the great tower — Caerleon upon Usk —
Nay, truly we were hidden : this fair lord,
The flower of all their vestal knight-hood, knelt
In amorous homage — knelt — what else ? — O ay
Knelt, and drew down from out his night-black hair
And mumbled that white hand whose ring'd caress
Had wander'd from her own King's golden head,
And lost itself in darkness, till she cried —
I thought the great tower would crash down on both —
' Rise, my sweet king, and kiss me on the lips,
Thou art my King.' This lad, whose lightest word
Is mere white truth in simple naked-ness,
Saw them embrace : he reddens, can-not speak,

So bashful, he ! but all the **maiden** Saints,
The deathless mother-maidenhood of Heaven
Cry out upon her. Up then, ride with me !
Talk not of shame ! thou canst not, an thou would'st,
Do these more shame than these have done themselves."
She lied with ease; but horror stricken he,
Remembering that dark bower at Camelot,
Breathed in a dismal whisper " It is truth."
Sunnily she smiled " And even in this lone wood
Sweet lord, ye do right well to whis-per this.
Fools prate, and perish traitors. Woods have tongues,
As walls have ears : but thou shalt go with me,
And we will speak at first exceeding low.
Meet is it the good King be not de-ceived.
See now, I set thee high on vantage ground,
From whence to watch the time, and eagle-like
Stoop at thy will on Lancelot and the Queen."
She ceased; his evil spirit upon him leapt,
He ground his teeth together, sprang with a yell,
Tore from the branch, and cast on earth, the shield,
Drove his mail'd heel athwart the royal crown,
Stampt all into defacement, hurl'd it from him
Among the forest weeds, and cursed the tale,
The told-of, and the teller.
                      That weird yell,
Unearthlier than all shriek of bird or beast,
Thrill'd thro' the woods; and Balan lurking there

(His quest was unaccomplish'd) heard
  and thought
"The scream of that Wood-devil I
  came to quell!"
Then nearing "Lo! he hath slain some
  brother-knight,
And tramples on the goodly shield to
  show
His loathing of our Order and the
  Queen.
My quest, meseems, is here. Or devil
  or man
Guard thou thine head." Sir Balin
  spake not word,
But snatch'd a sudden buckler from
  the Squire,
And vaulted on his horse, and so they
  crash'd
In onset, and King Pellam's holy
  spear,
Reputed to be red with sinless
  blood,
Redden'd at once with sinful, for the
  point
Across the maiden shield of Balan
  prick'd
The hauberk to the flesh; and Balin's
  horse
Was wearied to the death, and, when
  they clash'd,
Rolling back upon Balin, crush'd the
  man
Inward, and either fell, and swoon'd
  away.
  Then to her Squire mutter'd the
  damsel "Fools!
This fellow hath wrought some foul-
  ness with his Queen:
Else never had he borne her crown,
  nor raved
And thus foam'd over at a rival
  name:
But thou, Sir Chick, that scarce hast
  broken shell,
Art yet half-yolk, not even come to
  down—
Who never sawest Caerleon upon
  Usk—
And yet hast often pleaded for my
  love—
See what I see, be thou where I have
  been,

Or else Sir Chick — dismount and
  loose their casques
I fain would know what manner of
  men they be."
And when the Squire had loosed them,
  "Goodly! — look!
They might have cropt the myriad
  flower of May,
And butt each other here, like brain-
  less bulls,
Dead for one heifer!"
          Then the gentle Squire
"I hold them happy, so they died for
  love:
And, Vivien, tho' ye beat me like
  your dog,
I too could die, as now I live, for
  thee."
  "Live on, Sir Boy," she cried. "I
  better prize
The living dog than the dead lion:
  away!
I cannot brook to gaze upon the
  dead."
Then leapt her palfrey o'er the fallen
  oak,
And bounding forward "Leave them
  to the wolves."
  But when their foreheads felt the
  cooling air,
Balin first woke, and seeing that true
  face,
Familiar up from cradle-time, so
  wan,
Crawl'd slowly with low moans to
  where he lay,
And on his dying brother cast himself
Dying; and *he* lifted faint eyes; he
  felt
One near him; all at once they found
  the world,
Staring wild-wide; then with a childlike wail,
And drawing down the dim disastrous
  brow
That o'er him hung, he kiss'd it,
  moan'd and spake,
  "O Balin, Balin, I that fain had
  died
To save thy life, have brought thee
  to thy death.

Why had ye not the shield I knew?
  and why
Trampled ye thus on that which bare
  the Crown?"
  Then Balin told him brokenly, and
    in gasps,
All that had chanced, and Balan
  moan'd again.
  "Brother, I dwelt a day in Pellam's
    hall:
This Garlon mock'd me, but I heeded
  not.
And one said 'Eat in peace! a liar
  is he,
And hates thee for the tribute!' this
  good knight
Told me, that twice a wanton damsel
  came,
And sought for Garlon at the castle-
    gates,
Whom Pellam drove away with holy
  heat.
I well believe this damsel, and the
  one
Who stood beside thee even now, the
  same.
'She dwells among the woods' he
  said 'and meets
And dallies with him in the Mouth of
  Hell.'
Foul are their lives; foul are their
  lips; they lied.
Pure as our own true Mother is our
  Queen."
  "O brother" answer'd Balin "Woe
    is me!
My madness all thy life has been thy
  doom,
Thy curse, and darken'd all thy day;
  and now
The night has come. I scarce can
  see thee now.
Goodnight! for we shall never bid
  again
Goodmorrow — Dark my doom was
  here, and dark
It will be there. I see thee now no
  more.
I would not mine again should darken
  thine,
Goodnight, true brother."

            Balan answer'd low
"Goodnight, true brother here! good-
  morrow there!
We two were born together, and we
  die
Together by one doom:" and while
  he spoke
Closed his death-drowsing eyes, and
  slept the sleep
With Balin, either lock'd in either's
  arm.

            ─────

PROLOGUE TO GENERAL
HAMLEY.

OUR birches yellowing and from each
  The light leaf falling fast,
While squirrels from our fiery beech
  Were bearing off the mast,
You came, and look'd and loved the
    view
  Long-known and loved by me,
Green Sussex fading into blue
  With one gray glimpse of sea;
And, gazing from this height alone,
  We spoke of what had been
Most marvellous in the wars your
    own
  Crimean eyes had seen;
And now — like old-world inns that
    take
  Some warrior for a sign
That therewithin a guest may make
  True cheer with honest wine —
Because you heard the lines I read
  Nor utter'd word of blame,
I dare without your leave to head
  These rhymings with your name,
Who know you but as one of those
  I fain would meet again,
Yet know you, as your England knows
  That you and all your men
Were soldiers to her heart's desire,
  When, in the vanish'd year,
You saw the league-long rampart-fire
  Flare from Tel-el-Kebir
Thro' darkness, and the foe was driven,
  And Wolseley overthrew
Arâbi, and the stars in heaven
  Paled, and the glory grew.

THE CHARGE OF THE HEAVY BRIGADE AT BALACLAVA.

October 25, 1854.

I.

The charge of the gallant three hundred, the Heavy Brigade!
Down the hill, down the hill, thousands
of Russians,
Thousands of horsemen, drew to the
valley — and stay'd;
For Scarlett and Scarlett's three hundred were riding by
When the points of the Russian lances
arose in the sky;
And he call'd "Left wheel into line!"
and they wheel'd and obey'd.
Then he look'd at the host that had
halted he knew not why,
And he turn'd half round, and he bad
his trumpeter sound
To the charge, and he rode on ahead,
as he waved his blade
To the gallant three hundred whose
glory will never die —
"Follow," and up the hill, up the hill,
up the hill,
Follow'd the Heavy Brigade.

II.

The trumpet, the gallop, the charge,
and the might of the fight!
Thousands of horsemen had gather'd
there on the height,
With a wing push'd out to the left,
and a wing to the right,
And who shall escape if they close?
but he dash'd up alone
Thro' the great gray slope of men,
Sway'd his sabre, and held his own
Like an Englishman there and then;
All in a moment follow'd with force
Three that were next in their fiery
course,
Wedged themselves in between horse
and horse,
Fought for their lives in the narrow
gap they had made —

Four amid thousands! and up the hill,
up the hill,
Gallopt the gallant three hundred, the
Heavy Brigade.

III.

Fell like a cannonshot,
Burst like a thunderbolt,
Crash'd like a hurricane,
Broke thro' the mass from below,
Drove thro' the midst of the foe,
Plunged up and down, to and fro.
Rode flashing blow upon blow,
Brave Inniskillens and Greys
Whirling their sabres in circles of
light!
And some of us, all in amaze,
Who were held for a while from the
fight,
And were only standing at gaze,
When the dark-muffled Russian crowd
Folded its wings from the left and the
right,
And roll'd them around like a cloud,—
O mad for the charge and the battle
were we,
When our own good redcoats sank
from sight,
Like drops of blood in a dark-gray sea,
And we turn'd to each other, whisper-
ing, all dismay'd,
"Lost are the gallant three hundred
of Scarlett's Brigade!"

IV.

"Lost one and all" were the words
Mutter'd in our dismay;
But they rode like Victors and Lords
Thro' the forest of lances and swords
In the heart of the Russian hordes,
They rode, or they stood at bay —
Struck with the sword-hand and slew,
Down with the bridle-hand drew
The foe from the saddle and threw
Underfoot there in the fray —
Ranged like a storm or stood like a
rock
In the wave of a stormy day;
Till suddenly shock upon shock
Stagger'd the mass from without,
Drove it in wild disarray,

For our men gallopt up with a cheer
      and a shout,
And the foeman surged, and waver'd,
      and reel'd
Up the hill, up the hill, up the hill,
      out of the field,
And over the brow and away.

v.

Glory to each and to all, and the charge
      that they made!
Glory to all the three hundred, and all
      the Brigade!

NOTE.— The "three hundred" of the "Heavy Brigade" who made this famous charge were the Scots Greys and the 2nd squadron of Inniskillings; the remainder of the "Heavy Brigade" subsequently dashing up to their support.

The "three" were Scarlett's aide-de-camp, Elliot, and the trumpeter and Shegog the orderly, who had been close behind him.

EPILOGUE.

IRENE.

NOT this way will you set your name
      A star among the stars.

POET.

What way?

IRENE.

      You praise when you should blame
The barbarism of wars.
A juster epoch has begun.

POET.

Yet tho' this cheek be gray,
And that bright hair the modern sun,
      Those eyes the blue to-day,
You wrong me, passionate little friend.
      I would that wars should cease,
I would the globe from end to end
      Might sow and reap in peace,
And some new Spirit o'erbear the old,
      Or Trade re-frain the Powers
From war with kindly links of gold,
      Or Love with wreaths of flowers.
Slav, Teuton, Kelt, I count them all
      My friends and brother souls,
With all the peoples, great and small,
      That wheel between the poles.
But since, our mortal shadow, Ill
      To waste this earth began —
Perchance from some abuse of Will
      In worlds before the man

Involving ours — he needs must fight
      To make true peace his own,
He needs must combat might with
      might,
      Or Might would rule alone;
And who loves War for War's own
      sake
      Is fool, or crazed, or worse;
But let the patriot-soldier take
      His meed of fame in verse;
Nay — tho' that realm were in the
      wrong
      For which her warriors bleed,
It still were right to crown with song
      The warrior's noble deed —
A crown the Singer hopes may last,
      For so the deed endures;
But Song will vanish in the Vast;
      And that large phrase of yours
"A Star among the stars," my dear,
      Is girlish talk at best;
For dare we dally with the sphere
      As he did half in jest,
Old Horace? "I will strike" said he
      "The stars with head sublime,"
But scarce could see, as now we see,
      The man in Space and Time,
So drew perchance a happier lot
      Than ours, who rhyme to-day.
The fires that arch this dusky dot —
      Yon myriad-worlded way —
The vast sun-clusters' gather'd blaze,
      World-isles in lonely skies,
Whole heavens within themselves,
      amaze
      Our brief humanities;

And so does Earth; for Homer's
fame,
 Tho' carved in harder stone —
The falling drop will make his name
As mortal as my own.

IRENE.

No!

POET.

 Let it live then — ay, till when?
 Earth passes, all is lost
In what they prophesy, our wise men,
 Sun-flame or sunless frost,
And deed and song alike are swept
 Away, and all in vain
As far as man can see, except
 The man himself remain;
And tho', in this lean age forlorn,
 Too many a voice may cry
That man can have no after-morn,
 Not yet of these am I.
The man remains, and whatsoe'er
 He wrought of good or brave
Will mould him thro' the cycle-year
 That dawns behind the grave.

And here the Singer for his Art
 Not all in vain may plead
"The song that nerves a nation's
heart,
 Is in itself a deed."

TO VIRGIL.

WRITTEN AT THE REQUEST OF THE
MANTUANS FOR THE NINETEENTH
CENTENARY OF VIRGIL'S DEATH.

I.

ROMAN VIRGIL, thou that singest
 Ilion's lofty temples robed in fire,
Ilion falling, Rome arising,
 wars, and filial faith, and Dido's
pyre;

II.

Landscape-lover, lord of language
 more than he that sang the Works
and Days,

All the chosen coin of fancy
 flashing out from many a golden
phrase;

III.

Thou that singest wheat and woodland,
 tilth and vineyard, hive and horse
and herd;
All the charm of all the Muses
 often flowering in a lonely word;

IV.

Poet of the happy Tityrus
 piping underneath his beechen
bowers;
Poet of the poet-satyr
 whom the laughing shepherd
bound with flowers;

V.

Chanter of the Pollio, glorying
 in the blissful years again to be,
Summers of the snakeless meadow,
 unlaborious earth and oarless sea;

VI.

Thou that seëst Universal
 Nature moved by Universal
Mind;
Thou majestic in thy sadness
 at the doubtful doom of human
kind;

VII.

Light among the vanish'd ages;
 star that gildest yet this phantom
shore;
Golden branch amid the shadows,
 kings and realms that pass to
rise no more;

VIII.

Now thy Forum roars no longer,
 fallen every purple Cæsar's
dome —
Tho' thine ocean-roll of rhythm
 sound forever of Imperial
Rome —

IX.

Now the Rome of slaves hath perish'd,
　　and the Rome of freemen holds
　　her place,
I, from out the Northern Island
　　sunder'd once from all the hu-
　　man race,

X.

I salute thee, Mantovano,
　　I that loved thee since my day
　　began,
Wielder of the stateliest measure
　　ever moulded by the lips of man.

THE DEAD PROPHET.

182–.

I.

Dead!
　　And the Muses cried with a stormy
　　cry
"Send them no more, forevermore.
Let the people die."

II.

Dead!
　　"Is it *he* then brought so low?"
And a careless people flock'd from
　　the fields
With a purse to pay for the show.

III.

Dead, who had served his time,
　　Was one of the people's kings,
Had labor'd in lifting them out of
　　slime,
　　And showing them, souls have
　　wings!

IV.

Dumb on the winter heath he lay.
　　His friends had stript him bare,
And roll'd his nakedness everyway
　　That all the crowd might stare.

V.

A storm-worn signpost not to be read,
　　And a tree with a moulder'd nest

On its barkless bones, stood stark by
　　the dead;
　　And behind him, low in the West,

VI.

With shifting ladders of shadow and
　　light,
　　And blurr'd in color and form,
The sun hung over the gates of Night,
　　And glared at a coming storm.

VII.

Then glided a vulturous Beldam forth,
　　That on dumb death had thriven;
They call'd her "Reverence" here
　　upon earth,
　　And "The Curse of the Prophet"
　　in Heaven.

VIII.

She knelt—"We worship him"—
　　all but wept—
"So great so noble was he!"
She clear'd her sight, she arose, she
　　swept
　　The dust of earth from her knee.

IX.

"Great! for he spoke and the people
　　heard,
　　And his eloquence caught like a
　　flame
From zone to zone of the world, till
　　his Word
　　Had won him a noble name.

X.

"Noble! he sung, and the sweet sound
　　ran
　　Thro' palace and cottage door,
For he touch'd on the whole sad
　　planet of man,
　　The kings and the rich and the
　　poor;

XI.

"And he sung not alone of an old sun
　　set,
　　But a sun coming up in his youth!
Great and noble—O yes—but yet—
　　For man is a lover of Truth,

XII.

" And bound to follow, wherever she go
    Stark-naked, and up or down,
Thro' her high hill-passes of stainless
    snow,
    Or the foulest sewer of the town —

XIII.

" Noble and great — O ay — but then,
    Tho' a prophet should have his due,
Was he noblier-fashion'd than other
    men?
    Shall we see to it, I and you?

XIV.

" For since he would sit on a Prophet's
    seat,
    As a lord of the Human soul,
We needs must scan him from head
    to feet
    Were it but for a wart or a mole?"

XV.

His wife and his child stood by him
    in tears,
    But she — she push'd them aside.
" Tho' a name may last for a thou-
    sand years,
    Yet a truth is a truth," she cried.

XVI.

And she that had haunted his path-
    way still,
    Had often truckled and cower'd
When he rose in his wrath, and had
    yielded her will
    To the master, as overpower'd,

XVII.

She tumbled his helpless corpse
    about.
" Small blemish upon the skin!
But I think we know what is fair
    without
    Is often as foul within."

XVIII.

She crouch'd, she tore him part from
    part,
    And out of his body she drew

The red " Blood-eagle " [1] of liver and
    heart;
    She held them up to the view;

XIX.

She gabbled, as she groped in the
    dead,
    And all the people were pleased;
" See, what a little heart," she said,
    " And the liver is half-diseased!"

XX.

She tore the Prophet after death,
    And the people paid her well.
Lightnings flicker'd along the heath,
    One shriek'd "The fires of Hell!"

EARLY SPRING.

I.

ONCE more the Heavenly Power
    Makes all things new,
And domes the red-plow'd hills
    With loving blue;
The blackbirds have their wills,
    The throstles too.

II.

Opens a door in Heaven;
    From skies of glass
A Jacob's ladder falls
    On greening grass,
And o'er the mountain-walls
    Young angels pass.

III.

Before them fleets the shower,
    And burst the buds,
And shine the level lands,
    And flash the floods;
The stars are from their hands
    Flung thro' the woods,

[1] Old Viking term for lungs, liver, etc.,
when torn by the conqueror out of the body
of the conquered.

IV.

The woods with living airs
  How softly fann'd,
Light airs from where the deep,
  All down the sand,
Is breathing in his sleep,
  Heard by the land.

V.

O follow, leaping blood,
  The season's lure!
O heart, look down and up
  Serene, secure,
Warm as the crocus cup,
  Like snowdrops, pure!

VI.

Past, Future glimpse and fade
  Thro' some slight spell,
A gleam from yonder vale,
  Some far blue fell,
And sympathies, how frail,
  In sound and smell!

VII.

Till at thy chuckled note,
  Thou twinkling bird,
The fairy fancies range,
  And, lightly stirr'd,
Ring little bells of change
  From word to word.

VIII.

For now the Heavenly Power
  Makes all things new,
And thaws the cold, and fills
  The flower with dew;
The blackbirds have their wills,
  The poets too.

PREFATORY POEM TO MY
BROTHER'S SONNETS.

Midnight, June 30, 1879.

I.

MIDNIGHT — in no midsummer tune
The breakers lash the shores:
The cuckoo of a joyless June
Is calling out of doors:

And thou hast vanish'd from thine own
To that which looks like rest,
True brother, only to be known
By those who love thee best.

II.

Midnight — and joyless June gone by,
And from the deluged park
The cuckoo of a worse July
Is calling thro' the dark:

But thou art silent underground,
And o'er thee streams the rain,
True poet, surely to be found
When Truth is found again.

III.

And, now to these unsummer'd skies
The summer bird is still,
Far off a phantom cuckoo cries
From out a phantom hill;

And thro' this midnight breaks the
    sun
Of sixty years away,
The light of days when life begun,
The days that seem to-day,

When all my griefs were shared with
    thee,
As all my hopes were thine —
As all thou wert was one with me,
May all thou art be mine!

"FRATER AVE ATQUE VALE."

Row us out from Desenzano, to your
    Sirmione row!
So they row'd, and there we landed —
    "O venusta Sirmio!"
There to me thro' all the groves of
    olive in the summer glow,
There beneath the Roman ruin where
    the purple flowers grow,
Came that "Ave atque Vale" of the
    Poet's hopeless woe,
Tenderest of Roman poets nineteen-
    hundred years ago,
"Frater Ave atque Vale" — as we
    wander'd to and fro

Gazing at the Lydian laughter of the
    Garda Lake below
Sweet Catullus's all-but-island, olive-
    silvery Sirmio !

HELEN'S TOWER.[1]

HELEN'S TOWER, here I stand,
Dominant over sea and land.
Son's love built me, and I hold
Mother's love engrav'n in gold.
Love is in and out of time,
I am mortal stone and lime.
Would my granite girth were strong
As either love, to last as long !
I should wear my crown entire
To and thro' the Doomsday fire,
And be found of angel eyes
In earth's recurring Paradise.

EPITAPH ON LORD STRAT-
FORD DE REDCLIFFE.

IN WESTMINSTER ABBEY.

THOU third great Canning, stand
    among our best
    And noblest, now thy long day's
      work hath ceased,
Here silent in our Minster of the
    West
    Who wert the voice of England in
      the East.

EPITAPH ON GENERAL GOR-
DON.

FOR A CENOTAPH.

WARRIOR of God, man's friend, not
    laid below,
    But somewhere dead far in the
      waste Soudan,
Thou livest in all hearts, for all
    men know
    This earth has borne no simpler,
      nobler man.

[1] Written at the request of my friend,
Lord Dufferin.

EPITAPH ON CAXTON.

IN ST. MARGARET'S, WESTMINSTER.

FIAT LUX (his motto).

THY prayer was "Light — more Light
    — while Time shall last ! "
Thou sawest a glory growing on the
    night,
But not the shadows which that light
    would cast,
Till shadows vanish in the Light of
    Light.

TO THE DUKE OF ARGYLL.

O PATRIOT Statesman, be thou wise
    to know
The limits of resistance, and the
    bounds
Determining concession; still be bold
Not only to slight praise but suffer
    scorn;
And be thy heart a fortress to main-
    tain
The day against the moment, and the
    year
Against the day; thy voice, a music
    heard
Thro' all the yells and counter-yells
    of feud
And faction, and thy will, a power to
    make
This ever-changing world of circum-
    stance,
In changing, chime with never-chang-
    ing Law.

HANDS ALL ROUND.

FIRST pledge our Queen this solemn
    night,
    Then drink to England, every guest;
That man's the true Cosmopolite
    Who loves his native country best.
May freedom's oak forever live
    With stronger life from day to day ;
That man's the best Conservative
    Who lops the moulder'd branch
    away.

Hands all round!
  God the traitor's hope confound!
To this great cause of Freedom drink,
    my friends,
  And the great name of England,
    round and round.
To all the loyal hearts who long
  To keep our English Empire whole!
To all our noble sons, the strong
  New England of the Southern Pole!
To England under Indian skies,
  To those dark millions of her realm!
To Canada whom we love and prize,
  Whatever statesman hold the helm.
    Hands all round!
  God the traitor's hope confound!
To this great name of England drink,
    my friends,
  And all her glorious empire, round
    and round.

To all our statesmen so they be
  True leaders of the land's desire!
To both our Houses, may they see
  Beyond the borough and the shire!
We sail'd wherever ship could sail,
  We founded many a mighty state;
Pray God our greatness may not fail
  Through craven fears of being great.
    Hands all round!
  God the traitor's hope confound!
To this great cause of Freedom drink,
    my friends,
  And the great name of England,
    round and round.

FREEDOM.

I.

O THOU so fair in summers gone,
  While yet thy fresh and virgin soul
Inform'd the pillar'd Parthenon,
  The glittering Capitol;

II.

So fair in southern sunshine bathed,
  But scarce of such majestic mien
As here with forehead vapor-swathed
  In meadows ever green;

III.

For thou — when Athens reign'd and
    Rome,
  Thy glorious eyes were dimm'd
    with pain
To mark in many a freeman's home
  The slave, the scourge, the chain;

IV.

O follower of the Vision, still
  In motion to the distant gleam,
Howe'er blind force and brainless
    will
  May jar thy golden dream

V.

Of Knowledge fusing class with class,
  Of civic Hate no more to be,
Of Love to leaven all the mass,
  Till every Soul be free;

VI.

Who yet, like Nature, wouldst not
    mar
  By changes all too fierce and fast
This order of Her Human Star,
  This heritage of the past;

VII.

O scorner of the party cry
  That wanders from the public good,
Thou — when the nations rear on high
  Their idol smear'd with blood,

VIII.

And when they roll their idol down —
  Of saner worship sanely proud;
Thou loather of the lawless crown
  As of the lawless crowd;

IX.

How long thine ever-growing mind
  Hath still'd the blast and strown
    the wave,
Tho' some of late would raise a wind
  To sing thee to thy grave,

x.

Men loud against all forms of power—
   Unfurnish'd brows, tempestuous tongues—
Expecting all things in an hour—
   Brass mouths and iron lungs!

TO H.R.H. PRINCESS BEATRICE.

Two Suns of Love make day of human life,
Which else with all its pains, and griefs, and deaths,
Were utter darkness—one, the Sun of dawn
That brightens thro' the Mother's tender eyes,
And warms the child's awakening world—and one
The later-rising Sun of spousal Love,
Which from her household orbit draws the child
To move in other spheres. The Mother weeps
At that white funeral of the single life,
Her maiden daughter's marriage; and her tears
Are half of pleasure, half of pain—the child
Is happy—ev'n 'in leaving *her!* but Thou,
True daughter, whose all-faithful, filial eyes
Have seen the loneliness of earthly thrones,
Wilt neither quit the widow'd Crown, nor let
This later light of Love have risen in vain,
But moving thro' the Mother's home, between

The two that love thee, lead a summer life,
Sway'd by each Love, and swaying to each Love,
Like some conjectured planet in mid heaven
Between two Suns, and drawing down from both
The light and genial warmth of double day.

POETS AND THEIR BIBLIOG-
RAPHIES.

OLD poets foster'd under friendlier skies,
   Old Virgil who would write ten lines, they say,
   At dawn, and lavish all the golden day
To make them wealthier in his readers' eyes;
And you, old popular Horace, you the wise
   Adviser of the nine-years-ponder'd lay,
   And you, that wear a wreath of sweeter bay,
Catullus, whose dead songster never dies;
If, glancing downward on the kindly sphere
   That once had roll'd you round and round the Sun,
   You see your Art still shrined in human shelves,
You should be jubilant that you flourish'd here
   Before the Love of Letters, overdone,
Had swampt the sacred poets with themselves.

LOCKSLEY HALL SIXTY YEARS AFTER.

LATE, my grandson! half the morning have I paced these sandy tracts,
Watch'd again the hollow ridges roaring into cataracts,

Wander'd back to living boyhood while I heard the curlews call,
I myself so close on death, and death itself in Locksley Hall.

So — your happy suit was blasted — she the faultless, the divine;
And you liken — boyish babble — this boy-love of yours with mine.

I myself have often babbled doubtless of a foolish past;
Babble, babble; our old England may go down in babble at last.

"Curse him!" curse your fellow-victim? call him dotard in your rage?
Eyes that lured a doting boyhood well might fool a dotard's age.

Jilted for a wealthier! wealthier? yet perhaps she was not wise;
I remember how you kiss'd the miniature with those sweet eyes.

In the hall there hangs a painting — Amy's arms about my neck —
Happy children in a sunbeam sitting on the ribs of wreck.

In my life there was a picture, she that clasp'd my neck had flown;
I was left within the shadow sitting on the wreck alone.

Yours has been a slighter ailment, will you sicken for her sake?
You, not you! your modern amourist is of easier, earthlier make.

Amy loved me, Amy fail'd me, Amy was a timid child;
But your Judith — but your worldling — *she* had never driven me wild.

She that holds the diamond necklace dearer than the golden ring,
She that finds a winter sunset fairer than a morn of Spring.

She that in her heart is brooding on his briefer lease of life,
While she vows "till death shall part us," she the would-be-widow wife.

She the worldling born of worldlings — father, mother — be content,
Ev'n the homely farm can teach us there is something in descent.

Yonder in that chapel, slowly sinking now into the ground,
Lies the warrior, my forefather, with his feet upon the hound.

Cross'd! for once he sail'd the sea to crush the Moslem in his pride;
Dead the warrior, dead his glory, dead the cause in which he died.

Yet how often I and Amy in the mouldering aisle have stood,
Gazing for one pensive moment on that founder of our blood.

There again I stood to-day, and where of old we knelt in prayer,
Close beneath the casement crimson with the shield of Locksley — there,

All in white Italian marble, looking still as if she smiled,
Lies my Amy dead in child-birth, dead the mother, dead the child.

Dead — and sixty years ago, and dead her aged husband now,
I this old white-headed dreamer stoopt and kiss'd her marble brow.

Gone the fires of youth, the follies, furies, curses, passionate tears,
Gone like fires and floods and earthquakes of the planet's dawning years.

Fires that shook me once, but now to silent ashes fall'n away.
Cold upon the dead volcano sleeps the gleam of dying day.

Gone the tyrant of my youth, and mute below the chancel stones,
All his virtues — I forgive them — black in white above his bones.

Gone the comrades of my bivouac, some in fight against the foe,
Some thro' age and slow diseases, gone as all on earth will go.

Gone with whom for forty years my life in golden sequence ran,
She with all the charm of woman, she with all the breadth of man,

Strong in will and rich in wisdom, Edith, loyal, lowly, sweet,
Feminine to her inmost heart, and feminine to her tender feet,

Very woman of very woman, nurse of ailing body and mind,
She that link'd again the broken chain that bound me to my kind.

Here to-day was Amy with me, while I wander'd down the coast,
Near us Edith's holy shadow, smiling at the slighter ghost.

Gone our sailor son thy father, Leonard early lost at sea;
Thou alone, my boy, of Amy's kin and mine art left to me.

Gone thy tender-natured mother, wearying to be left alone,
Pining for the stronger heart that once had beat beside her own.

Truth, for Truth is Truth, he worshipt, being true as he was brave;
Good, for Good is Good, he follow'd, yet he look'd beyond the grave,

Wiser there than you, that crowning barren Death as lord of all,
Deem this over-tragic drama's closing curtain is the pall!

Beautiful was death in him who saw the death but kept the deck,
Saving women and their babes, and sinking with the sinking wreck,

Gone forever! Ever? no — for since our dying race began,
Ever, ever, and forever was the leading light of man.

Those that in barbarian burials kill'd the slave, and slew the wife,
Felt within themselves the sacred passion of the second life.

Indian warriors dream of ampler hunting grounds beyond the night;
Ev'n the black Australian dying hopes he shall return, a white.

Truth for truth, and good for good! The Good, the True, the Pure, the Just;
Take the charm "Forever" from them, and they crumble into dust.

Gone the cry of "Forward, Forward," lost within a growing gloom;
Lost, or only heard in silence from the silence of a tomb.

Half the marvels of my morning, triumphs over time and space,
Staled by frequence, shrunk by usage into commonest commonplace!

"Forward" rang the voices then, and of the many mine was one.
Let us hush this cry of "Forward" till ten thousand years have gone.

Far among the vanish'd races, old Assyrian kings would flay
Captives whom they caught in battle — iron-hearted victors they.

Ages after, while in Asia, he that led the wild Moguls,
Timur built his ghastly tower of eighty thousand human skulls,

Then, and here in Edward's time, an age of noblest English names,
Christian conquerors took and flung the conquer'd Christian into flames.

Love your enemy, bless your haters, said the Greatest of the great;
Christian love among the Churches look'd the twin of heathen hate.

From the golden alms of Blessing man had coin'd himself a curse:
Rome of Cæsar, Rome of Peter, which was crueller? which was worse?

France had shown a light to all men, preach'd a Gospel, all men's good;
Celtic Demos rose a Demon, shriek'd and slaked the light with blood.

Hope was ever on her mountain, watching till the day begun,
Crown'd with sunlight — over darkness — from the still unrisen sun.

Have we grown at last beyond the passions of the primal clan?
"Kill your enemy, for you hate him," still, "your enemy" was a man.

Have we sunk below them? peasants maim the helpless horse, and drive
Innocent cattle under thatch, and burn the kindlier brutes alive.

Brutes, the brutes are not your wrongers — burnt at midnight, found at morn,
Twisted hard in mortal agony with their offspring, born-unborn,

Clinging to the silent mother! Are we devils? are we men?
Sweet St. Francis of Assisi, would that he were here again,

He that in his Catholic wholeness used to call the very flowers
Sisters, brothers — and the beasts — whose pains are hardly less than ours!

Chaos, Cosmos! Cosmos, Chaos! who can tell how all will end!
Read the wide world's annals, you, and take their wisdom for your friend.

Hope the best, but hold the Present fatal daughter of the Past,
Shape your heart to front the hour, but dream not that the hour will last.

Ay, if dynamite and revolver leave you courage to be wise:
When was age so cramm'd with menace? madness? written, spoken lies?

Envy wears the mask of Love, and, laughing sober fact to scorn,
Cries to Weakest as to Strongest, " Ye are equals, equal-born."

Equal-born?   O yes, if yonder hill be level with the flat.
Charm us, Orator, till the Lion look no larger than the Cat.

Till the Cat thro' that mirage of overheated language loom
Larger than the Lion, — Demos end in working its own doom.

Russia bursts our Indian barrier, shall we fight her? shall we yield?
Pause, before you sound the trumpet, hear the voices from the field.

Those three hundred millions under one Imperial sceptre now,
Shall we hold them? shall we loose them? take the suffrage of the plow.

Nay, but these would feel and follow Truth if only you and you,
Rivals of realm-ruining party, when you speak were wholly true.

Plowmen, Shepherds, have I found, and more than once, and still could find,
Sons of God, and kings of men in utter nobleness of mind,

Truthful, trustful, looking upward to the practised hustings-liar;
So the Higher wields the Lower, while the Lower is the Higher.

Here and there a cotter's babe is royal-born by right divine;
Here and there my lord is lower than his oxen or his swine.

Chaos, Cosmos! Cosmos, Chaos! once again the sickening game;
Freedom, free to slay herself, and dying while they shout her name.

Step by step we gain'd a freedom known to Europe, known to all;
Step by step we rose to greatness, — thro' the tonguesters we may fall.

You that woo the Voices — tell them " old experience is a fool,"
Teach your flatter'd kings that only those who cannot read can rule.

Pluck the mighty from their seat, but set no meek ones in their place;
Pillory Wisdom in your markets, pelt your offal at her face.

Tumble Nature heel o'er head, and, yelling with the yelling street,
Set the feet above the brain and swear the brain is in the feet.

Bring the old dark ages back without the faith, without the hope,
Break the State, the Church, the Throne, and roll their ruins down the slope.

Authors — atheist, essayist, novelist, realist, rhymester, play your part,
Paint the mortal shame of nature with the living hues of Art.

Rip your brothers' vices open, strip your own foul passions bare;
Down with Reticence, down with Reverence — forward — naked — let them stare.

Feed the budding rose of boyhood with the drainage of your sewer;
Send the drain into the fountain, lest the stream should issue pure.

Set the maiden fancies wallowing in the troughs of Zolaism, —
Forward, forward, ay and backward, downward too into the abysm.

Do your best to charm the worst, to lower the rising race of men;
Have we risen from out the beast, then back into the beast again?

Only "dust to dust" for me that sicken at your lawless din,
Dust in wholesome old-world dust before the newer world begin.

Heated am I? you — you wonder — well, it scarce becomes mine age —
Patience! let the dying actor mouth his last upon the stage.

Cries of unprogressive dotage ere the dotard fall asleep?
Noises of a current narrowing, not the music of a deep?

Ay, for doubtless I am old, and think gray thoughts, for I am gray:
After all the stormy changes shall we find a changeless May?

After madness, after massacre, Jacobinism and Jacquerie,
Some diviner force to guide us thro' the days I shall not see?

When the schemes and all the systems, Kingdoms and Republics fall,
Something kindlier, higher, holier — all for each and each for all?

All the full-brain, half-brain races, led by Justice, Love, and Truth;
All the millions one at length, with all the visions of my youth?

All diseases quench'd by Science, no man halt, or deaf or blind;
Stronger ever born of weaker, lustier body, larger mind?

Earth at last a warless world, a single race, a single tongue,
I have seen her far away — for is not Earth as yet so young? —

Every tiger madness muzzled, every serpent passion kill'd,
Every grim ravine a garden, every blazing desert till'd,

Robed in universal harvest up to either pole she smiles,
Universal ocean softly washing all her warless Isles.

Warless ? when her tens are thousands, and her thousands millions, then —
All her harvest all too narrow — who can fancy warless men ?

Warless ? war will die out late then.   Will it ever ? late or soon ?
Can it, till this outworn earth be dead as yon dead world the moon ?

Dead the new astronomy calls her. . . .   On this day and at this hour,
In this gap between the sandhills, whence you see the Locksley tower,

Here we met, our latest meeting — Amy — sixty years ago —
She and I — the moon was falling greenish thro' a rosy glow,

Just above the gateway tower, and even where you see her now —
Here we stood and claspt each other, swore the seeming-deathless vow. . . .

Dead, but how her living glory lights the hall, the dune, the grass !
Yet the moonlight is the sunlight, and the sun himself will pass.

Venus near her ! smiling downward at this earthlier earth of ours,
Closer on the Sun, perhaps a world of never fading flowers.

Hesper, whom the poet call'd the Bringer home of all good things.
All good things may move in Hesper, perfect peoples, perfect kings.

Hesper — Venus — were we native to that splendor or in Mars,
We should see the Globe we groan in, fairest of their evening stars.

Could we dream of wars and carnage, craft and madness, lust and spite,
Roaring London, raving Paris, in that point of peaceful light ?

Might we not in glancing heavenward on a star so silver-fair,
Yearn, and clasp the hands and murmur, " Would to God that we were
    there " ?

Forward, backward, backward, forward, in the immeasurable sea,
Sway'd by vaster ebbs and flows than can be known to you or me.

All the suns — are these but symbols of innumerable man,
Man or Mind that sees a shadow of the planner or the plan ?

Is there evil but on earth ? or pain in every peopled sphere ?
Well be grateful for the sounding watchword, " Evolution " here.

Evolution ever climbing after some ideal good,
And Reversion ever dragging Evolution in the mud.

What are men that He should heed us ? cried the king of sacred song;
Insects of an hour, that hourly work their brother insect wrong,

While the silent Heavens roll, and Suns along their fiery way,
All their planets whirling round them, flash a million miles a day.

Many an Æon moulded earth before her highest, man, was born,
Many an Æon too may pass when earth is manless and forlorn,

Earth so huge, and yet so bounded — pools of salt, and plots of land —
Shallow skin of green and azure — chains of mountain, grains of sand!

Only That which made us, meant us to be mightier by and by,
Set the sphere of all the boundless Heavens within the human eye,

Sent the shadow of Himself, the boundless, thro' the human soul;
Boundless inward, in the atom, boundless outward, in the Whole.

*   *   *   *   *   *   *   *

Here is Locksley Hall, my grandson, here the lion-guarded gate.
Not to-night in Locksley Hall — to-morrow — you, you come so late.

Wreck'd — your train — or all but wreck'd? a shatter'd wheel? a vicious
    boy!
Good, this forward, you that preach it, is it well to wish you joy?

Is it well that while we range with Science, glorying in the Time,
City children soak and blacken soul and sense in city slime?

There among the glooming alleys Progress halts on palsied feet,
Crime and hunger cast our maidens by the thousand on the street.

There the Master scrimps his haggard sempstress of her daily bread,
There a single sordid attic holds the living and the dead.

There the smouldering fire of fever creeps across the rotted floor,
And the crowded couch of incest in the warrens of the poor.

Nay, your pardon, cry your "forward," yours are hope and youth, but I —
Eighty winters leave the dog too lame to follow with the cry,

Lame and old, and past his time, and passing now into the night;
Yet I would the rising race were half as eager for the light.

Light the fading gleam of Even? light the glimmer of the dawn?
Aged eyes may take the growing glimmer for the gleam withdrawn.

Far away beyond her myriad coming changes earth will be
Something other than the wildest modern guess of you and me.

Earth may reach her earthly-worst, or if she gain her earthly-best,
Would she find her human offspring this ideal man at rest?

Forward then, but still remember how the course of Time will swerve,
Crook and turn upon itself in many a backward streaming curve.

Not the Hall to-night, my grandson! Death and Silence hold their own.
Leave the Master in the first dark hour of his last sleep alone.

Worthier soul was he than I am, sound and honest, rustic Squire,
Kindly landlord, boon companion — youthful jealousy is a liar.

Cast the poison from your bosom, oust the madness from your brain.
Let the trampled serpent show you that you have not lived in vain.

Youthful! youth and age are scholars yet but in the lower school,
Nor is he the wisest man who never proved himself a fool.

Yonder lies our young sea-village — Art and Grace are less and less :
Science grows and Beauty dwindles — roofs of slated hideousness !

There is one old Hostel left us where they swing the Locksley shield,
Till the peasant cow shall butt the " Lion passant " from his field.

Poor old Heraldry, poor old History, poor old Poetry, passing hence,
In the common deluge drowning old political common-sense !

Poor old voice of eighty crying after voices that have fled !
All I loved are vanish'd voices, all my steps are on the dead.

All the world is ghost to me, and as the phantom disappears,
Forward far and far from here is all the hope of eighty years.

  *   *   *   *   *   *   *   *

In this Hostel — I remember — I repent it o'er his grave —
Like a clown — by chance he met me — I refused the hand he gave.

From that casement where the trailer mantles all the mouldering bricks —
I was then in early boyhood, Edith but a child of six —

While I shelter'd in this archway from a day of driving showers —
Peept the winsome face of Edith like a flower among the flowers.

Here to-night! the Hall to-morrow, when they toll the Chapel bell !
Shall I hear in one dark room a wailing, " I have loved thee well."

Then a peal that shakes the portal — one has come to claim his bride,
Her that shrank, and put me from her, shriek'd, and started from my side —

Silent echoes ! you, my Leonard, use and not abuse your day,
Move among your people, know them, follow him who led the way,

Strove for sixty widow'd years to help his homelier brother men,
Served the poor, and built the cottage, raised the school, and drain'd the fen.

Hears he now the Voice that wrong'd him ? who shall swear it cannot be ?
Earth would never touch her worst, were one in fifty such as he.

Ere she gain her Heavenly-best, a God must mingle with the game:
Nay, there may be those about us whom we neither see nor name,

Felt within us as ourselves, the Powers of Good, the Powers of Ill,
Strowing balm, or shedding poison in the fountains of the Will.

Follow you the Star that lights a desert pathway, yours or mine.
Forward, till you see the highest Human Nature is divine.

Follow Light, and do the Right — for man can half-control his doom —
Till you find the deathless Angel seated in the vacant tomb.

Forward, let the stormy moment fly and mingle with the Past.
I that loathed, have come to love him. Love will conquer at the last.

Gone at eighty, mine own age, and I and you will bear the pall;
Then I leave thee Lord and Master, latest Lord of Locksley Hall.

THE FLEET.[1]

I.

You, you, *if* you shall fail to under-
    stand
  What England is, and what her all-
    in-all,
On you will come the curse of all the
    land,
  Should this old England fall
    Which Nelson left so great.

II.

His isle, the mightiest Ocean-power
    on earth,
  Our own fair isle, the lord of every
    sea —
Her fuller franchise — what would
    that be worth —
  Her ancient fame of Free —
    Were she . . . a fallen state ?

[1] The speaker said that "he should like to be assured that other outlying portions of the Empire, the Crown colonies, and important coaling stations were being as promptly and as thoroughly fortified as the various capitals of the self-governing colonies. He was credibly informed this was not so. It was impossible, also, not to feel some degree of anxiety about the efficacy of present provision to defend and protect, by means of swift, well-armed cruisers, the immense mercantile fleet of the Empire. A third source of anxiety, so far as the colonies were concerned, was the apparently insufficient provision for the rapid manufacture of armaments and their prompt despatch when ordered to their colonial destination. Hence the necessity for manufacturing appliances equal to the requirements, not of Great Britain alone, but of the whole Empire. But the keystone of the whole was the necessity for an overwhelmingly powerful fleet and efficient defence for all necessary coaling sta- tions. This was as essential for the colonies as for Great Britain. It was the one condition for the continuance of the Empire. All that Continental Powers did with respect to armies England should effect with her navy. It was essentially a defensive force, and could be moved rapidly from point to point, but it should be equal to all that was expected from it. It was to strengthen the fleet that colonists would first readily tax themselves, because they realized how essential a powerful fleet was to the safety, not only of that extensive commerce sailing in every sea, but ultimately to the security of the distant portions of the Empire. Who could estimate the loss involved in even a brief period of disaster to the Imperial Navy. Any amount of money timely expended in preparation would be quite insignificant when compared with the possible calamity he had referred to." — *Extract from Sir Graham Berry's Speech at the Colonial Institute, 9th November,* 1886.

III.

Her dauntless army scatter'd, and so
 small,
 Her island-myriads fed from alien
 lands —
The fleet of England is her all-in-all;
 Her fleet is in your hands,
 And in her fleet her Fate.

IV.

You, you, that have the ordering of
 her fleet,
 If you should only compass her
 disgrace,
When all men starve, the wild mob's
 million feet
 Will kick you from your place,
 But then too late, too late.

OPENING OF THE INDIAN AND
COLONIAL EXHIBITION BY
THE QUEEN.

I.

Welcome, welcome with one voice!
In your welfare we rejoice,
Sons and brothers that have sent,
From isle and cape and continent,
Produce of your field and flood,
Mount and mine, and primal wood;
Works of subtle brain and hand,
And splendors of the morning land,
Gifts from every British zone;
 Britons, hold your own!

II.

May we find, as ages run,
The mother featured in the son;
And may yours forever be
That old strength and constancy
Which has made your fathers great
In our ancient island State,
And wherever her flag fly,
Glorying between sea and sky,
Makes the might of Britain known;
 Britons, hold your own!

III.

Britain fought her sons of yore —
Britain failed; and never more,
Careless of our growing kin,
Shall we sin our fathers' sin,
Men that in a narrower day —
Unprophetic rulers they —
Drove from out the mother's nest
That young eagle of the West
To forage for herself alone;
 Britons, hold your own!

IV.

Sharers of our glorious past,
Brothers, must we part at last?
Shall we not thro' good and ill
Cleave to one another still?
Britain's myriad voices call,
"Sons, be wedded each and all,
Into one imperial whole,
One with Britain, heart and soul!
One life, one flag, one fleet, one
 Throne!"
 Britons, hold your own!

TO THE MARQUIS OF DUF-
FERIN AND AVA.

I.

At times our Britain cannot rest,
 At times her steps are swift and
 rash;
 She moving, at her girdle clash
The golden keys of East and West.

II.

Not swift or rash, when late she lent
 The sceptres of her West, her East,
 To one, that ruling has increased
Her greatness and her self-content.

III.

Your rule has made the people love
 Their ruler. Your viceregal days
 Have added fulness to the phrase
Of "Gauntlet in the velvet glove."

IV.

But since your name will grow with
      Time,
   Not all, as honoring your fair fame
   Of Statesman, have I made the
      name
A golden portal to my rhyme :

V.

But more, that you and yours may
      know
   From me and mine, how dear a debt
   We owed you, and are owing yet
To you and yours, and still would owe.

VI.

For he — your India was his Fate,
   And drew him over sea to you —
   He fain had ranged her thro' and
      thro',
To serve her myriads and the State,—

VII

A soul that, watch'd from earliest
      youth,
   And on thro' many a brightening
      year,
   Had never swerved for craft or fear,
By one side-path, from simple truth ;

VIII.

Who might have chased and claspt
      Renown
   And caught her chaplet here — and
      there
   In haunts of jungle-poison'd air
The flame of life went wavering down ;

IX.

But ere he left your fatal shore,
   And lay on that funereal boat,
   Dying, " Unspeakable " he wrote
" Their kindness," and he wrote no
      more ;

X.

And sacred is the latest word ;
   And now The was, the Might-have-
      been,

And those lone rites I have not seen,
And one drear sound I have not heard,

XI.

Are dreams that scarce will let me be,
   Not there to bid my boy farewell,
   When That within the coffin fell,
Fell and flash'd into the Red Sea,

XII.

Beneath a hard Arabian moon
   And alien stars.   To question, why
   The sons before the fathers die,
Not mine! and I may meet him soon;

XIII.

But while my life's late eve endures,
   Nor settles into hueless gray,
   My memories of his briefer day
Will mix with love for you and yours.

ON THE JUBILEE OF QUEEN VICTORIA.

I.

FIFTY times the rose has flower'd
      and faded,
Fifty times the golden harvest fallen,
Since our Queen assumed the globe,
      the sceptre.

II.

She beloved for a kindliness
Rare in Fable or History,
Queen and Empress of India,
Crown'd so long with a diadem
Never worn by a worthier,
Now with prosperous auguries
Comes at last to the bounteous
Crowning year of her Jubilee.

III.

Nothing of the lawless, of the Despot,
Nothing of the vulgar, or vainglori-
      ous,
All is gracious, gentle, great and
      Queenly.

IV.

You then joyfully, all of you,
Set the mountain aflame to-night,
Shoot your stars to the firmament,
Deck your houses, illuminate
All your towns for a festival,
And in each let a multiude
Loyal, each, to the heart of it,
One full voice of allegiance,
Hail the fair Ceremonial
Of this year of her Jubilee.

V.

Queen, as true to womanhood as
   Queenhood,
Glorying in the glories of her people,
Sorrowing with the sorrows of the
   lowest!

VI.

You, that wanton in affluence,
Spare not now to be bountiful,
Call your poor to regale with you,
All the lowly, the destitute,
Make their neighborhood health-
   fuller,
Give your gold to the Hospital,
Let the weary be comforted,
Let the needy be banqueted,
Let the maim'd in his heart rejoice
At this glad Ceremonial,
And this year of her Jubilee.

VII.

Henry's fifty years are all in shadow,
Gray with distance Edward's fifty
   summers,
Ev'n her Grandsire's fifty half forgotten.

VIII.

You, the Patriot Architect,
You that shape for Eternity,
Raise a stately memorial,
Make it regally gorgeous,
Some Imperial Institute,
Rich in symbol, in ornament,
Which may speak to the centuries,
All the centuries after us,

Of this great Ceremonial,
And this year of her Jubilee.

IX.

Fifty years of ever-broadening Commerce!
Fifty years of ever-brightening Science!
Fifty years of ever-widening Empire!

X.

You, the Mighty, the Fortunate,
You, the Lord-territorial,
You, the Lord-manufacturer,
You, the hardy, laborious,
Patient children of Albion,
You, Canadian, Indian,
Australasian, African,
All your hearts be in harmony,
All your voices in unison,
Singing " Hail to the glorious
Golden year of her Jubilee ! "

XI.

Are there thunders moaning in the
   distance ?
Are there spectres moving in the
   darkness ?
Trust the Hand of Light will lead
   her people,
Till the thunders pass, the spectres
   vanish,
And the Light is the Victor, and
   the darkness
Dawns into the Jubilee of the Ages.

———

TO PROFESSOR JEBB,

WITH THE FOLLOWING POEM.

FAIR things are slow to fade away,
Bear witness you, that yesterday [1]
   From out the Ghost of Pindar in
     you
Roll'd an Olympian ; and they say [2]

[1] In Bologna.
[2] They say, for the fact is doubtful.

That here the torpid mummy wheat
Of Egypt bore a grain as sweet
    As that which gilds the glebe of
      England,
Sunn'd with a summer of milder heat.

So may this legend for awhile
If greeted by your classic smile,
    Tho' dead in its Trinacrian Enna,
Blossom again on a colder isle.

DEMETER AND PERSEPHONE.

(IN ENNA.)

FAINT as a climate-changing bird that
    flies
All night across the darkness, and at
    dawn
Falls on the threshold of her native
    land,
And can no more, thou camest, O my
    child,
Led upward by the God of ghosts
    and dreams,
Who laid thee at Eleusis, dazed and
    dumb
With passing thro' at once from state
    to state,
Until I brought thee hither, that the
    day,
When here thy hands let fall the
    gather'd flower,
Might break thro' clouded memories
    once again
On thy lost self. A sudden nightin-
    gale
Saw thee, and flash'd into a frolic of
    song
And welcome; and a gleam as of the
    moon,
When first she peers along the tremu-
    lous deep,
Fled wavering o'er thy face, and
    chased away
That shadow of a likeness to the king
Of shadows, thy dark mate. Per-
    sephone!
Queen of the dead no more — my
    child! Thine eyes

Again were human-godlike, and the
    Sun
Burst from a swimming fleece of win-
    ter gray,
And robed thee in his day from head
    to feet —
"Mother!" and I was folded in thine
    arms.

Child, those imperial, disimpas-
    sion'd, eyes
Awed even me at first, thy mother —
    eyes
That oft had seen the serpent-wanded
    power
Draw downward into Hades with his
    drift
Of flickering spectres, lighted from
    below
By the red race of fiery Phlegethon;
But when before have Gods or men
    beheld
The Life that had descended re-arise,
And lighted from above him by the
    Sun?
So mighty was the mother's childless
    cry,
A cry that rang thro' Hades, Earth,
    and Heaven!

So in this pleasant vale we stand
    again,
The field of Enna, now once more
    ablaze
With flowers that brighten as thy
    footstep falls,
All flowers — but for one black blur
    of earth
Left by that closing chasm, thro'
    which the car
Of dark Aïdoneus rising rapt thee
    hence.
And here, my child, tho' folded in
    thine arms,
I feel the deathless heart of mother-
    hood
Within me shudder, lest the naked
    glebe
Should yawn once more into the
    gulf, and thence
The shrilly whinnyings of the team
    of Hell,

Ascending, pierce the glad and song-
ful air,
And all at once their arch'd necks,
midnight-maned,
Jet upward thro' the mid-day blossom. No!
For, see, thy foot has touch'd it; all
the space
Of blank earth-baldness clothes itself
afresh,
And breaks into the crocus-purple
hour
That saw thee vanish.

         Child, when thou wert gone,
I envied human wives, and nested
birds,
Yea, the cubb'd lioness; went in
search of thee
Thro' many a palace, many a cot,
and gave
Thy breast to ailing infants in the
night,
And set the mother waking in amaze
To find her sick one whole; and forth
again
Among the wail of midnight winds,
and cried,
"Where is my loved one? Where-
fore do ye wail?"
And out from all the night an answer
shrill'd,
"We know not, and we know not why
we wail."
I climb'd on all the cliffs of all the
seas,
And ask'd the waves that moan about
the world
"Where? do ye make your moaning
for my child?"
And round from all the world the
voices came
"We know not, and we know not why
we moan."
"Where"? and I stared from every
eagle-peak,
I thridded the black heart of all the
woods,
I peer'd thro' tomb and cave, and in
the storms
Of Autumn swept across the city,
and heard

The murmur of their temples chant-
ing me,
Me, me, the desolate Mother!
"Where"? — and turn'd,
And fled by many a waste, forlorn of
man,
And grieved for man thro' all my
grief for thee, —
The jungle rooted in his shatter'd
hearth,
The serpent coil'd about his broken
shaft,
The scorpion crawling over naked
skulls; —
I saw the tiger in the ruin'd fane
Spring from his fallen God, but trace
of thee
I saw not; and far on, and, following
out
A league of labyrinthine darkness,
came
On three gray heads beneath a gleam-
ing rift.
"Where"? and I heard one voice
from all the three
"We know not, for we spin the lives
of men,
And not of Gods, and know not why
we spin!
There is a Fate beyond us." Nothing
knew.

     Last as the likeness of a dying
man,
Without his knowledge, from him
flits to warn
A far-off friendship that he comes no
more,
So he, the God of dreams, who heard
my cry,
Drew from thyself the likeness of
thyself
Without thy knowledge, and thy
shadow past
Before me, crying "The Bright one
in the highest
Is brother of the Dark one in the
lowest,
And Bright and Dark have sworn
that I, the child
Of thee, the great Earth-Mother,
thee, the Power

That lifts her buried life from gloom
  to bloom,
Should be forever and forevermore
The Bride of Darkness."

      So the Shadow wail'd.
Then I, Earth-Goddess, cursed the
  Gods of Heaven.
I would not mingle with their feasts;
  to me
Their nectar smack'd of hemlock on
  the lips,
Their rich ambrosia tasted aconite.
The man, that only lives and loves an
  hour,
Seem'd nobler than their hard Eter-
  nities.
My quick tears kill'd the flower, my
  ravings hush'd
The bird, and lost in utter grief I
  fail'd
To send my life thro' olive-yard and
  vine
And golden grain, my gift to helpless
  man.
Rain-rotten died the wheat, the bar-
  ley-spears
Were hollow-husk'd, the leaf fell,
  and the sun,
Pale at my grief, drew down before
  his time
Sickening, and Ætna kept her winter
  snow.
  Then He, the brother of this Darkness, He
Who still is highest, glancing from
  his height
On earth a fruitless fallow, when he
  miss'd
The wonted steam of sacrifice, the
  praise
And prayer of men, decreed that thou
  should'st dwell
For nine white moons of each whole
  year with me,
The three dark ones in the shadow
  with thy King.

Once more the reaper in the gleam
  of dawn
Will see me by the landmark far away,
Blessing his field, or seated in the dusk

Of even, by the lonely threshing-floor,
Rejoicing in the harvest and the
  grange.
  Yet I, Earth-Goddess, am but ill-
  content
With them, who still are highest.
  Those gray heads,
What meant they by their "Fate
  beyond the Fates"
But younger kindlier Gods to bear
  us down,
As we bore down the Gods before us?
  Gods,
To quench, not hurl the thunderbolt,
  to stay,
Not spread the plague, the famine;
  Gods indeed,
To send the noon into the night and
  break
The sunless halls of Hades into
  Heaven?
Till thy dark lord accept and love
  the Sun,
And all the Shadow die into the
  Light,
When thou shalt dwell the whole
  bright year with me,
And souls of men, who grew beyond
  their race,
And made themselves as Gods against
  the fear
Of Death and Hell; and thou that
  hast from men,
As Queen of Death, that worship
  which is Fear,
Henceforth, as having risen from out
  the dead,
Shalt eversend thy life along with mine
From buried grain thro' springing
  blade, and bless
Their garner'd Autumn also, reap
  with me,
Earth-mother, in the harvest hymns
  of Earth
The worship which is Love, and see
  no more
The Stone, the Wheel, the dimly-
  glimmering lawns
Of that Elysium, all the hateful fires
Of torment, and the shadowy warrior
  glide
Along the silent field of Asphodel.

OWD ROÄ.[1]

Naäy, noä mander [2] o' use to be callin' 'm Roä, Roä, Roä,
Fo' the dog's stoän-deäf, an' e's blind, 'e can neither stan' nor goä.

But I meäns fur to maäke 'is owd aäge as 'appy as iver I can,
Fur I owäs owd Roäver moor nor I iver owäd mottal man.

Thou's rode of 'is back when a babby, afoor thou was gotten too owd,
For 'e'd fetch an' carry like owt, 'e was allus as good as gowd.

Eh, but 'e'd fight wi' a will *when* 'e fowt; 'e could howd [3] 'is oan,
An' Roä was the dog as knaw'd when an' wheere to bury his boane.

An' 'e kep his heäd hoop like a king, an' 'e'd niver not down wi' 'is täail,
Fur 'e'd niver done nowt to be shäamed on, when we was i' Howlaby Daäle.

An' 'e sarved me sa well when 'e lived, that, Dick, when 'e cooms to be deäd,
I thinks as I'd like fur to hev soom soort of a sarvice reäd.

Fur 'e's moor good sense na the Parliament man 'at stans fur us 'ere,
An' I'd voät fur 'im, my oän sen, if 'e could but stan fur the Shere.

"Faäithful an' True " — them words be 'Scriptur — an' Faäithful an' True
Ull be fun' [4] upo' four short legs ten times fur one upo' two.

An' maäybe they'll walk upo' two but I knaws they runs upo' four,[5] —
Bedtime, Dicky! but waäit till tha 'eärs it be strikin' the hour.

Fur I wants to tell tha o' Roä when we lived i' Howlaby Daäle,
Ten year sin — Naäy — naäy! tha mun nobbut hev' one glass of aäle.

Straänge an' owd-farran'd [6] the 'ouse, an' belt [7] long afoor my daäy
Wi' haäfe o' the chimleys a-twizzen'd [8] an' twined like a band o' haäy.

The fellers as maäkes them picturs, 'ud coom at the fall o' the year,
An' settle their ends upo stools to pictur the door-poorch theere,

An' the Heagle 'as hed two heäds stannin' theere o' the brokken stick; [9]
An' they niver 'ed seed sich ivin' [10] as graw'd hall ower the brick;

An' theere i' the 'ouse one night — but it's down, an' all on it now
Goan into mangles an' tonups,[11] an' raäved slick thruf by the plow —

Theere, when the 'ouse wur a house, one night I wur sittin' aloän,
Wi' Roäver athurt my feeät, an' sleeäpin still as a stoän,

---

[1] Old Rover.   [2] Manner.   [3] Hold.   [4] Found.   [5] "Ou " as in "house."
[6] "Owd-farran'd," old-fashioned.   [7] Built.   [8] "Twizzen'd," twisted.
[9] On a staff *ragulé*.   [10] Ivy.   [11] Mangolds and turnips.

Of a Christmas Eäve, an' as cowd as this, an' the midders [1] as white,
An' the fences all on 'em bolster'd oop wi' the windle [2] that night;

An' the cat wur a-sleeäpin alongside Roäver, but I wur awaäke,
An' smoäkin' an' thinkin' o' things — Doänt maäke thysen sick wi' the caäke.

Fur the men ater supper 'ed sung their songs an' 'ed 'ed their beer,
An' 'ed goän their waäys; ther was nobbut three, an' noän on 'em theere.

They was all on 'em fear'd o' the Ghoäst an' dussn't not sleeäp i' the 'ouse,
But Dicky, the Ghoäst moästlins [3] was nobbut a rat or a mouse.

An' I looökt out wonst [4] at the night, an' the daäle was all of a thaw,
Fur I seed the beck coomin' down like a long black snaäke i' the snaw,

An' I heärd greät heäps o' the snaw slushin' down fro' the bank to the beck,
An' then as I stood i' the doorwaäy, I feeäld it drip o' my neck.

Saw I turn'd in ageän, an' I thowt o' the good owd times 'at was goan,
An' the munney they maäde by the war, an' the times 'at was coomin' on;

Fur I thowt if the Staäte was a gawin' to let in furriners wheät,
Howiver was British farmers to stan' ageän o' their feeät.

Howiver was I fur to find my rent an' to paäy my men ?
An' all along o' the feller [5] as turn'd 'is back of hissen.

Thou slep i' the chaumber above us, we couldn't ha' 'eärd tha call,
Sa Moother 'ed tell'd ma to bring tha down, an' thy craädle an' all;

Fur the gell o' the farm 'at slep wi' tha then 'ed gotten wer leäve,
Fur to goä that night to 'er foälk by cause o' the Christmas Eäve;

But I cleän forgot tha, my lad, when Moother 'ed gotten to bed,
An' I slep i' my chair hup-on-end, an' the Freeä Traäde runn'd i' my 'ead,

Till I dreäm'd 'at Squire walkt in, an' I says to him " Squire, ya're laäte,"
Then I seed at 'is faäce wur as red as the Yuleblock theer i' the graäte.

An' 'e says " can ya paäy me the rent to-night ? " an' I says to 'im " Noä,"
An' 'e cotch'd howd hard o' my hairm, [6] " Then hout to-night tha shall goä."

" Tha'll niver," says I, " be a-turnin ma hout upo' Christmas Eäve ? "
Then I waäked an' I fun it was Roäver a-tuggin' an' teärin' my slieäve.

An' I thowt as 'e'd goän cleän-wud, [7] fur I noäwaeys knaw'd 'is intent;
An' I says " Git awaäy, ya beäst," an' I fetcht 'im a kick an' 'e went.

Then 'e tummled up stairs, fur I 'eärd 'im, as if 'e'd 'a brokken 'is neck,
An' I'd cleär forgot, little Dicky, thy chaumber door wouldn't sneck ; [8]

[1] Meadows.　　　[2] Drifted snow.　　　[3] " Moästlins," for the most part, generally.
[4] Once.　　　[5] Peel.　　　[6] Arm.　　　[7] Mad.　　　[8] Latch.

An' I slep' i' my chair ageän wi' my hairm hingin' down to the floor,
An' I thowt it was Roäver a-tuggin' an' teärin' me wuss nor afoor,

An' I thowt 'at I kick'd 'im ageän, but I kick'd thy Moother istead.
" What arta snorin' theere fur ? the house is afire," she said.

Thy Moother 'ed beän a-naggin' about the gell o' the farm,
She offens 'ud spy summut wrong when there warn't not a mossel o' harm;

An' she didn't not solidly meän I wur gawin' that waäy to the bad,
Fur the gell [1] was as howry a trollope as iver traäps'd i' the squad.

But Moother was free of 'er tongue, as I offens 'ev tell'd 'er mysen,
Sa I kep i' my chair, fur I thowt she was nobbut a-rilin' ma then.

An' I says "I'd be good to tha, Bess, if tha'd onywaäys let ma be good,"
But she skelpt ma haäfe ower i' the chair, an' screeäd like a Howl gone wud [2] —

" Ya mun run fur the lether. [3] Git oop, if ya're onywaäys good for owt."
And I says " If I beänt noäwaäys — not nowadaäys — good fur nowt —

" Yit I beänt sich a Nowt [4] of all Nowts as 'ull hallus do as 'e's bid."
" But the stairs is afire," she said; then I seed 'er a-cryin', I did.

An' she beäld " Ya mun saäve little Dick, an' be sharp about it an' all,"
Sa I runs to the yard fur a lether, an' sets 'im ageän the wall,

An' I claums an' I mashes the winder hin, when I gits to the top,
But the heät druv hout i' my heyes till I feäld mysen ready to drop.

Thy Moother was howdin' the lether, an' tellin' me not to be skeärd,
An' I wasn't afeärd, or I thinks leästwaäys as I wasn't afeärd;

But I couldn't see for the smoäke wheere thou was a-liggin, my lad,
An' Roäver was theere i' the chaumber a-yowlin' an' yaupin' like mad;

An' thou was a-beälin' likewise, an' a-squeälin', as if tha was bit,
An' it wasn't a bite but a burn, fur the merk's [5] o' thy shou'der yit;

Then I call'd out Roä, Roä, Roä, thaw I didn't haäfe think as 'e'd 'ear,
But 'e coom'd thruf the fire wi' my bairn i' 's mouth to the winder theere !

He coom'd like a Hangel o' marcy as soon as 'e 'eärd 'is naäme,
Or like tother Hangel i' Scriptur 'at summun seed i' the flaäme,

When summun 'ed hax'd fur a son, an' 'e promised a son to she,
An' Roä was as good as the Hangel i' saävin' a son fur me.

---

[1] The girl was as dirty a slut as ever trudged in the mud, but there is a sense of slatternliness in " traäpes'd " which is not expressed in " trudged."
[2] She half overturned me and shrieked like an owl gone mad.   [3] Ladder.
[4] A thoroughly insignificant or worthless person.   [5] Mark.

Sa I browt tha down, an' I says "I mun gaw up ageän fur Roä."
"Gaw up ageän fur the varmint?" I tell'd 'er "Yeäs I maun goä."

An' I claumb'd up ageän to the winder, an' clemm'd[1] owd Roä by the 'eäd,
An' 'is 'air coom'd off i' my 'ands an' I taäked 'im at fust fur deäd;

Fur 'e smell'd like a herse a-singein', an' seeäm'd as blind as a poop,
An' haäfe on 'im bare as a bublin'.[2] I couldn't wakken 'im oop,

But I browt 'im down, an' we got to the barn, fur the barn wouldn't burn
Wi' the wind blawin' hard tother waäy, an' the wind wasn't like to turn.

An' *I* kep a-callin' o' Roä till 'e waggled 'is taäil fur a bit,
But the cocks kep a-crawin' an' crawin' all night, an' I 'ears 'em yit;

An' the dogs was a-yowlin' all round, and thou was a-squeälin' thysen,
An' Moother was naggin' an' groänin an' moänin' an' naggin' ageän;

An' I 'eärd the bricks an' the baulks[3] rummle down when the roof gev waäy,
Fur the fire was a-raägin' an' raävin' an' roarin' like judgment daäy.

Warm enew theere sewer-ly, but the barn was as cowd as owt,
An' we cuddled and huddled togither, an' happt[4] wersens oop as we mowt.

An' I browt Roä round, but Moother 'ed beän sa soäk'd wi' the thaw
'At she cotch'd 'er death o' cowd that night, poor soul, i' the straw.

Haäfe o' the parish runn'd oop when the rigtree[5] was tummlin' in —
Too laäte — but it's all ower now — hall hower — an' ten year sin;

Too laäte, tha mun git tha to bed, but I'll coom an' I'll squench the light,
Fur we moänt 'ev naw moor fires — and soa little Dick, good-night.

VASTNESS.

I.

Many a hearth upon our dark globe sighs after many a vanish'd face,
Many a planet by many a sun may roll with the dust of a vanish'd race.

II.

Raving politics, never at rest — as this poor earth's pale history runs, —
What is it all but a trouble of ants in the gleam of a million million of suns?

III.

Lies upon this side, lies upon that side, truthless violence mourn'd by the Wise,
Thousands of voices drowning his own in a popular torrent of lies upon lies;

---

[1] Clutched. [2] "Bubbling," a young unfledged bird. [3] Beams. [4] Wrapt ourselves.
[5] The beam that runs along the roof of the house just beneath the ridge.

IV.

Stately purposes, valor in battle, glorious annals of army and fleet,
Death for the right cause, death for the wrong cause, trumpets of victory, groans of defeat;

V.

Innocence seethed in her mother's milk, and Charity setting the martyr aflame;
Thraldom who walks with the banner of Freedom, and recks not to ruin a realm in her name.

VI.

Faith at her zenith, or all but lost in the gloom of doubts that darken the schools;
Craft with a bunch of all-heal in her hand, follow'd up by her vassal legion of fools;

VII.

Trade flying over a thousand seas with her spice and her vintage, her silk and her corn;
Desolate offing, sailorless harbors, famishing populace, wharves forlorn;

VIII.

Star of the morning, Hope in the sunrise; gloom of the evening, Life at a close;
Pleasure who flaunts on her wide down-way with her flying robe and her poison'd rose;

IX.

Pain, that has crawl'd from the corpse of Pleasure, a worm which writhes all day, and at night
Stirs up again in the heart of the sleeper, and stings him back to the curse of the light;

X.

Wealth with his wines and his wedded harlots; honest Poverty, bare to the bone;
Opulent Avarice, lean as Poverty; Flattery gilding the rift in a throne;

XI.

Fame blowing out from her golden trumpet a jubilant challenge to Time and to Fate;
Slander, her shadow, sowing the nettle on all the laurel'd graves of the Great;

XII.

Love for the maiden, crown'd with marriage, no regrets for aught that has been,
Household happiness, gracious children, debtless competence, golden mean;

XIII.

National hatreds of whole generations, and pigmy spites of the village spire;
Vows that will last to the last death-ruckle, and vows that are snapt in a moment of fire;

XIV.

He that has lived for the lust of the minute, and died in the doing it, flesh
  without mind;
He that has nail'd all flesh to the Cross, till Self died out in the love of his
  kind;

XV.

Spring and Summer and Autumn and Winter, and all these old revolutions of
  earth;
All new-old revolutions of Empire — change of the tide — what is all of
  it worth?

XVI.

What the philosophies, all the sciences, poesy, varying voices of prayer?
All that is noblest, all that is basest, all that is filthy with all that is fair?

XVII.

What is it all, if we all of us end but in being our own corpse-coffins at last,
Swallow'd in Vastness, lost in Silence, drown'd in the deeps of a meaningless
  Past?

XVIII.

What but a murmur of gnats in the gloom, or a moment's anger of bees in
  their hive? —

   *   *   *   *   *   *   *   *

Peace, let it be! for I loved him, and love him forever: the dead are not
  dead but alive.

Dedicated to the Hon. J. Russell Lowell.

THE RING.

MIRIAM AND HER FATHER.

MIRIAM (*singing*).

MELLOW moon of heaven,
 Bright in blue,
Moon of married hearts,
 Hear me, you!

Twelve times in the year
 Bring me bliss,
Globing Honey Moons
 Bright as this.

Moon, you fade at times
 From the night.
Young again you grow
 Out of sight.

Silver crescent-curve,
 Coming soon,
Globe again, and make
 Honey Moon.

Shall not *my* love last,
 Moon, with you,
For ten thousand years
 Old and new?

FATHER.

And who was he with such love-
 drunken eyes
They made a thousand honey moons
 of one?

MIRIAM.

The prophet of his own, my Hubert
 — his

The words, and mine the setting.
  "Air and Words,"
Said Hubert, when I sang the song,
  "are bride
And bridegroom." Does it please
  you?

FATHER.

            Mainly, child,
Because I hear your Mother's voice
  in yours.
She——, why, you shiver tho' the
  wind is west
With all the warmth of summer.

MIRIAM.

            Well, I felt
On a sudden I know not what, a
  breath that past
With all the cold of winter.

FATHER (*muttering to himself*).

            Even so.
The Ghost in Man, the Ghost that
  once was Man,
But cannot wholly free itself from
  Man,
Are calling to each other thro' a dawn
Stranger than earth has ever seen;
  the veil
Is rending, and the Voices of the day
Are heard across the Voices of the dark.
No sudden heaven, nor sudden hell,
  for man,
But thro' the Will of One who knows
  and rules —
And utter knowledge is but utter
  love —
Æonian Evolution, swift or slow,
Thro' all the Spheres — an ever open-
  ing height,
An ever lessening earth — and she
  perhaps,
My Miriam, breaks her latest earthly
  link
With me to-day.

MIRIAM.

      You speak so low, what is it?
Your "Miriam breaks" — is making
  a new link
Breaking an old one?

FATHER.

            No, for we, my child,
Have been till now each other's all-
  in-all.

MIRIAM.

And you the lifelong guardian of the
  child.

FATHER.

I, and one other whom you have not
  known.

MIRIAM.

And who? what other?

FATHER.

            Whither are you bound?
For Naples which we only left in
  May?

MIRIAM.

No! father, Spain, but Hubert brings
  me home
With April and the swallow. Wish
  me joy!

FATHER.

What need to wish when Hubert
  weds in you
The heart of Love, and you the soul
  of Truth
In Hubert?

MIRIAM.

            Tho' you used to call me once
The lonely maiden-Princess of the
  wood,
Who meant to sleep her hundred
  summers out
Before a kiss should wake her.

FATHER.

          '   Ay, but now
Your fairy Prince has found you,
  take this ring.

MIRIAM.

"Io t'amo " — and these diamonds —
    beautiful!
"From Walter," and for me from
    you then ?

FATHER.

              Well,
One way for Miriam.

MIRIAM.

       Miriam am I not ?

FATHER.

This ring bequeath'd you by your
    mother, child,
Was to be given you — such her
    dying wish —
Given on the morning when you came
    of age
Or on the day you married. Both
    the days
Now close in one. The ring is doubly
    yours.
Why do you look so gravely at the
    tower ?

MIRIAM.

I never saw it yet so all ablaze
With creepers crimsoning to the pin-
    nacles,
As if perpetual sunset linger'd there,
And all ablaze too in the lake below !
And how the birds that circle round
    the tower
Are cheeping to each other of their
    flight
To summer lands !

FATHER.

       And that has made you grave?
Fly — care not. Birds and brides
    must leave the nest.
Child, I am happier in your happi-
    ness
Than in mine own.

MIRIAM.

       It is not that !

FATHER.

             What else?

MIRIAM.

That chamber in the tower.

FATHER.

       What chamber, child ?
Your nurse is here ?

MIRIAM.

       My Mother's nurse and mine.
She comes to dress me in my bridal
    veil.

FATHER.

What did she say ?

MIRIAM.

          She said, that you and I
Had been abroad for my poor health
    so long
She fear'd I had forgotten her, and I
    ask'd
About my Mother, and she said,
    "Thy hair
Is golden like thy Mother's, not so
    fine."

FATHER.

What then ? what more ?

MIRIAM.

         She said — perhaps indeed
She wander'd, having wander'd now
    so far
Beyond the common date of death —
    that you,
When I was smaller than the statuette
Of my dear Mother on your bracket
    here —
You took me to that chamber in the
    tower,
The topmost — a chest there, by which
    you knelt —
And there were books and dresses —
    left to me,
A ring too which you kiss'd, and I,
    she said,

I babbled, Mother, Mother — as I used
To prattle to her picture — stretch'd
   my hands
As if I saw her; then a woman came
And caught me from my nurse. I
   hear her yet —
A sound of anger like a distant storm.

FATHER.

Garrulous old crone.

MIRIAM.

                  Poor nurse!

FATHER.

                  I bad her keep,
Like a seal'd book, all mention of
   the ring,
For I myself would tell you all to-day.

MIRIAM.

"She too might speak to-day," she
   mumbled. Still,
I scarce have learnt the title of your
   book,
But you will turn the pages.

FATHER.

                  Ay, to-day!
I brought you to that chamber on
   your third
September birthday with your nurse,
   and felt
An icy breath play on me, while I
   stoopt
To take and kiss the ring.

MIRIAM.

                  This very ring
Io t'amo?

FATHER.

   Yes, for some wild hope was mine
That, in the misery of my married life,
Miriam your Mother might appear to
   me.
She came to you, not me. The storm,
   you hear
Far-off, is Muriel — your step-
   mother's voice.

MIRIAM.

Vext, that you thought my Mother
   came to me?
Or at my crying "Mother?" or to find
My Mother's diamonds hidden from
   her there,
Like worldly beauties in the Cell,
   not shown
To dazzle all that see them?

FATHER.

                  Wait a while.
Your Mother and step-mother —
   Miriam Erne
And Muriel Erne — the two were
   cousins — lived
With Muriel's mother on the down,
   that sees
A thousand squares of corn and
   meadow, far
As the gray deep, a landscape which
   your eyes
Have many a time ranged over when
   a babe.

MIRIAM.

I climb'd the hill with Hubert yester-
   day,
And from the thousand squares, one
   silent voice
Came on the wind, and seem'd to
   say "Again."
We saw far off an old forsaken house,
Then home, and past the ruin'd mill.

FATHER.

                  And there
I found these cousins often by the
   brook,
For Miriam sketch'd and Muriel
   threw the fly;
The girls of equal age, but one was
   fair,
And one was dark, and both were
   beautiful.
No voice for either spoke within my
   heart
Then, for the surface eye, that only
   doats
On outward beauty, glancing from
   the one

To the other, knew not that which
    pleased it most,
The raven ringlet or the gold; but
    both
Were dowerless, and myself, I used
    to walk
This Terrace — morbid, melancholy;
    mine
And yet not mine the hall, the farm,
    the field;
For all that ample woodland whis-
    per'd "debt,"
The brook that. feeds this lakelet
    murmur'd "debt,"
And in yon arching avenue of old
    elms,
Tho' mine, not mine, I heard the
    sober rook
And carrion crow cry "Mortgage."

MIRIAM.
               Father's fault
Visited on the children!

FATHER.
               Ay, but then
A kinsman, dying, summon'd me to
    Rome —
He left me wealth — and while I
    journey'd hence,
And saw the world fly by me like a
    dream,
And while I communed with my
    truest self,
I woke to all of truest in myself,
Till, in the gleam of those mid-sum-
    mer dawns,
The form of Muriel faded, and the face
Of Miriam grew upon me, till I knew;
And past and future mix'd in Heaven
    and made
The rosy twilight of a perfect day.

MIRIAM.
So glad? no tear for him, who left
    you wealth,
Your kinsman?

FATHER.
         I had seen the man but once;
He loved my name not me; and then
    I pass'd

Home, and thro' Venice, where a
    jeweller,
So far gone down, or so far up in life,
That he was nearing his own hundred,
    sold
This ring to me, then laugh'd "the
    ring is weird."
And weird and worn and wizard-like
    was he.
"Why weird?" I ask'd him; and he
    said "The souls
Of two repentant Lovers guard the
    ring;"
Then with a ribald twinkle in his
    bleak eyes —
"And if you give the ring to any maid,
They still remember what it cost
    them here,
And bind the maid to love you by
    the ring;
And if the ring were stolen from the
    maid,
The theft were death or madness to
    the thief,
So sacred those Ghost Lovers hold
    the gift."
And then he told their legend:

                 "Long ago
Two lovers parted by a scurrilous tale
Had quarrell'd, till the man repenting
    sent
This ring 'Io t'amo' to his best be-
    loved,
And sent it on her birthday. She in
    wrath
Return'd it on her birthday, and that
    day
His death-day, when, half-frenzied by
    the ring,
He wildly fought a rival suitor, him
The causer of that scandal, fought
    and fell;
And she that came to part them all
    too late,
And found a corpse and silence, drew
    the ring
From his dead finger, wore it till her
    death,
Shrined him within the temple of her
    heart,
Made every moment of her after life

A virgin victim to his memory,
And dying rose, and rear'd her arms,
    and cried
' I see him, Io t'amo, Io t'amo.' "

MIRIAM.

Legend or true ? so tender should be
    true !
Did *he* believe it ? did you ask him ?

FATHER.

                                    Ay !
But that half skeleton, like a barren
    ghost
From out the fleshless world of spirits,
    laugh'd :
A hollow laughter !

MIRIAM.

                    Vile, so near the ghost
Himself, to laugh at love in death !
But you?

FATHER.

Well, as the bygone lover thro' this
    ring
Had sent his cry for her forgiveness, I
Would call thro' this " Io t'amo " to
    the heart
Of Miriam ; then I bad the man en-
    grave
" From Walter " on the ring, and send
    it — wrote
Name, surname, all as clear as noon,
    but he —
Some younger hand must have en-
    graven the ring —
His fingers were so stiffen'd by the
    frost
Of seven and ninety winters, that he
    scrawl'd
A " Miriam " that might seem a
    " Muriel ";
And Muriel claim'd and open'd what
    I meant
For Miriam, took the ring, and
    flaunted it
Before that other whom I loved and
    love.
    A mountain stay'd me here, a min-
        ster there,

A galleried palace, or a battlefield,
Where stood the sheaf of Peace : but
    — coming home —
And on your Mother's birthday — all
    but yours —
A week betwixt — and when the tower
    as now
Was all ablaze with crimson to the
    roof,
And all ablaze too plunging in the lake
Head-foremost — who were those that
    stood between
The tower and that rich phantom of
    the tower ?
Muriel and Miriam, each in white,
    and like
May-blossoms in mid autumn — was
    it they ?
A light shot upward on them from
    the lake.
What sparkled there ? whose hand
    was that ? they stood
So close together.   I am not keen of
    sight,
But coming nearer — Muriel had the
    ring —
" O Miriam ! have you given your
    ring to her ?
O Miriam ! " Miriam redden'd, Muriel
    clench'd
The hand that wore it, till I cried
    again :
" O Miriam, if you love me take the
    ring ! "
She glanced at me, at Muriel, and
    was mute.
" Nay, if you cannot love me, let it be."
Then — Muriel standing ever statue-
    like —
She turn'd, and in her soft imperial
    way
And saying gently : " Muriel, by your
    leave,"
Unclosed the hand, and from it drew
    the ring,
And gave it me, who pass'd it down
    her own,
" Io t'amo, all is well then." Muriel
    fled.

MIRIAM.

Poor Muriel !

FATHER.

Ay, poor Muriel when you hear
What follows!   Miriam loved me
    from the first,
Not thro' the ring; but on her mar-
    riage-morn
This birthday, death-day, and be-
    trothal ring,
Laid on her table overnight, was gone;
And after hours of search and doubt
    and threats,
And hubbub, Muriel enter'd with it,
    "See!—
Found in a chink of that old moulder'd
    floor!"
My Miriam nodded with a pitying
    smile,
As who should say "that those who
    lose can find."
    Then I and she were married for a
        year,
One year without a storm, or even a
    cloud;
And you my Miriam born within the
    year;
And she my Miriam dead within the
    year.
    I sat beside her dying, and she gaspt:
"The books, the miniature, the lace
    are hers,
My ring too when she comes of age,
    or when
She marries; you—you loved me,
    kept your word.
You love me still 'Io t'amo.'—Muriel
    —no—
She cannot love; she loves her own
    hard self,
Her firm will, her fix'd purpose.
    Promise me,
Miriam not Muriel — she shall have
    the ring."
And there the light of other life,
    which lives
Beyond our burial and our buried eyes,
Gleam'd for a moment in her own on
    earth.
I swore the vow, then with my latest
    kiss
Upon them, closed her eyes, which
    would not close,

But kept their watch upon the ring
    and you.
Your birthday was her death-day.

MIRIAM.

                    O poor Mother!
And you, poor desolate Father, and
    poor me,
The little senseless, worthless, word-
    less babe,
Saved when your life was wreck'd!

FATHER.

                    Desolate? yes!
Desolate as that sailor whom the
    storm
Had parted from his comrade in the
    boat,
And dash'd half dead on barren
    sands, was I.
Nay, you were my one solace; only
    —you
Were always ailing.   Muriel's mother
    sent,
And sure am I, by Muriel, one day
    came
And saw you, shook her head, and
    patted yours,
And smiled, and making with a kindly
    pinch
Each poor pale cheek a momentary
    rose—
"*That* should be fix'd," she said;
    "your pretty bud,
So blighted here, would flower into
    full health
Among our heath and bracken.   Let
    her come!
And we will feed her with our moun-
    tain air,
And send her home to you rejoicing."
    No—
We could not part.   And once, when
    you my girl
Rode on my shoulder home—the
    tiny fist
Had graspt a daisy from your Mother's
    grave—
By the lych-gate was Muriel.   "Ay,"
    she said,
"Among the tombs in this damp vale
    of yours!

You scorn my Mother's warning, but
  the child
Is paler than before. We often walk
In open sun, and see beneath our
  feet
The mist of autumn gather from your
  lake,
And shroud the tower; and once we
  only saw
Your gilded vane, a light above the
  mist "—
(Our old bright bird that still is
  veering there
Above his four gold letters) "and
  the light,"
She said, "was like that light"—and
  there she paused,
And long; till I believing that the
  girl's
Lean fancy, groping for it, could not
  find
One likeness, laugh'd a little and
  found her two—
" A warrior's crest above the cloud of
  war"—
" A fiery phœnix rising from the
  smoke,
The pyre he burnt in."—"Nay," she
  said, "the light
That glimmers on the marsh and on
  the grave."
And spoke no more, but turn'd and
  pass'd away.
  Miriam, I am not surely one of
  those
Caught by the flower that closes on
  the fly,
But after ten slow weeks her fix'd
  intent,
In aiming at an all but hopeless mark
To strike it, struck; I took, I left
  you there;
I came, I went, was happier day by
  day;
For Muriel nursed you with a mother's care;
Till on that clear and heather-scented
  height
The rounder cheek had brighten'd
  into bloom.
She always came to meet me carrying
  you,

And all her talk was of the babe she
  loved;
So, following her old pastime of the
  brook,
She threw the fly for me; but oftener
  left
That angling to the mother. " Muriel's
  health
Had weaken'd, nursing little Miriam.
  Strange !
She used to shun the wailing babe,
  and doats
On this of yours." But when the
  matron saw
That hinted love was only wasted
  bait,
Not risen to, she was bolder. " Ever
  since
You sent the fatal ring"— I told her
  " sent
To Miriam," "Doubtless — ay, but
  ever since
In all the world my dear one sees
  but you —
In your sweet babe she finds but you
  —she makes
Her heart a mirror that reflects but
  you."
And then the tear fell, the voice
  broke. *Her* heart !
I gazed into the mirror, as a man
Who sees his face in water, and a stone,
That glances from the bottom of the
  pool,
Strike upward thro' the shadow; yet
  at last,
Gratitude — loneliness — desire to
  keep
So skilled a nurse about you always
  — nay !
Some half remorseful kind of pity
  too —
Well ! well, you know I married
  Muriel Erne.
  " I take thee Muriel for my wedded
  wife "—
I had forgotten it was your birthday,
  child —
When all at once with some electric
  thrill
A cold air pass'd between us, and the
  hands

Fell from each other, and were join'd
     again.
   No second cloudless honeymoon
        was mine.
For by and by she sicken'd of the
     farce,
She dropt the gracious mask of
     motherhood,
She came no more to meet me, carry-
     ing you,
Nor ever cared to set you on her knee,
Nor ever let you gambol in her sight,
Nor ever cheer'd you with a kindly
     smile,
Nor ever ceased to clamor for the
     ring;
Why had I sent the ring at first to
     her?
Why had I made her love me thro'
     the ring,
And then had changed? so fickle are
     men — the best!
Not she — but now my love was hers
     again,
The ring by right, she said, was hers
     again.
At times too shrilling in her angrier
     moods,
"That weak and watery nature love
     you? No!
'*Io* t'amo, *Io* t'amo'!" flung herself
Against my heart, but often while
     her lips
Were warm upon my cheek, an icy
     breath,
As from the grating of a sepulchre,
Past over both. I told her of my
     vow,
No pliable idiot I to break my vow;
But still she made her outcry for the
     ring;
For one monotonous fancy madden'd
     her,
Till I myself was madden'd with her
     cry,
And even that "Io t'amo," those
     three sweet
Italian words became a weariness.
   My people too were scared with
        eerie sounds,
A footstep, a low throbbing in the
     walls,

A noise of falling weights that never
     fell,
Weird whispers, bells that rang with-
     out a hand,
Door-handles turn'd when none was
     at the door,
And bolted doors that open'd of them-
     selves:
And one betwixt the dark and light
     had seen
Her, bending by the cradle of her
     babe.

MIRIAM.

And I remember once that being
     waked
By noises in the house — and no one
     near —
I cried for nurse, and felt a gentle
     hand
Fall on my forehead, and a sudden
     face
Look'd in upon me like a gleam and
     pass'd,
And I was quieted, and slept again.
Or is it some half memory of a dream?

FATHER.

Your fifth September birthday.

MIRIAM.
                         And the face,
The hand, — my Mother.

FATHER.
                         Miriam, on that day
Two lovers parted by no scurrilous
     tale —
Mere want of gold — and still for
     twenty years
Bound by the golden cord of their
     first love —
Had ask'd us to their marriage, and
     to share
Their marriage-banquet. Muriel,
     paler then
Than ever you were in your cradle,
     moan'd,
"I am fitter for my bed, or for my
     grave,
I cannot go, go you." And then she
     rose,

She clung to me with such a hard
    embrace,
So lingeringly long, that half-amazed
I parted from her, and I went alone.
And when the bridegroom murmur'd,
    " With this ring,"
I felt for what I could not find, the
    key,
The guardian of her relics, of *her*
    ring.
I kept it as a sacred amulet
About me, — gone! and gone in that
    embrace!
Then, hurrying home, I found her
    not in house
Or garden — up the tower — an icy
    air
Fled by me. — There, the chest was
    open — all
The sacred relics tost about the
    floor —
Among them Muriel lying on her
    face —
I raised her, call'd her " Muriel,
    Muriel wake!"
The fatal ring lay near her; the
    glazed eye
Glared at me as in horror. Dead!
    I took
And chafed the freezing hand. A red
    mark ran
All round one finger pointed straight,
    the rest
Were crumpled inwards. Dead! —
    and maybe stung
With some remorse, had stolen, worn
    the ring —
Then torn it from her finger, or as
    if —
For never had I seen her show
    remorse —
As if —

MIRIAM.

— those two Ghost lovers —

FATHER.
        Lovers yet —

MIRIAM.

Yes, yes!

FATHER.

— but dead so long, gone up so far,
That now their ever-rising life has
    dwarf'd
Or lost the moment of their past on
    earth,
As we forget our wail at being born.
As if —

MIRIAM.

a dearer ghost had —

FATHER.
        — wrench'd it away.

MIRIAM.

Had floated in with sad reproachful
    eyes,
Till from her own hand she had torn
    the ring
In fright, and fallen dead. And I
    myself
Am half afraid to wear it.

FATHER.
        Well, no more!
No bridal music this! but fear not you!
You have the ring she guarded; that
    poor link
With earth is broken, and has left her
    free,
Except that, still drawn downward
    for an hour,
Her spirit hovering by the church,
    where she
Was married too, may linger, till she
    sees
Her maiden coming like a Queen, who
    leaves
Some colder province in the North to
    gain
Her capital city, where the loyal bells
Clash welcome — linger, till her own,
    the babe
She lean'd to from her Spiritual sphere,
Her lonely maiden-Princess, crown'd
    with flowers,
Has enter'd on the larger woman-world
Of wives and mothers.

        But the bridal veil —
Your nurse is waiting. Kiss me child
    and go.

FORLORN.

I.

" He is fled — I wish him dead —
He that wrought my ruin —
O the flattery and the craft
　Which were my undoing . . .
　In the night, in the night,
　When the storms are blowing.

II.

" Who was witness of the crime ?
Who shall now reveal it ?
He is fled, or he is dead,
　Marriage will conceal it . . .
　In the night, in the night,
　While the gloom is growing."

III.

Catherine, Catherine, in the night
What is this you're dreaming ?
There is laughter down in Hell
　At your simple scheming . . .
　In the night, in the night,
　When the ghosts are fleeting.

IV.

You to place a hand in his
Like an honest woman's,
You that lie with wasted lung
　Waiting for your summons . . .
　In the night, O the night !
　O the deathwatch beating !

V.

There will come a witness soon
Hard to be confuted,
All the world will hear a voice
　Scream you are polluted . . .
　In the night ! O the night,
　When the owls are wailing !

VI.

Shame and marriage, Shame and
　marriage,
Fright and foul dissembling,
Bantering bridesman, reddening
　priest,
　Tower and altar trembling . . .
　In the night, O the night,
　When the mind is failing !

VII.

Mother, dare you kill your child ?
　How your hand is shaking !
Daughter of the seed of Cain,
　What is this you're taking ? . . .
　In the night, O the night,
　While the house is sleeping.

VIII.

Dreadful ! has it come to this,
　O unhappy creature ?
You that would not tread on a worm
　For your gentle nature . . .
　In the night, O the night,
　O the night of weeping !

IX.

Murder would not veil your sin,
　Marriage will not hide it,
Earth and Hell will brand your name,
　Wretch you must abide it . . .
　In the night, O the night,
　Long before the dawning.

X.

Up, get up, and tell him all,
　Tell him you were lying !
Do not die with a lie in your mouth,
　You that know you're dying . . .
　In the night, O the night,
　While the grave is yawning.

XI.

No — you will not die before,
　Tho' you'll ne'er be stronger ;
You will live till *that* is born,
　Then a little longer . . .
　In the night, O the night,
　While the Fiend is prowling.

XII.

Death and marriage, Death and mar-
　riage !
Funeral hearses rolling !
Black with bridal favors mixt !
　Bridal bells with tolling ! . . .
　In the night, O the night,
　When the wolves are howling.

XIII.

Up, get up, the time is short,
   Tell him now or never!
Tell him all before you die,
   Lest you die for ever . . .
   In the night, O the night,
   Where there's no forgetting.

XIV.

Up she got, and wrote him all,
   All her tale of sadness,
Blister'd every word with tears,
   And eased her heart of madness . . .
   In the night, and nigh the dawn,
   And while the moon was setting.

HAPPY.

THE LEPER'S BRIDE.

I.

Why wail you, pretty plover? and what is it that you fear?
   Is he sick your mate like mine? have you lost him, is he fled?
And there — the heron rises from his watch beside the mere,
   And flies above the leper's hut, where lives the living-dead.

II.

Come back, nor let me know it! would he live and die alone?
   And has he not forgiven me yet, his over-jealous bride,
Who am, and was, and will be his, his own and only own,
   To share his living death with him, die with him side by side?

III.

Is that the leper's hut on the solitary moor,
   Where noble Ulric dwells forlorn, and wears the leper's weed?
The door is open.   He! is he standing at the door,
   My soldier of the Cross? it is he and he indeed!

IV.

My roses — will he take them *now* — mine, his — from off the tree
   We planted both together, happy in our marriage morn?
O God, I could blaspheme, for he fought Thy fight for Thee,
   And Thou hast made him leper to compass him with scorn —

V.

Hast spared the flesh of thousands, the coward and the base,
   And set a crueller mark than Cain's on him, the good and brave!
He sees me, waves me from him.   I will front him face to face.
   You need not wave me from you.   I would leap into your grave.

   *   *   *   *   *   *   *   *

VI.

My warrior of the Holy Cross and of the conquering sword,
   The roses that you cast aside — once more I bring you these.
No nearer? do you scorn me when you tell me O my lord,
   You would not mar the beauty of your bride with your disease.

VII.

You say your body is so foul — then here I stand apart,
  Who yearn to lay my loving head upon your leprous breast.
The leper plague may scale my skin but never taint my heart;
  Your body is not foul to me, and body is foul at best.

VIII.

I loved you first when young and fair, but now I love you most;
  The fairest flesh at last is filth on which the worm will feast;
This poor rib-grated dungeon of the holy human ghost,
  This house with all its hateful needs no cleaner than the beast,

IX.

This coarse diseaseful creature which in Eden was divine,
  This Satan-haunted ruin, this little city of sewers,
This wall of solid flesh that comes between your soul and mine,
  Will vanish and give place to the beauty that endures,

X.

The beauty that endures on the Spiritual height,
  When we shall stand transfigured, like Christ on Hermon hill,
And moving each to music, soul in soul and light in light,
  Shall flash thro' one another in a moment as we will.

XI.

Foul! foul! the word was yours not mine, I worship that right hand
  Which fell'd the foes before you as the woodman fells the wood,
And sway'd the sword that lighten'd back the sun of Holy land,
  And clove the Moslem crescent moon, and changed it into blood.

XII.

And once I worshipt all too well this creature of decay,
  For Age will chink the face, and Death will freeze the supplest limbs —
Yet you in your mid manhood — O the grief when yesterday
  They bore the Cross before you to the chant of funeral hymns.

XIII.

"Libera me, Domine!" you sang the Psalm, and when
  The Priest pronounced you dead, and flung the mould upon your feet,
A beauty came upon your face, not that of living men,
  But seen upon the silent brow when life has ceased to beat.

XIV.

"Libera *nos*, Domine" — you knew not one was there
  Who saw you kneel beside your bier, and weeping scarce could see;
May I come a little nearer, I that heard, and changed the prayer
  And sang the married "nos" for the solitary "me."

XV.

My beauty marred by you? by you! so be it. All is well
    If I lose it and myself in the higher beauty, yours.
My beauty lured that falcon from his eyry on the fell,
    Who never caught one gleam of the beauty which endures —

XVI.

The Count who sought to snap the bond that link'd us life to life,
    Who whisper'd me "your Ulric loves" — a little nearer still —
He hiss'd, "Let us revenge ourselves, your Ulric woos my wife" —
    A lie by which he thought he could subdue me to his will.

XVII.

I knew that you were near me when I let him kiss my brow;
    Well, he kiss'd me on the lips, I was jealous, anger'd, vain,
And I meant to make *you* jealous. Are you jealous of me now?
    Your pardon, O my love, if I ever gave you pain.

XVIII.

You never once accused me, but I wept alone, and sigh'd
    In the winter of the Present for the summer of the Past;
That icy winter silence — how it froze you from your bride,
    Tho' I made one barren effort to break it at the last.

XIX.

I brought you, you remember, these roses, when I knew
    You were parting for the war, and you took them tho' you frown'd;
You frown'd and yet you kiss'd them. All at once the trumpet blew,
    And you spurr'd your fiery horse, and you hurl'd them to the ground.

XX.

You parted for the Holy War without a word to me,
    And clear myself unask'd — not I. My nature was too proud.
And him I saw but once again, and far away was he,
    When I was praying in a storm — the crash was long and loud —

XXI.

That God would ever slant His bolt from falling on your head —
    Then I lifted up my eyes, he was coming down the fell —
I clapt my hands. The sudden fire from Heaven had dash'd him dead,
    And sent him charr'd and blasted to the deathless fire of Hell.

XXII.

See, I sinn'd but for a moment. I repented and repent,
    And trust myself forgiven by the God to whom I kneel.
A little nearer? Yes. I shall hardly be content
    Till I be leper like yourself, my love, from head to heel.

XXIII.

O foolish dreams, that you, that I, would slight our marriage oath :
  I held you at that moment even dearer than before ;
Now God has made you leper in His loving care for both,
  That we might cling together, never doubt each other more.

XXIV.

The Priest, who join'd you to the dead, has join'd our hands of old ;
  If man and wife be but one flesh, let mine be leprous too,
As dead from all the human race as if beneath the mould ;
  If you be dead, then I am dead, who only live for you.

XXV.

Would Earth tho' hid in cloud not be follow'd by the Moon ?
  The leech forsake the dying bed for terror of his life ?
The shadow leave the Substance in the brooding light of noon ?
  Or if *I* had been the leper would you have left the wife ?

XXVI.

Not take them ?   Still you wave me off — poor roses — must I go —
  I have worn them year by year — from the bush we both had set —
What ? fling them to you ? — well — that were hardly gracious.   No !
  Your plague but passes by the touch.   A little nearer yet !

XXVII.

There, there ! he buried you, the Priest ; the Priest is not to blame,
  He joins us once again, to his either office true :
I thank him.   I am happy, happy.   Kiss me.   In the name
  Of the everlasting God, I will live and die with you.

[DEAN MILMAN has remarked that the protection and care afforded by the Church to this blighted race of lepers was among the most beautiful of its offices during the Middle Ages. The leprosy of the thirteenth and fourteenth centuries was supposed to be a legacy of the crusades, but was in all probability the offspring of meagre and unwholesome diet, miserable lodging and clothing, physical and moral degradation.   The services of the Church in the seclusion of these unhappy sufferers were most affecting.   The stern duty of looking to the public welfare is tempered with exquisite compassion for the victims of this loathsome disease.   The ritual for the sequestration of the leprous differed little from the burial service.   After the leper had been sprinkled with holy water, the priest conducted him into the church, the leper singing the psalm "Libera me domine," and the crucifix and bearer going before.   In the church a black cloth was stretched over two trestles in front of the altar, and the leper leaning at its side devoutly heard mass.   The priest, taking up a little earth in his cloak, threw it on one of the leper's feet, and put him out of the church, if it did not rain too heavily ; took him to his hut in the midst of the fields, and then uttered the prohibitions : "I forbid you entering the church . . . or entering the company of others.   I forbid you quitting your home without your leper's dress."   He concluded : "Take this dress, and wear it in token of humility ; take these gloves, take this clapper, as a sign that you are forbidden to speak to any one.   You are not to be indignant at being thus separated from others, and as to your little wants, good people will provide for you, and God will not desert you."   Then in this old ritual follow these sad words : "When it shall come to pass that the leper shall pass out of this world, he shall be buried in his hut, and not in the church-yard."   At first there was a doubt whether wives should follow their husbands who had been leprous, or remain in the world and marry again.   The Church decided that the marriage-tie was indissoluble, and so bestowed on these unhappy beings this immense source of con-solation.   With a love stronger than this living death, lepers were followed into banishment from the haunts of men by their faithful wives.   Readers of Sir J. Stephen's *Essays on Ecclesiastical Biography* will recollect the description of the founder of the Franciscan order, how, controlling his involuntary disgust, St. Francis of Assisi washed the feet and dressed the sores of the lepers, once at least reverently applying his lips to their wounds. — BOUCHER-JAMES.]

  This ceremony of *quasi*-burial varied considerably at different times and in different places. In some cases a grave was dug, and the leper's face was often covered during the service.

TO ULYSSES.

"Ulysses," the title of a number of essays by W. G. Palgrave. He died at Monte Video before seeing either this volume or my poem.

I.

Ulysses, much-experienced man,
  Whose eyes have known this globe
    of ours,
  Her tribes of men, and trees, and
    flowers,
From Corrientes to Japan.

II.

To you that bask below the Line,
  I soaking here in winter wet —
  The century's three strong eights
    have met
To drag me down to seventy-nine.

III.

In summer if I reach my day —
  To you, yet young, who breathe the
    balm
Of summer-winters by the palm
And orange grove of Paraguay,

IV.

I tolerant of the colder time,
  Who love the winter woods, to trace
  On paler heavens the branching
    grace
Of leafless elm, or naked lime,

V.

And see my cedar green, and there
  My giant ilex keeping leaf
  When frost is keen and days are
    brief —
Or marvel how in English air

VI.

My yucca, which no winter quells,
  Altho' the months have scarce be-
    gun,
  Has push'd toward our faintest sun
A spike of half-accomplish'd bells —

VII.

Or watch the waving pine which here
  The warrior of Caprera set,[1]

[1] Garibaldi said to me, alluding to his barren island, " I wish I had your trees."

A name that earth will not forget
Till earth has roll'd her latest year —

VIII.

I, once half-crazed for larger light
  On broader zones beyond the foam,
  But chaining fancy now at home
Among the quarried downs of Wight,

IX.

Not less would yield full thanks to
    you
  For your rich gift, your tale of
    lands
  I know not,[1] your Arabian sands ;
Your cane, your palm, tree-fern, bam-
    boo,

X.

The wealth of tropic bower and
    brake ;
  Your Oriental Eden-isles,[2]
  Where man, nor only Nature smiles ;
Your wonder of the boiling lake ;[3]

XI.

Phra-Chai, the Shadow of the Best,[4]
  Phra-bat[5] the step ; your Pontic
    coast ;
  Crag-cloister ;[6] Anatolian Ghost ;[7]
Hong-Kong,[8] Karnac,[9] and all the
    rest.

XII.

Thro' which I follow'd line by line
  Your leading hand, and came, my
    friend,
  To prize your various book, and
    send
A gift of slenderer value, mine.

[1] The tale of Nejd.
[2] The Philippines.
[3] In Dominica.
[4] The shadow of the Lord. Certain obscure markings on a rock in Siam, which express the image of Budda to the Buddhist more or less distinctly according to his faith and his moral worth.
[5] The footstep of the Lord on another rock.
[6] The monastery of Sumelas.
[7] Anatolian Spectre stories.
[8] The three cities.
[9] Travels in Egypt.

TO MARY BOYLE.

WITH THE FOLLOWING POEM.

I.

"SPRING-FLOWERS"! While you still
        delay to take
    Your leave of Town,
Our elmtree's ruddy-hearted blossom-
        flake
    Is fluttering down.

II.

Be truer to your promise. There! I
        heard
    One cuckoo call.
Be needle to the magnet of your word,
    Nor wait, till all

III.

Our vernal bloom from every vale and
        plain
    And garden pass,
And all the gold from each laburnum
        chain
    Drop to the grass.

IV.

Is memory with your Marian gone to
        rest,
    Dead with the dead?
For ere she left us, when we met, you
        prest
    My hand, and said

V.

"I come with your spring-flowers."
        You came not, friend;
    My birds would sing,
You heard not. Take then this spring-
        flower I send,
    This song of spring,

VI.

Found yesterday — forgotten mine
        own rhyme
    By mine old self,
As I shall be forgotten by old Time,
    Laid on the shelf —

VII.

A rhyme that flower'd betwixt the
        whitening sloe
    And kingcup blaze,
And more than half a hundred years
        ago,
    In rick-fire days,

VIII.

When Dives loathed the times, and
        paced his land
    In fear of worse,
And sanguine Lazarus felt a vacant
        hand
    Fill with *his* purse.

IX.

For lowly minds were madden'd to
        the height
    By tonguester tricks,
And once — I well remember that red
        night
    When thirty ricks,

X.

All flaming, made an English home-
        stead Hell —
    These hands of mine
Have helpt to pass a bucket from the
        well
    Along the line,

XI.

When this bare dome had not begun
        to gleam
    Thro' youthful curls,
And you were then a lover's fairy
        dream,
    His girl of girls;

XII.

And you, that now are lonely, and
        with Grief
    Sit face to face,
Might find a flickering glimmer of
        relief
    In change of place.

XIII.

What use to brood ? this life of mingled pains
    And joys to me,
Despite of every Faith and Creed,
remains
    The Mystery.

XIV.

Let golden youth bewail the friend,
the wife,
    For ever gone.
He dreams of that long walk thro'
desert life
    Without the one.

XV.

The silver year should cease to mourn
and sigh —
    Not long to wait —
So close are we, dear Mary, you and
I
    To that dim gate.

XVI.

Take, read ! and be the faults your
Poet makes
    Or many or few,
He rests content, if his young music
wakes
    A wish in you

XVII.

To change our dark Queen-city, all
her realm
    Of sound and smoke,
For his clear heaven, and these few
lanes of elm
    And whispering oak.

THE PROGRESS OF SPRING.

I.

The groundflame of the crocus breaks
the mould,
    Fair Spring slides hither o'er the
    Southern sea,
Wavers on her thin stem the snowdrop cold

That trembles not to kisses of the
bee :
Come Spring, for now from all the
dripping eaves
    The spear of ice has wept itself
    away,
And hour by hour unfolding wood-
bine leaves
    O'er his uncertain shadow droops
    the day.
She comes ! The loosen'd rivulets
run ;
    The frost-bead melts upon her
    golden hair ;
Her mantle, slowly greening in the
Sun,
    Now wraps her close, now arching
    leaves her bare
    To breaths of balmier air ;

II.

Up leaps the lark, gone wild to welcome her,
    About her glance the tits, and
    shriek the jays,
Before her skims the jubilant woodpecker,
    The linnet's bosom blushes at her
    gaze,
While round her brows a woodland
culver flits,
    Watching her large light eyes and
    gracious looks,
And in her open palm a halcyon sits
    Patient — the secret splendor of
    the brooks.
Come Spring ! She comes on waste
and wood,
    On farm and field : but enter also
    here,
Diffuse thyself at will thro' all my
blood,
    And, tho' thy violet sicken into sere,
    Lodge with me all the year !

III.

Once more a downy drift against the
brakes,
    Self-darken'd in the sky, descend-
    ing slow !
But gladly see I thro' the wavering
flakes

Yon blanching apricot like snow in
  snow.
These will thine eyes not brook in
    forest-paths,
  On their perpetual pine, nor round
    the beech;
They fuse themselves to little spicy
    baths,
  Solved in the tender blushes of the
    peach;
They lose themselves and die
  On that new life that gems the
    hawthorn line;
Thy gay lent-lilies wave and put
    them by,
  And out once more in varnish'd
    glory shine
  Thy stars of celandine.

IV.

She floats across the hamlet.   Heaven
    lours,
  But in the tearful splendor of her
    smiles
I see the slowly-thickening chestnut
    towers
  Fill out the spaces by the barren
    tiles.
Now past her feet the swallow cir-
    cling flies,
  A clamorous cuckoo stoops to meet
    her hand;
Her light makes rainbows in my
    closing eyes,
  I hear a charm of song thro' all
    the land.
Come, Spring! She comes, and Earth
    is glad
  To roll her North below thy deep-
    ening dome,
But ere thy maiden birk be wholly
    clad,
  And these low bushes dip their
    twigs in foam,
  Make all true hearths thy home.

V.

Across my garden! and the thicket
    stirs,
  The fountain pulses high in sunnier
    jets,

The blackcap warbles, and the turtle
    purrs,
  The starling claps his tiny casta-
    nets.
Still round her forehead wheels the
    woodland dove,
  And scatters on her throat the
    sparks of dew,
The kingcup fills her footprint, and
    above
  Broaden the glowing isles of ver-
    nal blue.
Hail ample presence of a Queen,
  Bountiful, beautiful, apparell'd gay,
Whose mantle, every shade of glanc-
    ing green,
  Flies back in fragrant breezes to
    display
  A tunic white as May!

VI.

She whispers, "From the South I
    bring you balm,
  For on a tropic mountain was I
    born,
While some dark dweller by the coco-
    palm
  Watch'd my far meadow zoned
    with airy morn;
From under rose a muffled moan of
    floods;
  I sat beneath a solitude of snow;
There no one came, the turf was
    fresh, the woods
  Plunged gulf on gulf thro' all their
    vales below.
I saw beyond their silent tops
  The steaming marshes of the scar-
    let cranes,
The slant seas leaning on the man-
    grove copse,
  And summer basking in the sultry
    plains
  About a land of canes;

VII.

"Then from my vapor-girdle soar-
    ing forth
  I scaled the buoyant highway of
    the birds,

And drank the dews and drizzle of
the North,
  That I might mix with men, and
  hear their words
On pathway'd plains; for — while my
hand exults
  Within the bloodless heart of lowly
  flowers
To work old laws of Love to fresh
results,
  Thro' manifold effect of simple
  powers —
I too would teach the man
  Beyond the darker hour to see the
  bright,
That his fresh life may close as it
began,
  The still-fulfilling promise of a
  light
  Narrowing the bounds of night."

VIII.

So wed thee with my soul, that I may
mark
  The coming year's great good and
  varied ills,
And new developments, whatever
spark
  Be struck from out the clash of
  warring wills;
Or whether, since our nature cannot
rest,
  The smoke of war's volcano burst
  again
From hoary deeps that belt the
changeful West,
  Old Empires, dwellings of the
  kings of men;
Or should those fail, that hold the
helm,
  While the long day of knowledge
  grows and warms,
And in the heart of this most ancient
realm
  A hateful voice be utter'd, and
  alarms
  Sounding "To arms! to arms!"

IX.

A simpler, saner lesson might he
learn

Who reads thy gradual process,
Holy Spring.
Thy leaves possess the season in their
turn,
  And in their time thy warblers rise
  on wing.
How surely glidest thou from March
to May,
  And changest, breathing it, the
  sullen wind,
Thy scope of operation, day by day,
  Larger and fuller, like the human
  mind!
Thy warmths from bud to bud
Accomplish that blind model in the
seed,
And men have hopes, which race the
restless blood,
  That after many changes may suc-
  ceed
  Life, which is Life indeed.

MERLIN AND THE GLEAM.

I.

O young Mariner,
You from the haven
Under the sea-cliff,
You that are watching
The gray Magician
With eyes of wonder,
I am Merlin,
And *I* am dying,
I am Merlin
Who follow The Gleam.

II.

Mighty the Wizard
Who found me at sunrise
Sleeping, and woke me
And learn'd me Magic!
Great the Master,
And sweet the Magic,
When over the valley,
In early summers,
Over the mountain,
On human faces,
And all around me,
Moving to melody,
Floated The Gleam.

III.

Once at the croak of a Raven
    who crost it,
A barbarous people,
Blind to the magic,
And deaf to the melody,
Snarl'd at and cursed me.
A demon vext me,
The light retreated,
The landskip darken'd,
The melody deaden'd,
The Master whisper'd
" Follow The Gleam."

IV.

Then to the melody,
Over a wilderness
Gliding, and glancing at
Elf of the woodland,
Gnome of the cavern,
Griffin and Giant,
And dancing of Fairies
In desolate hollows,
And wraiths of the mountain,
And rolling of dragons
By warble of water,
Or cataract music
Of falling torrents,
Flitted The Gleam.

V.

Down from the mountain
And over the level,
And streaming and shining on
Silent river,
Silvery willow,
Pasture and plowland,
Horses and oxen,
Innocent maidens,
Garrulous children,
Homestead and harvest,
Reaper and gleaner,
And rough-ruddy faces
Of lowly labor,
Slided The Gleam. —

VI.

Then, with a melody
Stronger and statelier,
Led me at length
To the city and palace
Of Arthur the king;
Touch'd at the golden
Cross of the churches,
Flash'd on the Tournament,
Flicker'd and bicker'd
From helmet to helmet,
And last on the forehead
Of Arthur the blameless
Rested The Gleam.

VII.

Clouds and darkness
Closed upon Camelot;
Arthur had vanish'd
I knew not whither,
The king who loved me,
And cannot die;
For out of the darkness
Silent and slowly
The Gleam, that had waned to a
    wintry glimmer
On icy fallow
And faded forest,
Drew to the valley
Named of the shadow,
And slowly brightening
Out of the glimmer,
And slowly moving again to a
    melody
Yearningly tender,
Fell on the shadow,
No longer a shadow,
But clothed with The Gleam.

VIII.

And broader and brighter
The Gleam flying onward,
Wed to the melody,
Sang thro' the world;
And slower and fainter,
Old and weary,
But eager to follow,
I saw, whenever
In passing it glanced upon
Hamlet or city,
That under the Crosses
The dead man's garden,
The mortal hillock,
Would break into blossom;
And so to the land's
Last limit I came —
And can no longer,

But die rejoicing,
For thro' the Magic
Of Him the Mighty,
Who taught me in childhood,
There on the border
Of boundless Ocean,
And all but in Heaven
Hovers The Gleam.

IX.

Not of the sunlight,
Not of the moonlight,
Not of the starlight!
O young Mariner,
Down to the haven,
Call your companions,
Launch your vessel,
And crowd your canvas,
And, ere it vanishes
Over the margin,
After it, follow it,
Follow The Gleam.

ROMNEY'S REMORSE.

"I read Hayley's Life of Romney the other day — Romney wanted but education and reading to make him a very fine painter; but his ideal was not high nor fixed. How touching is the close of his lif ! He married at nineteen, and because Sir Joshua and others had said that 'marriage spoilt an artist' almost immediately left his wife in the North and scarce saw her till the end of his life; when old, nearly mad and quite desolate, he went back to her and she received him and nursed him till he died. This quiet act of hers is worth all Romney's pictures! even as a matter of Art, I am sure." (*Letters and Literary Remains of Edward Fitzgerald*, vol. i.)

"BEAT, little heart — I give you this
    and this " —
  Who are you? What! the Lady
    Hamilton?
Good, I am never weary painting you.
To sit once more? Cassandra, Hebe,
    Joan,
Or spinning at your wheel beside the
    vine —
Bacchante, what you will; and if I
    fail
To conjure and concentrate into form
And color all you are, the fault is less

In me than Art. What Artist ever
    yet
Could make pure light live on the
    canvas? Art!
Why should I so disrelish that short
    word?
  Where am I? snow on all the hills!
    so hot,
So fever'd! never colt would more
    delight
To roll himself in meadow grass
    than I
To wallow in that winter of the hills.
  Nurse, were you hired? or came of
    your own will
To wait on one so broken, so forlorn?
Have I not met you somewhere long
    ago?
I am all but sure I have — in Kendal
    church —
O yes! I hired you for a season
    there,   •
And then we parted; but you look so
    kind
That you will not deny my sultry
    throat
One draught of icy water. There —
    you spill
The drops upon my forehead. Your
    hand shakes.
I am ashamed. I am a trouble to
    you,
Could kneel for your forgiveness.
    Are they tears?
For me — they do me too much grace
    — for me?
O Mary, Mary!
        Vexing you with words!
Words only, born of fever, or the
    fumes
Of that dark opiate dose you gave
    me, — words,
Wild babble. I have stumbled back
    again
Into the common day, the sounder
    self.
God stay me there, if only for your
    sake,
The truest, kindliest, noblest-hearted
    wife
That ever wore a Christian marriage-
    ring.

My curse upon the Master's apo-
　　thegm,
That wife and children drag an Artist
　　down!
This seem'd my lodestar in the
　　Heaven of Art,
And lured me from the household
　　fire on earth.
To you my days have been a life-long
　　lie,
Grafted on half a truth, and tho' you
　　say
"Take comfort, you have won the
　　Painter's fame;"
The best in me that sees the worst in
　　me,
And groans to see it, finds no com-
　　fort there.
　　　　What fame? I am not Raphaël,
　　Titian — no
Nor even a Sir Joshua, some will cry.
Wrong there! The painter's fame?
　　but mine, that grew
Blown into glittering by the popular
　　breath,
May float awhile beneath the sun,
　　may roll
The rainbow hues of heaven about
　　it —
　　　　　　　　　　There!
The color'd bubble bursts above the
　　abyss
Of Darkness, utter Lethe.

　　　　　　　　Is it so?
Her sad eyes plead for my own fame
　　with me
To make it dearer.

　　　　　　Look, the sun has risen
To flame along another dreary day.
Your hand. How bright you keep
　　your marriage-ring!
Raise me. I thank you.

　　　　　　Has your opiate then
Bred this black mood? or am I con-
　　scious, more
Than other Masters, of the chasm
　　between
Work and Ideal? Or does the gloom
　　of Age

And suffering cloud the height I
　　stand upon
Even from myself? stand? stood . . .
　　no more.
　　　　　　　　　　And yet
The world would lose, if such a wife
　　as you
Should vanish unrecorded. Might I
　　crave
One favor? I am bankrupt of all
　　claim
On your obedience, and my strongest
　　wish
Falls flat before your least unwilling-
　　ness.
Still would you — if it please you —
　　sit to me?
　　I dream'd last night of that clear
　　summer noon,
When seated on a rock, and foot to
　　foot
With your own shadow in the placid
　　lake,
You claspt our infant daughter, heart
　　to heart.
I had been among the hills, and
　　brought you down
A length of staghorn-moss, and this
　　you twined
About her cap. I see the picture yet,
Mother and child. A sound from far
　　away,
No louder than a bee among the
　　flowers,
A fall of water lull'd the noon asleep.
You still'd it for the moment with a
　　song
Which often echo'd in me, while I
　　stood
Before the great Madonna-master-
　　pieces
Of ancient Art in Paris, or in Rome.
　　Mary, my crayons! if I can, I will.
You should have been — I might have
　　made you once,
Had I but known you as I know you
　　now —
The true Alcestis of the time. Your
　　song —
Sit, listen! I remember it, a proof
That I — even I — at times remem-
　　ber'd *you.*

"Beat upon mine, little heart! beat,
 beat!
Beat upon mine! you are mine, my
 sweet!
All mine from your pretty blue eyes
 to your feet,
     My sweet."
Less profile! turn to me — three-
 quarter face.
"Sleep, little blossom, my honey,
 my bliss!
For I give you this, and I give you
 this!
And I blind your pretty blue eyes
 with a kiss!
     Sleep!"
Too early blinded by the kiss of
 death —
"Father and Mother will watch
 you grow " —
You watch'd, not I, she did not grow,
 she died.

"Father and Mother will watch
 you grow,
And gather the roses whenever
 they blow,
And find the white heather wherever
 you go,
     My sweet."

Ah, my white heather only grows in
 heaven
With Milton's amaranth. There,
 there, there! a child
Had shamed me at it — Down, you
 idle tools,
Stampt into dust — tremulous, all
 awry,
Blurr'd like a landskip in a ruffled
 pool, —
Not one stroke firm. This Art, that
 harlot-like
Seduced me from you, leaves me
 harlot-like,
Who love her still, and whimper,
 impotent
To win her back before I die — and
 then —
Then, in the loud world's bastard
 judgment-day,

One truth will damn me with the
 mindless mob,
Who feel no touch of my temptation,
 more
More than all the myriad lies, that
 blacken round
The corpse of every man that gains a
 name;
"This model husband, this fine Art-
 ist"! Fool,
What matters? Six foot deep of
 burial mould
Will dull their comments! Ay, but
 when the shout
Of His descending peals from Heaven,
 and throbs
Thro' earth, and all her graves, if *He*
 should ask
"Why left you wife and children?
 for my sake,
According to my word?" and I replied
"Nay, Lord, for *Art*," why, that would
 sound so mean
That all the dead, who wait the doom
 of Hell
For bolder sins than mine, adulteries,
Wife-murders, — nay, the ruthless
 Mussulman
Who flings his bowstrung Harem in
 the sea,
Would turn, and glare at me, and
 point and jeer,
And gibber at the worm, who, living,
 made
The wife of wives a widow-bride, and
 lost
Salvation for a sketch.
     I am wild again!
The coals of fire you heap upon my
 head
Have crazed me. Someone knocking
 there without?
No! Will my Indian brother come?
 to find
Me or my coffin? Should I know the
 man?
This worn-out Reason dying in her
 house
May leave the windows blinded, and
 if so,
Bid him farewell for me, and tell
 him —

Hope !
I hear a death-bed Angel whisper
    " Hope."
" The miserable have no medicine
But only Hope ! " He said it . . .
    in the play.
His crime was of the senses ; of the
    mind
Mine ; worse, cold, calculated.
           Tell my son —
O let me lean my head upon your
    breast.

" Beat little heart " on this fool brain
    of mine.
I once had friends — and many —
    none like you.
I love you more than when we mar-
    ried. Hope !
O yes, I hope, or fancy that, perhaps,
Human forgiveness touches heaven,
    and thence —
For you forgive me, you are sure of
    that —
Reflected, sends a light on the forgiven.

PARNASSUS.

Exegi monumentum . . .
Quod non . . .
Possit diruere . . .
    . . . innumerabilis.
Annorum series et fuga temporum. — HORACE.

I.

WHAT be those crown'd forms high over the sacred fountain ?
Bards, that the mighty Muses have raised to the heights of the mountain,
And over the flight of the Ages ! O Goddesses, help me up thither !
Lightning may shrivel the laurel of Cæsar, but mine would not wither.
Steep is the mountain, but you, you will help me to overcome it,
And stand with my head in the zenith, and roll my voice from the summit
Sounding forever and ever thro' Earth and her listening nations,
And mixt with the great Sphere-music of stars and of constellations.

II.

What be those two shapes high over the sacred fountain,
Taller than all the Muses, and huger than all the mountain ?
On those two known peaks they stand ever spreading and heightening ;
Poet, that evergreen laurel is blasted by more than lightning !
Look, in their deep double shadow the crown'd ones all disappearing !
Sing like a bird and be happy, nor hope for a deathless hearing !
" Sounding forever and ever ? " pass on ! the sight confuses —
These are Astronomy and Geology, terrible Muses !

III.

If the lips were touch'd with fire from off a pure Pierian altar,
Tho' their music here be mortal need the singer greatly care ?
Other songs for other worlds ! the fire within him would not falter ;
Let the golden Iliad vanish, Homer here is Homer there.

BY AN EVOLUTIONIST.

THE Lord let the house of a brute to the soul of a man,
  And the man said "Am I your debtor?"
And the Lord — "Not yet: but make it as clean as you can,
  And then I will let you a better."

I.

If my body come from brutes, my soul uncertain, or a fable,
  Why not bask amid the senses while the sun of morning shines,
I, the finer brute rejoicing in my hounds, and in my stable,
  Youth and Health, and birth and wealth, and choice of women and of wines?

II.

What hast thou done for me, grim Old Age, save breaking my bones on the
    rack?
  Would I had past in the morning that looks so bright from afar!

OLD AGE.

Done for thee? starved the wild beast that was linkt with thee eighty years
    back.
  Less weight now for the ladder-of-heaven that hangs on a star.

I.

If my body come from brutes, tho' somewhat finer than their own,
  I am heir, and this my kingdom.   Shall the royal voice be mute?
No, but if the rebel subject seek to drag me from the throne,
  Hold the sceptre, Human Soul, and rule thy Province of the brute.

II.

I have climb'd to the snows of Age, and I gaze at a field in the Past,
  Where I sank with the body at times in the sloughs of a low desire,
But I hear no yelp of the beast, and the Man is quiet at last
  As he stands on the heights of his life with a glimpse of a height that is
    higher.

FAR — FAR — AWAY.

(FOR MUSIC.)

WHAT sight so lured him thro' the
    fields he knew
As where earth's green stole into
    heaven's own hue,
      Far — far — away?

What sound was dearest in his native
    dells?
The mellow lin-lan-lone of evening
    bells
      Far — far — away.

What vague world-whisper, mystic
    pain or joy,
Thro' those three words would haunt
    him when a boy
      Far — far — away?

A whisper from his dawn of life? a
    breath
From some fair dawn beyond the
    doors of death
      Far — far — away?

Far, far, how far? from o'er the
    gates of Birth,
The faint horizons, all the bounds of
    earth,
      Far — far — away?

What charm in words, a charm no
    words could give ?
O dying words, can **Music** make you
    live
            Far — far — away ?

POLITICS.

WE move, the wheel must always
    move,
    Nor always on the plain,
And if we move to such a goal
    As Wisdom hopes to gain,
Then you that drive, and know your
    Craft,
    Will firmly hold the rein,
Nor lend an ear to random cries,
    Or you may drive in vain,
For some cry " Quick " and some cry
    " Slow,"
    But, while the hills remain,
Up hill " Too-slow " will need the
    whip,
    Down hill " Too-quick " the chain.

BEAUTIFUL CITY.

BEAUTIFUL city, the centre and crater
    of European confusion,
O you with your passionate shriek
    for the rights of an equal hu-
    manity,
How often your Re-volution has
    proven but E-volution
Roll'd again back on itself in the
    tides of a civic insanity!

THE ROSES ON THE TERRACE.

ROSE, on this terrace fifty years ago,
    When I was in my June, you in
    your May,
Two words, " *My* Rose " set all your
    face aglow,
    And now that I am white, and you
    are gray,
That blush of fifty years ago, my
    dear,
    Blooms in the Past, but close to
    me to-day

As this red rose, which on our terrace
    here
    Glows in the blue of fifty miles
    away.

THE PLAY.

ACT first, this Earth, a stage so
    gloom'd with woe
    You all but sicken at the shifting
    scenes.
And yet be patient. Our Playwright
    may show
    In some fifth Act what this wild
    Drama means.

ON ONE WHO AFFECTED AN EFFEMINATE MANNER.

WHILE man and woman still are in-
    complete,
I prize that soul where man and
    woman meet,
Which types all Nature's male and
    female plan,
But, friend, man-woman is not
    woman-man.

TO ONE WHO RAN DOWN THE ENGLISH.

YOU make our faults too gross, and
    thence maintain
Our darker future. May your fears
    be vain !
At times the small black fly upon
    the pane
May seem the black ox of the dis-
    tant plain.

THE SNOWDROP.

MANY, many welcomes
    February fair-maid,
    Ever as of old time,
    Solitary firstling,
    Coming in the cold time,
    Prophet of the gay time,
    Prophet of the May time,
    Prophet of the roses,
    Many, many welcomes
    February fair-maid!

THE THROSTLE.

"SUMMER is coming, summer is
    coming.
I know it, I know it, I know it.
Light again, leaf again, life again,
    love again,"
Yes, my wild little Poet.

Sing the new year in under the blue.
    Last year you sang it as gladly.
"New, new, new, new!" Is it then
    so new
That you should carol so madly?

"Love again, song again, nest again,
    young again,"
Never a prophet so crazy!
And hardly a daisy as yet, little
    friend,
See, there is hardly a daisy.

"Here again, here, here, here, happy
    year!"
O warble unchidden, unbidden!
Summer is coming, is coming, my
    dear,
And all the winters are hidden.

THE OAK.

LIVE thy Life,
    Young and old,
Like yon oak,
Bright in spring,
    Living gold;

Summer-rich
    Then; and then
Autumn-changed,
Soberer-hued
    Gold again.

All his leaves
    Fall'n at length,
Look, he stands,
Trunk and bough,
    Naked strength.

IN MEMORIAM.

W. G. WARD.

FAREWELL, whose like on earth I
    shall not find,
    Whose Faith and Work were bells
        of full accord,
My friend, the most unworldly of
    mankind,
    Most generous of all Ultramon-
        tanes, Ward,
How subtle at tierce and quart of
    mind with mind,
    How loyal in the following of thy
        Lord!

CROSSING THE BAR.

SUNSET and evening star,
    And one clear call for me!
And may there be no moaning of the
    bar,
    When I put out to sea,

But such a tide as moving seems
    asleep,
    Too full for sound and foam,
When that which drew from out the
    boundless deep
    Turns again home.

Twilight and evening bell,
    And after that the dark!
And may there be no sadness of fare-
    well,
    When I embark;

For tho' from out our bourne of Time
    and Place
    The flood may bear me far,
I hope to see my Pilot face to face
    When I have crost the bar.

QUEEN MARY:

A DRAMA.

DRAMATIS PERSONÆ.

QUEEN MARY.
PHILIP, *King of Naples and Sicily, afterwards King of Spain.*
THE PRINCESS ELIZABETH.
REGINALD POLE, *Cardinal and Papal Legate.*
SIMON RENARD, *Spanish Ambassador.*
LE SIEUR DE NOAILLES, *French Ambassador.*
THOMAS CRANMER, *Archbishop of Canterbury.*
SIR NICHOLAS HEATH, *Archbishop of York; Lord Chancellor after Gardiner.*
EDWARD COURTENAY, *Earl of Devon.*
LORD WILLIAM HOWARD, *afterwards Lord Howard, and Lord High Admiral.*
LORD WILLIAMS OF THAME.　　LORD PAGET.　　LORD PETRE.
STEPHEN GARDINER, *Bishop of Winchester and Lord Chancellor.*
EDMUND BONNER, *Bishop of London.*　　THOMAS THIRLBY, *Bishop of Ely.*
SIR THOMAS WYATT } *Insurrectionary Leaders.*
SIR THOMAS STAFFORD
SIR RALPH BAGENHALL.　　　SIR ROBERT SOUTHWELL.
SIR HENRY BEDINGFIELD.　　SIR WILLIAM CECIL.
SIR THOMAS WHITE, *Lord Mayor of London.*
THE DUKE OF ALVA } *attending on Philip.*
THE COUNT DE FERIA
PETER MARTYR.　　FATHER COLE.　　FATHER BOURNE.
VILLA GARCIA.　　SOTO.
CAPTAIN BRETT } *Adherents of Wyatt.*
ANTHONY KNYVETT
PETERS, *Gentleman of Lord Howard.*
ROGER, *Servant to Noailles.*　　WILLIAM, *Servant to Wyatt.*
STEWARD OF HOUSEHOLD *to the Princess Elizabeth.*
OLD NOKES *and* NOKES.
MARCHIONESS OF EXETER, *Mother of Courtenay.*
LADY CLARENCE } *Ladies in Waiting to the Queen.*
LADY MAGDALEN DACRES
ALICE.
MAID OF HONOR *to the Princess Elizabeth.*
JOAN } *two Country Wives.*
TIB

Lords *and other* Attendants, Members *of the* Privy Council, Members *of*
　　Parliament, Two Gentlemen, Aldermen, Citizens, Peasants, Ushers,
　　Messengers, Guards, Pages, Gospellers, Marshalmen, *etc.*

ACT I.

SCENE I. — ALDGATE RICHLY DECORATED.

CROWD. MARSHALMEN.

Marshalman. Stand back, keep a clear lane! When will her Majesty pass, sayst thou? why now, even now; wherefore draw back your heads and your horns before I break them, and make what noise you will with your tongues, so it be not treason. Long live Queen Mary, the lawful and legitimate daughter of Harry the Eighth! Shout, knaves!

Citizens. Long live Queen Mary!

First Citizen. That's a hard word, legitimate; what does it mean?

Second Citizen. It means a bastard.

Third Citizen. Nay, it means true-born.

First Citizen. Why, didn't the Parliament make her a bastard?

Second Citizen. No; it was the Lady Elizabeth.

Third Citizen. That was after, man; that was after.

First Citizen. Then which is the bastard?

Second Citizen. Troth, they be both bastards by Act of Parliament and Council.

Third Citizen. Ay, the Parliament can make every true-born man of us a bastard. Old Nokes, can't it make thee a bastard? thou shouldst know, for thou art as white as three Christmasses.

Old Nokes (dreamily). Who's a-passing? King Edward or King Richard?

Third Citizen. No, old Nokes.

Old Nokes. It's Harry!

Third Citizen. It's Queen Mary.

Old Nokes. The blessed Mary's a-passing! [*Falls on his knees.*

Nokes. Let father alone, my masters! he's past your questioning.

Third Citizen. Answer thou for him, then! thou'rt no such cockerel thyself, for thou was born i' the tail end of old Harry the Seventh.

Nokes. Eh! that was afore bastard-making began. I was born true man at five in the forenoon i' the tail of old Harry, and so they can't make me a bastard.

Third Citizen. But if Parliament can make the Queen a bastard, why, it follows all the more that they can make thee one, who art fray'd i' the knees, and out at the elbow, and bald o' the back, and bursten at the toes, and down at heels.

Nokes. I was born of a true man and a ring'd wife, and I can't argue upon it; but I and my old woman 'ud burn upon it, that would we.

Marshalman. What are you cackling of bastardy under the Queen's own nose? I'll have you flogg'd and burnt too, by the Rood I will.

First Citizen. He swears by the Rood. Whew!

Second Citizen. Hark! the trumpets.

[*The Procession passes,* Mary *and* Elizabeth *riding side by side, and disappears under the gate.*

Citizens. Long live Queen Mary! down with all traitors! God save her Grace; and death to Northumberland! [*Exeunt.*

Manent TWO GENTLEMEN.

First Gentleman. By God's light a noble creature, right royal!

Second Gentleman. She looks comelier than ordinary to-day; but to my mind the Lady Elizabeth is the more noble and royal.

First Gentleman. I mean the Lady Elizabeth. Did you hear (I have a daughter in her service who reported it) that she met the Queen at Wanstead with five hundred horse, and the Queen (tho' some say they be much divided) took her hand, call'd her sweet sister, and kiss'd not her alone, but all the ladies of her following.

Second Gentleman. Ay, that was in

her hour of joy; there will be plenty to sunder and unsister them again: this Gardiner for one, who is to be made Lord Chancellor, and will pounce like a wild beast out of his cage to worry Cranmer.

First Gentleman. And furthermore, my daughter said that when there rose a talk of the late rebellion, she spoke even of Northumberland pitifully, and of the good Lady Jane as a poor innocent child who had but obeyed her father; and furthermore, she said that no one in her time should be burnt for heresy.

Second Gentleman. Well, sir, I look for happy times.

First Gentleman. There is but one thing against them. I know not if you know.

Second Gentleman. I suppose you touch upon the rumor that Charles, the master of the world, has offer'd her his son Philip, the Pope and the Devil. I trust it is but a rumor.

First Gentleman. She is going now to the Tower to loose the prisoners there, and among them Courtenay, to be made Earl of Devon, of royal blood, of splendid feature, whom the council and all her people wish her to marry. May it be so, for we are many of us Catholics, but few Papists, and the Hot Gospellers will go mad upon it.

Second Gentleman. Was she not betroth'd in her babyhood to the Great Emperor himself?

First Gentleman. Ay, but he's too old.

Second Gentleman. And again to her cousin Reginald Pole, now Cardinal; but I hear that he too is full of aches and broken before his day.

First Gentleman. O, the Pope could dispense with his Cardinalate, and his achage, and his breakage, if that were all: will you not follow the procession?

Second Gentleman. No; I have seen enough for this day.

First Gentleman. Well, I shall follow; if I can get near enough I shall judge with my own eyes whether her Grace incline to this splendid scion of Plantagenet.   [*Exeunt.*

SCENE II.

A ROOM IN LAMBETH PALACE.

Cranmer. To Strasburg, Antwerp, Frankfort, Zurich, Worms,
Geneva, Basle — our Bishops from their sees
Or fled, they say, or flying — Poinet, Barlow,
Bale, Scory, Coverdale; besides the Deans
Of Christchurch, Durham, Exeter, and Wells —
Ailmer and Bullingham, and hundreds more;
So they report: I shall be left alone.
No: Hooper, Ridley, Latimer will not fly.

Enter PETER MARTYR.

Peter Martyr. Fly, Cranmer! were there nothing else, your name
Stands first of those who sign'd the Letters Patent
That gave her royal crown to Lady Jane.

Cranmer. Stand first it may, but it was written last:
Those that are now her Privy Council, sign'd
Before me: nay, the Judges had pronounced
That our young Edward might bequeath the crown
Of England, putting by his father's will.
Yet I stood out, till Edward sent for me.
The wan boy-king, with his fast-fading eyes
Fixt hard on mine, his frail transparent hand,
Damp with the sweat of death, and griping mine,
Whisper'd me, if I loved him, not to yield

His Church of England to the Papal
    wolf
And Mary; then I could no more —
    I sign'd.
Nay, for bare shame of inconsis-
    tency,
She cannot pass her traitor council by,
To make me headless.
    Peter Martyr. That might be for-
    given.
I tell you, fly, my Lord. You do not
    own
The bodily presence in the Eucharist,
Their wafer and perpetual sacrifice:
Your creed will be your death.
    Cranmer.   Step after step,
Thro' many voices crying right and
    left,
Have I climb'd back into the primal
    church,
And stand within the porch, and
    Christ with me:
My flight were such a scandal to the
    faith,
The downfall of so many simple souls,
I dare not leave my post.
    Peter Martyr. But you divorced
Queen Catharine and her father;
    hence, her hate
Will burn till you are burn'd.
    Cranmer.   I cannot help it.
The Canonists and Schoolmen were
    with me.
" Thou shalt not wed thy brother's
    wife." — 'Tis written,
"They shall be childless." True,
    Mary was born,
But France would not accept her for
    a bride
As being born from incest; and this
    wrought
Upon the king; and child by child,
    you know,
Were momentary sparkles out as
    quick
Almost as kindled; and he brought
    his doubts
And fears to me. Peter, I'll swear
    for him
He *did* believe the bond incestuous.
But wherefore am I trenching on the
    time

That should already have seen your
    steps a mile
From me and Lambeth? God be
    with you! Go.
    Peter Martyr. Ah, but how fierce a
    letter you wrote against
Their superstition when they slander'd
    you
For setting up a mass at Canterbury
To please the Queen.
    Cranmer. It was a wheedling monk
Set up the mass.
    Peter Martyr. I know it, my good
    Lord.
But you so bubbled over with hot
    terms
Of Satan, liars, blasphemy, Anti-
    christ,
She never will forgive you. Fly, my
    Lord, fly!
    Cranmer. I wrote it, and God grant
    me power to burn!
    Peter Martyr. They have given me
    a safe conduct: for all that
I dare not stay. I fear, I fear, I see
    you,
Dear friend, for the last time; fare-
    well, and fly.
    Cranmer. Fly and farewell, and let
    me die the death.
                 [*Exit* Peter Martyr.

Enter OLD SERVANT.

O, kind and gentle master, the Queen's
    Officers
Are here in force to take you to the
    Tower.
    Cranmer. Ay, gentle friend, admit
    them. I will go.
I thank my God it is too late to fly.
                     [*Exeunt.*

SCENE III. — ST. PAUL'S CROSS.

FATHER BOURNE *in the pulpit. A
    crowd.* MARCHIONESS OF EXETER,
COURTENAY. *The* SIEUR DE
NOAILLES *and his man* ROGER *in
front of the stage. Hubbub.*

    Noailles. Hast thou let fall those
    papers in the palace?

Roger. Ay, sir.

Noailles. "There will be no peace for Mary till Elizabeth lose her head."

Roger. Ay, sir.

Noailles. And the other, " Long live Elizabeth the Queen !"

Roger. Ay, sir ; she needs must tread upon them.

Noailles. Well.
These beastly swine make such a grunting here,
I cannot catch what Father Bourne is saying.

Roger. Quiet a moment, my masters ; hear what the shaveling has to say for himself.

Crowd. Hush — hear !

Bourne. — and so this unhappy land, long divided in itself, and sever'd from the faith, will return into the one true fold, seeing that our gracious Virgin Queen hath ——

Crowd. No pope ! no pope !

Roger (*to those about him, mimicking* Bourne). — hath sent for the holy legate of the holy father the Pope, Cardinal Pole, to give us all that holy absolution which ——

First Citizen. Old Bourne to the life !

Second Citizen. Holy absolution ! holy Inquisition !

Third Citizen. Down with the Papist !

[*Hubbub.*

Bourne. — and now that your good bishop, Bonner, who hath lain so long under bonds for the faith — [*Hubbub.*

Noailles. Friend Roger, steal thou in among the crowd,
And get the swine to shout Elizabeth. Yon gray old Gospeller, sour as mid-winter,
Begin with him.

Roger (*goes*). By the mass, old friend, we'll have no pope here while the Lady Elizabeth lives.

Gospeller. Art thou of the true faith, fellow, that swearest by the mass ?

Roger. Ay, that am I, new con-verted, but the old leaven sticks to my tongue yet.

First Citizen. He says right ; by the mass we'll have no mass here.

Voices of the crowd. Peace ! hear him ; let his own words damn the Papist. From thine own mouth I judge thee — tear him down !

Bourne. — and since our Gracious Queen, let me call her our second Virgin Mary, hath begun to re-edify the true temple ——

First Citizen. Virgin Mary ! we'll have no virgins here — we'll have the Lady Elizabeth !

[*Swords are drawn, a knife is hurled and sticks in the pulpit. The mob throng to the pulpit stairs.*

Marchioness of Exeter. Son Courte-nay, wilt thou see the holy father
Murdered before thy face ? up, son, and save him !
They love thee, and thou canst not come to harm.

Courtenay (*in the pulpit*). Shame, shame, my masters ! are you English-born,
And set yourselves by hundreds against one ?

Crowd. A Courtenay ! a Courtenay !

[*A train of Spanish servants crosses at the back of the stage.*

Noailles. These birds of passage come before their time :
Stave off the crowd upon the Spaniard there.

Roger. My masters, yonder's fatter game for you
Than this old gaping gurgoyle : look you there —
The prince of Spain coming to wed our Queen !
After him, boys ! and pelt him from the city.

[*They seize stones and follow the Spaniards. Exeunt on the other side* Marchioness of Exeter *and* Attendants.

Noailles (*to* Roger). Stand from me. If Elizabeth lose her head —
That makes for France.

And if her people, anger'd thereupon,
Arise against her and dethrone the
    Queen —
That makes for France.
And if I breed confusion anyway —
That makes for France.
            Good-day, my Lord of Devon;
A bold heart yours to beard that rag-
    ing mob!
    Courtenay. My mother said, Go up;
        and up I went.
I knew they would not do me any
    wrong,
For I am mighty popular with them,
    Noailles.
    Noailles. You look'd a king.
    Courtenay.   Why not? I am
        king's blood.
    Noailles. And in the whirl of change
        may come to be one.
    Courtenay. Ah!
    Noailles. But does your gracious
        Queen entreat you kinglike?
    Courtenay. 'Fore God, I think she
        entreats me like a child.
    Noailles. You've but a dull life in
        this maiden court,
I fear, my Lord?
    Courtenay. A life of nods and yawns.
    Noailles. So you would honor my
        poor house to-night.
We might enliven you. Divers honest
    fellows,
The Duke of Suffolk lately freed from
    prison,
Sir Peter Carew and Sir Thomas
    Wyatt,
Sir Thomas Stafford, and some more
    — we play.
    Courtenay. At what?
    Noailles.   The Game of Chess.
    Courtenay.   The Game of Chess!
I can play well, and I shall beat you
    there.
    Noailles. Ay, but we play with
        Henry, King of France,
And certain of his court.
His Highness makes his moves across
    the Channel,
We answer him with ours, and there
    are messengers
That go between us.

    Courtenay. Why, such a game, sir,
        were whole years a playing.
    Noailles. Nay; not so long I trust.
        That all depends
Upon the skill and swiftness of the
    players.
    Courtenay. The King is skilful at it?
    Noailles.   Very, my Lord.
    Courtenay. And the stakes high?
    Noailles. But not beyond your
        means.
    Courtenay. Well, I'm the first of
        players. I shall win.
    Noailles. With our advice and in
        our company,
And so you well attend to the king's
    moves,
I think you may.
    Courtenay.   When do you meet?
    Noailles.   To-night.
    Courtenay (aside). I will be there;
        the fellow's at his tricks —
Deep — I shall fathom him.   (*Aloud.*)
    Good morning, Noailles.
                        [*Exit* Courtenay.
    Noailles. Good-day, my Lord.
        Strange game of chess! a King
That with her own pawns plays against
    a Queen,
Whose play is all to find herself a
    King.
Ay; but this fine blue-blooded Courte-
    nay seems
Too princely for a pawn. Call him a
    Knight,
That, with an ass's, not a horse's head,
Skips every way, from levity or from
    fear.
Well, we shall use him somehow, so
    that Gardiner
And Simon Renard spy not out our
    game
Too early. Roger, thinkest thou that
    anyone
Suspected thee to be my man?
    Roger.   Not one, sir.
    Noailles. No! the disguise was per-
        fect. Let's away.   [*Exeunt.*

SCENE IV.

London. A Room in the Palace.

Elizabeth. *Enter* Courtenay.

Courtenay. So yet am I,
Unless my friends and mirrors lie to
    me,
A goodlier-looking fellow than this
    Philip.
Pah !
The Queen is ill advised : shall I turn
    traitor ?
They've almost talked me into it : yet
    the word
Affrights me somewhat : to be such a
    one
As Harry Bolingbroke hath a lure in
    it.
Good now, my Lady Queen, tho' by
    your age,
And by your looks you are not worth
    the having,
Yet by your crown you are.
         [*Seeing* Elizabeth.
    The Princess there ?
If I tried her and la — she's amor-
    ous.
Have we not heard of her in Edward's
    time,
Her freaks and frolics with the late
    Lord Admiral ?
I do believe she'd yield. I should be
    still
A party in the state ; and then, who
    knows —
    Elizabeth. What are you musing on,
    my Lord of Devon ?
    Courtenay. Has not the Queen —
    Elizabeth.   Done what, Sir ?
    Courtenay.   — made you follow
The Lady Suffolk and the Lady Len-
    nox ? —
You,
The heir presumptive.
    Elizabeth. Why do you ask ? you
    know it.
    Courtenay. You needs must bear it
    hardly.
    Elizabeth.   No, indeed !
I am utterly submissive to the Queen.

    Courtenay. Well, I was musing up-
    on that ; the Queen
Is both my foe and yours . we should
    be friends.
    Elizabeth. My Lord, the hatred of
    another to us
Is no true bond of friendship.
    Courtenay.   Might it not
Be the rough preface of some closer
    bond ?
    Elizabeth. My Lord, you late were
    loosed from out the Tower,
Where, like a butterfly in a chrysalis,
You spent your life ; that broken, out
    you flutter
Thro' the new world, go zigzag, now
    would settle
Upon this flower, now that ; but all
    things here
At court are known ; you have solicited
The Queen, and been rejected.
    Courtenay.   Flower, she !
Half faded ! but you, cousin, are fresh
    and sweet
As the first flower no bee has ever
    tried.
    Elizabeth. Are you the bee to try
    me ? why, but now
I called you butterfly.
    Courtenay.   You did me wrong,
I love not to be called a butterfly :
Why do you call me butterfly ?
    Elizabeth. Why do you go so gay
    then ?
    Courtenay.   Velvet and gold.
This dress was made me as the Earl
    of Devon
To take my seat in ; looks it not right
    royal ?
    Elizabeth. So royal that the Queen
    forbad you wearing it.
    Courtenay. I wear it then to spite
    her.
    Elizabeth.   My Lord, my Lord ;
I see you in the Tower again. Her
    Majesty
Hears you affect the Prince — prelates
    kneel to you. —
    Courtenay. I am the noblest blood
    in Europe, Madam,
A Courtenay of Devon, and her
    cousin.

Elizabeth. She hears you make
your boast that after all
She means to wed you. Folly, my
good Lord.
Courtenay. How folly? a great
party in the state
Wills me to wed her.
Elizabeth. Failing her, my Lord,
Doth not as great a party in the
state
Will you to wed me?
Courtenay. Even so, fair lady.
Elizabeth. You know to flatter
ladies.
Courtenay. Nay, I meant
True matters of the heart.
Elizabeth. My heart, my Lord,
Is no great party in the state as yet.
Courtenay. Great, said you? nay,
you shall be great. I love you,
Lay my life in your hands. Can you
be close?
Elizabeth. Can you, my Lord?
Courtenay. Close as a miser's casket.
Listen:
The King of France, Noailles the
Ambassador,
The Duke of Suffolk and Sir Peter
Carew,
Sir Thomas Wyatt, I myself, some
others,
Have sworn this Spanish marriage
shall not be.
If Mary will not hear us — well —
conjecture —
Were I in Devon with my wedded
bride,
The people there so worship me —
Your ear;
You shall be Queen.
Elizabeth. You speak too low,
my Lord;
I cannot hear you.
Courtenay. I'll repeat it.
Elizabeth. No!
Stand further off, or you may lose
your head.
Courtenay. I have a head to lose
for your sweet sake.
Elizabeth. Have you, my Lord?
Best keep it for your own.
Nay, pout not, cousin.

Not many friends are mine, except
indeed
Among the many. I believe you
mine;
And so you may continue mine, farewell,
And that at once.

Enter MARY, *behind.*

Mary. Whispering — leagued to-
gether
To bar me from my Philip.
Courtenay. Pray — consider —
Elizabeth (*seeing the* Queen). Well,
that's a noble horse of yours,
my Lord.
I trust that he will carry you well
to-day,
And heal your headache.
Courtenay. You are wild; what
headache?
Heartache, perchance; not headache.
Elizabeth (*aside to* Courtenay.) Are
you blind?
[Courtenay *sees the* Queen *and exit.*
Exit Mary.

Enter LORD WILLIAM HOWARD.

Howard. Was that my Lord of
Devon? do not you
Be seen in corners with my Lord of
Devon.
He hath fallen out of favor with the
Queen.
She fears the Lords may side with
you and him
Against her marriage; therefore is he
dangerous.
And if this Prince of fluff and feather
come
To woo you, niece, he is dangerous
everyway.
Elizabeth. Not very dangerous that
way, my good uncle.
Howard. But your own state is full
of danger here.
The disaffected, heretics, reformers,
Look to you as the one to crown their
ends.
Mix not yourself with any plot I pray
you;

Nay, if by chance you hear of any such,
Speak not thereof — no, not to your
    best friend,
Lest you should be confounded with
    it. Still —
Perinde ac cadaver — as the priest
    says,
You know your Latin — quiet as a
    dead body.
What was my Lord of Devon telling
    you?
    Elizabeth. Whether he told me any-
      thing or not,
I follow your good counsel, gracious
    uncle.
Quiet as a dead body.
    Howard.   You do right well.
I do not care to know; but this I
    charge you,
Tell Courtenay nothing. The Lord
    Chancellor
(I count it as a kind of virtue in him,
He hath not many), as a mastiff dog
May love a puppy cur for no more
    reason
Than that the twain have been tied
    up together,
Thus Gardiner — for the two were
    fellow-prisoners
So many years in yon accursed
    Tower —
Hath taken to this Courtenay. Look
    to it, niece,
He hath no fence when Gardiner
    questions him;
All oozes out; yet him — because
    they know him
The last White Rose, the last Plan-
    tagenet
(Nay, there is Cardinal Pole, too), the
    people
Claim as their natural leader — ay,
    some say,
That you shall marry him, make him
    King belike.
    Elizabeth. Do they say so, good
    uncle?
    Howard.   Ay, good niece!
You should be plain and open with
    me, niece,
You should not play upon me.
    Elizabeth.   No, good uncle.

Enter GARDINER.

    Gardiner. The Queen would see
    your Grace upon the moment.
    Elizabeth. Why, my lord Bishop?
    Gardiner. I think she means to
    counsel your withdrawing
To Ashridge, or some other country
    house.
    Elizabeth. Why, my lord Bishop?
    Gardiner. I do but bring the mes-
    sage, know no more.
Your Grace will hear her reasons
    from herself.
    Elizabeth. 'Tis mine own wish ful-
    fill'd before the word
Was spoken, for in truth I had meant
    to crave
Permission of her Highness to retire
To Ashridge, and pursue my studies
    there.
    Gardiner. Madam, to have the wish
    before the word
Is man's good Fairy — and the Queen
    is yours.
I left her with rich jewels in her hand,
Whereof 'tis like enough she means
    to make
A farewell present to your Grace.
    Elizabeth.   My Lord,
I have the jewel of a loyal heart.
    Gardiner. I doubt it not, Madam,
    most loyal. [*Bows low and exit.*
    Howard.   See,
This comes of parleying with my Lord
    of Devon.
Well, well, you must obey; and I my-
    self
Believe it will be better for your wel-
    fare.
Your time will come.
    Elizabeth. I think my time will
    come.
Uncle,
I am of sovereign nature, that I know,
Not to be quell'd; and I have felt
    within me
Stirrings of some great doom when
    God's just hour
Peals — but this fierce old Gardiner
    — his big baldness,
That irritable forelock which he rubs,

His buzzard beak and deep-incavern'd
    eyes
Half fright me.
   Howard. You've a bold heart; keep
    it so.
He cannot touch you save that you
    turn traitor;
And so take heed I pray you — you
    are one
Who love that men should smile up-
    on you, niece.
They'd smile you into treason — some
    of them.
   Elizabeth. I spy the rock beneath
    the smiling sea.
But if this Philip, the proud Catholic
    prince,
And this bald priest, and she that
    hates me, seek
In that lone house, to practise on my
    life,
By poison, fire, shot, stab —
   Howard.   They will not, niece.
Mine is the fleet and all the power at
    sea —
Or will be in a moment. If they dared
To harm you, I would blow this Philip
    and all
Your trouble to the dogstar and the
    devil.
   Elizabeth. To the Pleiads, uncle;
    they have lost a sister.
   Howard. But why say that? what
    have you done to lose her?
Come, come, I will go with you to the
    Queen.   [*Exeunt*.

SCENE V.

A ROOM IN THE PALACE.

MARY *with* PHILIP'S *miniature*. ALICE.

   Mary (*kissing the miniature*). Most
    goodly, Kinglike and an Em-
    peror's son, —
A king to be, — is he not noble, girl?
   Alice. Goodly enough, your Grace,
    and yet, methinks,
I have seen goodlier.
   Mary.   Ay; some waxen doll

Thy baby eyes have rested on, belike;
All red and white, the fashion of our
    land.
But my good mother came (God rest
    her soul)
Of Spain, and I am Spanish in myself,
And in my likings.
   Alice.   By your Grace's leave
Your royal mother came of Spain,
    but took
To the English red and white. Your
    royal father
(For so they say) was all pure lily and
    rose
In his youth, and like a lady.
   Mary.   O, just God!
Sweet mother, you had time and cause
    enough
To sicken of his lilies and his roses.
Cast off, betray'd, defamed, divorced,
    forlorn!
And then the King — that traitor past
    forgiveness,
The false archbishop fawning on him,
    married
The mother of Elizabeth — a heretic
Ev'n as *she* is; but God hath sent me
    here
To take such order with all heretics
That it shall be, before I die, as tho'
My father and my brother had not
    lived.
What wast thou saying of this Lady
    Jane
Now in the Tower?
   Alice. Why, Madam, she was pass-
    ing
Some chapel down in Essex, and with
    her
Lady Anne Wharton, and the Lady
    Anne
Bow'd to the Pyx; but Lady Jane
    stood up
Stiff as the very backbone of heresy.
And wherefore bow ye not, says Lady
    Anne,
To him within there who made Heav-
    en and Earth?
I cannot, and I dare not, tell your
    Grace
What Lady Jane replied.
   Mary.   But I will have it.

Alice. She said — pray pardon me, and pity her —
She hath hearken'd evil counsel — ah! she said,
The baker made him.

    Mary. Monstrous! blasphemous!
She ought to burn. Hence, thou (*Exit* Alice). No — being traitor
Her head will fall: shall it? she is but a child.
We do not kill the child for doing that
His father whipt him into doing — a head
So full of grace and beauty! would that mine
Were half as gracious! O, my lord to be,
My love, for thy sake only.
I am eleven years older than he is.
But will he care for that?
No, by the holy Virgin, being noble,
But love me only: then the bastard sprout,
My sister, is far fairer than myself.
Will he be drawn to her?
No, being of the true faith with myself.
Paget is for him — for to wed with Spain
Would treble England — Gardiner is against him;
The Council, people, Parliament against him;
But I will have him! My hard father hated me;
My brother rather hated me than loved;
My sister cowers and hates me. Holy Virgin,
Plead with thy blessed Son; grant me my prayer:
Give me my Philip; and we two will lead
The living waters of the Faith again
Back thro' their widow'd channel here, and watch
The parch'd banks rolling incense, as of old,
To heaven, and kindled with the palms of Christ!

    Enter USHER.

Who waits, sir?

    Usher. Madam, the Lord Chancellor.

    Mary. Bid him come in. (*Enter* GARDINER.) Good morning, my good Lord. [*Exit* Usher.

    Gardiner. That every morning of your Majesty
May be most good, is every morning's prayer
Of your most loyal subject, Stephen Gardiner.

    Mary. Come you to tell me this, my Lord?

    Gardiner. And more.
Your people have begun to learn your worth.
Your pious wish to pay King Edward's debts,
Your lavish household curb'd, and the remission
Of half that subsidy levied on the people,
Make all tongues praise and all hearts beat for you.
I'd have you yet more loved: the realm is poor,
The exchequer at neap-tide: we might withdraw
Part of our garrison at Calais.

    Mary. Calais!
Our one point on the main, the gate of France!
I am Queen of England; take mine eyes, mine heart,
But do not lose me Calais.

    Gardiner. Do not fear it.
Of that hereafter. I say your Grace is loved.
That I may keep you thus, who am your friend
And ever faithful counsellor, might I speak?

    Mary. I can forespeak your speaking. Would I marry
Prince Philip, if all England hate him? That is
Your question, and I front it with another:
Is it England, or a party? Now, your answer.

    Gardiner. My answer is, I wear beneath my dress

A shirt of mail: my house hath been
    assaulted,
And when I walk abroad, the popu-
    lace,
With fingers pointed like so many
    daggers,
Stab me in fancy, hissing Spain and
    Philip;
And when I sleep, a hundred men-at-
    arms
Guard my poor dreams for England.
    Men would murder me,
Because they think me favorer of this
    marriage.
  Mary. And that were hard upon
    you, my Lord Chancellor.
  Gardiner. But our young Earl of
    Devon —
  Mary.   Earl of Devon?
I freed him from the Tower, placed
    him at Court;
I made him Earl of Devon, and — the
    fool —
He wrecks his health and wealth on
    courtesans,
And rolls himself in carrion like a
    dog.
  Gardiner. More like a school-boy
    that hath broken bounds,
Sickening himself with sweets.
  Mary.   I will not hear of him.
Good, then, they will revolt: but I am
    Tudor,
And shall control them.
  Gardiner. I will help you, Madam,
Even to the utmost. All the church
    is grateful.
You have ousted the mock priest, re-
    pulpited
The shepherd of St. Peter, raised the
    rood again,
And brought us back the mass. I am
    all thanks
To God and to your Grace: yet I
    know well,
Your people, and I go with them so
    far,
Will brook nor Pope nor Spaniard
    here to play
The tyrant, or in commonwealth or
    church.

  Mary (showing the picture). Is this
    the face of one who plays the
    tyrant?
Peruse it; is it not goodly, ay, and
    gentle?
  Gardiner. Madam, methinks a cold
    face and a haughty.
And when your Highness talks of
    Courtenay —
Ay, true — a goodly one. I would
    his life
Were half as goodly *(aside).*
  Mary.   What is that you mutter?
  Gardiner. Oh, Madam, take it
    bluntly; marry Philip,
And be stepmother of a score of
    sons!
The prince is known in Spain, in
    Flanders, ha!
For Philip —
  Mary. You offend us; you may
    leave us.
You see thro' warping glasses.
  Gardiner.   If your Majesty —
  Mary. I have sworn upon the body
    and blood of Christ
I'll none but Philip.
  Gardiner. Hath your Grace so
    sworn?
  Mary. Ay, Simon Renard knows it.
  Gardiner.   News to me!
It then remains for your poor Gardi-
    ner,
So you still care to trust him some-
    what less
Than Simon Renard, to compose the
    event
In some such form as least may harm
    your Grace.
  Mary. I'll have the scandal sounded
    to the mud.
I know it a scandal.
  Gardiner.   All my hope is now
It may be found a scandal.
  Mary.   You offend us.
  Gardiner (aside). These princes are
    like children, must be phys-
    ick'd,
The bitter in the sweet. I have lost
    mine office,
It may be, thro' mine honesty, like a
    fool.   *[Exit.*

Enter USHER.

Mary. Who waits?

Usher. The Ambassador from France, your Grace.

Mary (sits down). Bid him come in. Good morning, Sir de Noailles.
                                    [*Exit* Usher.

Noailles (entering). A happy morning to your Majesty.

Mary. And I should some time have a happy morning;
I have had none yet. What says the King your Master?

Noailles. Madam, my master hears with much alarm,
That you may marry Philip, Prince of Spain—
Foreseeing, with whate'er unwillingness,
That if this Philip be the titular king
Of England, and at war with him, your Grace
And kingdom will be suck'd into the war,
Ay, tho' you long for peace; wherefore, my master,
If but to prove your Majesty's goodwill,
Would fain have some fresh treaty drawn between you.

Mary. Why some fresh treaty? wherefore should I do it?
Sir, if we marry, we shall still maintain
All former treaties with his Majesty.
Our royal word for that! and your good master,
Pray God he do not be the first to break them,
Must be content with that; and so, farewell.

Noailles (going, returns). I would your answer had been other, Madam,
For I foresee dark days.

Mary.   And so do I, sir;
Your master works against me in the dark.
I do believe he holp Northumberland
Against me.

Noailles. Nay, pure phantasy, your Grace.
Why should he move against you?

Mary.   Will you hear why?
Mary of Scotland,—for I have not own'd
My sister, and I will not,—after me
Is heir of England; and my royal father,
To make the crown of Scotland one with ours,
Had mark'd her for my brother Edward's bride;
Ay, but your king stole her a babe from Scotland
In order to betroth her to your Dauphin.
See then:
Mary of Scotland, married to your Dauphin,
Would make our England, France:
Mary of England, joining hands with Spain,
Would be too strong for France.
Yea, were there issue born to her, Spain and we,
One crown, might rule the world.
                There lies your fear.
That is your drift. You play at hide and seek.
Show me your faces!

Noailles. Madam, I am amazed:
French, I must needs wish all good things for France.
That must be pardon'd me; but I protest
Your Grace's policy hath a farther flight
Than mine into the future. We but seek
Some settled ground for peace to stand upon.

Mary. Well, we will leave all this, sir, to our council.
Have you seen Philip ever?

Noailles.   Only once.

Mary. Is this like Philip?

Noailles. Ay, but nobler-looking.

Mary. Hath he the large ability of Emperor?

Noailles. No, surely.

Mary. I can make allowance for thee,
Thou speakest of the enemy of thy king.
Noailles. Make no allowance for the naked truth.
He is every way a lesser man than Charles ;
Stone-hard, ice-cold — no dash of daring in him.
Mary. If cold, his life is pure.
Noailles. Why (*smiling*), no, indeed.
Mary. Sayst thou ?
Noailles. A very wanton life indeed (*smiling*).
Mary. Your audience is concluded, sir.   [*Exit* Noailles.
      You cannot
Learn a man's nature from his natural foe.

Enter USHER.

Who waits ?
Usher. The Ambassador of Spain, your Grace.   [*Exit.*

Enter SIMON RENARD.

Mary (*rising to meet him*). Thou art ever welcome, Simon Renard. Hast thou
Brought me the letter which thine Emperor promised
Long since, a formal offer of the hand
Of Philip ?
Renard. Nay, your Grace, it hath not reach'd me.
I know not wherefore — some mischance of flood,
And broken bridge, or spavin'd horse, or wave
And wind at their old battle : he must have written.
Mary. But Philip never writes me one poor word,
Which in his absence had been all my wealth.
Strange in a wooer !
Renard.   Yet I know the Prince,
So your king-parliament suffer him to land,
Yearns to set foot upon your island shore.

Mary. God change the pebble which his kingly foot
First presses into some more costly stone
Than ever blinded eye. I'll have one mark it
And bring it me. I'll have it burnish'd firelike ;
I'll set it round with gold, with pearl, with diamond.
Let the great angel of the church come with him ;
Stand on the deck and spread his wings for sail !
God lay the waves and strow the storms at sea,
And here at land among the people !
    O Renard,
I am much beset, I am almost in despair.
Paget is ours. Gardiner perchance is ours ;
But for our heretic Parliament —
Renard.   O Madam,
You fly your thoughts like kites. My master, Charles,
Bade you go softly with your heretics here,
Until your throne had ceased to tremble. Then
Spit them like larks for aught I care. Besides,
When Henry broke the carcase of your church
To pieces, there were many wolves among you
Who dragg'd the scatter'd limbs into their den.
The Pope would have you make them render these ;
So would your cousin, Cardinal Pole ; ill counsel !
These let them keep at present ; stir not yet
This matter of the Church lands. At his coming
Your star will rise.
Mary.   My star ! a baleful one.
I see but the black night, and hear the wolf.
What star ?

Renard. Your star will be your
    princely son,
Heir of this England and the Nether-
    lands!
And if your wolf the while should
    howl for more,
We'll dust him from a bag of Spanish
    gold.
I do believe, I have dusted some al-
    ready,
That, soon or late, your Parliament is
    ours.
    Mary. Why do they talk so foully
    of your Prince,
Renard?
    Renard. The lot of Princes. To sit
    high
Is to be lied about.
    Mary.   They call him cold,
Haughty, ay, worse.
    Renard. Why, doubtless, Philip
    shows
Some of the bearing of your blue
    blood — still
All within measure — nay, it well
    becomes him.
    Mary. Hath he the large ability of
    his father?
    Renard. Nay, some believe that he
    will go beyond him.
    Mary. Is this like him?
    Renard. Ay, somewhat; but your
    Philip
Is the most princelike Prince beneath
    the sun.
This is a daub to Philip.
    Mary.   Of a pure life?
    Renard. As an angel among angels.
    Yea, by Heaven,
The text — Your Highness knows it,
    "Whosoever
Looketh after a woman," would not
    graze
The Prince of Spain. You are happy
    in him there,
Chaste as your Grace!
    Mary.   I am happy in him there.
    Renard. And would be altogether
    happy, Madam,
So that your sister were but look'd to
    closer.

You have sent her from the court, but
    then she goes,
I warrant, not to hear the nightingales,
But hatch you some new treason in
    the woods.
    Mary. We have our spies abroad
    to catch her tripping,
And then if caught, to the Tower.
    Renard.   The Tower! the block!
The word has turn'd your Highness
    pale; the thing
Was no such scarecrow in your father's
    time.
I have heard, the tongue yet quiver'd
    with the jest
When the head leapt — so common!
    I do think
To save your crown that it must come
    to this.
    Mary. No, Renard; it must never
    come to this.
    Renard. Not yet; but your old
    Traitors of the Tower —
Why, when you put Northumberland
    to death,
The sentence having past upon them
    all,
Spared you the Duke of Suffolk,
    Guildford Dudley,
Ev'n that young girl who dared to
    wear your crown?
    Mary. Dared? nay, not so; the
    child obey'd her father.
Spite of her tears her father forced it
    on her.
    Renard. Good Madam, when the
    Roman wish'd to reign,
He slew not him alone who wore the
    purple,
But his assessor in the throne, per-
    chance
A child more innocent than Lady Jane.
    Mary. I am English Queen, not
    Roman Emperor.
    Renard. Yet too much mercy is a
    want of mercy,
And wastes more life. Stamp out the
    fire, or this
Will smoulder and re-flame, and burn
    the throne
Where you should sit with Philip: he
    will not come

Till she be gone.
Mary. Indeed, if that were true —
For Philip comes, one hand in mine, and one
Steadying the tremulous pillars of the Church —
But no, no, no. Farewell. I am somewhat faint
With our long talk. Tho' Queen, I am not Queen
Of mine own heart, which every now and then
Beats me half dead: yet stay, this golden chain —
My father on a birthday gave it me,
And I have broken with my father — take
And wear it as a memorial of a morning
Which found me full of foolish doubts, and leaves me
As hopeful.
Renard (aside). Whew — the folly of all follies
Is to be love-sick for a shadow.
(*Aloud*) Madam,
This chains me to your service, not with gold,
But dearest links of love. Farewell, and trust me,
Philip is yours. [*Exit.*
Mary. Mine — but not yet all mine.

Enter USHER.

Usher. Your Council is in Session, please your Majesty.
Mary. Sir, let them sit. I must have time to breathe.
No, say I come. (*Exit* Usher.) I won by boldness once.
The Emperor counsell'd me to fly to Flanders.
I would not; but a hundred miles I rode,
Sent out my letters, call'd my friends together,
Struck home and won.
And when the Council would not crown me — thought
To bind me first by oaths I could not keep,

And keep with Christ and conscience
— was it boldness
Or weakness that won there? when I, their Queen,
Cast myself down upon my knees before them,
And those hard men brake into woman tears,
Ev'n Gardiner, all amazed, and in that passion
Gave me my Crown.

Enter ALICE.

Girl; hast thou ever heard
Slanders against Prince Philip in our Court?
Alice. What slanders? I, your Grace; no, never.
Mary. Nothing?
Alice. Never, your Grace.
Mary. See that you neither hear them nor repeat!
Alice (aside). Good Lord! but I have heard a thousand such.
Ay, and repeated them as often — mum!
Why comes that old fox-Fleming back again?

Enter RENARD.

Renard. Madam, I scarce had left your Grace's presence
Before I chanced upon the messenger
Who brings that letter which we waited for —
The formal offer of Prince Philip's hand.
It craves an instant answer, Ay or No.
Mary. An instant Ay or No! the Council sits.
Give it me quick.
Alice (stepping before her). Your Highness is all trembling.
Mary. Make way.
[*Exit into the Council Chamber.*
Alice. O, Master Renard, Master Renard,
If you have falsely painted your fine Prince;
Praised, where you should have blamed him, I pray God

No woman ever love you, Master
    Renard.
It breaks my heart to hear her moan
    at night
As tho' the nightmare never left her
    bed.
  Renard. My pretty maiden, tell me,
    did you ever
Sigh for a beard ?
  Alice. That's not a pretty question.
  Renard. Not prettily put ? I mean,
    my pretty maiden,
A pretty man for such a pretty
    maiden.
  Alice. My Lord of Devon is a pretty
    man.
I hate him. Well, but if I have, what
    then ?
  Renard. Then, pretty maiden, you
    should know that whether
A wind be warm or cold, it serves to
    fan
A kindled fire.
  Alice. According to the song.

His friends would praise him, I believed 'em,
  His foes would blame him, and I scorn'd
    'em,
His friends — as Angels I received 'em,
  His foes — the Devil had suborn'd 'em.

  Renard. Peace, pretty maiden.
I hear them stirring in the Council
    Chamber.
Lord Paget's "Ay" is sure — who
    else ? and yet,
They are all too much at odds to close
    at once
In one full-throated No ! Her High-
    ness comes.

Enter MARY.

  Alice. How deathly pale ! — a chair,
    your Highness.
        [*Bringing one to the* Queen.
  Renard.   Madam,
The Council ?
  Mary. Ay ! My Philip is all mine.
    [*Sinks into chair, half fainting.*

ACT II.

SCENE I. — ALLINGTON CASTLE.

  Sir Thomas Wyatt. I do not hear
    from Carew or the Duke
Of Suffolk, and till then I should not
    move.
The Duke hath gone to Leicester;
    Carew stirs
In Devon : that fine porcelain Courte-
    nay,
Save that he fears he might be crack'd
    in using,
(I have known a semi-madman in my
    time
So fancy-ridd'n) should be in Devon
    too.

Enter WILLIAM.
News abroad, William ?
  William. None so new, Sir Thomas,
and none so old, Sir Thomas. No
new news that Philip comes to wed
Mary, no old news that all men hate
it. Old Sir Thomas would have hated
it. The bells are ringing at Maidstone.
Doesn't your worship hear ?
  Wyatt. Ay, for the Saints are come
    to reign again.
Most like it is a Saint's-day. There's
    no call
As yet for me ; so in this pause, before
The mine be fired, it were a pious
    work
To string my father's sonnets, left
    about
Like loosely-scatter'd jewels, in fair
    order,
And head them with a lamer rhyme
    of mine,
To grace his memory.
  William. Ay, why not, Sir Thomas ?
He was a fine courtier, he ; Queen
Anne loved him. All the women
loved him. I loved him, I was in
Spain with him. I couldn't eat in
Spain, I couldn't sleep in Spain. I
hate Spain, Sir Thomas.
  Wyatt. But thou could'st drink in
    Spain if I remember.

William. Sir Thomas, we may grant the wine. Old Sir Thomas always granted the wine.

Wyatt. Hand me the casket with my father's sonnets.

William. Ay — sonnets — a fine courtier of the old Court, old Sir Thomas. [*Exit.*

Wyatt. Courtier of many courts, he loved the more
His own gray towers, plain life and letter'd peace,
To read and rhyme in solitary fields,
The lark above, the nightingale below,
And answer them in song. The sire begets
Not half his likeness in the son. I fail
Where he was fullest: yet — to write it down. [*He writes.*

Re-enter WILLIAM.

William. There *is* news, there *is* news, and no call for sonnet-sorting now, nor for sonnet-making either, but ten thousand men on Penenden Heath all calling after your worship, and your worship's name heard into Maidstone market, and your worship the first man in Kent and Christendom, for the Queen's down, and the world's up, and your worship a-top of it.

Wyatt. Inverted Æsop — mountain out of mouse.
Say for ten thousand ten — and pot-house knaves,
Brain-dizzied with a draught of morning ale.

Enter ANTONY KNYVETT.

William. Here's Antony Knyvett.

Knyvett. Look you, Master Wyatt, Tear up that woman's work there.

Wyatt. No; not these,
Dumb children of my father, that will speak
When I and thou and all rebellions lie
Dead bodies without voice. Song flies you know
For ages.

Knyvett. Tut, your sonnet's a flying ant,
Wing'd for a moment.

Wyatt. Well, for mine own work,
[*Tearing the paper.*
It lies there in six pieces at your feet;
For all that I can carry it in my head.

Knyvett. If you can carry your head upon your shoulders.

Wyatt. I fear you come to carry it off my shoulders,
And sonnet-making's safer.

Knyvett. Why, good Lord,
Write you as many sonnets as you will.
Ay, but not now; what, have you eyes, ears, brains?
This Philip and the black-faced swarms of Spain,
The hardest, cruellest people in the world,
Come locusting upon us, eat us up,
Confiscate lands, goods, money — Wyatt, Wyatt,
Wake, or the stout old island will become
A rotten limb of Spain. They roar for you
On Penenden Heath, a thousand of them — more —
All arm'd, waiting a leader; there's no glory
Like his who saves his country: and you sit
Sing-songing here; but, if I'm any judge,
By God, you are as poor a poet, Wyatt,
As a good soldier.

Wyatt. You as poor a critic
As an honest friend: you stroke me on one cheek,
Buffet the other. Come, you bluster, Antony!
You know I know all this. I must not move
Until I hear from Carew and the Duke.
I fear the mine is fired before the time.

Knyvett (*showing a paper*). But here's some Hebrew. Faith, I half forgot it.

Look ; can you make it English ?   A
   strange youth
Suddenly thrust it on me, whisper'd,
   "Wyatt,"
And whisking round a corner, show'd
   his back
Before I read his face.
  Wyatt. Ha ! Courtenay's cipher.
                    [*Reads.*
  " Sir Peter Carew fled to France : it
is thought the Duke will be taken.
I am with you still ; but, for appear-
ance sake, stay with the Queen. Gardiner knows, but the Council are all at
odds, and the Queen hath no force for
resistance. Move, if you move, at
once."

Is Peter Carew fled ?   Is the Duke
   taken ?
Down scabbard, and out sword ! and
   let Rebellion
Roar till throne rock, and crown fall.
   No ; not that ;
But we will teach Queen Mary how to
   reign.
Who are those that shout below there ?
  Knyvett.   Why, some fifty
That follow'd me from Penenden
   Heath in hope
To hear you speak.
  Wyatt. Open the window, Knyvett ;
The mine is fired, and I will speak to
   them.

Men of Kent ; England of England ;
you that have kept your old customs
upright, while all the rest of England
bow'd theirs to the Norman, the cause
that hath brought us together is not
the cause of a county or a shire, but
of this England, in whose crown our
Kent is the fairest jewel. Philip shall
not wed Mary ; and ye have called me
to be your leader. I know Spain. I
have been there with my father ; I
have seen them in their own land ; I
have marked the haughtiness of their
nobles ; the cruelty of their priests.
If this man marry our Queen, however
the Council and the Commons may
fence round his power with restriction,

he will be King, King of England, my
masters ; and the Queen, and the laws,
and the people, his slaves. What ?
shall we have Spain on the throne and
in the parliament ; Spain in the pulpit
and on the law-bench ; Spain in all the
great offices of state ; Spain in our
ships, in our forts, in our houses, in
our beds ?
  Crowd. No ! no ! no Spain !
  William. No Spain in our beds —
that were worse than all. I have been
there with old Sir Thomas, and the
beds I know. I hate Spain.
  A Peasant. But, Sir Thomas, must we
levy war against the Queen's Grace ?
  Wyatt. No, my friend ; war *for* the
Queen's Grace — to save her from herself and Philip — war against Spain.
And think not we shall be alone —
thousands will flock to us. The
Council, the Court itself, is on our side.
The Lord Chancellor himself is on our
side. The King of France is with us ;
the King of Denmark is with us ; the
world is with us — war against Spain !
And if we move not now, yet it will be
known that we have moved ; and if
Philip come to be King, O, my God !
the rope, the rack, the thumbscrew,
the stake, the fire. If we move not
now, Spain moves, bribes our nobles
with her gold, and creeps, creeps
snake-like about our legs till we cannot move at all ; and ye know, my
masters, that wherever Spain hath
ruled she hath wither'd all beneath
her. Look at the New World — a
paradise made hell ; the red man, that
good helpless creature, starved,
maim'd, flogg'd, flay'd, burn'd, boil'd,
buried alive, worried by dogs ; and
here, nearer home, the Netherlands,
Sicily, Naples, Lombardy. I say no
more — only this, their lot is yours.
Forward to London with me ! forward
to London ! If ye love your liberties
or your skins, forward to London !
  Crowd. Forward to London !   A
    Wyatt ! a Wyatt !
  Wyatt. But first to Rochester, to
    take the guns

From out the vessels lying in the river.

Then on.

    A Peasant. Ay, but I fear we be too few, Sir Thomas.

    Wyatt. Not many yet. The world as yet, my friend,

Is not half-waked; but every parish tower

Shall clang and clash alarum as we pass,

And pour along the land, and swoll'n and fed

With indraughts and side-currents, in full force

Roll upon London.

    Crowd. A Wyatt! a Wyatt! Forward!

    Knyvett. Wyatt, shall we proclaim Elizabeth ?

    Wyatt. I'll think upon it, Knyvett.

    Knyvett.   Or Lady Jane ?

    Wyatt. No, poor soul ; no.

Ah, gray old castle of Allington, green field

Beside the brimming Medway, it may chance

That I shall never look upon you more.

    Knyvett. Come, now, you're sonnetting again.

    Wyatt.   Not I.

I'll have my head set higher in the state ;

Or — if the Lord God will it — on the stake.   [*Exeunt.*

SCENE II. — GUILDHALL.

SIR THOMAS WHITE (The Lord Mayor), LORD WILLIAM HOWARD, SIR RALPH BAGENHALL, ALDERMEN *and* CITIZENS.

    White. I trust the Queen comes hither with her guards.

    Howard. Ay, all in arms.

    [*Several of the citizens move hastily out of the hall.*

Why do they hurry out there ?

    White. My Lord, cut out the rotten from your apple,

Your apple eats the better. Let them go.

They go like those old Pharisees in John

Convicted by their conscience, arrant cowards,

Or tamperers with that treason out of Kent.

When will her Grace be here ?

    Howard.   In some few minutes.

She will address your guilds and companies.

I have striven in vain to raise a man for her.

But help her in this exigency, make

Your city loyal, and be the mightiest man

This day in England.

    White.   I am Thomas White.

Few things have fail'd to which I set my will.

I do my most and best.

    Howard.   You know that after

The Captain Brett, who went with your train bands

To fight with Wyatt, had gone over to him

With all his men, the Queen in that distress

Sent Cornwallis and Hastings to the traitor,

Feigning to treat with him about her marriage —

Know too what Wyatt said.

    White.   He'd sooner be,

While this same marriage question was being argued,

Trusted than trust — the scoundrel — and demanded

Possession of her person and the Tower.

    Howard. And four of her poor Council too, my Lord,

As hostages.

    White. I know it. What do and say

Your Council at this hour ?

    Howard.   I will trust you.

We fling ourselves on you, my Lord. The Council,

The Parliament as well, are troubled waters ;

And yet like waters of the fen they
    know not
Which way to flow. All hangs on her
    address,
And upon you, Lord Mayor.
    White.   How look'd the city
When now you past it? Quiet?
    Howard.   Like our Council,
Your city is divided. As we past,
Some hail'd, some hiss'd us. There
    were citizens
Stood each before his shut-up booth,
    and look'd
As grim and grave as from a funeral.
And here a knot of ruffians all in
    rags,
With execrating execrable eyes,
Glared at the citizen. Here was a
    young mother,
Her face on flame, her red hair all
    blown back,
She shrilling " Wyatt," while the boy
    she held
Mimick'd and piped her " Wyatt," as
    red as she
In hair and cheek; and almost elbow-
    ing her,
So close they stood, another, mute as
    death,
And white as her own milk; her babe
    in arms
Had felt the faltering of his mother's
    heart,
And look'd as bloodless. Here a pious
    Catholic,
Mumbling and mixing up in his scared
    prayers
Heaven and earth's Maries; over his
    bow'd shoulder
Scowl'd that world-hated and world-
    hating beast,
A haggard Anabaptist. Many such
    groups.
The names of Wyatt, Elizabeth,
    Courtenay,
Nay the Queen's right to reign—'fore
    God, the rogues —
Were freely buzzed among them. So
    I say
Your city is divided, and I fear
One scruple, this or that way, of suc-
    cess

Would turn it thither. Wherefore
    now the Queen
In this low pulse and palsy of the
    state,
Bade me to tell you that she counts on
    you
And on myself as her two hands; on
    you,
In your own city, as her right, my
    Lord,
For you are loyal.
    White.   Am I Thomas White?
One word before she comes. Eliza-
    beth —
Her name is much abused among
    these traitors.
Where is she? She is loved by all
    of us.
I scarce have heart to mingle in this
    matter,
If she should be mishandled.
    Howard.   No; she shall not.
The Queen had written her word to
    come to court:
Methought I smelt out Renard in the
    letter,
And fearing for her, sent a secret mis-
    sive,
Which told her to be sick. Happily
    or not,
It found her sick indeed.
    White.   God send her well;
Here comes her Royal Grace.

Enter Guards, Mary, *and* Gardiner.
    Sir Thomas White *leads her to a
    raised seat on the daïs.*

    White. I, the Lord Mayor, and
    these our companies
And guilds of London, gathered here,
    beseech
Your Highness to accept our lowliest
    thanks
For your most princely presence; and
    we pray
That we, your true and loyal citizens,
From your own royal lips, at once
    may know
The wherefore of this coming, and so
    learn
Your royal will, and do it. — I, Lord
    Mayor

Of London, and our guilds and companies.

Mary. In mine own person am I
come to you,
To tell you what indeed ye see and
know,
How traitorously these rebels out of
Kent
Have made strong head against our-
selves and you.
They would not have me wed the
Prince of Spain ;
That was their pretext — so they
spake at first —
But we sent divers of our Council to
them,
And by their answers to the question
ask'd,
It doth appear this marriage is the
least
Of all their quarrel.
They have betrayed the treason of
their hearts :
Seek to possess our person, hold our
Tower,
Place and displace our councillors, and
use
Both us and them according as they
will.
Now what I am ye know right well —
your Queen ;
To whom, when I was wedded to the
realm
And the realm's laws (the spousal
ring whereof,
Not ever to be laid aside, I wear
Upon this finger), ye did promise
full
Allegiance and obedience to the death.
Ye know my father was the rightful
heir
Of England, and his right came down
to me,
Corroborate by your acts of Parlia-
ment :
And as ye were most loving unto him,
So doubtless will ye show yourselves
to me.
Wherefore, ye will not brook that
anyone
Should seize our person, occupy our
state,

More specially a traitor so presumptu-
ous
As this same Wyatt, who hath tam-
per'd with
A public ignorance, and, under color
Of such a cause as hath no color, seeks
To bend the laws to his own will, and
yield
Full scope to persons rascal and for-
lorn,
To make free spoil and havock of
your goods.
Now as your Prince, I say,
I, that was never mother, cannot tell
How mothers love their children ; yet,
methinks,
A prince as naturally may love his
people
As these their children ; and be sure
your Queen
So loves you, and so loving, needs
must deem
This love by you return'd as heartily ;
And thro' this common knot and bond
of love,
Doubt not they will be speedily over-
thrown.
As to this marriage, ye shall under-
stand
We made thereto no treaty of ourselves,
And set no foot theretoward unadvised
Of all our Privy Council ; furthermore,
This marriage had the assent of those
to whom
The king, my father, did commit his
trust ;
Who not alone esteem'd it honorable,
But for the wealth and glory of our
realm,
And all our loving subjects, most ex-
pedient.
As to myself,
I am not so set on wedlock as to choose
But where I list, nor yet so amorous
That I must needs be husbanded ; I
thank God,
I have lived a virgin, and I noway doubt
But that with God's grace, I can live
so still.
Yet if it might please God that I
should leave
Some fruit of mine own body after me,

To be your king, ye would rejoice
    thereat,
And it would be your comfort, as I
    trust;
And truly, if I either thought or knew
This marriage should bring loss or
    danger to you,
My subjects, or impair in any way
This royal state of England, I would
    never
Consent thereto, nor marry while I live:
Moreover, if this marriage should not
    seem,
Before our own High Court of Parlia-
    ment,
To be of rich advantage to our realm,
We will refrain, and not alone from
    this,
Likewise from any other, out of which
Looms the least chance of peril to our
    realm.
Wherefore be bold, and with your law-
    ful Prince
Stand fast against our enemies and
    yours,
And fear them not.   I fear them not.
        My Lord,
I leave Lord William Howard in your
    city,
To guard and keep you whole and
    safe from all
The spoil and sackage aim'd at by
    these rebels,
Who mouth and foam against the
    Prince of Spain.
  Voices. Long live Queen Mary!   .
            Down with Wyatt!
                The Queen!
  White. Three voices from our guilds
    and companies!
You are shy and proud like English-
    men, my masters,
And will not trust your voices. Under-
    stand:
Your lawful Prince hath come to cast
    herself
On loyal hearts and bosoms, hoped to
    fall
Into the wide-spread arms of fealty,
And finds you statues.   Speak at once
    — and all!
For whom ?

Our sovereign Lady by King Harry's
    will;
The Queen of England — or the Kent-
    ish Squire ?
I know you loyal. Speak! in the
    name of God!
The Queen of England or the rabble
    of Kent ?
The reeking dungfork master of the
    mace !
Your havings wasted by the scythe
    and spade —
Your rights and charters hobnail'd
    into slush —
Your houses fired — your gutters
    bubbling blood ——
  Acclamation. No! No! The Queen!
    the Queen!
  White.   Your Highness hears
This burst and bass of loyal harmony,
And how we each and all of us abhor
The venomous, bestial, devilish revolt
Of Thomas Wyatt. Hear us now
    make oath
To raise your Highness thirty thou-
    sand men,
And arm and strike as with one hand,
    and brush
This Wyatt from our shoulders, like
    a flea
That might have leapt upon us un-
    awares.
Swear with me, noble fellow-citizens,
    all,
With all your trades, and guilds, and
    companies.
  Citizens. We swear !
  Mary. We thank your Lordship and
    your loyal city.
            [*Exit* Mary *attended.*
  White. I trust this day, thro' God,
    I have saved the crown.
  First Alderman. Ay, so my Lord
    of Pembroke in command
Of all her force be safe ; but there are
    doubts.
  Second Alderman. I hear that Gar-
    diner, coming with the Queen,
And meeting Pembroke, bent to his
    saddle-bow,
As if to win the man by flattering him.
Is he so safe to fight upon her side ?

First Alderman. If not, there's no
man safe.

White. Yes, Thomas White.
I am safe enough; no man need flatter me.

Second Alderman. Nay, no man
need; but did you mark our
Queen?
The color freely play'd into her
face,
And the half sight which makes her
look so stern,
Seem'd thro' that dim dilated world
of hers,
To read our faces; I have never seen
her
So queenly or so goodly.

White. Courage, sir,
That makes or man or woman look
their goodliest.
Die like the torn fox dumb, but never
whine
Like that poor heart, Northumberland,
at the block.

Bagenhall. The man had children,
and he whined for those.
Methinks most men are but poor-
hearted, else
Should we so dote on courage, were
it commoner?
The Queen stands up, and speaks for
her own self;
And all men cry, She is queenly, she
is goodly.
Yet she's no goodlier; tho' my Lord
Mayor here,
By his own rule, he hath been so bold
to-day,
Should look more goodly than the
rest of us.

White. Goodly? I feel most goodly heart and hand,
And strong to throw ten Wyatts and
all Kent.
Ha! ha! sir; but you jest; I love it
a jest
In time of danger shows the pulses
even.
Be merry! yet, Sir Ralph, you look
but sad.
I dare avouch you'd stand up for
yourself,

Tho' all the world should bay like
winter wolves.

Bagenhall. Who knows? the man
is proven by the hour.

White. The man should make the
hour, not this the man;
And Thomas White will prove this
Thomas Wyatt,
And he will prove an Iden to this
Cade,
And he will play the Walworth to
this Wat;
Come, sirs, we prate; hence all —
gather your men —
Myself must bustle. Wyatt comes
to Southwark;
I'll have the drawbridge hewn into
the Thames,
And see the citizens arm'd. Good
day; good day. [*Exit* White.

Bagenhall. One of much outdoor
bluster.

Howard. For all that,
Most honest, brave, and skilful; and
his wealth
A fountain of perennial alms — his
fault
So thoroughly to believe in his own
self.

Bagenhall. Yet thoroughly to believe in one's own self,
So one's own self be thorough, were
to do
Great things, my Lord.

Howard. It may be.

Bagenhall. I have heard
One of your Council fleer and jeer at
him.

Howard. The nursery-cocker'd child
will jeer at aught
That may seem strange beyond his
nursery.
The statesman that shall jeer and fleer
at men,
Makes enemies for himself and for his
king;
And if he jeer not seeing the true
man
Behind his folly, he is thrice the
fool;
And if he see the man and still will
jeer,

He is child and fool, and traitor to the
State.
Who is he? let me shun him.
   Bagenhall.   Nay, my Lord,
He is damn'd enough already.
   Howard.   I must set
The guard at Ludgate.   Fare you
well, Sir Ralph.
   Bagenhall. "Who knows?" I am for
    England. But who knows,
That knows the Queen, the Spaniard,
   and the Pope,
Whether I be for Wyatt, or the
   Queen?   [*Exeunt.*

SCENE III. — London Bridge.

Enter Sir Thomas Wyatt *and*
Brett.

   Wyatt. Brett, when the Duke of
   Norfolk moved against us
Thou cried'st "A Wyatt!" and flying
   to our side
Left his all bare, for which I love
   thee, Brett.
Have for thine asking aught that I
   can give,
For thro' thine help we are come to
   London Bridge;
But how to cross it balks me. I fear
   we cannot.
   Brett. Nay, hardly, save by boat,
   swimming, or wings.
   Wyatt. Last night I climb'd into
   the gate-house, Brett,
And scared the gray old porter and
   his wife.
And then I crept along the gloom and
   saw
They had hewn the drawbridge down
   into the river.
It roll'd as black as death; and that
   same tide
Which, coming with our coming,
   seem'd to smile
And sparkle like our fortune as thou
   saidest,
Ran sunless down, and moan'd against
   the piers.
But o'er the chasm I saw Lord William Howard

By torchlight, and his guard; four
   guns gaped at me,
Black, silent mouths: had Howard
   spied me there
And made them speak, as well he
   might have done,
Their voice had left me none to tell
   you this.
What shall we do?
   Brett. On somehow. To go back
Were to lose all.
   Wyatt. On over London Bridge
We cannot: stay we cannot; there is
   ordnance
On the White Tower and on the Devil's
   Tower,
And pointed full at Southwark; we
   must round
By Kingston Bridge.
   Brett.   Ten miles about.
   Wyatt.   Ev'n so.
But I have notice from our partisans
Within the city that they will stand
   by us
If Ludgate can be reach'd by dawn to-
   morrow.

Enter one of Wyatt's *men.*

   Man. Sir Thomas, I've found this
paper; pray your worship read it; I
know not my letters; the old priests
taught me nothing.
   Wyatt (*reads*). "Whosoever will
apprehend the traitor Thomas Wyatt
shall have a hundred pounds for reward."
   Man. Is that it? That's a big lot
of money.
   Wyatt. Ay, ay, my friend; not read
it? 'tis not written
Half plain enough. Give me a piece
   of paper!
   [*Writes* "Thomas Wyatt" *large.*
There, any man can read that.
         [*Sticks it in his cap.*
   Brett.   But that's foolhardy.
   Wyatt. No! boldness, which will
give my followers boldness.

Enter Man *with a prisoner.*

   Man. We found him, your worship,
a plundering o' Bishop Winchester's

house; he says he's a poor gentleman.

Wyatt. Gentleman! a thief! Go
hang him. Shall we make
Those that we come to serve our
sharpest foes?

Brett. Sir Thomas —
Wyatt. Hang him, I say.
Brett. Wyatt, but now you promised
me a boon.

Wyatt. Ay, and I warrant this fine
fellow's life.

Brett. Ev'n so; he was my neighbor
once in Kent.
He's poor enough, has drunk and
gambled out
All that he had, and gentleman he
was.
We have been glad together; let him
live.

Wyatt. He has gambled for his
life, and lost, he hangs.
No, no, my word's my word. Take thy
poor gentleman!
Gamble thyself at once out of my
sight,
Or I will dig thee with my dagger.
Away!
Women and children!

Enter a Crowd *of* WOMEN *and*
Children.

First Woman. O Sir Thomas, Sir
Thomas, pray you go away, Sir
Thomas, or you'll make the White
Tower a black 'un for us this blessed
day. He'll be the death on us;
and you'll set the Divil's Tower a-
spitting, and he'll smash all our bits
o' things worse than Philip o' Spain.

Second Woman. Don't ye now go to
think that we be for Philip o' Spain.

Third Woman. No, we know that
ye be come to kill the Queen, and
we'll pray for you all on our bended
knees. But o' God's mercy don't ye
kill the Queen here, Sir Thomas; look
ye, here's little Dickon, and little
Robin, and little Jenny — though she's
but a side-cousin — and all on our
knees, we pray you to kill the Queen
further off, Sir Thomas.

Wyatt. My friends, I have not come
to kill the Queen
Or here or there: I come to save you
all,
And I'll go further off.

Crowd. Thanks, Sir Thomas, we be
beholden to you, and we'll pray for
you on our bended knees till our lives'
end.

Wyatt. Be happy, I am your friend.
To Kingston, forward! [*Exeunt.*

SCENE IV. — ROOM IN THE GATE-
HOUSE OF WESTMINSTER PALACE.

MARY, ALICE, GARDINER, RENARD,
LADIES.

Gardiner. Their cry is, Philip never
shall be king.

Mary. Lord Pembroke in command
of all our force
Will front their cry and shatter them
into dust.

Alice. Was not Lord Pembroke
with Northumberland?
O madam, if this Pembroke should be
false?

Mary. No, girl; most brave and
loyal, brave and loyal.
His breaking with Northumberland
broke Northumberland.
At the park gate he hovers with our
guards.
These Kentish ploughmen cannot
break the guards.

Enter MESSENGER.

Messenger. Wyatt, your Grace, hath
broken thro' the guards,
And gone to Ludgate.

Gardiner. Madam, I much fear
That all is lost; but we can save your
Grace.
The river still is free. I do beseech
you,
There yet is time, take boat and pass
to Windsor.

Mary. I pass to Windsor and I lose
my crown.

Gardiner. Pass, then, I pray your
Highness, to the Tower.

Mary. I shall but be their prisoner
　in the Tower.
Cries without. The traitor! treason!
　Pembroke!
Ladies. 　　　　　Treason! treason!
Mary. Peace.
False to Northumberland, is he false
　to me?
Bear witness, Renard, that I live and
　die
The true and faithful bride of Philip
　— A sound
Of feet and voices thickening hither
　— blows —
Hark, there is battle at the palace
　gates,
And I will out upon the gallery.
Ladies. No, no, your Grace; see
　there the arrows flying.
Mary. I am Harry's daughter, Tu-
　dor, and not fear.
　　　　　　[*Goes out on the gallery.*
The guards are all driven in, skulk
　into corners
Like rabbits to their holes. A gra-
　cious guard
Truly; shame on them! they have
　shut the gates!

Enter SIR ROBERT SOUTHWELL.

Southwell. The porter, please your
　Grace, hath shut the gates
On friend and foe. Your gentlemen-
　at-arms,
If this be not your Grace's order, cry
To have the gates set wide again, and
　they
With their good battleaxes will do you
　right
Against all traitors.
Mary. They are the flower of Eng-
　land; set the gates wide.
　　　　　　　　[*Exit* Southwell.

Enter COURTENAY.

Courtenay. All lost, all lost, all
　yielded! a barge, a barge!
The Queen must to the Tower.
Mary. 　　Whence come you, sir?
Courtenay. From Charing Cross;
　the rebels broke us there,

And I sped hither with what haste I
　might
To save my royal cousin.
Mary. 　　　Where is Pembroke?
Courtenay. I left him somewhere in
　the thick of it.
Mary. Left him and fled; and thou
　that would'st be King,
And hast nor heart nor honor. I my-
　self
Will down into the battle and there
　bide
The upshot of my quarrel, or die with
　those
That are no cowards and no Courte-
　nays.
Courtenay. I do not love your Grace
　should call me coward.

Enter another MESSENGER.

Messenger. Over, your Grace, all
　crush'd; the brave Lord Wil-
　liam
Thrust him from Ludgate, and the
　traitor flying
To Temple Bar, there by Sir Maurice
　Berkeley
Was taken prisoner.
Mary. 　　To the Tower with *him!*
Messenger. 'Tis said he told Sir
　Maurice there was one
Cognizant of this, and party thereunto,
My Lord of Devon.
Mary. 　　To the Tower with *him!*
Courtenay. O la, the Tower, the
　Tower, always the Tower,
I shall grow into it — I shall be the
　Tower.
Mary. Your lordship may not have
　so long to wait.
Remove him!
Courtenay. La, to whistle out my
　life,
And carve my coat upon the walls
　again!
　　　　　[*Exit* Courtenay *guarded.*
Messenger. Also this Wyatt did
　confess the Princess
Cognizant thereof, and party there-
　unto.
Mary. What? whom — whom did
　you say?

Messenger.　　Elizabeth,
Your Royal sister.
　　Mary.　　To the Tower with *her !*
My foes are at my feet and I am
　　Queen.
[*Gardiner and her* Ladies *kneel to her.*
　　Gardiner (*rising*).　There let them
　　lie, your footstool! (*Aside.*) Can
　　I strike
Elizabeth ? — not now and save the
　　life
Of Devon : if I save him, he and his
Are bound to me — may strike here-
　　after. (*Aloud.*) Madam,
What Wyatt said, or what they said
　　he said,
Cries of the moment and the street —
　　Mary.　　　　　　　He said it.
　　Gardiner. Your courts of justice
　　will determine that.
　　Renard (*advancing*). I trust by this
　　your Highness will allow
Some spice of wisdom in my telling
　　you,
When last we talk'd, that Philip would
　　not come
Till Guildford Dudley and the Duke of
　　Suffolk,
And Lady Jane had left us.
　　Mary.　　　　　They shall die.
　　Renard. And your so loving sister ?
　　Mary.　　　　　She shall die.
My foes are at my feet, and Philip
　　King.　　　　　　　[*Exeunt.*

ACT III.

SCENE I. — The Conduit in Grace-
　　　　church,

Painted with the Nine Worthies, among
　them King Henry VIII. holding a
　book, on it inscribed " Verbum Dei.*"*

Enter Sir Ralph Bagenhall *and* Sir
　　Thomas Stafford.
　　Bagenhall. A hundred here and
　　hundreds hang'd in Kent.
The tigress had unsheath'd her nails
　　at last,

And Renard and the Chancellor sharp-
　　en'd them.
In every London street a gibbet
　　stood.
They are down to-day. Here by this
　　house was one ;
The traitor husband dangled at the
　　door,
And when the traitor wife came out
　　for bread
To still the petty treason therewithin,
Her cap would brush his heels.
　　Stafford.　　　　It is Sir Ralph,
And muttering to himself as hereto-
　　fore.
Sir, see you aught up yonder ?
　　Bagenhall.　　I miss something.
The tree that only bears dead fruit is
　　gone.
　　Stafford. What tree, sir ?
　　Bagenhall.　　Well, the tree in
　　Virgil, sir,
That bears not its own apples.
　　Stafford.　　What ! the gallows ?
　　Bagenhall. Sir, this dead fruit was
　　ripening overmuch,
And had to be removed lest living
　　Spain
Should sicken at dead England.
　　Stafford.　　　　Not so dead,
But that a shock may rouse her.
　　Bagenhall.　　　　I believe
Sir Thomas Stafford ?
　　Stafford.　　I am ill disguised.
　　Bagenhall. Well, are you not in
　　peril here ?
　　Stafford.　　I think so.
I came to feel the pulse of England,
　　whether
It beats hard at this marriage.　Did
　　you see it ?
　　Bagenhall. Stafford, I am a sad man
　　and a serious.
Far liefer had I in my country hall
Been reading some old book, with
　　mine old hound
Couch'd at my hearth, and mine old
　　flask of wine
Beside me, than have seen it : yet I
　　saw it.
　　Stafford. Good, was it splendid ?
　　Bagenhall. Ay, if Dukes, and Earls.

And Counts, and sixty Spanish cava-
    liers,
Some six or seven Bishops, diamonds,
    pearls,
That royal commonplace too, cloth
    of gold,
Could make it so.
    Stafford. And what was Mary's
    dress ?
    Bagenhall. Good faith, I was too
    sorry for the woman
To mark the dress. She wore red
    shoes !
    Stafford.   Red shoes !
    Bagenhall. Scarlet, as if her feet
    were wash'd in blood,
As if she had waded in it.
    Stafford.   Were your eyes
So bashful that you look'd no higher ?
    Bagenhall.   A diamond,
And Philip's gift, as proof of Philip's
    love,
Who hath not any for any, — tho' a
    true one,
Blazed false upon her heart.
    Stafford. But this proud Prince —
    Bagenhall. Nay, he is King, you
    know, the King of Naples.
The father ceded Naples, that the son
Being a King, might wed a Queen —
    O he
Flamed in brocade — white satin his
    trunkhose,
Inwrought with silver, — on his neck
    a collar,
Gold, thick with diamonds ; hanging
    down from this
The Golden Fleece — and round his
    knee, misplaced,
Our English Garter, studded with
    great emeralds,
Rubies, I know not what. Have you
    had enough
Of all this gear ?
    Stafford. Ay, since you hate the
    telling it.
How look'd the Queen ?
    Bagenhall. No fairer for her jewels.
And I could see that as the new-made
    couple
Came from the Minster, moving side
    by side

Beneath one canopy, ever and anon
She cast on him a vassal smile of
    love,
Which Philip with a glance of some
    distaste,
Or so methought, return'd. I may be
    wrong, sir.
This marriage will not hold.
    Stafford.   I think with you.
The King of France will help to break
    it.
    Bagenhall.   France !
We once had half of France, and
    hurl'd our battles
Into the heart of Spain ; but England
    now
Is but a ball chuck'd between France
    and Spain,
His in whose hand she drops ; Harry
    of Bolingbroke
Had holpen Richard's tottering
    throne to stand,
Could Harry have foreseen that all
    our nobles
Would perish on the civil slaughter-
    field,
And leave the people naked to the
    crown,
And the crown naked to the people ;
    the crown
Female, too ! Sir, no woman's regimen
Can save us. We are fallen, and as I
    think,
Never to rise again.
    Stafford. You are too black-
    blooded.
I'd make a move myself to hinder
    that :
I know some lusty fellows there in
    France.
    Bagenhall. You would but make us
    weaker, Thomas Stafford.
Wyatt was a good soldier, yet he
    fail'd,
And strengthen'd Philip.
    Stafford. Did not his last breath
Clear Courtenay and the Princess
    from the charge
Of being his co-rebels ?
    Bagenhall.   Ay, but then
What such a one as Wyatt says is
    nothing :

We have no men among us. The new
    Lords
Are quieted with their sop of Abbey-
    lands,
And ev'n before the Queen's face
    Gardiner buys them
With Philip's gold. All greed, no
    faith, no courage!
Why, ev'n the haughty prince, North-
    umberland,
The leader of our Reformation, knelt
And blubber'd like a lad, and on the
    scaffold
Recanted, and resold himself to Rome.
    Stafford. I swear you do your
        country wrong, Sir Ralph.
I know a set of exiles over there,
Dare-devils, that would eat fire and
    spit it out
At Philip's beard : they pillage Spain
    already.
The French King winks at it. An
    hour will come
When they will sweep her from the
    seas. No men?
Did not Lord Suffolk die like a true
    man?
Is not Lord William Howard a true
    man?
Yea, you yourself, altho' you are
    black-blooded :
And I, by gold, believe myself a man.
Ay, even in the church there is a
    man —
Cranmer.
Fly would he not, when all men bade
    him fly.
And what a letter he wrote against
    the Pope!
There's a brave man, if any.
    Bagenhall.   Ay ; if it hold.
    Crowd (coming on). God save their
        Graces!
    Stafford.   Bagenhall, I see
The Tudor green and white. (*Trum-*
    pets.) They are coming now.
And here's a crowd as thick as her-
    ring-shoals.
    Bagenhall. Be limpets to this pillar,
        or we are torn
Down the strong wave of brawlers.
    Crowd. God save their Graces!

    [*Procession of Trumpeters, Jave-*
    lin-men, etc. ; then Spanish and
    Flemish Nobles intermingled.
    Stafford. Worth seeing, Bagenhall!
    These black dog-Dons
Garb themselves bravely. Who's the
    long-face there,
Looks very Spain of very Spain?
    Bagenhall.   The Duke
Of Alva, an iron soldier.
    Stafford.   And the Dutchman,
Now laughing at some jest?
    Bagenhall.   William of Orange,
William the Silent.
    Stafford. Why do they call him so?
    Bagenhall. He keeps, they say,
        some secret that may cost
Philip his life.
    Stafford. But then he looks so
        merry.
    Bagenhall. I cannot tell you why
        they call him so.
    [*The* King *and* Queen *pass, at-*
    tended by Peers of the Realm,
    Officers of State, etc. Cannon
    shot off.
    Crowd. Philip and Mary, Philip
        and Mary!
Long live the King and Queen, Philip
    and Mary!
    Stafford. They smile as if content
        with one another.
    Bagenhall. A smile abroad is oft a
        scowl at home.
    [King *and* Queen *pass on. Pro-*
    cession.
    First Citizen. I thought this Philip
had been one of those black devils of
Spain, but he hath a yellow beard.
    Second Citizen. Not red like
Iscariot's.
    First Citizen. Like a carrot's, as
thou say'st, and English carrot's better
than Spanish licorice; but I thought
he was a beast.
    Third Citizen. Certain I had heard
that every Spaniard carries a tail like
a devil under his trunk-hose.
    Tailor. Ay, but see what trunk-
hoses! Lord! they be fine; I never
stitch'd none such. They make amends
for the tails.

Fourth Citizen. Tut! every Spanish priest will tell you that all English heretics have tails.

Fifth Citizen. Death and the Devil — if he find I have one —

Fourth Citizen. Lo! thou hast call'd them up! here they come — a pale horse for Death and Gardiner for the Devil.

Enter GARDINER (*turning back from the procession*).

Gardiner. Knave, wilt thou wear thy cap before the Queen?

Man. My Lord, I stand so squeezed among the crowd
I cannot lift my hands unto my head.

Gardiner. Knock off his cap there, some of you about him!
See there be others that can use their hands.
Thou art one of Wyatt's men?

Man.   No, my Lord, no.

Gardiner. Thy name, thou knave?

Man.   I am nobody, my Lord.

Gardiner (*shouting*). God's passion! knave, thy name?

Man.   I have ears to hear.

Gardiner. Ay, rascal, if I leave thee ears to hear.
Find out his name and bring it me (*to Attendant*).

Attendant.   Ay, my Lord.

Gardiner. Knave, thou shalt lose thine ears and find thy tongue,
And shalt be thankful if I leave thee that. [*Coming before the Conduit.*
The conduit painted — the nine worthies — ay!
But then what's here? King Harry with a scroll.
Ha — Verbum Dei — verbum — word of God!
God's passion! do you know the knave that painted it?

Attendant. I do, my Lord.

Gardiner. Tell him to paint it out,
And put some fresh device in lieu of it —
A pair of gloves, a pair of gloves, sir; ha?
There is no heresy there.

Attendant.   I will, my Lord;
The man shall paint a pair of gloves.
    I am sure
(Knowing the man) he wrought it ignorantly,
And not from any malice.

Gardiner.   Word of God
In English! over this the brainless loons
That cannot spell Esaïas from St. Paul,
Make themselves drunk and mad, fly out and flare
Into rebellions. I'll have their bibles burnt.
The bible is the priest's. Ay! fellow, what!
Stand staring at me! shout, you gaping rogue!

Man. I have, my Lord, shouted till I am hoarse.

Gardiner. What hast thou shouted, knave?

Man.   ' Long live Queen Mary!

Gardiner. Knave, there be two.
There be both King and Queen,
Philip and Mary. Shout!

Man.   Nay, but, my Lord,
The Queen comes first, Mary and Philip.

Gardiner.   Shout, then,
Mary and Philip!

Man.   Mary and Philip!

Gardiner.   Now,
Thou hast shouted for thy pleasure, shout for mine!
Philip and Mary!

Man.   Must it be so, my Lord?

Gardiner. Ay, knave.

Man.   Philip and Mary!

Gardiner.   I distrust thee.
Thine is a half voice and a lean assent.
What is thy name?

Man.   Sanders.

Gardiner.   What else?

Man.   Zerubbabel.

Gardiner. Where dost thou live?

Man.   In Cornhill.

Gardiner. Where, knave, where?

Man. Sign of the Talbot.

Gardiner. Come to me to-morrow. —

Rascal! this land is like a hill of fire,
One crater opens when another shuts.
But so I get the laws against the heretic,
Spite of Lord Paget and Lord William Howard,
And others of our Parliament, revived,
I will show fire on my side — stake and fire —
Sharp work and short. The knaves are easily cow'd.
Follow their Majesties.

    [*Exit. The crowd following.*
Bagenhall.   As proud as Becket.
Stafford. You would not have him murder'd as Becket was?
Bagenhall. No — murder fathers murder: but I say
There is no man — there was one woman with us —
It was a sin to love her married, dead
I cannot choose but love her.
   Stafford.   Lady Jane?
   Crowd (*going off*). God save their Graces!
   Stafford.   Did you see her die?
   Bagenhall. No, no; her innocent blood had blinded me.
You call me too black-blooded — true enough
Her dark dead blood is in my heart with mine.
If ever I cry out against the Pope
Her dark dead blood that ever moves with mine
Will stir the living tongue and make the cry.
   Stafford. Yet doubtless you can tell me how she died?
   Bagenhall. Seventeen — and knew eight languages — in music
Peerless — her needle perfect, and her learning
Beyond the churchmen; yet so meek, so modest,
So wife-like humble to the trivial boy
Mismatch'd with her for policy! I have heard
She would not take a last farewell of him,
She fear'd it might unman him for his end.

She could not be unmann'd — no, nor outwoman'd —
Seventeen — a rose of grace!
Girl never breathed to rival such a rose;
Rose never blew that equall'd such a bud.
   Stafford. Pray you go on.
   Bagenhall. She came upon the scaffold,
And said she was condemn'd to die for treason;
She had but follow'd the device of those
Her nearest kin: she thought they knew the laws.
But for herself, she knew but little law,
And nothing of the titles to the crown;
She had no desire for that, and wrung her hands,
And trusted God would save her thro' the blood
Of Jesus Christ alone.
   Stafford.   Pray you go on.
   Bagenhall. Then knelt and said the Miserere Mei —
But all in English, mark you; rose again,
And, when the headsman pray'd to be forgiven,
Said " You will give me my true crown at last,
But do it quickly; " then all wept but she,
Who changed not color when she saw the block,
But ask'd him, childlike: " Will you take it off
Before I lay me down? " "No, madam," he said,
Gasping; and when her innocent eyes were bound,
She, with her poor blind hands feeling — "where is it?
Where is it? " — You must fancy that which follow'd,
If you have heart to do it!
   Crowd (*in the distance*). God save their Graces!
   Stafford. Their Graces, our disgraces! God confound them!

Why, she's grown bloodier! when I
last was here,
This was against her conscience —
would be murder!
  Bagenhall. The "Thou shalt do no
murder," which God's hand
Wrote on her conscience, Mary rubb'd
out pale —
She could not make it white — and
over that,
Traced in the blackest text of Hell —
"Thou shalt!"
And sign'd it — Mary!
  Stafford. Philip and the Pope
Must have sign'd too. I hear this
Legate's coming
To bring us absolution from the Pope.
The Lords and Commons will bow
down before him —
You are of the house? what will you
do, Sir Ralph?
  Bagenhall. And why should I be
bolder than the rest,
Or honester than all?
  Stafford. But, sir, if I —
And oversea they say this state of
yours
Hath no more mortice than a tower of
cards;
And that a puff would do it — then
if I
And others made that move I touch'd
upon,
Back'd by the power of France, and
landing here,
Came with a sudden splendor, shout,
and show,
And dazzled men and deafen'd by
some bright
Loud venture, and the people so un-
quiet —
And I the race of murder'd Bucking-
ham —
Not for myself, but for the kingdom
— Sir,
I trust that you would fight along
with us.
  Bagenhall. No; you would fling
your lives into the gulf.
  Stafford. But if this Philip, as he's
like to do,
Left Mary a wife-widow here alone,

Set up a viceroy, sent his myriads
hither
To seize upon the forts and fleet, and
make us
A Spanish province; would you not
fight then?
  Bagenhall. I think I should fight
then.
  Stafford. I am sure of it.
Hist! there's the face coming on here
of one
Who knows me. I must leave you.
Fare you well,
You'll hear of me again.
  Bagenhall. Upon the scaffold.
      [*Exeunt.*

SCENE II. — Room in Whitehall
Palace.

    Mary. *Enter* Philip *and*
    Cardinal Pole.

  Pole. Ave Maria, gratia plena, Bene-
dicta tu in mulieribus.
  Mary. Loyal and royal cousin,
humblest thanks.
Had you a pleasant voyage up the
river?
  Pole. We had your royal barge, and
that same chair,
Or rather throne of purple, on the deck.
Our silver cross sparkled before the
prow,
The ripples twinkled at their diamond-
dance,
The boats that follow'd, were as glow-
ing-gay
As regal gardens; and your flocks of
swans,
As fair and white as angels; and your
shores
Wore in mine eyes the green of Para-
dise.
My foreign friends, who dream'd us
blanketed
In ever-closing fog, were much amazed
To find as fair a sun as might have
flash'd
Upon their lake of Garda, fire the
Thames;
Our voyage by sea was all but miracle;

And here the river flowing from the sea,
Not toward it (for they thought not of our tides),
Seem'd as a happy miracle to make glide —
In quiet — home your banish'd countryman.

Mary. We heard that you were sick in Flanders, cousin.

Pole. A dizziness.

Mary. And how came you round again ?

Pole. The scarlet thread of Rahab saved her life ;
And mine, a little letting of the blood.

Mary. Well ? now ?

Pole. Ay, cousin, as the heathen giant
Had but to touch the ground, his force return'd —
Thus, after twenty years of banishment,
Feeling my native land beneath my foot,
I said thereto : " Ah, native land of mine,
Thou art much beholden to this foot of mine,
That hastes with full commission from the Pope
To absolve thee from thy guilt of heresy.
Thou hast disgraced me and attainted me,
And mark'd me ev'n as Cain, and I return
As Peter, but to bless thee : make me well."
Methinks the good land heard me, for to-day
My heart beats twenty, when I see you, cousin.
Ah, gentle cousin, since your Herod's death,
How oft hath Peter knock'd at Mary's gate !
And Mary would have risen and let him in,
But, Mary, there were those within the house
Who would not have it.

Mary. True, good cousin Pole ;
And there were also those without the house
Who would not have it.

Pole. I believe so, cousin.
State-policy and church-policy are conjoint,
But Janus-faces looking diverse ways.
I fear the Emperor much misvalued me.
But all is well ; 'twas ev'n the will of God,
Who, waiting till the time had ripen'd, now,
Makes me his mouth of holy greeting. " Hail,
Daughter of God, and saver of the faith,
Sit benedictus fructus ventris tui ! "

Mary. Ah, heaven !

Pole. Unwell, your Grace ?

Mary. No, cousin, happy —
Happy to see you ; never yet so happy
Since I was crown'd.

Pole. Sweet cousin, you forget
That long low minster where you gave your hand
To this great Catholic King.

Philip. Well said, Lord Legate.

Mary. Nay, not well said ; I thought of you my liege,
Ev'n as I spoke.

Philip. Ay, Madam ; my Lord Paget
Waits to present our Council to the Legate.
Sit down here, all ; Madam, between us you.

Pole. Lo, now you are enclosed with boards of cedar,
Our little sister of the Song of Songs !
You are doubly fenced and shielded sitting here
Between the two most high-set thrones on earth,
The Emperor's highness happily symboll'd by
The King your husband, the Pope's Holiness
By mine own self.

Mary. True, cousin, I am happy.
When will you that we summon both our houses

To take this absolution from your lips,
And be regather'd to the Papal fold?

Pole. In Britain's calendar the brightest day
Beheld our rough forefathers break their Gods,
And clasp the faith in Christ; but after that
Might not St. Andrew's be her happiest day?

Mary. Then these shall meet upon St. Andrew's day.

Enter PAGET, *who presents the Council. Dumb show.*

Pole. I am an old man wearied with my journey,
Ev'n with my joy. Permit me to withdraw.
To Lambeth?

Philip. Ay, Lambeth has ousted Cranmer.
It was not meet the heretic swine should live
In Lambeth.

Mary. There or anywhere, or at all.

Philip. We have had it swept and garnish'd after him.

Pole. Not for the seven devils to enter in?

Philip. No, for we trust they parted in the swine.

Pole. True, and I am the Angel of the Pope.
Farewell, your Graces.

Philip. Nay, not here — to me;
I will go with you to the waterside.

Pole. Not be my Charon to the counter side?

Philip. No, my Lord Legate, the Lord Chancellor goes.

Pole. And unto no dead world; but Lambeth palace,
Henceforth a centre of the living faith.
[*Exeunt* Philip, Pole, Paget, *etc.*

Manet Mary.

Mary. He hath awaked! he hath awaked!
He stirs within the darkness!

Oh, Philip, husband! now thy love to mine
Will cling more close, and those bleak manners thaw,
That make me shamed and tongue-tied in my love.
The second Prince of Peace —
The great unborn defender of the Faith,
Who will avenge me of mine enemies —
He comes, and my star rises.
The stormy Wyatts and Northumberlands,
The proud ambitions of Elizabeth,
And all her fieriest partisans — are pale
Before my star!
The light of this new learning wanes and dies:
The ghosts of Luther and Zuinglius fade
Into the deathless hell which is their doom
Before my star!
His sceptre shall go forth from Ind to Ind!
His sword shall hew the heretic peoples down!
His faith shall clothe the world that will be his,
Like universal air and sunshine! Open,
Ye everlasting gates! The King is here! —
My star, my son!

Enter PHILIP, DUKE OF ALVA, *etc.*

Oh, Philip, come with me;
Good news have I to tell you, news to make
Both of us happy — ay, the Kingdom too.
Nay come with me — one moment!

Philip (*to* Alva). More than that:
There was one here of late — William the Silent
They call him — he is free enough in talk,
But tells me nothing. You will be, we trust,
Sometime the viceroy of those provinces —

He must deserve his surname better.
Alva.   Ay, sir;
Inherit the Great Silence.
Philip.   True; the provinces
Are hard to rule and must be hardly
ruled;
Most fruitful, yet, indeed, an empty
rind,
All hollow'd out with stinging heresies;
And for their heresies, Alva, they will
fight;
You must break them or they break
you.
Alva (proudly).   The first.
Philip. Good!
Well, Madam, this new happiness of
mine?   [*Exeunt.*

Enter THREE PAGES.

First Page. News, mates! a miracle,
a miracle! news!
The bell must ring; Te Deums must
be sung;
The Queen hath felt the motion of her
babe!
Second Page. Ay; but see here!
First Page.   See what?
Second Page. This paper, Dickon.
I found it fluttering at the palace
gates: —
" The Queen of England is delivered
of a dead dog!"
Third Page. These are the things
that madden her. Fie upon it!
First Page. Ay; but I hear she
hath a dropsy, lad,
Or a high-dropsy, as the doctors call it.
Third Page. Fie on her dropsy, so
she have a dropsy!
I know that she was ever sweet to me.
First Page. For thou and thine are
Roman to the core.
Third Page. So thou and thine must
be. Take heed!
First Page.   Not I,
And whether this flash of news be
false or true,
So the wine run, and there be revelry,
Content am I. Let all the steeples
clash,
Till the sun dance, as upon Easter Day.
                         [*Exeunt.*

SCENE III. — GREAT HALL IN
WHITEHALL.

*At the far end a daïs. On this three
chairs, two under one canopy for* MARY
and PHILIP, *another on the right of
these for* POLE. *Under the daïs on
POLE's side, ranged along the wall, sit
all the Spiritual Peers, and along the
wall opposite, all the Temporal. The
Commons on cross benches in front, a
line of approach to the daïs between
them. In the foreground,* SIR RALPH
BAGENHALL *and other Members of
the* Commons.

First Member. St. Andrew's day;
sit close, sit close, we are friends.
Is reconciled the word? the Pope
again?
It must be thus; and yet, cocksbody!
how strange
That Gardiner, once so one with all of us
Against this foreign marriage, should
have yielded
So utterly! — strange! but stranger
still that he,
So fierce against the Headship of the
Pope,
Should play the second actor in this
pageant
That brings him in; such a cameleon
he!
Second Member. This Gardiner
turn'd his coat in Henry's time;
The serpent that hath slough'd will
slough again.
Third Member. Tut, then we all are
serpents.
Second Member. Speak for yourself.
Third Member. Ay, and for Gar-
diner! being English citizen,
How should he bear a bridegroom
out of Spain?
The Queen would have him! being
English churchman
How should he bear the headship of
the Pope?
The Queen would have it! Statesmen
that are wise
Shape a necessity, as a sculptor clay,
To their own model.

Second Member. Statesmen that are
    wise
Take truth herself for model. What
    say you ?   [*To* Sir Ralph
    Bagenhall.
Bagenhall. We talk and talk.
First Member. Ay, and what use to
    talk ?
Philip's no sudden alien — the Queen's
    husband,
He's here, and king, or will be — yet
    cocksbody !
So hated here ! I watch'd a hive of
    late ;
My seven-years' friend was with me,
    my young boy ;
Out crept a wasp, with half the swarm
    behind.
" Philip ! " says he. I had to cuff the
    rogue
For infant treason.
    Third Member. But they say that
    bees,
If any creeping life invade their hive
Too gross to be thrust out, will build
    him round,
And bind him in from harming of
    their combs.
And Philip by these articles is bound
From stirring hand or foot to wrong
    the realm.
    Second Member. By bonds of bees-
    wax, like your creeping thing ;
But your wise bees had stung him first
    to death.
    Third Member. Hush, hush !
You wrong the Chancellor: the clauses
    added
To that same treaty which the em-
    peror sent us
Were mainly Gardiner's : that no for-
    eigner
Hold office in the household, fleet,
    forts, army ;
That if the Queen should die without
    a child,
The bond between the kingdoms be
    dissolved ;
That Philip should not mix us any way
With his French wars —
    Second Member. Ay, ay, but what
    security,

Good sir, for this, if Philip ——
    Third Member. Peace — the Queen,
Philip, and Pole.   [*All rise, and stand.*

Enter MARY, PHILIP, *and* POLE.

    [Gardiner *conducts them to the three
    chairs of state.* Philip *sits on the*
    Queen's *left,* Pole *on her right.*
Gardiner. Our short-lived sun, before
    his winter plunge,
Laughs at the last red leaf, and An-
    drew's Day.
    Mary. Should not this day be held
    in after years
More solemn than of old ?
    Philip.   Madam, my wish
Echoes your Majesty's.
    Pole.   It shall be so.
    Gardiner. Mine echoes both your
    Graces' ;   (*aside*)   but   the
    Pope —
Can we not have the Catholic church
    as well
Without as with the Italian ? if we
    cannot,
Why then the Pope.
         My lords of the upper house,
And ye, my masters, of the lower
    house,
Do ye stand fast by that which ye re-
    solved ?
    Voices. We do.
    Gardiner. And be you all one mind
    to supplicate
The Legate here for pardon, and ac-
    knowledge
The primacy of the Pope ?
    Voices.   We are all one mind.
    Gardiner. Then must I play the
    vassal to this Pole.   [*Aside.*
    [*He draws a paper from under his
    robes and presents it to the* King
    and Queen, *who look through it
    and return it to him ; then as-
    cends a tribune, and reads.*
We, the Lords Spiritual and Tempo-
    ral,
And Commons here in Parliament as-
    sembled,
Presenting the whole body of this
    realm

Of England, and dominions of the same,

Do make most humble suit unto your Majesties,

In our own name and that of all the state,

That by your gracious means and intercession

Our supplication be exhibited

To the Lord Cardinal Pole, sent here as Legate

From our most Holy Father Julius, Pope,

And from the Apostolic see of Rome ;

And do declare our penitence and grief

For our long schism and disobedience,

Either in making laws and ordinances

Against the Holy Father's primacy,

Or else by doing or by speaking aught

Which might impugn or prejudice the same ;

By this our supplication promising,

As well for our own selves as all the realm,

That now we be and ever shall be quick,

Under and with your Majesties' authorities,

To do to the utmost all that in us lies

Towards the abrogation and repeal

Of all such laws and ordinances made ;

Whereon we humbly pray your Majesties,

As persons undefiled with our offence,

So to set forth this humble suit of ours

That we the rather by your intercession

May from the Apostolic see obtain,

Thro' this most reverend Father, absolution,

And full release from danger of all censures

Of Holy Church that we be fall'n into,

So that we may, as children penitent,

Be once again received into the bosom

And unity of Universal Church ;

And that this noble realm thro' after years

May in this unity and obedience

Unto the holy see and reigning Pope

Serve God and both your Majesties.

Voices. Amen. [*All sit.*

[*He again presents the petition to the* King *and* Queen, *who hand it reverentially to* Pole.

Pole (*sitting*). This is the loveliest day that ever smiled

On England. All her breath should, incenselike,

Rise to the heavens in grateful praise of Him

Who now recalls her to His ancient fold.

Lo! once again God to this realm hath given

A token of His more especial Grace ;

For as this people were the first of all

The islands call'd into the dawning church

Out of the dead, deep night of heathendom,

So now are these the first whom God hath given

Grace to repent and sorrow for their schism ;

And if your penitence be not mockery,

Oh how the blessed angels who rejoice

Over one saved do triumph at this hour

In the reborn salvation of a land

So noble. [*A pause.*

       For ourselves we do protest

That our commission is to heal, not harm ;

We come not to condemn, but reconcile ;

We come not to compel, but call again ;

We come not to destroy, but edify ;

Nor yet to question things already done ;

These are forgiven — matters of the past —

And range with jetsam and with offal thrown

Into the blind sea of forgetfulness.

               [*A pause.*

Ye have reversed the attainder laid on us

By him who sack'd the house of God ; and we,

Amplier than any field on our poor earth

Can render thanks in fruit for being sown,

Do here and now repay you sixty-fold,
A hundred, yea, a thousand thousand-
    fold,
With heaven for earth.
        [*Rising and stretching forth his
        hands. All kneel but* Sir Ralph
        Bagenhall, *who rises and re-
        mains standing.*
    The Lord who hath redeem'd us
With His own blood, and wash'd us
    from our sins,
To purchase for Himself a stainless
    bride;
He, whom the Father hath appointed
    Head
Of all his church, He by His mercy
    absolve you!   [*A pause.*
And we by that authority Apostolic
Given unto us, his Legate, by the Pope,
Our Lord and Holy Father, Julius,
God's Vicar and Vicegerent upon
    earth,
Do here absolve you and deliver you
And every one of you, and all the
    realm
And its dominions from all heresy,
All schism, and from all and every
    censure,
Judgment, and pain accruing there-
    upon;
And also we restore you to the bosom
And unity of Universal Church.
            [*Turning to* Gardiner.
Our letters of commission will declare
    this plainlier.
        [Queen *heard sobbing. Cries of
        Amen! Amen! Some of the
        Members embrace one another.
        All but* Sir Ralph Bagenhall
        *pass out into the neighboring
        chapel, whence is heard the* Te
        Deum.
Bagenhall. We strove against the
    papacy from the first,
In William's time, in our first Ed-
    ward's time,
And in my master Henry's time; but
    now,
The unity of Universal Church,
Mary would have it; and this Gardi-
    ner follows;
The unity of Universal Hell,

Philip would have it; and this Gardi-
    ner follows!
A Parliament of imitative apes!
Sheep at the gap which Gardiner
    takes, who not
Believes the Pope, nor any of them
    believe —
These spaniel-Spaniard English of the
    time,
Who rub their fawning noses in the
    dust,
For that is Philip's gold-dust, and adore
This Vicar of their Vicar. Would I
    had been
Born Spaniard! I had held my head
    up then.
I am ashamed that I am Bagenhall,
English.
            Enter OFFICER.
Officer. Sir Ralph Bagenhall!
Bagenhall.   What of that?
Officer. You were the one sole man
    in either house
Who stood upright when both the
    houses fell.
Bagenhall. The houses fell!
Officer. I mean the houses knelt
Before the Legate.
Bagenhall. Do not scrimp your
    phrase,
But stretch it wider; say when Eng-
    land fell.
Officer. I say you were the one sole
    man who stood.
Bagenhall. I am the one sole man
    in either house,
Perchance in England, loves her like
    a son.
Officer. Well, you one man, because
    you stood upright,
Her Grace the Queen commands you
    to the Tower.
Bagenhall. As traitor, or as heretic,
    or for what?
Officer. If any man in any way
    would be
The one man, he shall be so to his cost.
Bagenhall. What! will she have
    my head?
Officer.   A round fine likelier.
Your pardon.   [*Calling to Attendant.*
    By the river to the Tower. [*Exeunt.*

SCENE IV. — WHITEHALL. A ROOM
IN THE PALACE.

MARY, GARDINER, POLE, PAGET,
BONNER, *etc.*

Mary. The King and I, my Lords,
now that all traitors
Against our royal state have lost the
heads
Wherewith they plotted in their trea-
sonous malice,
Have talk'd together, and are well
agreed
That those old statutes touching
Lollardism
To bring the heretic to the stake,
should be
No longer a dead letter, but requick-
en'd.
One of the Council. Why, what hath
fluster'd Gardiner ? how he rubs
His forelock !
Paget. I have changed a word with
him
In coming, and may change a word
again.
Gardiner. Madam, your Highness
is our sun, the King
And you together our two suns in one ;
And so the beams of both may shine
upon us,
The faith that seem'd to droop will
feel your light,
Lift head, and flourish ; yet not light
alone,
There must be heat — there must be
heat enough
To scorch and wither heresy to the
root.
For what saith Christ ? "Compel
them to come in."
And what saith Paul ? "I would
they were cut off
That trouble you." Let the dead letter live !
Trace it in fire, that all the louts to
whom
Their A B C is darkness, clowns and
grooms
May read it ! so you quash rebellion
too,

For heretic and traitor are all one :
Two vipers of one breed — an amphis-
bœna,
Each end a sting. Let the dead letter
burn !
Paget. Yet there be some disloyal
Catholics,
And many heretics loyal ; heretic
throats
Cried no God-bless-her to the Lady
Jane,
But shouted in Queen Mary. So there
be
Some traitor-heretic, there is axe and
cord.
To take the lives of others that are
loyal,
And by the churchman's pitiless doom
of fire,
Were but a thankless policy in the
crown,
Ay, and against itself ; for there are
many.
Mary. If we could burn out here-
sy, my Lord Paget,
We reck not tho' we lost this crown
of England —
Ay ! tho' it were ten Englands !
Gardiner. Right, your Grace.
Paget, you are all for this poor life of
ours,
And care but little for the life to
be.
Paget. I have some time, for curi-
ousness, my Lord,
Watch'd children playing at *their* life
to be,
And cruel at it, killing helpless flies ;
Such is our time — all times for aught
I know.
Gardiner. We kill the heretics
that sting the soul —
They, with right reason, flies that
prick the flesh.
Paget. They had not reach'd right
reason ; little children !
They kill'd but for their pleasure and
the power
They felt in killing.
Gardiner. A spice of Satan, ha !
Why, good ! what then ? granted ! —
we are fallen creatures ;

Look to your Bible, Paget! we are
   fallen.
  Paget. I am but of the laity, my
    Lord Bishop,
And may not read your Bible, yet I
   found
One day, a wholesome scripture,
  " Little children,
Love one another."
  Gardiner. Did you find a scripture,
" I come not to bring peace but a
   sword " ? The sword
Is in her Grace's hand to smite with.
   Paget,
You stand up here to fight for heresy,
You are more than guess'd at as a
   heretic,
And on the steep-up track of the true
   faith
Your lapses are far seen.
  Paget.   The faultless Gardiner!
  Mary. You brawl beyond the ques-
    tion; speak, Lord Legate!
  Pole. Indeed, I cannot follow with
    your Grace :
Rather would say — the shepherd
   doth not kill
The sheep that wander from his flock,
   but sends
His careful dog to bring them to the
   fold.
Look to the Netherlands, wherein
   have been
Such holocausts of heresy! to what
   end ?
For yet the faith is not established
   there.
  Gardiner. The end's not come.
  Pole.   No — nor this way
    will come,
Seeing there lie two ways to every
   end,
A better and a worse — the worse is
   here
To persecute, because to persecute
Makes a faith hated, and is further-
   more
No perfect witness of a perfect faith
In him who persecutes : when men are
   tost
On tides of strange opinion, and not
   sure

Of their own selves, they are wroth
   with their own selves,
And thence with others ; then, who
   lights the faggot ?
Not the full faith, no, but the lurking
   doubt.
Old Rome, that first made martyrs in
   the Church,
Trembled for her own gods, for these
   were trembling —
But when did our Rome tremble ?
  Paget.   Did she not
In Henry's time and Edward's ?
  Pole.   What, my Lord !
The Church on Peter's rock ? never !
   I have seen
A pine in Italy that cast its shadow
Athwart a cataract ; firm stood the
   pine —
The cataract shook the shadow. To
   my mind,
The cataract typed the headlong
   plunge and fall
Of heresy to the pit : the pine was
   Rome.
You see, my Lords,
It was the shadow of the Church that
   trembled ;
Your church was but the shadow of a
   church ;
Wanting the Papal mitre.
  Gardiner (*muttering*). Here be tropes.
  Pole. And tropes are good to clothe
    a naked truth,
And make it look more seemly.
  Gardiner.   Tropes again !
  Pole. You are hard to please. Then
    without tropes, my Lord,
An overmuch severeness, I repeat,
When faith is wavering makes the
   waverer pass
Into more settled hatred of the doc-
   trines
Of those who rule, which hatred by
   and by
Involves the ruler (thus there springs
   to light
That Centaur of a monstrous Com-
   monweal,
The traitor-heretic) then tho' some
   may quail,

Yet others are that dare the stake and
    fire,
And their strong torment bravely
    borne, begets
An admiration and an indignation,
And hot desire to imitate; so the
    plague
Of schism spreads; were there but
    three or four
Of these misleaders, yet I would not say
Burn! and we cannot burn whole
    towns; they are many,
As my Lord Paget says.
    Gardiner. Yet my Lord Cardinal —
    Pole. I am your Legate; please you
    let me finish.
Methinks that under our Queen's
    regimen
We might go softlier than with crim-
    son rowel
And streaming lash. When Herod-
    Henry first
Began to batter at your English
    Church,
This was the cause, and hence the
    judgment on her.
She seethed with such adulteries, and
    the lives
Of many among your churchmen were
    so foul .
That heaven wept and earth blush'd.
    I would advise
That we should thoroughly cleanse
    the Church within
Before these bitter statutes be requick-
    en'd.
So after that when she once more is
    seen
White as the light, the spotless bride
    of Christ,
Like Christ himself on Tabor, pos-
    sibly
The Lutheran may be won to her
    again;
Till when, my Lords, I counsel toler-
    ance.
    Gardiner. What, if a mad dog bit
    your hand, my Lord,
Would you not chop the bitten finger
    off,
Lest your whole body should madden
    with the poison?

I would not, were I Queen, tolerate
    the heretic,
No, not an hour. The ruler of a
    land
Is bounden by his power and place to
    see
His people be not poison'd. Tolerate
    them!
Why? do they tolerate you? Nay,
    many of them
Would burn — have burnt each other;
    call they not
The one true faith, a loathsome idol-
    worship?
Beware, Lord Legate, of a heavier
    crime
Than heresy is itself; beware, I say,
Lest men accuse you of indifference
To all faiths, all religion; for you
    know
Right well that you yourself have been
    supposed
Tainted with Lutheranism it Italy.
    Pole (angered). But you, my Lord,
    beyond all supposition,
In clear and open day were congruent
With that vile Cranmer in the ac-
    cursed lie
Of good Queen Catherine's divorce —
    the spring
Of all those evils that have flow'd
    upon us;
For you yourself have truckled to the
    tyrant,
And done your best to bastardize our
    Queen,
For which God's righteous judgment
    fell upon you
In your five years of imprisonment,
    my Lord,
Under young Edward. Who so bol-
    ster'd up
The gross King's headship of the
    Church, or more
Denied the Holy Father!
    Gardiner.   Ha! what! eh?
But you, my Lord, a polish'd gentle-
    man,
A bookman, flying from the heat and
    tussle,
You lived among your vines and
    oranges,

In your soft Italy yonder! You were
  sent for,
You were appeal'd to, but you still
  preferr'd
Your learned leisure.   As for what I
  did
I suffer'd and repented.   You, Lord
  Legate
And Cardinal-Deacon, have not now
  to learn
That ev'n St. Peter in his time of fear
Denied his Master, ay, and thrice, my
  Lord.
  Pole.   But not for five-and-twenty
    years, my Lord.
  Gardiner.   Ha! good! it seems then
    I was summon'd hither
But to be mock'd and baited.   Speak,
  friend Bonner,
And tell this learned Legate he lacks
  zeal.
The Church's evil is not as the
  King's,
Cannot be heal'd by stroking.   The
  mad bite
Must have the cautery — tell him —
  and at once.
What would'st thou do hadst thou his
  power, thou
That layest so long in heretic bonds
  with me;
Would'st thou not burn and blast them
  root and branch?
  Bonner.   Ay, after you, my Lord.
  Gardiner.   Nay, God's passion, be-
    fore me! speak!
  Bonner.   I am on fire until I see
    them flame.
  Gardiner.   Ay, the psalm-singing
    weavers, cobblers, scum —
But this most noble prince Planta-
  genet,
Our good Queen's cousin — dallying
  over seas
Even when his brother's, nay, his
  noble mother's,
Head fell —
  Pole.   Peace, madman!
Thou stirrest up a grief thou canst
  not fathom.
Thou Christian Bishop, thou Lord
  Chancellor

Of England! no more rein upon thine
  anger
Than any child! Thou mak'st me
  much ashamed
That I was for a moment wroth at thee.
  Mary.   I come for counsel and ye
    give me feuds,
Like dogs that set to watch their mas-
  ter's gate,
Fall, when the thief is ev'n within the
  walls,
To worrying one another.   My Lord
  Chancellor,
You have an old trick of offending
  us;
And but that you are art and part
  with us
In purging heresy, well we might, for
  this
Your violence and much roughness to
  the Legate,
Have shut you from our counsels.
  Cousin Pole,
You are fresh from brighter lands.
  Retire with me.
His Highness and myself (so you
  allow us)
Will let you learn in peace and pri-
  vacy
What power this cooler sun of Eng-
  land hath
In breeding godless vermin.   And
  pray Heaven
That you may see according to our
  sight.
Come, cousin.
          [*Exeunt* Queen *and* Pole, *etc.*
  Gardiner.   Pole has the Plantagenet
    face,
But not the force made them our
  mightiest kings.
Fine eyes — but melancholy, irreso-
  lute —
A fine beard, Bonner, a very full fine
  beard.
But a weak mouth, an indeterminate
  — ha?
  Bonner.   Well, a weak mouth, per-
    chance.
  Gardiner.   And not like thine
To gorge a heretic whole, roasted or
  raw.

" ' Much suspected, of me
   Nothing proven can be,'
Quoth Elizabeth, prisoner."

Page 732.

Bonner. I'd do my best, my Lord;
but yet the Legate
Is here as Pope and Master of the
Church,
And if he go not with you —
    Gardiner. Tut, Master Bishop,
Our bashful Legate, saw'st not how he
flush'd ?
Touch him upon his old heretical
talk,
He'll burn a diocese to prove his or-
thodoxy.
And let him call me truckler. In
those times,
Thou knowest we had to dodge, or
duck, or die ;
I kept my head for use of Holy
Church ;
And see you, we shall have to dodge
again,
And let the Pope trample our rights,
and plunge
His foreign fist into our island Church
To plump the leaner pouch of Italy.
For a time, for a time.
Why ? that these statutes may be put
in force,
And that his fan may thoroughly
purge his floor.
    Bonner. So then you hold the
Pope —
    Gardiner. I hold the Pope !
What do I hold him ? what do I hold
the Pope ?
Come, come, the morsel stuck — this
Cardinal's fault —
I have gulpt it down. I am wholly
for the Pope,
Utterly and altogether for the Pope,
The Eternal Peter of the changeless
chair,
Crown'd slave of slaves, and mitred
king of kings,
God upon earth ! what more ? what
would you have ?
Hence, let's be gone.

Enter USHER.

    Usher. Well that you be not gone,
My lord. The Queen, most wroth at
first with you,
Is now content to grant you full for-
giveness,
So that you crave full pardon of the
Legate.
I am sent to fetch you.
    Gardiner. Doth Pole yield, sir,
ha !
Did you hear 'em ? were you by ?
    Usher. I cannot tell you,
His bearing is so courtly-delicate ;
And yet methinks he falters : their
two Graces
Do so dear-cousin and royal-cousin
him,
So press on him the duty which as
Legate
He owes himself, and with such royal
smiles —
    Gardiner. Smiles that burn men.
Bonner, it will be carried.
He falters, ha ? 'fore God, we change
and change ;
Men now are bow'd and old, the doc-
tors tell you,
At three-score years; then if we
change at all
We needs must do it quickly ; it is an
age
Of brief life, and brief purpose, and
brief patience,
As I have shown to-day. I am sorry
for it
If Pole be like to turn. Our old
friend Cranmer,
Your more especial love, hath turn'd
so often,
He knows not where he stands, which,
if this pass,
We two shall have to teach him ; let
'em look to it,
Cranmer and Hooper, Ridley and
Latimer,
Rogers and Ferrar, for their time is
come,
Their hour is hard at hand, their
"dies Iræ,"
Their "dies Illa," which will test
their sect.
I feel it but a duty — you will find in
it
Pleasure as well as duty, worthy
Bonner, —

To test their sect. Sir, I attend the
    Queen
To crave most humble pardon — of
    her most
Royal, Infallible, Papal Legate-cousin,
                 [Exeunt.

SCENE V. — WOODSTOCK.

ELIZABETH, LADY IN WAITING.

Elizabeth. So they have sent poor
    Courtenay over sea.
Lady. And banish'd us to Wood-
    stock, and the fields.
The colors of our Queen are green and
    white,
These fields are only green, they make
    me gape.
Elizabeth. There's whitethorn, girl.
Lady.   Ay, for an hour in May.
But court is always May, buds out in
    masques,
Breaks into feather'd merriments, and
    flowers
In silken pageants. Why do they
    keep us here ?
Why still suspect your Grace ?
Elizabeth.   Hard upon both.
[Writes on the window with a diamond.

> Much suspected, of me
> Nothing proven can be.
>   Quoth Elizabeth, prisoner.

Lady. What hath your Highness
    written ?
Elizabeth.   A true rhyme.
Lady. Cut with a diamond ; so to
    last like truth.
Elizabeth. Ay, if truth last.
Lady. But truth, they say, will out,
So it must last. It is not like a word,
That comes and goes in uttering.
Elizabeth.   Truth, a word !
The very Truth and very Word are
    one.
But truth of story, which I glanced
    at, girl,
Is like a word that comes from olden
    days,
And passes thro' the peoples : every
    tongue

Alters it passing, till it spells and
    speaks
Quite other than at first.
Lady.   I do not follow.
Elizabeth. How many names in the
    long sweep of time
That so foreshortens greatness, may
    but hang
On the chance mention of some fool
    that once
Brake bread with us, perhaps: and
    my poor chronicle
Is but of glass. Sir Henry Beding-
    field
May split it for a spite.
Lady.   God grant it last,
And witness to your Grace's innocence,
Till doomsday melt it.
Elizabeth.   Or a second fire,
Like that which lately crackled under-
    foot
And in this very chamber, fuse the glass,
And char us back again into the dust
We spring from. Never peacock
    against rain
Scream'd as you did for water.
Lady.   And I got it.
I woke Sir Henry — and he's true to
    you —
I read his honest horror in his eyes.
Elizabeth. Or true to you ?
Lady.   Sir Henry Bedingfield !
I will have no man true to me, your
    Grace,
But one that pares his nails ; to me ?
    the clown !
Elizabeth. Out, girl ! you wrong a
    noble gentleman.
Lady. For, like his cloak, his man-
    ners want the nap
And gloss of court ; but of this fire he
    says,
Nay swears, it was no wicked wilful-
    ness,
Only a natural chance.
Elizabeth.   A chance — perchance
One of those wicked wilfuls that men
    make,
Nor shame to call it nature. Nay, I
    know
They hunt my blood. Save for my
    daily range

Among the pleasant fields of Holy
    Writ
I might despair. But there hath
    some one come ;
The house is all in movement. Hence,
    and see.   [*Exit* Lady.

   Milkmaid (*singing without*).

Shame upon you, Robin,
   Shame upon you now!
Kiss me would you? with my hands
   Milking the cow?
   Daisies grow again,
   Kingcups blow again,
And you came and kiss'd me milking the cow.

Robin came behind me,
   Kiss'd me well I vow;
Cuff him could I? with my hands
   Milking the cow?
   Swallows fly again,
   Cuckoos cry again,
And you came and kiss'd me milking the cow.

Come, Robin, Robin,
   Come and kiss me now;
Help it can I? with my hands
   Milking the cow?
   Ringdoves coo again,
   All things woo again.
Come behind and kiss me milking the cow!

  Elizabeth. Right honest and red-
    cheek'd; Robin was violent,
And she was crafty — a sweet vio-
    lence,
And a sweet craft. I would I were a
    milkmaid,
To sing, love, marry, churn, brew,
    bake, and die,
Then have my simple headstone by
    the church,
And all things lived and ended hon-
    estly.
I could not if I would. I am Harry's
    daughter :
Gardiner would have my head. They
    are not sweet,
The violence and the craft that do
    divide
The world of nature ; what is weak
    must lie;
The lion needs but roar to guard his
    young;
The lapwing lies, says "here" when
    they are there.
Threaten the child ; "I'll scourge you
    if you did it :"

What weapon hath the child, save his
    soft tongue,
To say "I did not ?" and my rod's the
    block.
I never lay my head upon the pillow
But that I think, "Wilt thou lie there
    to-morrow ?"
How oft the falling axe, that never
    fell,
Hath shock'd me back into the day-
    light truth
That it may fall to-day ! Those
    damp, black, dead
Nights in the Tower ; dead — with the
    fear of death
Too dead ev'n for a death-watch !
    Toll of a bell,
Stroke of a clock, the scurrying of a
    rat
Affrighted me, and then delighted me,
For there was life — And there was
    life in death —
The little murder'd princes, in a pale
    light,
Rose hand in hand, and whisper'd,
    "come away !
The civil wars are gone for ever-
    more :
Thou last of all the Tudors, come
    away !
With us is peace !" The last ? It
    was a dream ;
I must not dream, not wink, but watch.
    She has gone,
Maid Marian to her Robin — by and
    by
Both happy ! a fox may filch a hen by
    night,
And make a morning outcry in the
    yard ;
But there's no Renard here to "catch
    her tripping."
Catch me who can; yet, sometime I
    have wish'd
That I were caught, and kill'd away
    at once
Out of the flutter. The gray rogue,
    Gardiner,
Went on his knees, and pray'd me to
    confess
In Wyatt's business, and to cast my-
    self

Upon the good Queen's mercy; ay,
    when, my Lord ?
God save the Queen ! My jailor —

Enter SIR HENRY BEDINGFIELD.

Bedingfield.　　　One, whose bolts,
That jail you from free life, bar you
    from death.
There haunt some Papist ruffians
    here about
Would murder you.
    Elizabeth. I thank you heartily, sir,
But I am royal, tho' your prisoner,
And God hath blest or cursed me with
    a nose —
Your boots are from the horses.
    Bedingfield.　　　Ay, my Lady.
When next there comes a missive
    from the Queen
It shall be all my study for one hour
To rose and lavender my horsiness,
Before I dare to glance upon your
    Grace.
    Elizabeth. A missive from the
    Queen: last time she wrote,
I had like to have lost my life: it
    takes my breath:
O God, sir, do you look upon your
    boots,
Are you so small a man ? Help me :
    what think you,
Is it life or death ?
    Bedingfield. I thought not on my
    boots ;
The devil take all boots were ever
    made
Since man went barefoot. See, I lay
    it here,
For I will come no nearer to your
    Grace ;
                [Laying down the letter.
And, whether it bring you bitter news
    or sweet,
And God hath given your grace a
    nose, or not,
I'll help you, if I may.
    Elizabeth.　　Your pardon, then ;
It is the heat and narrowness of the
    cage
That makes the captive testy; with
    free wing

The world were all one Araby. Leave
    me now,
Will you, companion to myself, sir ?
    Bedingfield.　　　　　Will I ?
With most exceeding willingness, I
    will ;
You know I never come till I be call'd.
                        [Exit.
    Elizabeth. It lies there folded : is
    there venom in it ?
A snake — and if I touch it, it may
    sting.
Come, come, the worst !
Best wisdom is to know the worst at
    once.　　　　　*[Reads :*

"It is the King's wish, that
you should wed Prince Philibert of
Savoy. You are to come to Court on
the instant; and think of this in your
coming.

            "MARY THE QUEEN."

Think ! I have many thoughts ;
I think there may be birdlime here for
    me ;
I think they fain would have me from
    the realm ;
I think the Queen may never bear a
    child ;
I think that I may be some time the
    Queen,
Then, Queen indeed : no foreign prince
    or priest
Should fill my throne, myself upon
    the steps.
I think I will not marry anyone,
Specially not this landless Philibert
Of Savoy ; but, if Philip menace me,
I think that I will play with Phili-
    bert, —
As once the Holy Father did with
    mine,
Before my father married my good
    mother, —
For fear of Spain.

            Enter LADY.

    Lady. O Lord ! your Grace, your
    Grace,
I feel so happy : it seems that we shall
    fly

These bald, blank fields, and dance
    into the sun
That shines on princes.

    Elizabeth.   Yet, a moment since,
I wish'd myself the milkmaid singing
    here,
To kiss and cuff among the birds and
    flowers —
A right rough life and healthful.

    Lady.   But the wench
Hath her own troubles; she is weep-
    ing now;
For the wrong Robin took her at her
    word.
Then the cow kick'd, and all her milk
    was spilt.
Your highness such a milkmaid?

    Elizabeth.   I had kept
My Robins and my cows in sweeter
    order
Had I been such.

    Lady (slyly).   And had your Grace
    a Robin?

    Elizabeth.   Come, come, you are
    chill here; you want the sun
That shines at court; make ready for
    the journey.
Pray God, we 'scape the sunstroke.
    Ready at once.   [*Exeunt.*

SCENE VI. — London. A Room in
    the Palace.

Lord Petre *and* Lord William
    Howard.

    Petre. You cannot see the Queen.
    Renard denied her,
Ev'n now to me.

    Howard. Their Flemish go-between
And all-in-all. I came to thank her
    Majesty
For freeing my friend Bagenhall
    from the Tower;
A grace to me! Mercy, that herb-of-
    grace,
Flowers now but seldom.

    Petre.   Only now perhaps.
Because the Queen hath been three
    days in tears
For Philip's going — like the wild
    hedge-rose

Of a soft winter, possible, not prob-
    able,
However you have prov'n it.

    Howard.   I must see her.

Enter Renard.

    Renard. My Lords, you cannot see
    her Majesty.

    Howard. Why then the King! for
    I would have him bring it
Home to the leisure wisdom of his
    Queen,
Before he go, that since these statutes
    past,
Gardiner out-Gardiners Gardiner in
    his heat,
Bonner cannot out-Bonner his own
    self —
Beast! — but they play with fire as
    children do,
And burn the house. I know that
    these are breeding
A fierce resolve and fixt heart-hate in
    men
Against the King, the Queen, the
    Holy Father,
The faith itself. Can I not see him?

    Renard.   Not now.
And in all this, my Lord, her Majesty
Is flint of flint, you may strike fire
    from her,
Not hope to melt her. I will give
    your message.
    [*Exeunt* Petre *and* Howard.

Enter Philip (*musing*).

    Philip. She will not have Prince
    Philibert of Savoy,
I talk'd with her in vain — says she
    will live
And die true maid — a goodly crea-
    ture too.
Would *she* had been the Queen! yet
    she must have him;
She troubles England: that she
    breathes in England
Is life and lungs to every rebel birth
That passes out of embryo.
        Simon Renard! —
This Howard, whom they fear, what
    was he saying?

Renard. What your imperial father said, my liege,
To deal with heresy gentlier. Gardiner burns,
And Bonner burns; and it would seem this people
Care more for our brief life in their wet land,
Than yours in happier Spain. I told my Lord
He should not vex her Highness; she would say
These are the means God works with, that His church
May flourish.
    Philip. Ay, sir, but in statesmanship
To strike too soon is oft to miss the blow.
Thou knowest I bade my chaplain, Castro, preach
Against these burnings.
    Renard.   And the Emperor
Approved you, and when last he wrote, declared
His comfort in your Grace that you were bland
And affable to men of all estates,
In hope to charm them from their hate of Spain.
    Philip. In hope to crush all heresy under Spain.
But, Renard, I am sicker staying here
Than any sea could make me passing hence,
Tho' I be ever deadly sick at sea.
So sick am I with biding for this child.
Is it the fashion in this clime for women
To go twelve months in bearing of a child?
The nurses yawn'd, the cradle gaped, they led
Processions, chanted litanies, clash'd their bells,
Shot off their lying cannon, and her priests
Have preach'd, the fools, of this fair prince to come;
Till, by St. James, I find myself the fool.
Why do you lift your eyebrow at me thus?

Renard. I never saw your Highness moved till now.
Philip. So weary am I of this wet land of theirs,
And every soul of man that breathes therein.
    Renard. My liege, we must not drop the mask before
The masquerade is over —
    Philip.   — Have I dropt it?
I have but shown a loathing face to you,
Who knew it from the first.

Enter MARY.

Mary (aside). With Renard. Still
Parleying with Renard, all the day with Renard,
And scarce a greeting all the day for me —
And goes to-morrow.   [*Exit* Mary.
    Philip (to Renard, *who advances to him).* Well, sir, is there more?
    Renard (who has perceived the Queen).
May Simon Renard speak a single word?
    Philip. Ay.
    Renard. And be forgiven for it?
    Philip.   Simon Renard
Knows me too well to speak a single word
That could not be forgiven.
    Renard.   Well, my liege,
Your Grace hath a most chaste and loving wife.
    Philip. Why not? The Queen of Philip should be chaste.
    Renard. Ay, but, my Lord, you know what Virgil sings,
Woman is various and most mutable.
    Philip. She play the harlot! never.
    Renard.   No, sire, no,
Not dream'd of by the rabidest gospeller.
There was a paper thrown into the palace,
"The King hath wearied of his barren bride."
She came upon it, read it, and then rent it,
With all the rage of one who hates a truth

He cannot but allow. Sire, I would
    have you —
What should I say, I cannot pick my
    words —
Be somewhat less — majestic to your
    Queen.
    Philip. Am I to change my man-
    ners, Simon Renard,
Because these islanders are brutal
    beasts ?
Or would you have me turn a son-
    neteer,
And warble those brief-sighted eyes
    of hers ?
    Renard. Brief-sighted tho' they be,
    I have seen them, sire,
When you perchance were trifling
    royally
With some fair dame of court, sud-
    denly fill
With such fierce fire — had it been
    fire indeed
It would have burnt both speakers.
    Philip.   Ay, and then ?
    Renard. Sire, might it not be policy
    in some matter
Of small importance now and then to
    cede
A point to her demand ?
    Philip.   Well, I am going.
    Renard. For should her love when
    you are gone, my liege,
Witness these papers, there will not
    be wanting
Those that will urge her injury —
    should her love —
And I have known such women more
    than one —
Veer to the counterpoint, and jeal-
    ousy
Hath in it an alchemic force to fuse
Almost into one metal love and hate,—
And she impress her wrongs upon her
    Council,
And these again upon her Parlia-
    ment —
We are not loved here, and would be
    then perhaps
Not so well holpen in our wars with
    France,
As else we might be — here she comes.

Enter MARY.

    Mary.   O Philip !
Nay, must you go indeed ?
    Philip.   Madam, I must.
    Mary. The parting of a husband
    and a wife
Is like the cleaving of a heart ; one half
Will flutter here, one there.
    Philip.   You say true, Madam.
    Mary. The Holy Virgin will not
    have me yet
Lose the sweet hope that I may bear
    a prince.
If such a prince were born and you
    not here !
    Philip. I should be here if such a
    prince were born.
    Mary. But must you go ?
    Philip. Madam, you know my fa-
    ther,
Retiring into cloistral solitude
To yield the remnant of his years to
    heaven,
Will shift the yoke and weight of all
    the world
From off his neck to mine. We meet
    at Brussels.
But since mine absence will not be for
    long,
Your Majesty shall go to Dover with
    me,
And wait my coming back.
    Mary.   To Dover ? no,
I am too feeble. I will go to Green-
    wich,
So you will have me with you ; and
    there watch
All that is gracious in the breath of
    heaven
Draw with your sails from our poor
    land, and pass
And leave me, Philip, with my prayers
    for you.
    Philip. And doubtless I shall profit
    by your prayers.
    Mary. Methinks that would you
    tarry one day more
(The news was sudden) I could mould
    myself
To bear your going better ; will you
    do it ?

Philip. Madam, a day may sink or
   save a realm.
Mary. A day may save a heart
   from breaking too.
Philip. Well, Simon Renard, shall
   we stop a day ?
Renard. Your Grace's business will
   not suffer, sire,
For one day more, so far as I can tell.
Philip. Then one day more to please
   her Majesty.
Mary. The sunshine sweeps across
   my life again.
O if I knew you felt this parting,
   Philip,
As I do !
Philip. By St. James I do protest,
Upon the faith and honor of a Span-
   iard,
I am vastly grieved to leave your
   Majesty.
Simon, is supper ready ?
Renard.   Ay, my liege,
I saw the covers laying.
Philip. Let us have it.   [*Exeunt.*

ACT IV.

SCENE I.— A Room in the Palace.

Mary, Cardinal Pole.

Mary. What have you there?
Pole.   So please your Majesty,
A long petition from the foreign
   exiles
To spare the life of Cranmer. Bishop
   Thirlby,
And my Lord Paget and Lord Wil-
   liam Howard,
Crave, in the same cause, hearing of
   your Grace.
Hath he not written himself — in-
   fatuated —
To sue you for his life ?
Mary.   His life ? Oh, no ;
Not sued for that — he knows it were
   in vain.
But so much of the anti-papal leaven
Works in him yet, he hath pray'd me
   not to sully

Mine own prerogative, and degrade
   the realm
By seeking justice at a stranger's
   hand
Against my natural subject. King
   and Queen,
To whom he owes his loyalty after
   God,
Shall these accuse him to a foreign
   prince ?
Death would not grieve him more. I
   cannot be
True to this realm of England and
   the Pope
Together, says the heretic.
Pole.   And there errs ;
As he hath ever err'd thro' vanity.
A secular kingdom is but as the body
Lacking a soul ; and in itself a beast.
The Holy Father in a secular kingdom
Is as the soul descending out of
   heaven
Into a body generate.
Mary.   Write to him, then.
Pole. I will.
Mary.   And sharply, Pole.
Pole. Here come the Cranmerites !

Enter Thirlby, Lord Paget, Lord
William Howard.

Howard. Health to your Grace !
   Good morrow, my Lord Cardi-
   nal ;
We make our humble prayer unto
   your Grace
That Cranmer may withdraw to
   foreign parts,
Or into private life within the realm.
In several bills and declarations,
   Madam,
He hath recanted all his heresies.
Paget. Ay, ay ; if Bonner have not
   forged the bills.   [*Aside.*
Mary. Did not More die, and
   Fisher ? he must burn.
Howard. He hath recanted, Madam.
Mary.   The better for him.
He burns in Purgatory, not in Hell.
Howard. Ay, ay, your Grace ; but
   it was never seen
That any one recanting thus at full,

As Cranmer hath, came to the fire on earth.

Mary. It will be seen now, then.

Thirlby.   O Madam, Madam!
I thus implore you, low upon my knees,
To reach the hand of mercy to my friend.
I have err'd with him; with him I have recanted.
What human reason is there why my friend
Should meet with lesser mercy than myself?

Mary. My Lord of Ely, this. After a riot
We hang the leaders, let their following go.
Cranmer is head and father of these heresies,
New learning as they call it; yea, may God
Forget me at most need when I forget
Her foul divorce — my sainted mother — No! —

Howard. Ay, ay, but mighty doctors doubted there.
The Pope himself waver'd; and more than one
Row'd in that galley — Gardiner to wit,
Whom truly I deny not to have been
Your faithful friend and trusty councillor.
Hath not your Highness ever read his book,
His tractate upon True Obedience,
Writ by himself and Bonner?

Mary.   I will take
Such order with all bad, heretical books
That none shall hold them in his house and live,
Henceforward. No, my Lord.

Howard.   Then never read it.
The truth is here. Your father was a man
Of such colossal kinghood, yet so courteous,
Except when wroth, you scarce could meet his eye

And hold your own; and were he wroth indeed,
You held it less, or not at all. I say,
Your father had a will that beat men down;
Your father had a brain that beat men down —

Pole. Not me, my Lord.

Howard. No, for you were not here;
You sit upon this fallen Cranmer's throne;
And it would more become you, my Lord Legate,
To join a voice, so potent with her Highness,
To ours in plea for Cranmer than to stand
On naked self-assertion.

Mary.   All your voices
Are waves on flint. The heretic must burn.

Howard. Yet once he saved your Majesty's own life;
Stood out against the King in your behalf,
At his own peril.

Mary.   I know not if he did;
And if he did I care not, my Lord Howard.
My life is not so happy, no such boon,
That I should spare to take a heretic priest's,
Who saved it or not saved. Why do you vex me?

Paget. Yet to save Cranmer were to serve the Church,
Your Majesty's I mean; he is effaced,
Self-blotted out; so wounded in his honor,
He can but creep down into some dark hole
Like a hurt beast, and hide himself and die;
But if you burn him, — well, your Highness knows
The saying, " Martyr's blood — seed of the Church."

Mary. Of the true Church; but his is none, nor will be.
You are too politic for me, my Lord Paget.

And if he have to live so loath'd a life,
It were more merciful to burn him now.
  Thirlby. O yet relent. O, Madam, if you knew him
As I do, ever gentle, and so gracious,
With all his learning —
  Mary.   Yet a heretic still.
His learning makes his burning the more just.
  Thirlby. So worshipt of all those that came across him;
The stranger at his hearth, and all his house—
  Mary. His children and his concubine, belike.
  Thirlby. To do him any wrong was to beget
A kindness from him, for his heart was rich,
Of such fine mould, that if you sow'd therein
The seed of Hate, it blossom'd Charity.
  Pole. "After his kind it costs him nothing," there's
An old world English adage to the point.
These are but natural graces, my good Bishop,
Which in the Catholic garden are as flowers,
But on the heretic dunghill only weeds.
  Howard. Such weeds make dunghills gracious.
  Mary.   Enough, my Lords.
It is God's will, the Holy Father's will,
And Philip's will, and mine, that he should burn.
He is pronounced anathema.
  Howard.   Farewell, Madam,
God grant you ampler mercy at your call
Than you have shown to Cranmer.
               [Exeunt Lords.
  Pole.   After this,
Your Grace will hardly care to overlook
This same petition of the foreign exiles
For Cranmer's life.
  Mary. Make out the writ to-night.
               [Exeunt.

SCENE II.— OXFORD. CRANMER IN PRISON.

  Cranmer. Last night, I dream'd the faggots were alight,
And that myself was fasten'd to the stake,
And found it all a visionary flame,
Cool as the light in old decaying wood;
And then King Harry look'd from out a cloud,
And bade me have good courage; and I heard
An angel cry "There is more joy in Heaven,"—
And after that, the trumpet of the dead.
        [Trumpets without.
Why, there are trumpets blowing now: what is it?

Enter FATHER COLE.

  Cole. Cranmer, I come to question you again;
Have you remain'd in the true Catholic faith
I left you in?
  Cranmer. In the true Catholic faith,
By Heaven's grace, I am more and more confirm'd.
Why are the trumpets blowing, Father Cole?
  Cole. Cranmer, it is decided by the Council
That you to-day should read your recantation
Before the people in St. Mary's Church.
And there be many heretics in the town,
Who loathe you for your late return to Rome,
And might assail you passing through the street,
And tear you piecemeal: so you have a guard.
  Cranmer. Or seek to rescue me. I thank the Council.
  Cole. Do you lack any money?

Cranmer.   Nay, why should I ?
The prison fare is good enough for me.
Cole. Ay, but to give the poor
Cranmer.   Hand it me, then !
I thank you.
Cole.   For a little space, farewell ;
Until I see you in St. Mary's Church.
                            [*Exit* Cole.
Cranmer. It is against all prece-
    dent to burn
One who recants ; they mean to par-
    don me.
To give the poor — they give the poor
    who die.
Well, burn me or not burn me I am
    fixt ;
It is but a communion, not a mass :
A holy supper, not a sacrifice ;
No man can make his Maker — Villa
    Garcia.

Enter VILLA GARCIA.

Villa Garcia. Pray you write out
    this paper for me, Cranmer.
Cranmer. Have I not writ enough
    to satisfy you ?
Villa Garcia. It is the last.
Cranmer.   Give it me, then.
                            [*He writes.*
Villa Garcia.   Now sign.
Cranmer. I have sign'd enough,
    and I will sign no more.
Villa Garcia. It is no more than
    what you have sign'd already,
The public form thereof.
Cranmer.   It may be so ;
I sign it with my presence, if I read it.
Villa Garcia. But this is idle of
    you. Well, sir, well,
You are to beg the people to pray for
    you ;
Exhort them to a pure and virtuous
    life ;
Declare the Queen's right to the
    throne ; confess
Your faith before all hearers ; and
    retract
That Eucharistic doctrine in your
    book.
Will you not sign it now ?
Cranmer.   No, Villa Garcia,

I sign no more.   Will they have mercy
    on me ?
Villa Garcia. Have you good hopes
    of mercy ! So farewell. [*Exit.*
Cranmer. Good hopes, not theirs,
    have I that I am fixt,
Fixt beyond fall ; however, in strange
    hours,
After the long brain-dazing colloquies,
And thousand-times recurring argu-
    ment
Of those two friars ever in my prison,
When left alone in my despondency,
Without a friend, a book, my faith
    would seem
Dead or half-drown'd, or else swam
    heavily
Against the huge corruptions of the
    Church,
Monsters of mistradition, old enough
To scare me into dreaming, " what
    am I,
Cranmer, against whole ages ? " was
    it so,
Or am I slandering my most inward
    friend,
To veil the fault of my most outward
    foe —
The soft and tremulous coward in the
    flesh ?
O higher, holier, earlier, purer church,
I have found thee and not leave thee
    any more.
It is but a communion, not a mass —
No sacrifice, but a life-giving feast !
(*Writes.*) So, so ; this will I say —
    thus will I pray. [*Puts up the
    paper.*

Enter BONNER.

Bonner. Good day, old friend ;
    what, you look somewhat worn ;
And yet it is a day to test your health
Ev'n at the best : I scarce have spoken
    with you
Since when ? — your degradation. At
    your trial
Never stood up a bolder man than
    you ;
You would not cap the Pope's com-
    missioner —

Your learning, and your stoutness, and your heresy,
Dumbfounded half of us. So, after that,
We had to dis-archbishop and unlord,
And make you simple Cranmer once again.
The common barber clipt your hair, and I
Scraped from your finger-points the holy oil ;
And worse than all, you had to kneel to *me;*
Which was not pleasant for you, Master Cranmer.
Now you, that would not recognize the Pope,
And you, that would not own the Real Presence,
Have found a real presence in the stake,
Which frights you back into the ancient faith ;
And so you have recanted to the Pope.
How are the mighty fallen, Master Cranmer !
    Cranmer. You have been more fierce against the Pope than I ;
But why fling back the stone he strikes me with ?   [*Aside.*
O Bonner, if I ever did you kindness —
Power hath been given you to try faith by fire —
Pray you, remembering how yourself have changed,
Be somewhat pitiful, after I have gone,
To the poor flock — to women and to children —
That when I was archbishop held with me.
    Bonner. Ay — gentle as they call you — live or die !
Pitiful to this pitiful heresy ?
I must obey the Queen and Council, man.
Win thro' this day with honor to yourself,
And I'll say something for you — so — good-bye.   [*Exit.*
    Cranmer. This hard coarse man of old hath crouch'd to me

Till I myself was half ashamed for him.

Enter THIRLBY.

Weep not, good Thirlby.
    Thirlby.   Oh, my Lord, my Lord !
My heart is no such block as Bonner's is :
Who would not weep ?
    Cranmer. Why do you so my-lord me,
Who am disgraced ?
    Thirlby. On earth ; but saved in heaven
By your recanting.
    Cranmer.   Will they burn me, Thirlby ?
    Thirlby. Alas, they will ; these burnings will not help
The purpose of the faith ; but my poor voice
Against them is a whisper to the roar
Of a spring-tide.
    Cranmer.   And they will surely burn me ?
    Thirlby. Ay ; and besides, will have you in the church
Repeat your recantation in the ears
Of all men, to the saving of their souls,
Before your execution.   May God help you
Thro' that hard hour !
    Cranmer. And may God bless you, Thirlby !
Well, they shall hear my recantation there.   [*Exit* Thirlby.
Disgraced, dishonor'd ! — not by them, indeed,
By mine own self — by mine own hand !
O thin-skinn'd hand and jutting veins, 'twas you
That sign'd the burning of poor Joan of Kent ;
But then she was a witch.   You have written much,
But you were never raised to plead for Frith,
Whose dogmas I have reach'd : he was deliver'd

To the secular arm to burn; and there
    was Lambert;
Who can foresee himself? truly these
    burnings,
As Thirlby says, are profitless to the
    burners,
And help the other side. You shall
    burn too,
Burn first when I am burnt.
Fire — inch by inch to die in agony!
    Latimer
Had a brief end — not Ridley.
    Hooper burn'd
Three-quarters of an hour. Will my
    faggots
Be wet as his were? It is a day of
    rain.
I will not muse upon it.
My fancy takes the burner's part, and
    makes
The fire seem even crueller than it
    is.
No, I not doubt that God will give
    me strength,
Albeit I have denied him.

Enter SOTO *and* VILLA GARCIA.

Villa Garcia.   We are ready
To take you to St. Mary's, Master
    Cranmer.
    Cranmer. And I : lead on ; ye loose
    me from my bonds.   [*Exeunt.*

SCENE III. — ST. MARY'S CHURCH.

COLE *in the Pulpit,* LORD WILLIAMS
OF THAME *presiding.* LORD WIL-
LIAM HOWARD, LORD PAGET, *and
others.* CRANMER *enters between*
SOTO *and* VILLA GARCIA, *and the
whole Choir strike up* "Nunc Dimit-
tis." CRANMER *is set upon a Scaffold before the people.*

    Cole. Behold him —
[*A pause : people in the foreground.*
People. Oh, unhappy sight !
First Protestant. See how the tears
    run down his fatherly face.
Second Protestant. James, didst thou
    ever see a carrion crow

Stand watching a sick beast before he
    dies ?
    First Protestant. Him perch'd up
    there ? I wish some thunder-
    bolt
Would make this Cole a cinder, pulpit
    and all.
    Cole. Behold him, brethren : he
    hath cause to weep ! —
So have we all : weep with him if ye
    will,
Yet ——
It is expedient for one man to die,
Yea, for the people, lest the people
    die.
Yet wherefore should he die that hath
    return'd
To the one Catholic Universal Church,
Repentant of his errors ?
    Protestant murmurs. Ay, tell us
    that.
    Cole. Those of the wrong side will
    despise the man,
Deeming him one that thro' the fear
    of death
Gave up his cause, except he seal his
    faith
In sight of all with flaming martyr-
    dom.
    Cranmer. Ay.
    Cole. Ye hear him, and albeit there
    may seem
According to the canons pardon due
To him that so repents, yet are there
    causes
Wherefore our Queen and Council at
    this time
Adjudge him to the death. He hath
    been a traitor,
A shaker and confounder of the
    realm ;
And when the King's divorce was
    sued at Rome,
He here, this heretic metropolitan,
As if he had been the Holy Father,
    sat
And judged it. Did I call him
    heretic ?
A huge heresiarch ! never was it
    known
That any man so writing, preaching
    so,

So poisoning the Church, so long con-
tinuing,
Hath found his pardon; therefore he
must die,
For warning and example.
                        Other reasons
There be for this man's ending, which
our Queen
And Council at this present deem it
not
Expedient to be known.
    Protestant murmurs. I warrant you.
    Cole. Take therefore, all, example
by this man,
For if our Holy Queen not pardon him,
Much less shall others in like cause
escape,
That all of you, the highest as the
lowest,
May learn there is no power against
the Lord.
There stands a man, once of so high
degree,
Chief prelate of our Church, arch-
bishop, first
In Council, second person in the
realm,
Friend for so long time of a mighty
King;
And now ye see downfallen and de-
based
From councillor to caitiff — fallen so
low,
The leprous flutterings of the byway,
scum
And offal of the city would not
change
Estates with him; in brief, so miser-
able,
There is no hope of better left for him,
No place for worse.
                Yet, Cranmer, be thou glad.
This is the work of God. He is glori-
fied
In thy conversion: lo! thou art re-
claim'd;
He brings thee home: nor fear but
that to-day
Thou shalt receive the penitent thief's
award,
And be with Christ the Lord in Para-
dise.

Remember how God made the fierce
fire seem
To those three children like a pleasant dew.
Remember, too,
The triumph of St. Andrew on his
cross,
The patience of St. Lawrence in the
fire.
Thus, if thou call on God and all the
saints,
God will beat down the fury of the
flame,
Or give thee saintly strength to under-
go.
And for thy soul shall masses here be
sung
By every priest in Oxford. Pray for
him.
    Cranmer. Ay, one and all, dear
brothers, pray for me;
Pray with one breath, one heart, one
soul for me.
    Cole. And now, lest anyone among
you doubt
The man's conversion and remorse of
heart,
Yourselves shall hear him speak.
Speak, Master Cranmer,
Fulfil your promise made me, and
proclaim
Your true undoubted faith, that all
may hear.
    Cranmer. And that I will. O God,
Father of Heaven!
O Son of God, Redeemer of the world!
O Holy Ghost! proceeding from them
both,
Three persons and one God, have
mercy on me,
Most miserable sinner, wretched man.
I have offended against heaven and
earth
More grievously than any tongue can
tell.
Then whither should I flee for any
help?
I am ashamed to lift my eyes to heaven,
And I can find no refuge upon earth.
Shall I despair then? — God forbid!
O God,
For thou art merciful, refusing none

That come to Thee for succor, unto
Thee,
Therefore, I come; humble myself to
Thee;
Saying, O Lord God, although my sins
be great,
For thy great mercy have mercy! O
God the Son,
Not for slight faults alone, when thou
becamest
Man in the Flesh, was the great mys-
tery wrought;
O God the Father, not for little sins
Didst thou yield up thy Son to human
death;
But for the greatest sin that can be
sinn'd,
Yea, even such as mine, incalculable,
Unpardonable, — sin against the light,
The truth of God, which I had proven
and known.
Thy mercy must be greater than all
sin.
Forgive me, Father, for no merit of
mine,
But that Thy name by man be glori-
fied,
And Thy most blessed Son's, who died
for man.
    Good people, every man at time of
death
Would fain set forth some saying that
may live
After his death and better humankind;
For death gives life's last word a
power to live,
And, like the stone-cut epitaph, remain
After the vanish'd voice, and speak
to men.
God grant me grace to glorify my God!
And first I say it is a grievous case,
Many so dote upon this bubble world,
Whose colors in a moment break and
fly,
They care for nothing else. What
saith St. John: —
"Love of this world is hatred against
God."
Again, I pray you all that, next to God,
You do unmurmuringly and willingly
Obey your King and Queen, and not
for dread

Of these alone, but from the fear of
Him
Whose ministers they be to govern
you.
Thirdly, I pray you all to live together
Like brethren; yet what hatred
Christian men
Bear to each other, seeming not as
brethren,
But mortal foes! But do you good to
all
As much as in you lieth. Hurt no
man more
Than you would harm your loving
natural brother
Of the same roof, same breast. If any
do,
Albeit he think himself at home with
God,
Of this be sure, he is whole worlds
away.
    Protestant murmurs. What sort of
brothers then be those that lust
To burn each other?
    Williams. Peace be among you,
there!
    Cranmer. Fourthly, to those that
own exceeding wealth,
Remember that sore saying spoken
once
By Him that was the truth, "How
hard it is
For the rich man to enter into
Heaven;"
Let all rich men remember that hard
word.
I have not time for more: if ever, now
Let them flow forth in charity, seeing
now
The poor so many, and all food so
dear.
Long have I lain in prison, yet have
heard
Of all their wretchedness. Give to
the poor,
Ye give to God. He is with us in the
poor.
    And now, forasmuch as I have
come
To the last end of life, and thereupon
Hangs all my past, and all my life to
be,

Either to live with Christ in Heaven
    with joy,
Or to be still in pain with devils in
    hell ;
And, seeing in a moment, I shall find
                    [Pointing upwards.
Heaven or else hell ready to swallow
    me,   *[Pointing downwards.*
I shall declare to you my very faith
Without all color.
    Cole. Hear him, my good brethren.
    Cranmer. I do believe in God, Father
    of all ;
In every article of the Catholic faith,
And every syllable taught us by our
    Lord,
His prophets, and apostles, in the
    Testaments,
Both Old and New.
    Cole. Be plainer, Master Cranmer.
    Cranmer. And now I come to the
    great cause that weighs
Upon my conscience more than any-
    thing
Or said or done in all my life by me;
For there be writings I have set abroad
Against the truth I knew within my
    heart,
Written for fear of death, to save my
    life,
If that might be ; the papers by my
    hand
Sign'd since my degradation — by this
    hand
           [Holding out his right hand.
Written and sign'd — I here renounce
    them all ;
And, since my hand offended, having
    written
Against my heart, my hand shall first
    be burnt,
So I may come to the fire.
                [Dead silence.
    Protestant murmurs.
    First Protestant. I knew it would be
    so.
    Second Protestant. Our prayers are
    heard !
    Third Protestant. God bless him !
    Catholic murmurs. Out upon him !
    out upon him !
Liar ! dissembler ! traitor ! to the fire !

    Williams (raising his voice). You
    know that you recanted all you
    said
Touching the sacrament in that same
    book
You wrote against my Lord of Win-
    chester ;
Dissemble not ; play the plain Chris-
    tian man.
    Cranmer. Alas, my Lord,
I have been a man loved plainness all
    my life ;
I *did* dissemble, but the hour has come
For utter truth and plainness ; where-
    fore, I say,
I hold by all I wrote within that book.
Moreover,
As for the Pope I count him Anti-
    christ,
With all his devil's doctrines ; and
    refuse,
Reject him, and abhor him. I have
    said.   *[Cries on all sides,*
    "Pull him down ! Away with
    him ! "
    Cole. Ay, stop the heretic's mouth !
    Hale him away !
    Williams. Harm him not, harm him
    not ! have him to the fire !
    *[*Cranmer *goes out between Two*
    Friars, smiling; hands are reached
    to him from the crowd. Lord
    William Howard *and* Lord
    Paget *are left alone in the church.*
    Paget. The nave and aisles all
    empty as a fool's jest !
No, here's Lord William Howard.
    What, my Lord,
You have not gone to see the burning ?
    Howard.   Fie !
To stand at ease, and stare as at a
    show,
And watch a good man burn. Never
    again.
I saw the deaths of Latimer and Rid-
    ley.
Moreover, tho' a Catholic, I would not,
For the pure honor of our common
    nature,
Hear what I might — another recanta-
    tion
Of Cranmer at the stake.

Paget.   You'd not hear that.
He pass'd out smiling, and he walk'd
     upright;
His eye was like a soldier's, whom the
     general
He looks to and he leans on as his
     God,
Hath rated for some backwardness
     and bidd'n him
Charge one against a thousand, and
     the man
Hurls his soil'd life against the pikes
     and dies.
     Howard. Yet that he might not
     after all those papers
Of recantation yield again, who
     knows ?
     Paget. Papers of recantation!
     Think you then
That Cranmer read all papers that he
     sign'd ?
Or sign'd all those they tell us that he
     sign'd ?
Nay, I trow not: and you shall see,
     my Lord,
That howsoever hero-like the man
Dies in the fire, this Bonner or another
Will in some lying fashion misreport
His ending to the glory of their
     church.
And you saw Latimer and Ridley die ?
Latimer was eighty, was he not ? his
     best
Of life was over then.
     Howard.   His eighty years
Look'd somewhat crooked on him in
     his frieze ;
But after they had stript him to his
     shroud,
He stood upright, a lad of twenty-one,
And gather'd with his hands the start-
     ing flame,
And wash'd his hands and all his face
     therein,
Until the powder suddenly blew him
     dead.
Ridley was longer burning; but he
     died
As manfully and boldly, and, 'fore
     God,
I know them heretics, but right Eng-
     lish ones.

If ever, as heaven grant, we clash
     with Spain,
Our Ridley-soldiers and our Latimer-
     sailors
Will teach her something.
     Paget.   Your mild Legate Pole
Will tell you that the devil helpt them
     thro' it.
     [*A murmur of the Crowd in the
          distance.*
Hark, how those Roman wolfdogs
     howl and bay him !
     Howard. Might it not be the other
     side rejoicing
In his brave end ?
     Paget.   They are too crush'd, too
     broken,
They can but weep in silence.
     Howard.   Ay, ay, Paget,
They have brought it in large measure
     on themselves.
Have I not heard them mock the
     blessed Host
In songs so lewd, the beast might roar
     his claim
To being in God's image, more than
     they ?
Have I not seen the gamekeeper, the
     groom,
Gardener, and huntsman, in the par-
     son's place,
The parson from his own spire swung
     out dead,
And Ignorance crying in the streets,
     and all men
Regarding her ? I say they have
     drawn the fire
On their own heads : yet, Paget, I do
     hold
The Catholic, if he have the greater
     right,
Hath been the crueller.
     Paget.   Action and re-action,
The miserable see-saw of our child-
     world,
Make us despise it at odd hours, my
     Lord.
Heaven help that this re-action not
     re-act
Yet fiercelier under Queen Elizabeth,
So that she come to rule us.
     Howard.   The world's mad

Paget. My Lord, the world is like
     a drunken man,
Who cannot move straight to his end
     — but reels
Now to the right, then as far to the
     left,
Push'd by the crowd beside — and
     underfoot
An earthquake; for since Henry for
     a doubt —
Which a young lust had clapt upon
     the back,
Crying, " Forward ! " — set our old
     church rocking, men
Have hardly known what to believe,
     or whether
They should believe in anything; the
     currents
So shift and change, they see not
     how they are borne,
Nor whither. I conclude the King a
     beast;
Verily a lion if you will — the world
A most obedient beast and fool —
     myself
Half beast and fool as appertaining
     to it ;
Altho' your Lordship hath as little of
     each
Cleaving to your original Adam-clay,
As may be consonant with mortality.
     Howard. We talk and Cranmer
     suffers.
The kindliest man I ever knew; see,
     see,
I speak of him in the past. Unhappy
     land !
Hard-natured Queen, half-Spanish in
     herself,
And grafted on the hard-grain'd stock
     of Spain —
Her life, since Philip left her, and she
     lost
Her fierce desire of bearing him a
     child,
Hath, like a brief and bitter winter's
     day,
Gone narrowing down and darkening
     to a close.
There will be more conspiracies, I
     fear.
     Paget. Ay, ay, beware of France.

Howard.   O Paget, Paget !
I have seen heretics of the poorer
     sort,
Expectant of the rack from day to
     day,
To whom the fire were welcome, lying
     chain'd
In breathless dungeons over steaming
     sewers,
Fed with rank bread that crawl'd upon
     the tongue,
And putrid water, every drop a worm,
Until they died of rotted limbs ; and
     then
Cast on the dunghill naked, and
     become
Hideously alive again from head to
     heel,
Made even the carrion-nosing mongrel
     vomit
With hate and horror.
     Paget.   Nay, you sicken *me*
To hear you.
     Howard. Fancy-sick ; these things
     are done,
Done right against the promise of this
     Queen
Twice given.
     Paget. No faith with heretics, my
     Lord !
Hist ! there be two old gossips — gos-
     pellers,
I take it ; stand behind the pillar here ;
I warrant you they talk about the
     burning.

Enter TWO OLD WOMEN. JOAN, *and
     after her* TIB.

     Joan. Why, it be Tib !
     Tib. I cum behind tha, gall, and
couldn't make tha hear. Eh, the wind
and the wet ! What a day, what a
day ! nigh upo' judgement daay loike.
Pwoaps be pretty things, Joan, but
they wunt set i' the Lord's cheer o'
that daay.
     Joan. I must set down myself, Tib ;
it be a var waay vor my owld legs up
vro' Islip. Eh, my rheumatizy be that
bad howiver be I to win to the burnin'.
     Tib. I should saay 'twur ower by

now. I'd ha' been here avore, but Dumble wur blow'd wi' the wind, and Dumble's the best milcher in Islip.

Joan. Our Daisy's as good 'z her.

Tib. Noa, Joan.

Joan. Our Daisy's butter's as good 'z hern.

Tib. Noa, Joan.

Joan. Our Daisy's cheeses be better.

Tib. Noa, Joan.

Joan. Eh, then ha' thy waay wi' me, Tib ; ez thou hast wi' thy owld man.

Tib. Ay, Joan, and my owld man wur up and awaay betimes wi' dree hard eggs for a good pleace at the burnin' ; and barrin' the wet, Hodge 'ud ha' been a-harrowin' o' white peasen i' the outfield — and barrin' the wind, Dumble wur blow'd wi' the wind, so 'z we was forced to stick her, but we fetched her round at last. Thank the Lord therevore. Dumble's the best milcher in Islip.

Joan. Thou's thy way wi' man and beast, Tib. I wonder at tha', it beats me ! Eh, but I do know ez Pwoaps and vires be bad things ; tell 'ee now, I heerd summat as summun towld summun o' owld Bishop Gardiner's end ; there wur an owld lord a-cum to dine wi' un, and a wur so owld a couldn't bide vor his dinner, but a had to bide howsomiver, vor "I wunt dine," says my Lord Bishop, says he, "not till I hears ez Latimer and Ridley be a-vire ; " and so they bided on and on till vour o' the clock, till his man cum in post vro' here, and tells un ez the vire has tuk holt. "Now," says the Bishop, says he, "we'll gwo to dinner ; " and the owld lord fell to 's meat wi' a will, God bless un ! but Gardiner wur struck down like by the hand o' God avore a could taste a mossel, and a set un all a-vire, so 'z the tongue on un cum a-lolluping out o' 'is mouth as black as a rat. Thank the Lord, therevore.

Paget. The fools !

Tib. Ay, Joan ; and Queen Mary gwoes on a-burnin' and a-burnin', to get her baaby born ; but all her burnins' 'ill never burn out the hypocrisy that makes the water in her. There's nought but the vire of God's hell ez can burn out that.

Joan. Thank the Lord, therevore.

Paget. The fools !

Tib. A-burnin' and a-burnin', and a-makin' o' volk madder and madder ; but tek thou my word vor't, Joan, — and I bean't wrong not twice i' ten year — the burnin' o' the owld archbishop 'll burn the Pwoap out o' this 'ere land vor iver and iver.

Howard. Out of the church, you brace of cursed crones,
Or I will have you duck'd ! (*Women hurry out.*) Said I not right ?
For how should reverend prelate or throned prince
Brook for an hour such brute malignity ?
Ah, what an acrid wine has Luther brew'd !

Paget. Pooh, pooh, my Lord ! poor garrulous country-wives.
Buy you their cheeses, and they'll side with you ;
You cannot judge the liquor from the lees.

Howard. I think that in some sort we may. But see,

Enter PETERS.

Peters, my gentleman, an honest Catholic,
Who follow'd with the crowd to Cranmer's fire.
One that would neither misreport nor lie,
Not to gain paradise : no, nor if the Pope,
Charged him to do it — he is white as death.
Peters, how pale you look ! you bring the smoke
Of Cranmer's burning with you,
    Peters.   Twice or thrice
The smoke of Cranmer's burning wrapt me round.

Howard. Peters, you know me
  Catholic, but English.
Did he die bravely ? Tell me that, or
  leave
All else untold.
  Peters.   My Lord, he died most
    bravely.
  Howard. Then tell me all.
  Paget. Ay, Master Peters, tell us.
  Peters. You saw him how he past
    among the crowd ;
And ever as he walk'd the Spanish
    friars
Still plied him with entreaty and re-
    proach :
But Cranmer, as the helmsman at the
    helm
Steers, ever looking to the happy ha-
    ven
Where he shall rest at night, moved
    to his death ;
And I could see that many silent
    hands
Came from the crowd and met his
    own ; and thus,
When we had come where Ridley
    burnt with Latimer,
He, with a cheerful smile, as one
    whose mind
Is all made up, in haste put off the
    rags
They had mock'd his misery with, and
    all in white,
His long white beard, which he had
    never shaven
Since Henry's death, down-sweeping
    to the chain
Wherewith they bound him to the
    stake, he stood
More like an ancient father of the
    Church,
Than heretic of these times ; and still
    the friars
Plied him, but Cranmer only shook
    his head,
Or answer'd them in smiling negatives ;
Whereat Lord Williams gave a sud-
    den cry : —
" Make short ! make short !" and so
    they lit the wood.
Then Cranmer lifted his left hand to
    heaven,

And thrust his right into the bitter
    flame ;
And crying, in his deep voice, more
    than once,
" This hath offended — this unworthy
    hand ! "
So held it till it all was burn'd, before
The flame had reach'd his body ; I
    stood near —
Mark'd him — he never uttered moan
    of pain :
He never stirr'd or writhed, but, like a
    statue,
Unmoving in the greatness of the
    flame,
Gave up the ghost ; and so past mar-
    tyr-like —
Martyr I may not call him — past —
    but whither ?
  Paget. To purgatory, man, to pur-
    gatory.
  Peters. Nay, but, my Lord, he de-
    nied purgatory.
  Paget. Why then to heaven, and
    God ha' mercy on him.
  Howard. Paget, despite his fearful
    heresies,
I loved the man, and needs must
    moan for him ;
O Cranmer !
  Paget. But your moan is useless
    now :
Come out, my Lord, it is a world of
    fools.   [*Exeunt.*

ACT V.

SCENE I. — LONDON.   HALL IN THE
        PALACE.

  QUEEN, SIR NICHOLAS HEATH.

Heath. Madam,
I do assure you, that it must be look'd
    to :
Calais is but ill-garrison'd, in Guisnes
Are scarce two hundred men, and the
    French fleet
Rule in the narrow seas. It must be
    look'd to,
If war should fall between yourself
    and France ;
Or you will lose your Calais.

Mary. It shall be look'd to;
I wish you a good morning, good Sir
    Nicholas :
Here is the King.   [*Exit* Heath.

Enter PHILIP.

Philip. Sir Nicholas tells you true,
And you must look to Calais when I go.
    Mary. Go ? must you go, indeed —
    again — so soon ?
Why, nature's licensed vagabond, the
    swallow,
That might live always in the sun's
    warm heart,
Stays longer here in our poor north
    than you : —
Knows where he nested — ever comes
    again.
    Philip. And, Madam, so shall I.
    Mary. O, will you ? will you ?
I am faint with fear that you will
    come no more.
    Philip. Ay, ay; but many voices
    call me hence.
    Mary. Voices — I hear unhappy
    rumors — nay,
I say not, I believe. What voices
    call you
Dearer than mine that should be dear-
    est to you ?
Alas, my Lord ! what voices and how
    many ?
    Philip. The voices of Castile and
    Aragon,
Granada, Naples, Sicily, and Milan,—
The voices of Franche-Comté, and the
    Netherlands,
The voices of Peru and Mexico,
Tunis, and Oran, and the Philippines,
And all the fair spice-islands of the
    East.
    Mary (*admiringly*). You are the
    mightiest monarch upon earth,
I but a little Queen : and, so indeed,
Need you the more.
    Philip. A little Queen ! but when
I came to wed your Majesty, Lord
    Howard,
Sending an insolent shot that dash'd
    the seas
Upon us, made us lower our kingly flag
To yours of England.

    Mary. Howard is all English !
There is no king, not were he ten times
    king,
Ten times our husband, but must
    lower his flag
To that of England in the seas of
    England.
    Philip. Is that your answer ?
    Mary. Being Queen of England,
I have none other.
    Philip. So.
    Mary. But wherefore not
Helm the huge vessel of your state,
    my liege,   ●
Here by the side of her who loves you
    most ?
    Philip. No, Madam, no ! a candle in
    the sun
Is all but smoke — a star beside the
    moon
Is all but lost; your people will not
    crown me —
Your people are as cheerless as your
    clime ;
Hate me and mine : witness the brawls,
    the gibbets.
Here swings a Spaniard — there an
    Englishman ;
The peoples are unlike as their com-
    plexion ;
Yet will I be your swallow and re-
    turn —
But now I cannot bide.
    Mary. Not to help *me* ?
They hate *me* also for my love to you,
My Philip ; and these judgments on
    the land —
Harvestless autumns, horrible agues,
    plague —
    Philip. The blood and sweat of
    heretics at the stake
Is God's best dew upon the barren field.
Burn more !
    Mary. I will, I will; and you will
    stay ?
    Philip. Have I not said ? Madam,
    I came to sue
Your Council and yourself to declare
    war.
    Mary. Sir, there are many English
    in your ranks
To help your battle.

Philip.   So far, good.   I say
I came to sue your Council and your-
    self
To declare war against the King of
    France.
    Mary.   Not to see me ?
    Philip.   Ay, Madam, to see you.
Unalterably and pesteringly fond!
                              [*Aside.*
But, soon or late you must have war
    with France ;
King Henry warms your traitors at
    his hearth.
Carew is there, and Thomas Stafford
    there.
Courtenay, belike —
    Mary.   A fool and featherhead !
    Philip.   Ay, but they use his name.
    In brief, this Henry
Stirs up your land against you to the
    intent
That you may lose your English her-
    itage.
And then, your Scottish namesake
    marrying
The Dauphin, he would weld France,
    England, Scotland,
Into one sword to hack at Spain and
    me.
    Mary.   And yet the Pope is now
    colleagued with France ;
You make your wars upon him down
    in Italy : —
Philip, can that be well ?
    Philip.   Content you, Madam ;
You must abide my judgment, and
    my father's,
Who deems it a most just and holy
    war.
The Pope would cast the Spaniard
    out of Naples :
He calls us worse than Jews, Moors,
    Saracens.
The Pope has pushed his horns be-
    yond his mitre —
Beyond his province. Now,
Duke Alva will but touch him on the
    horns,
And he withdraws ; and of his holy
    head —
For Alva is true son of the true
    church —

No hair is harm'd.   Will you not help
    me here ?
    Mary.   Alas ! the Council will not
    hear of war.
They say your wars are not the wars
    of England.
They will not lay more taxes on a
    land
So hunger-nipt and wretched; and
    you know
The crown is poor. We have given
    the church-lands back :
The nobles would not ; nay, they clapt
    their hands
Upon their swords when ask'd ; and
    therefore God
Is hard upon the people. What's to
    be done ?
Sir, I will move them in your cause
    again,
And we will raise us loans and subsidies
Among the merchants ; and Sir
    Thomas Gresham
Will aid us. There is Antwerp and
    the Jews.
    Philip.   Madam, my thanks.
    Mary.   And you will stay your
    going ?
    Philip.   And further to discourage
    and lay lame
The plots of France, altho' you love
    her not,
You must proclaim Elizabeth your
    heir.
She stands between you and the
    Queen of Scots.
    Mary.   The Queen of Scots at least
    is Catholic.
    Philip.   Ay, Madam, Catholic ; but
    I will not have
The King of France the King of Eng-
    land too.
    Mary.   But she's a heretic, and,
    when I am gone,
Brings the new learning back.
    Philip.   It must be done.
You must proclaim Elizabeth your
    heir.
    Mary.   Then it is done ; but you will
    stay your going
Somewhat beyond your settled pur-
    pose ?

Philip.   No !
Mary. What, not one day ?
Philip.   You beat upon the rock.
Mary. And I am broken there.
Philip.   Is this a place
To wail in, Madam ? what ! a public
      hall.
Go in, I pray you.
Mary.   Do not seem so changed.
Say go; but only say it lovingly.
Philip. You do mistake.   I am not
      one to change.
I never loved you more.
Mary.   Sire, I obey you.
Come quickly.
Philip.   Ay.   [*Exit* Mary.

Enter COUNT DE FERIA.

Feria (*aside*). The Queen in tears !
Philip.   Feria !
Hast thou not mark'd — come closer
      to mine ear —
How doubly aged this Queen of ours
      hath grown
Since she lost hope of bearing us a
      child ?
Feria. Sire, if your Grace hath
      mark'd it, so have I.
Philip. Hast thou not likewise
      mark'd Elizabeth,
How fair and royal — like a Queen,
      indeed ?
Feria. Allow me the same answer
      as before —
That if your Grace hath mark'd her,
      so have I.
Philip. Good, now; methinks my
      Queen is like enough
To leave me by and by.
Feria.   To leave you, sire ?
Philip. I mean not like to live.
      Elizabeth —
To Philibert of Savoy, as you know,
We meant to wed her; but I am not
      sure
She will not serve me better — so my
      Queen
Would leave me — as — my wife.
Feria.   Sire, even so.
Philip. She will not have Prince
      Philibert of Savoy.

Feria. No, sire.
Philip.   I have to pray you,
      some odd time,
To sound the Princess carelessly on
      this ;
Not as from me, but as your phantasy ;
And tell me how she takes it.
Feria.   Sire, I will.
Philip. I am not certain but that
      Philibert
Shall be the man ; and I shall urge
      his suit
Upon the Queen, because I am not
      certain :
You understand, Feria.
Feria.   Sire, I do.
Philip. And if you be not secret
      in this matter,
You understand me there, too ?
Feria.   Sire, I do.
Philip. You must be sweet and
      supple, like a Frenchman.
She is none of those who loathe the
      honeycomb.   [*Exit* Feria.

Enter RENARD.

Renard. My liege, I bring you
      goodly tidings.
Philip.   Well ?
Renard. There *will* be war with
      France, at last, my liege ;
Sir Thomas Stafford, a bull-headed
      ass,
Sailing from France, with thirty Eng-
      lishmen,
Hath taken Scarboro' Castle, north of
      York ;
Proclaims himself protector, and af-
      firms
The Queen has forfeited her right to
      reign
By marriage with an alien — other
      things
As idle ; a weak Wyatt ! Little doubt
This buzz will soon be silenced ; but
      the Council
(I have talk'd with some already) are
      for war.
This the fifth conspiracy hatch'd in
      France ;
They show their teeth upon it ; and
      your Grace,

So you will take advice of mine,
   should stay
Yet for awhile, to shape and guide the
   event.
  Philip.   Good! Renard, I will stay
   then.
  Renard.   Also, sire,
Might I not say — to please your wife,
   the Queen ?
  Philip. Ay, Renard, if you care to
   put it so.   [*Exeunt.*

SCENE II.— A ROOM IN THE
PALACE.

MARY, *sitting: a rose in her hand.*
LADY CLARENCE. ALICE *in the back-
ground.*

  Mary. Look ! I have play'd with
   this poor rose so long
I have broken off the head.
  Lady Clarence. Your Grace hath
   been
More merciful to many a rebel head
That should have fallen, and may rise
   again.
  Mary. There were not many hang'd
   for Wyatt's rising.
  Lady Clarence. Nay, not two hun-
   dred.
  Mary.   I could weep for them
And her, and mine own self and all
   the world.
  Lady Clarence. For her ? for whom,
   your Grace ?

Enter USHER.

  Usher. The Cardinal.

Enter CARDINAL POLE. (MARY *rises.*)

  Mary. Reginald Pole, what news
   hath plagued thy heart ?
What makes thy favor like the blood-
   less head
Fall'n on the block, and held up by
   the hair ?
Philip ? —
  Pole. No, Philip is as warm in life
As ever.
  Mary. Ay, and then as cold as
   ever.
Is Calais taken ?

  Pole.   Cousin, there hath chanced
A sharper harm to England and to
   Rome,
Than Calais taken. Julius the Third
Was ever just, and mild, and father-
   like ;
But this new Pope Caraffa, Paul the
   Fourth,
Not only reft me of that legateship
Which Julius gave me, and the legate-
   ship
Annex'd to Canterbury — nay, but
   worse —
And yet I must obey the Holy Father,
And so must you, good cousin ; —
   worse than all,
A passing bell toll'd in a dying ear —
He hath cited me to Rome, for heresy,
Before his Inquisition.
  Mary.   I knew it, cousin,
But held from you all papers sent by
   Rome,
That you might rest among us, till
   the Pope,
To compass which I wrote myself to
   Rome,
Reversed his doom, and that you
   might not seem
To disobey his Holiness.
  Pole.   He hates Philip ;
He is all Italian, and he hates the
   Spaniard ;
He cannot dream that *I* advised the
   war ;
He strikes thro' me at Philip and
   yourself.
Nay, but I know it of old, he hates
   me too ;
So brands me in the stare of Christen-
   dom
A heretic !
Now, even now, when bow'd before
   my time,
The house half-ruin'd ere the lease be
   out ;
When I should guide the Church in
   peace at home,
After my twenty years of banishment,
And all my lifelong labor to uphold
The primacy — a heretic. Long ago,
When I was ruler in the patrimony,
I was too lenient to the Lutheran,

And I and learned friends among our-
selves
Would freely canvass certain Luther-
anisms.
What then, he knew I was no Lutheran.
A heretic!
He drew this shaft against me to the
head,
When it was thought I might be
chosen Pope,
But then withdrew it. In full con-
sistory,
When I was made Archbishop, he
approved me.
And how should he have sent me
Legate hither,
Deeming me heretic? and what heresy
since?
But he was evermore mine enemy,
And hates the Spaniard — fiery-chol-
eric,
A drinker of black, strong, volcanic
wines,
That ever make him fierier. I, a
heretic?
Your Highness knows that in pursu-
ing heresy
I have gone beyond your late Lord
Chancellor, —
He cried Enough! enough! before
his death. —
Gone beyond him and mine own nat-
ural man
(It was God's cause); so far they call
me now,
The scourge and butcher of their Eng-
lish church.
Mary. Have courage, your reward
is Heaven itself.
Pole. They groan amen; they
swarm into the fire
Like flies — for what? no dogma.
They know nothing;
They burn for nothing.
Mary. You have done your best.
Pole. Have done my best, and as a
faithful son,
That all day long hath wrought his
father's work,
When back he comes at evening hath
the door

Shut on him by the father whom he
loved,
His early follies cast into his teeth,
And the poor son turn'd out into the
street
To sleep, to die — I shall die of it,
cousin.
Mary. I pray you be not so discon-
solate;
I still will do mine utmost with the
Pope.
Poor cousin!
Have not I been the fast friend of
your life
Since mine began, and it was thought
we two
Might make one flesh, and cleave
unto each other
As man and wife?
Pole. Ah, cousin, I remember
How I would dandle you upon my
knee
At lisping-age. I watch'd you danc-
ing once
With your huge father; he look'd the
Great Harry,
You but his cockboat; prettily you
did it,
And innocently. No — we were not
made
One flesh in happiness, no happiness
here;
But now we are made one flesh in
misery;
Our bridemaids are not lovely — Dis-
appointment,
Ingratitude, Injustice, Evil-tongue,
Labor-in-vain.
Mary. Surely, not all in vain.
Peace, cousin, peace! I am sad at
heart myself.
Pole. Our altar is a mound of dead
men's clay,
Dug from the grave that yawns for
us beyond;
And there is one Death stands behind
the Groom,
And there is one Death stands behind
the Bride —
Mary. Have you been looking at
the "Dance of Death"?

Pole. No; but these libellous papers
    which I found
Strewn in your palace.   Look you
    here — the Pope
Pointing at me with " Pole, the here-
    tic,
Thou hast burnt others, do thou burn
    thyself,
Or I will burn thee;" and this other;
    see !—
" We pray continually for the death
Of our accursed Queen and Cardinal
    Pole."
This last — I dare not read it her.
                            [*Aside.*
    Mary.   Away !
Why do you bring me these ?
I thought you knew me better.   I
    never read,
I tear them; they come back upon my
    dreams.
The hands that write them should be
    burnt clean off
As Cranmer's, and the fiends that
    utter them
Tongue-torn with pincers, lash'd to
    death, or lie
Famishing in black cells, while fam-
    ish'd rats
Eat them alive.   Why do they bring
    me these ?
Do you mean to drive me mad ?
    Pole.   I had forgotten
How these poor libels trouble you.
    Your pardon,
Sweet cousin, and farewell !   " O bub-
    ble world,
Whose colors in a moment break and
    fly ! "
Why, who said that ?   I know not —
    true enough !
    [*Puts up the papers, all but the last,
    which falls.   Exit Pole.*
    Alice. If Cranmer's spirit were a
    mocking one,
And heard these two, there might be
    sport for him.   [*Aside.*
    Mary. Clarence, they hate me ;
    even while I speak
There lurks a silent dagger, listening
In some dark closet, some long gal-
    lery, drawn,

And panting for my blood as I go by.
    Lady Clarence. Nay, Madam, there
    be loyal papers too,
And I have often found them.
    Mary.   Find me one !
    Lady Clarence. Ay, Madam; but
    Sir Nicholas Heath, the Chan-
    cellor,
Would see your Highness.
    Mary. Wherefore should I see
    him ?
    Lady Clarence. Well, Madam, he
    may bring you news from
    Philip.
    Mary. So, Clarence.
    Lady Clarence.   Let me first put
    up your hair ;
It tumbles all abroad.
    Mary.   And the gray dawn
Of an old age that never will be mine
Is all the clearer seen.   No, no ; what
    matters ?
Forlorn I am, and let me look forlorn.

    Enter Sir Nicholas Heath.

    Heath. I bring your Majesty such
    grievous news
I grieve to bring it.   Madam, Calais
    is taken.
    Mary. What traitor spoke ?   Here,
    let my cousin Pole
Seize him and burn him for a Lu-
    theran.
    Heath. Her Highness is unwell.   I
    will retire.
    Lady Clarence. Madam, your Chan-
    cellor, Sir Nicholas Heath.
    Mary. Sir Nicholas !   I am stunn'd
    — Nicholas Heath ?
Methought some traitor smote me on
    the head.
What said you, my good Lord, that
    our brave English
Had sallied out from Calais and
    driven back
The Frenchmen from their trenches ?
    Heath.   Alas ! no.
That gateway to the mainland over
    which
Our flag hath floated for two hundred
    years
Is France again.

Mary.   So ; but it is not lost —
Not yet.   Send out : let England as of
    old
Rise lionlike, strike hard and deep
    into
The prey they are rending from her
    — ay, and rend
The renders too.   Send out, send out,
    and make
Musters in all the counties ; gather
    all
From sixteen years to sixty ; collect
    the fleet ;
Let every craft that carries sail and
    gun
Steer toward Calais.   Guisnes is not
    taken yet ?
    Heath. Guisnes is not taken yet.
    Mary.   There is yet hope.
    Heath. Ah, Madam, but your peo-
    ple are so cold ;
I do much fear that England will not
    care.
Methinks there is no manhood left
    among us.
    Mary. Send out ; I am too weak to
    stir abroad :
Tell my mind to the Council — to the
    Parliament :
Proclaim it to the winds.   Thou art
    cold thyself
To babble of their coldness.   O would
    I were
My father for an hour !   Away now —
    Quick !   [*Exit* Heath.
I hoped I had served God with all my
    might !
It seems I have not.   Ah ! much
    heresy
Shelter'd in Calais.   Saints, I have
    rebuilt
Your shrines, set up your broken
    images ;
Be comfortable to me.   Suffer not
That my brief reign in England be
    defamed
Thro' all her angry chronicles here-
    after
By loss of Calais.   Grant me Calais.
    Philip,
We have made war upon the Holy
    Father

All for your sake : what good could
    come of that ?
    Lady Clarence. No, Madam, not
    against the Holy Father ;
You did but help King Philip's war
    with France,
Your troops were never down in Italy.
    Mary. I am a byword.   Heretic and
    rebel
Point at me and make merry.   Philip
    gone !
And Calais gone !   Time that I were
    gone too !
    Lady Clarence. Nay, if the fetid
    gutter had a voice
And cried I was not clean, what
    should I care ?
Or you, for heretic cries ?   And I
    believe,
Spite of your melancholy Sir Nicholas,
Your England is as loyal as myself.
    Mary (*seeing the paper dropt by* Pole).
    There ! there ! another paper !
    Said you not
Many of these were loyal ?   Shall I
    try
If this be one of such ?
    Lady Clarence. Let it be, let it be.
God pardon me !   I have never yet
    found one.   [*Aside.*
    Mary (*reads*). " Your people hate
    you as your husband hates you."
Clarence, Clarence, what have I done ?
    what sin
Beyond all grace, all pardon ?   Mother
    of God,
Thou knowest woman never meant so
    well,
And fared so ill in this disastrous
    world.
My people hate me and desire my
    death.
    Lady Clarence. No, Madam, no.
    Mary. My husband hates me, and
    desires my death.
    Lady Clarence. No, Madam ; these
    are libels.
    Mary. I hate myself, and I desire
    my death.
    Lady Clarence. Long live your
    Majesty !   Shall Alice sing
    you

One of her pleasant songs ? Alice,
  my child,
Bring us your lute (*Alice goes*). They
  say the gloom of Saul
Was lighten'd by young David's harp.
  Mary.   Too young !
And never knew a Philip.

Re-enter Alice.

                    Give *me* the lute.
He hates me !

(*She sings.*)

Hapless doom of woman happy in betroth-
  ing !
Beauty passes like a breath and love is lost
  in loathing :
Low, my lute ; speak low, my lute, but say
  the world is nothing —
          Low, lute, low !
Love will hover round the flowers when they
  first awaken ;
Love will fly the fallen leaf, and not be overtaken ;
Low, my lute ! oh low, my lute ! we fade and
  are forsaken —
          Low, dear lute, low !

Take it away ! not low enough for me !
  Alice. Your Grace hath a low voice.
  Mary.   How dare you say it ?
Even for that he hates me. A low
  voice
Lost in a wilderness where none can
  hear !
A voice of shipwreck on a shoreless
  sea !
A low voice from the dust and from
  the grave
(*Sitting on the ground*). There, am I
  low enough now ?
  Alice. Good Lord ! how grim and
  ghastly looks her Grace,
With both her knees drawn upward to
  her chin.
There was an old-world tomb beside
  my father's,
And this was open'd, and the dead
  were found
Sitting, and in this fashion ; she looks
  a corpse.

Enter LADY MAGDALEN DACRES.

  Lady Magdalen. Madam, the Count
  de Feria waits without,
In hopes to see your Highness.

  Lady Clarence (*pointing to* Mary).
          Wait he must —
Her trance again. She neither sees
  nor hears,
And may not speak for hours.
  Lady Magdalen.   Unhappiest
Of Queens and wives and women !
  Alice (*in the foreground with* Lady
  Magdalen.)   And all along
Of Philip.
  Lady Magdalen. Not so loud ! Our
  Clarence there
Sees ever such an aureole round the
  Queen,
It gilds the greatest wronger of her
  peace,
Who stands the nearest to her.
  Alice.   Ay, this Philip ;
I used to love the Queen with all my
  heart —
God help me, but methinks I love her
  less
For such a dotage upon such a man.
I would I were as tall and strong as
  you.
  Lady Magdalen. I seem half-shamed
  at times to be so tall.
  Alice. You are the stateliest deer in
  all the herd —
Beyond his aim — but I am small and
  scandalous,
And love to hear bad tales of Philip.
  Lady Magdalen.   Why ?
I never heard him utter worse of you
Than that you were low-statured.
  Alice.   Does he think
Low stature is low nature, or all wom-
  en's
Low as his own ?
  Lady Magdalen. There you strike
  in the nail.
This coarseness is a want of phantasy.
It is the low man thinks the woman
  low ;
Sin is too dull to see beyond himself.
  Alice. Ah, Magdalen, sin is bold as
  well as dull.
How dared he ?
  Lady Magdalen. Stupid soldiers oft
  are bold.
Poor lads, they see not what the gen-
  eral sees,

A risk of utter ruin. I am *not*
Beyond his aim, or was not.
    Alice.   Who? Not you?
Tell, tell me; save my credit with
    myself.
    Lady Magdalen. I never breathed
    it to a bird in the eaves,
Would not for all the stars and
    maiden moon
Our drooping Queen should know! In
    Hampton Court
My window look'd upon the corri-
    dor;
And I was robing; — this poor throat
    of mine,
Barer than I should wish a man to see
    it, —
When he we speak of drove the win-
    dow back,
And, like a thief, push'd in his royal
    hand;
But by God's providence a good stout
    staff
Lay near me; and you know me
    strong of arm;
I do believe I lamed his Majesty's
For a day or two, tho', give the Devil
    his due,
I never found he bore me any spite.
    Alice. I would she could have wed-
    ded that poor youth,
My Lord of Devon — light enough,
    God knows,
And mixt with Wyatt's rising — and
    the boy
Not out of him — but neither cold,
    coarse, cruel,
And more than all — no Spaniard.
    Lady Clarence.   Not so loud.
Lord Devon, girls! what are you
    whispering here?
    Alice. Probing an old state-secret—
    how it chanced
That this young Earl was sent on
    foreign travel,
Not lost his head.
    Lady Clarence. There was no proof
    against him.
    Alice. Nay, Madam; did not Gardi-
    ner intercept
A letter which the Count de Noailles
    wrote

To that dead traitor Wyatt, with full
    proof
Of Courtenay's treason? What be-
    came of that?
    Lady Clarence. Some say that
    Gardiner, out of love for him,
Burnt it, and some relate that it was
    lost
When Wyatt sack'd the Chancellor's
    house in Southwark.
Let dead things rest.
    Alice. Ay, and with him who died
Alone in Italy.
    Lady Clarence. Much changed, I
    hear,
Had put off levity and put graveness
    on.
The foreign courts report him in his
    manner
Noble as his young person and old
    shield.
It might be so — but all is over
    now;
He caught a chill in the lagoons of
    Venice,
And died in Padua.
    Mary (*looking up suddenly*). Died
    in the true faith?
    Lady Clarence. Ay, Madam, happily.
    Mary.   Happier he than I.
    Lady Magdalen. It seems her High-
    ness hath awaken'd. Think you
That I might dare to tell her that the
    Count——
    Mary. I will see no man hence for
    evermore,
Saving my confessor and my cousin
    Pole.
    Lady Magdalen. It is the Count de
    Feria, my dear lady.
    Mary.   What Count?
    Lady Magdalen. The Count de
    Feria, from his Majesty
King Philip.
    Mary. Philip! quick! loop up my
    hair!
Throw cushions on that seat, and make
    it throne-like.
Arrange my dress — the gorgeous
    Indian shawl
That Philip brought me in our happy
    days! —

That covers all.   So — am I somewhat
    Queenlike,
Bride of the mightiest sovereign upon
    earth ?
    Lady Clarence. Ay, so your Grace
        would bide a moment yet.
    Mary. No, no, he brings a letter.
        I may die
Before I read it.   Let me see him at
    once.

    Enter COUNT DE FERIA (*kneels*).

    Feria. I trust your Grace is well.
        (*Aside*) How her hand burns !
    Mary. I am not well, but it will
        better me,
Sir Count, to read the letter which
    you bring.
    Feria. Madam, I bring no letter.
    Mary.   How ! no letter ?
    Feria. His Highness is so vex'd with
        strange affairs —
    Mary. That his own wife is no affair
        of his.
    Feria. Nay, Madam, nay ! he sends
        his veriest love,
And says, he will come quickly.
    Mary.   Doth he, indeed ?
You, sir, do *you* remember what *you*
    said
When last you came to England ?
    Feria.   Madam, I brought
My King's congratulations ; it was
    hoped
Your Highness was once more in happy
    state
To give him an heir male.
    Mary.   Sir, you said more ;
You said he would come quickly.   I
    had horses
On all the road from Dover, day and
    night ;
On all the road from Harwich, night
    and day ;
But the child came not, and the hus-
    band came not ;
And yet he will come quickly. . .
        Thou hast learnt
Thy lesson, and I mine.   There is no
    need
For Philip so to shame himself again.
Return,

And tell him that I know he comes no
    more.
Tell him at last I know his love is
    dead,
And that I am in state to bring forth
    death —
Thou art commission'd to Elizabeth,
And not to me !
    Feria. Mere compliments and
        wishes.
But shall I take some message from
    your Grace ?
    Mary. Tell her to come and close
        my dying eyes,
And wear my crown, and dance upon
    my grave.
    Feria. Then I may say your Grace
        will see your sister ?
Your Grace is too low-spirited.   Air
    and sunshine.
I would we had you, Madam, in our
    warm Spain.
You droop in your dim London.
    Mary.   Have him away !
I sicken of his readiness.
    Lady Clarence.   My Lord Count,
Her Highness is too ill for colloquy.
    Feria (*kneels, and kisses her hand*).
        I wish her Highness better.
        (*Aside*) How her hand burns !
                        [*Exeunt.*

SCENE III. — A HOUSE NEAR
            LONDON.

ELIZABETH, STEWARD OF THE HOUSE-
        HOLD, ATTENDANTS.

    Elizabeth. There's half an angel
        wrong'd in your account ;
Methinks I am all angel, that I bear
    it
Without more ruffling.   Cast it o'er
    again.
    Steward. I were whole devil if I
        wrong'd you, Madam.
                        [*Exit* Steward.
    Attendant. The Count de Feria from
        the King of Spain.
    Elizabeth. Ah ! — let him enter.
        Nay, you need not go :
                        [*To her* Ladies

Remain within the chamber, but apart.
We'll have no private conference.
Welcome to England!

Enter FERIA.

Feria. Fair island star!
Elizabeth. I shine! What else, Sir
  Count?
Feria. As far as France, and into
  Philip's heart.
My King would know if you be fairly
  served,
And lodged, and treated.
Elizabeth. You see the lodging, sir,
I am well-served, and am in everything
Most loyal and most grateful to the
  Queen.
Feria. You should be grateful to
  my master, too.
He spoke of this; and unto him you
  owe
That Mary hath acknowledged you
  her heir.
Elizabeth. No, not to her nor him;
  but to the people,
Who know my right, and love me, as
  I love
The people! whom God aid!
Feria. You will be Queen,
And, were I Philip —
Elizabeth. Wherefore pause you —
  what?
Feria. Nay, but I speak from mine
  own self, not him;
Your royal sister cannot last; your
  hand
Will be much coveted! What a deli-
  cate one!
Our Spanish ladies have none such —
  and there,
Were you in Spain, this fine fair gos-
  samer gold —
Like sun-gilt breathings on a frosty
  dawn —
That hovers round your shoulder —
Elizabeth. Is it so fine?
Troth, some have said so.
Feria. —would be deemed a mira-
  cle.
Elizabeth. Your Philip hath gold
  hair and golden beard;

There must be ladies many with hair
  like mine.
Feria. Some few of Gothic blood
  have golden hair,
But none like yours.
Elizabeth. I am happy you approve
  it.
Feria. But as to Philip and your
  Grace — consider, —
If such a one as you should match
  with Spain,
What hinders but that Spain and
  England join'd,
Should make the mightiest empire
  earth has known.
Spain would be England on her seas,
  and England
Mistress of the Indies.
Elizabeth. It may chance, that
  England
Will be the Mistress of the Indies yet,
Without the help of Spain.
Feria. Impossible;
Except you put Spain down.
Wide of the mark ev'n for a madman's
  dream.
Elizabeth. Perhaps; but we have
  seamen. Count de Feria,
I take it that the King hath spoken
  to you;
But is Don Carlos such a goodly
  match?
Feria. Don Carlos, Madam, is but
  twelve years old.
Elizabeth. Ay, tell the King that I
  will muse upon it;
He is my good friend, and I would
  keep him so;
But — he would have me Catholic of
  Rome,
And that I scarce can be; and, sir, till
  now
My sister's marriage, and my father's
  marriages,
Make me full fain to live and die a
  maid.
But I am much beholden to your
  King.
Have you aught else to tell me?
Feria. Nothing, Madam,
Save that methought I gather'd from
  the Queen

That she would see your Grace before
she — died.

Elizabeth. God's death! and where-
fore spake you not before ?
We dally with our lazy moments here,
And hers are number'd. Horses
there, without!
I am much beholden to the King, your
master.
Why did you keep me prating?
Horses, there!
[*Exit* Elizabeth, *etc.*

Feria. So from a clear sky falls the
thunderbolt!

Don Carlos? Madam, if you marry
Philip,
Then I and he will snaffle your "God's
death,"
And brake your paces in, and make
you tame;
God's death, forsooth — you do not
know King Philip. [*Exit.*

SCENE IV. — London. Before
the Palace.

*A light burning within. Voices of the
night passing.*

First. Is not yon light in the
Queen's chamber ?
Second. Ay,
They say she's dying.
First. So is Cardinal Pole.
May the great angels join their wings,
and make
Down for their heads to heaven!
Second. Ame— Come on.
[*Exeunt.*

Two Others.

First. There's the Queen's light.
I hear she cannot live.
Second. God curse her and her
Legate! Gardiner burns
Already; but to pay them full in kind,
The hottest hold in all the devil's den
Were but a sort of winter; sir, in
Guernsey,
I watch'd a woman burn; and in her
agony

The mother came upon her — a child
was born —
And, sir, they hurl'd it back into the
fire,
That, being but baptised in fire, the
babe
Might be in fire for ever. Ah, good
neighbor,
There should be something fiercer than
fire
To yield them their deserts.
First. Amen to all.
Your wish, and further.
A Third Voice. Deserts! Amen to
what ? Whose deserts ? Yours ?
You have a gold ring on your finger,
and soft raiment about your body;
and is not the woman up yonder sleeping after all she has done, in peace and
quietness, on a soft bed, in a closed
room, with light, fire, physic, tendance; and I have seen the true men
of Christ lying famine-dead by scores,
and under no ceiling but the cloud that
wept on them, not for them.
First. Friend, tho' so late, it is not
safe to preach.
You had best go home. What are
you ?
Third. What am I? One who cries
continually with sweat and tears to
the Lord God that it would please Him
out of His infinite love to break down
all kingship and queenship, all priesthood and prelacy; to cancel and
abolish all bonds of human allegiance,
all the magistracy, all the nobles, and
all the wealthy; and to send us again,
according to His promise, the one King,
the Christ, and all things in common,
as in the day of the first church, when
Christ Jesus was King.
First. If ever I heard a madman,
— let's away!
Why, you long-winded —— Sir, you
go beyond me.
I pride myself on being moderate.
Good night! Go home. Besides, you
curse so loud,
The watch will hear you. Get you
home at once. [*Exeunt.*

SCENE V. — LONDON. A ROOM IN
THE PALACE.

*A Gallery on one side. The moonlight
streaming through a range of windows
on the wall opposite.* MARY, LADY
CLARENCE, LADY MAGDALEN
DACRES, ALICE. QUEEN *pacing the
Gallery. A writing-table in front.*
QUEEN *comes to the table and writes
and goes again, pacing the Gallery.*

Lady Clarence. Mine eyes are dim :
what hath she written ? read.
Alice. " I am dying, Philip ; come
to me."
Lady Magdalen. There — up and
down, poor lady, up and down.
Alice. And how her shadow crosses
one by one
The moonlight casements pattern'd on
the wall,
Following her like her sorrow. She
turns again.
[Queen *sits and writes, and goes again.*
Lady Clarence. What hath she
written now ?
Alice. Nothing ; but "come, come,
come," and all awry,
And blotted by her tears. This can-
not last. [Queen *returns.*
Mary. I whistle to the bird has
broken cage,
And all in vain. [*Sitting down.*
Calais gone — Guisnes gone, too —
and Philip gone !
Lady Clarence. Dear Madam, Philip
is but at the wars ;
I cannot doubt but that he comes
again ;
And he is with you in a measure still.
I never look'd upon so fair a likeness
As your great King in armor there,
his hand
Upon his helmet.
[*Pointing to the portrait of* Philip *on
the wall.*
Mary. Doth he not look noble ?
I had heard of him in battle over
seas,
And I would have my warrior all in
arms.

He said it was not courtly to stand
helmeted
Before the Queen. He had his gra-
cious moment,
Altho' you'll not believe me. How
he smiles
As if he loved me yet !
Lady Clarence. And so he does.
Mary. He never loved me — nay,
he could not love me.
It was his father's policy against
France.
I am eleven years older than he,
Poor boy ! [*Weeps.*
Alice. That was a lusty boy of
twenty-seven ; [*Aside.*
Poor enough in God's grace !
Mary. — And all in vain
The Queen of Scots is married to the
Dauphin,
And Charles, the lord of this low
world, is gone ;
And all his wars and wisdoms past
away ;
And in a moment I shall follow
him.
Lady Clarence. Nay, dearest Lady,
see your good physician.
Mary, Drugs — but he knows they
cannot help me — says
That rest is all — tells me I must not
think —
That I must rest — I shall rest by and
by.
Catch the wild cat, cage him, and when
he springs
And maims himself against the bars,
say " rest " :
Why, you must kill him if you would
have him rest —
Dead or alive you cannot make him
happy.
Lady Clarence. Your Majesty has
lived so pure a life,
And done such mighty things by Holy
Church,
I trust that God will make you happy
yet.
Mary. What is the strange thing
happiness ? Sit down here :
Tell me thine happiest hour.
Lady Clarence. I will, if that

May make your Grace forget yourself
a little.
There runs a shallow brook across our
field
For twenty miles, where the black
crow flies five,
And doth so bound and babble all the
way
As if itself were happy. It was May-
time,
And I was walking with the man I
loved.
I loved him, but I thought I was not
loved.
And both were silent, letting the wild
brook
Speak for us — till he stoop'd and
gather'd one
From out a bed of thick forget-me-nots,
Look'd hard and sweet at me, and
gave it me.
I took it, tho' I did not know I took it,
And put it in my bosom, and all at
once
I felt his arms about me, and his lips —
Mary. O God! I have been too
slack, too slack;
There are Hot Gospellers even among
our guards —
Nobles we dared not touch. We have
but burnt
The heretic priest, workmen, and
women and children.
Wet, famine, ague, fever, storm,
wreck, wrath, —
We have so play'd the coward; but by
God's grace,
We'll follow Philip's leading, and set
up
The Holy Office here — garner the
wheat,
And burn the tares with unquenchable
fire!
Burn! —
Fie, what a savor! tell the cooks to
close
The doors of all the offices below.
Latimer!
Sir, we are private with our women
here —
Ever a rough, blunt, and uncourtly
fellow —

Thou light a torch that never will go
out!
'Tis out — mine flames. Women, the
Holy Father
Has ta'en the legateship from our
cousin Pole —
Was that well done? and poor Pole
pines of it,
As I do, to the death. I am but a
woman,
I have no power. — Ah, weak and
meek old man,
Seven-fold dishonor'd even in the
sight
Of thine own sectaries — No, no. No
pardon! —
Why that was false: there is the right
hand still
Beckons me hence.
Sir, you were burnt for heresy, not for
treason,
Remember that! 'twas I and Bonner
did it,
And Pole; we are three to one — Have
you found mercy there,
Grant it me here: and see, he smiles
and goes,
Gentle as in life.
Alice. Madam, who goes? King
Philip?
Mary. No, Philip comes and goes,
but never goes.
Women, when I am dead,
Open my heart, and there you will
find written
Two names, Philip and Calais; open
his, —
So that he have one, —
You will find Philip only, policy, pol-
icy, —
Ay, worse than that — not one hour
true to me!
Foul maggots crawling in a fester'd
vice!
Adulterous to the very heart of Hell.
Hast thou a knife?
Alice. Ay, Madam, but o' God's
mercy —
Mary. Fool, think'st thou I would
peril mine own soul
By slaughter of the body? I could
not, girl,

Not this way — callous with a constant stripe,
Unwoundable. The knife!
  Alice.   Take heed, take heed!
The blade is keen as death.
  Mary.   This Philip shall not
Stare in upon me in my haggardness;
Old, miserable, diseased,
Incapable of children. Come thou down.
[*Cuts out the picture and throws it down.*
Lie there. (*Wails*) O God, I have kill'd my Philip!
  Alice.   No,
Madam, you have but cut the canvas out;
We can replace it.
  Mary.   All is well then; rest —
I will to rest; he said, I must have rest. [*Cries of* "Elizabeth" *in the street.*
A cry! What's that? Elizabeth? revolt?
A new Northumberland, another Wyatt?
I'll fight it on the threshold of the grave.
  Lady Clarence. Madam, your royal sister comes to see you.
  Mary. I will not see her.
Who knows if Boleyn's daughter be my sister?
I will see none except the priest. Your arm. [*To* Lady Clarence.
O Saint of Aragon, with that sweet worn smile
Among thy patient wrinkles — Help me hence. [*Exeunt.*

The PRIEST *passes. Enter* ELIZABETH *and* SIR WILLIAM CECIL.

  Elizabeth. Good counsel yours —
       No one in waiting? still,
As if the chamberlain were Death himself!
The room she sleeps in — is not this the way?
No, that way there are voices. Am I too late?
Cecil . . . God guide me lest I lose the way. [*Exit* Elizabeth.

  Cecil. Many points weather'd, many perilous ones,
At last a harbor opens; but therein
Sunk rocks — they need fine steering — much it is
To be nor mad, nor bigot — have a mind —
Nor let the Priests talk, or dream of worlds to be,
Miscolor things about her — sudden touches
For him, or him — sunk rocks; no passionate faith —
But — if let be — balance and compromise;
Brave, wary, sane to the heart of her — a Tudor
School'd by the shadow of death — a Boleyn, too,
Glancing across the Tudor — not so well.

Enter ALICE.

How is the good Queen now?
  Alice.   Away from Philip.
Back in her childhood — prattling to her mother
Of her betrothal to the Emperor Charles,
And childlike-jealous of him again — and once
She thank'd her father sweetly for his book
Against that godless German. Ah, those days
Were happy. It was never merry world
In England, since the Bible came among us.
  Cecil. And who says that?
  Alice. It is a saying among the Catholics.
  Cecil. It never will be merry world in England,
Till all men have their Bible, rich and poor.
  Alice. The Queen is dying, or you dare not say it.

Enter ELIZABETH.

  Elizabeth. The Queen is dead.
  Cecil. Then here she stands! my homage.

Elizabeth. She knew me, and acknowledged me her heir,
Pray'd me to pay her debts, and keep
the Faith ;
Then claspt the cross, and pass'd
away in peace.
I left her lying still and beautiful,
More beautiful than in life. Why would
you vex yourself,
Poor sister ? Sir, I swear I have no
heart
To be your Queen. To reign is restless fence,
Tierce, quart, and trickery. Peace is
with the dead.
Her life was winter, for her spring
was nipt :
And she loved much : pray God she
be forgiven.
   Cecil. Peace with the dead, who
never were at peace !

Yet she loved one so much — I needs
must say —
That never English monarch dying left
England so little.
   Elizabeth.   But with Cecil's aid
And others, if our person be secured
From traitor stabs — we will make
England great.

Enter PAGET, *and other* LORDS OF THE
COUNCIL, SIR RALPH BAGENHALL,
etc.

   Lords. God save Elizabeth, the
Queen of England !
   Bagenhall. God save the Crown !
the Papacy is no more.
   Paget (*aside*). Are we so sure of
that ?
   Acclamation. God save the Queen !

HAROLD:

A DRAMA.

To His Excellency
THE RIGHT HON. LORD LYTTON,
Viceroy and Governor-General of India.

MY DEAR LORD LYTTON, — After old-world records — such as the Bayeux tapestry and the Roman de Rou, — Edward Freeman's History of the Norman Conquest, and your father's Historical Romance treating of the same times, have been mainly helpful to me in writing this Drama. Your father dedicated his "Harold" to my father's brother; allow me to dedicate my "Harold" to yourself.   A. TENNYSON.

SHOW-DAY AT BATTLE ABBEY, 1876.

A GARDEN here — May breath and bloom of spring —
The cuckoo yonder from an English elm
Crying "with my false egg I overwhelm
The native nest :" and fancy hears the ring
Of harness, and that deathful arrow sing,
And Saxon battleaxe clang on Norman helm.
Here rose the dragon-banner of our realm :
Here fought, here fell, our Norman slander'd king.
O Garden blossoming out of English blood!
O strange hate-healer Time ! We stroll and stare
Where might made right eight hundred years ago;
Might, right ? ay good, so all things make for good —
But he and he, if soul be soul, are where
Each stands full face with all he did below.

DRAMATIS PERSONÆ.

KING EDWARD THE CONFESSOR.
STIGAND, *created Archbishop of Canterbury by the Antipope Benedict.*
ALDRED, *Archbishop of York.*   THE NORMAN BISHOP OF LONDON.
HAROLD, *Earl of Wessex, afterwards King of England* ⎫
TOSTIG, *Earl of Northumbria*   ⎪
GURTH, *Earl of East Anglia*   ⎬ *Sons of*
LEOFWIN, *Earl of Kent and Essex*   ⎪ *Godwin.*
WULFNOTH   ⎭
COUNT WILLIAM OF NORMANDY.   WILLIAM RUFUS.
WILLIAM MALET, *a Norman Noble.*[1]
EDWIN, *Earl of Mercia*   ⎱ *Sons of Alfgar of*
MORCAR, *Earl of Northumbria after Tostig* ⎰ *Mercia.*
GAMEL, *a Northumbrian Thane.*   GUY, *Count of Ponthieu.*
ROLF, *a Ponthieu Fisherman.*   HUGH MARGOT, *a Norman Monk.*
OSGOD *and* ATHELRIC, *Canons from Waltham.*
THE QUEEN, *Edward the Confessor's Wife, Daughter of Godwin.*
ALDWYTH, *Daughter of Alfgar and Widow of Griffyth, King of Wales.*
EDITH, *Ward of King Edward.*

Courtiers, Earls and Thanes, Men-at-Arms, Canons of Waltham,
Fishermen, etc.

---

[1] . . . quidam partim Normannus et Anglus
Compater Heraldi. (*Guy of Amiens*, 587.)

ACT I.

SCENE I. — LONDON. THE KING'S
PALACE.

(*A comet seen through the open window.*)

ALDWYTH, GAMEL, COURTIERS *talking
together.*

First Courtier. Lo! there once more
— this is the seventh night!
You grimly-glaring, treble-brandish'd
scourge
Of England!
  Second Courtier. Horrible!
  First Courtier. Look you, there's
a star
That dances in it as mad with agony!
  Third Courtier. Ay, like a spirit in
Hell who skips and flies
To right and left, and cannot scape
the flame.
  Second Courtier. Steam'd upward
from the undescendable
Abysm.
  First Courtier. Or floated down-
ward from the throne
Of God Almighty.
  Aldwyth.   Gamel, son of Orm,
What thinkest thou this means?
  Gamel.   War, my dear lady!
  Aldwyth. Doth this affright thee?
  Gamel.   Mightily, my dear lady!
  Aldwyth. Stand by me then, and
look upon my face,
Not on the comet.

(*Enter* MORCAR.)

           Brother! why so pale?
  Morcar. It glares in heaven, it
flares upon the Thames,
The people are as thick as bees below,
They hum like bees, — they cannot
speak — for awe;
Look to the skies, then to the river,
strike
Their hearts, and hold their babies up
to it.
I think that they would Molochize
them too,
To have the heavens clear.

  Aldwyth.   They fright not me

(*Enter* LEOFWIN, *after him* GURTH.)

Ask thou Lord Leofwin what he
thinks of this!
  Morcar. Lord Leofwin, dost thou
believe, that these
Three rods of blood-red fire up yon-
der mean
The doom of England and the wrath
of Heaven?
  Bishop of London (*passing*). Did ye
not cast with bestial violence
Our holy Norman bishops down from
all
Their thrones in England? I alone
remain.
Why should not Heaven be wroth?
  Leofwin.   With us, or thee?
  Bishop of London. Did ye not out-
law your archbishop Robert,
Robert of Jumiéges — well-nigh mur-
der him too?
Is there no reason for the wrath of
Heaven?
  Leofwin. Why then the wrath of
Heaven hath three tails,
The devil only one.
         [*Exit* Bishop of London.

(*Enter* ARCHBISHOP STIGAND.)

           Ask *our* Archbishop.
Stigand should know the purposes of
Heaven.
  Stigand. Not I. I cannot read the
face of heaven;
Perhaps our vines will grow the better
for it.
  Leofwin (*laughing*). He can but read
the king's face on his coins.
  Stigand. Ay, ay, young lord, *there*
the king's face is power.
  Gurth. O father, mock not at a
public fear,
But tell us, is this pendent hell in
heaven
A harm to England?
  Stigand. Ask it of King Edward!
And he may tell thee, *I* am a harm to
England.
Old uncanonical Stigand — ask of *me*

Who had my pallium from an Anti-
pope!
Not he the man — for in our windy
world
What's up is faith, what's down is
heresy.
Our friends, the Normans, holp to
shake his chair.
I have a Norman fever on me, son,
And cannot answer sanely . . . What
it means?
Ask our broad Earl.
    [*Pointing to* HAROLD, *who enters.*
  Harold (*seeing* Gamel). Hail, Ga-
mel, son of Orm!
Albeit no rolling stone, my good friend
Gamel,
Thou hast rounded since we met.
Thy life at home
Is easier than mine here. Look! am
I not
Work-wan, flesh-fallen?
  Gamel. Art thou sick, good
Earl?
  Harold. Sick as an autumn swal-
low for a voyage,
Sick for an idle week of hawk and
hound
Beyond the seas — a change! When
camest thou hither?
  Gamel. To-day, good Earl.
  Harold. Is the North quiet, Gamel?
  Gamel. Nay, there be murmurs, for
thy brother breaks us
With over-taxing — quiet, ay, as yet —
Nothing as yet.
  Harold. Stand by him, mine old
friend,
Thou art a great voice in Northum-
berland!
Advise him: speak him sweetly, he
will hear thee.
He is passionate but honest. Stand
thou by him!
More talk of this to-morrow, if yon
weird sign
Not blast us in our dreams. — Well,
father Stigand —
    [*To* Stigand, *who advances to him.*
  Stigand (*pointing to the comet*). War
there, my son? is that the doom
of England?

  Harold. Why not the doom of all
the world as well?
For all the world sees it as well as
England.
These meteors came and went before
our day,
Not harming any: it threatens us no
more
Than French or Norman. War? the
worst that follows
Things that seem'd jerk'd out of the
common rut
Of Nature is the hot religious fool,
Who, seeing war in heaven, for
heaven's credit
Makes it on earth: but look, where
Edward draws
A faint foot hither, leaning upon Tos-
tig.
He hath learnt to love our Tostig
much of late.
  Leofwin. And *he* hath learnt, de-
spite the tiger in him,
To sleek and supple himself to the
king's hand.
  Gurth. I trust the kingly touch
that cures the evil
May serve to charm the tiger out of
him.
  Leofwin. He hath as much of cat
as tiger in him.
Our Tostig loves the hand and not
the man.
  Harold. Nay! Better die than lie!

Enter KING, QUEEN, *and* TOSTIG.

  Edward.   In heaven signs!
Signs upon earth! signs everywhere!
your Priests
Gross, worldly, simoniacal, unlearn'd!
They scarce can read their Psalter;
and your churches
Uncouth, unhandsome, while in Nor-
manland
God speaks thro' abler voices, as He
dwells
In statelier shrines. I say not this,
as being
Half Norman-blooded, nor as some
have held,
Because I love the Norman better —
no,

But dreading God's revenge upon this realm

For narrowness and coldness : and I say it

For the last time perchance, before I go

To find the sweet refreshment of the Saints.

I have lived a life of utter purity:

I have builded the great church of Holy Peter :

I have wrought miracles — to God the glory —

And miracles will in my name be wrought

Hereafter. — I have fought the fight and go —

I see the flashing of the gates of pearl —

And it is well with me, tho' some of you

Have scorn'd me — ay — but after I am gone

Woe, woe to England! I have had a vision ;

The seven sleepers in the cave at Ephesus

Have turn'd from right to left.

Harold. My most dear Master,

What matters ? let them turn from left to right

And sleep again.

Tostig. Too hardy with thy king!

A life of prayer and fasting well may see

Deeper into the mysteries of heaven

Than thou, good brother.

Aldwyth (aside). Sees he into thine,

That thou wouldst have his promise for the crown ?

Edward. Tostig says true ; my son, thou art too hard,

Not stagger'd by this ominous earth and heaven :

But heaven and earth are threads of the same loom,

Play into one another, and weave the web

That may confound thee yet.

Harold. Nay, I trust not,

For I have served thee long and honestly.

Edward. I know it, son ; I am not thankless : thou

Hast broken all my foes, lighten'd for me

The weight of this poor crown, and left me time

And peace for prayer to gain a better one.

Twelve years of service ! England loves thee for it.

Thou art the man to rule her !

Aldwyth (aside). So, not Tostig !

Harold. And after those twelve years a boon, my king,

Respite, a holiday : thyself wast wont

To love the chase : thy leave to set my feet

On board, and hunt and hawk beyond the seas !

Edward. What with this flaming horror overhead ?

Harold. Well, when it passes then.

Edward. Ay, if it pass.

Go not to Normandy — go not to Normandy.

Harold. And wherefore not, my king, to Normandy ?

Is not my brother Wulfnoth hostage there

For my dead father's loyalty to thee ?

I pray thee, let me hence and bring him home.

Edward. Not thee, my son : some other messenger.

Harold. And why not me, my lord, to Normandy ?

Is not the Norman Count thy friend and mine ?

Edward. I pray thee, do not go to Normandy.

Harold. Because my father drove the Normans out

Of England ? — That was many a summer gone —

Forgotten and forgiven by them and thee.

Edward. Harold, I will not yield thee leave to go.

Harold. Why then to Flanders. I will hawk and hunt

In Flanders.

Edward. Be there not fair woods
and fields
In England ? Wilful, wilful. Go —
the Saints
Pilot and prosper all thy wandering
out
And homeward. Tostig, I am faint
again.
Son Harold, I will in and pray for
thee.
[*Exit, leaning on* Tostig, *and fol-
lowed by* Stigand, Morcar, *and*
Courtiers.
Harold. What lies upon the mind of
our good king
That he should harp this way on
Normandy ?
Queen. Brother, the king is wiser
than he seems ;
And Tostig knows it ; Tostig loves
the king.
Harold. And love should know ; and
— be the king so wise, —
Then Tostig too were wiser than he
seems.
I love the man but not his phantasies.

(*Re-enter* TOSTIG.)

Well, brother,
When didst thou hear from thy
Northumbria ?
Tostig. When did I hear aught but
this " *When* " from thee ?
Leave me alone, brother, with my
Northumbria :
She is *my* mistress, let *me* look to her !
The King hath made me Earl ; make
me not fool !
Nor make the King a fool, who made
me Earl !
Harold. No, Tostig — lest I make
myself a fool
Who made the King who made thee,
make thee Earl.
Tostig. Why chafe me then ? Thou
knowest I soon go wild.
Gurth. Come, come ! as yet thou art
not gone so wild
But thou canst hear the best and
wisest of us.
Harold. So says old Gurth, not I :
yet hear ! thine earldom,

Tostig, hath been a kingdom. Their
old crown
Is yet a force among them, a sun
set
But leaving light enough for Alfgar's
house
To strike thee down by — nay, this
ghastly glare
May heat their fancies.
Tostig. My most worthy brother,
Thou art the quietest man in all the
world —
Ay, ay and wise in peace and great in
war —
Pray God the people choose thee for
their king !
But all the powers of the house of
Godwin
Are not enframed in thee.
Harold. Thank the Saints, no !
But thou hast drain'd them shallow
by thy tolls,
And thou art ever here about the
King :
Thine absence well may seem a want
of care.
Cling to their love ; for, now the sons
of Godwin
Sit topmost in the field of England,
envy,
Like the rough bear beneath the tree,
good brother,
Waits till the man let go.
Tostig. Good counsel truly !
I heard from my Northumbria yester-
day.
Harold. How goes it then with thy
Northumbria ? Well ?
Tostig. And wouldst thou that it
went aught else than well ?
Harold. I would it went as well as
with mine earldom,
Leofwin's and Gurth's.
Tostig. Ye govern milder men.
Gurth. We have made them milder
by just government.
Tostig. Ay, ever give yourselves
your own good word.
Leofwin. An honest gift, by all the
Saints, if giver
And taker be but honest ! but they
bribe

Each other, and so often, an honest
　　world
Will not believe them.

　Harold.　　I may tell thee, Tostig,
I heard from thy Northumberland
　to-day.

　Tostig. From spies of thine to spy
　my nakedness
In my poor North!

　Harold. There is a movement there,
A blind one — nothing yet.

　Tostig.　　　　　Crush it at once
With all the power I have! — I must
　— I will! —
Crush it half-born! Fool still? or
　wisdom there,
My wise head-shaking Harold?

　Harold.　　　　Make not thou
The nothing something. Wisdom
　when in power
And wisest, should not frown as
　Power, but smile
As kindness, watching all, till the true
　must
Shall make her strike as Power: but
　when to strike —
O Tostig, O dear brother — If they
　prance,
Rein in, not lash them, lest they rear
　and run,
And break both neck and axle.

　Tostig.　　　　　Good again!
Good counsel tho' scarce needed. Pour
　not water
In the full vessel running out at
　top
To swamp the house.

　Leofwin. Nor thou be a wild thing
Out of the waste, to turn and bite the
　hand
Would help thee from the trap.

　Tostig.　　Thou playest in tune.

　Leofwin. To the deaf adder thee,
　that wilt not dance
However wisely charm'd.

　Tostig.　　No more, no more!

　Gurth. I likewise cry "no more."
　Unwholesome talk
For Godwin's house! Leofwin, thou
　hast a tongue!
Tostig, thou look'st as thou wouldst
　spring upon him.

St. Olaf, not while I am by! Come,
　come,
Join hands, let brethren dwell in unity;
Let kith and kin stand close as our
　shield-wall,
Who breaks us then? I say, thou hast
　a tongue,
And Tostig is not stout enough to bear
　it.
Vex him not, Leofwin.

　Tostig.　　　No, I am not vext, —
Altho' ye seek to vex me, one and all.
I have to make report of my good
　earldom
To the good king who gave it — not
　to you —
Not any of you. — I am not vext at all.

　Harold. The king? the king is ever
　at his prayers;
In all that handles matter of the
　state
I am the king.

　Tostig.　　That shalt thou never be
If I can thwart thee.

　Harold.　　Brother, brother!

　Tostig.　　　　　Away!
　　　　　　　　[*Exit* Tostig.

　Queen. Spite of this grisly star ye
　three must gall
Poor Tostig.

　Leofwin. Tostig, sister, galls him-
　self;
He cannot smell a rose but pricks his
　nose
Against the thorn, and rails against
　the rose.

　Queen. I am the only rose of all the
　stock
That never thorn'd him; Edward
　loves him, so
Ye hate him. Harold always hated
　him.
Why — how they fought when boys
　— and, Holy Mary!
How Harold used to beat him!

　Harold.　　Why, boys will fight.
Leofwin would often fight me, and I
　beat him.
Even old Gurth would fight. I had
　much ado
To hold mine own against old Gurth.
　Old Gurth,

We fought like great states for grave cause; but Tostig —
On a sudden — at a something — for a nothing —
The boy would fist me hard, and when we fought
I conquer'd, and he loved me none the less,
Till thou wouldst get him all apart, and tell him
That where he was but worsted, he was wrong'd.
Ah! thou hast taught the king to spoil him too;
Now the spoilt child sways both. Take heed, take heed;
Thou art the Queen; ye are boy and girl no more:
Side not with Tostig in any violence,
Lest thou be sideways guilty of the violence.

Queen. Come fall not foul on me. I leave thee, brother.

Harold. Nay, my good sister —

[*Exeunt* Queen, Harold, Gurth, *and* Leofwin.

Aldwyth.   Gamel, son of Orm,
What thinkest thou this means?

[*Pointing to the comet.*

Gamel.   War, my dear lady,
War, waste, plague, famine, all malignities.

Aldwyth. It means the fall of Tostig from his earldom.

Gamel. That were too small a matter for a comet!

Aldwyth. It means the lifting of the house of Alfgar.

Gamel. Too small! a comet would not show for that!

Aldwyth. Not small for thee, if thou canst compass it.

Gamel. Thy love?

Aldwyth.   As much as I can give thee, man;
This Tostig is, or like to be, a tyrant;
Stir up thy people: oust him!

Gamel.   And thy love?

Aldwyth. As much as thou canst bear.

Gamel.   I can bear all,
And not be giddy.

Aldwyth. No more now: to-morrow.

SCENE II. — In the Garden. The King's House near London. Sunset.

Edith. Mad for thy mate, passionate nightingale . . .
I love thee for it — ay, but stay a moment;
He can but stay a moment: he is going.
I fain would hear him coming! . . . near me . . near,
Somewhere — To draw him nearer with a charm
Like thine to thine.

(*Singing.*)

Love is come with a song and a smile,
Welcome Love with a smile and a song:
Love can stay but a little while.
Why cannot he stay? They call him away:
Ye do him wrong, ye do him wrong;
Love will stay for a whole life long.

Enter Harold.

Harold. The nightingales at Havering-in-the-bower
Sang out their loves so loud, that Edward's prayers
Were deafen'd and he pray'd them dumb, and thus
I dumb thee too, my wingless nightingale!   [*Kissing her.*

Edith. Thou art my music! Would their wings were mine
To follow thee to Flanders! Must thou go?

Harold. Not must, but will. It is but for one moon.

Edith. Leaving so many foes in Edward's hall
To league against thy weal. The Lady Aldwyth
Was here to-day, and when she touch'd on thee,
She stammer'd in her hate; I am sure she hates thee,
Pants for thy blood.

Harold.   Well, I have given her cause —
I fear no woman.

Edith.   Hate not one who felt
Some pity for thy hater!   I am sure
Her morning wanted sunlight, she so
    praised
The convent and lone life — within
    the pale —
Beyond the passion.   Nay — she held
    with Edward,
At least methought she held with holy
    Edward,
That marriage was half sin.
    Harold.   A lesson worth
Finger and thumb — thus (*snaps his
    fingers*). And my answer to it —
See here — an interwoven H and E!
Take thou this ring; I will demand
    his ward
From Edward when I come again.
    Ay, would she?
She to shut up my blossom in the dark!
Thou art *my* nun, thy cloister in mine
    arms.
    Edith (*taking the ring*). Yea, but
        Earl Tostig —
    Harold.   That's a truer fear!
For if the North take fire, I should be
    back;
I shall be, soon enough.
    Edith.   Ay, but last night
An evil dream that ever came and
    went —
    Harold. A gnat that vext thy pil-
        low!   Had I been by,
I would have spoil'd his horn.   My
    girl, what was it?
    Edith. Oh! that thou wert not go-
        ing!
For so methought it was our marriage-
    morn,
And while we stood together, a dead
    man
Rose from behind the altar, tore away
My marriage ring, and rent my bridal
    veil;
And then I turn'd, and saw the church
    all fill'd
With dead men upright from their
    graves, and all
The dead men made at thee to murder
    thee,
But thou didst back thyself against a
    pillar,

And strike among them with thy bat-
    tle-axe —
There, what a dream!
    Harold.   Well, well — a dream —
        no more!
    Edith.   Did not Heaven speak to
        men in dreams of old?
    Harold.   Ay — well — of old.   I
        tell thee what, my child;
Thou hast misread this merry dream
    of thine,
Taken the rifted pillars of the wood
For smooth stone columns of the sanc-
    tuary,
The shadows of a hundred fat dead deer
For dead men's ghosts.   True, that the
    battle-axe
Was out of place; it should have been
    the bow. —
Come, thou shalt dream no more such
    dreams; I swear it,
By mine own eyes — and these two
    sapphires — these
Twin rubies, that are amulets against all
The kisses of all kind of womankind
In Flanders, till the sea shall roll me
    back
To tumble at thy feet.
    Edith.   That would but shame me,
Rather than make me vain.   The sea
    may roll
Sand, shingle, shore-weed, not the liv-
    ing rock
Which guards the land.
    Harold.   Except it be a soft one
And undereaten to the fall.   Mine
    amulet . . .
This last . . . upon thine eyelids, to
    shut in
A happier dream.   Sleep, sleep, and
    thou shalt see
My greyhounds fleeting like a beam
    of light,
And hear my peregrine and her bells
    in heaven;
And other bells on earth, which yet
    are heaven's;
Guess what they be.
    Edith. He cannot guess who knows.
Farewell, my king.
    Harold.   Not yet, but then — my
        queen.   [*Exeunt.*

Enter ALDWYTH *from the thicket.*

Aldwyth.   The kiss that charms
    thine eyelids into sleep,
Will hold mine waking.   Hate him ?
    I could love him
More, tenfold, than this fearful child
    can do ;
Griffyth I hated: why not hate the foe
Of England ?   Griffyth when I saw
    him flee,
Chased deer-like up his mountains, all
    the blood
That should have only pulsed for Grif-
    fyth, beat
For his pursuer.   I love him or think
    I love him.
If he were King of England, I his queen,
I might be sure of it.   Nay, I do love
    him. —
She must be cloister'd somehow, lest
    the king
Should yield his ward to Harold's will.
    What harm ?
She hath but blood enough to live, not
    love. —
When Harold goes and Tostig, shall
    I play
The craftier Tostig with him ? fawn
    upon him ?
Chime in with all ?   " O thou more
    saint than king ! "
And that were true enough.   " O
    blessed relics ! "
" O Holy Peter ! " If he found me thus,
Harold might hate me ; he is broad
    and honest,
Breathing an easy gladness . . . not
    like Aldwyth . . .
For which I strangely love him.
    Should not England
Love Aldwyth, if she stays the feuds
    that part
The sons of Godwin from the sons of
    Alfgar
By such a marrying ?   Courage, noble
    Aldwyth !
Let all thy people bless thee !
            Our wild Tostig,
Edward hath made him Earl: he
    would be king : —

The dog that snapt the shadow, dropt
    the bone. —
I trust he may do well, this Gamel,
    whom
I play upon, that he may play the note
Whereat the dog shall howl and run,
    and Harold
Hear the king's music, all alone with
    him,
Pronounced his heir of England.
I see the goal and half the way to it. —
Peace-lover is our Harold for the
    sake
Of England's wholeness — so — to
    shake the North
With earthquake and disruption —
    some division —
Then fling mine own fair person in the
    gap
A sacrifice to Harold, a peace-offering,
A scape-goat marriage — all the sins
    of both
The houses on mine head — then a
    fair life
And bless the Queen of England.
    Morcar (coming from the thicket). Art
    thou assured
By this, that Harold loves but Edith ?
    Aldwyth.   Morcar !
Why creep'st thou like a timorous
    beast of prey
Out of the bush by night ?
    Morcar.   I follow'd thee.
    Aldwyth.   Follow my lead, and I
    will make thee earl.
    Morcar.   What lead then ?
    Aldwyth.   Thou shalt flash it secretly
Among the good Northumbrian folk,
    that I —
That Harold loves me — yea, and pres-
    ently
That I and Harold are betroth'd — and
    last —
Perchance that Harold wrongs me ;
    tho' I would not
That it should come to that.
    Morcar.   I will both flash
And thunder for thee.
    Aldwyth.   I said " secretly " ;
It is the flash that murders, the poor
    thunder
Never harm'd head.

Morcar. But thunder may bring down
That which the flash hath stricken.
Aldwyth. Down with Tostig!
That first of all. — And when doth Harold go?
Morcar. To-morrow — first to Bosham, then to Flanders.
Aldwyth. Not to come back till Tostig shall have shown
And redden'd with his people's blood the teeth
That shall be broken by us — yea, and thou
Chair'd in his place. Good-night, and dream thyself
Their chosen Earl. [*Exit* Aldwyth.
Morcar. Earl first, and after that
Who knows I may not dream myself their king!

ACT II.

SCENE I. — SEASHORE. PONTHIEU. NIGHT.

HAROLD *and his* Men, *wrecked.*

Harold. Friends, in that last inhospitable plunge
Our boat hath burst her ribs; but ours are whole;
I have but bark'd my hands.
Attendant. I dug mine into
My old fast friend the shore, and clinging thus
Felt the remorseless outdraught of the deep
Haul like a great strong fellow at my legs,
And then I rose and ran. The blast that came
So suddenly hath fallen as suddenly —
Put thou the comet and this blast together —
Harold. Put thou thyself and mother-wit together.
Be not a fool!

(*Enter* Fishermen *with torches,* HAROLD *going up to one of them,* ROLF.)

Wicked sea-will-o'-the-wisp!
Wolf of the shore! dog, with thy lying lights
Thou hast betray'd us on these rocks of thine!
Rolf. Ay, but thou liest as loud as the black herring-pond behind thee. We be fishermen; I came to see after my nets.
Harold. To drag us into them. Fishermen? devils!
Who, while ye fish for men with your false fires,
Let the great Devil fish for your own souls.
Rolf. Nay then, we be liker the blessed Apostles; *they* were fishers of men, Father Jean says.
Harold. I had liefer that the fish had swallowed me,
Like Jonah, than have known there were such devils.
What's to be done?
[*To his* Men — *goes apart with them.*
Fisherman. Rolf, what fish did swallow Jonah?
Rolf. A whale!
Fisherman. Then a whale to a whelk we have swallowed the King of England. I saw him over there. Look thee, Rolf, when I was down in the fever, *she* was down with the hunger, and thou didst stand by her and give her thy crabs, and set her up again, till now, by the patient Saints, she's as crabb'd as ever.
Rolf. And I'll give her my crabs again, when thou art down again.
Fisherman. I thank thee, Rolf. Run thou to Count Guy; he is hard at hand. Tell him what hath crept into our creel, and he will fee thee as freely as he will wrench this outlander's ransom out of him — and why not? for what right had he to get himself wrecked on another man's land?
Rolf. Thou art the human-heartedest, Christian-charitiest of all crab-catchers. Share and share alike!
[*Exit.*
Harold (*to* Fisherman). Fellow, dost thou catch crabs?

Fisherman. As few as I may in a wind, and less than I would in a calm. Ay!

    Harold. I have a mind that thou shalt catch no more.

    Fisherman. How?

    Harold. I have a mind to brain thee with mine axe.

    Fisherman. Ay, do, do, and our great Count-crab will make his nippers meet in thine heart; he'll sweat it out of thee, he'll sweat it out of thee. Look, he's here! He'll speak for himself! Hold thine own, if thou canst!

Enter GUY, COUNT OF PONTHIEU.

    Harold. Guy, Count of Ponthieu?

    Guy. Harold, Earl of Wessex!

    Harold. Thy villains with their lying lights have wreck'd us!

    Guy. Art thou not Earl of Wessex?

    Harold. In mine earldom
A man may hang gold bracelets on a bush,
And leave them for a year, and coming back
Find them again.

    Guy. Thou art a mighty man
In thine own earldom!

    Harold. Were such murderous liars
In Wessex — if I caught them, they should hang
Cliff-gibbeted for sea-marks; our sea-mew
Winging their only wail!

    Guy. Ay, but my men
Hold that the shipwreckt are accursed of God; —
What hinders me to hold with mine own men?

    Harold. The Christian manhood of the man who reigns!

    Guy. Ay, rave thy worst, but in our oubliettes
Thou shalt or rot or ransom. Hale him hence!
       [*To one of his* Attendants.
Fly thou to William; tell him we have Harold.

SCENE II. — BAYEUX. PALACE.

COUNT WILLIAM *and* WILLIAM MALET.

    William. We hold our Saxon woodcock in the springe,
But he begins to flutter. As I think
He was thine host in England when I went
To visit Edward.

    Malet. Yea, and there, my lord,
To make allowance for their rougher fashions,
I found him all a noble host should be.

    William. Thou art his friend: thou know'st my claim on England
Thro' Edward's promise: we have him in the toils.
And it were well, if thou shouldst let him feel,
How dense a fold of danger nets him round,
So that he bristle himself against my will.

    Malet. What would I do, my lord, if I were you?

    William. What wouldst thou do?

    Malet. My lord, he is thy guest

    William. Nay, by the splendor of God, no guest of mine.
He came not to see me, had past me by
To hunt and hawk elsewhere, save for the fate
Which hunted *him* when that un-Saxon blast,
And bolts of thunder moulded in high heaven
To serve the Norman purpose, drave and crack'd
His boat on Ponthieu beach; where our friend Guy
Had wrung his ransom from him by the rack,
But that I stept between and purchased him,
Translating his captivity from Guy
To mine own hearth at Bayeux, where he sits
My ransom'd prisoner.

    Malet. Well, if not with gold,

With golden deeds and iron strokes
    that brought
Thy war with Brittany to a goodlier
    close
Than else had been, he paid his ran-
    som back.
    William. So that henceforth they
    are not like to league
With Harold against *me*.
    Malet.   A marvel, how
He from the liquid sands of Coesnon
Haled thy shore-swallow'd, armor'd
    Normans up
To fight for thee again!
    William.   Perchance against
Their saver, save thou save him from
    himself.
    Malet. But I should let him home
    again, my lord.
    William. Simple! let fly the bird
    within the hand,
To catch the bird again within the
    bush!
No.
Smooth thou my way, before he clash
    with me;
I want his voice in England for the
    crown,
I want thy voice with him to bring him
    round;
And being brave he must be subtly
    cow'd,
And being truthful wrought upon to
    swear
Vows that he dare not break. Eng-
    land our own
Thro' Harold's help, he shall be my
    dear friend
As well as thine, and thou thyself
    shalt have
Large lordship there of lands and ter-
    ritory.
    Malet. I knew thy purpose; he and
    Wulfnoth never
Have met, except in public; shall
    they meet
In private? I have often talk'd with
    Wulfnoth,
And stuff'd the boy with fears that
    these may act
On Harold when they meet.
    William.   Then let them meet!

    Malet. I can but love this noble,
    honest Harold.
    William. Love him! why not?
    thine is a loving office,
I have commission'd thee to save the
    man:
Help the good ship, showing the
    sunken rock,
Or he is wreckt for ever.

    Enter WILLIAM RUFUS.

    William Rufus.   Father.
    William.   Well, boy.
    William Rufus. They have taken
    away the toy thou gavest me,
The Norman knight.
    William.   Why, boy?
    William Rufus.   Because I broke
The horse's leg — it was mine own to
    break;
I like to have my toys, and break them
    too.
    William. Well, thou shalt have
    another Norman knight!
    William Rufus. And may I break
    his legs?
    William. Yea, — get thee gone!
    William Rufus. I'll tell them I have
    had my way with thee. [*Exit.*
    Malet. I never knew thee check thy
    will for ought
Save for the prattling of thy little ones.
    William. Who shall be kings of
    England. I am heir
Of England by the promise of her king.
    Malet. But there the great As-
    sembly choose their king,
The choice of England is the voice of
    England.
    William. I will be king of England
    by the laws,
The choice, and voice of England.
    Malet.   Can that be?
    William. The voice of any people
    is the sword
That guards them, or the sword that
    beats them down.
Here comes the would-be what I will
    be . . . kinglike . . .
Tho' scarce at ease; for, save our
    meshes break,

More kinglike he than like to prove a
· king.

(*Enter* HAROLD, *musing, with his eyes
on the ground.*)

He sees me not — and yet he dreams
of me.
Earl, wilt thou fly my falcons this
fair day ?
They are of the best, strong-wing'd
against the wind.
Harold (*looking up suddenly, having
caught but the last word*). Which
way does it blow ?
William. Blowing for England,
ha ?
Not yet. Thou hast not learnt thy
quarters here.
The winds so cross and jostle among
these towers.
Harold. Count of the Normans,
thou hast ransom'd us,
Maintain'd, and entertain'd us royally !
William. And thou for us hast
fought as loyally,
Which binds us friendship-fast for
ever !
Harold. Good !
But lest we turn the scale of courtesy
By too much pressure on it, I would
fain,
Since thou has promised Wulfnoth
home with us,
Be home again with Wulfnoth.
William. Stay — as yet
Thou hast but seen how Norman
hands can strike,
But walk'd our Norman field, scarce
touch'd or tasted
The splendors of our Court.
Harold. I am in no mood :
I should be as the shadow of a cloud
Crossing your light.
William. Nay, rest a week or two,
And we will fill thee full of Norman
sun,
And send thee back among thine
island mists
With laughter.
Harold. Count, I thank thee, but
had rather

Breathe the free wind from off our
Saxon downs,
Tho' charged with all the wet of all
the west.
William. Why if thou wilt, so let it
be — thou shalt.
That were a graceless hospitality
To chain the free guest to the banquet-
board ;
To-morrow we will ride with thee to
Harfleur,
And see thee shipt, and pray in thy
behalf
For happier homeward winds than
that which crack'd
Thy bark at Ponthieu, — yet to us, in
faith,
A happy one — whereby we came to
know
Thy valor and thy value, noble earl.
Ay, and perchance a happy one for
thee,
Provided — I will go with thee to-
morrow —
Nay — but there be conditions, easy
ones,
So thou, fair friend, will take them
easily.

Enter PAGE.

Page. My lord, there is a post from
over seas
With news for thee. [*Exit* Page.
William. Come, Malet, let us hear !
[*Exeunt* Count William *and* Malet.
Harold. Conditions ? What condi-
tions ? pay him back
His ransom ? "easy" — that were
easy — nay —
No money-lover he ! What said the
King ?
"I pray you do not go to Normandy."
And fate hath blown me hither, bound
me too
With bitter obligation to the Count —
Have I not fought it out ? What did
he mean ?
There lodged a gleaming grimness in
his eyes,
Gave his shorn smile the lie. The
walls oppress me,

And yon huge keep that hinders half
    the heaven.
Free air! free field!
    [*Moves to go out. A* Man-at-arms
    follows him.
    Harold (*to the* Man-at-arms). I need
    thee not. Why dost thou fol-
    low me?
    Man-at-arms. I have the Count's
    commands to follow thee.
    Harold. What then? Am I in dan-
    ger in this court?
    Man-at-arms. I cannot tell. I have
    the Count's commands.
    Harold. Stand out of earshot then,
    and keep me still
In eyeshot.
    Man-at-arms.   Yea, Lord Harold.
                  [*Withdraws.*
    Harold.   And arm'd men
Ever keep watch beside my chamber
    door,
And if I walk within the lonely wood,
There is an arm'd man ever glides be-
    hind!

(*Enter* MALET.)

Why am I follow'd, haunted, harass'd,
    watch'd?
See yonder!
    [*Pointing to the* Man-at-arms.
    Malet. 'Tis the good Count's care
    for thee!
The Normans love thee not, nor thou
    the Normans,
Or — so they deem.
    Harold. But wherefore is the wind,
Which way soever the vane-arrow
    swing,
Not ever fair for England? Why but
    now
He said (thou heardst him) that I
    must not hence
Save on conditions.
    Malet.   So in truth he said.
    Harold. Malet, thy mother was an
    Englishwoman;
There somewhere beats an English
    pulse in thee!
    Malet. Well — for my mother's
    sake I love your England,
But for my father I love Normandy.

    Harold. Speak for thy mother's
    sake, and tell me true.
    Malet. Then for my mother's sake,
    and England's sake
That suffers in the daily want of
    thee,
Obey the Count's conditions, my good
    friend.
    Harold. How, Malet, if they be not
    honorable!
    Malet. Seem to obey them.
    Harold.   Better die than lie!
    Malet. Choose therefore whether
    thou wilt have thy conscience
White as a maiden's hand, or whether
    England
Be shatter'd into fragments.
    Harold. News from England?
    Malet. Morcar and Edwin have
    stirr'd up the Thanes
Against thy brother Tostig's govern-
    ance;
And all the North of Humber is one
    storm.
    Harold. I should be there, Malet, I
    should be there!
    Malet. And Tostig in his own hall
    on suspicion
Hath massacred the Thane that was
    his guest,
Gamel, the son of Orm: and there be
    more
As villanously slain.
    Harold.   The wolf! the beast!
Ill news for guests, ha, Malet! More?
    What more?
What do they say? did Edward know
    of this?
    Malet. They say, his wife was know-
    ing and abetting.
    Harold. They say, his wife! — To
    marry and have no husband
Makes the wife fool. My God, I
    should be there.
I'll hack my way to the sea.
    Malet.   Thou canst not, Harold;
Our Duke is all between thee and the
    sea,
Our Duke is all about thee like a God;
All passes block'd. Obey him, speak
    him fair,
For he is only debonair to those

That follow where he leads, but stark
    as death
To those that cross him. — Look thou,
    here is Wulfnoth!
I leave thee to thy talk with him
    alone;
How wan, poor lad! how sick and sad
    for home!   [*Exit* Malet.
    Harold (*muttering*). Go not to Nor-
    mandy — go not to Normandy!

(*Enter* WULFNOTH.)

Poor brother! still a hostage!
    Wulfnoth.   Yea, and I
Shall see the dewy kiss of dawn no
    more
Make blush the maiden-white of our
    tall cliffs,
Nor mark the sea-bird rouse himself
    and hover
Above the windy ripple, and fill the sky
With free sea-laughter — never —
    save indeed
Thou canst make yield this iron-
    mooded Duke
To let me go.
    Harold. Why, brother, so he will;
But on conditions. Canst thou guess
    at them?
    Wulfnoth. Draw nearer, — I was in
    the corridor,
I saw him coming with his brother Odo
The Bayeux bishop, and I hid myself.
    Harold. They did thee wrong who
    made thee hostage; thou
Wast ever fearful.
    Wulfnoth.   And he spoke — I
    heard him —
" This Harold is not of the royal blood,
Can have no right to the crown," and
    Odo said,
" Thine is the right, for thine the
    might; he is here,
And yonder is thy keep."
    Harold.   No, Wulfnoth, no.
    Wulfnoth. And William laugh'd and
    swore that might was right,
Far as he knew in this poor world of
    ours —
" Marry, the Saints must go along with
    us,

And, brother, we will find a way," said
    he —
Yea, yea, he would be king of England.
    Harold.   Never!
    Wulfnoth. Yea, but thou must not
    this way answer *him*.
    Harold. Is it not better still to
    speak the truth?
    Wulfnoth. Not here, or thou wilt
    never hence nor I:
For in the racing toward this golden
    goal
He turns not right or left, but tram-
    ples flat
Whatever thwarts him; hast thou
    never heard
His savagery at Alençon, — the town
Hung out raw hides along their walls,
    and cried
" Work for the tanner."
    Harold.   That had anger'd *me*
Had I been William.
    Wulfnoth. Nay, but he had prison-
    ers,
He tore their eyes out, sliced their
    hands away,
And flung them streaming o'er the
    battlements
Upon the heads of those who walk'd
    within —
O speak him fair, Harold, for thine
    own sake.
    Harold. Your Welshman says,
    " The   Truth   against   the
    World,"
Much more the truth against myself.
    Wulfnoth.   Thyself?
But for my sake, oh brother! oh! for
    my sake!
    Harold. Poor Wulfnoth! do they
    not entreat thee well?
    Wulfnoth. I see the blackness of
    my dungeon loom
Across their lamps of revel, and be-
    yond
The merriest murmurs of their ban-
    quet clank
The shackles that will bind me to the
    wall.
    Harold. Too fearful still!
    Wulfnoth.   Oh no, no — speak
    him fair!

Call it to temporize ; and not to lie ;
Harold, I do not counsel thee to lie.
The man that hath to foil a murder-
ous aim
May, surely, play with words.
    Harold.   Words are the man.
Not ev'n for thy sake, brother, would
I lie.
    Wulfnoth. Then for thine Edith ?
    Harold.   There thou prick'st me
deep.
    Wulfnoth. And for our Mother
England ?
    Harold.   Deeper still.
    Wulfnoth. And deeper still the
deep-down oubliette,
Down thirty feet below the smiling
day —
In blackness — dogs' food thrown upon
thy head.
And over thee the suns arise and set,
And the lark sings, the sweet stars
come and go,
And men are at their markets, in their
fields,
And woo their loves and have forgot-
ten thee ;
And thou art upright in thy living
grave,
Where there is barely room to shift
thy side,
And all thine England hath forgotten
thee ;
And he our lazy-pious Norman King,
With all his Normans round him once
again,
Counts his old beads, and hath for-
gotten thee.
    Harold. Thou art of my blood, and
so methinks, my boy,
Thy fears infect me beyond reason.
Peace !
    Wulfnoth. And then our fiery Tos-
tig, while thy hands
Are palsied here, if his Northumbri-
ans rise
And hurl him from them, — I have
heard the Normans
Count upon this confusion — may he
not make
A league with William, so to bring
him back ?

    Harold. That lies within the
shadow of the chance.
    Wulfnoth. And like a river in flood
thro' a burst dam
Descends the ruthless Norman — our
good King
Kneels mumbling some old bone —
our helpless folk
Are wash'd away, wailing, in their
own blood —
    Harold. Wailing ! not warring ?
Boy, thou hast forgotten
That thou art English.
    Wulfnoth. Then our modest wo-
men —
I know the Norman license — thine
own Edith —
    Harold. No more! I will not hear
thee — William comes.
    Wulfnoth. I dare not well be seen
in talk with thee.
Make thou not mention that I spake
with thee.
    [*Moves away to the back of the stage.*

Enter WILLIAM, MALET, *and* Officer.

    Officer. We have the man that
rail'd against thy birth.
    William. Tear out his tongue.
    Officer.   He shall not rail again.
He said that he should see confusion
fall
On thee and on thine house.
    William.   Tear out his eyes,
And plunge him into prison.
    Officer.   It shall be done.
    [*Exit* Officer.
    William. Look not amazed, fair
earl ! Better leave undone
Than do by halves — tongueless and
eyeless, prison'd —
    Harold. Better methinks have
slain the man at once!
    William. We have respect for
man's immortal soul,
We seldom take man's life, except in
war ;
It frights the traitor more to maim
and blind.
    Harold. In mine own land I should
have scorn'd the man,

Or lash'd his rascal back, and let him
    go.
  William. And let him go ? To
slander thee again !
Yet in thine own land in thy father's
   · day
They blinded my young kinsman,
  Alfred — ay,
Some said it was thy father's deed.
  Harold. They lied.
  William. But thou and he — whom
  at thy word, for thou
Art known a speaker of the truth, I
  free
From this foul charge —
  Harold. Nay, nay, he freed himself
By oath and compurgation from the
  charge.
The king, the lords, the people clear'd
  him of it.
  William. But thou and he drove
  our good Normans out
From England, and this rankles in
  us yet.
Archbishop Robert hardly scaped
  with life.
  Harold. Archbishop Robert! Rob-
ert the Archbishop!
Robert of Jumiéges, he that —
  Malet. Quiet ! quiet !
  Harold. Count! if there sat with-
in the Norman chair
A ruler all for England — one who
  fill'd
All offices, all bishopricks with Eng-
lish —
We could not move from Dover to
  the Humber
Saving thro' Norman bishopricks — I
  say
Ye would applaud that Norman who
  should drive
The stranger to the fiends !
  William. Why, that is reason !
Warrior thou art, and mighty wise
  withal !
Ay, ay, but many among our Norman
  lords
Hate thee for this, and press upon
  me — saying
God and the sea have given thee to
  our hands —

To plunge thee into life-long prison
  here : —
Yet I hold out against them, as I may,
Yea — would hold out, yea, tho' they
  should revolt —
For thou hast done the battle in my
  cause ;
I am thy fastest friend in Normandy.
  Harold. I am doubly bound to thee
  . . . if this be so.
  William. And I would bind thee
  more, and would myself
Be bounden to thee more.
  Harold. Then let me hence
With Wulfnoth to King Edward.
  William. So we will.
We hear he hath not long to live.
  Harold. It may be.
  William. Why then the heir of
  England, who is he ?
  Harold. The Atheling is nearest
  to the throne.
  William. But sickly, slight, half-
  witted and a child,
Will England have him king ?
  Harold. It may be, no.
  William. And hath King Edward
  not pronounced his heir ?
  Harold. Not that I know.
  William. When he was here
  in Normandy,
He loved us and we him, because we
  found him
A Norman of the Normans.
  Harold. So did we.
  William. A gentle, gracious, pure
  and saintly man !
And grateful to the hand that shielded
  him,
He promised that if ever he were king
In England, he would give his kingly
  voice
To me as his successor. Knowest
  thou this ?
  Harold. I learn it now.
  William. Thou knowest I am
  his cousin,
And that my wife descends from
  Alfred ?
  Harold. Ay.
  William. Who hath a better claim
  then to the crown

So that ye will not crown the Atheling ?

Harold. None that I know . . . if
that but hung upon
King Edward's will.

William. Wilt *thou* uphold my
claim ?

Malet (*aside to* Harold). Be careful
of thine answer, my good friend.

Wulfnoth (*aside to* Harold). Oh !
Harold, for my sake and for
thine own !

Harold. Ay . . . if the king have
not revoked his promise.

William. But hath he done it
then ?

Harold. Not that I know.

William. Good, good, and thou
wilt help me to the crown ?

Harold. Ay . . . if the Witan will
consent to this.

William. Thou art the mightiest
voice in England, man,
Thy voice will lead the Witan —
shall I have it ?

Wulfnoth (*aside to* Harold). Oh !
Harold, if thou love thine Edith,
ay.

Harold. Ay, if —

Malet (*aside to* Harold). Thine
" ifs " will sear thine eyes out
— ay.

William. I ask thee, wilt thou help
me to the crown ?
And I will make thee my great Earl
of Earls,
Foremost in England and in Normandy ;
Thou shalt be verily king — all but
the name —
For I shall most sojourn in Normandy ;
And thou be my vice-king in England. Speak.

Wulfnoth (*aside to* Harold). Ay,
brother — for the sake of England — ay.

Harold. My lord —

Malet (*aside to* Harold). Take heed
now.

Harold. Ay.

William. I am content,

For thou art truthful, and thy word
thy bond.
To-morrow will we ride with thee to
Harfleur. [*Exit* William.

Malet. Harold, I am thy friend,
one life with thee,
And even as I should bless thee saving
mine,
I thank thee now for having saved
thyself. [*Exit* Malet.

Harold. For having lost myself
to save myself,
Said " ay " when I meant " no," lied
like a lad
That dreads the pendent scourge,
said " ay " for " no " !
Ay ! No ! — he hath not bound me by
an oath —
Is " ay " an oath ? is " ay " strong as
an oath ?
Or is it the same sin to break my word
As break mine oath ? He call'd my
word my bond !
He is a liar who knows I am a liar,
And makes me believe that he believes
my word —
The crime be on his head — not
bounden — no.
[*Suddenly doors are flung open, discovering in an inner hall* COUNT
WILLIAM *in his state robes, seated
upon his throne, between two
Bishops,* ODO OF BAYEUX *being
one : in the centre of the hall an
ark covered with cloth of gold ;
and on either side of it the Norman barons.*

Enter a JAILOR *before* William's *throne.*

William (*to* Jailor). Knave, hast
let thy prisoner scape ?

Jailor. Sir Count,
He had but one foot, he must have
hopt away,
Yea, some familiar spirit must have
help'd him.

William. Woe knave to thy familiar
and to thee !
Give me thy keys. [*They fall clashing.*
Nay let them lie. Stand there and
wait my will.
[*The* Jailor *stands aside.*

William (*to* Harold). Hast thou such trustless jailors in thy North ?

Harold. We have few prisoners in mine earldom there,

So less chance for false keepers.

William. We have heard Of thy just, mild, and equal governance ;

Honor to thee ! thou art perfect in all honor !

Thy naked word thy bond ! confirm it now

Before our gather'd Norman baronage,

For they will not believe me — as I believe.

[*Descends from his throne and stands by the ark.*

Let all men here bear witness of our bond !

[*Beckons to* Harold, *who advances.*

Enter MALET *behind him.*

Lay thou thy hand upon this golden pall !

Behold the jewel of St. Pancratius

Woven into the gold. Swear thou on this !

Harold. What should I swear ? Why should I swear on this ?

William (*savagely*). Swear thou to help me to the crown of England.

Malet (*whispering* Harold). My friend, thou hast gone too far to palter now.

Wulfnoth (*whispering* Harold). Swear thou to-day, to-morrow is thine own.

Harold. I swear to help thee to the crown of England . . .

According as King Edward promises.

William. Thou must swear absolutely, noble Earl.

Malet (*whispering*). Delay is death to thee, ruin to England.

Wulfnoth (*whispering*). Swear, dearest brother, I beseech thee, swear !

Harold (*putting his hand on the jewel*). I swear to help thee to the crown of England.

William. Thanks, truthful Earl; I did not doubt thy word,

But that my barons might believe thy word,

And that the Holy Saints of Normandy When thou art home in England, with thine own,

Might strengthen thee in keeping of thy word,

I made thee swear. — Show him by whom he hath sworn.

[*The two* Bishops *advance, and raise the cloth of gold. The bodies and bones of Saints are seen lying in the ark.*

The holy bones of all the Canonized From all the holiest shrines in Normandy !

Harold. Horrible ! [*They let the cloth fall again.*

William. Ay, for thou hast sworn an oath

Which, if not kept, would make the hard earth rive

To the very Devil's horns, the bright sky cleave

To the very feet of God, and send her hosts

Of injured Saints to scatter sparks of plague

Thro' all your cities, blast your infants, dash

The torch of war among your standing corn,

Dabble your hearths with your own blood. — Enough !

Thou wilt not break it ! I, the Count — the King —

Thy friend — am grateful for thine honest oath,

Not coming fiercely like a conqueror, now,

But softly as a bridegroom to his own For I shall rule according to your laws,

And make your ever-jarring Earldoms move

To music and in order — Angle, Jute, Dane, Saxon, Norman, help to build a throne

Out-towering hers of France . . . The wind is fair

For England now . . . To-night we
  will be merry.
To-morrow will I ride with thee to
  Harfleur.
    [*Exeunt* William *and all the Nor-
    man barons, etc.*
  Harold. To-night we will be merry
    — and to-morrow —
Juggler and bastard — bastard — he
  hates that most —
William the tanner's bastard! Would
  he heard me!
O God, that I were in some wide,
  waste field
With nothing but my battle-axe and
  him
To spatter his brains! Why let earth
  rive, gulf in
These cursed Normans — yea and
  mine own self.
Cleave heaven, and send thy saints
  that I may say
Ev'n to their faces, "If ye side with
  William
Ye are not noble." How their pointed
  fingers
Glared at me! Am I Harold, Harold,
  son
Of our great Godwin? Lo! I touch
  mine arms,
My limbs — they are not mine — they
  are a liar's —
I mean to be a liar — I am not bound —
Stigand shall give me absolution for
  it —
Did the chest move? did it move?
  I am utter craven!
O Wulfnoth, Wulfnoth, brother, thou
  hast betray'd me!
  Wulfnoth. Forgive me, brother, I
    will live here and die.

Enter PAGE.

  Page. My lord! the Duke awaits
    thee at the banquet.
  Harold. Where they eat dead men's
    flesh, and drink their blood.
  Page. My lord —
  Harold. I know your Norman
    cookery is so spiced,
It masks all this.

  Page.   My lord! thou art white
    as death.
  Harold. With looking on the dead.
    Am I so white?
Thy Duke will seem the darker.
    Hence, I follow.   [*Exeunt.*

ACT III.

SCENE I. — THE KING'S PALACE.
         LONDON.

KING EDWARD *dying on a couch, and
  by him standing the* QUEEN, HAROLD,
  ARCHBISHOP STIGAND, GURTH,
  LEOFWIN, ARCHBISHOP ALDRED,
  ALDWYTH, *and* EDITH.

  Stigand. Sleeping or dying there?
    If this be death,
Then our great Council wait to crown
    thee King —
Come hither, I have a power;
                      [*To* Harold.
They call me near, for I am close to
    thee
And England — I, old shrivell'd
    Stigand, I,
Dry as an old wood-fungus on a dead
    tree,
I have a power!
See here this little key about my neck!
There lies a treasure buried down in
    Ely:
If e'er the Norman grow too hard for
    thee,
Ask me for this at thy most need,
    son Harold,
At thy most need — not sooner.
  Harold.   So I will.
  Stigand. Red gold — a hundred
    purses — yea, and more!
If thou canst make a wholesome use
    of these
To chink against the Norman, I do
    believe
My old crook'd spine would bud out
    two young wings
To fly to heaven straight with.
  Harold.   Thank thee, father!
Thou art English, Edward too is Eng-
    lish now,

He hath clean repented of his Nor-
manism.
Stigand. **Ay,** as the libertine re-
pents who cannot
Make done undone, when thro' his
dying sense
Shrills "lost thro' thee." They have
built their castles here;
Our priories are Norman; the Norman
adder
Hath bitten us; we are poison'd: our
dear England
Is demi-Norman. He!—
[*Pointing to* King Edward, *sleeping.*
Harold. I would I were
As holy and as passionless as he!
That I might rest as calmly! Look
at him —
The rosy face, and long down-silver-
ing beard,
The brows unwrinkled as a summer
mere. —
Stigand. A summer mere with sud-
den wreckful gusts
From a side-gorge. Passionless? How
he flamed
When Tostig's anger'd earldom flung
him, nay,
He fain had calcined all Northumbria
To one black ash, but that thy patriot
passion
Siding with our great Council against
Tostig,
Outpassion'd his! Holy? ay, ay, for-
sooth,
A conscience for his own soul, not his
realm;
A twilight conscience lighted thro' a
chink;
Thine by the sun; nay, by some sun
to be,
When all the world hath learnt to
speak the truth,
And lying were self-murder by that
state
Which was the exception.
Harold. That sun may God speed!
Stigand. Come, Harold shake the
cloud off!
Harold. Can I, father?
Our Tostig parted cursing me and
England;

Our sister hates us for his banish-
ment;
He hath gone to kindle Norway against
England,
And Wulfnoth is alone in Normandy.
For when I rode with William down
to Harfleur,
"Wulfnoth is sick," he said; "he
cannot follow;"
Then with that friendly-fiendly smile
of his,
"We have learnt to love him, let him
a little longer
Remain a hostage for the loyalty
Of Godwin's house." As far as
touches Wulfnoth
I that so prized plain word and naked
truth
Have sinn'd against it — all in vain.
Leofwin. Good brother,
By all the truths that ever priest hath
preach'd,
Of all the lies that ever men have lied,
Thine is the pardonablest.
Harold. May be so!
I think it so, I think I am a fool
To think it can be otherwise than so.
Stigand. Tut, tut, I have absolved
thee: dost thou scorn me,
Because I had my Canterbury pallium
From one whom they dispoped?
Harold. No, Stigand, no!
Stigand. Is naked truth actable in
true life?
I have heard a saying of thy father
Godwin,
That, were a man of state nakedly
true,
Men would but take him for the
craftier liar.
Leofwin. Be men less delicate than
the Devil himself?
I thought that naked Truth would
shame the Devil
The Devil is so modest.
Gurth. He never said it!
Leofwin. Be thou not stupid-honest,
brother Gurth!
Harold. Better to be a liar's dog,
and hold
My master honest, than believe that
lying

And ruling men are fatal twins that
　cannot
Move one without the other.　Ed-
　ward wakes! —
Dazed — he hath seen a vision.
　　Edward.　　　　　　The green tree!
Then a great Angel past along the
　highest
Crying "the doom of England," and
　at once
He stood beside me, in his grasp a
　sword
Of lightnings, wherewithal he cleft
　the tree
From off the bearing trunk, and
　hurl'd it from him
Three fields away, and then he dash'd
　and drench'd,
He dyed, he soak'd the trunk with
　human blood,
And brought the sunder'd tree again,
　and set it
Straight on the trunk, that thus bap-
　tized in blood
Grew ever high and higher, beyond
　my seeing,
And shot out sidelong boughs across
　the deep
That dropt themselves, and rooted in
　far isles
Beyond my seeing: and the great
　Angel rose
And past again along the highest cry-
　ing
"The doom of England!" — Tostig,
　raise my head!
　　　　　　　[*Falls back senseless.*
　Harold (*raising him*).　Let Harold
　serve for Tostig!
　Queen.　　　　　　Harold served
Tostig so ill, he cannot serve for Tos-
　tig!
Ay, raise his head, for thou hast laid
　it low!
The sickness of our saintly king, for
　whom
My prayers go up as fast as my tears
　fall,
I well believe, hath mainly drawn it-
　self
From lack of Tostig — thou hast ban-
　ish'd him.

　Harold.　Nay — but the council, and
　the king himself.
　Queen.　Thou hatest him, hatest
　him.
　Harold (*coldly*).　　　Ay — Stigand,
　unriddle
This vision, canst thou?
　Stigand.　　　　　　　　Dotage!
　Edward (*starting up*).　It is finish'd!
I have built the Lord a house — the
　Lord hath dwelt
In darkness.　I have built the Lord a
　house —
Palms, flowers, pomegranates, golden
　cherubim
With twenty-cubit wings from wall to
　wall —
I have built the Lord a house — sing,
　Asaph! clash
The cymbal, Heman! blow the trum-
　pet, priest!
Fall, cloud, and fill the house — lo!
　my two pillars,
Jachin and Boaz! —
　　　　　[*Seeing Harold and Gurth.*
　　Harold, Gurth, — where am I?
Where is the charter of our Westmin-
　ster?
　Stigand.　It lies beside thee, king,
　upon thy bed.
　Edward.　Sign, sign at once — take,
　sign it, Stigand, Aldred!
Sign it, my good son Harold, Gurth,
　and Leofwin,
Sign it, my queen!
　All.　　　　We have sign'd it.
　Edward.　　　　　　It is finish'd!
The kingliest Abbey in all Christian
　lands,
The lordliest, loftiest minster ever
　built
To Holy Peter in our English isle!
Let me be buried there, and all our
　kings,
And all our just and wise and holy
　men
That shall be born hereafter.　It is
　finish'd!
Hast thou had absolution for thine
　oath?　　　　　　　　[*To* Harold.
　Harold.　Stigand hath given me
　absolution for it.

Edward. Stigand is not canonical
  enough
To save thee from the wrath of Nor-
  man Saints.
  Stigand. Norman enough! Be
  there no Saints of England
To help us from their brethren yon-
  der?
  Edward.   Prelate,
The Saints are one, but those of Nor-
  manland
Are mightier than our own. Ask it of
  Aldred.   [*To* Harold.
  Aldred. It shall be granted him,
  my king; for he
Who vows a vow to strangle his own
  mother
Is guiltier keeping this, than breaking
  it.
  Edward. O friends, I shall not over-
  live the day.
  Stigand. Why then the throne is
  empty. Who inherits?
For tho' we be not bound by the king's
  voice
In making of a king, yet the king's
  voice
Is much toward his making. Who
  inherits?
Edgar the Atheling?
  Edward.   No, no, but Harold.
I love him : he hath served me : none
  but he
Can rule all England. Yet the curse
  is on him
For swearing falsely by those blessed
  bones;
He did not mean to keep his vow.
  Harold.   Not mean
To make our England Norman.
  Edward.   There spake Godwin,
Who hated all the Normans; but their
  Saints
Have heard thee, Harold.
  Edith.   Oh! my lord, my king!
He knew not whom he sware by.
  Edward.   Yea, I know
He knew not, but those heavenly ears
  have heard,
Their curse is on him; wilt thou bring
  another,
Edith, upon his head?

Edith.   No, no, not I.
  Edward. Why then, thou must not
  wed him.
  Harold.   Wherefore, wherefore?
  Edward. O son, when thou didst
  tell me of thine oath,
I sorrow'd for my random promise
  given
To yon fox-lion. I did not dream
  then
I should be king. — My son, the Saints
  are virgins;
They love the white rose of virginity,
The cold, white lily blowing in her
  cell :
I have been myself a virgin; and I
  sware
To consecrate my virgin here to
  heaven —
The silent, cloister'd, solitary life,
A life of life-long prayer against the
  curse
That lies on thee and England.
  Harold.   No, no, no.
  Edward. Treble denial of the
  tongue of flesh,
Like Peter's when he fell, and thou
  wilt have
To wail for it like Peter. O my
  son!
Are all oaths to be broken then, all
  promises
Made in our agony for help from
  heaven?
Son, there is one who loves thee :
  and a wife,
What matters who, so she be service-
  able
In all obedience, as mine own hath
  been :
God bless thee, wedded daughter.
  [*Laying his hand on the* Queen's *head.*
  Queen.   Bless thou too
That brother whom I love beyond the
  rest,
My banish'd Tostig.
  Edward.   All the sweet Saints
  bless him!
Spare and forbear him, Harold, if he
  comes!
And let him pass unscathed; he loves
  me, Harold!

Be kindly to the Normans left among
    us,
Who follow'd me for love! and dear
    son, swear
When thou art king, to see my solemn
    vow
Accomplish'd.
    Harold. Nay, dear lord, for I have
    sworn
Not to swear falsely twice.
    Edward.   Thou wilt not swear?
    Harold. I cannot.
    Edward.   Then on thee remains
    the curse,
Harold, if thou embrace her: and on
    thee,
Edith, if thou abide it, —
    [*The* King *swoons;* Edith *falls and*
    kneels by the couch.
    Stigand.   He hath swoon'd!
Death? . . . no, as yet a breath.
    Harold.   Look up! look up!
Edith!
    Aldred. Confuse her not; she hath
    begun
Her life-long prayer for thee.
    Aldwyth.   O noble Harold,
I would thou couldst have sworn.
    Harold. For thine own pleasure?
    Aldwyth. No, but to please our
    dying king, and those
Who make thy good their own — all
    England, Earl.
    Aldred. *I* would thou couldst have
    sworn. Our holy king
Hath given his virgin lamb to Holy
    Church
To save thee from the curse.
    Harold.   Alas! poor man,
His promise brought it on me.
    Aldred.   O good son!
That knowledge made him all the
    carefuller
To find a means whereby the curse
    might glance
From thee and England.
    Harold. Father, we so loved —
    Aldred. The more the love, the
    mightier is the prayer;
The more the love, the more acceptable
The sacrifice of both your loves to
    heaven.

No sacrifice to heaven, no help from
    heaven;
That runs thro' all the faiths of all
    the world.
And sacrifice there must be, for the
    king
Is holy, and hath talk'd with God,
    and seen
A shadowing horror; there are signs
    in heaven —
    Harold. Your comet came and went.
    Aldred.   And signs on earth!
Knowest thou Senlac hill?
    Harold.   I know all Sussex;
A good entrenchment for a perilous
    hour!
    Aldred. Pray God that come not
    suddenly! There is one
Who passing by that hill three nights
    ago —
He shook so that he scarce could out
    with it —
Heard, heard —
    Harold.   The wind in his hair?
    Aldred.   A ghostly horn
Blowing continually, and faint battle-
    hymns,
And cries, and clashes, and the groans
    of men;
And dreadful shadows strove upon
    the hill,
And dreadful lights crept up from out
    the marsh —
Corpse-candles gliding over nameless
    graves —
    Harold. At Senlac?
    Aldred.   Senlac.
    Edward (*waking*). Senlac! Sangue-
    lac,
The Lake of Blood!
    Stigand. This lightning before
    death
Plays on the word, — and Normanizes
    too!
    Harold. Hush, father, hush!
    Edward.   Thou uncanonical fool,
Wilt *thou* play with the thunder?
    North and South
Thunder together, showers of blood
    are blown
Before a never ending blast, and
    hiss

Against the blaze they cannot quench
  — a lake,
A sea of blood — we are drown'd in
  blood — for God
Has fill'd the quiver, and Death has
  drawn the bow —
Sanguelac! Sanguelac! the arrow! the
  arrow!   [*Dies.*
  Stigand. It is the arrow of death in
    his own heart —
And our great Council wait to crown
  thee King.

SCENE II. — In the Garden. The
  King's House near London.

  Edith. Crown'd, crown'd and lost,
    crown'd King — and lost to me!
(*Singing.*)
Two young lovers in winter weather,
      None to guide them,
Walk'd at night on the misty heather;
Night, as black as a raven's feather;
Both were lost and found together,
      None beside them.

That is the burthen of it — lost and
  found
Together in the cruel river Swale
A hundred years ago; and there's
  another,

    Lost, lost, the light of day,

To which the lover answers lovingly

      " I am beside thee."
  Lost, lost, we have lost the way.
  " Love, I will guide thee."
Whither, O whither ? into the river,
Where we two may be lost together,
And lost for ever ? " Oh ! never, oh !
    never,
Tho' we be lost and be found to-
    gether."

Some think they loved within the pale
  forbidden
By Holy Church : but who shall say ?
  the truth
Was lost in that fierce North, where
  they were lost,

Where all good things are lost, where
  Tostig lost
The good hearts of his people. It is
  Harold !

(*Enter* Harold.)

Harold the King !
  Harold.   Call me not King,
    but Harold.
  Edith. Nay, thou art King !
  Harold.   Thine, thine, or King
    or churl !
My girl, thou hast been weeping : turn
  not thou
Thy face away, but rather let me be
King of the moment to thee, and com-
  mand
That kiss my due when subject, which
  will make
My kingship kinglier to me than to
  reign
King of the world without it.
  Edith.   Ask me not,
Lest I should yield it, and the second
  curse
Descend upon thine head, and thou
  be only
King of the moment over England.
  Harold.   Edith,
Tho' somewhat less a king to my true
  self
Than ere they crown'd me one, for I
  have lost
Somewhat of upright stature thro'
  mine oath,
Yet thee I would not lose, and sell
  not thou
Our living passion for a dead man's
  dream ;
Stigand believed he knew not what he
  spake.
Oh God ! I cannot help it, but at
  times
They seem to me too narrow, all the
  faiths
Of this grown world of ours, whose
  baby eye
Saw them sufficient. Fool and wise,
  I fear
This curse, and scorn it. But a little
  light ! —

And on it falls the shadow of the priest;
Heaven yield us more! for better, Woden, all
Our cancell'd warrior-gods, our grim Walhalla,
Eternal war, than that the Saints at peace
The Holiest of our Holiest one should be
This William's fellow-tricksters; — better die
Than credit this, for death is death, or else
Lifts us beyond the lie. Kiss me — thou art not
A holy sister yet, my girl, to fear
There might be more than brother in my kiss,
And more than sister in thine own.

   Edith.   I dare not.

   Harold. Scared by the church —
"Love for a whole life long"
When was that sung?

   Edith.   Here to the nightingales.

   Harold. Their anthems of no church, how sweet they are!
Nor kingly priest, nor priestly king to cross
Their billings ere they nest.

   Edith.   They are but of spring,
They fly the winter change — not so with us —
No wings to come and go.

   Harold.   But wing'd souls flying
Beyond all change and in the eternal distance
To settle on the Truth.

   Edith.   They are not so true,
They change their mates.

   Harold. Do they? I did not know it.

   Edith. They say thou art to wed the Lady Aldwyth.

   Harold. They say, they say.

   Edith.   If this be politic,
And well for thee and England — and for her —
Care not for me who love thee.

   Gurth (calling).   Harold, Harold!

   Harold. The voice of Gurth! (*Enter* GURTH.) Good even, my good brother!

   Gurth. Good even, gentle Edith.

   Edith.   Good even, Gurth.

   Gurth. Ill news hath come! Our hapless brother, Tostig —
He, and the giant King of Norway, Harold
Hardrada — Scotland, Ireland, Iceland, Orkney,
Are landed North of Humber, and in a field
So packt with carnage that the dykes and brooks
Were bridged and damm'd with dead, have overthrown
Morcar and Edwin.

   Harold.   Well then, we must fight.
How blows the wind?

   Gurth.   Against St. Valery
And William.

   Harold. Well then, we will to the North.

   Gurth. Ay, but worse news: this William sent to Rome,
Swearing thou swarest falsely by his Saints:
The Pope and that Archdeacon Hildebrand
His master, heard him, and have sent him back
A holy gonfanon, and a blessed hair
Of Peter, and all France, all Burgundy,
Poitou, all Christendom is raised against thee;
He hath cursed thee, and all those who fight for thee,
And given thy realm of England to the bastard.

   Harold. Ha! ha!

   Edith. Oh! laugh not! . . . Strange and ghastly in the gloom
And shadowing of this double thunder-cloud
That lours on England — laughter!

   Harold.   No, not strange!
This was old human laughter in old Rome
Before a Pope was born, when that which reign'd
Call'd itself God. — A kindly rendering

Of "Render unto Cæsar." . . . The Good Shepherd!
Take this, and render that.

Gurth. They have taken York.

Harold. The Lord was God and came as man — the Pope
Is man and comes as God. — York taken?

Gurth. Yea, Tostig hath taken York!

Harold. To York then. Edith, Hadst thou been braver, I had better braved
All — but I love thee and thou me — and that
Remains beyond all chances and all churches,
And that thou knowest.

Edith. Ay, but take back thy ring.
It burns my hand — a curse to thee and me.
I dare not wear it.

[*Proffers Harold the ring, which he takes.*

Harold. But I dare. God with thee!

[*Exeunt Harold and Gurth.*

Edith. The King hath cursed him, if he marry me;
The Pope hath cursed him, marry me or no!
God help me! I know nothing — can but pray
For Harold — pray, pray, pray — no help but prayer,
A breath that fleets beyond this iron world,
And touches Him that made it.

ACT IV.

SCENE I. — In Northumbria.

Archbishop Aldred, Morcar, Edwin, *and* Forces. *Enter* Harold. *The standard of the golden Dragon of Wessex preceding him.*

Harold. What! are thy people sullen from defeat?
Our Wessex dragon flies beyond the Humber,
No voice to greet it.

Edwin. Let not our great king
Believe us sullen — only shamed to the quick
Before the king — as having been so bruised
By Harold, king of Norway; but our help
Is Harold, king of England. Pardon us, thou!
Our silence is our reverence for the king!

Harold. Earl of the Mercians! if the truth be gall,
Cram me not thou with honey, when our good hive
Needs every sting to save it.

Voices. Aldwyth! Aldwyth!

Harold. Why cry thy people on thy sister's name?

Morcar. She hath won upon our people thro' her beauty,
And pleasantness among them.

Voices. Aldwyth, Aldwyth!

Harold. They shout as they would have her for a queen.

Morcar. She hath followed with our host, and suffer'd all.

Harold. What would ye, men?

Voice. Our old Northumbrian crown,
And kings of our own choosing.

Harold. Your old crown
Were little help without our Saxon carle
Against Hardrada.

Voice. Little! we are Danes.
Who conquer'd what we walk on, our own field.

Harold. They have been plotting here! [*Aside.*

Voice. He calls us little!

Harold. The kingdoms of this world began with little,
A hill, a fort, a city — that reach'd a hand
Down to the field beneath it, "Be thou mine,"
Then to the next, "Thou also!" If the field
Cried out "I am mine own;" another hill
Or fort, or city, took it, and the first
Fell, and the next became an Empire.

Voice.   Yet
Thou art but a West Saxon: *we* are
    Danes!
    Harold. My mother is a Dane, and
        I am English;
There is a pleasant fable in old books,
Ye take a stick, and break it; bind a
    score
All in one faggot, snap it over knee,
Ye cannot.
    Voice.   Hear King Harold! he
        says true!
    Harold. Would ye be Norsemen?
    Voices.   No!
    Harold.   Or Norman?
    Voices.   No!
    Harold. Snap not the faggot-band
        then.
    Voice.   That is true!
    Voice. Ah, but thou art not kingly,
        only grandson
To Wulfnoth, a poor cow-herd.
    Harold.   This old Wulfnoth
Would take me on his knees and tell
    me tales
Of Alfred and of Athelstan the Great
Who drove you Danes; and yet he
    held that Dane,
Jute, Angle, Saxon, were or should
    be all
One England, for this cow-herd, like
    my father,
Who shook the Norman scoundrels
    off the throne,
Had in him kingly thoughts — a king
    of men,
Not made but born, like the great
    king of all,
A light among the oxen.
    Voice.   That is true!
    Voice. Ah, and I love him now, for
        mine own father
Was great, and cobbled.
    Voice.   Thou art Tostig's brother,
Who wastes the land.
    Harold. This brother comes to save
Your land from waste; I saved it
    once before,
For when your people banish'd Tostig
    hence,
And Edward would have sent a host
    against you,

Then I, who loved my brother, bade
    the king
Who doted on him, sanction your de-
    cree
Of Tostig's banishment, and choice
    of Morcar,
To help the realm from scattering.
    Voice.   King! thy brother,
If one may dare to speak the truth,
    was wrong'd.
Wild was he, born so: but the plots
    against him
Had madden'd tamer men.
    Morcar.   Thou art one of those
Who brake into Lord Tostig's treas-
    ure-house
And slew two hundred of his following,
And now, when Tostig hath come back
    with power,
Are frighted back to Tostig.
    Old Thane. Ugh! Plots and feuds!
This is my ninetieth birthday. Can
    ye not
Be brethren? Godwin still at feud
    with Alfgar,
And Alfgar hates King Harold. Plots
    and feuds!
This is my ninetieth birthday!
    Harold.   Old man, Harold
Hates nothing; not *his* fault, if our
    two houses
Be less than brothers.
    Voices. Aldwyth, Harold, Aldwyth!
    Harold. Again! Morcar! Edwin!
        What do they mean?
    Edwin. So the good king would
        deign to lend an ear
Not overscornful, we might chance —
    perchance —
To guess their meaning.
    Morcar. Thine own meaning, Har-
        old,
To make all England one, to close all
    feuds,
Mixing our bloods, that thence a king
    may rise
Half-Godwin and half-Alfgar, one to
    rule
All England beyond question, beyond
    quarrel.
    Harold. Who sow'd this fancy here
        among the people?

Morcar. Who knows what sows
itself among the people ?
A goodly flower at times.
Harold. The Queen of Wales ?
Why, Morcar, it is all but duty in
her
To hate me ; I have heard she hates
me.
Morcar. No !
For I can swear to that, but cannot
swear
That these will follow thee against
the Norsemen,
If thou deny them this.
Harold. Morcar and Edwin,
When will ye cease to plot against
my house ?
Edwin. The king can scarcely
dream that we, who know
His prowess in the mountains of the
West,
Should care to plot against him in
the North.
Morcar. Who dares arraign us,
king, of such a plot ?
Harold. Ye heard one witness even
now.
Morcar. The craven !
There is a faction risen again for
Tostig,
Since Tostig came with Norway —
fright not love.
Harold. Morcar and Edwin, will ye,
if I yield,
Follow against the Norseman ?
Morcar. Surely, surely !
Harold. Morcar and Edwin, will ye
upon oath,
Help us against the Norman ?
Morcar. With good will ;
Yea, take the Sacrament upon it, king.
Harold. Where is thy sister ?
Morcar. Somewhere hard at hand.
Call and she comes.
[*One goes out, then enter* Aldwyth.
Harold. I doubt not but thou knowest
Why thou art summon'd.
Aldwyth. Why ? — I stay with these,
Lest thy fierce Tostig spy me out
alone,
And flay me all alive.
Harold. Canst thou love one

Who did discrown thine husband, un-
queen thee ?
Didst thou not love thine husband ?
Aldwyth. Oh ! my lord,
The nimble, wild, red, wiry, savage
king —
That was, my lord, a match of policy.
Harold. Was it ?
I knew him brave : he loved his land :
he fain
Had made her great : his finger on her
harp
(I heard him more than once) had in
it Wales,
Her floods, her woods, her hills : had
I been his,
I had been all Welsh.
Aldwyth. Oh, ay — all Welsh —
and yet
I saw thee drive him up his hills —
and women
Cling to the conquer'd, if they love,
the more ;
If not, they cannot hate the conqueror.
We never — oh ! good Morcar, speak
for us,
His conqueror conquer'd Aldwyth.
Harold. Goodly news !
Morcar. Doubt it not thou ! Since
Griffyth's head was sent
To Edward, she hath said it.
Harold. I had rather
She would have loved her husband.
Aldwyth, Aldwyth,
Canst thou love me, thou knowing
where I love ?
Aldwyth. I can, my lord, for mine
own sake, for thine,
For England, for thy poor white dove,
who flutters
Between thee and the porch, but then
would find
Her nest within the cloister, and be
still.
Harold. Canst thou love one, who
cannot love again ?
Aldwyth. Full hope have I that love
will answer love.
Harold. Then in the name of the
great God, so be it !
Come, Aldred, join our hands before
the hosts,

That all may see.
   [Aldred *joins the hands of* Harold
   and Aldwyth *and blesses them.*
  Voices. Harold, Harold and Ald-
    wyth!
  Harold. Set forth our golden Dra-
    gon, let him flap
The wings that beat down Wales!
Advance our Standard of the Warrior,
Dark among gems and gold; and
    thou, brave banner,
Blaze like a night of fatal stars on
    those
Who read their doom and die.
Where lie the Norsemen? on the
    Derwent? ay
At Stamford-bridge.
Morcar, collect thy men; Edwin, my
    friend —
Thou lingerest. — Gurth, —
Last night King Edward came to me
    in dreams —
The rosy face and long down-silvering
    beard —
He told me I should conquer: —
I am no woman to put faith in dreams.
        (*To his army.*)
Last night King Edward came to me
    in dreams,
And told me we should conquer.
  Voices.   Forward! Forward!
Harold and Holy Cross!
  Aldwyth.   The day is won!

SCENE II. — A Plain. Before the
  Battle of Stamford-Bridge.

    Harold *and his* Guard.

  Harold. Who is it comes this way?
    Tostig? (*Enter* Tostig *with a
    small force.*) O brother,
What art thou doing here?
  Tostig.   I am foraging
For Norway's army.
  Harold. I could take and slay thee.
Thou art in arms against us.
  Tostig.   Take and slay me,
For Edward loved me.
  Harold. Edward bade me spare
    thee.
  Tostig. I hate King Edward, for he
    join'd with thee

To drive me outlaw'd. Take and slay
    me, I say,
Or I shall count thee fool.
  Harold. Take thee, or free thee,
Free thee or slay thee, Norway will
    have war;
No man would strike with Tostig, save
    for Norway.
Thou art nothing in thine England,
    save for Norway,
Who loves not thee but war. What
    dost thou here,
Trampling thy mother's bosom into
    blood?
  Tostig. She hath wean'd me from
    it with such bitterness.
I come for mine own Earldom, my
    Northumbria;
Thou hast given it to the enemy of
    our house.
  Harold. Northumbria threw thee
    off, she will not have thee,
Thou hast misused her: and, O crown-
    ing crime!
Hast murder'd thine own guest, the
    son of Orm,
Gamel, at thine own hearth.
  Tostig.   The slow, fat fool!
He drawl'd and prated so, I smote
    him suddenly,
I knew not what I did. He held with
    Morcar. —
I hate myself for all things that I
    do.
  Harold. And Morcar holds with
    us. Come back with him.
Know what thou dost; and we may
    find for thee,
So thou be chasten'd by thy banish-
    ment,
Some easier earldom.
  Tostig.   What for Norway then?
He looks for land among us, he and
    his.
  Harold. Seven feet of English land,
    or something more,
Seeing he is a giant.
  Tostig.   That is noble!
That sounds of Godwin.
  Harold.   Come thou back, and
    be
Once more a son of Godwin.

Tostig (turns away). O brother,
brother,
O Harold —
Harold (laying his hand on Tostig's
shoulder). Nay then, come thou
back to us!
Tostig (after a pause turning to him).
Never shall any man say that I,
that Tostig
Conjured the mightier Harold from
his North
To do the battle for me here in Eng-
land,
Then left him for the meaner!
thee! —
Thou hast no passion for the House
of Godwin —
Thou hast but cared to make thyself
a king —
Thou hast sold me for a cry. —
Thou gavest thy voice against me in
the Council —
I hate thee, and despise thee, and defy
thee.
Farewell for ever!   [*Exit.*
Harold.   On to Stamford-bridge!

SCENE III.

After the Battle of Stamford-
Bridge. Banquet.

Harold *and* Aldwyth.   Gurth,
Leofwin, Morcar, Edwin, *and
other* Earls *and* Thanes.

Voices. Hail! Harold! Aldwyth!
hail, bridegroom and bride!
Aldwyth (talking with Harold). Answer them thou!
Is this our marriage-banquet? Would
the wines
Of wedding had been dash'd into the
cups
Of victory, and our marriage and thy
glory
Been drunk together! these poor
hands but sew,
Spin, broider — would that they were
man's to have held
The battle-axe by thee!

Harold.   There *was* a moment
When being forced aloof from all my
guard,
And striking at Hardrada and his
madmen
I had wish'd for any weapon.
Aldwyth.   Why art thou sad?
Harold. I have lost the boy who
play'd at ball with me,
With whom I fought another fight
than this
Of Stamford-bridge.
Aldwyth.   Ay! ay! thy victories
Over our own poor Wales, when at
thy side
He conquer'd with thee.
Harold.   No — the childish fist
That cannot strike again.
Aldwyth.   Thou art too kindly.
Why didst thou let so many Norse-
men hence?
Thy fierce forekings had clench'd
their pirate hides
To the bleak church doors, like kites
upon a barn.
Harold. Is there so great a need to
tell thee why?
Aldwyth. Yea, am I not thy wife?
Voices.   Hail, Harold, Aldwyth!
Bridegroom and bride!
Aldwyth. Answer them!
                [*To* Harold.
Harold (to all). Earls and Thanes!
Full thanks for your fair greeting of
my bride!
Earls, Thanes, and all our country-
men! the day,
Our day beside the Derwent will not
shine
Less than a star among the goldenest
hours
Of Alfred, or of Edward his great
son,
Or Athelstan, or English Ironside
Who fought with Knut, or Knut who
coming Dane
Died English. Every man about his
king
Fought like a king; the king like his
own man,
No better; one for all, and all for
one,

One soul! and therefore have we shat-
　ter'd back
The hugest wave from Norseland ever
　yet
Surged on us, and our battle-axes
　broken
The Raven's wing, and dumb'd his
　carrion croak
From the gray sea for ever. Many
　are gone —
Drink to the dead who died for us, the
　living
Who fought and would have died, but
　happier lived,
If happier be to live; they both have
　life
In the large mouth of England, till
　her voice
Die with the world. Hail — hail!
　Morcar. May all invaders perish
like Hardrada!
All traitors fail like Tostig!
　　　　　　　[*All drink but* Harold.
　Aldwyth.　　　　Thy cup's full!
　Harold. I saw the hand of Tostig
cover it.
Our dear, dead, traitor-brother, Tostig,
　him
Reverently we buried. Friends, had
　I been here,
Without too large self-lauding I must
　hold
The sequel had been other than his
　league
With Norway, and this battle. Peace
　be with him!
He was not of the worst. If there be
　those
At banquet in this hall, and hearing
　me —
For there be those I fear who prick'd
　the lion
To make him spring, that sight of
　Danish blood
Might serve an end not English —
　peace with them
Likewise, if *they* can be at peace with
　what
God gave us to divide us from the wolf!
　Aldwyth (*aside to* Harold). Make
not our Morcar sullen: it is not
wise.

Harold. Hail to the living who
　fought, the dead who fell!
Voices. Hail, hail!
First Thane. How ran that answer
　which King Harold gave
To his dead namesake, when he ask'd
　for England?
　Leofwin. "Seven feet of English
earth, or something more,
Seeing he is a giant!"
　First Thane. Then for the bastard
Six feet and nothing more!
　Leofwin.　　　　Ay, but belike
Thou hast not learnt his measure.
　First Thane.　　　By St. Edmund
I over-measure him. Sound sleep to
　the man
Here by dead Norway without dream
　or dawn!
　Second Thane. What is he brag-
　ging still that he will come
To thrust our Harold's throne from
　under him?
My nurse would tell me of a molehill
　crying
To a mountain "Stand aside and room
　for me!"
　First Thane. Let him come! let him
　come. Here's to him, sink or
　swim!　　　　　　　　[*Drinks.*
Second Thane. God sink him!
First Thane. Cannot hands which
　had the strength
To shove that stranded iceberg off
　our shores,
And send the shatter'd North again
　to sea,
Scuttle his cockle-shell? What's
　Brunanburg
To Stamford-bridge? a war-crash, and
　so hard,
So loud, that, by St. Dunstan, old St.
　Thor —
By God, we thought him dead — but
　our old Thor
Heard his own thunder again, and
　woke and came
Among us again, and mark'd the sons
　of those
Who made this Britain England,
　break the North:

Mark'd how the war-axe swang,
Heard how the war-horn sang,
Mark'd how the spear-head sprang,
Heard how the shield-wall rang,
Iron on iron clang,
Anvil on hammer bang —

Second Thane. Hammer on anvil,
hammer on anvil. Old dog,
Thou art drunk, old dog!
First Thane. Too drunk to fight
with thee!
Second Thane. Fight thou with
thine own double, not with me,
Keep that for Norman William!
First Thane. Down with William!
Third Thane. The washerwoman's
brat!
Fourth Thane. The tanner's bas-
tard!
Fifth Thane. The Falaise byblow!

[*Enter a* Thane *from Pevensey,
spatter'd with mud.*

Harold. Ay, but what late guest,
As haggard as a fast of forty days,
And caked and plaster'd with a hun-
dred mires,
Hath stumbled on our cups?
Thane from Pevensey. My lord the
King!
William the Norman, for the wind had
changed —
Harold. I felt it in the middle of
that fierce fight
At Stamford-bridge. William hath
landed, ha?
Thane from Pevensey. Landed at
Pevensey — I am from Peven-
sey —
Hath wasted all the land at Peven-
sey —
Hath harried mine own cattle — God
confound him!
I have ridden night and day from
Pevensey —
A thousand ships — a hundred thou-
sand men —
Thousands of horses, like as many
lions
Neighing and roaring as they leapt to
land —

Harold. How oft in coming hast
thou broken bread?
Thane from Pevensey. Some thrice,
or so.
Harold. Bring not thy hollowness
On our full feast. Famine is fear,
were it but
Of being starved. Sit down, sit down,
and eat,
And, when again red-blooded, speak
again;
(*Aside.*) The men that guarded
England to the South
Were scatter'd to the harvest. . . .
No power mine
To hold their force together. . . .
Many are fallen
At Stamford-bridge . . . the people
stupid-sure
Sleep like their swine . . . in South
and North at once
I could not be.
(*Aloud.*) Gurth, Leofwin, Morcar,
Edwin!
(*Pointing to the revellers.*) The curse
of England! these are drown'd
in wassail,
And cannot see the world but thro'
their wines!
Leave them! and thee too, Aldwyth,
must I leave —
Harsh is the news! hard is our honey-
moon!
Thy pardon. (*Turning round to his
attendants.*) Break the banquet
up . . . Ye four!
And thou, my carrier-pigeon of black
news,
Cram thy crop full, but come when
thou art call'd. [*Exit* Harold.

ACT V.

SCENE I. — A TENT ON A MOUND,
FROM WHICH CAN BE SEEN THE
FIELD OF SENLAC.

HAROLD, *sitting; by him standing* HUGH
MARGOT *the* Monk, GURTH, LEOF-
WIN.

Harold. Refer my cause, my crown
to Rome! . . . The wolf

Mudded the brook and predetermined all.

Monk,
Thou hast said thy say, and had my constant "No"
For all but instant battle. I hear no more.

Margot. Hear me again — for the last time. Arise,
Scatter thy people home, descend the hill,
Lay hands of full allegiance in thy Lord's
And crave his mercy, for the Holy Father
Hath given this realm of England to the Norman.

Harold. Then for the last time, monk, I ask again
When had the Lateran and the Holy Father
To do with England's choice of her own king ?

Margot. Earl, the first Christian Cæsar drew to the East
To leave the Pope dominion in the West.
He gave him all the kingdoms of the West.

Harold. So ! — did he ? — Earl — I have a mind to play
The William with thine eyesight and thy tongue.

Earl—ay—thou art but but a messenger of William.
I am weary — go : make me not wroth with thee !

Margot. Mock-king, I am the messenger of God,
His Norman Daniel ! Mene, Mene, Tekel !
Is thy wrath Hell, that I should spare to cry,
Yon heaven is wroth with *thee* ? Hear me again !
Our Saints have moved the Church that moves the world,
And all the Heavens and very God : they heard —
They know King Edward's promise and thine — thine.

Harold. Should they not know free England crowns herself ?
Not know that he nor I had power to promise ?
Not know that Edward cancell'd his own promise ?
And for *my* part therein — Back to that juggler,   [*Rising.*
Tell him the Saints are nobler than he dreams,
Tell him that God is nobler than the Saints,
And tell him we stand arm'd on Senlac Hill,
And bide the doom of God.

Margot. Hear it thro' me.
The realm for which thou art forsworn is cursed,
The babe enwomb'd and at the breast is cursed,
The corpse thou whelmest with thine earth is cursed,
The soul who fighteth on thy side is cursed,
The seed thou sowest in thy field is cursed,
The steer wherewith thou plowest thy field is cursed,
The fowl that fleeth o'er thy field is cursed,
And thou, usurper, liar —

Harold. Out, beast monk !
     [*Lifting his hand to strike him.*
     Gurth *stops the blow.*
I ever hated monks.

Margot. I am but a voice
Among you : murder, martyr me if ye will —

Harold. Thanks, Gurth ! The simple, selfless man
Is worth a world of tonguesters. (*To* Margot.) Get thee gone !
He means the thing he says. See him out safe !

Leofwin. He hath blown himself as red as fire with curses.
An honest fool ! Follow me, honest fool,
But if thou blurt thy curse among our folk,
I know not — I may give that egg-bald head
The tap that silences.

Harold.   See him out safe.

[*Exeunt* Leofwin *and* Margot.

Gurth. Thou hast lost thine even
     temper, brother Harold!

Harold. Gurth, when I past by
     Waltham, my foundation
For men who serve the neighbor, not
     themselves,
I cast me down prone, praying; and,
     when I rose,
They told me that the Holy Rood had
     lean'd
And bow'd above me; whether that
     which held it
Had weaken'd, and the Rood itself
     were bound
To that necessity which binds us down;
Whether it bow'd at all but in their
     fancy;
Or if it bow'd, whether it symbol'd ruin
Or glory, who shall tell? but they
     were sad,
And somewhat sadden'd me.

Gurth.   Yet if a fear,
Or shadow of a fear, lest the strange
     Saints
By whom thou swarest, should have
     power to balk
Thy puissance in this fight with him,
     who made
And heard thee swear — brother — *I*
     have not sworn —
If the king fall, may not the kingdom
     fall?
But if I fall, I fall, and thou art king;
And, if I win, I win, and thou art king;
Draw thou to London, there make
     strength to breast
Whatever chance, but leave this day
     to me.

Leofwin (*entering*). And waste the
     land about thee as thou goest,
And be thy hand as winter on the field,
To leave the foe no forage.

Harold.   Noble Gurth!
Best son of Godwin! If I fall, I fall —
The doom of God! How should the
     people fight
When the king flies? And, Leofwin,
     art thou mad?
How should the King of England
     waste the fields

Of England, his own people? — No
     glance yet
Of the Northumbrian helmet on the
     heath?

Leofwin. No, but a shoal of wives
     upon the heath,
And someone saw thy willy-nilly nun
Vying a tress against our golden
     fern.

Harold. Vying a tear with our cold
     dews, a sigh
With these low-moaning heavens.
     Let her be fetch'd.
We have parted from our wife without
     reproach,
Tho' we have dived thro' all her prac-
     tices;
And that is well.

Leofwin.   I saw her even now:
She hath not left us.

Harold. Nought of Morcar then?

Gurth. Nor seen, nor heard; thine,
     William's or his own
As wind blows, or tide flows: belike
     he watches,
If this war-storm in one of its rough
     rolls
Wash up that old crown of Northum-
     berland.

Harold. I had married her for
     Morcar — a sin against
The truth of love. Evil for good, it
     seems,
Is oft as childless of the good as evil
For evil.

Leofwin. Good for good hath borne
     at times
A bastard false as William.

Harold.   Ay, if Wisdom
Pair'd not with Good. But I am
     somewhat worn,
A snatch of sleep were like the peace
     of God.
Gurth, Leofwin, go once more about
     the hill —
What did the dead man call it — San-
     guelac,
The lake of blood?

Leofwin. A lake that dips in Wil-
     liam
As well as Harold.

Harold. Like enough. I have seen

The trenches dug, the palisades up-
rear'd
And wattled thick with ash and wil-
low-wands ;
Yea, wrought at them myself. Go
round once more ;
See all be sound and whole. No Nor-
man horse
Can shatter England, standing shield
by shield ;
Tell that again to all.
   Gurth.   I will, good brother.
   Harold. Our guardsman hath but
toil'd his hand and foot,
I hand, foot, heart and head. Some
wine ! (*One pours wine into a
goblet which he hands to* Harold.)
                  Too much !
What ? we must use our battle-axe
to-day.
Our guardsmen have slept well, since
we came in ?
   Leofwin. Ay, slept and snored.
Your second-sighted man
That scared the dying conscience of
the king,
Misheard their snores for groans.
They are up again
And chanting that old song of Brunan-
burg
Where England conquer'd.
   Harold. That is well. The Norman,
What is he doing ?
   Leofwin. Praying for Normandy ;
Our scouts have heard the tinkle of
their bells.
   Harold. And our old songs are
prayers for England too !
But by all Saints —
   Leofwin. Barring the Norman !
   Harold.   Nay,
Were the great trumpet blowing
doomsday dawn,
I needs must rest. Call when the
Norman moves —
          [*Exeunt all but* Harold.
No horse — thousand of horses — our
shield wall —
Wall — break it not — break not —
break —   [*Sleeps.*
   Vision of Edward. Son Harold, I
thy king, who came before

To tell thee thou shouldst win at
Stamford-bridge,
Come yet once more, from where I am
at peace,
Because I loved thee in my mortal
day,
To tell thee thou shalt die on Senlac
hill —
Sanguelac !
   Vision of Wulfnoth. O brother, from
my ghastly oubliette
I send my voice across the narrow
seas —
No more, no more, dear brother,
nevermore —
Sanguelac !
   Vision of Tostig. O brother, most
unbrotherlike to me,
Thou gavest thy voice against me in
my life,
I give my voice against thee from the
grave —
Sanguelac !
   Vision of Norman Saints. O hapless
Harold ! King but for an hour !
Thou swarest falsely by our blessed
bones,
We give our voice against thee out of
heaven !
Sanguelac ! Sanguelac ! The arrow :
the arrow !
   Harold (*starting up, battle-axe in
hand*).   Away !
My battle-axe against your voices.
Peace !
The king's last word — " the arrow ! "
I shall die —
I die for England then, who lived for
England —
What nobler ? men must die.
I cannot fall into a falser world —
I have done no man wrong. Tostig,
poor brother,
Art *thou* so anger'd ?
Fain had I kept thine earldom in thy
hands
Save for thy wild and violent will
that wrench'd
All hearts of freemen from thee. I
could do
No other than this way advise the
king

Against the race of Godwin. Is it
  possible
That mortal men should bear their
  earthly heats
Into yon bloodless world, and threaten
  us thence
Unschool'd of Death? Thus then
  thou art revenged —
I left our England naked to the South
To meet thee in the North. The
  Norseman's raid
Hath helpt the Norman, and the race
  of Godwin
Hath ruin'd Godwin. No — our wak-
  ing thoughts
Suffer a stormless shipwreck in the
  pools
Of sullen slumber, and arise again
Disjointed: only dreams — where
  mine own self
Takes part against myself! Why?
  for a spark
Of self-disdain born in me when I
  sware
Falsely to him, the falser Norman,
  over
His gilded ark of mummy-saints, by
  whom
I knew not that I sware, — not for my-
  self —
For England — yet not wholly —

(*Enter* EDITH.)

             Edith, Edith,
Get thou into thy cloister as the king
Will'd it: be safe: the perjury-mon-
  gering Count
Hath made too good an use of Holy
  Church
To break her close! There the great
  God of truth
Fill all thine hours with peace! — A
  lying devil
Hath haunted me — mine oath — my
  wife — I fain
Had made my marriage not a lie; I
  could not:
Thou art my bride! and thou in after
  years
Praying perchance for this poor soul
  of mine

In cold, white cells beneath an icy
  moon —
This memory to thee! — and this to
  England,
My legacy of war against the Pope
From child to child, from Pope to
  Pope, from age to age,
Till the sea wash her level with her
  shores,
Or till the Pope be Christ's.

Enter ALDWYTH.

  Aldwyth (*to* Edith). Away from
  him!
  Edith. I will . . . I have not spoken
  to the king
One word; and one I must. Farewell!
             [*Going.*
  Harold.   Not yet.
Stay.
  Edith. To what use?
  Harold. The king commands thee,
  woman!
      (*To* Aldwyth.)
Have thy two brethren sent their forces
  in?
  Aldwyth. Nay, I fear not.
  Harold. Then there's no force in
  thee!
Thou didst possess thyself of Edward's
  ear
To part me from the woman that I
  loved!
Thou didst arouse the fierce Northum-
  brians!
Thou hast been false to England and
  to me! —
As . . . in some sort . . . I have been
  false to thee.
Leave me. No more — Pardon on both
  sides — go!
  Aldwyth. Alas, my lord, I loved thee!
  Harold (*bitterly*).   With a love
Passing thy love for Griffyth! where-
  fore now
Obey my first and last commandment.
  Go!
  Aldwyth. O Harold! husband! Shall
  we meet again?
  Harold. After the battle — after
  the battle. Go.

Aldwyth. I go. (*Aside.*) That I
could stab her standing there!
[*Exit* Aldwyth.

Edith. Alas, my lord, she loved thee.
Harold.   Never! never!
Edith. I saw it in her eyes!
Harold.   I see it in thine.
And not on thee — nor England — fall
God's doom!
Edith. On *thee?* on me. And thou
art England! Alfred
Was England. Ethelred was nothing.
England
Is but her king, and thou art Harold!
Harold.   Edith,
The sign in heaven — the sudden blast
at sea —
My fatal oath — the dead Saints — the
dark dreams —
The Pope's Anathema — the Holy
Rood
That bow'd to me at Waltham — Edith,
if
I, the last English king of England —
Edith.   No,
First of a line that coming from the
people,
And chosen by the people —
Harold.   And fighting for
And dying for the people —
Edith.   Living! living!
Harold. Yea so, good cheer! thou
art Harold, I am Edith!
Look not thus wan!
Edith. What matters how I look?
Have we not broken Wales and Norse-
land? slain,
Whose life was all one battle, incar-
nate war,
Their giant-king, a mightier man-in-
arms
Than William.
Harold. Ay, my girl, no tricks in
him —
No bastard he! when all was lost, he
yell'd,
And bit his shield, and dash'd it on the
ground,
And swaying his two-handed sword
about him,
Two deaths at every swing, ran in upon
us

And died so, and I loved him as I hate
This liar who made me liar. If Hate
can kill,
And Loathing wield a Saxon battle-
axe —
Edith. Waste not thy might before
the battle!
Harold.   No,
And thou must hence. Stigand will
see thee safe,
And so — Farewell.
[*He is going, but turns back.*
The ring thou darest not wear,
I have had it fashion'd, see, to meet
my hand.
[HAROLD *shows the ring which is on
his finger.*
Farewell!
[*He is going, but turns back again.*
I am as dead as Death this day to ought
of earth's
Save William's death or mine.
Edith.   Thy death! — to-day!
Is it not thy birthday?
Harold.   Ay, that happy day!
A birthday welcome! happy days and
many!
One — this!   [*They embrace.*
Look, I will bear thy blessing into the
battle
And front the doom of God.
Norman cries (*heard in the distance*).
Ha Rou! Ha Rou!

Enter GURTH.

Gurth. The Norman moves!
Harold. Harold and Holy Cross!
[*Exeunt* Harold *and* Gurth.

Enter STIGAND.

Stigand. Our Church in arms — the
lamb the lion — not
Spear into pruning-hook — the counter
way —
Cowl, helm; and crozier, battle-axe.
Abbot Alfwig,
Leofric, and all the monks of Peter-
boro'
Strike for the king; but I, old wretch,
old Stigand,
With hands too limp to brandish iron
— and yet

I have a power — would Harold ask
me for it —
I have a power.
    Edith. What power, holy father?
    Stigand. Power now from Harold
to command thee hence
And see thee safe from Senlac.
    Edith.   I remain!
    Stigand. Yea, so will I, daughter,
until I find
Which way the battle balance. I can
see it
From where we stand : and, live or
die, I would
I were among them!

Canons from Waltham (singing without).

        Salva patriam
        Sancte Pater,
        Salva Fili,
        Salva Spiritus,
        Salva patriam,
        Sancta Mater.[1]

    Edith. Are those the blessed angels
quiring, father?
    Stigand. No, daughter, but the
canons out of Waltham,
The king's foundation, that have follow'd him.
    Edith. O God of battles, make their
wall of shields
Firm as thy cliffs, strengthen their
palisades!
What is that whirring sound?
    Stigand.   The Norman arrow!
    Edith. Look out upon the battle —
is he safe?
    Stigand. The king of England
stands between his banners.
He glitters on the crowning of the hill.
God save King Harold!
    Edith.   — chosen by his people
And fighting for his people!
    Stigand.   There is one
Come as Goliath came of yore — he
flings
His brand in air and catches it again,
He is chanting some old warsong.
    Edith.   And no David

---

[1] The *a* throughout these Latin hymns
should be sounded broad, as in "father."

To meet him?
    Stigand. Ay, there springs a Saxon
on him,
Falls — and another falls.
    Edith.   Have mercy on us!
    Stigand. Lo! our good Gurth hath
smitten him to the death.
    Edith. So perish all the enemies of
Harold!
    Canons (singing).

        Hostis in Angliam
        Ruit prædator,
        Illorum, Domine,
        Scutum scindatur!
        Hostis per Angliæ
        Plagas bacchatur;
        Casa crematur
        Pastor fugatur
        Grex trucidatur —

    Stigand. Illos trucida, Domine.
    Edith.   Ay, good father.
    Canons (singing).

        Illorum scelera
        Pœna sequatur!

    English cries.   Harold and Holy
Cross! Out! out!
    Stigand.   Our javelins
Answer their arrows. All the Norman foot
Are storming up the hill. The range
of knights
Sit, each a statue on his horse, and
wait.
    English cries. Harold and God Al-
mighty!
    Norman cries. Ha Rou! Ha Rou!
    Canons (singing).

        Eques cum pedite
        Præpediatur!
        Illorum in lacrymas
        Cruor fundatur!
        Pereant, pereant,
        Anglia precatur.

    Stigand. Look, daughter, look.
    Edith. Nay, father, look for *me!*
    Stigand. Our axes lighten with a sin-
gle flash
About the summit of the hill, and heads
And arms are sliver'd off and splinter'd by

Their lightning — and they fly — the
　　Norman flies.

Edith. Stigand, O father, have we
　　won the day ?

Stigand. No, daughter, no — they
　　fall behind the horse —

Their horse are thronging to the bar-
　　ricades ;

I see the gonfanon of Holy Peter

Floating above their helmets — ha !
　　he is down !

Edith. He down ! Who down ?

Stigand. The Norman Count is
　　down.

Edith. So perish all the enemies of
　　England !

Stigand. No, no, he hath risen
　　again — he bares his face —

Shouts something — he points onward
　　— all their horse

Swallow the hill locust-like, swarming
　　up.

Edith. O God of battles, make his
　　battle-axe keen

As thine own sharp-dividing justice,
　　heavy

As thine own bolts that fall on crime-
　　ful heads

Charged with the weight of heaven
　　wherefrom they fall !

Canons (*singing*).

　　　Jacta tonitrua
　　　　Deus bellator !
　　　Surgas e tenebris,
　　　　Sis vindicator !
　　　Fulmina, fulmina,
　　　　Deus vastator !

Edith. O God of battles, they are
　　three to one,

Make thou one man as three to roll
　　them down !

Canons (*singing*).

　　　Equus cum equite
　　　　Dejiciatur !
　　　Acies, Acies
　　　　Prona sternatur !
　　　Illorum lanceas
　　　　Frange Creator !

Stigand. Yea, yea, for how their
　　lances snap and shiver

Against the shifting blaze of Harold's
　　axe !

War-woodman of old Woden, how he
　　fells

The mortal copse of faces ! There !
　　And there !

The horse and horseman cannot meet
　　the shield,

The blow that brains the horseman
　　cleaves the horse,

The horse and horseman roll along
　　the hill,

They fly once more, they fly, the Nor-
　　man flies !

　　　Equus cum equite
　　　　Præcipitatur.

Edith. O God, the God of truth hath
　　heard my cry.

Follow them, follow them, drive them
　　to the sea !

　　　Illorum scelera
　　　　Pœna sequatur !

Stigand. Truth ! no ; a lie ; a trick,
　　a Norman trick !

They turn on the pursuer, horse against
　　foot,

They murder all that follow.

Edith. 　　　　Have mercy on us !

Stigand. Hot-headed fools — to burst
　　the wall of shields !

They have broken the commandment
　　of the king !

Edith. *His* oath was broken — O
　　holy Norman Saints,

Ye that now are of heaven, and see
　　beyond

Your Norman shrines, pardon it, par-
　　don it,

That he forsware himself for all he
　　loved,

Me, me and all !　Look out upon the
　　battle !

Stigand. They thunder again upon
　　the barricades.

My sight is eagle, but the strife so
　　thick —

This is the hottest of it : hold, ash !
　　hold, willow !

English cries. Out, out !

Norman cries. 　　　　Ha Rou !

Stigand. Ha! Gurth hath leapt upon
   him
And slain him : he hath fallen.
   Edith.   And I am heard.
Glory to God in the Highest! fallen,
   fallen !
   Stigand.   No, no, his horse — he
   mounts another — wields
His war-club, dashes it on Gurth, and
   Gurth,
Our noble Gurth, is down !
   Edith.   Have mercy on us !
   Stigand. And Leofwin is down !
   Edith.   Have mercy on us !
O Thou that knowest, let not my strong
   prayer
Be weaken'd in thy sight, because I
   love
The husband of another !
   Norman cries.   Ha Rou ! Ha Rou !
   Edith.   I do not hear our English
   war-cry.
   Stigand.   No.
   Edith. Look out upon the battle —
   is he safe ?
   Stigand. He stands between the
   banners with the dead
So piled about him he can hardly
   move.
   Edith (*takes up the war-cry*). Out!
   out!
   Norman cries. Ha Rou !
   Edith (*cries out*). Harold and Holy
   Cross !
   Norman cries. Ha Rou ! Ha Rou !
   Edith. What is that whirring sound?
   Stigand. The Norman sends his ar-
   rows up to Heaven,
They fall on those within the palisade !
   Edith. Look out upon the hill — is
   Harold there ?
   Stigand. Sanguelac — Sanguelac —
   the arrow — the arrow ! — away !

SCENE II. — FIELD OF THE DEAD.
   NIGHT.

ALDWYTH *and* EDITH.

   Aldwyth. O Edith, art thou here ?
   O Harold, Harold —
Our Harold — we shall never see him
   more.

   Edith. For there was more than sis-
   ter in my kiss,
And so the saints were wroth.   I can-
   not love them,
For they are Norman saints — and yet
   I should —
They are so much holier than their
   harlot's son
With whom they play'd their game
   against the king !
   Aldwyth. The king is slain, the
   kingdom overthrown !
   Edith. No matter !
   Aldwyth.   How no matter, Harold
   slain ? —
I cannot find his body. O help me
   thou !
O Edith, if I ever wrought against
   thee,
Forgive me thou, and help me here !
   Edith.   No matter !
   Aldwyth. Not help me, nor forgive
   me ?
   Edith.   So thou saidest.
   Aldwyth. I say it now, forgive me !
   Edith.   Cross me not !
I am seeking one who wedded me in
   secret.
Whisper ! God's angels only know it.
   Ha !
What art *thou* doing here among the
   dead ?
They are stripping the dead bodies
   naked yonder,
And thou art come to rob them of
   their rings !
   Aldwyth. O Edith, Edith, I have
   lost both crown
And husband.
   Edith.   So have I.
   Aldwyth.   I tell thee, girl,
I am seeking my dead Harold.
   Edith.   And I mine !
The Holy Father strangled him with
   a hair
Of Peter, and his brother Tostig helpt;
The wicked sister clapt her hands and
   laugh'd ;
Then all the dead fell on him.
   Aldwyth.   Edith, Edith —
   Edith. What was he like, this hus-
   band ? like to thee ?

Call not for help from me. I knew
    him not.
He lies not here : not close beside the
    standard.
Here fell the truest, manliest hearts
    of England.
Go further hence and find him.
    Aldwyth.   She is crazed !
    Edith. That doth not matter either.
        Lower the light.
He must be here.

> *Enter two* Canons, Osgod *and*
> Athelric, *with torches. They
> turn over the dead bodies and
> examine them as they pass.*

Osgod. I think that this is Thurkill.
Athelric. More likely Godric.
Osgod.   I am sure this body
Is Alfwig, the king's uncle.
Athelric.   So it is !
No, no — brave Gurth, one gash from
    brow to knee !
Osgod. And here is Leofwin.
Edith.   And here is *He !*
Aldwyth. Harold ? Oh no — nay, if
    it were — my God,
They have so maim'd and murder'd
    all his face
There is no man can swear to him.
Edith.   But one woman !
Look you, we never mean to part again.
I have found him, I am happy.
Was there not someone ask'd me for
    forgiveness ?
I yield it freely, being the true wife
Of this dead King, who never bore
    revenge.

Enter Count William *and* William
    Malet.

William. Who be these women ?
    And what body is this ?
Edith. Harold, thy better !
William. Ay, and what art thou ?
Edith. His wife !
Malet. Not true, my girl, here is the
    Queen ! [*Pointing out* Aldwyth.
William (*to* Aldwyth). Wast thou
    his Queen ?
Aldwyth. I was the Queen of Wales.

William. Why then of England.
    Madam, fear us not.
(*To* Malet.) Knowest thou this
    other ?
Malet.   When I visited England,
Some held she was his wife in secret
    — some —
Well — some believed she was his
    paramour.
Edith. Norman, thou liest ! liars all
    of you,
Your Saints and all ! *I* am his wife !
    and she —
For look, our marriage ring !
    [*She draws it off the finger of* Harold.
            I lost it somehow —
I lost it, playing with it when I was
    wild.
That bred the doubt ! but I am wiser
    now . . .
I am too wise . . . Will none among
    you all
Bear me true witness — only for this
    once —
That I have found it here again ?
                [*She puts it on.*
            And thou,
Thy wife am I for ever and evermore.
            [*Falls on the body and dies.*
William. Death ! — and enough of
    death for this one day,
The day of St. Calixtus, and the day,
My day when I was born.
Malet.   And this dead king's
Who, king or not, hath kinglike
    fought and fallen,
His birthday, too. It seems but yes-
    ter-even
I held it with him in his English halls,
His day, with all his rooftree ringing
    "Harold,"
Before he fell into the snare of Guy ;
When all men counted Harold would
    be king,
And Harold was most happy.
William.   Thou art half English.
Take them away !
Malet, I vow to build a church to God
Here on the hill of battle ; let our
    high altar
Stand where their standard fell . . .
    where these two lie.

Take them away, I do not love to see
    them.
Pluck the dead woman off the dead
    man, Malet!
  Malet. Faster than ivy. Must I
    hack her arms off ?
How shall I part them ?
  William. Leave them. Let them be !
Bury him and his paramour together.
He that was false in oath to me, it
    seems
Was false to his own wife. We will
    not give him
A Christian burial : yet he was a war-
    rior,
And wise, yea truthful, till that
    blighted vow
Which God avenged to-day.
Wrap them together in a purple cloak
And lay them both upon the waste
    sea-shore
At Hastings, there to guard the land
    for which
He did forswear himself — a warrior
    — ay,
And but that Holy Peter fought for us,
And that the false Northumbrian held
    aloof,
And save for that chance arrow which
    the Saints
Sharpen'd and sent against him —
    who can tell ? —

Three horses had I slain beneath me :
    twice
I thought that all was lost. Since I
    knew battle,
And that was from my boyhood,
    never yet —
No, by the splendor of God — have I
    fought men
Like Harold and his brethren, and his
    guard
Of English. Every man about his king
Fell where he stood. They loved him;
    and, pray God
My Normans may but move as true
    with me
To the door of death. Of one self-
    stock at first,
Make them again one people — Nor-
    man, English ;
And English, Norman; we should
    have a hand
To grasp the world with, and a foot
    to stamp it . . .
  Flat. Praise the Saints. It is over.
    No more blood !
I am king of England, so they thwart
    me not,
And I will rule according to their laws.
  (*To* Aldwyth.) Madam, we will en-
    treat thee with all honor.
  Aldwyth. My punishment is more
    than I can bear.

THE CUP;

A TRAGEDY.

ACT I.

SCENE I. — DISTANT VIEW OF A CITY OF GALATIA. AFTERNOON.

As the curtain rises, Priestesses *are heard singing in the Temple.* Boy *discovered on a pathway among Rocks picking grapes. A party of* Roman Soldiers, *guarding a prisoner in chains, come down the pathway and exeunt.*

Enter SYNORIX (*looking round*). *Singing ceases.*

Synorix. Pine, beech and plane, oak, walnut, apricot,
Vine, cypress, poplar, myrtle, bowering in
The city where she dwells. She past me here
Three years ago when I was flying from
My Tetrarchy to Rome. I almost touch'd her —
A maiden slowly moving on to music
Among her maidens to this Temple — O Gods !
She is my fate — else wherefore has my fate
Brought me again to her own city ? — married
Since — married Sinnatus, the Tetrarch here —
But if he be conspirator, Rome will chain,
Or slay him. I may trust to gain her then
When I shall have my tetrarchy restored
By Rome, our mistress, grateful that I show'd her
The weakness and the dissonance of our clans,
And how to crush them easily. Wretched race !
And once I wish'd to scourge them to the bones.
But in this narrow breathing-time of life
Is vengeance for its own sake worth the while,
If once our ends are gain'd ? and now this cup —
I never felt such passion for a woman.
[*Brings out a cup and scroll from under his cloak.*
What have I written to her?

THE CUP. 811

[Reading the scroll.

"To the admired Camma, wife of Sinnatus, the Tetrarch, one who years ago, himself an adorer of our great goddess, Artemis, beheld you afar off worshipping in her Temple, and loved you for it, sends you this cup rescued from the burning of one of her shrines in a city thro' which he past with the Roman army : it is the cup we use in our marriages. Receive it from one who cannot at present write himself other than

"A Galatian serving by force in the Roman Legion."

[Turns and looks up to boy.

Boy, dost thou know the house of Sinnatus ?

Boy. These grapes are for the house of Sinnatus —

Close to the Temple.

Synorix. Yonder ?

Boy. Yes.

Synorix (Aside). That I
With all my range of women should yet shun
To meet her face to face at once! My boy,

[Boy comes down rocks to him.

Take thou this letter and this cup to Camma,

The wife of Sinnatus.

Boy. Going or gone to-day
To hunt with Sinnatus.

Synorix. That matters not.
Take thou this cup and leave it at her doors.

[Gives the cup and scroll to the boy.

Boy. I will, my lord.

[Takes his basket of grapes and exit.

Enter Antonius.

Antonius (meeting the Boy as he goes out). Why, whither runs the boy ?
Is that the cup you rescued from the fire ?

Synorix. I send it to the wife of Sinnatus,
One half besotted in religious rites.
You come here with your soldiers to enforce

The long-withholden tribute : you suspect
This Sinnatus of playing patriotism,
Which in your sense is treason. You have yet
No proof against him : now this pious cup
Is passport to their house, and open arms
To him who gave it; and once there I warrant
I worm thro' all their windings.

Antonius. If you prosper,
Our Senate, wearied of their tetrarchies,
Their quarrels with themselves, their spites at Rome,
Is like enough to cancel them, and throne
One king above them all, who shall be true
To the Roman : and from what I heard in Rome,
This tributary crown may fall to you.

Synorix. The king, the crown! their talk in Rome ? is it so ?

[Antonius nods.

Well — I shall serve Galatia taking it,
And save her from herself, and be to Rome
More faithful than a Roman.

*[Turns and sees Camma coming.
Stand aside,*

Stand aside ; here she comes !

[Watching Camma as she enters with her Maid.

Camma (to Maid.) Where is he, girl?

Maid. You know the waterfall
That in the summer keeps the mountain side,
But after rain o'erleaps a jutting rock
And shoots three hundred feet.

Camma. The stag is there ?

Maid. Seen in the thicket at the bottom there
But yester-even.

Camma. Good then, we will climb
The mountain opposite and watch the chase.

[They descend the rocks and exeunt.

Synorix (watching her. Aside.). The bust of Juno and the brows and eyes

Of Venus; face and form unmatchable!

Antonius. Why do you look at her
so lingeringly ?

Synorix. To see if years have
changed her.

Antonius (*sarcastically*). Love her,
do you ?

Synorix. I envied Sinnatus when
he married her.

Antonius. She knows it ? Ha!

Synorix. She — no, nor ev'n my
face.

Antonius. Nor Sinnatus either ?

Synorix. No, nor Sinnatus.

Antonius. Hot-blooded! I have
heard them say in Rome,
That your own people cast you from
their bounds,
From some unprincely violence to a
woman,
As Rome did Tarquin.

Synorix. Well, if this were so,
I here return like Tarquin — for a
crown.

Antonius. And may be foil'd like
Tarquin, if you follow
Not the dry light of Rome's straight-
going policy,
But the fool-fire of love or lust, which
well
May make you lose yourself, may
even drown you
In the good regard of Rome.

Synorix. Tut — fear me not;
I ever had my victories among women.
I am most true to Rome.

Antonius (*aside*). I hate the man !
What filthy tools our Senate works
with ! Still
I must obey them. (*Aloud.*) Fare you
well. [*Going.*

Synorix. Farewell !

Antonius (*stopping*). A moment! If
you track this Sinnatus
In any treason, I give you here an
order [*Produces a paper.*
To seize upon him. Let me sign it.
(*Signs it.*) There
"Antonius leader of the Roman
Legion."
[*Hands the paper to* Synorix. *Goes
up pathway and exit.*

Synorix. Woman again ! — but I am
wiser now.
No rushing on the game — the net, —
the net.
[*Shouts of "* Sinnatus! Sinnatus!"
Then horn.
(*Looking off stage.*) He comes, a rough,
bluff, simple-looking fellow.
If we may judge the kernel by the husk,
Not one to keep a woman's fealty when
Assailed by Craft and Love. I'll join
with him:
I may reap something from him —
come upon *her*
Again, perhaps, to-day — *her.* Who
are with him ?
I see no face that knows me. Shall
I risk it ?
I am a Roman now, they dare not
touch me.
I will.

Enter SINNATUS, *Huntsmen and
hounds.*

Fair Sir, a happy day to you !
You reck but little of the Roman here,
While you can take your pastime in
the woods.

Sinnatus. Ay, ay, why not ? What
would you with me, man ?

Synorix. I am a life-long lover of
the chase,
And tho' a stranger fain would be
allow'd
To join the hunt.

Sinnatus. Your name ?

Synorix. Strato, my name.

Sinnatus. No Roman name ?

Synorix. A Greek, my lord; you
know
That we Galatians are both Greek
and Gaul.
[*Shouts and horns in the distance.*

Sinnatus. Hillo, the stag! (*To*
Synorix.) What, you are all
unfurnish'd ?
Give him a bow and arrows — follow
— follow.
[*Exit, followed by* Huntsmen.

Synorix. Slowly but surely — till
I see my way.

It is the one step in the dark beyond
Our expectation, that amazes us.
                    [*Distant shouts and horns.*
Hillo! Hillo!
    [*Exit* Synorix. *Shouts and horns.*

SCENE II. — A ROOM IN THE TE-
        TRARCH'S HOUSE.

*Frescoed figures on the wall. Evening.
    Moonlight outside.   A couch with
    cushions on it.   A small table with
    flagon of wine, cups, plate of grapes,
    etc., also the cup of Scene I. A chair
    with drapery on it.*

CAMMA *enters and opens curtains of
        window.*

    Camma. No Sinnatus yet — and
        there the rising moon.
        [*Takes up a cithern and sits on
            couch. Plays and sings.*
" Moon on the field and the foam,
    Moon on the waste and the wold,
Moon bring him home, bring him
        home
    Safe from the dark and the cold,
Home, sweet home, bring him home,
    Home with the flock to the fold —
Safe from the wolf " ——
(*Listening.*) Is he coming? I thought
        I heard
A footstep. No not yet. They say
        that Rome
Sprang from a wolf. I fear my dear
        lord mixt
With some conspiracy against the
        wolf.
This mountain shepherd never dream'd
        of Rome.
(*Sings.*) "Safe from the wolf to the
        fold " ——
And that great break of precipice
        that runs
Thro' all the wood, where twenty
        years ago
Huntsman, and hound, and deer were
        all neck-broken!
Nay, here he comes.

Enter SINNATUS *followed by* SYNORIX.

    Sinnatus (*angrily*). I tell thee, my
        good fellow,
My arrow struck the stag.
    Synorix.   But was it so?
Nay, you were further off: besides
        the wind
Went with *my* arrow.
    Sinnatus. I am sure *I* struck him.
    Synorix. And I am just as sure,
        my lord, *I* struck him.
(*Aside.*)   And I may strike your
        game when you are gone.
    Camma. Come, come, we will not
        quarrel about the stag.
I have had a weary day in watching
        you.
Yours must have been a wearier. Sit
        and eat,
And take a hunter's vengeance on the
        meats.
    Sinnatus. No, no — we have eaten
        — we are heated. Wine!
    Camma. Who is our guest?
    Sinnatus. Strato he calls himself.
        [Camma *offers wine to* Synorix,
            while Sinnatus *helps himself.*]
    Sinnatus. I pledge you, Strato.
                            [*Drinks.*
    Synorix. And I you, my lord.
                            [*Drinks.*
    Sinnatus (*seeing the cup sent to* Cam-
        ma). What's here?
    Camma. A strange gift sent to me
        to-day.
A sacred cup saved from a blazing
        shrine
Of our great Goddess, in some city
        where
Antonius past. I had believed that
        Rome
Made war upon the peoples not the
        Gods.
    Synorix. Most like the city rose
        against Antonius,
Whereon he fired it, and the sacred
        shrine
By chance was burnt along with it.
    Sinnatus.   Had you then
No message with the cup?

Camma. Why, yes, see here.
　　　　　　[Gives him the scroll.
Sinnatus (*reads*). " To the admired
Camma, — beheld you afar off —
loved you — sends you this cup —
the cup we use in our marriages
— cannot at present write himself
other than

" A GALATIAN SERVING BY FORCE
　　　IN THE ROMAN LEGION."

Serving by force ! Were there no
　　boughs to hang on,
Rivers to drown in ? Serve by force ?
　　No force
Could make me serve by force.
　　Synorix.　　　How then, my lord ?
The Roman is encamped without your
　　city —
The force of Rome a thousand-fold
　　our own.
Must all Galatia hang or drown her-
　　self ?
And you a Prince and Tetrarch in this
　　province ——
　　Sinnatus. Province !
　　Synorix. Well, well, they call it so
　　in Rome.
　　Sinnatus (*angrily*). Province !
　　Synorix. A noble anger ! but An-
　　tonius
To-morrow will demand your tribute
　　— you,
Can you make war ? Have you al-
　　liances ?
Bithynia, Pontus, Paphlagonia ?
We have had our leagues of old with
　　Eastern kings.
There is my hand — if such a league
　　there be.
What will you do ?
　　Sinnatus. Not set myself abroach
And run my mind out to a random
　　guest
Who join'd me in the hunt. You saw
　　my hounds
True to the scent ; and we have two-
　　legg'd dogs
Among us who can smell a true oc-
　　casion,
And when to bark and how.
　　Synorix. My good Lord Sinnatus,

I once was at the hunting of a lion.
Roused by the clamor of the chase he
　　woke,
Came to the front of the wood — his
　　monarch mane
Bristled about his quick ears — he
　　stood there
Staring upon the hunter. A score of
　　dogs
Gnaw'd at his ankles : at the last he
　　felt
The trouble of his feet, put forth one
　　paw,
Slew four, and knew it not, and so re-
　　main'd
Staring upon the hunter : and this
　　Rome
Will crush you if you wrestle with
　　her ; then
Save for some slight report in her
　　own Senate
Scarce know what she has done.
　　(*Aside.*) Would I could move him,
Provoke him any way ! (*Aloud.*) The
　　Lady Camma,
Wise I am sure as she is beautiful,
Will close with me that to submit at
　　once
Is better than a wholly-hopeless war,
Our gallant citizens murder'd all in
　　vain,
Son, husband, brother gash'd to death
　　in vain,
And the small state more cruelly
　　trampled on
Than had she never moved.
　　Camma.　　　　Sir, I had once
A boy who died a babe ; but were he
　　living
And grown to man and Sinnatus will'd
　　it, I
Would set him in the front rank of
　　the fight
With scarce a pang. (*Rises.*) Sir, if
　　a state submit
At once, she may be blotted out at once
And swallow'd in the conqueror's
　　chronicle.
Whereas in wars of freedom and de-
　　fence
The glory and grief of battle won or
　　lost

Solders a race together — yea — tho'
 they fail,
The names of those who fought and
 fell are like
A bank'd-up fire that flashes out
 again
From century to century, and at last
May lead them on to victory — I hope
 so —
Like phantoms of the Gods.
 Sinnatus. Well spoken, wife.
 Synorix (bowing). Madam, so well I
 yield.
 Sinnatus. I should not wonder
If Synorix, who has dwelt three years
 in Rome
And wrought his worst against his
 native land,
Returns with this Antonius.
 Synorix. What is Synorix ?
 Sinnatus. Galatian, and not know ?
 This Synorix.
Was Tetrarch here, and tyrant also —
 did
Dishonor to our wives.
 Synorix. Perhaps you judge him
With feeble charity : being as you tell
 me
Tetrarch, there might be willing wives
 enough
To feel dishonor, honor.
 Camma. Do not say so.
I know of no such wives in all Ga-
 latia.
There may be courtesans for aught I
 know
Whose life is one dishonor.

Enter ATTENDANT.

 Attendant (aside). My lord, the men !
 Sinnatus (aside). Our anti-Roman
 faction ?
 Attendant (aside). Ay, my lord.
 Synorix (overhearing). (*Aside.*) I
 have enough — their anti-Roman faction.
 Sinnatus (aloud). Some friends of
 mine would speak with me
 without.
You, Strato, make good cheer till I
 return. [*Exit.*

 Synorix. I have much to say, no
 time to say it in.
First, lady, know myself am that
 Galatian
Who sent the cup.
 Camma. I thank you from my heart.
 Synorix. Then that I serve with
 Rome to serve Galatia.
That is my secret: keep it, or you sell me
To torment and to death. [*Coming closer.*
 For your ear only —
I love you — for your love to the
 great Goddess.
The Romans sent me here a spy upon
 you,
To draw you and your husband to your
 doom.
I'd sooner die than do it.
 [*Takes out paper given him by* An-
 tonius.
 This paper sign'd
Antonius — will you take it, read it ?
 there !
 Camma (reads). " You are to seize
 on Sinnatus, — if — "
 Synorix (snatches paper). No more.
What follows is for no wife's eyes. O
 Camma,
Rome has a glimpse of this con-
 spiracy ;
Rome never yet hath spar'd con-
 spirator.
Horrible ! flaying, scourging, crucify-
 ing —
 Camma. I am tender enough. Why
 do you practise on me ?
 Synorix. Why should I practise on
 you ? How you wrong me !
I am sure of being every way malign'd.
And if you should betray me to your
 husband —
 Camma. Will *you* betray him by
 this order ?
 Synorix. See,
I tear it all to pieces, never dream'd
Of acting on it. [*Tears the paper.*
 Camma. I owe you thanks for ever.
 Synorix. Hath Sinnatus never told
 you of this plot ?
 Camma. What plot ?
 Synorix. A child's sand-castle on
 the beach

For the next wave — all seen, — all calculated,
All known by Rome. No chance for Sinnatus.
　Camma. Why, said you not as much to my brave Sinnatus ?
　Synorix. Brave — ay — too brave, too over-confident,
Too like to ruin himself, and you, and me !
Who else, with this black thunderbolt of Rome
Above him, would have chased the stag to-day
In the full face of all the Roman camp ?
A miracle that they let him home again,
Not caught, maim'd, blinded him.
　　　　　　　　[*Camma shudders.*
　(*Aside.*) I have made her tremble.
(*Aloud.*) I know they mean to torture him to death.
I dare not tell him how I came to know it ;
I durst not trust him with — my serving Rome
To serve Galatia : you heard him on the letter.
Not say as much ? I all but said as much.
I am sure I told him that his plot was folly.
I say it to you — you are wiser — Rome knows all,
But you know not the savagery of Rome.
　Camma. O — have you power with Rome ? use it for him !
　Synorix. Alas ! I have no such power with Rome. All that
Lies with Antonius.
　　　[*As if struck by a sudden thought. Comes over to her.*
　　　　　　　　　　He will pass to-morrow
In the gray dawn before the Temple doors.
You have beauty, — O great beauty, — and Antonius,
So gracious toward women, never yet
Flung back a woman's prayer. Plead to him,

I am sure you will prevail.
　Camma.　　　Still — I should tell
My husband.
　Synorix. Will he let you plead for him
To a Roman ?
　Camma. I fear not.
　Synorix.　　Then do not tell him.
Or tell him, if you will, when you return,
When you have charm'd our general into mercy,
And all is safe again. O dearest lady,
　　　[*Murmurs of* "Synorix ! Synorix !" *heard outside.*
Think,— torture,— death,— and come.
　Camma.　　　　I will, I will.
And I will not betray you.
　Synorix (*aside. As* Sinnatus *enters.*).
　　　Stand apart.

Enter SINNATUS *and* ATTENDANT.

　Sinnatus. Thou art that Synorix !
One whom thou hast wrong'd
Without there, knew thee with Antonius.
They howl for thee, to rend thee head from limb.
　Synorix. I am much malign'd. I thought to serve Galatia.
　Sinnatus. Serve thyself first, villain ! They shall not harm
My guest within my house. There !
　(*points to door*) there ! this door
Opens upon the forest ! Out, begone !
Henceforth I am thy mortal enemy.
　Synorix. However I thank thee (*draws his sword*) ; thou hast saved my life.　　　　　[*Exit.*
　Sinnatus (*to* Attendant). Return and tell them Synorix is not here.
　　　　　　　　　　[*Exit* Attendant.
What did that villain Synorix say to you ?
　Camma. Is *he* — *that* — Synorix ?
　Sinnatus. Wherefore should you doubt it ?
One of the men there knew him.
　Camma.　　　　　　Only one,
And he perhaps mistaken in the face.
　Sinnatus. Come, come, could he deny it ? What did he say ?

Camma. What *should* he say ?

Sinnatus. What *should* he say, my wife !
He should say this, that being Tetrarch once
His own true people cast him from their doors
Like a base coin.

Camma. Not kindly to them ?

Sinnatus. Kindly ?
O the most kindly Prince in all the world !
Would clap his honest citizens on the back,
Bandy their own rude jests with them, be curious
About the welfare of their babes, their wives,
O ay — their wives — their wives.
What should he say ?
He should say nothing to my wife if I
Were by to throttle him ! He steep'd himself
In all the lust of Rome. How should *you* guess
What manner of beast it is ?

Camma. Yet he seem'd kindly,
And said he loathed the cruelties that Rome
Wrought on her vassals.

Sinnatus. Did he, *honest* man ?

Camma. And you, that seldom brook the stranger here,
Have let him hunt the stag with you to-day.

Sinnatus. I warrant you now, he said *he* struck the stag.

Camma. Why no, he never touch'd upon the stag.

Sinnatus. Why so I said, *my* arrow.
Well, to sleep.
          [*Goes to close door.*

Camma. Nay, close not yet the door upon a night
That looks half day.

Sinnatus. True ; and my friends may spy him
And slay him as he runs.

Camma. He is gone already.
Oh look, — yon grove upon the mountain, — white

In the sweet moon as with a lovelier snow !
But what a blotch of blackness underneath !
Sinnatus, you remember — yea, you must,
That there three years ago — the vast vine-bowers
Ran to the summit of the trees, and dropt
Their streamers earthward, which a breeze of May
Took ever and anon, and open'd out
The purple zone of hill and heaven ; there
You told your love ; and like the swaying vines —
Yea, — with our eyes, — our hearts, our prophet hopes
Let in the happy distance, and that all
But cloudless heaven which we have found together
In our three married years ! You kiss'd me there
For the first time. Sinnatus, kiss me now.

Sinnatus. First kiss. (*Kisses her.*)
There then. You talk almost as if it
Might be the last.

Camma. Will you not eat a little ?

Sinnatus. No, no, we found a goat-herd's hut and shared
His fruits and milk. Liar ! You will believe
Now that he never struck the stag — a brave one
Which you shall see to-morrow.

Camma. I rise to-morrow
In the gray dawn, and take this holy cup
To lodge it in the shrine of Artemis.

Sinnatus. Good !

Camma. If I be not back in half an hour,
Come after me.

Sinnatus. What ! is there danger ?

Camma. Nay,
None that I know : 'tis but a step from here
To the Temple.

Sinnatus.   All my brain is full of
    sleep.
Wake me before you go, I'll after
    you —
After *me* now !   [*Closes door and exit.*
    Camma (*drawing curtains*). Your
    shadow. Synorix —
His face was not malignant,and he said
That men malign'd him. Shall I go ?
    Shall I go ?
Death, torture —
" He never yet flung back a woman's
    prayer " —
I go, but I will have my dagger with
    me.   [*Exit.*

SCENE III. — SAME AS SCENE I.
    DAWN.

Music and Singing in the Temple.

Enter SYNORIX *watchfully, after him*
    PUBLIUS *and* Soldiers.

Synorix. Publius !
Publius.   Here !
Synorix.   Do you remember what
I told you ?
Publius.   When you cry " Rome,
    Rome," to seize
On whomsoever may be talking with
    you,
Or man, or woman, as traitors unto
    Rome.
Synorix. Right. Back again. How
    many of you are there ?
Publius. Some half a score.
              [*Exeunt* Soldiers *and* Publius.
Synorix.   I have my guard
    about me.
I need not fear the crowd that hunted
    me
Across the woods, last night. I hardly
    gain'd
The camp at midnight. Will she
    come to me
Now that she knows me Synorix ?
    Not if Sinnatus
Has told her all the truth about me.
    Well,
I cannot help the mould that I was
    cast in.

I fling all that upon my fate, my
    star.
I know that I am genial, I would be
Happy, and make all others happy so
They did not thwart me. Nay, she
    will not come.
Yet if she be a true and loving wife
She may, perchance, to save this
    husband. Ay !
See, see, my white bird stepping
    toward the snare.
Why now I count it all but miracle,
That this brave heart of mine should
    shake me so,
As helplessly as some unbearded boy's
When first he meets his maiden in a
    bower.

    Enter CAMMA (*with cup*).

Synorix. The lark first takes the
    sunlight on his wing,
But you, twin sister of the morning
    star,
Forelead the sun.
    Camma.   Where is Antonius ?
    Synorix. Not here as yet. You are
    too early for him.
              [*She crosses towards Temple.*
Synorix. Nay, whither go you now ?
Camma.   To lodge this cup
Within the holy shrine of Artemis,
And so return.
Synorix.   To find Antonius here.
    [*She goes into the Temple, he looks
    after her.*
The loveliest life that ever drew the
    light
From heaven to brood upon her, and
    enrich
Earth with her shadow ! I trust she
    will return.
These Romans dare not violate the
    Temple.
No, I must lure my game into the
    camp.
A woman I could live and die for
    What !
Die for a woman, what new faith is
    this ?
I am not mad, not sick, not old enough
To doat on one alone. Yes, mad for
    her,

Camma the stately, Camma the great-
hearted,
So mad, I fear some strange and evil
chance
Coming upon me, for by the Gods I
seem
Strange to myself.

Re-enter CAMMA.

Camma. Where is Antonius ?
Synorix. Where? As I said before,
you are still too early.
Camma. Too early to be here alone
with thee ;
For whether men malign thy name, or
no,
It bears an evil savor among women.
Where is Antonius ? (*Loud.*)
Synorix. Madam, as you know,
The camp is half a league without the
city ;
If you will walk with me we needs
must meet
Antonius coming, or at least shall
find him
There in the camp.
Camma. No, not one step with
thee.
Where is Antonius ? (*Louder.*)
Synorix (*advancing towards her*).
Then for your own sake,
Lady, I say it with all gentleness,
And for the sake of Sinnatus your
husband,
I must compel you.
Camma (*drawing her dagger*). Stay !
— too near is death.
Synorix (*disarming her*). Is it not
easy to disarm a woman ?

Enter SINNATUS (*seizes him from behind
by the throat*).

Synorix (*throttled and scarce audible*).
Rome ! Rome !
Sinnatus. Adulterous dog !
Synorix (*stabbing him with Camma's
dagger*). What ! will you have
it ?
[*Camma* utters a cry and runs to
Sinnatus.

Sinnatus (*falls backward*). I have it
in my heart — to the Temple —
fly —
For *my* sake — or they seize on thee.
Remember !
Away — farewell ! [*Dies.*
Camma (*runs up the steps into the
Temple, looking back*). Fare-
well !
Synorix (*seeing her escape*). The
women of the Temple drag her
in.
Publius ! Publius ! No,
Antonius would not suffer me to
break
Into the sanctuary. She hath escaped.
[*Looking down at* Sinnatus.
"Adulterous dog!" that red-faced
rage at me !
Then with one quick short stab —
eternal peace.
So end all passions. Then what use
in passions ?
To warm the cold bounds of our dying
life
And, lest we freeze in mortal apathy,
Employ us, heat us, quicken us, help
us, keep us
From seeing all too near that urn,
those ashes
Which all must be. Well used, they
serve us well.
I heard a saying in Egypt, that am-
bition
Is like the sea wave, which the more
you drink,
The more you thirst — yea — drink
too much, as men
Have done on rafts of wreck — it
drives you mad.
I will be no such wreck, am no such
gamester
As, having won the stake, would dare
the chance
Of double, or losing all. The Roman
Senate,
For I have always play'd into their
hands,
Means me the crown. And Camma
for my bride —
The people love her — if I win her
love,

They too will cleave to me, as one
    with her.
There then I rest, Rome's tributary
    king.
        [*Looking down on* Sinnatus.
Why did I strike him? — having
    proof enough
Against the man, I surely should have
    left
That stroke to Rome. He saved my
    life too.   Did he?
It seem'd so.   I have play'd the sud-
    den fool.
And that sets her against me — for the
    moment.
Camma — well, well, I never found
    the woman
I could not force or wheedle to my
    will.
She will be glad at last to wear my
    crown.
And I will make Galatia prosperous
    too,
And we will chirp among our vines,
    and smile
At bygone things till that (*pointing to*
    Sinnatus) eternal peace.
Rome! Rome!

Enter PUBLIUS *and* Soldiers.

Twice I cried Rome. Why came ye
    not before?
    Publius.   Why come we now?
Whom shall we seize upon?
Synorix (*pointing to the body of*
    Sinnatus).   The body of that
    dead traitor Sinnatus.
Bear him away.
        [*Music and Singing in Temple.*

ACT II.

SCENE. — INTERIOR OF THE TEMPLE
        OF ARTEMIS.

*Small gold gates on platform in front of
the veil before the colossal statue of the
Goddess, and in the centre of the
Temple a tripod altar, on which is a*
*lighted lamp. Lamps (lighted) sus-
pended between each pillar. Tripods,
vases, garlands of flowers, etc., about
stage. Altar at back close to Goddess, with two cups. Solemn music.
Priestesses decorating the Temple.*

Enter a PRIESTESS.

Priestess.   Phœbe, that man from
    Synorix, who has been
So oft to see the Priestess, waits once
    more
Before the Temple.
    Phœbe.   We will let her know.
        [*Signs to one of the* Priestesses,
            who goes out.
Since Camma fled from Synorix to our
    Temple,
And for her beauty, stateliness, and
    power,
Was chosen Priestess here, have you
    not mark'd
Her eyes were ever on the marble
    floor?
To-day they are fixt and bright —
    they look straight out.
Hath she made up her mind to marry
    him?
    Priestess.   To marry him who stabb'd
    her Sinnatus.
You will not easily make me credit
    that.
    Phœbe.   Ask her.

Enter CAMMA *as Priestess* (*in front of
        the curtains*).

    Priestess.   You will not marry
        Synorix?
    Camma.   My girl, I am the bride of
        Death, and only
Marry the dead.
    Priestess.   Not Synorix then?
    Camma.   My girl,
At times this oracle of great Artemis
Has no more power than other oracles
To speak directly.
    Phœbe.   Will you speak to him,
The messenger from Synorix who waits
Before the Temple?
    Camma.   Why not?   Let him enter.
        [*Comes forward on to step by tripod.*

Enter a MESSENGER.

Messenger (*kneels*). Greeting and
  health from Synorix! More
  than once
You have refused his hand. When
  last I saw you,
You all but yielded. He entreats
  you now
For your last answer. When he
  struck at Sinnatus —
As I have many a time declared to
  you —
He knew not at the moment who had
  fasten'd
About his throat — he begs you to
  forget it
As scarce his act : — a random stroke :
  all else
Was love for you: he prays you to
  believe him.
  Camma. I pray him to believe —
    that I believe him.
  Messenger. Why that is well. You
    mean to marry him ?
  Camma I mean to marry him — if
    that be well.
  Messenger. This very day the Ro-
    mans crown him king
For all his faithful services to Rome.
He wills you then this day to marry
  him,
And so be throned together in the
  sight
Of all the people, that the world may
  know
You twain are reconciled, and no
  more feuds
Disturb our peaceful vassalage to
  Rome.
  Camma. To-day ? Too sudden. I
    will brood upon it.
When do they crown him ?
  Messenger. Even now.
  Camma.   And where ?
  Messenger. Here by your temple.
  Camma.   Come once more to me
Before the crowning, — I will answer
  you.
                    [*Exit* Messenger.
  Phœbe. Great Artemis ! O Camma,
    can it be well,

Or good, or wise, that you should
  clasp a hand
Red with the sacred blood of Sinnatus ?
  Camma. Good ! mine own dagger
    driven by Synorix found
All good in the true heart of Sinnatus,
And quench'd it there for ever. Wise !
Life yields to death and wisdom bows
  to Fate,
Is wisest, doing so. Did not this man
Speak well ? We cannot fight impe-
  rial Rome,
But he and I are both Galatian-born,
And tributary sovereigns, he and I,
Might teach this Rome — from knowl-
  edge of our people —
Where to lay on her tribute — heavily
  here
And lightly there. Might I not live
  for that,
And drown all poor self-passion in
  the sense
Of public good ?
  Phœbe. I am sure you will not mar-
    ry him.
  Camma. Are you so sure ? I pray
    you wait and see.
    [*Shouts* (*from the distance*),
     "Synorix!" "Synorix!"
  Camma. Synorix, Synorix! So they
    cried Sinnatus
Not so long since — they sicken me.
  The One
Who shifts his policy suffers some-
  thing, must
Accuse himself, excuse himself; the
  Many
Will feel no shame to give themselves
  the lie.
  Phœbe. Most like it was the Roman
    soldier shouted.
  Camma. Their shield-borne patriot
    of the morning star
Hang'd at mid-day, their traitor of
  the dawn
The clamor'd darling of their after-
  noon !
And that same head they would have
  play'd at ball with,
And kick'd it featureless — they now
  would crown.
                    [*Flourish of trumpets.*

Enter a Galatian NOBLEMAN *with crown on a cushion.*

Noble (kneels). Greeting and health
from Synorix. He sends you
This diadem of the first Galatian
Queen,
That you may feed your fancy on the
glory of it,
And join your life this day with his,
and wear it
Beside him on his throne. He waits
your answer.
Camma. Tell him there is one
shadow among the shadows,
One ghost of all the ghosts — as yet
so new,
So strange among them — such an
alien there,
So much of husband in it still — that if
The shout of Synorix and Camma sit-
ting
Upon one throne, should reach it, *it*
would rise.
HE! . . . HE, with that red star be-
tween the ribs,
And my knife there — and blast the
king and me,
And blanch the crowd with horror. I
dare not, sir!
Throne him — and then the marriage
— ay and tell him
That I accept the diadem of Galatia —
                    [*All are amazed.*
Yea, that ye saw me crown myself
withal.   [*Puts on the crown.*
I wait him his crown'd queen.
Noble.   So will I tell him.
                                [*Exit.*

Music. Two Priestesses *go up the steps
before the shrine, draw the curtains on
either side (discovering the Goddess),
then open the gates and remain on
steps, one on either side, and kneel.
A Priestess goes off and returns with
a veil of marriage, then assists* PHŒBE
to veil Camma. *At the same time
Priestesses enter and stand on either
side of the Temple.* CAMMA *and all
the* Priestesses *kneel, raise their*
hands to the Goddess, *and bow
down.*

        [*Shouts,* "Synorix! Synorix!"
        All rise.
Camma. Fling wide the doors, and
let the new-made children
Of our imperial mother see the show.
        [*Sunlight pours through the doors.*
I have no heart to do it. (*To Phœbe.*)
Look for me!
        [*Crouches. Phœbe looks out.*
        [*Shouts,* "Synorix! Synorix!"
Phœbe. He climbs the throne.
Hot blood, ambition, pride
So bloat and redden his face — O
would it were
His third last apoplexy! O bestial!
O how unlike our goodly Sinnatus.
Camma (on the ground). You wrong
him surely; far as the face goes
A goodlier-looking man than Sinnatus.
Phœbe (aside). How dare she say
it? I could hate her for it
But that she is distracted.
        [*A flourish of trumpets.*
Camma.   Is he crown'd?
Phœbe. Ay, there they crown him.
        [*Crowd without shout,* "Synorix!
        Synorix!"
Camma (rises).
        [*A* Priestess *brings a box of spices
        to* Camma *who throws them on the
        altar flame.*
Rouse the dead altar-flame, fling in
the spices,
Nard, Cinnamon, amomum, benzoin.
Let all the air reel into a mist of odor,
As in the midmost heart of Paradise.
Lay down the Lydian carpets for the
king.
The king should pace on purple to his
bride,
And music there to greet my lord the
king.   [*Music.*
(*To Phœbe.*) Dost thou remember
when I wedded Sinnatus?
Ay, thou wast there — whether from
maiden fears
Or reverential love for him I loved,
Or some strange second-sight, the
marriage-cup

Wherefrom we make libation to the Goddess
So shook within my hand, that the red wine
Ran down the marble and lookt like blood, like blood.

    Phœbe. I do remember your first-marriage fears.

    Camma. I have no fears at this my second marriage.

See here — I stretch my hand out — hold it there.

How steady it is!

    Phœbe. Steady enough to stab him!

    Camma. O hush! O peace! This violence ill becomes

The silence of our Temple. Gentleness, Low words best chime with this solemnity.

Enter a procession of Priestesses *and* Children *bearing garlands and golden goblets, and strewing flowers.*

Enter SYNORIX (*as King, with gold laurel-wreath crown and purple robes*), *followed by* ANTONIUS, PUBLIUS, Noblemen, Guards, *and the* Populace.

    Camma. Hail, King!

    Synorix.   Hail, Queen!

The wheel of Fate has roll'd me. to the top.

I would that happiness were gold, that I

Might cast my largess of it to the crowd!

I would that every man made feast to-day

Beneath the shadow of our pines and planes!

For all my truer life begins to-day.

The past is like a travell'd land now sunk

Below the horizon — like a barren shore

That grew salt weeds, but now all drown'd in love

And glittering at full tide — the bounteous bays

And havens filling with a blissful sea.

Nor speak I now too mightily, being King

And happy! happiest, Lady, in my power

To make you happy.

    Camma.   Yes, sir.

    Synorix.   Our Antonius,

Our faithful friend of Rome, tho' Rome may set

A free foot where she will, yet of his courtesy

Entreats he may be present at our marriage.

    Camma. Let him come — a legion with him, if he will.

(*To* Antonius.) Welcome, my lord Antonius, to our Temple.

(*To* Synorix.) You on this side the altar. (*To* Antonius.) You on that.

Call first upon the Goddess, Synorix.

    [*All face the* Goddess. *Priestesses, Children, Populace and Guards kneel—the others remain standing.*

    Synorix. O Thou, that dost inspire the germ with life,

The child, a thread within the house of birth,

And give him limbs, then air, and send him forth

The glory of his father — Thou whose breath

Is balmy wind to robe our hills with grass,

And kindle all our vales with myrtle-blossom,

And roll the golden oceans of our grain,

And sway the long grape-bunches of our vines,

And fill all hearts with fatness and the lust

Of plenty — make me happy in my marriage!

    Chorus (*chanting*). Artemis, Artemis, hear him, Ionian Artemis!

    Camma. O Thou that slayest the babe within the womb

Or in the being born, or after slayest him

As boy or man, great Goddess, whose storm-voice

Unsockets the strong oak, and rears his root

Beyond his head, and strows our fruits, and lays

Our golden grain, and runs to sea and
    makes it
Foam over all the fleeted wealth of
    kings
And peoples, hear.
Whose arrow is the plague — whose
    quick flash splits
The mid-sea mast, and rifts the tower
    to the rock,
And hurls the victor's column down
    with him
That crowns it, hear.
Who causest the safe earth to shud-
    der and gape,
And gulf and flatten in her closing
    chasm
Domed cities, hear.
Whose lava-torrents blast and blacken
    a province
To a cinder, hear.
Whose winter-cataracts find a realm
    and leave it
A waste of rock and ruin, hear. I
    call thee
To make my marriage prosper to my
    wish!
  Chorus. Artemis, Artemis, hear her,
    Ephesian Artemis!
  Camma. Artemis, Artemis, hear me,
    Galatian Artemis!
I call on our own Goddess in our own
    Temple.
  Chorus. Artemis, Artemis, hear her,
    Galatian Artemis!
              [*Thunder. All rise.*
  Synorix (*aside*). Thunder! Ay, ay,
    the storm was drawing hither
Across the hills when I was being
    crown'd.
I wonder if I look as pale as she?
  Camma. Art thou — still bent —
    on marrying?
  Synorix.   Surely — yet
These are strange words to speak to
    Artemis.
  Camma. Words are not always what
    they seem, my King.
I will be faithful to thee till thou die.
  Synorix. I thank thee, Camma, — I
    thank thee.
  Camma (*turning to* Antonius). An-
    tonius,

Much graced are we that our Queen
    Rome in you
Deigns to look in upon our barbarisms.
    [*Turns, goes up steps to altar before
    the* Goddess. *Takes a cup from
    off the altar. Holds it towards*
    Antonius. Antonius *goes up
    to the foot of the steps, opposite to*
    Synorix.
You see this cup, my lord.
              [*Gives it to him.*
  Antonius.   Most curious!
The many-breasted mother Artemis
Emboss'd upon it.
  Camma. It is old, I know not
How many hundred years. Give it
    me again.
It is the cup belonging our own Temple.
    [*Puts it back on altar, and takes
    up the cup of Act* I. *Showing
    it to* Antonius.
Here is another sacred to the Goddess,
The gift of Synorix; and the Goddess,
    being
For this most grateful, wills, thro'
    me her Priestess,
In honor of his gift and of our marriage,
That Synorix should drink from his
    own cup.
  Synorix. I thank thee, Camma, — I
    thank thee.
  Camma.   For — my lord —
It is our ancient custom in Galatia
That ere two souls be knit for life and
    death,
They two should drink together from
    one cup,
In symbol of their married unity,
Making libation to the Goddess.
    Bring me
The costly wines we use in marriages.
    [*They bring in a large jar of wine.*
    Camma *pours wine into cup.*
(*To* Synorix.) See here, I fill it. (*To*
    Antonius.) Will you drink,
    my lord?
  Antonius. I? Why should I? I
    am not to be married.
  Camma. But that might bring a
    Roman blessing on us.
  Antonius (*refusing cup*). Thy pardon,
    Priestess!

Camma. Thou art in the right.
This blessing is for Synorix and for
me.
See first I make libation to the God-
dess,   [*Makes libation.*
And now I drink.
          [*Drinks and fills the cup again.*
Thy turn, Galatian King.
Drink and drink deep — our marriage
will be fruitful.
Drink and drink deep, and thou wilt
make me happy.
          [*Synorix goes up to her. She
          hands him the cup. He drinks.*
Synorix. There, Camma! I have
almost drain'd the cup —
A few drops left.
     Camma. Libation to the Goddess.
          [*He throws the remaining drops on
          the altar and gives* Camma *the cup.*
Camma (placing the cup on the altar).
Why then the Goddess hears.
          [*Comes down and forward to
          tripod.* Antonius *follows.*
                              Antonius,
Where wast thou on that morning when
I came
To plead to thee for Sinnatus's life,
Beside this temple half a year ago?
     Antonius. I never heard of this re-
quest of thine.
*Synorix (coming forward hastily to
foot of tripod steps).* I sought
him and I could not find him.
Pray you,
Go on with the marriage rites.
     Camma.   Antonius ——
" Camma !" who spake?
     Antonius. Not I.
     Phœbe.   Nor any here.
     Camma. I am all but sure that some
one spake. Antonius,
If you had found him plotting against
Rome,
Would you have tortured Sinnatus to
death?
     Antonius. No thought was mine of
torture or of death,
But had I found him plotting, I had
counsell'd him
To rest from vain resistance. Rome
is fated

To rule the world. Then, if he had
not listen'd,
I might have sent him prisoner to
Rome.
     Synorix. Why do you palter with
the ceremony?
Go with the marriage rites.
     Camma.   They are finish'd.
     Synorix.   How!
     Camma. Thou hast drunk deep
enough to make me happy.
Dost thou not feel the love I bear to
thee
Glow thro' thy veins?
     Synorix. The love I bear to thee
Glows thro' my veins since first I
look'd on thee.
But wherefore slur the perfect cere-
mony?
The sovereign of Galatia weds his
Queen.
Let all be done to the fullest in the
sight
Of all the Gods. (*Starts.*) This pain
— what is it? — again?
I had a touch of this last year — in —
Rome.
Yes, yes. (*To* Antonius.) Your arm
— a moment — It will pass.
I reel beneath the weight of utter
joy —
This all too happy day, crown —
queen at once. [*Staggers.*
O all ye Gods — Jupiter! — Jupiter!
                              [*Falls backward.*
     Camma. Dost thou cry out upon
the Gods of Rome!
Thou art Galatian-born? Our Artemis
Has vanquish'd their Diana.
     Synorix (on the ground). I am
poison'd.
She — close the Temple doors. Let
her not fly.
     Camma (leaning on tripod). Have I
not drunk of the same cup with
thee?
     Synorix. Ay, by the Gods of Rome
and all the world,
She too — she too — the bride! the
Queen! and I —
Monstrous! I that loved her.
     Camma.   I loved *him.*

Synorix. O murderous mad-woman!
    I pray you lift me
And make me walk awhile. I have
    heard these poisons
May be walk'd down.
    [*Antonius and Publius raise
    him up.*
        My feet are tons of lead,
They will break in the earth — I am
    sinking — hold me —
Let me alone.
    [*They leave him; he sinks down
    on ground.*
    Too late — thought myself wise —
A woman's dupe. Antonius, tell the
    Senate
I have been most true to Rome —
    would have been true
To *her* — if — if ——
                    [*Falls as if dead.*
Camma (*coming and leaning over him*).
    So falls the throne of an
    hour.
Synorix (*half rising*). Throne? is it
    thou? the Fates are throned,
    not we —
Not guilty of ourselves — thy doom
    and mine —
Thou — coming my way too — Camma
    — good-night.   [*Dies.*
Camma (*upheld by weeping* Priest-
    esses). Thy way? poor worm,
    crawl down thine own black
    hole
To the lowest Hell. Antonius, is *he*
    there?
I meant thee to have follow'd — better
    thus.
Nay, if my people must be thralls of
    Rome,

He is gentle, tho' a Roman.
    [*Sinks back into the arms of the*
    Priestesses.
Antonius.   Thou art one
With thine own people, and tho' a
    Roman I
Forgive thee, Camma.
    Camma (*raising herself*). "CAMMA!"
    why there again
I am most sure that some one call'd.
    O women,
Ye will have Roman masters. I am glad
I shall not see it. Did not some old
    Greek
Say death was the chief good? He
    had my fate for it,
Poison'd. (*Sinks back again.*) Have
    I the crown on? I will go
To meet him, crown'd! crown'd victor
    of my will —
On my last voyage — but the wind has
    fail'd —
Growing dark too — but light enough
    to row.
Row to the blessed Isles! the blessed
    Isles! —
Sinnatus!
Why comes he not to meet me? It is
    the crown
Offends him — and my hands are too
    sleepy
To lift it off.
    [*Phœbe takes the crown off.*
Who touch'd me then? I thank you.
    [*Rises, with outspread arms.*
There — league on league of ever-
    shining shore
Beneath an ever-rising sun — I see him —
"Camma, Camma!" Sinnatus, Sin-
    natus!   [*Dies.*

THE FALCON.

—◦◦❈◦◦—

DRAMATIS PERSONÆ.

THE COUNT FEDERIGO DEGLI ALBERIGHI.
FILIPPO, *Count's foster-brother*.
THE LADY GIOVANNA.
ELISABETTA, *the Count's nurse*.

SCENE. — AN ITALIAN COTTAGE. CASTLE AND MOUNTAINS SEEN THROUGH WINDOW.

ELISABETTA *discovered seated on stool in window darning. The* COUNT *with Falcon on his hand comes down through the door at back. A withered wreath on the wall.*

Elisabetta. So, my lord, the Lady Giovanna, who hath been away so long, came back last night with her son to the castle.

Count. Hear that, my bird! Art thou not jealous of her?
My princess of the cloud, my plumed purveyor,
My far-eyed queen of the winds — thou that canst soar
Beyond the morning lark, and howsoe'er
Thy quarry wind and wheel, swoop down upon him
Eagle-like, lightning-like — strike, make his feathers
Glance in mid heaven.
         [Crosses to chair.
    I would thou hadst a mate!
Thy breed will die with thee, and mine with me:
I am as lone and loveless as thyself.
         [Sits in chair.

Giovanna here! Ay, ruffle thyself — be jealous!
Thou should'st be jealous of her.
Tho' I bred thee
The full-train'd marvel of all falconry,
And love thee and thou me, yet if Giovanna
Be here again — No, no! Buss me, my bird!
The stately widow has no heart for me.
Thou art the last friend left me upon earth —
No, no again to that.
         [Rises and turns.
         My good old nurse,
I had forgotten thou wast sitting there.
Elisabetta. Ay, and forgotten thy foster-brother too.
Count. Bird-babble for my falcon! Let it pass.
What art thou doing there?
Elisabetta. Darning, your lordship.
We cannot flaunt it in new feathers now:
Nay, if we *will* buy diamond necklaces
To please our lady, we must darn, my lord.
This old thing here (*points to necklace round her neck*), they are but blue beads — my Piero,
God rest his honest soul, he bought 'em for me,

Ay, but he knew I meant to marry
   him.
How couldst thou do it, my son?
   How couldst thou do it?
   Count.   She saw it at a dance, upon
   a neck
Less lovely than her own, and long'd
   for it.
   Elisabetta.   She told thee as much?
   Count.   No, no — a friend of hers.
   Elisabetta.   Shame on her that she
   took it at thy hands,
She rich enough to have bought it for
   herself!
   Count.   She would have robb'd me
   then of a great pleasure.
   Elisabetta.   But hath she yet re-
   turn'd thy love?
   Count.   Not yet!
   Elisabetta.   She should return thy
   necklace then.
   Count.   Ay, if
She knew the giver; but I bound the
   seller
To silence, and I left it privily
At Florence, in her palace.
   Elisabetta.   And sold thine own
To buy it for her.   She not know?
   She knows
There's none such other ——
   Count.   Madman anywhere.
Speak freely, tho' to call a madman
   mad
Will hardly help to make him sane
   again.

Enter FILIPPO.

   Filippo.   Ah, the women, the women!   Ah, Monna Giovanna, you
here again! you that have the face of
an angel and the heart of a — that's
too positive!   You that have a score
of lovers and have not a heart for any
of them — that's positive-negative:
you that have *not* the head of a toad,
and *not* a heart like the jewel in it —
that's too negative; you that have a
cheek like a peach and a heart like
the stone in it — that's positive again
— that's better!
   Elisabetta.   Sh — sh — Filippo!

   Filippo (*turns half round*).   Here has
our master been a-glorifying and
a-velveting and a-silking himself, and
a-peacocking and a-spreading to catch
her eye for a dozen year, till he hasn't
an eye left in his own tail to flourish
among the peahens, and all along o'
you, Monna Giovanna, all along o'
you!
   Elisabetta.   Sh—sh—Filippo!   Can't
you hear that you are saying behind
his back what you see you are saying
afore his face?
   Count.   Let him — he never spares
me to my face!
   Filippo.   No, my lord, I never spare
your lordship to your lordship's face,
nor behind your lordship's back, nor
to right, nor to left, nor to round
about and back to your lordship's
face again, for I'm honest, your lordship.
   Count.   Come, come, Filippo, what
is there in the larder?
   [*Elisabetta crosses to fireplace and
      puts on wood.*
   Filippo.   Shelves and hooks, shelves
and hooks, and when I see the shelves
I am like to hang myself on the
hooks.
   Count.   No bread?
   Filippo.   Half a breakfast for a rat!
   Count.   Milk?
   Filippo.   Three laps for a cat!
   Count.   Cheese?
   Filippo.   A supper for twelve mites.
   Count.   Eggs?
   Filippo.   One, but addled.
   Count.   No bird?
   Filippo.   Half a tit and a hern's bill.
   Count.   Let be thy jokes and thy
jerks, man!   Anything or nothing?
   Filippo.   Well, my lord, if all-but-
nothing be anything, and one plate of
dried prunes be all-but-nothing, then
there is anything in your lordship's
larder at your lordship's service, if
your lordship care to call for it.
   Count.   Good mother, happy was
         the prodigal son,
For he return'd to the rich father; I
But add my poverty to thine.   And all

Thro' following of my fancy. Pray
  thee make
Thy slender meal out of those scraps
  and shreds
Filippo spoke of. As for him and me,
There sprouts a salad in the garden
  still.
(*To the Falcon.*) Why didst thou
  miss thy quarry yester-even?
To-day, my beauty, thou must dash
  us down
Our dinner from the skies. Away,
  Filippo!
          [*Exit followed by* Filippo.
Elisabetta. I knew it would come
to this. She has beggared him. I
always knew it would come to this!
(*Goes up to table as if to resume darning, and looks out of window.*) Why,
as I live, there is Monna Giovanna
coming down the hill from the castle.
Stops and stares at our cottage. Ay,
ay! stare at it: it's all you have left
us. Shame upon you! *She* beautiful! sleek as a miller's mouse! Meal
enough, meat enough, well fed; but
beautiful — bah! Nay, see, why she
turns down the path through our little
vineyard, and I sneezed three times
this morning. Coming to visit my
lord, for the first time in her life too!
Why, bless the saints! I'll be bound
to confess her love to him at last. I
forgive her, I forgive her! I knew
it would come to this — I always
knew it must come to this! (*Going
up to door during latter part of
speech and opens it.*) Come in, Madonna, come in. (*Retires to front of
table and curtseys as the* Lady Giovanna *enters, then moves chair towards
the hearth.*) Nay, let me place this
chair for your ladyship.
          [Lady Giovanna *moves slowly
          down stage, then crosses to chair,
          looking about her, bows as she
          sees the Madonna over fireplace,
          then sits in chair.*
Lady Giovanna. Can I speak with
  the Count?
Elisabetta. Ay, my lady, but won't
you speak with the old woman first,

and tell her all about it and make her
happy? for I've been on my knees
every day for these half-dozen years
in hope that the saints would send us
this blessed morning; and he always
took you so kindly, he always took
the world so kindly. When he was a
little one, and I put the bitters on my
breast to wean him, he made a wry
mouth at it, but he took it so kindly,
and your ladyship has given him bitters enough in this world, and he
never made a wry mouth at you, he
always took you so kindly — which is
more than I did, my lady, more than
I did — and he so handsome — and
bless your sweet face, you look as
beautiful this morning as the very
Madonna her own self — and better
late than never — but come when they
will — then or now — it's all for the
best, come when they will — they are
made by the blessed saints — these
marriages.   [*Raises her hands.*
  Lady Giovanna. Marriages? I shall
    never marry again!
  Elisabetta (*rises and turns*). Shame
    on her then!
  Lady Giovanna. Where is the
    Count?
Elisabetta.   Just gone
To fly his falcon.
  Lady Giovanna. Call him back and
    say
I come to breakfast with him.
  Elisabetta.   Holy mother!
To breakfast! Oh sweet saints! one
    plate of prunes!
Well, Madam, I will give your mes-
    sage to him.   [*Exit.*
  Lady Giovanna. His falcon, and I
    come to ask for his falcon,
The pleasure of his eyes — boast of
    his hand —
Pride of his heart — the solace of his
    hours —
His one companion here — nay, I have
    heard
That, thro' his late magnificence of
    living
And this last costly gift to mine own
    self,   [*Shows diamond necklace.*

He hath become so beggar'd, that his
    falcon
Ev'n wins his dinner for him in the
    field.
That must be talk, not truth, but
    truth or talk,
How can I ask for his falcon?
        [Rises and moves as she speaks.
                O my sick boy!
My daily fading Florio, it is thou
Hath set me this hard task, for when
    I say
What can I do — what can I get for
    thee?
He answers, " Get the Count to give
    me his falcon,
And that will make me well." Yet if
    I ask,
He loves me, and he knows I know he
    loves me!
Will he not pray me to return his
    love —
To marry him? — (*pause*) — I can
    never marry him.
His grandsire struck my grandsire in
    a brawl
At Florence, and my grandsire stabb'd
    him there.
The feud between our houses is the
    bar
I cannot cross; I dare not brave my
    brother,
Break with my kin. My brother
    hates him, scorns
The noblest-natured man alive, and I—
Who have that reverence for him that
    I scarce
Dare beg him to receive his diamonds
    back —
How can I, dare I, ask him for his
    falcon?
        [Puts diamonds in her casket.

Re-enter COUNT *and* FILIPPO. COUNT
    turns to FILIPPO.

  Count. Do what I said; I cannot
    do it myself.
  Filippo. Why then, my lord, we are
    pauper'd out and out.
  Count. Do what I said!
        [Advances and bows low.

Welcome to this poor cottage, my
    dear lady.
  Lady Giovanna. And welcome turns
a cottage to a palace.
  Count. 'Tis long since we have met!
  Lady Giovanna. To make amends
I come this day to break my fast with
    you.
  Count. I am much honor'd — yes —
        [Turns to Filippo.
Do what I told thee. Must I do it
    myself?
  Filippo. I will, I will. (*Sighs.*)
    Poor fellow!   *[Exit.*
  Count. Lady, you bring your light
into my cottage
Who never deign'd to shine into my
    palace.
My palace wanting you was but a
    cottage;
My cottage, while you grace it, is a
    palace.
  Lady Giovanna. In cottage or in
    palace, being still
Beyond your fortunes, you are still
    the king
Of courtesy and liberality.
  Count. I trust I still maintain my
    courtesy;
My liberality perforce is dead.
Thro' lack of means of giving.
  Lady Giovanna.   Yet I come
To ask a gift.
        [Moves toward him a little.
  Count.   It will be hard, I fear,
To find one shock upon the field when
    all
The harvest has been carried.
  Lady Giovanna.   But my boy —
(*Aside.*) No, no! not yet — I cannot!
  Count.   Ay, how is he,
That bright inheritor of your eyes —
    your boy?
  Lady Giovanna. Alas, my Lord
Federigo, he hath fallen
Into a sickness, and it troubles me.
  Count. Sick! is it so? why, when
    he came last year
To see me hawking, he was well
    enough:
And then I taught him all our hawk-
    ing-phrases.

Lady Giovanna. Oh yes, and once
  you let him fly your falcon.
Count. How charm'd he was! what
  wonder ? — A gallant boy,
A noble bird, each perfect of the
  breed.
Lady Giovanna (*sinks in chair*).
  What do you rate her at ?
Count. My bird ? a hundred
Gold pieces once were offer'd by the
  Duke.
I had no heart to part with her for
  money.
Lady Giovanna. No, not for money.
  [*Count turns away and sighs.*
  Wherefore do you sigh ?
Count. I have lost a friend of
  late.
Lady Giovanna. I could sigh with
  you
For fear of losing more than friend,
  a son ;
And if he leave me — all the rest of
  life —
That wither'd wreath were of more
  worth to me.
  [*Looking at wreath on wall.*
Count. That wither'd wreath is of
  more worth to me
Than all the blossom, all the leaf of
  this
New-wakening year.
  [*Goes and takes down wreath.*
Lady Giovanna. And yet I never
  saw
The land so rich in blossom as this
  year.
Count (*holding wreath toward her*).
  Was not the year when this
  was gather'd richer ?
Lady Giovanna. How long ago was
  that ?
Count. Alas, ten summers !
A lady that was beautiful as day
Sat by me at a rustic festival
With other beauties on a mountain
  meadow,
And she was the most beautiful of
  all ;
Then but fifteen, and still as beautiful.
The mountain flowers grew thickly
  round about.

I made a wreath with some of these ;
  I ask'd
A ribbon from her hair to bind it
  with ;
I whisper'd, Let me crown you Queen
  of Beauty,
And softly placed the chaplet on her
  head.
A color, which has color'd all my life,
Flush'd in her face ; then I was call'd
  away ;
And presently all rose, and so de-
  parted.
Ah ! she had thrown my chaplet on
  the grass,
And there I found it.
  [*Lets his hands fall, holding wreath
  despondingly.*
Lady Giovanna (*after pause*). How
  long since do you say ?
Count. That was the very year be-
  fore you married.
Lady Giovanna. When I was mar-
  ried you were at the wars.
Count. Had she not thrown my
  chaplet on the grass,
It may be I had never seen the wars.
  [*Replaces wreath whence he had
  taken it.*
Lady Giovanna. Ah, but, my lord,
  there ran a rumor then
That you were kill'd in battle. I can
  tell you
True tears that year were shed for
  you in Florence.
Count. It might have been as well
  for me. Unhappily
I was but wounded by the enemy
  there
And then imprison'd.
Lady Giovanna. Happily, however,
I see you quite recover'd of your
  wound.
Count. No, no, not quite, Madonna,
  not yet, not yet

Re-enter FILIPPO.

Filippo. My lord, a word with you.
Count. Pray, pardon me !
  [*Lady Giovanna crosses, and passes
  behind chair and takes down*

wreath ; then goes to chair by table.

Count (to Filippo). What is it, Filippo ?

Filippo. Spoons, your lordship.

Count. Spoons !

Filippo. Yes, my lord, for wasn't my lady born with a golden spoon in her ladyship's mouth, and we haven't never so much as a silver one for the golden lips of her ladyship.

Count. Have we not half a score of silver spoons ?

Filippo. Half o' one, my lord !

Count. How half of one ?

Filippo. I trod upon him even now, my lord, in my hurry, and broke him.

Count. And the other nine ?

Filippo. Sold ! but shall I not mount with your lordship's leave to her ladyship's castle, in your lordship's and her ladyship's name, and confer with her ladyship's seneschal, and so descend again with some of her ladyship's own appurtenances ?

Count. Why — no, man. Only see your cloth be clean.

[*Exit* Filippo.

Lady Giovanna. Ay, ay, this faded ribbon was the mode
In Florence ten years back. What's here ? a scroll
Pinn'd to the wreath.
    My lord, you have said so much
Of this poor wreath that I was bold enough
To take it down, if but to guess what flowers
Had made it; and I find a written scroll
That seems to run in rhymings. Might I read ?

Count. Ay, if you will.

Lady Giovanna. It should be if you can.

(*Reads.*) " Dead mountain." Nay, for who could trace a hand
So wild and staggering ?

Count. This was penn'd, Madonna,
Close to the grating on a winter morn
In the perpetual twilight of a prison,

When he that made it, having his right hand
Lamed in the battle, wrote it with his left.

Lady Giovanna. Oh heavens ! the very letters seem to shake
With cold, with pain perhaps, poor prisoner ! Well,
Tell me the words — or better — for I see
There goes a musical score along with them,
Repeat them to their music.

Count. You can touch
No chord in me that would not answer you
In music.

Lady Giovanna. That is musically said.

[*Count takes guitar.* Lady Giovanna *sits listening with wreath in her hand, and quietly removes scroll and places it on table at the end of song.*

Count (sings, playing guitar). " Dead mountain flowers, dead mountain-meadow flowers,
Dearer than when you made your mountain gay,
Sweeter than any violet of to-day,
Richer than all the wide world-wealth of May,
To me, tho' all your bloom has died away,
You bloom again, dead mountain-meadow flowers."

Enter ELISABETTA *with cloth.*

Elisabetta. A word with you, my lord !

Count (singing). " O mountain flowers ! "

Elisabetta. A word, my lord ! (*Louder.*)

Count (sings). " Dead flowers ! "

Elisabetta. A word, my lord ! (*Louder.*)

Count. I pray you pardon me again !

[Lady Giovanna, *looking at wreath.*

Count (to Elisabetta). What is it ?

Elisabetta. My lord, we have but

one piece of earthenware to serve the salad in to my lady, and that cracked!

Count. Why then, that flower'd bowl my ancestor
Fetch'd from the farthest east — we never use it
For fear of breakage — but this day has brought
A great occasion. You can take it, nurse!

Elisabetta. I did take it, my lord, but what with my lady's coming that had so flurried me, and what with the fear of breaking it, I did break it, my lord: it is broken!

Count. My one thing left of value in the world!
No matter! see your cloth be white as snow!

Elisabetta (*pointing thro' window*). White? I warrant thee, my son, as the snow yonder on the very tip-top o' the mountain.

Count. And yet to speak white truth, my good old mother,
I have seen it like the snow on the moraine.

Elisabetta. How can your lordship say so? There, my lord!
[*Lays cloth.*
O my dear son, be not unkind to me. And one word more.
[*Going — returns.*

Count (*touching guitar*). Good! let it be but one.

Elisabetta. Hath she return'd thy love?

Count.   Not yet!

Elisabetta.   And will she?

Count (*looking at* Lady Giovanna). I scarce believe it!

Elisabetta. Shame upon her then!
[*Exit.*

Count (*sings.*) " Dead mountain flowers " —
Ah well, my nurse has broken
The thread of my dead flowers, as she has broken
My china bowl. My memory is as dead. [*Goes and replaces guitar.*
Strange that the words at home with me so long

Should fly like bosom friends when needed most.
So by your leave if you would hear the rest,
The writing.

Lady Giovanna (*holding wreath toward him*). There! my lord, you are a poet,
And can you not imagine that the wreath,
Set, as you say, so lightly on her head,
Fell with her motion as she rose, and she,
A girl, a child, then but fifteen, however
Flutter'd or flatter'd by your notice of her,
Was yet too bashful to return for it?

Count. Was it so indeed? was it so? was it so?
[*Leans forward to take wreath, and touches* Lady Giovanna's *hand, which she withdraws hastily; he places wreath on corner of chair.*

Lady Giovanna (*with dignity*). I did not say, my lord, that it was so;
I said you might imagine it was so.

Enter FILIPPO *with bowl of salad, which he places on table.*

Filippo. Here's a fine salad for my lady, for tho' we have been a soldier, and ridden by his lordship's side, and seen the red of the battle-field, yet are we now drill-sergeant to his lordship's lettuces, and profess to be great in green things and in garden-stuff.

Lady Giovanna. I thank you, good Filippo.   [*Exit* Filippo.

Enter ELISABETTA *with bird on a dish which she places on table.*

Elisabetta (*close to table*). Here's a fine fowl for my lady; I had scant time to do him in. I hope he be not underdone, for we be undone in the doing of him.

Lady Giovanna. I thank you, my good nurse.

Filippo (*re-entering with plate of prunes*). And here are fine fruits for my lady — prunes, my lady, from the tree that my lord himself planted here in the blossom of his boyhood — and so I, Filippo, being, with your ladyship's pardon, and as your ladyship knows, his lordship's own foster-brother, would commend them to your ladyship's most peculiar appreciation. [*Puts plate on table.*

Elisabetta. Filippo!

Lady Giovanna (Count *leads her to table*). Will you not eat with me, my lord?

Count. I cannot, Not a morsel, not one morsel. I have broken
My fast already. I will pledge you. Wine! Filippo, wine!

[*Sits near table; Filippo brings flask, fills the* Count's *goblet, then* Lady Giovanna's; Elisabetta *stands at the back of* Lady Giovanna's *chair.*

Count. It is but thin and cold, Not like the vintage blowing round your castle.
We lie too deep down in the shadow here.
Your ladyship lives higher in the sun. [*They pledge each other and drink.*

Lady Giovanna. If I might send• you down a flask or two
Of that same vintage? There is iron in it.
It has been much commended as a medicine.
I give it my sick son, and if you be
Not quite recover'd of your wound, the wine
Might help you. None has ever told me yet
The story of your battle and your wound.

Filippo (*coming forward*). I can tell you, my lady, I can tell you.

Elisabetta. Filippo! will you take the word out of your master's own mouth?

Filippo. Was it there to take? Put it there, my lord.

Count. Giovanna, my dear lady, in this same battle
We had been beaten — they were ten to one.
The trumpets of the fight had echo'd down,
I and Filippo here had done our best,
And, having passed unwounded from the field,
Were seated sadly at a fountain side,
Our horses grazing by us, when a troop,
Laden with booty and with a flag of ours
Ta'en in the fight ——

Filippo. Ay, but we fought for it back,
And kill'd ——

Elisabetta. Filippo!

Count. A troop of horse ——

Filippo. Five hundred!

Count. Say fifty!

Filippo. And we kill'd 'em by the score!

Elisabetta. Filippo!

Filippo. Well, well, well! I bite my tongue.

Count. We may have left their fifty less by five.
However, staying not to count how many,
But anger'd at their flaunting of our flag,
We mounted, and we dashed into the heart of 'em.
I wore the lady's chaplet round my neck;
It served me for a blessed rosary.
I am sure that more than one brave fellow owed
His death to the charm in it.

Elisabetta. Hear that, my lady!

Count. I cannot tell how long we strove before
Our horses fell beneath us; down we went
Crush'd, hack'd at, trampled under-foot. The night,
As some cold-manner'd friend may strangely do us
The truest service, had a touch of frost

That help'd to check the flowing of
the blood.
My last sight ere I swoon'd was one
sweet face
Crown'd with the wreath. *That* seem'd
to come and go.
They left us there for dead !
   Elisabetta.   Hear that, my lady !
   Filippo. Ay, and I left two fingers
there for dead. See, my lady!
              [*Showing his hand.*
   Lady Giovanna. I see, Filippo !
   Filippo. And I have small hope of
the gentleman gout in my great toe.
   Lady Giovanna. And why, Filippo ?
              [*Smiling absently.*
   Filippo. I left him there for dead
too!
   Elisabetta. She smiles at him — how
hard the woman is !
My lady, if your ladyship were not
Too proud to look upon the garland,
   you
Would find it stain'd —
   Count (*rising*). Silence, Elisabetta !
   Elisabetta. Stain'd with the blood of
the best heart that ever
Beat for one woman.
          [*Points to wreath on chair.*
   Lady Giovanna (*rising slowly*). I can
eat no more !
   Count. You have but trifled with
our homely salad,
But dallied with a single lettuce-leaf;
Not eaten anything.
   Lady Giovanna. Nay, nay, I cannot.
You know, my lord, I told you I was
troubled.
My one child Florio lying still so
sick,
I bound myself, and by a solemn
vow,
That I would touch no flesh till he
were well
Here, or else well in Heaven, where all
is well.
   [*Elisabetta clears table of bird and
salad: Filippo snatches up the
plate of prunes and holds them to*
   Lady Giovanna.
   Filippo. But the prunes, my lady,
from the tree that his lordship ——

   Lady Giovanna. Not now, Filippo.
      My lord Federigo,
Can I not speak with you once more
alone ?
   Count. You hear, Filippo ? My
good fellow, go !
   Filippo. But the prunes that your
lordship ——
   Elisabetta. Filippo !
   Count. Ay, prune our company of
thine own and go !
   Elisabetta. Filippo !
   Filippo (*turning*). Well, well ! the
women !   [*Exit.*
   Count. And thou too leave us, my
dear nurse, alone.
   Elisabetta (*folding up cloth and going*).
And me too ! Ay, the dear nurse will
leave you alone ; but, for all that, she
that has eaten the yolk is scarce like
to swallow the shell.
   [*Turns and curtseys stiffly to* Lady
    Giovanna, *then exit.* Lady
    Giovanna *takes out diamond
    necklace from casket.*
   Lady Giovanna. I have anger'd your
good nurse; these old-world ser-
vants
Are all but flesh and blood with those
they serve.
My lord, I have a present to return
you,
And afterwards a boon to crave of
you.
   Count. No, my most honor'd and
long-worshipt lady,
Poor Federigo degli Alberighi
Takes nothing in return from you
except
Return of his affection — can deny
Nothing to you that you require of
him.
   Lady Giovanna. Then I require you
to take back your diamonds —
            [*Offering necklace.*
I doubt not they are yours. No other
heart
Of such magnificence in courtesy
Beats — out of heaven. They seem'd
too rich a prize
To trust with any messenger. I came

In person to return them.

    [*Count draws back.*

     If the phrase
"Return" displease you, we will say
  — exchange them
For your — for your ——
Count (*takes a step toward her and then
  back*)　For mine — and what of
  mine ?
  Lady Giovanna.　Well, shall we say
  this wreath and your sweet
  rhymes ?
  Count.　But have you ever worn my
  diamonds ?
  Lady Giovanna.   No !
For that would seem accepting of your
  love.
I cannot brave my brother — but be
  sure
That I shall never marry again, my
  lord!
  Count.　Sure ?
  Lady Giovanna.　Yes!
  Count.　Is this your brother's order ?
  Lady Giovanna.   No !
For he would marry me to the richest
  man
In Florence ; but I think you know
  the saying —
"Better a man without riches, than
  riches without a man."
  Count.　A noble saying — and acted
  on would yield
A nobler breed of men and women.
  Lady,
I find you a shrewd bargainer.　The
  wreath
That once you wore outvalues twenty-
  fold
The diamonds that you never deign'd
  to wear.
But lay them there for a moment !

  [*Points to table.*　Lady Giovanna
  places necklace on table.

     And be you
Gracious enough to let me know the
  boon
By granting which, if aught be mine
  to grant,
I should be made more happy than I
  hoped
Ever to be again.

  Lady Giovanna.　Then keep your
  wreath,
But you will find me a shrewd bar-
  gainer still.
I cannot keep your diamonds, for the
  gift
I ask for, to *my* mind and at this
  present
Outvalues all the jewels upon earth.
  Count.　It should be love that thus
  outvalues all.
You speak like love, and yet you love
  me not.
I have nothing in this world but love
  for you.
  Lady Giovanna.　Love ? it *is* love,
  love for my dying boy,
Moves me to ask it of you.
  Count.   What ? my time ?
Is it my time ?　Well, I can give my
  time
To him that is a part of you, your son.
Shall I return to the castle with you ?
  Shall I
Sit by him, read to him, tell him my
  tales,
Sing him my songs ?　You know that
  I can touch
The ghittern to some purpose.
  Lady Giovanna. No, not that !
I thank you heartily for that — and you,
I doubt not from your nobleness of
  nature,
Will pardon me for asking what I ask.
  Count.　Giovanna, dear Giovanna, I
  that once
The wildest of the random youth of
  Florence
Before I saw you — all my nobleness
Of nature, as you deign to call it,
  draws
From you, and from my constancy to
  you.
No more, but speak.
  Lady Giovanna.　I will.　You know
  sick people,
More specially sick children, have
  strange fancies,
Strange longings ; and to thwart them
  in their mood
May work them grievous harm at
  times, may even

Hasten their end.   I would you had a
 son!
It might be easier then for you to
 make
Allowance for a mother — her — who
 comes
To rob you of your one delight on
 earth.
How often has my sick boy yearn'd
 for this!
I have put him off as often ; but to-
 day
I dared not — so much weaker, so
 much worse
For last day's journey.   I was weep-
 ing for him ;
He gave me his hand: " I should be
 well again
If the good Count would give me —— "
 Count.   Give me.
 Lady Giovanna.   His falcon.
 Count (*starts back*).   My falcon !
 Lady Giovanna.   Yes, your falcon,
  Federigo !
 Count.   Alas, I cannot !
 Lady Giovanna.   Cannot ? Even so !
I fear'd as much.   O this unhappy
 world !
How shall I break it to him ? how
 shall I tell him ?
The boy may die: more blessed were
 the rags
Of some pale beggar-woman seeking
 alms
For her sick son, if he were like to
 live,
Than all my childless wealth, if mine
 must die.
I was to blame — the love you said
 you bore me —
My lord, we thank you for your
 entertainment,
    [*With a stately curtsey.*
And so return — Heaven help him ! —
 to our son.   [*Turns.*
 Count (*rushes forward*).   Stay, stay,
  I am most unlucky, most un-
  happy.
You never had look'd in on me be-
 fore,
And when you came and dipt your
 sovereign head

Thro' these low doors, you ask'd to
 eat with me.
I had but emptiness to set before
 you,
No not a draught of milk, no not an
 egg,
Nothing but my brave bird, my noble
 falcon,
My comrade of the house, and of the
 field.
She had to die for it — she died for
 you.
Perhaps I thought with those of old,
 the nobler
The victim was, the more acceptable
Might be the sacrifice.   I fear you
 scarce
Will thank me for your entertain-
 ment now.
 Lady Giovanna (*returning*).   I bear
  with him no longer.
 Count.   No, Madonna !
And he will have to bear with it as he
 may.
 Lady Giovanna.   I break with him
  for ever !
 Count.   Yes, Giovanna,
But he will keep his love to you for
 ever !
 Lady Giovanna.   You ? you ? not
  you !   My brother ! my hard
  brother !
O Federigo, Federigo, I love you !
Spite of ten thousand brothers, Fed-
 erigo.   [*Falls at his feet.*
 Count (*impetuously*).   Why then the
  dying of my noble bird
Hath served me better than her living
 — then
    [*Takes diamonds from table.*
These diamonds are both yours and
 mine — have won
Their value again — beyond all mar-
 kets — there
I lay them for the first time round
 your neck.
    [*Lays necklace round her neck.*
And then this chaplet — No more
 feuds, but peace,
Peace and conciliation !   I will make
Your brother love me.   See, I tear
 away

The leaves were darken'd by the battle —
  *[Pulls leaves off and throws them
  down.*
                        — crown you
Again with the same crown my Queen
  of Beauty.
            [Places wreath on her head.
Rise — I could almost think that the
  dead garland
Will break once more into living blossom.

Nay, nay, I pray you rise.
            [Raises her with both hands.
                  We two together
Will help to heal your son — your
  son and mine —
We shall do it — we shall do it.
                        [Embraces her.
The purpose of my being is accom-
  plish'd,
And I am happy!
  Lady Giovanna. And I too, Fed-
  erigo.

BECKET.

To the Lord Chancellor,

THE RIGHT HONORABLE EARL OF SELBORNE.

My Dear Selborne, — To you, the honored Chancellor of our own day, I dedicate this dramatic memorial of your great predecessor; — which, altho' not intended in its present form to meet the exigencies of our modern theatre, has nevertheless — for so you have assured me — won your approbation.   Ever yours,

TENNYSON.

DRAMATIS PERSONÆ.

Henry II. (*son of the Earl of Anjou*).
Thomas Becket, *Chancellor of England, afterwards Archbishop of Canterbury.*
Gilbert Foliot, *Bishop of London.*
Roger, *Archbishop of York.*
    Bishop of Hereford.
Hilary, *Bishop of Chichester.*
Jocelyn, *Bishop of Salisbury.*
John of Salisbury } *friends of Becket.*
Herbert of Bosham }
Walter Map, *reputed author of* " Golias," *Latin poems against the priesthood.*
King Louis of France.
Geoffrey, *son of Rosamund and Henry.*
Grim, *a monk of Cambridge.*
Sir Reginald Fitzurse }
Sir Richard de Brito } *the four knights of the King's household, enemies of*
Sir William de Tracy } *Becket.*
Sir Hugh de Morville }
De Broc of Saltwood Castle.
Lord Leicester.
Philip de Eleemosyna.
Two Knight Templars.
John of Oxford (*called the Swearer*).
Eleanor of Aquitaine, *Queen of England* (*divorced from Louis of France*).
Rosamund de Clifford.
Margery.

Knights, Monks, Beggars, *etc.*

PROLOGUE.

A Castle in Normandy. Interior
of the Hall. Roofs of a City
seen thro' Windows.

Henry *and* Becket *at chess.*

Henry. So then our good Arch-
  bishop Theobald
Lies dying.
  Becket. I am grieved to know as
    much.
  Henry. But we must have a
    mightier man than he
For his successor.
  Becket. Have you thought of one ?
  Henry. A cleric lately poison'd his
    own mother,
And being brought before the courts
  of the Church,
They but degraded him. I hope they
  whipt him.
I would have hang'd him.
  Becket.   It is your move.
  Henry.   Well — there. [*Moves.*
The Church in the pell-mell of
  Stephen's time
Hath climb'd the throne and almost
  clutch'd the crown;
But by the royal customs of our realm
The Church should hold her baronies
  of me,
Like other lords amenable to law.
I'll have them written down and made
  the law. ·
  Becket. My liege, I move my bishop.
  Henry.   And if I live,
No man without my leave shall ex-
  communicate
My tenants or my household.
  Becket.   Look to your king.
  Henry. No man without my leave
    shall cross the seas
To · set the Pope against me — I pray
  your pardon.
  Becket. Well — will you move ?
  Henry.   There.   [*Moves.*
  Becket.   Check — you
    move so wildly.
  Henry. There then !   [*Moves.*

  Becket. Why — there then, for you
    see my bishop
Hath brought your king to a stand-
  still. You are beaten.
  Henry (*kicks over the board*). Why,
    there then — down go bishop
    and king together.
I loathe being beaten ; had I fixt my
  fancy
Upon the game I should have beaten
  thee,
But that was vagabond.
  Becket.   Where, my liege ?
    With Phryne,
Or Lais, or thy Rosamund, or another ?
  Henry. My Rosamund is no Lais,
    Thomas Becket ;
And yet she plagues me too — no
  fault in her —
But that I fear the Queen would have
  her life.
  Becket. Put her away, put her away,
    my liege !
Put her away into a nunnery !
Safe enough there from her to whom
  thou art bound
By Holy Church. And wherefore
  should she seek
The life of Rosamund de Clifford more
Than that of other paramours of
  thine ?
  Henry. How dost thou know I am
    not wedded to her ?
  Becket. How should I know ?
  Henry. That is my secret, Thomas.
  Becket. State secrets should be pa-
    tent to the statesman
Who serves and loves his king, and
  whom the king
Loves not as statesman, but true lover
  and friend.
  Henry. Come, come, thou art but
    deacon, not yet bishop,
No, nor archbishop, nor my confessor
  yet.
I would to God thou wert, for I should
  find
An easy father confessor in thee.
  Becket. St. Denis, that thou shouldst
    not. I should beat
Thy kingship as my bishop hath
  beaten it.

Henry. Hell take thy bishop then,
    and my kingship too!
Come, come, I love thee and I know
    thee, I know thee,
A doter on white pheasant-flesh at
    feasts,
A sauce-deviser for thy days of fish,
A dish-designer, and most amorous
Of good old red sound liberal Gascon
    wine:
Will not thy body rebel, man, if thou
    flatter it?
    Becket. That palate is insane which
    cannot tell
A good dish from a bad, new wine
    from old.
    Henry. Well, who loves wine loves
    woman.
    Becket. So I do.
Men are God's trees, and women are
    God's flowers;
And when the Gascon wine mounts to
    my head,
The trees are all the statelier, and the
    flowers
Are all the fairer.
    Henry.   And thy thoughts,
    thy fancies?
    Becket. Good dogs, my liege, well
    train'd, and easily call'd
Off from the game.
    Henry. Save for some once or twice,
When they ran down the game and
    worried it.
    Becket. No, my liege, no!—not
    once—in God's name, no!
    Henry. Nay, then, I take thee at
    thy word—believe thee
The veriest Galahad of old Arthur's
    hall.
And so this Rosamund, my true heart-
    wife,
Not Eleanor—she whom I love indeed
As a woman should be loved—Why
    dost thou smile
So dolorously?
    Becket. My good liege, if a man
Wastes himself among women, how
    should he love
A woman, as a woman should be loved?
    Henry. How shouldst thou know
    that never hast loved one?

Come, I would give her to thy care in
    England
When I am out in Normandy or Anjou.
    Becket. My lord, I am your subject,
    not your——
    Henry.   Pander.
God's eyes! I know all that—not my
    purveyor
Of pleasures, but to save a life—her
    life;
Ay, and the soul of Eleanor from hell-
    fire.
I have built a secret bower in Eng-
    land, Thomas,
A nest in a bush.
    Becket. And where, my liege?
    Henry (*whispers*).   Thine ear.
    Becket. That's lone enough.
    Henry (*laying paper on table*). This
    chart here mark'd "*Her Bower,*"
Take, keep it, friend. See, first, a
    circling wood,
A hundred pathways running every-
    way,
And then a brook, a bridge; and after
    that
This labyrinthine brickwork maze in
    maze,
And then another wood, and in the
    midst
A garden and my Rosamund. Look,
    this line—
The rest you see is color'd green—
    but this
Draws thro' the chart to her.
    Becket.   This blood-red line?
    Henry. Ay! blood, perchance, ex-
    cept thou see to her.
    Becket. And where is she? There
    in her English nest?
    Henry. Would God she were—no,
    here within the city.
We take her from her secret bower in
    Anjou
And pass her to her secret bower in
    England.
She is ignorant of all but that I love
    her.
    Becket. My liege, I pray thee let me
    hence: a widow
And orphan child, whom one of thy
    wild barons——

Henry. Ay, ay, but swear to see her in England.

Becket. Well, well, I swear, but not to please myself.

Henry. Whatever come between us?

Becket. What should come Between us, Henry?

Henry. Nay — I know not, Thomas.

Becket. What need then? Well — whatever come between us.

[*Going.*

Henry. A moment! thou didst help me to my throne
In Theobald's time, and after by thy wisdom
Hast kept it firm from shaking; but now I,
For my realm's sake, myself must be the wizard
To raise that tempest which will set it trembling
Only to base it deeper. I, true son
Of Holy Church — no croucher to the Gregories
That tread the kings their children underheel —
Must curb her; and the Holy Father, while
This Barbarossa butts him from his chair,
Will need my help — be facile to my hands.
Now is my time. Yet — lest there should be flashes
And fulminations from the side of Rome,
An interdict on England — I will have
My young son Henry crown'd the King of England,
That so the Papal bolt may pass by England,
As seeming his, not mine, and fall abroad.
I'll have it done — and now.

Becket. Surely too young
Even for this shadow of a crown; and tho'
I love him heartily, I can spy already
A strain of hard and headstrong in him. Say,
The Queen should play his kingship against thine!

Henry. I will not think so, Thomas.
Who shall crown him?
Canterbury is dying.

Becket. The next Canterbury.

Henry. And who shall he be, my friend Thomas? Who?

Becket. Name him; the Holy Father will confirm him.

Henry (*lays his hand on* Becket's *shoulder*). Here!

Becket. Mock me not. I am not even a monk.
Thy jest — no more. Why — look — is this a sleeve
For an archbishop?

Henry. But the arm within
Is Becket's, who hath beaten down my foes.

Becket. A soldier's, not a spiritual arm.

Henry. I lack a spiritual soldier, Thomas —
A man of this world and the next to boot.

Becket. There's Gilbert Foliot.

Henry. He! too thin, too thin.
Thou art the man to fill out the Church robe;
Your Foliot fasts and fawns too much for me.

Becket. Roger of York.

Henry. Roger is Roger of York.
King, Church, and State to him but foils wherein
To set that precious jewel, Roger of York.
No.

Becket. Henry of Winchester?

Henry. Him who crown'd Stephen —
King Stephen's brother! No; too royal for me.
And I'll have no more Anselms.

Becket. Sire, the business
Of thy whole kingdom waits me: let me go.

Henry. Answer me first.

Becket. Then for thy barren jest
Take thou mine answer in bare com monplace —
Nolo episcopari.

Henry. Ay, but *Nolo Archiepiscopari*, my good friend,

Is quite another matter.
   Becket.   A more lawful one.
Make *me* archbishop ! Why, my
   liege, I know
Some three or four poor priests a
   thousand times
Fitter for this grand function. *Me*
   archbishop !
God's favor and king's favor might so
   clash
That thou and I —— That were a
   jest indeed !
   Henry. Thou angerest me, man : I
do not jest.

Enter ELEANOR *and* SIR REGINALD
        FITZURSE.

   Eleanor (*singing*). Over! the sweet
     summer closes,
     The reign of the roses is done ——
   Henry (*to* Becket, *who is going*).
Thou shalt not go. I have not ended
   with thee.
   Eleanor (*seeing chart on table*). This
chart with the red line ! her bower !
whose bower ?
   Henry. The chart is not mine, but
Becket's : take it, Thomas.
   Eleanor. Becket! O — ay — and
these chessmen on the floor — the
king's crown broken ! Becket hath
beaten thee again — and thou hast
kicked down the board. I know thee
of old.
   Henry. True enough, my mind was
set upon other matters.
   Eleanor. What matters ? State
matters ? love matters ?
   Henry. My love for thee, and thine
for me.
   Eleanor. Over! the sweet summer
     closes,
     The reign of the roses is done ;
   Over and gone with the roses,
     And over and gone with the sun.
   Here ; but our sun in Aquitaine
lasts longer. I would I were in Aquitaine again — your north chills me.
     Over! the sweet summer closes,
     And never a flower at the close ;
   Over and gone with the roses,
     And winter again and the snows.

That was not the way I ended it first
— but unsymmetrically, preposter-
ously, illogically, out of passion, without art — like a song of the people.
Will you have it ? The last Parthian
shaft of a forlorn Cupid at the King's
left breast, and all left-handedness
and under-handedness.
     And never a flower at the close,
     Over and gone with the roses,
     Not over and gone with the rose.
True, one rose will outblossom the
rest, one rose in a bower. I speak
after my fancies, for I am a Trouba-
dour, you know, and won the violet at
Toulouse ; but my voice is harsh
here, not in tune, a nightingale out of
season ; for marriage, rose or no rose,
has killed the golden violet.
   Becket. Madam, you do ill to scorn
wedded love.
   Eleanor. So I do. Louis of France
loved me, and I dreamed that I loved
Louis of France : and I loved Henry of
England, and Henry of England
dreamed that he loved me ; but the
marriage-garland withers even with
the putting on, the bright link rusts
with the breath of the first after-
marriage kiss, the harvest moon is
the ripening of the harvest, and the
honeymoon is the gall of love ; he
dies of his honeymoon. I could pity
this poor world myself that is no better ordered.
   Henry. Dead is he, my Queen ?
What, altogether ? Let me swear
nay to that by this cross on thy neck.
God's eyes ! what a lovely cross ! what
jewels !
   Eleanor. Doth it please you ? Take
it and wear it on that hard heart of
yours — there.   [*Gives it to him.*
   Henry (*puts it on*). On this left
     breast before so hard a heart,
To hide the scar left by thy Parthian
   dart.
   Eleanor. Has my simple song set
you jingling ? Nay, if I took and
translated that hard heart into our
Provençal facilities, I could so play
about it with the rhyme ——

Henry. That the heart were lost in the rhyme and the matter in the metre. May we not pray you, Madam, to spare us the hardness of your facility ?

Eleanor. The wells of Castaly are not wasted upon the desert. We did but jest.

Henry. There's no jest on the brows of Herbert there. What is it, Herbert ?

Enter HERBERT OF BOSHAM.

Herbert. My liege, the good Archbishop is no more.

Henry. Peace to his soul !

Herbert. I left him with peace on his face — that sweet other-world smile, which will be reflected in the spiritual body among the angels. But he longed much to see your Grace and the Chancellor ere he past, and his last words were a commendation of Thomas Becket to your Grace as his successor in the archbishoprick.

Henry. Ha, Becket ! thou rememberest our talk !

Becket. My heart is full of tears — I have no answer.

Henry. Well, well, old men must die, or the world would grow mouldy, would only breed the past again. Come to me to-morrow. Thou hast but to hold out thy hand. Meanwhile the revenues are mine. A-hawking, a-hawking ! If I sit, I grow fat.

[*Leaps over the table, and exit.*

Becket. He did prefer me to the chancellorship,

Believing I should ever aid the Church —

But have I done it ? He commends me now

From out his grave to this archbishoprick.

Herbert. A dead man's dying wish should be of weight.

Becket. *His* should. Come with me. Let me learn at full

The manner of his death, and all he said.

[*Exeunt* Herbert *and* Becket.

Eleanor. Fitzurse, that chart with the red line — thou sawest it — her bower.

Fitzurse. Rosamund's ?

Eleanor. Ay — there lies the secret of her whereabouts, and the King gave it to his Chancellor.

Fitzurse. To this son of a London merchant — how your Grace must hate him.

Eleanor. Hate him ? as brave a soldier as Henry and a goodlier man : but thou — dost thou love this Chancellor, that thou hast sworn a voluntary allegiance to him ?

Fitzurse. Not for my love toward him, but because he had the love of the King. How should a baron love a beggar on horseback, with the retinue of three kings behind him, outroyalling royalty ? Besides, he holp the King to break down our castles, for the which I hate him.

Eleanor. For the which I honor him. Statesman not Churchman he. A great and sound policy that : I could embrace him for it : you could not see the King for the kinglings.

Fitzurse. Ay, but he speaks to a noble as tho' he were a churl, and to a churl as if he were a noble.

Eleanor. Pride of the plebeian !

Fitzurse. And this plebeian like to be Archbishop !

Eleanor. True, and I have an inherited loathing of these black sheep of the Papacy. Archbishop ? I can see further into a man than our hot-headed Henry, and if there ever come feud between Church and Crown, and I do not then charm this secret out of our loyal Thomas, I am not Eleanor.

Fitzurse. Last night I followed a woman in the city here. Her face was veiled, but the back methought was Rosamund — his paramour, thy rival. I can feel for thee.

Eleanor. Thou feel for me ! — paramour — rival ! King Louis had no paramours, and I loved him none the more. Henry had many, and I loved him none the less — now neither more nor less — not at all ; the cup's empty.

I would she were but his paramour, for men tire of their fancies; but I fear this one fancy hath taken root, and borne blossom too, and she, whom the King loves indeed, is a power in the State. Rival!—ay, and when the King passes, there may come a crash and embroilment as in Stephen's time; and her children—canst thou not—that secret matter which would heat the King against thee (*whispers him and he starts*). Nay, that is safe with me as with thyself: but canst thou not—thou art drowned in debt—thou shalt have our love, our silence, and our gold—canst thou not—if thou light upon her—free me from her?

Fitzurse. Well, Madam, I have loved her in my time.

Eleanor. No, my bear, thou hast not. My Courts of Love would have held thee guiltless of love—the fine attractions and repulses, the delicacies, the subtleties.

Fitzurse. Madam, I loved according to the main purpose and intent of nature.

Eleanor. I warrant thee! thou wouldst hug thy Cupid till his ribs cracked—enough of this. Follow me this Rosamund day and night, whithersoever she goes; track her, if thou canst, even into the King's lodging, that I may (*clenches her fist*)—may at least have my cry against him and her,—and thou in my way shouldst be jealous of the King, for thou in thy way didst once, what shall I call it, affect her thine own self.

Fitzurse. Ay, but the young colt winced and whinnied and flung up her heels; and then the King came honeying about her, and this Becket, her father's friend, like enough staved us from her.

Eleanor. Us!

Fitzurse. Yea, by the Blessed Virgin! There were more than I buzzing round the blossom—De Tracy—even that flint De Brito.

Eleanor. Carry her off among you; run in upon her and devour her, one and all of you; make her as hateful to herself and to the King, as she is to me.

Fitzurse. I and all would be glad to wreak our spite on the rosefaced minion of the King, and bring her to the level of the dust, so that the King ——

Eleanor. Let her eat it like the serpent, and be driven out of her paradise.

ACT I.

SCENE 1.—BECKET'S HOUSE IN LONDON. CHAMBER BARELY FURNISHED. BECKET UNROBING. HERBERT OF BOSHAM AND SERVANT.

Servant. Shall I not help your lordship to your rest?

Becket. Friend, am I so much better than thyself
That thou shouldst help me? Thou art wearied out
With this day's work, get thee to thine own bed.
Leave me with Herbert, friend.
                    [*Exit* Servant.
Help me off, Herbert, with this—and this.

Herbert. Was not the people's blessing as we past
Heart-comfort and a balsam to thy blood?

Becket. The people know their Church a tower of strength,
A bulwark against Throne and Baronage.
Too heavy for me, this; off with it, Herbert!

Herbert. Is it so much heavier than thy Chancellor's robe?

Becket. No; but the Chancellor's and the Archbishop's
Together more than mortal man can bear.

Herbert. Not heavier than thine armor at Thoulouse?

Becket. O Herbert, Herbert, in my chancellorship

I more than once have gone against
the Church.

Herbert. To please the King?

Becket. Ay, and the King of kings,
Or justice; for it seem'd to me but just
The Church should pay her scutage
like the lords.
But hast thou heard this cry of Gil-
bert Foliot
That I am not the man to be your
Primate,
For Henry could not work a miracle—
Make an Archbishop of a soldier?

Herbert.   Ay,
For Gilbert Foliot held himself the
man.

Becket. Am I the man? My
mother, ere she bore me,
Dream'd that twelve stars fell glittering out of heaven
Into her bosom.

Herbert. Ay, the fire, the light,
The spirit of the twelve Apostles
enter'd
Into thy making.

Becket. And when I was a child,
The Virgin, in a vision of my sleep,
Gave me the golden keys of Paradise.
Dream,
Or prophecy, that?

Herbert. Well dream and prophecy
both.

Becket. And when I was of Theobald's household, once—
The good old man would sometimes
have his jest—
He took his mitre off, and set it on me,
And said, "My young Archbishop—
thou wouldst make
A stately Archbishop!" Jest or
prophecy there?

Herbert. Both, Thomas, both.

Becket. Am I the man? That rang
Within my head last night, and when
I slept
Methought I stood in Canterbury
Minster,
And spake to the Lord God, and said,
"O Lord,
I have been a lover of wines, and
delicate meats,
And secular splendors, and a favorer

Of players, and a courtier, and a
feeder
Of dogs and hawks, and apes, and
lions, and lynxes.
Am I the man?" And the Lord an-
swer'd me,
"Thou art the man, and all the more
the man."
And then I asked again, "O Lord my
God,
Henry the King hath been my friend,
my brother,
And mine uplifter in this world, and
chosen me
For this thy great archbishoprick,
believing
That I should go against the Church
with him,
And I shall go against him with the
Church,
And I have said no word of this to
him:
"Am I the man?" And the Lord
answer'd me,
"Thou art the man, and all the more
the man."
And thereupon, methought, He drew
toward me,
And smote me down upon the Minster
floor.
I fell.

Herbert. God make not thee, but
thy foes, fall.

Becket. I fell. Why fall? Why
did He smite me? What?
Shall I fall off—to please the King
once more?
Not fight—tho' somehow traitor to
the King—
My truest and mine utmost for the
Church?

Herbert. Thou canst not fall that
way. Let traitor be;
For how have fought thine utmost for
the Church,
Save from the throne of thine arch-
bishoprick?
And how been made Archbishop
hadst thou told him,
"I mean to fight mine utmost for the
Church,
Against the King?"

Becket. But dost thou think the King
Forced mine election ?
  Herbert. I do think the King
Was potent in the election, and why
  not ?
Why should not Heaven have so
  inspired the King ?
Be comforted. Thou art the man —
  be thou
A mightier Anselm.
  Becket. I do believe thee, then. I
  am the man.
And yet I seem appall'd — on such a
  sudden
At such an eagle-height I stand and
  see
The rift that runs between me and the
  King.
I served our Theobald well when I
  was with him ;
I served King Henry well as Chan-
  cellor ;
I am his no more, and I must serve
  the Church.
This Canterbury is only less than
  Rome,
And all my doubts I fling from me
  like dust,
Winnow and scatter all scruples to
  the wind,
And all the puissance of the warrior,
And all the wisdom of the Chancellor,
And all the heap'd experiences of
  life,
I cast upon the side of Canterbury —
Our holy mother Canterbury, who
  sits
With tatter'd robes. Laics and
  barons, thro'
The random gifts of careless kings,
  have graspt
Her livings, her advowsons, granges,
  farms,
And goodly acres — we will make her
  whole ;
Not one rood lost. And for these
  Royal customs,
These ancient Royal customs — they
  are Royal,
Not of the Church — and let them be
  anathema,

And all that speak for them ana-
  thema.
  Herbert. Thomas, thou art moved
  too much.
  Becket. O Herbert, here
I gash myself asunder from the King,
Tho' leaving each, a wound ; mine
  own, a grief
To show the scar for ever — his, a
  hate
Not ever to be heal'd.

Enter ROSAMUND DE CLIFFORD, *flying
  from* SIR REGINALD FITZURSE.
  Drops her veil.*

  Becket. Rosamund de Clifford !
  Rosamund. Save me, father, hide
me — they follow me — and I must
not be known.
  Becket. Pass in with Herbert there.
    [*Exeunt* Rosamund *and* Herbert
    by side door.

Enter FITZURSE.

  Fitzurse. The Archbishop !
  Becket. Ay ! what wouldst thou,
  Reginald ?
  Fitzurse. Why — why, my lord, I
  follow'd — follow'd one ——
  Becket. And then what follows ?
  Let me follow thee.
  Fitzurse. It much imports me I
  should know her name.
  Becket. What her ?
  Fitzurse. The woman that I fol-
  low'd hither.
  Becket. Perhaps it may import her
  all as much
Not to be known.
  Fitzurse. And what care I for that ?
Come, come, my lord Archbishop ; I
  saw that door
Close even now upon the woman.
  Becket. Well ?
  Fitzurse (*making for the door*). Nay,
  let me pass, my lord, for I must
  know.
  Becket. Back, man !
  Fitzurse. Then tell me who and
  what she is.
  Becket. Art thou so sure thou fol-
  lowedst anything ?

Go home, and sleep thy wine off, for
    thine eyes
Glare stupid-wild with wine.
    Fitzurse (*making to the door*). I
    must and will.
I care not for thy new archbishoprick.
    Becket. Back, man, I tell thee!
    What!
Shall I forget my new archbishoprick
And smite thee with my crozier on the
    skull?
'Fore God, I am a mightier man than
    thou.
    Fitzurse. It well befits thy new
    archbishoprick
To take the vagabond woman of the
    street
Into thine arms!
    Becket.   O drunken ribaldry!
Out, beast! out, bear!
    Fitzurse. I shall remember this.
    Becket. Do, and begone!
                   [*Exit* Fitzurse.
    [*Going to the door sees* De Tracy.
    Tracy, what dost thou here?
    De Tracy. My lord, I follow'd
    Reginald Fitzurse.
    Becket. Follow him out!
    De Tracy. I shall remember this
Discourtesy.   [*Exit.*
    Becket. Do. These be those baron-
    brutes
That havock'd all the land in Stephen's
    day.
Rosamund de Clifford.

Re-enter ROSAMUND *and* HERBERT.

    Rosamund.   Here am I.
    Becket.   Why here?
We gave thee to the charge of John
    of Salisbury,
To pass thee to thy secret bower to-
    morrow.
Wast thou not told to keep thyself
    from sight?
    Rosamund. Poor bird of passage!
    so I was; but, father,
They say that you are wise in winged
    things,
And know the ways of Nature. Bar
    the bird

From following the fled summer — a
    chink — he's out,
Gone! And there stole into the city
    a breath
Full of the meadows, and it minded
    me
Of the sweet woods of Clifford, and
    the walks
Where I could move at pleasure, and
    I thought
Lo! I must out or die.
    Becket.   Or out *and* die.
And what hast thou to do with this
    Fitzurse?
    Rosamund. Nothing. He sued my
    hand. I shook at him.
He found me once alone. Nay —
    nay — I cannot
Tell you: my father drove him and
    his friends,
De Tracy and De Brito, from our
    castle.
I was but fourteen and an April
    then.
I heard him swear revenge.
    Becket.   Why will you court it
By self-exposure? flutter out at night?
Make it so hard to save a moth from
    the fire?
    Rosamund. I have saved many of
    'em. You catch 'em, so,
Softly, and fling them out to the free
    air.
They burn themselves *within*-door.
    Becket.   Our good John
Must speed you to your bower at
    once. The child
Is there already.
    Rosamund. Yes — the child — the
    child —
O rare, a whole long day of open field.
    Becket. Ay, but you go disguised.
    Rosamund. O rare again!
We'll baffle them, I warrant. What
    shall it be?
I'll go as a nun.
    Becket.   No.
    Rosamund. What, not good enough
Even to play at nun?
    Becket.   Dan John with a nun,
That Map, and these new railers at
    the Church

May plaister his clean name with
  scurrilous rhymes!
No!
Go like a monk, cowling and clouding
  up
That fatal star, thy Beauty, from the
  squint
Of lust and glare of malice. Good
  night! good night!

    Rosamund. Father, I am so tender
  to all hardness!
Nay, father, first thy blessing.
    Becket.   Wedded?
    Rosamund.   Father!
    Becket. Well, well! I ask no more.
  Heaven bless thee! hence!
    Rosamund. O, holy father, when
  thou seest him next,
Commend me to thy friend.
    Becket.   What friend?
    Rosamund.   The King.
    Becket. Herbert, take out a score of
  armed men
To guard this bird of passage to her
  cage;
And watch Fitzurse, and if he follow
  thee,
Make him thy prisoner. I am Chan-
  cellor yet.

    [*Exeunt* Herbert *and* Rosamund.
Poor soul! poor soul!
My friend, the King! . . . O thou Great
  Seal of England,
Given me by my dear friend the King
  of England —
We long have wrought together, thou
  and I —
Now must I send thee as a common
  friend
To tell the King, my friend, I am
  against him.
We are friends no more: he will say
  that, not I.
The worldly bond between us is dis-
  solved,
Not yet the love: can I be under him
As Chancellor? as Archbishop over
  him?
Go therefore like a friend slighted by
  one
That hath climb'd up to nobler
  company.

Not slighted — all but moan'd for:
  thou must go.
I have not dishonor'd thee — I trust I
  have not;
Not mangled justice. May the hand
  that next
Inherits thee be but as true to thee
As mine hath been! O, my dear
  friend, the King!
O brother! — I may come to martyr-
  dom.
I am martyr in myself already. —
  Herbert!
    Herbert (re-entering). My lord, the
  town is quiet, and the moon
Divides the whole long street with
  light and shade.
No footfall — no Fitzurse. We have
  seen her home.
    Becket. The hog hath tumbled him-
  self into some corner,
Some ditch, to snore away his drunk-
  enness
Into the sober headache, — Nature's
  moral
Against excess. Let the Great Seal
  be sent
Back to the King to-morrow.
    Herbert.   Must that be?
The King may rend the bearer limb
  from limb.
Think on it again.
    Becket.   Against the moral excess
No physical ache, but failure it may
  be
Of all we aim'd at. John of Salisbury
Hath often laid a cold hand on my
  heats,
And Herbert hath rebuked me even
  now.
I will be wise and wary, not the
  soldier
As Foliot swears it. — John, and out
  of breath!

    Enter JOHN OF SALISBURY.

    John of Salisbury. Thomas, thou
  wast not happy taking charge
Of this wild Rosamund to please the
  King,
Nor am I happy having charge of
  her —

The included Danaë has escaped again
Her tower, and her Acrisius — where
    to seek ?
I have been about the city.

    Becket.   Thou wilt find her
Back in her lodging. Go with her —
    at once —
To-night — my men will guard you to
    the gates.
Be sweet to her, she has many ene-
    mies.
Send the Great Seal by daybreak.
    Both, good night !

SCENE II.

ELEANOR'S RETAINERS *and* BECKET'S
RETAINERS *fighting. Enter* ELEA-
NOR *and* BECKET *from opposite
streets.*

    Eleanor. Peace, fools !
    Becket. Peace, friends ! what idle
    brawl is this ?
    Retainer of Becket. They said — her
    Grace's people — thou wast
    found —
Liars ! I shame to quote 'em — caught,
    my lord,
With a wanton in thy lodging — Hell
    requite 'em !
    Retainer of Eleanor. My liege, the
    Lord Fitzurse reported this
In passing to the Castle even now.
    Retainer of Becket. And then they
    mock'd us and we fell upon
    'em,
For we would live and die for thee,
    my lord,
However kings and queens may frown
    on thee.
    Becket (*to his* Retainers). Go, go —
    no more of this !
    Eleanor (*to her* Retainers). Away ! —
    (*Exeunt* Retainers.) Fitz-
    urse——
    Becket. Nay, let him be.
    Eleanor.   No, no, my Lord Arch-
    bishop,

'Tis known you are midwinter to all
    women,
But often in your chancellorship you
    served
The follies of the King.
    Becket.   No, not these follies !
    Eleanor. My lord, Fitzurse beheld
    her in your lodging.
    Becket. Whom ?
    Eleanor. Well — you know — the
    minion, Rosamund.
    Becket. He had good eyes !
    Eleanor. Then hidden in the street
He watch'd her pass with John of
    Salisbury
And heard her cry " Where is this
    bower of mine ? "
    Becket. Good ears too !
    Eleanor.   You are going to the
    Castle,
Will you subscribe the customs ?
    Becket.   I leave that,
Knowing how much you reverence
    Holy Church,
My liege, to your conjecture.
    Eleanor.   I and mine —
And many a baron holds along with
    me —
Are not so much at feud with Holy
    Church
But we might take your side against
    the customs —
So that you grant me one slight favor.
    Becket.   What ?
    Eleanor. A sight of that same chart
    which Henry gave you
With the red line — " her bower."
    Becket.   And to what end ?
    Eleanor. That Church must scorn
    herself whose fearful Priest
Sits winking at the license of a king,
Altho' we grant when kings are dan-
    gerous
The Church must play into the hands
    of kings ;
Look ! I would move this wanton
    from his sight
And take the Church's danger on
    myself.
    Becket. For which she should be
    duly grateful.
    Eleanor.   True !

Tho' she that binds the bond, herself
    should see
That kings are faithful to their mar-
    riage vow.
  Becket. Ay, Madam, and queens
    also.
  Eleanor.   And queens also !
What is your drift ?
  Becket.   My drift is to the Castle,
Where I shall meet the Barons and
    my King.   [*Exit.*

DE BROC, DE TRACY, DE BRITO, DE
    MORVILLE (*passing*).

  Eleanor. To the Castle ?
  De Broc.   Ay !
  Eleanor.   Stir up the King, the
    Lords !
Set all on fire against him !
  De Brito.   Ay, good Madam !
               [*Exeunt.*
  Eleanor. Fool! I will make thee
    hateful to thy King.
Churl ! I will have thee frighted
    into France,
And I shall live to trample on thy
    grave.

SCENE III. — THE HALL IN NORTH-
    AMPTON CASTLE.

*On one side of the stage the doors of an
inner Council-chamber, half-open. At
the bottom, the great doors of the Hall.*
ROGER ARCHBISHOP OF YORK, FO-
LIOT BISHOP OF LONDON, HILARY
OF CHICHESTER, BISHOP OF HERE-
FORD, RICHARD DE HASTINGS
(*Grand Prior of Templars*), PHILIP
DE ELEEMOSYNA (*The Pope's Al-
moner*), *and others.* DE BROC,
FITZURSE, DE BRITO, DE MOR-
VILLE, DE TRACY, *and other
Barons assembled — a table before
them.* JOHN OF OXFORD, *President
of the Council.*

Enter BECKET *and* HERBERT OF
    BOSHAM.

  Becket. Where is the King ?
  Roger of York. Gone hawking on
    the Nene,

His heart so gall'd with thine ingrati-
    tude,
He will not see thy face till thou hast
    sign'd
These ancient laws and customs of
    the realm.
Thy sending back the Great Seal
    madden'd him,
He all but pluck'd the bearer's eyes
    away.
Take heed, lest he destroy thee ut-
    terly.
  Becket. Then shalt thou step into
    my place and sign.
  Roger of York. Didst thou not
    promise Henry to obey
These ancient laws and customs of
    the realm ?
  Becket. Saving the honor of my
    order — ay.
Customs, traditions, — clouds that
    come and go ;
The customs of the Church are Peter's
    rock.
  Roger of York. Saving thine order !
    But King Henry sware
That, saving his King's kingship, he
    would grant thee
The crown itself. Saving thine order,
    Thomas,
Is black and white at once, and comes
    to nought.
O bolster'd up with stubbornness and
    pride,
Wilt thou destroy the Church in fight-
    ing for it,
And bring us all to shame ?
  Becket.   Roger of York,
When I and thou were youths in
    Theobald's house,
Twice did thy malice and thy calum-
    nies
Exile me from the face of Theo-
    bald.
Now I am Canterbury and thou art
    York.
  Roger of York. And is not York the
    peer of Canterbury ?
Did not Great Gregory bid St. Austin
    here
Found two archbishopricks, London
    and York ?

Becket. What came of that ? The first archbishop fled,
And York lay barren for a hundred years.
Why, by this rule, Foliot may claim the pall
For London too.
    Foliot. And with good reason too,
For London had a temple and a priest
When Canterbury hardly bore a name.
    Becket. The pagan temple of a pagan Rome !
The heathen priesthood of a heathen creed !
Thou goest beyond thyself in petulancy !
Who made thee London ? Who, but Canterbury ?
    John of Oxford. Peace, peace, my lords ! these customs are no longer
As Canterbury calls them, wandering clouds,
But by the King's command are written down,
And by the King's command I, John of Oxford,
The President of this Council, read them.
    Becket.   Read !
    John of Oxford (reads). "All causes of advowsons and presentations, whether between laymen or clerics, shall be tried in the King's court."
    Becket. But that I cannot sign : for that would drag
The cleric before the civil judgment-seat,
And on a matter wholly spiritual.
    John of Oxford. "If any cleric be accused of felony, the Church shall not protect him ; but he shall answer to the summons of the King's court to be tried therein."
    Becket. And that I cannot sign.
Is not the Church the visible Lord on earth ?
Shall hands that do create the Lord be bound
Behind the back like laymen-criminals ?

The Lord be judged again by Pilate ? No !
    John of Oxford. "When a bishoprick falls vacant, the King, till another be appointed, shall receive the revenues thereof."
    Becket. And that I cannot sign. Is the King's treasury
A fit place for the monies of the Church,
That be the patrimony of the poor ?
    John of Oxford. "And when the vacancy is to be filled up, the King shall summon the chapter of that church to court, and the election shall be made in the Chapel Royal, with the consent of our lord the King, and by the advice of his Government."
    Becket. And that I cannot sign : for that would make
Our island-Church a schism from Christendom,
And weight down all free choice beneath the throne.
    Foliot. And was thine own election so canonical,
Good father ?
    Becket. If it were not, Gilbert Foliot,
I mean to cross the sea to France, and lay
My crozier in the Holy Father's hands,
And bid him re-create me, Gilbert Foliot.
    Foliot. Nay ; by another of these customs thou
Wilt not be suffer'd so to cross the seas
Without the license of our lord the King.
    Becket. That, too, I cannot sign.

DE BROC, DE BRITO, DE TRACY, FITZURSE, DE MORVILLE, *start up — a clash of swords.*

              Sign and obey !

    Becket. My lords, is this a combat or a council ?
Are ye my masters, or my lord the King ?

Ye make this clashing for no love o'
   the customs
Or constitutions, or whate'er ye call
   them,
But that there be among you those
   that hold
Lands reft from Canterbury.
   De Broc. And mean to keep them,
In spite of thee!
     Lords (shouting). Sign, and obey the
     crown!
   Becket. The crown? Shall I do less
   for Canterbury
Than Henry for the crown? King
   Stephen gave
Many of the crown lands to those that
   helpt him;
So did Matilda, the King's mother.
   Mark,
When Henry came into his own
   again,
Then he took back not only Stephen's
   gifts,
But his own mother's, lest the crown
   should be
Shorn of ancestral splendor. This
   did Henry.
Shall I do less for mine own Canter-
   bury?
And thou, De Broc, that holdest Salt-
   wood Castle——
   De Broc. And mean to hold it,
   or——
   Becket. To have my life.
   De Broc. The King is quick to
   anger; if thou anger him,
We wait but the King's word to strike
   thee dead.
   Becket. Strike, and I die the death
   of martyrdom;
Strike, and ye set these customs by
   my death
Ringing their own death-knell thro'
   all the realm.
   Herbert. And I can tell you, lords,
   ye are all as like
To lodge a fear in Thomas Becket's
   heart
As find a hare's form in a lion's cave.
   John of Oxford. Ay, sheathe your
   swords, ye will displease the
   King.

   De Broc. Why down then thou!
   but an he come to Saltwood,
By God's death, thou shalt stick him
   like a calf! [*Sheathing his sword.*
   Hilary. O my good lord, I do en-
   treat thee — sign.
Save the King's honor here before his
   barons.
He hath sworn that thou shouldst
   sign, and now but shuns
The semblance of defeat; I have
   heard him say
He means no more; so if thou sign,
   my lord,
That were but as the shadow of an
   assent.
   Becket. 'Twould seem too like the
   substance, if I sign'd.
   Philip de Eleemosyna. My lord, thine
   ear! I have the ear of the Pope.
As thou hast honor for the Pope our
   master,
Have pity on him, sorely prest upon
By the fierce Emperor and his Anti-
   pope.
Thou knowest he was forced to fly to
   France;
He pray'd me to pray thee to pacify
Thy King; for if thou go against thy
   King,
Then must he likewise go against thy
   King,
And then thy King might join the
   Antipope,
And that would shake the Papacy as
   it stands.
Besides, thy King swore to our car-
   dinals
He meant no harm nor damage to the
   Church.
Smoothe thou his pride — thy signing
   is but form;
Nay, and should harm come of it it
   is the Pope
Will be to blame — not thou. Over
   and over
He told me thou shouldst pacify the
   King,
Lest there be battle between Heaven
   and Earth,
And Earth should get the better —
   for the time.

Cannot the Pope absolve thee if thou
  sign?
 Becket. Have I the orders of the
  Holy Father?
 Philip de Eleemosyna. Orders, my
  lord — why, no; for what am I?
The secret whisper of the Holy
  Father.
Thou, that hast been a statesman,
  couldst thou always
Blurt thy free mind to the air?
 Becket. If Rome be feeble, then
  should I be firm.
 Philip. Take it not that way —
  balk not the Pope's will.
When he hath shaken off the Em-
  peror,
He heads the Church against the King
  with thee.
 Richard de Hastings (kneeling).
  Becket, I am the oldest of the
  Templars;
I knew thy father; he would be mine
  age
Had he lived now; think of me as
  thy father!
Behold thy father kneeling to thee,
  Becket.
Submit; I promise thee on my salva-
  tion
That thou wilt hear no more o' the
  customs.
 Becket.   What!
Hath Henry told thee? hast thou
  talk'd with him?
 Another Templar (kneeling). Father,
  I am the youngest of the Tem-
  plars,
Look on me as I were thy bodily son,
For, like a son, I lift my hands to
  thee.
 Philip. Wilt thou hold out for ever,
  Thomas Becket?
Dost thou not hear?
 Becket (signs). Why — there then
  — there — I sign,
And swear to obey the customs.
 Foliot.   Is it thy will,
My lord Archbishop, that we too
  should sign?
 Becket. O ay, by that canonical
  obedience

Thou still hast owed thy father, Gil-
  bert Foliot.
 Foliot. Loyally and with good faith,
  my lord Archbishop?
 Becket. O ay, with all that loyalty
  and good faith
Thou still hast shown thy primate,
  Gilbert Foliot.
  [*Becket draws apart with* Herbert.
Herbert, Herbert, have I betray'd the
  Church?
I'll have the paper back — blot out
  my name.
 Herbert. Too late, my lord: you see
  they are signing there.
 Becket. False to myself — it is the
  will of God
To break me, prove me nothing of
  myself!
This Almoner hath tasted Henry's
  gold.
The cardinals have finger'd Henry's
  gold.
And Rome is venal ev'n to rotten-
  ness.
I see it, I see it.
I am no soldier, as he said — at least
No leader. Herbert, till I hear from
  the Pope
I will suspend myself from all my func-
  tions.
If fast and prayer, the lacerating
  scourge ——
 Foliot (from the table). My lord
  Archbishop, thou hast yet to
  seal.
 Becket. First, Foliot, let me see
  what I have sign'd.
        [*Goes to the table.*
What, this! and this! — what! new
  and old together!
Seal? If a seraph shouted from the
  sun,
And bade me seal against the rights of
  the Church,
I would anathematize him. I will
  not seal. [*Exit with* Herbert.

     Enter KING HENRY.

 Henry. Where's Thomas? hath he
  sign'd? show me the papers!
Sign'd and not seal'd! How's that?

John of Oxford. He would not seal.
And when he sign'd, his face was
    stormy-red —
Shame, wrath, I know not what. He
    sat down there
And dropt it in his hands, and then a
    paleness,
Like the wan twilight after sunset,
    crept
Up even to the tonsure, and he
    groan'd,
" False to myself ! It is the will of
    God ! "
    Henry. God's will be what it will,
    the man shall seal,
Or I will seal his doom. My burgher's
    son —
Nay, if I cannot break him as the
    prelate,
I'll crush him as the subject. Send
    for him back.
    [*Sits on his throne.*
Barons and bishops of our realm of
    England,
After the nineteen winters of King
    Stephen —
A reign which was no reign, when none
    could sit
By his own hearth in peace ; when
    murder common
As nature's death, like Egypt's plague,
    had fill'd
All things with blood ; when every
    doorway blush'd,
Dash'd red with that unhallow'd pass-
    over ;
When every baron ground his blade
    in blood ;
The household dough was kneaded up
    with blood ;
The millwheel turn'd in blood ; the
    wholesome plow
Lay rusting in the furrow's yellow
    weeds,
Till famine dwarft the race — I came,
    your King !
Nor dwelt alone, like a soft lord of
    the East,
In mine own hall, and sucking thro'
    fools' ears
The flatteries of corruption — went
    abroad

Thro' all my counties, spied my peo-
    ple's ways ;
Yea, heard the churl against the baron
    — yea,
And did him justice ; sat in mine own
    courts
Judging my judges, that had found a
    King
Who ranged confusions, made the
    twilight day,
And struck a shape from out the
    vague, and law
From madness. And the event — our
    fallows till'd,
Much corn, repeopled towns, a realm
    again.
So far my course, albeit not glassy-
    smooth,
Had prosper'd in the main, but sud-
    denly
Jarr'd on this rock. A cleric violated
The daughter of his host, and mur-
    der'd him.
Bishops — York, London, Chichester,
    Westminster —
Ye haled this tonsured devil into your
    courts ;
But since your canon will not let you
    take
Life for a life, ye but degraded him
Where I had hang'd him. What doth
    hard murder care
For degradation ? and that made me
    muse,
Being bounden by my coronation oath
To do men justice. Look to it, your
    own selves !
Say that a cleric murder'd an arch-
    bishop,
What could ye do ? Degrade, imprison
    him —
Not death for death.
    John of Oxford. But I, my liege,
    could swear,
To death for death.
    Henry. And, looking thro' my reign,
I found a hundred ghastly murders
    done
By men, the scum and offal of the
    Church ;
Then, glancing thro' the story of this
    realm,

I came on certain wholesome usages,
Lost in desuetude, of my grandsire's
day,
Good royal customs — had them writ-
ten fair
For John of Oxford here to read to
you.
  John of Oxford. And I can easily
    swear to these as being
The King's will and God's will and
justice; yet
I could but read a part to-day, be-
cause ——
  Fitzurse. Because my lord of Can-
    terbury ——
  De Tracy.   Ay,
This lord of Canterbury ——
  De Brito.   As is his wont
Too much of late whene'er your royal
rights
Are mooted in our councils ——
  Fitzurse.   — made an uproar.
  Henry. And Becket had my bosom
on all this;
If ever man by bonds of grateful-
ness —
I raised him from the puddle of the
gutter,
I made him porcelain from the clay
of the city —
Thought that I knew him, err'd thro'
love of him,
Hoped, were he chosen archbishop,
Church and Crown,
Two sisters gliding in an equal
dance,
Two rivers gently flowing side by
side —
But no!
The bird that moults sings the same
song again,
The snake that sloughs comes out a
snake again.
Snake — ay, but he that lookt a fang-
less one,
Issues a venomous adder.
For he, when having dofft the Chan-
cellor's robe —
Flung the Great Seal of England in
my face —
Claim'd some of our crown lands for
Canterbury —

My comrade, boon companion, my co-
reveller,
The master of his master, the King's
king. —
God's eyes! I had meant to make him
all but king.
Chancellor-Archbishop, he might well
have sway'd
All England under Henry, the young
King,
When I was hence. What did the
traitor say?
False to himself, but ten-fold false to
me!
The will of God — why, then it is my
will —
Is he coming?
  Messenger (*entering*). With a crowd
    of worshippers,
And holds his cross before him thro'
the crowd,
As one that puts himself in sanctuary.
  Henry. His cross!
  Roger of York. His cross! I'll front
    him, cross to cross.
                    [*Exit* Roger of York.
  Henry. His cross! it is the traitor
that imputes
Treachery to his King!
It is not safe for me to look upon
him.
Away — with me!
    [*Goes in with his* Barons *to the
    Council Chamber, the door of
    which is left open.*

Enter BECKET, *holding his cross of silver
before him. The* BISHOPS *come round
him.*

  Hereford. The King will not abide
thee with thy cross.
Permit me, my good lord, to bear it
for thee,
Being thy chaplain.
  Becket. No: it must protect me.
  Herbert. As once he bore the stand-
ard of the Angles,
So now he bears the standard of the
angels.
  Foliot. I am the Dean of the prov-
ince: let me bear it.

Make not thy King a traitorous murderer.

Becket. Did not your barons draw their swords against me ?

Enter ROGER OF YORK, *with his cross, advancing to* BECKET.

Becket. Wherefore dost thou presume to bear thy cross,
Against the solemn ordinance from Rome,
Out of thy province ?

Roger of York. Why dost thou presume,
Arm'd with thy cross, to come before the King ?
If Canterbury bring his cross to court,
Let York bear his to mate with Canterbury.

Foliot (seizing hold of Becket's *cross).*
Nay, nay, my lord, thou must not brave the King.

Nay, let me have it. I will have it !

Becket. Away ! [*Flinging him off.*

Foliot. He fasts, they say, this mitred Hercules !

He fast ! is that an arm of fast ? My lord,
Hadst thou not sign'd, I had gone along with thee ;
But thou the shepherd hast betray'd the sheep,
And thou art perjured, and thou wilt not seal.
As Chancellor thou wast against the Church,
Now as Archbishop goest against the King ;
For, like a fool, thou knowst no middle way.
Ay, ay ! but art thou stronger than the King ?

Becket. Strong — not in mine own self, but Heaven ; true
To either function, holding it ; and thou
Fast, scourge thyself, and mortify thy flesh,
Not spirit — thou remainest Gilbert Foliot,
A worldly follower of the worldly strong.

I, bearing this great ensign, make it clear
Under what Prince I fight.

Foliot. My lord of York,
Let us go in to the Council, where our bishops
And our great lords will sit in judgment on him.

Becket. Sons sit in judgment on their father ! — then
The spire of the Holy Church may prick the graves —
Her crypt among the stars. Sign ? seal ? I promised
The King to obey these customs, not yet written,
Saving mine order ; true too, that when written
I sign'd them — being a fool, as Foliot call'd me.
I hold not by my signing. Get ye hence,
Tell what I say to the King.
[*Exeunt* Hereford, Foliot, *and other* Bishops.

Roger of York. The Church will hate thee. [*Exit.*

Becket. Serve my best friend and make him my worst foe ;
Fight for the Church, and set the Church against me !

Herbert. To be honest is to set all knaves against thee.

Ah ! Thomas, excommunicate them all !

Hereford (re-entering). I cannot brook the turmoil thou hast raised.
I would, my lord Thomas of Canterbury,
Thou wert plain Thomas and not Canterbury,
Or that thou wouldst deliver Canterbury
To our King's hands again, and be at peace.

Hilary (re-entering). For hath not thine ambition set the Church
This day between the hammer and the anvil —
Fealty to the King, obedience to thyself ?

Herbert. What say the bishops?

Hilary. Some have pleaded for him,
But the King rages — most are with
 the King;
And some are reeds, that one time
 sway to the current,
And to the wind another. But we hold
Thou art forsworn; and no forsworn
  Archbishop
Shall helm the Church. We therefore
 place ourselves
Under the shield and safeguard of the
 Pope,
And cite thee to appear before the
 Pope,
And answer thine accusers. . . . Art
 thou deaf?

Becket. I hear you. [*Clash of arms.*

Hilary.   Dost thou hear
 those others?

Becket. Ay!

Roger of York (*re-entering*). The
 King's "God's eyes!" come now
 so thick and fast,
We fear that he may reave thee of
 thine own.
Come on, come on! it is not fit for us
To see the proud Archbishop muti-
 lated.
Say that he blind thee and tear out
 thy tongue.

Becket. So be it. He begins at top
 with me;
They crucified St. Peter downward.

Roger of York.   Nay,
But for their sake who stagger betwixt
 thine
Appeal, and Henry's anger, yield.

Becket.   Hence, Satan!
    [*Exit* Roger of York.

Fitzurse (*re-entering*). My lord, the
 King demands three hundred
 marks,
Due from his castles of Berkham-
 stead and Eye
When thou thereof wast warden.

Becket.   Tell the King
I spent thrice that in fortifying his
 castles.

De Tracy (*re-entering*). My lord,
 the King demands seven hundred marks,

Lent at the siege of Thoulouse by the
 King.

Becket. I led seven hundred knights
 and fought his wars.

De Brito (*re-entering*). My lord, the
 King demands five hundred
 marks,
Advanced thee at his instance by the
 Jews,
For which the King was bound secu-
 rity.

Becket. I thought it was a gift; I
 thought it was a gift.

Enter LORD LEICESTER (*followed by*
 Barons *and* Bishops).

Lord Leicester. My lord, I come
 unwillingly. The King
Demands a strict account of all those
 revenues
From all the vacant sees and abbacies,
Which came into thy hands when
 Chancellor.

Becket. How much might that
 amount to, my lord Leicester?

Leicester. Some thirty — forty thousand silver marks.

Becket. Are these your customs? O
 my good lord Leicester,
The King and I were brothers. All I
 had
I lavish'd for the glory of the
 King;
I shone from him, for him, his glory,
 his
Reflection: now the glory of the
 Church
Hath swallow'd up the glory of the
 King;
I am his no more, but hers. Grant
 me one day
To ponder these demands.

Leicester. Hear first thy sentence!
The King and all his lords ——

Becket. Son, first hear *me*!

Leicester. Nay, nay, canst thou, that
 holdest thine estates
In fee and barony of the King, decline
The judgment of the King?

Becket. The King! I hold
Nothing in fee and barony of the
 King.

Whatever the Church owns — she
  holds it in
Free and perpetual alms, unsubject to
One earthly sceptre.
    Leicester.   Nay, but hear
      thy judgment.
The King and all his barons ——
    Becket.   Judgment! Barons!
Who but the bridegroom dares to
      judge the bride,
Or he the bridegroom may appoint?
      Not he
That is not of the house, but from the
      street
Stain'd with the mire thereof.
              I had been so true
To Henry and mine office that the
      King
Would throne me in the great Arch-
      bishoprick:
And I, that knew mine own infirmity,
For the King's pleasure rather than
      God's cause
Took it upon me — err'd thro' love of
      him.
Now therefore God from me withdraws
      Himself,
And the King too.
What! forty thousand marks!
Why thou, the King, the Pope, the
      Saints, the world,
Know that when made Archbishop I
      was freed,
Before the Prince and chief Justiciary,
From every bond and debt and obli-
      gation
Incurr'd as Chancellor.
              Hear me, son.
              As gold
Outvalues dross, light darkness, Abel
      Cain,
The soul the body, and the Church
      the Throne,
I charge thee, upon pain of mine
      anathema,
That thou obey, not me, but God in
      me,
Rather than Henry. I refuse to stand
By the King's censure, make my cry
      to the Pope,
By whom I will be judged; refer my-
      self,

The King, these customs, all the
      Church, to him,
And under his authority — I depart.
              [*Going.*
      [*Leicester looks at him doubtingly.*
Am I a prisoner?
    Leicester.   By St. Lazarus, no!
I am confounded by thee. Go in
      peace.
De Broc. In peace now — but after.
Take that for earnest.
    [*Flings a bone at him from the rushes.*

DE BRITO, FITZURSE, DE TRACY *and
    others* (*flinging wisps of rushes*).

Ay, go in peace, caitiff, caitiff! And
that too, perjured prelate — and that,
turncoat shaveling! There, there,
there! traitor, traitor, traitor!
    Becket. Mannerless wolves!
              [*Turning and facing them.*
    Herbert. Enough, my lord, enough!
    Becket. Barons of England and of
      Normandy,
When what ye shake at doth but
      seem to fly,
True test of coward, ye follow with
      a yell.
But I that threw the mightiest knight
      of France,
Sir Engelram de Trie, ——
    Herbert.   Enough, my lord.
    Becket. More than enough. I play
      the fool again.

Enter HERALD.

    Herald. The King commands you,
      upon pain of death,
That none should wrong or injure
      your Archbishop.
    Foliot. Deal gently with the young
      man Absalom.
    [*Great doors of the Hall at the back
      open, and discover a crowd.*
    They shout: Blessed is he that
      cometh in the name of the
      Lord!

SCENE IV. — Refectory of the Monastery at Northampton. A Banquet on the Tables.

Enter Becket. Becket's Retainers.

First Retainer. Do thou speak first.

Second Retainer. Nay, thou! Nay, thou! Hast not thou drawn the short straw ?

First Retainer. My lord Archbishop, wilt thou permit us——

Becket. To speak without stammering and like a free man ? Ay.

First Retainer. My lord, permit us then to leave thy service.

Becket. When ?

First Retainer. Now.

Becket. To-night ?

First Retainer. To-night, my lord.

Becket. And why ?

First Retainer. My lord, we leave thee not without tears.

Becket. Tears ? Why not stay with me then ?

First Retainer. My lord, we cannot yield thee an answer altogether to thy satisfaction.

Becket. I warrant you, or your own either. Shall I find you one ? The King hath frowned upon me.

First Retainer. That is not altogether our answer, my lord.

Becket. No; yet all but all. Go, go ! Ye have eaten of my dish and drunken of my cup for a dozen years.

First Retainer. And so we have. We mean thee no wrong. Wilt thou not say, " God bless you," ere we go ?

Becket. God bless you all ! God redden your pale blood! But mine is human-red ; and when ye shall hear it is poured out upon earth, and see it mounting to Heaven, may God bless you, that seems sweet to you now, will blast and blind you like a curse.

First Retainer. We hope not, my lord. Our humblest thanks for your blessing. Farewell!

[*Exeunt* Retainers.

Becket. Farewell, friends ! farewell, swallows ! I wrong the bird; she leaves only the nest she built, they leave the builder. Why ? Am I to be murdered to-night ?

[*Knocking at the door.*

Attendant. Here is a missive left at the gate by one from the castle.

Becket. Cornwall's hand or Leicester's : they write marvellously alike.

[*Reading.*

" Fly at once to France, to King Louis of France : there be those about our King who would have thy blood."

Was not my lord of Leicester bidden to our supper ?

Attendant. Ay, my lord, and divers other earls and barons. But the hour is past, and our brother, Master Cook, he makes moan that all be a-getting cold.

Becket. And I make my moan along with him. Cold after warm, winter after summer, and the golden leaves, these earls and barons, that clung to me, frosted off me by the first cold frown of the King. Cold, but look how the table steams, like a heathen altar ; nay, like the altar at Jerusalem. Shall God's good gifts be wasted ? None of them here ! Call in the poor from the streets, and let them feast.

Herbert. That is the parable of our blessed Lord.

Becket. And why should not the parable of our blessed Lord be acted again ? Call in the poor ! The Church is ever at variance with the kings, and ever at one with the poor. I marked a group of lazars in the market-place — half-rag, half-sore — beggars, poor rogues (Heaven bless 'em) who never saw or dreamed of such a banquet. I will amaze them. Call them in, I say. They shall henceforward be my earls and barons — our lords and masters in Christ Jesus. [*Exit* Herbert.

If the King hold his purpose, I am myself a beggar. Forty thousand marks ! forty thousand devils — and these craven bishops !

A Poor Man (entering) with his dog. My lord Archbishop, may I come in with my poor friend, my dog ? The

King's verdurer caught him a-hunting in the forest, and cut off his paws. The dog followed his calling, my lord. I ha' carried him ever so many miles in my arms, and he licks my face and moans and cries out against the King.

Becket. Better thy dog than thee. The King's courts would use thee worse than thy dog — they are too bloody. Were the Church king, it would be otherwise. Poor beast! poor beast! set him down. I will bind up his wounds with my napkin. Give him a bone, give him a bone! Who misuses a dog would misuse a child — they cannot speak for themselves. Past help! his paws are past help. God help him!

Enter the BEGGARS *(and seat themselves at the Tables)*. BECKET *and* HERBERT *wait upon them.*

First Beggar. Swine, sheep, ox — here's a French supper. When thieves fall out, honest men ——

Second Beggar. Is the Archbishop a thief who gives thee thy supper?

First Beggar. Well, then, how does it go? When honest men fall out, thieves — no, it can't be that.

Second Beggar. Who stole the widow's one sitting hen o' Sunday, when she was at mass?

First Beggar. Come, come! thou hadst thy share on her. Sitting hen! Our Lord Becket's our great sitting-hen cock, and we shouldn't ha' been sitting here if the barons and bishops hadn't been a-sitting on the Archbishop.

Becket. Ay, the princes sat in judgment against me, and the Lord hath prepared your table — *Sederunt principes, ederunt pauperes.*

A Voice. Becket, beware of the knife!

Becket. Who spoke?

Third Beggar. Nobody, my lord. What's that, my lord?

Becket. Venison.

Third Beggar. Venison?

Becket. Buck; deer, as you call it.

Third Beggar. King's meat! By the Lord, won't we pray for your lordship!

Becket. And, my children, your prayers will do more for me in the day of peril that dawns darkly and drearily over the house of God — yea, and in the day of judgment also, than the swords of the craven sycophants would have done had they remained true to me whose bread they have partaken. I must leave you to your banquet. Feed, feast, and be merry. Herbert, for the sake of the Church itself, if not for my own, I must fly to France to-night. Come with me.

[*Exit with* Herbert.

Third Beggar. Here — all of you — my lord's health (*they drink*). Well — if that isn't goodly wine ——

First Beggar. Then there isn't a goodly wench to serve him with it: they were fighting for her to-day in the street.

Third Beggar. Peace!

First Beggar. The black sheep baaed to the miller's ewe-lamb,
The miller's away for to-night.
Black sheep, quoth she, too black a sin for me.
And what said the black sheep, my masters?
We can make a black sin white.

Third Beggar. Peace!

First Beggar. "Ewe lamb, ewe lamb, I am here by the dam."
But the miller came home that night,
And so dusted his back with the meal in his sack,
That he made the black sheep white.

Third Beggar. Be we not of the family? be we not a-supping with the head of the family? be we not in my lord's own refractory? Out from among us; thou art our black sheep.

Enter the four KNIGHTS.

Fitzurse. Sheep, said he? And sheep without the shepherd, too. Where is my lord Archbishop? Thou the lustiest and lousiest of this Cain's brotherhood, answer.

Third Beggar. With Cain's answer, my lord. Am I his keeper? Thou shouldst call him Cain, not me.

Fitzurse. So I do, for he would murder his brother the State.

Third Beggar (rising and advancing). No, my lord; but because the Lord hath set his mark upon him that no man should murder him.

Fitzurse. Where is he? where is he?

Third Beggar. With Cain belike, in the land of Nod, or in the land of France for aught I know.

Fitzurse. France! Ha! De Morville, Tracy, Brito — fled is he? Cross swords all of you! swear to follow him! Remember the Queen!

[*The four* Knights *cross their swords.*

De Brito. They mock us; he is here.

[*All the* Beggars *rise and advance upon them.*

Fitzurse. Come, you filthy knaves, let us pass.

Third Beggar. Nay, my lord, let *us* pass. We be a-going home after our supper in all humbleness, my lord; for the Archbishop loves humbleness, my lord; and though we be fifty to four, we daren't fight you with our crutches, my lord. There now, if thou hast not laid hands upon me! and my fellows know that I am all one scale like a fish. I pray God I haven't given thee my leprosy, my lord.

[*Fitzurse shrinks from him and another presses upon* De Brito.

De Brito. Away, dog!

Fourth Beggar. And I was bit by a mad dog o' Friday, an' I be half dog already by this token, that tho' I can drink wine I cannot bide water, my lord; and I want to bite, I want to bite, and they do say the very breath catches.

De Brito. Insolent clown. Shall I smite him with the edge of the sword?

De Morville. No, nor with the flat of it either. Smite the shepherd and the sheep are scattered. Smite the sheep and the shepherd will excommunicate thee.

De Brito. Yet my fingers itch to beat him into nothing.

Fifth Beggar. So do mine, my lord. I was born with it, and sulphur won't bring it out o' me. But for all that the Archbishop washed my feet o' Tuesday. He likes it, my lord.

Sixth Beggar. And see here, my lord, this rag fro' the gangrene i' my leg. It's humbling — it smells o' human natur'. Wilt thou smell it, my lord? for the Archbishop likes the smell on it, my lord; for I be his lord and master i' Christ, my lord.

De Morville. Faugh! we shall all be poisoned. Let us go.

[*They draw back,* Beggars *following.*

Seventh Beggar. My lord, I ha' three sisters a-dying at home o' the sweating sickness. They be dead while I be a-supping.

Eighth Beggar. And I ha' nine darters i' the spital that be dead ten times o'er i' one day wi' the putrid fever; and I bring the taint on it along wi' me, for the Archbishop likes it, my lord.

[*Pressing upon the* Knights *till they disappear thro' the door.*

Third Beggar. Crutches, and itches, and leprosies, and ulcers, and gangrenes, and running sores, praise ye the Lord, for to-night ye have saved our Archbishop!

First Beggar. I'll go back again. I hain't half done yet.

Herbert of Bosham (entering). My friends, the Archbishop bids you goodnight. He hath retired to rest, and being in great jeopardy of his life, he hath made his bed between the altars, from whence he sends me to bid you this night pray for him who hath fed you in the wilderness.

Third Beggar. So we will — so we will, I warrant thee. Becket shall be king and the Holy Father shall be king, and the world shall live by the King's venison and the bread o' the Lord, and there shall be no more poor for ever. Hurrah! Vive le roy! That's the English of it.

ACT II.

SCENE I. — ROSAMUND'S BOWER. A GARDEN OF FLOWERS. IN THE MIDST A BANK OF WILD-FLOWERS WITH A BENCH BEFORE IT.

Voices heard singing among the trees.

DUET.

1. Is it the wind of the dawn that I hear in the pine overhead ?
2. No ; but the voice of the deep as it hollows the cliffs of the land.
1. Is there a voice coming up with the voice of the deep from the strand,

One coming up with a song in the flush of the glimmering red ?
2. Love that is born of the deep coming up with the sun from the sea.
1. Love that can shape or can shatter a life till the life shall have fled?
2. Nay, let us welcome him, Love that can lift up a life from the dead.
1. Keep him away from the lone little isle. Let us be, let us be.
2. Nay, let him make it his own, let him reign in it — he, it is he,

Love that is born of the deep coming up with the sun from the sea.

Enter HENRY *and* ROSAMUND.

Rosamund. Be friends with him again — I do beseech thee.
Henry. With Becket ? I have but one hour with thee —
Sceptre and crozier clashing, and the mitre
Grappling the crown — and when I flee from this
For a gasp of freer air, a breathing-while
To rest upon thy bosom and forget him —
Why thou, my bird, thou pipest Becket, Becket —
Yea, thou my golden dream of Love's own bower,

Must be the nightmare breaking on my peace
With " Becket."
Rosamund. O my life's life, not to smile
Is all but death to me. My sun, no cloud !
Let there not be one frown in this one hour.
Out of the many thine, let this be mine !
Look rather thou all-royal as when first
I met thee.
Henry. Where was that ?
Rosamund. Forgetting that
Forgets me too.
Henry. Nay, I remember it well.
There on the moors.
Rosamund. And in a narrow path.
A plover flew before thee. Then I saw
Thy high black steed among the flaming furze,
Like sudden night in the main glare of day.
And from that height something was said to me
I knew not what.
Henry. I ask'd the way.
Rosamund. I think so.
So I lost mine.
Henry. Thou wast too shamed to answer.
Rosamund. Too scared — so young !
Henry. The rosebud of my rose ! —
Well, well, no more of *him* — I have sent his folk,
His kin, all his belongings, overseas ;
Age, orphans, and babe-breasting mothers — all
By hundreds to him — there to beg, starve, die —
So that the fool King Louis feed them not.
The man shall feel that I can strike him yet.
Rosamund. Babes, orphans, mothers ! is that royal, Sire ?
Henry. And I have been as royal with the Church.
He shelter'd in the Abbey of Pontigny.

There wore his time studying the canon law
To work it against me. But since he cursed
My friends at Veselay, I have let them know,
That if they keep him longer as their guest,
I scatter all their cowls to all the hells.

Rosamund. And is that altogether royal ?

Henry. Traitress !

Rosamund. A faithful traitress to thy royal fame.

Henry. Fame ! what care I for fame ? Spite, ignorance, envy,
Yea, honesty too, paint her what way they will.
Fame of to-day is infamy to-morrow ;
Infamy of to-day is fame to-morrow ;
And round and round again. What matters ? Royal —
I mean to leave the royalty of my crown
Unlessen'd to mine heirs.

Rosamund. Still — thy fame too :
I say that should be royal.

Henry. And I say,
I care not for thy saying.

Rosamund. And I say,
I care not for *thy* saying. A greater King
Than thou art, Love, who cares not for the word,
Makes " care not " — care. There have I spoken true ?

Henry. Care dwell with me for ever, when I cease
To care for thee as ever !

Rosamund. No need ! no need ! . . .
There is a bench. Come, wilt thou sit ? . . . My bank
Of wild-flowers. [*He sits.*] At thy feet !
[*She sits at his feet.*

Henry. I bade them clear
A royal pleasaunce for thee, in the wood,
Not leave these countryfolk at court.

Rosamund. I brought them
In from the wood, and set them here. I love them

More than the garden flowers, that seem at most
Sweet guests, or foreign cousins, not half speaking
The language of the land. I love *them* too,
Yes. But, my liege, I am sure, of all the roses —
Shame fall on those who gave it a dog's name —
This wild one (*picking a briar-rose*) — nay, I shall not prick myself —
Is sweetest. Do but smell !

Henry. Thou rose of the world !
Thou rose of all the roses !
[*Muttering.*
I am not worthy of her — this beast-body
That God has plunged my soul in — I, that taking
The Fiend's advantage of a throne, so long
Have wander'd among women, — a foul stream
Thro' fever-breeding levels, — at her side,
Among these happy dales, run clearer, drop
The mud I carried, like yon brook, and glass
The faithful face of heaven —
[*Looking at her and unconsciously aloud.*
— Thine ! thine !

Rosamund. I know it.

Henry (*muttering*). Not hers. We have but one bond, her hate of Becket.

Rosamund (*half hearing*). Nay ! nay ! what art thou muttering ? *I* hate Becket ?

Henry (*muttering*). A sane and natural loathing for a soul
Purer, and truer and nobler than herself ;
And mine a bitterer illegitimate hate,
A bastard hate born of a former love.

Rosamund. My fault to name him !
O let the hand of one
To whom thy voice is all her music, stay it
But for a breath.
[*Puts her hand before his lips.*

Speak only of thy love.
Why there — like some loud beggar
    at thy gate —
The happy boldness of this hand hath
    won it
Love's alms, thy kiss (*looking at her
    hand*) — Sacred! I'll kiss it
    too.   [*Kissing it.*
There! wherefore dost thou so peruse
    it? Nay,
There may be crosses in my line of
    life.
    Henry. Not half *her* hand — no hand
    to mate with *her,*
If it should come to that.
    Rosamund. With her? with whom?
    Henry. Life on the hand is naked
    gipsy-stuff;
Life on the face, the brows — clear
    innocence!
Vein'd marble — not a furrow yet —
    and hers   [*Muttering.*
Crost and recrost, a venomous spider's
    web ——
    Rosamund (*springing up*). Out of the
    cloud, my Sun — out of the
    eclipse
Narrowing my golden hour!
    Henry.   O Rosamund,
I would be true — would tell thee all
    — and something
I had to say — I love thee none the
    less —
Which will so vex thee.
    Rosamund. Something against *me?*
    Henry. No, no, against myself.
    Rosamund. I will not hear it.
Come, come, mine hour! I bargain
    for mine hour.
I'll call thee little Geoffrey.
    Henry.   Call him!
    Rosamund.   Geoffrey!

    Enter GEOFFREY.

    Henry. How the boy grows!
    Rosamund. Ay, and his brows are
    thine;
The mouth is only Clifford, my dear
    father.
    Geoffrey. My liege, what hast thou
    brought me?
    Henry.   Venal imp!

What say'st thou to the Chancellor-
    ship of England?
    Geoffrey. O yes, my liege.
    Henry. "O yes, my liege!" He
    speaks
As if it were a cake of gingerbread.
Dost thou know, my boy, what it is
to be Chancellor of England?
    Geoffrey. Something good, or thou
wouldst not give it me.
    Henry. It is, my boy, to side with
the King when Chancellor, and then
to be made Archbishop and go against
the King who made him, and turn the
world upside down.
    Geoffrey. I won't have it then.
Nay, but give it me, and I promise
thee not to turn the world upside down.
    Henry (*giving him a ball*). Here is
a ball, my boy, thy world, to turn
anyway and play with as thou wilt —
which is more than I can do with
mine. Go try it, play. [*Exit* Geoffrey.
A pretty lusty boy.
    Rosamund.   So like to thee;
Like to be liker.
    Henry.   Not in my chin, I hope!
That threatens double.
    Rosamund. Thou art manlike per-
    fect.
    Henry. Ay, ay, no doubt; and were
    I humpt behind,
Thou'd say as much — the goodly
    way of women
Who love, for which I love them.
    May God grant
No ill befall or him or thee when I
Am gone.
    Rosamund. Is *he* thy enemy?
    Henry.   He? who? ay!
    Rosamund. Thine enemy knows the
    secret of my bower.
    Henry. And I could tear him
    asunder with wild horses
Before he would betray it. Nay —
    no fear!
More like is he to excommunicate me.
    Rosamund. And I would creep,
    crawl over knife-edge flint
Barefoot, a hundred leagues, to stay
    his hand
Before he flash'd the bolt.

Henry.   And when he flash'd it
Shrink from me, like a daughter of
  the Church.
Rosamund.   Ay, but he will not.
Henry.   Ay! but if he did?
Rosamund.   O then! O then! I
  almost fear to say
That my poor heretic heart would
  excommunicate
His excommunication, clinging to thee
Closer than ever.
Henry (*raising* Rosamund *and kiss-
  ing her*).   My brave-hearted
  Rose!
Hath he ever been to see thee?
Rosamund.   Here? not he.
And it is so lonely here — no con-
  fessor.
Henry.   Thou shalt confess all thy
  sweet sins to me.
Rosamund.   Besides, we came away
  in such a heat,
I brought not ev'n my crucifix.
Henry.   Take this.
  [*Giving her the Crucifix which*
  Eleanor *gave him.*
Rosamund.   O beautiful! May I
  have it as mine, till mine
Be mine again?
Henry (*throwing it round her neck*).
  Thine — as I am — till death!
Rosamund.   Death? no! I'll have
  it with me in my shroud,
And wake with it, and show it to all
  the Saints.
Henry.   Nay — I must go; but when
  thou layest thy lip
To this, remembering One who died
  for thee,
Remember also one who lives for thee
Out there in France; for I must hence
  to brave
The Pope, King Louis, and this turbu-
  lent priest.
Rosamund (*kneeling*).   O by thy love
  for me, all mine for thee,
Fling not thy soul into the flames of
  hell:
I kneel to thee — be friends with him
  again.
Henry.   Look, look! if little Geof-
  frey have not tost

His ball into the brook! makes after
  it too
To find it.   Why, the child will drown
  himself.
Rosamund.   Geoffrey! Geoffrey!
                              [*Exeunt.*

SCENE II. — MONTMIRAIL. "THE
  MEETING OF THE KINGS." JOHN
  OF OXFORD AND HENRY. CROWD
  IN THE DISTANCE.

John of Oxford.   You have not
  crown'd young Henry yet, my
  liege?
Henry.   Crown'd! by God's eyes,
  we will not have him crown'd.
I spoke of late to the boy, he an-
  swer'd me,
As if he wore the crown already —
  No,
We will not have him crown'd.
'Tis true what Becket told me, that
  the mother
Would make him play his kingship
  against mine.
John of Oxford.   Not have him
  crown'd?
Henry.   Not now — not yet! and
  Becket —
Becket should crown him were he
  crown'd at all:
But, since we would be lord of our
  own manor,
This Canterbury, like a wounded deer,
Has fled our presence and our feeding-
  grounds.
John of Oxford.   Cannot a smooth
  tongue lick him whole again
To serve your will?
Henry.   He hates my will, not me.
John of Oxford.   There's York, my
  liege.
Henry.   But England scarce would
  hold
Young Henry king, if only crown'd
  by York,
And that would stilt up York to twice
  himself.
There is a movement yonder in the
  crowd —

See if our pious — what shall I call
  him, John ? —
Husband-in-law, our smooth-shorn
  suzerain,
Be yet within the field.
  John of Oxford. I will. [*Exit.*
  Henry.   Ay ! Ay !
Mince and go back ! his politic Holi-
  ness
Hath all but climb'd the Roman perch
  again,
And we shall hear him presently with
  clapt wing
Crow over Barbarossa — at last
  tongue-free
To blast my realms with excommuni-
  cation
And interdict. I must patch up a
  peace —
A piece in this long-tugged at, thread-
  bare worn
Quarrel of Crown and Church — to
  rend again.
His Holiness cannot steer straight
  thro' shoals,
Nor I. The citizen's heir hath con-
  quer'd me
For the moment. So we make our
  peace with him.

Enter Louis.

Brother of France, what shall be done
  with Becket ?
  Louis. The holy Thomas ! Brother,
  you have traffick'd
Between the Emperor and the Pope,
  between
The Pope and Antipope — a perilous
  game
For men to play with God.
  Henry.   Ay, ay, good brother,
They call you the Monk-King.
  Louis.   Who calls me ? she
That was my wife, now yours ? You
  have her Duchy,
The point you aim'd at, and pray
  God she prove
True wife to you. You have had the
  better of us
In secular matters.
  Henry. Come, confess, goodbrother,

You did your best or worst to keep
  her Duchy.
Only the golden Leopard printed in it
Such hold-fast claws that you per-
  force again
Shrank into France. Tut, tut ! did
  we convene
This conference but to babble of our
  wives ?
They are plagues enough in-door.
  Louis. We fought in the East,
And felt the sun of Antioch scald our
  mail,
And push'd our lances into Saracen
  hearts.
We never hounded on the State at
  home
To spoil the Church.
  Henry. How should you see this
  rightly ?
  Louis. Well, well, no more ! I am
  proud of my " Monk-King,"
Whoever named me ; and, brother,
  Holy Church
May rock, but will not wreck, nor our
  Archbishop
Stagger on the slope decks for any
  rough sea
Blown by the breath of kings. We
  do forgive you
For aught you wrought against us.
          [*Henry holds up his hand.*
          Nay, I pray you,
Do not defend yourself. You will do
  much
To rake out old dying heats, if
  you,
At my requesting, will but look into
The wrongs you did him, and restore
  his kin,
Reseat him on his throne of Canter-
  bury,
Be, both, the friends you were.
  Henry.   The friends we were !
Co-mates we were, and had our sport
  together,
Co-kings we were, and made the laws
  together.
The world had never seen the like
  before.
You are too cold to know the fashion
  of it.

Well, well, we will be gentle with
    him, gracious —
Most gracious.

Enter BECKET, *after him*, JOHN OF
    OXFORD, ROGER OF YORK, GIL-
    BERT FOLIOT, DE BROC, FITZURSE,
    etc.

            Only that the rift he made
May close between us, here I am
    wholly king,
The word should come from him.
    Becket (*kneeling*). Then, my dear
    liege,
I here deliver all this controversy
Into your royal hands.
    Henry.   Ah, Thomas, Thomas,
Thou art thyself again, Thomas again.
    Becket (*rising*). Saving God's honor!
    Henry.   Out upon thee, man!
Saving the Devil's honor, his yes and
    no.
Knights, bishops, earls, this London
    spawn — by Mahound,
I had sooner have been born a Mus-
    sulman —
Less clashing with their priests —
I am half-way down the slope — will
    no man stay me ?
I dash myself to pieces — I stay my-
    self —
Puff — it is gone. You, Master
    Becket, you
That owe to me your power over me—
    Nay, nay —
Brother of France, you have taken,
    cherish'd him
Who thief-like fled from his own
    church by night,
No man pursuing. I would have had
    him back.
Take heed he do not turn and rend
    you too :
For whatsoever may displease him —
    that
Is clean against God's honor — a shift,
    a trick
Whereby to challenge, face me out of
    all
My regal rights. Yet, yet — that
    none may dream

I go against God's honor — ay, or him-
    self
In any reason, choose
A hundred of the wisest heads from
    England,
A hundred, too, from Normandy and
    Anjou :
Let these decide on what was cus-
    tomary
In olden days, and all the Church of
    France
Decide on their decision, I am con
    tent.
More, what the mightiest and the
    holiest
Of all his predecessors may have done
Ev'n to the least and meanest of my
    own,
Let him do the same to me — I am
    content.
    Louis. Ay, ay! the King humbles
    himself enough.
    Becket (*aside*). Words! he will
    wriggle out of them like an eel
When the time serves. (*Aloud.*) My
    lieges and my lords,
The thanks of Holy Church are due
    to those
That went before us for their work,
    which we
Inheriting reap an easier harvest.
    Yet ——
    Louis. My lord, will you be greater
    than the Saints,
More than St. Peter ? whom ——
    what is it you doubt ?
Behold your peace at hand.
    Becket.   I say that those
Who went before us did not wholly
    clear
The deadly growths of earth, which
    Hell's own heat
So dwelt on that they rose and dark-
    en'd Heaven.
Yet they did much. Would God they
    had torn up all
By the hard root, which shoots again,
    our trial
Had so been less ; but, seeing they
    were men
Defective or excessive, must we fol-
    low

All that they overdid or underdid ?
Nay, if they were defective as St.
    Peter
Denying Christ, who yet defied the
    tyrant,
We hold by his defiance, not his de-
    fect.
O good son Louis, do not counsel me,
No, to suppress God's honor for the
    sake
Of any king that breathes. No, God
    forbid!
   Henry. No! God forbid! and turn
    me Mussulman!
No God but one, and Mahound is his
    prophet.
But for your Christian, look you, you
    shall have
None other God but me—me, Thomas,
    son
Of Gilbert Becket, London merchant.
    Out!
I hear no more.   [*Exit.*
   Louis. Our brother's anger puts
    him,
Poor man, beside himself — not wise.
    My lord,
We have claspt your cause, believing
    that our brother
Had wrong'd you; but this day he
    proffer'd peace.
You will have war; and tho' we grant
    the Church
King over this world's kings, yet, my
    good lord,
We that are kings are something in
    this world,
And so we pray you, draw yourself
    from under
The wings of France. We shelter
    you no more.   [*Exit.*
   John of Oxford. I am glad that
    France hath scouted him at
    last:
I told the Pope what manner of man
    he was.   [*Exit.*
   Roger of York. Yea, since he flouts
    the will of either realm,
Let either cast him away like a dead
    dog!   [*Exit.*
   Foliot. Yea, let a stranger spoil his
    heritage,

And let another take his bishoprick!
       [*Exit.*
   De Broc. Our castle, my lord, be-
    longs to Canterbury.
I pray you come and take it. [*Exit.*
   Fitzurse. When you will. [*Exit.*
   Becket. Cursed be John of Oxford,
    Roger of York,
And Gilbert Foliot! cursed those De
    Brocs
That hold our Saltwood Castle from
    our see!
Cursed Fitzurse, and all the rest of
    them
That sow this hate between my lord
    and me!
   Voices from the Crowd. Blessed be
the Lord Archbishop, who hath with-
stood two Kings to their faces for the
honor of God.
   Becket. Out of the mouths of babes
    and sucklings, praise!
I thank you, sons; when kings but
    hold by crowns,
The crowd that hungers for a crown
    in Heaven
Is my true king.
   Herbert. Thy true King bade thee be
A fisher of men; thou hast them in
    thy net.
   Becket. I am too like the King
    here ; both of us
Too headlong for our office. Better
    have been
A fisherman at Bosham, my good
    Herbert,
Thy birthplace — the sea-creek — the
    petty rill
That falls into it — the green field —
    the gray church —
The simple lobster-basket, and the
    mesh —
The more or less of daily labor done —
The pretty gaping bills in the home-
    nest
Piping for bread — the daily want
    supplied—
The daily pleasure to supply it.
   Herbert.   Ah, Thomas,
You had not borne it, no, not for a
    day.
   Becket. Well, maybe, no.

Herbert. But bear with Walter Map,
For here he comes to comment on
the time.

Enter WALTER MAP.

Walter Map. Pity, my lord, that
you have quenched the warmth of
France toward you, tho' His Holiness,
after much smouldering and smoking,
be kindled again upon your quarter.

Becket. Ay, if he do not end in
smoke again.

Walter Map. My lord, the fire,
when first kindled, said to the smoke,
"Go up, my son, straight to Heaven."
And the smoke said, "I go"; but
anon the North-east took and turned
him South-west, then the South-west
turned him North-east, and so of the
other winds; but it was in him to go
up straight if the time had been
quieter. Your lordship affects the
unwavering perpendicular; but His
Holiness, pushed one way by the Empire and another by England, if he
move at all, Heaven stay him, is fain
to diagonalize.

Herbert. Diagonalize! thou art a
word-monger!
Our Thomas never will diagonalize.
Thou art a jester and a verse-maker.
Diagonalize!

Walter Map. Is the world any the
worse for my verses if the Latin
rhymes be rolled out from a full
mouth? or any harm done to the
people if my jest be in defence of the
Truth?

Becket. Ay, if the jest be so done
that the people
Delight to wallow in the grossness of it,
Till Truth herself be shamed of her
defender.
Non defensoribus istis, Walter Map.

Walter Map. Is that my case? so if
the city be sick, and I cannot call the
kennel sweet, your lordship would suspend me from verse-writing, as you
suspended yourself after sub-writing
to the customs.

Becket. I pray God pardon mine infirmity.

Walter Map. Nay, my lord, take
heart; for tho' you suspended yourself,
the Pope let you down again; and tho'
you suspend Foliot or another, the
Pope will not leave them in suspense,
for the Pope himself is always in suspense, like Mahound's coffin hung between heaven and earth — always in
suspense, like the scales, till the weight
of Germany or the gold of England
brings one of them down to the dust
— always in suspense, like the tail of
the horologe — to and fro — tick-tack
— we make the time, we keep the time,
ay, and we serve the time; for I have
heard say that if you boxed the Pope's
ears with a purse, you might stagger
him, but he would pocket the purse.
No saying of mine — Jocelyn of Salisbury. But the King hath bought half
the College of Redhats. He warmed
to you to-day, and you have chilled
him again. Yet you both love God.
Agree with him quickly again, even
for the sake of the Church. My one
grain of good counsel which you will
not swallow. I hate a split between
old friendships as I hate the dirty gap
in the face of a Cistercian monk, that
will swallow anything. Farewell.
　　　　　　　　　　　　　　　[Exit.

Becket. Map scoffs at Rome. I all
but hold with Map.
Save for myself no Rome were left in
England,
All had been his. Why should this
Rome, this Rome,
Still choose Barabbas rather than the
Christ,
Absolve the left-hand thief and damn
the right?
Take fees of tyranny, wink at sacri-
lege,
Which even Peter had not dared?
condemn
The blameless exile? —

Herbert. Thee, thou holy Thomas!
I would that thou hadst been the Holy
Father.

Becket. I would have done my most
to keep Rome holy,

I would have made Rome know she
    still is Rome —
Who stands aghast at her eternal self
And shakes at mortal kings — her
    vacillation,
Avarice, craft — O God, how many an
    innocent
Has left his bones upon the way to
    Rome
Unwept, uncared for. Yea — on mine
    own self
The King had had no power except
    for Rome.
'Tis not the King who is guilty of
    mine exile,
But Rome, Rome, Rome!
  Herbert. My lord, I see this Louis
Returning, ah! to drive thee from his
    realm.
  Becket. He said as much before.
    Thou art no prophet.
Nor yet a prophet's son.
  Herbert.   Whatever he say,
Deny not thou God's honor for a king.
The King looks troubled.

Re-enter KING LOUIS.

  Louis. My dear lord Archbishop,
I learn but now that those poor Poite-
    vins,
That in thy cause were stirr'd against
    King Henry,
Have been, despite his kingly promise
    given
To our own self of pardon, evilly used
And put to pain. I have lost all trust
    in him.
The Church alone hath eyes — and
    now I see
That I was blind — suffer the phrase
    — surrendering
God's honor to the pleasure of a man.
Forgive me and absolve me, holy
    father.   [*Kneels.*
  Becket. Son, I absolve thee in the
    name of God.
  Louis (*rising*). Return to Sens, where
    we will care for you.
The wine and wealth of all our France
    are yours;
Rest in our realm, and be at peace
    with all.   [*Exeunt.*

  Voices from the Crowd. Long live the
good King Louis! God bless the
great Archbishop!

Re-enter HENRY *and* JOHN OF OXFORD.

  Henry (*looking after* King Louis *and*
    Becket). Ay, there they go—
    both backs are turn'd to me —
Why then I strike into my former
    path
For England, crown young Henry
    there, and make
Our waning Eleanor all but love me!
                        John,
Thou hast served me heretofore with
    Rome — and well.
They call thee John the Swearer.
  John of Oxford.   For this reason,
That, being ever duteous to the King,
I evermore have sworn upon his side,
And ever mean to do it.
  Henry (*claps him on shoulder*). Honest
    John!
To Rome again! the storm begins
    again.
Spare not thy tongue! be lavish with
    our coins,
Threaten our junction with the Em-
    peror — flatter
And fright the Pope — bribe all the
    Cardinals — leave
Lateran and Vatican in one dust of
    gold —
Swear and unswear, state and misstate
    thy best!
I go to have young Henry crown'd by
    York.

ACT III.

SCENE I. — THE BOWER.

HENRY *and* ROSAMUND.

  Henry. All that you say is just. I
    cannot answer it
Till better times, when I shall put
    away ——
  Rosamund. What will you put
    away?

Henry.   That which you ask me
Till better times.   Let it content you
    now
There is no woman that I love so
    well.
  Rosamund. No woman but should
    be content with that —
  Henry. And one fair child to fon-
    dle!
  Rosamund.   O yes, the child
We waited for so long — heaven's gift
    at last —
And how you doated on him then! To-
    day
I almost fear'd your kiss was colder
    — yes —
But then the child *is* such a child.
    What chance
That he should ever spread into the
    man
Here in our silence?   I have done my
    best.
I am not learn'd.
  Henry.   I am the King, his father,
And I will look to it. Is our secret
    ours?
Have you had any alarm? no stranger?
  Rosamund.   No.
The warder of the bower hath given
    himself
Of late to wine.   I sometimes think
    he sleeps
When he should watch; and yet what
    fear? the people
Believe the wood enchanted.   No one
    comes,
Nor foe nor friend; his fond excess of
    wine
Springs from the loneliness of my
    poor bower,
Which weighs even on me.
  Henry.   Yet these tree-towers,
Their long bird-echoing minster-aisles,
    — the voice
Of the perpetual brook, these golden
    slopes
Of Solomon-shaming flowers — that
    was your saying,
All pleased you so at first.
  Rosamund.   Not now so much.
My Anjou bower was scarce as beau-
    tiful.

But you were oftener there.   I have
    none but you.
The brook's voice is not yours, and no
    flower, not
The sun himself, should he be changed
    to one,
Could shine away the darkness of that
    gap
Left by the lack of love.
  Henry.   The lack of love!
  Rosamund. Of one we love.   Nay,
    I would not be bold,
Yet hoped ere this you might ——
          [*Looks earnestly at him.*
  Henry.   Anything further?
  Rosamund. Only my best bower-
    maiden died of late,
And that old priest whom John of
    Salisbury trusted
Hath sent another.
  Henry.   Secret?
  Rosamund.   I but ask'd her
One question, and she primm'd her
    mouth and put
Her hands together — thus — and said,
    God help her,
That she was sworn to silence.
  Henry.   What did you ask her?
  Rosamund. Some daily something-
    nothing.
  Henry.   Secret, then?
  Rosamund. I do not love her.   Must
    you go, my liege,
So suddenly?
  Henry. I came to England suddenly
And on a great occasion sure to
    wake
As great a wrath in Becket ——
  Rosamund.   Always Becket!
He always comes between us.
  Henry.   — And to meet it
I needs must leave as suddenly.   It is
    raining,
Put on your hood and see me to the
    bounds.   [*Exeunt.*

    Margery (*singing behind scene*).

    Babble in bower
      Under the rose!
    Bee mustn't buzz,
      Whoop — but he knows.

Kiss me, little one,
  Nobody near!
Grasshopper, grasshopper,
  Whoop — you can hear.

Kiss in the bower,
  Tit on the tree!
Bird mustn't tell,
  Whoop — he can see.

Enter MARGERY.

I ha' been but a week here and I ha' seen what I ha' seen, for to be sure it's no more than a week since our old Father Philip that has confessed our mother for twenty years, and she was hard put to it, and to speak truth, nigh at the end of our last crust, and that mouldy, and she cried out to him to put me forth in the world and to make me a woman of the world, and to win my own bread, whereupon he asked our mother if I could keep a quiet tongue i' my head, and not speak till I was spoke to, and I answered for myself that I never spoke more than was needed, and he told me he would advance me to the service of a great lady, and took me ever so far away, and gave me a great pat o' the cheek for a pretty wench, and said it was a pity to blindfold such eyes as mine, and such to be sure they be, but he blinded 'em for all that, and so brought me no-hows as I may say, and the more shame to him after his promise, into a garden and not into the world, and bade me whatever I saw not to speak one word, an' it 'ud be well for me in the end, for there were great ones who would look after me, and to be sure I ha' seen great ones to-day — and then not to speak one word, for that's the rule o' the garden, tho' to be sure if I had been Eve i' the garden I shouldn't ha' minded the apple, for what's an apple, you know, save to a child, and I'm no child, but more a woman o' the world than my lady here, and I ha' seen what I ha' seen — tho' to be sure if I hadn't minded it we should all on us ha' had to go, bless the Saints, wi'

bare backs, but the backs 'ud ha' countenanced one another, and belike it 'ud ha' been always summer, and anyhow I am as well-shaped as my lady here, and I ha' seen what I ha' seen, and what's the good of my talking to myself, for here comes my lady (*enter* ROSAMUND), and, my lady, tho' I shouldn't speak one word, I wish you joy o' the King's brother.

Rosamund. What is it you mean?

Margery. I mean your goodman, your husband, my lady, for I saw your ladyship a-parting wi' him even now i' the coppice, when I was a-getting o' bluebells for your ladyship's nose to smell on — and I ha' seen the King once at Oxford, and he's as like the King as fingernail to fingernail, and I thought at first it was the King, only you know the King's married, for King Louis ——

Rosamund. Married!

Margery. Years and years, my lady, for her husband, King Louis ——

Rosamund. Hush!

Margery. — And I thought if it were the King's brother he had a better bride than the King, for the people do say that his is bad beyond all reckoning, and ——

Rosamund. The people lie.

Margery. Very like, my lady, but most on 'em know an honest woman and a lady when they see her, and besides they say, she makes songs, and that's against her, for I never knew an honest woman that could make songs, tho' to be sure our mother 'ill sing me old songs by the hour, but then, God help her, she had 'em from her mother, and her mother from her mother back and back for ever so long, but none on 'em ever made songs, and they were all honest.

Rosamund. Go, you shall tell me of her some other time.

Margery. There's none so much to tell on her, my lady, only she kept the seventh commandment better than some I know on, or I couldn't look your ladyship i' the face, and she brew'd the best ale in all Glo'ster, that is to say in her time when she had the " Crown."

Rosamund. The crown! who ?

Margery. Mother.

Rosamund. I mean her whom you call — fancy — my husband's brother's wife.

Margery. Oh, Queen Eleanor. Yes, my lady ; and tho' I be sworn not to speak a word, I can tell you all about her, if ——

Rosamund. No word now. I am faint and sleepy. Leave me.
Nay — go. What! will you anger me.
　　　　　　　　　　　[*Exit* Margery.
He charged me not to question any of those
About me. Have I? no! she question'd *me*.
Did she not slander *him?* Should she stay here ?
May she not tempt me, being at my side,
To question *her ?* Nay, can I send her hence
Without his kingly leave ! I am in the dark.
I have lived, poor bird, from cage to cage, and known
Nothing but him — happy to know no more,
So that he loved me — and he loves me — yes,
And bound me by his love to secrecy
Till his own time.
　　　　　Eleanor, Eleanor, have I
Not heard ill things of her in France ? Oh, she's
The Queen of France. I see it — some confusion,
Some strange mistake. I did not hear aright,
Myself confused with parting from the King.

Margery (behind scene).
　　Bee mustn't buzz,
　　Whoop — but he knows.

Rosamund. Yet her — what her? he hinted of some her —
When he was here before —
Something that would displease me. Hath he stray'd

From love's clear path into the common bush,
And, being scratch'd, returns to his true rose,
Who hath not thorn enough to prick him for it,
Ev'n with a word ?

Margery (behind scene).
　　Bird mustn't tell,
　　Whoop — he can see.

Rosamund. I would not hear him.
　　Nay—there's more—he frown'd
" No mate for her, if it should come to that " —
To that — to what ?

Margery (behind scene).
　　Whoop — but he knows,
　　Whoop — but he knows.

Rosamund. O God! some dreadful truth is breaking on me —
Some dreadful thing is coming on me.

Enter GEOFFREY.
　　　　　　　　Geoffrey !

Geoffrey. What are you crying for, when the sun shines ?

Rosamund. Hath not thy father left us to ourselves ?

Geoffrey. Ay, but he's taken the rain with him. I hear Margery : I'll go play with her.
　　　　　　　　[*Exit* Geoffrey.

Rosamund. Rainbow, stay,
　　Gleam upon gloom,
　　Bright as my dream,
　　Rainbow, stay !
　　But it passes away,
　　Gloom upon gleam,
　　Dark as my doom —
　　O rainbow, stay.

SCENE II. — OUTSIDE THE WOODS NEAR ROSAMUND'S BOWER.

ELEANOR. FITZURSE.

Eleanor. Up from the salt lips of the land we two
Have track'd the King to this dark inland wood :
And somewhere hereabouts he vanish'd. Here

His turtle builds: his exit is our
    adit :
Watch! he will out again, and pres-
    ently,
Seeing he must to Westminster and
    crown
Young Henry there to-morrow.
   Fitzurse.   We have watch'd
So long in vain, he hath pass'd out
    again,
And on the other side.
              [A great horn winded.
              Hark! Madam!
   Eleanor.   Ah,
How ghostly sounds that horn in the
    back wood!
              [A countryman flying.
Whither away, man? what are you
    flying from?
   Countryman. The witch! the witch!
she sits naked by a great heap of
gold in the middle of the wood, and
when the horn sounds she comes out
as a wolf. Get you hence! a man
passed in there to-day: I holla'd to
him, but he didn't hear me: he'll
never out again, the witch has got
him. I daren't stay — I daren't stay!
   Eleanor. Kind of the witch to give
thee warning tho'.   *[Man flies.*
Is not this wood-witch of the rustic's
    fear
Our woodland Circe that hath witch'd
    the King?
       [Horn sounded. Another flying.
   Fitzurse. Again! stay, fool, and tell
me why thou fliest.
   Countryman. Fly thou too. The
King keeps his forest head of game
here, and when that horn sounds, a
score of wolf-dogs are let loose that
will tear thee piecemeal. Linger not
till the third horn. Fly!   *[Exit.*
   Eleanor. This is the likelier tale.
We have hit the place.
Now let the King's fine game look to
    itself.   *[Horn.*
   Fitzurse. Again! —
And far on in the dark heart of the
    wood
I hear the yelping of the hounds of
    hell.

   Eleanor. I have my dagger here to
    still their throats.
   Fitzurse. Nay, Madam, not to-night
    — the night is falling.
What can be done to-night?
   Eleanor.   Well — well — away.

SCENE III. — TRAITOR'S MEADOW
AT FRÉTEVAL. PAVILIONS AND
TENTS OF THE ENGLISH AND
FRENCH BARONAGE.

BECKET *and* HERBERT OF BOSHAM.

   Becket. See here!
   Herbert. What's here?
   Becket.   A notice from the priest,
To whom our John of Salisbury com-
    mitted
The secret of the bower, that our
    wolf-Queen
Is prowling round the fold. I should
    be back
In England ev'n for this.
   Herbert.   These are by-things
In the great cause.
   Becket. The by-things of the Lord
Are the wrong'd innocences that will
    cry
From all the hidden by-ways of the
    world
In the great day against the wronger.
    I know
Thy meaning. Perish she, I, all, be-
    fore
The Church should suffer wrong!
   Herbert.   Do you see, my lord,
There is the King talking with Wal-
    ter Map?
   Becket. He hath the Pope's last let-
    ters, and they threaten
The immediate thunder-blast of inter-
    dict :
Yet he can scarce be touching upon
    those,
Or scarce would smile that fashion.
   Herbert.   Winter sunshine!
Beware of opening out thy bosom to it,
Lest thou, myself, and all thy flock
    should catch
An after ague-fit of trembling. Look!

He bows, he bares his head, he is
  coming hither,
Still with a smile.

Enter KING HENRY *and* WALTER
            MAP.

Henry. We have had so many hours
    together, Thomas,
So many happy hours alone together,
That I would speak with you once
    more alone.
  Becket. My liege, your will and
    happiness are mine.
        [*Exeunt* King *and* Becket.
  Herbert. The same smile still.
  Walter Map. Do you see that great
black cloud that hath come over the
sun and cast us all into shadow ?
  Herbert. And feel it too.
  Walter Map. And see you yon side-
beam that is forced from under it,
and sets the church-tower over there
all a-hell-fire as it were ?
  Herbert. Ay.
  Walter Map. It is this black, bell-
silencing, anti-marrying, burial-hin-
dering interdict that hath squeezed
out this side-smile upon Canterbury,
whereof may come conflagration.
Were I Thomas, I wouldn't trust it.
Sudden change is a house on sand ;
and tho' I count Henry honest enough,
yet when fear creeps in at the front,
honesty steals out at the back, and
the King at last is fairly scared by
by this cloud — this interdict. I have
been more for the King than the
Church in this matter — yea, even for
the sake of the Church : for, truly, as
the case stood, you had safelier have
slain an archbishop than a she-goat :
but our recoverer and upholder of customs hath in this crowning of young
Henry by York and London so violated
the immemorial usage of the Church,
that, like the gravedigger's child I have
heard of, trying to ring the bell, he
hath half-hanged himself in the rope
of the Church, or rather pulled all
the Church with the Holy Father
astride of it down upon his own head.

  Herbert. Were you tnere ?
  Walter Map. In the church rope ?
— no. I was at the crowning, for I
have pleasure in the pleasure of
crowds, and to read the faces of men
at a great show.
  Herbert. And how did Roger of
York comport himself ?
  Water Map. As magnificently and
archiepiscopally as our Thomas would
have done : only there was a dare-
devil in his eye — I should say a dare-
Becket. He thought less of two
kings than of one Roger the king of
the occasion. Foliot is the holier
man, perhaps the better. Once or
twice there ran a twitch across his
face as who should say what's to follow ? but Salisbury was a calf cowed
by Mother Church, and every now
and then glancing about him like a
thief at night when he hears a door
open in the house and thinks "the
master."
  Herbert. And the father-king ?
  Walter Map. The father's eye was
so tender it would have called a goose
off the green, and once he strove to
hide his face, like the Greek king
when his daughter was sacrificed, but
he thought better of it : it was but
the sacrifice of a kingdom to his son,
a smaller matter ; but as to the young
crownling himself, he looked so mala-
pert in the eyes, that had I fathered
him I had given him more of the rod
than the sceptre. Then followed the
thunder of the captains and the shouting, and so we came on to the banquet, from whence there puffed out
such an incense of unctuosity into
the nostrils of our Gods of Church
and State, that Lucullus or Apicius
might have sniffed it in their Hades
of heathenism, so that the smell of
their own roast had not come across
it ——
  Herbert. Map, tho' you make your
butt too big, you overshoot it.
  Walter Map. —For as to the fish,
they de-miracled the miraculous

draught, and might have sunk a navy ——

Herbert. There again, Goliasing and Goliathising!

Walter Map. — And as for the flesh at table, a whole Peter's sheet, with all manner of game, and four-footed things, and fowls ——

Herbert. And all manner of creeping things too?

Walter Map. — Well, there were Abbots — but they did not bring their women; and so we were dull enough at first, but in the end we flourished out into a merriment; for the old King would act servitor and hand a dish to his son; whereupon my Lord of York — his fine-cut face bowing and beaming with all that courtesy which hath less loyalty in it than the backward scrape of the clown's heel — "great honor," says he, "from the King's self to the King's son." Did you hear the young King's quip?

Herbert. No, what was it?

Walter Map. Glancing at the days when his father was only Earl of Anjou, he answered : — "Should not an earl's son wait on a king's son?" And when the cold corners of the King's mouth began to thaw, there was a great motion of laughter among us, part real, part childlike, to be freed from the dulness — part royal, for King and kingling both laughed, and so we could not but laugh, as by a royal necessity — part childlike again — when we felt we had laughed too long and could not stay ourselves — many midriff-shaken even to tears, as springs gush out after earthquakes — but from those, as I said before, there may come a conflagration — tho', to keep the figure moist and make it hold water, I should say rather, the lacrymation of a lamentation; but look if Thomas have not flung himself at the King's feet. They have made it up again — for the moment.

Herbert. Thanks to the blessed Magdalen, whose day it is.

Re-enter HENRY *and* BECKET. (*During their conference the* Barons *and* Bishops *of* France *and* England *come in at back of stage.*)

Becket. Ay, King! for in thy kingdom, as thou knowest,
The spouse of the Great King, thy King, hath fallen —
The daughter of Zion lies beside the way —
The priests of Baal tread her underfoot—
The golden ornaments are stolen from her ——

Henry. Have I not promised to restore her, Thomas,
And send thee back again to Canterbury?

Becket. Send back again those exiles of my kin
Who wander famine-wasted thro' the world.

Henry. Have I not promised, man, to send them back?

Becket. Yet one thing more. Thou hast broken thro' the pales
Of privilege, crowning thy young son by York,
London and Salisbury — not Canterbury.

Henry. York crown'd the Conqueror — not Canterbury.

Becket. There was no Canterbury in William's time.

Henry. But Hereford, you know, crown'd the first Henry.

Becket. But Anselm crown'd this Henry o'er again.

Henry. And thou shalt crown my Henry o'er again.

Becket. And is it then with thy goodwill that I
Proceed against thine evil councillors,
And hurl the dread ban of the Church on those
Who made the second mitre play the first,
And acted me?

Henry. Well, well, then — have thy way!
[It may be they were evil councillors.

What more, my lord Archbishop?
　　What more, Thomas?
I make thee full amends. Say all
　　thy say,
But blaze not out before the French-
　　men here.
　　Becket. More? Nothing, so thy
　　　promise be thy deed.
　　Henry (*holding out his hand*). Give
　　　me thy hand. My Lords of
　　　France and England,
My friend of Canterbury and my-
　　self
Are now once more at perfect amity.
Unkingly should I be, and most un-
　　knightly,
Not striving still, however much in
　　vain,
To rival him in Christian charity.
　　Herbert. All praise to Heaven, and
　　　sweet St. Magdalen!
　　Henry. And so farewell until we
　　　meet in England.
　　Becket. I fear, my liege, we may not
　　　meet in England.
　　Henry. How, do you make me a
　　　traitor?
　　Becket.　　　　　　No, indeed!
That be far from thee.
　　Henry.　Come, stay with us, then,
Before you part for England.
　　Becket.　　I am bound
For that one hour to stay with good
　　King Louis,
Who helpt me when none else.
　　Herbert.　　He said thy life
Was not one hour's worth in England
　　save
King Henry gave thee first the kiss of
　　peace.
　　Henry. He said so? Louis, did he?
　　　look you, Herbert.
When I was in mine anger with King
　　Louis,
I sware I would not give the kiss of
　　peace,
Not on French ground, nor any ground
　　but English,
Where his cathedral stands. Mine
　　old friend, Thomas,
I would there were that perfect trust
　　between us,

That health of heart, once ours, ere
　　Pope or King
Had come between us! Even now —
　　who knows? —
I might deliver all things to thy hand —
If . . . but I say no more . . . fare-
　　well, my lord.
　　Becket. Farewell, my liege!
　　　[*Exit* Henry, *then the* Barons *and*
　　　Bishops.
　　Walter Map. There again! when the
full fruit of the royal promise might
have dropt into thy mouth hadst thou
but opened it to thank him.
　　Becket. He fenced his royal promise
with an *if.*
　　Walter Map. And is the King's *if* too
high a stile for your lordship to over-
step and come at all things in the next
field?
　　Becket. Ay, if this *if* be like the
　　　Devil's "*if*
Thou wilt fall down and worship me."
　　Herbert.　　　Oh, Thomas,
I could fall down and worship thee,
　　my Thomas,
For thou hast trodden this wine-press
　　alone.
　　Becket. Nay, of the people there are
　　　many with me.
　　Walter Map. I am not altogether
with you, my lord, tho' I am none of
those that would raise a storm between
you, lest ye should draw together like
two ships in a calm. You wrong the
King: he meant what he said to-day.
Who shall vouch for his to-morrows?
One word further. Doth not the *few-
ness* of anything make the fulness of
it in estimation? Is not virtue prized
mainly for its rarity and great baseness loathed as an exception: for were
all, my lord, as noble as yourself, who
would look up to you? and were all
as base as — who shall I say —Fitzurse
and his following — who would look
down upon them? My lord, you have
put so many of the King's household
out of communion, that they begin to
smile at it.
　　Becket. At their peril, at their
　　　peril——

Walter Map. — For tho' the drop may hollow out the dead stone, doth not the living skin thicken against perpetual whippings ? This is the second grain of good counsel I ever proffered thee, and so cannot suffer by the rule of frequency. Have I sown it in salt ? I trust not, for before God I promise you the King hath many more wolves than he can tame in his woods of England, and if it suit their purpose to howl for the King, and you still move against him, you may have no less than to die for it ; but God and his free wind grant your lordship a happy home-return and the King's kiss of peace in Kent. Farewell ! I must follow the King.

[*Exit.*

Herbert. Ay, and I warrant the customs. Did the King Speak of the customs ?

Becket. No ! — to die for it — I live to die for it, I die to live for it. The State will die, the Church can never die. The King's not like to die for that which dies ; But I must die for that which never dies. It will be so — my visions in the Lord : It must be so, my friend ! the wolves of England Must murder her one shepherd, that the sheep May feed in peace. False figure, Map would say. Earth's falses are heaven's truths. And when my voice Is martyr'd mute, and this man disappears, That perfect trust may come again between us, And there, there, there, not here I shall rejoice To find my stray sheep back within the fold. The crowd are scattering, let us move away ! And thence to England.

[*Exeunt.*

ACT IV.

SCENE I. — THE OUTSKIRTS OF THE BOWER.

Geoffrey (*coming out of the wood*). Light again! light again! Margery ? no, that's a finer thing there. How it glitters !

Eleanor (*entering*). Come to me, little one. How camest thou hither ?

Geoffrey. On my legs.

Eleanor. And mighty pretty legs too. Thou art the prettiest child I ever saw. Wilt thou love me ?

Geoffrey. No ; I only love mother.

Eleanor. Ay ; and who is thy mother ?

Geoffrey. They call her —— But she lives secret, you see.

Eleanor. Why ?

Geoffrey. Don't know why.

Eleanor. Ay, but some one comes to see her now and then. Who is he ?

Geoffrey. Can't tell.

Eleanor. What does she call him ?

Geoffrey. My liege.

Eleanor. Pretty one, how camest thou ?

Geoffrey. There was a bit of yellow silk here and there, and it looked pretty like a glowworm, and I thought if I followed it I should find the fairies.

Eleanor. I am the fairy, pretty one, a good fairy to thy mother. Take me to her.

Geoffrey. There are good fairies and bad fairies, and sometimes she cries, and can't sleep sound o' nights because of the bad fairies.

Eleanor. She shall cry no more; she shall sleep sound enough if thou wilt take me to her. I am her good fairy.

Geoffrey. But you don't look like a good fairy. Mother does. You are not pretty, like mother.

Eleanor. We can't all of us be as pretty as thou art — (*aside*) little bastard. Come, here is a golden chain I will give thee if thou wilt lead me to thy mother.

Geoffrey. No — no gold. Mother

says gold spoils all. Love is the only gold.

Eleanor. I love thy mother, my pretty boy. Show me where thou camest out of the wood.

Geoffrey. By this tree; but I don't know if I can find the way back again.

Eleanor. Where's the warder?

Geoffrey. Very bad. Somebody struck him.

Eleanor. Ay? who was that?

Geoffrey. Can't tell. But I heard say he had had a stroke, or you'd have heard his horn before now. Come along, then; we shall see the silk here and there, and I want my supper. [*Exeunt.*

SCENE II. — ROSAMUND'S BOWER.

Rosamund. The boy so late; pray God, he be not lost.
I sent this Margery, and she comes not back;
I sent another, and she comes not back.
I go myself — so many alleys, crossings,
Paths, avenues — nay, if I lost him, now
The folds have fallen from the mystery,
And left all naked, I were lost indeed.

Enter GEOFFREY *and* ELEANOR.

Geoffrey, the pain thou hast put me to !
[*Seeing* Eleanor.
Ha, you!
How came you hither ?

Eleanor. Your own child brought me hither !

Geoffrey. You said you couldn't trust Margery, and I watched her and followed her into the woods, and I lost her and went on and on till I found the light and the lady, and she says she can make you sleep o' nights.

Rosamund. How dared you ? Know you not this bower is secret,
Of and belonging to the King of England,

More sacred than his forests for the chase ?
Nay, nay, Heaven help you ; get you hence in haste
Lest worse befall you.

Eleanor. Child, I am mine own self
Of and belonging to the King. The King
Hath divers ofs and ons, ofs and belongings,
Almost as many as your true Mussulman —
Belongings, paramours, whom it pleases him
To call his wives ; but so it chances, child,
That I am his main paramour, his sultana.
But since the fondest pair of doves will jar,
Ev'n in a cage of gold, we had words of late,
And thereupon he call'd my children bastards.
Do you believe that you are married to him ?

Rosamund. I *should* believe it.

Eleanor. You must not believe it,
Because I have a wholesome medicine here
Puts that belief asleep. Your answer, beauty !
Do you believe that you are marrried to him?

Rosamund. Geoffrey, my boy, I saw the ball you lost in the fork of the great willow over the brook. Go. See that you do not fall in. Go.

Geoffrey. And leave you alone with the good fairy. She calls you beauty, but I don't like her looks. Well, you bid me go, and I'll have my ball anyhow. Shall I find you asleep when I come back ?

Rosamund. Go. [*Exit* Geoffrey.

Eleanor. He is easily found again.
Do you believe it ?
I pray you then to take my sleeping-draught ;
But if you should not care to take it — see ! [*Draws a dagger.*
What ! have I scared the red rose from your face

Into your heart. But this will find it
there,
And dig it from the root for ever.
Rosamund. Help! help!
Eleanor. They say that walls have
ears; but these, it seems,
Have none! and I have none — to
pity thee.
Rosamund. I do beseech you — my
child is so young,
So backward too; I cannot leave him
yet.
I am not so happy I could not die my-
self,
But the child is so young. You have
children — his;
And mine is the King's child; so, if
you love him —
Nay, if you love him, there is great
wrong done
Somehow; but if you do not — there
are those
Who say you do not love him — let
me go
With my young boy, and I will hide
my face,
Blacken and gipsyfy it; none shall
know me;
The King shall never hear of me
again,
But I will beg my bread along the
world
With my young boy, and God will be
our guide.
I never meant you harm in any way.
See, I can say no more.
Eleanor. Will you not say you are not
married to him?
Rosamund. Ay, Madam, I can *say*
it, if you will.
Eleanor. Then is thy pretty boy a
bastard?
Rosamund. No.
Eleanor. And thou thyself a proven
wanton?
Rosamund. No.
I am none such. I never loved but
one.
I have heard of such that range from
love to love,
Like the wild beast — if you can call
it love.

I have heard of such — yea, even
among those
Who sit on thrones — I never saw any
such,
Never knew any such, and howsoever
You do misname me, match'd with any
such,
I am snow to mud.
Eleanor. The more the pity then
That thy true home — the heavens —
cry out for thee
Who art too pure for earth.

Enter FITZURSE.

Fitzurse. Give her to me.
Eleanor. The Judas-lover of our
passion-play
Hath track'd us hither.
Fitzurse. Well, why not? I follow'd
You and the child: he babbled all the
way.
Give her to me to make my honey-
moon.
Eleanor. Ay, as the bears love honey.
Could you keep her
Indungeon'd from one whisper of the
wind,
Dark even from a side glance of the
moon,
And oublietted in the centre — No!
I follow out my hate and thy revenge.
Fitzurse. You bade me take revenge
another way —
To bring her to the dust. . . . Come
with me, love,
And I will love thee. . . . Madam,
let her live.
I have a far-off burrow where the King
Would miss her and for ever.
Eleanor. How sayest thou, sweet-
heart?
Wilt thou go with him? he will marry
thee.
Rosamund. Give me the poison;
set me free of him!
[*Eleanor offers the vial.*
No, no! I will not have it.
Eleanor. Then this other,
The wiser choice, because my sleep-
ing-draught
May bloat thy beauty out of shape,
and make

Thy body loathsome even to thy child;
While this but leaves thee with a bro-
    ken heart,
A doll-face blanch'd and bloodless,
    over which
If pretty Geoffrey do not break his
    own,
It must be broken for him.
　　Rosamund.　　　　　　O I see now
Your purpose is to fright me — a
    troubadour
You play with words. You had
    never used so many,
Not if you meant it, I am sure. The
    child . . .
No . . . mercy ! No !　　　[*Kneels.*
　　Eleanor. Play ! . . . that bosom
    never
Heaved under the King's hand with
    such true passion
As at this loveless knife that stirs the
    riot,
Which it will quench in blood ! Slave,
    if he love thee,
Thy life is worth the wrestle for it :
    arise,
And dash thyself against me that I
    may slay thee !
The worm ! shall I let her go ? But
    ha ! what's here ?
By very God, the cross I gave the
    King !
His village darling in some lewd
    caress
Has wheedled it off the King's neck
    to her own.
By thy leave, beauty. Ay, the same !
    I warrant
Thou hast sworn on this my cross a
    hundred times
Never to leave him — and that merits
    death,
False oath on holy cross — for thou
    must leave him
To-day, but not quite yet. My good
    Fitzurse,
The running down the chase is kind-
    lier sport
Ev'n than the death. Who knows
    but that thy lover
May plead so pitifully, that I may
    spare thee ?

Come hither, man ; stand there.　(*To*
    Rosamund.)　Take thy one
    chance ;
Catch at the last straw. Kneel to
    thy lord Fitzurse ;
Crouch even because thou hatest him ;
    fawn upon him
For thy life and thy son's.
　　Rosamund (*rising*). I am a Clifford,
My son a Clifford and Plantagenet.
I am to die then, tho' there stand
    beside thee
One who might grapple with thy dag-
    ger, if he
Had aught of man, or thou of
    woman ; or I
Would bow to such a baseness as
    would make me
Most worthy of it : both of us will die,
And I will fly with my sweet boy to
    heaven,
And shriek to all the saints among
    the stars :
"Eleanor of Aquitaine, Eleanor of
    England !
Murder'd by that adulteress Eleanor,
Whose doings are a horror to the east,
A hissing in the west !" Have we
    not heard
Raymond of Poitou, thine own uncle
    — nay,
Geoffrey Plantagenet, thine own hus
    band's father —
Nay, ev'n the accursed heathen Sal-
    addeen ——
Strike !
I challenge thee to meet me before
    God.
Answer me there.
　　Eleanor (*raising the dagger*). This
    in thy bosom, fool,
And after in thy bastard's !

Enter BECKET *from behind. Catches
    hold of her arm.*

　　Becket.　　　　　　　Murderess !
[*The dagger falls ; they stare at one an-
    other　After a pause.*
　　Eleanor. My lord, we know you
    proud of your fine hand,
But having now admired it long
    enough,

We find that it is mightier than it seems —
At least mine own is frailer: you are laming it.
    Becket. And lamed and maim'd to dislocation, better
Than raised to take a life which Henry bade me
Guard from the stroke that dooms thee after death
To wail in deathless flame.
    Eleanor.   Nor you, nor I
Have now to learn, my lord, that our good Henry
Says many a thing in sudden heats, which he
Gainsays by next sunrising — often ready
To tear himself for having said as much.
My lord, Fitzurse ——
    Becket. He too! what dost thou here?
Dares the bear slouch into the lion's den?
One downward plunge of his paw would rend away
Eyesight and manhood, life itself, from thee.
Go, lest I blast thee with anathema,
And make thee a world's horror.
    Fitzurse.   My lord, I shall
Remember this.
    Becket. I *do* remember thee;
Lest I remember thee to the lion, go.
            [*Exit* Fitzurse.
Take up your dagger; put it in the sheath.
    Eleanor. Might not your courtesy stoop to hand it me?
But crowns must bow when mitres sit so high.
Well — well — too costly to be left or lost.   [*Picks up the dagger.*
I had it from an Arab soldan, who,
When I was there in Antioch, marvell'd at
Our unfamiliar beauties of the west;
But wonder'd more at my much constancy
To the monk-king, Louis, our former burthen,

From whom, as being too kin, you know, my lord,
God's grace and Holy Church deliver'd us.
I think, time given, I could have talk'd him out of
His ten wives into one. Look at the hilt.
What excellent workmanship. In our poor west
We cannot do it so well.
    Becket.   We can do worse.
Madam, I saw your dagger at her throat;
I heard your savage cry.
    Eleanor.   Well acted, was it?
A comedy meant to seem a tragedy —
A feint, a farce. My honest lord, you are known
Thro' all the courts of Christendom as one
That mars a cause with over-violence.
You have wrong'd Fitzurse. I speak not of myself.
We thought to scare this minion of the King
Back from her churchless commerce with the King
To the fond arms of her first love, Fitzurse,
Who swore to marry her. You have spoilt the farce.
My savage cry? Why, she — she — when I strove
To work against her license for her good,
Bark'd out at me such monstrous charges, that
The King himself, for love of his own sons,
If hearing, would have spurn'd her; whereupon
I menaced her with this, as when we threaten
A yelper with a stick. Nay, I deny not
That I was somewhat anger'd. Do you hear me?
Believe or no, I care not. You have lost
The ear of the King. I have it. . . .
My lord Paramount,

Our great High-priest, will not your
    Holiness
Vouchsafe a gracious answer to your
    Queen ?
    Becket. Rosamund hath not an-
swer'd you one word ;
Madam, I will not answer you one
    word.
Daughter, the world hath trick'd thee.
    Leave it, daughter ;
Come thou with me to Godstow nun-
    nery,
And live what may be left thee of a
    life
Saved as by miracle alone with Him
    Who gave it.

      Re-enter GEOFFREY.

    Geoffrey. Mother, you told me a
    great fib : it wasn't in the willow.
    Becket. Follow us, my son, and we
    will find it for thee —
Or something manlier.
    [*Exeunt* Becket, Rosamund, *and*
    Geoffrey.
    Eleanor. The world hath trick'd her
    — that's the King ; if so,
There was the farce, the feint — not
    mine. And yet
I am all but sure my dagger was a
    feint
Till the worm turn'd — not life shot
    up in blood,
But death drawn in ; — (*looking at the
    vial*) *this* was no feint then ? no.
But can I swear to that, had she but
    given
Plain answer to plain query ? nay,
    methinks
Had she but bow'd herself to meet the
    wave
Of humiliation, worshipt whom she
    loathed,
I should have let her be, scorn'd her
    too much
To harm her. Henry — Becket tells
    him this —
To take my life might lose him
    Aquitaine.
Too politic for that. Imprison me ?
No, for it came to nothing — only a
    feint.

Did she not tell me I was playing on
    her ?
I'll swear to mine own self it was a
    feint.
Why should I swear, Eleanor, who
    am, or was,
A sovereign power ? The King plucks
    out their eyes
Who anger him, and shall not I, the
    Queen,
Tear out her heart — kill, kill with
    knife or venom
One of his slanderous harlots ? "None
    of such ? "
I love her none the more. Tut, the
    chance gone,
She lives — but not for him ; one point
    is gain'd.
O I, that thro' the Pope divorced King
    Louis,
Scorning his monkery, — I that wedded
    Henry,
Honoring his manhood — will he not
    mock at me
The jealous fool balk'd of her will —
    with *him* ?
But he and he must never meet again.
Reginald Fitzurse !

      Re-enter FITZURSE.

    Fitzurse. Here, Madam, at your
    pleasure.
    Eleanor. My pleasure is to have a
    man about me.
Why did you slink away so like a
    cur ?
    Fitzurse. Madam, I am as much
    man as the King.
Madam, I fear Church-censures like
    your King.
    Eleanor. He grovels to the Church
    when he's black-blooded,
But kinglike fought the proud arch-
    bishop, — kinglike
Defied the Pope, and, like his kingly
    sires,
The Normans, striving still to break or
    bind
The spiritual giant with our island
    laws
And customs, made me for the moment
    proud

Ev'n of that stale Church-bond which link'd me with him
To bear him kingly sons. I am not so sure
But that I love him still. Thou as much man!
No more of that; we will to France and be
Beforehand with the King, and brew from out
This Godstow-Becket intermeddling such
A strong hate-philtre as may madden him — madden
Against his priest beyond all hellebore.

ACT V.

SCENE I. — CASTLE IN NORMANDY. KING'S CHAMBER.

HENRY, ROGER OF YORK, FOLIOT, JOCELYN OF SALISBURY.

Roger of York. Nay, nay, my liege,
He rides abroad with armed followers,
Hath broken all his promises to thyself,
Cursed and anathematized us right and left,
Stirr'd up a party there against your son —
  Henry. Roger of York, you always hated him,
Even when you both were boys at Theobald's.
  Roger of York. I always hated boundless arrogance.
In mine own cause I strove against him there,
And in thy cause I strive against him now.
  Henry. I cannot think he moves against my son,
Knowing right well with what a tenderness
He loved my son.
  Roger of York. Before you made him king.
But Becket ever moves against a king.
The Church is all — the crime to be a king.

We trust your Royal Grace, lord of more land
Than any crown in Europe, will not yield
To lay your neck beneath your citizens' heel.
  Henry. Not to a Gregory of my throning! No.
  Foliot. My royal liege, in aiming at your love,
It may be sometimes I have overshot
My duties to our Holy Mother Church,
Tho' all the world allows I fall no inch
Behind this Becket, rather go beyond
In scourgings, macerations, mortifyings,
Fasts, disciplines that clear the spiritual eye,
And break the soul from earth. Let all that be.
I boast not: but you know thro' all this quarrel
I still have cleaved to the crown, in hope the crown
Would cleave to me that but obey'd the crown,
Crowning your son; for which our loyal service,
And since we likewise swore to obey the customs,
York and myself, and our good Salisbury here,
Are push'd from out communion of the Church.
  Jocelyn of Salisbury. Becket hath trodden on us like worms, my liege;
Trodden one half dead; one half, but half-alive,
Cries to the King.
  Henry (aside). Take care o' thyself, O King.
  Jocelyn of Salisbury. Being so crush'd and so humiliated
We scarcely dare to bless the food we eat
Because of Becket.
  Henry. What would ye have me do?
  Roger of York. Summon your barons; take their counsel: yet

I know — could swear — as long as Becket breathes,

Your Grace will never have one quiet hour.

Henry. What ? . . . Ay . . . but pray you do not work upon me.

I see your drift . . . it may be so . . . and yet

You know me easily anger'd. Will you hence ?

He shall absolve you . . . you shall have redress.

I have a dizzying headache. Let me rest.

I'll call you by and by.

[*Exeunt* Roger of York, Foliot, *and* Jocelyn of Salisbury.

Would he were dead! I have lost all love for him.

If God would take him in some sudden way —

Would he were dead. [*Lies down.*

Page (entering). My liege, the Queen of England.

Henry. God's eyes! [*Starting up.*

Enter ELEANOR.

Eleanor. Of England ? Say of Aquitaine.

I am no Queen of England. I had dream'd

I was the bride of England, and a queen.

Henry. And, — while you dream'd you were the bride of England, —

Stirring her baby-king against me ? ha!

Eleanor. The brideless Becket is thy king and mine :

I will go live and die in Aquitaine.

Henry. Except I clap thee into prison here,

Lest thou shouldst play the wanton there again.

Ha, you of Aquitaine! O you of Aquitaine!

You were but Aquitaine to Louis — no wife ;

You are only Aquitaine to me — no wife.

Eleanor. And why, my lord, should I be wife to one

That only wedded me for Aquitaine ?

Yet this no wife — her six and thirty sail

Of Provence blew you to your English throne ;

And this no wife has borne you four brave sons,

And one of them at least is like to prove

Bigger in our small world than thou art.

Henry. Ay —

Richard, if he *be* mine — I hope him mine.

But thou art like enough to make him thine.

Eleanor. Becket is like enough to make all his.

Henry. Methought I had recover'd of the Becket,

That all was planed and bevell'd smooth again,

Save from some hateful cantrip of thine own.

Eleanor. I will go live and die in Aquitaine.

I dream'd I was the consort of a king,

Not one whose back his priest has broken.

Henry. What !

Is the end come ? You, will you crown my foe

My victor in mid-battle ? I will be

Sole master of my house. The end is mine.

What game, what juggle, what devilry are you playing ?

Why do you thrust this Becket on me again ?

Eleanor. Why ? for I *am* true wife, and have my fears

Lest Becket thrust you even from your throne.

Do you know this cross, my liege ?

Henry (turning his head). Away! Not I.

Eleanor. Not ev'n the central diamond, worth, I think,

Half of the Antioch whence I had it.

Henry. That ?

Eleanor. I gave it to you, and you
  your paramour;
She sends it back, as being dead to
  earth,
So dead henceforth to you.
  Henry. Dead! you have murder'd
    her,
Found out her secret bower and mur-
  der'd her.
  Eleanor. Your Becket knew the
    secret of your bower.
  Henry (calling out). Ho there! thy
    rest of life is hopeless prison.
  Eleanor. And what would my own
    Aquitaine say to that?
First, free thy captive from *her* hope-
  less prison.
  Henry. O devil, can I free her from
    the grave?
  Eleanor. You are too tragic: both
    of us are players
In such a comedy as our court of
  Provence
Had laugh'd at. That's a delicate
  Latin lay
Of Walter Map: the lady holds the
  cleric
Lovelier than any soldier, his poor
  tonsure
A crown of Empire. Will you have
  it again?
  [*Offering the cross. He dashes it
    down.*
St. Cupid, that is too irreverent.
Then mine once more. (*Puts it on.*)
    Your cleric hath your lady.
Nay, what uncomely faces, could he
  see you!
Foam at the mouth because King
  Thomas, lord
Not only of your vassals but
  amours,
Thro' chastest honor of the Decalogue
Hath used the full authority of his
  Church
To put her into Godstow nunnery.
  Henry. To put her into Godstow
    nunnery!
He dared not — liar! yet, yet I
  remember —
I do remember.
He bade me put her into a nunnery —

Into Godstow, into Hellstow, Devil-
  stow!
The Church! the Church!
God's eyes! I would the Church
  were down in hell!   [*Exit.*
  Eleanor. Aha!

  Enter the four KNIGHTS.

  Fitzurse. What made the King cry
    out so furiously?
  Eleanor. Our Becket, who will not
    absolve the Bishops.
I think ye four have cause to love
  this Becket.
  Fitzurse. I hate him for his inso-
    lence to all.
  De Tracy. And I for his insolence
    to thee.
  De Brito. I hate him for I hate
    him is my reason,
And yet I hate him for a hypocrite.
  De Morville. I do not love him, for
    he did his best
To break the barons, and now braves
  the King.
  Eleanor. Strike, then, at once, the
    King would have him — See!

  Re-enter HENRY.

  Henry. No man to love me, honor
    me, obey me!
Sluggards and fools!
The slave that eat my bread has
  kick'd his King!
The dog I cramm'd with dainties wor-
  ried me!
The fellow that on a lame jade came
  to court,
A ragged cloak for saddle — he, he,
  he,
To shake my throne, to push into my
  chamber —
My bed, where ev'n the slave is pri-
  vate — he —
I'll have her out again, he shall ab-
  solve
The bishops — they but did my will
  — not you —
Sluggards and fools, why do you stand
  and stare?
You are no king's men — you — you
  — you are Becket's men.

Down with King Henry! up with the
    Archbishop!
Will no man free me from this pesti-
    lent priest?   [*Exit.*
    [*The* Knights *draw their swords.*
Eleanor. Are ye king's men? I am
    king's woman, I.
The Knights. King's men! King's
    men!

SCENE II.

A ROOM IN CANTERBURY MONAS-
TERY.

BECKET *and* JOHN OF SALISBURY.

Becket. York said so?
John of Salisbury. Yes: a man may
    take good counsel
Ev'n from his foe.
Becket.   York will say anything.
What is he saying now? gone to the
    King
And taken our anathema with him.
    York!
Can the King de-anathematize this
    York?
John of Salisbury. Thomas, I would
    thou hadst return'd to England,
Like some wise prince of this world
    from his wars,
With more of olive-branch and am-
    nesty
For foes at home — thou hast raised
    the world against thee.
Becket. Why, John, my kingdom is
    not of this world.
John of Salisbury. If it were more
    of this world it might be
More of the next. A policy of wise
    pardon
Wins here as well as there. To bless
    thine enemies ——
Becket. Ay, mine, not Heaven's.
John of Salisbury. And may there
    not be something
Of this world's leaven in thee too,
    when crying
On Holy Church to thunder out her
    rights

And thine own wrong so pitilessly?
    Ah, Thomas,
The lightnings that we think are only
    Heaven's
Flash sometimes out of earth against
    the heavens.
The soldier, when he lets his whole
    self go
Lost in the common good, the com-
    mon wrong,
Strikes truest ev'n for his own self.
    I crave
Thy pardon — I have still thy leave
    to speak.
Thou hast waged God's war against
    the King; and yet
We are self-uncertain creatures, and
    we may,
Yea, even when we know not, mix our
    spites
And private hates with our defence of
    Heaven.

Enter EDWARD GRIM.

Becket. Thou art but yesterday
    from Cambridge, Grim;
What say ye there of Becket?
Grim.   *I* believe him
The bravest in our roll of Primates
    down
From Austin — there are some — for
    there are men
Of canker'd judgment everywhere——
Becket.   Who hold
With York, with York against me.
Grim.   Well, my lord,
A stranger monk desires access to you.
Becket. York against Canterbury,
    York against God!
I am open to him.   [*Exit* Grim.

Enter ROSAMUND *as a Monk.*

Rosamund.   Can I speak with you
Alone, my father?
Becket.   Come you to confess?
Rosamund. Not now.
Becket. Then speak; this is my
    other self,
Who like my conscience never lets
    me be.

Rosamund (*throwing back the cowl*).
  I know him; our good John of
  Salisbury.
Becket. Breaking already from thy
  novitiate
To plunge into this bitter world
  again —
These wells of Marah. I am grieved,
  my daughter.
I thought that I had made a peace for
  thee.
  Rosamund. Small peace was mine
  in my novitiate, father.
Thro' all closed doors a dreadful
  whisper crept
That thou wouldst excommunicate the
  King.
I could not eat, sleep, pray: I had
  with me
The monk's disguise thou gavest me
  for my bower:
I think our Abbess knew it and
  allow'd it.
I fled, and found thy name a charm to
  get me
Food, roof, and rest. I met a robber
  once,
I told him I was bound to see the
  Archbishop;
"Pass on," he said, and in thy name
  I pass'd
From house to house. In one a son
  stone-blind
Sat by his mother's hearth: he had
  gone too far
Into the King's own woods; and the
  poor mother,
Soon as she learnt I was a friend of
  thine,
Cried out against the cruelty of the
  King.
I said it was the King's courts, not
  the King;
But she would not believe me, and
  she wish'd
The Church were King: she had seen
  the Archbishop once,
So mild, so kind. The people love
  thee, father.
  Becket. Alas! when I was Chancel-
  lor to the King,
I fear I was as cruel as the King.

  Rosamund. Cruel? Oh, no — it is
  the law, not he;
The customs of the realm.
  Becket.   The customs! customs!
  Rosamund. My lord, you have not
  excommunicated him?
Oh, if you have, absolve him!
  Becket.   Daughter, daughter,
Deal not with things you know
  not.
  Rosamund.   I know *him*.
Then you have done it, and I call *you*
  cruel.
  John of Salisbury. No, daughter,
  you mistake our good Arch-
  bishop;
For once in France the King had been
  so harsh,
He thought to excommunicate him —
  Thomas,
You could not — old affection mas-
  ter'd you,
You falter'd into tears.
  Rosamund.   God bless him for it.
  Becket. Nay, make me not a
  woman, John of Salisbury,
Nor make me traitor to my holy
  office.
Did not a man's voice ring along the
  aisle,
"The King is sick and almost unto
  death."
How could I excommunicate him
  then?
  Rosamund. And wilt thou excom-
  municate him now?
  Becket. Daughter, my time is short,
  I shall not do it.
And were it longer — well — I should
  not do it.
  Rosamund. Thanks in this life, and
  in the life to come.
  Becket. Get thee back to thy nun-
  nery with all haste;
Let this be thy last trespass. But
  one question —
How fares thy pretty boy, the little
  Geoffrey?
No fever, cough, croup, sickness?
  Rosamund.   No, but saved
From all that by our solitude. The
  plagues

That smite the city spare the solitudes.

Becket. God save him from all sickness of the soul!
Thee too, thy solitude among thy nuns,
May that save thee! Doth he remember me?

Rosamund. I warrant him.

Becket. He is marvellously like thee.

Rosamund. Liker the King.

Becket. No, daughter.

Rosamund. Ay, but wait
Till his nose rises; he will be very king.

Becket. Ev'n so: but think not of the King: farewell!

Rosamund. My lord, the city is full of armed men.

Becket. Ev'n so: farewell!

Rosamund. I will but pass to vespers,
And breathe one prayer for my liege-lord the King,
His child and mine own soul, and so return.

Becket. Pray for me too: much need of prayer have I.

[*Rosamund kneels and goes.*

Dan John, how much we lose, we celibates,
Lacking the love of woman and of child.

John of Salisbury. More gain than loss; for of your wives you shall
Find one a slut whose fairest linen seems
Foul as her dust-cloth, if she used it — one
So charged with tongue, that every thread of thought
Is broken ere it joins — a shrew to boot,
Whose evil song far on into the night
Thrills to the topmost tile — no hope but death;
One slow, fat, white, a burthen of the hearth;
And one that being thwarted ever swoons
And weeps herself into the place of power;
And one an *uxor pauperis Ibyci.*
So rare the household honeymaking bee,
Man's help! but we, we have the Blessed Virgin
For worship, and our Mother Church for bride;
And all the souls we saved and father'd here
Will greet us as our babes in Paradise.
What noise was that? she told us of arm'd men
Here in the city. Will you not withdraw?

Becket. I once was out with Henry in the days
When Henry loved me, and we came upon
A wild-fowl sitting on her nest, so still
I reach'd my hand and touch'd; she did not stir;
The snow had frozen round her, and she sat
Stone-dead upon a heap of ice-cold eggs.
Look! how this love, this mother, runs thro' all
The world God made — even the beast — the bird!

John of Salisbury. Ay, still a lover of the beast and bird?
But these arm'd men — will you not hide yourself?
Perchance the fierce De Brocs from Saltwood Castle,
To assail our Holy Mother lest she brood
Too long o'er this hard egg, the world, and send
Her whole heart's heat into it, till it break
Into young angels. Pray you, hide yourself.

Becket. There was a little fair-hair'd Norman maid
Lived in my mother's house: if Rosamund is
The world's rose, as her name imports her — she
Was the world's lily.

John of Salisbury. Ay, and what of her?

Becket. She died of leprosy.

John of Salisbury. I know not why You call these old things back again, my lord.

Becket. The drowning man, they say, remembers all The chances of his life, just ere he dies.

John of Salisbury. Ay — but these arm'd men — will *you* drown *yourself?*

He loses half the meed of martyrdom Who will be martyr when he might escape.

Becket. What day of the week? Tuesday?

John of Salisbury. Tuesday, my lord.

Becket. On a Tuesday was I born, and on a Tuesday Baptized; and on a Tuesday did I fly Forth from Northampton; on a Tuesday pass'd From England into bitter banishment; On a Tuesday at Pontigny came to me The ghostly warning of my martyrdom; On a Tuesday from mine exile I return'd, And on a Tuesday ——

[*Tracy enters, then* Fitzurse, De Brito, *and* De Morville. *Monks following.*

— on a Tuesday —— Tracy!

[*A long silence, broken by* Fitzurse *saying, contemptuously,*

God help thee!

John of Salisbury (*aside*). How the good Archbishop reddens!

He never yet could brook the note of scorn.

Fitzurse. My lord, we bring a message from the King Beyond the water; will you have it alone, Or with these listeners near you?

Becket. As you will.

Fitzurse. Nay, as *you* will.

Becket. Nay, as *you* will.

John of Salisbury. Why then Better perhaps to speak with them apart.

Let us withdraw.

[*All go out except the four* Knights *and* Becket.

Fitzurse. We are all alone with him.

Shall I not smite him with his own cross-staff?

De Morville. No, look! the door is open: let him be.

Fitzurse. The King condemns your excommunicating ——

Becket. This is no secret, but a public matter.

In here again!

[John of Salisbury *and* Monks *return.*

Now, sirs, the King's commands!

Fitzurse. The King beyond the water, thro' our voices, Commands you to be dutiful and leal To your young King on this side of the water, Not scorn him for the foibles of his youth. What! you would make his coronation void By cursing those who crown'd him. Out upon you!

Becket. Reginald, all men know I loved the Prince.

His father gave him to my care, and I Became his second father: he had his faults, For which I would have laid my own life down To help him from them, since indeed I loved him, And love him next after my lord his father. Rather than dim the splendor of his crown I fain would treble and quadruple it With revenues, realms, and golden provinces So that were done in equity.

Fitzurse. You have broken

Your bond of peace, your treaty with
  the King —
Wakening such brawls and loud dis-
  turbances
In England, that he calls you oversea
To answer for it in his Norman courts.
  Becket. Prate not of bonds, for
    never, oh, never again
Shall the waste voice of the bond-
  breaking sea
Divide me from the mother church of
  England,
My Canterbury. Loud disturbances!
Oh, ay — the bells rang out even to
  deafening,
Organ and pipe, and dulcimer, chants
  and hymns
In all the churches, trumpets in the
  halls,
Sobs, laughter, cries : they spread
  their raiment down
Before me — would have made my
  pathway flowers,
Save that it was mid-winter in the
  street,
But full mid-summer in those honest
  hearts.
  Fitzurse. The King commands you
    to absolve the bishops
Whom you have excommunicated.
  Becket.   I ?
Not I, the Pope. Ask *him* for absolu-
  tion.
  Fitzurse. But you advised the Pope.
  Becket.   And so I did.
They have but to submit.
  The Four Knights. The King com-
    mands you.
We are all King's men.
  Becket. King's men at least should
    know
That their own King closed with me
  last July
That I should pass the censures of
  the Church
On those that crown'd young Henry
  in this realm,
And trampled on the rights of Can-
  terbury.
  Fitzurse. What! dare you charge
    the King with treachery ?
He sanction thee to excommunicate

The prelates whom he chose to crown
  his son !
  Becket. I spake no word of treach-
    ery, Reginald.
But for the truth of this I make appeal
To all the archbishops, bishops, pre-
  lates, barons,
Monks, knights, five hundred, that
  were there and heard.
Nay, you yourself were there: you
  heard yourself.
  Fitzurse. I was not there.
  Becket.   I saw you there.
  Fitzurse.   I was not.
  Becket. You were. I never forget
    anything.
  Fitzurse. He makes the King a
    traitor, me a liar.
How long shall we forbear him ?
  John of Salisbury (*drawing* Becket
    aside). O my good lord,
Speak with them privately on this
  hereafter.
You see they have been revelling,
  and I fear
Are braced and brazen'd up with
  Christmas wines
For any murderous brawl.
  Becket.   And yet they prate
Of mine, my brawls, when those, that
  name themselves
Of the King's part, have broken down
  our barns,
Wasted our diocese, outraged our ten-
  ants.
Lifted our produce, driven our clerics
  out —
Why they, your friends, these ruffians,
  the De Brocs,
They stood on Dover beach to mur-
  der me,
They slew my stags in mine own manor
  here,
Mutilated, poor brute, my sumpter-
  mule,
Plunder'd the vessel full of Gascon
  wine,
The old King's present, carried off the
  casks,
Kill'd half the crew, dungeon'd the
  other half
In Pevensey Castle ——

De Morville. Why not rather then,
If this be so, complain to your young
    King,
Not punish of your own authority ?
Becket. Mine enemies barr'd all ac-
    cess to the boy.
They knew he loved me.
Hugh, Hugh, how proudly you exalt
    your head !
Nay, when they seek to overturn our
    rights,
I ask no leave of king, or mortal
    man,
To set them straight again. Alone I
    do it.
Give to the King the things that are
    the King's,
And those of God to God.
Fitzurse.   Threats ! threats !
    ye hear him.
What! will he excommunicate all the
    world ?
    [*The* Knights *come round* Becket.
De Tracy. He shall not.
De Brito.   Well, as yet
    — I should be grateful —
He hath not excommunicated *me.*
Becket. Because thou was *born* ex-
    communicate.
I never spied in thee one gleam of
    grace.
De Brito. Your Christian's Chris-
    tian charity.
Becket.   By St. Denis——
De Brito. Ay, by St. Denis, now will
    he flame out,
And lose his head as old St. Denis
    did.
Becket. Ye think to scare me from
    my loyalty
To God and to the Holy Father.
    No !
Tho' all the swords in England flash'd
    above me
Ready to fall at Henry's word or
    yours —
Tho' all the loud-lung'd trumpets
    upon earth
Blared from the heights of all the
    thrones of her kings,
Blowing the world against me, I would
    stand

Clothed with the full authority of
    Rome,
Mail'd in the perfect panoply of faith,
First of the foremost of their files,
    who die
For God, to people heaven in the great
    day
When God makes up his jewels. Once
    I fled —
Never again, and you — I marvel at
    you —
Ye know what is between us. Ye
    have sworn
Yourselves my men when I was Chan-
    cellor —
My vassals — and yet threaten your
    Archbishop
In his own house.
Knights. Nothing can be between us
That goes against our fealty to the
    King.
Fitzurse. And in his name we charge
    you that ye keep
This traitor from escaping.
Becket.   Rest you easy,
For I am easy to keep. I shall not fly.
Here, here, here will you find me.
De Morville.   Know you not
You have spoken to the peril of your
    life ?
Becket. As I shall speak again.
Fitzurse, De Tracy, and De Brito. To
    arms !
    [*They rush out,* De Morville *lingers.*
Becket.   De Morville,
I had thought so well of you ; and
    even now
You seem the least assassin of the
    four.
Oh, do not damn yourself for com-
    pany !
Is it too late for me to save your soul ?
I pray you for one moment stay and
    speak.
De Morville. Becket, it *is* too late.
    [*Exit.*
Becket.   Is it too late ?
Too late on earth may be too soon in
    hell.
Knights (in the distance). Close the
    great gate — ho, there — upon
    the town.

Becket's Retainers. Shut the hall-
　　doors. 　　　　　　[*A pause.*

Becket. You hear them, brother
　　John ;
Why do you stand so silent, brother
　　John ?

John of Salisbury. For I was mus-
　　ing on an ancient saw,

Suaviter in modo, fortiter in re,
Is strength less strong when hand-in-
　　hand with grace ?

Gratior in pulchro corpore virtus.
　　Thomas,
Why should you heat yourself for
　　such as these ?

Becket. Methought I answer'd mod-
　　erately enough.

John of Salisbury. As one that
　　blows the coal to cool the fire.
My lord, I marvel why you never lean
On any man's advising but your own.

Becket. Is it so, Dan John ? well,
　　what should I have done ?

John of Salisbury. You should have
　　taken counsel with your friends
Before these bandits brake into your
　　presence.
They seek — you make — occasion for
　　your death.

Becket. My counsel is already taken,
　　John.
I am prepared to die.

John of Salisbury. We are sinners
　　all,
The best of all not all-prepared to die.

Becket. God's will be done !

John of Salisbury. Ay, well. God's
　　will be done !

GRIM (*re-entering*).

Grim. My lord, the knights are
　　arming in the garden
Beneath the sycamore.

Becket. 　　　　Good ! let them arm.

Grim. And one of the De Brocs is
　　with them, Robert,
The apostate monk that was with
　　Randulf here.
He knows the twists and turnings of
　　the place.

Becket. No fear !

Grim. 　　　　No fear, my lord.
　　[*Crashes on the hall-doors.　The
　　Monks flee.*

Becket (*rising*). Our dovecote flown !
I cannot tell why monks should all
　　be cowards.

John of Salisbury. Take refuge in
　　your own cathedral, Thomas.

Becket. Do they not fight the Great
　　Fiend day by day ?
Valor and holy life should go together.
Why should all monks be cowards ?

John of Salisbury. 　　Are they so ?
I say, take refuge in your own cathe-
　　dral.

Becket. Ay, but I told them I would
　　wait them here.

Grim. May they not say you dared
　　not show yourself
In your old place ? and vespers are
　　beginning.
[*Bell rings for vespers till end of scene.*
You should attend the office, give
　　them heart.
They fear you slain : they dread they
　　know not what.

Becket. Ay, monks, not men.

Grim. I am a monk, my lord.
Perhaps, my lord, you wrong us.
Some would stand by you to the death.

Becket. 　　　　Your pardon.

John of Salisbury. He said, "At-
　　tend the office."

Becket. 　　　　Attend the office ?
Why then — The Cross ! — who bears
　　my Cross before me ?
Methought they would have brain'd
　　me with it, John.
　　　　　　[*Grim takes it.*

Grim. I ! Would that I could bear
　　thy cross indeed !

Becket. The Mitre !

John of Salisbury. 　　Will you wear
　　it ? — there !
　　　[*Becket puts on the mitre.*

Becket. 　　　　The Pall !
I go to meet my King !
　　　　[*Puts on the pall.*

Grim. To meet the King ?
　　[*Crashes on the doors as they go out.*

John of Salisbury. Why do you
　　move with such a stateliness ?

Can you not hear them yonder like a
    storm,
Battering the doors, and breaking
    thro' the walls ?

  Becket. Why do the heathen rage ?
    My two good friends,
What matters murder'd here or mur-
    der'd there ?
And yet my dream foretold my mar-
    tyrdom
In mine own church. It is God's will.
    Go on.
Nay, drag me not. We must not seem
    to fly.

SCENE III. — NORTH TRANSEPT OF
  CANTERBURY CATHEDRAL. ON THE
  RIGHT HAND A FLIGHT OF STEPS
  LEADING TO THE CHOIR, ANOTHER
  FLIGHT ON THE LEFT, LEADING TO
  THE NORTH AISLE. WINTER AF-
  TERNOON SLOWLY DARKENING. LOW
  THUNDER NOW AND THEN OF AN AP-
  PROACHING STORM. MONKS HEARD
  CHANTING THE SERVICE. ROSA-
  MUND KNEELING.

  Rosamund. O blessed saint, O glori-
    ous Benedict, —
These arm'd men in the city, these
    fierce faces —
Thy holy follower founded Canter-
    bury —
Save that dear head which now is
    Canterbury,
Save him, he saved my life, he saved
    my child,
Save him, his blood would darken
    Henry's name ;
Save him till all as saintly as thyself
He miss the searching flame of purga-
    tory, and pass at once perfect
    to Paradise.
  [*Noise of steps and voices in the cloisters.*
Hark ! Is it they ? Coming ! He is
    not here —
Not yet, thank heaven. O save him !
    [*Goes up steps leading to choir.*

BECKET (*entering, forced along by* JOHN
  OF SALISBURY *and* GRIM).

  Becket.   No, I tell you !
I cannot bear a hand upon my person,

Why do you force me thus against
    my will ?
  Grim. My lord, we force you from
    your enemies.
  Becket. As you would force a king
    from being crown'd.
  John of Salisbury. We must not
    force the crown of martyrdom.
    [*Service stops.* Monks *come down
    from the stairs that lead to the
    choir.*
  Monks. Here is the great Arch-
    bishop ! He lives ! he lives !
Die with him, and be glorified to-
    gether.
  Becket. Together ? . . . get you
    back ! go on with the office.
  Monks. Come, then, with us to ves-
    pers.
  Becket.   How can I come
When you so block the entry ? Back,
    I say !
Go on with the office. Shall not
    Heaven be served
Tho' earth's last earthquake clash'd
    the minster-bells,
And the great deeps were broken up
    again,
And hiss'd against the sun ?
    [*Noise in the cloisters.*
  Monks.   The murderers, hark !
Let us hide ! let us hide !
  Becket. What do these people fear ?
  Monks. Those arm'd men in the
    cloister.
  Becket.   Be not such cravens !
I will go out and meet them.
  Grim and others.   Shut the doors !
We will not have him slain before
    our face.
    [*They close the doors of the transept.
    Knocking.*
Fly, fly, my lord, before they burst
    the doors !   [*Knocking.*
  Becket. Why, these are our own
    monks who follow'd us !
And will you bolt them out, and have
    them slain ?
Undo the doors : the church is not a
    castle :
Knock, and it shall be open'd. Are
    you deaf ?

What, have I lost authority among
    you ?
Stand by, make way !
    [*Opens the doors.* Enter Monks
    from cloister.
    Come in, my friends, come in !
Nay, faster, faster !
  Monks. Oh, my lord Archbishop,
A score of knights all arm'd with
    swords and axes —
To the choir, to the choir !
    [*Monks divide, part flying by the
    stairs on the right, part by those
    on the left. The rush of these last
    bears* Becket *along with them
    some way up the steps, where he
    is left standing alone.*
  Becket. Shall I too pass to the choir,
And die upon the Patriarchal throne
Of all my predecessors ?
  John of Salisbury. No, to the crypt !
Twenty steps down. Stumble not in
    the darkness,
Lest they should seize thee.
  Grim.   To the crypt ? no — no,
To the chapel of St. Blaise beneath
    the roof !
  John of Salisbury (*pointing upward
    and downward*). That way, or
    this ! Save thyself either way.
  Becket. Oh, no, not either way, nor
    any way
Save by that way which leads thro'
    night to light.
Not twenty steps, but one.
And fear not I should stumble in the
    darkness,
Nor tho' it be their hour, the power of
    darkness,
But my hour too, the power of light
    in darkness !
I am not in the darkness but the light,
Seen by the Church in Heaven, the
    Church on earth —
The power of life in death to make
    her free !
    [*Enter the four* Knights. John of
    Salisbury *flies to the altar of St.
    Benedict.*
  Fitzurse. Here, here, King's men !
    [*Catches hold of the last flying* Monk.
    Where is the traitor Becket ?

  Monk. I am not he ! I am not he,
    my lord.
I am not he indeed !
  Fitzurse. Hence to the fiend !
                [*Pushes him away.*
Where is this treble traitor to the King ?
  De Tracy. Where is the Archbishop,
    Thomas Becket ?
  Becket.   Here.
No traitor to the King, but Priest of
    God,
Primate of England.
    [*Descending into the transept.*
                I am he ye seek.
What would ye have of me ?
  Fitzurse.   Your life.
  De Tracy.   Your life.
  De Morville. Save that you will
    absolve the bishops.
  Becket.   Never, —
Except they make submission to the
    Church.
You had my answer to that cry before.
  De Morville. Why, then you are a
    dead man ; flee !
  Becket.   I will not.
I am readier to be slain, than thou to
    slay.
Hugh, I know well thou hast but half
    a heart
To bathe this sacred pavement with
    my blood.
God pardon thee and these, but God's
    full curse
Shatter you all to pieces if ye harm
One of my flock !
  Fitzurse. Was not the great gate
    shut ?
They are thronging in to vespers —
    half the town.
We shall be overwhelm'd. Seize him
    and carry him !
Come with us — nay — thou art our
    prisoner — come !
  De Morville. Ay, make him prisoner,
    do not harm the man.
    [Fitzurse *lays hold of the* Arch-
    bishop's *pall.*
  Becket. Touch me not !
  De Brito. How the good priest gods
    himself !
He is not yet ascended to the Father.

Fitzurse. I will not only touch, but drag thee hence.

Becket. Thou art my man, thou art my vassal. Away!

   [Flings him off till he reels, almost to falling.

De Tracy (lays hold of the pall). Come; as he said, thou art our prisoner.

Becket.   Down!

   [Throws him headlong.

Fitzurse (advances with drawn sword). I told thee that I should remember thee!

Becket. Profligate pander!

Fitzurse. Do you hear that? strike, strike.

   [Strikes off the Archbishop's *mitre, and wounds him in the forehead.*

Becket (covers his eyes with his hand). I do commend my cause to God, the Virgin,

St. Denis of France and St. Alphege of England,

And all the tutelar Saints of Canterbury.

   [Grim wraps his arms about the Archbishop.

Spare this defence, dear brother.

   [Tracy has arisen, and approaches, hesitatingly, with his sword raised.

Fitzurse. Strike him, Tracy!

Rosamund (rushing down steps from choir). No, No, No, No!

Fitzurse. This wanton here. De Morville,

Hold her away.

De Morville. I hold her.

Rosamund (held back by De Morville, *and stretching out her arms).* Mercy, mercy,

As you would hope for mercy.

Fitzurse.   Strike, I say.

Grim. O God, O noble knights, O sacrilege!

Strike our Archbishop in his own cathedral!

The Pope, the King, will curse you — the whole world

Abhor you; ye will die the death of dogs!

Nay, nay, good Tracy. *[Lifts his arm.*

Fitzurse.   Answer not, but strike.

De Tracy. There is my answer then.

   [Sword falls on Grim's *arm, and glances from it, wounding* Becket.

Grim.   Mine arm is sever'd.

I can no more — fight out the good fight — die

Conqueror.

   [Staggers into the chapel of St. Benedict.

Becket (falling on his knees). At the right hand of Power —

Power and great glory — for thy Church, O Lord —

Into Thy hands, O Lord — into Thy hands! ——   *[Sinks prone.*

De Brito. This last to rid thee of a world of brawls!   *[Kills him.*

The traitor's dead, and will arise no more.

Fitzurse. Nay, have we still'd him? What! the great Archbishop!

Does he breathe? No?

De Tracy. No, Reginald, he is dead.

   [Storm bursts.[1]

De Morville. Will the earth gape and swallow us?

De Brito.   The deed's done. — Away!

   [De Brito, De Tracy, Fitzurse, rush out, crying "King's men!" De Morville *follows slowly. Flashes of lightning thro' the Cathedral.* Rosamund *seen kneeling by the body of* Becket.

---

[1] A tremendous thunderstorm actually broke over the Cathedral as the murderers were leaving it.

THE PROMISE OF MAY.

DRAMATIS PERSONÆ.

FARMER DOBSON.
Mr. PHILIP EDGAR, *afterwards* Mr. HAROLD.
FARMER STEER, DORA and EVA's *Father.*
Mr. WILSON, *a Schoolmaster.*
HIGGINS ⎫
JAMES ⎪
DAN SMITH ⎬ *Farm Laborers.*
JACKSON ⎪
ALLEN ⎭
DORA STEER.
EVA STEER.
SALLY ALLEN ⎫ *Farm Servants.*
MILLY ⎭

Farm Servants, Laborers, etc.

ACT I.

SCENE. — BEFORE FARMHOUSE.

Farming Men and Women. Farming Men carrying forms, etc., Women carrying baskets of knives and forks, etc.

1ST FARMING MAN.
Be thou a-gawin' to the long barn?

2D FARMING MAN.
Ay, to be sewer! Be thou?

1ST FARMING MAN.
Why, o' coorse, fur it be the owd man's birthdaäy. He be heighty this very daäy, and 'e telled all on us to be i' the long barn by one o'clock, fur he'll gie us a big dinner, and haäfe th' parish 'll be theer, an' Miss Dora, an' Miss Eva, an' all!

2D FARMING MAN.
Miss Dora be coomed back, then?

1ST FARMING MAN.
Ay, haäfe an hour ago. She be in theer now. (*Pointing to house.*) Owd Steer wur afeärd she wouldn't be back i' time to keep his birthdaäy, and he wur in a tew about it all the murnin'; and he sent me wi' the gig to Littlechester to fetch 'er; and 'er an' the owd man they fell a kissin' o' one another like two sweet'arts i' the poorch as soon as he clapt eyes of 'er.

2D FARMING MAN.
Foälks says he likes Miss Eva the best.

1ST FARMING MAN.
Naäy, I knaws nowt o' what foälks says, an' I caäres nowt neither. Foälks doesn't hallus knaw thessens; but sewer I be, they be two o' the purtiest gels ye can see of a summer murnin'.

2D FARMING MAN.

Beänt Miss Eva gone off a bit of
'er good looks o' laäte ?

1ST FARMING MAN.

Noä, not a bit.

2D FARMING MAN.

Why coöm awaäy, then, to the long
barn.
[*Exeunt.*

DORA *looks out of window.* *Enter*
DOBSON.

DORA (*singing*).

The town lay still in the low sun-light,
The hen cluckt late by the white farm
     gate,
The maid to her dairy came in from
     the cow,
The stock-dove coo'd at the fall of
     night,
The blossom had open'd on every
     bough ;
     O joy for the promise of May, of
     May,
     O joy for the promise of May.

(*Nodding at* DOBSON.) I'm coming
down, Mr. Dobson. I haven't seen
Eva yet. Is she anywhere in the
garden ?

DOBSON.

Noä, Miss. I ha'n't seed 'er neither.

DORA (*enters singing*).

But a red fire woke in the heart of
     the town,
And a fox from the glen ran away
     with the hen,
And a cat to the cream, and a rat to
     the cheese ;
And the stock-dove coo'd, till a kite
     dropt down,
And a salt wind burnt the blossoming
     trees ;
     O grief for the promise of May,
     of May,
     O grief for the promise of May.

I don't know why I sing that song;
I don't love it.

DOBSON.

Blessings on your pretty voice, Miss
Dora. Wheer did they larn ye that ?

DORA.

In Cumberland, Mr. Dobson.

DOBSON.

An' how did ye leäve the owd uncle
i' Coomberland ?

DORA.

Getting better, Mr. Dobson. But
he'll never be the same man again.

DOBSON.

An' how d'ye find the owd man
'ere ?

DORA.

As well as ever. I came back to
keep his birthday.

DOBSON.

Well, I be coomed to keep his
birthdaäy an' all. The owd man be
heighty to-daäy, beänt he ?

DORA.

Yes, Mr. Dobson. And the day's
bright like a friend, but the wind east
like an enemy. Help me to move
this bench for him into the sun.
(*They move bench.*) No, not that
way — here, under the apple tree.
Thank you. Look how full of rosy
blossom it is. [*Pointing to apple tree.*

DOBSON.

Theer be redder blossoms nor them,
Miss Dora.

DORA.

Where do they blow, Mr. Dobson ?

DOBSON.

Under your eyes, Miss Dora.

DORA.

Do they?

DOBSON.

And your eyes be as blue as ——

DORA.

What, Mr. Dobson? A butcher's frock?

DOBSON.

Noä, Miss Dora; as blue as ——

DORA.

Bluebell, harebell, speedwell, blue-bottle, succory, forget-me-not?

DOBSON.

Noä, Miss Dora; as blue as ——

DORA.

The sky? or the sea on a blue day?

DOBSON.

Naäy then. I meän'd they be as blue as violets.

DORA.

Are they?

DOBSON.

Theer ye goäs ageän, Miss, niver believing owt I says to ye — hallus a-fobbing ma off, tho' ye knaws I love ye. I warrants ye'll think moor o' this young Squire Edgar as ha' coomed among us — the Lord knaws how — ye'll think more on 'is little finger than hall my hand at the haltar.

DORA.

Perhaps, Master Dobson. I can't tell, for I have never seen him. But my sister wrote that he was mighty pleasant, and had no pride in him.

DOBSON.

He'll be arter you now, Miss Dora.

DORA.

Will he? How can I tell?

DOBSON.

He's been arter Miss Eva, haän't he?

DORA.

Not that I know.

DOBSON.

Didn't I spy 'em a-sitting i' the woodbine harbor togither?

DORA.

What of that? Eva told me that he was taking her likeness. He's an artist.

DOBSON.

What's a hartist? I doänt believe he's iver a 'eart under his waistcoat. And I tells ye what, Miss Dora: he's no respect for the Queen, or the parson, or the justice o' peace, or owt. I ha' heärd 'im a-gawin' on 'ud make your 'air — God bless it! — stan' on end. And wuss nor that. When theer wur a meeting o' farmers at Littlechester t'other daäy, and they was all a-crying out at the bad times, he cooms up, and he calls out among our oän men, "The land belongs to the people!"

DORA.

And what did *you* say to that?

DOBSON.

Well, I says, s'pose my pig's the land, and you says it belongs to the parish, and theer be a thousand i' the parish, taäkin' in the women and childer; and s'pose I kills my pig, and gi'es it among 'em, why there wudn't be a dinner for nawbody, and I should ha' lost the pig.

DORA.

And what did he say to that?

DOBSON.

Nowt — what could he saäy ? But I taäkes 'im fur a bad lot and a burn fool, and I haätes the very sight on him.

DORA.

(*Looking at* DOBSON.) Master Dobson, you are a comely man to look at.

DOBSON.

I thank you for that, Miss Dora, onyhow.

DORA.

Ay, but you turn right ugly when you're in an ill temper; and I promise you that if you forget yourself in your behavior to this gentleman, my father's friend, I will never change word with you again.

Enter FARMING MAN *from barn.*

FARMING MAN.

Miss, the farming men 'ull hev their dinner i' the long barn, and the master 'ud be straänge an' pleased if you'd step in fust, and see that all be right and reg'lar fur 'em afoor he coöm.

[*Exit.*

DORA.

I go. Master Dobson, did you hear what I said ?

DOBSON.

Yeas, yeas ! I'll not meddle wi' 'im if he doänt meddle wi' meä. (*Exit* DORA.) Coomly, says she. I niver thowt o' mysen i' that waäy ; but if she'd taäke to ma i' that waäy, or ony waäy, I'd slaäve out my life fur 'er. "Coomly to look at," says she — but she said it spiteful-like. To look at — yeas, "coomly"; and she mayn't be so fur out theer. But if that be nowt to she, then it be nowt to me. (*Looking off stage.*) Schoolmaster ! Why if Steer han't haxed school-master to dinner, thaw 'e knaws I

was hallus ageän heving schoolmaster i' the parish ! fur him as be handy wi' a book bean't but haäfe a hand at a pitchfork.

Enter WILSON.

Well, Wilson. I seed that one cow o' thine i' the pinfold ageän as I wur a-coomin' 'ere.

WILSON.

Very likely, Mr. Dobson. She *will* break fence. I can't keep her in order.

DOBSON.

An' if tha can't keep thy one cow i' horder, how can tha keep all thy scholards i' horder ? But let that goä by. What dost a knaw o' this Mr. Hedgar as be a-lodgin' wi' ye ? I coom'd upon 'im t'other daäy lookin' at the coontry, then a-scrattin upon a bit o' paäper, then a-lookin' agean ; and I taäked 'im fur soom sort of a land-surveyor — but a beänt.

WILSON.

He's a Somersetshire man, and a very civil-spoken gentleman.

DOBSON.

Gentleman ! What be he a-doing here ten mile an' moor fro' a raäil ? We laäys out o' the waäy fur gentle-foälk altogither — leästwaäys they niver cooms 'ere but fur the trout i' our beck, fur they be knaw'd as far as Littlechester. But 'e doänt fish neither.

WILSON.

Well, it's no sin in a gentleman not to fish.

DOBSON.

Noä, but I haätes 'im.

WILSON.

Better step out of his road, then, for he's walking to us, and with a book in his hand.

DOBSON.

An' I haätes booöks an' all, fur they puts foälk off the owd waäys.

Enter EDGAR, *reading — not seeing* DOBSON *and* WILSON.

EDGAR.

This author, with his charm of simple style
And close dialectic, all but proving man
An automatic series of sensations,
Has often numb'd me into apathy
Against the unpleasant jolts of this rough road
That breaks off short into the abysses — made me
A Quietist taking all things easily.

DOBSON.

(*Aside.*) There mun be summut wrong theer, Wilson, fur I doänt understan' it.

WILSON.

(*Aside.*) Nor I either, Mr. Dobson.

DOBSON.

(*Scornfully.*) An' thou doänt understan' it neither — and thou schoolmaster an' all.

EDGAR.

What can a man, then, live for but sensations,
Pleasant ones? men of old would undergo
Unpleasant for the sake of pleasant ones
Hereafter, like the Moslem beauties waiting
To clasp their lovers by the golden gates.
For me, whose cheerless Houris after death
Are Night and Silence, pleasant ones — the while —
If possible, here! to crop the flower and pass.

DOBSON.

Well, I never 'eärd the likes o' that afoor.

WILSON.

(*Aside.*) But I have, Mr. Dobson. It's the old Scripture text, "Let us eat and drink, for to-morrow we die." I'm sorry for it, for, tho' he never comes to church, I thought better of him.

EDGAR.

"What are we," says the blind old man in Lear?
"As flies to the Gods; they kill us for their sport."

DOBSON.

(*Aside.*) Then the owd man i' Lear should be shaämed of hissen, but noän o' the parishes goäs by that naäme 'ereabouts.

EDGAR.

The Gods! but they, the shadows of ourselves,
Have past forever. It is Nature kills,
And not for *her* sport either. She knows nothing.
Man only knows, the worse for him! for why
Cannot *he* take his pastime like the flies?
And if my pleasure breed another's pain,
Well — is not that the course of Nature too,
From the dim dawn of Being — her main law
Whereby she grows in beauty — that her flies
Must massacre each other? this poor Nature!

DOBSON.

Natur! Natur! Well, it be i' *my* natur to knock 'im o' the 'eäd now; but I weänt.

EDGAR.

A Quietest taking all things easily —
   why —
Have I been dipping into this again
To steel myself against the leaving
   her ?

(*Closes book, seeing* WILSON.)
Good day!

WILSON.

Good day, sir.

(DOBSON *looks hard at* EDGAR.)

EDGAR.

(*To* DOBSON.) Have I the pleasure,
friend, of knowing you ?

DOBSON.

Dobson.

EDGAR.

Good day, then, Dobson.   [*Exit.*

DOBSON.

" Good daäy then, Dobson ! " Civil-
spoken i'deed ! Why, Wilson, tha
'eärd 'im thysen — the feller couldn't
find a Mister in his mouth fur me, as
farms five hoonderd haäcre.

WILSON.

You never find one for me, Mr.
Dobson.

DOBSON.

Noä, fur thou be nobbut schoolmaster ; but I taäkes 'im fur a Lunnun
swindler, and a burn fool.

WILSON.

He can hardly be both, and he pays
me regular every Saturday.

DOBSON.

Yeas ; but I haätes 'im.

Enter STEER, FARM MEN *and* WOMEN.

STEER.

(*Goes and sits under apple tree.*)
Hev' ony o' ye seen Eva ?

DOBSON.

Noä, Mr. Steer.

STEER.

Well, I reckons they'll hev' a fine
cider-crop to-year if the blossom 'owds.
Good murnin', neighbors, and the
saäme to you, my men. I taäkes it
kindly of all o' you that you be
coomed — what's the newspaäper
word, Wilson ? — celebrate — to celebrate my birthdaäy i' this fashion.
Niver man 'ed better friends, and I will
saäy niver master 'ed better men : fur
thaw I may ha' fallen out wi' ye sometimes, the fault, mebbe, wur as much
mine as yours ; and, thaw I says it
mysen, niver men 'ed a better master
— and I knaws what men be, and
what masters be, fur I wur nobbut a
laäborer, and now I be a landlord —
burn a plowman, and now, as far as
money goäs, I be a gentleman, thaw
I beänt naw scholard, fur I 'ednt naw
time to maäke mysen a scholard while
I wur maäkin' mysen a gentleman,
but I ha taäen good care to turn out
boäth my darters right down fine
laädies.

DOBSON.

An' soä they be.

1ST FARMING MAN.

Soä they be ! soä they be !

2D FARMING MAN.

The Lord bless boath on 'em !

3D FARMING MAN.

An' the saäme to you, Master.

4TH FARMING MAN.

And long life to boath on 'em. An'
the saäme to you, Master Steer, likewise.

STEER.

Thank ye !

Enter EVA.

Wheer 'asta been ?

EVA.

(*Timidly.*) Many happy returns of the day, father.

STEER.

They can't be many, my dear, but I 'oäpes they'll be 'appy.

DOBSON.

Why, tha looks haäle anew to last to a hoonderd.

STEER.

An' why shouldn't I last to a hoonderd? Haäle! why shouldn't I be haäle? fur thaw I be heighty this very daäy, I niver 'es sa much as one pin's prick of paäin; an' I can taäke my glass along wi' the youngest, fur I niver touched a drop of owt till my oän wedding-daäy, an' then I wur turned huppads o' sixty. Why shouldn't I be haäle? I ha' plowed the ten-aäcre — it be mine now — afoor ony o' ye wur burn — ye all knaws the ten-aäcre — I mun ha' plowed it moor nor a hoonderd times; hallus hup at sunrise, and I'd drive the plow straäit as a line right i' the faäce o' the sun, then back ageän, a-follering my oän shadder — then hup ageän i' the faäce o' the sun. Eh! how the sun 'ud shine, and the larks 'ud sing i' them daäys, and the smell o' the mou'd an' all. Eh! if I could ha' gone on wi' the plowin' nobbut the smell o' the mou'd 'ud ha' maäde ma live as long as Jerusalem.

EVA.

Methusaleh, father.

STEER.

Ay, lass, but when thou be as owd as me thou'll put one word fur another as I does.

DOBSON.

But, Steer, thaw thou be haäle anew I seed tha a-limpin' up just now wi' the roomatics i' the knee.

STEER.

Roomatics! Noä; I laäme't my knee last night running arter a thief. Beänt there house-breäkers down i' Littlechester, Dobson — doänt ye hear of ony?

DOBSON.

Ay, that there be. Immanuel Goldsmiths was broke into o' Monday night, and ower a hoonderd pounds worth o' rings stolen.

STEER.

So I thowt, and I heärd the winder — that's the winder at the end o' the passage, that goäs by thy chaumber. (*Turning to* EVA.) Why, lass, what maäkes tha sa red? Did 'e git into thy chaumber?

EVA.

Father!

STEER.

Well, I runned arter thief i' the dark, and fell ageän coalscuttle and my kneeä gev waäy, or I'd ha' cotched 'im, but afoor I coomed up he got thruff the winder ageän.

EVA.

Got thro' the window again?

STEER.

Ay, but he left the mark of 'is foot i' the flower-bed; now theer be noän o' my men, thinks I to mysen, 'ud ha' done it 'cep' it were Dan Smith, fur I cotched 'im once a-steälin' coäls, an' I sent fur 'im, an' I measured his foot wi' the mark i' the bed, but it wouldn't fit — seeäms to me the mark wur maäde by a Lunnun boot. (*Looks at* EVA.) Why, now, what maäkes tha sa white?

EVA.

Fright, father!

STEER.

Maäke thysen eäsy. I'll hev the winder naäiled up, and put Towser under it.

EVA.

(*Clasping her hands.*) No, no, father! Towser'll tear him all to pieces.

STEER.

Let him keep awaäy, then; but coom, coom! let's be gawin. They ha' broached a barrel of aäle i' the long barn, and the fiddler be theer, and the lads and lasses 'ull hev a dance.

EVA.

(*Aside.*) Dance! small heart have I to dance. I should seem to be dancing upon a grave.

STEER.

Wheer be Mr. Edgar? about the premises?

DOBSON.

Hallus about the premises!

STEER.

So much the better, so much the better. I likes 'im, and Eva likes 'im. Eva can do owt wi' 'im; look for 'im, Eva, and bring 'im to the barn. He 'ant naw pride in 'im, and we'll git 'im to speechify for us arter dinner.

EVA.

Yes, father!   [*Exit.*

STEER.

Coom along then, all the rest o' ye! Church-warden be a coomin, thaw me and 'im we niver 'grees about the tithe; and Parson mebbe, thaw he niver mended that gap i' the glebe fence as I telled 'im; and Blacksmith, thaw he niver shoes a herse to my likings; and Baäker, thaw I sticks to hoämmaäde — but all on 'em welcome,

all on 'em welcome; and I've hed the long barn cleared out of all the machines, and the sacks, and the taäters, and the mangles, and theer'll be room anew for all o' ye. Foller me.

ALL.

Yeas, yeas! Three cheers for Mr. Steer!
          [*All exeunt except* DOBSON *into barn.*

Enter EDGAR.

DOBSON (*who is going, turns*).

Squire! — if so be you be a squire.

EDGAR.

Dobbins, I think.

DOBSON.

Dobbins, you thinks; and I thinks ye weärs a Lunnun boot.

EDGAR.

Well?

DOBSON.

And I thinks I'd like to taäke the measure o' your foot.

EDGAR.

Ay, if you'd like to measure your own length upon the grass.

DOBSON.

Coom, coom, that's a good un. Why, I could throw four o' ye; but I promised one of the Misses I wouldn't meddle wi' ye, and I weänt.
          [*Exit into barn.*

EDGAR.

Jealous of me with Eva! Is it so?
Well, tho' I grudge the pretty jewel, that I
Have worn, to such a clod, yet that might be
The best way out of it, if the child could keep

Her counsel. I am sure I wish her
    happy.
But I must free myself from this
    entanglement.
I have all my life before me — so has
    she —
Give her a month or two, and her
    affections
Will flower toward the light in some
    new face.
Still I am half afraid to meet her
    now.
She will urge marriage on me. I hate
    tears.
Marriage is but an old tradition. I
    hate
Traditions, ever since my narrow
    father,
After my frolic with his tenant's
    girl,
Made younger elder son, violated the
    whole
Tradition of our land, and left his
    heir,
Born, happily, with some sense of art,
    to live
By brush and pencil. By and by,
    when Thought
Comes down among the crowd, and
    man perceives that
The lost gleam of an after-life but
    leaves him
A beast of prey in the dark, why then
    the crowd
May wreak my wrongs upon my
    wrongers. Marriage!
That fine, fat, hook-nosed uncle of
    mine, old Harold,
Who leaves me all his land at Little-
    chester,
He, too, would oust me from his will,
    if I
Made such a marriage. And marriage
    in itself —
The storm is hard at hand will sweep
    away
Thrones, churches, ranks, traditions,
    customs, marriage
One of the feeblest! Then the man,
    the woman,
Following their best affinities, will
    each

Bid their old bond farewell with
    smiles, not tears ;
Good wishes, not reproaches ; with no
    fear
Of the world's gossiping clamor, and
    no need
Of veiling their desires.
                        Conventionalism,
Who shrieks by day at what she does
    by night,
Would call this vice ; but one time's
    vice may be
The virtue of another ; and Vice and
    Virtue
Are but two masks of self ; and what
    hereafter
Shall mark out Vice from Virtue in
    the gulf
Of never-dawning darkness ?

Enter EVA.

                        My sweet Eva,
Where have you lain in ambush all
    the morning ?
They say your sister, Dora, has re-
    turn'd,
And that should make you happy, if
    you love her!
But you look troubled.

EVA.

                        Oh, I love her so,
I was afraid of her, and I hid myself.
We never kept a secret from each
    other ;
She would have seen at once into my
    trouble,
And ask'd me what I could not
    answer. Oh, Philip,
Father heard you last night. Our
    savage mastiff,
That all but kill'd the beggar, will be
    placed
Beneath the window, Philip.

EDGAR.

                        Savage, is he ?
What matters ? Come, give me your
    hand and kiss me
This beautiful May-morning.

EVA.

The most beautiful
May we have had for many years!

EDGAR.

And here
Is the most beautiful morning of this
May.
Nay, you must smile upon me! There
— you make
The May and morning still more beau-
tiful,
You, the most beautiful blossom of
the May.

EVA.

Dear Philip, all the world is beautiful
If we were happy, and could chime in
with it.

EDGAR.

True; for the senses, love, are for the
world;
That for the senses.

EVA.

Yes.

EDGAR.

And when the man,
The child of evolution, flings aside
His swaddling-bands, the morals of
the tribe,
He, following his own instincts as his
God,
Will enter on the larger golden age;
No pleasure then taboo'd: for when
the tide
Of full democracy has overwhelm'd
This Old world, from that flood will
rise the New,
Like the Love-goddess with no bridal
veil,
Ring, trinket of the Church, but naked
Nature
In all her loveliness.

EVA.

What are you saying?

EDGAR.

That, if we did not strain to make
ourselves
Better and higher than Nature, we
might be
As happy as the bees there at their
honey
In these sweet blossoms.

EVA.

Yes; how sweet they smell!

EDGAR.

There! let me break some off for you.
[*Breaking branch off.*

EVA.

My thanks.
But, look, how wasteful of the blos-
som you are!
One, two, three, four, five, six — you
have robb'd poor father
Of ten good apples. Oh, I forgot to
tell you
He wishes you to dine along with us,
And speak for him after — you that
are so clever!

EDGAR.

I grieve I cannot; but, indeed ——

EVA.

What is it?

EDGAR.

Well, business. I must leave you,
love, to-day.

EVA.

Leave me, to-day! And when will
you return?

EDGAR.

I cannot tell precisely; but ——

EVA.

But what?

EDGAR.

I trust, my dear, we shall be always friends.

EVA.

After all that has gone between us — friends!

What, only friends?   [*Drops branch.*

EDGAR.

All that has gone between us
Should surely make us friends.

EVA.

But keep us lovers.

EDGAR.

Child, do you love me now?

EVA.

Yes, now and ever.

EDGAR.

Then you should wish us both to love forever.
But, if you *will* bind love to one forever,
Altho' at first he take his bonds for flowers,
As years go on, he feels them press upon him,
Begins to flutter in them, and at last
Breaks thro' them, and so flies away forever;
While, had you left him free use of his wings,
Who knows that he had ever dream'd of flying?

EVA.

But all that sounds so wicked and so strange;
" Till death us part " — those are the only words,
The true ones — nay, and those not true enough,
For they that love do not believe that death

Will part them. Why do you jest with me, and try
To fright me? Tho' you are a gentleman,
I but a farmer's daughter ——

EDGAR.

Tut! you talk
Old feudalism. When the great Democracy
Makes a new world——

EVA.

And if you be not jesting,
Neither the old world, nor the new, nor father,
Sister, nor you, shall ever see me more.

EDGAR (*moved*).

Then — (*aside*) Shall I say it? — (*aloud*) fly with me to-day.

EVA.

No! Philip, Philip, if you do not marry me,
I shall go mad for utter shame and die.

EDGAR.

Then, if we needs must be conventional,
When shall your parish-parson bawl our banns
Before your gaping clowns?

EVA.

Not in our church —
I think I scarce could hold my head up there.
Is there no other way?

EDGAR.

Yes, if you cared
To fee an over-opulent superstition,
Then they would grant you what they call a license
To marry.   Do you wish it?

EVA.

Do I wish it?

EDGAR.

In London.

EVA.

You will write to me ?

EDGAR.

I will.

EVA.

And I will fly to you thro' the night,
the storm —
Yes, tho' the fire should run along the
ground,
As once it did in Egypt. Oh, you
see,
I was just out of school, I had no
mother —
My sister far away — and you, a
gentleman,
Told me to trust you : yes, in everything —
That was the only *true* love; and I
trusted —
Oh, yes, indeed, I would have died for
you.
How could you — Oh, how could you ?
— nay, how could I ?
But now you will set all right again,
and I
Shall not be made the laughter of the
village,
And poor old father not die miserable.

DORA (*singing in the distance*).

"O joy for the promise of May, of May,
O joy for the promise of May."

EDGAR.

Speak not so loudly; that must be
your sister.
You never told her, then, of what has
past
Between us.

EVA.

Never !

EDGAR.

Do not till I bid you.

EVA.

No, Philip, no.   [*Turns away.*

EDGAR (*moved*).

How gracefully there she stands
Weeping — the little Niobe ! What !
we prize
The statue or the picture all the
more
When we have made them ours ! Is
she less loveable,
Less lovely, being wholly mine ?   To
stay —
Follow my art among these quiet
fields,
Live with these honest folk ——
                    And play the fool !
No ! she that gave herself to me so
easily
Will yield herself as easily to another.

EVA.

Did you speak, Philip ?

EDGAR.

Nothing more, farewell.
                    [*They embrace.*

DORA (*coming nearer*).

"O grief for the promise of May, of
May,
O grief for the promise of May."

EDGAR (*still embracing her*).

Keep up your heart till we meet
again.

EVA.

If that should break before we meet
again ?

EDGAR.

Break ! nay, but call for Philip when
you will,
And he returns.

EVA.

Heaven hears you, Philip Edgar !

EDGAR (*moved*).

And *he* would hear you even from the
grave.
Heaven curse him if he come not at
your call
                    [*Exit.*

Enter DORA.

DORA.

Well, Eva!

EVA.

Oh, Dora, Dora, how long you have been away from home! Oh, how often I have wished for you! It seemed to me that we were parted forever.

DORA.

Forever, you foolish child! What's come over you? We parted like the brook yonder about the alder island, to come together again in a moment and to go on together again, till one of us be married. But where is this Mr. Edgar whom you praised so in your first letters? You haven't even mentioned him in your last?

EVA.

He has gone to London.

DORA.

Ay, child; and you look thin and pale. Is it for his absence? Have you fancied yourself in love with him? That's all nonsense, you know, such a baby as you are. But you shall tell me all about it.

EVA.

Not now — presently. Yes, I have been in trouble, but I am happy — I think, quite happy now.

DORA *(taking* EVA's *hand)*.

Come, then, and make them happy in the long barn, for father is in his glory, and there is a piece of beef like a house-side, and a plum-pudding as big as the round haystack. But see they are coming out for the dance already. Well, my child, let us join them.

Enter all from barn laughing. EVA *sits reluctantly under apple tree.* STEER *enters smoking, sits by* EVA.

Dance.

ACT II.

Five years have elapsed between Acts I. and II.

SCENE. — A MEADOW. ON ONE SIDE A PATHWAY GOING OVER A RUSTIC BRIDGE. AT BACK THE FARMHOUSE AMONG TREES. IN THE DISTANCE A CHURCH SPIRE.

DOBSON *and* DORA.

DOBSON.

So the owd uncle i' Coomberland be deäd, Miss Dora, beänt he?

DORA.

Yes, Mr. Dobson, I've been attending on his death-bed and his burial.

DOBSON.

It be five year sin' ye went afoor to him, and it seems to me nobbut t'other day. Hesn't he left ye nowt?

DORA.

No, Mr. Dobson.

DOBSON.

But he were mighty fond o' ye, warn't he?

DORA.

Fonder of poor Eva — like everybody else.

DOBSON *(handing* DORA *basket of roses)*.

Not like me, Miss Dora; and I ha' browt these roses to ye — I forgits what they calls 'em, but I hallus gi'ed soom on 'em to Miss Eva at this time o' year. Will ya taäke 'em? fur Miss Eva, she set the bush by my dairy winder afoor she went to school at Littlechester — so I allus browt soom on 'em to her; and now she be gone, will ye taäke 'em, Miss Dora?

DORA.

I thank you. They tell me that yesterday you mentioned her name too suddenly before my father. See that you do not do so again!

DOBSON.

Noä; I knaws a deäl better now. I seed how the owd man wur vext.

DORA.

I take them, then, for Eva's sake. [*Takes basket, places some in her dress.*

DOBSON.

Eva's saäke. Yeas. Poor gel, poor gel! I can't abeär to think on 'er now, fur I'd ha' done owt fur 'er mysen; an' ony o' Steer's men, an' ony o' my men 'ud ha' done owt fur 'er, an' all the parish 'ud ha' done owt fur 'er, fur we was all on us proud on 'er, an' them theer be soom of her oän roses, an' she wur as sweet as ony on 'em — the Lord bless 'er — 'er oän sen; an' weänt ye taäke 'em now, Miss Dora, fur 'er saäke an' fur my saäke an' all?

DORA.

Do you want them back again?

DOBSON.

Noä, noä! Keep 'em. But I hed a word to saäy to ye.

DORA.

Why, Farmer, you should be in the hayfield looking after your men; you couldn't have more splendid weather.

DOBSON.

I be a going theer; but I thowt I'd bring tha them roses fust. The weather's well anew, but the glass be a bit shaäky. S'iver we've led moäst on it.

DORA.

Ay! but you must not be too sudden with it either, as you were last year, when you put it in green, and your stack caught fire.

DOBSON.

I were insured, Miss, an' I lost nowt by it. But I weänt be too sudden wi' it; and I feel sewer, Miss Dora, that I ha' been noän too sudden wi' you, fur I ha' sarved for ye well nigh as long as the man sarved for 'is sweet-'art i' Scriptur'. Weänt ye gi'e me a kind answer at last?

DORA.

I have no thought of marriage, my friend. We have been in such grief these five years, not only on my sister's account, but the ill success of the farm, and the debts, and my father's breaking down, and his blindness. How could I think of leaving him?

DOBSON.

Eh, but I be well to do; and if ye would nobbut hev me, I would taäke the owd blind man to my oän fireside. You should hev him allus wi' ye.

DORA.

You are generous, but it cannot be. I cannot love you; nay, I think I never can be brought to love any man. It seems to me that I hate men, ever since my sister left us. Oh, see here. (*Pulls out a letter.*) I wear it next my heart. Poor sister, I had it five years ago. "Dearest Dora, — I have lost myself, and am lost forever to you and my poor father. I thought Mr. Edgar the best of men, and he has proved himself the worst. Seek not for me, or you may find me at the bottom of the river. — EVA."

DOBSON.

Be that my fault?

DORA.

No; but how should I, with this grief still at my heart, take to the milking of your cows, the fatting of your calves, the making of your butter, and the managing of your poultry?

DOBSON.

Naäy, but I hev an owd woman as 'ud see to all that; and you should sit i' your oän parlor quite like a laädy, ye should!

DORA.

It cannot be.

DOBSON.

And plaäy the pianner, if ye liked, all daäy long, like a laädy, ye should an' all.

DORA.

It cannot be.

DOBSON.

And I would loove tha moor nor ony gentleman 'ud loove tha.

DORA.

No, no; it cannot be.

DOBSON.

And p'raps ye hears 'at I soomtimes taäkes a drop too much; but that be all along o' you, Miss, because ye weänt hev me; but, if ye would, I could put all that o' one side eäsy anew.

DORA.

Cannot you understand plain words, Mr. Dobson? I tell you, it cannot be.

DOBSON.

Eh, lass! Thy feyther eddicated his darters to marry gentlefoälk, and see what's coomed on it.

DORA.

That is enough, Farmer Dobson. You have shown me that, though fortune had born *you* into the estate of a gentleman, you would still have been Farmer Dobson. You had better attend to your hayfield. Good afternoon.   [*Exit.*

DOBSON.

"Farmer Dobson"! Well, I be Farmer Dobson; but I thinks Farmer Dobson's dog 'ud ha' knaw'd better nor to cast her sister's misfortin inter 'er teeth arter she'd been a-reädin' me the letter wi' 'er voice a-shaäkin', and the drop in 'er eye. Theer she goäs! Shall I foller 'er and ax 'er to maäke it up? Noä, not yet. Let 'er cool upon it; I likes 'er all the better fur taäkin' me down, like a laädy, as she be. Farmer Dobson! I be Farmer Dobson, sewer anew; but if iver I cooms upo' Gentleman Hedgarageän, and doänt laäy my cartwhip athurt 'is shou'ders, why then I beänt Farmer Dobson, but summun else — blaäme't if I beänt!

Enter HAYMAKERS *with a load of hay.*

The last on it, eh?

1ST HAYMAKER.

Yeas.

DOBSON.

Hoäm wi' it, then.   [*Exit surlily.*

1ST HAYMAKER.

Well, it be the last loäd hoäm.

2D HAYMAKER.

Yeas, an' owd Dobson should be glad on it. What maäkes 'im allus sa glum?

SALLY ALLEN.

Glum! he be wus nor glum. He coom'd up to me yisterdaäy i' the haäyfield, when meä and my sweet'art was a workin' along o' one side wi' one another, and he sent 'im awaäy to t'other end o' the field; and when I axed 'im why, he telled me 'at sweet-'arts niver worked well togither; and I telled *'im* 'at sweet'arts allus worked best togither; and then he called me a rude naäme, and I can't abide 'im.

JAMES.

Why, lass, doänt tha knaw he be sweet upo' Dora Steer, and she weänt sa much as look at 'im? And wheniver 'e sees two sweet'arts togither like thou and me, Sally, he be fit to bust hissen wi' spites and jealousies.

SALLY.

Let 'im bust hissen, then, for owt *I* cares.

1ST HAYMAKER. *

Well but, as I said afoor, it be the last loäd hoäm; do thou and thy sweet'art sing us hoäm to supper — "The Last Loäd Hoäm."

ALL.

Ay ! "The Last Loäd Hoäm."

Song.

What did ye do, and what did ye saäy,
Wi' the wild white rose, and the woodbine sa gaäy,
An' the midders all mow'd, and the sky sa blue —
What did ye saäy, and what did ye do,
When ye thowt there were nawbody watchin' o' you,
And you and your Sally was forkin' the haäy,
    At the end of the daäy,
    For the last loäd hoäm ?

What did we do, and what did we saäy,
Wi' the briar sa green, and the willer sa graäy,
An' the midders all mow'd, and the sky sa blue —
Do ye think I be gawin' to tell it to you,
What we mowt saäy, and what we mowt do,
When me and my Sally was forkin' the haäy,
    At the end of the daäy,
    For the last loäd hoäm ?

But what did ye saäy, and what did ye do,
Wi' the butterflies out, and the swallers at plaäy,
An' the midders all mow'd, and the sky sa blue ?
Why, coom then, owd feller, I'll tell it to you;
For me and my Sally we sweär'd to be true,
To be true to each other, let 'appen what maäy,
    Till the end of the daäy
    And the last loäd hoäm.

ALL.

Well sung !

JAMES.

Fanny be the naäme i' the song, but I swopt it fur *she*.
    [*Pointing to* SALLY.

SALLY.

Let ma aloän afoor foälk, wilt tha ?

1ST HAYMAKER.

Ye shall sing that ageän to-night, fur owd Dobson 'll gi'e us a bit o' supper.

SALLY.

I weänt goä to owd Dobson; he wur rude to me i' tha haäyfield, and he'll be rude to me ageän to-night. Owd Steer's gotten all his grass down and wants a hand, and I'll goä to him.

1ST HAYMAKER.

Owd Steer gi'es nubbut cowd tea to '*is* men, and owd Dobson gi'es beer.

SALLY.

But I'd like owd Steer's cowd tea better nor Dobson's beer. Good-bye.
    [*Going.*

JAMES.

Gi'e us a buss fust, lass.

SALLY.

I tell'd tha to let ma aloän !

JAMES.

Why, wasn't thou and me a-bussin'
o' one another t'other side o' the haäy-
cock, when owd Dobson coom'd upo'
us ? I can't let thaa aloän if I would,
Sally. [*Offering to kiss her.*

SALLY.

Git along wi' ye, do ! [*Exit.*
[*All laugh; exeunt singing.*

" To be true to each other, let 'appen
what maäy,
Till the end o' the daäy
An' the last loäd hoäm."

Enter HAROLD.

HAROLD.

Not Harold ! " Philip Edgar, Philip
Edgar ! "
Her phantom call'd me by the name
she loved.
I told her I should hear her from the
grave.
Ay ! yonder is her casement. I re-
member
Her bright face beaming starlike
down upon me
Thro' that rich cloud of blossom.
Since I left her
Here weeping, I have ranged the
world, and sat
Thro' every sensual course of that
full feast
That leaves but emptiness.

Song.

" To be true to each other, let 'appen
what maäy,
To the end o' the daäy
An' the last loäd hoäm."

HAROLD.

Poor Eva ! O my God, if man be only
A willy-nilly current of sensations —
Reaction needs must follow revel —
yet —

Why feel remorse, he, knowing that
he *must* have
Moved in the iron grooves of Destiny ?
Remorse then is a part of Destiny,
Nature a liar, making us feel guilty
Of her own faults.
    My grandfather — of him
They say, that women —
      O this mortal house,
Which we are born into, is haunted by
The ghosts of the dead passions of
dead men ;
And these take flesh again with our
own flesh,
And bring us to confusion.
      He was only
A poor philosopher who call'd the
mind
Of children a blank page, a *tabula
rasa.*
There, there, is written in invisible
inks
" Lust, Prodigality, Covetousness,
Craft,
Cowardice, Murder " — and the heat
and fire
Of life will bring them out, and black
enough,
So the child grow to manhood : better
death
With our first wail than life —

Song (further off).

" Till the end o' the daäy
An' the last loäd hoäm,
Loäd hoäm."

This bridge again ! (*Steps on the
bridge.*)
    How often have I stood
With Eva here ! The brook among
its flowers !
Forget-me-not, meadowsweet, willow-
herb.
I had some smattering of science then,
Taught her the learned names, anato-
mized
The flowers for her — and now I only
wish
This pool were deep enough, that I
might plunge
And lose myself forever.

Enter DAN SMITH (*singing*).

Gee oop! whoä! Gee oop! whoä!
Scizzars an' Pumpy was good uns to
    goä
    Thruf slush an' squad
    When roäds was bad,
But hallus ud stop at the Vine-an'-
    the-Hop,
    Fur boäth on 'em knaw'd as well as
      mysen
That beer be as good fur 'erses as
    men.
Gee oop! whoä! Gee oop! whoä!
Scizzars an' Pumpy was good uns to
    goä.

The beer's gotten oop into my 'eäd.
S'iver I mun git along back to the
farm, fur she tell'd ma to taäke the
cart to Littlechester.

Enter DORA.

Half an hour late! why are you
loitering here? Away with you at
once.   [*Exit* DAN SMITH.

(*Seeing* HAROLD *on bridge.*)
           Some madman, is it,
Gesticulating there upon the bridge?
I am half afraid to pass.

HAROLD.

           Sometimes I wonder,
When man has surely learnt at last
    that all
His old-world faith, the blossom of
    his youth,
Has faded, falling fruitless — whether
    then
All of us, all at once, may not be
    seized
With some fierce passion, not so much
    for Death
As against Life! all, all, into the
    dark —
No more! — and science now could
    drug and balm us
Back into nescience with as little pain
As it is to fall asleep.
           This beggarly life,
This poor, flat, hedged-in field — no
    distance — this

Hollow Pandora-box,
With all the pleasures flown, not even
    Hope
Left at the bottom!
           Superstitious fool,
What brought me here? To see her
    grave? her ghost?
Her ghost is everyway about me here.

DORA (*coming forward*).

Allow me, sir, to pass you.

HAROLD.

Eva!

DORA.

           Eva!

HAROLD.

What are you? Where do you come
    from?

DORA.

           From the farm
Here, close at hand.

HAROLD.

Are you — you are — that Dora,
The sister. I have heard of you. The
    likeness
Is very striking

DORA.

          You knew Eva, then?

HAROLD.

Yes — I was thinking of her when —
    O yes,
Many years back, and never since
    have met
Her equal for pure innocence of na-
    ture,
And loveliness of feature.

DORA.

           No, nor I.

HAROLD.

Except, indeed, I have found it once
    again
In your own self.

DORA.

You flatter me.   Dear Eva
Was always thought the prettier.

HAROLD.

And *her* charm
Of voice is also yours; and I was
brooding
Upon a great unhappiness when you
spoke.

DORA.

Indeed, you seem'd in trouble, sir.

HAROLD.

And you
Seem my good angel who may help
me from it.

DORA (*aside*).

How worn he looks, poor man! who
is it, I wonder.
How can I help him? (*Aloud.*)
Might I ask your name?

HAROLD.

Harold.

DORA.

I never heard her mention you.

HAROLD.

I met her first at a farm in Cumberland —
Her uncle's.

DORA.

She was there six years ago.

HAROLD.

And if she never mention'd me, perhaps
The painful circumstances which I
heard —
I will not vex you by repeating them —
Only last week at Littlechester, drove
me
From out her memory.   She has disappear'd,
They told me, from the farm — and
darker news.

DORA.

She has disappear'd, poor darling,
from the world —
Left but one dreadful line to say, that
we
Should find her in the river; and we
dragg'd
The Littlechester river all in vain:
Have sorrow'd for her all these years
in vain.
And my poor father, utterly broken
down
By losing her — she was his favorite
child —
Has let his farm, all his affairs, I fear,
But for the slender help that I can
give,
Fall into ruin.   Ah! that villain, Ed-
gar,
If he should ever show his face among
us,
Our men and boys would hoot him,
stone him, hunt him
With pitchforks off the farm, for all
of them
Loved her, and she was worthy of all
love.

HAROLD.

They say, we should forgive our
enemies.

DORA.

Ay, if the wretch were dead I might
forgive him;
We know not whether he be dead or
living.

HAROLD.

What Edgar?

DORA.

Philip Edgar of Toft Hall
In Somerset.   Perhaps you know him?

HAROLD.

Slightly.
(*Aside.*) Ay, for how slightly have
I known myself.

DORA.

This Edgar, then, is living?

HAROLD.

Living ? well —
One Philip Edgar of Toft Hall in
   Somerset
Is lately dead.

DORA.

Dead ! — is there more than one ?

HAROLD.

Nay — now — not one, (*aside*) for I
   am Philip Harold.

DORA.

That one, is he then — dead !

HAROLD.

(*Aside.*) My father's death,
Let her believe it mine; this, for the
   moment,
Will leave me a free field.

DORA.

Dead! and this world
Is brighter for his absence as that other
Is darker for his presence.

HAROLD.

Is not this
To speak too pitilessly of the dead ?

DORA.

My five-years' anger cannot die at
   once,
Not all at once with death and him.
   I trust
I shall forgive him — by-and-by — not
   now.
O sir, you seem to have a heart; if
   you
Had seen us that wild morning when
   we found
Her bed unslept in, storm and shower
   lashing
Her casement, her poor spaniel wail-
   ing for her,
That desolate letter, blotted with her
   tears,
Which told us we should never see
   her more —

Our old nurse crying as if for her own
   child,
My father stricken with his first
   paralysis,
And then with blindness — had you
   been one of us
And seen all this, then you would
   know it is not
So easy to forgive — even the dead.

HAROLD.

But sure am I that of your gentleness
You will forgive him. She, you mourn
   for, seem'd
A miracle of gentleness — would not
   blur
A moth's wing by the touching; would
   not crush
The fly that drew her blood; and,
   were she living,
Would not — if penitent — have denied
   him *her*
Forgiveness. And perhaps the man
   himself,
When hearing of that piteous death,
   has suffer'd
More than we know. But wherefore
   waste your heart
In looking on a chill and changeless
   Past ?
Iron will fuse, and marble melt; the
   Past
Remains the Past. But you are young,
   and — pardon me —
As lovely as your sister. Who can
   tell
What golden hours, with what full
   hands, may be
Waiting you in the distance ? Might
   I call
Upon your father — I have seen the
   world —
And cheer his blindness with a travel-
   ler's tales ?

DORA.

Call if you will, and when you will.
   I cannot
Well answer for my father; but if
   you
Can tell me anything of our sweet Eva

When in her brighter girlhood, I at
    least
Will bid you welcome, and will listen
    to you.
Now I must go.

HAROLD.

    But give me first your hand:
I do not dare, like an old friend, to
    shake it.
I kiss it as a prelude to that privilege
When you shall know me better.

DORA.

    (*Aside.*) How beautiful
His manners are, and how unlike the
    farmer's !
You are staying here ?

HAROLD.

    Yes, at the wayside inn
Close by that alder-island in your
    brook,
" The Angler's Home."

DORA.

    Are *you* one ?

HAROLD.

    No, but I
Take some delight in sketching, and
    the country
Has many charms, altho' the inhabi-
    tants
Seem semi-barbarous.

DORA.

    I am glad it pleases you;
Yet I, born here, not only love the
    country,
But its inhabitants too; and you, I
    doubt not,
Would take to them as kindly, if you
    cared
To live some time among them.

HAROLD.

    If I did,
Then one at least of its inhabitants
Might have more charm for me than
    all the country.

DORA.

That one, then, should be grateful
    for your preference.

HAROLD.

I cannot tell, tho' standing in her
    presence.
(*Aside.*) She colors !

DORA.

    Sir !

HAROLD.

    Be not afraid of me,
For these are no conventional flour-
    ishes.
I do most earnestly assure you that
Your likeness ——
        [*Shouts and cries without.*

DORA.

What was that ? my poor blind
    father —

Enter FARMING MAN.

FARMING MAN.

    Miss Dora, Dan Smith's cart hes
runned ower a laädy i' the holler
laäne, and they ha' ta'en the body
up inter your chaumber, and they be
all a-callin' for ye.

DORA.

The body ! — Heavens ! I come !

HAROLD.

    But you are trembling.
Allow me to go with you to the farm.
        [*Exeunt.*

Enter DOBSON.

DOBSON.

    What feller wur it as 'a' been a-
talkin' fur haäfe an hour wi' my
Dora ? (*Looking after him.*) Seeäms
I ommost knaws the back on 'im —
drest like a gentleman, too. Damn
all gentlemen, says I ! I should ha'
thowt they'd hed anew of gentlefoälk,
as I telled 'er to-daäy when she fell
foul upo' me.

Minds ma o' summun. I could sweär to that; but that be all one, fur I haätes 'im afoor I knaws what 'e be. Theer! he turns round. Philip Hedgar o' Soomerset! Philip Hedgar o' Soomerset! — Noä — yeas — thaw the feller's gone and maäde such a litter of his faäce.

Eh lad, if it be thou, I'll Philip tha! a-plaäyin' the saäme gaäme wi' my Dora — I'll Soomerset tha.

I'd like to drag 'im thruff the herse-pond, and she to be a-lookin' at it. I'd like to leather 'im black and blue, and she to be a-laughin' at it. I'd like to fell 'im as deäd as a bullock! (*Clenching his fist.*)

But what 'ud she saäy to that ? She telled me once not to meddle wi' 'im, and now she be fallen out wi' ma, and I can't coom at 'er.

It mun be *him*. Noä! Fur she'd niver 'a been talkin' haäfe an hour wi' the divil 'at killed her oän sister, or she beänt Dora Steer.

Yeas! Fur she niver knawed 'is faäce when 'e wur 'ere afoor ; but I'll maäke 'er knaw! I'll maäke 'er knaw!

Enter HAROLD.

Naäy, but I mun git out on 'is waäy now, or I shall be the death on 'im.

[*Exit.*

HAROLD.

How the clown glared at me! that Dobbins, is it,
With whom I used to jar? but can he trace me
Thro' five years' absence, and my change of name,
The tan of southern summers and the beard.
I may as well avoid him.
             Ladylike!
Lilylike in her stateliness and sweetness!
How came she by it ? — a daughter of the fields,
This Dora!
She gave her hand, unask'd, at the farm-gate ;

I almost think she half-return'd the pressure
Of mine. What, I that held the orange blossom
Dark as the yew ? but may not those, who march
Before their age, turn back at times, and make
Courtesy to custom ? and now the stronger motive,
Misnamed free-will — the crowd would call it conscience —
Moves me — to what ? I am dreaming ; for the past
Look'd thro' the present, Eva's eyes thro' hers —
A spell upon me! Surely I loved Eva
More than I knew! or is it but the past
That brightens in retiring ? Oh, last night,
Tired, pacing my new lands at Littlechester,
I dozed upon the bridge, and the black river
Flow'd thro' my dreams — if dreams they were. She rose
From the foul flood and pointed toward the farm,
And her cry rang to me across the years,
" I call you, Philip Edgar, Philip Edgar!
Come, you will set all right again, and father
Will not die miserable." I could make his age
A comfort to him — so be more at peace
With mine own self. Some of my former friends
Would find my logic faulty; let them. Color
Flows thro' my life again, and I have lighted
On a new pleasure. Anyhow we must
Move in the line of least resistance when
The stronger motive rules.
             But she hates Edgar.
May not this Dobbins, or some other, spy

Edgar in Harold?   Well then, I must
  make her
Love Harold first, and then she will
  forgive
Edgar for Harold's sake.   She said
  herself
She would forgive him, by-and-by, not
  now —
For her own sake *then*, if not for mine
  — not now —
But by-and-by.

Enter DOBSON *behind.*

DOBSON.

By-and-by — eh, lad, dosta knaw
this paäper?   Ye dropt it upo' the
roäd.   "Philip Edgar, Esq."   Ay, you
be a pretty squire.   I ha' fun' ye out,
I hev.   Eh, lad, dosta knaw what tha
meäns wi' by-and-by?   Fur if ye be
goin' to sarve our Dora as ye sarved
our Eva — then, by-and-by, if she
weänt listen to me when I be a-tryin'
to saäve 'er — if she weänt — look to
thysen, for, by the Lord, I'd think na
moor o' maäkin' an end o' tha nor
a carrion craw — noä — thaw they
hanged ma at 'Size fur it.

HAROLD.

Dobbins, I think!

DOBSON.

I beänt Dobbins.

HAROLD.

Nor am I Edgar, my good fellow.

DOBSON.

Tha lies!   What hasta been saäyin' to *my* Dora?

HAROLD.

I have been telling her of the death
of one Philip Edgar of Toft Hall,
Somerset.

DOBSON.

Tha lies!

HAROLD (*pulling out a newspaper*).

Well, my man, it seems that you
can read.   Look there — under the
deaths.

DOBSON.

"O' the 17th, Philip Edgar, o' Toft
Hall, Soomerset."   How coom thou
to be sa like 'im, then?

HAROLD.

Naturally enough; for I am closely
related to the dead man's family.

DOBSON.

An' 'ow coom thou by the letter to
'im?

HAROLD.

Naturally again; for as I used to
transact all his business for him, I
had to look over his letters.   Now
then, see these (*takes out letters*).
Half a score of them, all directed to
me — Harold.

DOBSON.

'Arold! 'Arold! 'Arold, so they be.

HAROLD.

My name is Harold!   Good day,
Dobbins!   [*Exit.*

DOBSON.

'Arold!   The feller's cleän daäzed,
an' maäzed, an' maäted, an' muddled
ma.   Deäd!   It mun be true, fur it
wur i' print as black as owt.   Naäy,
but "Good daäy, Dobbins."   Why,
that wur the very twang on 'im.   Eh,
lad, but whether thou be Hedgar, or
Hedgar's business man, thou hesn't
naw business 'ere wi' *my* Dora, as I
knaws on, an' whether thou calls thysen Hedgar or Harold, if thou stick
to she I'll stick to thee — stick to
tha like a weasel to a rabbit, I will.
Ay! and I'd like to shoot tha like a
rabbit an' all.   "Good daäy, Dobbins."   Dang tha!

ACT III.

SCENE.—A Room in Steer's House. Door leading into Bedroom at the Back.

Dora (*ringing a handbell*).
Milly!

Enter Milly.

MILLY.

The little 'ymn? Yeäs, Miss; but I wur so ta'en up wi' leädin' the owd man about all the blessed murnin' 'at I ha' nobbut larned mysen haäfe on it.

"O man, forgive thy mortal foe,
Nor ever strike him blow for blow;
For all the souls on earth that live
To be forgiven must forgive.
Forgive him seventy times and seven:
For all the blessed souls in Heaven
Are both forgivers and forgiven."

But I'll git the book ageän, and larn mysen the rest, and saäy it to ye afoor dark; ye ringed fur that, Miss, didn't ye?

DORA.

No, Milly; but if the farming men be come for their wages, to send them up to me.

MILLY.

Yeäs, Miss. [*Exit.*

Dora (*sitting at desk counting money*).

Enough at any rate for the present. (*Enter* Farming Men.) Good afternoon, my friends. I am sorry Mr. Steer still continues too unwell to attend to you, but the schoolmaster looked to the paying you your wages when I was away, didn't he?

MEN.

Yeäs; and thanks to ye.

DORA.

Some of our workmen have left us, but he sent me an alphabetical list of those that remain, so, Allen, I may as well begin with you.

ALLEN (*with his hand to his ear*).

Halfabitical! Taäke one o' the young ones fust, Miss, fur I be a bit deaf, and I wur hallus scaäred by a big word; leästwaäys, I should be wi' a lawyer.

DORA.

I spoke of your names, Allen, as they are arranged here (*shows book*) — according to their first letters.

ALLEN.

Letters! Yeas, I sees now. Them be what they larns the childer' at school, but I were burn afoor school-in-time.

DORA.

But, Allen, tho' you can't read, you could whitewash that cottage of yours where your grandson had the fever.

ALLEN.

I'll hev it done o' Monday.

DORA.

Else if the fever spread, the parish will have to thank you for it.

ALLEN.

Meä? why, it be the Lord's doin', noän o' mine; d'ye think *I'd* gi'e 'em the fever? But I thanks ye all the saäme, Miss. (*Takes money.*)

Dora (*calling out names*).

Higgins, J a c k s o n, L u s c o m b e, Nokes, Oldham, Skipworth! (*All take money.*) Did you find that you worked at all the worse upon the cold tea than you would have done upon the beer?

HIGGINS.

Noä, Miss; we worked naw wuss upo' the cowd tea; but we'd ha' worked better upo' the beer.

DORA.

Come, come, you worked well enough, and I am much obliged to all of you. There's for you, and you, and you. Count the money and see if it's all right.

MEN.

All right, Miss; and thank ye kindly.

[*Exeunt* LUSCOMBE, NOKES, OLDHAM, SKIPWORTH.

DORA.

Dan Smith, my father and I forgave you stealing our coals.

[DAN SMITH *advances to* DORA.

DAN SMITH (*bellowing*).

Whoy, O lor, Miss! that wur sa long back, and the walls sa thin, and the winders brokken, and the weather sa cowd, and my missus a-gittin' ower 'er lyin'-in.

DORA.

Didn't I say that we had forgiven you? But, Dan Smith, they tell me that you — and you have six children — spent all your last Saturday's wages at the ale-house; that you were stupid drunk all Sunday, and so ill in consequence all Monday, that you did not come into the hayfield. Why should I pay you your full wages?

DAN SMITH.

I be ready to taäke the pledge.

DORA.

And as ready to break it again. Besides it was you that were driving the cart — and I fear you were tipsy then, too — when you lamed the lady in the hollow lane.

DAN SMITH (*bellowing*).

O lor, Miss! noä, noä, noä! Ye sees the holler laäne be hallus sa dark i' the arternoon, and wheere the big eshtree cuts athurt it, it gi'es a turn like, and 'ow should I see to laäme the laädy, and meä coomin' along pretty sharp an' all?

DORA.

Well, there are your wages; the next time you waste them at a pot-house you get no more from me. (*Exit* DAN SMITH.) Sally Allen, you worked for Mr. Dobson, didn't you?

SALLY (*advancing*).

Yeäs, Miss; but he wur so rough wi' ma, I couldn't abide 'im.

DORA.

Why should he be rough with you? You are as good as a man in the hayfield. What's become of your brother?

SALLY.

'Listed for a soädger, Miss, i' the Queen's Real Hard Tillery.

DORA.

And your sweetheart — when are you and he to be married?

SALLY.

At Michaelmas, Miss, please God.

DORA.

You are an honest pair. I will come to your wedding.

SALLY.

An' I thanks ye fur that, Miss, moor nor fur the waäge.

(*Going — returns.*)

'A cotched ma about the waäist, Miss, when 'e wur 'ere afoor, an' axed ma to be 'is little sweet-art, an' soä I knaw'd 'im when I seed 'im ageän an I telled feyther on 'im.

DORA.

What is all this, Allen?

ALLEN.

Why, Miss Dora, meä and my maätes, us three, we wants to hev three words wi' ye.

HIGGINS.

That be 'im, and meä, Miss.

JACKSON.

An' meä, Miss.

ALLEN.

An' we weänt mention naw naämes, we'd as lief talk o' the Divil afoor ye as 'im, fur they says the master goäs cleän off his 'eäd when he 'eärs the naäme on 'im; but us three, arter Sally'd telled us o' 'im, we fun' 'im out a-walkin' i' West Field wi' a white 'at, nine o'clock, upo' Tuesday murnin', and all on us, wi' your leave, we wants to leather 'im.

DORA.

Who?

ALLEN.

Him as did the mischief here, five year' sin'.

DORA.

Mr. Edgar?

ALLEN.

Theer, Miss! You ha' naämed 'im — not me.

DORA.

He's dead, man — dead; gone to his account — dead and buried.

ALLEN.

I beänt sa sewer o' that, fur Sally knaw'd 'im; Now then?

DORA.

Yes; it was in the Somersetshire papers.

ALLEN.

Then yon mun be his brother, an' we'll leather *'im.*

DORA.

I never heard that he had a brother. Some foolish mistake of Sally's; but what! would you beat a man for his brother's fault? That were a wild justice indeed. Let bygones be bygones. Go home! Good-night! (*All exeunt.*) I have once more paid them all. The work of the farm will go on still, but for how long? We are almost at the bottom of the well: little more to be drawn from it — and what then? Encumbered as we are, who would lend us anything? We shall have to sell all the land, which Father, for a whole life, has been getting together, again, and that, I am sure, would be the death of him. What am I to do? Farmer Dobson, were I to marry him, has promised to keep our heads above water; and the man has doubtless a good heart, and a true and lasting love for me: yet — though I can be sorry for him — as the good Sally says, "I can't abide him" — almost brutal, and matched with my Harold is like a hedge thistle by a garden rose. But then, he, too — will he ever be of one faith with his wife? which is my dream of a true marriage. Can I fancy him kneeling with me, and uttering the same prayer; standing up side by side with me, and singing the same hymn? I fear not. Have I done wisely, then, in accepting him? But may not a girl's love-dream have too much romance in it to be realized all at once, or altogether, or anywhere but in Heaven? And yet I had once a vision of a pure and perfect marriage, where the man and the woman, only differing as the stronger and the weaker, should walk hand in hand together down this valley of tears, as they call it so truly, to the grave at the bottom, and lie down there together in the darkness which would seem but for a moment, to be wakened again together by the light of the resurrection, and no more partings forever and forever. (*Walks up and down. She sings.*)

" O happy lark, that warblest high
　　Above thy lowly nest,
O brook, that brawlest merrily by
　　Thro' fields that once were blest,
O tower spiring to the sky,
　　O graves in daisies drest,
O Love and Life, how weary am I,
　　And how I long for rest."

There, there, I am a fool! Tears! I have sometimes been moved to tears by a chapter of fine writing in a novel; but what have I to do with tears now? All depends on me — Father, this poor girl, the farm, everything; and they both love me — I am all in all to both; and he loves me too, I am quite sure of that. Courage, courage! and all will go well. (*Goes to bedroom door; opens it.*) How dark your room is! Let me bring you in here where there is still full daylight. (*Brings* Eva *forward.*) Why, you look better.

Eva.

And I feel so much better that I trust I may be able by-and-by to help you in the business of the farm; but I must not be known yet. Has anyone found me out, Dora?

Dora.

Oh, no; you kept your veil too close for that when they carried you in; since then, no one has seen you but myself.

Eva.

Yes — this Milly.

Dora.

Poor blind Father's little guide, Milly, who came to us three years after you were gone, how should she know you? But now that you have been brought to us as it were from the grave, dearest Eva, and have been here so long, will you nöt speak with Father to-day?

Eva.

Do you think that I may? No, not yet. I am not equal to it yet.

Dora.

Why? Do you still suffer from your fall in the hollow lane?

Eva.

Bruised; but no bones broken.

Dora.

I have always told Father that the huge old ashtree there would cause an accident some day; but he would never cut it down, because one of the Steers had planted it there in former times.

Eva.

If it had killed one of the Steers there the other day, it might have been better for her, for him, and for you.

Dora.

Come, come, keep a good heart! Better for me! That's good. How better for me?

Eva.

You tell me you have a lover. Will he not fly from you if he learn the story of my shame and that I am still living?

Dora.

No; I am sure that when we are married he will be willing that you and Father should live with us; for, indeed, he tells me that he met you once in the old times, and was much taken with you, my dear.

EVA.

Taken with me; who was he? Have you told him I am here?

DORA.

No; do you wish it?

EVA.

See, Dora; you yourself are ashamed of me (*weeps*), and I do not wonder at it.

DORA.

But I should wonder at myself if it were so. Have we not been all in all to one another from the time when we first peeped into the bird's nest, waded in the brook, ran after the butterflies, and prattled to each other that we would marry fine gentlemen, and played at being fine ladies?

EVA.

That last was my Father's fault, poor man. And this lover of yours — this Mr. Harold — is a gentleman?

DORA.

That he is, from head to foot. I do believe I lost my heart to him the very first time we met, and I love him so much ——

EVA.

Poor Dora!

DORA.

That I dare not tell him how much I love him.

EVA.

Better not. Has he offered you marriage, this gentleman?

DORA.

Could I love him else?

EVA.

And are you quite sure that after marriage this gentleman will not be shamed of his poor farmer's daughter among the ladies in his drawing-room?

DORA.

Shamed of me in a drawing-room! Wasn't Miss Vavasour, our schoolmistress at Littlechester, a lady born? Were not our fellow-pupils all ladies? Wasn't dear mother herself at least by one side a lady? Can't I speak like a lady; pen a letter like a lady; talk a little French like a lady; play a little like a lady? Can't a girl when she loves her husband, and he her, make herself anything he wishes her to be? Shamed of me in a drawing-room, indeed! See here! "I hope your Lordship is quite recovered of your gout?" (*Curtsies.*) "Will your Ladyship ride to cover to-day?" (*Curtsies.*) I can recommend our Voltigeur." "I am sorry that we could not attend your Grace's party on the 10th!" (*Curtsies.*) There, I am glad my nonsense has made you smile!

EVA.

I have heard that "your Lordship," and "your Ladyship," and "your Grace" are all growing old-fashioned!

DORA.

But the love of sister for sister can never be old-fashioned. I have been unwilling to trouble you with questions, but you seem somewhat better to-day. We found a letter in your bedroom torn into bits. I couldn't make it out. What was it?

EVA.

From him! from him! He said we had been most happy together, and he trusted that some time we should meet again, for he had not forgotten his promise to come when I called him. But that was a mockery, you know, for he gave me no address, and there was no word of marriage; and,

O Dora, he signed himself "Yours gratefully" — fancy, Dora, "gratefully"! "Yours gratefully"!

DORA.

Infamous wretch! (*Aside.*) Shall I tell her he is dead? No; she is still too feeble.

EVA.

Hark! Dora, some one is coming. I cannot and I will not see anybody.

DORA.

It is only Milly.

Enter MILLY, *with basket of roses.*

DORA.

Well, Milly, why do you come in so roughly? The sick lady here might have been asleep.

MILLY.

Pleäse, Miss, Mr. Dobson told me to saäy he's browt some of Miss Eva's roses for the sick laädy to smell on.

DORA.

Take them, dear. Say that the sick lady thanks him! Is he here?

MILLY.

Yeäs, Miss; and he wants to speak to ye partic'lar.

DORA.

Tell him I cannot leave the sick lady just yet.

MILLY.

Yeäs, Miss; but he says he wants to tell ye summut very partic'lar.

DORA.

Not to-day. What are you staying for?

MILLY.

Why, Miss, I be afeard I shall set him a-sweäring like onythink.

DORA.

And what harm will that do you, so that you do not copy his bad manners? Go, child. (*Exit* MILLY.) But, Eva, why did you write "Seek me at the bottom of the river"?

EVA.

Why? because I meant it! — that dreadful night! that lonely walk to Littlechester, the rain beating in my face all the way, dead midnight when I came upon the bridge; the river, black, slimy, swirling under me in the lamplight, by the rotten wharfs — but I was so mad, that I mounted upon the parapet ——

DORA.

You make me shudder!

EVA.

To fling myself over, when I heard a voice, "Girl, what are you doing there?" It was a Sister of Mercy, come from the death-bed of a pauper, who had died in his misery blessing God, and the Sister took me to her house, and bit by bit — for she promised secrecy — I told her all.

DORA.

And what then?

EVA.

She would have persuaded me to come back here, but I couldn't. Then she got me a place as nursery governess, and when the children grew too old for me, and I asked her once more to help me, once more she said, "Go home;" but I hadn't the heart or face to do it. And then — what would Father say? I sank so low that I went into service — the drudge of a lodging-house — and when the mistress died, and I appealed to the Sister again, her answer — I think I have it about me — yes, there it is!

DORA (*reads*).

"My dear Child, — I can do no more for you. I have done wrong in keeping your secret; your Father must be now in extreme old age. Go back to him and ask his forgiveness before he dies. — SISTER AGATHA." Sister Agatha is right. Don't you long for Father's forgiveness?

EVA.

I would almost die to have it!

DORA.

And he may die before he gives it; may drop off any day, any hour. You must see him at once. (*Rings bell. Enter* MILLY.) Milly, my dear, how did you leave Mr. Steer?

MILLY.

He's been a-moänin' and a-groänin' in 'is sleep, but I thinks he be wakken-in' oop.

DORA.

Tell him that I and the lady here wish to see him. You see she is lamed, and cannot go down to him.

MILLY.

Yeäs, Miss, I will.   [*Exit* MILLY.

DORA.

I ought to prepare you. You must not expect to find our Father as he was five years ago. He is much al-tered; but I trust that your return — for you know, my dear, you were always his favorite — will give him, as they say, a new lease of life.

EVA (*clinging to* DORA).

Oh, Dora, Dora!

Enter STEER, *led by* MILLY.

STEER.

Hes the cow cawved?

DORA.

No, Father.

STEER.

Be the colt deäd?

DORA.

No, Father.

STEER.

He wur sa bellows'd out wi' the wind this murnin', 'at I tell'd 'em to gallop 'im. Be he deäd?

DORA.

Not that I know.

STEER.

What hasta sent fur me, then, fur?

DORA (*taking* STEER's *arm*).

Well, Father, I have a surprise for you.

STEER.

I ha niver been surprised but once i' my life, and I went blind upon it.

DORA.

Eva has come home.

STEER.

Hoäm? fro' the bottom o' the river?

DORA.

No, Father, that was a mistake. She's here again.

STEER.

The Steers was all gentlefoälks i' the owd times, an' I worked early an' laäte to maäke 'em all gentlefoälks ageän. The land belonged to the Steers i' the owd times, an' it belongs to the Steers ageän: I bowt it back ageän; but I couldn't buy my darter back ageän when she lost hersen, could I? I eddicated boäth on 'em to marry gentlemen, an' one on 'em went an' lost hersen i' the river.

DORA.

No, father, she's here.

STEER.

Here! she moänt coom here. What would her mother saäy? If it be her ghoäst, we mun abide it. We can't keep a ghoäst out.

EVA (*falling at his feet*).

O forgive me! forgive me!

STEER.

Who said that? Taäke me awaäy, little gell. It be one o' my bad daäys.
[*Exit* STEER *led by* MILLY.

DORA (*smoothing* EVA's *forehead*).

Be not so cast down, my sweet Eva. You heard him say it was one of his bad days. He will be sure to know you to-morrow.

EVA.

It is almost the last of my bad days, I think. I am very faint. I must lie down. Give me your arm. Lead me back again.
[DORA *takes* EVA *into inner room.*

Enter MILLY.

MILLY.

Miss Dora! Miss Dora!

DORA (*returning and leaving the bed-room door ajar*).

Quiet! quiet! What is it?

MILLY.

Mr. 'Arold, Miss.

DORA.

Below?

MILLY.

Yeäs, Miss. He be saäyin' a word to the owd man, but he'll coom up if ye lets 'im.

DORA.

Tell him, then, that I'm waiting for him.

MILLY.

Yeäs, Miss.
[*Exit.* DORA *sits pensively and waits.*

Enter HAROLD.

HAROLD.

You are pale, my Dora! but the ruddiest cheek
That ever charm'd the plowman of your wolds
Might wish its rose a lily, could it look
But half as lovely. I was speaking with
Your father, asking his consent — you wish'd me —
That we should marry: he would answer nothing,
I could make nothing of him; but, my flower,
You look so weary and so worn! What is it
Has put you out of heart?

DORA.

It puts me in heart
Again to see you; but indeed the state
Of my poor father puts me out of heart.
Is yours yet living?

HAROLD.

No — I told you.

DORA.

When?

HAROLD.

Confusion! — Ah well, well! the state we all
Must come to in our spring-and-winter world
If we live long enough! and poor Steer looks
The very type of Age in a picture, bow'd

To the earth he came from, to the
    grave he goes to,
Beneath the burthen of years.

DORA.

        More like the picture
Of Christian in my " Pilgrim's Prog-
    ress " here,
Bow'd to the dust beneath the burthen
    of sin.

HAROLD.

Sin!. What sin ?

DORA.

    Not his own.

HAROLD.

        That nursery-tale
Still read, then ?

DORA.

Yes ; our carters and our shepherds
Still find a comfort there.

HAROLD.

        Carters and shepherds !

DORA.

Scorn! I hate scorn. A soul with no
    religion —
My mother used to say that such a
    one
Was without rudder, anchor, compass
    — might be
Blown everyway with every gust and
    wreck
On any rock ; and tho' you are good
    and gentle,
Yet if thro' any want ——

HAROLD.

        Of this religion ?
Child, read a little history, you will
    find
The common brotherhood of man has
    been
Wrong'd by the cruelties of his re-
    ligions

More than could ever have happen'd
    thro' the want
Of any or all of them.

DORA.

        — But, O dear friend,
If thro' the want of any — I mean the
    true one —
And pardon me for saying it — you
    should ever
Be tempted into doing what might
    seem
Not altogether worthy of you, I
    think
That I should break my heart, for
    you have taught me
To love you.

HAROLD.

What is this ? some one been stirring
Against me ? he, your rustic amourist,
The polish'd Damon of your pastoral
    here,
This Dobson of your idyll ?

DORA.

        No, Sir, no !
Did you not tell me he was crazed
    with jealousy,
Had threaten'd ev'n your life, and
    would say anything ?
Did *I* not promise not to listen to
    him,
Not ev'n to see the man ?

HAROLD.

        Good ; then what is it
That makes you talk so dolefully ?

DORA.

        I told you —
My father. Well, indeed, a friend
    just now,
One that has been much wrong'd,
    whose griefs are mine,
Was warning me that if a gentleman
Should wed a farmer's daughter, he
    would be
Sooner or later shamed of her among
The ladies, born his equals.

HAROLD.

　　　　　　More fool he !
What I that have been call'd a Socialist,
A Communist, a Nihilist — what you will ! —

DORA.

What are all these ?

HAROLD.

　　　　　Utopian idiotcies.
They did not last three Junes.　Such rampant weeds
Strangle each other, die, and make the soil
For Cæsars, Cromwells, and Napoleons
To root their power in.　I have freed myself
From all such dreams, and some will say because
I have inherited my Uncle.　Let them.
But — shamed of you, my Empress !
I should prize
The pearl of Beauty, even if I found it
Dark with the soot of slums.

DORA.

　　　　　　But I can tell you,
We Steers are of old blood, tho' we be fallen.
See there our shield.　(*Pointing to arms on mantelpiece.*)　For I have heard the Steers
Had land in Saxon times ; and your own name
Of Harold sounds so English and so old
I am sure you must be proud of it.

HAROLD.

　　　　　　　Not I !
As yet I scarcely feel it mine.　I took it
For some three thousand acres.　I have land now
And wealth, and lay both at your feet.

DORA.

　　　　　　And *what* was
Your name before ?

HAROLD.

　　Come, come, my girl, enough
Of this strange talk.　I love you and you me.
True, I have held opinions, hold some still,
Which you would scarce approve of : for all that,
I am a man not prone to jealousies,
Caprices, humors, moods ; but very ready
To make allowances, and mighty slow
To feel offences.　Nay, I do believe
I could forgive — well, almost anything —
And that more freely than your formal priest,
Because I know more fully than *he* can
What poor earthworms are all and each of us,
Here crawling in this boundless Nature.　Dora,
If marriage ever brought a woman happiness
I doubt not I can make you happy.

DORA.

　　　　　　You make me
Happy already.

HAROLD.

　　　　And I never said
As much before to any woman living.

DORA.

No ?

HAROLD.

No ! by this true kiss, *you* are the first
I ever have loved truly.
　　　　　　[*They kiss each other.*

EVA (*with a wild cry*).

　　　　　Philip Edgar !

HAROLD.

The phantom cry! *You* — did *you* hear a cry?

DORA.

She must be crying out "Edgar" in her sleep.

HAROLD.

Who must be crying out "Edgar" in her sleep?

DORA.

Your pardon for a minute. She must be waked.

HAROLD.

Who must be waked?

DORA.

I am not deaf: you fright me. What ails you?

HAROLD.

Speak.

DORA.

You know her, Eva.

HAROLD.

Eva!
[Eva *opens the door and stands in the entry.*

She!

EVA.

Make her happy, then, and I forgive you.
[*Falls dead.*

DORA.

Happy! What? Edgar? Is it so? Can it be?
They told me so. Yes, yes! I see it all now.
O she has fainted. Sister, Eva, sister!

He is yours again — he will love *you* again;
I give him back to you again. Look up!
One word, or do but smile! Sweet, do you hear me?
[*Puts her hand on* EVA's *heart.*
There, there — the heart, O God! — the poor young heart
Broken at last — all still — and nothing left
To live for.
[*Falls on body of her sister.*

HAROLD.

Living . . . dead . . . She said "all still.
Nothing to live for."
She — she knows me — now . . .

(*A pause.*)

She knew me from the first, she juggled with me,
She hid this sister, told me she was dead —
I have wasted pity on her — not dead now —
No! acting, playing on me, both of them.
They drag the river for her! no, not they!
Playing on me — not dead now — a swoon — a scene —
Yet — how she made her wail as for the dead!

Enter MILLY.

MILLY.

Pleäse, Mister 'Arold

HAROLD (*roughly*).

Well?

MILLY.

The owd man's coom'd ageän to 'issen, an' wants
To hev a word wi' ye about the marriage.

HAROLD.

The what?

MILLY.

The marriage.

HAROLD.

The marriage?

MILLY.

Yeäs, the marriage.
Granny says marriages be maäde i'
'eaven.

HAROLD.

She lies! They are made in Hell.
Child, can't you see?
Tell them to fly for a doctor.

MILLY.

O law — yeäs, Sir!
I'll run fur 'im mysen.

HAROLD.

All silent there,
Yes, deathlike! Dead? I dare not
look: if dead,
Were it best to steal away, to spare
myself,
And her too, pain, pain, pain?
My curse on all
This world of mud, on all its idiot
gleams
Of pleasure, all the foul fatalities
That blast our natural passions into
pains!

Enter DOBSON.

DOBSON.

You, Master Hedgar, Harold, or
whativer
They calls ye, for I warrants that ye
goäs
By haäfe a scoor o' naämes — out o'
the chaumber.
[*Dragging him past the body.*

HAROLD.

Not that way, man! Curse on your
brutal strength!
I cannot pass that way.

DOBSON.

Out o' the chaumber!
I'll mash tha into nowt.

HAROLD.

The mere wild-beast!

DOBSON.

Out o' the chaumber, dang tha!

HAROLD.

Lout, churl, clown!
[*While they are shouting and strug-
gling* DORA *rises and comes between them.*

DORA (*to* DOBSON).

Peace, let him be: it is the chamber
of Death!
Sir, you are tenfold more a gentleman,
A hundred times more worth a
woman's love,
Than this, this — but I waste no
words upon him:
His wickedness is like my wretchedness —
Beyond all language.

(*To* HAROLD.)

You — you see her there!
Only fifteen when first you came on
her,
And then the sweetest flower of all
the wolds,
So lovely in the promise of her May,
So winsome in her grace and gaiety,
So loved by all the village people
here,
So happy in herself and in her
home ——

DOBSON (*agitated*).

Theer, theer! ha' done. I can't abeär to see her.
                     [*Exit.*

DORA.

A child, and all as trustful as a child!
Five years of shame and suffering broke the heart
That only beat for you; and he, the father,
Thro' that dishonor which you brought upon us,
Has lost his health, his eyesight, even his mind.

HAROLD (*covering his face*).

Enough!

DORA.

    It seem'd so; only there was left
A second daughter, and to her you came
Veiling one sin to act another.

HAROLD.

                     No!
You wrong me there! hear, hear me!
    I wish'd, if you ——
                     [*Pauses.*

DORA.

If I ——

HAROLD.

Could love me, could be brought to love me
As I loved you ——

DORA.

What then?

HAROLD.

            I wish'd, I hoped
To make, to make ——

DORA.

What did you hope to make?

HAROLD.

'Twere best to make an end of my lost life.
O Dora, Dora!

DORA.

What did you hope to make?

HAROLD.

Make, make! I cannot find the word —forgive it—
Amends.

DORA.

For what? to whom?

HAROLD.

            To him, to you!
             [*Falling at her feet.*

DORA.

To *him!* to *me!*
          No, not with all your wealth,
Your land, your life! Out in the fiercest storm
That ever made earth tremble — he, nor I —
The shelter of *your* roof — not for one moment —
Nothing from *you!*
Sunk in the deepest pit of pauperism,
Push'd from all doors as if we bore the plague,
Smitten with fever in the open field,
Laid famine-stricken at the gates of Death —
Nothing from you!
         But she there — her last word
Forgave — and I forgive you. If you ever
Forgive yourself, you are even lower and baser
Than even I can well believe you. Go!
         [*He lies at her feet. Curtain falls.*